international marketing

thirteenth edition

Philip R. Cateora
FELLOW, ACADEMY OF INTERNATIONAL BUSINESS
UNIVERSITY OF COLORADO

John L. Graham
UNIVERSITY OF CALIFORNIA, IRVINE

 McGraw-Hill
Irwin

Boston   Burr Ridge, IL   Dubuque, IA   Madison, WI   New York   San Francisco   St. Louis
Bangkok   Bogotá   Caracas   Kuala Lumpur   Lisbon   London   Madrid   Mexico City
Milan   Montreal   New Delhi   Santiago   Seoul   Singapore   Sydney   Taipei   Toronto

McGraw-Hill
Irwin

INTERNATIONAL MARKETING

Published by McGraw-Hill/Irwin, a business unit of The McGraw-Hill Companies, Inc., 1221 Avenue of the Americas, New York, NY, 10020. Copyright © 2007 by The McGraw-Hill Companies, Inc. All rights reserved. No part of this publication may be reproduced or distributed in any form or by any means, or stored in a database or retrieval system, without the prior written consent of The McGraw-Hill Companies, Inc., including, but not limited to, in any network or other electronic storage or transmission, or broadcast for distance learning.

Some ancillaries, including electronic and print components, may not be available to customers outside the United States.

This book is printed on acid-free paper.

4 5 6 7 8 9 0 VNH/VNH 0 9 8 7

ISBN-13: 978-0-07-110594-1
ISBN-10: 0-07-110594-8

Photo credits (chapter openers): page 2, AP/Wide World Photos; page 26, © AFP/Getty Images; page 54, © Dave G. Houser/CORBIS; page 156, © Reuters NewMedia Inc./CORBIS; page 244, © AFP/Getty Images; page 278, © AFP/Getty Images; page 394, © AFP/Getty Images; page 432, © Macduff Everton/CORBIS; page 466, © AFP/Getty Images; page 500, © Roger Ressmeyer/CORBIS; page 526, AP/Wide World Photos; page 556, Copyrighted and used by permission of KARRASS, LTD. Beverly Hills, California.

www.mhhe.com

To Thomas, Maggie, and Angela
To Greta, Emily, Jack, and Grace

Philip R. Cateora, Professor Emeritus, The University of Colorado at Boulder, received his Ph.D. from the University of Texas at Austin where he was elected to Beta Gamma Sigma. In his academic career at the University of Colorado he has served as Division Head of Marketing, Coordinator of International Business Programs, Associate Dean, and Interim Dean. His teaching has spanned a range of courses in marketing and international business from fundamentals through the doctoral level. He received the University of Colorado Teaching Excellence Award and the Western Marketing Educator's Association's Educator of the Year Award.

Professor Cateora has conducted faculty workshops on internationalizing principles of marketing courses for the AACSB and participated in designing and offering similar faculty workshops under a grant by the Department of Education. In conjunction with these efforts, he co-authored *Marketing: An International Perspective,* a supplement to accompany principles of marketing texts. Professor Cateora has served as consultant to small export companies as well as multinational companies, served on the Rocky Mountain Export Council, and taught in management development programs. He is a Fellow of the Academy of International Business.

John L. Graham, Professor of International Business and Marketing and Associate Dean at the Graduate School of Management at the University of California, Irvine, has been Director, UCI Center for Citizen Peacebuilding, Visiting Scholar, Georgetown University School of Business, Visiting Professor at Madrid Business School in Spain, and Associate Professor, University of Southern California. Before beginning his doctoral studies at U.C. Berkeley, he worked for a division of Caterpillar Tractor Co. and served as an officer in the U.S. Navy Underwater Demolition Teams. Professor Graham is the author (with N. Mark Lam), of *China Now,* (McGraw-Hill 2006); with Yoshihiro Sano and James Hodgson, former U.S. ambassador to Japan, of *Doing Business with the New Japan* (Rowman & Littlefield, 3rd edition, 2000); author, with Philip Cateora, of *International Marketing* (McGraw-Hill, 10th, 11th, and 12th editions, 1999); and editor, with Taylor Meloan, of *Global and International Marketing* (Irwin, 2nd edition, 1997). He has also written more than 50 articles and chapters for publications such as the *Harvard Business Review, Sloan Management Review, Journal of Marketing, Journal of International Business Studies, Journal of Consumer Research, Strategic Management Review, Marketing Science, Journal of Higher Education,* the *Los Angeles Times,* and *The New York Times;* excerpts of his work have been read into the Congressional Record and his research of business negotiation styles in 20 cultures was the subject of an article in the January 1988 issue of *Smithsonian;* his 1994 paper in *Management Science* received a citation of excellence from the Lauder Institute at the Wharton School of Business.

At the start of the last millennium the Chinese were the preeminent international traders. Although a truly global trading system would not evolve until some 500 years later, Chinese silk was available in Europe.

At the start of the last century the British military, merchants, and manufacturers dominated the seas and international commerce. Literally, the sun did not set on the British Empire.

At the start of the last decade, Japan's economic successes had rendered the military competition between the United States and the Soviet Union obsolete. Pundits circa 1990 predicted a Pacific Century, wherein trans-Pacific trade would surpass trans-Atlantic trade. Other Asian economies would follow the lead of Japan. No one then foresaw the ascendancy and impact of the American-created information technology revolution.

What surprises do the new decade, century, and millennium hold in store for all of us? Halfway through the decade natural disasters and wars have hampered commerce and human progress. The battle to balance economic growth and stewardship of the environment continues. The globalization of markets has certainly accelerated through almost universal acceptance of the democratic free enterprise model and new communication technologies, including cell phones and the Internet. Which will prove the better, Chinese gradualism or the Russian big-bang approach to economic and political reform? Will the information technology boom of the previous decade be followed by a demographics bust when American baby boomers try to retire in 2010? Or will NAFTA and the young folks in Mexico provide a much needed demographic balance? Ten years out the debate about global warming should be settled—more data and better science will yield the answers. What unforeseen advances or disasters will the biological sciences bring us? Will we conquer AIDS/HIV in Africa? Will weapons and warfare become obsolete?

International marketing will play a key role in providing positive answers to all these questions. We know that trade causes peace and prosperity by promoting creativity, mutual understanding, and interdependence. Markets are burgeoning in emerging economies in eastern Europe, the Commonwealth of Independent States, China, Indonesia, Korea, India, Mexico, Chile, Brazil, and Argentina—in short, globally. These emerging economies hold the promise of huge markets in the future. In the more mature markets of the industrialized world, opportunity and challenge also abound as consumers' tastes become more sophisticated and complex and as increases in purchasing power provide consumers with new means of satisfying new demands.

Opportunities in today's global markets are on a par with the global economic expansion that existed after World War II. Today, however, the competitive environment within which these opportunities exist is vastly different from that earlier period when United States multinationals dominated world markets. From the late 1940s through the 1960s, multinational corporations (MNCs) from the United States had little competition; today, companies from almost all the world's nations vie for global markets.

There is no better illustration of the changes that have occurred in the competition for global markets in the last quarter century than that experienced by General Electric Lighting (GEL). GEL, begun in 1887, dominated the U.S. lighting market until traditional rival Westinghouse sold its lamp operations to Philips Electronics of Holland in 1983. "Suddenly," reflected GEL's chief, "we have bigger, stronger competition. They're coming to our market, but we're not in theirs. So we're on the defensive." Not long after, GEL acquired Tungsram, a Hungarian lighting company, and Thorn EMI in Britain, and then moved into Asia via a joint venture with Hitachi. As recently as 1988, GE Lighting got less than 20 percent of its sales from outside the United States; in 2000, more than half came from abroad. What happened at GE Lighting has occurred over and over again to MNCs in the United States, Europe, and Asia. The companies that succeed in the 21st century will be those capable of adapting to constant change and adjusting to new challenges.

The economic, political, and social changes that have occurred over the last decade have dramatically altered the landscape of global business. Consider the present and future impact of the following:

- The ever-present threat of global terrorism as represented by the September 11, 2001, attacks
- Major armed conflicts in sub-Saharan Africa and the Middle East
- The looming global recession
- The emerging markets in eastern Europe, Asia, and Latin America, where more than 75 percent of the growth in world trade over the next 20 years is expected to occur
- The reunification of Hong Kong, Macau, and China, which finally puts all of Asia under the control of Asians for the first time in over a century
- The European Monetary Union and the successful switch from local-country currencies to one monetary unit for Europe, the euro
- The rapid move away from traditional distribution structures in Japan, Europe, and many emerging markets
- The growth of middle-income households the world over
- The continued strengthening and creation of regional market groups such as the European Union (EU), the North American Free Trade Area (NAFTA), the Central American Free Trade Area (CAFTA), ASEAN Free Trade Area (AFTA), the Southern Cone Free Trade Area (Mercosur), and the Asian-Pacific Economic Cooperation (APEC)
- The successful completion of the Uruguay Round of the General Agreement on Tariffs and Trade (GATT) and the creation of the World Trade Organization (WTO), the latter now including China and Taiwan
- The restructuring, reorganizing, and refocusing of companies in telecommunications, entertainment, and biotechnology, as well as in traditional smokestack industries around the world
- The continuing integration of the Internet and cell phones into all aspects of companies' operations and consumers' lives

These are not simply news reports. These changes affect the practice of business worldwide, and they mean that companies will have to constantly examine the way they do business and remain flexible enough to react rapidly to changing global trends to be competitive.

As global economic growth occurs, understanding marketing in all cultures is increasingly important. *International Marketing* addresses global issues and describes concepts relevant to all international marketers, regardless of the extent of their international involvement. Not all firms engaged in overseas marketing have a global perspective, nor do they need to. Some companies' foreign marketing is limited to one country; others market in a number of countries, treating each as a separate market; and still others, the global enterprises, look for market segments with common needs and wants across political and economic boundaries. All, however, are affected by competitive activity in the global marketplace. It is with this future that the thirteenth edition of *International Marketing* is concerned.

Emphasis is on the strategic implications of competition in different country markets. An environmental/cultural approach to international marketing permits a truly global orientation. The reader's horizons are not limited to any specific nation or to the particular ways of doing business in a single nation. Instead, the book provides an approach and framework for identifying and analyzing the important cultural and environmental uniqueness of any nation or global region. Thus, when surveying the tasks of marketing in a foreign milieu, the reader will not overlook the impact of crucial cultural issues.

The text is designed to stimulate curiosity about management practices of companies, large and small, seeking market opportunities outside the home country and to raise the reader's consciousness about the importance of viewing international marketing management strategies from a global perspective.

Although this revised edition is infused throughout with a global orientation, export marketing and the operations of smaller companies are not overlooked. Issues specific to exporting are discussed where strategies applicable to exporting arise, and examples of marketing practices of smaller companies are examined.

New and Expanded Topics in This Edition

The new and expanded topics in this thirteenth edition reflect issues in competition, changing marketing structures, ethics and social responsibility, negotiations, and the development of the manager for the 21st century. Competition is raising the global standards for quality, increasing the demand for advanced technology and innovation, and increasing the value of customer satisfaction. The global market is swiftly changing from a seller's market to a buyer's market. This is a period of profound social, economic, and political change. To remain competitive globally, companies must be aware of all aspects of the emerging global economic order.

Additionally, the evolution of global communications and its known and unknown impact on how international business is conducted cannot be minimized. In the third millennium people in the "global village" will grow closer than ever, and will hear and see each other as a matter of course. An executive in Germany will be able to routinely pick up his or her videophone to hear and see his or her counterpart in an Australian company or anywhere else in the world. In many respects, geographic distance is becoming irrelevant.

Telecommunications, videophones, facsimile machines, the Internet, and satellites are helping companies optimize their planning, production, and procurement processes. Information—and, in its wake, the flow of goods—is moving around the globe at lightning speed. Increasingly powerful networks spanning the globe enable the delivery of services that reach far beyond national and continental boundaries, fueling and fostering international trade. The connections of global communications bring people all around the world together in new and better forms of dialogue and understanding.

This dynamic nature of the international marketplace is reflected in the number of substantially improved and expanded topics in this thirteenth edition, including the following:

- A deeper look at the causes of cultural differences
- The Internet and cell phones and their expanding role in international marketing
- Negotiations with customers, partners, and regulators
- Big emerging markets (BEMs)
- Evolving global middle-income households
- Bottom of the pyramid markets
- World Trade Organization
- Free trade agreements
- Asia-Pacific Economic Cooperation
- Multicultural research
- Qualitative and quantitative research
- Country-of-origin effect and global brands
- Industrial trade shows
- A growing emphasis on both consumer and industrial services
- Trends in channel structures in Europe, Japan, and developing countries
- Ethics and socially responsible decisions
- Green marketing
- Changing profiles of global managers

Structure of the Text

The text is divided into six parts. The first two chapters, Part 1, introduce the reader to the environmental/cultural approach to international marketing and to three international marketing management concepts: domestic market expansion, multidomestic marketing, and global marketing. As companies restructure for the global competitive rigors of the 21st century, so too must tomorrow's managers. The successful manager must be globally aware and have a frame of reference that goes beyond a country, or even a region, and encompasses the world. What global awareness means and how it is acquired is discussed early in the text; it is at the foundation of global marketing.

Chapter 2 focuses on the dynamic environment of international trade and the competitive challenges and opportunities confronting today's international marketer. The importance of the creation of the World Trade Organization, the successor to GATT, is fully explored. The growing importance of cell phones and the Internet in conducting international business is considered, creating a foundation on which specific applications in subsequent chapters are presented.

The five chapters in Part 2 deal with the cultural environment of global marketing. A global orientation requires the recognition of cultural differences and the critical decision of whether it is necessary to accommodate them.

Geography and history (Chapter 3) are included as important dimensions in understanding cultural and market differences among countries. Not to be overlooked is concern for the deterioration of the global ecological environment and the multinational company's critical responsibility to protect it.

Chapter 4 presents a broad review of culture and its impact on human behavior as it relates to international marketing. Specific attention is paid to Geert Hofstede's study of cultural values and behavior. The elements of culture reviewed in Chapter 4 set the stage for the in-depth analyses in Chapters 5, 6, and 7 of business customs and the political and legal environments. Ethics and social responsibility are presented in the context of the dilemma that often confronts the international manager, that is, balancing corporate profits against the social and ethical consequences of his or her decisions.

The three chapters in Part 3 are concerned with assessing global market opportunities. As markets expand, segments grow within markets; as market segments across country markets evolve, marketers are forced to understand market behavior within and across different cultural contexts. Multicultural research, qualitative and quantitative research, and the Internet as a tool in the research task are explored in Chapter 8.

Chapters 9 and 10 in Part 3 explore the impact of the three important trends in global marketing: the growth and expansion of the world's big emerging markets; the rapid growth of middle-income market segments; and the steady creation of regional market groups that include NAFTA, the European Union, CAFTA, APEC, and the evolving Free Trade Area of the Americas (FTAA). Also discussed is the growing number of trade agreements that have been executed by the European Union and Japan with the FTAA and some Latin American countries.

The strategic implications of the dissolution of the Soviet Union the emergence of new independent republics, the shift from socialist-based to market-based economies in Eastern Europe, and the return of South Africa and Vietnam to international commerce are examined. Attention is also given to the efforts of the governments of India and many Latin American countries to reduce or eliminate barriers to trade, open their countries to foreign investment, and privatize state-owned enterprises.

These political, social, and economic changes that are sweeping the world are creating new markets and opportunities, making some markets more accessible while creating the potential for greater protectionism in others.

In Part 4, Developing Global Marketing Strategies, planning and organizing for global marketing is the subject of Chapter 11. The discussion of collaborative relationships, including strategic alliances, recognizes the importance of relational collaborations among firms, suppliers, and customers in the success of the global marketer. Many multinational companies realize that to fully capitalize on opportunities offered by global markets, they must have strengths that often exceed their capabilities. Collaborative relationships can provide technology, innovations, productivity, capital, and market access that strengthen a company's competitive position.

Chapters 12 and 13 focus on product and services management, reflecting the differences in strategies between consumer and industrial offerings and the growing importance in world markets for both consumer and business services. Additionally, the discussion on the development of global offerings stresses the importance of approaching the adaptation issue from the viewpoint of building a standardized product/service platform that can be adapted to reflect cultural differences. The competitive importance in today's global market for quality, innovation, and technology as the keys to marketing success is explored.

Chapter 14 takes the reader through the distribution process, from home country to the consumer in the target country market. The structural impediments to market entry imposed by a country's distribution system are examined in the framework of a detailed presentation of the Japanese distribution system. Additionally, the rapid changes in channel structure that are occurring in Japan, as well as in other countries, and the emergence of the World Wide Web as a distribution channel are presented.

In Chapter 15, the special issues involved in moving a product from one country market to another, and the accompanying mechanics of exporting, are addressed. The importance of the Internet in assisting the exporter to wade through the details of exporting is discussed in the context of the revised export regulations.

Chapter 16 covers advertising and addresses the promotional element of the international marketing mix. Included in the discussion of global market segmentation are recognition of the rapid growth of market segments across country markets and the importance of market segmentation as a strategic competitive tool in creating an effective promotional message. Chapter 17 discusses personal selling and sales management and the critical nature of training, evaluating, and controlling sales representatives.

Price escalation and ways it can be lessened, countertrade practices, and price strategies to employ when the dollar is strong or weak relative to foreign currencies are concepts presented in Chapter 18.

In Part 5, Chapter 19 is a thorough presentation of negotiating with customers, partners, and regulators. The discussion stresses the varying negotiation styles found among cultures and the importance of recognizing these differences at the negotiation table.

Pedagogical Features of the Text

The text portion of the book provides a thorough coverage of its subject, with subject emphasis on the planning and strategic problems confronting companies that market across cultural boundaries.

The use of the Internet as a tool of international marketing is stressed throughout the text. On all occasions where data used in the text originated from an Internet source, the Web address is given. Problems that require the student to access the Internet are included with end-of-chapter questions. Internet-related problems are designed to familiarize the student with the power of the Internet in his or her research, to illustrate data available on the Internet, and to challenge the reader to solve problems using the Internet. Many of the examples, illustrations, and exhibits found in the text can be explored in more detail by accessing the Web addresses that are included.

Current, pithy, sometimes humorous, and always relevant examples are used to stimulate interest and increase understanding of the ideas, concepts, and strategies presented in emphasizing the importance of understanding cultural uniqueness and relevant business practices and strategies.

Each chapter is introduced with a Global Perspective, a real-life example of company experiences that illustrates salient issues discussed in the chapter. Companies featured in the Global Perspectives range from exporters to global enterprises.

The boxed "Crossing Borders," an innovation of the first edition of *International Marketing,* have always been popular with students. They reflect contemporary issues in international marketing and can be used to illustrate real-life situations and as the basis for class discussion. They are selected to be unique, humorous, and of general interest to the reader.

The book is presented in full color, allowing maps to depict of geographical, cultural, and political boundaries and features more easily. Color also allows us to better communicate through that medium the intricacies of international symbols and meanings in marketing communications. New photographs of current and relevant international marketing events are found throughout the text—all in color.

"The Country Notebook—A Guide for Developing a Marketing Plan," found in Part 6, Supplementary Material, is a detailed outline that provides both a format for a complete cultural and economic analysis of a country and guidelines for developing a marketing plan.

In addition to "The Country Notebook," Part 6 comprises a selection of short and long cases. The short cases focus on a single problem, serving as the basis for discussion of a specific concept or issue. The longer, more integrated cases are broader in scope and focus on more than one marketing management problem; new cases focus on services marketing, and marketing strategy. The cases can be analyzed by using the information provided. They also lend themselves to more in-depth analysis, requiring the student to engage in additional research and data collection.

Supplements
We have taken great care to offer new features and improvements to every part of the teaching aid package. Following is a list of specific features:

- **Instructor's Manual and Test Bank.** The Instructor's Manual, prepared by the authors, contains lecture notes or teaching suggestions for each chapter. A section called "Changes to This Edition" is included to help instructors adapt their teaching notes to the thirteenth edition. A case correlation grid at the beginning of the case note offers alternative uses for the cases.

The Test Bank, prepared by Davis Folsom, *University of South Carolina–Beaufort,* is bound with the Instructor's Manual for ease of use. The Test Bank contains more than 2,000 questions, including true/false, critical thinking, and essay formats. Computerized testing software with an online testing feature is also available on the instructor's CD-ROM.

- **Videos.** The video program has been revised for the thirteenth edition and contains new footage of companies, topics videos, and unique training materials for international negotiations. Teaching notes and questions relevant to each chapter in the text are available in the IM and at the Web site.

- **PowerPoint slides.** This edition has PowerPoint slides for both the instructor and students, the latter of which are narrated. The PowerPoint presentation that accompanies *International Marketing,* thirteenth edition, contains exhibits from the text and other sources. The PowerPoint slides are prepared by Caroline Juszczak.

- **Instructor's CD-ROM.** This presentation manager, available to adopters of the textbook, contains the Instructor's Manual, Test Bank, and PowerPoint. Instructors have the ability to customize their lectures with this powerful tool.

- **Web site:** www.mhhe.com/cateora07. Included on the site are instructor resources such as downloadable files for the complete Instructor's Manual, PowerPoint slides, video clips, and links to current events and additional resources for the classroom. Instructors can also link to PageOut to create their own course Web site and access the complete Test Bank. For students, our site provides links to Web sites, an interactive version of the Country Notebook, online quizzing, and narrated chapter PowerPoint Slides.

Acknowledgments
The success of a text depends on the contributions of many people, especially those who take the time to share their thoughtful criticisms and suggestions to improve the text.

We would especially like to thank the following reviewers who gave us valuable insights into this revision:

Francisco Coronel
Hampton University

Steven Engel
University of Colorado–Boulder

Randy Howell
Kirkwood Community College

Joe H. Kim
Rider University

Susan D. Peters
California State University–Pomona

Kristen Regine
Johnson & Wales University

Ye Sheng
Florida Atlantic University

Tanuja Singh
Northern Illinois University

Bronis Verhage
Georgia State University

We appreciate the help of all the many students and professors who have shared their opinions of past editions, and we welcome their comments and suggestions on this and future editions of *International Marketing*.

A very special thanks to Andy Winston, Amy Luck, Dan Silverburg, Rhonda Seelinger, Harvey Yep, Sesha Bolisetty, Cara David, Sue Lombardi, Kathy Shive, and Janna Martin from McGraw-Hill/Irwin, whose enthusiasm, creativity, constructive criticisms, and commitment to excellence have made this edition possible.

Philip R. Cateora
John L. Graham

WALKTHROUGH
A quick look at the new edition

International Marketing by Cateora and Graham has always been a pioneer in the field of international marketing. The authors continue to set the standard in this edition with new and expanded topics that reflect the swift changes of an expanding competitive global market as well as an increased coverage of technology's impact on the international market arena.

1 The World

ALB.	Albania
AUS.	Austria
BELG.	Belgium
BOS.–HER.	Bosnia and Herzegovina
CZECH REP.	Czech Republic
CR.	Croatia
DEN.	Denmark
SERB-MONT.	Serbia-Montenegro
HUN.	Hungary
MAC.	Macedonia
NETH.	The Netherlands
SWITZ.	Switzerland
SLOV.	Slovakia
SLOVE.	Slovenia

MICROSOFT

MICROSOFT annually spends more than a billion dollars on its global advertising. The company has 75 subsidiaries around the world. The management processes used to develop the "Windows Office" campaign are instructive.

Things begin with marketing research in individual countries regarding key market segments, most attractive product features, and potential themes. The data collected by the international subsidiaries are then sent to McCann-Erickson's San Francisco offices for the development of a set of universal themes. McCann-Erickson Worldwide has more than 200 offices in 111 countries and is ideally suited for global clients such as Microsoft, Coca-Cola, DuPont, and Lucent Technologies. The San Francisco office is closest to Redmond, Washington, where Microsoft is headquartered, and, of course, it is also adjacent to the Silicon Valley.

The agency sends the appropriate core concepts, video footage, photographic layouts, and copy themes that comprise the set of universal materials. Then, in cooperation with their local agencies, managers at each subsidiary choose the most appropriate materials for their particular consumers and markets. The most customization is required in Brazil, China, India, and Russia—all are plagued by major piracy problems. Also, since Japan is the firm's second largest market behind only the United States, executives there are given more freedom to adapt to local requirements and tastes.

corporate/brand image campaign

The purpose behind this corporate campaign is to complement the firm's heavy product-oriented marketing with a program that explains Microsoft's broader corporate mission. That is, "to help people and businesses throughout the world reach their full potential." The campaign serves to soften the image of the firm and emphasizes the contribution its products and services have made to technology and the practical applications of personal computing in business, science, education, and so on. The program runs in more than 30 countries (here you see the versions used in the United States, Japan, and Mexico) including TV ads with local copy, voice-over, and other adaptations to the global theme. The majority of the ads are pre- and post-tested in multiple countries to check for cultural nuance. Some $19 million a year is spent just on this aspect of the research. The print and TV ads are complemented by an associated PR, government, and community affairs campaign. The campaign is in its third year with positive results reflected in measured improving consumers' views about the company.

product-specific advertising

Here Microsoft Office is pitted against its toughest competitor—earlier versions of itself. So the goal of the campaign is to break up the inertia and facilitate an upgrade cycle. The key message is the way the world (of information workers) works is much different today than it was three to five years ago, or one or two versions ago of Office. The ads focus on scenarios around mobility, collaboration, and controlling sensitive data.

Since there is so much complacency (85 percent satisfaction with Office), the firm needs to do something different or risk just reinforcing with customers the previous version of Office. The dinosaur heads proved to do that in most markets, but they needed local adaptations—photos were used in the United States, cartoons in Korea, and other treatments based on local cultures. This theme was supplemented by a heavy public relations campaign including speeches by Bill Gates about the changing information worker environment. The program was run in more than 30 countries, but not in China. Companies in that market are often in the "product trial" (that is, piracy) stage of the buyer–seller relationship, and different programs are therefore appropriate.

Notice the similarity of the campaigns across the countries, and notice the differences. For the Mexican version, after the "We See," "the king of the skies" is transformed into "imagine what heights you can reach." The tagline for all the ads was developed originally for the corporate campaign. You will also notice that the ad targeting French buyers is the only one with no English in it (except for the product name).

The translations are done locally, so, for example, the copy is different between Mexico and Spain. A variety of themes and media (print and outdoor) are used across countries. And, in any one country, several themes and media may be used, particularly in the larger, more diverse markets.

Finally, the executions are then tested in each market and adjustments are made. This global approach makes sense for Microsoft because the product, its uses, and its market share are virtually the same across markets. This integrated approach has saved some $30 million in worker-hours and production costs over previous similar campaigns.

(Courtesy Microsoft Corporation)

4-Color Design

New color maps and exhibits allow for improved pedagogy and a clearer presentation of international symbols and cultural meanings in marketing and advertising. In addition, photos that depend on full color for maximum impact easily bring many global examples to life. This visually stimulating combination works together to make the text material reader-friendly and accessible for both instructors and students.

Chapter Openers

Chapter Outline provides students an at-a-glance overview of chapter topics, while Chapter Objectives summarize the chapter's goals and focus. Each chapter is introduced with a Global Perspective, a real-life example of company experiences that illustrates significant issues discussed in the chapter. Companies featured in the Global Perspective vignettes range from exporters to global enterprises.

1

the scope and challenge
of international marketing

CHAPTER OUTLINE

Global Perspective: Global Commerce Causes Peace

The Internationalization of U.S. Business

International Marketing Defined

The International Marketing Task
    Marketing Decision Factors
    Aspects of the Domestic Environment
    Aspects of the Foreign Environment

Environmental Adaptation Needed

The Self-Reference Criterion and Ethnocentrism:
    Major Obstacles

Developing a Global Awareness

Stages of International Marketing Involvement
    No Direct Foreign Marketing
    Infrequent Foreign Marketing
    Regular Foreign Marketing
    International Marketing
    Global Marketing

Strategic Orientation
    Domestic Market Extension Orientation
    Multidomestic Market Orientation
    Global Market Orientation

The Orientation of International Marketing

CHAPTER LEARNING OBJECTIVES

What you should learn from Chapter 1:

- The changing face of U.S. business
- The scope of the international marketing task
- The importance of the self-reference criterion (SRC) in international marketing
- The progression of becoming a global marketer
- The increasing importance of global awareness

Global Perspective

GLOBAL COMMERCE CAUSES PEACE

Global commerce thrives during peacetime. The economic boom in North America during the late 1990s was in large part due to the end of the Cold War and the opening of the formerly communist countries to the world trading system. However, we should also understand the important role that trade and international marketing play in producing peace.

Boeing Company, America's largest exporter, is perhaps the most prominent example. Although many would argue that Boeing's military sales (aircraft and missiles) do not exactly promote peace, over the years that business has constituted only about 20 percent of the company's commercial activity. Up until 2002, of Boeing's some $60 billion in annual revenues, about 65 percent came from sales of commercial jets around the world and another 15 percent from space and communications technologies. Unfortunately, these historical numbers are being skewed by American military spending and the damage done to tourism by terrorism.[1] Even so, the company still counts customers in 145 countries, and its 159,000 employees work in 67 countries. Its more than 11,000 commercial jets in service around the world carry about one billion travelers per year. Its NASA Services division is the lead contractor in the construction and operation of the 16-country International Space Station. In the fall of 2006 The Space and Intelligence Systems Division also produces and launches communications satellites affecting people in every country.

All the activity associated with the development, production, and marketing of commercial aircraft and space vehicles requires millions of people from around the world to work together. Moreover, no company does more[2] to enable people from all countries to meet face to face for both recreation and commerce. All this interaction yields not just the mutual gain associated with business relationships but also personal relationships and mutual understanding. The latter are the foundation of global peace and prosperity.

Another class of companies that promotes global dialogue and therefore peace is the mobile phone industry. During 2005 more than 700 million new mobile phones were purchased around the world connecting more than one-quarter of all people on the planet. Nokia (Finland), the market leader, is well ahead of American manufacturer Motorola, Samsung (S. Korea), LG (S. Korea), Siemens (Germany), and Sony Ericsson (Japan/Sweden).

Individual and small companies also make a difference, perhaps a subtler one than large multinational companies, but one just as important in the aggregate. Our favorite example is Daniel Lubetzky's company, PeaceWorks. Mr. Lubetzky used a fellowship at Stanford Law School to study how to foster joint ventures between Arabs and Israelis. Then, following his own advice, he created a company that combines basil pesto from Israel with other raw materials and glass jars supplied by an Arab partner to produce the first product in a line he calls Moshe & Ali's Gourmet Foods. The company now sells some 60 products in 3,000 stores in the United States and has its headquarters on Park Avenue in New York and business operations in Israel, Egypt, Indonesia, Turkey, Sri Lanka, and South Africa. Again, beyond the measurable commercial benefits of cooperation between the involved Arabs, Israelis, and others is the longer-lasting and more fundamental appreciation for one another's circumstances and character.

International marketing is hard work. Making sales calls is no vacation even in Paris when you've been there 10 times before. But international marketing is important work. It can enrich you, your family, your company, and your country. And ultimately, when international marketing is done well, by large companies or small, the needs and wants of customers in other lands are well understood, and prosperity and peace are promoted along the way.[3]

Sources: www.boeing.com and www.peaceworks.com – both are worth a visit, and *The Economist*, "Nokia, the Giant's Makeover," June 18, 2005, p. 59.

[1] Circa 2006 about half of Boeing's business is defense related (www.boeing.com).

[2] European commercial aircraft manufacturer Airbus is beginning to catch up, employing 52,000 people around the world (www.airbus.com).

[3] In response to the criticism of globalization catalyzed by the riots in Seattle in 1999 a growing literature argues for trade as a fundamental cause of peace. For a variety of such arguments, see *The Economist*, "Human Evolution, Homo Economicus?" April 9, 2005, pp. 67–68; James Flanigan, "Globalization Is Doing a World of Good for the U.S.," *Los Angeles Times*, April 24, 2005, pp. C1, C4; Jagdish Bhatwati, *In Defense of Globalization* (Oxford: Oxford University Press, 2004); Pietra Rivoli, *The Travels of a T-Shirt in the Global Economy* (New York: Wiley, 2005); Thomas L. Friedman, *The World Is Flat* (New York: Farrar, Straus, and Giroux, 2005); Jared Diamond, *Collapse* (New York: Viking, 2005); Clifford J. Schultz III, Timothy J. Burkink, Bruno Grbac, and Natasa Renko, "When Policies and Marketing Systems Explode: An Assessment of Food Marketing in the War-Ravaged Balkans and Implications for Recovery, Sustainable Peace, and Prosperity," *Journal of Public Policy and Marketing* 24, no. 1 (2005), pp. 24–37; John L. Graham, "Trade Brings Peace," in J. Ranzo and N. Martin, *War and Reconciliation* (Cambridge: Cambridge University Press, 2006).

6

the political environment:

A CRITICAL CONCERN

CHAPTER OUTLINE

Global Perspective: Chiquita Bananas and Prosciutto di Parma, Louis Vuitton Handbags, Scented Bath Oils and Soaps, and Batteries—Strange Bedfellows from the World of Politics

The Sovereignty of Nations

Stability of Government Policies
    Forms of Government
    Political Parties
    Nationalism
    Targeted Fear and/or Animosity
    Trade Disputes

Political Risks of Global Business
    Confiscation, Expropriation, and Domestication
    Economic Risks
    Political Sanctions
    Political and Social Activists and Nongovernmental Organizations
    Violence and Terrorism
    Cyberterrorism and Cybercrime

Assessing Political Vulnerability
    Politically Sensitive Products and Issues
    Forecasting Political Risk

Lessening Political Vulnerability
    Joint Ventures
    Expanding the Investment Base
    Licensing
    Planned Domestication
    Political Bargaining
    Political Payoffs

Government Encouragement

CHAPTER LEARNING OBJECTIVES

What you should learn from Chapter 6:

- What the sovereignty of nations means and how it can affect the stability of government policies
- How different governmental types, political parties, nationalism, targeted fear/animosity, and trade disputes can affect the environment for marketing in foreign countries
- The political risks of global business and the factors that affect stability
- The importance of the political system to international marketing and its effect on foreign investments
- The impact of political and social activists, violence, and terrorism on international business
- How to assess and reduce the effect of political vulnerability
- How and why governments encourage foreign investment

Global Perspective

CHIQUITA BANANAS AND PROSCIUTTO DI PARMA, LOUIS VUITTON HANDBAGS, SCENTED BATH OILS AND SOAPS, AND BATTERIES—STRANGE BEDFELLOWS FROM THE WORLD OF POLITICS

As the old saying goes, "Politics makes strange bedfellows," but in this case the only one making out is Miss Chiquita Banana. Prosciutto di Parma ham from Italy, handbags from France, bath oils and soaps from Germany, and a host of other imported products from Europe were all slapped with a 100 percent import tariff as retaliation by the U.S. government against European Union banana-import rules that favor Caribbean bananas over Latin American bananas. First imported from the United States, yet the United States has been engaged in a trade war over the last seven years that has cost numerous small businesses on both sides of the Atlantic millions of dollars. But how can this be, you ask? Politics, that's how!

One small business, Reha Enterprises, for example, sells bath oil, soap, and other supplies imported from Germany. The tariff on its most popular product, an herbal foam bath, was raised from 5 percent to 100 percent. The customs bill for six months spiraled to $37,783 from just $1,851—a 1,941 percent tax increase. For a small business whose gross sales are less than $1 million annually, it was crippling. When Mr. Rhea heard of the impending "banana war" he called everyone—his congressman, his senator, the United States Trade Representative (USTR). When he described his plight to a USTR representative, the official expressed amazement, "They were surprised I was still importing," because they thought the tariff would cut off the industry entirely. That was their intention, which, of course, would have meant killing Reha Enterprises as well.

In effect, he was told it was his fault that he got caught up in the trade war. He should have attended the hearings in Washington just like Gillette and Mattel, and maybe his products would have been dropped from the targeted list just as theirs were. Scores of European products, from clothing to stoves to glass Christmas ornaments, dolls, and ballpoint pens, that were originally targeted for the retaliatory tariffs escaped the tariff. Aggressive lobbying by large corporations, trade groups, and members of Congress got most of the threatened imported products off the list. The USTR had published a list of the targeted imports in the *Federal Register* inviting affected companies to testify. Unfortunately, the *Federal Register* was not on Rhea's reading list.

In that case, he was told, he should have hired a lobbyist in Washington to keep him briefed. Good advice—but it doesn't make much sense to a company that grosses less than $1 million a year. Other advice received from an official of the USTR included the off-the-record suggestion that he might want to change the custom number on the invoice so it would appear that he was importing goods not subject to the tariff, a decision that could, if he were caught, result in a hefty fine or jail. Smaller businesses in Europe faced similar problems as their export business dries up because of the tariffs.

How did this banana war start? The European Union imposed a quota and tariffs that favored imports from former colonies in the Caribbean and Africa, distributed by European firms, over Latin American bananas distributed by U.S. firms. Chiquita Brands International and Dole Food Company, contending that the EU's "illegal trade barriers" were costing $520 million annually in lost sales to Europe, asked the U.S. government for help. The government agreed that unfair trade barriers were damaging their business, and 100 percent tariffs on selected European imports were levied. Coincidentally, Chiquita Brands' annual campaign contributions increased from barely over $40,000 in 1991 to $1.3 million in 1998.

The European Union complained about the proposed U.S. tariffs and took a grievance to the World Trade Organization (WTO), which ruled in favor of the United States. The EU ignored the WTO and continued the banana tariffs, and the United States continued with its high tariffs—the banana war continued. Because of lack of compliance, the USTR imposed a "carousel" provision that allowed it to rotate, every six months, products that were to be targeted for the 100 percent tariffs. Like all trade disputes, this one was apparently settled, but at what cost to those caught in the middle between two nations and a giant MNC? The biggest losers were the African and Caribbean countries that Europe favored in the dispute. A glut in production has driven prices down and farmers are selling fewer bananas at lower prices. Most recently, the European Union proposed new tariffs in anticipation of Congress passing the Central American Free Trade Agreement. Will bananas be bruised again?

Sources: "U.S. Sets Import Tariffs in Latest Salvo in Ongoing Battle over Banana Trade," *Minneapolis Star Tribune*, March 4, 1999; Timothy Dove, "His by a $200,000 Bill from the Blue," *Time*, February 7, 2000, p. 54; "How to Become a Top Banana," *Time*, February 7, 2000, p. 42; Sarah Ryle, "Banana War Leaves the Caribbean a Casualty," *The Observer*, November 24, 2002; Irwin Stelzer, "Opening Shots in a New Style of Trade Warfare," *Sunday Times*, June 5, 2005, B4.

Crossing Borders Boxes

These invaluable boxes offer anecdotal company examples. These entertaining examples are designed to encourage critical thinking and guide students through topics ranging from ethical to cultural to global issues facing marketers today.

CROSSING BORDERS 3.5 The World's Breadbasket to the World's Lungs

As nations prosper and economic development is sought, building roads and dams and digging tunnels to overcome physical barriers become a necessity but often at an unintended cost. For example, a 1,097-mile trip on BR-163, the road between Santarém, a port on the Amazon River, and Cuiabá, capital of the state of Mato Grosso, Brazil, can take 14 days during the rainy season. The road joins what Brazilians call the "world's breadbasket" to the "world's lungs"—the crop fields and pastures of Mato Grosso to the Amazonian rain forest. You drive on whichever bit of the road seems least likely to tear off the undercarriage of your vehicle. During the six-month rainy season, when the road becomes a river of mud, men with tractors wait for you to founder and then haul you out for a fee. Within four years, the BR-163 will become a superhighway, launching commodities toward markets in Europe and Asia, speeding computers and cell phones from Manaus to São Paulo, thus ending the near-isolation of hundreds of thousands of people living along its unpaved stretches. But at what cost?

If the past is any guide, the "lungs" will suffer. Paving the BR-163 could lay waste to thousands of square kilometers of forest, carrying deep into the jungle the "arc of deforestation" through which it passes. In general, some 85 percent of deforestation takes place within 50 kilometers of a road, because a road makes it more profitable to fell trees, first for timber and then for pasture.

According the head of the union of rural workers, "On the one hand paving BR-163 will bring development—on the other hand it will bring ruin to the region—more land grabbing, more drug trafficking. Total violence will arrive." According to a report by two research institutes, paving the BR-163 could destroy 22,000 to 49,000 [amazon] forest by 2020.

A farmer rubs his eyes while surveying land that was deforested for agricultural use in northern Brazil. At the behest of environmentalists, the government pledged new controls to reduce deforestation of Brazil's Amazon rain forest which is home to up to 30 percent of the world's animal and plant life. (© Reuters NewMedia Inc./CORBIS)

chaotic growth, reducing social inequities rather than exacerbating them, preserving the Amazon rather than despoiling it. Getting it right has now become a global project, involving NGOs,* multinationals, and grassroots groups, as well as all levels of Brazil's government. The miracle will be a road that promotes Brazil's growth while protecting the indispensable Amazon.

*NGOs are nongovernmental organizations associated with the United Nations and include such organizations as Earth Charter Initiative and Society for Conservation and Protection of Environment (SCOPE). See www.ngo.org.

Sources: "Asphalt the Jungle," *The Economist*, July 22, 2004; Steve Connor, "How a Century of Destruction Has Laid Bare the World's Rainforests," *The (London) Independent*, July 2004; Leandru V. Ferreira, "Amazonian Deforestation Models," *Science*, February 18, 2005.

CROSSING BORDERS 7.2 Ceské Budějovice, Privatization, Trademarks, and Taste Tests—What Do They Have in Common with Anheuser-Busch? Budweiser, That's What!

Anheuser-Busch (AB) launched a massive public relations program in the small Czech town of Ceské Budějovice, where a local brewery produces "Budweiser Budvar." Anheuser-Busch planted trees along main avenues, opened a new cultural center offering free English courses to citizens and management advice to budding entrepreneurs, and ran newspaper ads touting the possibilities of future cooperation.

NEW Cases

New cases, both in the book and on video, accompany the new edition, enlivening the material in the book and class discussions while broadening a student's critical thinking skills. These cases bring forth many of the topics discussed in the chapters and demonstrate how these concepts are dealt with in the real world.

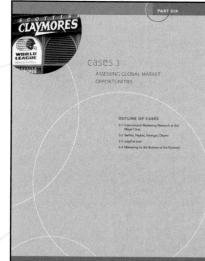

CASE 3-3 easyCar.com

Global Perspectives

At the beginning of each chapter, Global Perspectives give examples of current company experiences in global marketing. Illustrating chapter concepts, these profiles help students to combine the theory they read about with real-life application.

Video Segment

In a segment produced by author John Graham, the video takes a look at JL Design, a U.S.-based manufacturer of athletic apparel. This segment examines how a small business grew to marketing their products internationally and how it has managed its growth within a global market.

Online Learning Center

Numerous resources available for both Instructors and Students are online at www.mhhe.com/cateora07. Instructor resources include downloadable versions of the Instructor's Manual, PowerPoint presentation, and Instructor Notes to accompany the videos. Student study tools include Chapter Quizzes, PowerPoint International Resource Links, and the Country Notebook Online with an interactive component so students can complete this popular marketing plan project online.

BRIEF CONTENTS

Part One
An Overview

1 The Scope and Challenge of International Marketing 2

2 The Dynamic Environment of International Trade 26

Part Two
The Cultural Environment of Global Markets

3 History and Geography: The Foundations of Culture 54

4 Cultural Dynamics in Assessing Global Markets 92

5 Culture, Management Style, and Business Systems 122

6 The Political Environment: A Critical Concern 156

7 The International Legal Environment: Playing by the Rules 180

Part Three
Assessing Global Market Opportunities

8 Developing a Global Vision through Marketing Research 212

9 Emerging Markets 244

10 Multinational Market Regions and Market Groups 278

Part Four
Developing Global Marketing Strategies

11 Global Marketing Management: Planning and Organization 310

12 Products and Services for Consumers 336

13 Products and Services for Businesses 368

14 International Marketing Channels 394

15 Exporting and Logistics: Special Issues for Business 432

16 Integrated Marketing Communications and International Advertising 466

17 Personal Selling and Sales Management 500

18 Pricing for International Markets 526

Part Five
Implementing Global Marketing Strategies

19 Negotiating with International Customers, Partners, and Regulators 556

Part Six
Supplementary Material

THE COUNTRY NOTEBOOK—A Guide for Developing a Marketing Plan 585

CASES

1 An Overview 595

1-1 Starbucks—Going Global Fast 596
1-2 Nestlé: The Infant Formula Controversy 600
1-3 Coke and Pepsi Learn to Compete in India 604
1-4 Marketing Microwave Ovens to a New Market Segment 610

2 The Cultural Environment of Global Marketing 613

2-1 The Not-So-Wonderful World of EuroDisney— Things Are Better Now at Paris Disneyland 614
2-2 Cultural Norms, Fair & Lovely, and Advertising 618
2-3 Starnes-Brenner Machine Tool Company: To Bribe or Not to Bribe? 621
2-4 Ethics and Airbus 624
2-5 Coping with Corruption in Trading with China 629
2-6 When International Buyers and Sellers Disagree 631
2-7 McDonald's and Obesity 632

3 Assessing Global Market Opportunities 635

3-1 International Marketing Research at the Mayo Clinic 636
3-2 Swifter, Higher, Stronger, Dearer 640
3-3 easyCar.com 644
3-4 Marketing to the Bottom of the Pyramid 650

4 Developing Global Marketing Strategies 653

4-1 McDonald's Great Britain— The Turnaround 654
4-2 Tambrands: Overcoming Cultural Resistance 656
4-3 Iberia Airlines Builds a BATNA 659
4-4 Sales Negotiations Abroad for MRI Systems 662

4-5 *National Office Machines—Motivating*
   Japanese Salespeople: Straight Salary or
   Commission? 663
4-6 *AIDS, Condoms, and Carnival* 666
4-7 *Making Socially Responsible and Ethical*
   Marketing Decisions: Selling Tobacco to Third
   World Countries 670

Glossary 675
Name Index 683
Subject Index 689

PART ONE

AN OVERVIEW

The Scope and
Challenge of International
Marketing   2

Global Perspective: Global
    Commerce Causes Peace   3
The Internationalization of U.S.
    Business   6
International Marketing Defined   9
The International Marketing
    Task   10
    Marketing Decision
        Factors   10
    Aspects of the Domestic
        Environment   11
    Aspects of the Foreign
        Environment   12
Environmental Adaptation
    Needed   14
The Self-Reference Criterion and
    Ethnocentrism: Major
    Obstacles   15
Developing a Global Awareness   17
Stages of International Marketing
    Involvement   18
    No Direct Foreign
        Marketing   19

Infrequent Foreign
    Marketing   19
Regular Foreign
    Marketing   19
International Marketing   19
Global Marketing   20
Strategic Orientation   22
    Domestic Market Extension
        Orientation   22
    Multidomestic Market
        Orientation   22
    Global Market Orientation   23
The Orientation of International
    Marketing   23

The Dynamic Environment
of International Trade   26

Global Perspective: Trade
    Barriers—An International
    Marketer's Minefield   27
The Twentieth to the Twenty-First
    Century   29
    World Trade and U.S.
        Multinationals   30

The First Decade of the
    Twenty-First Century and
    Beyond   33
Balance of Payments   35
Protectionism   37
    Protection Logic and
        Illogic   37
    Trade Barriers   39
Easing Trade Restrictions   45
    The Omnibus Trade and
        Competitiveness Act   45
    General Agreement on Tariffs
        and Trade   46
    World Trade Organization   48
    Skirting the Spirit of GATT and
        WTO   49
The International Monetary Fund
    and World Bank Group   49
Protests against Global
    Institutions   51

PART TWO

THE CULTURAL ENVIRONMENT OF GLOBAL MARKETS

3 History and Geography: The Foundations of Culture **54**

Global Perspective: Birth of a Nation—Panama in 67 Hours **55**
Historical Perspective in Global Business **56**
History and Contemporary Behavior **56**
History Is Subjective **57**
Manifest Destiny and the Monroe Doctrine **59**
Geography and Global Markets **62**
Climate and Topography **63**
Geography, Nature, and Economic Growth **65**
Social Responsibility and Environmental Management **67**
Resources **70**
Dynamics of Global Population Trends **71**
Controlling Population Growth **72**
Rural/Urban Migration **73**
Population Decline and Aging **74**
Worker Shortage and Immigration **76**
World Trade Routes **77**
Communication Links **78**

World Maps **81**

4 Cultural Dynamics in Assessing Global Markets **92**

Global Perspective: Equities and eBay—Culture Gets in the Way **93**

Culture's Pervasive Impact **94**
Definitions and Origins of Culture **98**
Geography **99**
History **102**
The Political Economy **102**
Technology **102**
Social Institutions **103**
Elements of Culture **105**
Cultural Values **106**
Rituals **108**
Symbols **109**
Beliefs **112**
Thought Processes **113**
Cultural Knowledge **113**
Factual versus Interpretive Knowledge **114**
Cultural Sensitivity and Tolerance **115**
Cultural Change **115**
Cultural Borrowing **116**
Similarities: An Illusion **116**
Resistance to Change **117**
Planned and Unplanned Cultural Change **118**
Consequences of Innovation **119**

5 Culture, Management Style, and Business Systems **122**

Global Perspective: Do Blondes Have More Fun in Japan? **123**
Required Adaptation **124**
Degree of Adaptation **125**
Imperatives, Electives, and Exclusives **125**
The Impact of American Culture on Management Style **127**

Management Styles around the World **130**
Authority and Decision Making **130**
Management Objectives and Aspirations **132**
Communication Styles **134**
Formality and Tempo **137**
P-Time versus M-Time **138**
Negotiations Emphasis **140**
Gender Bias in International Business **140**
Business Ethics **142**
Corruption Defined **142**
The Western Focus on Bribery **143**
Bribery: Variations on a Theme **146**
Ethical and Socially Responsible Decisions **148**
Culture's Influence on Strategic Thinking **149**
A Synthesis, Relationship-Oriented versus Information-Oriented Cultures **151**

6 The Political Environment: A Critical Concern **156**

Global Perspective: Chiquita Bananas and Prosciutto di Parma, Louis Vuitton Handbags, Scented Bath Oils and Soaps, and Batteries— Strange Bedfollows from the World of Politics **157**
The Sovereignty of Nations **158**
Stability of Government Policies **159**
Forms of Government **161**

Political Parties   162

Nationalism   163

*Targeted Fear and/or
   Animosity   164*

Trade Disputes   165

Political Risks of Global
   Business   166

*Confiscation, Expropriation,
   and Domestication   166*

Economic Risks   167

Political Sanctions   169

*Political and Social Activists
   and Nongovernmental
   Organizations   169*

Violence and Terrorism   172

*Cyberterrorism and
   Cybercrime   172*

Assessing Political
   Vulnerability   173

*Politically Sensitive Products
   and Issues   173*

Forecasting Political Risk   174

Lessening Political
   Vulnerability   176

Joint Ventures   177

*Expanding the Investment
   Base   177*

Licensing   177

Planned Domestication   177

Political Bargaining   177

Political Payoffs   178

Government Encouragement   178

7 The International Legal
Environment: Playing by the
Rules   180

Global Perspective: The Pajama
   Caper   181

Bases for Legal Systems   182

Common and Code Law   183

Islamic Law   185

Marxist-Socialist Tenets   186

Jurisdiction in International Legal
   Disputes   186

International Dispute
   Resolution   187

Conciliation   187

Arbitration   189

Litigation   190

Protection of Intellectual Property
   Rights: A Special
   Problem   191

Counterfeiting and Piracy   191

Inadequate Protection   194

*Prior Use versus
   Registration   194*

International Conventions   196

Commercial Law within
   Countries   198

Marketing Laws   198

*Green Marketing
   Legislation   201*

Antitrust   202

U.S. Laws Apply in Host
   Countries   203

*Foreign Corrupt Practices
   Act   203*

National Security Laws   204

Antitrust Laws   205

Antiboycott Law   205

*Extraterritoriality of U.S.
   Laws   206*

Cyberlaw: Unresolved Issues   207

*Domain Names and
   Cybersquatters   207*

Taxes   209

*Jurisdiction of Disputes and
   Validity of Contracts   209*

PART THREE

ASSESSING GLOBAL MARKET OPPORTUNITIES

Developing a Global Vision
through Marketing
Research   212

Global Perspective: Selling Apples
   in Japan Can Be a Bruising
   Business   213
Breadth and Scope of International
   Marketing Research   215
The Research Process   216
Defining the Problem and
   Establishing Research
   Objectives   217
Problems of Availability and Use of
   Secondary Data   218
   Availability of Data   *218*
   Reliability of Data   *219*
   Comparability of Data   *220*
   *Validating Secondary
      Data*   *220*
Gathering Primary Data:
   Quantitative and Qualitative
   Research   221
Problems of Gathering Primary
   Data   224
   *Ability to Communicate
      Opinions*   *224*
Willingness to Respond   224
   Sampling in Field Surveys   *225*
   *Language and
      Comprehension*   *226*
Multicultural Research: A Special
   Problem   229
Research on the Internet: A
   Growing Opportunity   230
Estimating Market Demand   232
   Expert Opinion   *232*
   Analogy   *232*
Problems in Analyzing and
   Interpreting Research
   Information   234

Responsibility for Conducting
   Marketing Research   235
Communicating with Decision
   Makers   236
Appendix: Sources of Secondary
   Data   238

Emerging Markets   244

Global Perspective: Wal-Mart,
   Tide, and Three-Snake
   Wine   245
Marketing and Economic
   Development   246
   *Stages of Economic
      Development*   *247*
   NIC Growth Factors   *249*
   *Information Technology, the
      Internet, and Economic
      Development*   *251*
   *Objectives of Developing
      Countries*   *252*
   *Infrastructure and
      Development*   *253*
   Marketing's Contributions   *254*
Marketing in a Developing
   Country   256
   *Level of Market
      Development*   *256*
   *Demand in a Developing
      Country*   *256*
   *Bottom of the Pyramid Markets
      (BOPMs)*   *259*
Developing Countries and Emerging
   Markets   261
   Latin America   *263*
   *Eastern Europe and the
      Baltic States*   *265*
   Asia   *267*
   Newest Emerging Markets   *273*

Strategic Implications for
   Marketing   274

Multinational Market
Regions and Market
Groups   278

Global Perspective: Might Free
   Trade Bring Peace to the
   Middle East?   279
La Raison d'Etre   280
   Economic Factors   *281*
   Political Factors   *281*
   *Geographic and Temporal
      Proximity*   *282*
   Cultural Factors   *282*
Patterns of Multinational
   Cooperation   282
Global Markets and Multinational
   Market Groups   284
Europe   285
   *A Brief History of European
      Integration*   *286*
   European Union   *289*
   *Strategic Implications for
      Marketing in Europe*   *292*
   *Marketing Mix
      Implications*   *294*
   *The Commonwealth of
      Independent States*   *294*
The Americas   296
   *North American Free Trade
      Agreement*   *296*
   United States–Central
      American Free Trade
      Agreement–Dominican
      Republic Free Trade
      Agreement (CAFTA)   300
   *Southern Cone Free Trade Area
      (Mercosur)*   *300*

Latin American Economic
Cooperation 301
NAFTA to FTAA or
SAFTA? 303
Asian-Pacific Rim 303

Association of Southeast Asian
States 303
Asia-Pacific Economic
Cooperation 305
Africa 305

Middle East 306
Regional Trading Groups and
Emerging Markets 308

PART FOUR

DEVELOPING GLOBAL MARKETING STRATEGIES

Global Marketing
Management: Planning and
Organization 310

Global Perspective: Global
Gateways 311
Global Marketing Management 312
The Nestlé Way: Evolution Not
Revolution 314
Benefits of Global
Marketing 315
Planning for Global Markets 317
Company Objectives and
Resources 317
International Commitment 318
The Planning Process 318
Alternative Market-Entry
Strategies 322
Exporting 323
Contractual Agreements 325
Strategic International
Alliances 327
Direct Foreign Investment 332
Organizing for Global
Competition 333
Locus of Decision 334

Centralized versus
Decentralized
Organizations 334

Products and Services for
Consumers 336

Global Perspective: Hong Kong—
Disney Rolls the Dice
Again 337
Quality 338
Quality Defined 339
Maintaining Quality 340
Physical or Mandatory
Requirements and
Adaptation 341
Green Marketing and Product
Development 341
Products and Culture 343
Innovative Products and
Adaptation 345
Diffusion of Innovations 346
Production of Innovations 349
Analyzing Product Components for
Adaptation 350
Core Component 350

Packaging Component 351
Support Services
Component 353
Marketing Consumer Services
Globally 355
Services Opportunities in
Global Markets 355
Barriers to Entering Global
Markets for Consumer
Services 357
Brands in International
Markets 360
Global Brands 362
National Brands 363
Country-of-Origin Effect and
Global Brands 364
Private Brands 366

Products and Services for
Businesses 368

Global Perspective: Intel, the Boom
and the Inescapable Bust 369
Demand in Global Business-to-
Business Markets 371
The Volatility of Industrial
Demand 372

Stages of Economic
Development   375
Technology and Market
Demand   375
Quality and Global Standards   376
Quality Is Defined by the
Buyer   376
ISO 9000 Certification: An
International Standard of
Quality   380
Business Services   381
After-Sale Services   382
Other Business Services   384
Trade Shows: A Crucial Part of
Business-to-Business
Marketing   385
Relationship Marketing in
Business-to-Business
Contexts   388

14 International Marketing
Channels   394

Global Perspective: A Single Stick
of Doublemint Today—
18 Billion Tomorrow   395
Channel-of-Distribution
Structures   396
Import-Oriented Distribution
Structure   396
Japanese Distribution
Structure   397
Trends: From Traditional to
Modern Channel
Structures   402
Distribution Patterns   405
General Patterns   405
Retail Patterns   407
Alternative Middleman
Choices   409
Home-Country
Middlemen   411
Foreign-Country
Middlemen   415
Government-Affiliated
Middlemen   417
Factors Affecting Choice of
Channels   419
Cost   419
Capital Requirements   420
Control   420
Coverage   420

Character   420
Continuity   421
Locating, Selecting, and Motivating
Channel Members   422
Locating Middlemen   422
Selecting Middlemen   422
Motivating Middlemen   423
Terminating Middlemen   423
Controlling Middlemen   424
The Internet   425

15 Exporting and Logistics:
Special Issues for
Business   432

Global Perspective: An Export Sale:
From Trade Show to
Installation   433
Export Restrictions   436
Determining Export
Requirements   436
ELAIN, STELA, ERIC, and
SNAP   440
Import Restrictions   441
Tariffs   441
Exchange Permits   442
Quotas   442
Import Licenses   442
Standards   443
Boycotts   444
Voluntary Agreements   444
Other Restrictions   444
Terms of Sale   445
Getting Paid: Foreign Commercial
Payments   446
Letters of Credit   446
Bills of Exchange   448
Cash in Advance   449
Open Accounts   449
Forfaiting   449
Export Documents   449
Packing and Marking   451
Customs-Privileged Facilities   451
Foreign Trade Zones   451
Offshore Assembly
(Maquiladoras)   452
Logistics   453
Interdependence of Physical
Distribution
Activities   453

Benefits of a Physical
Distribution System   456
Export Shipping and
Warehousing   456
Foreign Freight
Forwarder   459
International Logistics and
Supply Chain
Management   459
Terrorism and Logistics   460
Cargo and Container Security
Initiative   461
Customs–Trade Partnership
against Terrorism   462
Electronic Tracking   462

16 Integrated Marketing
Communications and
International
Advertising   466

Global Perspective: Barbie versus
Mulan   467
Sales Promotions in International
Markets   468
International Public
Relations   470
International Advertising   471
Advertising Strategy and
Goals   474
Product Attribute and Benefit
Segmentation   475
Regional Segmentation   478
The Message: Creative
Challenges   479
Global Advertising and the
Communications
Process   479
Legal Constraints   483
Linguistic Limitations   485
Cultural Diversity   486
Media Limitations   487
Production and Cost
Limitations   487
Media Planning and
Analysis   488
Tactical Considerations   488
Campaign Execution and
Advertising Agencies   496
International Control of Advertising:
Broader Issues   497

17 Personal Selling and Sales Management   500

Global Perspective: International Assignments Are Glamorous, Right?   501
Designing the Sales Force   502
Recruiting Marketing and Sales Personnel   504
  Expatriates   *504*
  Virtual Expatriates   *505*
  Local Nationals   *506*
  Third-Country Nationals   *509*
  Host-Country Restrictions   *509*
Selecting Sales and Marketing Personnel   509
Training for International Marketing   512
Motivating Sales Personnel   513
Designing Compensation Systems   515
  For Expatriates   *515*
  For a Global Sales Force   *516*
Evaluating and Controlling Sales Representatives   518
Preparing U.S. Personnel for Foreign Assignments   518
  Overcoming Reluctance to Accept a Foreign Assignment   *519*
  Reducing the Rate of Early Returns   *519*

Successful Expatriate Repatriation   *520*
Developing Cultural Awareness   521
The Changing Profile of the Global Manager   522
Foreign-Language Skills   524

18 Pricing for International Markets   526

Global Perspective: The Price War   527
Pricing Policy   528
  Pricing Objectives   *528*
  Parallel Imports   *529*
Approaches to International Pricing   532
  Full-Cost versus Variable-Cost Pricing   *532*
  Skimming versus Penetration Pricing   *533*
Price Escalation   534
  Costs of Exporting   *535*
  Taxes, Tariffs, and Administrative Costs   *535*
  Inflation   *535*
  Deflation   *536*
  Exchange Rate Fluctuations   *536*
  Varying Currency Values   *537*

Middleman and Transportation Costs   *538*
Sample Effects of Price Escalation   539
Approaches to Reducing Price Escalation   540
  Lowering Cost of Goods   *540*
  Lowering Tariffs   *541*
  Lowering Distribution Costs   *543*
  Using Foreign Trade Zones to Lessen Price Escalation   *543*
  Dumping   *544*
Leasing in International Markets   545
Countertrade as a Pricing Tool   546
  Types of Countertrade   *547*
  Problems of Countertrading   *548*
  The Internet and Countertrading   *549*
  Proactive Countertrade Strategy   *549*
Transfer Pricing Strategy   550
Price Quotations   551
Administered Pricing   552
  Cartels   *552*
  Government-Influenced Pricing   *554*

PART FIVE

En los negocios no se consi
lo que se merece, se consig
lo que se negocia.

IMPLEMENTING GLOBAL MARKETING STRATEGIES

19 Negotiating with International Customers, Partners, and Regulators 556

Global Perspective: A Japanese
  Aisatsu 557
The Dangers of Stereotypes 559
The Pervasive Impact of Culture on
  Negotiation Behavior 560

Differences in Language and
  Nonverbal
  Behaviors 561
Differences in Values 567
Differences in Thinking and
  Decision-Making
  Processes 569
Implications for Managers and
  Negotiators 570

Negotiation Teams 570
Negotiation Preliminaries 572
At the Negotiation Table 575
After Negotiations 581
Conclusions 582

PART SIX

SUPPLEMENTARY MATERIAL

THE COUNTRY NOTEBOOK—
A Guide for Developing a
Marketing Plan   585

CASES

1 An Overview   595

*1-1 Starbucks—Going Global
Fast   596*

*1-2 Nestlé: The Infant Formula
Controversy   600*

*1-3 Coke and Pepsi Learn to
Compete in India   604*

*1-4 Marketing Microwave Ovens to
a New Market Segment   610*

2 The Cultural Environment of
Global Marketing   613

*2-1 The Not-So-Wonderful World of
EuroDisney—Things Are Better
Now at Paris Disneyland   614*

*2-2 Cultural Norms, Fair & Lovely,
and Advertising   618*

*2-3 Starnes-Brenner Machine Tool
Company: To Bribe or Not to
Bribe?   621*

2-4 Ethics and Airbus   624

*2-5 Coping with Corruption in
Trading with China   629*

*2-6 When International Buyers and
Sellers Disagree   631*

2-7 McDonald's and Obesity   632

3 Assessing Global Market
Opportunities   635

*3-1 International Marketing Research
at the Mayo Clinic   636*

*3-2 Swifter, Higher, Stronger,
Dearer   640*

3-3 easyCar.com   644

*3-4 Marketing to the Bottom of the
Pyramid   650*

4 Developing Global
Marketing Strategies   653

*4-1 McDonald's Great Britain—The
Turnaround   654*

*4-2 Tambrands: Overcoming
Cultural Resistance   656*

*4-3 Iberia Airlines Builds a
BATNA   659*

*4-4 Sales Negotiations Abroad for
MRI Systems   662*

*4-5 National Office Machines—
Motivating Japanese Salespeople:
Straight Salary or
Commission?   663*

*4-6 AIDS, Condoms, and
Carnival   666*

*4-7 Making Socially Responsible
and Ethical Marketing
Decisions: Selling Tobacco to
Third World Countries   670*

Glossary   675

Name Index   683

Subject Index   689

LIST OF "CROSSING BORDERS" BOXES

PART ONE

An Overview

1 The Scope and Challenge of International Marketing 2

  1.1 What Do French Farmers, Chinese Fisherman, and Russian Hackers Have in Common? 6
  1.2 Blanca Nieves, La Cenicienta y Bimbo (Snow White, Cinderella, and Bimbo) 8
  1.3 Mobile Phones, Economic Development, and Shrinking the Digital Divide 13
  1.4 Napster Lost the Battle, But the War over Intellectual Property Rights Rages On Worldwide 16
  1.5 Orange County, CA, Travels East and West 21

2 The Dynamic Environment of International Trade 26

  2.1 Trade Barriers, Hypocrisy, and the United States 38
  2.2 A Word for Open Markets 39
  2.3 Crossing Borders with Monkeys in His Pants 41
  2.4 The Dumper Becomes the Dumped Upon and Vice-Versa 44

PART TWO

The Cultural Environment of Global Markets

3 History and Geography: The Foundations of Culture 54

  3.1 Welcome to the Land of the Father of Aviation 57
  3.2 What Do the Mexican-American War, Ireland, and Gringo Have in Common? 60
  3.3 Microsoft Adapts Encarta to "Local History" 62
  3.4 Fog, Fog Everywhere and Water to Drink 63
  3.5 The World's Breadbasket to the World's Lungs 68
  3.6 Garbage without a Country—The Final Solution 69
  3.7 Where Have All the Women Gone? 76

4 Cultural Dynamics in Assessing Global Markets 92

  4.1 It's Not the Gift That Counts, but How You Present It 108
  4.2 Ici on Parle Français 110
  4.3 Gaining Cultural Awareness in 17th- and 18th-Century England: The Grand Tour 114
  4.4 Cultures Are Just Different, Not Right or Wrong, Better or Worse 115

5 Culture, Management Style, and Business Systems 122

  5.1 Don't Beat Your Mother-in-Law! 131
  5.2 The American Tourist and the Mexican Fisherman 133
  5.3 A Classic—Edward T. Hall's the Language [Symbolism] of Space 134
  5.4 Time: A Many-Cultured Thing 138
  5.5 Bangladesh at the Bottom of the Corruption List? Uganda is Moving Up. 147

6 The Political Environment: A Critical Concern 156

  6.1 Coke's Back and It Still Has the Secret 164
  6.2 Trade Does Not Work as a Stick, Only as a Carrot 170
  6.3 Curbing Child Labor—Boycotts, Rallies, and Demonstrations Get Attention, but Is There a Better Way? 171
  6.4 When States Fail: Dodging the Bullet in Former Yugoslavia 175

7 The International Legal Environment: Playing by the Rules 180

  7.1 Patent Law: The United States versus Japan—Differences in Culture Do Matter 184
  7.2 České Budějovice, Privatization, Trademarks, and Taste Tests—What Do They Have in Common with Anheuser-Busch? Budweiser, That's What! 188
  7.3 Counterfeit, Pirated, or the Original—Take Your Choice 192
  7.4 Aspirin in Russia, Bayer in the United States—It's Enough to Give You a Headache 195

PART THREE

Assessing Global Market Opportunities

8 Developing a Global Vision through Marketing Research 212

    8.1 Headache? Take Two Aspirin and Lie Down 219
    8.2 Oops! Even the Best Companies Can Make Mistakes 222
    8.3 China Handcuffs Marketing Researcher 223
    8.4 Forecasting the Global Health Care Market 233

9 Emerging Markets 244

    9.1 The Benefits of Information Technology in Village Life 253
    9.2 Infrastructure: India 255
    9.3 Got Distribution Problems? Call Grandma or Your Local University! 258
    9.4 Marketing in the Third World: Teaching, Pricing, and Community Usage 263
    9.5 In Developing Countries, Opportunity Means Creating It 270

10 Multinational Market Regions and Market Groups 278

    10.1 Free Trade Means Losing Jobs— Or Does It? 283
    10.2 There Are Myths and Then There Are Euromyths 290
    10.3 The Death of the Drachma 292
    10.4 Americans Obey European Rules 297

PART FOUR

Developing Global Marketing Strategies

11 Global Marketing Management: Planning and Organization 310

    11.1 Swedish Takeout 316
    11.2 There Was a Guy Riding a Bike and Talking on His Cell Phone 318
    11.3 The Men Who Would Be Pizza Kings 326
    11.4 The Consortium Goes Corporate—Bad News for Boeing? 331

12 Products and Services for Consumers 336

    12.1 The Quality of Food Is a Matter of Taste 340
    12.2 In Germany, Video Games Showing Frontal Nudity Are OK, but Blood Is Verboten 342
    12.3 So This Is What Is Called an Innovation—But Does It Flush? 348
    12.4 D'oh! Or Just Dough In Dubai? 352
    12.5 So Your Computer Isn't Working? 354
    12.6 Even the Old Technology and a Telemarketer Can Save Your Life 357
    12.7 Just To Go To School 358

13 Products and Services for Businesses 368

    13.1 Trade Statistics Don't Tell the Whole Story 371
    13.2 Your Hoses Are a Threat to Public Security! 378
    13.3 Yes, Opinions Do Differ about the Metric System 379
    13.4 Garbage Collection an International Service? Perhaps! 382
    13.5 No More Aching Feet, but What about the 15-Ton Russian Tank? 387

14 International Marketing Channels 394

    14.1 Mitsukoshi Department Store, Established 1611—But Will It Be there in 2011? 401
    14.2 Big-Box Bookie-Cutter Stores Don't Always Work 403
    14.3 It Depends on What "Not Satisfied" Means 409
    14.4 No More Roses for My Miami Broker 424
    14.5 Mariott.com, Marriotte.ie, Marriot.co.uk, etc. 428

15 Exporting and Logistics: Special Issues for Business 432

    15.1 Major Smuggling Ring Busted—A Sweet Deal 443
    15.2 Underwear, Outerwear, Sony Playstations and Pointed Ears—What Do They Have in Common? 452
    15.3 If the Shoe Fits, Wear It . . . or Abandon It 457
    15.4 Global Trade Compliance 460

16 Integrated Marketing Communications and International Advertising 466

    16.1 PR in the PRC 471
    16.2 Arnold Terminates Site Leaking Foreign TV Ads 482
    16.3 Joe Canack Bashes America 484
    16.4 Objections to Indian Ad Not Taken Lightly 487
    16.5 Advertising Themes That Work in Japan, Including a Polite Duck 491
    16.6 Subliminal Advertising in Russia 498

17 Personal Selling and Sales Management 500

    17.1 Sales Force Management and Global Customers 503
    17.2 The New Risks of International Travel 505
    17.3 Avon Calling—or Not? 508
    17.4 How Important Are Those Meetings? 514
    17.5 Iberia Grinds Airbus and Boeing 523
    17.6 A Look Into the Future: Tomorrow's International Leaders? An Education for the 21st Century 524

18 Pricing for International Markets 526

    18.1 How Do Levi's 501s Get to International Markets? 529
    18.2 Don't Squeeze the Charmin, Mr. Whipple— Or Change the Color 533
    18.3 When Is a Care a Truck and a Daily Planner a Diary? When the U.S. Customs Says So 541
    18.4 What Does It Mean To Be Human? 5.2 Percent, That's What 542

PART FIVE

Implementing Global Marketing Strategies

19 Negotiating with International Customers, Partners, and Regulators 556

19.1 *Poker Faces and Botox Injections* 565

19.2 *A Russian and an Indonesian Manager Talk about Negotiations* 569

19.3 *Ford Trains Executives for Negotiations with Japanese* 753

19.4 *The Digital Impact on International Negotiations* 576

19.5 *Fishing for Business in Brazil* 579

international marketing

1

The scope and challenge of international marketing

CHAPTER OUTLINE

Global Perspective: Global Commerce Causes Peace

The Internationalization of U.S. Business

International Marketing Defined

The International Marketing Task

    Marketing Decision Factors
    Aspects of the Domestic Environment
    Aspects of the Foreign Environment

Environmental Adaptation Needed

The Self-Reference Criterion and Ethnocentrism:
  Major Obstacles

Developing a Global Awareness

Stages of International Marketing Involvement

    No Direct Foreign Marketing
    Infrequent Foreign Marketing
    Regular Foreign Marketing
    International Marketing
    Global Marketing

Strategic Orientation

    Domestic Market Extension Orientation
    Multidomestic Market Orientation
    Global Market Orientation

The Orientation of *International Marketing*

CHAPTER LEARNING OBJECTIVES

What you should learn from Chapter 1:

- The changing face of U.S. business

- The scope of the international marketing task

- The importance of the self-reference criterion (SRC) in international marketing

- The progression of becoming a global marketer

- The increasing importance of global awareness

Global Perspective

GLOBAL COMMERCE CAUSES PEACE

Global commerce thrives during peacetime. The economic boom in North America during the late 1990s was in large part due to the end of the Cold War and the opening of the formerly communist countries to the world trading system. However, we should also understand the important role that trade and international marketing play in producing peace.

Boeing Company, America's largest exporter, is perhaps the most prominent example. Although many would argue that Boeing's military sales (aircraft and missiles) do not exactly promote peace, over the years that business has constituted only about 20 percent of the company's commercial activity. Up until 2002, of Boeing's some $60 billion in annual revenues, about 65 percent came from sales of commercial jets around the world and another 15 percent from space and communications technologies. Unfortunately, these historical numbers are being skewed by American military spending and the damage done to tourism by terrorism.[1] Even so, the company still counts customers in 145 countries, and its 159,000 employees work in 67 countries. Its more than 11,000 commercial jets in service around the world carry about one billion travelers per year. Its NASA Services division is the lead contractor in the construction and operation of the 16-country International Space Station, first manned by an American and two Russians in the fall of 2000. The Space and Intelligence Systems Division also produces and launches communications satellites affecting people in every country.

All the activity associated with the development, production, and marketing of commercial aircraft and space vehicles requires millions of people from around the world to work together. Moreover, no company does more[2] to enable people from all countries to meet face to face for both recreation and commerce. All this interaction yields not just the mutual gain associated with business relationships but also personal relationships and mutual understanding. The latter are the foundation of global peace and prosperity.

Another class of companies that promotes global dialogue and therefore peace is the mobile phone industry. During 2005 more than 700 million new mobile phones were purchased around the world connecting more than one-quarter of all people on the planet. Nokia (Finland), the market leader, is well ahead of American manufacturer Motorola, Samsung (S. Korea), LG (S. Korea), Siemens (Germany), and Sony Ericsson (Japan/Sweden).

Individuals and small companies also make a difference, perhaps a subtler one than large multinational companies, but one just as important in the aggregate. Our favorite example is Daniel Lubetzky's company, PeaceWorks. Mr. Lubetzky used a fellowship at Stanford Law School to study how to foster joint ventures between Arabs and Israelis. Then, following his own advice, he created a company that combines basil pesto from Israel with other raw materials and glass jars supplied by an Arab partner to produce the first product in a line he calls Moshe & Ali's Gourmet Foods. The company now sells some 60 products in 3,000 stores in the United States and has its headquarters on Park Avenue in New York and business operations in Israel, Egypt, Indonesia, Turkey, Sri Lanka, and South Africa. Again, beyond the measurable commercial benefits of cooperation between the involved Arabs, Israelis, and others is the longer-lasting and more fundamental appreciation for one another's circumstances and character.

International marketing is hard work. Making sales calls is no vacation even in Paris when you've been there 10 times before. But international marketing is important work. It can enrich you, your family, your company, and your country. And ultimately, when international marketing is done well, by large companies or small, the needs and wants of customers in other lands are well understood, and prosperity and peace are promoted along the way.[3]

Sources: www.boeing.com and www.peaceworks.com—both are worth a visit; and *The Economist*, "Nokia, the Giant's Makeover," June 18, 2005, p. 59.

---

[1]Circa 2006 about half of Boeing's business is defense related (www.boeing.com).

[2]European commercial aircraft manufacturer Airbus is beginning to catch up, employing 52,000 people around the world (www.airbus.com).

[3]In response to the criticism of globalization catalyzed by the riots in Seattle in 1999 a growing literature argues for trade as a fundamental cause of peace. For a variety of such arguments, see *The Economist*, "Human Evolution, Homo Economicus?" April 9, 2005, pp. 67–68; James Flanigan, "Globalization Is Doing a World of Good for the U.S.," *Los Angeles Times*, April 24, 2005, pp. C1, C4; Jagdish Bhabwati, *In Defense of Globalization* (Oxford: Oxford University Press, 2004); Pietra Rivoli, *The Travels of a T-Shirt in the Global Economy* (New York: Wiley, 2005); Thomas L. Friedman, *The World Is Flat* (New York: Farrar, Straus, and Giroux, 2005); Jared Diamond, *Collapse* (New York: Viking, 2005); Clifford J. Schultz III, Timothy J. Burkink, Bruno Grbac, and Natasa Renko, "When Policies and Marketing Systems Explode: An Assessment of Food Marketing in the War-Ravaged Balkans and Implications for Recovery, Sustainable Peace, and Prosperity," *Journal of Public Policy and Marketing* 24, no. 1 (2005), pp. 24–37; John L. Graham, "Trade Brings Peace," in J. Runzo and N. Martin, *War and Reconciliation* (Cambridge: Cambridge University Press, 2006).

"Never before in American history have U.S. businesses, large and small, been so deeply involved in and affected by international business. A global economic boom, unprecedented in modern economic history, has been under way as the drive for efficiency, productivity, and open, unregulated markets sweeps the world. Powerful economic, technological, industrial, political, and demographic forces are converging to build the foundation of a new global economic order on which the structure of a one-world economic and market system will be built."

When we wrote those words five years ago to open the eleventh edition of this book the world was a very different place. The nation was still mesmerized by the information technology boom of the late 1990s. Most did not visualize the high-tech bust of 2001 or the associated Enron and WorldCom scandals. No one could have imagined the September 11, 2001, disasters, not even the perpetrators. Wars in Afghanistan and Iraq were not on the horizon. The major international conflict grabbing headlines then was the series of diplomatic dustups among China, Taiwan, and the United States. Who could have predicted the disruptions associated with the 2003 SARS outbreak in Asia? The great Indian Ocean tsunami of 2004 was perhaps impossible to anticipate.[4] Oil at over $60 per barrel was unthinkable then. We wrote about the promise of the space program and the international space station whose future was dramatically jeopardized by the Columbia shuttle tragedy and associated NASA budget cuts.

Through all these major events American consumers continued to spend, keeping the world economy afloat. Layoffs at industrial icons such as United Airlines and Boeing and a generally tough job market didn't slow the booming American housing market. Lower government interest rates meant a refinancing stampede, throwing the cash that fueled the consumer spending. And seeing into the future is harder than ever. Most experts expect global terrorism to increase, and the carnage in Bali, Madrid, and London seem to prove the point. Many predict a global housing price collapse and the associated economic disruptions.[5] Finally, as the global economy continues to wobble, international trade tensions take on new importance.[6] Competition from new Chinese companies has begun to raise concerns in the United States.[7] The steady growth of the U.S. trade and balance of payments deficits is particularly worrisome,[8] particularly those with China.[9]

Aside from the tragic loss of life resulting from the terrorism of September 11, the event also represents a direct attack on the world trading system. Hopefully, the destruction of the New York City World Trade Center will be the low point for global commerce and peace as the remainder of the second millennium unfolds. (© Reuters NewMedia Inc./CORBIS)

International marketing is affected by and affects all these things. For the first time in history McDonald's pulled out of international markets in both Latin America and the Middle East.[10] Slow economies, increasing competition, and anti-Americanism have impacted their sales in both regions. Moreover, recall that the September 11 attacks were on the *World Trade* Center in New York City. Indeed, the salient lesson for those involved in international commerce at the turn of the 21st century is to expect the unexpected. Any executive experienced in international business will verify that things never go as planned in global commerce. You still have to plan and forecast, but markets, particularly international ones, are ultimately unpredictable. The natural fluctuations in markets are best managed through building strong interpersonal and commercial relationships and broad portfolios of businesses. Flexibility means survival.

---

[4]Jim Gomez, "Indonesia Starts to Push U.S. Away, American Carrier Retreats from Nation Hit by Tsunami," *Chicago Sun-Times*, January 13, 2005, p. 30.

[5]*The Economist*, "In Come the Waves, The Worldwide Rise in House Prices Is the Biggest Bubble in History," June 18, 2005, pp. 66–68.

[6]Evelyn Iritani, "Trade Tension May Be Rising," *Los Angeles Times*, June 2, 2005, pp. C1, C6.

[7]Brian Bremmer and Kathleen Kerwin, "Here Come the Chinese Cars," *BusinessWeek*, June 6, 2005, pp. 34–37.

[8]Associated Press, "U.S. Trade Gap Increases by 3.6%," *Los Angeles Times*, June 18, 2005, p. C3.

[9]Heather Stewart, "Chinese Walls: The West Sees Red," *The Observer*, June 12, 2005, p. 3.

[10]"McDonald's Posts Its First Loss and Lowers Outlook for Growth," *New York Times*, January 24, 2003, p. C18.

Here the planet grows a little closer together. The European Parliament votes to start discussions with Turkey about joining the EU. Trade is beginning to bridge the religious divide between Christian Europe and Muslim Asia Minor. *(AP/Wide World Photos)*

Perhaps now, more than ever, whether or not a U.S. company wants to participate directly in international business, it cannot escape the effects of the ever-increasing number of North American firms exporting, importing, and manufacturing abroad. Nor can it ignore the number of foreign-based firms operating in U.S. markets, the growth of regional trade areas, the rapid growth of world markets, and the increasing number of competitors for global markets.

Of all the events and trends affecting global business today, four stand out as the most dynamic, the ones that will influence the shape of international business beyond today's "bumpy roads" and far into the future: (1) the rapid growth of the World Trade Organization[11] and regional free trade areas such as the North American Free Trade Area and the European Union; (2) the trend toward the acceptance of the free market system among developing countries in Latin America,[12] Asia, and eastern Europe; (3) the burgeoning impact of the Internet,[13] mobile phones, and other global media on the dissolution of national borders; and (4) the mandate to properly manage the resources[14] and global environment for the generations to come.[15]

Today most business activities are global in scope. Technology, research, capital investment, production, and marketing, distribution, and communications networks all have global dimensions. Every business must be prepared to compete in an increasingly interdependent global economic and physical environment, and all businesspeople must be aware of the effects of these trends when managing a domestic company that exports or a multinational conglomerate. As one international expert noted, every American company is international, at least to the extent that its business performance is conditioned in part by events that occur abroad. Even companies that do not operate in the international arena are affected to some degree by the success of the European Union, the export-led growth in South Korea, the revitalized Mexican economy, the economic changes taking place in China, military conflicts in the Middle East, and global warming.

Businesses are increasingly less able to avoid the influence of the internationalization of the U.S. economy, the globalization of the world's markets, and the growth of emerging markets. As competition for world markets intensifies, the number of companies operating solely in domestic markets will decrease. Or, to put it another way, it is increasingly true that the business of American business is international business.

The challenge of international marketing is to develop strategic plans that are competitive in the intensifying global markets. For a growing number of companies, being international is no longer a luxury but a necessity for economic survival. These and other issues affecting the world economy, trade, markets, and competition are discussed throughout this text.

---

[11]Elaine Sciolino, "WTO to Start Talks on Admitting Iran, U.S. Relents after Nuclear Concession," *International Herald Tribune*, May 27, 2005, p. 3.

[12]Geri Smith with Paul Magnusson, "Central America Is Holding Its Breath," *BusinessWeek*, June 20, 2005, p. 32.

[13]Thomas L. Friedman, *The World Is Flat* (New York: Farrar, Straus, and Giroux, 2005).

[14]Kenneth R. Weiss, "Seas Being Stripped of Big Fish, Study Finds," *Los Angeles Times*, May 15, 2003, p. A1.

[15]John Carey, "Global Warming; Suddenly the Climate in Washington Is Changing," *BusinessWeek*, June 27, 2005, p. 91.

CROSSING BORDERS 1.1   What Do French Farmers, Chinese Fishermen, and Russian Hackers Have in Common?

They can all disrupt American firms' international marketing efforts.

Thousands of supporters and activists gathered recently to show support for a French sheep farmer on trial for vandalizing a local McDonald's. Jose Bove has become an international legend of antiglobalization. Leader of the French Peasant Confederation, he has demonized the fast-food chain as the symbol of American trade "hegemony" and economic globalization. He and nine other farmers served six weeks in jail and paid fines for partially destroying the restaurant. Most recently, Bove has been thrown in jail again, this time for ten months, for damaging fields of genetically modified rice and corn.

Local fishermen demanded suspension of reclamation and dredging of a bay near Hong Kong where Disney has built Hong Kong Disneyland. The fishermen claim that the work has plunged water quality near the site to levels much worse than predicted, killing huge numbers of fish. The spokesman for the fishermen claims they have lost some $30 million between July and September because of depleted and diseased fish stocks.

St. Petersburg has in a decade become the capital of Russian computer hackers. These are the same folks that are reputed to have invaded Microsoft's internal network. Russia's science city has become the natural hub for high-tech computer crime. Dozens of students, teachers, and computer specialists hack into computers, seeing themselves as members of an exciting subculture that has flourished since the fall of communism. Before *glasnost* and *perestroika*, those who were dissatisfied with official Soviet culture turned to samizdat literature and bootleg tapes of Western pop music. But the Gorbachev era left little to rebel against. Today Russia's hackers, who even have their own magazine, titled *Khacker*, have created a new underground culture that perhaps offers more excitement than passing around banned poetry. The city also benefits from being near the Baltic states. Programs are copied on the black market; the latest Windows pirate always arrives in Russia months before it appears in the West. Yes, fines and prison terms are consequences if caught. But computers are readily accessible at the universities and increasingly in homes.

Sources: Agnes Lam, "Disney Dredging Killing Fish," *South China Morning Post,* November 5, 2000, p. 4; Alice Lagnado, "Russians Turn to Hacking as the New Subversion," *The Times of London,* October 28, 2000, p. 4; John Tagliabue, "Activist Jailed in Attack on Modified Crops," *New York Times,* February 27, 2003, p. 6; Brian Grow, "Hacker Hunters," *BusinessWeek,* May 30, 2005, p. 74.

The Internationalization of U.S. Business

Current interest in international marketing can be explained by changing competitive structures coupled with shifts in demand characteristics in markets throughout the world. With the increasing globalization of markets, companies find they are unavoidably enmeshed with foreign customers, competitors, and suppliers, even within their own borders. They face competition on all fronts—from domestic firms and from foreign firms. A significant portion of all CD players, computers, apparel, and dinnerware sold in the United States is foreign made. Sony, Laura Ashley, Norelco, Samsung, Toyota, and Nescafé are familiar brands in the United States, and for U.S. industry they are formidable opponents in a competitive struggle for U.S. and world markets.

Many familiar U.S. companies are now foreign controlled or headed in that direction.[16] When you drop in at a 7-Eleven convenience store or buy Firestone tires, you are buying directly from a Japanese company. Some well-known brands no longer owned by U.S. companies are Carnation (Swiss), Chrysler (German), and the all-American Smith and Wesson handgun that won the U.S. West, which is owned by a British firm. The last U.S.-owned company to manufacture TV sets was Zenith, but even it was acquired by South Korea's LG Electronics, Inc., which manufactures Goldstar TVs and other products. Pearle Vision, Universal Studios, and many more are currently owned or controlled by foreign multinational businesses (see Exhibit 1.1). Foreign investment in the United States is more than $9.6 trillion, some $2.6 trillion more than American overseas investment. Companies from the

---

[16]Evelyn Iritani, "China Showing Bigger Interest in U.S.," *Los Angeles Times,* June 22, 2005, p. C1, C6.

U.S. Companies	Foreign Owner
Firestone (tires)	Japan
Ben & Jerry's (ice cream)	U.K.
Alpo (pet food)	Switzerland
Burger King (fast food)	U.K.
Random House (publishing)	Germany
Chrysler (autos)	Germany
TV Guide (magazine)	Australia
New York Post (newspaper)	Australia
Oroweat (breads)	Mexico
Smith and Wesson (guns)	U.K.
RCA (televisions)	France/China
Chef America ("Hot Pockets" and other foods)	Switzerland
[IBM] ThinkPad (personal computers)	China
Huffy Corp. (bicycles)	China

United Kingdom lead the group of investors, with companies from the Netherlands, Japan, Germany, and Switzerland following in that order.[17]

Other foreign companies that entered the U.S. market through exporting their products into the United States realized sufficient market share to justify building and buying manufacturing plants in the United States.[18] Fuji Photo Film invested more than $300 million in a plant to service its 12 percent share of the U.S. film market. Honda, BMW, and Mercedes are all manufacturing in the United States. Investments go the other way as well. Ford bought Jaguar; PacifiCorp acquired Energy Group, the United Kingdom's largest electricity supplier and second-largest gas distributor; and Wisconsin Central Transportation, a medium-sized U.S. railroad, controls all U.K. rail freight business and runs the queen's private train via its English, Welsh & Scottish Railway unit. It has also acquired the

[17]United Press International, "Foreign Investment Increases in the U.S.," July 22, 2004; and David H. Levey and Stuart S. Brown, "The Overstretch Myth," *Foreign Affairs*, March/April 2005, pp. 1–4.

[18]Denise M. Bonilla, "Latino Market Arrives with Giant Aspirations," *Los Angeles Times*, May 7, 2003, p. B6.

Along with NAFTA have come two of Mexico's most prominent brand names. Gigante, one of Mexico's largest supermarket chains, now has several stores in southern California including this one in Anaheim. On store shelves are a variety of Bimbo bakery products. Grupo Bimbo, a growing Mexican multinational, has recently purchased American brand-named firms such as Oroweat, Webers, and Mrs. Baird's Bread.

CROSSING BORDERS 1.2

Blanca Nieves, La Cenicienta y Bimbo (Snow White, Cinderella, and Bimbo)

Bimbo is a wonderful brand name. It so well demonstrates the difficulties of marketing across borders. Of course, to middle America "bimbo" is slang for a dumb blonde. Even in *Webster's Dictionary* it's defined as ". . . a term of disparagement, a tramp."

Meanwhile in Spain, Mexico, and other Spanish-speaking countries, the word "bimbo" has no pejorative meaning. Indeed, it is often simply associated with the little white bear logo of Bimbo brand bread. Bimbo is the most popular brand of bread in Mexico and, with NAFTA, is stretching its corporate arms north and south. For example, the Mexican firm most recently acquired Mrs. Baird's Bread, the most popular local brand in Dallas, Texas, and Fargo, the most popular bread brand in Argentina. And you can now see 18-wheelers pulling truckloads of Bimbo products north on Interstate 5 toward Latino neighborhoods in Southern California.

Perhaps Bimbo is the reason the city fathers in Anaheim so feared Gigante's entrance into their city. Gigante, the Mexican-owned supermarket chain, features Bimbo buns, tomatillos, cactus pears, and other Latino favorites. Gigante already has three stores in Los Angeles County. But it was denied the city's permission to open a new market near the "Happiest Place on Earth." One has to wonder if Disneyland, Anaheim's biggest employer, may have been fretting over the juxtaposition of the Bimbo brand and its key characters, blonde little all-American Alice and her cinema sisters.

Actually, the better case can be made that the Gigante–Anaheim imbroglio was more a matter of a mix of nationalism, xenophobia, and even racism. And the city council eventually was forced to allow Gigante to open. American firms have often run into similar problems as they have expanded around the world.

Consider French nationalism. French farmers are famous for their protests—throwing lamb chops at their trade ministers and such. Or better yet, Culture Minister Jack Lang's comments about the U.S. Cartoon Network: "We must fight back against this American aggression. It is intolerable that certain North American audiovisual groups shamelessly colonize our countries."

Consider our own fear and loathing of "Japanese colonization" in both the 1920s and the 1980s. This apparent xenophobia turned to racism when Americans stoned Toyotas and Hondas but not Volkswagens and BMWs; when we decried Japanese takeovers of American firms and ignored Germany's recent gorging on the likes of Bankers Trust, Random House, and Chrysler.

PEMEX's current ban on American investments in the oil and gas industry in Mexico is a good example of nationalism. However, when British Petroleum buying ARCO is no problem, but Mexican cement giant CEMEX buying Houston's Southdown is, that's racism at work.

A cruel irony regarding Gigante's problems in Anaheim is well revealed by a quick drive around Tijuana. During the last decade the change in Tijuana's retail facade has been remarkable. In this border town, after the North American Free Trade Agreement (NAFTA), Blockbuster Video, Burger King, COSTCO, Smart & Final, and other American brands now dominate the signage.

Sources: John L. Graham, "Blanca Nieves, La Cenicienta, Y Bimbo," *La Opinion*, February 22, 2002, p. C1 (translated from the Spanish); Denise M. Bonilla, "Latino Market Arrives with Giant Aspirations," *Los Angeles Times*, May 7, 2003, p. B6; *Reuters News*, "Argentina Regulator OKs Bimbo Bread Acquisition," July 29, 2004.

company that runs rail shuttles through the Channel Tunnel. Investments by U.S. multinationals abroad are nothing new. They have been roaming the world en masse since the end of World War II, buying companies and investing in manufacturing plants. What is relatively new for U.S. companies is having their global competitors competing with them in "their" market, the United States. One of the more interesting new entrants is Chivas USA, a Mexican-owned soccer team that will play its matches in southern California.[19]

Once the private domain of domestic businesses, the vast U.S. market that provided an opportunity for continued growth must now be shared with a variety of foreign companies and products. Companies with only domestic markets have found increasing difficulty in sustaining customary rates of growth, and many are seeking foreign markets in which to expand. Companies with foreign operations find that foreign earnings are making an important overall contribution to total corporate profits. A four-year Conference Board study of

---

[19] David Davis, "Conquistador in Cleats," *Los Angeles Times Magazine*, March 13, 2005, pp. 8–11, 29–30.

Exhibit 1.2
Selected U.S. Companies
and Their International
Sales

Source: Compiled from annual reports
of listed firms, 2005

Company	Global Revenues (billions)	Percent Revenues from Outside the U.S.
Wal-Mart	$285.2	19.7
Ford Motor	171.6	49.2
General Electric	152.4	46.8
CitiGroup	86.2	58.1
Hewlett-Packard	73.1	60.3
Boeing	52.5	28.7
Intel	34.2	76.8
Disney	30.8	28.8
Coca-Cola	22.0	73.1
Apple	8.3	40.7

1,250 U.S. manufacturing companies found that multinationals of all sizes and in all industries outperformed their strictly domestic U.S. counterparts. They grew twice as fast in sales and earned significantly higher returns on equity and assets. Further, the U.S. multinationals reduced their manufacturing employment, both at home and abroad, more than domestic companies.

Exhibit 1.2 illustrates how important revenues generated on investments abroad are to U.S. companies. In many cases, foreign sales were greater than U.S. sales, demonstrating the global reach of these American brands.

Companies that never ventured abroad until recently are now seeking foreign markets. Companies with existing foreign operations realize they must be more competitive to succeed against foreign multinationals. They have found it necessary to spend more money and time improving their marketing positions abroad because competition for these growing markets is intensifying. For firms venturing into international marketing for the first time and for those already experienced, the requirement is generally the same: a thorough and complete commitment to foreign markets and, for many, new ways of operating.

International Marketing Defined

International marketing is the performance of business activities designed to plan, price, promote, and direct the flow of a company's goods and services to consumers or users in more than one nation for a profit. The only difference between the definitions of domestic marketing and international marketing is that in the latter case marketing activities take place in more than one country. This apparently minor difference, "in more than one country," accounts for the complexity and diversity found in international marketing operations. Marketing concepts, processes, and principles are universally applicable, and the marketer's task is the same whether doing business in Dimebox, Texas, or Dar es Salaam, Tanzania. Business's goal is to make a profit by promoting, pricing, and distributing products for which there is a market. If this is the case, what is the difference between domestic and international marketing?

The answer lies not with different concepts of marketing but with the environment within which marketing plans must be implemented. The uniqueness of foreign marketing comes from the range of unfamiliar problems and the variety of strategies necessary to cope with different levels of uncertainty encountered in foreign markets.

Competition, legal restraints, government controls, weather, fickle consumers, and any number of other uncontrollable elements can, and frequently do, affect the profitable outcome of good, sound marketing plans. Generally speaking, the marketer cannot control or influence these uncontrollable elements, but instead must adjust or adapt to them in a manner consistent with a successful outcome. What makes marketing interesting is the challenge of molding the controllable elements of marketing decisions (product, price, promotion, distribution, and research) within the framework of the uncontrollable elements of the marketplace (competition, politics, laws, consumer behavior, level of technology, and so forth) in such a way that marketing objectives are achieved. Even though marketing principles and concepts are universally applicable, the environment within which the marketer must implement marketing plans can change dramatically from country to country or region to region. The difficulties created by different environments are the international marketer's primary concern.

The International Marketing Task

The international marketer's task is more complicated than that of the domestic marketer because the international marketer must deal with at least two levels of uncontrollable uncertainty instead of one. Uncertainty is created by the uncontrollable elements of all business environments, but each foreign country in which a company operates adds its own unique set of uncontrollable factors.

Exhibit 1.3 illustrates the total environment of an international marketer. The inner circle depicts the controllable elements that constitute a marketer's decision area, the second circle encompasses those environmental elements at home that have some effect on foreign-operation decisions, and the outer circles represent the elements of the foreign environment for each foreign market within which the marketer operates. As the outer circles illustrate, each foreign market in which the company does business can (and usually does) present separate problems involving some or all of the uncontrollable elements. Thus, the more foreign markets in which a company operates, the greater is the possible variety of foreign environmental factors with which to contend. Frequently, a solution to a problem in country market A is not applicable to a problem in country market B.

Marketing Decision Factors

The successful manager constructs a marketing program designed for optimal adjustment to the uncertainty of the business climate. The inner circle in Exhibit 1.3 represents the area under control of the marketing manager. Assuming the necessary overall corporate resources,

Exhibit 1.3
The International Marketing Task

structures, and competencies that can limit or promote strategic choice,[20] the marketing manager blends price, product, promotion, channels-of-distribution, and research activities to capitalize on anticipated demand. The controllable elements can be altered in the long run and, usually, in the short run to adjust to changing market conditions, consumer tastes, or corporate objectives.

The outer circles surrounding the marketing decision factors represent the levels of uncertainty that are created by the domestic and foreign environments. Although the marketer can blend a marketing mix from the controllable elements, the uncontrollable factors are precisely that; the marketer must actively evaluate and, if needed, adapt. That effort, the adaptation of the marketing mix to these environmental factors, determines the outcome of the marketing enterprise.

Aspects of the Domestic Environment

The second circle in Exhibit 1.3 represents the aspects of the domestic environment that are often beyond the control of companies. These include home-country elements that can have a direct effect on the success of a foreign venture: political and legal forces, economic climate, and competition.

A political decision involving domestic foreign policy can have a direct effect on a firm's international marketing success. For example, the U.S. government placed a total ban on trade with Libya to condemn Libyan support for terrorist attacks, imposed restrictions on trade with South Africa to protest apartheid, and placed a total ban on trade with Iraq, whose actions constituted a threat to the national security of the United States and its allies. In each case, the international marketing programs of the U.S. company, whether it was IBM, Exxon, or Hawg Heaven Bait Company, were restricted by these political decisions. The U.S. government has the constitutional right to restrict foreign trade when such trade adversely affects the security or economy of the country, or when such trade is in conflict with U.S. foreign policy.

Conversely, positive effects occur when changes in foreign policy offer countries favored treatment. Such were the cases when South Africa abolished apartheid and the embargo was lifted and when the U.S. government decided to uncouple human rights issues from foreign trade policy and grant permanently normalized trade relations (PNTR) status to China, paving the way for entry into the World Trade Organization (WTO). In both cases, opportunities were created for U.S. companies. Finally, note that on occasion companies can exercise some degree of influence over such legislation in the United States. Indeed, in the case of PNTR for China, companies with substantial interests there, such as Boeing and Motorola, lobbied hard for the easing of trade restrictions.

The domestic economic climate is another important home-based uncontrollable variable with far-reaching effects on a company's competitive position in foreign markets. The capacity to invest in plants and facilities, either in domestic or foreign markets, is to a large extent a function of domestic economic vitality. It is generally true that capital tends to flow toward optimum use; however, capital must be generated before it can have mobility. Furthermore, if internal economic conditions deteriorate, restrictions against foreign investment and purchasing may be imposed to strengthen the domestic economy.

Competition within the home country can also have a profound effect on the international marketer's task.[21] For more than a century, Eastman Kodak dominated the U.S. film market and could depend on achieving profit goals that provided capital to invest in foreign markets. Without having to worry about the company's lucrative base, management had the time and resources to devise aggressive international marketing programs. However, the competitive structure changed when Fuji Photo Film became a formidable competitor by lowering film prices in the United States, opening a $300 million plant, and gaining 12 percent of the U.S. market. Then the acceptance of digital photography, with Canon[22] from Japan leading the market, has further disrupted Kodak's domestic business. As a result,

---

[20]A. Verbke, "The Evolutionary View of the MNE and the Future of Internationalization Theory," *Journal of International Business Studies* 34, no. 6 (2003), pp. 498–504.

[21]G.R.G. Benito, B. Grogaard, and R. Narula, "Environmental Influences on MNE Subsidiary Roles: Economic Integration and the Nordic Countries," *Journal of International Business Studies* 34, no. 5 (2003), pp. 443–456.

[22]*Business Wire*, "Canon Named 'America's Choice' for Digital Cameras in 2004," February 1, 2005.

Kodak has had to direct energy and resources back to the United States. Competition within its home country affects a company's domestic as well as international plans. Inextricably entwined with the effects of the domestic environment are the constraints imposed by the environment of each foreign country.

Aspects of the Foreign Environment

In addition to uncontrollable domestic elements, a significant source of uncertainty is the number of factors in the foreign environment that are often uncontrollable (depicted in Exhibit 1.3 by the outer circles). A business operating in its home country undoubtedly feels comfortable in forecasting the business climate and adjusting business decisions to these elements. The process of evaluating the uncontrollable elements in an international marketing program, however, often involves substantial doses of cultural, political, and economic shock.

A business operating in a number of foreign countries might find polar extremes in political stability, class structure, and economic climate—critical elements in business decisions. The dynamic upheavals in some countries further illustrate the problems of dramatic change in cultural, political, and economic climates over relatively short periods of time. A case in point is China, which has moved from a communist legal system in which all business was done with the state to a transitional period while a commercial legal system is developing. In this transitional phase, new laws are passed but left to be interpreted by local authorities, where confusion prevails as to what rules are still in force and what rules are no longer applicable.

For example, commercial contracts can be entered into with a Chinese company or individual only if that company or person is considered a "legal person." To be a legal person in China, the company or person must have registered as such with the Chinese government. To complicate matters further, binding negotiations may take place only with "legal representatives" of the "legal person." So if your company enters into negotiations with a Chinese company or person, you must ask for signed legal documents establishing the right to do business. The formalities of the signature must also be considered. Will a signature on a contract be binding or is it necessary to place a traditional Chinese seal on the document? Even when all is done properly, the government still might change its mind. Coca-Cola had won approval for its plan to build a new facility to produce product for its increasing Chinese market share, but before construction began the Chinese parliament objected that Coca-Cola appeared to be too successful in China, so negotiations continue. Such are the uncertainties of the uncontrollable political and legal factors of international business.

The more significant elements in the uncontrollable international environment, shown in the outer circles of Exhibit 1.3, include political/legal forces; economic forces; competitive forces, level of technology,[23] structure of distribution, geography and infrastructure; and cultural forces.[24] These constitute the principal elements of uncertainty an international marketer must cope with in designing a marketing program. Although each will be discussed in depth in subsequent chapters, consider the level of technology and political/legal forces as illustrations of the uncontrollable nature of the foreign environment.

The level of technology is an uncontrollable element that can often be misread because of the vast differences that may exist between developed and undeveloped countries. A marketer cannot assume that the understanding of the concept of preventive maintenance for machinery is the same in other countries as in the United States. Technical expertise may not be available at a level necessary for product support, and the general population may not have an adequate level of technical knowledge to properly maintain equipment. In such situations, a marketer will have to take extra steps to make sure that the importance of routine maintenance is understood and carried out. Further, if technical support is not readily available, local people will have to be specially trained or the company will have to provide the support.

Political and legal issues face a business whether it operates at home or in a foreign country. However, the issues abroad are often amplified by the "alien status" of the company,

---

[23]Shih-Fen S. Chen, "Extending Internationalization Theory: A New Perspective on International Technology Transfer and Its Generalization," *Journal of International Business Studies,* 2005, advance published online.

[24]Laszlo Tihany, David A. Griffith, and Craig J. Russell, "The Effect of Cultural Distance on Entry Mode Choice, International Diversification, and MNE Performance: A Meta-Analysis," *Journal of International Business Studies* 36, no. 3 (2005), pp. 270–283.

CROSSING BORDERS 1.3 | Mobile Phones, Economic Development, and Shrinking the Digital Divide

Wedged between stalls of dried fish and mounds of plastic goods, a red shipping container is loaded with Coca-Cola bottles. The local distributor for Soweto market, located in a tatty corner of Zambia's capital city, Lusaka, sells all its stock every few days. A full load costs 10m kwacha (about $2,000). In cash, this amount can be hard to get hold of, takes ages to count and—being 10 times the average annual wage—is tempting to thieves. So Coca-Cola now tells its 300 Zambian distributors to pay for deliveries not in cash, but by sending text messages from their mobile phones. The process takes about 30 seconds, and the driver issues a receipt. Faraway computers record the movement of money and stock. Coca-Cola is not alone. Around the corner from the market, a small dry-cleaning firm lets customers pay for laundry using their phones. So do Zambian petrol stations and dozens of bigger shops and restaurants.

This is just one example of the many innovative ways in which mobile phones are being used in the poorest parts of the world. Anecdotal evidence for mobile phones' ability to boost economic activity is abundant: They enable fishermen or farmers to check prices at different markets before selling produce, make it easier for

people to look for jobs, and prevent wasted journeys. Mobile phones reduce transaction costs, broaden trade networks, and substitute for costly physical transport. They are of particular value when other means of communication (such as roads, post, or fixed-line phones) are poor or nonexistent.

This can be hard for people in the rich world to understand, because the ways in which mobile phones are used in the poor world are so different. In particular, phones are widely shared. One person in a village buys a mobile phone, perhaps using a microcredit loan. Others then rent it out by the minute; the small profit margin enables its owner to pay back the loan and make a living. When the phone rings, its owner carries it to the home of the person being called, who then takes the call. Other entrepreneurs can set up as "text message interpreters," sending and receiving text messages (which are generally cheaper than voice calls) on behalf of their customers, who may be illiterate. So although the number of phones per 100 people is low by rich-world standards, they still make a big difference.

Source: *The Economist*, "Economics Focus, Calling across the Divide," March 12, 2005, p. 74.

which increases the difficulty of properly assessing and forecasting the dynamic international business climate. The alien status of a foreign business has two dimensions: It is alien in that foreigners control the business and in that the culture of the host country is alien to management. The alien status of a business means that, when viewed as an outsider, it can be seen as an exploiter and receive prejudiced or unfair treatment at the hands of politicians, legal authorities, or both. Political activists can rally support by advocating the expulsion of the "foreign exploiters," often with open or tacit approval of authorities. The Indian government, for example, gave Coca-Cola the choice of either revealing its secret formula or leaving the country. The company chose to leave. When it was welcomed back several years later, it faced harassment and constant interference with its operations from political activists, inspired by competing soft drink companies.

Furthermore, in a domestic situation political details and the ramifications of political and legal events are often more transparent than they are in some foreign countries. For instance, whereas in the United States each party in a dispute has access to established legal procedures and due process, legal systems in many other countries are still evolving. In many foreign countries corruption may prevail, foreigners may receive unfair treatment, or the laws may be so different from those in the home country that they are misinterpreted. The point is that a foreign company is foreign and thus always subject to the political whims of the local government to a greater degree than a domestic firm.

Political/legal forces and the level of technology are only two of the uncontrollable aspects of the foreign environment that are discussed in subsequent chapters. The uncertainty of different foreign business environments creates the need for a close study of the uncontrollable elements within each new country. Thus a strategy successful in one country can be rendered ineffective in another by differences in political climate, stages of economic development, level of technology, or other cultural variation.

Japanese consumers have been fast to adopt both vending-machine and cell-phone technologies. This is so despite a wide variance in views about the importance of tradition as represented by these two views of Japanese women's dress. (left: © Paul Chesley/Network Aspen; right:© Thomas Hoepker/ Magnum Photos)

Environmental Adaptation Needed

To adjust and adapt a marketing program to foreign markets, marketers must be able to interpret effectively the influence and impact of each of the uncontrollable environmental elements on the marketing plan for each foreign market in which they hope to do business. In a broad sense, the uncontrollable elements constitute the culture; the difficulty facing the marketer in adjusting to the culture lies in recognizing their impact. In a domestic market the reaction to much of the environment's (cultural) impact on the marketer's activities is automatic; the various cultural influences that fill our lives are simply a part of our socialization, and we react in a manner acceptable to our society without thinking about it because we are culturally responsive to our environment. The experiences we have gained throughout life have become second nature and serve as the basis for our behavior.

The task of cultural adjustment, however, is the most challenging and important one confronting international marketers; they must adjust their marketing efforts to cultures to which they are not attuned. In dealing with unfamiliar markets, marketers must be aware of the frames of reference they are using in making their decisions or evaluating the potential of a market, because judgments are derived from experience that is the result of acculturation in the home country. Once a frame of reference is established, it becomes an important factor in determining or modifying a marketer's reaction to situations—social and even nonsocial.

For example, a Westerner must learn that white is a symbol of mourning in parts of Asia, which is quite different from Western culture's use of white for bridal gowns. Also, time-conscious Americans are not culturally prepared to understand the meaning of time to Latin Americans. These differences must be learned to avoid misunderstandings that can lead to marketing failures. Such a failure actually occurred in one situation when ignorance led to ineffective advertising on the part of an American firm; a second misunderstanding resulted in lost sales when a "long waiting period" in the outer office of a Latin American customer was misinterpreted by an American sales executive. Cross-cultural misunderstandings can also occur when a simple hand gesture has a number of different meanings in different parts of the world. When wanting to signify something is OK, many people in the United States raise a hand and make a circle with the thumb and forefinger. However, this same hand gesture means "zero" or "worthless" to the French, "money" to the Japanese, and a general sexual insult in Sardinia and Greece. A U.S. president sent an unintentional message to some Australian protesters when he held up his first two fingers with the back of his hand to the protesters. Meaning to give the "victory" sign, he was unaware that in Australia the same hand gesture is equivalent to holding up the middle finger in the United States.

Cultural conditioning is like an iceberg—we are not aware of nine-tenths of it. In any study of the market systems of different peoples, their political and economic structures, religions, and other elements of culture, foreign marketers must constantly guard against measuring and assessing the markets against the fixed values and assumptions of their own cultures. They must take specific steps to make themselves aware of the home cultural reference in their analyses and decision making.

The Self-Reference Criterion and Ethnocentrism: Major Obstacles

The key to successful international marketing is adaptation to the environmental differences from one market to another. Adaptation is a conscious effort on the part of the international marketer to anticipate the influences of both the foreign and domestic uncontrollable factors on a marketing mix and then to adjust the marketing mix to minimize the effects.

The primary obstacles to success in international marketing are a person's self-reference criterion (SRC) and an associated ethnocentrism. SRC is an unconscious reference to one's own cultural values, experiences, and knowledge as a basis for decisions. Closely connected is ethnocentrism, that is, the notion that one's own culture or company knows best how to do things. Ethnocentrism is particularly a problem for American managers at the beginning of the 21st century because of America's dominance in the world economy during the late 1990s. Ethnocentrism is generally a problem when managers from affluent countries work with managers and markets in less affluent countries. Both the SRC and ethnocentrism impede the ability to assess a foreign market in its true light.

When confronted with a set of facts, we react spontaneously on the basis of knowledge assimilated over a lifetime—knowledge that is a product of the history of our culture. We seldom stop to think about a reaction; we simply react. Thus when faced with a problem in another culture, the tendency is to react instinctively and refer to our SRC for a solution. Our reaction, however, is based on meanings, values, symbols, and behavior relevant to our own culture and usually different from those of the foreign culture. Such decisions are often not good ones.

To illustrate the impact of the SRC, consider misunderstandings that can occur about personal space between people of different cultures. In the United States, unrelated individuals keep a certain physical distance between themselves and others when talking or in groups. We do not consciously think about that distance; we just know what feels right without thinking. When someone is too close or too far away, we feel uncomfortable and either move farther away or get closer to correct the distance. In doing so, we are relying on our SRC. In some cultures the acceptable distance between individuals is substantially less than that which is comfortable for Americans. When someone from another culture approaches an American too closely, the American, unaware of that culture's acceptable distance, unconsciously reacts by backing away to restore the proper distance (i.e., proper by American standards), and confusion results for both parties. Americans assume foreigners are pushy, while foreigners assume Americans are unfriendly and literally "standoffish." Both react according to the values of their own SRCs, making both victims of a cultural misunderstanding.

Your self-reference criterion can prevent you from being aware of cultural differences or from recognizing the importance of those differences. Thus you might fail to recognize the need to take action, you might discount the cultural differences that exist among countries, or you might react to a situation in a way offensive to your hosts. A common mistake made by Americans is to refuse food or drink when offered. In the United States, a polite refusal is certainly acceptable, but in Asia or the Middle East, a host is offended if you refuse hospitality. Although you do not have to eat or drink much, you do have to accept the offering of hospitality. Understanding and dealing with the self-reference criterion are two of the more important facets of international marketing.

Ethnocentrism and the SRC can influence an evaluation of the appropriateness of a domestically designed marketing mix for a foreign market. If U.S. marketers are not aware, they might evaluate a marketing mix based on U.S. experiences (i.e., their SRC) without fully appreciating the cultural differences that require adaptation. Esso, the brand name of a gasoline, was a successful name in the United States and would seem harmless enough for foreign countries; however, in Japan, the name phonetically means "stalled car," an undesirable image

CROSSING BORDERS 1.4 Napster Lost the Battle, But the War over Intellectual Property Rights Rages On Worldwide

Perhaps the worst loan ever made was the $50 million Thomas Middlehoff, charismatic but recently fired CEO of Germany's Bertelsmann (BMG Entertainment is their music division), made to Shawn Fanning and Napster in 2000. Three years later Bertelsmann was being sued for $17 billion by recording artists and BMG's competitors, arguing that the loan allowed Napster to continue ripping them off. Of course, Napster first went bankrupt, then went to legitimate file sharing for a fee globally.

In 2003 Rock 'n' rap band Linkin Park and their *Meteora* album brought a new weapon into the war. Super new prerelease security measures worked, and so did interviews disguised as songs from the album promulgated over the Net designed to inoculate the Net against the likes of Kazaa and the other second-generation Napsters. Some have argued that the innovative intellectual property protection strategies lead to sales of 810,000 copies in the first week of release, easily yielding Linkin Park a number 1 spot on the pop charts and fat wallets as well. We assume the music was excellent, too. Kazaa and Grokster may be dead, but the battle goes on with the latest forms of Internet piracy such as LimeWire and the abuse of BitTorrent.

Similar battles are being fought in China and sub-Sahara Africa. The intellectual property is more likely to be computer software in the former and pharmaceutical products in the latter. But the war involves the same institutions—multinational companies trying to protect their ideas from the piracy of the public. China's entry into the World Trade Organization means more enforcement of copyright laws in that country. But it will be at least a decade before the Chinese begin to develop enough of their own proprietary technology to make the standard transition from pirates to policemen.

Finally, the AIDS/HIV epidemic in Africa is forcing the American and European pharmaceutical companies to relent on their high prices for drugs they've developed to fight the disease. Protests, shareholder lobbying, and social responsibility have all started a general relaxation of an intellectual property rights regime that many said was killing millions of people.

Sources: Joseph Menn, "Piracy Battle Shifts to Bertelsmann," *Los Angeles Times*, February 20, 2003, p. C1; Jeff Leeds, "Unheard-Of Security: With a Massive Lockdown, Warner Bros. Records and Linkin Park All but Stop Early Leaks of the Album 'Meteora,'" *Los Angeles Times*, April 2, 2003, p. C1; Ginger Thompson, "In the Grip of AIDS, South Africa Cries for Equity," *New York Times*, May 10, 2003, p. 4; Roben Farzad, "File Swappers Get Creative as Wheels of Justice Turn," *New York Times*, June 18, 2005, p. 13; Terrance H. Witkowski, "Antiglobal Challenges to Marketing in Developing Countries," *Journal of Public Policy and Marketing* 24, no. 1 (2005), pp. 7–23.

for gasoline. Another example is "Pet" in Pet Milk. The name has been used for decades, yet in France the word *pet* means, among other things, "flatulence"—again, not the desired image for canned milk. Both of these examples were real mistakes made by major companies stemming from reliance on their SRC in making a decision. In U.S. culture, a person's SRC would not reveal a problem with either Esso or Pet, but in international marketing, relying on one's SRC could produce an inadequately adapted marketing program that ends in failure.

When marketers take the time to look beyond their own self-reference criteria the results are more positive. A British manufacturer of chocolate biscuits (cookies in American English), ignoring its SRC, knows that it must package its biscuits differently to accommodate the Japanese market. Thus, in Japan, McVitie's chocolate biscuits are wrapped individually, packed in presentation cardboard boxes, and priced about three times higher than in the United Kingdom—the cookies are used as gifts in Japan and thus must look and be perceived as special. Unilever, appreciating the uniqueness of its markets, repackaged and reformulated its detergent for Brazil. One reason was that the lack of washing machines among poorer Brazilians made a simpler soap formula necessary. Also, since people wash their clothes in rivers, the powder was packaged in plastic rather than paper so it would not get soggy. Finally, because the Brazilian poor are price conscious and buy in small quantities, the soap was packaged in small, low-priced packages. Even McDonald's modifies its traditional Big Mac in India, where it is known as the Maharaja Mac. This burger features two mutton patties because most Indians consider cows sacred and don't eat beef. In each of these examples, had the marketers' own self-reference criteria been the basis for decisions, none of the changes would have been readily apparent based on home-market experience.

The most effective way to control the influence of ethnocentrism and the SRC is to recognize their effects on our behavior. Although learning every culture in depth and being aware of every important difference is almost humanly impossible, an awareness of the need to be sensitive to differences and to ask questions when doing business in another culture can help one avoid many of the mistakes possible in international marketing. Asking the appropriate question helped the Vicks Company avoid making a mistake in Germany. It discovered that in German "Vicks" sounds like the crudest slang equivalent of "intercourse," so they changed the name to "Wicks" before introducing the product.

Be aware, also, that not every activity within a marketing program is different from one country to another; indeed, there probably are more similarities than differences. For example, the McVitie's chocolate biscuits mentioned earlier are sold in the United States in the same package as in the United Kingdom. Such similarities, however, may lull the marketer into a false sense of apparent sameness. This apparent sameness, coupled with the self-reference criterion, is often the cause of international marketing problems. Undetected similarities do not cause problems; however, the one difference that goes undetected can create a marketing failure.

To avoid errors in business decisions, the knowledgeable marketer will conduct a cross-cultural analysis that isolates the SRC influences and will maintain a vigilance regarding ethnocentrism. The following steps are suggested as a framework for such an analysis.

1. Define the business problem or goal in home-country cultural traits, habits, or norms.

2. Define the business problem or goal in foreign-country cultural traits, habits, or norms through consultation with natives of the target country. Make no value judgments.

3. Isolate the SRC influence in the problem and examine it carefully to see how it complicates the problem.

4. Redefine the problem without the SRC influence and solve for the optimum business goal situation.

An American sales manager newly posted to Japan decided that his Japanese sales representatives did not need to come into the office every day for an early morning meeting before beginning calls on clients in Tokyo. After all, that was how things were done in the United States. However, the new policy, based on both the American's SRC and a modicum of ethnocentrism, produced a precipitous decline in sales performance. In his subsequent discussions with his Japanese staff he determined that Japanese sales representatives are motivated mostly by peer pressure. Fortunately he was able to recognize that his SRC and his American "business acumen" did not apply in this case in Tokyo. A return to the proven system of daily meetings brought sales performance back to previous levels.

The cross-cultural analysis approach requires an understanding of the culture of the foreign market as well as one's own culture. Surprisingly, understanding one's own culture may require additional study because much of the cultural influence on market behavior remains at a subconscious level and is not clearly defined.

Developing a Global Awareness

Opportunities in global business abound for those who are prepared to confront myriad obstacles with optimism and a willingness to continue learning new ways. The successful businessperson in the 21st century will have global awareness and a frame of reference that goes beyond a region or even a country and encompasses the world. To be globally aware is to have (1) tolerance of cultural differences and (2) knowledge of cultures, history, world market potential, and global economic, social, and political trends.

To be globally aware is to have tolerance for cultural differences. Tolerance is understanding cultural differences and accepting and working with others whose behaviors may be different from yours. You do not have to accept as your own the cultural ways of another, but you must allow others to be different and equal. For example, the fact that punctuality is less important in some cultures does not make them less productive, only different. The tolerant person understands the differences that may exist between cultures and uses that knowledge to relate effectively.

A globally aware person is knowledgeable about cultures and history. Knowledge of cultures is important in understanding behavior in the marketplace or in the boardroom. Knowledge of history is important because the way people think and act is influenced by their history. Some Latin Americans' reluctance about foreign investment or Chinese reluctance to open completely to outsiders can be understood better if you have a historical perspective.

Global awareness also involves knowledge of world market potentials and global economic, social, and political trends. Over the next few decades enormous changes will take place in market potentials in almost every region of the world, all of which a globally aware person must continuously monitor. Finally, a globally aware person will keep abreast of the global economic, social, and political trends because a country's prospects can change as these trends shift direction or accelerate. The former republics of the Soviet Union, along with Russia, eastern Europe, China, India, Africa, and Latin America, are undergoing economic, social, and political changes that have already altered the course of trade and defined new economic powers. The knowledgeable marketer will identify opportunity long before it becomes evident to others. It is the authors' goal in this text to guide the reader toward acquiring a global awareness.

Global awareness can and should be built in organizations using several approaches. The obvious strategy is to select individual managers specifically for their demonstrated global awareness. Global awareness can also be obtained through personal relationships in other countries. Indeed, market entry is very often facilitated through previously established social ties. Certainly, successful long-term business relationships with foreign customers often result in an organizational global awareness based on the series of interactions required by commerce. Foreign agents and partners can also help directly in this regard. But perhaps the most effective approach is to have a culturally diverse senior executive staff or board of directors. Unfortunately, American managers seem to see relatively less value in this last approach than managers in most other countries.

Stages of International Marketing Involvement

Once a company has decided to go international, it has to decide the degree of marketing involvement and commitment it is prepared to make. These decisions should reflect considerable study and analysis of market potential and company capabilities—a process not always followed. Many companies begin tentatively in international marketing, growing as they gain experience and gradually changing strategy and tactics as they become more committed.[25] Others enter international marketing after much research and with fully developed long-range plans, prepared to make investments to acquire a market position and often evincing bursts of international activities.[26]

Regardless of the means employed to gain entry into a foreign market, a company may make little or no actual market investment—that is, its marketing involvement may be limited to selling a product with little or no thought given to development of market control. Alternatively, a company may become totally involved and invest large sums of money and effort to capture and maintain a permanent, specific position in the market. In general, one of five (sometimes overlapping) stages can describe the international marketing involvement of a company.[27] Although the stages of international marketing involvement are presented here in a linear order, the reader should not infer that a firm progresses from one stage to another; quite to the contrary, a firm may begin its international involvement at any

[25]Marian V. Jones and Nicole E. Coviello, "Internationalisation: Conceptualising an Entrepreneurial Process of Behaviour in Time," *Journal of International Business Studies* 36, no. 3 (2005), pp. 284–303.

[26]Elizabeth Maitland, Elizabeth L. Rose, and Stephen Nicholas, "How Firms Grow: Clustering as a Dynamic Model of Internationalization," *Journal of International Business Studies*, 2005, advance online publication.

[27]Alan M. Rugman and Alain Verbeke, "Extending the Theory of the Multinational Enterprise: Internationalization and Strategic Management Perspectives," *Journal of International Business Studies* 3 (2003), pp. 125–137.

one stage or be in more than one stage simultaneously. For example, because of a short product life cycle and a thin but widespread market for many technology products, many high-tech companies large and small see the entire world, including their home market, as a single market and strive to reach all possible customers as rapidly as possible.

No Direct Foreign Marketing

A company in this stage does not actively cultivate customers outside national boundaries; however, this company's products may reach foreign markets. Sales may be made to trading companies as well as foreign customers who come directly to the firm. Or products may reach foreign markets via domestic wholesalers or distributors who sell abroad without explicit encouragement or even knowledge of the producer. As companies develop Web sites on the Internet, many receive orders from international Web surfers. Often an unsolicited order from a foreign buyer is what piques the interest of a company to seek additional international sales.

Infrequent Foreign Marketing

Temporary surpluses caused by variations in production levels or demand may result in infrequent marketing overseas. The surpluses are characterized by their temporary nature; therefore, sales to foreign markets are made as goods are available, with little or no intention of maintaining continuous market representation. As domestic demand increases and absorbs surpluses, foreign sales activity is withdrawn. In this stage, little or no change is seen in company organization or product lines. However, few companies today fit this model because customers around the world increasingly seek long-term commercial relationships. Further, evidence exists that financial returns from initial international expansions are limited.[28]

Regular Foreign Marketing

At this level, the firm has permanent productive capacity devoted to the production of goods to be marketed in foreign markets. A firm may employ foreign or domestic overseas intermediaries or it may have its own sales force or sales subsidiaries in important foreign markets. The primary focus of operations and production is to service domestic market needs. However, as overseas demand grows, production is allocated for foreign markets, and products may be adapted to meet the needs of individual foreign markets. Profit expectations from foreign markets move from being seen as a bonus to regular domestic profits to a position in which the company becomes dependent on foreign sales and profits to meet its goals.

Meter-Man, a small company (25 employees) in southern Minnesota that manufactures agricultural measuring devices, is a good example of a company in this stage.[29] In 1989, the 35-year-old company began exploring the idea of exporting; by 1992 the company was shipping product to Europe. Today, a third of Meter-Man's sales are in 35 countries, and soon the company expects international sales to account for about half of its business. "When you start exporting, you say to yourself, this will be icing on the cake," says the director of sales and marketing. "But now I say going international has become critical to our existence."

International Marketing

Companies in this stage are fully committed and involved in international marketing activities. Such companies seek markets all over the world and sell products that are a result of planned production for markets in various countries. This generally entails not only the marketing but also the production of goods outside the home market. At this point a company becomes an international or multinational marketing firm.

The experience of Fedders, a manufacturer of room air conditioners, typifies that of a company that begins its international business at this stage.[30] Even though it is the largest manufacturer of air conditioners in the United States, the firm faced constraints in its

---

[28]Farok J. Contractor, Sumit K. Kundu, and Chin-Chun Hsu, "A Three-Stage Theory of International Expansion: The Link between Multinationality and Performance in the Service Sector," *Journal of International Business Studies* 34, no. 1 (2003), pp. 5–18.

[29]See www.meter-man.com for its product line and other details.

[30]See www.fedders.com for details about the company.

North of Beijing, China, the new development is marketed as Orange County, China. The gardens and stucco and tile exteriors are all intended to replicate the Mediterranean look and feel of homes in Newport Beach, CA. (© AFP/Getty Images)

domestic market. Its sales were growing steadily, but sales of air conditioners (the company's only product) are seasonal and thus domestic sales at times do not even cover fixed costs. Furthermore, the U.S. market is mature, with most customers buying only replacement units. Any growth would have to come from a rival's market share, and the rivals, Whirlpool and Matsushita, are formidable. Fedders decided that the only way to grow was to venture abroad.

Fedders decided that Asia, with its steamy climate and expanding middle class, offered the best opportunity. China, India, and Indonesia were seen as the best prospects. China was selected because sales of room air conditioners had grown from 500,000 units to over 4 million in five years, which still accounted for only 12 percent of the homes in cities like Beijing, Shanghai, and Guangzhou. The company saw China as a market with terrific growth potential. After careful study, Fedders entered a joint venture with a small Chinese air conditioner company that was looking for a partner; a new company, Fedders Xinle, was formed. The company immediately found that it needed to redesign its product for this market. In China, air conditioners are a major purchase seen as a status symbol, not as a box to keep a room cool, as in the United States. The Chinese also prefer a split-type air conditioner, with the unit containing the fan inside the room and the heat exchanger mounted on a wall outside. Since Fedders did not manufacture split models, it designed a new product that is lightweight, energy efficient, and packed with features such as a remote control and an automatic air-sweeping mechanism.

The joint venture appears to be successful, and the company is exploring the possibility of marketing to other Asian markets and Japan and maybe even back to the United States with the new product that it developed for the Chinese market. As Fedders expands into other markets and makes other commitments internationally, it continues to evolve as an international or multinational company. The company may remain in this stage, as most companies do, or go through a change in orientation and become a global company.

Global Marketing

At the global marketing level, the most profound change is the orientation of the company toward markets and associated planning activities. At this stage, companies treat the world, including their home market, as one market. Market segmentation decisions are no longer focused on national borders. Instead, market segments are defined by income levels, usage patterns, or other factors that often span countries and regions.[31] Often this transition from international marketing to global marketing is catalyzed by a company's crossing the threshold of more than half its sales revenues coming from abroad. The best people in the company begin to seek international assignments, and the entire operation—organizational structure, sources of finance, production, marketing, and so forth—begins to take on a global perspective.[32]

The example of Coca-Cola's transition from international to global is instructive. Coca-Cola had actually been a global company for years; the mid-1990s organizational change was the last step in recognizing the changes that had already occurred. Initially, all international divisions reported to an executive vice president in charge of international operations, who, along with the vice president of U.S. operations, reported to the president. The new organization consists of six international divisions—five Coca-Cola divisions and one Coca-Cola Foods division. The U.S. business unit accounts for about 20 percent of profits and has been downgraded to just part of one of the six international business units in the company's global geographic regions. The new structure does not reduce the importance of the company's North American business; it just puts other areas on an equal footing. It is recognition, however, that future growth is going to come from emerging markets outside the United States.

[31]Frenkel Ter Hofstede, Jan-Benedict E. M. Steenkamp, and Michel Wedel, "International Market Segmentation Based on Consumer-Product Relations," *Journal of Marketing Research* 36 (February 1999), pp. 1–17.

[32]One author argues for a middle ground on the issue of global markets: Pankaj Ghemawat, "Semiglobalization and International Business Strategy," *Journal of International Business Studies* 34 (2003), pp. 139–152.

CROSSING **BORDERS 1.5**   Orange County, CA, Travels East and West

For $500,000 you can now buy a four-bedroom house in Orange County, in China!

The homes are designed by Southern California architects and built with American features, but are located in a new development an hour's drive north of Beijing. The country road can be icy and is lined by fields and populated by trucks and sheep. The landscape is a far cry from palm-ringed golf courses and "Surfin' USA." A bit after Sun City, another half-built gated community, the tidy homes of Orange County come into view. Finally, you drive through a stone portal, past advertisements showing men fly-fishing in cowboy hats and such, and pull up before the impressive mansions of Watermark-Longbeach, the epicenter of *faux* L.A. in China. Says homeowner Nasha Wei, a former army doctor turned businesswoman, "I liked it immediately—it is just like a house in California."

And, apparently in France, the waves can actually be better than California. Check out the 60-footers at Belharra Reef off St. Jean de Luz. Or hang 10 along the surfwear shops nearby in the hamlet of Hossegor in southwest France. They're all there: Roxy, Rip Curl Girl,

Billabong, and Quicksilver Boardriders Club. And the kids in the neighborhoods and sidewalk cafés are decked out in Volcom sweatshirts, Vans sneakers, and jeans.

The $4.5-billion surfwear industry, rooted in Orange County, CA, has established a beachhead in Europe. So many U.S. surfwear companies have international headquarters, subsidiaries, and stores in Pays Basque that it has a new nickname: *la petite Californie*. "This is the best place to observe the market," says Petra Holtschneider, who is organizing the first Action Sports Retailer trade show in the area this summer. "So if you're not here, you're not getting it."

Finally, perhaps the scariest OC export is the television program so named. It is now showing an entire new generation of Europeans the latest kinds of misbehavior going on in "paradise" while influencing teen fashions globally.

Sources: Elisabeth Rosenthal, "North of Beijing, California Dreams Come True," *New York Times*, February 3, 2003, p. A3; Leslie Earnest, "Riding a French New Wave," *Los Angeles Times*, May 11, 2003, p. C1; Kitty Bean Yancey, "Teen Concierges Help Reduce the 'Whatever' Factor," *USA Today*, July 1, 2005, p. 8D.

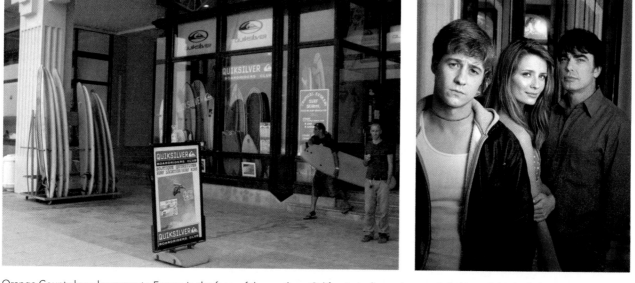

Orange County has also come to France in the form of the southern California surfing culture and clothiers. OC's Quiksilver opened its European headquarters in southwest France in 1984. Last year European sales amounted to some $300 million. Part of the firm's success in Europe can be attributed to hiring local nationals in key marketing positions. Maritxu Darrigrand, former French women's surfing champion, is now Quiksilver's marketing director for Europe. The OC has also come to the UK. The Fox TV program brings California beach culture—clothes, music, and misbehavior—to Europe. *(right: Photofest/© 2003 FOX BROADCASTING)*

International operations of businesses in global marketing reflect the heightened competitiveness brought about by the globalization of markets, interdependence of the world's economies, and the growing number of competing firms from developed and developing countries vying for the world's markets. *Global companies* and *global marketing* are terms frequently used to describe the scope of operations and marketing management orientation of companies in this stage.

Strategic Orientation

The stages of international marketing involvement described above do not necessarily coincide with managers' thinking and strategic orientations. Often companies are led into international and even global markets by burgeoning consumer or customer demands, and strategic thinking is secondary to "filling the next order." But putting strategic thinking on the back burner has resulted in marketing failures for even the largest companies.

The consensus of the researchers and authors[33] in the area reveals three relatively distinctive approaches that seem to dominate strategic thinking in firms involved in international markets:

1. Domestic market extension concept
2. Multidomestic market concept
3. Global marketing concept

Differences in the complexity and sophistication of a company's marketing activity depend on which orientation guides its operations. The ideas expressed in each strategic orientation reflect the philosophical orientation that also should be associated with successive stages in the evolution of the international operations in a company.

Domestic Market Extension Orientation

The domestic company seeking sales extension of its domestic products into foreign markets illustrates this orientation to international marketing. It views its international operations as secondary to and an extension of its domestic operations; the primary motive is to market excess domestic production. Domestic business is its priority, and foreign sales are seen as a profitable extension of domestic operations. Even though foreign markets may be vigorously pursued, the firm's orientation remains basically domestic. Its attitude toward international sales is typified by the belief that if it sells in St. Louis it will sell anywhere else in the world. Minimal, if any, efforts are made to adapt the marketing mix to foreign markets; the firm's orientation is to market to foreign customers in the same manner in which the company markets to domestic customers. It seeks markets where demand is similar to the home market and its domestic product will be acceptable. This domestic market extension strategy can be very profitable; large and small exporting companies approach international marketing from this perspective. Firms with this marketing approach are classified as ethnocentric. Meter-Man, discussed earlier, could be said to follow this orientation.

Multidomestic Market Orientation

Once a company recognizes the importance of differences in overseas markets and the importance of offshore business to the organization, its orientation toward international business may shift to a multidomestic market strategy. A company guided by this concept has a strong sense that country markets are vastly different (and they may be, depending on the product) and that market success requires an almost independent program for each country. Firms with this orientation market on a country-by-country basis, with separate marketing strategies for each country.

Subsidiaries operate independently of one another in establishing marketing objectives and plans, and the domestic market and each of the country markets have separate marketing mixes with little interaction among them. Products are adapted for each market with little coordination with other country markets; advertising campaigns are localized, as are the

---

[33]A seminal paper in this genre is Yorum Wind, Susan P. Douglas, and Howard V. Perlmutter, "Guidelines for Developing International Marketing Strategy," *Journal of Marketing*, April 1973, pp. 14–23; also important is Anne-Wil Harzing, "An Empirical Analysis and Extension of the Bartlett and Ghoshal Typology of Multinational Companies," *Journal of International Business Studies* 31, no. 1 (2000), pp. 101–120.

pricing and distribution decisions. A company with this concept does not look for similarity among elements of the marketing mix that might respond to standardization; rather, it aims for adaptation to local country markets. Control is typically decentralized to reflect the belief that the uniqueness of each market requires local marketing input and control. Firms with this orientation would be classified as polycentric. Fedders, as it progresses in its plans, fits this orientation.

Global Market Orientation

A company guided by the global marketing orientation or philosophy is generally referred to as a global company; its marketing activity is global, and its market coverage is the world. A company employing a global marketing strategy strives for efficiencies of scale by developing a standardized marketing mix applicable across national boundaries. Markets are still segmented, but country or region is considered side by side with a variety of other segmentation variables, such as consumer characteristics (age, income, language group), usage patterns, and legal constraints. The world as a whole is viewed as the market, and the firm develops a global marketing strategy. The global marketing company would fit the regiocentric or geocentric classifications. Coca-Cola Company, Ford Motor Company, and Intel are among the companies that can be described as global companies.

The global marketing concept views an entire set of country markets (whether the home market and only 1 other country or the home market and 100 other countries) as a unit, identifying groups of prospective buyers with similar needs as a global market segment and developing a marketing plan that strives for standardization wherever it is cost and culturally effective. This might mean a company's global marketing plan has a standardized product but country-specific advertising, or has a standardized theme in all countries with country- or cultural-specific appeals to a unique market characteristic, or has a standardized brand or image but has adapted products to meet specific country needs, and so on. In other words, the marketing planning and marketing mix are approached from a global perspective, and where feasible in the marketing mix, efficiencies of standardization are sought. Wherever cultural uniqueness dictates the need for adaptation of the product, its image, and so on, it is accommodated. For example, McDonald's standardizes its processes, logo, most of its advertising, and store decor and layouts whenever and wherever possible. However, you will find wine on the menu in France and beer in Germany, a Filipino-style spicy burger in Manila, and pork burgers in Thailand—all to accommodate local tastes and customs. The point is, being global is a mindset, a way of looking at the market for commonalties that can be standardized across regions or country-market groups. And such a global mindset can work alike for the largest companies and small companies[34] that take aggressive strategies toward learning.[35]

As the competitive environment facing U.S. businesses becomes more internationalized—and it surely will—the most effective orientation for many firms engaged in marketing into another country will be a global orientation. This means operating as if all the country markets in a company's scope of operations (including the domestic market) were approachable as a single global market and standardizing the marketing mix where culturally feasible and cost effective. This does not, however, mean a slavish adherence to one strategic orientation. Depending on the product and market, other orientations may make more marketing sense. For example, Procter & Gamble may pursue a global strategy for disposable diapers but a multidomestic strategy in Asian markets for detergents.

The Orientation of *International Marketing*

Most problems encountered by the foreign marketer result from the strangeness of the environment within which marketing programs must be implemented. Success hinges, in part, on the ability to assess and adjust properly to the impact of a strange environment. The successful international marketer possesses the best qualities of the anthropologist, sociologist, psychologist, diplomat, lawyer, prophet, and businessperson.

---

[34]Gary A. Knight and S. Tamer Cavusgil, "Innovation, Organizational Capabilities, and the Born-Global Firm," *Journal of International Business Studies* 35, no. 2 (2004), pp. 124–141.

[35]Sylvie Chetty and Colin Campbell-Hunt, "A Strategic Approach to Internationalization: A Traditional versus a 'Born-Global' Approach," *Journal of International Marketing* 12, no. 1 (2004), pp. 57–81.

Exhibit 1.4
Foreign Policy's Global Top 20

The countries that top the charts in trade, travel, technology, and links to the rest of the world

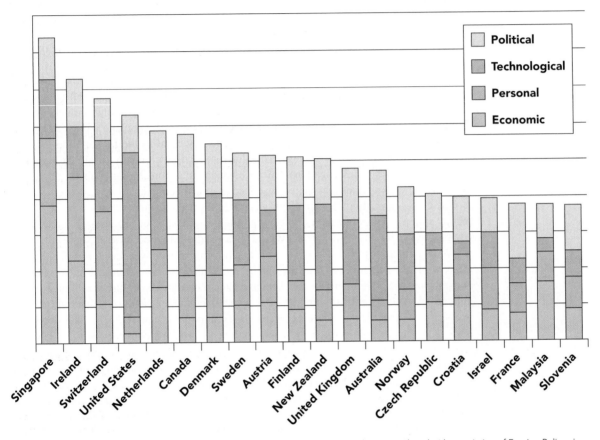

Legend:
- ☐ Political
- ☐ Technological
- ☐ Personal
- ☐ Economic

Countries (left to right): Singapore, Ireland, Switzerland, United States, Netherlands, Canada, Denmark, Sweden, Austria, Finland, New Zealand, United Kingdom, Australia, Norway, Czech Republic, Croatia, Israel, France, Malaysia, Slovenia

Source: From *Foreign Policy*, May/June 2005, pp. 52–60. Copyright 2005 by Foreign Policy. Reproduced with permission of Foreign Policy via Copyright Clearance Center.

In light of all the variables involved, with what should a text in foreign marketing be concerned? It is the opinion of the authors that a study of foreign marketing environments, people, and cultures[36] and their influences on the total marketing process is of primary concern and is the most effective approach to a meaningful presentation. Our views are supported by the most recent ranking of countries on their extent of globalization—see Exhibit 1.4.[37] Yes, the United States is near the top of the list and most of the "Global Top 20" are small countries. However, the key conclusion to be drawn from the graph is the dominance of "technological connectivity" for America. In particular, notice that as a country the United States is weakest on the "personal contact" dimension. Compared to folks in other countries, Americans generally do not experience foreign environments. This lack is the gap our book focuses on.

Consequently, the orientation of this text can best be described as an environmental/cultural approach to international strategic marketing.[38] By no means is it intended to present principles of marketing; rather, it is intended to demonstrate the unique problems of international marketing. It attempts to relate the foreign environment to the marketing process and to illustrate the many ways in which culture can influence the marketing task. Although

---

[36]A multiyear survey of high-tech executives in the southern California area has continuously mentioned cultural differences as one of the most prominent obstacles to international commerce. See Dennis J. Aigner, *The 2005 Orange County Executive Survey*, annually published form 1986 to 2005, Chapman University.

[37]"Measuring Globalization," *Foreign Policy*, May/June 2005, pp. 52–60.

[38]Lawrence E. Harrison and Samuel P. Huntington (eds.), *Culture Matters* (New York: Basic Books, 2000).

marketing principles are universally applicable, the cultural environment within which the marketer must implement marketing plans can change dramatically from country to country. It is with the difficulties created by different environments that this text is primarily concerned.

The text is concerned with any company marketing in or into any other country or groups of countries, however slight the involvement or the method of involvement. Hence this discussion of international marketing ranges from the marketing and business practices of small exporters, such as a Colorado-based company that generates more than 50 percent of its $40,000 annual sales of fish-egg sorters in Canada, Germany, and Australia, to the practices of global companies such as Motorola, Avon, and Johnson & Johnson, all of which generate more than 50 percent of their annual profits from the sales of multiple products to multiple country-market segments all over the world.

The first section of *International Marketing* offers an overview of international marketing, including a brief discussion of the global business environment confronting the marketer. The next section deals exclusively with the uncontrollable elements of the environment and their assessment, followed by chapters on assessing global market opportunities. Then, management issues in developing global marketing strategies are discussed. In each chapter, the impact of the environment on the marketing process is illustrated.

Space prohibits an encyclopedic approach to all the issues of international marketing; nevertheless, the authors have tried to present sufficient detail so that readers will appreciate the real need to make a thorough analysis whenever the challenge arises. The text provides a framework for this task.

Summary

The internationalization of American business is proceeding with increasing pace. The globalization of markets and competition necessitates all managers to pay attention to the global environment. International marketing is defined as the performance of business activities including pricing, promotion, product, and distribution decisions across national borders. The international marketing task is made more daunting because environmental factors such as laws, customs, and cultures vary from country to country. These environmental differences must be taken into account if firms are to market products and services at a profit in other countries.

Key obstacles facing international marketers are not limited to environmental issues. Just as important are difficulties associated with the marketer's own self-reference criteria and ethnocentrism.

Both limit the international marketer's abilities to understand and adapt to differences prevalent in foreign markets. A global awareness and sensitivity are the best solutions to these problems, and these should be nurtured in international marketing organizations.

Three different strategic orientations are found among managers of international marketing operations. Some see international marketing as ancillary to the domestic operations. A second kind of company sees international marketing as a crucial aspect of sales revenue generation but treats each market as a separate entity. Finally, a global orientation views the globe as the marketplace and market segments are no longer based solely on national borders—common consumer characteristics and behaviors come into play as key segmentation variables applied across countries.

Questions

1. Define the following terms:

international marketing	foreign uncontrollables
controllable elements	marketing relativism
uncontrollable elements	self-reference criterion (SRC)
domestic uncontrollables	global awareness

2. "The marketer's task is the same whether applied in Dimebox, Texas, or Dar es Salaam, Tanzania." Discuss.

3. How can the increased interest in international marketing on the part of U.S. firms be explained?

4. Discuss the four phases of international marketing involvement.

5. Discuss the conditions that have led to the development of global markets.

6. Differentiate between a global company and a multinational company.

7. Differentiate among the three international marketing concepts.

8. Prepare your lifelong plan to be globally aware.

9. Discuss the three factors necessary to achieve global awareness.

10. Define and discuss the idea of global orientation.

11. Visit the Bureau of Economic Analysis homepage (www.bea.doc.gov). Select the section "International articles" and find the most recent information on foreign direct investments in the United States. Which country has the highest dollar amount of investment in the United States? Second highest?

www.sina.com.cn

2

The Dynamic Environment of international Trade

CHAPTER OUTLINE

Global Perspective: Trade Barriers—An International
   Marketer's Minefield

The Twentieth to the Twenty-First Century

   World Trade and U.S. Multinationals
   The First Decade of the Twenty-First Century and Beyond

Balance of Payments

Protectionism

   Protection Logic and Illogic
   Trade Barriers

Easing Trade Restrictions

   The Omnibus Trade and Competitiveness Act
   General Agreement on Tariffs and Trade
   World Trade Organization
   Skirting the Spirit of GATT and WTO

The International Monetary Fund and
   World Bank Group

Protests against Global Institutions

CHAPTER LEARNING OBJECTIVES

What you should learn from Chapter 2:

- The basis for the reestablishment of world trade following World War II

- The importance of balance-of-payment figures to a country's economy

- The effects of protectionism on world trade

- The seven types of trade barriers

- The provisions of the Omnibus Trade and Competitiveness Act

- The importance of GATT and the World Trade Organization

- The emergence of the International Monetary Fund and the World Bank Group

Global Perspective

TRADE BARRIERS—AN INTERNATIONAL MARKETER'S MINEFIELD

We all know the story about our trade disputes with Japan. Japan has so many trade barriers and high tariffs that U.S. manufacturers are unable to sell in Japan as much as Japanese companies sell in the United States. The Japanese claim that "unique" Japanese snow requires skis made in Japan, and U.S. baseballs are not good enough for Japanese baseball. Even when Japan opened its rice market, the popular California rice had to be mixed and sold with inferior grades of Japanese rice.

However, the Japanese are not alone; every country seems to take advantage of the open U.S. market while putting barriers in the way of U.S. exports. The French, for example, protect their film and broadcast industry from foreign competition by limiting the number of American shows that can appear on television, the percentage of American songs broadcast on radio, and the proportion of U.S. movies that can be shown in French theaters. Most recently France launched its own "French" version of CNN with strong government financial support. Not only do these barriers and high tariffs limit how much U.S. companies can sell; they also raise prices for imported products much higher than they sell for in the United States.

Consider the fiscal hazards facing international marketing managers at a company like Neutrogena[1] contemplating exporting its products to Russia. Upon arrival there the firm's products might be classified by Russian customs officers into any one of three separate categories for the purposes of assigning tariffs: pharmaceuticals at a 5 percent duty, soap at 15 percent, or cosmetics at 20 percent. Of course, Neutrogena managers would argue for the lowest tariff by pointing out that their "hypoallergenic soaps are recommended by dermatologists." And, as long as shipments remain relatively small, the customs officers might not argue. However, as exports to Russia grow from cartons to container loads, the product classification receives more scrutiny. Simple statements on packaging, such as "Pure Neutrogena skin and hair care products are available at drug stores and *cosmetic counters*," would give the Russians reason to claim the highest duty of 20 percent.

Barriers to trade, both tariff and nontariff, are one of the major issues confronting international marketers. Fortunately, tariffs generally have been reduced to record lows and substantial progress has been made on eliminating nontariff barriers. However, nations continue to use trade barriers for a variety of reasons: some rational, some not so rational.

Sources: Adapted from Todd G. Buchholz, "Free Trade Keeps Prices Down," *Consumers' Research Magazine*, October 1995, p. 22; Tomas Kellner, "What Gaul!" *Forbes*, April 28, 2003, p. 52; "Russia Blames Canada for Obstructing WTO Accession Talks," *Dow Jones Newswires*, July 7, 2005; www.neutrogena.com.

---

[1]Neutrogena has been a division of Johnson & Johnson since 1994. See Susan Warner, "From Band-Aids to Biotech," *New York Times*, April 10, 2005, p. 1.

Exhibit 2.1
Top Ten 2004 U.S. Trading Partners ($ billions, merchandise trade)

Source: www.census.gov/foreign-trade/top

Country	Total Trade	Exports	Imports	Balance
Canada	446.1	190.2	255.9	−65.7
Mexico	266.6	110.8	155.8	−45.0
China	231.4	34.7	196.7	−132.0
Japan	184.0	54.4	129.6	−75.2
Germany	108.6	31.4	77.2	−45.8
United Kingdom	82.4	36.0	46.4	−10.4
South Korea	72.5	26.3	46.2	−19.9
Taiwan	56.3	21.7	34.6	−12.9
France	53.1	21.2	31.8	−10.6
Malaysia	39.1	10.9	28.2	−17.3

Yesterday's competitive market battles were fought in western Europe, Japan, and the United States; tomorrow's competitive battles will extend to Latin America, eastern Europe, Russia, China, India, Asia, and Africa as these emerging markets continue to open to trade. More of the world's people, from the richest to the poorest, will participate in the world's wealth through global trade. The emerging global economy in which we live brings us into worldwide competition with significant advantages for both marketers and consumers. Marketers benefit from new markets opening and smaller markets growing large enough to become viable business opportunities. Consumers benefit by being able to select from the widest range of goods produced anywhere in the world at the lowest prices.

Bound together by satellite communications and global companies, consumers in every corner of the world are demanding an ever-expanding variety of goods. As Exhibit 2.1 illustrates, world trade is an important economic activity. Because of this importance, the inclination is for countries to control international trade to their own advantage. As competition intensifies, the tendency toward protectionism gains momentum. If the benefits of the social, political, and economic changes now taking place are to be fully realized, free trade must prevail throughout the global marketplace. The creation of the World Trade Organization (WTO) is one of the biggest victories for free trade in decades.

This chapter briefly surveys the United States' past and present role in global trade and some concepts important in understanding the relationship between international trade and national economic policy. A discussion of the logic and illogic of protectionism, the major impediment to trade, is followed by a review of the General Agreement on Tariffs and Trade (GATT) and its successor, the World Trade Organization (WTO), two multinational agreements designed to advance free trade.

1000 First millennium ends; Y1K problem overblown—widespread fear of the end of the world proved unfounded
1000 Vikings settle Newfoundland
1004 Chinese unity crumbles with treaty between the Song and the Liao giving the Liao full autonomy; China will remain fractured until the Mongol invasion in the 13th century (see 1206)
1025 Navy of Cholas in southern India crushes the empire of Srivijaya in modern Myanmar to protect their trade with China

1054 Italy and Egypt formalize commercial relations
1066 William the Conqueror is victorious over Harold II in the Battle of Hastings, establishing Norman rule in England and forever linking the country with the continent
1081 Venice and Byzantium conclude a commercial treaty (renewed in 1126)
1095 First of the crusades begins; Pope Urban II calls on Europe's noblemen to help the Byzantines repel the Turks; the crusaders' travel, stories, and goods acquired along the way help increased trade across

Europe and with the Mediterranean and Asia; eighth major crusade ends, Syria expels the Christians
1100 Japan begins to isolate itself from the rest of the world, not really opening up again until the mid-19th century (see 1858)
1100 China invents the mariner's compass and becomes a force in trade; widespread use of paper money also helps increase trade and prosperity
1100 Inca Empire in the Andes begins to develop, eventually encompassing about

12 million people until its destruction by the Spanish in 1553; cities specialize in certain farming and trade with others for what they don't make
1132 Corporate towns in France granted charters by Henry I to protect commerce
1189 German merchants conclude treaty with Novgorod in Russia
1200 Islam is introduced by spice traders to Southeast Asia
1200 More than 60,000 Italian merchants work and live in Constantinople
1206 Genghis Khan becomes the Great Khan, controlling

The Twentieth to the Twenty-First Century

At no time in modern economic history have countries been more economically interdependent, have greater opportunities for international trade existed, or has the potential for increased demand existed than now, at the opening of the 21st century. In the preceding 100 years, world economic development was erratic.

Bicycles and Web sites are both part of marketing in China.
(© AFP/Getty Images)

The first half of the 20th century was marred by a major worldwide economic depression that occurred between two world wars that all but destroyed most of the industrialized world. The last half of the century, while free of a world war, was marred by struggles between countries espousing the socialist Marxist approach and those following a democratic capitalist approach to economic development. As a result of this ideological split, traditional trade patterns were disrupted.

After World War II, as a means to dampen the spread of communism, the United States set out to infuse the ideal of capitalism throughout as much of the world as possible. The Marshall Plan to assist in rebuilding Europe, financial and industrial development assistance to rebuild Japan, and funds channeled through the Agency for International Development and other groups designed to foster economic growth in the underdeveloped world were used to help create a strong world economy. The dissolution of colonial powers created scores of new countries in Asia and Africa. With the striving of these countries to gain economic independence and the financial assistance offered by the United States, most of the noncommunist world's economies grew and new markets were created.

The benefits from the foreign economic assistance given by the United States flowed both ways. For every dollar the United States invested in the economic development and rebuilding of other countries after World War II, hundreds of dollars more returned in the form of purchases of U.S. agricultural products, manufactured goods, and services. This overseas demand created by the Marshall Plan and other programs[2] was important to the U.S. economy since the vast manufacturing base built to supply World War II and the swelling labor supply of returning military created a production capacity well beyond domestic needs. The major economic

---

[2]The Organization for Economic Cooperation and Development (OECD) was a direct result of the Marshall Plan. See Pam Casellas, "America Does Earn Its Stripes," *West Australian*, January 6, 2005, p. 15.

---

most of northern China; after his death in 1227, the Khan clan conquers much of Asia by midcentury and promotes trade and commerce, reviving the ancient Silk Road that linked Chinese and Western traders
1215 Magna Carta, a pact between the English king and his subjects, is signed by King John, who becomes subject to the rule of law
1229 German merchants sign trade treaty with the Prince of Smolensk in Russia
1252 First gold coins issued in the West since the fall of Rome, in Florence

1269 England institutes toll roads
1270 Venetian Marco Polo and his father travel through Asia and the Middle East, becoming the first European traders to establish extensive links with the region
1279 Kublai Khan unites China and creates the Yuan (Origin) dynasty; by the time he dies in 1294, he has created a unified Mongol Empire extending from China to eastern Europe
1300 The early stirrings of the Renaissance begin in Europe as people are exposed to other

cultures, primarily through merchants and trade; trade fairs are held in numerous European cities
1315 A great famine hits Europe, lasting two years, more widespread and longer than any before
1348 The Plague (the Black Death) kills one-fourth to one-third of the population in Europe (25 million people) in just three years, disrupting trade as cities try to prevent the spread of the disease by restricting visitors; it likely started in Asia in the 1320s; massive inflation took hold, since goods

could only be obtained locally; serfs were in high demand and began moving to higher wage payers, forever altering Europe's labor landscape
1358 German Hanseatic league officially formed by the Hansa companies of merchants for trade and mutual protection, eventually encompassing more than 70 cities and lasting nearly 300 years
1375 Timur Lang the Turk conquers lands from Moscow to Delhi
1381 English rioters kill foreign Flemish traders as part of the 100,000-strong peasant

boom and increased standard of living the United States experienced after World War II were fueled by fulfilling pent-up demand in the United States and demand created by the rebuilding of war-torn countries of Europe and Asia. In short, the United States helped to make the world's economies stronger, which enabled them to buy more from us.

In addition to U.S. economic assistance, a move toward international cooperation among trading nations was manifest in the negotiation of the General Agreement on Tariffs and Trade (GATT). International trade had ground to a halt following World War I when nations followed the example set by the U.S. passage of the Smoot-Hawley Act (1930), which raised average U.S. tariffs on more than 20,000 imported goods to levels in excess of 60 percent. In retaliation, 60 countries erected high tariff walls and international trade was stalled, along with most economies. A major worldwide recession catapulted the world's economies into the Great Depression when trade all but dried up after tariffs and other trade barriers were raised to intolerable heights.[3]

Determined not to repeat the economic disaster that followed World War I, world leaders created GATT, a forum for member countries to negotiate a reduction of tariffs and other barriers to trade. The forum proved successful in reaching those objectives. With the ratification of the Uruguay Round agreements, the GATT became part of the World Trade Organization (WTO) and its 117 original members moved into a new era of free trade.

World Trade and U.S. Multinationals

The rapid growth of war-torn economies and previously underdeveloped countries, coupled with large-scale economic cooperation and assistance, led to new global marketing opportunities. Rising standards of living and broad-based consumer and industrial markets abroad created opportunities for American companies to expand exports and investment worldwide. During the 1950s, many U.S. companies that had never before marketed outside the United States began to export, and others made significant investments in marketing and production facilities overseas.

At the close of the 1960s, U.S. multinational corporations (MNCs) were facing major challenges on two fronts: resistance to direct investment and increasing competition in export markets. Large investments by U.S. businesses in Europe and Latin America heightened the concern of these countries about the growing domination of U.S. multinationals. The reaction in Latin American countries was to expropriate direct U.S. investments or to force companies to sell controlling interests to nationals. In Europe, apprehension manifested itself in strong public demand to limit foreign investment. Concern there that Britain might become a satellite with manufacturing but no determination of policy led to specific guidelines for joint ventures between British and U.S. companies. In the European Community, U.S. multinationals were rebuffed in ways ranging from tight control over proposed

---

[3]David M. Kennedy, Lizabeth Cohen, and Thomas A. Bailey, *The American Pageant*, 13th ed. (Boston: Houghton Mifflin, 2005).

---

rebellion against Richard II, which was led by Wat Tyler in a failed attempt to throw off the yoke of feudalism

1392 England prohibits foreigners from retailing goods in the country

1400 Koreans develop movable-type printing (see 1450)

1404 Chinese prohibit private trading in foreign countries, but foreign ships may trade in China with official permission

1415 Chinese begin significant trading with Africa through government expeditions—some believe they sailed to North America as well in 1421

1425 Hanseatic city of Brugge becomes the first Atlantic seaport to be a major trading center

1427 Aztec Empire is created by Itzcotl; it will encompass about 6 million people until its destruction in 1519

1430 Portuguese Prince Henry the Navigator explores west African coast to promote trade

1441 Mayan Empire collapses as the city of Mayapán is destroyed in a revolt

1450 Renaissance takes hold in Florence, its traditional birthplace

1450 Gutenberg Bible is first book printed with movable type; the ability to mass produce books creates an information revolution

1453 Byzantine Empire is destroyed as Muhammad II sacks Constantinople (renaming it Istanbul)

1464 French royal mail service established by Louis XI

1470 Early trademark piracy committed by Persians who copy mass-produced Chinese porcelain to capitalize on its popularity in foreign countries

1479 Under the Treaty of Constantinople, in exchange

for trading rights in the Black Sea, Venice agrees to pay tribute to the Ottoman Empire

1482 English organize a postal system that features fresh relays of horses every 20 miles

1488 Bartolomeu Dias sails around the coast of Africa; this, along with the voyages of Christopher Columbus, ushers in the era of sea travel

1492 Christopher Columbus "discovers" the New World

1494 Portugal and Spain divide the unexplored world between them with the Treaty of Tordesillas joint ventures and regulations covering U.S. acquisitions of European firms to strong protectionism laws.

The threat felt by Europeans was best expressed in the popular book *The American Challenge*, published in 1968, in which the French author J. J. Servan-Schreiber wrote:

> Fifteen years from now it is quite possible that the world's third greatest industrial power, just after the United States and Russia, will not be Europe but American Industry in Europe. Already, in the ninth year of the Common Market, this European market is basically American in organization.[4]

Servan-Schreiber's prediction did not come true for many reasons, but one of the more important reasons was that American MNCs were confronted by a resurgence of competition from all over the world. The worldwide economic growth and rebuilding after World War II was beginning to surface in competition that challenged the supremacy of American industry. Competition arose on all fronts; Japan, Germany, most of the industrialized world, and many developing countries were competing for demand in their own countries and were looking for world markets as well. Countries once classified as less developed were reclassified as newly industrialized countries (NICs). NICs such as Brazil, Mexico, South Korea, Taiwan, Singapore, and Hong Kong experienced rapid industrialization in selected industries and became aggressive world competitors in steel, shipbuilding, consumer electronics, automobiles, light aircraft, shoes, textiles, apparel, and so forth. In addition to the NICs, developing countries such as Venezuela, Chile, and Bangladesh established state-owned enterprises (SOEs) that operated in other countries. One state-owned Venezuelan company has a subsidiary in Puerto Rico that produces canvas, cosmetics, chairs, and zippers; there are also Chilean and Colombian companies in Puerto Rico; in the U.S. state of Georgia, a Venezuelan company engages in agribusiness; and Bangladesh, the sixth largest exporter of garments to the United States, also owns a mattress company in Georgia.

In short, economic power and potential became more evenly distributed among countries than was the case when Servan-Schreiber warned Europe about U.S. multinational domination. Instead, the U.S. position in world trade is now shared with other countries. For example, in 1950 the United States represented 39 percent of world gross national product (GNP), but by 2000 it represented 23 percent. In the meantime, however, the global GNP was much larger, as was the world's manufacturing output—all countries shared in a much larger economic pie. This change was reflected in the fluctuations in growth of MNCs from other countries as well. Exhibit 2.2 shows the dramatic changes between 1963 and 2005. In 1963, the United States had 67 of the world's largest industrial corporations. By 1996, that number had dropped to a low of 24 while Japan moved from having 3 of the largest to 29

---

[4]J. J. Servan-Schreiber, *The American Challenge* (New York: Atheneum Publishers, 1968), p. 3.

1500   Rise of mercantilism, the accumulation of wealth by the state to increase power, in western Europe; states without gold or silver mines try to control trade to maintain a surplus and accumulate gold and silver; Englishman Thomas Mun was one of the great proponents in 1600, who realized that the overall balance of trade was the important factor, not whether each individual trade resulted in a surplus

1500   Slave trade becomes a major component of commerce

1504   Regular postal service established between Vienna, Brussels, and Madrid

1520   First chocolate brought from Mexico to Spain

1521   Mexico is conquered by Hernán Cortés after Aztec ruler, Montezuma, is accidentally killed

1522   Magellan's expedition completes its three-year sail around the world; it is the first successful circumnavigation

1531   Antwerp stock exchange is the first exchange to move into its own building, signifying its importance in financing commercial enterprises throughout Europe and the rising importance of private trade and commerce;

Antwerp emerges as a trading capital

1532   Brazil is colonized by the Portuguese

1534   English break from the Catholic Church, ending its dominance of politics and trade throughout Europe, as Henry VIII creates the Church of England

1553   South American Incan Empire ends with conquest by Spanish; the Incas had created an extensive area of trade, complete with an infrastructure of roads and canals

1555   Tobacco trade begins after its introduction to Europe

by Spanish and Portuguese traders

1557   Spanish crown suffers first of numerous bankruptcies, discouraging cross-border lending

1561   Via Dutch traders, tulips come to Europe from Near East for first time

1564   William Shakespeare is born; many of his plays are stories of merchant traders

1567   Typhoid fever, imported from Europe, kills two million Indians in South America

1588   Spanish Armada defeated by British, heralding Britain's emergence as the

Exhibit 2.2
The Nationality of the World's 100 Largest Industrial Corporations (size measured by annual revenues)

Source: For 2005 data, *2005 Global 500, Fortune,* www.fortune.com

	1963	1979	1984	1990	1996	2000	2003	2005
US	67	47	47	33	24	36	42	33
Germany	13	13	8	12	13	12	11	15
Britain	7	7	5	6	2	5	3	10
France	4	11	5	10	13	11	7	10
Japan	3	7	12	18	29	22	20	12
Italy	2	3	3	4	4	3	3	3
Netherlands–United Kingdom	2	2	2	2	2	—	2	2
Netherlands	1	3	1	1	2	5	4	2
Switzerland	1	1	2	3	5	3	4	4
Argentina	—	—	1	—	—	—	—	—
Belgium	—	1	1	1	—	1	—	—
Belgium–Netherlands	—	—	—	—	—	—	—	1
Brazil	—	1	—	1	—	—	—	—
Canada	—	2	3	—	—	—	—	—
India	—	—	1	—	—	—	—	—
Kuwait	—	—	1	—	—	—	—	—
Mexico	—	1	1	1	1	—	—	1
Venezuela	—	1	1	1	1	—	—	—
South Korea	—	—	4	2	4	—	—	1
Sweden	—	—	1	2	—	—	—	—
South Africa	—	—	1	1	—	—	—	—
Spain	—	—	—	2	—	—	1	1
Turkey	—	—	—	—	—	—	—	—
China	—	—	—	—	—	2	3	1
Norway	—	—	—	—	—	—	—	1

and South Korea from none to four. And following the great economic boom in the late 1990s in the United States, 42 of the largest companies were American, only 20 Japanese, and none were Korean.

Another dimension of world economic power, the balance of merchandise trade, reflected the changing role of the United States in world trade. Between 1888 and 1971, the United States sold more to other countries than it bought from them; that is, the United States had a favorable balance of trade. By 1971, however, the United States had a trade deficit of $2 billion that grew steadily until it peaked at $160 billion in 1987. After that, the deficit in merchandise trade declined to $74 billion in 1991 but began increasing again and by 2005 had surpassed $650 billion.

world's greatest naval power; this power will enable Britain to colonize many regions of the globe and lead to its becoming the world's commercially dominant power for the next 300 years
1596 First flush toilet is developed for Britain's Queen Elizabeth I
1597 Holy Roman Empire expels English merchants in retaliation for English treatment of Hanseatic League
1600 Potatoes are brought from South America to Europe where they quickly spread to the rest of world and become a staple of agricultural production
1600 Japan begins trading silver for foreign goods
1600 Britain's Queen Elizabeth I grants charter to the East India Company, which will dominate trade with the East until its demise in 1857
1601 France makes postal agreements with neighboring states
1602 Dutch charter their own East India Company, which will dominate the South Asian coffee and spice trade
1607 British colony of Jamestown built
1609 Dutch begin fur trade through Manhattan
1611 Japan gives Dutch limited permission to trade
1612 British East India Company builds its first factory in India
1620 *Mayflower* sails for the New World
1620 Father of the Scientific Revolution, Francis Bacon, publishes *Novum Organum,* promoting inductive reasoning through experimentation and observation
1625 Dutch jurist Hugo Grotius, sometimes called the father of international law, publishes *On the Laws of War and Peace*
1636 Harvard University founded
1637 Dutch "tulip mania" results in history's first boom–bust market crash
1651 English pass first of so-called Navigation Acts to restrict Dutch trade by forcing colonies to trade only with English ships
1654 Spain and Germany develop hereditary land rights, a concept which will help lead to the creation of great wealth in single families and thus to the development of private commercial empires

The heightened competition for U.S. businesses during the 1980s and early 1990s raised questions similar to those heard in Europe two decades earlier: how to maintain the competitive strength of American business, to avoid the domination of U.S. markets by foreign multinationals, and to forestall the buying of America. In the 1980s, the United States saw its competitive position in capital goods such as computers and machinery erode sharply. From 1983 to 1987, almost 70 percent of the growth of the merchandise trade deficit was in capital goods and automobiles. At the time, those were America's high-wage, high-skill industries. U.S. industry got a wake-up call and responded by restructuring its industries, in essence, "getting lean and mean." By the late 1990s, the United States was once again holding its own in capital goods, particularly with trade surpluses in the high-tech category.

Among the more important questions raised were those concerning the ability of U.S. firms to compete in foreign markets and the fairness of international trade policies of some countries. Trade friction revolved around Japan's sales of autos and electronics in the United States and Japan's restrictive trade practices. The United States, a strong advocate of free trade, was confronted with the dilemma of how to encourage trading partners to reciprocate with open access to their markets without provoking increased protectionism. Besides successfully pressuring Japan to open its markets for some types of trade and investment, the United States was a driving force behind the establishment of the WTO.

By the last decade of the 20th century profound changes in the way the world would trade were already under way. The continuing integration of the countries of the European Union, the creation of NAFTA and the American Free Trade Area (AFTA), and the rapid evolution of the Asia-Pacific Economic Cooperation Conference (APEC) are the beginnings of global trading blocks that many experts expect to dominate trade patterns in the future. With the return of Hong Kong in 1997 and Macao in 2000 to China, all of Asia is now controlled and managed by Asians for the first time in 400 years. During the decades since World War II, the West set the patterns for trade, but increasingly Asia will be a major force, if not the leading force.

The First Decade of the Twenty-First Century and Beyond

The unprecedented and precipitous growth of the U.S. economy in the late 1990s has slowed dramatically in the last few years. Growth in most of the rest of the world has followed suit with the exception of China. The Organization for Economic Cooperation and Development (OECD) estimates that the economies of member countries will expand an average of 3 percent annually for the next 25 years, the same rate as in the past 25 years. Conversely, the economies of the developing world will grow at faster rates—from an annual rate of 4 percent in the past quarter century to a rate of 6 percent for the next 25 years. Their share of world output will rise from about one-sixth to nearly one-third over the same period. The World Bank estimates that five countries—Brazil, China, India, Indonesia, and Russia—whose share of world trade is barely a third of that of the European Union will by 2020 be 50 percent higher than that of the European Union. As a consequence, economic

---

1687 Apple falling on Newton's head leads to his publication of the law of gravity

1694 The Bank of England is established; it offers loans to private individuals at 8 percent interest

1698 First steam engine is invented

1719 French consolidate their trade in Asia into one company, the French East India Company; rival British East India Company maintains its grip on the region's trade, however, and French revert to individual company trading 60 years later

1725 Rise of Physiocrats, followers of the economic philosopher François Quesnay, who believed that production, not trade, created wealth and that natural law should rule, which meant producers should be able to exchange goods freely; movement influenced Adam Smith's ideas promoting free trade

1740 Maria Theresa becomes empress of the Holy Roman Empire (until 1780); she ends serfdom and strengthens the power of the state

1748 First modern, scientifically drawn map, the Carte

Géométrique de la France, comprising 182 sheets, was authorized and subsequently drawn by the French Academy; Louis XV proclaimed that the new map, with more accurate data, lost more territory than his wars of conquest had gained

1750 Benjamin Franklin shows that lightning is a form of electricity by conducting it through the wet string of a kite

1750 Industrial revolution begins and takes off with the manufacture, in 1780, of the steam engine to drive machines—increased productivity and

consumption follow (as do poor working conditions and increased hardships for workers)

1760 Chinese begin strict regulation of foreign trade to last nearly a century when they permit Europeans to do business only in a small area outside Canton and only with appointed Chinese traders

1764 British victories in India begin Britain's dominance of India, Eastern trade, and trade routes

1764 British begin numbering houses, making mail delivery more efficient and providing the means for the development power and influence will move away from industrialized countries—Japan, the United States, and the European Union—to countries in Latin America, eastern Europe, Asia, and Africa.

This does not mean that markets in Europe, Japan, and the United States will cease to be important; those economies will continue to produce large, lucrative markets and the companies established in those markets will benefit. It does mean that if a company is to be a major player in the 21st century, now is the time to begin laying the groundwork. How will these changes that are taking place in the global marketplace impact international business? For one thing, the level and intensity of competition will change as companies focus on gaining entry into or maintaining their position in emerging markets, regional trade areas, and the established markets in Europe, Japan, and the United States.

Companies are looking for ways to become more efficient, improve productivity, and expand their global reach while maintaining an ability to respond quickly to deliver a product that the market demands. For example, large multinational companies such as Matsushita of Japan continue to expand their global reach. Nestlé is consolidating its dominance in global consumer markets by acquiring and vigorously marketing local-country major brands. Samsung of South Korea has invested $500 million in Mexico to secure access to markets in the North American Free Trade Area. Whirlpool, the U.S. appliance manufacturer which secured first place in the global appliance business by acquiring the European division of the appliance maker N. V. Philips, immediately began restructuring itself into its version of a global company. These are a few examples of changes that are sweeping multinational companies as they gear up for the 21st century.

Global companies are not the only ones aggressively seeking new market opportunities. Smaller companies are using novel approaches to marketing and seeking ways to apply their technological expertise to exporting goods and services not previously sold abroad. A small Midwestern company that manufactures and freezes bagel dough for supermarkets to bake and sell as their own saw opportunities abroad and began to export to Japan. International sales, though small initially, showed such potential that the company sold its U.S. business in order to concentrate on international operations. Other examples of smaller companies include Nochar Inc., which makes a fire retardant it developed a decade ago for the Indianapolis 500. The company now gets 32 percent of its sales overseas, in 29 countries. The owner of Buztronics Inc., a maker of promotional lapel buttons, heard from a friend that his buttons, with their red blinking lights, would "do great" in Japan. He made his first entry in exporting to Japan and after only a year, 10 percent of Buztronics sales come from overseas. While 50 of the largest exporters account for 30 percent of U.S. merchandise exports, the rest come from middle and small firms like those just mentioned. The business world is weathering a flurry of activity as companies large and small adjust to the internationalization of the marketplace at home and abroad.

As is always true in business, the best-laid plans can fail or be slowed by dramatic changes in the economy. When the U.S. economy was less involved in international trade, economic upheavals abroad often went unnoticed except by the very largest companies. But

of direct mail merchants centuries later

1773 Boston Tea Party symbolizes start of American Revolution; impetus comes from American merchants trying to take control of distribution of goods that were being controlled exclusively by Britain

1776 American Declaration of Independence proclaims the colonies' rights to determine their own destiny, particularly their own economic destiny

1776 Theory of modern capitalism and free trade expressed by Adam Smith in *The Wealth of Nations*; he theorized that

countries would only produce and export goods which they were able to produce more cheaply than could trading partners; he demonstrates that mercantilists were wrong: It is not gold or silver that will enhance the state, but the *material* that can be purchased with it

1787 U.S. Constitution approved; it becomes a model document for constitutions for at least the next two centuries; written constitutions will help to stabilize many countries and encourage foreign investment and trade with them

1783 Treaty of Paris officially ends the American Revolution following British surrender to American troops at Yorktown in 1781

1789 French Revolution begins; it will alter the power structure in Europe and help lead to the introduction of laws protecting the individual and to limited democracy in the region

1792 Gas lighting introduced; within three decades most major European and U.S. cities will use gas lights

1804 Steam locomotive introduced; it will become the dominant form of transport of goods

and people until the 20th century when trucks and airplanes become commercially viable

1804 Napoleon crowns himself emperor, overthrowing the French revolutionary government, and tries to conquer Europe (after already occupying Egypt as a means of cutting off British trade with the East), the failure of which results in the redrawing of national boundaries in Europe and Latin America

1807 Robert Fulton's steamboat is the first to usher in a new age of transport when his *Clermont* sails from New York to Albany in 1997, when the stock market in Hong Kong dropped precipitously and South Korea and several Southeast Asia economies faltered shortly thereafter, the U.S. stock market reacted with its largest daily drop in several years. The fear was the potential negative impact on U.S. technology industries if the economies of Asian customers slowed. Four years later most of the world's emerging markets were on a somewhat slower but nevertheless positive growth path than before the financial crisis of 1997.

Balance of Payments

When countries trade, financial transactions among businesses or consumers of different nations occur. Products and services are exported and imported, monetary gifts are exchanged, investments are made, cash payments are made and cash receipts received, and vacation and foreign travel occurs. In short, over a period of time, there is a constant flow of money into and out of a country. The system of accounts that records a nation's international financial transactions is called its *balance of payments*.

A nation's balance-of-payments statement records all financial transactions between its residents and those of the rest of the world during a given period of time—usually one year. Because the balance-of-payments record is maintained on a double-entry bookkeeping system, it must always be in balance. As on an individual's financial statement, the assets and liabilities or the credits and debits must offset each other. And like an individual's statement, the fact that they balance does not mean a nation is in particularly good or poor financial condition. A balance of payments is a record of condition, not a determinant of condition. Each of the nation's financial transactions with other countries is reflected in its balance of payments.

A nation's balance-of-payments presents an overall view of its international economic position and is an important economic measure used by treasuries, central banks, and other government agencies whose responsibility is to maintain external and internal economic stability. A balance of payments represents the difference between receipts from foreign countries on one side and payments to them on the other. On the plus side of the U.S. balance of payments are merchandise export sales, money spent by foreign tourists, payments to the United States for insurance, transportation, and similar services, payments of dividends and interest on investments abroad, return on capital invested abroad, new foreign investments in the United States, and foreign government payments to the United States.

On the minus side are costs of goods imported, spending by American tourists overseas, new overseas investments, and the cost of foreign military and economic aid. A deficit results when international payments are greater than receipts. It can be reduced or eliminated by increasing a country's international receipts (i.e., gain more exports to other countries or more tourists from other countries) and/or reducing expenditures in other countries. A balance-of-payments statement includes three accounts: the *current account*—a record of all merchandise exports, imports, and services plus unilateral transfers of funds; the *capital account*—a record of direct investment, portfolio investment, and short-term capital movements to and from countries; and the official *reserves account*—a record of exports and imports of gold,

---

1807   French Napoleonic Code issued and eventually becomes a model of civil law adopted by many nations around the world
1807   U.S. President Thomas Jefferson bans trade with Europe in an effort to convince warring British and French ships to leave neutral U.S. trading ships alone
1810   Frenchman Nicolas Appert successfully cans food and prevents spoilage
1810   Following Napoleon's invasion of Spain and Portugal, Simón Bolivar begins wars of independence for Spanish

colonies in Latin America, leading to new governments in Bolivia, Columbia, Ecuador, Peru, and Venezuela
1814   First practical steam locomotive is built by George Stephenson in England, leading to the birth of railroad transportation in 1825 with the first train carrying 450 passengers at 15 miles per hour
1815   Napoleon defeated at Battle of Waterloo and gives up throne days later
1815   British build roads of crushed stone, greatly improving the quality and speed of road travel

1817   David Ricardo publishes *Principles of Political Economy and Taxation*, in which he proposes modern trade theory: that comparative advantage drives trade; that countries will produce and export goods for which they have a *comparative* advantage as opposed to Adam Smith's *absolute* advantage (see 1776)
1821   Britain is first to adopt gold standard to back value of its currency
1823   U.S. President James Monroe promulgates the doctrine bearing his name that declares the Americas closed to

colonization in an attempt to assert U.S. influence over the region
1837   Reign of Britain's Queen Victoria begins; she oversees the growth of the British Empire and Britain's emergence as an industrial power (she dies in 1901)
1837   Electronic telegraph begins wide commercial use, transmitting information, including production orders, swiftly
1839   Process for recording negative images on paper is introduced in England, the precursor to modern film technology

Exhibit 2.3
U.S. Current Account by Major Components, 2004 ($ billions)

Exports	
Goods	808
Services	344
Income receipts	380
Imports	
Goods	−1,473
Services	−296
Income payments	−349
Unilateral current transfers, net	−81
Current account balance	−666

increases or decreases in foreign exchange, and increases or decreases in liabilities to foreign central banks. Of the three, the current account is of primary interest to international business.

The *current account* is important because it includes all international merchandise trade and service accounts, that is, accounts for the value of all merchandise and services imported and exported and all receipts and payments from investments.[5] Exhibit 2.3 gives the current account calculations for the United States in 2004.[6]

Since 1971 the United States has had a favorable current account balance (as a percentage of GDP) in only a few years—see Exhibit 2.4. The imbalances resulted primarily from

---

[5]Rich Miller, "Too Much Money," *BusinessWeek*, July 11, 2005, pp. 59–64.
[6]"Wise Men at Ease," *The Economist*, April 30, 2005, pp. 69–70.

Exhibit 2.4
United States Current Account Balance (% of GDP)

Percent

*IMF estimate

Exhibit 2.5
What Would One U.S.
Dollar Buy?

Source: Euromonitor International,
2005.

	1985	1988	1992	1995	1999	2000	2003	2005
British pound	0.86	0.54	0.56	0.63	0.62	0.68	0.61	0.57
French franc	9.6	5.4	5.29	4.95	6.49	7.28	—	—
Japanese yen	250.23	123.7	126.7	93.96	102.58	112.21	118.7	112.3
Swiss franc	2.25	1.29	1.41	1.18	1.58	1.68	1.31	1.31
EURO					1.01	.90	.85	.84
Mexico peso	0.37	2.28	3.12	6.45	9.43	9.47	10.6	10.8

U.S. demand for oil,[7] petroleum products, cars, consumer durables, and other merchandise. Indeed, the merchandise trade deficit for 2004 was $665 billion.[8] Such imbalances have drastic effects on the balance of payments, and, therefore, the value of U.S. currency in the world marketplace. Factors such as these eventually require an adjustment through a change in exchange rate, prices, and/or incomes.[9] In short, once the wealth of a country whose expenditures exceed its income has been exhausted that country, like an individual, must reduce its standard of living. If its residents do not do so voluntarily, the rate of exchange of its money for foreign moneys declines; and through the medium of the foreign exchange market, the purchasing power of foreign goods is transferred from that country to another. As can be seen in Exhibit 2.5, the U.S. dollar strengthened against most of the other major currencies during the 1990s but has weakened recently.

As the U.S. trade deficit grows pressures should begin to push the value of the dollar to lower levels. And when foreign currencies can be traded for more dollars, U.S. products (and companies)[10] are less expensive for the foreign customer and exports increase, and foreign products are more expensive for the U.S. customer and the demand for imported goods is dampened.

Protectionism

International business must face the reality that this is a world of tariffs, quotas, and nontariff barriers designed to protect a country's markets from intrusion by foreign companies. Although the World Trade Organization has been effective in reducing tariffs, countries still resort to measures of protectionism. Nations utilize legal barriers, exchange barriers, and psychological barriers to restrain entry of unwanted goods.[11] Businesses work together to establish private market barriers while the market structure itself may provide formidable barriers to imported goods. The complex distribution system in Japan is a good example of a market structure creating a barrier to trade. However, as effective as it is in keeping some products out of the market, in a legal sense it cannot be viewed as a trade barrier.

Protection Logic and Illogic

Countless reasons to maintain government restrictions on trade are espoused by protectionists, but essentially all arguments can be classified as follows: (1) protection of an infant industry, (2) protection of the home market,[12] (3) need to keep money at home, (4) encouragement of

---

[7]Sudeep Reddy, "$60.54 per Barrel," *Dallas Morning News*, June 28, 2005, p. D1.

[8]Associated Press, "U.S. Trade Gap Increases 3.6%," June 18, 2005.

[9]Some disagree with this conventional wisdom. See Diana Farrell, "America's External Deficit," *Milken Institute Review* 2 (2005), pp. 10–17.

[10]Katherine Yung, "Chinese See USA as Land of Opportunity," *Dallas Morning News*, June 26, 2005, pp. D1, D6.

[11]"Europe's New Protectionism," *The Economist*, July 2, 2005, p. 49.

[12]Even Japan is facing uncomfortable competition from China. See Chester Dawson and Karen Nickel Anhalt, "A 'China Price' for Toyota," *BusinessWeek*, February 21, 2005, pp. 50–52

1856 Declaration of Paris recognizes the principle of free movement for trade, even in wartime—blockades could only extend along the enemy's coast; it also establishes the practice of allowing the accession to treaties of nations other than the original signatories

1857 Russia and France sign trade treaty
1858 Ansei Commercial Treaties with Japan open the formerly closed country to trade with the West (treaties follow "opening" of Japan to the West by American Matthew Perry in 1854)

1860 The Cobden Treaty aims to create free trade by reducing or eliminating tariffs between Britain and France; also leads to most-favored-nation status in bilateral agreements and eventually to multilateral agreements

1860 Passports are introduced in the United States to regulate foreign travel
1866 The principle of the electric dynamo is found by German Werner Siemens, who will produce the first electric power transmission system

CROSSING BORDERS 2.1   Trade Barriers, Hypocrisy, and the United States

The United States thinks of itself as the leader in free trade and frequently brings actions against nations as unfair trade partners. Section 301* of the Omnibus Trade and Competitiveness Act authorizes the U.S. government to investigate and retaliate against specific foreign trade barriers judged to be unfair and to impose up to 100 percent tariffs on exports to the United States from guilty nations unless they satisfy U.S. domestic demands. But critics say the United States is somewhat hypocritical in some of the stands taken since it is just as guilty of protecting its markets with trade barriers. A Japanese government study alleges that the United States engages in unfair trade practices in 10 of 12 policy areas reviewed in the study. Notably, the United States imposes quotas on imports, has high tariffs, and abuses antidumping measures. Are the critics correct? Is the United States being hypocritical when it comes to free trade? You be the judge.

The United States launched a Section 301 investigation of Japanese citrus quotas. "The removal of Japan's unfair barriers could cut the price of oranges for Japanese consumers by one third," said the U.S. trade representative. Coincidentally, the United States had a 40 percent tariff on Brazilian orange juice imports when the investigation was initiated.

The United States brought a 301 case against Korea for its beef import quotas even though the United States has beef import quotas that are estimated to cost U.S. consumers $873 million annually in higher prices. Another 301 case was brought against Brazil, Korea, and Taiwan for trade barriers on footwear even though the United States maintains tariffs as high as 67 percent on footwear imports.

Can you believe that we have two phone book–sized volumes of the U.S. customs code that includes restrictions on such innocuous items as scissors, sweaters, leather, costume jewelry, tampons, pizzas, cotton swabs, ice cream from Jamaica, and even products we do not produce such as vitamin B_{12}. We also have restrictions on more sensitive products such as cars, supercomputers, lumber, and every type of clothing imaginable. Would-be Latin American exporters find hundreds of their most promising export products such as grapes, tomatoes, onions, steel, cement, asparagus, and shoes on the customs list. Visit www.usitc.gov/taffairs.htm and select the Interactive Tariff Database to see some other examples.

So, is the U.S. as guilty as the rest or not?

*Section 301, a provision of U.S. trade law, enables the U.S. government to take action against countries deemed to have engaged in "unreasonable, unjustifiable, or discriminatory" practices that restrict U.S. commerce.

Sources: Abstracted from James Bovard, "A U.S. History of Trade Hypocrisy," *Wall Street Journal*, March 8, 1994, p. A10; Paul Glader, "U.S. Imports of Steel Increase 23%," *Asian Wall Street Journal*, June 23, 2005, p. A1.

---

capital accumulation, (5) maintenance of the standard of living and real wages, (6) conservation of natural resources, (7) industrialization of a low-wage nation, (8) maintenance of employment and reduction of unemployment, (9) national defense, (10) increase of business size, and (11) retaliation and bargaining. Economists in general recognize as valid only the arguments for infant industry, national defense, and industrialization of underdeveloped countries. The resource conservation argument becomes increasingly valid in an era of environmental consciousness[13] and worldwide shortages of raw materials and agricultural commodities. A case might be made for temporary protection of markets with excess pro-

---

[13]John Carey, "Global Warming, Suddenly the Climate in Washington Is Changing," *BusinessWeek*, June 27, 2005, p. 91.

1866 The trans-Atlantic cable is completed, allowing nearly instant (telegraphic) communication between the United States and Europe
1869 Suez Canal completed after 11 years of construction; the canal significantly cuts the time for travel between Europe and Asia, shortening, for example, the trip between Britain and India by 4,000 miles
1869 First U.S. transcontinental rail route is completed, heralding a boon for commerce; first commercially viable typewriter patented; until computer word processing becomes common more than a century later, the typewriter enables anyone to produce documents quickly and legibly
1873 United States adopts the gold standard to fix the international value of the dollar
1875 Universal Postal Union created in Switzerland to provide for an international mail service
1876 Alexander Graham Bell is granted a patent for the telephone, which will revolutionize communications
1880 Thomas Edison creates first electric power station, after

CROSSING **BORDERS 2.2**   A Word for Open Markets

Bastiat's century-old farcical letter to the French Chamber of Deputies points up the ultimate folly of tariffs and the advantages of utilizing the superior production advantage of others.

To the Chamber of Deputies:

We are subjected to the intolerable competition of a foreign rival, who enjoys such superior facilities for the production of light that he can inundate our national market at reduced price. This rival is no other than the sun. Our petition is to pass a law shutting up all windows, openings, and fissures through which the light of the sun is used to penetrate our dwellings, to the prejudice of the profitable manufacture we have been enabled to bestow on the country.

Signed: Candlestick Makers,
    F. Bastiat

ductive capacity or excess labor when such protection could facilitate an orderly transition. Unfortunately such protection becomes long term and contributes to industrial inefficiency while detracting from a nation's realistic adjustment to its world situation.

Most protectionists argue the need for tariffs on one of the three premises recognized by economists—whether or not they are relevant to their products. Proponents are likely also to call on the maintenance-of-employment argument because it has substantial political appeal. When arguing for protection, the basic economic advantages of international trade are ignored. The fact that the consumer ultimately bears the cost of tariffs and other protective measures is conveniently overlooked. Sugar and textiles are good examples of protected industries in the United States that could not be justified by any of the three arguments, and U.S. government protections of both industries are eroding quickly.

To give you some idea of the cost to the consumer, consider the results of a recent study of 21 protected industries. The research showed that U.S. consumers pay about $70 billion per year in higher prices because of tariffs and other protective restrictions. On average, the cost to consumers for saving one job in these protected industries was $170,000 per year, or six times the average pay (wages and benefits) for manufacturing workers. Those figures represent the average of 21 protected industries, but the cost is much higher in selected industries. In the steel industry, for example, countervailing duties and antidumping penalties on foreign suppliers of steel since 1992 have saved the jobs of 1,239 steelworkers at a cost of $835,351 each. Unfortunately, protectionism is politically popular, but it rarely leads to renewed growth in a declining industry. And the jobs that are saved are saved at a very high cost, which constitutes a hidden tax that consumers unknowingly pay.

Trade Barriers   To encourage development of domestic industry and protect existing industry, governments may establish such barriers to trade as tariffs, quotas, boycotts, monetary barriers, nontariff barriers, and market barriers. Barriers are imposed against imports and against foreign businesses. While the inspiration for such barriers may be economic or political, they are encouraged by local industry. Whether or not the barriers are economically logical, the fact is they exist.

inventing the electric light in 1878, which lights New York City and starts a revolution in culture and business—making a truly 24-hour day and paving the way for electronic machines
1881 Zoopraxiscope, which shows pictures in motion, is developed

1884 The basis for establishing standard time and measuring the longitude of any spot in the world is created with the designation of Greenwich, England, as the prime meridian (0° longitude)
1886 American Federation of Labor founded, becoming a

model for workers around the world to unite against management and gain higher pay and better working conditions
1901 Italian Guglielmo Marconi sends the first radio message; the radio could be said to spark the start of globalization because of the speed with

which information is able to be transmitted
1903 First successful flight of an airplane, piloted by Orville Wright, takes place at Kitty Hawk, North Carolina
1904 First vacuum tube is developed by John Fleming, allowing alternating current to

Exhibit 2.6
Types of Nontariff Barriers

Specific Limitations on Trade Quotas Import licensing requirements Proportional restrictions of foreign to domestic goods (local-content requirements) Minimum import price limits Embargoes	**Governmental Participation in Trade** Government procurement policies Export subsidies Countervailing duties Domestic assistance programs
Customs and Administrative Entry Procedures Valuation systems Antidumping practices Tariff classifications Documentation requirements Fees	**Charges on Imports** Prior import deposit requirements Administrative fees Special supplementary duties Import credit discriminations Variable levies Border taxes
Standards Standards disparities Intergovernmental acceptances of testing methods and standards Packaging, labeling, marking standards	**Others** Voluntary export restraints Orderly marketing agreements

Source: Reprinted from *Journal of World Business*, A. D. Cao, "Nontariff Barriers to U.S. Manufactured Exports," vol. 15, p. 94. Copyright © 1980, with permission from Elsevier.

Tariffs.   A tariff, simply defined, is a tax imposed by a government on goods entering at its borders. Tariffs may be used as a revenue-generating tax or to discourage the importation of goods, or for both reasons.[14] In general, tariffs:

Increase	Inflationary pressures. Special interests' privileges. Government control and political considerations in economic matters. The number of tariffs (they beget other tariffs via reciprocity).
Weaken	Balance-of-payments positions. Supply-and-demand patterns. International relations (they can start trade wars).
Restrict	Manufacturers' supply sources. Choices available to consumers. Competition.

In addition, tariffs are arbitrary, are discriminatory, and require constant administration and supervision. They often are used as reprisals against protectionist moves of trading partners. In a dispute with the European Union over pasta export subsidies, the United States ordered a 40 percent increase in tariffs on European spaghetti and fancy pasta. The EU retaliated against U.S. walnuts and lemons. The pasta war raged on as Europe increased tariffs on U.S. fertilizer, paper products, and beef tallow, and the United States responded in kind. The war ended when the Europeans finally dropped pasta export subsidies. The EU and the United States also fought a similar trade war over bananas! Most recently less

---

[14]Jordan Ryan, "A Changed Vietnam, American Support Vital to Expand Reforms," *Dallas Morning News*, June 27, 2005, p. 17A.

become direct current and helping to create widespread use of the radio
1913 Assembly line introduced by Henry Ford; it will revolutionize manufacturing
1914 The first war to involve much of the world begins with the assassination of Archduke

Francis Ferdinand and lasts four years; construction of Panama Canal is completed, making trade faster and easier
1917 Lenin and Trotsky lead Russian revolution, creating a living economic model which will affect trade (adversely) for the rest of the century

1919 First nonstop transAtlantic flight completed, paving the way for cargo to be transported quickly around the globe
1920 League of Nations created, establishing a model for international cooperation (though it failed to keep the peace)

1923 Vladimir Zworykin creates first electronic television, which will eventually help integrate cultures and consumers across the world
1929 Great Depression starts with crash of U.S. stock market
1930 Hawley-Smoot Tariff passed by U.S. Senate,

CROSSING BORDERS 2.3   Crossing Borders with Monkeys in His Pants

Robert Cusack smuggled a pair of endangered pygmy monkeys into the United States. In his pants! On June 13, 2002, a U.S. Fish and Wildlife Service special agent was called to Los Angeles International Airport after Cusack was detained by U.S. Customs on arrival from Thailand. Officials soon also discovered that Cusack had four endangered birds of paradise and 50 protected orchids with him. "When one of the inspectors opened up his luggage, one of the birds flew out," tells one official. "He had to go catch the bird." After finding the other purloined birds and exotic flowers, the inspectors asked, "Do you have anything else you should tell us about?" Cusack answered, "Yes, I have monkeys in my pants." The monkeys ended up in the Los Angeles Zoo, and the smuggler ended up in jail for 57 days. He also paid a five-figure fine.

Richard Connors, a Chicago lawyer, should have known better. He was caught smuggling thousands of Cuban cigars into the United States in violation of the 40-year-old trade embargo against Castro's Cuba. Connors, who had made monthly trips to Cuba via Canada and Mexico, faces up to five years in prison for his transgressions.

Smuggling isn't just a game played by sneaking individuals. Multinational companies can also get into

the act. During this last year alone convictions have come down for smuggling cell phones into Vietnam, cigarettes into Iraq and Canada, and platinum into China. In perhaps the biggest ever corporate case, after a nine-year lawsuit Amway Corporation agreed to pay the Canadian government $38.1 million to settle charges it had avoided customs duties by undervaluing merchandise it exported from the U.S. to Canadian distributors over a six-year period. As long as there have been trade barriers, smuggling has been a common response. Indeed, Rudyard Kipling wrote some 100 years ago:

> Five and twenty ponies trotting through the dark—
> Brandy for the Parson, 'baccy for the clerk;
> Laces for a lady, letters for a spy;
> And watch the wall, my darling, while the Gentlemen go by!

Sources: "Amway Pays $38-Million to Canada," *Los Angeles Times*, September 22, 1989, p. 3; "Conviction in Cigar Smuggling," *New York Times*, October 11, 2002, p. 27; Patricia Ward Biederman, "Smuggler to Pay for Pocketing Monkeys," *Los Angeles Times*, December 19, 2002, p. B1; Barry Wain, "Two Vietnamese Brothers Fall Victim to Their Success," *Wall Street Journal*, May 15, 2003, p. A15.

developed countries are increasingly voicing complaints about American and European tariffs on agricultural products.[15]

Quotas.   A quota is a specific unit or dollar limit applied to a particular type of good. Great Britain limits imported television sets, Germany established quotas on Japanese ball bearings, Italy restricts Japanese motorcycles, and the United States has quotas on sugar, textiles,[16] and, of all things, peanuts. Quotas put an absolute restriction on the quantity of a specific item that can be imported. When the Japanese first let foreign rice into their country it was on a quota basis, but since 2000 the quotas have been replaced by tariffs.[17] Even more complicated, the banana war between the United States and the EU resulted in a mixed system wherein a quota of bananas is allowed into the EU with a tariff, then a second quota comes in tariff-free. Like tariffs, quotas tend to increase prices. U.S. quotas on textiles are estimated to add 50 percent to the wholesale price of clothing.

---

[15]"Delivering on Doha's Promise," *The Economist*, January 8, 2005, p. 11.

[16]Ernesto Zedillo, "China—Wrong Whipping Boy," *Forbes*, July 25, 2005, p. 37.

[17]See the USA Rice Federation's Web site for details—www.usarice.com.

plunging the world deeper into the Great Depression
1935 Radar developed in Britain; it will allow travel on ships and planes even when there is no visibility, enabling the goods to keep to a transport schedule (eventually allow-

ing the development of just-in-time and other cost-savings processes)
1938 American Chester Carlson develops dry copying process for documents (xerography), which, among other things, will enable governments

to require that multiple forms be filled out to move goods
1939 World War II begins with German invasion of Poland; over 50 million people will die
1943 The first programmable computer, Colossus I, is created in England at Bletchley Park; it

helps to crack German codes
1944 Bretton Woods Conference creates basis for economic cooperation among 44 nations and the founding of the International Monetary Fund to help stabilize exchange rates

Voluntary Export Restraints.   Similar to quotas are the *voluntary export restraints* (VERs) or *orderly market agreements* (OMAs). Common in textiles, clothing, steel, agriculture, and automobiles, the VER is an agreement between the importing country and the exporting country for a restriction on the volume of exports. Japan has a VER on automobiles to the United States; that is, Japan has agreed to export a fixed number of automobiles annually. When televisions were still manufactured in the United States, Japan signed an OMA limiting Japanese color television exports to the United States to 1.56 million units per year. However, as a result of the OMA, Japanese companies began investing in television manufacturing in the United States and Mexico, and as a result they regained the entire market share that had been lost through the OMA, eventually dominating the entire market. A VER is called voluntary because the exporting country sets the limits; however, it is generally imposed under the threat of stiffer quotas and tariffs being set by the importing country if a VER is not established.

Boycotts and Embargoes.   A government boycott is an absolute restriction against the purchase and importation of certain goods from other countries. An embargo is a refusal to sell to a specific country. A public boycott can be either formal or informal and may be government sponsored or sponsored by an industry. The United States uses boycotts and embargoes against countries with which it has a dispute. For example, Cuba and Iran still have sanctions imposed by the United States. Among U.S. policy makers, there is rising concern, however, that government-sponsored sanctions cause unnecessary harm for both the United States and the country being boycotted without reaching desired results. It is not unusual for the citizens of a country to boycott goods of other countries at the urging of their government or civic groups. Nestlé products were boycotted by a citizens group that considered the way Nestlé promoted baby milk formula in less developed countries misleading to mothers and harmful to their babies.

Monetary Barriers.   A government can effectively regulate its international trade position by various forms of exchange-control restrictions. A government may enact such restrictions to preserve its balance-of-payments position or specifically for the advantage or encouragement of particular industries. Three barriers should be considered: blocked currency, differential exchange rates, and government approval requirements for securing foreign exchange.

Blocked currency is used as a political weapon or as a response to difficult balance-of-payments situations. In effect, blockage cuts off all importing or all importing above a certain level. Blockage is accomplished by refusing to allow an importer to exchange its national currency for the sellers' currency.

The *differential exchange rate* is a particularly ingenious method of controlling imports. It encourages the importation of goods the government deems desirable and discourages importation of goods the government does not want. The essential mechanism requires the importer to pay varying amounts of domestic currency for foreign exchange with which to purchase products in different categories. For example, the exchange rate for a desirable category of goods might be one unit of domestic money for one unit of a specific foreign currency. For a less desirable product, the rate might be two domestic currency units for one foreign unit. For an undesirable product, the rate might be three domestic units for one foreign unit. An importer of an undesirable product has to pay three times as much for the foreign exchange as the importer of a desired product.

Government approval to secure foreign exchange is often used by countries experiencing severe shortages of foreign exchange. At one time or another, most Latin American and East

1945   Atomic weapons introduced; World War II ends; United Nations founded
1947   General Agreement on Tariffs and Trade signed by 23 countries to try to reduce barriers to trade around the world
1948   Transistor is invented; it replaces the vacuum tube,

starting a technology revolution
1949   People's Republic of China founded by Mao Zedong, which will restrict access to the largest single consumer market on the globe
1957   European Economic Community (EEC) established by

Belgium, France, West Germany, Italy, Luxembourg, and the Netherlands, the precursor to today's European Union
1961   Berlin Wall is erected, creating Eastern and Western Europe with a physical and spiritual barrier

1964   Global satellite communications network established with INTELSAT (International Telecommunications Satellite Organization)
1965   *Unsafe at Any Speed* published by Ralph Nader, sparking a revolution in consumer information and rights

Cracker Jack invented the toy-with-candy promotion back in 1912. However, the Italian chocolatier Ferrero took things much further. Its milk chocolate Kinder eggs contain "sopresas" that kids enjoy in 37 countries around the world. The product is unavailable in the United States because of choking hazards. The product pictured is produced in Argentina for sale in Mexico, and it includes a warning label regarding kids under three. Cracker Jack has had to eliminate many of the cool little toys it put in the packages for the same reason. Nestlé introduced a product similar to Kinder eggs in the U.S. market in the late 1990s, but had to withdraw it for safety reasons. Wonderball is the latest version of that, but it has edible chocolate figures inside. See www.ferrero.com.ar and www.crackerjack.com for more details. Toys must be larger than the diameter of the plastic tube pictured on the right to meet the U.S. safety standard. *(left: © Sharon Hoogstraten; right: AP/Wide World Photos)*

European countries have required all foreign exchange transactions to be approved by a central minister. Thus, importers who want to buy a foreign good must apply for an exchange permit, that is, permission to exchange an amount of local currency for foreign currency.

The exchange permit may also stipulate the rate of exchange, which can be an unfavorable rate depending on the desires of the government. In addition, the exchange permit may stipulate that the amount to be exchanged must be deposited in a local bank for a set period prior to the transfer of goods. For example, Brazil has at times required funds to be deposited 360 days prior to the import date. This is extremely restrictive because funds are out of circulation and subject to the ravages of inflation. Such policies cause major cash flow problems for the importer and greatly increase the price of imports. Clearly, these currency-exchange barriers constitute a major deterrent to trade.

Standards. Nontariff barriers of this category include standards to protect health, safety, and product quality. The standards are sometimes used in an unduly stringent or discriminating way to restrict trade, but the sheer volume of regulations in this category is a problem in itself. A fruit content regulation for jam varies so much from country to country that one agricultural specialist says, "A jam exporter needs a computer to avoid one or another country's regulations." Different standards are one of the major disagreements between the United States and Japan. The size of knotholes in plywood shipped to Japan can determine whether or not the shipment is accepted; if a knothole is too large, the shipment is rejected because quality standards are not met.

The United States and other countries require some products (automobiles in particular) to contain a percentage of "local content" to gain admission to their markets. The North American Free Trade Agreement (NAFTA) stipulates that all automobiles coming from

1967 European Community (EC) established by uniting the EEC, the European Coal and Steel Community, and the European Atomic Energy Community
1971 First microprocessor produced by Intel, which leads to the personal computer; Communist China joins the

United Nations, making it a truly global representative body
1971 United States abandons gold standard, allowing the international monetary system to base exchange rates on perceived values instead of ones fixed in relation to gold

1972 One billion radios on the planet
1973 Arab oil embargo jolts industrial world into understanding the totally global nature of supply and demand
1980 CNN founded, providing instant and common information the world over, taking

another significant step in the process of globalization started by the radio in 1901
1987 ISO issues ISO 9000 to create a global quality standard
1988 One billion televisions on the planet
1989 Berlin Wall falls, symbolizing the opening of the East to

CROSSING BORDERS 2.4   The Dumper Becomes the Dumped Upon and Vice-Versa

Our favorite example of the difficulties of making dumping cases stick regards two typewriter companies. One of the most contentious and longest lasting dumping cases in history ended abruptly in 1994 when both parties realized the fight was futile. Smith Corona, a 120-year-old American firm, and Brother Industries Ltd. of Japan made a joint statement agreeing to end all litigation between them: "Both of our companies are better served by concentrating on the marketplace and serving our customers."

The 14-year legal battle started with the American firm accusing the Japanese of "dumping" portable typewriters into the U.S. market—that is, selling them for below manufacturing costs. However, Smith Corona during the mid-1990s shifted its production from Cortland, New York, to Mexico, Singapore, and other plants outside the United States. How could the American company claim Brother's imports from Japan were hurting an American company with no domestic production?

Meanwhile, Brother began moving production capacity from Nagoya, Japan, to Bartlett, Tennessee, qualifying it as an American manufacturer. Indeed, in 1991 Brother claimed it was the firm that represented the U.S. domestic typewriter industry and not Smith Corona, which in 1989 became a public company, with 48 percent British ownership. Brother filed a cross suit alleging that Smith Corona was "dumping" its Singapore-made typewriters in the United States. In 1993 the U.S. Commerce Department appeared to agree with Brother in a preliminary determination. At that point both firms decided to terminate their battle. After all, most consumers were dumping their typewriters in favor of computers anyway!

Source: Amal Kumar Jan, "Smith Corona, Brother Industries End 14 Years of Litigation over Dumping," *Wall Street Journal*, February 8, 1994. Check each company's Web site for a listing of current products—www.brother.com and www.smithcorona.com.

member countries must have at least 62.5 percent North American content to deter foreign car makers from using one member nation as the back door to another.

Trade restrictions abound, and the United States is among the governments applying them. According to one source, approximately 45 percent of U.S. manufactured imports are subject to some form of nontariff barrier. For more than a decade, U.S. government officials have arranged "voluntary" agreements with the Japanese steel and automobile industries to limit sales to the United States. Similar negotiations with the governments of major textile producers have limited textile imports into the United States. While countries create barriers to trade, they appreciate the growing interdependence of the world's economies and thus strive to lower barriers in a controlled and equitable manner. The General Agreement on Tariffs and Trade (GATT) and the World Trade Organization (WTO) both have as their goal the elimination of trade barriers.

Antidumping Penalties.   Historically tariffs and nontariff trade barriers have impeded free trade, but over the years they have been eliminated or lowered through the efforts of GATT and WTO. Now there is a new nontariff barrier: antidumping laws that have emerged as a way of keeping foreign goods out of a market. Antidumping laws were designed to prevent foreign producers from "predatory pricing," a practice whereby a foreign producer would intentionally sell its products in the United States for less than the cost of production in order to undermine the competition and take control of the market.[18]

---

[18]D. Morris, "All Countries Must Adhere to WTO Rules," *Financial Times*, July 8, 2005, p. 18.

the West for ideas and commerce
1991   Soviet Union formally abandons communism, as most formerly communist states move toward capitalism and the trade it fosters; Commonwealth of Independent States (CIF) established

between Russia, Ukraine, and Belarus
1993   NAFTA ratified by U.S. Congress; European Union created from the European Community, along with a framework for joint security and foreign policy action, by the 1991 Maastricht Treaty on

European Union; the EEC is renamed the EC
1994   The Chunnel (Channel Tunnel) is opened between France and Britain, providing a ground link for commerce between the continent and Britain
1995   World Trade Organization (WTO) set up as successor

at GATT; by 2000 more than 130 members will account for over 90 percent of world trade
1997   Hong Kong, a world trading and financial capital and bastion of capitalism, is returned to communist Chinese control; *Pathfinder* lands on Mars, and *Rover* goes for a

This was intended as a kind of antitrust law for international trade. Violators are assessed "antidumping" duties for selling below cost and/or assessed "countervailing duties" to prevent the use of foreign government subsidies to undermine American industry. Many countries have similar laws, and they are allowed under WTO rules.

Recent years have seen a staggering increase in antidumping cases in the United States. In one year, 12 U.S. steel manufacturers launched antidumping cases against 82 foreign steelmakers in 30 countries.[19] Many economists felt that these antidumping charges were unnecessary because of the number of companies and countries involved; supply and demand could have been left to sort out the best producers and prices. And, of course, targeted countries have complained as well. Nevertheless, antidumping cases are becoming de facto trade barriers. The investigations are very costly, they take a long time to resolve, and until they are resolved they effectively limit trade. Further, the threat of being hit by an antidumping charge is enough to keep some companies out of the market.

Easing Trade Restrictions

Lowering the trade deficit has been a priority of the U.S. government for a number of years. Of the many proposals brought forward, most deal with fairness of trade with some of our trading partners instead of reducing imports or adjusting other trade policies. Many believe that too many countries are allowed to trade freely in the United States without granting equal access to U.S. products in their countries. Japan was for two decades the trading partner with which we had the largest deficit and which elicited the most concern about fairness. The Omnibus Trade and Competitiveness Act of 1988 addressed the trade fairness issue and focused on ways to improve U.S. competitiveness. At the turn of the century China took over from Japan as America's number one "trade problem."

The Omnibus Trade and Competitiveness Act

The *Omnibus Trade and Competitiveness Act of 1988* is many faceted, focusing on assisting businesses to be more competitive in world markets as well as on correcting perceived injustice in trade practices. The trade act was designed to deal with trade deficits, protectionism, and the overall fairness of our trading partners. Congressional concern centered on the issue that U.S. markets were open to most of the world but markets in Japan, western Europe, and many Asian countries were relatively closed. The act reflected the realization that we must deal with our trading partners based on how they actually operate, not on how we want them to behave. Some see the act as a protectionist measure, but the government sees it as a means of providing stronger tools to open foreign markets and to help U.S. exporters be more competitive. The bill covers three areas considered critical in improving U.S. trade: market access, export expansion, and import relief.

The issue of the openness of markets for U.S. goods is addressed as *market access*. Many barriers restrict or prohibit goods from entering a foreign market. Unnecessarily restrictive technical standards, compulsory distribution systems, customs barriers, tariffs, quotas, and restrictive licensing requirements are just a few. The act gives the U.S. president authority to restrict sales of a country's products in the U.S. market if that country imposes unfair restrictions on U.S. products. Further, if a foreign government's procurement rules discriminate against U.S. firms, the U.S. president has the authority to impose a similar ban on U.S. government procurement of goods and services from the offending nation.

---

[19]Robert Guy Matthews, "U.S. Steel Tariffs Likely to Stay Despite WTO-Sanction Threat," *Wall Street Journal*, March 31, 2003, p. A2.

---

drive but finds no one with whom to trade
1999   Euro introduced in 11 European Union nations, paving the way for the creation of a true trade union and trade bloc
1999   Seattle Round of WTO negotiations pits U.S. vs. EU,

first great protest against globalization
1999   Control of the Panama Canal, a major trade lane, is returned to Panama
2000   Second millenium arrives, predicted computer problems are a non-event

2001   September 11 terrorist attack on the World Trade Center in New York City and the Pentagon in Washington, D.C. One billion mobile phones on the planet
2002   United States attacks Taliban in Afghanistan

2003   United States attacks regime of Saddam Hussein in Iraq
2004   Great Indian Ocean tsunami kills 500,000.
2006   One billion personal computers on the planet.

The billboard overlooking a busy shopping district in Beijing proclaims the importance of China's space technology to all passersby. Meanwhile, Boeing and Hughes have had to pay $32 million in a settlement with the U.S. government for allegedly giving the Chinese sensitive space technology in the middle 1990s. The restrictions on technology sales have rendered American high-tech firms less competitive in international markets even beyond China such as Canada.

Besides emphasizing market access, the act also recognizes that some problems with U.S. export competitiveness stem from impediments on trade imposed by U.S. regulations and export disincentives. Export controls, the Foreign Corrupt Practices Act (FCPA), and export promotion were specifically addressed in the *export expansion* section of the act. Export licenses could be obtained more easily and more quickly for products on the export control list. In addition, the act reaffirmed the government's role in being more responsive to the needs of the exporter. Two major contributions facilitating export trade were computer-based procedures to file for and track export license requests, and the creation of the National Trade Data Bank (NTDB) to improve access to trade data.

Export trade is a two-way street: We must be prepared to compete with imports in the home market if we force foreign markets to open to U.S. trade. Recognizing that foreign penetration of U.S. markets can cause serious competitive pressure, loss of market share, and, occasionally, severe financial harm, the *import relief* section of the Omnibus Trade and Competitiveness Act provides a menu of remedies for U.S. businesses adversely affected by imports. Companies seriously injured by fairly traded imports can petition the government for temporary relief while they adjust to import competition and regain their competitive edge.

The act has resulted in a much more flexible process for obtaining export licenses, in fewer products on the export control list, and in greater access to information, and has established a basis for negotiations with India, Japan, and other countries to remove or lower barriers to trade. However, since a 1999 congressional report (accusing China of espionage regarding defense technology) restrictions on exports of many high-tech products have again been tightened for national security reasons.[20]

As the global marketplace evolves, trading countries have focused attention on ways of eliminating tariffs, quotas, and other barriers to trade. Four ongoing activities to support the growth of international trade are GATT, the associated World Trade Organization (WTO), the International Monetary Fund (IMF), and the World Bank Group.

General Agreement on Tariffs and Trade

Historically, trade treaties were negotiated on a bilateral (between two nations) basis, with little attention given to relationships with other countries. Further, they tended to raise barriers rather than extend markets and restore world trade. The United States and 22 other countries signed the *General Agreement on Tariffs and Trade (GATT)* shortly after World War II. Although not all countries participated, this agreement paved the way for the first effective worldwide tariff agreement. The original agreement provided a process to reduce tariffs and created an agency to serve as watchdog over world trade. GATT's agency director and staff offer nations a forum for negotiating trade and related issues. Member nations seek to resolve their trade disputes bilaterally; if that fails, special GATT panels are set up to recommend action. The panels are only advisory and have no enforcement powers.

The GATT treaty and subsequent meetings have produced agreements significantly reducing tariffs on a wide range of goods. Periodically, member nations meet to reevaluate trade barriers and establish international codes designed to foster trade among members. In general, the agreement covers these basic elements: (1) trade shall be conducted on a nondiscriminatory basis; (2) protection shall be afforded domestic industries through customs tariffs, not through such commercial measures as import quotas; and (3) consultation shall be the primary method used to solve global trade problems.

Since GATT's inception, eight "rounds" of intergovernmental tariff negotiations have been held. The most recently completed was the Uruguay Round (1994), which built on the successes of the Tokyo Round (1974)—the most comprehensive and far-reaching round

---

[20]Elaine Kurtenbach, "China Says Bids Due from Three Global Nuclear Power Companies," *Associated Press*, February 25, 2005.

According to the U.S. government, you can't call it a "catfish" unless it's grown in America. Vietnamese are producing filets in flooded rice paddies at about $1.80 a pound at wholesale. American fish farmers are charging about $2.80. Neither consumers nor ichthyologists can tell the difference between the Asian and American fish, but Uncle Sam has stepped in anyway. The congressional claim on the "catfish" name has forced the United States to stifle its own protests about Europeans claiming exclusive rights to the name "herring." (© Tom McHugh/Photo Researchers, Inc.)

undertaken by GATT up to that time. The Tokyo Round resulted in tariff cuts and set out new international rules for subsidies and countervailing measures, antidumping, government procurement, technical barriers to trade (standards), customs valuation, and import licensing. While the Tokyo Round addressed nontariff barriers, some areas that were not covered continued to impede free trade.

In addition to market access, there were issues of trade in services, agriculture, and textiles; intellectual property rights; and investment and capital flows. The United States was especially interested in addressing services trade and intellectual property rights since neither had been well protected. Based on these concerns, the eighth set of negotiations (Uruguay Round) was begun in 1986 at a GATT Trade Minister's meeting in Punta del Este, Uruguay, and finally concluded in 1994. By 1995, eighty GATT members, including the United States, the European Union (and its member states), Japan, and Canada, had accepted the agreement.

The market access segment (tariff and nontariff measures) was initially considered to be of secondary importance in the negotiations, but the final outcome went well beyond the initial Uruguay Round goal of a one-third reduction in tariffs. Instead, virtually all tariffs in 10 vital industrial sectors with key trading partners were eliminated. This resulted in deep cuts (ranging from 50 to 100 percent) in tariffs on electronic items and scientific equipment and the harmonization of tariffs in the chemical sector at very low rates (5.5 to 0 percent).

U.S. exporters of paper products serve as a good example of the opportunities that opened as a result of these changes. Currently, U.S. companies competing for a share of the paper products market in the European Union have to pay tariffs as high as 9 percent while European competitors enjoy duty-free access within the EU. When the Uruguay Round market-access package was implemented, these high tariffs were eliminated. Another example is Korean tariffs as high as 20 percent on scientific equipment, which were reduced to an average of 7 percent, permitting U.S. exporters to be more competitive in that market.

An important objective of the United States in the Uruguay Round was to reduce or eliminate barriers to international trade in services. The *General Agreement on Trade in Services (GATS)* was the first multilateral, legally enforceable agreement covering trade and investment in the services sector. It provides a legal basis for future negotiations aimed at eliminating barriers that discriminate against foreign services and deny them market access. For the first time, comprehensive multilateral disciplines and procedures covering trade and investment in services have been established. Specific market-opening concessions from a wide range of individual countries were achieved, and provision was made for continued negotiations to further liberalize telecommunications and financial services.

Equally significant were the results of negotiations in the investment sector. *Trade-Related Investment Measures (TRIMs)* established the basic principle that investment restrictions can be major trade barriers and therefore are included, for the first time, under GATT procedures. As a result of TRIMs, restrictions in Indonesia which prohibit foreign firms from opening their own wholesale or retail distribution channels can be challenged. And so can investment restrictions in Brazil that require foreign-owned manufacturers to buy most of their components from high-cost local suppliers and that require affiliates of foreign multinationals to maintain a trade surplus in Brazil's favor by exporting more than they sell within.

Another objective of the United States for the Uruguay Round was achieved by an agreement on *Trade-Related Aspects of Intellectual Property Rights (TRIPs)*. The TRIPs agreement establishes substantially higher standards of protection for a full range of intellectual property rights (patents, copyrights, trademarks, trade secrets, industrial designs, and semiconductor chip mask works) than are embodied in current international agreements, and it provides for the effective enforcement of those standards both internally and at the border.

The Uruguay Round also provides for a better integration of the agricultural and textiles areas into the overall trading system. The reductions of export subsidies, internal supports, and actual import barriers for agricultural products are included in the agreement. The Uruguay Round also includes another set of improvements in rules covering antidumping, standards, safeguards, customs valuation, rules of origin, and import licensing. In each case, rules and procedures were made more open, equitable, and predictable, thus leading to a more level playing field for trade. Perhaps the most notable achievement of the Uruguay Round was the creation of a new institution as a successor to the GATT—the World Trade Organization.

World Trade Organization[21]

At the signing of the Uruguay Round trade agreement in Marrakech, Morocco, in April 1994, U.S. representatives pushed for an enormous expansion of the definition of trade issues. The result was the creation of the *World Trade Organization (WTO)*, which encompasses the current GATT structure and extends it to new areas not adequately covered in the past. The WTO is an institution, not an agreement as was GATT. It sets many rules governing trade between its 148 members, provides a panel of experts to hear and rule on trade disputes between members, and, unlike GATT, issues binding decisions. It will require, for the first time, the full participation of all members in all aspects of the current GATT and the Uruguay Round agreements, and, through its enhanced stature and scope, provide a permanent, comprehensive forum to address the trade issues of the 21st-century global market.

All member countries will have equal representation in the WTO's ministerial conference, which will meet at least every two years to vote for a director general, who will appoint other officials. Trade disputes such as that swirling around genetically modified foods[22] are heard by a panel of experts selected by the WTO from a list of trade experts provided by member countries. The panel hears both sides and issues a decision; the winning side will be authorized to retaliate with trade sanctions if the losing country does not change its practices. Although the WTO has no means of enforcement, international pressure to comply with WTO decisions from other member countries is expected to force compliance. The WTO ensures that member countries agree to the obligations of all the agreements, not just those they like. For the first time, member countries, including developing countries (the fastest-growing markets of the world), will undertake obligations to open their markets and to be bound by the rules of the multilateral trading system.

The World Trade Organization provision of the Uruguay Round encountered some resistance before it was finally ratified by the three super powers: Japan, the European Union (EU), and the United States. A legal wrangle between European Union countries centered on whether the EU's founding treaty gives the European Commission the sole right to negotiate for its members in all areas covered by the WTO.

In the United States, ratification was challenged because of concern for the possible loss of sovereignty over its trade laws to WTO, the lack of veto power (the U.S. could have a decision imposed on it by a majority of the WTO's members), and the role the United States would assume when a conflict arises over an individual state's laws that might be challenged by a WTO member. The GATT agreement was ratified by the U.S. Congress and soon after, the EU, Japan, and more than 60 other countries followed. All 117 members of the former GATT supported the Uruguay agreement. Since almost immediately after its inception on January 1, 1995, WTO's agenda has been full with issues ranging from threats of boycotts and sanctions and the membership of Iran[23] and Russia.[24] Indeed, a major event in international trade during recent years is China's 2001 entry into the WTO. Instead of waiting for various "rounds" to iron out problems, the WTO offers a framework for a continuous discussion and resolution of issues that retard trade.

---

[21]See http://wto.org.

[22]Thomas Fuller, "Farms, To Subsidize, or Not To Subsidize," *International Herald Tribune*, July 2, 2005, p. 2.

[23]Tom Wright, "WRTO to Open Talks on Iran's Membership," *International Herald Tribune*, May 27, 2005, p. 1.

[24]"Mexico Backs Russia's WTO Bid, Welcomes Russian Energy Investment, *Agence France-Presse*, June 21, 2005.

WTO has its detractors but from most indications it is gaining acceptance by the trading community. The number of countries that have joined and those that want to become members is a good measure of its importance. Another one is the accomplishments since its inception: It has been the forum for successful negotiations to opening markets in telecommunications and in information technology equipment, something the United States had sought for the last two rounds of GATT. It also has been active in settling trade disputes and it continues to oversee the implementation of the agreements reached in the Uruguay Round. But with its successes come other problems, namely, how to counter those countries that want all the benefits of belonging to WTO but also want to protect their markets.

Skirting the Spirit of GATT and WTO

Unfortunately, as is probably true of every law or agreement, since its inception there have been those who look for loopholes and ways to get around the provisions of the WTO. For example, China was asked to become a member of the WTO but to be accepted it had to show good faith in reducing tariffs and other restrictions on trade. To fulfill the requirements to join the WTO, China reduced tariffs on 5,000 product lines and eliminated a range of traditional nontariff barriers to trade, including quotas, licenses, and foreign exchange controls. At the same time, U.S. companies began to notice an increase in the number and scope of technical standards and inspection requirements. As a case in point, China recently applied safety and quality inspection requirements on such seemingly benign imported goods as jigsaw puzzles. It also has been insisting that a long list of electrical and mechanical imports undergo an expensive certification process that requires foreign companies but not domestic companies to pay for on-site visits by Chinese inspection officials. Under WTO rules, China now must justify the decision to impose certain standards and provide a rationale for the inspection criteria. However, the foreign companies will have to request a review before the WTO will investigate. The WTO recognizes the need for standards (safety, health, and so on) and it advocates worldwide harmonization of product standards.

The previously mentioned antidumping duties are becoming a favorite way for nations to impose new duties. Indeed, following the example of the United States, the region's most prolific user of antidumping cases, Mexico and other Latin American countries have increased their use as well. The WTO continues to fight these new, creative barriers to trade.

Finally, frustrated with the slow progress of the most recent round of WTO trade negotiations, several countries are negotiating bilateral trade agreements. For example, the United States is currently negotiating free-trade agreements with Singapore,[25] Morocco, Australia, and the remainder of the Americas.[26] The European Union is engaged in similar activities with Albania and South American countries. To the extent that the bilateral talks ultimately lead to multilateral concessions, such activities are not inconsistent with WTO goals and aspirations.

The International Monetary Fund and World Bank Group   The International Monetary Fund[27] and the World Bank[28] group are two global institutions created to assist nations in becoming and remaining economically viable. Each plays an important role in the environment of international trade by helping to maintain stability in the financial markets and by assisting countries that are seeking economic development and restructuring.[29]

Inadequate monetary reserves and unstable currencies are particularly vexing problems in global trade. So long as these conditions exist, world markets cannot develop and function as effectively as they should. To overcome these particular market barriers that plagued international trading before World War II, the *International Monetary Fund (IMF)* was formed.

---

[25]Evelyn Iritani, "Singapore Trade Deal Gives U.S. 'Full Access,'" *Los Angeles Times*, May 7, 2003, p. C1.

[26]"Support CAFTA," *Orlando Sentinel* editorial, July 11, 2005, p. A16.

[27]www.imf.org.

[28]www.worldbank.org.

[29]Augmenting such institutional approaches to economic development are important grassroots efforts. See Alan J. Patricof and Julie E. Sunderland, "In a Slew of Developing Countries," *Milken Institute Review* 2 (2005), pp. 90–94.

Originally 29 countries signed the agreement; now 184 countries are members. Among the objectives of the IMF are the stabilization of foreign exchange rates and the establishment of freely convertible currencies to facilitate the expansion and balanced growth of international trade. Member countries have voluntarily joined to consult with one another in order to maintain a stable system of buying and selling their currencies so that payments in foreign money can take place between countries smoothly and without delay. The IMF also lends money to members having trouble meeting financial obligations to other members. Argentina[30] and Turkey[31] have recently received such help from the IMF, but the results have been mixed.

To cope with universally floating exchange rates, the IMF developed *special drawing rights (SDRs)*, one of its more useful inventions. Because both gold and the U.S. dollar have lost their utility as the basic medium of financial exchange, most monetary statistics relate to SDRs rather than dollars. The SDR is in effect "paper gold" and represents an average base of value derived from the value of a group of major currencies. Rather than being denominated in the currency of any given country, trade contracts are frequently written in SDRs because they are much less susceptible to exchange-rate fluctuations. Even floating rates do not necessarily accurately reflect exchange relationships. Some countries permit their currencies to float cleanly without manipulation (clean float) whereas other nations systematically manipulate the value of their currency (dirty float), thus modifying the accuracy of the monetary marketplace. Although much has changed in the world's monetary system since the IMF was established, it still plays an important role in providing short-term financing to governments struggling to pay current-account debts, as well.

Although the International Monetary Fund has some severe critics,[32] most agree that it has performed a valuable service and at least partially achieved many of its objectives. To be sure, the IMF proved its value in the financial crisis among some Asian countries in 1997. The impact of the crisis was lessened substantially as a result of actions taken by the IMF. During the financial crisis, the IMF provided loans to several countries including Thailand, Indonesia, and South Korea. Had these countries not received aid ($60 billion to Korea alone), the economic reverberations might have led to a global recession. As it was, all the major equity markets reflected substantial reductions in market prices and the rate of economic growth in some countries was slowed.

Sometimes confused with the IMF, the *World Bank Group* is a separate institution that has as its goal the reduction of poverty and the improvement of living standards by promoting sustainable growth and investment in people. The bank provides loans, technical assistance, and policy guidance to developing-country members to achieve its objectives. The World Bank Group has five institutions, each of which performs the following services: (1) lending money to the governments of developing countries to finance development projects in education, health, and infrastructure; (2) providing assistance to governments for developmental projects to the poorest developing countries (per capita incomes of $925 or less); (3) lending directly to the private sector to help strengthen the private sector in developing countries with long-term loans, equity investments, and other financial assistance; (4) providing investors with investment guarantees against "noncommercial risk," such as expropriation and war, to create an environment in developing countries that will attract foreign investment; and (5) promoting increased flows of international investment by providing facilities for the conciliation and arbitration of disputes between governments and foreign investors. It also provides advice, carries out research, and produces publications in the area of foreign investment law. Since their inception, these institutions have played a

---

[30]Adam Thomson, "Agentina Moves Closer to Negotiations with IMF," *Financial Times* (www.FT.com), June 21, 2005.

[31]Claudia Rosett, "How the IMF Lost Turkey," *Wall Street Journal*, April 2, 2003, p. A14; Peter S. Goodman, "Turkey Chases Global Trade," *Pittsburgh Post-Gazette*, July 3, 2005, p. A6.

[32]Mary Locke, "Funding the IMF: The Debate in the U.S. Congress," *Finance & Development* 37, no. 3 (September 2000), pp. 56–59; Sadanand Dhume, "Calling the IMF," *Far Eastern Economic Review*, January 23, 2003, p. 18.

pivotal role in the economic development of countries throughout the world and thus contributed to the expansion of international trade since World War II.

Protests against Global Institutions[33]

Beginning in 1999 what some are calling "anticapitalist protesters" began to influence the workings of the major global institutions described above. The basic complaint against the WTO, IMF, and others is the amalgam of unintended consequences of globalization: environmental concerns, worker exploitation and domestic job losses, cultural extinction, higher oil prices, and diminished sovereignty of nations. The antiglobalization protests first caught the attention of the world press during a WTO meeting in Seattle in November 1999. Then came the World Bank and IMF meetings in April in Washington, DC, the World Economic Forum in Melbourne, Australia, in September, and IMF/World Bank meetings in Prague also in September 2000. Some 10,000 protesters faced some 11,000 police in Prague. The protesters have established Web sites associated with each event, labeled according to the respective dates. The Web sites and the Internet have proved to be important media aiding organizational efforts. And the protests and violence have continued at other meetings of world leaders regarding economic issues such as the G-8 meetings in Evian, France, in 2003 and in individual countries affected by the IMF. Tragically, the terrorism in London was most likely timed to coincide with the G-8 meetings in Scotland in 2005.[34]

---

[33]"Anti-Capitalist Protests: Angry and Effective," *The Economist*, September 23, 2000, pp. 85–87.

[34]Mark Rice-Osley, "Overshadowed by Terrorism, G-8 Summit Still Secures Debt Relief," *Christian Science Monitor*, July 11, 2005, p. 7.

Three kinds of anti-globalization protests: photo on this page and the two photos on the next.

Gifford Myers showed this sculpture "Object (Globalization)–2001" in Faenza, Italy, as a peaceful protest. (*"Globalization" by Gifford Myers, Altadena, CA, 2001.*)

Starbucks may be replacing McDonald's as the American brand foreigners most love to hate. Here local police fail to stop anti–World Trade Organization rioters in Seattle from breaking windows close to home. *(© AFP/Getty Images)*

And, finally, protest of the deadly sort. Terrorists maim and kill those aboard the classic red London double-deck bus (you can see the pieces in the street). *(AP/Wide World Photos)*

The protest groups, some of them with responsible intent, have affected policy. For example, "antisweatshop" campaigns, mostly in America and mostly student-led, have had effects beyond college campuses. A coalition of nongovernmental organizations, student groups, and UNITE (the textile workers' union) recently sued clothing importers, including Calvin Klein and Gap, over working conditions in the American commonwealth of Saipan in the Pacific. Faced with litigation and extended public campaigns against their brands, 17 companies settled, promising better working conditions. Similarly, a World Bank project in China, which involved moving poor ethnic Chinese into lands that were traditionally Tibetan, was abandoned after a political furor led by a relatively small group of pro-Tibetan activists.

Given the apparent previous successes associated with the generally peaceful grassroots efforts to influence policy at these global institutions, we can expect more of the same in the future. But to predict the consequences of terrorism apparently being added to the mix of protestation is impossible.

Summary

Regardless of the theoretical approach used in defense of international trade, the benefits from absolute or comparative advantage clearly can accrue to any nation. Heightened competitors from around the world have created increased pressure for protectionism from every region of the globe at a time when open markets are needed if world resources are to be developed and utilized in the most beneficial manner. And although market protection may be needed in light of certain circumstances and may be beneficial to national defense or the encouragement of infant industries in developing nations, the consumer seldom benefits from such protection.

Free international markets help underdeveloped countries become self-sufficient, and because open markets provide new customers, most industrialized nations have, since World War II, cooperated in working toward freer trade. Such trade will always be partially threatened by various governmental and market barriers that exist or are created for the protection of local businesses. However, the trend has been toward freer trade. The changing economic and political realities are producing unique business structures that continue to protect certain major industries. The future of open global markets lies with the controlled and equitable reduction of trade barriers.

Questions

1. Define the following terms:

   GATT

   balance of payments

   balance of trade

   current account

   tariff

   IMF

   nontariff barriers

   voluntary export restraint (VER)

   protectionism

   WTO

2. Discuss the globalization of the U.S. economy.

3. Differentiate among the current account, balance of trade, and balance of payments.

4. Explain the role of price as a free market regulator.

5. "Theoretically, the market is an automatic, competitive, self-regulating mechanism which provides for the maximum consumer welfare and which best regulates the use of the factors of production." Explain.

6. Interview several local businesspeople to determine their attitudes toward world trade. Further, learn if they buy or sell goods produced in foreign countries. Correlate the attitudes with their commercial experience and report on your findings.

7. What is the role of profit in international trade? Does profit replace or complement the regulatory function of pricing? Discuss.

8. Why does the balance of payments always balance even though the balance of trade does not?

9. Enumerate the ways in which a nation can overcome an unfavorable balance of trade.

10. Support or refute each of the various arguments commonly used in support of tariffs.

11. France exports about 18 percent of its gross domestic product, while neighboring Belgium exports 46 percent. What areas of economic policy are likely to be affected by such variations in exports?

12. Does widespread unemployment change the economic logic of protectionism?

13. Review the economic effects of major trade imbalances such as those caused by petroleum imports.

14. Discuss the main provisions of the Omnibus Trade and Competitiveness Act of 1988.

15. The Tokyo Round of GATT emphasized the reduction of nontariff barriers. How does the Uruguay Round differ?

16. Discuss the impact of GATS, TRIMs, and TRIPs on global trade.

17. Discuss the evolution of world trade that led to the formation of the WTO.

18. Visit www.usitc.gov/taffairs.htm (U.S. Customs tariff schedule) and look up the import duties on leather footwear. You will find a difference in the duties on shoes of different value, material composition, and quantity. Using what you have learned in this chapter, explain the reasoning behind these differences. Do the same for frozen and/or concentrated orange juice.

19. The GATT has had a long and eventful history. Visit www.wto.org/wto/about/about.htm and write a short report on the various rounds of GATT. What were the key issues addressed in each round?

3

history and geography:
THE FOUNDATIONS OF CULTURE

CHAPTER OUTLINE

Global Perspective: Birth of a Nation—Panama in 67 Hours

Historical Perspective in Global Business

    History and Contemporary Behavior
    History Is Subjective
    Manifest Destiny and the Monroe Doctrine

Geography and Global Markets

    Climate and Topography
    Geography, Nature, and Economic Growth
    Social Responsibility and Environmental Management
    Resources

Dynamics of Global Population Trends

    Controlling Population Growth
    Rural/Urban Migration
    Population Decline and Aging
    Worker Shortage and Immigration

World Trade Routes

Communication Links

CHAPTER LEARNING OBJECTIVES

What you should learn from Chapter 3:

- The importance of history and geography in the understanding of international markets

- The effects of history on a country's culture

- How culture interprets events through its own eyes

- How the United States moved west and how this move affected attitudes

- The effect of geographic diversity on economic profiles of a country

- Why marketers need to be responsive to geography of a country

- Economic effects of controlling population growth versus aging population

- Communications are an integral part of international commerce

Global Perspective

BIRTH OF A NATION—PANAMA IN 67 HOURS

The Stage Is Set

June 1902 United States offers to buy the Panama Canal Zone from Colombia for $10 million.

August 1903 The Colombian Senate refuses the offer. Theodore Roosevelt, angered by the refusal, referred to the Colombian Senate as "those contemptible little creatures in Bogotá." Roosevelt agrees to a plot, led by secessionist Dr. Manuel Amador, to assist a group planning to secede from Colombia.

October 17 Panamanian dissidents travel to Washington and agree to stage a U.S.-backed revolution. The revolution is set for November 3 at 6 p.m.

October 18 Flag, constitution, and declaration of independence are created over the weekend. Panama's first flag was designed and sewn by hand in Highland Falls, New York, using fabric bought at Macy's.

Philippe Jean Bunau-Varilla, a French engineer associated with the bankrupt French-Panama canal construction company and not a permanent resident in Panama, is named Panama's ambassador to the United States.

A Country Is Born

Tuesday, November 3 Precisely at 6 p.m., the Colombian garrison was bribed to lay down their arms. The revolution begins, the U.S.S. *Nashville* steams into Colón harbor, and the junta proclaims Panama's independence.

Friday, November 6 By 1:00 p.m., the United States recognizes the sovereign state of Panama.

Saturday, November 7 The new government sends an official delegation from Panama to the United States to instruct the Panamanian ambassador to the United States on provisions of the Panama Canal Treaty.

Wednesday, November 18 At 6:40 p.m., the Panamanian ambassador signs the Panama Canal Treaty. At 11:30 p.m., the official Panamanian delegation arrives at a Washington, DC, railroad station and is met by their ambassador, who informs them that the treaty was signed just hours earlier.

The Present

1977 The United States agrees to relinquish control of the Panama Canal Zone on December 31, 1999.

1997 Autoridad del Canal de Panama, the canal authority that will assume control from the U.S. Panama Canal Commission, is created.

1998 Panama gives a Chinese company the right to build new port facilities on both the Pacific and Atlantic sides, to control anchorages, to hire new pilots to guide ships through the canal, and to block all passage that interferes with the company's business.

January 1, 2000 "The canal is ours" is jubilant cry in Panama.

January 17, 2000 Pentagon sees potential Chinese threat to Panama Canal.

July 2002 China pressures Panama to extend diplomatic recognition to China and drop recognition of Taiwan.

2005 Panama Canal is expected to reach maximum capacity by 2010. The administrative board proposes a $5 billion expansion to add a parallel set of locks in response to the threat of a competing project to build canals or "multimodal" systems across Mexico's Tehuantepec isthmus. Either expand or "run the risk of eventually becoming just a regional canal."

2010 ????

This story is a good illustration of how history and geography can affect public and political attitudes in the present and far into the future. To the Panamanians and much of Latin America, the Panama Canal is but one example of the many U.S. intrusions during the early 20th century that have tainted U.S.–Latin American relations. For the United States, the geographical importance of the Panama Canal for trade (shipping between the two coasts via the canal is cut by 8,000 miles) makes control of the canal a sensitive issue, especially if that control could be potentially hostile. That a Chinese-owned company has operational control of both the Pacific and Atlantic ports and could pose an indirect threat to the Panama Canal Zone concerns the U.S. government. The recent history of U.S. conflict with China and the history of Western domination of parts of China create in the minds of many an adversarial relationship between the two countries. Further, some wonder if Panama would be reluctant to ask the United States to intervene at some future date, perhaps fearing that the Americans might stay another 98 years. Although the probability of China sabotaging the canal is slim at best, historical baggage makes one wonder what would happen should U.S. relations with China deteriorate to the point that the canal was considered to be in jeopardy.

Sources: Bernard A. Weisberger, "Panama: Made in U.S.A.," *American Heritage*, November 1989, pp. 24–25; Juanita Darling, "'The Canal Is Ours' Is Jubilant Cry in Panama," *Los Angeles Times*, January 1, 2000, p. A1; "Pentagon Sees Potential China Threat to Panama Canal," *Asian Political News*, January 17, 2000, p. 20; "Panama Canal at Crossroads," *The Wall Street Journal*, January 7, 2004, p. A1; and, Chris Kraul, "$5-Billion Expansion of Panama Canal Is Considered," *Los Angeles Times*, January 22, 2005, p. A15.

Culture is defined as a society's accepted basis for responding to external and internal events. To understand fully a society's actions and its points of view you must have an appreciation for the influence of historical events and the geographical uniqueness to which a culture has had to adapt. To interpret a culture's behavior and attitudes, a marketer must have some idea of a country's history and geography.

The goal of this chapter is to introduce the reader to the impact of history and geography on the marketing process. The influence of history on behavior and attitudes and the influence of geography on markets, trade, and environmental issues are examined.

Historical Perspective in Global Business

History helps define a nation's "mission," how it perceives its neighbors, how it sees its place in the world, and how it sees itself. Insights into the history of a country are important for understanding attitudes about the role of government and business, the relations between managers and the managed, the sources of management authority, and attitudes toward foreign corporations.

To understand, explain, and appreciate a people's image of itself and the attitudes and unconscious fears that are reflected in its view of foreign cultures, it is necessary to study the culture as it is now as well as to understand the culture as it was—that is, a country's history.[1]

History and Contemporary Behavior

Unless you have a historical sense of the many changes that have buffeted Japan—seven centuries under the shogun feudal system,[2] the isolation before the coming of Commodore Perry in 1853, the threat of domination by colonial powers,[3] the rise of new social classes, Western influences, the humiliation of World War II, and involvement in the international

---

[1]How can anyone understand the conflict that exists between Israel and the Palestinians without an appreciation for the long history of tension that exists there? See, for example, Romesh Ratnesar, "The Dawn of Israel," *Time Atlantic*, March 31, 2003; Bernard Gilland, "Zionism, Israel and the Arabs," *Contemporary Review*, January 2003, p. 27; Bashir Abu-Manneh, "Palestinian Self-Determination and the Israeli Occupation," *Palestine Chronicle*, April 16, 2005, p. 22; Andrea Stone, "Plan to Move Settlers Feeds Turmoil in Israel," *USA Today*, April 25, 2005.

[2]For an interesting discussion of aspects of Japan's political, economic, and social life that helps to explain how Japan is today and why it is like that, see Duncan McCargo, *Contemporary Japan*, 2nd ed. (New York: Palgrave Macmillan, 2004).

[3]For centuries, Japan sought isolation from the rest of the world, refusing to trade or become involved in any way. When Commodore Perry sailed to the Land of the Rising Sun, Japan was opened to the West. Treaties signed with the United States, Britain, Holland, Russia, and France extended jurisdiction onto Japanese soil and limited the country's right to impose taxes on imports. According to one account, these unequal and humiliating treaties had much to do with shaping Japan's goal to make itself the West's industrial and military equal. For a history of the period, see Ann Graham Gaines, *Commodore Perry Opens Japan to Trade in World History* (Berkeley Heights, NJ: Enslow Publishers, 2000).

CROSSING BORDERS 3.1   Welcome to the Land of the Father of Aviation

"Welcome to the Land of the Father of Aviation" proclaims a billboard on the outskirts of Santos Dumont. What? Is Santos Dumont near Kitty Hawk, North Carolina? No—in Brazil. As Brazilians see it, Orville and Wilbur Wright are not heroes or pioneers, but rather villains and frauds who stole credit for the invention of the airplane from the man after whom this quiet provincial town is named. Nearby stands a full-scale model of the 14bis, the boxy biplane that Alberto Santos-Dumont twice flew in Paris during the fall of 1906. Although what Brazilian textbooks call "the Wright Brothers' alleged flight" at Kitty Hawk on December 17, 1903, took place nearly three years before, they cannot be considered the first to fly according to Brazilians. Why? Because the airplane did not take off under its own power but used a ramp, and it had no wheels. Additionally, they argue, the Americans did not fly a predetermined distance before an independent and impartial panel of experts. It is just like the competition at the Olympics: "An athlete has to pass the test in front of judges, playing according to established rules, if he does it the night before, it doesn't count, and he doesn't win the gold medal," Dumont was quoted as saying.

The image of Santos-Dumont is almost omnipresent among Brazilians. He and his 14bis have appeared on banknotes and in dozens of songs, poems, paintings, and books that celebrate his feats. Rio's main in-town airport is named after him, as are streets, squares, plazas, and schools. At the municipal library in Santos Dumont, an extensive collection of memorabilia and books document his life and work, but there are no books about the Wright Brothers. "Even today, after so much proof to the contrary, Americans continue not to recognize Santos-Dumont as the true inventor of heavier-than-air flight . . . That's what they teach in the schools up there to children like you! Really, it's not honest and it's disrespectful to us," wrote the author of a school textbook still in print today.

Like beauty—"History is in the eyes of the beholder."

Sources: Larry Rohter, "Brazilians Intend to Ignore Centennial of Wrights' Flight," *New York Times News Service,* December 16, 2003; Thomas G. Donlan, "Following the Wrights," *Barron's Online,* December 15, 2003; Kyle Hedlund, "Who Is Santos Dumont?" www.gringoes.com, May 6, 2005,

community—you will have difficulty fully understanding its contemporary behavior. Why do the Japanese have such strong loyalty toward their companies? Why is the loyalty found among participants in the Japanese distribution systems so difficult for an outsider to develop? Why are decisions made by consensus? Answers to such questions can be explained in part by Japanese history.

Loyalty to family, to country, to company, and to social groups and the strong drive to cooperate, to work together for a common cause, permeate many facets of Japanese behavior and have historical roots that date back thousands of years. Historically, loyalty and service, a sense of responsibility, and respect for discipline, training, and artistry were stressed to maintain stability and order. Confucian philosophy, taught throughout Japan's history, emphasizes the basic virtue of loyalty "of friend to friend, of wife to husband, of child to parent, of brother to brother, but, above all, of subject to lord," that is, to country. A fundamental premise of Japanese ideology reflects the importance of cooperation for the collective good. Japanese achieve consensus by agreeing that all will unite against outside pressures that threaten the collective good. A historical perspective gives the foreigner in Japan a basis on which to begin developing cultural sensitivity and a better understanding of contemporary Japanese behavior.[4]

History Is Subjective   History is important in understanding why a country behaves as it does, but history from whose viewpoint? Historical events always are viewed from one's own biases and self reference criteria (SRC), and thus what is recorded by one historian may not be what another

---

[4]For an insightful report on the transformation of Japan from an isolated island shogunate into an expansive military empire and then into a pacified and prosperous democracy, see Ian Buruma, *Inventing Japan, 1853–1964* (New York: Modern Library, 2003).

The Monumento de los Niños Heroes honors six young cadets who during the Mexican-American War of 1847 chose death over surrender. The Mexican-American War is important in Mexican history and helps to explain, in part, the Mexican love-hate relationship with the United States. (© Dave G. Houser/CORBIS)

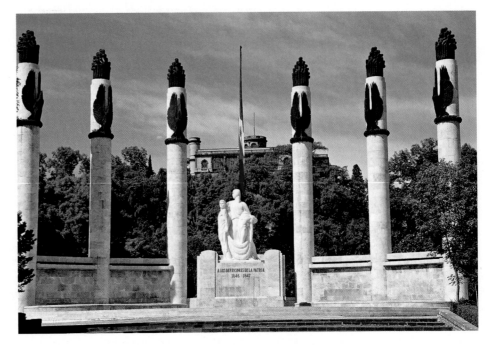

records, especially if the historians are from different cultures. Historians traditionally try to be objective, but few can help filtering events through their own cultural biases.[5]

Our perspective influences not only our view of history, but also subtly influences our view of many other matters. For example, maps of the world sold in the United States generally show the United States at the center, whereas maps in Britain show Britain at the center, and so on for other nations.[6]

A crucial element in understanding any nation's business and political culture is the subjective perception of its history. Why do Mexicans have a love–hate relationship with the United States? Why were Mexicans required to have majority ownership in most foreign investments until recently? Why did dictator General Porfírio Díaz lament, "Poor Mexico, so far from God, so near the United States"? Why? Because Mexicans see the United States as a threat to their political, economic, and cultural independence.

Most citizens of the United States are mystified by such feelings. After all, the United States has always been Mexico's good neighbor. Most would agree with President John F. Kennedy's proclamation during a visit to Mexico that "Geography has made us neighbors, tradition has made us friends." North Americans may be surprised to learn that most Mexicans "felt it more accurate to say 'Geography has made us closer, tradition has made us far apart.'"[7]

Citizens of the United States feel they have been good neighbors. They see the Monroe Doctrine as protection for Latin America from European colonization and the intervention of Europe in the governments of the Western Hemisphere. Latin Americans, on the other hand, tend to see the Monroe Doctrine as an offensive expression of U.S. influence in Latin America. To put it another way, "Europe keep your hands off—Latin America is only for the United States," an attitude perhaps typified by former U.S. president Ulysses S. Grant, who, in a speech in Mexico in 1880, described Mexico as a "magnificent mine" that lay waiting south of the border for North American interests.

---

[5]An example of such biases is the differing perceptions of Turkey by European Union members in deciding on Turkey's membership in the EU. "Which Turkey?" *The Economist*, March 17, 2005.

[6]Professor Lyn S. Amine of Saint Louis University brought this to our attention.

[7]For an insightful review of some of the issues that have affected relations between the United States and Mexico, see John Skirius, "Railroad, Oil and Other Foreign Interest in the Mexican Revolution, 1911–1914," *Journal of Latin American Studies*, February 2003, p. 25.

Exhibit 3.1
Territorial Expansion of United States from 1783

The United States expanded westward to the Pacific by a series of financial deals, negotiated settlements, and forcible annexations. The acquisition of territory from Mexico began with the Battle of San Jacinto in 1836 when Texas staged a successful revolt against the rule of Mexico and became The Republic of Texas—later to join the Union in 1845. The Mexican War (1846–1848) resulted in Mexico ceding California and a large part of the West to the United States.

Source: From *Oxford Atlas of the World*, 10th ed, 2002. Copyright © 2002 Philip's Cartography.

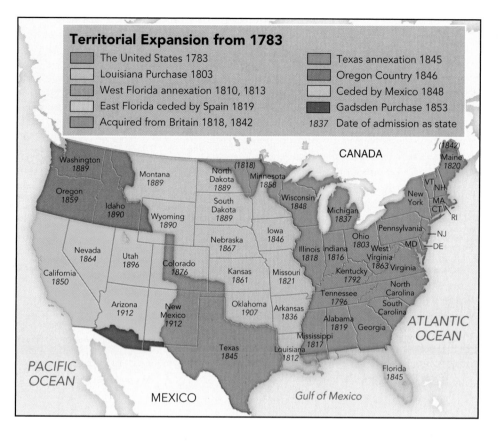

United States Marines sing with pride of their exploits "from the halls of Montezuma to the shores of Tripoli." To the Mexican, the exploit to which the "halls of Montezuma" refers is remembered as U.S. troops marching all the way to the center of Mexico City and extracting as tribute 890,000 square miles that became Arizona, California, New Mexico, and Texas (see Exhibit 3.1). A prominent monument at the entrance of Chapultepec Park recognizes *Los Niños Heroes* (the boy heroes), who resisted U.S. troops, wrapped themselves in Mexican flags, and jumped to their deaths rather than surrender. Mexicans recount the heroism of *Los Niños Heroes*[8] and the loss of Mexican territory to the United States every September 13, when the president of Mexico, his cabinet, and the diplomatic corps assemble at the Mexico City fortress to recall the defeat that led to the *"despojo territorial"* (territorial plunder).

The Mexican Revolution, which overthrew dictator Díaz and launched the modern Mexican state, is particularly remembered for the expulsion of foreigners—most notably North American businessmen who were the most visible of the wealthy and influential entrepreneurs in Mexico.

Manifest Destiny and the Monroe Doctrine

Manifest Destiny and the Monroe Doctrine were accepted as the basis for U.S. foreign policy during much of the 19th and 20th centuries.[9] Manifest Destiny, in its broadest interpretation, meant that Americans were a chosen people ordained by God to create a model society. More specifically, it referred to the territorial expansion of the United States from the Atlantic to the Pacific. The idea of Manifest Destiny was used to justify U.S. annexation of Texas, Oregon, New Mexico, and California and, later, U.S. involvement in Cuba, Alaska, Hawaii, and the Philippines. Exhibit 3.1 illustrates when and by what means the present United States was acquired.

---

[8]When the United Nations recommended that all countries set aside a single day each year to honor children, Mexico designated April 30 as "Dia de Los Niños." Interestingly, this holiday is often included with Saint Patrick's Day celebrations which include recognition of the San Patricios, the Irish-American battalion that fought with the Mexicans in the Mexican-American War. See Carol Sowers, "El Dia de Los Niños Adds International Touch to Celebration," *Arizona Republic*, April 29, 2005.

[9]Some say even into the 21st century. "Manifest Destiny Warmed Up?" *The Economist*, August 14, 2003.

CROSSING BORDERS 3.2

What Do the Mexican-American War, Ireland, and *Gringo* Have in Common?

Revered in Mexico, honored in Ireland, and all but forgotten in the United States are the San Patricios (St. Patrick's Battalion). During the Mexican-American War the San Patricios were approximately 250 men, mostly Irish, who made up a battalion of defectors from the U.S. Army and fought for Mexico. During the two-year conflict, the immigrant deserters forged a strong alliance with the Mexicans. For their pains, the Americans executed most, but they became a symbol of independence and defense against imperialism.

The San Patricios fought well, but when they ended up back in American hands, 50 of them died by hanging and many others were branded on the right cheek with a two-inch letter *D* for *deserter*. When the war ended, Mexico was forced to cede half its territory to the United States.

The Mexican-American conflict that lasted from 1846 to 1848 may be dismissed as irrelevant "history" north of the border, but not south of it. Every year the San Patricios are remembered with a ceremony in Mexico City and County Galway, Ireland, home of the brigade's commanding officer.

Now we know what Ireland and the Mexican-American War have in common, but what about the word *gringo*? According to some sources, at day's end the San Patricios would sit around their campfires singing a song called "Green Grow the Lilacs." The story goes that the Mexican soldiers began to refer to their comrades as "los gringos." To be fair, we should share the other explanation for the derivation of *gringo*: Some historians say the word was used in Spain prior to the discovery of America and was an alteration of *griego* ("Greek") to indicate foreign gibberish or "it's Greek to me."

Sources: James Callaghan, "The San Patricios," *American Heritage*, November 1995, p. 58; "The Irish Connection," *Hispanic*, March 2001, p. 20; Ellie Lopez-Bowlan, "Mexicans Have Reason to Celebrate St. Pat Too," *Reno Gazette-Journal*, March 17, 2005, p. 7.

The Monroe Doctrine, a cornerstone of early U.S. foreign policy, was enunciated by President James Monroe in a public statement proclaiming three basic dicta: no further European colonization in the New World, abstention of the United States from European political affairs, and nonintervention of European governments in the governments of the Western Hemisphere.

After 1870, interpretation of the Monroe Doctrine became increasingly broad. In 1881, its principles were evoked in discussing the development of a canal across the Isthmus of Panama. Theodore Roosevelt applied the Monroe Doctrine with an extension that became known as the Roosevelt Corollary.[10] The corollary stated that not only would the United States prohibit non-American intervention in Latin American affairs but it would also police the area and guarantee that Latin American nations met their international obligations. The corollary sanctioning American intervention was applied in 1905 when Roosevelt forced the Dominican Republic to accept the appointment of an American economic adviser, who quickly became the financial director of the small state. It was also used in the acquisition of the Panama Canal Zone from Colombia in 1903 and the formation of a provisional government in Cuba in 1906.

The manner in which the United States acquired the land for the Panama Canal Zone typifies the Roosevelt Corollary—whatever is good for the United States is justifiable. As the Global Perspective at the beginning of this chapter illustrates, the creation of the country of Panama was a total fabrication of the United States.[11]

According to U.S. history, these Latin American adventures were a justifiable part of our foreign policy; to Latin Americans, they were unwelcome intrusions in Latin-American affairs. This perspective has been constantly reinforced by U.S. intervention in Latin America since 1945 (see Exhibit 3.2). The way historical events are recorded and interpreted in one culture can differ substantially from the way those same events are recorded and interpreted in another. From the U.S. view, each of the interventions illustrated in Exhibit 3.2 was justified. A

---

[10]Michael Barone, "A Big Stick," *U.S. News and World Report*, February 25, 2002, p. 52.

[11]An interesting discussion of how past U.S. foreign interventions affect attitudes about U.S. involvement in Iraq, see "Anti-Americanism: The View from Abroad," *The Economist*, February 17, 2005.

Exhibit 3.2
U.S. Intervention in Latin America Since 1945

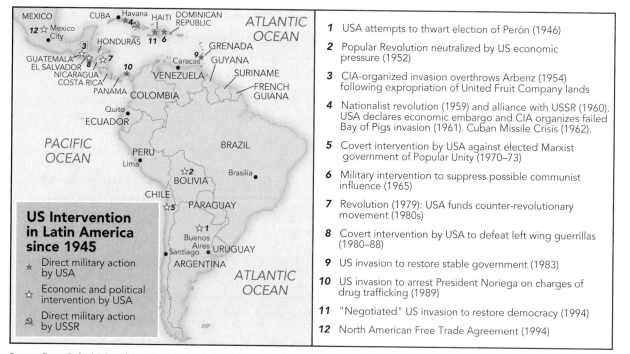

US Intervention in Latin America since 1945

★ Direct military action by USA

☆ Economic and political intervention by USA

⚒ Direct military action by USSR

1   USA attempts to thwart election of Perón (1946)

2   Popular Revolution neutralized by US economic pressure (1952)

3   CIA-organized invasion overthrows Arbenz (1954) following expropriation of United Fruit Company lands

4   Nationalist revolution (1959) and alliance with USSR (1960). USA declares economic embargo and CIA organizes failed Bay of Pigs invasion (1961). Cuban Missile Crisis (1962).

5   Covert intervention by USA against elected Marxist government of Popular Unity (1970–73)

6   Military intervention to suppress possible communist influence (1965)

7   Revolution (1979): USA funds counter-revolutionary movement (1980s)

8   Covert intervention by USA to defeat left wing guerrillas (1980–88)

9   US invasion to restore stable government (1983)

10 US invasion to arrest President Noriega on charges of drug trafficking (1989)

11 "Negotiated" US invasion to restore democracy (1994)

12 North American Free Trade Agreement (1994)

Source: From *Oxford Atlas of the World*, 10th ed., 2002. Copyright © 2002 Philip's Cartography.

Members of the San Antonio Living History Association, portraying Alamo defenders, fire a volley marking the final day of battle at the Alamo which fell after a 13-day siege in 1836. To many Texans, San Antonio is the self-proclaimed cradle of Texas freedom, and "Remember the Alamo" has the same emotional meaning as "Viva Mexico" has among many Mexicans. (*AP/Wide World Photos*)

comparison of histories goes a long way in explaining the differences in outlooks and behavior of people on both sides of the border. Many Mexicans believe that their "good neighbor" to the north is not reluctant to throw its weight around when it wants something. Suspicions that self-interest is the primary motivation for good relations with Mexico abound.[12]

History viewed from a Latin-American perspective explains how a national leader, under adverse economic conditions, can point a finger at the United States or a U.S. multinational corporation and evoke a special emotional, popular reaction to divert attention away from the government in power.[13] As a case in point, after the U.S. House of Representatives voted to censure Mexico for drug corruption, President Ernesto Zedillo was under pressure to take a hard stand with Washington. He used the anniversary of Mexico's 1938 expropriation of the oil industry from foreign companies to launch a strong nationalist attack. He praised the state oil monopoly Pemex as a "symbol of our historical struggles for sovereignty." Union members cheered him on, waving a huge banner that read: "In 1938 Mexico was 'decertified' because it expropriated its oil and it won—today we were decertified for defending our dignity and sovereignty."[14]

[12]Many Latin-Americans' elation with the Bush administration's first term pronouncements that the United States was looking south "not as an afterthought but as a fundamental commitment"—that a region "too often separated by history or rivalry and resentment" should prepare itself for the start of a "new era" of cooperation—soon became disappointment as the war on terror turned U.S. attention away from Latin America. Marcela Sanchez, "Bush, Looking Every Which Way but South," *Washington Post*, January 6, 2005.

[13]Richard Lambert, "Misunderstanding Each Other," *Foreign Affairs*, March 1, 2003, p. 62.

[14]Such attitudes continue to hamper relations between the United States and Mexico. See Mary Anastasia O'Grady, "Americas: Fears of Yankee Imperialism Inhibit Perimeter Security," *Wall Street Journal*, June 7, 2002, p. A11.

CROSSING BORDERS 3.3 | Microsoft Adapts Encarta to "Local History"

Adapting your product to the local culture is an important strategy for many products. Understanding a country's history helps to achieve that goal. Microsoft has nine different editions reflecting local "history" in order to be sure that its Encarta multimedia encyclopedia on CD-ROM does not contain cultural blunders. As a consequence, it often reflects different and sometimes contradictory understandings of the same historical events. For example, who invented the telephone? In the U.S., U.K., and German editions it is Alexander Graham Bell, but ask the question in the Italian edition and your answer is Antonio Meucci, an Italian-American candle maker who Italians believe beat Bell by five years. For electric light bulbs, it is Thomas Alva Edison in the United States, but in the United Kingdom, it is the British inventor Joseph Swan. Other historical events reflect local perceptions. The nationalization of the Suez Canal, for example, in the U.S. edition is a decisive intervention by superpowers. In the French and U.K. editions, it is summed up as a "humiliating reversal" for Britain and France—a phrase that does not appear in the U.S. edition.

While Microsoft is on the mark by adapting these events to their local historical context, it has, on occasion, missed the boat on geography. South Korean ire was raised when the South Korean island of Ullung-do was placed within Japan's borders and when the Chon-Ji Lake, where the first Korean is said to have descended from heaven, was located in China. And finally, an embarrassed Microsoft apologized to the people of Thailand for referring to Bangkok as a commercial sex center, assuring the women's activists group that protested that the revised version would "include all the great content that best reflects its rich culture and history."

Microsoft also bows to political pressure. The government of Turkey stopped distribution of an Encarta edition with the name Kurdistan used to denote a region of southeastern Turkey on a map. Hence Microsoft removed the name Kurdistan from the map. Governments frequently lobby the company to show their preferred boundaries on maps. When the border between Chile and Argentina in the southern Andes was in dispute, both countries lobbied for their preferred boundary, and the solution both countries agreed to was—no line.

Sources: Kevin J. Delaney, "Microsoft's Encarta Has Different Facts for Different Folks," *Wall Street Journal*, June 25, 1999, p. A1; "Microsoft Apologizes for the Thailand Sex Hub Reference," *Agence France-Presse*, February 23, 2000; Steve Young and Anand Naidoo, "Microsoft Criticized for Making Correction to Encarta Encyclopedia," *CNN International: World News*, August 22, 2000; "Why You Won't Find Kurdistan on a Microsoft Map of Turkey," *Geographical*, November 1, 2004.

The leader might be cheered for expropriation or confiscation of a foreign investment even though the investment was making an important contribution to the economy. To understand a country's attitudes, prejudices, and fears, it is necessary to look beyond the surface of current events to the inner subtleties of the country's entire past for clues. Three comments by Mexicans best summarize this section:

> History is taught one way in Mexico and another way in the United States—the United States robbed us but we are portrayed in U.S. textbooks as bandits who invaded Texas.

> We may not like gringos for historical reasons, but today the world is dividing into commercial blocks, and we are handcuffed to each other for better or worse.

> We always have been and we continue to be a colony of the United States.[15]

Geography and Global Markets

Geography, the study of Earth's surface, climate, continents, countries, peoples, industries, and resources, is an element of the uncontrollable environment that confronts every marketer but which receives scant attention.[16] The tendency is to study the aspects of geography as isolated entities rather than as important causal agents of

---

[15]"Amid Anti-War Feelings, U.S. Fighting War Myths in Mexico," *Dow Jones International News*, March 27, 2003.

[16]The importance of geography in understanding global challenges that exist today is discussed in Harm J. DeBlij, *Why Geography Matters* (New York: Oxford University Press, 2005).

CROSSING **BORDERS 3.4** Fog, Fog Everywhere and Water to Drink

When you live in Chungungo, Chile, one of the country's most arid regions with no nearby source of water, you drink fog. Of course! Thanks to a legend and resourceful Canadian and Chilean scientists, Chungungo now has its own supply of drinkable water after a 20-year drought. Before this new source of water, Chungungo depended on water trucks that came twice a week.

Chungungo has always been an arid area, and legend has it that the region's original inhabitants used to worship trees. They considered them sacred because a permanent flow of water sprang from the treetops, producing a constant interior rain. The legend was right—the trees produced rain! Thick fog forms along the coast. As it moves inland and is forced to rise against the hills, it changes into tiny raindrops, which are in turn retained by the tree leaves, producing the constant

source of rain. Scientists set out to take advantage of this natural phenomenon.

The nearby ancient eucalyptus forest of El Tofo hill provided the clue that scientists needed to create an ingenious water-supply system. To duplicate the water-bearing effect of the trees, they installed 86 "fog catchers" on the top of the hill—huge nets supported by 12-foot eucalyptus pillars, with water containers at their base. About 1,900 gallons of water are collected each day and then piped into town. This small-scale system is cheap (about one-fifth as expensive as having water trucked in), clean, and provides the local people with a steady supply of drinking water.

Sources: "Drinking Fog," *World Press Review;* "Silver Lining," *The Economist,* February 5, 2000, p. 75; "UNESCO Water Portal Weekly Update No. 89: Fog," April 15, 2005, www.unesco.org/water/news/newsletter/89.shtml.

the marketing environment. Geography is much more than memorizing countries, capitals, and rivers.[17] It also includes an understanding of how a society's culture and economy are affected as a nation struggles to supply its people's needs within the limits imposed by its physical makeup. Thus, the study of geography is important in the evaluation of markets and their environment.

This section discusses the important geographic characteristics the marketer needs to consider when assessing the environmental aspects of marketing. Examining the world as a whole provides the reader with a broad view of world markets and an awareness of the effects of geographic diversity on the economic profiles of various nations. Climate and topography are examined as facets of the broader and more important elements of geography. A brief look at Earth's resources and population—the building blocks of world markets—completes the presentation on geography and global markets.

Climate and Topography

Altitude, humidity, and temperature extremes are climatic features that affect the uses and functions of products and equipment.[18] Products that perform well in temperate zones may deteriorate rapidly or require special cooling or lubrication to function adequately in tropical zones. Manufacturers have found that construction equipment used in the United States requires extensive modifications to cope with the intense heat and dust of the Sahara Desert. A Taiwanese company sent a shipment of drinking glasses via ship to a buyer in the Middle East. The glasses were packed in wooden crates with hay used as dunnage to prevent breakage. The glasses arrived in shards. Why? When the crates moved to the warmer, less humid climate of the Middle East, the moisture content of the hay dropped significantly and shriveled to a point that it offered no protection.[19]

Within even a single national market, climate can be sufficiently diverse to require major adjustments. In Ghana, a product adaptable to the entire market must operate effectively

[17]Tony Burdett, "Geographic Ignorance," *Salt Lake Tribune,* March 3, 2000, p. A2.

[18]How Canada's geography affects distribution of computers is explored in Vawn Himmelsbach, "Direct/Indirect Littered with Pitfalls: Canada's Geography Lends Itself to Being a Channel-Friendly Country," *Computer Dealer News,* April 2005.

[19]Michael D. White, *International Marketing Blunders* (Novato, CA: World Trade Press, 2002), p. 79.

A young girl stands next to some personal possessions recovered from the debris left by the 2005 tsunami that devastated Aceh Besar, Indonesia. Indonesia's health ministry said the number of dead and missing exceeded 230,000. Even the most economically advanced countries cannot escape the destruction and human and economic loss caused by tsunamis, hurricanes, or other natural disasters. A case in point is hurricane Katrina that devastated the Gulf Coast of the United States in 2005. (© Adek Berry/AFP/Getty Images)

in extreme desert heat and low humidity and in tropical rain forests with consistently high humidity. Bosch-Siemens washing machines designed for European countries require spin cycles to range from a minimum spin cycle of 500 rpm to a maximum of 1,600 rpm: Because the sun does not shine regularly in Germany or in Scandinavia, washing machines must have a 1,600 rpm spin cycle because users do not have the luxury of hanging them out to dry. In Italy and Spain, however, clothes can be damp since the abundant sunshine is sufficient to justify a spin cycle speed of 500 rpm.

Different seasons between the northern and southern hemispheres also affect global strategies. JCPenney had planned to open five stores in Chile as part of its expansion into countries below the equator. It wanted to capitalize on its vast bulk buying might for its North American, Mexican, and Brazilian stores to provide low prices for its expansion into South America. After opening its first store in Chile, the company realized that the plan was not going to work—when it was buying winter merchandise in North America, it needed summer merchandise in South America. The company quickly sold its one store in Chile; its expansion into South America was limited to Brazil.[20]

South America represents an extreme but well-defined example of the importance of geography in marketing considerations. Economic and social systems are explained, in part, in terms of the geographical characteristics of the area. It is a continent 4,500 miles long and 3,000 miles wide at its broadest point. Two-thirds of it is comparable to Africa in its climate, 48 percent of its total area is made up of forest and jungle, and only 5 percent is arable. Mountain ranges cover South America's west coast for 4,500 miles, with an average height of 13,000 feet and a width of 300 to 400 miles. This natural, formidable barrier has precluded the establishment of commercial routes between the Pacific and Atlantic coasts. South America's natural barriers inhibit both national and regional growth, trade, and communication. It is a vast land area with population concentrations on the outer periphery and an isolated and almost uninhabited interior. In Colombia, mountain ranges are a major barrier to travel. The airtime from Bogotá to Medellín, the second-largest city in Colombia, is 30 minutes; by highway, the same trip takes 10 to 12 hours. Other regions of the world with extreme topographic and climatic variations are China, Russia, India, and Canada.

Mountains, oceans, seas, jungles, and other geographical features can pose serious impediments to economic growth and trade. Geographic hurdles have a direct effect on a

---

[20] Miriam Jordan, "Penney Blends Two Business Cultures," *Wall Street Journal*, April 5, 2001.

Waving banners of their Swiss cantons, engineers and workmen met after they broke through the final four meters of rock to complete the bore of the Loetschberg tunnel under the Swiss Alps between Goppenstein and Kandersteg. The first of two rail tunnels linking north and south Europe, the 34.6 kilometer tunnel is part of a massive construction project to move heavy European Union trucks off Switzerland's narrow highways and onto trains. *(AP/Wide World Photos)*

country's economy, markets, and the related activities of communication and distribution. As countries seek economic opportunities and the challenges of the global marketplace, they invest in infrastructure to overcome such barriers. Once seen as natural protection from potentially hostile neighbors, physical barriers that exist within Europe are now seen as impediments to efficient trade in an integrated economic union.

For 200 years the British resisted a tunnel under the English Channel—they did not trust the French or any other European country and saw the channel as protection. But when they became members of the European Union, economic reality meant the channel tunnel had to be built to facilitate trade with other EU members.

From the days of Hannibal, the Alps have served as an important physical barrier and provided European countries protection from one another. But with EU expansion the Alps became a major impediment to trade. Truck traffic between southern Germany and northern Italy, which choked highways through some of Switzerland's most treacherous mountain roads and pristine nature areas, was not only burdensome for all travelers but was becoming economically unacceptable. The solution, the 21-mile Loetschberg tunnel,[21] opening in 2007, burrows under the Alps and trims the time trains will need to cross between Germany and Italy from a three-and-a-half-hour trip to under two. By 2014 the 36-mile Gotthard Tunnel[22] will provide additional rail coverage for the area and be the world's longest rail tunnel.

Other projects that help to further integrate the European Union include the 10-mile-long Oresund Link, a bridge and tunnel across the Baltic Strait to continental Europe completed in 2000. It accommodates freight and high-speed passenger trains and reduces a five-hour trip between Copenhagen, Denmark, and Malmo, Sweden, to two and a half hours. Ultimately, it will be possible to drive from Lapland in northernmost Scandinavia to Calabria in southern Italy and then on to Sicily when the bridge over the Messina Strait connecting Calabria to Sicily is completed[23]—all tangible symbols that these nations are ending their political isolation from one another as they break down natural barriers in an increasingly borderless Europe.[24]

Geography, Nature, and Economic Growth

Always on the slim margin between subsistence and disaster, less-privileged countries suffer disproportionately from natural and human-assisted catastrophes.[25] Climate and topography coupled with civil wars, poor environmental policies, and natural disasters push these countries further into economic stagnation. Without irrigation and water management, droughts, floods, and soil erosion afflict them, often leading to creeping deserts that reduce the long-term fertility of the land.[26] Population increases, deforestation, and overgrazing intensify the impact of drought and lead to malnutrition and ill health, further undermining these countries' abilities to solve their problems.[27] Cyclones cannot be prevented, nor can inadequate rainfall, but means to control their effects are available. Unfortunately, each disaster seems to push developing countries further away from effective solutions. Countries that suffer the most from major calamities are among the poorest in the world. Many have

[21]"Lotschberg Tunnel Makes Rail History," *Swissinfo*, April 28, 2005.

[22]"New Swiss Rail Tunnel Removes Barriers," *The Oregonian*, April 29, 2005, p A4.

[23]Stephen Jewkes, "Messina Strait Project," *Europe*, October 2002, p. 26.

[24]Bradley S. Klapper, "Swiss Complete Digging Alpine Tunnel," *Washington Post*, April 28, 2005.

[25]"Asia's Tsunami: Helping the Survivors," *The Economist*, January 5, 2005.

[26]See the Map 2 Global Climate in the World Maps section for a view of the diversity of the world's climate. The climatic phenomenon of El Niño raises havoc with weather patterns and is linked to crop failures, famine, forest fires, dust and sand storms, and other disasters associated with either an overabundance or a lack of rain.

[27]Peter Moszynski, "Ethiopia: Can Famine Be Avoided?" *New African*, February 2003, p. 30.

Large trucks are dwarfed by the 185-meter-high sluice gates of the Three Gorges Dam. China began filling the reservoir in a major step toward completion of the world's largest hydroelectric project. The level is expected to reach 135 meters (446 feet), inundating thousands of acres including cities and farms along the Yangtze. *(AP/Wide World Photos)*

A woman sits in the remains of demolished buildings below a water level marker on the bank of the Yangtze River. Many residents along the banks of the river moved their homes and farmland to higher ground, but were, nevertheless, caught by rising water, which inundated their crops even though the high water level had been announced well in advance. *(AP/Wide World Photos)*

neither the capital nor the technical ability to minimize the effects of natural phenomena; they are at the mercy of nature.[28]

As countries prosper, natural barriers are overcome. Tunnels and canals are dug and bridges and dams are built in an effort to control or to adapt to climate, topography, and the recurring extremes of nature.[29] Humankind has been reasonably successful in overcoming or minimizing the effects of geographical barriers and natural disasters, but as they do so, they must contend with problems of their own making. The construction of dams is a good example of how an attempt to harness nature for good has a bad side. Developing countries consider dams a cost-effective solution to a host of problems. Dams create electricity, help control floods, provide water for irrigation during dry periods, and can be a rich source of fish. However, there are side effects; dams displace people (the Three Gorges dam in China will displace 1.2 million people), and silt that ultimately clogs the reservoir is no longer carried downstream to replenish the soil and add nutrients.[30] Similarly, the Narmada Valley Dam Project in India will provide electricity, flood control, and irrigation, but it has already displaced tens of thousands of people, and as the benefits are measured against social and environmental costs, questions of its efficacy are being raised. In short, the need for gigantic projects such as these must be measured against their social and environmental costs.[31]

As the global rush toward industrialization and economic growth accelerates, environmental issues become more apparent. Disruption of ecosystems, relocation of people, inadequate hazardous waste management, and industrial pollution are problems that must be addressed by the industrialized world and those seeking economic development.[32] The problems are mostly by-products of processes that have contributed significantly to economic

[28]As horrible as the tsunami was in East Asia, the economic devastation remains long after the physical damage is repaired. "After the Deluge," *The Economist,* January 6, 2005.

[29]"400,000 To Be Moved for Canals Network," *The Standard,* April 6, 2005.

[30]Beside the relocation of over a million, the Three Gorges Dam is also cited for various environmental problems, including silt accumulation and pollution controls. See "China Plans to Relocate 108,000 This Year to Make Way for the Three Gorges Dam," *Agence France Presse,* February 14, 2004.

[31]"Dams Control Most of the World's Largest Rivers," *Environmental News Service,* April 15, 2005.

[32]Robert Marquand, "China Makes Sudden Push to Protect Environment," *Christian Science Monitor,* February 2005.

development and improved lifestyles. During the last part of the 20th century, governments and industry expended considerable effort to develop better ways to control nature and to allow industry to grow while protecting the environment.[33]

Social Responsibility and Environmental Management

Nations, companies, and people reached a consensus during the close of the last decade: Environmental protection is not an optional extra—it is an essential part of the complex process of doing business. Many view the problem as a global issue rather than a national issue and as one that poses common threats to humankind and thus cannot be addressed by nations in isolation. Of special concern to governments and businesses are ways to stem the tide of pollution and to clean up decades of neglect.

Companies looking to build manufacturing plants in countries with more liberal pollution regulations than they have at home are finding that regulations everywhere have gotten stricter. Many governments are drafting new regulations and enforcing existing ones.[34] Electronic products contain numerous toxic substances that create a major disposal problem in landfills where inadequate disposal allows toxins to seep into groundwater. The EU, as well as other countries, has laws stipulating the amount and types of potentially toxic substances it will require a company to take back to recycle.[35] A strong motivator is the realization that pollution is on the verge of getting completely out of control.

An examination of rivers, lakes, and reservoirs in China revealed that toxic substances polluted 21 percent and that 16 percent of the rivers were seriously polluted with excrement. China has 16 of the world's 20 most polluted cities.[36] The very process of controlling industrial wastes leads to another and perhaps equally critical issue: the disposal of hazardous waste, a by-product of pollution controls. Estimates of hazardous wastes collected annually exceed 300 million tons; the critical issue is disposal that does not simply move the problem elsewhere. Countries encountering increasing difficulty in disposal of wastes at home are seeking countries willing to assume the burden of disposal. Waste disposal is legal in some developing countries as governments seek the revenues that are generated by offering sites for waste disposal. In other cases, illegal dumping is done clandestinely.[37] A treaty among members of the Basel Convention that required prior approval before dumping could occur was later revised to a total ban on the export of hazardous wastes by developed nations. The influence and leadership provided by this treaty are reflected in a broad awareness of pollution problems by businesses and people in general.[38]

A woman collects plastic bottles near a river where the water is polluted with reddish dye in east China's Jiangxi Province. The pollution comes from wastewater directly discharged from a small paper factory nearby. China's already severe water shortages are worsening due to the heavy pollution of lakes and aquifers and urban development projects with a big thirst for water. A survey in 2005 found that only 47 percent of water in China's major rivers is drinkable, while half of all lakes are heavily polluted. Unfortunately, excessive pollution is often the result in rapidly developing economies. *(AP/Wide World Photos)*

Governments, organizations, and businesses are becoming increasingly concerned with the social responsibility and ethical issues surrounding the problem of maintaining economic growth while protecting the environment for future generations. The Organization for Economic Cooperation and Development, the United Nations, the European Union, and international activist groups are undertaking programs to strengthen environmental policies.[39] The issue that concerns all is whether economic development and protection for the environment can coexist. *Sustainable development,* a joint approach among those (governments, businesses, environmentalists, and others) who seek economic growth with "wise resource management, equitable distribution of benefits and reduction of negative efforts on people

---

[33]Visit www.gemi.org for information on Global Environmental Management Initiative, an organization of U.S. multinational companies dedicated to environmental protection.

[34]"Impose Stiff Penalties in Toxic Waste Cases," *New Straits Times-Management News*, January 6, 2003.

[35]"Electronics, Unleaded," *The Economist*, March 10, 2005.

[36]"A Great Wall of Waste," *The Economist*, August 19, 2004.

[37]Barbie Nadeau, "Under the Volcano II: Italy's New 'eco-mafia' Makes Garbage into Gold," *Newsweek*, November 8, 2004.

[38]For a comprehensive view of OECD programs including environmental issues, visit www.oecd.org.

[39]William C. Clark, "Science and Policy for Sustainable Development," *Environment*, January–February 2005.

CROSSING BORDERS 3.5   The World's Breadbasket to the World's Lungs

As nations prosper and economic development is sought, building roads and dams and digging tunnels to overcome physical barriers becomes a necessity but often at an unintended cost. For example, a 1,097-mile trip on BR-163, the road between Santarém, a port on the Amazon River, and Cuiabá, capital of the state of Mato Grosso, Brazil, can take 14 days during the rainy season. The road joins what Brazilians call the "world's breadbasket" to the "world's lungs"—the crop fields and pastures of Mato Grosso to the Amazonian rain forest. You drive on whichever bit of the road seems least likely to tear off the undercarriage of your vehicle. During the six-month rainy season, when the road becomes a river of mud, men with tractors wait for you to founder and then haul you out for a fee. Within four years, the BR-163 will become a superhighway, launching commodities toward markets in Europe and Asia, speeding computers and cell phones from Manaus to São Paulo, thus ending the near-isolation of hundreds of thousands of people living along its unpaved stretches. But at what cost?

If the past is any guide, the "lungs" will suffer. Paving the BR-163 could lay waste to thousands of square kilometers of forest, carrying deep into the jungle the "arc of deforestation" through which it passes. In general, some 85 percent of deforestation takes place within 50 kilometers of a road, because a road makes it more profitable to fell trees, first for timber and then for pasture.

According to the head of the union of rural workers, "On the one hand paving BR-163 will bring development—on the other hand it will bring ruin to the region—more land grabbing, more drug trafficking. Total violence will arrive." According to a report by two research institutes, paving the BR-163 could destroy 22,000 to 49,000 square kilometers of the Amazon forest by 2020.

Proponents of paving argue that this paving will be a different sort of roadwork, bringing ordered rather than

A farmer rubs his eyes while surveying land that was deforested for agricultural use in northern Brazil. At the behest of environmentalists, the government pledged new controls to reduce deforestation of Brazil's Amazon rain forest which is home to up to 30 percent of the world's animal and plant life. (© Reuters NewMedia Inc./CORBIS)

chaotic growth, reducing social inequities rather than exacerbating them, preserving the Amazon rather than despoiling it. Getting it right has now become a global project, involving NGOs,* multinationals, and grassroots groups, as well as all levels of Brazil's government. The miracle will be a road that promotes Brazil's growth while protecting the indispensable Amazon.

*NGOs are nongovernmental organizations associated with the United Nations and include such organizations as Earth Charter Initiative and Society for Conservation and Protection of Environment (SCOPE). See www.ngo.org.

Sources: "Asphalt the Jungle," *The Economist*, July 22, 2004; Steve Connor, "How a Century of Destruction Has Laid Bare the World's Rainforests," *The (London) Independent*, July 2004; Leandro V. Ferreira, "Amazonian Deforestation Models," *Science*, February 18, 2005.

and the environment from the process of economic growth," is the concept that guides many governments and multinational companies today.[40] Sustainable development is not about the environment or the economy or society. It is about striking a lasting balance between all of these. More and more companies are embracing the idea of sustainable development as a "win-win" opportunity.[41] Responsibility for protecting the environment does not rest solely with governments, businesses, or activist groups, however; each citizen has a social and moral responsibility to include environmental protection among his or her highest goals.[42]

[40]Jeremy Rifkin, "The European Dream: Building Sustainable Development in a Globally Connected World," *The Environmental Magazine*, March–April 2005.

[41]Visit www.oecd.org; the OECD Web site, for a directory to complete coverage of sustainable development.

[42]Visit www.webdirectory.com for the *Amazing Environmental Organization Web Directory*, a search engine with links to an extensive list of environmental subjects.

CROSSING **BORDERS 3.6**   Garbage without a Country—The Final Solution

We have all read or heard the story of "the man without a country," who is sentenced to remain at sea for his entire life, aimlessly wandering the world. Of course, that is just fiction. In real life, however, there is a bargeload of garbage that aimlessly wanders the globe looking for a country that will accept it in its landfills.

Orange rinds, beer bottles, newspapers, and chicken bones—it was trash, like all trash, taken to an incinerator in Philadelphia for incineration. The ashes, like all ashes, were to be taken away to a landfill somewhere in Philadelphia. Joseph Paolino & Sons had a $6 million contract to remove the ash but kept having doors slammed in its face.

Paolino hired Amalgamated Shipping—operator of the *Khian Sea*, a 17-year-old, 466-foot rust bucket registered in Liberia—to dump the ash in the Bahamas, where Amalgamated was based. The Bahamian government rejected the ash, and the *Khian Sea* began its 16-year journey as the Flying Dutchman of debris.

Briefly returning to the United States, it took off for Puerto Rico, Bermuda, the Dominican Republic, Honduras, Guinea-Bissau, and the Netherlands Antilles, where it was turned away again and again. To make the cargo more appealing the ash was described as "topsoil fertilizer" and the Haitian government agreed to accept the ash. About two thirds of the ash (4,000 tons) had been unloaded when Greenpeace and local activists protested. The Haitian government then ordered the crew to reload the ash, but the ship departed leaving the ash.

The ship returned to Philadelphia hoping to find a place for the remaining ash but to no avail. It left again seeking a resting place. It sailed to Senegal and Cape Verde, Sri Lanka, Indonesia, and the Philippines, arriving in Singapore empty. Years later, the ship's captain admitted in court that the remaining ash, one third of the original load, had been dumped in the Atlantic and Indian oceans.

Meanwhile, in Haiti, where the 4,000 tons of ash had been left on the beach, Greenpeace found that only 2,500 tons of the original 4,000 tons remained. Most had been carried off by wind and water, and Haitians said goats were dying.

Enter an unlikely hero: New York City. In 1996, to end mob involvement in the city's waste industry, Mayor Rudolph Giuliani established a Trade Waste commission to oversee the awarding of trash removal. When Eastern Environmental Services applied to do business in New York, the Trade Waste Commission issued an ultimatum:

After a 16-year odyssey on the cargo ship *Khian Sea*, 2,500 tons of ash from Philadelphia incinerators is on its way back to a final resting place in Pennsylvania where it began its journey. *(AP/Wide World Photos)*

If Eastern wanted to haul trash in New York, it had to deal with the *Khian Sea* ash.

Eastern agreed to find a place in its landfills, and what was left of the ash, 2,500 tons, was loaded on the *Khian Sea* and departed Haiti. Finally, after a 16-year odyssey, Philadelphia agreed to give the ash a final resting place.

The saga of the *Khian Sea* is not an isolated case of wandering toxic waste, albeit the longest journey. In 1999 the MV *Ulla* was loaded with 2,200 tons of ash from coal-fired power stations in Spain bound for Algeria, where the ash was to be incorporated into the construction of a dam. The cargo was refused by Algeria and thus it began a journey that ended in 2004 with the ship sinking off the Turkish coast, where it lay rusting until 2005, when Spain agreed to remove the toxic waste and the ship.

Unfortunately, one of the by-products of economic and technological growth is toxic waste and, as countries such as China and India industrialize, toxic waste disposal will only become worse—there has to be a better solution than wandering ships.

Sources: "Wandering Waste's 14-Year Journey," *Toronto Star*, May 3, 2000; Molly Hennessy-Fiske, "Unwanted Ash Transferred to One Large, Covered Barge," *Palm Beach Post*, April 30, 2000, p. 1B; William M. Hartnett, "2,000 Tons of Ash Await Next Leg of 14-Year Odyssey," *Palm Beach Post*, January 7, 2001, p. 1B; "Toxic Waste Returns," *Earth Island Journal*, Winter 2002–2003, p. 12; "Spain to Remove Sunken Ship with Toxic Cargo Off Turkish Coast," *Agence France Presse*, February 2, 2005.

Resources

The availability of minerals and the ability to generate energy are the foundations of modern technology. The locations of Earth's resources, as well as the available sources of energy, are geographic accidents. The world's nations are not equally endowed, and no nation's demand for a particular mineral or energy source necessarily coincides with domestic supply.

In much of the underdeveloped world, human labor provides the preponderance of energy. The principal supplements to human energy are animals, wood, fossil fuel, nuclear power, and, to a lesser and more experimental extent, the ocean's tides, geothermal power, and the sun. Of all the energy sources, oil and gas contribute over 60 percent of world energy consumption.[43] Because of petroleum's versatility and the ease with which it is stored and transported, petroleum-related products continue to dominate energy usage.[44] (See Exhibit 3.3.)

After the immersion of hundreds of idols of Hindu goddess Durga into the River Yamuna to celebrate the final day of the festival of Durga Puja in New Delhi, Indians wade through white foam from chemical pollution and floating debris. The festival commemorates the slaying of a demon king by the lion-riding, 10-armed goddess Durga, marking the triumph of good over evil. One wonders if it was intentional for the festival to take place in polluted waters . . . are the men trying to call upon the goddess to help vanquish the pollution . . . or was that simply the nearest body of water for these celebrants? *(AP/Wide World Photos)*

Many countries that were self-sufficient during much of their early economic growth have become net importers of petroleum during the past several decades and continue to become increasingly dependent on foreign sources. A spectacular example is the United States, which was almost completely self-sufficient until 1942, became a major importer by 1950, and between 1973 and 2000 increased its dependency from 36 percent to over 66 percent of its annual requirements.[45] If present rates of consumption continue, predictions are that by the mid-2000s the United States will be importing more than 70 percent of its needs, that is, more than 17 million barrels of oil each day. Exhibit 3.3 compares North American domestic energy consumption with other world regions. It is interesting to note that although North America is currently a major consumer of energy, industrializing Asia and the three industrialized areas (as shown in Exhibit 3.3) do not lag far behind. In fact, China has become the world's second-largest oil importer after the United States and demand continues to grow rapidly.[46]

Since World War II, concern for the limitless availability of seemingly inexhaustible supplies of petroleum has become a prominent factor. The dramatic increase in economic growth in the industrialized world and the push for industrialization in the remaining world has put tremendous pressure on Earth's energy resources. Unfortunately, as countries industrialize, energy sources are not always efficiently utilized. China, for example, spends three times the world average on energy (all sources) to produce one dollar of gross national product (GNP). In comparison with Japan, possibly the world's most efficient user of energy, less than 5 ounces of oil is needed to generate $1 in GNP, whereas in China approximately 80 ounces of oil is needed.[47] The reasons for China's inefficient oil use are numerous but the worst culprit is outdated technology.[48]

The growth of market-driven economies and an increasing reliance on petroleum supplies from areas of political instability—the Middle East, the former Soviet Union, and Latin America—create a global interdependence of energy resources. The net result is a profound impact on oil prices[49] and on the economies of the industrialized and industrializing countries.

---

[43]Visit www.eia.doe.gov and search for "International Energy Outlook (most current year)" for details of production, use, etc.

[44]See Map 3, "Oil and Gas Production and Consumption," for a global view of the flow and uses of petroleum.

[45]"U.S. Energy Bill Won't End Dependence on Foreign Oil," *Reuters News Service*, April 21, 2005.

[46]Koh Chin Ling and Loretta Ng, "China's Crude Oil Imports Surge in March," *International Herald Tribune*, April 22, 2005.

[47]"Lessons from a Miser," *BusinessWeek*, April 11, 2005, p. 51.

[48]"Wasteful Ways," *BusinessWeek*, April 11, 2005, p. 50.

[49]The effect that the war in Iraq has had on oil prices is discussed in some detail in Gene Epstein, "Iraq Bites Back," *Barron's*, May 16, 2005, p. 36.

Exhibit 3.3
World Energy Consumption

Energy consumed by world regions, measured in quadrillion BTUs in 2001. Total world consumption was 381.8 quadrillion BTUs. The largest portion of the hydro/other category is hydroelectrical energy. Fuels such as wood, peat, animal waste, wind, solar, and geothermal account for less than 1.0 quadrillion BTUs in the other portion of the *hydro/other* category.

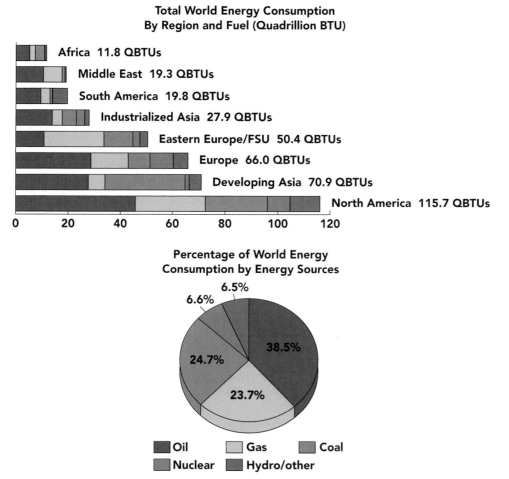

**Total World Energy Consumption
By Region and Fuel (Quadrillion BTU)**

Africa 11.8 QBTUs
Middle East 19.3 QBTUs
South America 19.8 QBTUs
Industrialized Asia 27.9 QBTUs
Eastern Europe/FSU 50.4 QBTUs
Europe 66.0 QBTUs
Developing Asia 70.9 QBTUs
North America 115.7 QBTUs

0   20   40   60   80   100   120

**Percentage of World Energy
Consumption by Energy Sources**

6.5%
6.6%
38.5%
24.7%
23.7%

Oil   Gas   Coal
Nuclear   Hydro/other

Sources: Data compiled from "Introduction to World Geography," *Oxford Atlas of the World* (New York: Oxford University Press, 2003) and Energy Information Administration (EIA), *International Energy Outlook 2004* (Washington, DC, 2005), www.eia.doe.gov/oiaf/ieo.

The location, quality, and availability of resources will affect the pattern of world economic development and trade well into the 21st century.[50] In addition to the raw materials of industrialization, an economically feasible energy supply must be available to transform resources into usable products. As the global demand for resources intensifies and prices rise, resources will continue to increase in importance among the uncontrollable elements of the international marketer's decisions.[51]

Dynamics of Global Population Trends
Current population, rural/urban population shifts, rates of growth, age levels, and population control help determine today's demand for various categories of goods. Although not the only determinant, the existence of sheer numbers of people is significant in appraising potential consumer markets. Changes in the

[50]"Consider the Alternatives," *The Economist*, April 28, 2005.

[51]For an interesting discussion on why one analyst believes the world is not running out of oil, see "The Bottomless Beer Mug," *The Economist*, April 28, 2005.

composition and distribution of population among the world's countries will profoundly affect future demand.

Recent estimates place world population at more than 6 billion people, and this is expected to grow to 9 billion by 2050. Further, 98 percent of the projected growth for 2050 will occur in less-developed regions.[52] Exhibit 3.4 shows that 84 percent of the population will be concentrated in less-developed regions by 2025 and, if growth rates continue, 86 percent by 2050. The International Labor Organization estimates that 1.2 billion jobs must be created worldwide by 2025 to accommodate these new entrants. Further, most of the new jobs will need to be created in urban areas where most of the population will reside.[53]

Controlling Population Growth

Faced with the ominous consequences of the population explosion, it would seem logical for countries to take appropriate steps to reduce growth to manageable rates, but procreation is one of the most culturally sensitive uncontrollable factors. Economics, self-esteem, religion, politics, and education all play a critical role in attitudes about family size.

The prerequisites to population control are adequate incomes, higher literacy levels, education for women, universal access to health care, family planning, improved nutrition, and, perhaps most important, a change in basic cultural beliefs regarding the importance of large families. Unfortunately, minimum progress in providing improved living conditions and changing beliefs has occurred. India serves as a good example of what is happening in much of the world. India's population was once stable, but with improved health conditions leading to greater longevity and lower infant mortality, its population will exceed that of China by 2050 and the two will account for about 50 percent of the world's inhabitants.[54] The government's attempts to institute change are hampered by a variety of factors, including political ineptitude[55] and slow change in cultural norms. Nevertheless, the government continues to pass laws with the intended purpose of limiting the number of births. The most recent attempt is a law that bars those with more than two children from election to the national Parliament and state assemblies. This would mean that many now in office could not seek reelection based on family size.[56]

Perhaps the most important deterrent to population control is cultural attitudes about the importance of large families.[57] In many cultures, the prestige of a man, whether alive or dead, depends on the number of his progeny, and a family's only wealth is its children. Such feelings are strong. Prime Minister Indira Gandhi found out how strong when she attempted mass sterilization of males, which reportedly was the main cause of her defeat in a subsequent election. Additionally, many religions discourage or ban family planning and thus serve as a deterrent to control.[58] Nigeria has a strong Muslim tradition in the north and a strong Roman Catholic tradition in the east, and both faiths favor large families. Most traditional religions in Africa encourage large families; in fact, the principal deity for many is the goddess of land and fertility.

Cattle dung, which is used both as farmyard manure and, dried into cakes, as household fuel, is being carried to a local market in India. India's cattle produce enormous quantities of dung, which some studies suggest provide the equivalent of 10,000 megawatts of energy annually.

[52]See "UNFPA State of World Population—2005," *UN Population Fund*, found at www.unfpa.org.

[53]Peter Auer and Mariangels Fortuny, "Ageing of the Labour Force in OECD Countries: Economic and Social Consequences," Employment Paper 2000/2, International Labour Organization, www.ilo.org/public/english/employment/strat/publ/ep00-2.htm.

[54]"India to Surpass China in Population," *ExpressIndia*, May 18, 2005.

[55]Anand Giridharadas, "A Buoyant India Dares to Ask: Is a Billion So Bad?" *International Herald Tribune*, May 4, 2005.

[56]V. K. Paghunathan, "3 Tykes and You're Out," *Straits Times*, April 11, 2003.

[57]See, for example, Jianghong Li and William Lovely, "Village Context, Women's Status, and Son Preference among Rural Chinese Women," *Rural Sociology*, March 2003, p. 87.

[58]Huma Aamir Malik, "Aziz Seeks Scholars' Support to Control Population," *Arab News*, May 5, 2005.

Exhibit 3.4

World Population by Region, 2005–2050, and Life Expectancy at Birth, 2005–2010 (millions)

Source: Compiled from "World Population Prospects: 2004 Revision," United Nations Population Division, Department of Economic and Social Information and Policy Analysis, 2005. www.un.org/popin/ (select "World Population").

| Regions | Population (in millions) | | | Life Expectancy at Birth |
	2005	2025	2050	2005–2010
World	6,465	7,905	9,076	66.5
More-developed regions*	1,211	1,249	1,236	76.2
Less-developed regions†	5,253	6,656	7,840	64.6
Least-developed regions‡	759	1,167	1,735	52.5
Africa	906	1,344	1,937	49.9
Asia	3,905	4,728	5,217	68.8
Europe	728	707	653	74.3
Latin America	561	697	783	72.9
Northern America	331	388	438	78.2
Oceania	33	41	48	75.1

*More-developed regions comprise all regions of Europe and Northern America, Australia–New Zealand, and Japan.
†Less-developed regions comprise all regions of Africa, Asia (excluding Japan), and Latin America and the regions of Melanesia, Micronesia, and Polynesia.
‡Least-developed regions as defined by the United Nations General Assembly include 48 countries, of which 33 are in Africa, 9 in Asia, 1 in Latin America, and 5 in Oceania. They are also included in less-developed regions.

Family planning and all that it entails is by far the most universal means governments use to control birthrates, but some economists believe that a decline in the fertility rate is a function of economic prosperity and will come only with economic development. Ample anecdotal evidence suggests that fertility rates decline as economies prosper. For example, before Spain's economy began its rapid growth in the 1980s, families had six or more children; now, Spain has one of the lowest birthrates in Europe, an average of 1.24 children per woman. Similar patterns have followed in other European countries as economies have prospered.[59]

Rural/Urban Migration

Migration from rural to urban areas is largely a result of a desire for greater access to sources of education, health care, and improved job opportunities. In the early 1800s, less than 3.5 percent of the world's people were living in cities of 20,000 or more and less than 2 percent in cities of 100,000 or more; today more than 40 percent of the world's people are urbanites, and the trend is accelerating. Once in the city, perhaps three out of four migrants achieve some economic gains. The family income of a manual worker in urban Brazil, for example, is almost five times that of a farm laborer in a rural area.

By 2030, estimates indicate that more than 61 percent of the world's population will live in urban areas (see Exhibit 3.5), and at least 27 cities will have populations of 10 million or

Exhibit 3.5

Rural and Urban Population, 2005–2030 (millions)

Source: Compiled from "World Population Prospects: 2004 Revision," United Nations Population Division, Department of Economic and Social Information and Policy Analysis, 2005. www.un.org/popin/ (select "World Population").

| Region | Urban | | Rural | | Percent Urban | |
	2005	2030	2005	2030	2005	2030
World	3,177	4,987	3,287	3,212	49	61
More-developed regions*	907	1,022	304	229	75	82
Less-developed regions†	2,270	3,964	2,983	2,984	43	57
Least-developed regions‡	210	555	549	726	28	43
Africa	360	783	546	680	40	48
Asia	1,557	2,657	2,348	2,216	40	55
Europe	534	555	195	143	73	80
Latin America	436	611	126	111	78	85
Northern America	87	267	348	63	52	81
Oceania	24	32	9	11	73	74

*More-developed regions comprise all regions of Europe and Northern America, Australia–New Zealand, and Japan.
†Less-developed regions comprise all regions of Africa, Asia (excluding Japan), and Latin America and the regions of Melanesia, Micronesia, and Polynesia.
‡Least-developed regions as defined by the United Nations General Assembly include 48 countries, of which 33 are in Africa, 9 in Asia, 1 in Latin America, and 5 in Oceania. They are also included in less-developed regions.

[59]Gautam Naik et al., "Global Baby Bust," *Wall Street Journal*, January 24, 2003, p. B1.

more, 23 of which will be in the less-developed regions. Tokyo has already overtaken Mexico City as the largest city on Earth, with a population of 26 million, a jump of almost 8 million since 1990.

Although migrants experience some relative improvement in their living standards, intense urban growth without investment in services eventually leads to serious problems. Slums populated with unskilled workers living hand to mouth put excessive pressure on sanitation systems, water supplies,[60] and other social services. At some point, the disadvantages of unregulated urban growth begin to outweigh the advantages for all concerned.

Consider the conditions that exist in Mexico City today. Besides smog, garbage, and pollution brought about by the increased population, Mexico City faces a severe water shortage. Local water supplies are nearly exhausted and in some cases unhealthy.[61] Water consumption from all sources is about 16,000 gallons per second, but the underground aquifers are producing only 2,640 gallons per second. Water comes from hundreds of miles away and has to be pumped up to an elevation of 7,444 feet to reach Mexico City. This is a grim picture of one of the most beautiful and sophisticated cities in Latin America. Such problems are not unique to Mexico; throughout the developing world, poor sanitation and inadequate water supplies are consequences of runaway population growth.[62] An estimated 1.1 billion people are currently without access to clean drinking water, and 2.8 billion lack access to sanitation services.[63] Estimates are that 40 percent of the world's population, 2.5 billion people, will be without clean water if more is not invested in water resources.[64] Prospects for improvement are not encouraging because most of the world's urban growth will take place in the already economically strained developing countries.[65]

Population Decline and Aging

While the developing world faces a rapidly growing population, the industrialized world's population is in decline and rapidly aging. Birthrates in western Europe and Japan have been decreasing since the early or mid-1960s; more women are choosing careers instead of children, and many working couples are electing to remain childless. As a result of these and other contemporary factors, population growth in many countries has dropped below the rate necessary to maintain present levels. Just to keep the population from falling, a nation needs a fertility rate of about 2.1 children per woman. Not one major country has sufficient internal population growth to maintain itself, and this trend is expected to continue for the next 50 years. Europe's population could decline by as much as 88 million (from 375 million to 287 million) people if present trends continue to 2015.[66]

At the same time that population growth is declining in the industrialized world, there are more aging people today than ever before. Global life expectancy has grown more in the last 50 years than over the previous 5,000 years. Until the Industrial Revolution, no more than 2 or 3 percent of the total population was over the age of 65. Today in the developed world, the over-age-65 group will amount to 14 percent, and by 2030, this group will reach 25 percent in some 30 different countries.[67] Further, the number of "old old" will grow much faster than the "young old." The United Nations projects that by 2050, the number of people aged 65 to 84 worldwide will grow from 400 million to 1.3 billion (a threefold increase), while the number of people aged 85 and over will grow from 26 million to 175 million (a sixfold increase)—and the number aged 100 and over will increase from

---

[60]"China Faces Worsening Water Woes," *Chicago Sun-Times*, March 24, 2005.

[61]"Nation Faces Water Shortage," *El Universal*, (Mexico City) March 23, 2005.

[62]Yoriko Kawaguchi, "Water Is Life," *OECD Observer*, March 19, 2003.

[63]For more details of global water problems, visit www.wateryear2003.org.

[64]David Usorne, "The Water Crisis: One Billion People Lack Clean Supplies," *The (London) Independent*, March 23, 2005.

[65]"An Unquenchable Thirst," *The Economist*, June 17, 2004.

[66]Mark Henderson, "Europe Shrinking as Birthrates Decline," *The Times* online (UK), March 28, 2003.

[67]Naik Gautam, "Leveraging the Age Gap," *Wall Street Journal*, February 27, 2003, p. B1.

Exhibit 3.6
Age Density for World and Selected Countries

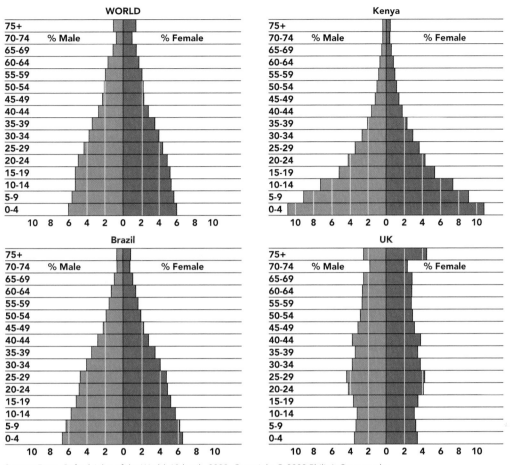

Source: From *Oxford Atlas of the World*, 10th ed., 2002. Copyright © 2002 Philip's Cartography.

135,000 to 2.2 million (a sixteenfold increase). Exhibit 3.6 illustrates the disparity in aging that is typical among lesser-developed countries (Kenya), developing countries (Brazil), and an economically developed country (United Kingdom). Countries like Kenya, with a high proportion of young, face high education and healthcare costs, whereas countries like the United Kingdom, with top-heavy population pyramids, face high pension and healthcare costs for the elderly with fewer wage earners to bear the burden.

Europe, Japan, and the United States epitomize the problems caused by an increasing percentage of elderly people who must be supported by a declining number of skilled workers. In 1998, Japan crossed a threshold anticipated with fear by the rest of the developed world: The point at which retirees withdrawing funds from the pension system exceeded those workers contributing to it.[68] The elderly require higher government outlays for health care and hospitals, special housing and nursing homes, and pension and welfare assistance, but the workforce that supports these costs is dwindling. The part of the world with the largest portion of people over 65 is also the part of the world with the fewest number of people under age 15. This means that there will be fewer workers to support future retirees, resulting in an intolerable tax burden on future workers, more of the over-65 group remaining in the labor force, or pressure to change existing laws to allow mass migration to stabilize the worker/retiree ratio. No one solution is without its problems.

---

[68]Sebastian Moffett, "Going Gray: For Ailing Japan, Longevity Begins to Take Its Toll," *Wall Street Journal*, February 11, 2003, p. A1.

CROSSING **BORDERS 3.7**   Where Have All the Women Gone?

Three converging issues in China have the potential of causing a serious gender imbalance:

- China, the world's most populous country, has a strict one-child policy to curb population growth.
- Traditional values dictate male superiority and a definite parental preference for boys.
- Prenatal scanning allows women to discover the sex of their fetuses and thereby abort unwanted female fetuses.

The first wave of children born under the one-child policy is reaching marriageable age and there are far too few brides to go around. The ratio of males to females is unnaturally high, hovering between 117 to 119 boys for every 100 girls in 2000. Thus men in their 20s have to deal with the harsh reality of six bachelors for every five potential brides. So what is a desperate bachelor to do?

The shortage has prompted some parents to acquire babies as future brides for their sons. Infants are considered more appealing because they are less likely to run away, will look on their buyers as their own parents, and are cheaper than buying a teenage bride. Buying a baby girl can cost as little as $100 and won't result in the fines imposed on couples who violate birth control limits. Such fines can equal as much as six years' income.

Another alternative is to marry a relative. At age 20, with his friends already paired off, Liu found himself the odd man out. His parents, farmers in a small backwater village, could not raise the $2,000 required to attract a bride for their son. Desperate, Liu's mother asked her sister for a favor: Could she ask Hai, her daughter, to be Liu's bride? Young women like Hai are not likely to defy their parents. And so Liu and Hai were wed.

Chinese officials are starting to worry about the imbalance and have announced a raft of new programs to reverse the trend. These include cash payments for couples who have a daughter and let her live, along with privileges in housing, employment, and job training. Some families with girls will also be exempted from paying school fees. Even though the government staunchly defends its one-child policy, it is experimenting with allowing couples whose firstborn is a girl to have a second child. In the meantime and until the new policy results in more girls, today's 20-year-old men will just have to compete if they want a wife.

Sources: "Sex Determination before Birth," *Reuters News Service*, May 3, 1994; "Seven Times as Many Men," *AP News Service*, March 31, 1994; "To Have Girls Is Glorious," *WSJ Opinion Journal*, August 22, 2004; "China Breeding Frustrated Bachelors," *Vietnam Investment Review*, March 2004; "China to Make Sex-Selective Abortions a Crime," *ITV.Com*, January 7, 2005.

Worker Shortage and Immigration

For most countries mass immigration is not well received by the resident population. However, a recent report from the United Nations makes the strongest argument for change in immigration as a viable solution. The free flow of immigration will help to ameliorate the dual problems of explosive population expansion in less-developed countries and worker shortage in industrialized regions. Europe is the region of the world most affected by aging and thus by a steadily decreasing worker/retiree ratio. The proportion of older persons will increase from 20 percent in 1998 to 35 percent in 2050. The country with the largest share of old people will be Spain, closely followed by Italy. Recognizing the problem, Spain has changed immigration laws to open its borders to all South Americans of Spanish descent.[69] To keep the worker/retiree ratio from falling, Europe will need 1.4 billion immigrants over the next 50 years, while Japan and the United States will need 600 million immigrants between now and 2050. Immigration will not help to ameliorate the problem if political and cultural opposition to immigration cannot be overcome.[70]

The trends of increasing population in the developing world[71] with substantial shifts from rural to urban areas, declining birthrates in the industrialized world, and global population aging will have profound effects on the state of world business and world economic conditions. Without successful adjustments to these trends,[72] many countries will experience slower eco-

[69]"Spain Grants Amnesty to 700,000 Migrants," *Guardian Unlimited*, May 9, 2005.

[70]Paolo Pontoniere, "Europe Needs More Immigrants, but Sees Spike in Racism," *Focus*, April 26, 2005.

[71]Girish Kuber, "Golden Years: UN Report Suggests India's Ageing Fast," *Economic Times*, April 27, 2005.

[72]Sylvia Hui, "Action Urged in Deepening Aging Crisis," *The Standard*, April 27, 2005.

Exhibit 3.7
500 Years of Trade

U.S. negotiators seem miffed that Latin American countries didn't trip all over themselves to forge a free trade zone of the Americas pact. Indeed, the U.S. team blamed Brazil for the pact's failure to move further along.

But the United States often fails to recognize that many Latin American countries have strong relationships with Europe, Asia, and the rest of the world—and these relationships were in place long before the United States even existed.

nomic growth, serious financial problems for senior retirement programs, and further deterioration of public and social services, leading to possible social unrest.[73]

World Trade Routes

Trade routes bind the world together, minimizing distance, natural barriers, lack of resources, and the fundamental differences between peoples and economies. As long as one group of people in the world wants something that another group somewhere else has and there is a means of travel between the two, there is trade. Early trade routes were overland;[74] later came sea routes, air routes, and, finally, some might say, the Internet to connect countries.

As Exhibit 3.7 illustrates, trade routes among Europe, Asia, and the Americas were well established by the 1500s. The Spanish empire founded the city of Manila in the

[73]David J. Lynch, "Looming Pension Crisis in China Stirs Fears of Chaos," *USA Today*, April 19, 2005

[74]For a short history of the Silk Road, see Ann Saccomano, "The Great Trade Routes," *World Trade*, January 1, 2002.

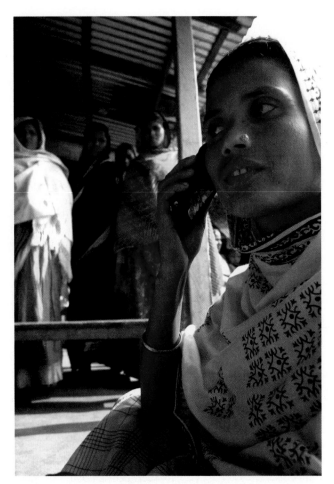

One of the "telephone ladies" at Kalampur, Bangladesh, talks over the phone. These entrepreneurs give globalization true meaning, promoting the cellular phone in remote villages that still have few telephone lines. The telephone lady, selling time on her cell phone, is one type of small business that is bringing goods and services to the Bottom of the Pyramid market segment in rural villages. *(AP/Wide World Photos)*

Philippines to receive its silver-laden galleons bound for China. On the return trip the ship's cargo of silk and other Chinese goods would be offloaded in Mexico, carried overland to the Atlantic, and put on Spanish ships to Spain. What we sometimes fail to recognize is that these same trades routes remain important today and that many Latin American countries have strong relationships with Europe, Asia, and the rest of the world that date back to the 1500s. The commodities traded have changed between 1500s and 2006 but trade and the trade routes continue to be important. Today, instead of offloading goods in Mexico and carrying them on mule carts overland to the Atlantic, ships travel from the Pacific to the Atlantic via the Panama Canal. And ships too large for the canal offload their containers onto a railroad that crosses the Isthmus of Panama to be met by another container ship.[75]

Trade routes represent the attempts of countries to overcome economic and social imbalances created in part by the influence of geography. The majority of world trade is among the most industrialized and industrializing countries of Europe, North America, and Asia. It is no surprise that the trade flow, as seen in Map 8, link these major trading areas.

Communication Links An underpinning of all commerce is effective communications—knowledge of where goods and services exist and where they are needed and the ability to communicate instantaneously across vast distances. Continuous improvements in electronic communications have facilitated the expansion of trade. First came the telegraph, then the telephone, television, satellites, the computer, and the Internet. Map 5 illustrates the importance of fiber-optic cable and satellites in providing global communications. Each revolution in electronic technology has had a profound effect on human conditions, economic growth, and the manner in which commerce functions. Each new communications technology has spawned new business models; some existing businesses have reinvented their practices to adapt to the new technology, while other businesses have failed to respond and thus ceased to exist.[76] The Internet revolution will be no different; it too affects human conditions, economic growth, and the manner in which commerce operates. As we discuss in subsequent chapters, the Internet has already begun to shape how international business is managed. However, as the Internet permeates the fabric of the world's cultures, the biggest changes are yet to come!

---

[75]Larry Luxner, "New Tracks for the Panama Canal," *Americas*, September/October 2001, p. 5.

[76]For an interesting and insightful review of the impact information and communication technology will have on how business operates, see Jose de la Torre and Richard W. Moxon, "Introduction to the Symposium E-Commerce and Global Business: The Impact of the Information and Communication Technology Revolution on the Conduct of International Business," *Journal of International Business Studies* 32, no. 4 (2001), p. 617.

Summary

One British authority admonishes foreign marketers to study the world until "the mere mention of a town, country, or river enables it to be picked out immediately on the map." Although it may not be necessary for the student of foreign marketing to memorize the world map to that extent, a prospective international marketer should be reasonably familiar with the world, its climate, and topographic differences. Otherwise, the important marketing characteristics of geography could be completely overlooked when marketing in another country. The need for geographical and historical knowledge goes deeper than being able to locate continents and their countries. Geographic hurdles must be recognized as having a direct effect on marketing and the related activities of communications and distribution. For someone who has never been in a tropical rain forest with an annual rainfall of at least 60 inches (and sometimes more than 200 inches), anticipating the need for protection against high humidity is difficult. Likewise, someone who has never encountered the difficult problems caused by dehydration in constant 100-degrees-plus heat in the Sahara region will find them hard to comprehend. Indirect effects from the geographical ramifications of a society and culture may be ultimately reflected in marketing activities. Many of the peculiarities of a country (i.e., peculiar to the foreigner) would be better understood and anticipated if its history and geography were studied more closely. Without a historical understanding of a culture, the attitudes within the marketplace may not be fully understood.

Aside from the simpler and more obvious ramifications of climate and topography, history and geography exert complex influences on the development of the general economy and society of a country. In this case, the study of history and geography is needed to provide the marketer with an understanding of why a country has developed as it has rather than as a guide for adapting marketing plans. History and geography are two of the environments of foreign marketing that should be thoroughly understood and that must be included in foreign marketing plans to a degree commensurate with their influence on marketing effort.

Questions

1. Define the following terms:

   Manifest Destiny   sustainable development

   Roosevelt Corollary   Monroe Doctrine

2. Why study geography in international marketing? Discuss.

3. Why study a country's history? Discuss.

4. How does an understanding of history help an international marketer?

5. Why is there a love–hate relationship between Mexico and the United States? Discuss.

6. Some say the global environment is a global issue rather than a national one. What does this mean? Discuss.

7. Pick a country and show how employment and topography affect marketing within the country.

8. Pick a country, other than Mexico, and show how significant historical events have affected the country's culture.

9. Discuss the bases of world trade. Give examples illustrating the different bases.

10. The marketer "should also examine the more complex effect of geography on general market characteristics, distribution systems, and the state of the economy." Comment.

11. The world population pattern trend is shifting from rural to urban areas. Discuss the marketing ramifications.

12. Select a country with a stable population and one with a rapidly growing population. Contrast the marketing implications of these two situations.

13. "World trade routes bind the world together." Discuss.

14. Discuss how your interpretations of Manifest Destiny and the Monroe Doctrine might differ from those of a native of Latin America.

15. The telegraph, the telephone, television, satellites, the computer, and the Internet have all had an effect on how international business operates. Discuss how each of these communications innovations affects international business management.

world maps

1   **The World**

2   **Global Climate**

3   **Oil and Gas Production and Consumption**

4   **Water**

5   **Global Communications**

6   **Global Terrorism**

7   **Religions**

8   **Global Economy and World Trade**

1 **The World**

POLAR EASTERLIES

POLAR EASTERLIES

POLAR EASTERLIES

Labrador Current

WESTERLIES

WESTERLIES

WESTERLIES

E U

NORTH AMERICA

Alaska Current

North Pacific Current

North Equatorial Current

California Current

NORTHEAST TRADE WINDS

Gulf Stream

Canary Current

NORTHEAST TRADE WINDS

North Equatorial Current

Equatorial Counter Current

South Equatorial Current

A

South Equatorial Current

SOUTH AMERICA

Peru (Humboldt) Current

El Niño

SOUTHEAST TRADE WINDS

Brazil Current

SOUTHEAST TRADE WINDS

El Niño

Up to 30 times in a century, the El Niño effect occurs, when east-to-west trade winds sweeping over the Pacific Ocean become unusually weak, allowing warm water, normally held back by the winds, to flow eastwards along the equator. The current creates a warm band of water and an area of low atmospheric pressure with violent storms right across the eastern Pacific. The global weather machine is thrown into chaos; random and unusual weather events, such as hurricanes, heatwaves, freak floods, and droughts, occur around the globe, bringing devastation in their wake.

Falkland Current

Benguela Current

WESTERLIES

WESTERLIES

West Wind Drift

West Wind Drift

POLAR EASTERLIES

WESTERLIES

POLAR EASTERLIES

WESTERLIES

EASTERLIES

lantic Drift

POLAR EASTERLIES

Winds and currents
The winds and currents that circulate across the surface of the planet act as a global heat exchange mechanism, transferring warmth from the tropics, which receive the most heat from the Sun, toward the cold polar regions. If air in one region of the globe is heated above the temperature of the surrounding air, it becomes less dense and rises. Cooler, denser air in another part of the atmosphere sinks—a constant cycle of heat exchange and air circulation, known as the prevailing winds. The surface currents of the ocean, which extend to depths of several hundred meters, are influenced by global wind patterns. The transfer of warm water polewards can have a strong influence on neighboring continents—the warm Gulf Stream in the Atlantic, for example, keeps northwestern Europe free of ice.

OPE

RICA

ASIA

SOUTHWEST MONSOON (APR.–SEPT.)

Kuro Siwo Current

North Equatorial Current

NORTHEAST TRADE WINDS

Equatorial Counter Current

Equatorial Counter Current

South Equatorial Current

NORTHEAST MONSOON (OCT.–MAR.)

SOUTHEAST TRADE WINDS

South Equatorial Current

AUSTRALIA

West Australian Current

WESTERLIES

Climate Zones

- Ice cap
- Tundra
- Subarctic
- Highlands
- Marine west coast
- Humid continental
- Humid subtropical
- Mediterranean
- Arid
- Semiarid
- Tropical wet and dry
- Tropical wet

West Wind Drift

West Wind Drift

WESTERLIES

WESTERLIES

POLAR EASTERLIES

POLAR EASTERLIES

POLAR EASTERLIES

WESTERLIES

- Warm current
- Cool current

3 Oil and Gas Production and Consumption

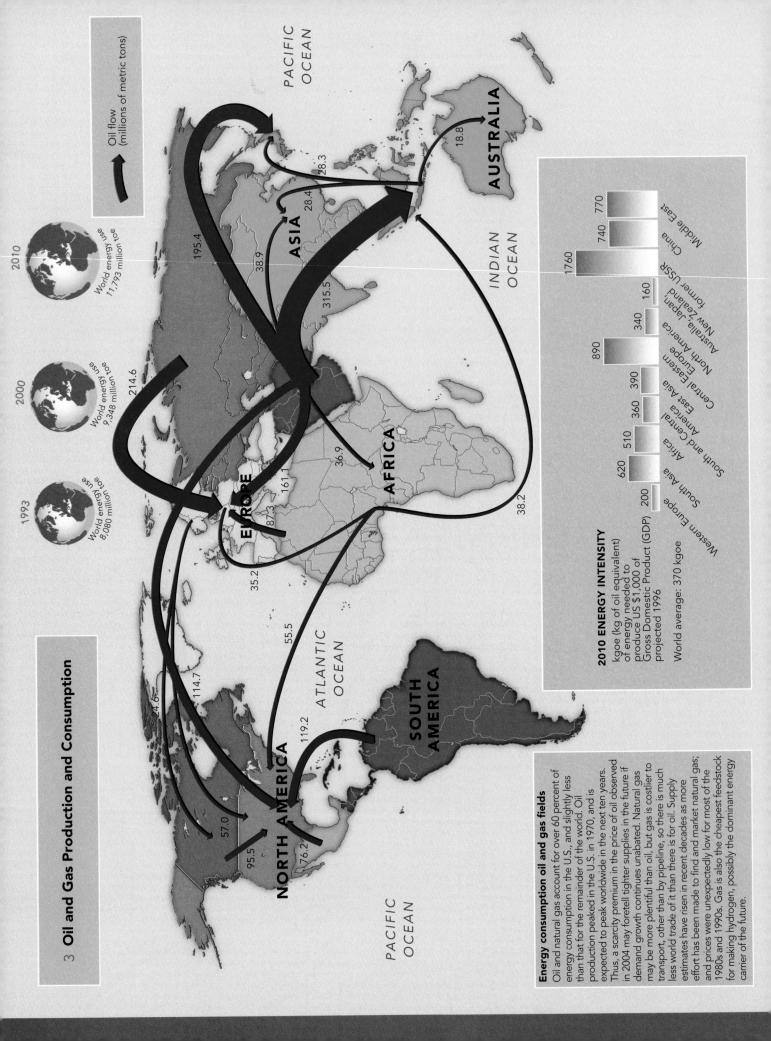

Oil flow
(millions of metric tons)

1993
World energy use
8,080 million toe

2000
World energy use
9,348 million toe

2010
World energy use
11,793 million toe

PACIFIC
OCEAN

ASIA

AUSTRALIA

EUROPE

AFRICA

INDIAN
OCEAN

NORTH
AMERICA

ATLANTIC
OCEAN

SOUTH
AMERICA

PACIFIC
OCEAN

195.4

214.6

28.3

28.4

38.9

315.5

36.9

161.1

87.3

35.2

55.5

114.7

24.6

57.0

95.5

76.2

119.2

18.8

38.2

2010 ENERGY INTENSITY

kgoe (kg of oil equivalent)
of energy needed to
produce US $1,000 of
Gross Domestic Product (GDP)
projected 1996

World average: 370 kgoe

	kgoe
Western Europe	200
South Asia	620
Africa	510
South and Central America	390
East Asia	360
Central Eastern Europe	890
North America	340
Australia, Japan, New Zealand	160
former USSR	1760
China	740
Middle East	770

Energy consumption oil and gas fields

Oil and natural gas account for over 60 percent of
energy consumption in the U.S., and slightly less
than that for the remainder of the world. Oil
production peaked in the U.S. in 1970, and is
expected to peak worldwide in the next ten years.
Thus, a scarcity premium in the price of oil observed
in 2004 may foretell tighter supplies in the future if
demand growth continues unabated. Natural gas
may be more plentiful than oil, but gas is costlier to
transport, other than by pipeline, so there is much
less world trade of it than there is for oil. Supply
estimates have risen in recent decades as more
effort has been made to find and market natural gas;
and prices were unexpectedly low for most of the
1980s and 1990s. Gas is also the cheapest feedstock
for making hydrogen, possibly the dominant energy
carrier of the future.

4 Water

THE WORLD'S WATER
1993 percentages

salt water
97.5%

fresh water
2.5%

69% glaciers
and permanent
snow cover

30% fresh
groundwater

0.3%
freshwater lakes
and river flows

0.9%
other, including
soil moisture,
ground ice and
swamp water

WATER SHORTAGES
proportion of world's population
facing water shortages
1995 and 2050

1995

stress 5%   scarcity 3%

relative
sufficiency
92%

world population 5.7 billion

2050

scarcity
18%

stress
24%

relative
sufficiency
58%

world population 9.4 billion

2050
FRESH WATER
Availability per person per year
cubic meters
projected 1997
borders 1998

water scarcity:
under 1,000 cubic
meters
per person
chronic water shortages
impede economic
development and cause
environmental degradation

water stress:
1,000–1,700 cubic meters
per person
chronic and widespread
water supply problems

relative water sufficiency:
over 1,700 cubic
meters
per person
intermittent or localized
shortages

relative sufficiency in 1995
although shortage predicted
for 2050

Note: Based on
UN population data 1996

CANADA

U.S.A.

MEXICO

CUBA
JAMAICA
BELIZE
GUATEMALA
EL SALVADOR
HONDURAS
NICARAGUA
COSTA RICA
PANAMA
DOM REP
HAITI

BARBADOS

VENEZUELA
GUYANA
SURINAME
FRENCH GUIANA (Fr.)
COLOMBIA
ECUADOR
PERU
BRAZIL
BOLIVIA
PARAGUAY
CHILE
ARGENTINA
URUGUAY

FALKLAND
ISLANDS
(U.K.)

ICELAND
IRELAND
U.K.
PORTUGAL
SPAIN
NORWAY
SWEDEN
FINLAND
DENMARK
NETH
BEL
GERMANY
FRANCE
LUX
SWITZ
ITALY
EST
LAT
LITH
POLAND
BELARUS
CZECH
SLOVAKIA
AUS
HUNG
SLOV
CRO
B-H
S-M
ALB
MACE
BULG
GREECE
ROMANIA
MOL
UKRAINE

RUSSIA

MOROCCO
WESTERN
SAHARA
(Morocco)
MAURITANIA
MALI
ALGERIA
LIBYA
NIGER
CHAD
SENEGAL
GAMBIA
GUINEA-BISSAU
CAPE VERDE
GUINEA
SIERRA LEONE
LIBERIA
CÔTE D'IVOIRE
BURKINA
FASO
GHANA
TOGO
BENIN
NIGERIA
CAMEROON
EQ. GUINEA
GABON
CONGO
CENT.
AFR. REP.
DEM. REP.
OF THE CONGO
ANGOLA
NAMIBIA
BOTSWANA
SOUTH
AFRICA
LESOTHO
SWAZILAND
ZIMB.
ZAMBIA
MALAWI
MOZAMBIQUE
MADAGASCAR
MAURITIUS
COMOROS
TANZANIA
BUR.
RWA.
UGA.
KENYA
SOMALIA
ETHIOPIA
ERITREA
DJIBOUTI
SUDAN
EGYPT
TUNISIA
MALTA

TURKEY
CYPRUS
LEB
ISRAEL
JOR
SYRIA
IRAQ
IRAN
GEORGIA
ARM
AZER
KUWAIT
BAHRAIN
QATAR
U.A.E.
SAUDI
ARABIA
YEMEN
OMAN
AFGHANISTAN
PAKISTAN
TAJ.
TURKMENISTAN
UZBEKISTAN
KYRGYSTAN
KAZAKHSTAN
MONGOLIA
CHINA
NEPAL
INDIA
SRI LANKA

RUSSIA

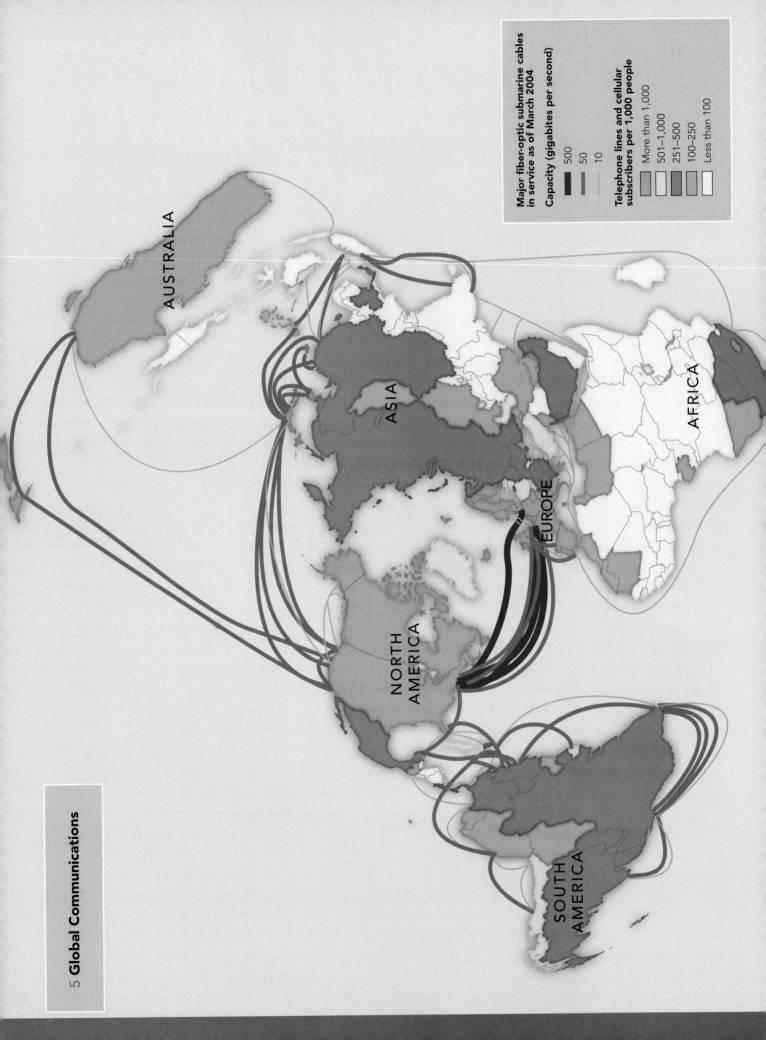

Major fiber-optic submarine cables
in service as of March 2004

Capacity (gigabites per second)

500

50

10

Telephone lines and cellular
subscribers per 1,000 people

More than 1,000

501–1,000

251–500

100–250

Less than 100

AUSTRALIA

ASIA

EUROPE

AFRICA

NORTH
AMERICA

SOUTH
AMERICA

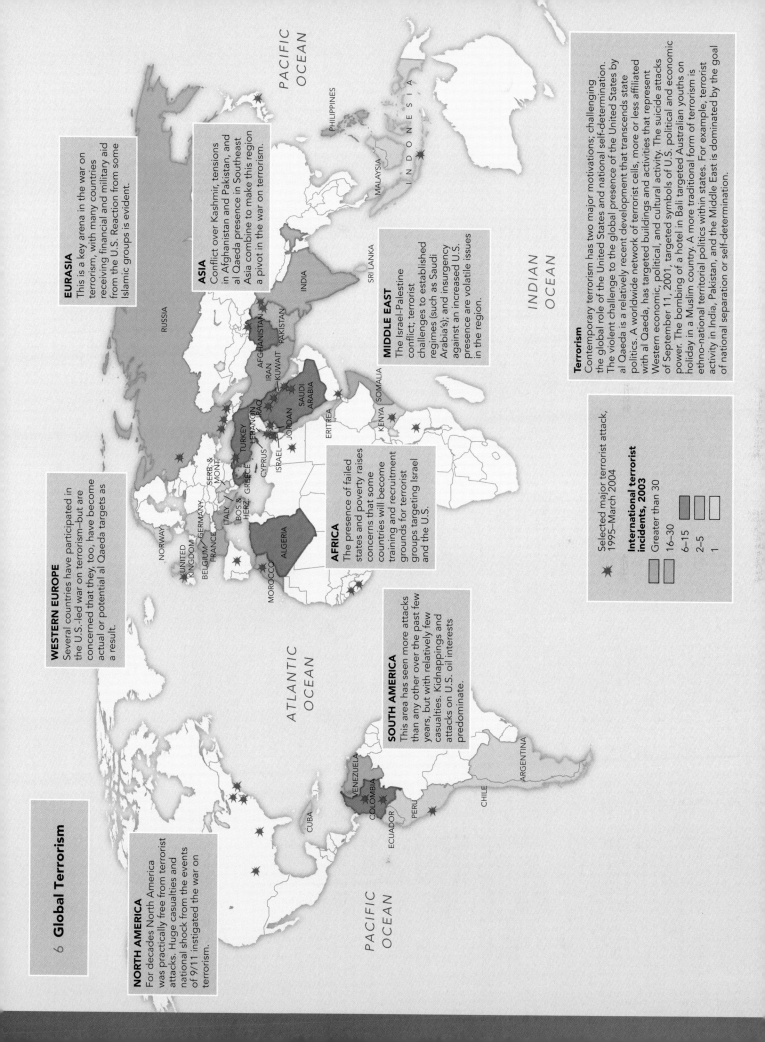

6 Global Terrorism

NORTH AMERICA
For decades North America was practically free from terrorist attacks. Huge casualties and national shock from the events of 9/11 instigated the war on terrorism.

WESTERN EUROPE
Several countries have participated in the U.S.-led war on terrorism—but are concerned that they, too, have become actual or potential al Qaeda targets as a result.

EURASIA
This is a key arena in the war on terrorism, with many countries receiving financial and military aid from the U.S. Reaction from some Islamic groups is evident.

ASIA
Conflict over Kashmir, tensions in Afghanistan and Pakistan, and al Qaeda presence in Southeast Asia combine to make this region a pivot in the war on terrorism.

MIDDLE EAST
The Israel-Palestine conflict; terrorist challenges to established regimes (such as Saudi Arabia's); and insurgency against an increased U.S. presence are volatile issues in the region.

AFRICA
The presence of failed states and poverty raises concerns that some countries will become training and recruitment grounds for terrorist groups targeting Israel and the U.S.

SOUTH AMERICA
This area has seen more attacks than any other over the past few years, but with relatively few casualties. Kidnappings and attacks on U.S. oil interests predominate.

Terrorism
Contemporary terrorism has two major motivations; challenging the global role of the United States and national self-determination. The violent challenge to the global presence of the United States by al Qaeda is a relatively recent development that transcends state politics. A worldwide network of terrorist cells, more or less affiliated with al Qaeda, has targeted buildings and activities that represent Western economic, political, and cultural activity. The suicide attacks of September 11, 2001, targeted symbols of U.S. political and economic power. The bombing of a hotel in Bali targeted Australian youths on holiday in a Muslim country. A more traditional form of terrorism is ethno-national territorial politics within states. For example, terrorist activity in India, Pakistan, and the Middle East is dominated by the goal of national separation or self-determination.

★ Selected major terrorist attack, 1995–March 2004

International terrorist incidents, 2003
Greater than 30
16–30
6–15
2–5
1

PACIFIC OCEAN

ATLANTIC OCEAN

PACIFIC OCEAN

INDIAN OCEAN

RUSSIA
NORWAY
UNITED KINGDOM
GERMANY
BELGIUM
FRANCE
ITALY
SERB. & MONT.
BOS. & HERZ.
GREECE
TURKEY
CYPRUS
LEBANON
ISRAEL
JORDAN
IRAQ
KUWAIT
IRAN
AFGHANISTAN
PAKISTAN
INDIA
SRI LANKA
SAUDI ARABIA
ERITREA
SOMALIA
KENYA
ALGERIA
MOROCCO
MALAYSIA
INDONESIA
PHILIPPINES

CUBA
VENEZUELA
COLOMBIA
ECUADOR
PERU
CHILE
ARGENTINA

PACIFIC
OCEAN

AUSTRALIA

ASIA

INDIAN
OCEAN

AFRICA

EUROPE

ATLANTIC
OCEAN

NORTH
AMERICA

SOUTH
AMERICA

PACIFIC
OCEAN

RELIGIONS

Atheism (and Communism)

Buddhism

Hindu

Muslim

Traditional/Tribal

Others

Christian (Orthodox)

Christian (no major sect)

Christian (Protestant)

Christian (Roman Catholic)

Christian (no major sect), Muslim, Hindu

Christian (no major sect), Traditional, Buddhism

Christian (no major sect), Traditional, Hindu, Muslim

Christian (no major sect), Christian (Roman Catholic), Hindu, Muslim, Others

Christian (Roman Catholic), Buddhism, Others

Christian (Roman Catholic), Muslim, Traditional

Christian (no major sect), Muslim, Traditional

Christian (Orthodox), Muslim, Atheism

Christian (Roman Catholic), Muslim, Others

Trade flow

The circling paths of trade between continents show just how inter-connected the world's economies truly are. The richest countries, such as those in North America, western Europe, and the Far East, trade mostly with each other, exchanging different varieties of similar goods such as automobiles. However, trade also flows between higher- and lower-income regions. In those cases, the high-income countries typically provide more complex goods, such as electronic equipment, while low-income countries provide primary goods such as minerals. Smaller, poorer countries are more likely to be dependent on exporting a single commodity, such as coffee or petroleum. In general, poor, labor-abundant countries tend to export labor-intensive goods, such as textiles and shoes, and the countries rich in arable land will export foods such as grains.

AUSTRALIA

ASIA

NORTH AMERICA

EUROPE

AFRICA

SOUTH AMERICA

World economies

High income
Upper-middle income
Lower-middle income
Low income
No income data

World merchandise trade
(in billions of U.S. dollars)

Greater than 200
101–200
31–100
5–30
Less than 5

4

cultural Dynamics in Assessing Global markets

CHAPTER OUTLINE

Global Perspective: Equities and eBay—Culture Gets
   in the Way

Culture's Pervasive Impact

Definitions and Origins of Culture

   Geography
   History
   The Political Economy
   Technology
   Social Institutions

Elements of Culture

   Cultural Values
   Rituals
   Symbols
   Beliefs
   Thought Processes

Cultural Knowledge

   Factual versus Interpretive Knowledge
   Cultural Sensitivity and Tolerance

Cultural Change

   Cultural Borrowing
   Similarities: An Illusion
   Resistance to Change
   Planned and Unplanned Cultural Change
   Consequences of Innovation

CHAPTER LEARNING OBJECTIVES

- The importance of culture to an international
  marketer

- The origins and elements of culture

- The impact of cultural borrowing

- The strategy of planned change and
  its consequences

Global Perspective

EQUITIES AND eBAY—CULTURE GETS IN THE WAY

Two trillion dollars! That's about 200 trillion yen. Either way you count, it's a lot of money. American brokerage houses such as Fidelity Investments, Goldman Sachs, and Merrill Lynch rushed new investment products and services to market in Japan to try to capture the huge capital outflow expected from 10-year time deposits then held in the Japanese postal system. Liberalization of Japan's capital markets in recent years now gives Japanese more freedom of choice in their investments. Post office time deposits still yield about a 2 percent return in Japan, and bank savings yields have been around zero. By American e-trading standards, that means an electronic flood of money moving out of the post offices and into the stock markets. Right?

However, Japan is not America. There is no American-style risk-taking culture among Japanese investors. The volume of stock trading in Japan is about one-sixth that of the United States. In Japan, only 9 percent of household financial assets are directly invested in stocks and a mere 2 percent in mutual funds. In contrast, about 50 percent of U.S. households own stock. Says one analyst, "Most of the population [in Japan] doesn't know what a mutual fund is." So will the flood be just a trickle? And what about online stock trading? Internet use in Japan has burgeoned—there are now some 75 million users in Japan. That's about the same percentage as in the United States. But the expected deluge into equities has been a dribble. Merrill Lynch and others are cutting back staff now as fast as they built it just a couple of years ago.

A French firm is trying to break through a similar aversion to both e-trading and equities in France. That is, only about 10 million adults use the Internet in France, and half that number own stocks. The French have long shied away from stock market investments, seeing them as schemes to enrich insiders while fleecing novices. Given the Enron and WorldCom scandals here, you can almost hear the chortling in the sidewalk cafés there.

eBay, the personal online auction site so successful in the United States, is running into comparable difficulties in both Japan and France. The relatively low rate of Internet use in France is just part of the problem. For Japanese it has been embarrassing to sell castoffs to anyone, much less buy them from strangers. Garage sales are unheard of. In France, company founder Pierre Omidyar's home country, eBay runs into French laws restricting operations to a few government-certified auctioneers.

Based on a knowledge of differences in cultural values between the United States and both Japan and France, we should expect a slower diffusion of these high-tech Internet services in the latter two countries. E-trading and e-auctions have both exploded on the American scene. However, compared with those in many other countries, U.S. investors are averse to neither the risk and uncertainties of equity investments nor the impersonal interactions of online transactions.

Sources: William D. Echikson, "Rough Crossing for eBay," *Business Week E.Biz*, February 7, 2000, p. EB48; Yukimo Ono, "Pizza Queen of Japan Turns Web Auctioneer," *Wall Street Journal*, March 6, 2000, p. B1; Euromonitor (2005); Sebastian Moffett, "Japan's Breakup of Postal System Clears Big Hurdle," *Wall Street Journal*, July 6, 2005, p. A13.

Culture deals with a group's design for living. It is pertinent to the study of marketing, especially international marketing. If you consider the scope of the marketing concept—the satisfaction of consumer needs and wants at a profit—the successful marketer clearly must be a student of culture. For example, when a promotional message is written, symbols recognizable and meaningful to the market (the culture) must be used. When designing a product, the style, uses, and other related marketing activities must be made culturally acceptable (i.e., acceptable to the present society) if they are to be operative and meaningful. In fact, culture is pervasive in all marketing activities—in pricing, promotion, channels of distribution, product, packaging, and styling—and the marketer's efforts actually become a part of the fabric of culture. The marketer's efforts are judged in a cultural context for acceptance, resistance, or rejection. How such efforts interact with a culture determines the degree of success or failure of the marketing effort.

The manner in which people consume, the priority of needs and the wants they attempt to satisfy, and the manner in which they satisfy them are functions of their culture that temper, mold, and dictate their style of living. Culture is the human-made part of human environment—the sum total of knowledge, beliefs, art, morals, laws, customs, and any other capabilities and habits acquired by humans as members of society.[1]

Markets constantly change; they are not static but evolve, expand, and contract in response to marketing effort, economic conditions, and other cultural influences. Markets and market behavior are part of a country's culture. One cannot truly understand how markets evolve or how they react to a marketer's effort without appreciating that markets are a result of culture. Markets are the result of the three-way interaction of a marketer's efforts, economic conditions, and all other elements of the culture. Marketers are constantly adjusting their efforts to cultural demands of the market, but they also are acting as *agents of change* whenever the product or idea being marketed is innovative. Whatever the degree of acceptance in whatever level of culture, the use of something new is the beginning of cultural change, and the marketer becomes a change agent.

This is the first of four chapters that focus on culture and international marketing. A discussion of the broad concept of culture as the foundation for international marketing is presented in this chapter. The next chapter, "Business Culture in Global Marketing," discusses culture and how it influences business practices and the behaviors and thinking of managers. Chapters 6 and 7 examine elements of culture essential to the study of international marketing: the political environment and the legal environment.

This chapter's purpose is to heighten the reader's sensitivity to the dynamics of culture. It is neither a treatise on cultural information about a particular country nor a thorough marketing science or epidemiological study of the various topics. Rather, it is designed to emphasize the importance of cultural differences to marketers and the need for study of each country's culture(s) and all its origins and elements, and to point out some relevant aspects on which to focus.

Culture's Pervasive Impact

Culture affects every part of our lives, every day, from birth to death,[2] and everything in between.[3] It affects how we spend money[4] and how we consume in general.[5] It even affects how we sleep. For example, we are told that Spaniards sleep less than other

---

[1] An interesting Web site that has information on various cultural traits, gestures, holidays, language, religions, and so forth is www.culturegrams.com.

[2] Funerals vary in style and cost around the world. See Hiroko Tashiro and Brian Bremner, "Bereaved, but Not Broke in Japan," *BusinessWeek*, February 14, 2005, p. 10.

[3] A most important summary of research in the area of culture's impact on consumption behavior is Eric J. Arnould and Craig J. Thompson, "Consumer Culture Theory (CCT): Twenty Years of Research," *Journal of Consumer Research* 3, no. 2 (March 2005), pp. 868–882.

[4] Marcus Walker, "Behind Slow Growth in Europe: Citizens' Tight Grip on Wallets," *Wall Street Journal*, December 10, 2004, pp. A1, A11.

[5] Robert J. Samuelson, "The Afflictions of Affluence," *Newsweek*, March 22, 2004, p. 45.

Exhibit 4.1
Birthrates (per 1,000 women)

Source: World Bank, *World Development Indicators*, 2004. Copyright © 2004 by World Bank. Reprinted with permission of World Bank via Copyright Clearance Center.

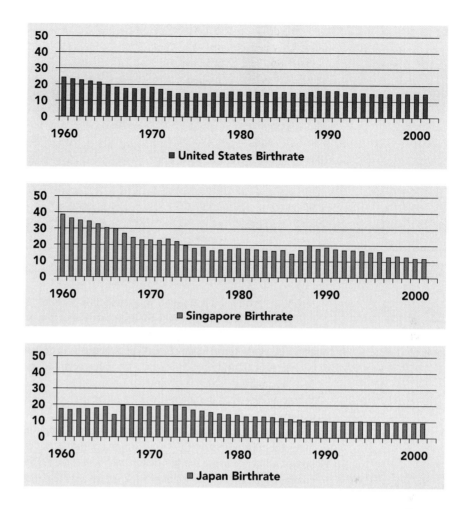

Europeans[6] and Japanese children often sleep with their parents.[7] You can clearly see culture operating in the birthrate tables in Exhibit 4.1. When you look across the data from the three countries, the gradual declines beginning in the 1960s are evident. As countries move from agricultural to industrial to services economies, birthrates decline. Immediate causes may be government policies and birth control technologies, but a global change in values is also occurring. Almost everywhere smaller families are becoming favored. This cultural change now leads experts to predict that the planet's population will actually begin to decline after 2050[8] unless major breakthroughs in longevity intervene, as some predict.[9]

But a closer look at the tables reveals even more interesting consequences of culture. Please notice the little peaks in 1976 and 1988 in the Singapore data. The same pattern can be seen in birthrate data from Taiwan. Those "extra" births are not a matter of random fluctuation. In Chinese cultures, being born in the Year of the Dragon (12 animals—dogs, rats, rabbits, pigs, etc.—correspond to specific years in the calendar) is considered good luck. Such birthrate spikes have implications for sellers of diapers, toys, schools, colleges, and so forth in successive years in Singapore. However, superstitions have an even stronger influence on the birthrates in Japan, shown in Exhibit 4.1. A one-year 20 percent drop in

---

[6]This seems a reasonable proposition to the authors given that the best restaurants in Madrid are still serving the main course after midnight!

[7]"Cultural Differences, You Say Tomato," *The Economist*, April 19, 2003, p. 68.

[8]Gautam Niak, Vanessa Fuhrmans, Jonathan Karp, Joel Millman, Farnaz Fassihi, and Joanna Slater, "Global Baby Bust," *Wall Street Journal*, January 24, 2003, p. B1; "Global Population at a Glance: 2002 and Beyond," *U.S. Census Bureau*, March 2004, pp. 1–4.

[9]Ray Kurzwell and Terry Grossman, *Fantastic Voyage: Live Long Enough to Live Forever* (Emmaus, PA: Rodale, 2004).

Exhibit 4.2
Patterns of Consumption (annual per capita)

Country	Cut Flowers (stems)	Chocolate (kg)	Fish (kg)	Pasta (kg)	Wine (lt)	Tobacco (sticks)
France	81	4.3	27.6	4.6	30.4	1375 (−1)*
Germany	120	8.7	10.2	5.1	21.3	1719 (+4)
Italy	87	2.5	22.2	**20.7**	**34.4**	1869 (+12)
Netherlands	**125**	5.0	22.6	2.5	17.9	1050 (+4)
Spain	33	1.7	**37.4**	4.4	13.1	**2288 (+10)**
United Kingdom	48	**10.5**	15.4	2.1	15.7	973 (−16)
Japan	110	1.8	37.8	10.9	6.9	2472 (−4)
United States	75	5.6	19.0	3.5	5.9	1428 (−18)

*5-year growth rate, percent.

Source: EuroMonitor International, 2004 and 2005.

Japanese fertility rates in 1966 was caused by a belief that women born in the Year of the Fire Horse, which occurs every 60 years, will lead unhappy lives and perhaps murder their husbands. This sudden and substantial decline in fertility, which has occurred historically every 60 years since Japan started keeping birth records, reflects abstinence, abortions, and birth certificate fudging. This superstition has resulted in the stigmatization of women born in 1966 and has had a large impact on market potential for a wide variety of consumer goods and services in Japan. It will be interesting to see how technological innovations and culture will interact in Japan in 2026, the next Year of the Fire Horse.[10]

Culture's influence is also illustrated in the consumption data presented in Exhibit 4.2. The focus there is on the six European Union countries, but data from the two other major markets of affluence in the world—Japan and the United States—are also included. The products compared are those that might be included in a typical (American) romantic dinner date.

First come the flowers and candy. The Dutch are the champion consumers of cut flowers,[11] and this particular preference for petals will be further explored in the pages to come. The British love their chocolate. Perhaps the higher consumption rate there is caused by Cadbury's[12] advertising, or perhaps the cooler temperatures have historically allowed for easier storage and better quality in the northern countries. At least among our six EU countries, per capita chocolate consumption appears to decline with latitude.

In Europe the Spaniards are the most likely to feast on fish. They even come close to the Japanese preference for seafood—in Japan they even eat it raw! From the data in the table one might conclude that being surrounded in Japan by water explains the preference for seafood. However, what about the British? The flat geography in England and Scotland allows for the efficient production of beef, and a bit later in this section we consider the consequences for their strong preference for red meat. The Italians eat more pasta—not a surprise. History is important. The product was actually invented in China and in 1270 Marco Polo brought the innovation back to Italy where it has flourished. Proximity to China also explains the high rate of Japanese pasta (noodle) consumption.

How about alcohol and tobacco? Grapes grow best in France and Italy, thus a combination of climate and soil conditions explains at least part of the pattern of wine consumption seen in Exhibit 4.2.[13] Culture also influences the laws, age limits, and such. The legal

[10]Robert W. Hodge and Naohiro Ogawa, *Fertility Change in Contemporary Japan* (Chicago: University of Chicago Press, 1991).

[11]Ken Wilkie, "The French Connection," *Holland Herald*, April 2005, pp. 11–15.

[12]See Cadbury's Web site for the history of chocolate, www.cadbury.co.uk. Chocolate is also an important product in Switzerland, where the consumption per capita is over 12 kg. The mountain climate is cooler and, of course, Nestlé has corporate headquarters there.

[13]Actually, Luxembourg, Hungary, and Ireland are the top three consuming countries (on a per capita basis) of alcohol. See "Emerging Market Indicators," *The Economist*, July 3, 2004, p. 102.

Finding horse or donkey as your entree would not be romantic or even appetizing in most places around the world. Even though horse consumption is generally declining in France, here in Paris you can still buy a steed steak at the local *bouchers chevaleries*. Escargot *oui*, Eeyore *non!*

environment also has implications for the consumption of cigarettes. Indeed, most striking in the table are not the current consumption numbers. The interesting data are the five-year growth rates. Demand is shrinking remarkably fast in the United States and the United Kingdom. Even the Japanese are succeeding in reducing the consumption of cigarettes. But the Italians and Spaniards are losing the battle.

Any discussion of tobacco consumption leads immediately to consideration of the consequences of consumption. One might expect that a high consumption of the romance products—flowers, candy, and wine—might lead to a high birthrate. Reference to Exhibit 4.3 doesn't yield any clear conclusions. The Germans have some of the highest consumption levels of the romantic three, but the lowest birthrate among the eight countries.

Perhaps the Japanese diet's[14] emphasis on fish yields them the longest life expectancy. But length of life among the eight affluent countries represented in the table shows little variation. How people die, however, does vary substantially across the countries. The influence of fish versus red meat consumption on the incidence of heart problems is easy to

---

[14]Notice we are not referring to the Japanese Diet, their legislature, although fishing rights are a hugely important international issue for that body.

Exhibit 4.3
Consequences of Consumption

Country	Birthrate (per 100,000)	Life Expectancy	Death Rate per 100,000			
			Ischemic Heart Disease	Chronic Liver Disease and Cirrhosis	Lung Cancer	Stomach Cancer
France	**12.3**	**79**	75	16	42	9
Germany	8.2	78	**241**	**22**	46	16
Italy	8.6	**79**	131	19	55	**19**
Netherlands	10.6	78	113	5	54	11
Spain	8.9	78	100	15	**59**	15
United Kingdom	10.6	77	162	9	57	12
Japan	9.2	81	59	11	42	41
United States	13.1	78	193	11	55	5

Source: World Health Organization (www3.who.int/whosis/menu.cfm, click on WHO Mortality Database, then Table 1), 2004.

see. Liver problems seem to be associated with greater wine consumption. And perhaps the high incidence of lung cancer in Spain is associated with high consumption of cigarettes.

The most interesting datum in the table is the extremely high incidence of stomach cancer in Japan. The latest studies suggest two culprits, (1) salty foods such as soy sauce and (2) the bacterium *Helicobacter pylori.* The latter is associated with the unsanitary conditions prevalent in Japan immediately after World War II, and it is still hurting health in Japan today. Finally, because stomach cancer in Japan is so prevalent, the Japanese have developed the most advanced treatment of the disease, that is, both procedures and instruments. Even though the death rate is highest, the treatment success rate is likewise the highest in Japan. Whether you are in Tacoma, Toronto, or Tehran, the best medicine for stomach cancer may be a ticket to Tokyo. Indeed, this last example well demonstrates that culture not only affects consumption, it also affects production (of medical services in this case) as well!

The point is that culture matters.[15] It is imperative for foreign marketers to learn to appreciate the intricacies of cultures different from their own if they are to be effective in foreign markets.

Definitions and Origins of Culture

There are many ways to think about culture. Dutch management professor Geert Hofstede refers to culture as the "software of the mind" and argues that it provides a guide for humans on how to think and behave; it is a problem-solving tool.[16] Anthropologist and business consultant Edward Hall provides a definition even more relevant to international marketing managers: "The people we were advising kept bumping their heads against an invisible barrier . . . We knew that what they were up against was a completely different way of organizing life, of thinking, and of conceiving the underlying assumptions about the family and the state, the economic system, and even Man himself."[17] The salient points in Hall's comments are that cultural differences are often invisible, and that marketers who ignore them often hurt both their companies and careers. Finally, James Day Hodgson, former U.S. ambassador to Japan, describes culture as a "thicket."[18] This last metaphor holds hope for struggling international marketers. According to the ambassador, thickets are tough to get through, but effort and patience often do lead to successes.

Most traditional definitions of culture center around the notion that culture is the sum of the *values, rituals, symbols, beliefs,* and *thought processes* that are *learned, shared* by a group of people, and *transmitted* from generation to generation.[19] So culture resides in the individual's mind. But the expression "a culture" recognizes that large collectives of people can to a great degree be like-minded.

The best international marketers will not only appreciate the cultural differences pertinent to their businesses, they will also understand the origins of these differences. Possession of the latter, deeper knowledge will help marketers notice cultural differences in new markets and foresee changes in current markets of operation. Exhibit 4.4 depicts the several causal factors and social processes that determine and form cultures and cultural differences. Simply stated, humans make *adaptations* to changing environments through *innovation.* Individuals learn culture from social institutions through *socialization* (growing up) and *acculturation* (adjusting to a new culture). Individuals also absorb culture through role

[15]Lawrence E. Harrison and Samuel P. Huntington (eds.), *Culture Matters* (New York: Basic Books, 2000).

[16]Geert Hofstede, *Culture's Consequences,* 2nd ed. (Thousand Oaks, CA: Sage, 2001); Susan P. Douglas, "Exploring New Worlds: The Challenge of Global Marketing," *Journal of Marketing,* January 2001, pp. 103–109.

[17]Edward T. Hall, *The Silent Language* (New York: Doubleday, 1959), p. 26.

[18]James D. Hodgson, Yoshihiro Sano, and John L. Graham, *Doing Business with the New Japan* (Boulder, CO: Rowman & Littlefield, 2000).

[19]Melvin Herskovitz, *Man and His Works* (New York: Alfred A. Knopf, 1952), p. 634. See also Chapter 10, "Culture," in Raymond Scupin and Christopher R. Decorse, *Anthropology: A Global Perspective,* 6th ed. (Engelwood Cliffs, NJ: Prentice Hall, 2005).

Exhibit 4.4
Origins, Elements, and Consequences of Culture

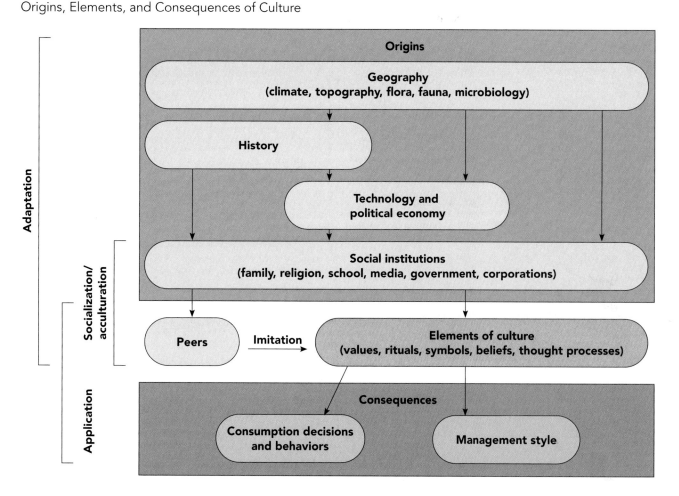

modeling, or imitation of their peers. Finally, people make decisions about consumption and production through *application* of their cultural-based knowledge. More details are provided below.

Geography   In the previous chapter we described the immediate effects of geography on consumer choice. But geography exercises a more profound influence than just affecting the sort of jacket you buy. Indeed, geography (broadly defined here to include climate, topography, flora, fauna, and microbiology) has influenced history, technology, economics, our social institutions, and yes, our ways of thinking.[20] Geographical influences manifest themselves in our deepest cultural values developed through the millennia, and as geography changes humans can adapt almost immediately. One sees the latter happening in the new etiquette evolving from the HIV/AIDS disaster, or more recently the SARS outbreak in China. The ongoing cultural divide across the English Channel is also representative of geography's historical salience in human affairs.

The ideas of two researchers are particularly pertinent to any discussion of geography's influence on everything from history to present-day cultural values. First, Jared Diamond,[21]

[20]Richard E. Nisbett, *The Geography of Thought: How Asians and Westerners Think Differently . . . and Why* (New York: Free Press, 2003).

[21]Jared Diamond's *Guns, Germs and Steel: The Fates of the Human Societies* (New York: Norton, 1999) is a Pulitzer Prize winner, recipient of the Phi Beta Kappa Award in Science, and a wonderful read for anyone interested in history and/or innovation. PBS also has produced a video version of *Guns, Germs and Steel.* And see Diamond's most recent book, *Collapse* (New York: Viking, 2005).

The Floriad, the biggest exhibition of flowers on earth, happens once every decade. You can go to the next one in 2012.

Outside the Aalsmeer Flower Auction—notice the jet landing at nearby Schiphol Airport, which serves both Amsterdam and Aalsmeer.

The Pope in St. Peter's Square on Easter Sunday surrounded by Dutch flowers. (© Giansanti Gianni/CORBIS SYGMA)

The Amsterdam flower market—a busy place for local consumers and tourists.

400 years later, the one-dollar black tulip is available in the Amsterdam flower market.

we all love flowers. But, for the Dutch, flowers are more important than that. For them, it's more like a national fascination, fixation, or even a fetish for flowers. **why?**

The answer is an instructive story about culture and international markets, the broader subjects of this chapter. The story starts with geography, goes through the origins and elements of culture, and ends with the Dutch being the masters of the exhibition, consumption, and production of flowers.

Geography. The rivers and the bays make the Netherlands a great trading country. The miserable weather, rain and snow more than 200 days per year, make it a colorless place, gray nearly year round. The flying Dutchmen not only went to the Spice Islands for spice for the palate, they also went to the eastern Mediterranean for spice for the eyes. That is, the vibrant colors of tulip first came to Europe from the Ottoman Empire on a Dutch ship in 1561.

History. The Dutch enthusiasm for the new "visual drug" was great. Its most potent form was, ironically, the black tulip. Prices exploded, and speculators bought and sold promissory notes guaranteeing the future delivery of black tulip bulbs. This derivatives market yielded prices in today's dollars of $1 million or more for a single bulb, enough to buy a 5-story house in central Amsterdam today. Not only did the tulip mania create futures markets, it also caused the first great market bust in recorded history. Prices plummeted when the government took control in 1637. Now at the Amsterdam flower market you can buy a black tulip bulb for about a dollar!

A view of a Dutch harbor with trading ships circa 1600. (© Archivo Iconografico, S.A./CORBIS)

Inside Aalsmeer, 150 football fields of cut flowers, 20 million per day, are readied for auction.

The bidders in four huge auction rooms pay attention to the "clock" as high starting prices tick down. The wholesale buyer that stops the clock pays the associated price in this the archetypical "Dutch auction."

technology and economics.

The technology in the story comes in the name of Carolus Clusius, a botanist who developed methods for manipulating the colors of the tulips in the early 1600s. This added to their appeal and value, and the tulip trade became international for the Dutch.

social institutions.

Every Easter Sunday the Pope addresses the world at St. Peter's Square in Rome reciting, "Bedankt voor bloemen." Thus, he thanks the Dutch nation for providing the flowers for this key Catholic ritual. The Dutch government once every tenth year sponsors the largest floriculture exhibition in the world, the Floriad. You can go next in 2012. Finally, at the Aalsmeer Flower Auction near Amsterdam, the prices are set for all flowers in all markets around the world. The Dutch remain the largest exporters of flowers (60% global market share) shipping them across Europe by trucks and worldwide by air freight.

Outside again at Aalsmeer, trucks are loaded for shipments by land across Europe and airfreight worldwide.

cultural values.

The high value the Dutch place on flowers is reflected in many ways, not the least of which is their high consumption rate as seen in Exhibit 4.2.

Aesthetics as symbols.

Rembrandt Van Rijn's paintings, including his most famous "Night Watch" (1642, Rijksmuseum, Amsterdam), reflect a dark palette. Artists generally paint in the colors of their surroundings. A quarter century later his compatriot Vincent Van Gogh used a similar bleak palette when he worked in Holland. Later, when Van Gogh went to the sunny and colorful south of France the colors begin to explode on his canvases. And, of course, there he painted flowers!

Rembrandt's "Night Watch."
(© Rijksmuseum, Amsterdam/SuperStock)

Van Gogh's "Vase with Fifteen Sunflowers" painted in the south of France in 1889, and sold to a Japanese insurance executive for some $40 million in 1987, at the time the highest price ever paid for a single work of art. The Japanese are also big flower consumers—see Exhibit 4.2! (AP/Wide World Photos)

Van Gogh's "Potato Eaters" painted in The Netherlands in 1885. (© Yves Forestier/CORBIS SYGMA)

a professor of physiology, tells us that historically innovations spread faster east to west than north to south. Before the advent of transoceanic shipping, ideas flowed over the Silk Road but not across the Sahara or the Isthmus of Panama. He uses this geographical approach to explain the dominance of Euro-Asian cultures, with their superior technology and more virulent germs, over African and American cultures. Indeed, Diamond's most important contribution is his material on the influence of microbiology on world history.

Second, Philip Parker,[22] a marketing professor, well argues for geography's deep influence on history, economics, and consumer behavior. For example, he reports strong correlations between the latitude (climate) and the per capita GDP of countries. Empirical support can be found as others report climate's apparent influence on workers' wages.[23] Parker, like Diamond before him, explains social phenomena using principles of physiology. The management implications of his treatise have to do with using ambient temperature as a market segmentation variable. We return to this issue in Chapter 8.

| History | The impact of specific events in history can be seen reflected in technology, social institutions, cultural values, and even consumer behavior.[24] Diamond's book is filled with examples. For instance, much of American trade policy has depended on the happenstance of tobacco (i.e., the technology of a new cash crop) being the original source of the Virginia colony's economic survival in the 1600s. In a like manner, the Declaration of Independence, and thereby Americans' values and institutions, was fundamentally influenced by the coincident 1776 publication of Adam Smith's *Wealth of Nations*. Notice too that the military conflicts in the Middle East in 2003 bred new cola brands—Mecca Cola, Muslim Up, Arab Cola, and ColaTurk.[25] |

History

The impact of specific events in history can be seen reflected in technology, social institutions, cultural values, and even consumer behavior.[24] Diamond's book is filled with examples. For instance, much of American trade policy has depended on the happenstance of tobacco (i.e., the technology of a new cash crop) being the original source of the Virginia colony's economic survival in the 1600s. In a like manner, the Declaration of Independence, and thereby Americans' values and institutions, was fundamentally influenced by the coincident 1776 publication of Adam Smith's *Wealth of Nations*. Notice too that the military conflicts in the Middle East in 2003 bred new cola brands—Mecca Cola, Muslim Up, Arab Cola, and ColaTurk.[25]

The Political Economy

For most of the 20th century three approaches to governance competed for world dominance: fascism, communism, and democracy/free enterprise. Fascism fell in 1945. Communism crumbled in the 1990s.[26] One pundit even declared the "end of history."[27] Unfortunately, we have September 11 and the conflicts in the Middle East to keep the list of bad things growing. Much more detail is included in Chapters 6 and 7 on the influences of politics and the legal environment on the culture of commerce and consumption, so we will leave this important topic until then. The main point here is for you to appreciate the influence of the political economy on social institutions and cultural values and ways of thinking.

Technology

Sit back for a moment and consider what technological innovation has had the greatest impact on institutions and cultural values in the last 50 years in the United States. Seriously, stop reading, look out your window, and for a moment consider the question.

There are many good answers, but only one best one. Certainly jet aircraft, air conditioning, televisions, computers, and the Internet all make the list. But the best answer is most likely the pill.[28] That is, the birth control pill or more broadly birth control techniques have had a huge effect on everyday life for most Americans. Mainly, it has freed women to have careers and freed men to spend more time with kids. Before the advent of the pill men's and women's roles were prescribed by reproductive responsibilities and roles. Now

---

[22]Philip Parker's *Physioeconomics* (Cambridge, MA: MIT Press, 2000) is a data-rich discussion of global economics well worth reading.

[23]Evert Van de Vliert, "Thermoclimate, Culture, and Poverty as Country-Level Roots of Workers' Wages," *Journal of International Business* 34, no. 1 (2003), pp. 40–52.

[24]A wonderful book on the influence of beverages on culture is *A History of the World in 6 Glasses* by Tom Standage (New York: Walker & Company, 2005).

[25]See www.colaturka.com.tr.

[26]Some might argue that communism has survived in North Korea, Cuba, or the Peoples' Republic of China, but at least in the last case free enterprise is on the ascendancy. The former look more like dictatorships to most.

[27]Francis Fukuyama, *The End of History and the Last Man* (New York: Free Press, 1992).

[28]Bernard Asbell, *The Pill: A Biography of the Drug that Changed the World* (New York: Random House, 1995).

half the marketing majors in the United States are women. Now 10 percent of the crews on American aircraft carriers are women. Before the pill this was unimaginable.

Obviously, not everyone is happy with these new "freedoms." For example, in 1968 the Roman Catholic church forbade use of the birth control pill. But the technology of birth control undeniably has deeply affected social institutions and cultural values. Families are smaller; and government and schools are forced to address issues such as abstinence and condom distribution.

Social Institutions

Social institutions including *family, religion, school, the media, government*, and *corporations* all affect the ways in which people relate to one another, organize their activities to live in harmony with one another, teach acceptable behavior to succeeding generations, and govern themselves. The positions of men and women in society, the family, social classes, group behavior, age groups, and how societies define decency[29] and civility are interpreted differently within every culture. In cultures where the social organizations result in close-knit family units, for example, a promotion campaign aimed at the family unit is usually more effective than one aimed at individual family members. Travel advertising in culturally divided Canada has pictured a wife alone for the English-speaking market segment but a man and wife together for the French-speaking segments of the population because the latter are traditionally more closely bound by family ties.

The roles and status positions found within a society are influenced by the dictates of social institutions. The caste system in India is one such institution. The election of a low-caste person—once called an "untouchable"—as president made international news because it was such a departure from traditional Indian culture. Decades ago, brushing against an untouchable or even glancing at one was considered enough to defile a Hindu of high status. Even though the caste system had been outlawed, it remains a part of the culture.

Family.

Family forms and functions vary substantially around the world, even around the country. For example, where nepotism is seen as a problem in American organizations, it is more often seen as an organizing principle in Chinese[30] and Mexican[31] firms. Or consider the Dutch executive who lives with his mother, wife, and kids in a home in Maastricht that his family has owned for the last 300 years. Then there's the common practice of the high-income folks in Cairo buying an apartment house and filling it up with the extended family—grandparents, married siblings, cousins, and kids. Or how about the Japanese mother caring for her two children pretty much by herself, often sleeping with them at night, while her husband catches up on sleep during his four hours a day commuting via train. And there's the American family in California—both parents work like dogs to support their cars, closets, and kids in college, all the while worrying about aging grandparents halfway across the country in Texas.

Even the ratio of male to female children is affected by culture. For example, the gender percentage of boys aged one to six is 52 in India, and aged one to four is 55 in China. Obviously these ratios have long-term implications for families and societies.[32] Moreover, the favoritism of boys is deep-seated in such cultures, as demonstrated by the Chinese *Book of Songs*, circa 800 B.C.:

> When a son is born
> Let him sleep on the bed,
> Clothe him with fine clothes.
> And give him jade to play with . . .

---

[29]Steve McKee, "Summer Olympics: An Olympic Pose Isn't What It Used to Be," *Wall Street Journal*, August 18, 2004, p. A8.

[30]Kathy Chen, "China's Growth Places Strains on Family Ties," *Wall Street Journal*, April 13, 2005, pp. A1, A15.

[31]Anabella Davila and Marta M. Elvira, "Culture and Human Resource Management in Latin America," in Marta M. Elvira and Anabella Davila (eds.), *Managing Human Resources in Latin America* (London: Routledge, 2005), pp. 3–24.

[32]David Glenn, "A Dangerous Surplus of Sons?" *Chronicle of Higher Education*, April 30, 2004, pp. A14–A16.

When a daughter is born,
Let her sleep on the ground,
Wrap her in common wrappings,
And give her broken tiles for playthings.

All these differences lead directly to differences in how children think and behave. For example, individualism is being taught the first night the American infant is tucked into her own separate bassinette. Values for egalitarianism are learned the first time Dad washes the dishes in front of the kids or Mom heads off to work or the toddler learns that both Grandpa and little brother are properly called "you."

Religion.   In most cultures the first social institution infants are exposed to outside the home takes the form of a church, mosque, shrine, or temple. The impact of religion on the value systems of a society and the effect of value systems on marketing must not be underestimated. For example, Protestants believe that one's relationship with God is a personal one, and confessions are made directly through prayer. Alternatively, Roman Catholics confess to priests setting up a hierarchy within the Church. Thus some scholars reason that Protestantism engenders egalitarian thinking. But no matter the details, religion clearly does affect people's habits, their outlook on life, the products they buy, the way they buy them, and even the newspapers they read.

The influence of religion is often quite strong.[33] So marketers with little or no understanding of a religion may readily offend deeply. One's own religion is often not a reliable guide to another's beliefs. Most people do not understand religions other than their own, and/or what is "known" about other religions is often incorrect. The Islamic religion is a good example of the need for a basic understanding of all major religions. Between 800 million and 1.2 billion people in the world embrace Islam, yet major multinational companies often offend Muslims. The French fashion house of Chanel unwittingly desecrated the Koran by embroidering verses from the sacred book of Islam on several dresses shown in its summer collections. The designer said he had taken the design, which was aesthetically pleasing to him, from a book on India's Taj Mahal and that he was unaware of its meaning. To placate a Muslim group that felt the use of the verses desecrated the Koran, Chanel had to destroy the dresses with the offending designs, along with negatives of the photos taken of the garments. Chanel certainly had no intention of offending Muslims, since some of its most important customers embrace Islam. This example shows how easy it is to offend if the marketer, in this case the designer, has not familiarized himself or herself with other religions.

School.   Education, one of the most important social institutions, affects all aspects of the culture, from economic development to consumer behavior. The literacy rate of a country is a potent force in economic development. Numerous studies indicate a direct link between the literacy rate of a country and its capability for rapid economic growth. According to the World Bank, no country has been successful economically with less than 50 percent literacy, but when countries have invested in education the economic rewards have been substantial. Literacy has a profound effect on marketing. To communicate with a literate market is much easier than communicating to one in which the marketer must depend on symbols and pictures.

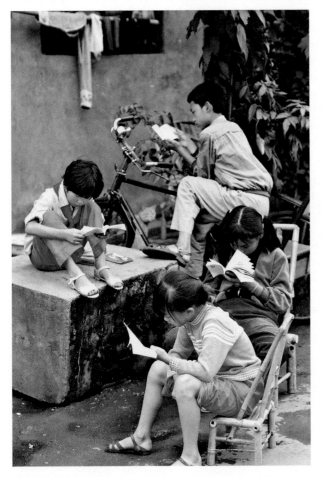

In the United States, kids attend school 180 days per year; in China, they attend 251 days—that's six days a week. There's a great thirst for the written word in China—here children read books rented from a street vendor. (© Cary Wolinsky)

---

[33]"Score One for the Vatican," *The Economist*, June 18, 2005, p. 48.

The Media.   The four social institutions that most strongly influence values and culture are schools, churches, families, and, most recently, the media. In the United States during the last 30 years, women have joined the workforce in growing numbers, substantially reducing the influence of family on American culture. Media time (TV and increasingly the Internet) has replaced family time—much to the detriment of American culture, some argue. At this time it is hard to gauge the long-term effects of the hours spent with Bart Simpson or an EverQuest cleric-class character. Indeed, the British Prime Minister's cameo on *The Simpsons* reflects its prominence around the world.[34]

American kids spend only 180 days per year in school. Contrast that with 251 days in China, 240 days in Japan, and 200 days in Germany. Indeed, Chinese officials are recognizing the national disadvantages of too much school—narrow minds. Likewise, Americans more and more complain about the detrimental effects of too much media.

Government.   Compared to the early (during childhood) and direct influences of family, religion, school, and the media during childhood, governments hold relatively little sway. Cultural values and thought patterns are pretty much set before and during adolescence. Most often governments try to influence the thinking and behaviors of adult citizens for the citizens' "own good." For example, the French government has been urging citizens to procreate since the time of Napoleon. Now the government is offering a new "birth bonus" of $800 given to women in their seventh month of pregnancy—despite France having the second highest fertility rate in the EU behind only Ireland (see Exhibit 4.1). Also, major changes in governments, such as the dissolution of the Soviet Union, can have noticeable impacts on personal beliefs and other aspects of culture.[35]

Of course, in some countries the government owns media and regularly uses propaganda to form "favorable" public opinions. Other countries prefer no separation of church and state—Iran is currently ruled by religious clerics, for example. Governments also affect ways of thinking indirectly, through their support of religious organizations and schools. For example, both the Japanese and Chinese governments are currently trying to promote more creative thinking among students through mandated changes in classroom activities and hours. Finally, governments influence thinking and behavior through the passage, promulgation, promotion, and enforcement of a variety of laws affecting consumption and marketing behaviors. The Irish government is newly concerned about its citizens' consumption of Guinness and other alcohol products. Their studies suggest excessive drinking costs the country 2 percent of GDP, so to discourage underage drinking the laws are being tightened again (see Chapter 16, page 493 for more details).

Corporations.   Of course, corporations get a grip on us early through the media. But, more important, most innovations are introduced to societies by companies, many times multinational companies. Indeed, merchants and traders have throughout history been the primary conduit for the diffusion of innovations, whether it be over the Silk Road or via today's air freight and/or the Internet. Multinational firms have access to ideas from around the world. Through the efficient distribution of new products and services based on these new ideas cultures are changed and new ways of thinking are stimulated. The crucial role of companies as change agents is discussed in detail in the last section of the chapter.

Elements of Culture

Earlier culture was defined by listing its five elements: values, rituals, symbols, beliefs, and thought processes. International marketers must design products, distribution systems, and promotional programs with due consideration of each of the five.

---

[34]"Britian: Blair vs. Bart, Politics and Comedy," *The Economist*, April 19, 2003, p. 49.

[35]Shawn T. Thelen and Earl D. Honeycutt Jr., "Assessing National Identity in Russia between Generations Using the National Identity Scale," *Journal of International Marketing* 12, no. 2 (2004), pp. 58–81.

Exhibit 4.5
Hofstede's Indexes,
Language, and Linguistic
Distance

Source: From Geert Hofstede,
Culture's Consequences, 2001, Sage
Publications. Used by permission of
Geert Hofstede.

Country	IDV Score	PDI Score	UAI Score	Primary Language	Distance from English
Arab countries	38	80	68	Arabic	5
Australia	90	36	51	English	0
Brazil	38	69	76	Portuguese	3
Canada	80	39	48	English (French)	0, 3
Colombia	13	67	80	Spanish	3
Finland	63	33	59	Finnish	4
France	71	68	86	French	3
Germany	67	35	65	German	1
Great Britain	89	35	35	English	0
Greece	35	60	112	Greek	3
Guatemala	6	95	101	Spanish	3
India	48	77	40	Dravidian	3
Indonesia	14	78	48	Bahasa	7
Iran	41	58	59	Farsi	3
Japan	46	54	92	Japanese	4
Mexico	30	81	82	Spanish	3
Netherlands	80	38	53	Dutch	1
New Zealand	79	22	49	English	0
Pakistan	14	55	70	Urdu	3
South Korea	18	60	85	Korean	4
Taiwan	17	58	69	Taiwanese	6
Turkey	37	66	85	Turkish	4
United States	91	40	46	English	0
Uruguay	36	61	100	Spanish	3
Venezuela	12	81	76	Spanish	3

Cultural Values

Underlying the cultural diversity that exists among countries are fundamental differences in cultural values.[36] The most useful information on how cultural values influence various types of business and market behavior comes from seminal work by Geert Hofstede.[37] Studying more than 90,000 people in 66 countries, he found that the cultures of the nations studied differed along four primary dimensions. Subsequently, he and hundreds of other researchers have determined that a wide variety of business and consumer behavior patterns are associated with three of those four dimensions.[38] The four[39] dimensions are as follows: the Individualism/Collective Index (IDV), which focuses on self-orientation; the Power Distance Index (PDI), which focuses on authority orientation; the Uncertainty Avoidance Index (UAI), which focuses on risk orientation; and the Masculinity/Femininity Index (MAS), which focuses on assertiveness and achievement. The Individualism/Collectivism dimension has proven the most useful of the four dimensions, justifying entire books on the subject.[40] Because MAS has proven least useful, we will not consider it further here. Please see Exhibit 4.5 for details.

---

[36]Ping Ping Fu, Jeff Kennedy, Jasmine Tata, Gary Yukl, Michael Harris Bond, Tai-Kuang Peng, Ekkirala S. Srinivas, Jon P. Howell, Leonel Prieto, Paul Koopman, Jaap J. Boonstra, Selda Pasa, Marie-Francoise Lacassagne, Hiro Higashide, and Adith Cheosakul, "The Impact of Societal Cultural Values and Individual Social Beliefs on the Perceived Effectiveness of Managerial Influence Strategies," *Journal of International Business Studies*, 35, no. 4 (2004), pp. 284–305.

[37]Geert Hofstede, *Culture's Consequences*, 2nd ed. (Thousand Oaks. CA: Sage; 2001).

[38]Debanjan Mitra and Peter N. Golder, "Whose Culture Matters? Near-Market Knowledge and Its Impact on Foreign Market Entry Timing," *Journal of Marketing Research* 39, no. 3 (August 2002), pp. 350–365; Boonghee Yoo and Naveen Donthu, "Culture's Consequences, a Book Review," *Journal of Marketing Research* 39, no. 3 (August 2002), pp. 388–389.

[39]In a subsequent study, a fifth dimension, Long-Term Orientation (LTO), was identified as focusing on temporal orientation. See Geert Hofstede and Michael Harris Bond, "The Confucius Connection," *Organizational Dynamics* 16, no. 4 (Spring 1988), pp. 4–21; and Hofstede, 2001.

[40]Harry C. Triandis, *Individualism and Collectivism* (Boulder, CO: Westview Press, 1995).

Individualism/Collectivism Index. The Individualism/Collective Index refers to the preference for behavior that promotes one's self-interest. Cultures that score high in IDV reflect an "I" mentality and tend to reward and accept individual initiative, whereas those low in individualism reflect a "we" mentality and generally subjugate the individual to the group. This does not mean that individuals fail to identify with groups when a culture scores high on IDV, but rather that personal initiative and independence are accepted and endorsed. Individualism pertains to societies in which the ties between individuals are loose; everyone is expected to look after himself or herself and his or her immediate family. Collectivism, as its opposite, pertains to societies in which people from birth onward are integrated into strong, cohesive groups, which throughout people's lifetimes continue to protect them in exchange for unquestioning loyalty.

Power Distance Index. The Power Distance Index measures the tolerance of social inequality, that is, power inequality between superiors and subordinates within a social system. Cultures with high PDI scores tend to be hierarchical, with members citing social role, manipulation, and inheritance as sources of power and social status. Those with low scores, on the other hand, tend to value equality and cite knowledge and respect as sources of power. Thus people from cultures with high PDI scores are more likely to have a general distrust of others (not in their groups) because power is seen to rest with individuals and is coercive rather than legitimate. High PDI scores tend to indicate a perception of differences between superior and subordinate and a belief that those who hold power are entitled to privileges. A low score reflects more egalitarian views.

Uncertainty Avoidance Index. The Uncertainty Avoidance Index measures the tolerance of uncertainty and ambiguity among members of a society. Cultures with high UAI scores are highly intolerant of ambiguity and as a result tend to be distrustful of new ideas or behaviors. They tend to have a high level of anxiety and stress and a concern with security and rule following. Accordingly, they dogmatically stick to historically tested patterns of behavior, which in the extreme become inviolable rules. Those with very high UAI scores thus accord a high level of authority to rules as a means of avoiding risk. Cultures scoring low in uncertainty avoidance are associated with a low level of anxiety and stress, a tolerance of deviance and dissent, and a willingness to take risks. Thus, those cultures low in UAI take a more empirical approach to understanding and knowledge, whereas those high in UAI seek absolute truth.

Cultural Values and Consumer Behavior. Let's go back to the e-trading example that opened this chapter and see how Hofstede's notions of cultural values might help us predict the speed of diffusion of such new consumer services as equity investments and electronic auctions in Japan and France. As shown in Exhibit 4.5, the United States scores the highest of all countries on individualism, at 91, with Japan at 46 and France at 71. Indeed, in America, where individualism reigns supreme, we might predict that the "virtually social" activity of sitting alone at one's computer might be most acceptable. In both Japan and France, where values favor group activities, face-to-face conversations with stockbrokers and neighbors might be preferred to impersonal electronic communications.

Similarly, both Japan (92) and France (86) score quite high on Hofstede's Uncertainty Avoidance Index, and America scores low (46). Based on these scores, both Japanese and French investors might be expected to be less willing to take the risks of stock market investments—and indeed, the security of post office deposits or bank savings accounts is preferred. So in both instances Hofstede's data on cultural values suggest that diffusion of these innovations will be slower in Japan and France than in the United States. Such predictions are consistent with research findings that cultures scoring higher on individualism and lower on uncertainty avoidance tend to be more innovative.[41]

---

[41]Jan-Benedict E. M. Steenkamp, Frenkel ter Hofstede, and Micel Wedel, "A Cross-National Investigation into the Individual and National Cultural Antecedents of Consumer Innovativeness," *Journal of Marketing* 63 (April 1999), pp. 55–69.

CROSSING BORDERS 4.1
It's Not the Gift That Counts, but How You Present It

Giving a gift in another country requires careful attention if it is to be done properly. Here are a few suggestions.

Japan

Do not open a gift in front of a Japanese counterpart unless asked, and do not expect the Japanese to open your gift.

Avoid ribbons and bows as part of the gift wrapping. Bows as we know them are considered unattractive, and ribbon colors can have different meanings.

Always offer the gift with both hands.

Europe

Avoid red roses and white flowers, even numbers, and the number 13. Do not wrap flowers in paper.

Do not risk the impression of bribery by spending too much on a gift.

Arab World

Do not give a gift when you first meet someone. It may be interpreted as a bribe.

Do not let it appear that you contrived to present the gift when the recipient is alone. It looks bad unless you know the person well. Give the gift in front of others in less-personal relationships.

Latin America

Do not give a gift until after a somewhat personal relationship has developed unless it is given to express appreciation for hospitality.

Gifts should be given during social encounters, not in the course of business.

Avoid the colors black and purple; both are associated with the Roman Catholic Lenten season.

China

Never make an issue of a gift presentation—publicly or privately. But always deliver gifts with two hands.

Gifts should be presented privately, with the exception of collective ceremonial gifts at banquets or after speeches.

United States

Gifts that are too ostentatious can cause big problems.

Source: www.executiveplanet.com; James Day Hodgson, Yoshiro Sano, and John L. Graham, *Doing Business with the New Japan* (Boulder, CO: Rowman and Littlefield, 2000); Michelle Archer, "From Nose Hair to Networking, a Word of Advice," *USA Today*, July 11, 2005, p. B5.

Perhaps the most interesting application of cultural values and consumer behavior regards a pair of experiments done with American and Chinese students.[42] Both groups were shown print ads using other-focused emotional appeals (that is, a couple pictured having fun on the beach) versus self-focused emotional appeals (an individual having fun on the beach). The researchers predicted that the individualistic Americans would respond more favorably to the self-focused appeals, and the collectivistic Chinese to the other-focused appeals. They found the opposite. The Americans responded better to the other-focused ads, and the Chinese vice versa. Their second experiment helped explain these unexpected results. That is, in both cases what the participants liked about the ads was their *novelty* vis-à-vis their own cultures. So, even in this circumstance, cultural values appear to provide useful information for marketers. However, the complexity of human behavior, values, and culture is manifest.

Rituals Life is filled with rituals, that is, patterns of behavior and interaction that are learned and repeated. The most obvious ones are associated with major events in life. Marriage ceremonies and funerals are good examples. Perhaps the one most important to most readers of this book is the hopefully proximate graduation ritual—*Pomp and Circumstance*, funny hats, long speeches, and all. Very often these rituals differ across cultures. Indeed, there is an entire *genre* of foreign films about weddings.[43] Perhaps best is *Monsoon Wedding*. Grooms on white horses and edible flowers are apparently part of the ceremony for

[42]Jennifer L. Aaker and Patti Williams, "Empathy vs. Pride: The Influence of Emotional Appeals across Cultures," *Journal of Consumer Research* 25 (December 1998), pp. 241–261.

[43]Other excellent films in this genre are *Cousin, Cousine* (French), *Four Weddings and a Funeral* (the U.K.), *Bend It Like Beckham* (the U.K., Asian immigrants), *Wedding in Galilee* (Palestine/Israel), and *The Wedding Banquet* (Taiwan).

Every Muslim is enjoined to make the hajj, or pilgrimage to Mecca, once in his or her lifetime if physically able. Here some 2 million faithful come from all over the world annually to participate in what is the largest ritual meeting on Earth. Meanwhile, televised rituals such as the Academy Awards and World Cup soccer draw billions in the form of virtual crowds. (© AFP/Getty Images)

high-income folks in New Delhi. We even know of at least one cross-cultural wedding in the United States that had the reception before the ceremony!

Life is also filled with little rituals such as dinner at a restaurant or a visit to a department store, or even grooming before heading off to work or class in the morning. In a nice restaurant in Madrid dessert may precede the entree, but dinner often starts at about midnight, and the entire process can be a three-hour affair. Walking into a department store in the United States often yields a search for an employee to answer questions. Not so in Japan, where the help bows at the door as you walk in. Visit a doctor in the States and a 15-minute wait in a cold exam room with nothing on but a paper gown is typical. In Spain the exams are often done in the doctor's office. There's no waiting because you find the doctor sitting at her desk.

Rituals are important. They coordinate everyday interactions and special occasions. They let people know what to expect. In the final chapter we discuss the ritual of business negotiations, and that ritual varies across cultures as well.

Symbols   Anthropologist Edward T. Hall tells us that culture is communication. In his seminal article about cultural differences in business settings he talks about the "languages" of time, space, things, friendships, and agreements.[44] Indeed, learning to interpret correctly the symbols that surround us is a key part of socialization. And this learning begins immediately after birth as we begin to hear the language spoken and see the facial expressions and feel the touch and taste the milk of our mothers.[45] We begin our discussion of symbolic systems with language, the most obvious part and the part that most often involves conscious communication.

Language.   We should mention that for some around the world language is itself thought of as a social institution often with political importance. Certainly the French go to extreme lengths and expense to preserve the purity of their *français*. In Canada the language has been the focus of political disputes including secession, although things seem to have calmed down there most recently. Unfortunately, as the number of spoken languages continues to decline worldwide, so does the interesting cultural diversity of the planet.

---

[44]Edward T. Hall, "The Silent in Overseas Business," *Harvard Business Review*, May–June, 1960, pp. 87–96. A discussion of the salience of Hall's work appears in John L. Graham, "Culture and Human Resources Management," in Alan M. Rugman and Thomas L. Brewer (eds.), *The Oxford Handbook of International Business* (Oxford: Oxford University Press, 2001), pp. 503–536.

[45]The spices a nursing mother consumes actually affect the flavor of the milk she produces.

CROSSING BORDERS 4.2   Ici on Parle Français

Frequently a conflict arises between a desire to borrow from another culture and the natural inclination not to pollute one's own culture by borrowing from others. France offers a good example of this conflict. On the one hand, the French accept such U.S. culture as Oprah Winfrey's television show, and they award Sylvester "Rambo" Stallone the Order of Arts and Letters, listen to Bruce Springsteen, and dine on all-American gastronomic delights such as the Big Mac and Kentucky Fried Chicken. At the same time, there is an uneasy feeling that accepting so much from America will somehow dilute the true French culture. Thus, in an attempt to somehow control cultural pollution, France embarked on a campaign to expunge examples of *"franglais"* from all walks of life, including television, billboards, and business contracts. If the culture ministry had its way, violators would be fined. Lists of correct translations included *heures de grande écoute* for "prime time," *coussin gonflable de protection* for "airbag," *sable américain* for "cookie," and some 3,500 other expressions. Although the demand for hamburgers and U.S. television shows could not be stemmed, perhaps the language could be saved.

With a tongue-in-cheek response, an English lawmaker said he would introduce a bill in Parliament to ban the use of French words in public. Order an aperitif in a British bar or demand an encore at the end of an opera and you might be in trouble—and so go the "language wars."

Perhaps the French *should* be concerned. After years of *Law and Order*-type TV dramas seen in France, it is reported that French prisoners address a judge in a courtroom as "Your Honor," rather than the traditionally acceptable "Mr. President." They also ask to have their "*Miranda* rights read to them" and routinely demand to see a warrant when police want to search their homes. Neither is part of the French legal code.

Postscript. The use of foreign words in media and advertising got a last-minute reprieve when France's highest constitutional authority struck down the most controversial parts of the law, saying it applies only to public services and not to private citizens.

Sources: Maarten Huygen, "The Invasion of the American Way," *World Press Review*, November 1992, pp. 28–29; "La Guerre Franglaise," *Fortune*, June 13, 1994, p. 14; "The Internet and Linguistic Diversity," *The American Prospect*, March 27–April 10, 2000; Mary Blume, "A Parisian Attempt to Tame the Tagueurs," *International Herald Tribune*, April 15, 2005, p. 18.

The importance of understanding the language of a country cannot be overestimated, particularly if you're selling your products in France! The successful international marketer must achieve expert communication, which requires a thorough understanding of the language as well as the ability to speak it. Advertising copywriters should be concerned less with obvious differences between languages and more with the idiomatic meanings expressed. It is not sufficient to say you want to translate into Spanish, for instance, because across Spanish-speaking Latin America the language vocabulary varies widely. *Tambo*, for example, means a roadside inn in Bolivia, Colombia, Ecuador, and Peru; a dairy farm in Argentina and Uruguay; and a brothel in Chile. If that gives you a problem, consider communicating with the people of Papua New Guinea. Some 750 languages, each distinct and mutually unintelligible, are spoken there. This crucial issue of accurate translations in marketing communications is discussed further in Chapters 8 and 16.

The relationship between language and international marketing is important in another way. Recent studies indicate that a new concept, *linguistic distance*, is proving useful to marketing researchers in market segmentation and strategic entry decisions. Linguistic distance has been shown to be an important factor in determining the amount of trade between countries.[46] The idea is that crossing "wider" language differences increases transaction costs.

---

[46]Pankaj Ghemawat, "Distance Still Matters: The Hard Reality of Global Expansion," *Harvard Business Review*, September 2001, pp. 137–147; Jennifer D. Chandler and John L. Graham, "Using Formative Indicators to Discern the Meaning of Corruption and Its Implications for International Marketing," working paper, University of California, Irvine, 2006.

Over the years linguistics researchers have determined that languages around the world conform to family trees[47] based on the similarity of their forms and development. For example, Spanish, Italian, French, and Portuguese are all classified as Romance languages because of their common roots in Latin. Distances can be measured on these linguistic trees. If we assume English[48] to be the starting point, German is one branch away, Danish two, Spanish three, Japanese four, Hebrew five, Chinese six, and Thai seven. These "distance from English" scores are listed for a sampling of cultures in Exhibit 4.5.

Other work in the area is demonstrating a direct influence of language on cultural values, expectations, and even conceptions of time.[49] For example, as linguistic distance from English increases, individualism decreases.[50] These studies are the first in this genre, and much more work needs to be done. However, the notion of linguistic distance appears to hold promise for better understanding and prediction of cultural differences in both consumer and management values, expectations, and behaviors.

Moreover, the relationship between language spoken and cultural values holds deeper implications. That is, as English spreads around the world via school systems and the Internet, cultural values of individualism and egalitarianism will spread with it. For example, both Chinese Mandarin speakers and Spanish speakers must learn two words for "you" (*ni* and *nin*, and *tu* and *usted*, respectively). The proper use of the two depends completely on knowledge of the social context of the conversation. Respect for status is communicated by the use of *nin* and *usted*. In English there is only one form for "you."[51] Speakers can ignore social context and status and still speak correctly. It's easier, and social status becomes less important. *Français* beware!

Aesthetics as Symbols.   Art communicates. Indeed, Confucius is reputed to have opined, "A picture is worth a thousand words." But, of course, so can a dance or a song. As we acquire our culture we learn the meaning of this wonderful symbolic system represented in the aesthetics, that is, the arts,[52] folklore, music, drama, and dance. Customers everywhere respond to images, myths, and metaphors that help them define their personal and national identities and relationships within a context of culture and product benefits. The uniqueness of a culture can be spotted quickly in symbols having distinct meanings. Think about the subtle earth tones of the typical Japanese restaurant compared with the bright reds and yellows in the décor of ethnic Chinese restaurants. Similarly, a long-standing rivalry between the Scottish Clan Lindsay and Clan Donald caused McDonald's Corporation some consternation when they chose the Lindsay tartan design for new uniforms for its restaurant hosts and hostesses. Godfrey Lord Macdonald, Chief of Clan Donald, was outraged and complained that McDonald's had a "complete lack of understanding of the name." Of course, the plaid in the uniforms is now the least of the firm's worries as British consumers are becoming more concerned about health-related matters.[53]

---

[47]For the most comprehensive representation of global linguistic trees, see Jiangtian Chen, Robert R. Sokal, and Merrit Ruhlen, "Worldwide Analysis of Genetic and Linguistic Relationships of Human Populations," *Human Biology* 67, no. 4 (August 1995), pp. 595–612.

[48]We appreciate the ethnocentricity in using English as the starting point. However, linguistic trees can be used to measure distance from any language. For example, analyses using French or Japanese as the starting point have proven useful as well.

[49]Lera Boroditsky, "Does Language Shape Thought? Mandarin and English Speakers' Conceptions of Time," *Cognitive Psychology* 43 (2001), pp. 1–22.

[50]Joel West and John L. Graham, "A Linguistics-Based Measure of Cultural Distance and Its Relationship to Managerial Values," *Management International Review* 44, no. 3 (2004), pp. 239–260.

[51]In English there was historically a second second-person form. That is, "thee" was the informal form up until the last century. Even in some Spanish-speaking countries such as Costa Rica the "tu" is being dropped in a similar manner.

[52]Japanese-style animation is making a strong entry to pop American culture. See Ian Rowley, Chester Dawson, and Hiroko Tashiro, "The Anime Biz: Still an Adolescent," *BusinessWeek*, June 27, 2005, pp. 50–52.

[53]"McDonald's Tartan Choice Upsets Scottish Clan," *Advertising Age*, May 12, 1997, p. 3; Victoria Furness, "Fast-Food Giants Face an Unhealthy Future," *Marketing Week*, January 9, 2003, p. 18.

Exhibit 4.6
Metaphorical Journeys
through 23 Nations

Source: From Martin J. Gannon,
*Understanding Global Cultures,
Metaphorical Journeys through
23 Nations*, 2nd ed. Copyright
© 2001. Reprinted by permission
of Sage Publications.

The Thai Kingdom	The Traditional British House
The Japanese Garden	The Malaysian *Balik Kampung*
India: The Dance of Shiva	The Nigerian Marketplace
Bedouin Jewelry and Saudi Arabia	The Israeli Kibbutzim and Moshavim
The Turkish Coffeehouse	The Italian Opera
The Brazilian Samba	Belgian Lace
The Polish Village Church	The Mexican Fiesta
Kimchi and Korea	The Russian Ballet
The German Symphony	The Spanish Bullfight
The Swedish *Stuga*	The Portuguese Bullfight
Irish Conversations	The Chinese Family Altar
American Football	

Without a culturally correct interpretation of a country's aesthetic values, a host of marketing problems can arise. Product styling must be aesthetically pleasing to be successful, as must advertisements and package designs. Insensitivity to aesthetic values can offend, create a negative impression, and, in general, render marketing efforts ineffective or even damaging. Strong symbolic meanings may be overlooked if one is not familiar with a culture's aesthetic values. The Japanese, for example, revere the crane as being very lucky because it is said to live a thousand years; however, the use of the number four should be avoided completely because the word for four, *shi*, is also the Japanese word for death. Thus teacups are sold in sets of five, not four, in Japan.

Finally, one author has suggested that understanding different cultures' metaphors is a key doorway to success. In Exhibit 4.6 we list the metaphors Martin Gannon[54] identified to represent cultures around the world. In the fascinating text he compares "American Football" (with its individualism, competitive specialization, huddling, and ceremonial celebration of perfection) to the "Spanish Bullfight" (with its pompous entrance parade, audience participation, and the ritual of the fight) to the "Indian Dance of the Shiva" (with its cycles of life, family, and social interaction). Empirical evidence is beginning to accumulate supporting the notion that metaphors matter.[55] Any good international marketer would see fine fodder for advertising campaigns in the insightful descriptions depicted.

Beliefs   Of course, much of what we learn to believe comes from religious training. But to adequately consider matters of true faith and spirituality here is certainly impossible. Moreover, the relationship between superstition and religion is not at all clear. For example, one explanation of the origin about the Western aversion to the number 13 has to do with Jesus sitting with his 12 disciples at the Last Supper.

However, many of our beliefs are secular in nature. What Westerners often call superstition may play quite a large role in a society's belief system in another part of the world. For example, in parts of Asia, ghosts, fortune telling, palmistry, blood types, head-bump reading, phases of the moon, faith healers, demons, and soothsayers can all be integral elements of society. Surveys of advertisements in Greater China show a preference for an "8" as the last digit in prices listed—the number connotes "prosperity" in Chinese culture.[56] And recall the Japanese concern about Year of the Fire Horse discussed earlier.

Called art, science, philosophy, or superstition—depending on who is talking—the Chinese practice of *feng shui* is an important ancient belief held by Chinese, among others. Feng shui is the process that links humans and the universe to *ch'i*, the energy that sustains life and flows through our bodies and surroundings, in and around our homes and workplaces. The idea is to harness this ch'i to enhance good luck, prosperity, good health, and

[54]Martin J. Gannon, *Understanding Global Cultures, Metaphorical Journeys through 23 Nations*, 2nd ed. (Thousand Oaks, CA: Sage, 2001).

[55]Cristina B. Gibson and Mary E. Zeller-Bruhn, "Metaphors and Meaning: An Intercultural Analysis of the Concept of Work," *Administrative Science Quarterly* 46, no. 2 (2001), pp. 274–303.

[56]Lee C. Simmons and Robert M. Schindler, "Cultural Superstitions and the Price Endings in Chinese Advertising," *Journal of International Marketing* 11, no. 2 (2003), pp. 101–111.

honor for the owner of a premise and to minimize the negative force, *sha ch'i*, and its effect. Feng shui requires engaging the services of a feng shui master to determine the positive orientation of a building in relation to the owner's horoscope, the date of establishment of the business, or the shape of the land and building. It is not a look or a style, and it is more than aesthetics: Feng shui is a strong belief in establishing a harmonious environment through the design and placement of furnishings and the avoidance of buildings facing northwest, the "devil's entrance," and southwest, the "devil's backdoor." Indeed, Disney has even "feng-shuied" all its new rides in Hong Kong Disneyland.[57]

Too often, one person's beliefs are another person's funny story. To discount the importance of myths, beliefs, superstitions, or other cultural beliefs, however strange they may appear, is a mistake because they are an important part of the cultural fabric of a society and influence all manner of behavior. For the marketer, to make light of superstitions in other cultures when doing business there can be an expensive mistake. Making a fuss about being born in the right year under the right phase of the moon or relying heavily on handwriting and palm-reading experts, as in Japan, can be difficult to comprehend for a Westerner who refuses to walk under a ladder, worries about the next seven years after breaking a mirror, buys a one-dollar lottery ticket, and seldom sees a 13th floor in a building.

Thought Processes

We are now learning in much more detail the degree to which ways of thinking vary across cultures. Richard Nisbett in his wonderful book *The Geography of Thought*[58] broadly discusses differences in "Asian and Western" thinking. He starts with Confucius and Aristotle and develops his arguments through consideration of historical and philosophical writings and findings from more recent behavioral science research including his own social-psychological experiments. While he acknowledges the dangers surrounding generalizations about Japanese, Chinese, and Korean cultures, on the one hand, and European and American cultures, on the other, many of his conclusions are consistent with our own work related to international negotiations, cultural values, and linguistic distance.

A good metaphor for his views involves going back to Confucius' picture. Asians tend to see the whole picture and can report details about the background and foreground. Westerners alternatively focus on the foreground and can provide great detail about central figures, but see relatively little in the background. This difference in perception—focus versus big picture—is associated with a wide variety of differences in values, preferences, and expectations about future events. Nisbett's book is essential reading for anyone marketing products and services internationally. His insights are pertinent to Japanese selling in Jacksonville or Belgians selling in Beijing.

Each of the five cultural elements must be evaluated in light of how they might affect a proposed marketing program. Newer products and services and more extensive programs involving the entire cycle from product development through promotion to final selling require greater consideration of cultural factors. Moreover, the separate origins and elements of culture we have presented interact, often in synergistic ways. Therefore, the marketer must also take a step back and consider larger cultural consequences of marketing actions.

Cultural Knowledge

There are two kinds of knowledge about cultures. One is factual knowledge about a culture; it is usually obvious and must be learned. Different meanings of colors, different tastes, and other traits indigenous to a culture are facts that a marketer can anticipate, study, and absorb. The other is interpretive knowledge—an ability to understand and to appreciate fully the nuances of different cultural traits and patterns. For example, the meaning of time, attitudes toward other people and certain objects, the understanding of one's role in

[57]Wayne Friedman, "Brand Management," *Variety.com*, April 28, 2005.

[58]Richard E. Nisbett, *The Geography of Thought: How Asians and Westerners Think Differently . . . and Why* (New York: Free Press, 2003).

CROSSING BORDERS 4.3

Gaining Cultural Awareness in 17th- and
18th-Century England: The Grand Tour

Gaining cultural awareness has been a centuries-old need for anyone involved in international relations. The concept of the *Grand Tour*, a term first applied over 300 years ago in England, was, by 1706, firmly established as the ideal preparation for soldiers, diplomats, and civil servants. It was seen as the best means of imparting to young men of fortune a modicum of taste and knowledge of other countries. By the summer of 1785, 40,000 English were estimated to be on the continent.

The Grand Tourist was expected to conduct a systematic survey of each country's language, history, geography, clothes, food, customs, politics, and laws. In particular, he was to study its most important buildings and their valuable contents, and he was encouraged to collect prints, paintings, drawings, and sculpture. All this could not be achieved in a few weeks, and several years were to lapse before some tourists saw England's shores again. Vast sums of money were spent. At times, touring was not the relatively secure affair of today. If the Grand Tourist managed to avoid the pirates of Dunkirk, he then had to run a gauntlet of highwaymen on Dutch roads, thieves in Italy and France, marauding

packs of disbanded soldiery everywhere, and the Inquisition in Spain, to say nothing of ravenous wolves and dogs.

He had to be self-contained; he carried with him not only the obligatory sword and pistols but also a box of medicines as well as spices and condiments, a means of securing hotel rooms at night, and an overall to protect his clothes while in bed. At the end of these Grand Tours, many returned with as many as 800 or 900 pieces of baggage. These collections of art, sculpture, and writings can be seen today in many of the mansions throughout the British Isles.

Nowadays, more than 150,000 American college students go on their own international "road trips" in the form of study abroad programs. This is double the number of 10 years ago. And a like number of Chinese are now studying abroad as well. A jolly good show!

Sources: Nigel Sale, *Historic Houses and Gardens of East Anglia* (Norwich, England: Jerrold Colour Publications, 1976), p. 1; Zhu Zhe, "Students More Prudent in Rush to Go Abroad," *China Daily*, July 16, 2005.

society, and the meanings of life can differ considerably from one culture to another and may require more than factual knowledge to be fully appreciated. In this case, interpretive knowledge is also necessary.

Factual versus Interpretive Knowledge

Frequently, factual knowledge[59] has meaning as a straightforward fact about a culture but assumes additional significance when interpreted within the context of the culture. For example, that Mexico is 98 percent Roman Catholic is an important bit of factual knowledge. But equally important is the meaning of being a Catholic within Mexican culture versus being Catholic in Spain or Italy. Each culture practices Catholicism in a slightly different way. For example, All Souls' Day is an important celebration among some Catholic countries. In Mexico, however, the celebration receives special emphasis. The Mexican observance is a unique combination of pagan (mostly Indian) influence and Catholic tradition. On the Day of the Dead, as All Souls' Day is called by many in Mexico, it is believed that the dead return to feast. Hence many Mexicans visit the graves of their departed, taking the dead's favorite foods to place on the graves for them to enjoy. Prior to All Souls' Day, bakeries pile their shelves with bread shaped like bones and coffins, and candy stores sell sugar skulls and other special treats to commemorate the day. As the souls feast on the food, so do the living celebrants. Although the prayers, candles, and the idea of the soul are Catholic, the idea of the dead feasting is pre-Christian Mexican. Thus a Catholic in Mexico observes All Souls' Day quite differently from a Catholic in Spain. The interpretive, as well as factual, knowledge about religion in Mexico is necessary to fully understand this part of Mexican culture.

Interpretive knowledge requires a degree of insight that may best be described as a feeling. It is the kind of knowledge most dependent on past experience for interpretation and

---

[59]The information provided in CultureGrams is a good example of readily available factual knowledge. See www.culturegrams.com.

CROSSING BORDERS 4.4 Cultures Are Just Different, Not Right or Wrong, Better or Worse

We must not make value judgments as to whether cultural behavior is good or bad, better or worse. There is no cultural right or wrong, just difference.

People around the world feel as strongly about their cultures as we do about ours. Every country thinks its culture is the best, and for every foreign peculiarity that amuses us, there is an American peculiarity that amuses others. The Chinese tell American dog jokes, reflecting their amazement that we could feel the way we do about an animal that the Chinese consider better for

eating than petting. (Actually, with growing affluence in China, dogs are surviving as pets more frequently, and pet food sales have increased 70 percent over the last five years.) And we're surprised that the French take their dogs to the finest restaurants, where the dogs themselves might be served sitting at the table.

Sources: Lennie Copeland and Lewis Griggs, *Going International* (New York: Plume, 1997), p. 7; "Bill Would Ban Killing Dogs for Human Consumption," *Associated Press*, February 12, 2005.

most frequently prone to misinterpretation if one's home-country frame of reference (SRC) is used. Ideally, the foreign marketer should possess both kinds of knowledge about a market. Many facts about a particular culture can be learned through research in published materials. This effort can also transmit a small degree of empathy, but to appreciate the culture fully it is necessary to live with the people for some time. Because this ideal solution is not practical for a marketer, other solutions must be sought. Consultation and cooperation with bilingual natives with marketing backgrounds is the most effective answer to the problem. This has the further advantage of helping the marketer acquire an increasing degree of empathy through association with people who understand the culture best—locals.

Cultural Sensitivity and Tolerance

Successful foreign marketing begins with cultural sensitivity—being attuned to the nuances of culture so that a new culture can be viewed objectively, evaluated, and appreciated. Cultural sensitivity, or cultural empathy, must be carefully cultivated. Perhaps the most important step is the recognition that cultures are not right or wrong, better or worse; they are simply different. As mentioned previously, for every amusing, annoying, peculiar, or repulsive cultural trait we find in a country, others see a similarly amusing, annoying, or repulsive trait in our culture. For example, we bathe, perfume, and deodorize our bodies in a daily ritual that is seen in many cultures as compulsive, while we often become annoyed with those cultures less concerned with natural body odor.

Just because a culture is different does not make it wrong. Marketers must understand how their own cultures influence their assumptions about another culture. The more exotic the situation, the more sensitive, tolerant, and flexible one needs to be. Being culturally sensitive will reduce conflict and improve communications, and thereby increase success in collaborative relationships.

Besides knowledge of the origins and elements of cultures, the international marketer also should have appreciation of how cultures change and accept or reject new ideas. Because the marketer usually is trying to introduce something completely new (such as e-trading), or to improve what is already in use, how cultures change and the manner in which resistance to change occurs should be thoroughly understood.

Cultural Change

Culture is dynamic in nature; it is a living process. But the fact that cultural change is constant seems paradoxical, because another important attribute of culture is that it is conservative and resists change. The dynamic character of culture is significant in assessing new markets even though changes face resistance. Societies change in a variety of ways. Some have change thrust upon them by war (for example, the changes in Japan after World War II) or by natural disaster. More frequently, change is a result of a society seeking ways to solve the problems created by changes in its environment. One view is that culture is the accumulation of a series of the best solutions to problems faced in common by members of a given society. In other words, culture is the means used in adjusting to the environmental and historical components of human existence.

Accident has provided solutions to some problems; invention has solved many others. Usually, however, societies have found answers by looking to other cultures from which they can borrow ideas. Cultural borrowing is common to all cultures. Although each society has a few unique situations facing it (such as stomach cancer in Japan), most problems confronting all societies are similar in nature.

Cultural Borrowing

Cultural borrowing is a responsible effort to learn from others' cultural ways in the quest for better solutions to a society's particular problems. Thus, cultures unique in their own right are the result, in part, of imitating a diversity of others.[60] Consider, for example, American (U.S.) culture and a typical U.S. citizen, who begins breakfast with an orange from the eastern Mediterranean, a cantaloupe from Persia, or perhaps a piece of African watermelon. After her fruit and first coffee she goes on to waffles, cakes made by a Scandinavian technique from wheat domesticated in Asia Minor. Over these she pours maple syrup, invented by the Indians of the eastern U.S. woodlands. As a side dish she may have the eggs of a species of bird domesticated in Indochina, or thin strips of the flesh of an animal domesticated in eastern Asia that have been salted and smoked by a process developed in northern Europe. While eating, she reads the news of the day, imprinted in characters invented by the ancient Semites upon a material invented in China by a process also invented in China. As she absorbs the accounts of foreign troubles, she will, if she is a good conservative citizen, thank a Hebrew deity in an Indo-European language that she is 100 percent American.[61]

Actually, this citizen is correct to assume that she is 100 percent American because each of the borrowed cultural facets has been adapted to fit her needs, molded into uniquely American habits, foods, and customs. Americans behave as they do because of the dictates of their culture. Regardless of how or where solutions are found, once a particular pattern of action is judged acceptable by society, it becomes the approved way and is passed on and taught as part of the group's cultural heritage. Cultural heritage is one of the fundamental differences between humans and other animals. Culture is learned; societies pass on to succeeding generations solutions to problems, constantly building on and expanding the culture so that a wide range of behavior is possible. The point is, of course, that although many behaviors are borrowed from other cultures, they are combined in a unique manner that becomes typical for a particular society. To the foreign marketer, this similar-but-different feature of cultures has important meaning in gaining cultural empathy.

Similarities: An Illusion

For the inexperienced marketer, the similar-but-different aspect of culture creates illusions of similarity that usually do not exist. Several nationalities can speak the same language or have similar race and heritage, but it does not follow that similarities exist in other respects—that a product acceptable to one culture will be readily acceptable to the other, or that a promotional message that succeeds in one country will succeed in the other. Even though people start with a common idea or approach, as is the case among English-speaking Americans and the British, cultural borrowing and assimilation to meet individual needs translate over time into quite distinct cultures. A common language does not guarantee a similar interpretation of words or phrases. Both British and Americans speak English, but their cultures are sufficiently different so that a single phrase has different meanings to each and can even be completely misunderstood. In England, one asks for a lift instead of an elevator, and an American, when speaking of a bathroom, generally refers to a toilet, whereas in England a bathroom is a place to take a tub bath. Also, the English "hoover"[62] a carpet

---

[60]See W. Scott Morton and J. Kenneth Olenik, *Japan and Its History and Culture* (New York: McGraw-Hill, 2005) for a discussion of the extent of Japan's cultural borrowing.

[61]Ralph Linton, *The Study of Man* (New York: Appleton-Century-Crofts, 1936), p. 327.

[62]This is also a good example of a brand name becoming generic, similar to asking someone to "Xerox" a letter instead of asking it to be photocopied. The Hoover brand vacuum cleaner was among the first popular brands in England; thus, "hoover" the carpet.

whereas Americans vacuum. The movie title *The Spy Who Shagged Me* means nothing to most Americans, but much to British consumers. Indeed, anthropologist Edward Hall warns that Americans and British have a harder time understanding each other because of *apparent* and *assumed* cultural similarities.

The growing economic unification of Europe has fostered a tendency to speak of the "European consumer." Many of the obstacles to doing business in Europe have been or will be eliminated as the European Union takes shape, but marketers, eager to enter the market, must not jump to the conclusion that an economically unified Europe means a common set of consumer wants and needs. Cultural differences among the members of the European Union are the product of centuries of history that will take centuries to erase. The United States itself has many subcultures that even today, with mass communications and rapid travel, defy complete homogenization. To suggest that the South is in all respects culturally the same as the northeastern or midwestern parts of the United States would be folly, just as it would be folly to assume that the unification of Germany has erased cultural differences that arose from over 40 years of political and social separation.

Marketers must assess each country thoroughly in terms of the proposed products or services and never rely on an often-used axiom that if it sells in one country, it will surely sell in another. As worldwide mass communications and increased economic and social interdependence of countries grow, similarities among countries will increase and common market behaviors, wants, and needs will continue to develop. As this process occurs, the tendency will be to rely more on apparent similarities when they may not exist. A marketer is wise to remember that a culture borrows and then adapts and customizes to its own needs and idiosyncrasies; thus, what may appear to be the same on the surface may be different in its cultural meaning.

The scope of culture is broad. It covers every aspect of behavior within a society. The task of foreign marketers is to adjust marketing strategies and plans to the needs of the culture in which they plan to operate. Whether innovations develop internally through invention, experimentation, or by accident, or are introduced from outside through a process of borrowing or immigration, cultural dynamics always seem to take on both positive and negative aspects.

Resistance to Change

A characteristic of human culture is that change occurs. That people's habits, tastes, styles, behavior, and values are not constant but are continually changing can be verified by reading 20-year-old magazines. However, this gradual cultural growth does not occur without some resistance; new methods, ideas, and products are held to be suspect before they are accepted, if ever.

The degree of resistance to new patterns varies. In some situations new elements are accepted completely and rapidly; in others, resistance is so strong that acceptance is never forthcoming. One study using Hofstede's data shows that consumers' acceptance of innovations varies across cultures—innovation was associated with higher individualism (IDV), and lower power distance (PDI) and uncertainty avoidance (UAI).[63] Others argue that culture also influences the production of innovations.[64]

Other studies show that the most important factors in determining what kind and how much of an innovation will be accepted is the degree of interest in the particular subject, as well as how drastically the new will change the old—that is, how disruptive the innovation will be to presently acceptable values and behavior patterns. Observations indicate that those innovations most readily accepted are those holding the greatest interest within the society and those least disruptive. For example, rapid industrialization in parts of Europe has changed many long-honored attitudes involving time and working women. Today, there is an interest in ways to save time and make life more productive; the leisurely continental life is rapidly disappearing. With this time-consciousness has come the very rapid acceptance of many innovations that might have been resisted by most just a few years ago. Instant foods,

---

[63]Idil Sayrac Yaveroglu and Naveen Donthu, "Cultural Influences on the Diffusion of New Products," *Journal of International Consumer Marketing* 14, no. 4 (2003), pp. 49–63.

[64]Thomas Friedman, "The Secret of Our Sauce," *New York Times*, March 7, 2004, p. 17.

The picture here demonstrates the imagery and symbolism used by protest groups in the battle of genetically modified foods or, as the protestors have labeled them, "Frankenfoods." Of course, the label attempts to associate some very benign innovations in food production with the fictional monster of movie lore—an effective public relations gambit on the part of the protestors. *(Illustration by Frances Jetter. Used by permission of Frances Jetter.)*

labor-saving devices, and fast-food establishments, all supportive of a changing attitude toward work and time, are rapidly gaining acceptance.

The resistance to genetically modified (GM) foods (some call it "Frankenfood") has become an important and interesting example. European ethnocentrism certainly entered into the equation early—Europeans protested in the streets the introduction of products such as tomatoes genetically designed to ripen slowly. Conversely, Asian governments labeled the foods as genetically altered, and Asian consumers ate them. In America, where this revolution in biotechnology first took hold, the government didn't bother labeling food and consumers didn't care—at least not until about 2000. Now the protests have begun in the United States. Companies such as Frito-Lay have responded by eliminating GM ingredients, and the federal government is debating new labeling laws.

Although cultures meet most newness with some resistance or rejection, that resistance can be overcome. Cultures are dynamic, and change occurs when resistance slowly yields to acceptance as the basis for resistance becomes unimportant or forgotten. Gradually there comes an awareness of the need for change, or ideas once too complex become less so because of cultural gains in understanding, or an idea is restructured in a less complex way, and so on. Once a need is recognized, even the establishment may be unable to prevent the acceptance of a new idea. For some ideas, solutions to problems, or new products, resistance can be overcome in months; for others, approval may come only after decades or centuries.

An understanding of the process of acceptance of innovations is of crucial importance to the marketer. The marketer cannot wait centuries or even decades for acceptance but must gain acceptance within the limits of financial resources and projected profitability periods. Possible methods and insights are offered by social scientists who are concerned with the concepts of planned social change. Historically, most cultural borrowing and the resulting change has occurred without a deliberate plan, but increasingly changes are occurring in societies as a result of purposeful attempts by some acceptable institution to bring about change, that is, planned change.

Planned and Unplanned Cultural Change

The first step in bringing about planned change in a society is to determine which cultural factors conflict with an innovation, thus creating resistance to its acceptance. The next step is an effort to change those factors from obstacles to acceptance into stimulants for change. The same deliberate approaches used by the social planner to gain acceptance for hybrid grains, better sanitation methods, improved farming techniques, or protein-rich diets among the peoples of underdeveloped societies can be adopted by marketers to achieve marketing goals.[65]

Marketers have two options when introducing an innovation to a culture: They can wait, or they can cause change. The former requires hopeful waiting for eventual cultural changes that prove their innovations of value to the culture; the latter involves introducing an idea or product and deliberately setting about to overcome resistance and to cause change that accelerates the rate of acceptance. The folks at Fidelity Investments in Japan, for example, pitched a tent in front of Tokyo's Shinjuku train station and showered commuters with investment brochures and demonstrations of its Japanese language WebXpress online stock trading services to cause faster changes in Japanese investor behavior. However, as mentioned earlier, the changes have not happened fast enough for most foreign firms targeting this business.

Obviously not all marketing efforts require change in order to be accepted. In fact, much successful and highly competitive marketing is accomplished by a strategy of *cultural congruence*. Essentially this involves marketing products similar to ones already on the market in a manner as congruent as possible with existing cultural norms, thereby minimizing resistance. However, when marketing programs depend on cultural change to be successful,

---

[65]Two very important books on this topic are Everett M. Rogers, *Diffusion of Innovations*, 4th ed. (New York: Free Press, 1995), and Gerald Zaltman and Robert Duncan, *Strategies for Planned Change* (New York: John Wiley & Sons, 1979).

MTV meets Mom in Mumbai (formerly Bombay), India. Culture does change—dress and even names of major cities! Even so, a local resident tells us everyone still calls it Bombay despite the official alteration. (© Joe McNally)

a company may decide to leave acceptance to a strategy of unplanned change—that is, introduce a product and hope for the best. Or a company may employ a strategy of planned change—that is, deliberately set out to change those aspects of the culture offering resistance to predetermined marketing goals.

As an example of unplanned cultural change, consider how the Japanese diet has changed since the introduction of milk and bread soon after World War II. Most Japanese, who were predominantly fish eaters, have increased their intake of animal fat and protein to the point that fat and protein now exceed vegetable intake. As many McDonald's hamburgers are likely to be eaten in Japan as the traditional rice ball wrapped in edible seaweed, and American hamburgers are replacing many traditional Japanese foods. Burger King purchased Japan's homegrown Morinaga Love restaurant chain, home of the salmon burger—a patty of salmon meat, a slice of cheese, and a layer of dried seaweed, spread with mayonnaise and stuck between two cakes of sticky Japanese rice pressed into the shape of a bun—an eggplant burger, and other treats. The chain was converted and sells Whoppers instead of the salmon-rice burger.[66]

The Westernized diet has caused many Japanese to become overweight. To counter this, the Japanese are buying low-calorie, low-fat foods to help shed excess weight and are flocking to health clubs. All this began when U.S. occupation forces introduced bread, milk, and steak to Japanese culture. The effect on the Japanese was unintentional, but nevertheless, change occurred. Had the intent been to introduce a new diet—that is, a strategy of planned change—specific steps could have been taken to identify resistance to dietary change and then to overcome these resistances, thus accelerating the process of change.

Marketing strategy is judged culturally in terms of acceptance, resistance, or rejection. How marketing efforts interact with a culture determines the degree of success or failure, but even failures leave their imprint on a culture. All too often marketers are not aware of the scope of their impact on a host culture. If a strategy of planned change is implemented, the marketer has some responsibility to determine the consequences of such action.

Consequences of Innovation

When product diffusion (acceptance) occurs, a process of social change may also occur. One issue frequently raised concerns the consequences of the changes that happen within a social system as a result of acceptance of an innovation. The marketer seeking product diffusion and adoption may inadvertently bring about change that affects the very fabric of

---

[66]Interestingly the articles we found did not mention this change in diet as a potential factor in the prevalence of stomach cancer in Japan. However, given that medical science has yet to completely understand the disease, one has to wonder. And the other major environmental catastrophe of the time, the atomic bombs, is not mentioned either.

a social system. Consequences of diffusion of an innovation may be functional or dysfunctional, depending on whether the effects on the social system are desirable or undesirable. In most instances, the marketer's concern is with perceived functional consequences—the positive benefits of product use. Indeed, in most situations innovative products for which the marketer purposely sets out to gain cultural acceptance have minimal, if any, dysfunctional consequences, but that cannot be taken for granted.

On the surface, it would appear that the introduction of a processed feeding formula into the diet of babies in underdeveloped countries where protein deficiency is a health problem would have all the functional consequences of better nutrition and health, stronger and faster growth, and so forth. Much evidence, however, suggests that in many situations the dysfunctional consequences far exceeded the benefits. In Nicaragua (and numerous other developing countries), as the result of the introduction of the formula, a significant number of babies annually were changed from breast feeding to bottle feeding before the age of six months. In the United States, with appropriate refrigeration and sanitation standards, a similar pattern exists with no apparent negative consequences. In Nicaragua, however, where sanitation methods are inadequate, a substantial increase in dysentery and diarrhea and a much higher infant mortality rate resulted.

A change from breast feeding to bottle feeding at an early age without the users' complete understanding of purification had caused dysfunctional consequences. This was the result of two factors: the impurity of the water used with the formula and the loss of the natural immunity to childhood disease that a mother's milk provides. This was a case of planned change that resulted in devastating consequences. The infant formula companies set out to purposely change traditional breast feeding to bottle feeding. Advertising, promotions of infant formula using testimonials from nurses and midwives, and abundant free samples were used to encourage a change in behavior. It was a very successful marketing program, but the consequences were unintentionally dysfunctional. An international boycott of infant formula products by several groups resulted in the company agreeing to alter its marketing programs to encourage breast feeding. This problem first occurred some 30 years ago and is still causing trouble for the company. The consequences of the introduction of an innovation can be serious for society and the company responsible, whether the act was intentional or not.[67]

Some marketers may question their responsibility beyond product safety as far as the consequences of their role as change agents are concerned. The authors' position is that the marketer has responsibility for the dysfunctional results of marketing efforts whether intentional or not. Foreign marketers may cause cultural changes that can create dysfunctional consequences. If proper analysis indicates that negative results can be anticipated from the acceptance of an innovation, it is the responsibility of the marketer to design programs not only to gain acceptance for a product but also to eliminate any negative cultural effects.

---

[67]See the Nestlé Infant Formula case toward the end of the book for complete details regarding the ongoing infant formula controversy.

Summary

A complete and thorough appreciation of the origins (geography, history, political economy, technology, and social institutions) and elements (cultural values, rituals, symbols, beliefs, and ways of thinking) of culture may well be the single most important gain to a foreign marketer in the preparation of marketing plans and strategies. Marketers can control the product offered to a market—its promotion, price, and eventual distribution methods—but they have only limited control over the cultural environment within which these plans must be implemented. Because they cannot control all the influences on their marketing plans, they must attempt to anticipate the eventual effect of the uncontrollable elements and plan in such a way that these elements do not preclude the achievement of marketing objectives. They can also set about to effect changes that lead to quicker acceptance of their products or marketing programs.

Planning marketing strategy in terms of the uncontrollable elements of a market is necessary in a domestic market as well, but when a company is operating internationally each new environment that is influenced by elements unfamiliar and sometimes unrecognizable to the marketer complicates the task. For these reasons, special effort and study are needed to absorb enough understanding of the foreign culture to cope with the uncontrollable features. Perhaps it is safe to generalize that of all the tools the foreign marketer must have, those that help generate empathy for another culture are the most valuable. Each of the cultural elements is explored in depth in subsequent chapters. Specific attention is given to business customs, political culture, and legal culture in the following chapters.

Questions

1. Define the following terms:

   culture

   cultural sensitivity

   social institutions

   factual knowledge

   ethnocentrism

   interpretive knowledge

   strategy of cultural
   congruence

   cultural values

   linguistic distance

   cultural borrowing

   strategy of unplanned
   change

   aesthetics

   strategy of planned
   change

2. Which role does the marketer play as a change agent?

3. Discuss the three cultural change strategies a foreign marketer can pursue.

4. "Culture is pervasive in all marketing activities." Discuss.

5. What is the importance of cultural empathy to foreign marketers? How do they acquire cultural empathy?

6. Why should a foreign marketer be concerned with the study of culture?

7. What is the popular definition of culture? Where does culture come from?

8. "Members of a society borrow from other cultures to solve problems that they face in common." What does this mean? What is the significance to marketing?

9. "For the inexperienced marketer, the 'similar-but-different' aspect of culture creates an illusion of similarity that usually does not exist." Discuss and give examples.

10. Outline the elements of culture as seen by an anthropologist. How can a marketer use this cultural scheme?

11. Social institutions affect culture and marketing in a variety of ways. Discuss, giving examples.

12. "Markets are the result of the three-way interaction of a marketer's efforts, economic conditions, and all other elements of the culture." Comment.

13. What are some particularly troublesome problems caused by language in foreign marketing? Discuss.

14. Suppose you were asked to prepare a cultural analysis for a potential market. What would you do? Outline the steps and comment briefly on each.

15. Cultures are dynamic. How do they change? Are there cases where changes are not resisted but actually preferred? Explain. What is the relevance to marketing?

16. How can resistance to cultural change influence product introduction? Are there any similarities in domestic marketing? Explain, giving examples.

17. Innovations are described as being either functional or dysfunctional. Explain and give examples of each.

18. Defend the proposition that a multinational corporation has no responsibility for the consequences of an innovation beyond the direct effects of the innovation, such as the product's safety, performance, and so forth.

19. Find a product whose introduction into a foreign culture may cause dysfunctional consequences and describe how the consequences might be eliminated and the product still profitably introduced.

5

culture, management style, and business systems

CHAPTER OUTLINE

Global Perspective: Do Blondes Have More Fun in Japan?

Required Adaptation

    Degree of Adaptation
    Imperatives, Electives, and Exclusives

The Impact of American Culture on Management Style

Management Styles around the World

    Authority and Decision Making
    Management Objectives and Aspirations
    Communication Styles
    Formality and Tempo
    P-Time versus M-Time
    Negotiations Emphasis

Gender Bias in International Business

Business Ethics

    Corruption Defined
    The Western Focus on Bribery
    Bribery: Variations on a Theme
    Ethical and Socially Responsible Decisions

Culture's Influence on Strategic Thinking

A Synthesis, Relationship-Oriented versus Information-Oriented Cultures

CHAPTER LEARNING OBJECTIVES

What you should learn from Chapter 5:

- The necessity for adapting to cultural differences

- How and why management styles vary around the world

- The extent and implications of gender bias in other countries

- The importance of cultural differences in business ethics

- The differences between relationship-oriented and information-oriented cultures

Global Perspective

DO BLONDES HAVE MORE FUN IN JAPAN?

On the one hand: Tells one American executive, "My first trip to Japan was pretty much a disaster for several reasons. The meetings didn't run smoothly because every day at least 20, if not more, people came walking in and out of the room just to look at me. It is one thing to see a woman at the negotiation table, but to see a woman who happens to be blonde, young and very tall by Japanese standards (5'8" with no shoes) leading the discussions was more than most of the Japanese men could handle.

"Even though I was the lead negotiator for the Ford team, the Japanese would go out of their way to avoid speaking directly to me. At the negotiation table I purposely sat in the center of my team, in the spokesperson's strategic position. Their key person would not sit across from me, but rather two places down. Also, no one would address questions and/or remarks to me—to everyone (all male) on our team—but none to me. They would never say my name or acknowledge my presence. And most disconcerting of all, they appeared to be laughing at me. We would be talking about a serious topic such as product liability, I would make a point or ask a question, and after a barrage of Japanese they would all start laughing."

On the other hand: For years, Barbie dolls sold in Japan looked different from their U.S. counterparts. They had Asian facial features, black hair, and Japanese-inspired fashions.

Then about five years ago Mattel Inc. conducted consumer research around the world and learned something surprising: The original Barbie, with her yellow hair and blue eyes, played as well in Hong Kong as it did in Hollywood. Girls didn't care if Barbie didn't look like them, at least if you believed their marketing research.

"It's all about fantasies and hair," says Peter Broegger, general manager of Mattel's Asian operations. "Blonde Barbie sells just as well in Asia as in the United States."

So Mattel began rethinking one of the basic tenets of its $55 billion global industry—that children in different countries want different playthings. The implications were significant for kids, parents, and particularly the company. In the past, giants such as Mattel, Hasbro Inc., and Lego Co. produced toys and gear in a variety of styles. But Mattel went the other direction, designing and marketing one version worldwide. Sales plummeted, forcing a Barbie makeover.

Sources: James D. Hodgson, Yoshihiro Sano, and John L. Graham, *Doing Business with the New Japan* (Boulder, CO: Rowman & Littlefield, 2000); Lisa Banon and Carlta Vitzthum, "One-Toy-Fits-All: How Industry Learned to Love the Global Kid," *Wall Street Journal*, April 29, 2003, p. A1; Melinda Fulmer, "Mattel Sees Results from Barbie Makeover," *Los Angeles Times*, February 1, 2005, pp. C1, C12.

Perhaps nothing causes more problems for Americans negotiating in other countries than their impatience. Everyone around the world knows that delaying tactics work well against time-conscious U.S. bargainers.

Culture, including all its elements, profoundly affects management style and overall business systems. This is not a new idea. German sociologist Max Weber made the first strong case back in 1930.[1] Culture not only establishes the criteria for day-to-day business behavior but also forms general patterns of values and motivations.[2] Executives are largely captives of their heritages and cannot totally escape the elements of culture they learned growing up.

In the United States, for example, the historical perspective of individualism and "winning the West" seems to be manifest in individual wealth or corporate profit being dominant measures of success. Japan's lack of frontiers and natural resources and its dependence on trade have focused individual and corporate success criteria on uniformity, subordination to the group, and society's ability to maintain high levels of employment. The feudal background of southern Europe tends to emphasize maintenance of both individual and corporate power and authority while blending those feudal traits with paternalistic concern for minimal welfare for workers and other members of society. Various studies identify North Americans as individualists, Japanese as consensus oriented and committed to the group, and central and southern Europeans as elitists and rank conscious. Although these descriptions are stereotypical, they illustrate cultural differences that are often manifest in business behavior and practices. Such differences also coincide quite well with Hofstede's scores listed in Exhibit 4.5 in the last chapter.[3]

A lack of empathy for and knowledge of foreign business practices can create insurmountable barriers to successful business relations. Some businesses plot their strategies with the idea that their counterparts from other business cultures are similar to themselves and are moved by similar interests, motivations, and goals—that they are "just like us." Even though that may be true in some respects, enough differences exist to cause frustration, miscommunication, and, ultimately, failed business opportunities if these differences are not understood and responded to properly.

Knowledge of the *management style*—that is, the business culture, management values, and business methods and behaviors—existing in a country and a willingness to accommodate the differences are important to success in an international market. Unless marketers remain flexible by accepting differences in basic patterns of thinking, local business tempo, religious practices, political structure, and family loyalty, they are hampered, if not prevented, from reaching satisfactory conclusions to business transactions. In such situations, obstacles take many forms, but it is not unusual to have one negotiator's business proposition accepted over another's simply because "that one understands us."

This chapter focuses on matters specifically related to management style. Besides an analysis of the need for adaptation, it reviews differences in management styles and ethics, and concludes with a discussion of culture's influence on strategic thinking.

Required Adaptation

Adaptation is a key concept in international marketing, and willingness to adapt is a crucial attitude. Adaptation, or at least accommodation, is required on small matters as well as large ones.[4] In fact, the small, seemingly insignificant situations are often the most

---

[1]Max Weber, *The Protestant Ethic and Spirit of Capitalism* (London: George Allen & Unwin, 1930, 1976).

[2]Rohit Deshpande and John U. Farley, "Organizational Culture, Market Orientation, Innovativeness, and Firm Performance: An International Odyssey," *International Journal of Research in Marketing* 21, no. 1 (2004), pp. 3–22.

[3]Geert Hofstede, *Culture's Consequences*, 2nd ed. (Thousand Oaks, CA: Sage, 2001).

[4]Including strategic approaches—see Leo Y. M. Sin, Alan C. B. Tse, Oliver H. M. Yau, Raymond P. M. Chow, and Jenny Lee, "Market Orientation, Relationship Marketing Orientation, and Business Performance: The Moderating Effects of Economic Ideology and Industry Type," *Journal of International Marketing* 13, no. 1 (2005), pp. 36–57.

crucial. More than tolerance of an alien culture is required. Affirmative acceptance, that is, open tolerance of the concept "different but equal" is needed as well. Through such affirmative acceptance, adaptation becomes easier because empathy for another's point of view naturally leads to ideas for meeting cultural differences.[5]

As a guide to adaptation, all who wish to deal with individuals, firms, or authorities in foreign countries should be able to meet 10 basic criteria: (1) open tolerance, (2) flexibility, (3) humility, (4) justice/fairness, (5) ability to adjust to varying tempos, (6) curiosity/interest, (7) knowledge of the country, (8) liking for others, (9) ability to command respect, and (10) ability to integrate oneself into the environment. In short, add the quality of adaptability to the qualities of a good executive for a composite of the successful international marketer. It is difficult to argue with these 10 items. As one critic commented, "They border on the 12 Boy Scout laws." However, as you read this chapter you will see that it is the obvious that we sometimes overlook.

Degree of Adaptation

Adaptation does not require business executives to forsake their ways and change to local customs; rather, executives must be aware of local customs and be willing to accommodate to those differences that can cause misunderstandings. Essential to effective adaptation is awareness of one's own culture and the recognition that differences in others can cause anxiety, frustration, and misunderstanding of the host's intentions. The self-reference criterion (SRC) is especially operative in business customs. If we do not understand our foreign counterpart's customs, we are more likely to evaluate that person's behavior in terms of what is acceptable to us.

The key to adaptation is to remain American but to develop an understanding of and willingness to accommodate the differences that exist. A successful marketer knows that in China it is important to make points without winning arguments; criticism, even if asked for, can cause a host to lose face. In Germany, it is considered discourteous to use first names unless specifically invited to do so. Instead, address a person as Herr, Frau, or Fraulein with the last name. In Brazil, do not be offended by the Brazilian inclination to touch during conversation. Such a custom is not a violation of your personal space but rather the Brazilian way of greeting, emphasizing a point, or making a gesture of goodwill and friendship. A Chinese, German, or Brazilian does not expect you to act like one of them. After all, you are American, not Chinese, German, or Brazilian, and it would be foolish for an American to give up the ways that have contributed so notably to American success. It would be equally foolish for others to give up their ways. When different cultures meet, open tolerance and a willingness to accommodate each other's differences are necessary. Once a marketer is aware of cultural differences and the probable consequences of failure to adapt or accommodate, the seemingly endless variety of customs must be assessed. Where does one begin? Which customs should be absolutely adhered to? Which others can be ignored? Fortunately, among the many obvious differences that exist between cultures, only a few are troubling.

Imperatives, Electives, and Exclusives

Business customs can be grouped into *imperatives,* customs that must be recognized and accommodated; *electives,* customs to which adaptation is helpful, but not necessary; and *exclusives,* customs in which an outsider must not participate. An international marketer must appreciate the nuances of cultural imperatives, cultural electives, and cultural exclusives.

Cultural Imperatives.

Cultural imperatives are the business customs and expectations that must be met and conformed to or avoided if relationships are to be successful. Successful businesspeople know the Chinese word *guanxi,* the Japanese *ningen kankei,* or the Latin American *compadre.* All refer to friendship, human relations, or attaining a level of trust. They also know there is no substitute for establishing friendship in some cultures before effective business negotiations can begin.

---

[5]P. Christopher Earley and Elaine Mosakowski, "Cultural Intelligence," *Harvard Business Review,* October 2004, pp. 139–146.

Informal discussions, entertaining, mutual friends, contacts, and just spending time with others are ways *guanxi, ningen kankei, compadre,* and other trusting relationships are developed. In those cultures where friendships are a key to success, the businessperson should not slight the time required for their development. Friendship motivates local agents to make more sales, and friendship helps establish the right relationship with end users, which leads to more sales over a longer period. Naturally, after-sales service, price, and the product must be competitive, but the marketer who has established *guanxi, ningen kankei,* or *compadre* has the edge. Establishing friendship is an imperative in many cultures. If friendship is not established, the marketer risks not earning trust and acceptance, the basic cultural prerequisites for developing and retaining effective business relationships.

The significance of establishing friendship cannot be overemphasized, especially in those countries where family relationships are close. In China, for example, the outsider is, at best, in fifth place in order of importance when deciding with whom to conduct business. The family is first, then the extended family, then neighbors from one's hometown, then former classmates, and only then, reluctantly, strangers—and the last only after a trusting relationship has been established.

In some cultures a person's demeanor is more critical than in other cultures. For example, it is probably never acceptable to lose your patience, raise your voice, or correct someone in public, no matter how frustrating the situation. In some cultures such behavior would only cast you as boorish, but in others it could end a business deal. In Asian cultures it is imperative to avoid causing your counterpart to lose face. In China, to raise your voice, to

BEIJING, CHINA: European Commission President Jose Manuel Barroso (Left), British Prime Minister Tony Blair (Center), and Chinese Premier Wen Jiabao toast after the EU-China Business Summit at the Great Hall of the People in Beijing on September 5, 2005. The summit was boosted by the settlement of a trade row that has left 80 million Chinese-made garments piled up in European seaports, unable to be delivered to shops under a quota pact agreed to in June. Drinking half a bottle is a cultural elective, but taking a symbolic sip is more of an imperative in this case. *(CLARO CORTESIV/AFP/Getty Images)*

shout at a Chinese person in public, or to correct one in front of his or her peers will cause that person to lose face.

A complicating factor in cultural awareness is that what may be an imperative to avoid in one culture is an imperative to do in another. For example, in Japan prolonged eye contact is considered offensive and it is imperative that it be avoided. However, with Arab and Latin American executives it is important to make strong eye contact or you run the risk of being seen as evasive and untrustworthy.

Cultural Electives.   Cultural electives relate to areas of behavior or to customs that cultural aliens may wish to conform to or participate in but that are not required. In other words, to follow the custom in question is not particularly important but is permissible. The majority of customs fit into this category. One need not greet another man with a kiss (a custom in some countries), eat foods that disagree with the digestive system (so long as the refusal is gracious), or drink alcoholic beverages (if for health, personal, or religious reasons). On the other hand, a symbolic attempt to participate in such options is not only acceptable but also may help to establish rapport. It demonstrates that the marketer has studied the culture. Japanese do not expect a Westerner to bow and to understand the ritual of bowing among Japanese, yet a symbolic bow indicates interest and some sensitivity to Japanese culture that is acknowledged as a gesture of goodwill. It may help pave the way to a strong, trusting relationship.

A cultural elective in one county may be an imperative in another. For example, in some cultures one can accept or tactfully and politely reject an offer of a beverage, whereas in other cases the offer of a beverage is a special ritual and to refuse it is an insult. In the Czech Republic an aperitif or other liqueur offered at the beginning of a business meeting, even in the morning, is a way to establish goodwill and trust. It is a sign that you are being welcomed as a friend. It is imperative that you accept unless you make it clear to your Czech counterpart that the refusal is because of health or religion. Chinese business negotiations often include banquets at which large quantities of alcohol are consumed in an endless series of toasts. It is imperative that you participate in the toasts with a raised glass of the offered beverage, but to drink is optional. Your Arab business associates will offer coffee as part of the important ritual of establishing a level of friendship and trust; you should accept even if you only take a ceremonial sip. Cultural electives are the most visibly different customs and thus more obvious. Often, it is compliance with the less obvious imperatives and exclusives that is more critical.

Cultural Exclusives. Cultural exclusives are those customs or behavior patterns reserved exclusively for the locals and from which the foreigner is barred. For example, a Christian attempting to act like a Muslim would be repugnant to a follower of Mohammed. Equally offensive is a foreigner criticizing or joking about a country's politics, mores, and peculiarities (that is, peculiar to the foreigner) even though locals may, among themselves, criticize such issues. There is truth in the old adage, "I'll curse my brother, but if you curse him, you'll have a fight." Few cultural traits are reserved exclusively for locals, but a foreigner must carefully refrain from participating in those that are reserved.

Foreign managers need to be perceptive enough to know when they are dealing with an imperative, an elective, or an exclusive and have the adaptability to respond to each. There are not many imperatives or exclusives, but most offensive behaviors result from not recognizing them. It is not necessary to obsess over committing a faux pas. Most sensible businesspeople will make allowances for the occasional misstep. But the fewer you make the smoother the relationship will be. By the way, you can ask for help. That is, if you have a good relationship with your foreign counterparts you can always ask them to tell you when and how you have "misbehaved."

The Impact of American Culture on Management Style

There are at least three reasons to briefly focus on American culture and management style. First, for American readers it is important to be aware of the elements of culture influencing decisions and behaviors. Such a self-awareness will help American readers adapt to working with associates in other cultures. Second, for readers new to American culture, it is useful to better understand your business associates from the States. The U.S. market is the biggest export market in the world. And, hopefully, this knowledge will help everyone be more patient while conducting business across borders. Third, since the late 1990s American business culture has been exported around the world, just as in the 1980s Japanese management practices were imitated almost everywhere. Management practices developed in the U.S. environment will not be appropriate and useful everywhere.[6] That is clear. So understanding their bases will help everyone make decisions about applying, adapting, or rejecting American practices. Indeed, most often Peter Drucker's advice will apply: "Different people have to be managed differently."[7]

There are many divergent views regarding the most important ideas on which normative U.S. cultural concepts are based. Those that occur most frequently in discussions of cross-cultural evaluations are represented by the following:

- "Master of destiny" viewpoint
- Independent enterprise as the instrument of social action
- Personnel selection and reward based on merit
- Decisions based on objective analysis
- Wide sharing in decision making
- Never-ending quest for improvement
- Competition producing efficiency

The *"master of destiny"* philosophy is fundamental to U.S. management thought. Simply stated, people can substantially influence the future; they are in control of their own

---

[6]See Michael Song, Jinhong Xie, and Barbara Dyer, "Antecedents and Consequences of Marketing Managers' Conflict-Handling Behaviors," *Journal of Marketing* 64 (January 2000), pp. 50–66, for an excellent discussion of differences among Chinese, Japanese, U.K., and U.S. managers.

[7]Peter F. Drucker, *Management Challenges for the 21st Century* (New York: HarperBusiness, 1999), p. 17.

destinies. This viewpoint also reflects the attitude that although luck may influence an individual's future, on balance, persistence, hard work, a commitment to fulfill expectations, and effective use of time give people control of their destinies. In contrast, many cultures have a more fatalistic approach to life. They believe individual destiny is determined by a higher order and that what happens cannot be controlled.

In the United States, approaches to planning, control, supervision, commitment, motivation, scheduling, and deadlines are all influenced by the concept that individuals can control their futures. Recall from Chapter 4 that the United States scored highest on Hofstede's individualism scale.[8] In cultures with more collectivistic and fatalistic beliefs, these good business practices may be followed, but concern for the final outcome is different. After all, if one believes the future is determined by an uncontrollable higher order, then what difference does individual effort really make?

The acceptance of the idea that *independent enterprise* is an instrument for social action is the fundamental concept of U.S. corporations. A corporation is recognized as an entity that has rules and continuity of existence, and is a separate and vital social institution. This recognition can result in strong feelings of obligation to serve the company. Indeed, the company may take precedence over family, friends, or activities that might detract from what is best for the company. This is in sharp contrast to the attitudes held by Mexicans, who feel strongly that personal relationships are more important in daily life than work and the company,[9] and Chinese, who consider a broader set of stakeholders as crucial.[10]

Consistent with the view that individuals control their own destinies is the belief that personnel selection and reward must be made on *merit*. The selection, promotion, motivation, or dismissal of personnel by U.S. managers emphasizes the need to select the best-qualified persons for jobs, retaining them as long as their performance meets standards of expectations, and continuing the opportunity for upward mobility as long as those standards are met. In other cultures where friendship or family ties may be more important than the vitality of the organization, the criteria for selection, organization, and motivation are substantially different from those in U.S. companies. In some cultures, organizations expand to accommodate the maximum number of friends and relatives. If one knows that promotions are made on the basis of personal ties and friendships rather than on merit, a fundamental motivating lever is lost. On the other hand, in many other cultures, social pressure from one's group often motivates strongly.

The very strong belief in the United States that business decisions are based on *objective analysis* and that managers strive to be scientific has a profound effect on the U.S. manager's attitudes toward objectivity in decision making and accuracy of data. While judgment and intuition are important criteria for making decisions, most U.S. managers believe decisions must be supported and based on accurate and relevant information. Thus, in U.S. business, great emphasis is placed on the collection and free flow of information to all levels within the organization and on frankness of expression in the evaluation of business opinions or decisions. In other cultures, such factual and rational support for decisions is not as important; the accuracy of data and even the proper reporting of data are not prime prerequisites. Further, existing data frequently are for the eyes of a select few. The frankness of expression and openness in dealing with data characteristic of U.S. businesses do not fit easily into some cultures.

Compatible with the views that one controls one's own destiny and that advancement is based on merit is the prevailing idea of *wide sharing in decision making*. Although decision making is not a democratic process in U.S. businesses, there is a strong belief that individuals in an organization require and, indeed, need the responsibility of making decisions for

[8]Geert Hofstede, *Culture's Consequences*, 2nd ed. (Thousand Oaks, CA: Sage, 2001).

[9]Eva S. Kras, *Management in Two Cultures: Bridging the Gap between U.S. and Mexican Managers* (Yarmouth, ME: Intercultural Press, 1995) provides a still useful description of the differences between managers' thinking in the two countries.

[10]Chung-Leung Luk, Oliver H. M. Yau, Alan C. B. Tse, Leo Y. M. Sin, and Raymond P. M. Chow, "Stakeholder Orientation and Business Performance: The Case of Service Companies in China," *Journal of International Marketing* 13, no. 1 (2005), pp. 89–110.

continued development. Thus decisions are frequently decentralized, and the ability as well as the responsibility for making decisions is pushed down to lower ranks of management. In many cultures, decisions are highly centralized, in part because of the belief that only a few in the company have the right or the ability to make decisions. In the Middle East, for example, only top executives make decisions.

A key value underlying the American business system is reflected in the notion of a *never-ending quest for improvement*. The United States has always been a relatively activist society; in many walks of life, the prevailing question is "Can it be done better?" Thus management concepts reflect the belief that change is not only normal but also necessary, that nothing is sacred or above improvement. In fact, the merit on which one achieves advancement is frequently tied to one's ability to make improvements. Results are what count; if practices must change to achieve results, then change is in order. In other cultures, the strength and power of those in command frequently rest not on change but on the premise that the status quo demands stable structure. To suggest improvement implies that those in power have failed; for someone in a lower position to suggest change would be viewed as a threat to another's private domain rather than as the suggestion of an alert and dynamic individual.

Perhaps most fundamental to Western management practices is the notion that *competition is crucial for efficiency*, improvement, and regeneration. Gordon Gekko put it most banally in the movie *Wall Street*: "Greed is good." Adam Smith in his *Wealth of Nations* wrote one of the most important sentences in the English language: "By pursuing his own interest he frequently promotes that of the society more effectually than when he really intended to promote it."[11] This is the "invisible hand" notion that justifies competitive behavior because it improves society and its organizations. Competition among salespeople (for example, sales contests) is a good thing because it promotes better individual performance and, consequently, better corporate performance. When companies compete, society is better off, according to this reasoning. However, managers and policy makers in other cultures often do not share this "greed is good" view.

---

[11] Adam Smith, *The Wealth of Nations*, Book IV (1776; reprint, New York: Modern Library, 1994), p. 485.

What's different about Adam Smith's "By pursuing his own interests he frequently promotes that of society more effactually than when he really intended to promote it" and Gordon Gekko's "Greed is good" statements? It's the adverb. Smith didn't say "always," "most of the time," or even "often." He said "frequently." Today many on Wall Street ignore this crucial difference. *(left: © Bettmann/CORBIS; right: 20th Century Fox/The Kobal Collection)*

Cooperation is more salient, and efficiencies are attained through reduced transaction costs. These latter views are more prevalent in collectivistic cultures such as China and Japan.

Management Styles Around the World[12]

Because of the diverse structures, management values,[13] and behaviors encountered in international business, there is considerable variation in the ways business is conducted.[14] No matter how thoroughly prepared a marketer may be when approaching a foreign market, a certain amount of cultural shock occurs when differences in the contact level, communications emphasis, tempo, and formality of foreign businesses are encountered. Ethical standards differ substantially across cultures, as do rituals such as sales interactions and negotiations. In most countries, the foreign trader is also likely to encounter a fairly high degree of government involvement. Among the four dimensions of Hofstede's cultural values discussed in Chapter 4, the Individualism/Collectivism Index (IDV)[15] and Power Distance Index (PDI) are especially relevant in examining methods of doing business cross-culturally.

Authority and Decision Making

Business size, ownership, public accountability, and cultural values that determine the prominence of status and position (PDI) combine to influence the authority structure of business.[16] In high-PDI countries such as Mexico and Malaysia, understanding the rank and status of clients and business partners is much more important than in more egalitarian (low PDI) societies such as Denmark and Israel. In high-PDI countries subordinates are not likely to contradict bosses, but in low-PDI countries they often do. Although the international businessperson is confronted with a variety of authority patterns, most are a variation of three typical patterns: top-level management decisions, decentralized decisions, and committee or group decisions.

Top-level management decision making is generally found in those situations where family or close ownership gives absolute control to owners and where businesses are small enough to allow such centralized decision making. In many European businesses, such as those in France, decision-making authority is guarded jealously by a few at the top, who exercise tight control. In other countries, such as Mexico and Venezuela, where a semifeudal, land-equals-power heritage exists, management styles are characterized as autocratic and paternalistic. Decision-making participation by middle management tends to be deemphasized; dominant family members make decisions that tend to please the family members more than to increase productivity. This is also true for government-owned companies where professional managers have to follow decisions made by politicians, who generally lack any working knowledge about management. In Middle Eastern countries, the top man makes all decisions and prefers to deal only with other executives with decision-making powers. There, one always does business with an individual per se rather than an office or title.

As businesses grow and professional management develops, there is a shift toward decentralized management decision making. Decentralized decision making allows executives

---

[12]A Web site that provides information about management styles around the world is www.executiveplanet.com.

[13]T. Lenartowich and J. P. Johnson, "A Cross-National Assessment of the Values of Latin American Managers: Contrasting Hues or Shades of Gray?" *Journal of International Business Studies* 34, no. 3 (2003), pp. 266–281.

[14]This includes how the notion of teamwork varies—see Cristina B. Gibson and Mary E. Zellmer-Bruhn, "Applying the Concept of Teamwork Metaphors to the Management of Teams in Multicultural Contexts," *Organizational Dynamics* 31, no. 2 (2002), pp. 101–116.

[15]Ping Ping Fu et al., "The Impact of Societal Cultural Values and Individual Social Beliefs on the Perceived Effectiveness of Managerial Influence Strategies: A Meso Approach," *Journal of International Business Studies* 35, no. 4 (2004), pp. 284–305.

[16]Michael K. Hui, Kevin Au, and Henry Fock, "Empowerment Effects across Cultures," *Journal of International Business Studies* 35, no. 1 (2004), pp. 46–60.

CROSSING BORDERS 5.1   Don't Beat Your Mother-in-Law!

The crowding and collectivism of Chinese culture provide fertile ground for hierarchy. Add in a little Confucian advice and status relationships become central for understanding Chinese business systems. Confucius' teachings were the foundation for Chinese education for 2,000 years, until 1911. He defined five cardinal relationships: between ruler and ruled, husband and wife, parents and children, older and younger brothers, and between friends. Except for the last, all relationships were hierarchical. The ruled, wives, children, and younger brothers were all counseled to trade obedience and loyalty for the benevolence of their ruler, husband, parents, and older brothers, respectively. Strict adherence to these vertical relations yielded social harmony, that being the antidote for the violence and civil war of his time.

Obedience and deference to one's superiors remain a strong value in Chinese culture. The story of the Cheng family illustrates the historical salience of social hierarchy and high power distance:

> In October 1865, Cheng Han-cheng's wife had the insolence to beat her mother-in-law. This was regarded as such a heinous crime that the following punishment was meted out. Cheng and his wife were both skinned alive, in front of the mother, their skin displayed at city gates in various towns and their bones burned to ashes. Cheng's granduncle, the eldest of his close relatives, was beheaded; his uncle and two brothers, and the head of the Cheng clan, were hanged. The wife's mother,

her face tattooed with the words "neglected the daughter's education," was paraded through seven provinces. Her father was beaten 80 strokes and banished to a distance of 3,000 *li*. The heads of the family in the houses to the right and left of Cheng's were beaten 80 strokes and banished to Heilungkiang. The educational officer in town was beaten 60 strokes and banished to a distance of 1,000 *li*. Cheng's nine-month-old boy was given a new name and put in the county magistrate's care. Cheng's land was to be left in waste "forever." All this was recorded on a stone stele and rubbings of the inscriptions were distributed throughout the empire.

We recommend you have your children read this story! But seriously, notice the authorities held responsible the entire social network for the woman's breach of hierarchy. Status is no joke among Chinese. Age and rank of executives and other status markers must be taken into account during business negotiations with Chinese. American informality and egalitarianism will not play well on the western side of the Pacific.

Sources: Hsu, Dau-lin, "The Myth of the 'Five Human Relations' of Confucius," *Monumenta Sinica*, 1970, pp. 29, 31, as quoted in Gary G. Hamilton, "Patriarchalism in Imperial China and Western Europe: A Revision of Weber's Sociology of Domination," *Theory and Society* 13, pp. 393–425; N. Mark Lam and John L. Graham, *China Now* (New York: McGraw-Hill, 2006).

at different levels of management to exercise authority over their own functions. As mentioned above, this is typical of large-scale businesses with highly developed management systems such as those found in the United States. A trader in the United States is likely to be dealing with middle management, and title or position generally takes precedence over the individual holding the job.

Committee decision making is by group or consensus. Committees may operate on a centralized or decentralized basis, but the concept of committee management implies something quite different from the individualized functioning of the top management and decentralized decision-making arrangements just discussed. Because Asian cultures and religions tend to emphasize harmony and collectivism, it is not surprising that group decision making predominates there. Despite the emphasis on rank and hierarchy in Japanese social structure, business emphasizes group participation, group harmony, and group decision making—but at the top management level.

The demands of these three types of authority systems on a marketer's ingenuity and adaptability are evident. In the case of the authoritative and delegated societies, the chief problem is to identify the individual with authority. In the committee decision setup, every committee member must be convinced of the merits of the proposition or product in question. The marketing approach to each of these situations differs.

Management Objectives and Aspirations

The training and background (i.e., cultural environment) of managers significantly affect their personal and business outlooks.[17] Society as a whole establishes the social rank or status of management, and cultural background dictates patterns of aspirations and objectives among businesspeople. These cultural influences affect the attitude of managers toward innovation, new products, and conducting business with foreigners. To fully understand another's management style, one must appreciate an individual's values, which are usually reflected in the goals of the business organization and in the practices that prevail within the company. In dealing with foreign business, a marketer must be particularly aware of the varying objectives and aspirations of management.

Security and Mobility.

Personal security and job mobility relate directly to basic human motivation and therefore have widespread economic and social implications. The word *security* is somewhat ambiguous, and this very ambiguity provides some clues to managerial variation. To some, security means a big paycheck and the training and ability required for moving from company to company within the business hierarchy; for others, it means the security of lifetime positions with their companies; to still others, it means adequate retirement plans and other welfare benefits. European companies, particularly in the more hierarchical (PDI) countries, such as France and Italy, have a strong paternalistic orientation, and it is assumed that individuals will work for one company for the majority of their lives. For example, in Britain managers place great importance on individual achievement and autonomy, whereas French managers place great importance on competent supervision, sound company policies, fringe benefits, security, and comfortable working conditions. French managers have much less mobility than British.

Personal Life.

For many individuals, a good personal and/or family life takes priority over profit, security, or any other goal. In his worldwide study of individual aspirations, David McClelland[18] discovered that the culture of some countries stressed the virtue of a good personal life as being far more important than profit or achievement. The hedonistic outlook of ancient Greece explicitly included work as an undesirable factor that got in the way of the search for pleasure or a good personal life. Alternatively, according to Max Weber,[19] at least part of the standard of living that we enjoy in the United States today can be attributed to the hard-working Protestant ethic from which we derive much of our business heritage.

To the Japanese, personal life is company life. Many Japanese workers regard their work as the most important part of their overall lives. Metaphorically speaking, such workers may even find themselves "working in a dream." The Japanese work ethic—maintenance of a sense of purpose—derives from company loyalty and frequently results in the Japanese employee maintaining identity with the corporation. Although this notion continues to be true for the majority, strong evidence indicates that the faltering Japanese economy has moved the position of the Japanese "salary man" from that of one of Japan's business elite to one of some derision. Japan's business culture is gradually shifting away from the lifelong employment that led to the intense company loyalty.

We can get some measure of the work–personal life trade-off made in different cultures with reference to Exhibit 5.1. As a point of reference, 40 hours per week times 50 weeks equals 2,000 hours. The Americans appear to be in the middle of hours worked, far above the Europeans and below the Southeast Asians. Most Americans are getting about two weeks of paid vacation, while in Europe they are taking between four and six weeks! In Singapore and Hong Kong Saturday is a workday. However, the scariest datum isn't in the table. While hours worked are decreasing almost everywhere, in the States the numbers are increasing, up 36 from 1990. Thank you Max Weber!

---

[17]Ted Baker, Eric Gedajlovic, and Michael Lubatkin, "A Framework for Comparing Entrepreneurship Processes across Nations," *Journal of International Business Studies*, 2005.

[18]David C. McClelland, *The Achieving Society* (New York: Free Press, 1985).

[19]Max Weber, *The Protestant Ethic and Spirit of Capitalism* (London: George Allen & Unwin, 1930, 1976).

CROSSING BORDERS 5.2   The American Tourist and the Mexican Fisherman

An American tourist was at the pier of a small coastal Mexican village when a small boat with just one fisherman docked. Inside the small boat were several large yellowfin tuna. The tourist complimented the Mexican on the quality of the fish and asked how long it took to catch them.

The Mexican replied, "Only a little while."

The tourist then asked, "Why didn't you stay out longer and catch more fish?"

The Mexican replied, "With this I have enough to support my family's needs."

The tourist then asked, "But what do you do with the rest of your time?"

The Mexican fisherman said, "I sleep late, fish a little, play with my children, take a siesta with my wife, Maria, stroll into the village each evening where I sip wine and play guitar with my amigos. I have a full and busy life."

The tourist scoffed, "I can help you. You should spend more time fishing and with the proceeds, buy a bigger boat. With the proceeds from the bigger boat you could buy several boats. Eventually you would have a fleet of fishing boats. Instead of selling your catch to a middleman you could sell directly to the processor, eventually opening your own cannery. You would control the product, processing, and distribution. You could leave this small village and move to Mexico City, then Los Angeles, and eventually to New York City where you could run your ever-expanding enterprise."

The Mexican fisherman asked, "But, how long will this take?"

The tourist replied, "15 to 20 years."

"But what then?" asked the Mexican.

The tourist laughed and said, "That's the best part. When the time is right you would sell your company stock to the public and become very rich, you would make millions."

"Millions? . . . Then what?"

The American said, "Then you would retire. Move to a small coastal fishing village where you would sleep late, fish a little, play with your grandkids, take a siesta with your wife, stroll to the village in the evenings where you could sip wine and play your guitar with your amigos."

Source: Author unknown.

By the way, the worst work–personal life trade-off seems to be among junior doctors. In the United States they work 80 hours per week[20] and because of the associated fatigue make many mistakes. In Ireland they work only 75 hours per week. In both countries pressure is being put on the medical community to cut down. Indeed, the Irish are being asked to comply with the 58-hour per week limit established by the European Union.[21]

Affiliation and Social Acceptance.   In some countries, acceptance by neighbors and fellow workers appears to be a predominant goal within business. The Asian outlook is reflected in the group decision making so important in Japan, and the Japanese place high importance on fitting in with their group. Group identification is so strong in Japan that when a worker is asked what he does for a living, he generally answers by telling you he works for Sumitomo or Mitsubishi or Matsushita, rather than that he is a chauffeur, an engineer, or a chemist.

---

[20]Laura Landro, "Push to Reduce Doctors' Hours Gets a Boost," *Wall Street Journal*, October 28, 2004, pp. D1, D12.

[21]Eithne Donnellan, "Talks Resume over Doctors' Hours," *Irish Times*, March 30, 2004, p. 1.

Exhibit 5.1
Annual Hours Worked

Source: International Labor Organization, 2004.

Britain	1,719
Canada	1,776
Germany	1,480
Hong Kong	2,287
Japan	1,842
Norway	1,399
Singapore	2,307
United States	1,979

CROSSING BORDERS 5.3

A Classic—Edward T. Hall's the Language [Symbolism] of Space

Like time, the language of space is different wherever one goes. The American businessman, familiar with the pattern of American corporate life, has no difficulty appraising the relative importance of someone else, simply by noting the size of his office in relation to other offices around him.

One pattern calls for the president or the chairman of the board to have the biggest office. The executive vice president will have the next largest, and so on down the line until you end up in the "bullpen." More important offices are usually located at the corners of and on the upper floors. Executive suites will be on the top floor. The relative rank of vice presidents will be reflected in where they are placed along "executive row." The French, on the other hand, are much more likely to lay out space as a network of connecting points of influence, activity, or interest. The French supervisor will ordinarily be found in the middle of his subordinates, where he can control them.

Americans who are crowded will often feel that their status in the organization is suffering. As one would expect in the Arab world, the location of an office and its size constitute a poor index of the importance of the man who occupies it. What we would experience as crowded, the Arab will often regard as spacious. The same is true in Spanish cultures. A Latin American official illustrated the Spanish view of this point while showing me around a plant. Opening the door to an 18-by-20-foot office in which 17 clerks and their desks were placed, he said, "See, we have nice, spacious offices. Lots of space for everyone."

In the Middle East and Latin America, the businessman is likely to feel left out in time and overcrowded in space. People get too close to him, lay their hands on him, and generally crowd his physical being. In Scandinavia and Germany, he feels more at home, but at the same time the people are a little cold and distant. It is space itself that conveys this feeling.

Source: Edwart T. Hall, "The Silent Language in Overseas Business," *Harvard Business Review*, May–June 1960, pp. 87–96.

Power and Achievement.   Although there is some power seeking by business managers throughout the world, power seems to be a more important motivating force in South American countries. In these countries, many business leaders are not only profit oriented but also use their business positions to become social and political leaders. Related, but different, are the motivations for achievement also identified by McClelland. One way to measure achievement is by money in the bank; another is high rank—both aspirations particularly relevant to the United States.

Communication Styles   Edward T. Hall, professor of anthropology and for decades a consultant to business and government on intercultural relations, tells us that communication involves much more than just words. His article "The Silent Language of Overseas Business," which appeared in the

Speaking of office space: Notice the individualism reflected in the American cubicles and the collectivism demonstrated by the Japanese office organization. *(left: © Ed Kashi/CORBIS; right: © Tom Wagner/CORBIS SABA)*

Exhibit 5.2
Contextual Background of
Various Countries

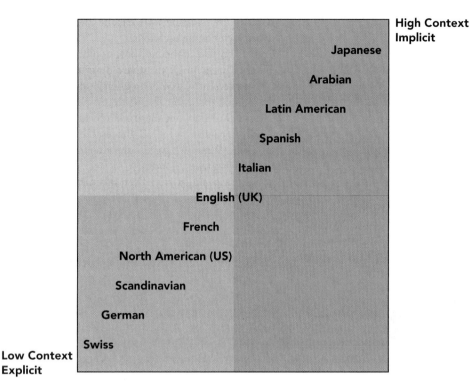

Note: Patterned after E. T. Hall.

Harvard Business Review in 1960,[22] remains a most worthwhile read. In it he describes symbolic meanings of *time, space, things, friendships,* and *agreements,* and how they vary across cultures. In 1960 Hall could not have anticipated the innovations brought on by the Internet. However, all of his ideas about cross-cultural communication apply to that medium as well.[23] We begin here with a discussion of communication in the face-to-face setting and then move to the electronic media.

Face-to-Face Communication.   No language readily translates into another because the meanings of words differ widely among languages. For example, the word "marriage," even when accurately translated, can connote very different things in different languages—in one it may mean love, in another restrictions. Though it is the basic communication tool of marketers trading in foreign lands, managers, particularly from the United States, often fail to develop even a basic understanding of just one other language, much less master the linguistic nuances that reveal unspoken attitudes and information.

Verbal communication, no matter how imprecise, is at least explicit. But much business communication depends on implicit messages that are not verbalized. Edward Hall goes on to say, "In some cultures, messages are explicit; the words carry most of the information. In other cultures . . . less information is contained in the verbal part of the message since more is in the context."

Based on decades of anthropological fieldwork, Hall[24] places 11 cultures along a high-context/low-context continuum (see Exhibit 5.2). Communication in a high-context culture depends heavily on the contextual (*who* says it, *when* it is said, *how* it is said) or nonverbal

---

[22]*Harvard Business Review,* May–June 1960, pp. 87–96.

[23]Some claim that the Internet is changing "offices" in a fundamental way, but we expect Hall's ideas to be worthwhile far into the future. See Brad Stone, "Designing Your Next Office," *Newsweek,* April 28, 2003, pp. 46–47.

[24]Edward T. Hall, "Learning the Arabs' Silent Language," *Psychology Today,* August 1979, pp. 45–53. Hall has several books that should be read by everyone involved in international business: *The Silent Language* (New York: Doubleday, 1959), *The Hidden Dimension* (New York: Doubleday, 1966), and *Beyond Culture* (New York: Anchor Press-Doubleday, 1976).

aspects of communication, whereas the low-context culture depends more on explicit, verbally expressed communications.

A brief exemplar of the high/low-context dimension of communication style regards an international marketing executive's description of a Los Angeles business entertainment event. "I picked him [a German client] up at his hotel near LAX and asked what kind of food he wanted for dinner. He said, 'Something local.' Now in LA local food is Mexican food. I'd never met anyone that hadn't had a taco before! We went to a great Mexican place in Santa Monica and had it all, guacamole, salsa, enchiladas, burritos, a real Alka-Seltzer kind of night. When we were done I asked how he liked the food. He responded rather blandly, 'It wasn't very good.'"

The American might have been taken aback by his client's honest, and perhaps too direct answer. However, the American knew well about German frankness[25] and just rolled with the "blow." Germans, being very low-context oriented, just deliver the information without any social padding. Most Americans would soften the blow some with an answer more like, "It was pretty good, but maybe a bit too spicy." And a high-context oriented Japanese would really pad the response with something like, "It was very good. Thanks." But then the Japanese would never order Mexican food again.

While an American or German might view the Japanese response as less than truthful, from the Japanese perspective, he was just preserving a harmonious relationship. Indeed, the Japanese have two words for truth, *honne* (true mind) and *tatemae* (official stance).[26] The former delivers the information and the latter preserves the relationship. And in high-context Japan the latter is often more important.

Internet Communications.   The message on a business-to-business Web site is an extension of the company and should be as sensitive to business customs as any other company representative would be. Once a message is posted, it can be read anywhere at any time. As a consequence, the opportunity to convey an unintended message is infinite. Nothing about the Web will change the extent to which people identify with their own languages and cultures; thus language should be at the top of the list when examining the viability of a company's Web site.

Estimates are that 78 percent of today's Web site content is written in English, but an English e-mail message cannot be understood by 35 percent of all Internet users. A study of businesses on the European continent highlights the need for companies to respond in the languages of their Web sites. One-third of the European senior managers surveyed said they would not tolerate English online. They do not believe that middle managers can use English well enough to transact business on the Internet. There is some support for such a belief. In a test of "perceived" versus "actual" English-language skills, 4,500 Europeans were asked to translate a series of English phrases or sentences. Less than half had an acceptable command of English, and in France, Spain, and Italy fewer than 3 percent had command of the language.

At the extreme are the French, who even ban the use of English terms. The French Ministry of Finance issued a directive that all official French civil service correspondence must avoid common English-language business words such as *start-up* and *e-mail;* instead, *jeune pousse* ("a young plant") and *courrier électronique* are recommended.

The solution to the problem is to have country-specific Web sites, like those of IBM and Marriott. Dell Computer, for example, makes its Premier Pages Web sites, built for its business clients, available in 12 languages. A host of companies specialize in Web site translations; in addition, software programs are available to translate the company message into another language. However, cultural and linguistic correctness remains a problem with machine translation. If not properly done, English phrases are likely to be translated in a way

---

[25]Interestingly, the etymology of the term "frankness" has to do with the Franks, an ancient Germanic tribe that settled along the Rhine. This is not mere coincidence; it's history again influencing symbols (that is, language)!

[26]James D. Hodgson, Yoshihiro Sano, and John L. Graham, *Doing Business with the New Japan.* (Boulder, CO: Rowman & Littlefield, 2000).

that will embarrass or even damage a company. One way to avoid this is to prepare the original source material in easy-to-translate English devoid of complicated phrases, idioms, or slang. Unfortunately, no machine translation is available that can manage all the nuances of language or syntax.

It would be ideal if every representative of your company spoke fluently the language of and understood the culture of your foreign customers or business associates; but that is an impossible goal for most companies. However, there is no reason why every person who accesses a company's Web site should not be able to communicate in his or her own language if a company wants to be truly global.

In addition to being language friendly, a Web site should be examined for any symbols, icons, and other nonverbal impressions that could convey an unwanted message. Icons that are frequently used on Web sites can be misunderstood. For example, an icon such as a hand making a high-five sign will be offensive in Greece; an image of a thumb-to-index finger, the A-OK gesture, will infuriate visitors in Brazil; a two-fingered peace sign when turned around has a very crude meaning to the British; and AOL's "You've Got Mail" looks a lot like a loaf of bread to a European. Colors can also pose a problem; green is a sacred color in some Middle Eastern cultures and should not be used for something frivolous like a Web background.

Finally, e-mail use and usage rates by managers are also affected by culture. That is, businesspeople in high-context cultures do not use the medium to the same extent as those in low-context cultures. Indeed, the structure of the Japanese language has at least hindered the diffusion of Internet technologies in that country.[27] Moreover, businesspeople in Hong Kong behave less cooperatively in negotiations using e-mail than in face-to-face encounters.[28] Much of the contextual information so important in high-context cultures simply cannot be signaled via the computer.

Formality and Tempo

The breezy informality and haste that seem to characterize American business relationships appear to be American exclusives that businesspeople from other countries not only fail to share but also fail to appreciate. A German executive commented that he was taken aback when employees of his Indiana client called him by his first name. He noted, "In Germany you don't do that until you know someone for 10 years—and never if you are at a lower rank." This apparent informality, however, does not indicate a lack of commitment to the job. Comparing British and American business managers, an English executive commented about the American manager's compelling involvement in business, "At a cocktail party or a dinner, the American is still on duty."

Even though Northern Europeans seem to have picked up some American attitudes in recent years, do not count on them being "Americanized." As one writer says, "While using first names in business encounters is regarded as an American vice in many countries, nowhere is it found more offensive than in France," where formality still reigns. Those who work side by side for years still address one another with formal pronouns. France is higher on Hofstede's Power Distance Index (PDI) than the United States, and such differences can lead to cultural misunderstandings. For example, the formalities of French business practices as opposed to Americans' casual manners are symbols of the French need to show rank and Americans' tendency to downplay it. Thus the French are dubbed snobbish by Americans, while the French consider Americans crude and unsophisticated.

Haste and impatience are probably the most common mistakes of North Americans attempting to trade in the Middle East. Most Arabs do not like to embark on serious business discussions until after two or three opportunities to meet the individual they are dealing with; negotiations are likely to be prolonged. Arabs may make rapid decisions once they are prepared to do so, but they do not like to be rushed and they do not like deadlines. The managing partner of the Kuwait office of KPMG Peat Marwick says of the "flying-visit"

---

[27]James D. Hodgson, Yoshihiro Sano, and John L. Graham, *Doing Business with the New Japan* (Boulder, CO: Rowman & Littlefield, 2000).

[28]Guang Yang and John L. Graham, "The Impact of Computer-Mediated Communications on the Process and Outcomes of Buyer-Seller Negotiations," working paper, University of California, Irvine, 2006.

CROSSING BORDERS 5.4   Time: A Many-Cultured Thing

Time is cultural, subjective, and variable. One of the most serious causes of frustration and friction in cross-cultural business dealings occurs when counterparts are out of sync with each other. Differences often appear with respect to the pace of time, its perceived nature, and its function. Insights into a culture's view of time may be found in its sayings and proverbs. For example:

- "Time is money." *United States*
- "Those who rush arrive first at the grave." *Spain*
- "The clock did not invent man." *Nigeria*
- "If you wait long enough, even an egg will walk." *Ethiopia*
- "Before the time, it is not yet the time; after the time, it's too late." *France*

The precision of clocks also tells a lot about a culture. In a study on how cultures keep time, the researcher found that clocks are slow or fast by an average of just 19 seconds in Switzerland. When a man in Brazil was queried about the time, however, he was more than three hours off when he said it was "exactly 2:14." When a postal employee in the central post office in Jakarta was asked the time, he responded that he didn't know the time but to go outside and ask a street vendor.

The perception of how much one works is typically overstated among different cultures. For example, American women tend to overestimate by 26 percent, and American men tend to overestimate by 15 percent the number of hours worked per week. Contrast this with a British study that reported that university teachers misstated the amount they worked by 39 percent, and that 72 percent of the estimates by Nigerian teachers were inaccurate.

Sources: Alan Zarembo, "What If There Weren't Any Clocks to Watch?" *Newsweek*, June 30, 1997; Robert Levine, *The Geography of Time* (New York: Basic Books, 1998); Max King, "Today You Can Forget Manana, Emerging Markets Are Defying the Old Stereotypes," *Daily Telegraph*, January 22, 2005, p. 6.

approach of many American businesspeople, "What in the West might be regarded as dynamic activity—the 'I've only got a day here' approach—may well be regarded here as merely rude."

Marketers who expect maximum success have to deal with foreign executives in ways that are acceptable to the foreigner. Latin Americans depend greatly on friendships but establish these friendships only in the South American way: slowly, over a considerable period of time. A typical Latin American is highly formal until a genuine relationship of respect and friendship is established. Even then the Latin American is slow to get down to business and will not be pushed. In keeping with the culture, *mañana* (tomorrow) is good enough. How people perceive time helps to explain some of the differences between U.S. managers and those from other cultures.

P-Time versus M-Time

North Americans are a more time-bound culture than Middle Eastern and Latin cultures. Our stereotype of those cultures is "they are always late," and their view of us is "you are always prompt." Neither statement is completely true though both contain some truth. What is true, however, is that we are a very time-oriented society—time is money to us—whereas in other cultures time is to be savored, not spent.

Edward T. Hall defines two time systems in the world: monochronic and polychronic time. *M-time,* or *monochronic time,* typifies most North Americans, Swiss, Germans, and Scandinavians. These Western cultures tend to concentrate on one thing at a time. They divide time into small units and are concerned with promptness. M-time is used in a linear way and it is experienced as being almost tangible in that one saves time, wastes time, bides time, spends time, and loses time. Most low-context cultures operate on M-time. *P-time,* or *polychronic time,* is more dominant in high-context cultures, where the completion of a human transaction is emphasized more than holding to schedules. P-time is characterized by the simultaneous occurrence of many things and by "a great involvement with people." P-time allows for relationships to build and context to be absorbed as parts of high-context cultures.

One study comparing perceptions of punctuality in the United States and Brazil found that Brazilian timepieces were less reliable and public clocks less available than in the United States. Researchers also found that Brazilians more often described themselves as

Exhibit 5.3
Speed Is Relative

Rank of 31 countries for overall pace of life [combination of three measures: (1) minutes downtown pedestrians take to walk 60 feet, (2) minutes it takes a postal clerk to complete a stamp-purchase transaction, and (3) accuracy in minutes of public clocks].

Source: From Robert Levine, "The Pace of Life in 31 Countries," *American Demographics*, November, 1997. Reprinted with permission from the November 1997 issue of *American Demographics*. Copyright, Crain Communications, Inc. 2004.

Overall Pace	Country	Walking 60 Feet	Postal Service	Public Clocks
1	Switzerland	3	2	1
2	Ireland	1	3	11
3	Germany	5	1	8
4	Japan	7	4	6
5	Italy	10	12	2
6	England	4	9	13
7	Sweden	13	5	7
8	Austria	23	8	9
9	Netherlands	2	14	25
10	Hong Kong	14	6	14
11	France	8	18	10
12	Poland	12	15	8
13	Costa Rica	16	10	15
14	Taiwan	18	7	21
15	Singapore	25	11	4
16	United States	6	23	20
17	Canada	11	21	22
18	South Korea	20	20	16
19	Hungary	19	19	18
20	Czech Republic	21	17	23
21	Greece	14	13	29
22	Kenya	9	30	24
23	China	24	25	12
24	Bulgaria	27	22	17
25	Romania	30	29	5
26	Jordan	28	27	19
27	Syria	29	28	27
28	El Salvador	22	16	31
29	Brazil	31	24	28
30	Indonesia	26	26	30
31	Mexico	17	31	26

late arrivers, allowed greater flexibility in defining *early* and *late,* were less concerned about being late, and were more likely to blame external factors for their lateness than were Americans.[29] Please see such comparisons of 31 countries in Exhibit 5.3.

The American desire to get straight to the point and get down to business is a manifestation of an M-time culture, as are other indications of directness. The P-time system gives rise to looser time schedules, deeper involvement with individuals, and a wait-and-see-what-develops attitude. For example, two Latins conversing would likely opt to be late for their next appointments rather than abruptly terminate the conversation before it came to a natural conclusion. P-time is characterized by a much looser notion of being on time or late. Interruptions are routine, delays to be expected. It is not so much putting things off until *mañana* as it is the concept that human activity is not expected to proceed like clockwork.

Most cultures offer a mix of P-time and M-time behavior, but have a tendency to be either more P-time or M-time in regard to the role time plays. Some are similar to Japan, where appointments are adhered to with the greatest M-time precision but P-time is followed once a meeting begins. The Japanese see U.S. businesspeople as too time bound and driven by schedules and deadlines that thwart the easy development of friendships. The differences between M-time and P-time are reflected in a variety of ways throughout a culture.

When businesspeople from M-time and P-time meet, adjustments need to be made for a harmonious relationship. Often clarity can be gained by specifying tactfully, for example, whether a meeting is to be on "Mexican time" or "American time." An American who has

---

[29]Robert Levine, *The Geography of Time* (New York: Basic Books, 1998).

been working successfully with the Saudis for many years says he has learned to take plenty of things to do when he travels. Others schedule appointments in their offices so they can work until their P-time friend arrives. The important thing for the U.S. manager to learn is adjustment to P-time in order to avoid the anxiety and frustration that comes from being out of synchronization with local time. As global markets expand, however, more businesspeople from P-time cultures are adapting to M-time.

Negotiations Emphasis   Business negotiations are perhaps the most fundamental commercial rituals.[30] All the just-discussed differences in business customs and culture come into play more frequently and are more obviously in the negotiating process than in any other aspect of business. The basic elements of business negotiations are the same in any country: They relate to the product, its price and terms, services associated with the product, and, finally, friendship between vendors and customers. But it is important to remember that the negotiating process is complicated, and the risk of misunderstanding increases when negotiating with someone from another culture.

Attitudes brought to the negotiating table by each individual are affected by many cultural factors and customs often unknown to the other participants and perhaps unrecognized by the individuals themselves. His or her cultural background conditions each negotiator's understanding and interpretation of what transpires in negotiating sessions. The possibility of offending one another or misinterpreting each other's motives is especially high when one's self-reference criteria (SRC) is the basis for assessing a situation. One standard rule in negotiating is "know thyself" first, and second, "know your counterpart." The SRC of both parties can come into play here if care is not taken. How business customs and culture influence negotiations is the focus of Chapter 19.

Gender Bias in International Business

The gender bias[31] against women managers that exists in some countries, coupled with myths harbored by male managers, creates hesitancy among U.S. multinational companies to offer women international assignments. Although women constitute nearly half of the U.S. workforce, they represent relatively small percentages of the employees who are chosen for international assignments—only 18 percent. Why? The most frequently cited reason, the inability of women to succeed abroad, might be more fiction than fact. As one executive was quoted as saying, "Overall, female American executives tend not to be as successful in extended foreign work assignments as are male American executives." Unfortunately, such attitudes are shared by many and probably stem from the belief that the traditional roles of women in male-dominated societies preclude women from establishing successful relationships with host-country associates. An often-asked question is whether it is appropriate to send women to conduct business with foreign customers in cultures where females are typically not in managerial positions. To some it appears logical that if women are not accepted in managerial roles within their own cultures, a foreign woman will not be any more acceptable.

It is true that in many cultures—Asian, Middle Eastern, and Latin American—women are not typically found in upper levels of management (see Exhibit 5.4), and men and women are treated very differently. Indeed, the scariest newspaper headline ever written may have been "Asia, Vanishing Point for as Many as 100 Million Women." The article, appearing in the *International Herald Tribune* in 1991,[32] points out that the birthrate in most countries around the world is about 105 boys for every 100 girls. However, in countries like the United States or Japan, where generally women outlive men, there are about 96 men per

---

[30]"Homo Economicus?" *The Economist*, April 9, 2005, pp. 67–68.

[31]Gender bias is now taking on a new character that has long-term implications for the workplace. In a reversal of historical patterns, in most of the industrialized countries women are now the majority on college campuses. Please see Michelle Colin, "The New Gender Gap," *BusinessWeek*, May 26, 2003, pp. 75–81; and "The Conundrum of the Glass Ceiling," *The Economist*, July 23, 2005, pp. 63–65.

[32]January 7, 1991, p. 1.

Exhibit 5.4
Few and Far Between

Source: Ethical Investment Research Service

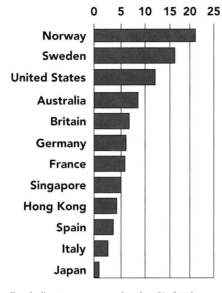

Female directors on corporate boards as % of total, March 2004

100 women in the population. The current numbers[33] of men per 100 women in other Asian countries are: Korea 102, China 103, India 109, and Pakistan 106. The article describes systematic discrimination against females from birth. Now illegal everywhere, ultrasound units are still being used for making gender-specific abortion decisions, and all this prejudice against females is creating disruptive shortages of women. In some provinces in China there are currently 120 men per 100 women.

Despite the substantial prejudices toward women in foreign countries, evidence suggests that prejudice toward foreign women executives may be exaggerated and that the treatment local women receive in their own cultures is not necessarily an indicator of how a foreign businesswoman is treated. It would be inaccurate to suggest that there is no difference in how male and female managers are perceived in different cultures. However, this does not mean that women are not successful in foreign postings.

A key to success for either men or women often hinges on the strength of a firm's backing. When a woman manager receives training and the strong backing of her firm, she usually receives the respect commensurate with the position she holds and the firm she represents. For success, a woman needs a title that gives immediate credibility in the culture in which she is working, and a support structure and reporting relationship that will help her get the job done.[34] In short, with the power of the corporate organization behind her, resistance to her as a woman either does not materialize or is less troublesome than anticipated. Once business negotiations begin, the willingness of a business host to engage in business transactions and the respect shown to a foreign businessperson grow or diminish depending on the business skills he or she demonstrates, regardless of gender. As one executive stated, "The most difficult aspect of an international assignment is getting sent, not succeeding once sent."

The number of women in managerial positions (all levels) in most European countries, with the exception of Germany, is comparable to the United States. The International Labor Organization notes that in the United States, 43 percent of managerial positions are held by women, in Britain 33 percent, and in Switzerland 28 percent. In Germany, however, the picture is less positive. According to one economic source, German female executives held just 9.2 percent of management jobs, and these meet stiff resistances from their male counterparts when they vie for upper-level positions. But the good news is the indication that some German businesses are attempting to remedy the situation. One step taken to help boost women up the executive ladder is a so-called cross-mentoring system organized by Lufthansa and seven other major corporations. High-ranking managers in one company offer advice to women managers in another firm in an effort to help them develop the kind of old-boy network that allows male managers to successfully climb the corporate ladder.

As world markets become more global and international competition intensifies, U.S. companies need to be represented by the most capable personnel available, from entry level to CEO. Research shows that global companies are requiring international experience for top executive positions. Executives who have had international experience are more likely

---

[33]Euromonitor, 2004.

[34]Nancy J. Adler, "Pacific Basin Managers: A Gaijin, Not a Woman," *Human Resource Management* 26, no. 2 (Summer 1987), pp. 169–191; Nancy J. Adler, *International Dimensions of Organizational Behavior*, 4th ed. (Mason, OH: Southwestern College Publishing, 2001).

to get promoted, have higher rewards, and have greater occupational tenure. The lack of international experience should not be a structural barrier to breaking through the glass ceiling in corporate America; to limit the talent pool simply because of gender seems shortsighted.

So what about our female Ford executive mentioned at the start of the chapter? She was having no fun in Japan when we left her story. However, by all accounts (from peers, supervisors, and even Japanese counterparts) that first encounter was not representative of her continuing successes with the Japanese. She attributes her subsequent effectiveness to the strong support of her male Ford team members and her own recognition of the importance of building personal relationships with the Japanese. She explains:

> My husband, also a Ford manager working with Japanese clients, and I decided to have a few of our Mazda associates over for an "All-American" dinner during their next trip to Detroit. So, we started out inviting three people to our home. We thought this would be a nice intimate way to get to know one another and provide the Japanese with an honest-to-goodness homemade American meal. By the eve of the dinner word had gotten out and we had thirteen for dinner. They sort of invited themselves, they changed their meetings around, and some even flew in from the Chicago Auto Show. We had a wonderful time and for the first time they saw me as a person. A mom and a wife as well as a business associate. We talked about families, some business, not particulars, but world economics and the auto industry in general. The dinner party was a key turning point in my relationships with Mazda.[35]

Business Ethics

The moral question of what is right or appropriate poses many dilemmas for domestic marketers. Even within a country, ethical standards are frequently not defined or always clear. The problem of business ethics is infinitely more complex in the international marketplace because value judgments differ widely among culturally diverse groups. That which is commonly accepted as right in one country may be completely unacceptable in another. Giving business gifts of high value, for example, is generally condemned in the United States, but in many countries of the world gifts are not only accepted but also expected.[36]

Corruption Defined

Indeed, consistent with the discussions about language above, the meaning of the word corruption varies considerably around the world. In formerly communist countries where Marxism was an important part of the educational system for many, *profits* can be seen as a kind of corruption. What American managers view as essential others view as a sign of exploitation. *Individualism* so important to Americans can also be seen as a kind of corruption. The Japanese have an expression, "The nail that sticks up gets hammered down." In India many attribute the decline in the society there to the *rampant consumerism*, such as that promoted on MTV. Of course, such rampant consumerism is what kept the American economy afloat right after the turn of the century. In some countries there is no greater Satan than *R-rated American movies* with their sex and violence. In China *missionaries* and religious movements are viewed by the government as being potentially dangerous and disruptive. Many in sub-Sahara Africa view Western *intellectual property laws* as a kind of exploitation that prevents treatment of AIDS for millions. During the 1997–1998 financial crisis many government leaders in Southeast Asia decried *currency speculation* as the worst kind of corruption.

Finally, please recall the 2003 homogenization of Barbie described at the beginning of the chapter. Here's what we predicted in the previous edition of this text: "And then there is *Barbie* having great fun in Japan these days. We hope the love affair lasts, but we are not confident it will. The article does describe the extensive marketing research Mattel did with kids. But there is no mention made about marketing research with their parents.[37] We guarantee that selling a big-busted, blonde doll to their daughters will be viewed as a kind of

---

[35]James D. Hodgson, Yoshihiro Sano, and John L. Graham, *Doing Business with the New Japan* (Boulder, CO: Rowman & Littlefield, 2000).

[36]See www.ethics.org and www.business-ethics.org for more pertinent information.

[37]Lisa Bannon and Carlta Vitzthum, "One-Toy-Fits-All," *Wall Street Journal*, April 29, 2003, p. A1.

corruption by some Asian parents, and perhaps governmental officials as well. Particularly, if America is perceived as pursuing military and economic hegemony, a strong reaction against symbols of America will follow. Watch out Barbie, GI Joe, and your other toy store friends."

Our criticism of Mattel then was on the mark in three ways. First, sales of Barbie declined worldwide after the global standardization. Second, parents and governments did react. Most scandalous was the Saudi Arabian Barbie ban underscored on the Web site of the Saudi Committee for the Propagation of Virtue and Prevention of Vice, "Jewish Barbie dolls, with their revealing clothes and shameful postures, accessories and tools are symbols of decadence of the perverted West. Let us beware of her dangers and be careful."[38] Third, Mattel's strategy boosted sales of its competitors, MGA Entertainment, Inc.'s, multiethnic Bratz,[39] Razanne,[40] and, in the Arabian Gulf states, Fulla.[41] Razanne and Fulla were both designed with Muslim girls and Muslim parents in mind. Fulla has waist-length black hair with red streaks, a round face with big brown eyes, a tan, a flatter chest than Barbie, and clothes that conceal her elbows and knees. We will again touch on this topic as it pertains to marketing research in Chapter 8. But for now we switch from Barbie to bribery, another kind of corruption.

The Western Focus on Bribery

Before the Enron and WorldCom crises, to most Americans the word corruption meant bribery. Now in the domestic context fraud has moved to the more prominent spot in the headlines. However, during the 1970s for U.S. companies engaged in international markets, bribery became a national issue with public disclosure of political payoffs to foreign recipients by U.S. firms. At the time, the United States had no laws against paying bribes in foreign countries. But for publicly held corporations, the Securities and Exchange Commission's (SEC) rules required accurate public reporting of all expenditures. Because the

Scantily clad, blonde Barbie (here in Jakarta, a predominantly Muslim country) or *Matrix Reloaded*, an R-rated American film (here advertised on the streets of Beijing), might be seen as "corrupting" forces in many countries. Indeed, many parents in the United States would see both in such terms. *(left © Reuters New Media Inc./CORBIS)*

---

[38]"Saudis Bust Barbie's 'Dangers,'" *CBS News*, September 10, 2003.

[39]Christopher Palmeri, "Hair-Pulling in the Dollhouse," *BusinessWeek*, May 2, 2005, pp. 76–77.

[40]Tarek El-Tablawy, "Razanne Offers Image of Modesty, Self-Esteem for Muslim Girls," *Associated Press*, September 6, 2003.

[41]Brooke Anderson and Simeon Kerr, "Arab Girls Like the Look of New Boy's Fulla Doll," *Dow Jones Newswires*, June 1, 2005.

Lubrication and Subornation.   Another variation of bribery is the difference between lubrication and subornation. *Lubrication* involves a relatively small sum of cash, a gift, or a service given to a low-ranking official in a country where such offerings are not prohibited by law. The purpose of such a gift is to facilitate or expedite the normal, lawful performance of a duty by that official. This is a practice common in many countries of the world. A small payment made to dock workers to speed up their pace so that unloading a truck takes a few hours rather than all day is an example of lubrication.

Subornation, on the other hand, generally involves giving large sums of money—frequently not properly accounted for—designed to entice an official to commit an illegal act on behalf of the one offering the bribe. Lubrication payments accompany requests for a person to do a job more rapidly or more efficiently; subornation is a request for officials to turn their heads, to not do their jobs, or to break the law.

Agent's Fees.   A third type of payment that can appear to be a bribe but may not be is an agent's fee. When a businessperson is uncertain of a country's rules and regulations, an agent may be hired to represent the company in that country. For example, an attorney may be hired to file an appeal for a variance in a building code on the basis that the attorney will do a more efficient and thorough job than someone unfamiliar with such procedures. While this is often a legal and useful procedure, if a part of that agent's fee is used to pay bribes, the intermediary's fees are being used unlawfully. Under U.S. law, an official who knows of an agent's intention to bribe may risk prosecution and jail time. The Foreign Corrupt Practices Act (FCPA) prohibits U.S. businesses from paying bribes openly or using intermediaries as conduits for a bribe when the U.S. manager knows that part of the intermediary's payment will be used as a bribe. Attorneys, agents, distributors, and so forth may function simply as conduits for illegal payments. The process is further complicated by legal codes that vary from country to country; what is illegal in one country may be winked at in another and be legal in a third.

The answer to the question of bribery is not an unqualified one. It is easy to generalize about the ethics of political payoffs and other types of payments; it is much more difficult to make the decision to withhold payment of money when the consequences of not making the payment may affect the company's ability to do business profitably or at all. With the variety of ethical standards and levels of morality that exist in different cultures, the dilemma of ethics and pragmatism that faces international business cannot be resolved until the anticorruption accords among the OECD and OAS members are fully implemented and multinational businesses refuse to pay extortion or offer bribes.

The Foreign Corrupt Practices Act has had a positive effect. According to the latest Department of Commerce figures, since 1994 American businesses have bowed out of 294 major overseas commercial contracts valued at $145 billion rather than pay a bribe. This information corroborates the academic evidences cited above. Even though there are numerous reports indicating a definite reduction in U.S. firms paying bribes, the lure of contracts is too strong for some companies. Lockheed Corporation made $22 million in questionable foreign payments during the 1970s. More recently the company pled guilty to paying $1.8 million in bribes to a member of the Egyptian national parliament, in exchange for lobbying for three air cargo planes worth $79 million to be sold to the military. Lockheed was caught and fined $25 million, and cargo plane exports by the company were banned for three years. Lockheed's actions during the 1970s were a major influence on the passing of the FCPA. The company now maintains one of the most comprehensive ethics and legal training programs of any major corporation in the United States.

It would be naïve to assume that laws and the resulting penalties alone will put an end to corruption. Change will come only from more ethically and socially responsible decisions by both buyers and sellers and by governments willing to take a stand.

Ethical and Socially Responsible Decisions

To behave in an ethically and socially responsible way should be the hallmark of every businessperson's behavior, domestic or international. Most of us know innately the socially responsible or ethically correct response to questions about knowingly breaking the law, harming the environment, denying someone his or her rights, taking unfair advantage, or behaving in a manner that would bring bodily harm or damage. Unfortunately, the difficult issues are not the obvious and simple right-or-wrong ones. In many countries the international marketer faces the dilemma of responding to sundry situations where local law does not exist, where local practices appear to condone a certain behavior, or where the company willing to "do what is necessary" is favored over the company that refuses to engage in certain practices. In short, being socially responsible and ethically correct are not simple tasks for the international marketer operating in countries whose cultural and social values and/or economic needs are different from those of the marketer.

In normal business operations, difficulties arise in making decisions, establishing policies, and engaging in business operations in five broad areas: (1) employment practices and policies, (2) consumer protection, (3) environmental protection, (4) political payments and involvement in political affairs of the country, and (5) basic human rights and fundamental freedoms. In many countries, laws may help define the borders of minimum ethical or social responsibility, but the law is only the floor above which one's social and personal morality is tested. The statement that "there is no controlling legal authority" may mean that the behavior is not illegal, but it does not mean that the behavior is morally correct or ethical. Ethical business conduct should normally exist at a level well above the minimum required by law or the "controlling legal authority." In fact, laws are the markers of past behavior that society has deemed unethical or socially irresponsible.

Perhaps the best guide to good business ethics is the examples set by ethical business leaders. However, three ethical principles also provide a framework to help the marketer distinguish between right and wrong, determine what ought to be done, and properly justify his or her actions. Simply stated they are as follows.

- **Utilitarian ethics**—Does the action optimize the "common good" or benefits of all constituencies? And who are the pertinent constituencies?
- **Rights of the parties**—Does the action respect the rights of the individuals involved?
- **Justice or fairness**—Does the action respect the canons of justice or fairness to all parties involved?

Answers to these questions can help the marketer ascertain the degree to which decisions are beneficial or harmful, right or wrong, or whether the consequences of actions are ethical or socially responsible. Perhaps the best framework to work within is defined by asking: Is it legal? Is it right? Can it withstand disclosure to stockholders, to company officials, to the public?[48]

While the United States has clearly led the campaign against international bribery, European firms and institutions are apparently putting more effort and money into the promotion of what they are calling "corporate social responsibility." For example, the watchdog group CSR (Corporate Social Responsibility) Europe in cooperation with the INSEAD (European Institute of Administrative Affairs) business school outside Paris is studying the relationship between investment attractiveness and positive corporate behaviors on several dimensions. Their studies find a strong link between firms' social responsibility and European institutional investors' choices for equity investments.[49] All this is not to say that European firms do not still have their own corporate misbehaviors.[50] However, we expect more efforts in the future to focus on measuring and monitoring corporate social responsibility around the world.

Culture's Influence on Strategic Thinking

Perhaps Lester Thurow provided the most articulate description of how culture influences managers' thinking about business strategy.[51] Others are now examining his ideas in even deeper detail.[52] Thurow distinguished between

---

[48]For a comprehensive study of social contracts and ethics, see Thomas W. Dunfee, N. Craig Smith, and William T. Ross, "Social Contracts and Marketing Ethics," *Journal of Marketing*, July 1999, p. 14.

[49]See www.csreurope.org.

[50]Carol Matlack, John Rossant, David Fairlamb, and Kerry Campbell, "The Year of Nasty Surprises: Suddenly the Continent Is Awash in Accounting Scandals," *BusinessWeek*, March 10. 2003, pp. 48–50.

[51]Lester Thurow, *Head to Head* (New York: William Morrow, 1992).

[52]Gordon Redding, "The Thick Description and Comparison of Societal Systems of Capitalism," *Journal of International Business Studies* 36, no. 2 (2005), pp. 123–155.

After a decade of stagnation in Japan, the social contract of lifetime employment is softening. This is reflected in more frequent corporate layoffs, frustrating job searches, and "tent villages" in public places such as Ueno Park in Tokyo. But even at their worst point in history, Japanese jobless are just a trickle compared to the torrent of pink slips and homeless folks when the American economy heads south. *(left: © Tom Wagner/CORBIS SABA)*

the British-American "individualistic" kind of capitalism and the "communitarian" form of capitalism in Japan and Germany.[53] The business systems in the latter two countries are typified by cooperation among government, management, and labor, particularly in Japan. Contrarily, adversarial relationships among labor, management, and government are more the norm in the United Kingdom, and particularly in the United States. We see these cultural differences reflected in Hofstede's results—on the IDV scale the United States is 91, the United Kingdom is 89, Germany is 67, and Japan is 46.

We also find evidence of these differences in a comparison of the performance of American, German, and Japanese firms.[54] In the less individualistic cultures labor and management cooperate—in Germany labor is represented on corporate boards, and in Japan management takes responsibility for the welfare of the labor force. Because the welfare of the workforce matters more to Japanese and German firms, their sales revenues are more stable over time. American-style layoffs are eschewed. The individualistic American approach to labor–management relations is adversarial—each side takes care of itself. So we see damaging strikes and huge layoffs that result in more volatile performance for American firms.

Circa 2000 the American emphasis on competition looked like the best approach, and business practices around the world appeared to be converging on the American model.[55] But it is important to recall that key word in Adam Smith's justification for competition— "frequently." It's worth repeating here: "By pursuing his own interest he frequently promotes that of society. . . " Smith wrote *frequently*, not *always*, *most of the time*, or even *often*. A competitive, individualistic approach works well in the context of an economic boom. During the late 1990s American firms dominated Japanese and European ones. The latter seemed stodgy, conservative, and slow in the then current hot global information economy. However, downturns in a competitive culture can be ugly things. A review of the performance and layoffs at Boeing during the commercial aircraft busts of the late 1990s and early 2000s is instructive.

---

[53]Trevor Buck and Azura Shahrim, "The Translation of Corporate Governance Changes across National Cultures: The Case of Germany," *Journal of International Business Studies* 36, no. 1 (2005), pp. 42–61.

[54]Cathy Anterasian, John L. Graham, and R. Bruce Money, "Are U.S. Managers Superstitious about Market Share?" *Sloan Management Review* 37, no. 4 (1996), pp. 67–77.

[55]Tarun Khanna and Krishna G. Palepu, "Globalization and Convergence in Corporate Governance: Evidence from Infosys and the Indian Software Industry," *Journal of International Business Studies* 35, no. 6 (2004), pp. 484–507; Kwok Leung, Rabi S. Bhagat, Nancy R. Buchan, Miriam Erez, and Cristina B. Gibson, "Culture and International Business: Recent Advances and Their Implications for Future Research," *Journal of International Business Studies* 36, no. 4 (2005), pp. 357–378.

It should also be mentioned that Thurow and the others writing in the area omitted a fourth kind of capitalism—that common in Chinese cultures.[56] Its distinguishing characteristics are a more entrepreneurial approach and an emphasis on *guanxi* (one's network of personal connections)[57] as the coordinating principle among firms. This fourth kind of capitalism is also predicted by culture. Chinese cultures are high on PDI and low on IDV and the strong reciprocity implied by the notion of *guanxi* fits the data well.

Synthesis, Relationship-Oriented versus Information-Oriented Cultures

With increasing frequency, studies are noting a strong relationship between Hall's high/low context and Hofstede's Individualism/Collective and Power Distance indexes. For example, low-context American culture scores relatively low on power distance and high on individualism, while high-context Arab cultures score high on power distance and low on individualism. This is not at all surprising given that Hofstede[58] leans heavily on Hall's ideas in developing and labeling the dimensions of culture revealed via his huge database. Indeed, the three dimensions—high/low context, IDV, and PDI—are correlated above the $r = 0.6$ level, suggesting all three dimensions are largely measuring the same thing.[59] Likewise, when we compare linguistic distance (to English) and Transparency International's Corruption Perception Index to the other three we see similar levels of correlations among all five dimensions. And while metrics for other dimensions of business culture do not yet exist, a pattern appears to be evident (see Exhibit 5.7).

The pattern displayed is not definitive, only suggestive. Not every culture fits every dimension of culture in a precise way. However, the synthesis is useful in many ways. Primarily, it gives us a simple yet logical way to think about many of the cultural differences described in Chapters 4 and 5. For example, American culture is low context, individualistic (IDV), low power distance (PDI), obviously close to English, bribery is less common, monochronic time oriented, linguistically direct, foreground focused,[60] and achieves efficiency through competition; therefore, it is categorized hereafter in this book as an *information-oriented culture*. Alternatively, Japanese culture is high context, collectivistic, high power distance, far from English, bribery is more common, polychronic (in part), linguistically indirect, background focused, and achieves efficiency through reduction of transaction costs; therefore, it is properly categorized as a *relationship culture*. All this is so even though both the United States and Japan are high-income democracies. Both cultures do achieve efficiency, but through different emphases.

---

[56]Don Y. Lee and Philip L. Dawes, "Guanxi, Trust, and Long-Term Orientation in Chinese Business Markets," *Journal of International Marketing* 13, no. 2 (2005), pp. 28–56.

[57]Mark Lam and John L. Graham, *Doing Business in the New China* (New York: McGraw-Hill, 2006).

[58]Geert Hofstede, *Culture's Consequences*, 2nd ed. (Thousand Oaks, CA: Sage, 2001).

[59]This continuum has also been labeled "social context salience" in H. Rika Houston and John L. Graham, "Culture and Corruption in International Markets: Implications for Policy Makers and Managers," *Consumption, Markets, and Culture* 4, no. 3 (2000), pp. 315–340.

[60]Richard E. Nisbett, *The Geography of Thought* (New York: Free Press, 2003).

Exhibit 5.7
Dimensions of Culture, A Synthesis

Information-Oriented (IO)	Relationship-Oriented (RO)
Low context	High context
Individualism	Collectivism
Low power distance	High power distance (including gender)
Bribery less common	Bribery more common
Low distance from English	High distance from English
Linguistic directness	Linguistic indirectness
Monochronic time	Polychronic time
Internet	Face-to-face
Foreground	Background
Competition	Reduce transaction costs

The American business system uses competition, whereas the Japanese depends more on reducing transaction costs.

The most managerially useful aspect of this synthesis of cultural differences is that it allows us to make predictions about unfamiliar cultures. Reference to the three metrics available give us some clues about how consumers and/or business partners will behave and think. Hofstede has provided scores for 78 countries and regions, and we have included them in the appendix to this chapter. Find a country on his lists and you have some information about that market and/or person. One might expect Trinidad to be an information-oriented culture and Russia to be a relationship-oriented culture and so on. Moreover, measures of linguistic distance (any language can be used as the focal one, not just English) are available for every country and, indeed, every person. Thus we would expect that someone who speaks Javanese as a first language to be relationship oriented.

In closing, we are quite encouraged by the publication of the important book *Culture Matters*.[61] We obviously agree with the sentiment of the title and hope that the book will help rekindle the interest in culture's pervasive influences that Max Weber and other initiated so long ago.

Summary

Management styles differ around the world. Some cultures appear to emphasize the importance of information and competition while others focus more on relationships and transaction cost reductions. However, there are no simple answers and the only safe generalization is that businesspersons working in another country must be sensitive to the business environment and must be willing to adapt when necessary. Unfortunately, to know when such adaptation is necessary is not always easy; in some instances adaptation is optional, whereas in others it is actually undesirable. Understanding the culture you are entering is the only sound basis for planning.

Business behavior is derived in large part from the basic cultural environment in which the business operates and, as such, is subject to the extreme diversity encountered among various cultures and subcultures. Environmental considerations significantly affect the attitudes, behavior, and outlook of foreign businesspeople. Motivational patterns of such businesspeople depend in part on their personal backgrounds, their business positions, their sources of authority, and their own personalities.

Varying motivational patterns inevitably affect methods of doing business in different countries. Marketers in some countries thrive on competition; in others they do all possible to eliminate it. The authoritarian, centralized decision-making orientation in some nations contrasts sharply with democratic decentralization in others. International variation characterizes contact level, ethical orientation, negotiation outlook, and nearly every part of doing business. The foreign marketer can take no phase of business behavior for granted.

The new breed of international businessperson that has emerged in recent years appears to have a heightened sensitivity to cultural variations. Sensitivity, however, is not enough; the international trader must be constantly alert and prepared to adapt when necessary. One must always realize that, no matter how long in a country, the outsider is not a local; in many countries that person may always be treated as an outsider. Finally, one must avoid the critical mistake of assuming that knowledge of one culture will provide acceptability in another.

Questions

1. Define the following terms:

   cultural imperative   M-time

   cultural elective   subornation

   cultural exclusive   principle of utilitarian ethics

   FCPA   principle of justice or fairness

   P-time   silent languages

2. "More than tolerance of an alien culture is required; there is a need for affirmative acceptance of the concept 'different but equal.'" Elaborate.

3. "We should also bear in mind that in today's business-oriented world economy, the cultures themselves are being significantly affected by business activities and business practices." Comment.

4. "In dealing with foreign businesses, the marketer must be particularly aware of the varying objectives and aspirations of management." Explain.

5. Suggest ways in which persons might prepare themselves to handle unique business customs that may be encountered in a trip abroad.

6. Business customs and national customs are closely interrelated. In which ways would one expect the two areas to coincide and in which ways would they show differences? How could such areas of similarity and difference be identified?

7. Identify both local and foreign examples of cultural imperatives, electives, and exclusives. Be prepared to explain why each example fits into the category you have selected.

---

[61]Lawrence I. Harrison and Samuel P. Huntington (eds.), *Culture Matters* (New York: Basic Books, 2000).

8. Contrast the authority roles of top management in different societies. How do the different views of authority affect marketing activities?

9. Do the same for aspirational patterns.

10. What effects on business customs might be anticipated from the recent rapid increases in the level of international business activity?

11. Interview some foreign students to determine the types of cultural shock they encountered when they first came to your country.

12. Differentiate between:

    Private ownership and family ownership

    Decentralized and committee decision making

13. In which ways does the size of a customer's business affect business behavior?

14. Compare three decision-making authority patterns in international business.

15. Explore the various ways in which business customs can affect the structure of competition.

16. Why is it important that the business executive be alert to the significance of differing management styles?

17. Suggest some cautions that an individual from a relationship-oriented culture should bear in mind when dealing with someone from an information-oriented culture.

18. Political payoffs are a problem. How would you react if you faced the prospect of paying a bribe? If you knew that by not paying you would not be able to complete a $10 million contract?

19. Differentiate among the following:

subornation	lubrication
extortion	bribery

20. Distinguish between P-time and M-time.

21. Discuss how a P-time person reacts differently from an M-time person in keeping an appointment.

22. What is meant by "laws are the markers of past behavior that society has deemed unethical or socially irresponsible"?

23. What are the three ethical principles that provide a framework to help distinguish between right and wrong? Explain.

24. Visit Transparency International's Web page and check to see how the CPI Index for countries listed in Exhibits 5.4 and 5.5 have changed. After searching TI's databank, explain why the changes have occurred. The site is found at www.transparency. org.

25. Discuss the pros and cons of "there is no controlling legal authority" as a basis for ethical behavior.

26. "The *company.com* page is a company's front door and that doorway should be global in scope." Discuss. Visit several Web pages of major multinational companies and evaluate their "front door" to the global world.

27. Visit the Web sites of Shell and Nike and compare their statements on corporate values. What are the major issues each addresses? Do you think their statements are useful as guides to ethical and socially responsible decision making?

28. Go to your favorite Web reference source and access some recent news articles on Nike and alleged human rights violations. Access the Nike statement on corporate values and write a brief statement on the alleged violations and Nike's statement of corporate values.

Appendix: Index Scores for Countries and Regions

Country	Power Distance	Uncertainty Avoidance	Individualism/ Collectivism	Masculinity/ Femininity	Long-Short-Term Orientation	Primary Language	Distance from English
Argentina	49	86	46	56	31	Spanish	3
Australia total	36	51	90	61	10	English	0
Aborigines	80	128	89	22	31	Australian	7
Austria	11	70	55	79		German	1
Bangladesh	80	60	20	55	40	Bengali	3
Belgium total	65	94	75	54	38	Dutch	1
Dutch speakers	61	97	78	43		Dutch	1
French speakers	67	93	72	60		French	3
Brazil	69	76	38	49	65	Portuguese	3
Bulgaria	70	85	30	40		Bulgarian	3
Canada total	39	48	80	52	23	English	0
French speakers	54	60	73	45	30	French	3
Chile	63	86	23	28		Spanish	3
China	80	30	20	66	118	Mandarin	6
Colombia	67	80	13	64		Spanish	3
Costa Rica	35	86	15	21		Spanish	3
Czech Republic	57	74	58	57	13	Czech	1
Denmark	18	23	74	16	46	Danish	3
Ecuador	78	67	8	63		Spanish	3
Estonia	40	60	60	30		Estonian	4
Finland	33	59	63	26	41	Finnish	4
France	68	86	71	43	39	French	3
Germany	35	65	67	66	31	German	1
Great Britain	35	35	89	66	25	English	0
Greece	60	112	35	57		Greek	3
Guatemala	95	101	6	37		Spanish	3
Hong Kong	68	29	25	57	96	Cantonese	6
Hungary	46	82	80	88	50	Hungarian	4
India	77	40	48	56	61	Dravidian	3
Indonesia	78	48	14	46		Bahasa	7
Iran	58	59	41	43	43	Farsi	3
Ireland	28	35	70	68		English	0
Israel	13	81	54	47		Hebrew	5
Italy	50	75	76	70	34	Italian	3
Jamaica	45	13	39	68		English	0
Japan	54	92	46	95	80	Japanese	4
Korea (South)	60	85	18	39	75	Korean	4
Luxembourg	40	70	60	50		Luxembourgish	1

Country	Power Distance	Uncertainty Avoidance	Individualism/ Collectivism	Masculinity/ Femininity	Long-Short-Term Orientation	Primary Language	Distance from English
Malaysia	104	36	26	50		Malay	7
Malta	56	96	59	47		Maltese	5
Mexico	81	82	30	69		Spanish	3
Morocco	70	68	46	53		Arabic	5
Netherlands	38	53	80	14	44	Dutch	1
New Zealand	22	49	79	58	30	English	0
Norway	31	50	69	8	44	Norwegian	1
Pakistan	55	70	14	50	0	Urdu	3
Panama	95	86	11	44		Spanish	3
Peru	64	87	16	42		Spanish	3
Philippines	94	44	32	64	19	Tagalog	7
Poland	68	93	60	64	32	Polish	3
Portugal	63	104	27	31	30	Portuguese	3
Romania	90	90	30	42		Romanian	3
Russia	93	95	39	36		Russian	3
Salvador	66	94	19	40		Spanish	3
Singapore	74	8	20	48	48	Mandarin	6
Slovakia	104	51	52	110	38	Slovak	3
South Africa	49	49	65	63		Afrikaans	1
Spain	57	86	51	42	19	Spanish	3
Surinam	85	92	47	37		Dutch	1
Sweden	31	29	71	5	33	Swedish	1
Switzerland total	34	58	68	70	40	German	1
German speakers	26	56	69	72		German	1
French speakers	70	70	64	58		French	3
Taiwan	58	69	17	45	87	Taiwanese	6
Thailand	64	64	20	34	56	Thai	7
Trinidad	47	55	16	58		English	0
Turkey	66	85	37	45		Turkish	4
United States	40	46	91	62	29	English	0
Uruguay	61	100	36	38		Spanish	3
Venezuela	81	76	12	73		Spanish	3
Vietnam	70	30	20	40	80	Vietnamese	7
Yugoslavia total	76	88	27	21		Serbo-Croatian	3
Croatia (Zagreb)	73	80	33	40		Serbo-Croatian	3
Serbia (Beograd)	86	92	25	43		Serbo-Croatian	3
Slovenia (Ljubljana)	71	88	27	19		Slovene	3
Regions							
Arab countries	80	68	38	53		Arabic	5
East Africa	64	52	27	41	25		8
West Africa	77	54	20	46	16		8

Source: Geert Hofstede, *Culture's Consequences*, 2nd edition (Thousand Oaks, CA: Sage, 2001).

6

the political environment:

A CRITICAL CONCERN

CHAPTER OUTLINE

Global Perspective: Chiquita Bananas and Prosciutto di Parma, Louis Vuitton Handbags, Scented Bath Oils and Soaps, and Batteries—Strange Bedfellows from the World of Politics

The Sovereignty of Nations

Stability of Government Policies

    Forms of Government
    Political Parties
    Nationalism
    Targeted Fear and/or Animosity
    Trade Disputes

Political Risks of Global Business

    Confiscation, Expropriation, and Domestication
    Economic Risks
    Political Sanctions
    Political and Social Activists and Nongovernmental
      Organizations
    Violence and Terrorism
    Cyberterrorism and Cybercrime

Assessing Political Vulnerability

    Politically Sensitive Products and Issues
    Forecasting Political Risk

Lessening Political Vulnerability

    Joint Ventures
    Expanding the Investment Base
    Licensing
    Planned Domestication
    Political Bargaining
    Political Payoffs

Government Encouragement

CHAPTER LEARNING OBJECTIVES

What you should learn from Chapter 6:

- What the sovereignty of nations means and how it can affect the stability of government policies

- How different governmental types, political parties, nationalism, targeted fear/animosity, and trade disputes can affect the environment for marketing in foreign countries

- The political risks of global business and the factors that affect stability

- The importance of the political system to international marketing and its effect on foreign investments

- The impact of political and social activists, violence, and terrorism on international business

- How to assess and reduce the effect of political vulnerabililty

- How and why governments encourage foreign investment

Global Perspective

CHIQUITA BANANAS AND PROSCIUTTO DI PARMA, LOUIS VUITTON HANDBAGS, SCENTED BATH OILS AND SOAPS, AND BATTERIES—STRANGE BEDFELLOWS FROM THE WORLD OF POLITICS

As the old saying goes, "Politics makes strange bedfellows," but in this case the only one making out is Miss Chiquita Banana. Prosciutto di Parma ham from Italy, handbags from France, bath oils and soaps from Germany, and a host of other imported products from Europe were all slapped with a 100 percent import tariff as retaliation by the U.S. government against European Union banana-import rules that favor Caribbean bananas over Latin American bananas. Keep in mind that no bananas are exported from the United States, yet the United States has been engaged in a trade war over the last seven years that has cost numerous small businesses on both sides of the Atlantic millions of dollars. But how can this be, you ask? Politics, that's how!

One small business, Reha Enterprises, for example, sells bath oil, soap, and other supplies imported from Germany. The tariff on its most popular product, an herbal foam bath, was raised from 5 percent to 100 percent. The customs bill for six months spiraled to $37,783 from just $1,851—a 1,941 percent tax increase. For a small business whose gross sales are less than $1 million annually, it was crippling. When Mr. Rhea heard of the impending "banana war" he called everyone—his congressman, his senator, the United States Trade Representative (USTR). When he described his plight to a USTR representative, the official expressed amazement. "They were surprised I was still importing," because they thought the tariff would cut off the industry entirely. That was their intention, which, of course, would have meant killing Reha Enterprises as well.

In effect, he was told it was his fault that he got caught up in the trade war. He should have attended the hearings in Washington just like Gillette and Mattel, and maybe his products would have been dropped from the targeted list just as theirs were. Scores of European products, from clothing to stoves to glass Christmas ornaments, dolls, and ballpoint pens, that were originally targeted for the retaliatory tariffs escaped the tariff. Aggressive lobbying by large corporations, trade groups, and members of Congress got most of the threatened imported products off the list. The USTR had published a list of the targeted imports in the *Federal Register* inviting affected companies to testify. Unfortunately, the *Federal Register* was not on Rhea's reading list.

In that case, he was told, he should have hired a lobbyist in Washington to keep him briefed. Good advice—but it doesn't make much sense to a company that grosses less than $1 million a year. Other advice received from an official of the USTR included the off-the-record suggestion that he might want to change the custom number on the invoice so it would appear that he was importing goods not subject to the tariff, a decision that could, if he were caught, result in a hefty fine or jail. Smaller businesses in Europe faced similar problems as their export business dries up because of the tariffs.

How did this banana war start? The European Union imposed a quota and tariffs that favored imports from former colonies in the Caribbean and Africa, distributed by European firms, over Latin American bananas distributed by U.S. firms. Chiquita Brands International and Dole Food Company, contending that the EU's "illegal trade barriers" were costing $520 million annually in lost sales to Europe, asked the U.S. government for help. The government agreed that unfair trade barriers were damaging their business, and 100 percent tariffs on selected European imports were levied. Coincidentally, Chiquita Brands' annual campaign contributions increased from barely over $40,000 in 1991 to $1.3 million in 1998.

The European Union complained about the proposed U.S. tariffs and took a grievance to the World Trade Organization (WTO), which ruled in favor of the United States. The EU ignored the WTO and continued the banana tariffs, and the United States continued with its high tariffs—the banana war continued. Because of lack of compliance, the USTR imposed a "carousel" provision that allowed it to rotate, every six months, products that were to be targeted for the 100 percent tariffs. Like all trade disputes, this one was apparently settled, but at what cost to those caught in the middle between two nations and a giant MNC? The biggest losers were the African and Caribbean countries that Europe favored in the dispute. A glut in production has driven prices down and farmers are selling fewer bananas at lower prices. Most recently, the European Union proposed new tariffs in anticipation of Congress passing the Central American Free Trade Agreement. Will bananas be bruised again?

Sources: "U.S. Sets Import Tariffs in Latest Salvo in Ongoing Battle over Banana Trade," *Minneapolis Star Tribune,* March 4, 1999; Timothy Dove, "Hit by a $200,000 Bill from the Blue," *Time,* February 7, 2000, p. 54; "How to Become a Top Banana," *Time,* February 7, 2000, p. 42; Sarah Ryle, "Banana War Leaves the Caribbean a Casualty," *The Observer,* November 24, 2002; Irwin Stelzer, "Opening Shots in a New Style of Trade Warfare," *Sunday Times,* June 5, 2005, B4.

No company, domestic or international, large or small, can conduct business without considering the influence of the political environment within which it will operate. One of the most undeniable and crucial realities of international business is that both host and home governments are integral partners. A government reacts to its environment by initiating and pursuing policies deemed necessary to solve the problems created by its particular circumstances. Reflected in its policies and attitudes toward business are a government's ideas of how best to promote the national interest, considering its own resources and political philosophy. A government controls and restricts a company's activities by encouraging and offering support or by discouraging and banning or restricting its activities—depending on the pleasure of the government.

International law recognizes the sovereign right of a nation to grant or withhold permission to do business within its political boundaries and to control where its citizens conduct business. Thus the political environment of countries is a critical concern for the international marketer. This chapter examines some of the more salient political considerations in assessing global markets.

The Sovereignty of Nations

In the context of international law, a *sovereign state* is independent and free from all external control; enjoys full legal equality with other states; governs its own territory; selects its own political, economic, and social systems; and has the power to enter into agreements with other nations. *Sovereignty* refers to both the powers exercised by a state in relation to other countries and the supreme powers exercised over its own members.[1] A state sets requirements for citizenship, defines geographical boundaries, and controls trade and the movement of people and goods across its borders. Additionally, a citizen is subject to the state's laws even when beyond national borders. It is with the extension of national laws beyond a country's borders that much of the conflict in international business arises. This is especially true when another country considers its own sovereignty to be compromised.

Nations can and do abridge specific aspects of their sovereign rights in order to coexist with other nations. The European Union, North American Free Trade Agreement (NAFTA), North Atlantic Treaty Organization (NATO), and World Trade Organization (WTO)[2] represent examples of nations voluntarily agreeing to give up some of their sovereign rights in order to participate with member nations for a common, mutually beneficial goal. As indicated in Exhibit 1.4 (page 24), the United States' involvement in international political affiliations is surprisingly low (i.e., it is largely sovereign). Indeed, when it comes to participation in international treaty regimes the United States is ranked near the bottom of the 62 countries included in the *Foreign Policy* magazine rankings, tied with Thailand, Indonesia, and Iran (at 57th) and ahead of only Malaysia and Taiwan. Most notably, the Kyoto Protocol[3] on global climate change and the International Criminal Court were rejected by the Bush administration, along with lesser known treaties such as the Basel Convention on the Control of Transboundary Movement of Hazardous Wastes.[4] This apparent lack of international political engagement is particularly hard to understand given the wide acceptance that such agreements lead to peace and mutual understanding.[5]

Countries that agree to relinquish some of their sovereignty often are subject to a nagging fear that too much has been given away. For example, the WTO is considered by some as the biggest threat so far to national sovereignty. Adherence to the WTO inevitably means

---

[1]For those interested in learning more about the concept of sovereignty, see Stephen D. Krasner (ed.), *Problematic Sovereignty* (New York: Columbia University Press, 2001).

[2]Sonni Efron, "Bush Softens Stance on Iran," *Los Angeles Times*, March 12, 2005, pp. A1, A12.

[3]"More Than Hot Air," *The Economist*, July 16, 2005, p. 77.

[4]"Measuring Globalization," *Foreign Policy*, May/June 2005, pp. 52–60.

[5]John L. Graham, "The Big Secret of World Peace," *Journal of Commerce*, February 13, 1995, OPED page; John L. Graham, "Trade Brings Peace," in J. Runzo and N. Martin (eds.), *War and Reconciliation* (Cambridge: Cambridge University Press, 2005); Thomas L. Friedman, *The World Is Flat* (New York: Farrar, Straus, and Giroux, 2005).

loss of some degree of national sovereignty because the member nations have pledged to abide by international covenants and arbitration procedures that can override national laws and have far-reaching ramifications for citizens. Sovereignty was one of the issues at the heart of the spat between the United States and the European Union over Europe's refusal to lower tariffs and quotas on bananas (see the Global Perspective). And critics of the free trade agreement with Central American countries (CAFTA) claim America's sacrifice of sovereignty is too great.[6]

Foreign investment can also be perceived as a threat to sovereignty and thus become a rallying cry by opposing factions. The Chinese national oil company's proposed purchase of Unocal was opposed on such grounds.[7] Ironically, Americans have criticized Mexico for hindering similar sorts of American investments. That is, Mexico badly needs privately financed electricity generating plants to meet electrical power demands and to upgrade the country's overloaded transmission network. The Mexican government entered into an agreement with a Belgian company to build a power plant that would bypass the state electricity monopoly and sell electricity directly to large Mexican manufacturers. But the Mexican constitution limits private ownership of utilities and any exception requires a two-thirds vote of the legislature. The Institutional Revolutionary Party saw the attempt to open Mexico's protected energy industry as an assault on Mexican sovereignty and blocked the agreement. What all this highlights is that national sovereignty is a critical issue in assessing the environment in which a firm operates.

Stability of Government Policies

The ideal political climate for a multinational firm is a stable, friendly government. Unfortunately, governments are not always stable and friendly, nor do stable, friendly governments remain so. Radical shifts in government philosophy when an opposing political party ascends to power, pressure from nationalist and self-interest groups, weakened economic conditions, bias against foreign investment, or conflicts between governments are all issues that can affect the stability of a government. Because foreign businesses are judged by standards as variable as there are nations, the stability and friendliness of the government in each country must be assessed as an ongoing business practice.

At the top of the list of political issues concerning foreign businesses is the stability or instability of prevailing government policies. Governments might change or new political parties might be elected, but the concern of the multinational corporation is the continuity of the set of rules or codes of behavior and the continuation of the rule of law—regardless of which government is in power. A change in government, whether by election or coup, does not always mean a change in the level of political risk. In Italy, for example, more than 50 different governments have been formed since the end of World War II. While the political turmoil in Italy continues, business goes on as usual. In contrast, India has had as many different governments since 1945 as Italy, with several in the past few years favorable to foreign investment and open markets. However, much government policy remains hostile to foreign investment. Senior civil servants who are not directly accountable to the electorate but who remain in place despite the change of the elected government continue with former policies. Even after elections of parties favoring economic reform, the bureaucracy continues to be staffed by old-style central planners in India.

Conversely, radical changes in policies toward foreign business can occur in the most stable governments. The same political party, the Institutional Revolutionary Party (PRI), controlled Mexico from 1929 to 2000. During that period, the political risk for foreign investors ranged from expropriation of foreign investments to Mexico's membership in NAFTA and an open door for foreign investment and trade. In recent years, the PRI created

---

[6]Geri Smith and Paul Magnusson, "Central America Is Holding Its Breath," *BusinessWeek*, June 20, 2005, pp. 52–54.

[7]Joel Havemann and Elizabeth Douglass, "Lawmakers Seek to Stop CNOOC Bid," *Los Angeles Times*, July 14, 2005, pp. C1, C9.

a stable political environment for foreign investment in contrast to earlier expropriations and harassment. Beginning with the elections in 2000, however, a new era in Mexican politics emerged as a result of profound changes within the PRI brought about by then-president Zedillo. Since 1929, the Mexican president had selected his successor, who, without effective challenge, was always elected. President Zedillo changed the process by refusing to nominate a candidate; instead he let the nomination be decided by an open primary—the first in seven decades. From a field of four candidates the PRI selected Labastida Ochoa and the opposing party PAN[8] selected Vicente Fox, who, although considered a long shot, won the presidency. Although the PAN had gained strength for several years in the congress and among state governments, its presidential candidates never had a winning chance until the 2000 election.

Seventy-one years of uninterrupted rule by the PRI ended in 2000. It was the first time in the country's long history of ancient kingdoms, colonialism, civil war, dictatorship, and revolution that one regime gave way to another peacefully. Further, this election went on record as the cleanest and tightest in Mexican history.

A new era in Mexico's economic and social history began when President Fox assumed office. President Fox was relatively successful in stabilizing the Mexican economy during his tenure in office. As the run-up to the 2006 election began, GDP growth, foreign investment, and inflation all were going in good directions.[9] However, other problems persist. The economic turmoil that erupted during past changes of government must be avoided, an entrenched bureaucracy with allegiance to an opposing political party must be won over or replaced, an escalating crime wave (estimated to cost at least 6.2 percent of Mexico's gross domestic product) must be controlled, and a favorable relationship must be maintained with members of the North American Free Trade Association (NAFTA).[10]

Some African countries are unstable, with seemingly unending civil wars, boundary disputes, and oppressive military regimes. Sierra Leone has had three changes in government in five years; the most recent coup d'etat (1997) ended the country's brief experiment with democracy. Shortly after the coup, a civil war erupted, and UN peacekeeping forces have had to maintain peace. Central Africa,[11] where ethnic wars have embroiled seven nations, is one of the most politically unstable regions in the world.[12] Africa is trapped in a vicious cycle. For its nations to prosper they need foreign investment. But investment is leery of unstable nations, which is the status of most of Africa.[13] A recent World Bank study showed that the 47 nations of sub-Saharan Africa were attracting less than $2 billion annually in direct foreign investment—about one-tenth of what a developing nation such as Mexico attracts.[14]

If there is potential for profit and if permitted to operate within a country, multinational companies can function under any type of government as long as there is some long-run predictability and stability. PepsiCo, for example, operated profitably in the Soviet Union when it had one of the world's most extreme political systems. Years before the disintegration

---

[8]PAN stands for Partido Accion National. PAN and PRI are the largest of eight political parties in Mexico.

[9]Marla Dickerson, "Fear of Political Unrest Roils Mexican Markets," *Los Angeles Times*, April 7, 2005, pp. C1, C5.

[10]As an aftermath of the Iraq–U.S. war there were hard feelings between Mexico and the United States when President Fox, facing Mexican antiwar sentiment, refused to back the United States vote in the U.N. Security Council. The hard feelings were only temporary as both sides took steps to mend the rift. Nevertheless, this is a good illustration of how international turbulence can affect relationships among countries and create a tenuous investment environment. Hugh Dellios, "Mexico's President Makes Public Appeals to Mend Rift with U.S.," *Chicago Tribune*, April 22, 2003.

[11]"Central African States Must Work Hard to Create Peace, U.S. Says," *African News Service,* October 30, 2002.

[12]Statement of Dr. Francois Grignon, Committee on House International Relations Subcommittee on Africa, "Conditions in The Congo," FDCH Congressional Testimony, House International Relations Committee, April 3, 2002.

[13]Visit www.eiu.com for abstracts of the Economist Intelligence Unit's country reports of current political and economic data. Some information on this site is fee only, but other sources are free.

[14]"The Regime Changes [at the World Bank]," *The Economist*, June 4, 2005, pp. 65–66.

of the USSR Communist Party, PepsiCo established a very profitable business with the USSR by exchanging Pepsi syrup for Russian vodka.[15]

Socioeconomic and political environments invariably change, as they have in the Soviet Union and Mexico. There are five main political causes of instability in international markets: (1) some forms of government seem to be inherently unstable; (2) changes in political parties during elections can have major effects on trade conditions; (3) nationalism; (4) animosity targeted toward specific countries; and (5) trade disputes themselves.

Forms of Government

Circa 500 B.C. the ancient Greeks conceived of and criticized three fundamental forms of government: rule by one, rule by the few, and rule by the many. The common terms for these in use today are monarchy (or dictatorship), aristocracy (or oligarchy), and democracy. About the same time in history Cyrus the Great, monarch of Persia, declared that the purpose of government was to serve the people, not vice versa. Cyrus's notion is embedded in the constitutions of most modern nations. Following the collapse of communism circa 1990 the world seemed to have agreed that free-enterprise democracy was the best solution to all the criticisms of government since the time of Aristotle, Cyrus, and the others.[16]

Thus of the more than 200 sovereign states on the planet almost all have at least nominally representative governments with universal suffrage for those 18 years and over. In about 10 percent of the states voting is required; in the rest it is voluntary. A few states have some unusual rules for suffrage: In Bolivia you can vote at 18 if you are married and at 21 if single; in Peru police and military personnel cannot vote; in Croatia you can vote at 16 if employed; in Lebanon only women with at least an elementary education can vote (although all men can vote); and Saudi Arabia precludes women from voting. The last appears to be the only state still completely in the dark ages with regards to suffrage. Exhibit 6.1 lists a sampling of the countries that are currently taking a different approach to the conventional wisdom of representational democracy.

---

[15]Visit the Pepsi Web site in Russia for a history of Pepsi in Russia, Pepsi advertising in Russia, and other information: www.pepsi.ru.

[16]Francis Fukuyama, *The End of History and the Last Man* (New York: Free Press, 1992).

Exhibit 6.1
A Sampling of Government Types

Source: www.cia.gov/cia/publications/factbook/, 2005.

Country	Government Type
Afghanistan	Islamic republic
Belarus	Republic in name, although in fact a dictatorship
Bosnia and Herzegovina	Emerging federal democratic republic
Burma (Myanmar)	Military junta
Canada	Confederation with parliamentary democracy
China	Communist state
Congo, Democratic Republic of the	Dictatorship, presumably undergoing a transition to representative government
Cuba	Communist state
Iran	Theocratic republic
Libya	Jamahiriya (a state of the masses) in theory, governed by the populace through local councils; in fact a military dictatorship
North Korea	Communist state, one-man dictatorship
Saudi Arabia	Monarchy
Somalia	No permanent national government; transitional, parliamentary federal government
Sudan	Authoritarian regime—ruling military junta
United Kingdom	Constitutional monarchy
United States	Constitutional federal republic
Uzbekistan	Republic; authoritarian presidential rule, with little power outside the executive branch
Vietnam	Communist state

Eyes on the polls. Portraits of Ayatollah Ali Khamenei (the Supreme Leader) and the late Ayatollah Ruhollah Khomeini loom over Iranian women lined up to vote at a mosque south of Tehran. As mandated by law, women and men waited in separate lines at polling places with more than one ballot box. The current government also specifies the public dress of the women pictured. *(© Behrouz Mehri/AFP/Getty Images)*

The Central Intelligence Agency[17] claims to have taken a look beyond the facade of constitutions in their descriptors. For example, Iran (modern Persia) is defined as a "theocratic republic" recognizing that the constitution codifies Islamic principles of government as interpreted from the Koran. Although political parties are allowed to function, they hold little political power.[18] Instead, the Supreme Leader controls all-important decisions of the government, including who is allowed to run for president in Iran.

Political Parties   For most countries around the world it is particularly important for the marketer to know the philosophies of all major political parties within a country, since any one of them might become dominant and alter prevailing attitudes and the overall business climate.[19] In countries where two strong political parties typically succeed one another in control of the government, it is important to know the direction each party is likely to take. In Great Britain, for example, the Labour Party traditionally has tended to be more restrictive regarding foreign trade than the Conservative Party. The Labour Party, when in control, has limited imports, whereas the Conservative Party has tended to liberalize foreign trade when it is in power. A foreign firm in Britain can expect to seesaw between the liberal trade policies of the Conservatives and the restrictive ones of the Liberals.

Even in Mexico, where a dominant party (PRI) maintained absolute control for seven decades, knowledge of the philosophies of all political parties is important. Over the years, the doctrines of opposing parties have had an influence on the direction of Mexican policy. With the recent election of the PAN party nominee for president, it is even more essential to know the philosophy and direction of both the PRI and PAN, the two major political parties in Mexico.

The election of Vladimir Putin as president of Russia was originally favorably received. By all accounts Russia's economy had been stagnant for over 20 years. Corruption, half-baked market policies, expansion of the ranks of petty civil servants, and a chaotic legal system produced an economy that in many ways is as dysfunctional as the old Soviet

[17]www.cia.gov/cia/publications/factbook/, 2005

[18]Associated Press, "A Rare Runoff," *Orange County Register*, June 18, 2005, p. 1.

[19]Paul M. Vaaler, Burkhard N. Schrage, and Steven A. Block, "Counting the Investor Vote: Political Business Cycle Effects on Sovereign Bond Spreads in Developing Countries," *Journal of International Business Studies* 36, no. 1 (2005), pp. 62–88.

system. Putin's apparent commitment to economic reform and his statement that "the only dictatorship Russia will obey is the dictatorship of the rule of law"[20] were seen as encouraging notes presaging reform in Russia. However, most agree that it will take time to unseat an entrenched bureaucracy and a court system infested with low-paid communist-era judges who are susceptible both to bribery and political pressure. And, more recently Putin has been under fire for apparent backsliding in the direction of authoritarian rule with regard to the press and free enterprise, and financial markets have reflected the associated fears.[21]

An astute international marketer must understand all aspects of the political landscape to be properly informed about the political environment. Unpredictable and drastic shifts in government policies deter investments, whatever the cause of the shift. In short, a current assessment of political philosophy and attitudes within a country is important in gauging the stability and attractiveness of a government in terms of market potential.

Nationalism

Economic and cultural nationalism, which exists to some degree within all countries, is another factor important in assessing business climate. *Nationalism* can best be described as an intense feeling of national pride and unity, an awakening of a nation's people to pride in their country. This pride can take an anti–foreign business bias, where minor harassment and controls of foreign investment are supported, if not applauded. Economic nationalism has as one of its central aims the preservation of national economic autonomy in that residents identify their interests with the preservation of the sovereignty of the state in which they reside. In other words, national interest and security are more important than international relations.

Feelings of nationalism are manifested in a variety of ways, including a call to "buy our country's products only" (e.g., "Buy American"),[22] restrictions on imports, restrictive tariffs, and other barriers to trade. They may also lead to control over foreign investment,[23] often regarded with suspicion, which then becomes the object of intensive scrutiny and control. Generally speaking, the more a country feels threatened by some outside force or as the domestic economy declines, the more nationalistic it becomes in protecting itself against intrusions.

During the period after World War II when many new countries were founded and many others were seeking economic independence, manifestations of militant nationalism were rampant. Expropriation of foreign companies, restrictive investment policies, and nationalization of industries were common practices in some parts of the world. This was the period when India imposed such restrictive practices on foreign investments that companies such as Coca-Cola, IBM, and many others chose to leave rather than face the uncertainty of a hostile economic climate. In many Latin American countries, similar attitudes prevailed and led to expropriations and even confiscation of foreign investments.

By the late 1980s, militant nationalism had subsided; today, the foreign investor, once feared as a dominant tyrant that threatened economic development, is often sought after as a source of needed capital investment.[24] Nationalism comes and goes as conditions and attitudes change, and foreign companies welcomed today may be harassed tomorrow and vice versa.

Although militant economic nationalism has subsided, nationalistic feelings can be found even in the most economically prosperous countries. When U.S. negotiators pushed

---

[20]"Putin Reaffirms Need to Protect Foreigners' Rights," *Interfax*, January 22, 2003.

[21]Guy Chazan, "In Putin's Russia, Business Struggles for a Foothold," *Wall Street Journal*, April 27, 2005, p. A1.

[22]Kent L. Granzin and John J. Painter, "Motivational Influences on 'Buy Domestic' Purchasing: Marketing Management Implications from a Study of Two Nations," *Journal of International Marketing* 9, no. 2 (2001), pp. 73–96.

[23]Laura D'Andrea Tyson, "Stop Scapegoating China—Before It's Too Late," *BusinessWeek*, May 2, 2005, p. 26.

[24]Muammar el Kadafi, leader of Libya, has changed his approach to international relations from supporting terrorism to supporting trade, for example. See "Time, Warped," *Baltimore Sun*, June 29, 2005, p. 16A.

CROSSING BORDERS 6.1 | Coke's Back and It Still Has the Secret

For almost 100 years, the formula for making Coca-Cola has been a closely guarded secret. Then the government of India ordered Coca-Cola to disclose it or cease operations in that country. A secret ingredient called 7-X supposedly gives Coke its distinctive flavor. The government's minister for industry told the Indian parliament that Coca-Cola's Indian branch would have to transfer 60 percent of its equity shares to Indians and hand over its know-how by April 1978 or shut down.

Indian sales accounted for less than 1 percent of Coca-Cola's worldwide sales, but the potential market in India, a country of 800 million, was tremendous. The government refused to let the branch import the necessary ingredients, and Coca-Cola—whose products were once as abundant as the bottled drinking water sold in almost every Indian town of more than 50,000—packed up its bags and left the country. The minister for industry said that Coca-Cola's activities in India "furnish a classic example of how multinational corporations operating in a low-priority, high-profit area in a developing country attain run-away growth and . . . trifle with the weaker indigenous industry."

Sixteen years later, India's attitudes toward foreign investment changed and Coca-Cola reentered the market without having to divulge its formula. During Coke's 16-year exile, however, Pepsi-Cola came to India and captured a 26 percent market share. Not to worry; there is plenty of growth potential for both considering that India's per capita consumption is just 3 eight-ounce bottles a year, versus about 12 for Pakistan and over 500 in Mexico. To forestall further political vulnerability, Coke sold 49 percent of its Indian bottler subsidiary to institutional investors and employees. The company hopes this will put to rest an issue that concerned the Indian government, which wanted Indians to own part of Coke's local operation—in other words, Coke took steps to domesticate its operations.

But India is still a tough market. Most recently, new domestic price competition, a pesticide scare, and cool weather have hurt Coke's sales in India, despite a general global rebound in revenues and profits.

Sources: "Indian Government Rejects Coke's Bid to Sell Soft Drinks," *Wall Street Journal*, March 16, 1990, p. B5; "Coke Adds Fizz to India," *Fortune*, January 10, 1994, pp. 14–15; Manjeet Kripalani, "Finally, Coke Gets It Right," *BusinessWeek*, February 10, 2003, p. 47; Carol Wilbert, "Strong International Results Help Coke Boost Quarterly Profit 9%," *Atlanta Journal-Constitution*, July 22, 2005, p. F1.

Japan to import more rice to help balance the trade deficit between the two countries, nationalistic feelings rose to a new high. Deeply rooted Japanese notions of self-sufficiency, self-respect, and concern for the welfare of Japanese farmers caused Japan to resist any change for several years. It was only after a shortfall in the Japanese rice harvests that restrictions on rice imports were temporarily eased. Even then, all imported foreign rice had to be mixed with Japanese rice before it could be sold.

Targeted Fear and/or Animosity

It is important for marketers not to confuse nationalism, whose animosity is directed generally toward *all* foreign countries, with a widespread fear or animosity directed at a particular country. This was a mistake made by Toyota in the United States in the late 1980s and early 1990s. Sales of Japanese cars were declining in the States and an advertising campaign was designed and delivered that assumed the problem was American nationalism. However, nationalism was clearly not the problem, because sales of German cars were not experiencing the same kinds of declines. The properly defined problem was "Americans' *fear* of Japan." Indeed, at the time Americans considered the economic threat from Japan greater than the military threat from the Soviet Union. So when Toyota spent millions on an advertising campaign showing Toyotas being made by Americans in a plant in Kentucky, it may well have exacerbated the fear that the Japanese were "colonizing" the United States.

In a similar manner, currently China is vilifying Japan over recent changes in Japanese history books that downplay atrocities committed by the latter during World War II. Of course, other issues have strained this crucial relationship over the years, including the growing economic and political clout of each.[25] Similarly, Americans' criticism of China's

---

[25]Mark Magnier, "China and Japan Try to Ease the Strain," *Los Angeles Times*, April 24, 2005, p. A3.

Anti-Japanese demonstrations in Beijing produce halfhearted smiles by Japanese Prime Minister Junichiro Koisumi and Chinese President Hu Jintao at a conference in Jakarta. (© *China Photos/Getty Images*; © *WEDA/AFP/Getty Images*)

"unfair" trade practices, currency manipulations,[26] and growing militarism[27] now are beginning to sound much like U.S. sentiments expressed about Japan in the late 1980s. American moms are even "banning" Chinese products from Christmas lists.[28]

The World Is Not Merchandise, Who Is Killing France? The American Strategy, and *No Thanks Uncle Sam* have been best-selling titles in France that epitomize animosity toward the United States in France. Although such attitudes may seem odd in a country that devours U.S. movies, eats U.S. fast foods, views U.S. soap operas, and shops at U.S. Wal-Mart stores, national animosity—whatever the cause—is a critical part of the political environment. The United States is not immune to the same kinds of directed negativism either. The rift between France and the United States over the Iraq–U.S. war led to hard feelings on both sides and an American backlash against French wine, French cheese, and even products Americans thought were French. French's mustard felt compelled to issue a press release stating that it is an "American company founded by an American named 'French.'"[29]

And, of course, circa 2005 the French are not alone in directing ire at the United States and the products of its companies.[30] Citizens and politicians in many other countries are also unhappy about the war in Iraq. Numerous public opinion polls have shown a recent worldwide decline in sentiment toward America.[31] It is important to appreciate that no nation-state, however secure, will tolerate penetration by a foreign company into its market and economy if it perceives a social, cultural, economic, or political threat to its well-being.

Trade Disputes   Finally, narrow trade disputes themselves can roil broader international markets. At the beginning of the chapter we discussed our favorite example—bananas. Three hot issues circa

---

[26]China has now relented to American criticism of its currency policy, for the first time. See Michael M. Phillips, "China Drops Yuan's Dollar Peg, Will Let Currency Float in Band," *Wall Street Journal,* July 21, 2005, p. 1.

[27]"The House of War," *The Economist,* March 12, 2005, pp. 43–44.

[28]Jonathan Eig, "Christmas Embargo: A Mom Bans China from under the Christmas Tree," *Wall Street Journal,* December 24, 2004, pp. A1, A5.

[29]Floyd Norris, "French's Has an Unmentioned British Flavor, "*New York Times,* March 28, 2003. The news released failed to mention that French's is a subsidiary of Reckitt Benckiser P.L.C., a British firm—but the British did support the U.S. position.

[30]Sarah Murray, "Brand Names under Attack," *Los Angeles Times,* February 9, 2004, p. C1.

[31]Anne Applebaum, "In Search of Pro Americanism," *Foreign Policy,* July/August 2005, pp. 32–40; Sonni Efron, "U.S. Image Abroad Still Bad, but Better," *Los Angeles Times,* June 24, 2005, p. A3.

2005 were the relaxation of quotas on textiles[32] mandated by WTO, farm subsidies in developed countries,[33] and the long-simmering AIRBUS–Boeing battle over subsidies. Any of the three might boil over and affect other aspects of international trade, but at least at this writing cooler heads[34] seem to be prevailing along with the WTO dispute resolution processes.[35]

Political Risks of Global Business

Issues of sovereignty, differing political philosophies, and nationalism are manifest in a host of governmental actions that enhance the risks of global business. Risks can range from confiscation, the harshest, to many lesser but still significant government rules and regulations such as exchange controls, import restrictions, and price controls that directly affect the performance of business activities. Although not always officially blessed initially, social or political activist groups can provoke governments into actions that prove harmful to business. Of all the political risks, the most costly are those actions that result in a transfer of equity from the company to the government, with or without adequate compensation.

Confiscation, Expropriation, and Domestication

The most severe political risk is _confiscation,_ that is, the seizing of a company's assets without payment. The two most notable recent confiscations of U.S. property occurred when Fidel Castro became the leader in Cuba and later when the Shah of Iran was overthrown. Confiscation was most prevalent in the 1950s and 1960s when many underdeveloped countries saw confiscation, albeit ineffective, as a means of economic growth.

Less drastic, but still severe, is _expropriation,_ where the government seizes an investment but some reimbursement for the assets is made. Often the expropriated investment is nationalized, that is, it becomes a government-run entity. A third type of risk is _domestication._ This occurs when host countries gradually cause the transfer of foreign investments to national control and ownership through a series of government decrees by mandating local ownership and greater national involvement in a company's management. The ultimate goal of domestication is to force foreign investors to share more of the ownership, management, and profits with nationals than was the case before domestication.

Rather than a quick answer to economic development, expropriation and nationalization have often led to nationalized businesses that were inefficient, technologically weak, and noncompetitive in world markets. Risks of confiscation and expropriation have lessened over the last two decades because experience has shown that few of the desired benefits materialize after government takeover. Today, countries often require prospective investors to agree to share ownership, use local content, enter into labor and management agreements, and share participation in export sales as a condition of entry, in effect; the company has to become domesticated as a condition for investment.

Countries now view foreign investment as a means of economic growth. As the world has become more economically interdependent, it has become obvious that much of the economic success of countries such as South Korea, Singapore, and Taiwan is tied to foreign investments. Nations throughout the world that only a few years ago restricted or forbade foreign investments are now courting foreign investors as a much-needed source of capital and technology. Additionally, they have begun to privatize telecommunications, broadcasting, airlines, banks, railroads, and other nationally owned companies as a means of enhancing competition and attracting foreign capital.

The benefits of privatizing are many. In Mexico, for example, privatization of the national telephone company resulted in almost immediate benefits when the government received hundreds of millions of dollars of much-needed capital from the sale and immediate

---

[32]Tyler Marshall and Evelyn Iritani, "Clothes Will Cost Less, but Some Nations Pay," _Los Angeles Times,_ January 16, 2005, pp. A1, A28.

[33]Jerry Hirsch, "Trade Battle with Brazil Threatens U.S. Copyrights," _Los Angeles Times,_ June 10, 2005, pp. C1, C10.

[34]Joseph Rebello and Elizabeth Price, "Greenspan Warns Congress against Trade Protectionism," _Wall Street Journal,_ June 23, 2005, p. A1.

[35]Peter Pae, "Trade Showdown over Boeing, Airbus Defused," _Los Angeles Times,_ January 12, 2005, pp. C1, C6.

Exhibit 6.2
How Complicated Things
Can Get!

Source: "Myanmar's Crumbling Kit,"
Asiaweek, March 2, 2001, p. 8;
"Kyatastrophe," *Economist.com,*
March 20, 2003; Michael Vatikiotis,
"Neighbors Lean on Myanmar," *International Herald Tribune,* February 2,
2005, p. 7.

Exchange controls also are extended to products by applying a system of multiple exchange rates to regulate trade in specific commodities classified as necessities or luxuries. Necessary products are placed in the most favorable (low) exchange categories, while luxuries are heavily penalized with high foreign exchange rates. Myanmar, for example, has three exchange rates for the kyat (Kt): the official rate (Kt6:U.S.$1), the market rate (Kt100–125:U.S.$1), and an import duty rate (Kt100:U.S.$1). Since the kyat is not convertible—that is, not officially exchangeable for currencies that can be spent outside the country—investors are severely affected by tax liability, and their ability to send profits outside the country is diminished. Under such exchange rates, tax liability can be very high. For instance, a profit of Kt135,000 is worth U.S.$22,500 at the official exchange rate of Kt6 to U.S.$1, but at the market rate, the investor has earned only U.S.$1,000. The exchange rate difference means that the investor has to pay tax on U.S.$21,500 of nonexistent, unearned income. It seems not much makes sense in Myanmar these days.

investment in new telecommunications systems. A similar scenario has played out in Brazil, Argentina, India, and many eastern European countries. Ironically, many of the businesses that were expropriated and nationalized in earlier periods are now being privatized.

Economic Risks   Even though expropriation and confiscation are waning as risks of doing business abroad, international companies are still confronted with a variety of economic risks that can occur with little warning. Restraints on business activity may be imposed under the banner of national security to protect an infant industry, to conserve scarce foreign exchange, to raise revenue, or to retaliate against unfair trade practices, among a score of other real or imagined reasons. These economic risks are an important and recurring part of the political environment that few international companies can avoid.

Exchange Controls.   Exchange controls stem from shortages of foreign exchange held by a country. When a nation faces shortages of foreign exchange and/or a substantial amount of capital is leaving the country, controls may be levied over all movements of capital or selectively against the most politically vulnerable companies to conserve the supply of foreign exchange for the most essential uses. A recurrent problem for the foreign investor is getting profits in and out of the host country without loss of value, which can occur when a currency is devalued. For example, Venezuela imposed currency controls after a two-month-long national strike, in an attempt to stem the flow of capital from the country. The bolivar was pegged at 1,598 to the dollar, a 53 percent loss in value from a year earlier.[36] Exhibit 6.2 illustrates how exchange controls can affect an international company's profits. Many countries maintain regulations for control of currency, and, should an economy suffer an economic setback or foreign exchange reserves decline severely, the controls on convertibility are imposed quickly, as was the case in Venezuela.

Local-Content Laws.   In addition to restricting imports of essential supplies to force local purchase, countries often require a portion of any product sold within the country to have local content, that is, to contain locally made parts. Thailand, for example, requires that all milk products contain at least 50 percent milk from local dairy farmers. Contrary to popular belief, local-content requirements are not restricted to Third World countries. The European Union has had a local-content requirement as high as 45 percent for "screwdriver operations," a name often given to foreign-owned assemblers, and NAFTA requires 62 percent local content for all cars coming from member countries.

Import Restrictions.   Selective restrictions on the import of raw materials, machines, and spare parts are fairly common strategies to force foreign industry to purchase more supplies within the host country and thereby create markets for local industry.

---

[36]Mike Esterl, "US Companies Face New Challenges in Post-Strike Venezuela," *Dow Jones International News,* February 20, 2003.

Union workers from Daewoo Motor and its marketing arm, Daewoo Motor Sales Co., burn effigies representing General Motors and the automakers' creditors at a protest in Seoul, South Korea. The protest was against the proposed sale of South Korea's Daewoo Motors Co. to General Motors Corp. Thousands of students and workers from the hard-line Korean Confederation of Trade Unions, including dismissed Daewoo Motor union workers, clashed with police after a peaceful rally to protest mass layoffs. (© *Reuters NewMedia Inc./CORBIS*)

Although this is done in an attempt to support the development of domestic industry, the result is often to hamstring and sometimes interrupt the operations of established industries.[37] The problem then becomes critical when there are no adequately developed sources of supply within the country.

Tax Controls.   Taxes must be classified as a political risk when used as a means of controlling foreign investments. In such cases, they are raised without warning and in violation of formal agreements. India, for example, taxes PepsiCo and the Coca-Cola Company 40 percent on all soda bottled in India. Its most recent assault on new business is the attempt to collect $40 million in taxes on travel tickets sold online from Sabre's (an airlines reservations service) data center in Tulsa, Oklahoma. The Indian government contends that Sabre has a permanent establishment in India in the form of data flows between Sabre's Tulsa processing center and the desktop computers of travel agents in India. To underdeveloped countries with economies constantly threatened with a shortage of funds, unreasonable taxation of successful foreign investments appeals to some government officials as the handiest and quickest means of finding operating funds. As the Internet grows in importance, countries will surely seize on Internet transactions as a lucrative source of revenue.

Price Controls.   Essential products that command considerable public interest, such as pharmaceuticals, food, gasoline, and cars, are often subjected to price controls. Such controls applied during inflationary periods can be used to control the cost of living. They also may be used to force foreign companies to sell equity to local interests. A side effect on the local economy can be to slow or even stop capital investment.

Labor Problems.   In many countries, labor unions have strong government support that they use effectively in obtaining special concessions from business. Layoffs may be forbidden, profits may have to be shared, and an extraordinary number of services may have to be provided. In fact, in many countries, foreign firms are considered fair game for the demands of the domestic labor supply. In France, the belief in full employment is almost religious in fervor; layoffs of any size, especially by foreign-owned companies, are regarded as national crises. We should also note that some multinational companies are more powerful than local labor unions. Wal-Mart closed a store in Quebec rather than letting it be unionized.[38]

---

[37]"Russia Mulls Rice Import Restrictions," *Interfax,* February 19, 2003.

[38]"Union Loses Bid to Reopen Wal-Mart," *Montreal Gazette,* May 12, 2005, p. A11.

Political Sanctions

In addition to economic risks, one or a group of nations may boycott another nation, thereby stopping all trade between the countries, or may issue sanctions against the trade of specific products. The United States has long-term boycotts of trade with Cuba and Iran. The United States has come under some criticism for its demand for continued sanctions against Cuba and its threats of future sanctions against countries that violate human rights issues.[39]

History indicates that sanctions are almost always unsuccessful in reaching desired goals, particularly when other major nations' traders ignore them. This is the case with Cuba, North Korea, and Iran, where the undesirable behavior that the sanctions were imposed to change continues and the only ones who seem to be hurt are the people and companies that get caught in the middle. Moreover, the Chinese recently signed an agreement with Iran that will bring $70 billion of natural gas to China.[40] Please see Crossing Borders 6.2 for more on this issue.

Political and Social Activists and Nongovernmental Organizations

Although not usually officially sanctioned by the government, the impact of political and social activists (PSAs) can also interrupt the normal flow of trade. PSAs can range from those who seek to bring about peaceful change to those who resort to violence and terrorism to effect change. When well organized, the actions of PSAs can succeed.

One of the most effective and best-known PSA actions was against Nestlé and the sale of baby formula in Third World markets. The worldwide boycott of Nestlé products resulted in substantial changes in the company's marketing. More recently, activists of the Free Burma Campaign (FBC) have applied enough pressure to cause several U.S. garment companies to stop importing textiles from Burma (now known as Myanmar). Furthermore, activists on several U.S. college campuses boycotted Pepsi-Cola drinks and PepsiCo-owned Pizza Hut and Taco Bell stores, saying that the company contributes to abysmal human rights in Myanmar. The results of the boycott were serious enough that PepsiCo sold its stake in its joint venture in Myanmar and withdrew from that market. The concern was that potential losses in the United States outweighed potential profits in Myanmar. Holland's Heineken and Denmark's Carlsberg beer companies withdrew from Myanmar for similar reasons.

PSA groups such as Greenpeace and Consumers International have been successful in raising doubts about the safety of genetically modified (GM) food. Europeans' fears about "Frankenfood," as it is sometimes called, have spread throughout much of the world and persuaded some famine-ridden countries in Africa to reject GM grains. In some areas in Uganda an airborne fungus is decimating 80 percent of the banana plants. Bananas are a food staple there. Ugandans eat banana pancakes, banana mash, and banana bread. They season their beans with banana salt and they guzzle banana beer and sip banana gin.[41] Although a genetically modified plant has been developed that is immune to the leaf fungus, because of the fear of GM food, Uganda's legislature has not enacted laws that will permit bioengineered banana plants into the country.

The rather broad issue of globalization is the also the focus of many PSA groups. The demonstrations in Seattle during a WTO meeting and in Washington, DC, against the World Bank and the International Monetary Fund (IMF), along with similar demonstrations in other countries, reflect a growing concern about a global economy. Whether misguided, uninformed, or just "wackos," as they have been described, PSAs can be a potent force in rallying public opinion and are an important political force that should not be dismissed, as companies such as Nike, McDonald's, and Nestlé know.

The Internet has become an effective tool of PSAs to spread the word on whatever cause they sponsor.[42] During protest rallies against the U.S.–Iraq war, organizers were able to

---

[39]Andrew Meadows, "Legal Trade with Cuba Gains Favor," *Tampa Tribune,* February 28, 2003.

[40]Vivienne Walt, "Iran Looks East," *Fortune,* February 21, 2005, pp. 88–95.

[41]Roger Thurow, "As U.S., EU Clash on Biotech Crops, Africa Goes Hungry," *Wall Street Journal,* February 26, 2002, p. A1.

[42]Steve Stecklow, "How a Global Web of Activists Gives Coke Problems in India," *Wall Street Journal,* June 7, 2005, pp. A1, A6.

CROSSING **BORDERS** 6.2   Trade Does Not Work as a Stick, Only as a Carrot

It was 1807 when Thomas Jefferson came up with trade sanctions as an innovation in diplomacy. The donkeys he endeavored to persuade then were quite big and quite stubborn, England and France. The goal was to get these warring nations to leave American ships alone on the high seas. Lacking a competitive navy, our third president dreamed up the trade embargo—rather than using trade as a carrot he planned to withhold trade and use it as a stick. However, instead of changing French or English policies and behaviors, Jefferson's policy actually endangered New England traders. They complained:

> Our ships all in motion, once whiten'd the ocean;
> They sail'd and return'd with a Cargo;
> Now doom'd to decay, they are fallen a prey,
> To Jefferson, worms, and EMBARGO.

Jefferson's embargo fell apart in just fifteen months. Only the War of 1812 settled the problems with English aggression at sea.

Consider the track record of trade sanctions in the last century. In 1940 the United States told the Japanese to get out of China—the ensuing embargo of gasoline and scrap metal led directly to the Pearl Harbor attack. Since 1948 Arab countries have boycotted Israel. Given that countries trade most with their close neighbors, you have to wonder how much this lack of trade has promoted the continuing conflicts in the area. Israel is still there. In 1959 Fidel Castro took over Cuba, for forty-six years the United States has boycotted sugar and cigars, and Castro is still there. OPEC's 1973 oil flow slowdown was intended to get America to stop supporting Israel. However, the dollars still flow fast to Israel and now Egypt as well.

In 1979 the United States told the Soviets to get out of Afghanistan. They refused. America boycotted the Moscow Olympics and stopped selling them grain and technology. The Soviet response—they continued to kill Afghans (and, by the way, Soviet soldiers) for another ten years. Moreover, in 1984 they and their allies' athletes stayed away from the Olympics in Los Angeles. And the high-tech embargo didn't work anyway. A San Diego divi-sion of Caterpillar I had worked for in the mid-1970s lost millions of dollars in service contracts for Soviet natural gas pipelines. These revenues were lost permanently, because the Soviets taught themselves how to do the maintenance and overhauls. In 1989 I walked through a Moscow weapons research facility—they had every brand of computer then available in the West: IBMs, Apples, and the best from Taiwan and Japan, as well.

Perhaps the 1980s multilateral trade sanctions imposed on South Africa hastened apartheid's demise. But look how well the world's ten-year embargo of Iraq changed policy there. Using trade as a weapon killed kids while Saddam Hussein celebrated at $12 million birthday parties. Indeed, the best prescription for Middle East peace (and American taxpayers' wallets, by the way) is all sides dropping all embargoes.

The end of the last century witnessed great strides in the elimination of ill-conceived trade sanctions. Perhaps most important was the U.S. Senate's and President's approvals of permanently normalized trade relations (PNTR) with China. However, other important steps were the relaxation of some of the trade restrictions on Vietnam, North Korea, Iran, and Cuba. Indeed, as a result of President Clinton's diplomacy, North and South Koreans marched together at Sydney Olympics; Americans can now buy pistachio nuts and carpets from Tehran; and U.S. firms can sell medical supplies and services in Havana. Remarkable!

These same kinds of carrots need to be thrown in the direction of the other countries on America's blacklist—Myanmar (Burma), Angola, Libya, Sudan, and Syria. And be certain that the chorus of criticism regarding human rights, freedom of the press, and democracy should continue loud and clear. But instead of dropping bombs (or threatening to), we should be giving them computers and Internet connections. The cost of a cruise missile is about the same as 2,000 Apple computers! And, at the most fundamental level, coercion does not work. Exchange does.

Source: John L. Graham, "Trade Brings Peace," in Joseph Runzo and Nancy M. Martin (eds.), *War and Reconciliation* (Cambridge: Cambridge University Press, 2006).

coordinate protest demonstrations in 600 cities worldwide and to disseminate information easily. A Google search for "peace protest" during that time resulted in 788,000 entries, including news briefs, Web sites for peace organizations, online petitions for peace, where to show up with your placard, where to send your dollars, and how to write your member of Congress.[43]

---

[43]Mary Brown Malouf, "Web Unites Peace Rallies across Globe," *Salt Lake Tribune*, February 18, 2003.

CROSSING BORDERS 6.3

Curbing Child Labor—Boycotts, Rallies, and Demonstrations Get Attention, but Is There a Better Way?

The image from Pakistan is heartrending: Ten-year-old children bend over soccer balls, stitching seams for ten hours a day. Poor families in Brazil, Mexico, Zaire, India, and many other nations put their children to work. Look around your house. Chances are, Mexican children helped make some products found there. Wire harnesses that go into some Whirlpool, General Electric, and Amana refrigerators, as well as the ribbons used to wrap boxes of Godiva chocolates, come from these child factory workers.

These kids are doing the same work as the adults—working night shifts and even graveyard shifts. In Mexico from Matamoros to Tijuana, children, sometimes as young as 12, fill labor-intensive jobs. A bus that takes them to work is referred to as *"El Kinde"* because so many of its occupants look like they belong in kindergarten.

This isn't a scene from centuries past. According to the International Labor Organization,* there are an estimated 250 million children worldwide between the ages of 4 and 15 who, for one reason or another, are obliged to work. In many parts of the world, child labor is "still very much condoned or accepted, and is directly tied to the issue of poverty."

A study by UNICEF (www.unicef.org) across nine Latin American countries found that if a family were to lose the income from their 13- to 17-year-old children, they would face a drop in income of 10 percent to 20 percent. Their meager earnings help provide basic food and medicine for themselves and young siblings. As one official commented, "Child labor is not always exploitation, but in many cases a necessity."

The attempt to curb reported child exploitation by product boycott campaigns in developed countries falls short of attacking the root of the problem. Unfortunately, boycotts often lead to the relocation or closure of sweatshop-style factories; without the jobs, the children are forced to look for other ways of earning money—ways that can be just as, if not more, unsavory than the original factory work.

Something well-meaning Americans, college students, religious organizations, countries, and organizations such as the World Bank can do is to introduce and support programs that pay poor mothers to keep their teenage and younger sons and daughters in school and out of the labor force. Mexico, Brazil, and Honduras have established such programs. This type of program in Mexico, called Progresa, pays poor Mexican families a monetary stipend (close to what the children would earn if working) if schools certify that their children attend classes regularly. Most families earn about $100 a month from the program, and the increase has had a noticeable effect on their behavior.

It's not just a giveaway program: Children are required to attend school regularly and get routine, free medical checkups, and mothers must attend seminars on hygiene and nutrition. The family's Progresa payments are suspended if a student misses more than 15 percent of classes.

This pioneering Mexican approach appears to be highly successful. An evaluation shows that after only a couple of years, Progresa significantly raised the schooling of children in very poor Mexican families. It has also narrowed the education gap between girls and boys and reduced the labor force participation of boys. A similar program in Brazil has helped boost secondary school enrollment by more than 50 percent in just five years.

*Visit www.ilo.org and search "child labor" for more details.

Sources: Gary S. Becker, "Bribe Third World Parents to Keep Their Kids in School," *BusinessWeek*, November 22, 1999; Nancy San Martin, "Overworked and Underage: Maquiladoras Say Hiring Minors against Policy but Hard to Halt," *Dallas Morning News*, March 5, 2000; Geri Smith, "Mexico: A Powerful Incentive to Keep Kids in School," *BusinessWeek*, May 1, 2000; and Virginia Postrel, "The Reasons Children Work," *New York Times*, July 15, 2005, p. 15.

Often associated with political activism, nongovernmental organizations (NGOs) are increasingly affecting policy decisions made by governments.[44] Many are involved in peaceful protests, lobbying, and even collaborations with governmental organizations. Many also are involved in mitigating much of the human misery plaguing parts of the planet. Some NGOs have received global recognition—the Red Cross and Red Crescent, Amnesty

---

[44]Hildy Teegen, Jonathan P. Doh, and Sushil Vachani, "The Importance of Non-Governmental Organizations (NGOs) in Global Governance and Value Creation: An International Business Research Agenda," *Journal of International Business Studies* 35, no. 6 (2004), pp. 463–483.

Exhibit 6.3
U.S. State Department
Travel Warnings (in order
of date of posting, most
recent first)

Source: http://travel.state.gov/
travel/, 2005

Uzbekistan	Nigeria	Zimbabwe
Kenya	Saudi Arabia	Liberia
Iran	Indonesia	Ivory Coast
Iraq	Yemen	Algeria
Congo-Kinshasa	Colombia	Libya
Nepal	Lebanon	Bosnia-Herzegovina
Israel, the West Bank,	Central African Republic	Sudan
and Gaza	Pakistan	Burundi
Afghanistan	Kyrgyzstan	Somalia
Haiti	Philippines	

International, Oxfam, UNICEF, Care, and Habitat for Humanity are examples—for their good works, political influence, and even their brand power.[45]

Violence and Terrorism

Although not usually government initiated, violence is another related risk for multinational companies to consider in assessing the political vulnerability of their activities. The State Department reported 3,200 terrorist incidents worldwide in 2004, up dramatically from previous years given a new approach to counting.[46] Terrorism has many different goals. Multinationals are targeted to embarrass a government and its relationship with firms, to generate funds by kidnapping executives to finance terrorist goals, to use as pawns in political or social disputes not specifically directed at them, and to inflict terror within a country as did September 11.

September 11 has raised the cost of doing business domestically and internationally. The dominance of the United States in world affairs exposes U.S. businesses to a multitude of uncertainties, from the growing danger of political violence to investment risks in emerging markets.[47] In the past 30 years, 80 percent of terrorist attacks against the United States have been aimed at American businesses. Since September 11, McDonald's, Kentucky Fried Chicken, and Pizza Hut combined have been bombed in more than 10 countries, including Turkey, Saudi Arabia, Russia, Lebanon, and China; most attacks have been linked with militant Islamic groups. There are reasons to expect that businesses will become increasingly attractive to terrorists, both because they are less well defended than government targets and because of what they symbolize. Based on the threats of terrorism and other violence the U.S. State Department posts travel warnings on its Web site (see Exhibit 6.3 for a recent listing). However, many international travelers appear to regularly ignore those warnings.[48]

Cyberterrorism and Cybercrime

New on the horizon is the growing potential for cyberterrorism and cybercrime.[49] Although in its infancy, the Internet is a vehicle for terrorist and criminal attacks by foreign and domestic antagonists wishing to inflict damage on a company with little chance of being caught. One problem in tracing cyberterrorists and criminals is that it is hard to determine if a cyber attack has been launched by a rogue state, a terrorist, or by a hacker as a prank. The "I Love You" worm, which caused an estimated $25 billion in damage, was probably just an out-of-control prank. However, the Melissa virus and the denial of service (DoS) attacks that overloaded the Web sites of CNN, ZDNet, Yahoo!, and Amazon.com with a flood of electronic messages that crippled them for hours were considered to be purposeful attacks on specific targets.

Each wave of viruses gets more damaging and spreads so rapidly that considerable harm is done before it can be stopped. The "Slammer,"[50] for example, brought Internet service to

[45]See the excellent book by John A. Quelch and Nathalie Laidler-Kylander, *The New Global Brands: Managing Non-Governmental Organizations in the 21st Century* (Mason, OH: South-Western, 2006).

[46]Tim Reid, "The 28,000 Victims of Terrorism," *The Times of London*, July 7, 2005, p. 36.

[47]"Doing Business in a Dangerous World," *Harvard Business Review*, April 2002.

[48]"Who Do We Trust?" *Conde Nast Traveler*, March 2005, pp. 53–62.

[49]Jay Solomon, "India Firms Step Up Data Security," *Wall Street Journal*, November 4, 2004, p. B6.

[50]"Internet Worm Hits Companies Globally," *Wall Street Journal*, January 27, 2003, p. B4.

a crawl. It doubled its numbers every 8.5 seconds during the first minute of its attack and infected more than 75,000 hosts within 10 minutes.[51] After infecting hundreds of thousands of computers in Europe and North America the "Goner worm" traveled to Australia overnight and brought down government agencies, financial and manufacturing sites, and at least 25 MNCs. This virus arrives in an e-mail message with an invitation to download a screen saver; it then infects the computer and sends the virus to everyone in the computer's address list. Whether perpetrated by pranksters or hackers out to do harm, these incidents show that tools for cyberterrorism can be developed to do considerable damage to a company, an entire industry, or a country's infrastructure.

Because of mounting concern over the rash of attacks, business leaders and government officials addressed a Group of Eight[52] conference convened to discuss cybercrime, expressing an urgent need for cooperation among governments, industry, and users to combat the growing menace of cybercrime. As the Internet grows, "it's only a matter of time before every terrorist, anarchist, thief, and prankster with a PC and a phone line will be waging a virtual war and inflicting real harm." The Internet is a potent tool for cybercrime, and, unless systems are designed to safeguard it against these intrusions, the costs to governments and industry will be enormous and may prevent the Internet from reaching its full potential.[53]

Assessing Political Vulnerability

There are at least as many reasons for a company's political vulnerability as there are political philosophies, economic variations, and cultural differences. Some companies appear to be more politically vulnerable than others, in that they receive special government attention. Depending on the desirability of a company, this special attention may result in positive actions toward the company or in negative attention.

Unfortunately, a marketer has no absolute guidelines to follow to determine whether a company and its products will be subject to political attention. Countries seeking investments in high-priority industries may well excuse companies from taxes, customs duties, quotas, exchange controls, and other impediments to investment. In a bid to attract foreign investment and increase exports, India announced a new trade policy that eases restraints and offers tax breaks for companies developing and maintaining infrastructure. Conversely, firms either marketing products not considered high priority or that fall from favor for some other reason often face unpredictable government restrictions.

As a case in point, Continental Can Company's joint venture to manufacture cans for the Chinese market faced a barrage of restrictions when the Chinese economy weakened. China decreed that canned beverages were wasteful and must be banned from all state functions and banquets. Tariffs on aluminum and other materials imported for producing cans were doubled and a new tax was imposed on canned-drink consumption. For Continental Can, an investment that had the potential for profit after a few years was rendered profitless by a change in the attitude of the Chinese government.

Politically Sensitive Products and Issues

Although there are no specific guidelines to determine a product's vulnerability at any point, there are some generalizations that help to identify the tendency for products to be politically sensitive. Products that have or are perceived to have an effect on the environment, exchange rates, national and economic security, and the welfare of people (and particularly children—recall the story of Barbie in Saudi Arabia from the previous chapter), and that are publicly visible or subject to public debate, are more likely to be politically sensitive.

Fast-food restaurants, which are intended to be visible, have often been lightning rods for groups opposed to foreign companies. Health authorities closed a Kentucky Fried

---

[51]For more information, see www.silicondefense.com.

[52] The Group of Eight consists of government representatives from Britain, Canada, France, Germany, Italy, Japan, Russia, and the United States who convene periodically to examine issues that affect the group.

[53]For a report on security steps that need to be taken to protect the government and business, see *Challenges for Selected Agencies and Industry Sectors* (Washington, DC: Government Accounting Office, February 28, 2003).

Activists of the Bharatiya Janata Party wearing "evil" masks shout antigovernment slogans near the Union Carbide plant in the central Indian city of Bhopal on the eve of World Environment Day, June 4, 2003. The activists protested to draw the attention of the government to chemical wastage and demanded the cleanup of hazardous waste in the area. The leak from the Union Carbide pesticide plant in 1984 was one of the world's worst industrial accidents, killing 3,000 people and leaving thousands of others with lifetime illnesses. (© *Reuters NewMedia Inc./CORBIS*)

Chicken (KFC) restaurant for health reasons (two flies were seen in the kitchen) after months of protesters arguing that foreign investment should be limited to high technology. "India does not need foreign investment in junk-food," said the leader of a protesting farmers' group. The store was later reopened by court order.

Health is often the subject of public debate, and products that affect or are affected by health issues can be sensitive to political concern. The European Union has banned hormone-treated beef for more than a decade. There is a question about whether the ban is a valid health issue or just protection for the European beef industry. The World Trade Organization concluded in 1989 that the ban had no scientific basis; nevertheless, Europe has yet to lift the ban. Reluctance to respond to the WTO directive may be the result of the recent outcry against genetically modified (GM) foods that has, for all practical purposes, caused GM foods to be banned in Europe. Public opinion against Frankenfood has been so strong that Unilever announced that it would stop using GM ingredients in all its products in Britain. Additionally, 11 leading restaurant chains, including McDonald's, Pizza Hut, Wimpy, and Burger King, have gone GM-free. The issue in the United States has not risen to the same level of concern as in Europe; to forestall such adverse public opinion, many U.S. companies are slowing the introduction of GM foods. Fearing a strong public reaction as in Europe, McDonald's has decided to stop using genetically modified potatoes for its french fries in its U.S stores.

Forecasting Political Risk

In addition to qualitative measures of political vulnerability, a number of firms are employing systematic methods of measuring political risk.[54] Political risk assessment is an attempt to forecast political instability to help management identify and evaluate political events and their potential influence on current and future international business decisions. Perhaps the greatest risk to international marketers is the threat of the government actually failing, causing chaos in the streets and markets. *Foreign Policy* magazine uses 12 criteria to rank countries on their "Failed States Index."[55] The list of criteria includes demographic pressures, human flight, uneven development, and the like. (See Exhibit 6.4.)

Risk assessment is used to estimate the level of risk a company is assuming when making an investment and to help determine the amount of risk it is prepared to accept. In the former Soviet Union and in China, the risk may be too high for some companies, but stronger and better-financed companies can make long-term investments in those countries that will be profitable in the future. Additionally, one study found that compared to American and Japanese managers, French managers' market entry decisions appear to be

---

[54]See www.prsgroup.com for a wealth of information on political risk assessments.

[55]"The Failed States Index," *Foreign Policy*, July/August 2005, pp. 56–65.

Exhibit 6.4
Top 20 States in Danger of Failing (Ranked)

Source: From *Foreign Policy*, "Failed States Index," July/August 2005, pp. 56–65. Copyright 2005 by Foreign Policy. Reproduced with permission of Foreign Policy via Copyright Clearance Center.

Ivory Coast	Yemen	Guinea
Democratic Republic of Congo	Liberia	Bangladesh
	Haiti	Burundi
Sudan	Afghanistan	Dominican Republic
Iraq	Rwanda	Central African Republic
Somalia	North Korea	
Sierra Leone	Colombia	
Chad	Zimbabwe	

CROSSING BORDERS 6.4 | When States Fail: Dodging the Bullet in Former Yugoslavia

One pundit suggested that nations with McDonald's don't attack one another. Perhaps Yugoslavia was the exception that proves the rule?

During most of the 78-day air war against Yugoslavia in 1999, McDonald's kept the burgers flipping while NATO kept the bombs dropping. After only one night of air strikes, mobs of youths, whipped to patriotic fervor by the state-controlled media's attacks on the "NATO criminals and aggressors," targeted six McDonald's stores, smashing windows and scribbling insults on doors and walls. McDonald's Corporation was forced to temporarily close its 15 restaurants in Yugoslavia. Weeks later, when local managers flung the doors open again, they accomplished an extraordinary comeback using an unusual marketing strategy: They put McDonald's U.S. citizenship on the back burner.

Within a week after the attacks, they had launched a campaign to identify the plight of ordinary Serbs with the Mac. "McDonald's is sharing the destiny of all people here," read a sign at one branch. A key aspect of the campaign was to present McDonald's as a Yugoslav company. Restaurants promoted the McCountry, a domestic pork burger with paprika garnish, and lowered its price. Pork is considered the most Serbian of meats.

In a national flourish to evoke Serbian identity and pride, McDonald's produced posters and lapel buttons showing the golden arches topped with a traditional Serbian cap called the *sajkaca* (pronounced shy-KACH-a). The managing director said McDonald's needed to get Serbs to view the company as their own. He masterminded the campaign to "Serbify" McDonald's. It was in this vein that he and his team decided to redesign the logo with the Serbian cap cocked at a haughty angle over one arch. Traditional national emblems, like the *sajkaca*, a strong, unique Serbian symbol, had undergone a revival in recent years with the rise of Serbian nationalism. "By adding this symbol of our cultural heritage, we hoped to denote our pride in being a local company."

Additionally, more than 3,000 free burgers were delivered to the participants of the Belgrade marathon, which was dominated by an anti-NATO theme. At the same time, the company announced that for every burger sold it would donate one dinar (about a nickel) to the Yugoslav Red Cross to help victims of NATO's air strikes. They also handed out free cheeseburgers at anti-NATO rallies.

Once the war was over, the company basked in its success. Cash registers were ringing at prewar levels. McDonald's restaurants around the country were thronged with Serbs hungry for Big Macs and fries. And why not, asks 16-year-old Jovan Stojanovic, munching on a burger. "I don't associate McDonald's with America," he says. "Mac is ours." This is music to McDonald's ears. "We managed to save our brand."

That was no easy task. McDonald's is a global symbol of Western pop culture, Yankee know-how, and American corporate cunning; such prominence on the world stage can be a lightning rod for trouble. "We have been in Yugoslavia for years, during which time we sponsored schools, sports clubs and children's hospitals," the managing director says. "We're part of the community. The Belgrade McDonald's, the first in Central Europe, quickly became a source of local pride. At soccer matches in the old Yugoslavia, when teams from Belgrade met opponents from Zagreb, the Croatian capital, Belgrade fans would taunt their rivals with chants of 'We have McDonald's and you don't!'"

The real success of the campaign can best be illustrated by customer comments when the restaurant reopened and unveiled its new approach. "We are so happy to see the campaign to help people hurt by the war. It's very humane and the only way to justify the business of an American restaurant in Yugoslavia." Another wrote: "McDonald's is the only American who wished to become a Serb."

Source: Robert Block, "How Big Mac Kept from Becoming a Serb Archenemy," *Wall Street Journal*, September 3, 1999; John Kozak, "McDonald's Can't Serve Up World Peace," *The Guardian*, April 26, 2005, p. 27.

more influenced by concerns about political risk in foreign markets.[56] Early risk is accepted in exchange for being in the country when the economy begins to grow and risk subsides.

During the chaos that arose after the political and economic changes in the Soviet Union, the newly formed republics were eager to make deals with foreign investors, yet the problems and uncertainty made many investors take a wait-and-see attitude. However, as one executive commented, "If U.S. companies wait until all the problems are solved, somebody

---

[56]Jennifer D. Chandler and John L. Graham, "Using Formative Indicators to Discern the Meaning of Corruption and Its Impact on International Marketing," working paper, University of California, Irvine.

else will get the business." Certainly the many companies that are investing in the former Soviet Union or China do not expect big returns immediately; they are betting on the future. For a marketer doing business in a foreign country, a necessary part of any market analysis is an assessment of the probable political consequences of a marketing plan, since some marketing activities are more susceptible to political considerations than others.

Lessening Political Vulnerability
Even though a company cannot directly control or alter the political environment of the country within which it operates, a specific business venture can take measures to lessen its degree of susceptibility to politically induced risks.

Foreign investors frequently are accused of exploiting a country's wealth at the expense of the national population and for the sole benefit of the foreign investor. This attitude is best summed up in a statement made by a recent president of Peru: "We have had massive foreign investment for decades but Peru has not achieved development. Foreign capital will now have to meet government and social goals." Such charges are not wholly unsupported by past experiences.

As long as these impressions persist, the political climate for foreign investors will continue to be hostile. Companies must manage external affairs in foreign markets to ensure that the host government and the public are aware of their contributions to the economic, social, and human development of the country. Relations between governments and MNCs are generally positive if the investment (1) improves the balance of payments by increasing exports or reducing imports through import substitution; (2) uses locally produced resources; (3) transfers capital, technology, and/or skills; (4) creates jobs; and/or (5) makes tax contributions.

In addition to the economic contributions a company makes, corporate philanthropy also helps to create positive images among the general population. Many MNCs strive to benefit countries through their social programs, which polish their image as well. For example, Microsoft, recognizing that developing countries need sophisticated technical assistance, pledged more than $100 million in technology and training as part of a deal to put government services online in Mexico. Cisco Systems, the leading maker of Internet hardware, relies on nonprofit organizations to run its 10,000 networking academies, which train college and high school students to create computer networks in 150 countries. In China, Procter & Gamble is helping local schools and universities to train and educate leaders. And in Malaysia, Motorola and Intel have instituted training programs to enhance the skills of local workers.

Merck, the pharmaceutical company, has developed a pill to fight river blindness in Africa and Latin America. River blindness is a parasitic disease transmitted to humans through the bite of the black fly commonly found along the riverbanks in some African countries. The parasite infiltrates, multiplies, and spreads throughout the body for as long as 15 years, causing acute skin rashes, terrible itching, and sometimes disfigurement or blindness. The pill is taken just once a year and has been proven to prevent the disease. Merck contributed millions of doses to fight the disease in developing countries.[57]

Lever Brothers has a strong commitment to corporate social responsibility with a focus toward children. It sponsors the Missionaries of Charity in Chittagong, Bangladesh. Similarly, it has completely renovated the children's ward of a hospital. The company also sponsors the National Polio Day. Its Pepsodent brand plays a pivotal role in oral hygiene awareness through its Dental Health Week and School Education Program. Lifebuoy sponsors the Lifebuoy Friendship Hospital, a floating hospital aimed to provide healthcare facilities and health education to the poor.[58] Although these philanthropic gestures may be seen as "enlightened self-interest," any activity that improves the welfare of the population will ultimately create a stronger economy benefiting the country as well as the MNC.

Even though companies strive to become good corporate citizens in their host countries, political parties seeking publicity or scapegoats for their failures often serve their own interests by focusing public opinion on the negative aspects of MNCs, whether true or false. Companies that establish deep local roots and show by example, rather than meaningless talk, that their strategies are aligned with the long-term goals of the host country stand the best chance of

---

[57]David Shook, "Merck Is Treating the Third World," *BusinessWeek Online,* October 10, 2002.

[58]"Company Profile: Lever Brothers," *The Independent* (London), June 3, 2002.

The most entertaining protest technique was pioneered by French farmers. Perhaps they were inspired by that American export *Animal House.* In any case, French farmers like to throw their food. Here they tossed tomatoes and such at McDonald's; they've also lobbed lamb chops at their own trade ministers. Apparently they pay attention in Taiwan. Most recently, fishermen pitched perch in Taipei to protest the Japanese fishing fleet's presence in their waters. *(AP/Wide World Photos; AP/Wide World Photos)*

overcoming a less than positive image. "In times like these," says one executive, "global citizenship is perhaps more important than ever." [59] An effective defense for the multinational company is to actively participate in improving the lives of local citizens.

In addition to corporate activities focused on the social and economic goals of the host country and good corporate citizenship, MNCs can use other strategies to minimize political vulnerability and risk.

Joint Ventures

Typically less susceptible to political harassment, joint ventures can be with locals or other third-country multinational companies; in both cases, a company's financial exposure is limited. A joint venture with locals helps minimize anti-MNC feelings, and a joint venture with another MNC adds the additional bargaining power of a third country.

Expanding the Investment Base

Including several investors and banks in financing an investment in the host country is another strategy. This has the advantage of engaging the power of the banks whenever any kind of government takeover or harassment is threatened. This strategy becomes especially powerful if the banks have made loans to the host country; if the government threatens expropriation or other types of takeover, the financing bank has substantial power with the government.

Licensing

A strategy that some firms find that eliminates almost all risks is to license technology for a fee. Licensing can be effective in situations where the technology is unique and the risk is high. Of course, there is some risk assumed because the licensee can refuse to pay the required fees while continuing to use the technology.

Planned Domestication

In those cases where a host country is demanding local participation, the most effective long-range solution is planned phasing out, that is, planned domestication. This is not the preferred business practice, but the alternative of government-initiated domestication can be as disastrous as confiscation. As a reasonable response to the potential of domestication, planned domestication can be profitable and operationally expedient for the foreign investor. Planned domestication is, in essence, a gradual process of participating with nationals in all phases of company operations.

---

[59]Susan E. Reed, "Business; Technology Companies Take Hope in Charity," *New York Times,* March 23, 2003, p. 17.

Political Bargaining   Multinational companies clearly engage in lobbying and other sorts of political bargaining to avoid potential political risks.[60] Indeed, Toyota has considered raising prices of its cars in the American market to "help" its ailing American competitors.[61] The Japanese government has set quotas on auto exports in the past as American car companies have struggled. And, in the face of growing American and European criticism, China has agreed to put quotas on its exports of textiles[62] and to float its currency.[63]

Political Payoffs   One approach to dealing with political vulnerability is the political payoff—an attempt to lessen political risks by paying those in power to intervene on behalf of the multinational company. This is not an approach we recommend in any way. However, your competitors may use such a tactic, so beware. Political payoffs, or bribery, have been used to lessen the negative effects of a variety of problems. Paying heads of state to avoid confiscatory taxes or expulsion, paying fees to agents to ensure the acceptance of sales contracts, and providing monetary encouragement to an assortment of people whose actions can affect the effectiveness of a company's programs are decisions that frequently confront multinational managers and raise ethical questions.

Bribery poses problems for the marketer at home and abroad since it is illegal for U.S. citizens to pay a bribe even if it is a common practice in the host country. Political payoffs may offer short-term benefits, but in the long run the risks are high and bribery is an untenable option. This issue is discussed in more detail in Chapter 7.

Government Encouragement

Governments, both foreign and U.S., encourage foreign investment as well as discourage it. In fact, within the same country some foreign businesses may fall prey to politically induced harassment while others may be placed under a government umbrella of protection and preferential treatment. The difference lies in the evaluation of a company's contribution to the nation's interest.

The most important reason to encourage foreign investment is to accelerate the development of an economy. An increasing number of countries are encouraging foreign investment with specific guidelines aimed toward economic goals. Multinational corporations may be expected to create local employment, transfer technology, generate export sales, stimulate growth and development of local industry, conserve foreign exchange, or meet a combination of these expectations as a requirement for market concessions. Recent investments in China, India, and the former republics of the Soviet Union include provisions stipulating specific contributions to economic goals of the country that must be made by foreign investors.

The U.S. government is motivated for economic as well as political reasons to encourage American firms to seek business opportunities in countries worldwide, including those that are politically risky. It seeks to create a favorable climate for overseas business by providing the assistance that helps minimize some of the more troublesome politically motivated financial risks of doing business abroad. The Department of Commerce (DOC) at www.doc.gov is the principal agency that supports U.S. business abroad. The International Trade Administration (ITA) at www.ita.gov, a bureau in the DOC, is dedicated to helping U.S. business compete in the global marketplace. Other agencies that provide assistance to U.S. companies include:

- Export-Import Bank (Ex-Im Bank) underwrites trade and investments for U.S. firms. www.exim.gov

- Foreign Credit Insurance Association (FCIA), an agency of the Ex-Im Bank, provides credit insurance that minimizes nonpayment risk caused by financial,

[60]Amy J. Hillman and William P. Wan, "The Determinants of MNE Subsidiaries' Political Strategies: Evidence of Institutional Duality," *Journal of International Business Studies* 36, no. 3 (2005), pp. 322–340.

[61]"Toyota May Raise Prices to Avoid Backlash," *Associated Press*, April 26, 2005.

[62]"China to Put Quotas on Textile Exports," *Reuters*, June 22, 2005.

[63]Don Lee and Ching-Ching Ni, "China Revalues Currency in Action Sought by U.S.," *Los Angeles Times*, July 22, 2005, pp. A1, A4.

economic, or political uncertainties. It includes insurance against confiscation, civil disturbances, and the cancellation or restriction of export or import licenses. www.fcia.com

- The Agency for International Development (AID) provides aid to underdeveloped countries and has limited protection in support of "essential" projects in approved countries and for approved products. www.usaid.gov
- The Overseas Private Investment Corporation (OPIC) provides risk insurance for companies investing in less-developed countries. www.opic.gov

Summary

Vital to every marketer's assessment of a foreign market is an appreciation for the political environment of the country within which he or she plans to operate. Government involvement in business activities abroad, especially foreign-controlled business, is generally much greater than business is accustomed to in the United States. The foreign firm must strive to make its activities politically acceptable or it may be subjected to a variety of politically condoned harassment. In addition to the harassment that can be imposed by a government, the foreign marketer frequently faces the problem of uncertainty of continuity in government policy. As

governments change political philosophies, a marketing firm accepted under one administration might find its activities undesirable under another. An unfamiliar or hostile political environment does not necessarily preclude success for a foreign marketer if the company becomes a local economic asset and responds creatively to the issues raised by political and social activists. The U.S. government may aid American business in its foreign operations, and if a company is considered vital to achieving national economic goals, the host country often provides an umbrella of protection not extended to others.

Questions

1. Define the following terms:
   sovereignty p.158
   nationalism
   expropriation
   NGOs
   confiscation
   domestication
   PSAs

2. Why would a country rather domesticate than expropriate?

3. "A crucial fact when doing business in a foreign country is that permission to conduct business is controlled by the government of the host country." Comment.

4. What are the main factors to consider in assessing the dominant political climate within a country?

5. Why is a working knowledge of political party philosophy so important in a political assessment of a market? Discuss.

6. How can a change in the political party in power affect an investor? Discuss and give examples.

7. What are the most common causes of instability in governments? Discuss.

8. Discuss how governmental instability can affect marketing.

9. What are the most frequently encountered political risks in foreign business? Discuss.

10. Expropriation is considered a major risk of foreign business. Discuss ways in which this particular type of risk can be minimized somewhat as a result of company activities. Explain how these risks have been minimized by the activities of the U.S. government.

11. How do exchange controls impede foreign business? Discuss.

12. How do foreign governments encourage foreign investment? Discuss.

13. How does the U.S. government encourage foreign investment?

14. What are the motives behind U.S. government encouragement for foreign investment? Explain.

15. Discuss measures a company might take to lessen its political vulnerability.

16. Select a country and analyze it politically from a marketing viewpoint.

17. The text suggests that violence is a politically motivated risk of international business. Comment.

18. There is evidence that expropriation and confiscation are less frequently encountered today than just a few years ago. Why? What other types of political risks have replaced expropriation and confiscation in importance?

19. You are an executive in a large domestic company with only minor interests in international markets; however, corporate plans call for major global expansion. Visit the home page of Control Risks Group (CRG) at www.crg.com. After thoroughly familiarizing yourself with the services offered by CRG, write a brief report to management describing how its services could possibly help with your global expansion.

20. Visit the Web site www.politicalresources.net/ and select the Political Site of the Week. Write a brief political analysis highlighting potential problem areas for a company interested in investing in that country.

21. Search the Web for information on the activities of PSAs outside the United States and write a briefing paper for international management on potential problems.

22. Discuss ways the companies discussed in the Global Perspective could have minimized their losses in the banana wars.

23. Discuss any ethical and socially responsible issues that may be implied in the Global Perspective.

7

The International Legal Environment

PLAYING BY THE RULES

CHAPTER OUTLINE

Global Perspective: The Pajama Caper

Bases for Legal Systems

> Common and Code Law
> Islamic Law
> Marxist-Socialist Tenets

Jurisdiction in International Legal Disputes

International Dispute Resolution

> Conciliation
> Arbitration
> Litigation

Protection of Intellectual Property Rights:
   A Special Problem

> Counterfeiting and Piracy
> Inadequate Protection
> Prior Use versus Registration
> International Conventions

Commercial Law within Countries

> Marketing Laws
> Green Marketing Legislation
> Antitrust

U.S. Laws Apply in Host Countries

> Foreign Corrupt Practices Act
> National Security Laws
> Antitrust Laws
> Antiboycott Law
> Extraterritoriality of U.S. Laws

Cyberlaw: Unresolved Issues

> Domain Names and Cybersquatters
> Taxes
> Jurisdiction of Disputes and Validity of Contracts

CHAPTER LEARNING OBJECTIVES

What you should learn from Chapter 7:

- The four heritages of today's legal systems

- The important factors in jurisdiction of legal disputes

- Issues associated with jurisdiction of legal disputes and the various methods of dispute resolution

- The unique problems of protecting intellectual property rights internationally

- How to protect against piracy and counterfeiting

- The legal differences between countries and how the differences can affect international marketing plans

- The different ways U.S. laws can be applied to U.S. companies operating outside the United States

- The many issues of evolving cyberlaw

Global Perspective

THE PAJAMA CAPER

Six headlines illustrate the entanglements possible when U.S. law, host-country law, and a multinational company collide:

- "Wal-Mart's Cuban-Made Pajamas Defy Embargo"
- "Wal-Mart Ignites Row by Pulling Cuban Pajamas off Shelves in Canada"
- "Canada, U.S. Wager Diplomatic Capital in a High-Stakes Pajama Game"
- "Cuban Quandary: Wal-Mart in Hot Water for Yanking Pajamas"
- "Canada Probes Wal-Mart Move against Cuban Pajamas"
- "Wal-Mart Puts Cuban Goods Back on Sale"

The controversy arose over a U.S. embargo forbidding U.S. businesses to trade with Cuba, and concerned whether or not the embargo could be enforced in Canada. Wal-Mart was selling Cuban-made pajamas in Canada. When Wal-Mart officials in the United States became aware of the origin of manufacture, they issued an order to remove all the offending pajamas because it is against U.S. law (the Helms-Burton Act) for a U.S. company or any of its foreign subsidiaries to trade with Cuba. Canada was incensed at the intrusion of U.S. law on Canadian citizens. The Canadians felt they should have the choice of buying Cuban-made pajamas.

Wal-Mart was thus caught in the middle of conflicting laws in Canada and the United States and a Canada–U.S. foreign policy feud over the extraterritoriality of U.S. law. Wal-Mart Canada would be breaking U.S. law if it continued to sell the pajamas, and it would be subject to a million-dollar fine and possible imprisonment of its managers. However, if the company pulled the pajamas out of Canadian stores as the home office ordered, it would be subject to a $1.2 million fine under Canadian law. After discussion with Canadian authorities, Wal-Mart resumed selling the pajamas. Canada was upset with the United States for attempting to impose its laws on Canadian companies (Wal-Mart Canada is a subsidiary of Wal-Mart U.S.), while the United States says that Wal-Mart was violating its laws in not abiding by the boycott with Cuba. The situation illustrates the reality of the legal environment and international marketing—companies are subject to both home-country laws and host-country laws when doing business in another country. The federal government finally settled with Wal-Mart in 2003 and the pajama caper was finally closed.

Sources: *Boston Globe*, March 3, 1997; *St. Louis Post-Dispatch*, March 9, 1997; *Washington Post*, March 14, 1997, p. A6; *Wall Street Journal*, March 14, 1997, p. B4; John W. Boscariol, "An Anatomy of a Cuban Pyjama Crisis," *Law and Policy in International Business*, Spring 1999, p. 439; Verne Kopytoff, "U.S. Firms Face Fines/Violations of Trade Sanctions Alleged," *San Francisco Chronicle*, April 18, 2003.

How would you like to play a game where the stakes were high, there was no standard set of rules to play by, the rules changed whenever a new player entered the game, and, when a dispute arose, the referee used the other players' rules to interpret who was right? This fairly well describes the international legal environment. Because no single, uniform international commercial law governing foreign business transactions exists, the international marketer must pay particular attention to the laws of each country within which it operates.[1] An American company doing business with a French customer has to contend with two jurisdictions (United States and France), two tax systems, two legal systems, and a third supranational set of European Union laws and regulations that may override French commercial law. The situation is similar when doing business in Japan, Germany, or any other country. Laws governing business activities within and between countries are an integral part of the legal environment of international business.

The legal systems of different countries are so disparate and complex that it is beyond the scope of this text to explore the laws of each country individually. There are, however, issues common to most international marketing transactions that need special attention when operating abroad. Jurisdiction, dispute resolution, intellectual property, the extraterritoriality of U.S. laws, cyberlaw, and associated problems are discussed in this chapter to provide a broad view of the international legal environment. Although space and focus limit an in-depth presentation, the material presented should be sufficient for the reader to conclude that securing expert legal advice is a wise decision when doing business in another country. The foundation of a legal system profoundly affects how the law is written, interpreted, and adjudicated. The place to begin is with a discussion of the different legal systems.

Bases for Legal Systems

Four heritages form the bases for the majority of the legal systems of the world: (1) common law, derived from English law and found in England, the United States, Canada,[2] and other countries once under English influence; (2) civil or code law, derived from Roman law and found in Germany, Japan, France, and in non-Islamic and non-Marxist countries; (3) Islamic law, derived from the interpretation of the Koran and found in Pakistan, Iran, Saudi Arabia,[3] and other Islamic states; and (4) a commercial legal system in the Marxist-socialist economies of Russia and the republics of the former Soviet Union, Eastern Europe, China, and other Marxist-socialist states whose legal system centered on the economic, political, and social policies of the state. As each country moves toward its own version of a free market system and enters the global market, a commercial legal system is also evolving from those Marxist-socialist tenets. China has announced that it will adopt a constitution-based socialist legal system with Chinese characteristics.[4]

The differences among these four systems are of more than theoretical importance because due process of law may vary considerably among and within these legal systems. Even though a country's laws may be based on the doctrine of one of the four legal systems, its individual interpretation may vary significantly—from a fundamentalist interpretation of Islamic law as found in Pakistan to a combination of several legal systems found in the United States, where both common and code law are reflected in the legal system.

One measure of the importance of the legal system in each country is the number of attorneys per capita. Please see Exhibit 7.1. Judging by that metric the legal system is called upon to settle commercial disputes much more frequently in the United States than in China. As Japan continues to become more integrated in the global market the need for attorneys is burgeoning. There are approximately 23,000 attorneys there now and the Japanese government intends to grow that number to 50,000 by 2018.[5]

---

[1]Der Hovanesian, "Scrambling to Save Face in Japan," *BusinessWeek*, February 14, 2005, p. 74.

[2]All the provinces of Canada have a common-law system with the exception of Quebec, which is a code-law province. All the states in the United States are common law except Louisiana, which is code law.

[3]Donna Abu-Nasr, "The Saudi's Strict Ways," *Oregonian*, April 23, 2004, p. A10.

[4]"Legal System with Chinese Characteristics Taking Form," *Xinhua News Agency*, March 10, 2003.

[5]Ichiko Fuyuno, "Japan Grooms New Lawyers," *Wall Street Journal*, April 13, 2004, pp. A18, A19.

Exhibit 7.1
Lawyers per 100,000 People in Selected Countries

Sources: Council of Bars and Law Societies of Europe (www.ccbe.org), 2005; Ichiko Fuyuno, "Japan Grooms New Lawyers," *Wall Street Journal*, March 13, 2004, pp. A18, A19; Qin Jize, "Lawyers Playing a Bigger Role," *China Daily*, June 17, 2005.

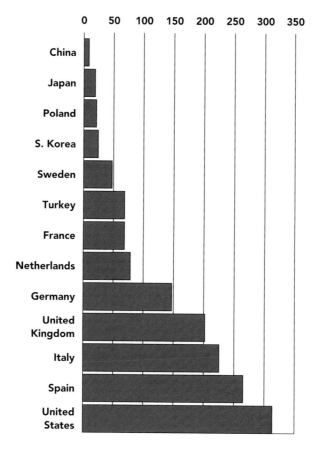

Common and Code Law

The basis for *common law*[6] is tradition, past practices, and legal precedents set by the courts through interpretations of statutes, legal legislation, and past rulings. Common law seeks "interpretation through the past decisions of higher courts which interpret the same statutes or apply established and customary principles of law to a similar set of facts." *Code law*,[7] on the other hand, is based on an all-inclusive system of written rules (codes) of law. Under code law, the legal system is generally divided into three separate codes: commercial, civil, and criminal.

Common law is recognized as not being all-inclusive, whereas code law is considered complete as a result of catchall provisions found in most code-law systems. For example, under the commercial code in a code-law country, the law governing contracts is made inclusive with the statement that "a person performing a contract shall do so in conformity with good faith as determined by custom and good morals." Although code law is considered all-inclusive, it is apparent from the foregoing statement that some broad interpretations are possible in order to include everything under the existing code.

Steps are being taken in common-law countries to codify commercial law even though the primary basis of commercial law is common law, that is, precedents set by court decisions. An example of the new uniformity is the acceptance of the Uniform Commercial Code by most states in the United States. Even though U.S. commercial law has been codified to some extent under the Uniform Commercial Code, the philosophy of interpretation is anchored in common law.

As discussed later in the section on protection of intellectual property, laws governing intellectual property offer the most striking differences between common-law and code-law

---

[6]Also known as English law.

[7]Also known as the Napoleonic Code.

CROSSING BORDERS 7.1 — Patent Law: The United States versus Japan—Differences in Culture Do Matter

The goal of Western patent systems is to protect and reward individual entrepreneurs and innovative businesses, to encourage invention, and to advance practical knowledge. The intent of the Japanese patent system is to share technology, not to protect it. In fact, it serves a larger, national goal: the rapid spread of technological know-how among competitors in a manner that avoids litigation, encourages broad-scale cooperation, and promotes Japanese industry as a whole. Even Japan's legal system is tilted against the inventor. Although Japanese patent law requires firms to compensate employees for their megabuck ideas, it doesn't specify how much. There's nothing to stop a company from giving a researcher only a few hundred dollars for a major invention.

This approach is entirely consistent with the broader characteristics of Japanese culture, which emphasizes harmony, cooperation, and hierarchy. It favors large companies over small ones, discourages Japanese entrepreneurship, and puts foreign companies that do not appreciate the true nature of the system at a substantial disadvantage. The following table compares patent laws in the United States and Japan.

United States	Japan
Operates under "first to invent" rule	Operates under "first to register" rule
Protects individual inventors	Promotes technology sharing
Patent applications secret	Patent applications public
Patents granted in up to 24 months	Patents granted in four to six years
Patents valid for 17 years from date issued	Patents valid 20 years from application

Sources: Yoshitaka Sonoda, "Constant Change to IP Laws Feeds Uncertainty," *Managing Intellectual Property*, September 2002, p. 72; "Matsushita, LG Settle Patent Dispute over Plasma Display Panels," *Associated Press*, April 4, 2005.

systems. Under common law, ownership is established by use; under code law, ownership is determined by registration. In some code-law countries, certain agreements may not be enforceable unless properly notarized or registered; in a common-law country, the same agreement may be binding so long as proof of the agreement can be established. Although every country has elements of both common and code law, the differences in interpretation between common- and code-law systems regarding contracts, sales agreements, and other legal issues are significant enough that an international marketer familiar with only one system must enlist the aid of legal counsel for the most basic legal questions.

Another illustration of where fundamental differences in the two systems can cause difficulty is in the performance of a contract. Under common law in the United States, the impossibility of performance does not necessarily excuse compliance with the provisions of a contract unless compliance is impossible for reason of an act of God, such as some extraordinary happening of nature not reasonably anticipated by either party of a contract. Hence floods, lightning, earthquakes, and similar occurrences are generally considered acts of God. Under code law, acts of God are not limited solely to acts of nature but are extended to include "unavoidable interference with performance, whether resulting from forces of nature or unforeseeable human acts," including such things as labor strikes and riots.

Consider the following situations: A contract was entered into to deliver a specific quantity of cloth. In one case, before the seller could make delivery an earthquake caused the destruction of the cloth and compliance was then impossible. In the second case, pipes in the sprinkler system where the material was stored froze and broke, spilling water on the cloth and destroying it. In each case, loss of the merchandise was sustained and delivery could not be made. Were the parties in these cases absolved of their obligations under the contract because of the impossibility of delivery? The answer depends on the system of law invoked.

In the first situation, the earthquake would be considered an act of God under both common and code law, and impossibility of performance would excuse compliance under the contract. In the second situation, courts in common-law countries would probably rule that the bursting of the water pipes did not constitute an act of God if it happened in a climate where freezing could be expected. Therefore, impossibility of delivery would not necessarily excuse compliance with the provisions of the contract. In code-law countries, where the scope of impossibility of performance is extended considerably, the destruction might very well be ruled an act of God, and thus release from compliance with the contract could be obtained.

Islamic Law

The basis for the *Shari'ah* (Islamic law) is interpretation of the Koran. It encompasses religious duties and obligations as well as the secular aspect of law regulating human acts.

Banking in Dubai, UAE, requires an understanding of Islamic law and customs. Prohibition against the payment of interest and prohibition against investments in businesses dealing with alcohol and gambling are two of the tenets of Islamic law that affect banking. (© *Derek Berwin/Getty Images*)

Broadly speaking, Islamic law defines a complete system that prescribes specific patterns of social and economic behavior for all individuals. It includes issues such as property rights, economic decision making, and types of economic freedom. The overriding objective of the Islamic system is social justice.

Among the unique aspects of Islamic law is the prohibition against the payment of interest. The Islamic law of contracts states that any given transaction should be devoid of *riba,* which is defined as unlawful advantage by way of excess of deferment, that is, interest or usury. Prohibiting the receipt and payment of interest is the nucleus of the Islamic system. However, other principles of Islamic doctrine advocate risk sharing, individuals' rights and duties, property rights, and the sanctity of contracts. The Islamic system places emphasis on the ethical, moral, social, and religious dimensions to enhance equality and fairness for the good of society. Another principle of the Islamic legal system is the prohibition against investment in those activities that violate the *Shari'ah*. For example, any investment in a business dealing with alcohol, gambling, and casinos would be prohibited.

Prohibition against the payment of interest affects banking and business practices severely.[8] However, certain acceptable practices adhere to Islamic law and permit the transaction of business. Mortgages for property are difficult because payment of interest is forbidden under Islamic law. Buyers of real property have to use a financier, who buys the property and then sells it to them in return for repayments of the capital. Instead of charging interest, a financier either sells the property at a higher price or sells it at the same price and takes additional payments to cover what would have been interest. Of the other ways to comply with Islamic law in financial transactions, trade with markup or cost-plus sale (*murabaha*) and leasing (*ijara*) are the most frequently used. In both *murabaha* and *ijara,* a mutually negotiated margin is included in the sale price or leasing payment. These practices meet the requirements of *Shari'ah* by enabling borrowers and lenders to share in the rewards as well as losses in an equitable fashion. They also ensure that the process of wealth accumulation and distribution in the economy is fair and representative of true productivity. Strict fundamentalists often frown on such an arrangement, but it is practiced and is an example of the way the strictness of Islamic law can be reconciled with the laws of non-Islamic legal systems.

Because the laws are based on interpretation of the Koran, the international marketer must have knowledge of the religion's tenets[9] and understand the way the law may be interpreted in each region. Regional courts can interpret Islamic law from the viewpoint of fundamentalists (those that adhere to a literal interpretation of the Koran) or they may use a more liberal translation. A company can find local authorities in one region willing to

[8]Sugata Ghosh, "Government Asks RBI to Draw up Roadmap for Islamic Banking," *Economic Times,* July 6, 2005.

[9]For an interesting discussion on Islamic beliefs about insurance and interest, see Khurshid Ahmad and Joseph A. Petrick, "The Challenge and Opportunity of Islamic Insurance," *Risk Management,* March 2003, p. 28.

allow payment of interest on deferred obligations as stipulated in a contract, while in another region all interest charges may be deleted and replaced with comparable "consulting fees." In yet another, authorities may void a contract and declare any payment of interest illegal. Marketers conducting business in Islamic-law countries must be knowledgeable about this important legal system.

Marxist-Socialist Tenets

As socialist countries become more directly involved in trade with non-Marxist countries, it has been necessary to develop a commercial legal system that permits them to engage in active international commerce. The pattern for development varies among the countries because each has a different background and each is at a different stage in its development of a market-driven economy. For example, central European countries such as the Czech Republic and Poland had comprehensive codified legal systems before communism took over, and their pre–World War II commercial legal codes have been revised and reinstituted. Consequently, they have moved toward a legal model with greater ease than some others have. Russia and most of the republics of the former Soviet Union and China, on the other hand, have had to build from scratch an entire commercial legal system. Under the premise that law, according to Marxist-socialist tenets, is strictly subordinate to prevailing economic conditions, such fundamental propositions as private ownership, contracts, due process, and other legal mechanisms have had to be developed. China and Russia differ, however, in that each has taken a different direction in its political economic growth. Russia is moving toward a democratic system. China is attempting to activate a private sector within a multicomponent, or mixed, economy in a socialist legal framework, that is, "perform its functions according to law and contribute to the development of socialist democracy and political civilization in China."

Both countries have actively passed laws, although the process has been slow and often disjointed. China has implemented more than 150 laws and regulations governing trade, yet the process is hampered by vaguely written laws, the lack of implementation mechanisms for the new laws, and an ineffective framework for dispute resolution and enforcement. A good example is China's attempt to control what goes on in Chinese cyberspace by applying the States Secrets Law to the Internet. The definition of a state secret is so broad that it can cover any information not cleared for publication with the relevant authorities.

Russia's experience has been similar to China's in that vaguely worded laws have been passed without mechanisms for implementation. The situation in Russia is often described as chaotic because of the laws' lack of precision. For example, to illegally receive or disseminate commercial secrets has become a crime, but the law provides no exact definition of a commercial secret. Copyright law violations that cause "great damage" are listed, but with no clear definition of how much damage constitutes "great." Both China and Russia are hampered by not having the heritage of a legal commercial code to build on as many of the Eastern-bloc European countries had.

The international marketer must be concerned with the differences among common law, code law, Islamic law, and socialist legal systems when operating between countries; the rights of the principals of a contract or some other legal document under one law may be significantly different from their rights under the other. It should be kept in mind that there could also be differences between the laws of two countries whose laws are based on the same legal system. Thus the problem of the marketer is one of anticipating the different laws regulating business, regardless of the legal system of the country.

Jurisdiction in International Legal Disputes

Determining whose legal system has jurisdiction when a commercial dispute arises is another problem of international marketing.[10] A frequent error is to assume that disputes between citizens of different nations are adjudicated under some supranational system of laws. Unfortunately, no judicial body exists to deal with legal commercial problems arising between citizens of different countries.

---

[10]"Chinese Court Says Nike Pirated Cartoon Figure," *Los Angeles Times*, December 31, 2004, p. C3.

Confusion probably stems from the existence of international courts such as the World Court at The Hague and the International Court of Justice, the principal judicial organ of the United Nations. These courts are operative in international disputes between sovereign nations of the world rather than between private citizens and/or companies.

Legal disputes can arise in three situations: between governments, between a company and a government, and between two companies. The World Court can adjudicate disputes between governments, whereas the other two situations must be handled in the courts of the country of one of the parties involved or through arbitration. Unless a commercial dispute involves a national issue between states, the International Court of Justice or any similar world court does not handle it. Because there is no "international commercial law," the foreign marketer must look to the legal system of each country involved—the laws of the home country or the laws of the countries within which business is conducted, or both.[11]

When international commercial disputes must be settled under the laws of one of the countries concerned, the paramount question in a dispute is: Which law governs? Jurisdiction is generally determined in one of three ways: (1) on the basis of jurisdictional clauses included in contracts, (2) on the basis of where a contract was entered into, or (3) on the basis of where the provisions of the contract were performed.

The most clear-cut decision can be made when the contracts or legal documents supporting a business transaction include a jurisdictional clause. A clause similar to the following establishes jurisdiction in the event of disagreements:

> That the parties hereby agree that the agreement is made in Oregon, USA, and that any question regarding this agreement shall be governed by the law of the state of Oregon, USA.

This clause establishes that the laws of the state of Oregon would be invoked should a dispute arise. If the complaint were brought in the court of another country, it is probable that the same Oregon laws would govern the decision. Cooperation and a definite desire to be judicious in foreign legal problems have led to the practice of foreign courts judging disputes on the basis of the law of another country or state whenever applicable. Thus, if an injured party from Oregon brings suit in the courts of Mexico against a Mexican over a contract that included the preceding clause, it would not be unusual for the Mexican courts to decide on the basis of Oregon law. This is assuming, of course, it was recognized that Oregon law prevailed in this dispute either as a result of the prior agreement by the parties or on some other basis.

International Dispute Resolution

When things go wrong in a commercial transaction—the buyer refuses to pay, the product is of inferior quality, the shipment arrives late, or any one of the myriad problems that can arise—what recourse does the international marketer have? The first step in any dispute is to try to resolve the issue informally, but if that fails the foreign marketer must resort to more resolute action. Such action can take the form of conciliation, arbitration, or as a last resort, litigation. Most international businesspeople prefer a settlement through arbitration rather than by suing a foreign company.

Conciliation

Most disputes that arise in commercial transactions are settled informally. When resolution is not forthcoming, however, conciliation can be an important first step in settling a dispute. *Conciliation* (also known as *mediation*) is a nonbinding agreement between parties to resolve disputes by asking a third party to mediate differences. The function of the mediator is to carefully listen to each party and to explore, clarify, and discuss the various practical options and possibilities for a solution with the intent that the parties will agree on a solution. Unlike arbitration and litigation, conciliation sessions are private and all conferences between parties and the mediator are confidential; the statements made by the parties may

---

[11]For a legal and thorough discussion of the globalization of jurisdiction, see Paul Schiff Berman, "The Globalization of Jurisdiction," *University of Pennsylvania Law Review*, December 2002, p.311; Yadong Luo, "Transactional Characteristics, Institutional Environment, and Joint Venture Contracts," *Journal of International Business Studies*, 2005.

CROSSING BORDERS 7.2   České Budějovice, Privatization, Trademarks, and Taste Tests—What Do They Have in Common with Anheuser-Busch? Budweiser, That's What!

Anheuser-Busch (AB) launched a massive public relations program in the small Czech town of České Budějovice, where a local brewery produces "Budweiser Budvar." Anheuser-Busch planted trees along main avenues, opened a new cultural center offering free English courses to citizens and management advice to budding entrepreneurs, and ran newspaper ads touting the possibilities of future cooperation.

Anheuser-Busch's goal was to win support for a minority stake in the Czech state-owned brewery, Budějovicky Budvar N.P., when the government privatized it. So why was AB interested in a brewery whose annual production of 500,000 barrels is the equivalent of two days' output for AB?

Part ownership is critically important to Anheuser-Busch for two reasons. It is in search of new markets in Europe, and it wants to be able to market the Budweiser brand in Europe. So what's the connection? AB doesn't have the rights to use the Budweiser brand in Europe because Budějovicky Budvar N.P. owns it. Its public relations plan didn't work because many Czechs see Budvar as the "family silver." Although the Czech prime minister asked publicly for American investors to put money into the Czech Republic, Czech Budweiser was not on the government's privatization list. "I believe in the strength of American investors, but I do not believe in the quality of American beer."

Anheuser-Busch established the name Budweiser in the United States when German immigrants founded the St. Louis family brewery and began selling under the Budweiser brand in 1876, which is 19 years before the Czech brewery opened. The Czechs claim they have been using the name since before Columbus discovered the New World and that Budweiser refers to Budwis, the original name of the city where Budvar is located. That is the name commonly referred to beer brewed in that area hundreds of years before Anheuser-Busch started brewing Budweiser.

The Anheuser-Busch Company markets Budweiser brand beer in North America, but in Europe it markets Busch brand beer because the Czechs have the rights to the use of the name Budweiser. Diplomacy and public relations didn't work, so what next? The parties have each other tied up in legal wrangling over who has the rights to the Budweiser name and to derivations of it, such as Bud. More than 40 lawsuits and 40 administrative cases are pending across Europe. U.S. law protects Anheuser-Busch's rights to the Budweiser label in the United States; the Czechs sell their beer as "Czechvar."

The Czech brewery exports to 37 countries, mainly in Europe, and AB has sales in more than 70 countries around the world. Anheuser-Busch sought a court order to have the Czech company's products taken off the shelves in Hong Kong, won a ruling in Hungary, and has launched similar lawsuits in the United Kingdom and the United States. AB said the Czech brewery had imported and sold beer in the United States labeled "Budweiser Budvar" in the state of Maryland. It says the Czech brewery is mimicking its name to confuse beer drinkers and cash in on the U.S. company's success.

The Czech government petitioned the WTO to grant beer regions the same kind of labeling protection that it gives to wine regions. Just as sparkling wines made in the Champagne region of France are the only ones legally entitled to call themselves champagne, it would mean that only beers brewed in Ceske Budejovice could call themselves Budweiser and only those brewed in Pilzen, another Czech town, could claim to be Pilsner. It seems unlikely that this will win approval since Pilsner has become a generic designation for a style of beer, and unlike the grapes that come from Champagne, the malt and the hops that go into its beer do not exclusively from České Budějovice.

The legal battle for the exclusive right to use the brand names Bud and Budweiser has spread worldwide. So far, this tactic hasn't worked too well either. Britain's high court allowed both companies to use the names Bud and Budweiser, whereas Switzerland's highest court banned Anheuser-Busch from selling beer under the Bud name.

We all know that the proof of who's best is in the tasting, right? Both lagers have legions of fans. The U.S. version lives up to its old slogan of "king of beers," at least as far as sales go: It's the top-selling beer in the world. The Czech version—nicknamed the "beer of kings" because it comes from a town that once brewed for royalty—has large followings in Germany and other parts of Europe. So the *St. Louis Post-Dispatch* hosted a blind taste test to determine which beer is better— Budvar won.

Visit the Budvar Web site (www.budvar.cz) for the history of Budvar and a tour of the plant, and visit the AB home page at www.anheuser-busch.com.

Sources: Stamborski, "Battle of the Buds: Taste Testers Say That Budvar Is Better," *St. Louis Post-Dispatch,* November 28, 1999, p. E1; "Prime Minister Says Budvar Will Stay Czech," *Modern Brewery,* March 2000; Gregory Cancelada, "Czech Brewery Retains Right to Use 'Budweiser' and 'Bud' Trademarks," *St. Louis Post-Dispatch,* February 17, 2003; Jim Salter, "A Victory for Bud Brewer," *Philadelphia Inquirer,* July 17, 2005, p. E12.

not be disclosed or used as evidence in any subsequent litigation or arbitration. The track record for the conciliation process is excellent, with a majority of disputes reaching settlement and leading to the resumption of business between the disputants.

Conciliation is considered to be especially effective when resolving disputes with Chinese business partners because they feel less threatened by conciliation than arbitration. The Chinese believe that when a dispute occurs, informal, friendly negotiation should be used first to solve the problem; if that fails, conciliation should be tried. In fact, some Chinese companies may avoid doing business with companies that resort first to arbitration. Conciliation can be either formal or informal. Both sides agreeing on a third party to mediate can establish informal conciliation. Formal conciliation is conducted under the auspices of some tribunal such as the Beijing Conciliation Center, which assigns one or two conciliators to mediate. If agreement is reached, a conciliation statement based on the signed agreement is recorded. Although conciliation may be the friendly route to resolving disputes in China, it is not legally binding; thus an arbitration clause should be included in all conciliation agreements. Experience has shown that having an arbitration clause in the conciliation agreement makes it easier to move to arbitration if necessary.

Arbitration If conciliation is not used or an agreement cannot be reached, the next step is *arbitration.* When all else fails, arbitration rather than litigation is the preferred method for resolving international commercial disputes. The usual arbitration procedure is for the parties involved to select a disinterested and informed party or parties as referee to determine the merits of the case and make a judgment that both parties agree to honor. Although informal arbitration is workable, most arbitration is conducted under the auspices of one of the more formal domestic and international arbitration groups organized specifically to facilitate the resolution of commercial disputes. These groups have formal rules for the process and experienced arbitrators to assist. In most countries, decisions reached in formal arbitration are enforceable under the law.

The popularity of arbitration has led to a proliferation of arbitral centers established by countries, organizations, and institutions. All have adopted standardized rules and procedures to administer cases, and each has its strengths and weaknesses. Some of the more active are the following:

- The Inter-American Commercial Arbitration Commission
- The Canadian-American Commercial Arbitration Commission (for disputes between Canadian and U.S. businesses)
- The London Court of Arbitration (decisions are enforceable under English law and English courts)
- The American Arbitration Association (www.adr.org/)
- The International Chamber of Commerce (www.iccwbo.org/; select Arbitration)

The procedures used by formal arbitration organizations are similar. Arbitration under the rules of the International Chamber of Commerce (ICC) affords an excellent example of how most organizations operate. When an initial request for arbitration is received, the chamber first attempts conciliation between the disputants. If this fails, the process of arbitration is started. The plaintiff and the defendant select one person each from among acceptable arbitrators to defend their case, and the ICC Court of Arbitration appoints a third member, generally chosen from a list of distinguished lawyers, jurists, and professors.

The history of ICC effectiveness in arbitration has been spectacular.[12] An example of a case that involved arbitration by the ICC concerned a contract between an English business and a Japanese manufacturer. The English business agreed to buy 100,000 plastic dolls for 80 cents each. On the strength of the contract, the English business sold the entire lot at $1.40 per doll. Before the dolls were delivered, the Japanese manufacturer had a strike; the

---

[12]"Ventana Receives Favorable Decision in HPV Intellectual Property Licensing Dispute with Institut Pasteur," *Market Wire*, April 29, 2005.

settlement of the strike increased costs, and the English business was informed that the delivery price of the dolls had increased from 80 cents to $1.50 each. The English business maintained that the Japanese firm had committed to make delivery at 80 cents and should deliver at that price. Each side was convinced that it was right.

The Japanese, accustomed to code law, felt that the strike was beyond control (an act of God) and thus compliance with the original provisions of the contract was excused. The English, accustomed to common law, did not accept the Japanese reasons for not complying because they considered a strike part of the normal course of doing business and not an act of God. The dispute could not be settled except through arbitration or litigation; they chose arbitration. The ICC appointed an arbitrator who heard both sides and ruled that the two parties would share proportionately in the loss. Both parties were satisfied with the arbitration decision, and costly litigation was avoided. Most arbitration is successful, but success depends on the willingness of both parties to accept the arbitrator's rulings.

Contracts and other legal documents should include clauses specifying the use of arbitration to settle disputes. Unless a provision for arbitration of any dispute is incorporated as part of a contract, the likelihood of securing agreement for arbitration after a dispute arises is reduced. A typical arbitration clause is as follows:

> Any controversy or claim arising out of or relating to this contract shall be determined by arbitration in accordance with the International Arbitration Rules of the American Arbitration Association.

Including the number of arbitrators, the place of arbitration (city and/or country), and the language of the arbitration in the clause is also useful.[13]

Although an arbitration clause in a contract can avert problems, sometimes enforcing arbitration agreements can be difficult. Arbitration clauses require agreement on two counts: (1) the parties agree to arbitrate in the case of a dispute according to the rules and procedures of some arbitration tribunal, and (2) they agree to abide by the awards resulting from the arbitration. Difficulty arises when the parties to a contract fail to honor the agreements. Companies may refuse to name arbitrators, refuse to arbitrate, or, after arbitration awards are made, they may refuse to honor the award. In most countries, arbitration clauses are recognized by the courts and are enforceable by law within those countries. More than 120 countries have ratified the Convention on the Recognition and Enforcement of Foreign Arbitral Awards, also known as the New York Convention, which binds them to uphold foreign arbitration awards. Under the New York Convention, the courts of the signatory countries automatically uphold foreign arbitral awards issued in member countries. In addition to the New York Convention, the United States is a signatory of the Inter-American Convention on International Arbitration, to which many Latin American countries are party. The United States is also party to a number of bilateral agreements containing clauses providing for enforcement of arbitral awards. When all else fails, the final step to solve a dispute is litigation.

Litigation   Lawsuits in public courts are avoided for many reasons. Most observers of lawsuits between citizens of different countries believe that almost all victories are spurious because the cost, frustrating delays, and extended aggravation that these cases produce are more oppressive by far than any matter of comparable size. In India, for instance, there is a backlog of more than three million cases, and litigating a breach of contract between private parties can take a decade or more. The best advice is to seek a settlement, if possible, rather than sue. Other deterrents to litigation are the following:

- Fear of creating a poor image and damaging public relations.
- Fear of unfair treatment in a foreign court. (Fear that a lawsuit can result in unfair treatment, perhaps intentionally, is justifiable since the decision could be made by either a jury or a judge not well versed in trade problems and the intricacies of international business transactions.)

---

[13]The American Arbitration Association, www.iccwbo.org (select Arbitration).

- Difficulty in collecting a judgment that may otherwise have been collected in a mutually agreed settlement through arbitration.

- The relatively high cost and time required when bringing legal action. The Rheem Manufacturing Company, a billion-dollar manufacturer of heating and air conditioning systems, estimates that by using arbitration over litigation, it has reduced the time and cost of commercial-dispute resolution in half.

- Loss of confidentiality. Unlike arbitration and conciliation proceedings, which are confidential, litigation is public.

One authority suggests that the settlement of every dispute should follow four steps: first, try to placate the injured party; if this does not work, conciliate, arbitrate, and, finally, litigate. The final step is typically taken only when all other methods fail. Actually, this advice is probably wise whether one is involved in an international dispute or a domestic one.

Protection of Intellectual Property Rights: A Special Problem

Companies spend millions of dollars establishing brand names or trademarks to symbolize quality and design a host of other product features meant to entice customers to buy their brands to the exclusion of all others.[14] Millions more are spent on research to develop products, processes, designs,[15] and formulas that provide companies with advantages over their competitors. Such intellectual or industrial properties are among the more valuable assets a company may possess. Brand names such as Kodak, Coca-Cola, and Gucci, processes such as xerography, and computer software are invaluable. One financial group estimated that the Marlboro brand had a value of $33 billion, Kellogg's $9 billion, Microsoft $9.8 billion, and Levi's $5 billion; all have experienced infringement of their intellectual property rights. Normally, property rights can be legally protected to prevent other companies from infringing on such assets. Companies must, however, keep a constant vigil against piracy and counterfeiting.

Counterfeiting and Piracy

Counterfeit and pirated goods come from a wide range of industries—apparel, automotive parts, agricultural chemicals, pharmaceuticals, books (yes, even management books such as the one you are reading right now),[16] records, films, computer software, baby formula to auto parts. Estimates are that more than 10 million fake Swiss timepieces carrying famous brand names such as Cartier and Rolex are sold every year, netting illegal profits of at least $500 million. Although difficult to pinpoint, lost sales from the unauthorized use of U.S. patents, trademarks, and copyrights amount to more than $300 billion annually. That translates into more than two million lost jobs. Software, music, and movies[17] are especially attractive targets for pirates because they are costly to develop but cheap[18] to reproduce and distribute over the Internet.[19] Pirated CD music sales are estimated to exceed $5 billion annually and are growing at 6 percent per year. And unauthorized U.S. software that sells for $500 in this country can be purchased for less than $10 in East Asia. The Business Software Alliance, a trade group, estimates that software companies lost over $7.9 billion in the

---

[14]The International Chamber of Commerce has published two comprehensive reports on intellectual property titled "What Is Intellectual Property?" and "Roadmaps on Current and Emerging Intellectual Property Issues 2002," available at www.iccwbo.org (select Intellectual Property). Also see Mira Serrill-Robins, "Harry Potter and the Cyberpirates," *BusinessWeek*, August 1, 2005, p. 9.

[15]Dexter Roberts, "Did Spark Spark a Copycat?" *BusinessWeek*, February 7, 2005, p. 64.

[16]Don Lee, "Ripping Off Good Reads in China," *Los Angeles Times*, April 24, 2005, pp. C1, C10.

[17]Steve Lohr, "Keeping Moviegoers away from the Dark Side," *New York Times*, June 18, 2005, p. 1.

[18]Joseph C. Nunes, Christopher K. Hsee, and Elke U. Weber, "Why Are People So Prone to Steal Software? The Effect of Cost Structure on Consumer Purchase and Payment Intentions," *Journal of Public Policy and Marketing* 23, no.1 (2004), pp. 43–53.

[19]Roben Farzad, "File Swappers Get Creative as Wheels of Justice Turn," *New York Times*, June 18, 2005, p. 13.

CROSSING BORDERS 7.3   Counterfeit, Pirated, or the Original—Take Your Choice

Intellectual properties—trademarks, brand names, designs, manufacturing processes, formulas—are valuable company assets that U.S. officials estimate are knocked off to the tune of $300 billion a year due to counterfeiting and pirating. Some examples from China:

- *Design rip-offs.* Estimates are that nearly 7 million of the 11 million motorcycles and scooters produced in China in one year were copies bearing the Yahama name. Some state-owned factories produce copies four months after a new model is launched.

- *Product rip-offs.* Exact copies of products made by Procter & Gamble, Colgate-Palmolive, Reebok, and Nike are common throughout southern China. Exact copies of any Madonna album are available for as little as $1, as are CDs and movies. Bestfoods estimates that one-quarter of its Skippy Peanut Butter is pirated.

- *Brand name rip-offs.* Bausch & Lomb's Ray Ban sunglasses become Ran Bans. Colgate in the familiar bright red tube becomes Cologate. The familiar red rooster on Kellogg's Corn Flakes appears on Kongalu Corn Strips packages that boast of "the trustworthy sign of quality that is famous around the world." Bogus Budweiser is sold in 640-ml bottles. Yameha, Suzaki, and Hondea motorcycles appear on nearly identical models of Yamaha, Suzuki, and Honda.

- *Book rip-offs.* Even the rich and powerful fall prey to pirating. Soon after *My Father, Deng Xiaoping,* a biography written by Deng Rong, daughter of Deng Xiaoping, was published, thousands of illegal copies flooded the market. The true owners also sell original versions of the products mentioned above in China.

In an attempt to control counterfeits, China passed a law that allows customers to demand a double refund for fake merchandise sold in department stores. This has led to bootleg "Vigilantes" who knowingly buy knockoffs and take them back demanding the double refund for violating the law. Wang Hai claimed to have made more than $10,000 buying bogus phones and fax machines and then getting a double refund "I couldn't believe it, every major department store was selling rip-offs," commented Wang, "If I had more money, I would have emptied out every store in Beijing." The Wang Hai phenomenon, as it is called, is spreading throughout China.

Sources: Marcus W. Brauchli, "Chinese Flagrantly Copy Trademarks of Foreigners," *Wall Street Journal,* June 26, 1994, p. B1; "How Heinz and Procter & Gamble Fight Counterfeiting," *Business China,* November 25, 1996, p. 6; Ching-Ching Ni, "Anti-Counterfeit Law Allows Chinese Consumers to Cash In," *Los Angeles Times,* September 14, 2002, p. A3; "Harry Potter Casts Spell over Asia but Faces New Foe—Pirates," *Agence France-Presse,* July 15, 2005.

Asia-Pacific region, $12.1 billion in Europe, and $7.5 billion in North America in 2004. One might conclude from perusing Exhibit 7.2 that China is the biggest piracy problem given its high ranking and large size. However, the dollars lost in the Unites States because of software piracy is almost double that of China, at $6.6 billion versus $3.6 billion, respectively. The good news in the data is that piracy rates are dropping in China (down 2 percent from the previous year) and globally (down 1 percent), due primarily to education programs and enforcement.[20]

The piracy industry has grown so sophisticated that many counterfeit goods are almost impossible to distinguish from the original. Toys, a popular knockoff candidate, are often counterfeited and sold before the original ones arrive in legitimate stores; copies are churned out in the same Chinese town where the originals are made. To thwart counterfeiters, Microsoft included a hologram on its software boxes and packaging, but it too has been duplicated to such perfection that the packages containing knockoff CDs of Windows NT are almost indistinguishable from the original. A genuine Chinese-language version of Windows XP comes in a shrink-wrapped box with the familiar logo and costs $245, about four months' salary for an average Chinese worker. The retail price is too much for the worker to pay "retail," but there is an alternative—a nearby stand sells illegally copied XP

---

[20]*Second Annual BSA and IDC Global Software Piracy Study* (Washington, DC: Business Software Alliance, 2005), www.bsa.org/globalstudy.

Exhibit 7.2

Piracy Rates for Computer Software, Top and Bottom 20

Source: From 2005 BSA and 100 Global Software Piracy Study, Business Software Alliance, May 2005. Reprinted with permission. *Second Annual BSA and IDC Global Software Piracy Study* (Washington, DC: Business Software Alliance, 2005), www.bsa.org/globalstudy. Ninety-three countries and regions are ranked.

Highest Piracy Rates		Lowest Piracy Rates	
Vietnam	92%	Unites States	22%
Ukraine	91	New Zealand	23
China	90	Austria	25
Zimbabwe	90	Sweden	26
Indonesia	87	United Kingdom	27
Russia	87	Denmark	27
Nigeria	84	Switzerland	28
Tunisia	84	Japan	28
Algeria	83	Finland	29
Kenya	83	Germany	29
Paraguay	83	Belgium	29
Pakistan	82	Netherlands	30
Bolivia	80	Norway	31
El Salvador	80	Australia	32
Nicaragua	80	Israel	33
Thailand	79	UAE	43
Venezuela	79	Canada	36
Guatemala	78	South Africa	37
Dominican Republic	77	Ireland	38
Lebanon	75	Portugal	40

CDs for $5.50 a CD. More than 90 percent of the application software used in China is estimated to come from illegal copies.

Note that recent research implies that for companies like Microsoft, some level of piracy actually can serve the company. It can be seen as a kind of product trial, building commitment. As updated versions of products become available, purchases may actually follow. Particularly as countries such as China begin to enforce WTO statutes on piracy, customers conditioned on pirated goods may indeed be willing and able to pay for the new versions.[21] In another way, at least in the short run, Apple's iPod strategy, which designs and prices products that take into consideration consumers' complaints regarding current intellectual property regimes, seems to be working well.[22]

While counterfeit CDs, toys, and similar products cost companies billions of dollars in lost revenue and have the potential of damaging the product's brand image, the counterfeiting of pharmaceuticals can do serious physical harm. In Colombia, investigators found an illegal operation making more than 20,000 counterfeit tablets a day of the flu drug Dristan, a generic aspirin known as Dolex, and Ponstan 500, a popular painkiller made by Pfizer. The counterfeited pills contained boric acid, cement, floor wax, talcum powder, and yellow paint with high lead levels, all used to replicate the genuine medications' appearance.

Counterfeit drugs range from copies that have the same efficacy as the original to those with few or no active ingredients to those made of harmful substances. A pharmaceutical manufacturers association estimates that 2 percent of the $327 billion worth of drugs sold each year are counterfeit, or about $6 billion worth. In some African and Latin American nations, as much as 60 percent are counterfeit. The World Health Organization thinks 8 percent of the bulk drugs imported into the United States are counterfeit, unapproved, or substandard.

Another problem is collusion between the contract manufacturer and illegitimate sellers. In China, exact copies of New Balance shoes are fabricated by contract manufacturers who are or were New Balance suppliers. They flood the market with genuine shoes that are sold for as little as $20. Uilever discovered that one of its suppliers in Shanghai made excess

---

[21]Ashutosh Rasad and Vijay Mahajan, "An Analysis of Piracy Protection on the Diffusion of Software," *International Journal of Research in Marketing* 20, no. 4 (2003), pp. 337–353.

[22]Brian Lavery, "Piracy Tops the Agenda at Copyright Conference," *International Herald Tribune*, June 28, 2004, p. 10.

cases of soap, which were sold directly to retailers. One of Procter & Gamble's Chinese suppliers sold empty P&G shampoo bottles to another company, which filled them with counterfeit shampoo. Counterfeiting and piracy of intellectual property constitute outright theft, but the possibility of legally losing the rights to intellectual property because of inadequate protection of property rights and/or a country's legal structure is another matter.[23]

Finally, it should be mentioned that some critics argue that MNCs have pushed the current intellectual property regime too far in favor of the firms, particularly with the most recent WTO TRIPS Agreement, to be discussed in more detail below.[24] The critics suggest that the so-called tight rein the firms hold on the production of intellectual property has actually served to limit creativity and the associated benefits to the people the intellectual property (IP) laws are intended to serve. Such arguments pitch antitrust laws against IP laws. The argument goes on.

Inadequate Protection

The failure to protect intellectual property rights adequately in the world marketplace can lead to the legal loss of rights in potentially profitable markets. Because patents, processes, trademarks, and copyrights are valuable in all countries, some companies have found their assets appropriated and profitably exploited in foreign countries without license or reimbursement.[25] Further, they often learn that not only are other firms producing and selling their products or using their trademarks, but that the foreign companies are the rightful owners in the countries where they operate.

There have been many cases where companies have legally lost the rights to trademarks and have had to buy back these rights or pay royalties for their use. The problems of inadequate protective measures taken by the owners of valuable assets stem from a variety of causes. One of the more frequent errors is assuming that because the company has established rights in the United States, they will be protected around the world, or that rightful ownership can be established should the need arise. This was the case with McDonald's in Japan, where enterprising Japanese registered its golden arches trademark. Only after a lengthy and costly legal action with a trip to the Japanese Supreme Court was McDonald's able to regain the exclusive right to use the trademark in Japan. After having to "buy" its trademark for an undisclosed amount, McDonald's maintains a very active program to protect its trademarks.

Similarly, a South Korean company legally uses the Coach brand on handbags and leather goods. The company registered the Coach trademark first and has the legal right to use that mark in Korea. The result is that a Coach-branded briefcase that is virtually identical to the U.S. product can be purchased for $135 in South Korea versus $320 in the United States. A U.S. attorney who practices with a South Korean firm noted that he has seen several instances in which a foreign company will come to Korea and naïvely start negotiating with a Korean company for distribution or licensing agreements, only to have the Korean company register the trademark in its own name. Later, the Korean company will use that registration as leverage in negotiations or, if the negotiations fall apart, will sell the trademark back to the company. Many businesses fail to take proper steps to legally protect their intellectual property. They fail to understand that some countries do not follow the common-law principle that ownership is established by prior use or to realize that registration and legal ownership in one country does not necessarily mean ownership in another.

Prior Use versus Registration

In the United States, a common-law country, ownership of intellectual property rights is established by prior use—whoever can establish first use is typically considered the rightful owner. In many code-law countries, however, ownership is established by registration rather than by prior use—the first to register a trademark or other property right is considered the

---

[23]"China Says GM Has Not Proved Piracy," *Associated Press*, September 7, 2004.

[24]Susan Sell, *Power and Ideas, North–South Politics of Intellectual Property and Antitrust* (Albany: State University of New York Press, 1998); Susan Sell, *Intellectual Property Rights: A Critical History* (Boulder, CO: Lynne Rienners Publishers, 2006).

[25]John Hagedoom, Danielle Cloodt, and Hans van Kranenburg, "Intellectual Property Rights and the Governance of International R&D Partnerships," *Journal of International Business Studies*, 2005.

CROSSING BORDERS 7.4   Aspirin in Russia, Bayer in the United States— It's Enough to Give You a Headache

Russia's patent office awarded the German chemical company Bayer AG the registered trademark to the word *aspirin*. If the trademark award holds, Bayer will have the exclusive right to market pain relievers under the brand name Aspirin in Russia. The word and labeling *aspirin* fell out of use in Russia in the 1970s, when the chemical name acetylsalicylic acid, aspirin's main ingredient, came into use. Bayer AG believes its trademark rights will be upheld and it will be the only company able to sell acetylsalicylic acid as Aspirin; the Russian patent office agrees. There are several reasons for granting Bayer the trademark: *Aspirin* has fallen out of popular use in Russia, Bayer was the world's first manufacturer of aspirin and marketed acetylsalicylic acid under the brand name Aspirin nearly a century ago, Bayer holds trademark rights to Aspirin in many countries, and it registered the name first.

In the United States it's a different story. Bayer AG lost the exclusive right to Aspirin when U.S. courts declared *aspirin* to be the generic term for acetylsalicylic acid. Later, Bayer AG lost the right to the name Bayer as well. Bayer AG did not sell the famous Bayer aspirin in the United States because Sterling Winthrop owned the Bayer trademark. The U.S. government confiscated the domestic assets of Bayer AG after World War I, and

in 1919 sold them along with the rights to the Bayer name. Although Sterling Winthrop had the exclusive use of the name Bayer, it did not have the exclusive use of the term *aspirin* because U.S. courts ruled it to be a generic term.

Ownership changes rapidly in international business. Bayer of Germany bought Sterling Winthrop, the U.S. owner of the Bayer brand, from the Kodak Company in 1994, and now Bayer of Germany once again owns the brand Bayer worldwide. The change in ownership in the United States, however, did not affect the trademark dispute over the brand name *Aspirin*, which remains generic in the United States.

The moral of the story: Patent and trademark protection is a complicated issue for international companies, and the value of Bayer and Aspirin are worth fighting for.

Sources: Marya Fogel, "Bayer Trademarks the Word 'Aspirin' in Russia, Leaving Rivals Apoplectic," *Wall Street Journal*, October 29, 1993, p. A9; Andrew Wood, "Companies: Bayer Corp.; New Recognition for an Old Name," *Chemical Week*, September 10, 1997, p. 51; Linda Wertheimer, "Dr. Mark Plummer Talks about Bayer's History Regarding Rights to Their Drugs," *All Things Considered (NPR)*, October 19, 2001; "Aspirin, It's a Growing Wonder Pill," *Canberra Times*, May 3, 2005, p. 4.

rightful owner. For example, a trademark in Jordan belongs to whoever registers it first in Jordan. Thus you can find "McDonald's" restaurants, "Microsoft" software, and "Safeway" groceries all legally belonging to a Jordanian. After a lengthy court battle that went to the Spanish Supreme Court, Nike lost its right to use the "Nike" brand name for sports apparel in Spain. Cidesport of Spain had been using Nike for sports apparel since 1932 and sued to block Nike (U.S.) sportswear sales. Since Cidesport does not sell shoes under the Nike label, Nike (U.S.) will be able to continue selling its brand of sports shoes in Spain. A company that believes it can always establish ownership in another country by proving it used the trademark or brand name first is wrong and risks the loss of these assets.

Besides the first-to-register issue, companies may encounter other problems with registering. China has improved intellectual property rights protection substantially and generally recognizes "first to invent." However, a Chinese company can capture the patent for a product invented elsewhere; it needs only to reverse-engineer or reproduce the product from published specifications and register it in China before the original inventor. Latvia and Lithuania permit duplicate registration of trademarks and brand names. A cosmetics maker registered Nivea and Niveja cosmetics brands in the former Soviet Union in 1986 and again in Latvia in 1992, but a Latvian firm had registered and had been selling a skin cream called Niveja since 1964. Neither the Soviet[26] nor the Latvian authorities notified either firm. Applicants are responsible for informing themselves about similar trademarks that are already registered. The case is being taken to the Supreme Court of Latvia. It is best to protect intellectual property rights through registration. Several international conventions provide for simultaneous registration in member countries.

---

[26]"Number of Counterfeit Products Growing in Russia," *Interfax*, February 26, 2003.

International Conventions

Many countries participate in international conventions designed for mutual recognition and protection of intellectual property rights. There are three major international conventions:

1. The Paris Convention for the Protection of Industrial Property, commonly referred to as the Paris Convention, includes the United States and 100 other countries.

2. The Inter-American Convention includes most of the Latin American nations and the United States.

3. The Madrid Arrangement, which established the Bureau for International Registration of Trademarks, includes 26 European countries.

In addition, the World Intellectual Property Organization (WIPO) of the United Nations is responsible for the promotion of the protection of intellectual property and for the administration of the various multilateral treaties through cooperation among its member states.[27] Furthermore, two multicountry patent arrangements have streamlined patent procedures in Europe. The first, the Patent Cooperation Treaty (PCT), facilitates the process for application for patents among its member countries. It provides comprehensive coverage in that a single application filed in the United States supplies the interested party with an international search report on other patents to help evaluate whether or not to seek protection in each of the countries cooperating under the PCT. The second, the European Patent Convention (EPC), established a regional patent system allowing any nationality to file a single international application for a European patent. Companies have a choice between relying on national systems when they want to protect a trademark or patent in just a few member countries and applying for protection in all 15 member states. Trademark protection is valid for 10 years and is renewable; however, if the mark is not used within five years, protection is forfeited. Once the patent or trademark is approved, it has the same effect as a national patent or trademark in each individual country designated on the application.

The Trade-Related Aspects of Intellectual Property Rights (TRIPs) agreement, a major provision of the World Trade Organization, is the most comprehensive multilateral agreement on intellectual property to date. TRIPs sets standards of protection for a full range of intellectual property rights that are embodied in current international agreements. The three main provisions of the TRIPs agreement require that participating members be in compliance with minimum standards of protection by 2006, set procedures and remedies for the enforcement of intellectual property rights, and make disputes between WTO members with respect to TRIPs obligations subject to the WTO's dispute settlement procedures.[28]

Once a trademark, patent, or other intellectual property right is registered, most countries require that these rights be worked and properly policed. The United States is one of the few countries in which an individual can hold a patent without the patented entity being manufactured and sold throughout the duration of the patent period. Other countries feel that in exchange for the monopoly provided by a patent, the holder must share the product with the citizens of the country. Hence, if patents are not produced within a specified period, usually from one to five years (the average is three years), the patent reverts to public domain.

This rule is also true for trademarks; products bearing the registered mark must be sold within the country or the company may forfeit its right to a particular trademark. McDonald's faced that problem in Venezuela. Even though the McDonald's trademark was properly registered in that code-law country, the company did not use it for more than two years. Under Venezuelan law, a trademark must be used within two years or it is lost. Thus a Venezuelan-owned "Mr. McDonalds," with accompanying golden arches, is operating in Venezuela. The U.S. McDonald's Corporation faces a potentially costly legal battle if it decides to challenge the Venezuelan company.

---

[27]Visit www.wipo.org, the home page of the WIPO, for detailed information on the various conventions and the activities of WIPO.

[28]For a discussion of TRIPs, visit www.wto.org and select Intellectual Property.

The three faces of piracy and/or reform, depending how you look at them. (1) American youths, particularly on college campuses, are protesting the current intellectual property laws and the associated enforcement tools. The fellow with the eyepatch was attending a seminar on the topic led by Attorney General Alberto Gonzales.[29] *(Photography by Rick Loomis, Los Angeles Times. Copyright, 2005, Los Angeles Times. Reprinted with permission.)* (2) Aside from the United States, the biggest piracy problem is China. Here Jackie Chan helps the Chinese government crack down. This well forecasts the probable path of IP piracy in China. That is, pirates have turned into policemen historically in the United States, Japan, and Taiwan as the production of intellectual property took off in each country.[30] The same will happen in China during the next decade as artists, researchers, and entrepreneurs there produce new ideas worth protecting. *(© Mike Clarke/AFP/Getty Images)* (3) The HIV/AIDS epidemic is an economic and health catastrophe which many in sub-Saharan Africa believe is exacerbated by drug companies' pricing policies and protection of intellectual property.[31] Here protestors march toward the U.S. embassy in Pretoria, South Africa. *(AP/Wide World Photos)*

Individual countries expect companies to actively police their intellectual property by bringing violators to court. Policing can be a difficult task, with success depending in large measure on the cooperation of the country within which the infringement or piracy takes place. A lack of cooperation in some countries may stem from cultural differences regarding how intellectual property is viewed. In the United States, the goal of protection of intellectual property is to encourage invention and to protect and reward innovative businesses. In Korea, the attitude is that the thoughts of one person should benefit all. In Japan, the intent is to share technology rather than protect it; an invention should serve a larger, national goal, with the rapid spread of technology among competitors in a manner that promotes cooperation. In light of such attitudes, the lack of enthusiasm toward protecting

[29]Lorenzo Munoz and Jon Healey, "Students Do Not Share Gonzales' View on Piracy," *Los Angeles Times*, April 29, 2005, pp. C1, C9.

[30]John L. Graham and N. Mark Lam, *Doing Business in the New China* (New York: McGraw-Hill, 2006).

[31]John E. Cook and Roger Bate, "Pharmaceuticals and the Worldwide HIV Epidemic: Can a Stakeholder Model Work?" *Journal of Public Policy and Marketing*, 2004, 23(2), pp. 140–152.

intellectual property is better understood. The United States is a strong advocate of protection, and at U.S. insistence many countries[32] are becoming more cooperative about policing cases of infringement and piracy. After decades of debate, European Union ministers agreed on a common continentwide system for patented inventions. Instead of being forced to submit an application in all EU countries' languages, inventors can submit only one, in English, French, or German.

Commercial Law within Countries

When doing business in more than one country, a marketer must remain alert to the different legal systems. This problem is especially troublesome for the marketer who formulates a common marketing plan to be implemented in several countries. Although differences in languages and customs may be accommodated, legal differences between countries may still present problems for a marketing program.

Marketing Laws   All countries have laws regulating marketing activities in promotion, product development,[33] labeling, pricing, and channels of distribution. Usually the discrepancies across markets cause problems for trade negotiators,[34] but particularly for managers and their firms. For example, the United States does not allow the buying or selling of human organs,[35] and it restricts the use of human stem cells in medical research to develop treatments for a variety of diseases.[36] Other nations have different laws. The ethics of both issues are quite controversial, and adding in an international dimension just complicates things even more. In the case of the current international trade in human organs, Europeans can legally travel to foreign countries for transplants. However, the European Union Parliament is considering making it a criminal offense to do so. Meanwhile, the U.S. government is considering relaxing laws regulating stem cell research as scientists in other nations, unfettered by similar restrictions, are making important advances in the field.

Some countries may have only a few marketing laws with lax enforcement; others may have detailed, complicated rules to follow that are stringently enforced. For example, Sweden banned all television advertising to children in 1991. Greece, Norway, Denmark, Austria, and the Netherlands all restrict advertising directed at children.[37] Recently, the European Commission threatened to restrict all advertising of soft drinks and snack foods to children, and PepsiCo volunteered to curb its advertising to kids in repsonse.[38] At the same time, the American food industry is arguing against such actions in the United States.[39] It is interesting to note that the U.S. Federal Trade Commission and the sugared food and toy manufactures went down a similar path on restricting advertising to children in the late 1970s. The industry made a few minor concessions at the time but began ignoring previous commitments during the 1980s. All this will be interesting to follow as childhood obesity continues to be a major public health issue in all affluent countries.

There often are vast differences in enforcement and interpretation among countries having laws covering the same activities. Laws governing sales promotions in the European Union offer good examples of such diversity. In Austria, premium offers, free gifts, or coupons are considered cash discounts and are prohibited. Premium offers in Finland are

---

[32]Paul Meller, "Europe Offers Plan to Fight Counterfeit Goods," *New York Times*, January 31, 2003; "China to Increase Piracy Prosecutions," *Bloomberg News*, July 12, 2005.

[33]Marilyn Chase and Gautam Naik, "Key AIDS Study in Cambodia Now in Jeopardy," *Wall Street Journal*, August 12, 2004, pp. B1–B2.

[34]Evelyn Iritani, "Another Snag for U.S.–Latin Trade Accord," *Los Angeles Times*, January 8, 2005, pp. C1, C8.

[35]Nancy Scheper-Hughes, "Organs without Borders," *Foreign Policy*, January/February 2005, pp. 26–27.

[36]Robert L. Paarlberg, "The Great Stem Cell Race," *Foreign Policy*, May/June 2005, pp. 44–51.

[37]Eric Schlosser, *Fast Food Nation* (New York: Perennial, 2002).

[38]Andrew Ward and Jeremy Grant, "PepsiCo Says It Has Curbed Advertising to Children," *Financial Times*, February 28, 2005, FT.com.

[39]Melanie Weber, "Food Industry Defends Marketing to Children," *New York Times*, July 15, 2005.

Laws regarding healthcare marketing differ substantially around the world. In Mexico prescriptions often are not required for powerful drugs. At this farmacia in the Cancun airport, tourists can buy the pictured antibiotic over the counter at bargain prices. Quality is an issue, but availability is not. In the Philippines and other developing countries you can buy yourself a kidney on the black market—the global price is around $2,000. U.S. laws prohibit the buying and selling of human organs. In South Korea the government supports stem cell research that is restricted in the United States by federal laws. *(right: AP/Wide World Photos; bottom right: AP/Wide World Photos)*

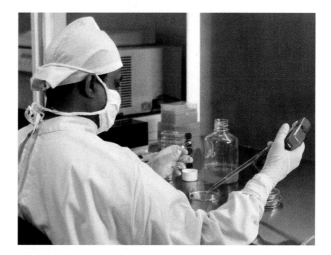

allowed with considerable scope as long as the word *free* is not used and consumers are not coerced into buying products. France also regulates premium offers, which are, for all practical purposes, illegal there because selling for less than cost price or offering a customer a gift or premium conditional on the purchase of another product is illegal. French law does permit sales twice a year, in January and August, which can legally last four to six weeks. This event is so popular that it is advertised on radio and TV, and special police are even required to control the crowds. One poll indicated that over 40 percent of the French set aside money during the year for sale time and 56 percent will spend less money on essentials to buy things on sale.[40]

The various product comparison laws, a natural and effective means of expression, are another major stumbling block. In Germany, comparisons in advertisements are always subject to the competitor's right to go to the courts and ask for proof of any implied or stated superiority. In Canada, the rulings are even more stringent: All claims and statements must be examined to ensure that any representation to the public is not false or misleading. Such representation cannot be made verbally in selling or be contained in or on anything that comes to the attention of the public (such as product labels, inserts in products, or any other form of advertising, including what may be expressed in a sales letter). Courts have been directed by Canadian law to take into account in determining whether a representation is false or misleading the "general impression" conveyed by the representation as well as its literal meaning.[41] The courts are expected to apply the "credulous person standard," which means that if any reasonable person could possibly misunderstand the representation, the representation is misleading. In essence, puffery, an acceptable practice in the United States, could be interpreted in Canada as false and misleading advertising. Thus a statement such as "the strongest drive shaft in Canada" would be judged misleading unless the advertiser had absolute evidence that the drive shaft was stronger than any other drive shaft for sale in Canada.

China is experimenting with a variety of laws to control how foreign companies do business. Some regulations are being relaxed, such as those controlling foreign advertising companies.[42] Censorship of advertising is a constant concern. TV ads for "offensive" products such as feminine-hygiene pads, hemorrhoid medications, and even athlete's food ointment are not allowed during the three daily mealtimes.[43] The Chinese authorities banned a LeBron James Nike TV ad because it "violates regulations that mandate all advertisements in China should uphold national dignity and interest and respect the motherland's culture."[44] Apparently LeBron battling a kung fu master isn't appropriate in the land of Confucius. Also, magazines have been ordered to use a direct translation of the often-obscure name that appears on their license or use no English name at all. Thus, *Cosmopolitan* would become "Trends Lady," *Woman's Day* would become "Friends of Health," and *Esquire* would become "Trends Man." Such diversity of laws among countries extends to advertising, pricing, sales agreements, and other commercial activities. Indeed, one study suggests that governmental policies actually forestall firms from taking a marketing orientation in their operations.[45]

There is some hope that the European Union will soon have a common commercial code. One step in that direction is the proposal to harmonize the pan-European regulation of promotions based on the conservative laws that cover promotions in Germany, Austria,

[40]Elaine Sciolino, "Battle Plans Go into Action as France Copes with a Twice-Yearly Onslaught," *Oregonian*, January 9, 2003, p. A6.

[41]Richard W. Pollay, "Considering the Evidence, No Wonder the Court Endorses Canada's Restrictions on Cigarette Advertising," *Journal of Public Policy and Marketing* 23, no. 1 (2004), pp. 80–88.

[42]Frederick Balfour and David Kiley, "Ad Agencies Unchained," *BusinessWeek*, April 25, 2005, pp. 50–51.

[43]Geoffrey A. Fowler, "China Cracks Down on Commercials," *Wall Street Journal*, February 19, 2004, p. B7.

[44]"China Bans Nike's LeBron Commercial," *Associated Press*, December 6, 2004.

[45]Rilian Qu and Christine T. Ennew, "Developing a Market Orientation in a Transitional Economy: The Role of Government Regulation and Ownership Structure," *Journal of Public Policy and Marketing* 24, no. 1 (2005), pp. 82–89.

A Greenpeace protester peers out from inside a plastic rubbish bin in Hong Kong, where activists were calling on the government to develop a comprehensive recycling industry which they claim will create 2,000 new jobs. A recent study by Greenpeace found that only 148 out of 18,200 rubbish bins in Hong Kong have waste separation compartments. It is calling on the government to revamp its current waste management procedures to facilitate a comprehensive system to reduce, recover, and recycle. (© AFP/Getty Images)

and Belgium. However, this proposal is meeting with strong resistance from several groups because of its severe restriction on promotions. Meanwhile, others push for even broader-based harmonization of marketing regulations involving the United States, United Nations, and the WTO.[46]

Although the European Union is a beautiful picture of economic cooperation, there is still the reality of dealing with 25 different countries, cultures, and languages, as well as 25 different legal systems. Even though some of Germany's complicated trade laws were revoked in 2000, groups such as the Center for Combating Unfair Competition, an industry-financed organization, continue to work to maintain the status quo. Before the German law was revoked, the Center's lawyers filed 1,000 lawsuits a year, going after, for example, a grocery store that offered discount coupons or a deli that gave a free cup of coffee to a customer who had already bought 10; its efforts will surely continue.

Although the goal of full integration and a common commercial code has not been totally achieved in the European Union, decisions by the European Court continue to strike down individual-country laws that impede competition across borders. In a recent decision, the European Court ruled that a French cosmetics company could sell its wares by mail in Germany and advertise them at a markdown from their original prices, a direct contradiction of German law. As the Single European Market Act is implemented, many of the legal and trade differences that have existed for decades will vanish. Surprisingly enough, standards set by the European Union for food, software, cars, and other items affect U.S. product standards as well. In many cases, the reconciliation of so many different consumer protection standards that existed in European countries prior to the European Union resulted in rules more rigorous than those for many U.S. products. Consequently, many U.S. products have had to be redesigned to comply with European standards. Once, a product designed for U.S. standards could be sold anywhere in the world; for many products this is no longer the case. For example, Carrier air conditioners have been redesigned to comply with European recycling rules; Microsoft has modified contracts with software makers; Internet service providers give consumers a wider choice of technologies; McDonald's has ceased including soft plastic toys with its Happy Meals and has withdrawn all genetically engineered potatoes from its restaurants worldwide. All this is because of the need to reconcile U.S. standards with those of the European Union. For many U.S. products with markets in Europe, meeting EU standards is less expensive than designing products especially for Europe.

Green Marketing Legislation

Multinational corporations also face a growing variety of legislation designed to address environmental issues.[47] Global concern for the environment extends beyond industrial pollution, hazardous waste disposal, and rampant deforestation to include issues that focus directly on consumer products. Green marketing laws focus on environmentally friendly products and on product packaging and its effect on solid waste management.

Germany has passed the most stringent green marketing laws that regulate the management and recycling of packaging waste.[48] The new packaging laws were introduced in three phases. The first phase required all transport packaging, such as crates, drums, pallets, and Styrofoam containers, to be accepted back by the manufacturers and distributors for recycling. The second phase required manufacturers, distributors, and retailers to accept all returned secondary packaging, including corrugated boxes, blister packs, packaging designed

---

[46]Paula Fitzgerald Boone and Karen Russo France, "International Harmonization of Food and Nutrition Regulation: The Good and The Bad," *Journal of Public Policy and Marketing* 22, no. 1 (2003), pp. 102–111.

[47]John Carey, "Global Warming: Suddenly the Climate in Washington Is Changing," *BusinessWeek*, June 27, 2005, p. 91.

[48]Jack Ewing, "A Cold Shoulder for Coca-Cola," *BusinessWeek*, May 2, 2005, p. 52.

to prevent theft, packaging for vending machine applications, and packaging for promotional purposes. The third phase requires all retailers, distributors, and manufacturers to accept returned sales packaging, including cans, plastic containers for dairy products, foil wrapping, Styrofoam packages, and folding cartons such as cereal boxes. The requirement for retailers to take back sales packaging has been suspended as long as the voluntary green dot program remains a viable substitute. A green dot on a package identifies manufacturers that have agreed to ensure a regular collection of used packaging materials directly from the consumer's home or from designated local collection points.

Reclaiming recyclables extends beyond packaging to automobiles. By 2006, manufacturers based in European Union nations must take back any cars they produced that no longer have resale value and pay for proper disposal. Further, by the same year, 85 percent of a scrapped car's material must be recovered for future use.

Many European countries also have devised schemes to identify products that comply with certain criteria that make them more environmentally friendly than similar products. Products that meet these criteria are awarded an "ecolabel" that the manufacturer can display on packaging to signal to customers that it is an environmentally friendly product. The EC is becoming more aggressive in issuing new directives and in harmonizing ecolabeling and other environmental laws across all member states. Ecolabeling and EU packaging laws are discussed in more detail in the chapter on consumer products (Chapter 12).[49]

Antitrust

With the exception of the United States, antitrust laws were either nonexistent or not enforced in most of the world's countries for the better part of the 20th century. However, the European Union,[50] Japan, and many other countries have begun to actively enforce their antitrust laws patterned after those in the United States.[51] Antimonopoly, price discrimination, supply restrictions, and full-line forcing are areas in which the European Court of Justice has dealt severe penalties. For example, before Procter & Gamble was allowed to buy VP-Schickedanz AG, a German hygiene products company, it had to agree to sell off one of the German company's divisions that produced Camelia, a brand of sanitary napkins. P&G already marketed a brand of sanitary napkins in Europe, and the commission was concerned that allowing P&G to keep Camelia would give the company a controlling 60 percent of the German sanitary products market and 81 percent of Spain's. In another instance, Coca-Cola was fined $1.8 million for anticompetitive practices by France's antitrust authority.

The United States also intervenes when non-U.S. companies attempt to acquire American companies. Nestlé's proposed $2.8 billion acquisition of Dreyer's Grand Ice Cream hit a roadblock as U.S. antitrust officials opposed the deal on grounds that it would lead to less competition and higher prices for gourmet ice cream in the United States.[52] At times, companies are subject to antitrust charges in more than one country. Microsoft had a partial victory against antitrust charges brought in the United States only to face similar anticompetitive charges against Microsoft's Windows 2000 operating system in the EU.[53] The probe is based on possible competitive benefits to European software concerns if legal limits are placed on Microsoft. American companies have faced antitrust violations since the trust-busting days of President Theodore Roosevelt but much less so in other parts of the world. Enforcement of antitrust in Europe was almost nonexistent until the early stages of the European Union established antitrust legislation.

---

[49]For information on the EU's environmental directives as well as other information about the European Union, visit www.europa.eu.int. This address will take you to the home page, where you can search for topics and visit various information sources about the European Union.

[50]Andy Reinhardt, "An Acid Test for Nickel Neelie," *BusinessWeek*, June 6, 2005, p. 46.

[51]Mark Landler and Paul Meller, "Europe Votes to Overhaul Antitrust Regulations," *New York Times*, November 11, 2002, p.W1; "EU Approves Starwood-Meridien-Lehman Deal," *Reuters*, July 20, 2005.

[52]William Hall, "Nestlé May Be Close to Dreyer's Deal," *Financial Times*, May 14, 2003.

[53]John R. Wilke and Brandon Mitchener, "Microsoft Rivals Allege Antitrust in New EU Case," *Wall Street Journal*, February 2, 2003, p. A1.

Competitive methods illegal in the United States can be legal in another country. If you go to one of the 15 Tony Roma franchises in Mexico, the only beer you can buy is Modelo, brewed by Grupo Modelo SA, maker of the top-selling imported beer in the United States, Corona Extra. "We used to have 28 different kinds of beer, including American beers," says the general manager of Tony Roma's, "but Modelo gave us money to sell only its beer." A Modelo distributor paid one town to ban stores from selling any other beer in exchange for cash, school uniforms, lighting for public parks, and free beer at city parties. That kind of tie-up, illegal in the United States, is common in restaurants, corner stores, and stadiums throughout Mexico. Such tactics have given Modelo and its rival, Fomento Economico Mexicano SA, 99 percent of the market. Such tactics, legal in Mexico but illegal in the United States, gives Modelo and other Mexican brewers an advantage in the U.S. market, where Corona accounts for 40 percent of all U.S. beer imports and 11 percent of the overall U.S. beer market compared to just 1 percent of the Mexican market for U.S. beer. Ironically, Pepsi-Cola and Coca-Cola dominate the Mexican soft drink market and have used similar tactics to compete with one another—that is, until a recent ruling that Coke is no longer allowed to make such tie-ins because it prevents Pepsi from competing.[54] Worldwide antitrust enforcement or lack thereof is just one more important areas of law that each multinational firm must consider in its strategic decision making.

U.S. Laws Apply in Host Countries

All governments are concerned with protecting their political and economic interests domestically and internationally; any activity or action, wherever it occurs, that adversely threatens national interests is subject to government control. Leaving the political boundaries of a home country does not exempt a business from home-country laws. Regardless of the nation where business is done, a U.S. citizen is subject to certain laws of the United States. What is illegal for an American business at home can also be illegal by U.S. law in foreign jurisdictions for the firm, its subsidiaries, and licensees of U.S. technology.

Laws that prohibit taking a bribe, trading with the enemy, participating in a commercial venture that negatively affects the U.S. economy, participating in an unauthorized boycott such as the Arab boycott, or any other activity deemed to be against the best interests of the United States apply to U.S. businesses and their subsidiaries and licensees regardless of where they operate. Thus at any given time a U.S. citizen in a foreign country must look not only at the laws of the host country, but at home law as well.

The question of jurisdiction of U.S. law over acts committed outside the territorial limits of the country has been settled by the courts through application of a long-established principle of international law, the "objective theory of jurisdiction." This concept holds that even if an act is committed outside the territorial jurisdiction of U.S. courts, those courts can nevertheless have jurisdiction if the act produces effects within the home country. The only possible exception may be when the violation is the result of enforced compliance with local law.

Foreign Corrupt Practices Act

Recall from Chapter 5 that the Foreign Corrupt Practices Act (FCPA) makes it illegal for companies to pay bribes to foreign officials, candidates, or political parties. Stiff penalties can be assessed against company officials, directors, employees, or agents found guilty of paying a bribe or of knowingly participating in or authorizing the payment of a bribe. However, also recall that bribery, which can range from lubrication to extortion, is a common business custom in many countries even though illegal.[55]

The original FCPA lacked clarity, and early interpretations were extremely narrow and confusing. Subsequent amendments in the Omnibus Trade and Competitiveness Act

---

[54]David Luhnow, "Why Corona Is Big Here, and Miller Is So Scarce in Mexico," *Wall Street Journal,* January 1, 2003, B1.

[55]For discussions of the FCPA, updates, and other information, visit the FCPA home page at www.usdoj.gov/criminal/fraud/fcpa.html.

clarified two of the most troubling issues. Corporate officers' liability was changed from having reason to know that illegal payments were made to knowing of or authorizing illegal payments. In addition, if it is customary in the culture, small (grease or lubrication) payments made to encourage officials to complete routine government actions such as processing papers, stamping visas, and scheduling inspections are not illegal per se.

The debate continues as to whether the FCPA puts U.S. businesses at a disadvantage. Some argue that U.S. businesses are at a disadvantage in international business transactions in those cases where bribery payments are customary, whereas others contend that it has little effect, indeed, that it helps companies to "just say no." The truth probably lies somewhere in between. The consensus is that most U.S. firms are operating within the law, and several studies indicate that the FCPA has not been as detrimental to MNC interest as originally feared because exports to developed and developing countries continue to be favorable.

U.S. firms seem to be able to compete and survive without resorting to corruption in the most corrupt societies. This does not mean, however, that violations do not occur or that companies are not penalized for violations. For example, a U.S. environmental engineering firm was found to have made corrupt payments to an Egyptian government official to assist the company in gaining a contract. The company agreed not to violate the FCPA in the future and agreed to pay a civil fine of $400,000 and to reimburse the Department of Justice for the costs of the investigation. Further, the company agreed to establish FCPA compliance procedures and to provide certifications of compliance annually for five years. Other firms have paid even larger fines in recent years, and the Justice Department has agreed not to prosecute firms with "excellent" training programs in place.

National Security Laws

U.S. firms, their foreign subsidiaries, or foreign firms that are licensees of U.S. technology cannot sell a product to a country in which the sale is considered by the U.S. government to affect national security. Further, responsibility extends to the final destination of the product regardless of the number of intermediaries that may be involved in the transfer of goods.

An extensive export control system was created to slow the spread of sensitive technologies to the former Soviet Union, China, and other communist countries that were viewed as major threats to U.S. security. The control of the sale of goods considered to have a strategic and military value was extremely strict. But with the end of the Cold War, export controls were systematically dismantled until 1999, when a congressional committee reported Chinese espionage activities and American aerospace companies transferring sensitive technology irresponsibly. Following the report, legislation was passed again restricting the export of products or technologies that might be used by other countries for defense applications.

The events of September 11, 2001, added another set of restrictions related to weapons of mass destruction (WMD). Unfortunately, many of the products used in WMD are difficult to control since they have dual purposes; that is, they have legitimate uses as well as being important in manufacturing WMD. For example, Iraq, which was allowed to import medical equipment despite a U.N. embargo, purchased, under the pretext of medical benefits, six machines that destroy kidney stones. The manufacturer accepted the claim that Saddam Hussein was concerned about kidney stones in the Iraqi population and began shipping the machines. However, integral components of these machines are high-precision electronic switches that are also used to set off the chain reaction in thermonuclear weapons. When 120 additional switches as "spare parts" were ordered, a red flag went up and the shipments were stopped.

Countless numbers of dual-purpose technologies are exported from the United States. A sticking point with dual-purpose exports is the intent of the buyer. Silicon Graphics Inc. (SGI) sold computer equipment to a Russian nuclear laboratory that contended it was for nonmilitary use, which would have been legal. However, the Department of Justice ruled that since the sale was made to a government-operated facility involved in both civil and noncivil activities, SGI should have applied for the correct export license. SGI paid a fine of $1 million plus a $500,000 fine for each of the export violations. National security laws prohibit a U.S. company, its subsidiaries, joint ventures, or licensees to sell controlled products without special permission from the U.S. government. The consequences of violation of the Trading with the Enemy Act can be severe: fines, prison sentences, and, in the case of foreign companies, economic sanctions.

Exports are controlled for the protection and promotion of human rights, as a means of enforcing foreign policy, because of national shortages, to control technology,[56] and for a host of other reasons the U.S. government deems necessary to protect its best interests. In years past, the government restricted trade with South Africa (human rights) and restricted the sale of wheat to the Soviet Union in retaliation for its invasion of Afghanistan (foreign policy). Currently, the government restricts trade with Iran (foreign policy)[57] and the sale of leading-edge electronics (control of technology), and it prohibits the export of pesticides that have not been approved for use in the United States (to avoid the return of residue of unauthorized pesticides in imported food and protect U.S. consumers from the so-called circle of poison). In each of these cases, U.S. law binds U.S. businesses regardless of where they operate.[58]

Antitrust Laws

Antitrust enforcement has two purposes in international commerce. The first is to protect American consumers by ensuring that they benefit from products and ideas produced by foreign competitors as well as by domestic competitors. Competition from foreign producers is important when imports are, or could be, a major source of a product or when a single firm dominates a domestic industry. This becomes relevant in many joint ventures, particularly if the joint venture creates a situation in which a U.S. firm entering a joint venture with a foreign competitor restricts competition for the U.S. parent in the U.S. market.

The second purpose of antitrust legislation is to protect American export and investment opportunities against any privately imposed restrictions. The concern is that all U.S.-based firms engaged in the export of goods, services, or capital should be allowed to compete on merit and not be shut out by restrictions imposed by bigger or less-principled competitors.

The questions of jurisdiction and how U.S. antitrust laws apply are frequently asked but only vaguely answered. The basis for determination ultimately rests with the interpretation of Sections I and II of the Sherman Act. Section I states that "every contract, combination . . . or conspiracy in restraint of trade or commerce among the several states or with foreign nations is hereby declared to be illegal." Section II makes it a violation to "monopolize, or attempt to monopolize, or combine or conspire with any other person or persons, to monopolize any part of the trade or commerce among the several states, or with foreign nations."

The Justice Department recognizes that application of U.S. antitrust laws to overseas activities raises some difficult questions of jurisdiction. It recognizes that U.S. antitrust-law enforcement should not interfere unnecessarily with the sovereign interest of a foreign nation. At the same time, however, the Antitrust Division is committed to controlling foreign transactions at home or abroad that have a substantial and foreseeable effect on U.S. commerce. When such business practices occur, there is no question in the Antitrust Division of the Department of Justice that U.S. laws apply.

Antiboycott Law

Under the antiboycott law,[59] U.S. companies are forbidden to participate in any unauthorized foreign boycott; further, they are required to report any request to cooperate with a boycott.

---

[56]Deborah Zabarenko, "U.S. Policy Curbs Global Space Cooperation," *Reuters*, June 23, 2005; "U.S. in Talks with Boeing over Sensor Sales to China," *Reuters*, July 7, 2005; "Space Station, No Plan B for Outer Space," *The Economist*, March 12, 2005, pp. 75–76.

[57]Kathryn Kranhod, "GE to Stop Seeking Business in Iran," *Wall Street Journal*, February 3, 2005, p. B3.

[58]Export controls will be discussed in more detail in Chapter 15.

[59]The antiboycott law applies only to those boycotts not sanctioned by the U.S. government. Sanctioned boycotts, such as the boycotts against trade with Cuba and Iran are initiated by the United States and must be honored by U.S. firms.

The antiboycott law was a response to the Arab League boycott of Israeli businesses.[60] The Arab League boycott of Israel has three levels: A primary boycott bans direct trade between Arab states and Israel, a secondary boycott bars Arab governments from doing business with companies that do business with Israel, and a tertiary boycott bans Arab governments from doing business with companies that do business with companies doing business with Israel.[61]

When companies do not comply with the Arab League's boycott directives, their names are placed on a blacklist and they are excluded from trade with members of the Arab League. U.S. companies are caught in the middle: If they trade with Israel, the Arab League will not do business with them, and if they refuse to do business with Israel in order to trade with an Arab League member, they will be in violation of U.S. law.[62] One hospital supply company that had been trading with Israel was charged with closing a plant in Israel in order to have the company taken off the Arab League blacklist. After an investigation, the company pleaded guilty, was fined $6.6 million, and was prohibited from doing business in Syria and Saudi Arabia for two years. A less costly fine of $12,000 was paid by a freight forwarder who certified that the goods shipped for a third party were not of Israeli origin, were not shipped from Israel, and did not contain any material from Israel.

Extraterritoriality of U.S. Laws

The issue of the extraterritoriality of U.S. laws is especially important to U.S. multinational firms because the long arm of U.S. legal jurisdiction causes anxiety for heads of state. Foreign governments fear the influence of American government policy on their economies through U.S. multinationals.[63]

Especially troublesome are those instances when U.S. law is in conflict with host countries' economic or political goals. Conflict arises when the host government requires joint ventures to do business within the country and the U.S. Justice Department restricts or forbids such ventures because of their U.S. anticompetitive effects. Host countries see this influence as evidence of U.S. interference. When U.S. MNCs' subsidiaries are prohibited from making a sale in violation of the U.S. Trading with the Enemy Act, host governments react with hostility toward the extraterritorial application of U.S. foreign policy. This chapter's Global Perspective is a good illustration of the extraterritoriality of U.S. law and how it has an impact on a friendly neighbor as well as a major multinational company.

In an interesting development, MNCs are being held liable for the human-rights abuses of foreign governments. Lawsuits are being brought in U.S. courts against U.S. MNCs, charging them with doing business with oppressive regimes. Unocal Corporation is being sued for doing business with Burma's military regime, which forced peasants at gunpoint to help build a pipeline for Unocal. Unocal denies the charges. This case was brought under the Alien Claims Act, originally intended to reassure Europe that the fledgling United States would not harbor pirates or assassins. It permits foreigners to sue in U.S. courts for violations of the "the law of nations." Businesses like IBM, Citibank, and Coca-Cola worry that they may be socked with huge jury damages for the misdeeds of oppressive governments. Employment lawyers warn that multinational companies are likely to face more lawsuits from the Third World.[64]

---

[60]Jannie Zacharia, "U.S Seeking Stiffer Penalties for Supporters of Arab Boycott," *Jerusalem Post*, November 7, 2002; Oanh Ha, "Ariba Chief in Line for U.S Commerce Post," *San Jose Mercury News*, June 30, 2005, p. MO1.

[61]For those non-U.S. companies trading with the Arab League and complying with the boycott, each was required to include a statement on the shipping invoices. On an invoice for 10 buses to be shipped from Brazil to Kuwait, the following statement appeared: "We certify that we are the producer and supplier of the shipped goods; we are neither blacklisted by the Arab Boycott of Israeli nor are we the head office branch or subsidiary of a boycotted company. No Israeli capital is invested in this firm, no company capital or capital of its owners is invested in any Israeli company; our products are not of Israeli origin and do not contain Israeli raw material or labor."

[62]For a list of current cases against firms violating the antiboycott law, see www.bxa.doc.gov and select Antiboycott Compliance and then Antiboycott Case Histories.

[63]Anthony Ferner, Phil Almond, and Trevor Colling, "Institutional Theory and the Cross-National Transfer of Employment Policy: The Case of 'Workforce Diversity' in U.S. Multinationals," *Journal of International Business Studies* 36, no. 3 (2005), pp. 304–321.

[64]"Global Law Suits to Increase," *People Management*, March 20, 2003, p. 9.

When the intent of any kind of overseas activity is to restrain trade, there is no question about the appropriateness of applying U.S. laws. There is a question, however, when the intent is to conclude a reasonable business transaction. If the U.S. government encourages U.S. firms to become multinational, then the government needs to make provisions for resolution of differences when conflict arises between U.S. law and host-government laws.

Cyberlaw: Unresolved Issues

The Internet is by its nature a global enterprise for which no political or national boundaries are closed. Although this is its strength, it also creates problems when existing laws do not clearly address the uniqueness of the Internet and its related activities.[65] Existing law is vague or does not completely cover such issues as gambling,[66] the protection of domain names,[67] taxes, jurisdiction in cross-border transactions, and contractual issues. The European Union, the United States, and many other countries are drafting legislation to address the myriad legal questions not clearly addressed by current law. But until these laws apply worldwide, companies will have to rely on individual-country laws, which may or may not provide protection.[68]

Domain Names and Cybersquatters

Unfortunately, the ease with which Web names can be registered and the low cost of registering has led to thousands being registered. Cybersquatters (CSQs) buy and register descriptive nouns, geographic names, names of ethnic groups and pharmaceutical substances, and other similar descriptors and hold them until they can be sold at an inflated price. For example, a cybersquatter sold "www.themortgage.com" for $500,000; the record price paid so far is $7.5 million for the domain name "www.business.com." If a cybersquatter has registered a generic domain name that a company wants, the only recourse is to buy it.

Another ploy of CSQs is to register familiar names and known trademarks that divert traffic from intended destinations or to sell competing products. eBay, the world's largest online auction house, was embroiled in a dispute with an entrepreneur in Nova Scotia who registered "www.ebay.ca," thus forcing the U.S. company to use "www.ca.ebay.com" for its newly launched Canadian Web site until it was successful in regaining the use of "www.ebay.ca"; both Web addresses now go to the same site.

CSQs register a well-known brand or trademark that misdirects a person to the CSQ's site or to a competing company's site. For example, an adult entertainment Web site registered "www.candyland.com." Hasbro, the toy company, markets a game for children called "Candy Land." Disturbed by the thought that customers might end up at an adult entertainment site, Hasbro wanted to have the site vacated. It had the option of suing to have it removed or buying the domain name. Hasbro elected to sue and, although the adult Web site was not directly infringing on its trademark, the courts deemed it to be damaging to the reputation of Hasbro and its children's game. The Web address now takes you directly to a Hasbro site.

Other cybersquatting abuses that can pose a serious threat to business include parody sites, protest sites, and hate sites. A good example is "www.walmartsucks.org," a site highly critical of Wal-Mart. This type of Web site may be difficult to prevent since the right to free speech is protected. The only defense Wal-Mart might have is to challenge the Web site's right to use a trade name to direct someone to the site.

A growing number of celebrity names have been hijacked. Julia Roberts had her name registered by a CSQ, "www.juliaroberts.com," and so did British Prime Minister Tony Blair's baby. Its name was registered, "www.leoblair.com," minutes after the name was made

[65]Alan Riding, "A French Call to Arms over Google Challenge," *International Herald Tribune*, March 31, 2005, p. 2.

[66]Willam R. Eadington, "The Future of Online Gambling in the United States and Elsewhere," *Journal of Public Policy and Marketing* 23, no. 2 (2004), pp. 214–219.

[67]Chip Cummins, "Shell Fights over Domain Name ahead of Parent Firms' Merger," *Wall Street Journal Europe*, June 2, 2005, p. A4.

[68]Jefferson Graham, "File-Sharing Beat Goes On," *USAToday*, June 29, 2005, p. 3B.

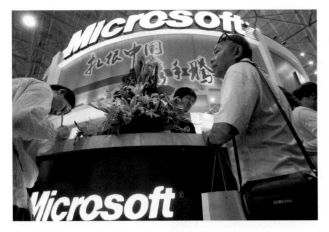

Potential customers visit a Microsoft booth in Beijing. When Chinese bloggers use Microsoft's service to post messages and type in such terms as "democracy," "capitalism," "liberty," or "human rights," they get a yellow light and a computer warning: "This message includes forbidden language. Please delete the prohibited expression." Microsoft has agreed to this sort of censorship, explaining that it is just following local laws and that the company still provides a most useful service to its Chinese clients. The critics disagree. The argument goes on. (AP/Wide World Photos)

public. Julia Roberts sued under the Anti–Cyber Squatting Consumer Protection Act (ACPA), a dispute resolution forum in the United States that facilitates action against domain name squatters if the domain name infringes on a trademark or personal name. Prime Minister Blair had "leoblair.com" evicted by his appeal to Nominet Dispute Resolution Service (DRS), a forum for resolving cybersquatting disputes in the United Kingdom. DRS requires the complainant to prove that it has rights in respect to name or mark identical or similar to the respondent's domain name, and that the domain name is an abusive registration. Abusive registration is defined as a domain name that either was registered or has been used in a manner which takes unfair advantage of or is unfairly detrimental to the complainant's rights.

In addition to CSQs hijacking trademarks, personal names, and other intellectual property, lawsuits involving libel, defamation, and product liability are creating legal quagmires for Internet users.[69] Consider a case involving Dow Jones and an Australian industrialist over an allegedly defamatory article that appeared on a U.S.-based Dow Jones Web site. The plaintiff sued Dow Jones, the Web site owner, as the author of the article.[70] Dow Jones argued that the suit should be tried in a New Jersey court, where its servers, the point of publication, are located. The Australian argued that the suit should be brought in Australia because that is where his reputation had been damaged. Australian law favors plaintiffs, whereas in the United States First Amendment rights demand a high burden of proof in libel cases. Australian courts sided with the plaintiff.

It is easy to imagine many situations where the actions of companies or information posted on a site can lead to a lawsuit when Internet content is unlawful in one country but not in the host country. For example, an American studio that makes a movie with nude scenes could be prosecuted in a country that bans nudity in movies. Not only would the movie studio be libel, but the Internet service provider could be liable for material posted on its Web site. Writers and publishers could face libel suits in countries with laws restrictive of free speech where weak or nonexistent free speech protections are tools to intimidate and censor.[71] Internet publishers or individual Web site owners fear they can be sued for defamation from any or many jurisdictions, merely because their articles can be downloaded anywhere in the world. Lawsuits involving libel, defamation, and product liability cause companies to voluntarily restrict their Web sites to selected countries rather than leave themselves open to legal action. The Internet is not a libel-free zone.

The United States has taken a giant step in dealing with domain name pirates by passing the Anti–Cyber Squatting Consumer Protection Act (ACPA), and the World Intellectual Property Organization (WIPO) established a structure through the Internet Corporation for Assigned Names and Numbers (ICANN) in which anyone registering a domain name with complying registries must agree to dispute resolution. This is known as the Uniform Dispute Resolution Policy (UDRP). Neither the ACPA nor the UDPR provides fail-safe ways of recovering a domain name once it has been cybersquatted.[72]

A study indicated that protection is needed for geographical names, ethnic groups, and pharmaceutical substances, all of which have been appropriated by CSQs. These abuses

[69]Brian Grow and Jason Bush, "Hacker Hunters, An Elite Force That Takes on the Dark Side of Computing," *BusinessWeek*, May 30, 2005, pp.74–76.

[70]Ralph Wragg, "Journalist to Test Right of Free Speech in Gutnick Case," *Australian Business News*, April 17, 2003.

[71]Mark Magnier and Joseph Menn, "As China Censors the Internet, Money Talks," *Los Angeles Times*, June 17, 2005, pp. A1, A14.

[72]Jonathan Robinson, "How to Prevent Cybersquatters," *Managing Internet Property,* March 2003, p. 25.

will continue unless preventive steps are taken. Agencies like the Artists Coalition against Piracy (ACAP), DRS, and WIPO[73] are useful, but, besides being costly, they only address disputes involving sites using names that are trademarked and have commercial value or are so well known they have common-law trademark rights. Even though protection from cybersquatters is not perfect, if a business has taken steps to properly defend its brand names, trade names, or product names and properly registers them, it greatly enhances its ability to defend against improper use of the name by a third party. Countries that recognize intellectual property will generally refer to those laws to resolve disputes.

Most country's courts are inclined to assert jurisdiction over online activity, where it originates, so long as harm is experienced locally and the sense is that the party responsible either knew or ought to have known that the harm was a likely consequence of its actions. Most agree, though, that laws that are expressly designed to apply not just in a single country but worldwide are necessary to untangle the legal hassles that are occurring.

Of 100 business leaders polled by the International Chamber of Commerce, more than one-third said legal uncertainty covering Internet operations affected "significant business decisions." The most immediate impact, according to the ICC, is clear: Many online merchants refuse to sell outside their home countries.[74]

Taxes

Another thorny issue in e-commerce concerns the collection of taxes. A typical tax system relies on knowing where a particular economic activity is located. But the Internet enables individual workers to operate in many different countries while sitting at the same desk. When taxes should be collected, where they should be collected, and by whom are all issues under consideration by countries around the world. In the past, a company was deemed to have a taxable presence in a country if it had a permanent establishment there. But whether the existence of a server or a Web site qualifies as such a presence is not clear. One proposal that has enthusiastic support from tax authorities is for servers to be designated as "virtual permanent establishments" and thus subject to local taxes.

To pinpoint when and where a sale takes place in cyberspace is difficult, and, unless elusive taxpayers can be pinpointed, any tax may be difficult to collect. In "brick-and-mortar" sales, the retailer collects, but when the Internet site is in one country and the customer is in another, who collects? One proposal is to have shipping companies such as FedEx or credit card companies collect—obviously, neither party is receiving this suggestion enthusiastically.

The EU Commission has announced plans for a directive to force foreign companies to levy value-added tax (VAT) on services delivered via the Internet, television, or radio to customers in the European Union. Foreign companies with sales via the Internet over €100,000 ($95,410) inside the European Union would have to register in at least one EU country and levy VAT at that country's rate, somewhere between 15 percent and 25 percent. The tax is justified on the basis of leveling the playing field. EU companies have to charge their EU customers VAT, whereas foreign companies supplying the same service to the same customers are duty free. U.S. companies are protesting, calling the proposal "e-protectionism." Although the EU plan is only a proposal now, as the value of Internet transactions increases, the taxman will sooner or later get his share.[75]

Jurisdiction of Disputes and Validity of Contracts

As countries realize that existing laws relating to commerce do not always clearly address the uniqueness of the Internet and its related activities, a body of cyberlaw is gradually being created. Two of the most troubling areas are determining whose laws will prevail in legal disputes between parties located in different countries and establishing the contractual

---

[73]The World Intellectual Property Organization is one of the 16 specialized agencies of the United Nations system of organizations. It administers 23 international treaties dealing with different aspects of intellectual property.

[74]Matthew Newman, "So Many Countries, So Many Laws," *Wall Street Journal,* April 28, 2003, p. R8.

[75]For a report on a resolution on cross-border tax issues proposed by OECD, see 'OECD Launches Project on Improving the Resolution of Cross-Border Tax Disputes," www.oecd.org and select Taxation. The OECD proposes a variety of issues related to the Internet, all of which can be found at this site.

validity of electronic communications. The European Union is having the most difficulty in reconciling the vast differences in the laws among its member states in order to create a uniform law. For example, a draft regulation debated in Brussels and other European capitals would have required vendors to comply with 25 different, and sometimes bizarre, sets of national rules on consumer protection—ranging from dozens of restrictions on advertising to France's requirement that all contracts must be concluded in French regardless of whether businesses intend to sell goods for export to France.

The EU Commission has adopted an e-commerce directive that will permit online retailers to trade by the rules of their home country unless the seller had enticed or approached the consumer by way of advertising. Then, any legal action is to take place in the consumer's country of residence. The rationale is that if a company actively seeks customers in a given country, it ought to be willing to abide by that country's consumer-protection laws. Whether the directive will be accepted by all 25 member states is still problematic.

The European Commission has begun to review the entire regulatory framework for the technological infrastructure of the information society. The commission is working on various pieces of legislation intended to place electronic commerce on an equal footing with conventional commerce.[76] One of the first steps was to introduce an EU–wide computer network dubbed EEJ-net that provides an easy way to resolve small-scale disputes out of court. Problems over deliveries, defective products, or products that do not fit their description can be dealt with by a single one-stop national contact point, or clearinghouse, in each member state. The consumer will be able to find information and support in making a claim to the out-of-court dispute-resolution system in the country where the product supplier is based.

Establishing the validity of contractual law for e-commerce is making substantial progress also. India, for example, recently passed a law that recognizes e-mail as a valid form of communication, electronic contracts as legal and enforceable, and digital signatures as binding. Several countries are preparing, or have passed, legislation similar to the United Kingdom's that allows digital signatures to be used in the creation of online contracts that are just as legally binding as any paper-based original document.

Summary

Businesses face a multitude of problems in their efforts to develop successful marketing programs. Not the least of these problems is the varying legal systems of the world and their effect on business transactions. Just as political climate, cultural differences, local geography, different business customs, and the stage of economic development must be taken into account, so must such legal questions as jurisdictional and legal recourse in disputes, protection of intellectual property rights, extended U.S. law enforcement, and enforcement of antitrust legislation by U.S. and foreign governments. A primary marketing task is to develop a plan that will be enhanced, or at least not adversely affected, by these and other environmental elements. New to the international legal scene is the Internet, which, by its nature, creates a new set of legal entanglements, many of which have yet to be properly addressed. One thing is certain: The freedom that now exists on the World Wide Web will be only a faint memory before long. The myriad questions created by different laws and different legal systems indicate that the prudent path to follow at all stages of foreign marketing operations is one leading to competent counsel, well versed in the intricacies of the international legal environment.

Questions

1. Define the following terms:

   common law

   Islamic law

   prior use versus registration

   arbitration

   cybersquatters

   code law

   Marxist-socialist tenets

   conciliation

   litigation

2. How does the international marketer determine which legal system will have jurisdiction when legal disputes arise?

3. Discuss the state of international commercial law.

4. Discuss the limitations of jurisdictional clauses in contracts.

5. What is the "objective theory of jurisdiction"? How does it apply to a firm doing business within a foreign country?

[76]Madeline Thomas, "Cross-Border Shoppers May Find Refunds Elusive," *Reuters*, July 14, 2005.

6. Discuss some of the reasons why seeking an out-of-court settlement in international commercial legal disputes is probably better than suing.

7. Illustrate the procedure generally followed in international commercial disputes when settled under the auspices of a formal arbitration tribunal.

8. What are intellectual property rights? Why should a company in international marketing take special steps to protect them?

9. In many code-law countries, registration rather than prior use establishes ownership of intellectual property rights. Comment.

10. Discuss the advantages to the international marketer arising from the existence of the various international conventions on trademarks, patents, and copyrights.

11. "The legal environment of the foreign marketer takes on an added dimension of importance since there is no single uniform international commercial law which governs foreign business transactions." Comment.

12. Why is conciliation a better way to resolve a commercial dispute than arbitration?

13. Differentiate between conciliation and arbitration.

14. Assume you are a vice president in charge of a new business-to-business e-commerce division of a well-known major international auto parts manufacturer. A cybersquatter has registered the company name as a domain Web name. What are your options to secure the domain name for your company? Discuss the steps you should take to ensure worldwide protection of your domain name.

15. Discuss the issues of a Web site owner being liable for information posted on the site.

16. Discuss the motives of a cybersquatter. What recourse does a company have to defend itself against a cybersquatter?

8

Developing a Global Vision through Marketing Research

CHAPTER OUTLINE

Global Perspective: Selling Apples in Japan Can Be a Bruising Business

Breadth and Scope of International Marketing Research

The Research Process

Defining the Problem and Establishing Research Objectives

Problems of Availability and Use of Secondary Data
>   Availability of Data
>   Reliability of Data
>   Comparability of Data
>   Validating Secondary Data

Gathering Primary Data: Quantitative and Qualitative Research

Problems of Gathering Primary Data
>   Ability to Communicate Opinions
>   Willingness to Respond
>   Sampling in Field Surveys
>   Language and Comprehension

Multicultural Research: A Special Problem

Research on the Internet: A Growing Opportunity

Estimating Market Demand
>   Expert Opinion
>   Analogy

Problems in Analyzing and Interpreting Research Information

Responsibility for Conducting Marketing Research

Communicating with Decision Makers

Appendix: Sources of Secondary Data

CHAPTER LEARNING OBJECTIVES

What you should learn from Chapter 8:

- The importance of problem definition in international research

- The problems of availability and use of secondary data

- Quantitative and qualitative research methods

- Multicultural sampling and its problems in less developed countries

- Sources of secondary data

- How to analyze and use research information

Global Perspective

SELLING APPLES IN JAPAN CAN BE A BRUISING BUSINESS

Selling apples in Japan—whether they are of the edible or computer variety—can be a bruising business. In both cases, designing effective and competitive marketing strategies requires a deep knowledge of buyer behavior that may be distinctly different from that which marketers encounter in the United States.

Washington State apple growers needed 24 years to get their fruit past customs inspectors in Japan. The door finally opened to Red and Golden Delicious apples in 1995, and Japanese consumers immediately gobbled up nearly 8,500 tons. But in 1996, sales dropped precipitously to only 800 tons. The slide in sales can be attributed in part to the fact that U.S. apple growers did not anticipate the strength of Japanese consumers' seasonal preferences; Americans buy and eat apples year round, but Japanese consumers do not. The growers also did not anticipate the lasting effects of nationalism among many Japanese. As one older Japanese woman wrote to her sister in the United States, "Younger Japanese people simply do not have any respect. They just buy those American apples with no shame. They do not have any loyalty to the Japanese farmers. All they care about is the lower price." The late 1990s recession in Asia also hurt sales of Washington apples. More recently a World Trade Organization ruling pried open the Japanese apple market to new varieties—Braeburn, Fuji, Gala, Granny Smith, and Jona Gold. However, the American apples have continued to move slower than anticipated due to lower prices on domestic varieties, competition from Tasmania, and most recently a new quarantine because of fire blight.

As for apples of the computer variety, Apple Computers traditionally has been a greater success in Japan than in the States. Its market share in Japan has jumped to nearly 8 percent since Steve Jobs again took the reins at Apple, and it hopes to maintain its industry-leading growth rate well into the 21st century. But it won't be easy to continue taking a big bite out of the $40 billion Japanese personal computer (PC) market. Apple continues to have mixed results at home, and the losses in market share and reputation in the United States certainly affected buyers' perceptions in Japan in the past. Indeed, during the 2001 computer bust, Apple's sales fell 47 percent in Japan compared to "only" 33 percent worldwide. Ouch! Now Apple PC sales are outpacing the competition worldwide once again with a recovering Japanese market leading the way.

Moreover, the Japanese PC market works differently than that in the United States. Japanese businesses have been relatively slow to use PCs to boost productivity, and managers prefer to network in face-to-face settings rather than via electronic hookups. Additionally, Japan has fewer information professionals than does the United States. Such circumstances suggest that the rate of adoption of PCs in the Japanese workplace will not parallel that in the United States, meaning Apple has a smaller market in which to operate. Indeed, its most recent successes in Japan have been in the consumer market, where its bright colors make a fashion statement. Of course, fashions come and fashions go. Let's hope these Apples don't become perishable!

Selling either kind of apple in Japan will require the best marketing research efforts of U.S. firms. The basis of a marketing budget is the all-important forecast of demand, which requires statistical analyses and macroeconomic data from Japan. But before those data are collected, consumer focus groups and surveys must be conducted. U.S. marketers must also travel across the Pacific for visits to grocery stores, consumers' homes, or office buildings to see firsthand these evolving markets at their cores.

Sources: Garry Barker, "Apple Rolls out More iThings," *The Age*, February 22, 2000, p. 1; John Zarocostas, "WTO Rules Japan Apple Restrictions Unfair to U.S.," *Lloyd's List*, July 22, 2005, p. 4. For the latest information on Apple Computer, Inc.'s, current performance see its latest annual report, 2005.

It's crucial for top executives to get away from their desks and spend time in the marketplace. While detailed marketing research reports are important, decisions at the very top of the largest corporations must still be informed by a sense of the market and customers only obtainable through direct contact by top executives. Here we see Bill Gates (left) and Steven Jobs (right) going east and west talking with and learning from their customers in the most direct way. Both have heavy international travel schedules and both find face-to-face meetings with foreign vendors, partners, customers, and regulators to be an inescapable part of trying to understand their international markets. *(AP/Wide World Photos; © Jim Watson/AFP/Getty Images)*

Information is the key component in developing successful marketing strategies and avoiding major marketing blunders. Information needs range from the general data required to assess market opportunities to specific market information for decisions about product, promotion, distribution, and price. Sometimes the information can be bought from trusted research vendors or supplied by internal marketing research staff. But sometimes even the highest-level executives have to "get their shoes dirty" by putting in the miles and talking to key customers and directly observing the marketplace in action.[1] As an enterprise broadens its scope of operations to include international markets, the need for current, accurate information is magnified. Indeed, some researchers maintain that entry into a fast-developing, new-to-the-firm foreign market is one of the most daunting and ambiguous strategic decisions an executive can face. A marketer must find the most accurate and reliable data possible within the limits imposed by time, cost, and the present state of the art. The measure of a competent researcher is twofold: the ability to utilize the most sophisticated and adequate techniques and methods available within these limits, and the effective communication of insights to the decision makers in the firm. The latter often requires involving senior executives directly in the research process itself.

Marketing research is traditionally defined as the systematic gathering, recording, and analyzing of data to provide information useful in marketing decision making. Although the research processes and methods are basically the same whether applied in Columbus, Ohio, or Colombo, Sri Lanka, international marketing research involves two additional complications. First, information must be communicated across cultural boundaries. That is, executives in Chicago must be able to "translate" their research questions into terms that consumers in Guangzhou, China, can understand. Then the Chinese answers must be put into terms (i.e., reports and data summaries) that American managers can comprehend. Fortunately, there are often internal staff and research agencies that are quite experienced in these kinds of cross-cultural communication tasks.

---

[1]Peter Drucker's wisdom improves with age. In his *Wall Street Journal* article of May 11, 1990 (p. A15), he eloquently makes the case for direct observation of the marketplace by even the most senior executives. For the most substantive argument in that same vein, see Gerald Zaltman's description of emotional aspects of managerial decision making in "Rethinking Market Research: Putting People Back In," *Journal of Marketing Research* 34, (November 1997), pp. 424–437.

Second, the environments within which the research tools are applied are often different in foreign markets. Rather than acquire new and exotic methods of research, the international marketing researcher must develop the ability for imaginative and deft application of tried and tested techniques in sometimes totally strange milieus. The mechanical problems of implementing foreign marketing research often vary from country to country. Within a foreign environment, the frequently differing emphases on the kinds of information needed, the often limited variety of appropriate tools and techniques available, and the difficulty of implementing the research process constitute the challenges facing most international marketing researchers.

This chapter deals with the operational problems encountered in gathering information in foreign countries for use by international marketers. Emphasis is on those elements of data generation that usually prove especially troublesome in conducting research in an environment other than the United States.

Breadth and Scope of International Marketing Research

The basic difference between domestic and foreign market research is the broader scope needed for foreign research, necessitated by higher levels of uncertainty. Research can be divided into three types based on information needs: (1) general information about the country, area, and/or market; (2) information necessary to forecast future marketing requirements by anticipating social, economic, consumer, and industry trends within specific markets or countries; and (3) specific market information used to make product, promotion, distribution, and price decisions and to develop marketing plans. In domestic operations, most emphasis is placed on the third type, gathering specific market information, because the other data are often available from secondary sources.

A country's political stability, cultural attributes, and geographical characteristics are some of the kinds of information not ordinarily gathered by domestic marketing research departments but which are required for a sound assessment of a foreign market. This broader scope of international marketing research is reflected in Unisys Corporation's planning steps, which call for collecting and assessing the following types of information:

1. **Economic.** General data on growth of the economy, inflation, business cycle trends, and the like; profitability analysis for the division's products; specific industry economic studies; analysis of overseas economies; and key economic indicators for the United States and major foreign countries.

2. **Cultural, sociological, and political climate.** A general noneconomic review of conditions affecting the division's business. In addition to the more obvious subjects, it covers ecology, safety, and leisure time and their potential impact on the division's business.[2]

3. **Overview of market conditions.** A detailed analysis of market conditions that the division faces, by market segment,[3] including international.

4. **Summary of the technological environment.** A summary of the state-of-the-art technology as it relates to the division's business, carefully broken down by product segments.

5. **Competitive situation.** A review of competitors' sales revenues, methods of market segmentation, products, and apparent strategies on an international scope.

Such in-depth information is necessary for sound marketing decisions.[4] For the domestic marketer, most such information has been acquired after years of experience with a single market, but in foreign markets this information must be gathered for each new market.

---

[2]Debanjan Mitra and Peter N. Golder, "Whose Culture Matters? Near-Market Knowledge and Its Impacts on Foreign Market Entry Timing," *Journal of Marketing Research* 39, no. 3 (August 2002), pp. 350–365.

[3]Tammo H.A. Bijmolt, Leo J. Paas, and Jeroen K. Vermunt, "Country and Consumer Segmentation: Multi-Level Latent Class Analysis of Financial Product Ownership," *International Journal of Research in Marketing* 21, no. 4 (2004), pp. 323–340.

[4]Apparently governments also get into the industrial competitive intelligence game as well. See Edward Iwata, "More U.S. Trade Secrets Walk out Door with Foreign Spies," *USA Today*, February 13, 2003, p. 5A; *The Economist*, "I Spy, You Spy," June 4, 2005, p. 61.

Exhibit 8.1

Top 20 Countries for Marketing Research Expenditures (millions of dollars)

Source: From *Marketing News*, July 12, 2005, pp. 24–25. Reprinted with permission of American Marketing Association.

United States	$6,660
United Kingdom	1,997
Germany	1,805
France	1,580
Japan	1,164
Italy	581
Canada	477
Spain	395
China	387
Australia	383
Netherlands	305
Sweden	273
Mexico	267
Brazil	195
Belgium	164
S. Korea	161
Switzerland	133
Finland	113
Denmark	106
Taiwan	81

There is a basic difference between information ideally needed and that which is collectible and/or used. Many firms engaged in foreign marketing do not make decisions with the benefit of the information listed. Cost, time, and human elements are critical variables. Some firms have neither the appreciation for information nor adequate time or money for implementation of research. As a firm becomes more committed to foreign marketing and the cost of possible failure increases, however, greater emphasis is placed on research. Indeed, marketing research expenditures reflect the size and growth of markets around the world. Please see Exhibit 8.1 for a listing of the top 20 markets for international marketing research.

The Research Process

A marketing research study is always a compromise dictated by limits of time, cost, and the present state of the art. The researcher must strive for the most accurate and reliable information within existing constraints. A key to successful research is a systematic and orderly approach to the collection and analysis of data.[5] Whether a research program is conducted in New York or New Delhi, the research process should follow these steps:

1. Define the research problem and establish research objectives.
2. Determine the sources of information to fulfill the research objectives.
3. Consider the costs and benefits of the research effort.
4. Gather the relevant data from secondary or primary sources, or both.
5. Analyze, interpret, and summarize the results.
6. Effectively communicate the results to decision makers.

Although the steps in a research program are similar for all countries, variations and problems in implementation occur because of differences in cultural and economic development. Whereas the problems of research in England or Canada may be similar to those in the United States, research in Germany, South Africa, or Mexico may offer a multitude of difficult distinctions. These distinctions become apparent with the first step in the research process—formulation of the problem. Subsequent text sections illustrate some frequently encountered difficulties facing the international marketing researcher.

---

[5]Thomas T. Semon provides an interesting description of how problems can crop up here in "Raw Numbers, Not Indexes, Tell Real Story," *Marketing News*, March 3, 2003, p. 11.

Defining the Problem and Establishing Research Objectives

The research process should begin with a definition of the research problem and the establishment of specific research objectives.[6] The major difficulty here is converting a series of often ambiguous business problems into tightly drawn and achievable research objectives. In this initial stage, researchers often embark on the research process with only a vague grasp of the total problem. A good example of such a loosely defined problem is that of Russian airline Aeroflot. The company undertook a branding study to inform marketing decisions regarding improving its long-standing reputation for poor safety standards and unreliable service. This is a tough challenge for international marketing researchers.[7]

This first, most crucial step in research is more critical in foreign markets because an unfamiliar environment tends to cloud problem definition. Researchers either fail to anticipate the influence of the local culture on the problem or fail to identify the self-reference criterion (SRC) and so treat the problem definition as if it were in the researcher's home environment. In assessing some foreign business failures it is apparent that research was conducted, but the questions asked were more appropriate for the U.S. market than for the foreign one. For example, all of Disney's years of research and experience in keeping people happy standing in long lines could not help Disney anticipate the scope of the problems it would run into at Disneyland Paris. The firm's experience had been that the relatively homogeneous clientele at both the American parks and Tokyo Disneyland were cooperative and orderly when it came to queuing up. Actually, so are most British and Germans. But the rules about queuing in other countries such as Spain and Italy are apparently quite different, creating the potential for a new kind of intra-European "warfare" in the lines. Understanding and managing this multinational customer service problem has required new ways of thinking. Isolating the SRC and asking the right questions are crucial steps in the problem formulation stage.

THE FAR SIDE® By GARY LARSON

"Say ... what's a mountain goat doing way up here in a cloud bank?"

The first step in marketing research is defining the problem. The pilots in Larson's cartoon eloquently reflect the major challenge in international marketing research. Defining the problem can be much more difficult in foreign markets, and more careful preliminary qualitative work is crucial in avoiding international marketing research "collisions with mountains"! By the way, this is not an Aeroflot joke. (The Far Side® by Gary Larson © 1983 FarWorks, Inc. All Rights Reserved. Used with permission.)

Other difficulties in foreign research stem from failures to establish problem limits broad enough to include all relevant variables. Information on a far greater range of factors is necessary to offset the unfamiliar cultural background of the foreign market. Consider proposed research about consumption patterns and attitudes toward hot milk-based drinks. In the United Kingdom, hot milk-based drinks are considered to have sleep-inducing, restful, and relaxing properties and are traditionally consumed prior to bedtime. People in Thailand, however, drink the same hot milk-based drinks in the morning on the way to work and see them as being invigorating, energy-giving, and stimulating. If one's only experience is the United States, the picture is further clouded since hot milk-based drinks are frequently associated with cold weather, either in the morning or the evening, and for different reasons each time of day. The market researcher must be certain the problem definition is sufficiently broad to cover the whole range of response possibilities and not be clouded by his or her self-reference criterion.

---

[6]Scholars in the field also struggle with defining the problem. See Mike W. Peng, "Identifying the Big Question in International Business Research," *Journal of International Business Studies* 35, no. 2 (2004), pp. 99–108.

[7]"Aeroflot Tries to Ditch Bad Image with Rebranding," *Marketing*, January 9, 2003, p. 3.

Indeed, this is a problem that Mattel Inc. ran into headlong. The company conducted a coordinated global research program using focus groups of children in several countries. Based on these findings the firm cut back on customization and ignored local managers' advice by selling an unmodified Barbie globally. Not only was it dangerous to ignore the advice of local managers; it was also dangerous to ignore parents' opinions involving toys. Kids may like a blonde Barbie, but parents may not.[8] Unfortunately, our predictions about Barbie in the last edition of this book proved correct. As we mentioned in previous chapters, sales of blonde Barbie dramatically declined in several foreign markets during the last two years. Only a 2004 "makeover" slowed—perhaps even reversed—the sagging sales of Mattel's most important product.[9]

Once the problem is adequately defined and research objectives established, the researcher must determine the availability of the information needed. If the data are available—that is, if they have been collected already by some other agency—the researcher should then consult these *secondary data* sources.

Problems of Availability and Use of Secondary Data

The U.S. government provides comprehensive statistics for the United States; periodic censuses of U.S. population, housing, business, and agriculture are conducted and, in some cases, have been taken for over 100 years. Commercial sources, trade associations, management groups, and state and local governments provide the researcher with additional sources of detailed U.S. market information. Often the problem for American marketing researchers is sorting through too much data!

Unfortunately, the quantity and quality of marketing-related data available on the United States is unmatched in other countries. The data available on and in Japan is a close second, and several European countries do a good job of collecting and reporting data. Indeed, on some dimensions the quality of data collected in these latter countries can actually exceed that in the United States. However, in many countries substantial data collection has been initiated only recently. Through the continuing efforts of organizations such as the United Nations and the Organization for Economic Cooperation and Development (OECD), improvements are being made worldwide.

In addition, with the emergence of eastern European countries as potentially viable markets, a number of private and public groups are funding the collection of information to offset a lack of comprehensive market data. Several Japanese consumer goods manufacturers are coordinating market research on a corporate level and have funded dozens of research centers throughout eastern Europe. As market activity continues in eastern Europe and elsewhere, market information will improve in quantity and quality. To build a database on Russian consumers, one Denver, Colorado, firm used a novel approach to conduct a survey: It ran a questionnaire in Moscow's *Komsomolskaya Pravda* newspaper asking for replies to be sent to the company. The 350,000 replies received (3,000 by registered mail) attested to the willingness of Russian consumers to respond to marketing inquiries. The problems of availability, reliability, and comparability of data and of validating secondary data are described in the following sections.

Availability of Data

Much of the secondary data that an American marketer is accustomed to having about U.S. markets is just not available for many countries. Detailed data on the numbers of wholesalers, retailers, manufacturers, and facilitating services, for example, are unavailable for many parts of the world, as are data on population and income. Most countries simply do not have governmental agencies that collect on a regular basis the kinds of secondary data readily available in the United States. If such information is important, the marketer must initiate the research or rely on private sources of data.

Another problem relating to the availability of data is researchers' language skills. For example, although data are often copious regarding the Japanese market, being able to read

---

[8]Lisa Bannon and Carlta Vitzhum, "One-Toy-Fits-All: How Industry Learned to Love the Global Kid," *Wall Street Journal*, April 29, 2003, p. A1.

[9]Melinda Fulmer, "Mattel Sees Results from Barbie Makeover," *Los Angeles Times*, February 1, 2005, pp. C1, C12.

CROSSING BORDERS 8.1   Headache? Take Two Aspirin and Lie Down

Such advice goes pretty far in countries such as Germany, where Bayer invented aspirin more than 100 years ago, and the United States. But people in many places around the world don't share such Western views about medicine and the causes of disease. Many Asians, including Chinese, Filipinos, Koreans, Japanese, and Southeast Asians, believe illnesses such as headaches are the result of the imbalance between *yin* and *yang*. *Yin* is the feminine, passive principle that is typified by darkness, cold, or wetness. Alternatively, *yang* is the masculine, active principle associated with light, heat, or dryness. All things result from their combination, and bad things like headaches result from too much of one or the other. Acupuncture and moxibustion (heating crushed wormwood or other herbs on the skin) are common cures for *yin* outweighing *yang*, or vice versa. Many Laotians believe pain can be caused by one of the body's 32 souls being lost or by sorcerers' spells. The exact cause is often determined by examining the yolk of a freshly broken egg. In other parts of the world, such as Mexico and Puerto Rico, illness is

believed to be caused by an imbalance of one of the four body humors: "blood—hot and wet; yellow bile—hot and dry; phlegm—cold and wet; and black bile—cold and dry." Even in the high-tech United States, many people believe that pain is often a "reminder from God" to behave properly.

Now Bayer is marketing aspirin as a preventive drug for other ailments such as intestinal cancer and heart attack. But in many foreign markets for companies such as Bayer, a key question to be addressed in marketing research is how and to what extent aspirin can be marketed as a supplement to the traditional remedies. That is, will little white pills mix well with phlegm and black bile?

Sources: Larry A. Samovar, Richard E. Porter, and Lisa A. Stefani, *Communication between Cultures*, 3rd ed. (Belmont, CA: Wadsworth Publishing, 1998), pp. 224–225; the direct quote is from N. Dresser, *Multicultural Manners: New Rules for Etiquette for a Changing Society* (New York: John Wiley & Sons, 1996), p. 236; "Bayer Says Aspirin Cuts Mortality Rate in Gut Cancer, *Reuters*, July 1, 2005.

Japanese is a requisite for accessing them, either online or in text. This may seem a rather innocuous problem, but only those who have tried to maneuver through foreign data can appreciate the value of having a native speaker of the appropriate language on the research team.

Reliability of Data   Available data may not have the level of reliability necessary for confident decision making for many reasons. Official statistics are sometimes too optimistic, reflecting national pride rather than practical reality, while tax structures and fear of the tax collector often adversely affect data.

Although not unique to them,[10] less-developed countries are particularly prone to being both overly optimistic and unreliable in reporting relevant economic data about their countries.[11] China's National Statistics Enforcement Office recently acknowledged that it had uncovered about 60,000 instances of false statistical reports since beginning a crackdown on false data reporting several months earlier.[12] Seeking advantages or hiding failures, local officials, factory managers, rural enterprises, and others filed fake numbers on everything from production levels to birthrates. For example, a petrochemical plant reported one year's output to be $20 million, 50 percent higher than its actual output of $13.4 million. Finally, if you believe the statistics, up until 2000 the Chinese in Hong Kong were the world-champion consumers of fresh oranges—64 pounds per year per person, twice as much as Americans. However, apparently about half of all the oranges imported into Hong Kong, some $30 million worth, were actually finding their way into the rest of China, where U.S. oranges were illegal. Indeed, one might predict a crash in citrus sales to Hong Kong now that WTO entry for China means that American oranges can be shipped there directly.

Willful errors in the reporting of marketing data are not uncommon in the most industrialized countries, either. Often print media circulation figures are purposely overestimated

---

[10]*The Economist*, "Britain: The Numbers Game," March 26, 2005, pp. 35–36.

[11]Don Lee, "China's GDP Figures in Doubt," *Los Angeles Times*, March 14, 2005, pp. C1, C5.

[12]Mark L. Clifford, "How Fast Is China Really Growing?" *BusinessWeek*, March 10, 2003, p. 65.

even in OECD countries. The European Union (EU) tax policies can affect the accuracy of reported data also. Production statistics are frequently inaccurate because these countries collect taxes on domestic sales. Thus some companies shave their production statistics a bit to match the sales reported to tax authorities. Conversely, foreign trade statistics may be blown up slightly because each country in the EU grants some form of export subsidy. Knowledge of such "adjusted reporting" is critical for a marketer who relies on secondary data for forecasting or estimating market demand.

Comparability of Data

— out of date

Comparability of available data is the third shortcoming faced by foreign marketers. In the United States, current sources of reliable and valid estimates of socioeconomic factors and business indicators are readily available. In other countries, especially those less developed, data can be many years out of date as well as having been collected on an infrequent and unpredictable schedule. Naturally, the rapid change in socioeconomic features being experienced in many of these countries makes the problem of currency a vital one. Further, even though many countries are now gathering reliable data, there are generally no historical series with which to compare the current information.

A related problem is the manner in which data are collected and reported. Too frequently, data are reported in different categories or in categories much too broad to be of specific value. The term *supermarket*, for example, has a variety of meanings around the world. In Japan a supermarket is quite different from its American counterpart. Japanese supermarkets usually occupy two- or three-story structures; they sell foodstuffs, daily necessities, and clothing on respective floors. Some even sell furniture, electric home appliances, stationery, and sporting goods; some have a restaurant. General merchandise stores, shopping centers, and department stores are different from stores of the same name in the United States.[13]

Validating Secondary Data

The shortcomings discussed here should be considered when using any source of information. Many countries have similarly high standards for the collection and preparation of data as those generally found in the United States, but secondary data from any source, including the United States, must be checked and interpreted carefully. As a practical matter, the following questions should be asked to effectively judge the reliability of secondary data sources:

1. Who collected the data? Would there be any reason for purposely misrepresenting the facts?
2. For what purposes were the data collected?
3. How (by what methodology) were the data collected?
4. Are the data internally consistent and logical in light of known data sources or market factors?

Checking the consistency of one set of secondary data with other data of known validity is an effective and often-used way of judging validity. For example, a researcher might check the sale of baby products with the number of women of childbearing age and with birthrates, or the number of patient beds in hospitals with the sale of related hospital equipment. Such correlations can also be useful in estimating demand and forecasting sales.

In general, the availability and accuracy of recorded secondary data increase as the level of economic development increases. There are exceptions; India is at a lower level of economic development than many countries but has accurate and relatively complete government-collected data.

Fortunately, interest in collecting high-quality statistical data rises as countries realize the value of extensive and accurate national statistics for orderly economic growth. This interest in improving the quality of national statistics has resulted in remarkable improvement in the

---

[13]Matthew B. Myers, Roger J. Calantone, Thomas J. Page Jr., and Charles R. Taylor, "An Application of Multiple-Group Causal Models in Assessing Cross-Cultural Measurement Equivalence," *Journal of International Marketing* 8, no. 4 (2000), pp. 108–121.

CROSSING BORDERS 8.2   Oops! Even the Best Companies Can Make Mistakes

Microsoft and Teléfonos de Mexico are joining forces to launch a new Spanish-language Internet portal—www.T1msn.com. Microsoft is also donating some $100 million to help the Mexican government go on-line. However, Microsoft hasn't always gotten along so well with Mexican consumers. At one time Mexican users of the Spanish-language version of Microsoft Word were quite angry. One might also say they were mad, burning, violent, bothered, steaming, raging, stormy, furious, irate, livid, frothy, piqued, annoyed, seething, resentful, infuriated, irked, vexed, roiled, enraged, ireful, ruffled, churlish, wrathful, and irritated.

The problem was the thesaurus, or synonym dictionary, that Microsoft included with its popular word processing program. When asked to provide alternatives for the word *Indian*, the thesaurus generated suggestions that included *cannibal* and *savage*. In Mexico, where most people can claim indigenous ancestry, that just wasn't right. It wasn't kosher or politically correct for that matter, either.

Similar problems arose with the words *lesbian*, whose suggested alternatives were *pervert* and *depraved person*, and *western*, whose suggested alternatives were *Aryan*, *white*, and *civilized*.

Critics minced no words. "I see this as profoundly dangerous because it is a lack of respect for our dignity as Mexicans and for our indigenous roots," said Adriana Luna, a Mexican congresswoman. Another deputy called the dictionary "fascist" and "conservative."

For Microsoft that translated into "public relations disaster." Its response, however, was swift. The company said the thesaurus was created by an outside contractor, but accepted full responsibility all the same. Calling the word suggestions "offensive" and "mistaken," it "asked for forgiveness of customers who have been offended." Microsoft also promised a revised dictionary, promised to make its Spanish-language products more sensitive to different countries' usage, and provided the new version to current users free of charge.

Microsoft seemed suitably embarrassed . . . as well as ashamed, humbled, distressed, disgraced, and chastened. But under the circumstances, we suggest that all avoid using another synonym for their situation: red-faced!

Source: *Latin Trade*, September 1996, p. 16; Elliot Spagat, "WRAP: Mexico's Telemex, Microsoft Launch Spanish Portal," *Dow Jones International News*, March 21, 2000; Susan E. Reed, "Technology Companies Take Hope in Charity," *New York Times*, March 23, 2003, p. 3.

availability of data over the last 25 years. However, where no data are available, or the secondary data sources are inadequate, it is necessary to begin the collection of primary data.

The appendix to this chapter includes a comprehensive listing of secondary data sources, including Web sites on a variety of international marketing topics. Indeed, almost all secondary data available on international markets can now be discovered or acquired via the Internet. For example, the most comprehensive statistics regarding international finances, demographics, consumption, exports, and imports are accessible through a single source, the U.S. Department of Commerce at www.stat-usa.gov. Many other governmental, institutional, and commercial sources of data can be tapped into on the Internet as well.

Gathering Primary Data: Quantitative and Qualitative Research
If, after seeking all reasonable secondary data sources, research questions are still not adequately answered, the market researcher must collect *primary data*—that is, data collected specifically for the particular research project at hand. The researcher may question the firm's sales representatives, distributors, middlemen, and/or customers to get appropriate market information. In most primary data collection, the researcher questions respondents to determine what they think about some topic or how they might behave under certain conditions. Marketing research methods can be grouped into two basic types: quantitative and qualitative research. In both methods, the marketer is interested in gaining knowledge about the market.

In *quantitative research,* usually a large number of respondents are asked to reply either verbally or in writing to structured questions using a specific response format (such as yes/no) or to select a response from a set of choices. Questions are designed to obtain specific responses regarding aspects of the respondents' behavior, intentions, attitudes, motives, and demographic characteristics.[14] Quantitative research provides the marketer with responses that can be presented with precise estimations. The structured responses received in a survey can be summarized in percentages, averages, or other statistics. For example, 76 percent of the respondents prefer product A over product B, and so on. Survey research is generally associated with quantitative research, and the typical instrument used is the questionnaire administered by personal interview, mail, telephone, and most recently over the Internet.

Scientific studies often are conducted by engineers and chemists in product-testing laboratories around the world.[15] There, product designs and formulas are developed and tested in consumer usage situations. Often those results are integrated with consumer opinions gathered in concurrent survey studies. One of the best examples of this kind of marketing research comes from Tokyo. You may not know it, but the Japanese are the world champions of bathroom and toilet technology. Japan's biggest company in that industry, Toto, has spent millions of dollars developing and testing consumer products. Thousands of people have collected data (using survey techniques) on the best features of a toilet, and at the company's "human engineering laboratory," volunteers sit in a Toto bathtub with electrodes strapped to their skulls, to measure brain waves and "the effects of bathing on the human body." Toto is now introducing one of its high-tech (actually low-tech compared with what it offers in Japan) toilets in the U.S. market. It's a $600 seat, lid, and control panel that attaches to the regular American bowl. It features a heated seat and deodorizing fan.

In *qualitative research,* if questions are asked, they are almost always open-ended or in-depth, and unstructured responses that reflect the person's thoughts and feelings on the subject are sought.[16] Consumers' first impressions about products may be useful.[16] Direct observation of consumers in choice or product usage situations is another important qualitative approach to marketing research. One researcher spent two months observing birthing practices in American and Japanese hospitals to gain insights into the export of healthcare services. Nissan Motors sent a researcher to live with an American family (renting a room in their house for six weeks) to directly observe how Americans use their cars. Anderson Worldwide, Nynex, and Texas Commerce Bank have all employed anthropologists who specialize in observational and in-depth interviews in their marketing research. Qualitative research seeks to interpret what the people in the sample are like—their outlooks, their feelings, the dynamic interplay of their feelings and ideas, their attitudes and opinions, and their resulting actions.[17] The most often used form of qualitative questioning is the focus group interview. However, oftentimes in-depth interviewing of individuals can be just as effective while consuming far fewer resources.

Qualitative research is used in international marketing research to formulate and define a problem more clearly and to determine relevant questions to be examined in subsequent research. It is also used where interest is centered on gaining an understanding of a market, rather than quantifying relevant aspects. For example, a small group of key executives at Solar Turbines International, a division of Caterpillar Tractor Company, called on key customers at their offices around the world. They discussed in great depth with both financial managers and production engineers potential applications and the demand for a new size of gas-turbine engine the company was considering developing. The data and insights gained during the interviews to a large degree confirmed the validity of the positive demand forecasts produced internally through macroeconomic modeling. The multimillion-dollar project was then implemented. Additionally, during the discussions new product features were suggested by the customer personnel that proved most useful in the development efforts.

Qualitative research is also helpful in revealing the impact of sociocultural factors on behavior patterns and in developing research hypotheses that can be tested in subsequent

---

[14]A good example of this sort of study involves a cross-cultural comparison of consumer panel data: Frederik T. Schut, Stefan Gress, and Juergen Wasem, "Consumer Price Sensitivity and Social Health Insurer Choice in Germany and the Netherlands," *Journal of Health Care Finance and Economics* 3, no. 2 (June 2003), p. 117.

[15]Patricia Sellers, "The World of Ideas: Where Do Good Ideas Come From? For Global 500 Companies, the Answer Could Be Anywhere," *Fortune*, July 25, 2005, special insert.

[16]Danielle Sacks, "The Accidental Guru," *Fast Company*, January 2005, pp. 64–68.

[17]Paul E. Green, Yoram Wind, Abba M. Krieger, and Paul Saatsoglou, "Applying Qualitative Data," *Marketing Research* 12, no. 1 (Spring 2000), pp. 17–25.

CROSSING **BORDERS 8.3**   China Handcuffs Marketing Researchers

China has announced that firms conducting market research must be officially licensed, and has claimed the right to halt any such projects deemed harmful to national security.

The new rules, unveiled at a government news conference, mark Beijing's most recent effort to control the country's freewheeling market research industry. In particular, projects conducted by foreign firms are receiving renewed scrutiny. Although the demand for marketing research is huge in China, officials appear worried that some surveys are addressing politically sensitive areas such as confidence in the government and economy or are investigating regional weaknesses within the country.

"Some foreign market research has been of poor quality. At other times, the research has been used to hurt our country's national security and the greater interest of the public," Zhai Ligong, deputy director of China's State Statistical Bureau, said to reporters.

Under the latest set of rules, companies seeking to conduct studies for foreign companies must obtain licenses. Companies are also required to give the State Statistical Bureau a detailed list of their research projects every two months, and may on occasion be required to reveal specific findings to the government officials. Firms have also been ordered to share survey questions and findings with the government before sharing them with their clients. The specter of forced partnerships with government-affiliated rivals has also been raised.

Thus far enforcement of such regulations has been slack, but arrests for similar "crimes" are being made. Finally, early signs are suggesting that WTO membership and a growing economy are starting to encourage the Chinese government to reconsider such efficiency-killing constraints on commerce. Let's hope this last trend continues.

Sources: Karby Leggett and Leslie Chang, "China Adds Limits for Researchers, Sparking Concern at Foreign Firms," *Wall Street Journal Interactive Edition*, July 28, 2000; Erik Eckholm, "China: Internet Operator Sentenced," *New York Times*, May 20, 2003, p. 8; Clarissa Oon, "Paying Lip Service to Opinion Polls," *The Straits Times*, April 18, 2005, p. 2.

studies designed to quantify the concepts and relevant relationships uncovered in qualitative data collection. Procter & Gamble has been one of the pioneers of this type of research—the company has systematically gathered consumer feedback for some 70 years. It was the first company to conduct in-depth consumer research in China. In the mid-1990s P&G began working with the Chinese Ministry of Health to develop dental hygiene programs and has now reached over one million children in 28 cities. The company now offers Crest toothpaste in two flavors and toothbrushes in four colors to Chinese consumers.

Oftentimes the combination of qualitative and quantitative research proves quite useful in consumer markets[18] and industrial and business-to-business marketing settings as well. In one study the number of personal referrals used in buying financial services in Japan was found to be much greater than in the United States.[19] The various comments made by the executives during the personal interviews in both countries proved invaluable in interpreting the quantitative results, suggesting implications for managers and providing ideas for further research. Likewise, the comments of sales managers in Tokyo during in-depth interviews helped researchers understand why individual financial incentives were found not to work with Japanese sales representatives.[20]

As we shall see later in this chapter, using either research method in international marketing research is subject to a number of difficulties brought about by the diversity of cultures and languages encountered.

---

[18]Nguyen Thi Thyet, Kwon Jung, Garold Lantz, and Sandra G. Loeb, "An Exploratory Investigation of Impulse Buying in a Transitional Economy: A Study of Urban Consumers in Vietnam," *Journal of International Business Studies* 11, no. 2 (2003), pp. 13–35.

[19]R. Bruce Money, "Word-of-Mouth Referral Sources for Buyers of International Corporate Financial Services," *Journal of World Business* 35, no. 3 (Fall 2000), pp. 314–329.

[20]R. Bruce Money and John L. Graham, "Sales Person Performance, Pay, and Job Satisfaction: Tests of a Model Using Data Collected in the U.S. and Japan," *Journal of International Business Studies* 30, no. 1 (1999), pp. 149–172.

Problems of Gathering Primary Data

The problems of collecting primary data in foreign countries are different only in degree from those encountered in the United States. Assuming the research problem is well defined and the objectives are properly formulated, the success of primary research hinges on the ability of the researcher to get correct and truthful information that addresses the research objectives. Most problems in collecting primary data in international marketing research stem from cultural differences among countries and range from the inability of respondents to communicate their opinions to inadequacies in questionnaire translation.

Ability to Communicate Opinions

The ability to express attitudes and opinions about a product or concept depends on the respondent's ability to recognize the usefulness and value of such a product or concept. It is difficult for a person to formulate needs, attitudes, and opinions about goods whose use may not be understood, that are not in common use within the community, or that have never been available. For example, someone who has never had the benefits of an office computer will be unable to express accurate feelings or provide any reasonable information about purchase intentions, likes, or dislikes concerning a new computer software package. The more complex the concept, the more difficult it is to design research that will help the respondent communicate meaningful opinions and reactions. Under these circumstances, the creative capabilities of the international marketing researcher are challenged.

No company has had more experience in trying to understand consumers with communication limitations than Gerber. Babies may be their business, but babies often can't talk, much less fill out a questionnaire. Over the years Gerber has found that talking to and observing both infants and their mothers are important in marketing research. In one study Gerber found that breast-fed babies adapted to solid food more quickly than bottle-fed babies because breast milk changes flavor depending on what the mother has eaten. For example, infants were found to suck longer and harder if their mother had recently eaten garlic. In another study, weaning practices were studied around the world. Indian babies were offered lentils served on a finger. Some Nigerian children got fermented sorghum, fed by the grandmother through the funnel of her hand. In some parts of tropical Asia mothers "food-kissed" prechewed vegetables into their babies' mouths. Hispanic mothers in the United States tend to introduce baby food much earlier than non-Hispanic mothers and continue it well beyond the first year. All this research helps the company decide which products are appropriate for which markets. For example, the Vegetable and Rabbit Meat and the Freeze-Dried Sardines and Rice flavors popular in Poland and Japan, respectively, most likely won't make it to American store shelves.

Willingness to Respond

Cultural differences offer the best explanation for the unwillingness or the inability of many to respond to research surveys.[21] The role of the male, the suitability of personal gender-based inquiries, and other gender-related issues can affect willingness to respond.

In some countries, the husband not only earns the money but also dictates exactly how it is to be spent. Because the husband controls the spending, it is he, not the wife, who should be questioned to determine preferences and demand for many consumer goods. In some countries, women would never consent to be interviewed by a male or a stranger. A French Canadian woman does not like to be questioned and is likely to be reticent in her responses. In some societies, a man would certainly consider it beneath his dignity to discuss shaving habits or brand preference in personal clothing with anyone—most emphatically not a female interviewer.

Anyone asking questions about any topic from which tax assessment could be inferred is immediately suspected of being a tax agent. Citizens of many countries do not feel the same legal and moral obligations to pay their taxes as do U.S. citizens. Tax evasion is thus an accepted practice for many and a source of pride for the more adept. Where such an attitude exists, taxes are often seemingly arbitrarily assessed by the government, which

---

[21]It should be noted that often data are collected whether or not consumers like it. Most consumers would be surprised to know to what degree hotels keep track of travelers' purchases. See Christina Binkley, "Soon, the Desk Clerk Will Know All About You—Hilton Hotels' New System Helps It Customize Service, Though Privacy May Suffer," *Wall Street Journal*, May 8, 2003, p. D4.

Midnight in New Delhi—both customer service and telephone survey research are being outsourced to lower-wage English-speaking countries. Cost savings of such outsourcing must be balanced with consumer reluctance in cross-cultural communication settings, particularly those involving voluntary responses to marketing research. (© *Brian Lee/CORBIS*)

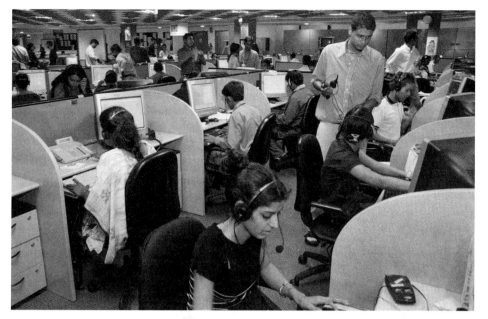

results in much incomplete or misleading information being reported. One of the problems revealed by the government of India in a recent population census was the underreporting of tenants by landlords trying to hide the actual number of people living in houses and flats. The landlords had been subletting accommodations illegally and were concealing their activities from the tax department.

In the United States, publicly held corporations are compelled by the Securities and Exchange Commission (SEC) to disclose certain operating figures on a periodic basis. In many European countries, however, such information is seldom if ever released and then most reluctantly. Attempts to enlist the cooperation of merchants in setting up an in-store study of shelf inventory and sales information ran into strong resistance because of suspicions and a tradition of competitive secrecy. The resistance was overcome by the researcher's willingness to approach the problem step by step. As the retailer gained confidence in the researcher and realized the value of the data gathered, more and more requested information was provided. Besides the reluctance of businesses to respond to surveys, local politicians in underdeveloped countries may interfere with studies in the belief that they could be subversive and must be stopped or hindered. A few moments with local politicians can prevent days of delay.

Although such cultural differences may make survey research more difficult to conduct, it is possible. In some communities, locally prominent people could open otherwise closed doors; in other situations, professional people and local students have been used as interviewers because of their knowledge of the market. Less direct measurement techniques and nontraditional data analysis methods may also be more appropriate. In one study, Japanese supermarket buyers rated the nationality of brands (foreign or domestic) as relatively unimportant in making stocking decisions when asked directly; however, when an indirect, paired-comparison questioning technique was used, brand nationality proved to be the most important factor.[22]

Sampling in Field Surveys

The greatest problem in sampling stems from the lack of adequate demographic data and available lists from which to draw meaningful samples.[23] If current, reliable lists are not available, sampling becomes more complex and generally less reliable. In many countries, telephone directories, cross-index street directories, census tract and block data, and

[22]Frank Alpert, Michael Kamins, Tomoaki Sakano, Naoto Onzo, and John L. Graham, "Retail Buyer Beliefs, Attitudes, and Behaviors toward Pioneer and Me-Too Follower Brands: A Comparative Study of Japan and the United States," *International Marketing Review* 18, no. 2 (2001), pp. 160–187.

[23]N. L. Reynolds, A. C. Simintiras, and A. Diamantopoulos, "Theoretical Justification of Sampling Choices in International Marketing Research: Key Issues and Guidelines for Researchers," *Journal of International Business Research* 34 (2003), pp. 80–89.

detailed social and economic characteristics of the population being studied are not available on a current basis, if at all. The researcher has to estimate characteristics and population parameters, sometimes with little basic data on which to build an accurate estimate.

To add to the confusion, in some South American, Mexican, and Asian cities, street maps are unavailable, and in some Asian metropolitan areas, streets are not identified and houses are not numbered. In contrast, one of the positive aspects of research in Japan and Taiwan is the availability and accuracy of census data on individuals. In these countries, when a household moves it is required to submit up-to-date information to a centralized government agency before it can use communal services such as water, gas, electricity, and education.

The effectiveness of various methods of communication (mail, telephone, personal interview, and Internet) in surveys is limited. In many countries, telephone ownership is extremely low, making telephone surveys virtually worthless unless the survey is intended to cover only the wealthy. In Sri Lanka, fewer than 5 percent of the residents—only the wealthy—have landline telephones.[24] Even if the respondent has a telephone, the researcher may still be unable to complete a call.

The adequacy of sampling techniques is also affected by a lack of detailed social and economic information. Without an age breakdown of the total population, for example, the researcher can never be certain of a representative sample requiring an age criterion because there is no basis of comparison for the age distribution in the sample. A lack of detailed information, however, does not prevent the use of sampling; it simply makes it more difficult. In place of probability techniques, many researchers in such situations rely on convenience samples taken in marketplaces and other public gathering places.

McDonald's got into trouble over sampling issues. The company was involved in a dispute in South Africa over the rights to its valuable brand name in that fast-emerging market. Part of the company's claim revolved around the recall of the McDonald's name among South Africans. In the two surveys the company conducted and provided as proof in the proceedings, the majority of those sampled had heard the company name and could recognize the logo. However, the Supreme Court judge hearing the case took a dim view of the evidence because the surveys were conducted in "posh, white" suburbs, whereas 76 percent of the South African population is black. Based in part on these sampling errors, the judge threw out McDonald's case.

Inadequate mailing lists and poor postal service can be problems for the market researcher using mail to conduct research. In Nicaragua, delays of weeks in delivery are not unusual, and expected returns are lowered considerably because a letter can be mailed only at a post office. In addition to the potentially poor mail service within countries, the extended length of time required for delivery and return when a mail survey is conducted from another country further hampers the use of mail surveys. Although airmail reduces this time drastically, it also increases costs considerably.

The kinds of problems encountered in drawing a random sample include the following:

- No officially recognized census of population.
- No other listings that can serve as sampling frames.
- Incomplete and out-of-date telephone directories.
- No accurate maps of population centers. Thus no cluster (area) samples can be developed.

Although all the conditions described do not exist in all countries, they illustrate why the collection of primary data requires creative applications of research techniques when firms expand into many foreign markets.

| **Language and Comprehension** | The most universal survey research problem in foreign countries is the language barrier. Differences in idiom and the difficulty of exact translation create problems in eliciting the specific information desired and in interpreting the respondents' answers.[25] Types of scales |

---

[24]World Bank, *World Development Indicators 2005* (Washington, DC: World Bank, 2005).
[25]Shi Zhang and Bernd H. Schmitt, "Creating Local Brands in Multilingual International Markets," *Journal of Marketing Research* 38 (August 2001), pp. 313–325.

appropriate in some cultures, such as reverse-worded items, are problematic in other cultures.[26] Equivalent concepts may not exist in all languages. Family, for example, has different connotations in different countries. In the United States, it generally means only the parents and children. In Italy and many Latin countries it could mean the parents, children, grandparents, uncles, aunts, cousins, and so forth. The meaning of names for family members can differ, depending on the context within which they are used. In the Italian culture, the words for aunt and uncle are different for the maternal and paternal sides of the family. The concept of affection is a universal idea, but the manner in which it is manifested in each culture may differ. Kissing, an expression of affection in the West, is alien to many Eastern cultures and even taboo in some.

Literacy poses yet another problem. In some less-developed countries with low literacy rates, written questionnaires are completely useless. Within countries, too, the problem of dialects and different languages can make a national questionnaire survey impractical. In India, there are 14 official languages and considerably more unofficial ones. One researcher has used pictures of products as stimuli and pictures of faces as response criteria in a study of eastern German brand preferences to avoid some of the difficulties associated with language differences and literacy in international research. Still others have used other nonverbal kinds of response elicitation techniques such as pictures and collages.[27]

Furthermore, a researcher cannot assume that a translation into one language will suffice in all areas where that language is spoken.[28] For example, one of the authors was in Mexico and requested a translation of the word *outlet,* as in *retail outlet,* to be used in Venezuela. It was read by Venezuelans to mean an electrical outlet, an outlet of a river into an ocean, and the passageway into a patio. Of course the responses were useless—although interesting. Thus it will always be necessary for a native speaker of the target country's language to take the "final cut" of any translated material.

All marketing communications, including research questionnaires, must be written *perfectly*. If not, consumers and customers will not respond with accuracy, or even at all. The obvious solution of having questionnaires prepared or reviewed by a native speaker of the language of the country is frequently overlooked. Even excellent companies such as American Airlines bring errors into their measurement of customer satisfaction by using the same questionnaire in Spanish for their surveys of passengers on routes to Spain and Mexico. To a Spaniard, orange juice is *zumo de naranja;* a Mexican would order *jugo de naranja.* These apparently subtle differences are no such things to Spanish speakers. In

[26]Nancy Wong, Aric Rindfleisch, and James E. Burroughs, "Do Reverse-Worded Items Confound Measures in Cross-Cultural Research? The Case of the Material Values Scale," *Journal of Consumer Research* 30, no. 1 (June 2003), pp. 72–91.

[27]Gerald Zaltman, "Rethinking Marketing Research: Putting the People Back In," *Journal of Marketing Research* 34 (November 1997), pp. 424–437.

[28]Subash Sharma and Danny Weathers, "Assessing Generalizability of Scales Used in Cross-National Research," *International Journal of Research in Marketing* 20, no. 3 (2003), pp. 287–295.

Marketing researchers in India have to consider the problems of language diversity in India. Here the primary 13 languages (besides English) are listed on a 20-rupee note.

another case, a German respondent was asked the number of washers (washing machines) produced in Germany for a particular year; the reply reflected the production of the flat metal disk. Marketers use three different techniques, back translation, parallel translation, and decentering, to help ferret out translation errors ahead of time.

Back Translation.

In *back translation* the questionnaire is translated from one language to another, and then a second party translates it back into the original.[29] This process pinpoints misinterpretations and misunderstandings before they reach the public. A soft-drink company wanted to use a very successful Australian advertising theme, "Baby, it's cold inside," in Hong Kong. It had the theme translated from English into Cantonese by one translator and then retranslated by another from Cantonese into English, in which the statement came out as "Small mosquito, on the inside it is very cold." Although "small mosquito" is the colloquial expression for "small child" in Hong Kong, the intended meaning was lost in translation.

Parallel Translation.

Back translations may not always ensure an accurate translation because of commonly used idioms in both languages. *Parallel translation* is used to overcome this problem. In this process, more than two translators are used for the back translation; the results are compared, differences discussed, and the most appropriate translation selected.

Decentering.

A third alternative, known as *decentering,* is a hybrid of back translation. It is a successive process of translation and retranslation of a questionnaire, each time by a different translator. For example, an English version is translated into French and then translated back to English by a different translator. The two English versions are compared and where there are differences, the original English version is modified and the process is repeated. If there are still differences between the two English versions, the original English version of the second iteration is modified and the process of translation and back translation is repeated. The process continues to be repeated until an English version can be translated into French and back translated, by a different translator, into the same English. In this process, the wording of the original instrument undergoes a change, and the version that is finally used and its translation have equally comprehensive and equivalent terminologies in both languages.

The complexities of the Japanese language confront second graders in Kyoto, where students write some of the 200-plus characters for the sound *shou*. The language commonly uses 15,000 kanji characters, which are borrowed from Chinese. The differences in the structure of the language from English make translation of questionnaires a most daunting task. (© Cary Wolinsky)

Regardless of the procedure used, proper translation and *perfect* use of the local language in a questionnaire are of critical importance to successful research design. Because of cultural and national differences, confusion can just as well be the problem of the researcher as of the respondent. The question itself may not be properly worded in the English version, or English slang or abbreviated words may be translated with a different or ambiguous meaning. This was the case mentioned earlier with the word *outlet* for *retail outlet*. The problem was not with the translation as much as with the term used in the question to be translated. In writing questions for translation, it is important that precise terms, not colloquialisms or slang, be used in the original to be translated. One classic misunderstanding that occurred in a *Reader's Digest* study of consumer behavior in western Europe resulted in a report that France and Germany consumed more spaghetti than did Italy. This rather curious and erroneous finding resulted from questions that asked about purchases of "packaged and branded spaghetti." Italians buy their spaghetti in bulk; the French and Germans buy branded and packaged spaghetti. Because of this crucial difference, the results underreported spaghetti purchases

---

[29]For example, see James P. Neelankavil, Anil Mathur, and Yong Zhang, "Determinants of Managerial Performance: A Cross-Cultural Comparison of Perceptions of Middle Managers in Four Countries," *Journal of International Business Studies* 31, no. 1 (2000), pp. 121–140.

by Italians. Had the goal of the research been to determine how much branded and packaged spaghetti was purchased, the results would have been correct. However, because the goal was to know about total spaghetti consumption, the data were incorrect. Researchers must always verify that they are asking the right question.

Some of the problems of cross-cultural marketing research can be addressed after data have been collected. For example, we know that consumers in some countries such as Japan tend to respond to rating scales more conservatively than Americans. That is, on a 1 to 7 scale anchored by "extremely satisfied" and "extremely dissatisfied," Japanese may tend to answer more toward the middle (more 3s and 5s), whereas Americans' responses may tend toward the extremes (more 1s and 7s). Such a response bias can be managed through statistical standardization procedures to maximize comparability.[30] Some translation problems can also be detected and mitigated post hoc through other statistical approaches as well.

Multicultural Research: A Special Problem

As companies become global marketers and seek to standardize various parts of the marketing mix across several countries, multicultural studies become more important. A company needs to determine to what extent adaptation of the marketing mix is appropriate.[31] Thus market characteristics across diverse cultures must be compared for similarities and differences before a company proceeds with standardization on any aspect of marketing strategy. The research difficulties discussed thus far have addressed problems of conducting research within a culture. When engaging in multicultural studies, many of these same problems further complicate the difficulty of cross-cultural comparisons.[32]

Multicultural research involves dealing with countries that have different languages, economies, social structures, behavior, and attitude patterns. When designing multicultural studies, it is essential that these differences be taken into account. An important point to keep in mind when designing research to be applied across cultures is to ensure comparability and equivalency of results. Different methods may have varying reliabilities in different countries. These differences must be taken into account in the design of a multicultural survey. Such differences may mean that different research methods should be applied in individual countries.

In some cases the entire research design may have to be different between countries to maximize the comparability of the results. For example, in Latin American countries it may be difficult to attract consumers to participate in either focus groups or in-depth interviews because of differences in the value for time.[33] And Japanese, compared with American businesspeople, tend not to respond to mail surveys. The latter problem was handled in two recent studies by using alternative methods of questionnaire distribution and collection in Japan. In one study, attitudes of retail buyers regarding pioneer brands were sought. In the U.S. setting a sample was drawn from a national list of supermarket buyers and questionnaires were distributed and collected by mail. Alternatively, in Japan questionnaires were distributed through contact people at 16 major supermarket chains and then returned by mail directly to the Japanese researchers. The second study sought to compare the job satisfaction of American and Japanese sales representatives. The questionnaires were delivered and collected via the company mail system for the U.S. firm. For the Japanese firm, participants in a sales training program were asked to complete the questionnaires during the program. Although the authors of both studies suggest that the use of different methods of data collection in comparative studies does threaten the quality of the results, the approaches taken were the best (only) practical methods of conducting the research.

The adaptations necessary to complete these cross-national studies serve as examples of the need for resourcefulness in international marketing research. However, they also

---

[30]Hans Baumgartner and Jan-Benedict E. M. Steenkamp, "Response Styles in Marketing Research: A Cross-National Investigation," *Journal of Marketing Research* 38 (May 2001), pp. 143–156.

[31]Erin White and Sarah Ellison, "Unilever Ads Offer a Tribute to Dirt—Campaign Signals Desire to Create Consistent Image for Global Array of Brands," *Wall Street Journal*, June 2, 2003, p. B3.

[32]Masaski Kotabe, "Contemporary Research Trends in International Marketing," Chapter 17 in Alan Rugman and Thomas Brewer (eds.), *Oxford Handbook of International Business* (Oxford: Oxford University Press, 2001).

[33]Carlos Denton, "Time Differentials in Latin America," *Marketing News*, March 15, 2004, pp. 52–53.

raise serious questions about the reliability of data gathered in cross-national research. Evidence suggests that often insufficient attention is given not only to nonsampling errors and other problems that can exist in improperly conducted multicultural studies, but also to the appropriateness of research measures that have not been tested in multicultural contexts.

Research on the Internet: A Growing Opportunity

To keep up with the worldwide growth in Internet use is literally impossible. We know that at this writing there are more than one billion users in more than 200 countries.[34] About one-sixth of the users are in the United States, but more than half of the hosts are there. The fastest growing market for the Internet is now China, with 100 milliion users.[35] International Internet use is growing almost twice as fast as American use. Growth in countries such as Costa Rica was dramatically spurred by the local government's decision to reclassify computers as "educational tools," thus eliminating all import tariffs on the hardware. The demographics of users worldwide are as follows: 60 percent male and 40 percent female; average age about 32; about 60 percent college educated; median income of about $60,000; usage time about 2.5 hours per week; and main activities are e-mail and finding information. The percentage of home pages by language is English, 80 percent; German, 3 percent; Japanese, 4 percent; French, 2 percent; Spanish, 1 percent; and all others less than 1 percent each.

For many companies the Internet provides a new and increasingly important medium for conducting a variety of international marketing research.[36] Indeed, a survey of marketing research professionals suggests that the most important influences on the industry are the Internet and globalization. New product concepts and advertising copy can be tested over the Internet for immediate feedback. Worldwide consumer panels[37] have been created to help test marketing programs across international samples. Indeed, it has been suggested that there are at least eight different uses for the Internet in international research:

1. **Online surveys and buyer panels.** These can include incentives for participation, and they have better "branching" capabilities (asking different questions based on previous answers) than more expensive mail and phone surveys.

2. **Online focus groups.** Bulletin boards can be used for this purpose.

3. **Web visitor tracking.** Servers automatically track and time visitors' travel through Web sites.

4. **Advertising measurement.** Servers track links to other sites, and their usefulness can therefore be assessed.[38]

5. **Customer identification systems.** Many companies are installing registration procedures that allow them to track visits and purchases over time, creating a "virtual panel."

6. **E-mail marketing lists.** Customers can be asked to sign up on e-mail lists to receive future direct marketing efforts via the Internet.

7. **Embedded research.** The Internet continues to automate traditional economic roles of customers, such as searching for information about products and services, comparison shopping among alternatives, interacting with service providers, and maintaining the customer brand relationship. More and more of these Internet processes look and feel like research processes themselves. The

---

[34] World Bank, *World Development Indicators 2005* (2005).

[35] "The Great Internet Race," *BusinessWeek,* June 13, 2005, pp. 54–55.

[36] Catherine Arnold, "Synovate Exec Discusses Future of International Research," *Marketing News*, May 15, 2004, p. 43.

[37] Information regarding worldwide Internet panels is available at www.decisionanalyst.com.

[38] *The Economist*, "Crowned at Last: A Survey of Consumer Power," April 2, 2005, pp. 1–16.

methods are often embedded directly into the actual purchase and use situations and are therefore more closely tied to actual economic behavior than traditional research methods can be. Some firms even provide the option of custom designing products online—the ultimate in applying research for product development purposes.

8. **Observational research.** Chat rooms, blogs, and personal Web sites can all be systematically monitored to assess consumers' opinions about products and services.

The city of Toronto, Canada, posts an online city guide. A pop-up survey was posted on it to solicit visitors' reactions and demographic information. The data were collected to help build visitor profiles, including browsing patterns, that can be used in promotional materials given to potential advertisers. A variety of online research applications are reported by SurveySite (www.surveysite.com), a Toronto-based company.

Clearly, as the Internet continues to grow, even more kinds of research will become feasible, and the extent to which new translation software has an impact on marketing communications and research over the Internet will be quite interesting to watch. Some companies now provide translation services for questionnaires, including commonly used phrases such as "rate your satisfaction level."[39] Surveys in multiple languages can be produced quickly, given the translation libraries now available from some application service providers. Finally, as is the case in so many international marketing contexts, privacy is and will continue to be a matter of personal and legal consideration. A vexing challenge facing international marketers will be the cross-cultural concerns about privacy and the enlistment of cooperative consumer and customer groups.

The ability to conduct primary research is one of the exciting aspects about the Internet. However, the potential bias of a sample universe composed solely of Internet respondents presents some severe limitations.[40] Nevertheless, as more of the general population in countries gain access to the Internet, this tool will be all the more powerful and accurate for conducting primary research. Also, the Internet can be used as one of several methods of collecting data offering more flexibility across countries.[41]

Today the real power of the Internet for international marketing research is the ability to easily access volumes of secondary data. These data have been available in print form for years, but now they are much easier to access and, in many cases, are more current. Instead of leafing through reference books to find two- or three-year-old data, as is the case with most printed sources, you can often find up-to-date data on the Internet. Such Internet sites as www.stat-usa.gov provide almost all data that are published by the U.S. government. If you want to know the quantity of a specific product being shipped to a country, the import duties on a product, and whether an export license is required, it's all there via your computer.

In addition to government sources, many private Web sites provide information free or for a nominal price. Visit www.exporthotline.com to find market research for 80 countries, directories of business listings, and imports and exports by product and country—just to name a few of the resources. For people interested in doing business in Japan, JETRO (www.jetro.go.jp), a Japanese trade organization, provides information ranging from how to do business in Japan to specific product studies. Similarly, many universities offer sites that have links to resources all over the world. One of the best is www.globaledge.msu.edu/ibrd/ibrd.asp.

Thus volumes of good secondary data can be accessed from your computer, making international marketing research much easier and more efficient than it has ever been. Keep in mind, however, that this information must be validated, just as any secondary information should.

---

[39]See, for example, www.markettools.com.

[40]Arundhati Parmar, "Net Research Is Not Quite Global," *Marketing News*, March 3, 2003, pp. 51–52.

[41]Janet Ilieva, Steve Baron, and Nigel M. Healey, "Online Surveys in Marketing Research; Pros and Cons," *International Journal of Marketing Research* 44, no. 3 (2002), pp. 361–376.

Estimating Market Demand

In assessing current product demand and forecasting future demand, reliable historical data are required.[42] As previously noted, the quality and availability of secondary data frequently are inadequate; nevertheless, estimates of market size must be attempted to plan effectively. Despite limitations, some approaches to demand estimation are usable with minimum information.[43] The success of these approaches relies on the ability of the researcher to find meaningful substitutes or approximations for the needed economic, geographic,[44] and demographic relationships.

When the desired statistics are not available, a close approximation can be made using local production figures plus imports, with adjustments for exports and current inventory levels. These data are more readily available because they are commonly reported by the United Nations and other international agencies. Once approximations for sales trends are established, historical series can be used as the basis for projections of growth. In any straight extrapolation, however, the estimator assumes that the trends of the immediate past will continue into the future. In a rapidly developing economy, extrapolated figures may not reflect rapid growth and must be adjusted accordingly. Given the greater uncertainties and data limitations associated with foreign markets, two methods of forecasting demand are particularly suitable for international marketers: expert opinion and analogy.

Expert Opinion

For many market estimation problems, particularly in foreign countries that are new to the marketer, expert opinion is advisable. In this method, experts are polled for their opinions about market size and growth rates. Such experts may be companies' own sales managers or outside consultants and government officials. The key in using expert opinion to help in forecasting demand is *triangulation,* that is, comparing estimates produced by different sources. One of the tricky parts is how best to combine the different opinions. Developing scenarios is useful in the most ambiguous situations, for example, predicting demand for accounting services in emerging markets such as China and Russia or trying to predict the impact of SARS on tourism to Hong Kong.

Analogy

Another technique is to estimate by analogy. This assumes that demand for a product develops in much the same way in all countries as comparable economic development occurs in each country. First, a relationship must be established between the item to be estimated and a measurable variable[45] in a country that is to serve as the basis for the analogy. Once a known relationship is established, the estimator then attempts to draw an analogy between the known situation and the country in question. For example, suppose a company wanted to estimate the market growth potential for a beverage in country X, for which it had inadequate sales figures, but the company had excellent beverage data for neighboring country Y. In country Y per capita consumption is known to increase at a predictable ratio as per capita gross domestic product (GDP) increases. If per capita GDP is known for country X, per capita consumption for the beverage can be estimated using the relationships established in country Y.

Caution must be used with analogy because the method assumes that factors other than the variable used (in the preceding example GDP) are similar in both countries, such as the

---

[42]Although almost 20 years old, still the best summary of forecasting methods and their advantages, disadvantages, and appropriate applications is David M. Georgoff and Robert G. Murdick, "Manager's Guide to Forecasting," *Harvard Business Review,* January–February 1986, pp. 110–120.

[43]Manoj K. Argawal, "Developing Global Segments and Forecasting Market Shares: A Simultaneous Approach Using Survey Data," *Journal of International Marketing* 11, no. 4 (2003), pp. 56–80.

[44]For a fascinating description of the potential role of ambient temperature (and latitude) in forecasting demand, see Philip M. Parker and Nader T. Tavassoli, "Homeostasis and Consumer Behavior across Cultures," *International Journal of Research in Marketing* 17, no. 1 (March 2000), pp. 33–53.

[45]These variables may be population and other demographics or usage rates or estimates, and so forth. Using combinations of such variables is also referred to as a *chain-ratio* approach to forecasting.

Exhibit 8.2
(a) Personal Computer and (b) Mobile Phone Diffusion Rate (per 1,000 people)

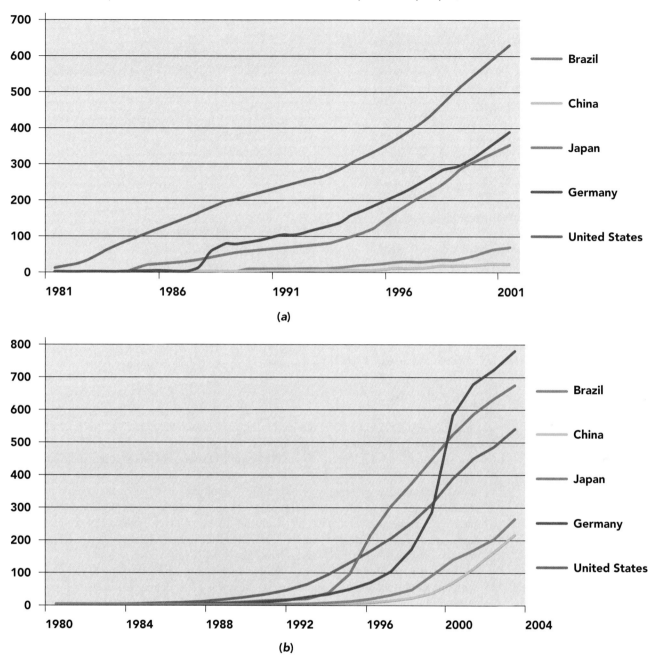

Source: World Bank, *World Development Indicators 2005* (Washington: World Bank, 2005).

same tastes, taxes, prices, selling methods, availability of products, consumption patterns,[46] and so forth. For example, the 13 million WAP (Wireless Access Protocol) users in Japan led to a serious overestimation of WAP adoptions in Europe—the actual figure of 2 million was less than the 10 million forecasted. Or, consider the relevance of the adoption rate of personal computers or cell phones in the Unites States as they help predict adoption rates in the other four countries listed in Exhibit 8.2. How might Apple Computer use the

---

[46]*The Economist*, "New Products: When Will It Fly?" August 9, 2003, p. 51; Gerard J. Tellis, Stefan Stremerch, and Eden Yin, "The International Takeoff of New Products: The Role of Economics, Culture, and Country Innovativeness," *Marketing Science* 22, no. 2 (2003), pp. 188–208.

CROSSING BORDERS 8.4   Forecasting the Global Healthcare Market

In 2000, Johns Hopkins Hospital in Baltimore treated more than 7,500 patients from foreign countries. That's up from just 600 in 1994. And there were no hassles with insurance companies and HMOs. In fact, many of these patients paid cash—even for $30,000 surgical procedures! The Mayo Clinic in Rochester, Minnesota, has been serving foreigners for decades. The number there has jumped by about 15 percent in five years to more than 1,000 per year. Similar growth is happening in places such as Mount Sinai Hospital in Miami, the University of Texas Cancer Center, and the UCLA Medical Center. The Mayo Clinic has even set up a Muslim prayer room to make patients and their families feel more comfortable. Fast growth, yes (some say exponential), but will it continue? Forecasting this demand so that decisions can be made about staffing and numbers of beds is a daunting project indeed.

Demand in Mexico and Latin America seems to be coming primarily for treatment of infectious and digestive diseases and cancer. Demand from the Middle East stems more from genetic diseases, heart diseases, cancer, and asthma. From Asia, wealthy patients are coming mainly to California for treatment of cancer and coronary diseases. Europeans travel to the United States for mental illness services, cancer and heart disease, and AIDS treatments. Given that Japan has the world's best success rate for treating stomach cancer, one would forecast that to be a growth sector in the future.

But perhaps the strangest market to forecast is global war wounded. Recently Johns Hopkins contracted to replace limbs for soldiers involved in a border clash between Ecuador and Peru at $35,000 per patient. The description in the *Wall Street Journal* article might have been a bit overzealous: "There are wars all over the world, bombs all over the world. Casualty patients are a new and enriching market niche."

Sources: "U.S. Hospitals Attracting Patients from Abroad," *USA Today*, July 22, 1997, p. 1A; Ron Hammerle, "Healthcare Becoming a Lot Less Local," *Modern Healthcare*, March 20, 2000, p. 40; Pamela Fayerman, "Risk of Blood Clots Jumps with Travel for Surgery," *National Post* (CanWest News Service), June 30, 2005, p. A8.

American data to help predict demand in Japan? Despite the apparent drawbacks to analogy, it can be useful where data are limited.

All the methods for market demand estimation described in this section are no substitute for original market research when it is economically feasible and time permits. Indeed, the best approach to forecasting is almost always a combination of such macroeconomic database approaches and interviews with potential and current customers. As more adequate data sources become available, as would be the situation in most of the economically developed countries, more technically advanced techniques such as multiple regression analysis or input-output analysis can be used.

Finally, it should go without saying that forecasting demand is one of the most difficult and important business activities. All business plans depend entirely on forecasts of a future that no one can see. Even the best companies make big mistakes. For example, Microsoft apparently didn't anticipate the waning interests of Japanese in video games in 2003 and suffered substantial financial losses in that market.[47]

Problems in Analyzing and Interpreting Research Information

Once data have been collected, the final steps in the research process are the analysis and interpretation of findings in light of the stated marketing problem. Both secondary and primary data collected by the market researcher are subject to the many limitations just discussed. In any final analysis, the researcher must take into consideration these factors and, despite their limitations, produce meaningful guides for management decisions.

Accepting information at face value in foreign markets is imprudent. The meanings of words, the consumer's attitude toward a product, the interviewer's attitude, or the interview situation can distort research findings. Just as culture and tradition influence the willingness to give information, so they also influence the information given. Newspaper circulation

[47]Mark Magnier, "Japanese Show Waning Interest in Video Games," *Los Angeles Times*, January 21, 2003, p. C1.

figures, readership and listenership studies, retail outlet figures, and sales volume can all be distorted through local business practice. To cope with such disparities, the foreign market researcher must possess three talents to generate meaningful marketing information.

First, the researcher must possess a high degree of cultural understanding of the market in which research is being conducted. To analyze research findings, the social customs, semantics, current attitudes, and business customs of a society or a subsegment of a society must be clearly understood. Indeed, at some level it will be absolutely necessary to have a native of the target country involved in the interpretation of the results of any research conducted in a foreign market.

Second, a creative talent for adapting research methods is necessary. A researcher in foreign markets often is called on to produce results under the most difficult circumstances and short deadlines. Ingenuity and resourcefulness, willingness to use "catch as catch can" methods to get facts, patience, a sense of humor, and a willingness to be guided by original research findings even when they conflict with popular opinion or prior assumptions are all considered prime assets in foreign marketing research.

Third, a skeptical attitude in handling both primary and secondary data is helpful. For example, it might be necessary to check a newspaper pressrun over a period of time to get accurate circulation figures or to deflate or inflate reported consumer income in some areas by 25 to 50 percent on the basis of observable socioeconomic characteristics. Indeed, where data are suspect, such triangulation through the use of multiple research methods will be crucial.

These essential traits suggest that a foreign marketing researcher should be a foreign national or should be advised by a foreign national who can accurately appraise the data collected in light of the local environment, thus validating secondary as well as primary data. Moreover, regardless of the sophistication of a research technique or analysis, there is no substitute for decision makers themselves getting into the field for personal observation.

Responsibility for Conducting Marketing Research

Depending on the size and degree of involvement in foreign marketing, a company in need of foreign market research can rely on an outside foreign-based agency or on a domestic company with a branch within the country in question. It can conduct research using its own facilities or employ a combination of its own research force with the assistance of an outside agency.

Both Ford and Philips keep track of European technology and consumers and develop products for global markets at their research centers in Aachen, Germany. The best technical universities are close by in Belgium, the Netherlands, and Germany.

Many companies have an executive specifically assigned to the research function in foreign operations; he or she selects the research method and works closely with foreign management, staff specialists, and outside research agencies. Other companies maintain separate research departments for foreign operations or assign a full-time research analyst to this activity. For many companies, a separate department is too costly; the diversity of markets would require a large department to provide a skilled analyst for each area or region of international business operations.

A trend toward decentralization of the research function is apparent. In terms of efficiency, local analysts appear to be able to provide information more rapidly and accurately than a staff research department. The obvious advantage to decentralization of the research function is that control rests in hands closer to the market. Field personnel, resident managers, and customers generally have a more intimate knowledge of the subtleties of the market and an appreciation of the diversity that characterizes most foreign markets. One disadvantage of decentralized research management is possible ineffective communications with home-office executives. Another is the potential unwarranted dominance of large-market studies in decisions about global standardization. That is to say, the larger markets, particularly the United States, justify more sophisticated research procedures and larger sample sizes, and results derived via simpler approaches that are appropriate in smaller countries are often erroneously discounted.

A comprehensive review of the different approaches to multicountry research suggests that the ideal approach is to have local researchers in each country, with close coordination between the client company and the local research companies. This cooperation is important at all stages of the research project, from research design to data collection to final analysis. Further, two stages of analysis are necessary. At the individual-country level, all issues involved in each country must be identified, and at the multicountry level, the information must be distilled into a format that addresses the client's objectives. Such recommendations are supported on the grounds that two heads are better than one and that multicultural input is essential to any understanding of multicultural data. With just one interpreter of multicultural data, there is the danger of one's self-reference criterion resulting in data being interpreted in terms of one's own cultural biases. Self-reference bias can affect the research design, questionnaire design, and interpretation of the data.

If a company wants to use a professional marketing research firm, many are available. Most major advertising agencies and many research firms have established branch offices worldwide. Moreover, foreign-based research and consulting firms have seen healthy growth. Of the 10 largest marketing research firms in the world (based on revenues), 4 are based in the United States, including the largest; 3 are in the United Kingdom; 1 is in France; 1 is in Germany; and 1 is in the Netherlands. The latest count of marketing research firms in China is more than 400 and growing fast. In Japan, where understanding the unique culture is essential, the quality of professional marketing research firms is among the best. A recent study reports that research methods applied by Japanese firms and American firms are generally similar, but with notable differences in the greater emphasis of the Japanese on forecasting, distribution channels, and sales research. A listing of international marketing research firms is printed annually in April as an advertising supplement in *Marketing News*.

An increasingly important issue related to international marketing research is the growing potential for governmental controls on the activity. In many countries consumer privacy issues are being given new scrutiny as the Internet expands companies' capabilities to gather data on consumers' behaviors. However, perhaps the most distressing development in this area is China's recent crackdown on marketing research activities there. Please see Crossing Borders 8.3 (page 223) for more details.

Communicating with Decision Makers
Most of the discussion in this chapter has regarded getting information from or about consumers, customers, and competitors. It should be clearly recognized, however, that getting the information is only half the job. That

Exhibit 8.3
Managing the Cultural Barrier in International Marketing Research

Cultural Barrier

information must also be given to decision makers in a timely manner.[48] High-quality international information systems design will be an increasingly important competitive tool as commerce continues to globalize, and resources must be invested accordingly.[49]

Decision makers, often top executives, should be directly involved not only in problem definition and question formulation, but also in the fieldwork of seeing the market and hearing the voice of the customers in the most direct ways when the occasion warrants (as in new foreign markets). Top managers should have a "feel" for their markets that even the best marketing reports cannot provide.

Finally, international marketers face an additional obstacle to obtaining the best information about customers. At the most basic level, marketing research is mostly a matter of talking to customers. Marketing decision makers have questions about how best to serve customers, and those questions are posed and answered often through the media of questionnaires and research agencies. Even when both managers and customers speak the same language and are from the same culture, communication can become garbled in either direction. That is, customers misunderstand the questions and/or managers misunderstand the answers. Throw in a language/cultural barrier, and the chances of misinformation expand dramatically.

The four kinds of company–agency–customer relationships possible are presented in Exhibit 8.3. Options B and C are better suited for managing the cultural barrier across the chain of communication. That is, in both cases the cultural barrier is bridged *within* a company wherein people that have a common corporate culture and work together on an everyday basis. In B the translation (in the broadest sense of the term—that is, of both questionnaires and reports) is worked out between employees of the international marketing research agency. In C the translation is managed within the company itself. In cases A and D both cultural and organizational barriers are being crossed simultaneously, thus maximizing the chances for miscommunication. Indeed, these same company–agency–customer considerations are also pertinent to the other kinds of communications between companies and customers such as advertising and distribution channel control, and this uniquely international topic will be addressed again in subsequent chapters.

---

[48]Anne L. Souchon, Adamantios Diamantopoulos, Hartmut H. Holzmuller, Catherine N. Axxin, James M. Sinkula, Heike Simmet, and Geoffrey R. Durden, "Export Information Use: A Five-Country Investigation of Key Determinants," *Journal of International Marketing* 11, no. 3 (2003), pp. 106–127.

[49]Nicoli Juul Foss and Torben Pedersen, "Organizing Knowledge Processes in the Multinational Corporation: An Introduction," *Journal of International Business Studies* 35, no. 5 (2004), pp. 340–349; Ram Mudambi and Pietro Navarra, "Is Knowledge Power? Knowledge Flows, Subsidiary Power and Rent-Seeking within MNCs," *Journal of International Business Studies* 35, no. 5 (2004), pp. 385–406.

Summary

The basic objective of the market research function is providing management with information for more accurate decision making. This objective is the same for domestic and international marketing. In foreign marketing research, however, achieving that objective presents some problems not encountered on the domestic front.

Customer attitudes about providing information to a researcher are culturally conditioned. Foreign market information surveys must be carefully designed to elicit the desired data and at the same time not offend the respondent's sense of privacy. Besides the cultural and managerial constraints involved in gathering information for primary data, many foreign markets have inadequate or unreliable bases of secondary information. Such challenges suggest three keys to successful international marketing research: (1) the inclusion of natives of the foreign culture on research teams; (2) the use of multiple methods and triangulation; and (3) the inclusion of decision makers, even top executives, who must on occasion talk directly to or directly observe customers in foreign markets.

Questions

1. Define the following terms:

   marketing research

   research process

   secondary data

   back translation

   expert opinion

   analogy

   international marketing research

   primary data

   multicultural research

   parallel translation

   decentering

2. Discuss how the shift from making "market entry" decisions to "continuous operations" decisions creates a need for different types of information and data.

3. Discuss the breadth and scope of international marketing research. Why is international marketing research generally broader in scope than domestic marketing research?

4. The measure of a competent researcher is the ability to utilize the most sophisticated and adequate techniques and methods available within the limits of time, cost, and the present state of the art. Comment.

5. What is the task of the international marketing researcher? How is it complicated by the foreign environment?

6. Discuss the stages of the research process in relation to the problems encountered. Give examples.

7. Why is the formulation of the research problem difficult in foreign market research?

8. Discuss the problems of gathering secondary data in foreign markets.

9. "In many cultures, personal information is inviolably private and absolutely not to be discussed with strangers." Discuss.

10. What are some problems created by language and the ability to comprehend the questions in collecting primary data? How can a foreign market researcher overcome these difficulties?

11. Discuss how decentering is used to get an accurate translation of a questionnaire.

12. Discuss when qualitative research may be more effective than quantitative research.

13. Sampling presents some major problems in market research. Discuss.

14. Select a country. From secondary sources found on the Internet compile the following information for at least a five-year period prior to the present:

    principal imports

    gross national product

    major cities and population

    principal exports

    chief of state

    principal agricultural crop

15. "The foreign market researcher must possess three essential capabilities to generate meaningful marketing information." What are they? Discuss.

Appendix: Sources of Secondary Data

For almost any marketing research project, an analysis of available secondary information is a useful and inexpensive first step. Although there are information gaps, particularly for detailed market information, the situation on data availability and reliability is improving. The principal agencies that collect and publish information useful in international business are presented here, with some notations regarding selected publications.

A. Web Sites for International Marketing

1. www.stat-usa.gov. STAT-USA/Internet is clearly the single most important source of data on the Internet. STAT-USA, a part of the U.S. Department of Commerce's Economics and Statistics Administration, produces and distributes at a nominal subscription fee the most extensive government-sponsored business, economic, and trade information databases in the world today, including the National Trade Data Bank (see section B6 of this appendix), Economic Bulletin Board, and Global Business Procurement Opportunities.

2. www.ita.doc.gov. The Web site of the Commerce Department's International Trade Administration provides export assistance, including information about trade events, trade statistics, tariffs and taxes, marketing research, and so forth.

3. www.usatradeonline.gov. Provides import and export information on more than 18,000 commodities, but the user must subscribe.

4. www.census.gov/foreign-trade/www/. The U.S. Census Bureau provides a variety of international trade statistics.

5. www.cia.gov/cia/publications/factbook/. Find the CIA *World Factbook* here, as well as other pertinent trade information.

6. www.customs.ustreas.gov. The U.S. Customs Service provides information regarding customs procedures and regulations.

7. www.opic.gov. The Overseas Private Investment Corporation (OPIC) provides information regarding its services.

8. www.exim.gov. The Export-Import Bank of the United States (Ex-Im Bank) provides information related to trade financing services provided by the U.S. government.

9. www.imf.org. The International Monetary Fund (IMF) provides information about the IMF and international banking and finance.

10. www.wto.org. The World Trade Organization (WTO) provides information regarding its operations.

11. www.oecd.org. The Organization of Economic Cooperation and Development (OECD) provides information regarding OECD policies and associated data for 29 member countries.

12. www.jetro.go.jp. The Japan External Trade Organization (JETRO) is the best source for data on the Japanese market.

13. www.euromonitor.com. Euromonitor is a company providing a variety of data and reports on international trade and marketing.

14. publications.worldbank.org. The World Development Indicators (WDI) Online offers the World Bank's comprehensive database on development data, covering more than 600 indicators, 208 economies, and 18 regional income groups.

15. University-based Web sites. The best such site is the Michigan State University Center for International Business Education and Research (http://globaledge.msu.edu/ibrd/ibrd.asp).

16. www.worldchambers.com. The World Network of Chambers of Commerce and Industry provides data and addresses regarding chambers of commerce around the world.

17. www.ipl.org/ref/RR/static/bus4700.html. The Internet Public Library provides Internet addresses for dozens of sources of trade data worldwide.

18. http://world.wtca.org. The World Trade Centers Association provides information about services provided by the World Trade Centers in the United States, including export assistance, trade leads, training programs, and trade missions.

19. www.worldtrademag.com. *World Trade* magazine provides online its annual Resource Guide to products, goods, and services for international trade.

B. U.S. Government Sources

The U.S. government actively promotes the expansion of U.S. business into international trade. In the process of keeping U.S. businesses informed of foreign opportunities, the U.S. government generates a considerable amount of general and specific market data for use by international market analysts. The principal source of information from the U.S. government is the Department of Commerce, which makes its services available to U.S. businesses in a variety of ways. First, information and assistance are available either through personal consultation in Washington, DC, or through any of the US&FCS (U.S. and Foreign Commercial Service) district offices of the International Trade Administration of the Department of Commerce located in key cities in the United States. Second, the Department of Commerce works closely with trade associations, chambers of commerce, and other interested associations in providing information, consultation, and assistance in developing international commerce. Third, the department publishes a wide range of information available to interested persons at nominal cost.

1. Foreign Trade Report FT410. U.S. exports—commodity by country. The FT410 provides a statistical record of all merchandise shipped from the United States to foreign countries, including both quantity and dollar value of these exports to each country during the month covered by the report. Additionally, it contains cumulative export statistics from the first of the calendar year. You can learn which of more than 150 countries have bought any of more than 3,000 U.S. products. By checking the FT410 over a period of three or four years, you can determine which countries have the largest and most consistent markets for specific products.

2. International Economic Indicators. Quarterly reports providing basic data on the economy of the United States and seven other principal industrial countries. Statistics included are gross national product, industrial production, trade, prices, finance, and labor. This report measures changes in key competitive indicators and highlights economic prospects and recent trends in the eight countries.

3. Market Share Reports. An annual publication prepared from special computer runs shows U.S. participation in foreign markets for manufactured products during the last five-year period. The 88 reports in a country's series represent import values for the United States and eight other leading suppliers, and the U.S. percentage share for about 900 manufactured products.

4. International Marketing Information Series. Publications that focus on foreign market opportunities for U.S. suppliers. This series is designed to assemble, under a common format, a diverse group of publications and reports available to the U.S. business community. The following publications are made available on a continuing basis under this program:

a. Global market surveys. Extensive foreign market research is conducted on target industries and target business opportunities identified by the Commerce Department. Findings are developed into global market surveys. Each survey condenses foreign market research conducted in 15 or more nations into individual-country market summaries.

b. Country market sectoral surveys. These in-depth reports cover the most promising U.S. export opportunities in a single foreign country. About 15 leading industrial sectors usually are included. Surveys currently available deal with Brazil, Nigeria, Venezuela, Indonesia, and Japan.

c. Overseas Business Reports (OBRs). These reports provide basic background data for businesspeople who are evaluating various export markets or are considering entering new areas. They include both developing and industrialized countries.

d. Foreign economic trends and their implications in the United States. This series gives in-depth reviews of current business conditions, current and near-term prospects, and the latest available data on the gross national product, foreign trade, wage and price indexes, unemployment rates, and construction starts.

e. Business America. The Department of Commerce's principal periodical, a monthly news magazine, is an up-to-date source on worldwide business activity, covering topics of general interest and new developments in world and domestic commerce.

5. Trade Opportunities Program (TOP). Overseas trade opportunities, private and government, are transmitted to the TOP computers through various American embassies and councils. U.S. business firms can indicate the product or products they wish to export and the types of opportunities desired (such as direct sales and representation) in countries of interest. The TOP computer matches the product interest of the foreign buyer's agent or distributor with the U.S. subscriber's interest. When a match occurs, a trade opportunity notice is mailed to the U.S. business subscriber.

6. National Trade Data Bank (NTDB). The Commerce Department provides a number of the data sources mentioned previously plus others in its computerized information system in the National Trade Data Bank. The NTDB is a one-step source for export promotion and international trade data collected by 17 U.S. government agencies. Updated each month and released on the Internet, the NTDB enables the reader to access more than 100,000 trade-related documents. The NTDB contains the latest census data on U.S. imports and exports by commodity and country; the complete CIA (Central Intelligence Agency) *World Factbook;* current market research reports compiled by the U.S. and Foreign Commercial Service; the complete *Foreign Traders Index,* which contains over 55,000 names and addresses of individuals and firms abroad that are interested in importing U.S. products; State Department country reports on economic policy and trade practices; the publications *Export Yellow Pages, A Basic Guide to Exporting,* and the *National Trade Estimates Report on Foreign Trade Barriers;* the *Export Promotion Calendar;* and many other data series. The NTDB is also available at over 900 federal depository libraries nationwide.

In addition, the Department of Commerce provides a host of other information services. Besides the material available through the Department of Commerce, consultation and information are available from a variety of other U.S. agencies. For example, the Department of State, Bureau of the Census, and Department of Agriculture can provide valuable assistance in the form of services and information for an American business interested in international operations.

C. Other Sources

1. Bibliographies

a. International Directory of Business Information Sources and Services, 2nd ed. London: Europa. Provides directory information on over 5,000 organizations, including details of libraries and publications.

b. Weekly, James K., *Information for International Marketing: An Annotated Guide to Sources* (Bibliographies and Indexes in Economics and Economic History, No. 3). Westport, CT: Greenwood. Lists and briefly annotates more than 190 government publications, databases, periodicals, and basic reference sources. Appendixes present brief directory listings for publishers, state trade contacts, U.S. foreign service offices in foreign countries, foreign embassies in the United States, the U.S. International Trade Administration, and international marketing journals.

c. World Directory of Marketing Information Sources. London: Euromonitor. (Also on CD-ROM.) Provides 6,000 entries, including libraries, market research companies, trade associations, trade journals, online sources, and international business contacts.

2. Directories

a. American Export Register. New York: Thomas Publishing, International Division. Annual. Includes an alphabetical product list with over 220,000 product and service listings in more than 4,200 separate categories as well as lists of U.S. and foreign embassies and consulates, chambers of commerce, world trade center clubs, U.S. and world ports, and banks.

b. D&B Principal International Businesses Directory. Wilton, CT: Dun's Marketing Services. Annual. (Also on CD-ROM.) Covers approximately 55,000 companies in 140 countries, listing businesses by product classification and alphabetically.

c. Directory of American Firms Operating in Foreign Countries, 14th ed. New York: World Trade Academy Press. Alphabetically lists U.S. firms with foreign subsidiaries and affiliates operating in over 125 countries; also lists the foreign operations grouped by countries.

d. Directory of United States Importers and *Directory of U.S. Exporters.* New York: Journal of Commerce. Annual. (Also on CD-ROM.) Contain verified business profiles on a total of 60,000 active trading companies. These annual guides also include a product index with the Harmonized Commodity Code numbers, customs information, foreign consulates, embassies, and international banks.

e. Encyclopedia of Global Industries. Detroit: Gale. Alphabetically covers 125 vital international industries, providing in-depth information including statistics, graphs, tables, charts, and market share.

f. Export Yellow Pages. Washington, DC: Venture Publishing North-America; produced in cooperation with the Office of Export Trading Company Affairs and International Trade Administration. Annual. Provides detailed information on over 12,000 export service providers and trading companies, agents, distributors, and companies outside the United States; also includes a product/service index and an alphabetical index.

g. FINDEX: The Worldwide Directory of Market Research Reports. London: Euromonitor. Annual. (Also on CD-ROM.) Abstracts and indexes more than 9,000 market research and company reports, spanning 12 broad product sectors.

h. International Brands and Their Companies. Detroit: Gale. Annual. Lists nearly 65,000 international consumer brand names attributed to 15,000 manufacturers, importers, and distributors, giving for each brand a description of the product, company name, and a code for the source from which the information was taken.

i. International Companies and Their Brands, 4th ed. Detroit: Gale. Lists 25,000 manufacturers, importers, and distributors and the nearly 80,000 brand names attributed to them, giving for each company the firm's address and telephone number and an alphabetical listing of its trade names.

j. International Directory of Corporate Affiliations. New Providence, NJ: National Register Publishing. Semiannual. Contains critical information on over 2,300 corporate parents with revenues of more than $50 million annually, 42,000 subsidiaries worldwide, and 54,000 key executives.

k. International Tradeshow. Frankfurt: m+a Publishers for Fairs, Exhibitions and Conventions. Semiannual. Contains detailed information on global trade fairs and exhibitions that are of national and international significance.

l. Trade Directories of the World. San Diego: Croner Publications. Looseleaf. Includes more than 3,000 trade, industrial, and professional directories in 1,000 categories in 175 countries.

m. World Directory of Consumer Brands and Their Owners. London: Euromonitor, 1996. Provides information on 17 market sectors, including consumer electronics, consumer health care, and leisure and entertainment.

n. World Directory of Trade and Business Associations. London: Euromonitor, 1995. (Also on CD-ROM.) Contains entries from a broad range of sectors, giving details of publications produced, aims and objectives of the association, and whether they provide assistance in further research.

o. World Retail Directory and Sourcebook, 2nd ed. London: Euromonitor. (Also on CD-ROM.) Identifies over 2,000 retailers, breaking them down by country and classifying them by organization and type of product sold.

p. Worldwide Franchise Directory. Detroit: Gale. Irregular. Provides information concerning some 1,574 franchising companies in 16 countries, arranged by type of business in more than 80 categories.

3. Marketing Guides

a. Export Market Locator. Wilton, CT: Dun & Bradstreet. Annual. (Also on CD-ROM.) Identifies the five largest and five fastest-growing global markets for a product; software version provides statistical information on more than 5,000 product lines, allowing searching by SIC code, Harmonized Commodity Code, or keyword commodity description. Reports available for single products.

b. Exporters Encyclopaedia. Wilton, CT: Dun & Bradstreet. Annual. Comprehensive world marketing guide, in five sections; section two, "Export Markets," gives important market information on 220 countries (import and exchange regulations, shipping services, communications data, postal information, currency, banks, and embassies); other sections contain general export information. Also available are regional guides for Asia-Pacific, Europe, and Latin America, and export guides for single countries.

c. International Business Handbook. Binghamton, NY: Haworth Press. Includes a global overview as well as separate chapters on 15 countries or regions, covering such topics as consumer cultures, business customs, methods of entry, and global strategies.

d. Reference Book for World Traders: A Guide for Exporters and Importers. San Diego: Croner Publications. Looseleaf. Provides information required for market research and for planning and executing exports and imports to and from all foreign countries; under each country it provides a listing of services to exporters and importers, including marketing research organizations, marketing publications, and custom brokers.

e. U.S. Custom House Guide. Hightstown, NJ: K-III Directory Co. Annual. Provides a comprehensive guide to importing, including seven main sections: import how-to, ports sections, directory of services, tariff schedules (Harmonized Tariff Schedules of the United States), special and administrative provisions, custom regulations, and samples of import documents.

4. Demographic Data

a. Consumer Europe. London: Euromonitor. Annual. Provides demographic data on consumer products for the major countries of Europe, totals for the European Union, and comparison among the European Union, Japan, and the United States.

b. European Marketing Data and Statistics. London: Euromonitor, Annual. (Also on CD-ROM.) Presents data from 32 European countries on everything from economic indicators to transport infrastructure in spreadsheet form, including 10-year trend data for each country and a full list of useful information sources.

c. International Marketing Data and Statistics. London: Euromonitor. Annual. (Also on CD-ROM.) Presents extensive marketing data for all countries outside Europe, including 10-year trend data for most series.

d. World Market Share Reporter, 2nd ed. Detroit: Gale. Provides market share data for hundreds of products, services, and commodities in countries of regions other than North America and Mexico.

5. Periodical Indexes

a. ABI/INFORM. Charlotte, NC: UMI/Data Courier. Weekly. (Computer file and CD-ROM.) Indexes and abstracts articles from some 1,000 business and management periodicals published worldwide. More than half the journals are indexed cover-to-cover, the others selectively. Abstracts are about 200 words long; available online on Data-Star, European Space Agency, Lexis-Nexis, Orbit Search Service, STN International, University Microfilm International, Ovid Technologies, and Knight-Ridder Information; and on CD-ROM as *ABI/INFORM Global Edition.*

b. Predicasts F & S Index Europe. Foster City, CA: Information Access Co. Monthly. (Print file, computer file, and CD-ROM.) Covers company, product, and industry information for the European Community (Common Market), Scandinavia, other regions in western Europe, the former Soviet Union, and eastern European countries in financial publications, business-oriented newspapers, trade magazines, and special reports; available online through Ovid Technologies, Data-Star, and Knight-Ridder Information and on CD-ROM as *Predicasts F & S Index Plus Text.* Abstracts in the computer file and on CD-ROM vary in length from 400 to 600 words and contain full text for many shorter articles.

c. Predicasts F & S Index International. Foster City, CA: Information Access Co. Monthly. (Print file, computer file, and CD-ROM.) Covers company, product, and industry information for Canada, Latin America, Africa, the Mideast, Asia, and Oceania in financial publications, business-oriented newspapers, trade magazines, and special reports; available online through Ovid Technologies, Data-Star, and Knight-Ridder Information and on CD-ROM as *Predicasts F & S Index Plus Text.* Abstracts in the computer file and on CD-ROM vary in length from 400 to 600 words and contain full text for many shorter articles.

6. Periodicals

a. Business Briefings. *Business Africa, Business Asia, Business China, Business Eastern Europe, Business Europe, Business Latin America, Business Middle East, Russia, India Business Intelligence, Crossborder Monitor, Ostwirtschafts-report.* New York: Business International. Biweekly or monthly. (Also on CD-ROM.) Reports issued for each title provide current news about companies, products, markets, and recent developments in laws and practices.

b. Business Operations Report. Eastern Europe, Middle East and Africa, Latin America, Asia. (Also on CD-ROM.) Provides hands-on operating information for setting up or operating a business, including information and commentary on new marketing and sales challenges and import and export policies.

c. China Hand. New York: Business International. Monthly. (Also on CD-ROM.) Provides comparative information on provinces and sites for setting up new operations and keeping up-to-date with regulatory changes and business developments.

d. East Asian Business Intelligence. Washington, DC: International Executive Reports. Biweekly. Provides sales and contracting opportunities for East Asian countries, including a brief description of the business opportunity, the person to contact, and the address, phone, and fax numbers.

e. Investing Licensing and Trading Abroad. New York: Business International. Semiannual. (Also on CD-ROM.) Directed toward companies that export directly or that have established subsidiaries, joint ventures, or licensing arrangements abroad; outlines business requirements for overcoming restrictions and other legal hurdles in 60 countries.

f. Marketing in Europe. New York: Economists Intelligence Unit. Monthly. Contains detailed studies of markets for consumer products in France, Germany, Italy, Belgium, and the Netherlands, including food, drink, tobacco, clothing, furniture, leisure goods, chemists' goods, household goods, and domestic appliances.

g. Market Research International. London: Euromonitor. Monthly. Each issue features diverse products and markets, focusing on international market review, global market trends and developments, U.S. market report, Japan market report, emerging market report, and market focus.

h. World Commodity Forecasts: Industrial Raw Materials and *Food, Feedstuffs and Beverages.* New York: Business International. Annual, with updates. Provide analysis of market trends, with specific price forecasts up to two years ahead for 28 commodities.

9

emerging markets

CHAPTER OUTLINE

Global Perspective: Wal-Mart, Tide, and Three-Snake Wine

Marketing and Economic Development

Stages of Economic Development
NIC Growth Factors
Information Technology, the Internet, and Economic Development
Objectives of Developing Countries
Infrastructure and Development
Marketing's Contributions

Marketing in a Developing Country

Level of Market Development
Demand in a Developing Country
Marketing in a Developing Country
Bottom-of-the-Pyramid Markets

Developing Countries and Emerging Markets

Latin America
Eastern Europe and the Baltic States
Asia
Newest Emerging Markets

Strategic Implications for Marketing

CHAPTER LEARNING OBJECTIVES

What you should learn from Chapter 9:

- The political and economic changes affecting global marketing

- The connection between the economic level of a country and the marketing task

- Marketing's contribution to the growth and development of a country's economy

- The growth of developing markets and their importance to regional trade

- The political and economic factors that affect stability of regional market groups

- The NIC growth factors and their role in economic development

Global Perspective

WAL-MART, TIDE, AND THREE-SNAKE WINE

Developing markets are experiencing rapid industrialization, growing industrial and consumer markets, and new opportunities for foreign investment. Consider the following illustration: In China, it is just a few shopping days before the advent of the Year of the Dog and the aisles at the local Wal-Mart supercenter are jammed with bargain hunters pushing carts loaded high with food, kitchen appliances, and clothing. It could be the preholiday shopping rush in any Wal-Mart in Middle America, but the shoppers here are China's nouveau riche. Superstores have proven popular with Chinese consumers, who devote a large part of their spending to food and daily necessities. Wal-Mart has been able to tap into the Chinese sense of social status by offering membership cards that confer not only eligibility for special discounts but social status as well.

Alongside Campbell's soup and Bounty paper towels are racks of dried fish and preserved plums. One shelf is stacked high with multiple brands of *congee,* a popular southern Chinese breakfast dish, and another has *nam yue* peanuts and packets of bamboo shoots. In the liquor section in the back of the store is three-snake rice wine, complete with the dead serpents' bodies coiled together in the potent liquid. About 95 percent of what Wal-Mart sells in China is sourced locally. Gone are the efforts to sell big extension ladders or a year's supply of soy sauce to customers living in tiny apartments.

At present Wal-Mart operates 1,600 units in nine foreign countries including more than 50 in China. Revenues and profits are growing nicely for its international operations, and overseas expansion is set to continue particularly in China since its entry into the World Trade Organization. As one executive commented, "It boggles the mind to think if everybody washed their hair every day, how much shampoo you would sell [in China]."

The China market can be difficult to tap and may not be profitable for many years. Most foreign retailers are in a learning mode about the ways and tastes of Asia, which are very different from those on Main Street U.S.A. Pricesmart

designed its Beijing store with two huge loading docks to accommodate full-sized diesel trucks in anticipation of the big deliveries needed to keep shelves well packed. What the company found was Chinese distributors arriving with goods in car trunks, on three-wheel pedicabs, or strapped to the backs of bicycles.

Procter & Gamble offered powdered Tide detergent in large quantities, but China's oppressive summer humidity turned it into unwieldy clumps. Stocking large quantities of paper towels and disposable diapers didn't work well either—most customers didn't know what a paper towel was, and disposable diapers were too expensive a luxury for most. Package sizes also posed a problem—small Chinese apartments could not handle the large American-sized packages.

On top of all that, foreign retailers have had to learn to deal with the uncertainty of China's complex and rapidly changing business climate, where personal connections matter more than business plans, and rules and regulations often are a matter of interpretation. "It doesn't matter what the law says," notes one retailer. "What matters is what the guy behind the desk interprets the law to say."

How do you sell $75 jeans or $150 wireless phones in a country where the per capita gross domestic product is only a couple of thousand dollars a year? Marketing researchers have found that extended families are showering their money on the kids, a common form of conspicuous consumption in the developing world. Even in China, the spending power of youth is nothing to discount. Studies have shown that the average 7- to 12-year-old in a large city has $182 a year in spending money—admittedly less than the $377 in France or $493 in the United States, but still a significant amount considering the huge population.

Sources: Keith B. Richburg, "Attention Shenzen Shoppers! U.S. Retail Giants Are Moving into China, and Finding the Learning Curve Formidable," *Washington Post*, February 12, 1997; David Barboza, "The Bold Struggle for China's Belly," *New York Times*, March 6, 2003, p. C1; www.walmartstores.com, 2005.

The distribution of Coca-Cola is often one of the first signs of a country transforming from a command economy to one of free enterprise. Here the cyclo driver transports a promotional refrigerator in Ho Chi Minh City (formerly Saigon), Vietnam. (© AFP/Getty Images)

Not many years ago, large parts of the developing world were hostile to foreign investment and imposed severe regulatory barriers to foreign trade. But few nations are content with the economic status quo; now, more than ever, they seek economic growth, improved standards of living, and an opportunity for the good life most people want as part of the global consumer world. China and other emerging markets throughout the world will account for 75 percent of the world's total growth in the next two decades and beyond, according to U.S. Department of Commerce estimates. The transition from socialist to market-driven economies, the liberalization of trade and investment policies in developing countries, the transfer of public-sector enterprises to the private sector, and the rapid development of regional market alliances are changing the way countries will trade and prosper in the 21st century.

China, South Korea, Poland, Argentina, Brazil, Mexico, Turkey, and India are some of the countries undergoing impressive changes in their economies and emerging as vast markets. These and other countries have an ever-expanding and changing demand for goods and services. As countries prosper and their people are exposed to new ideas and behavior patterns via global communications networks, old stereotypes, traditions, and habits are cast aside or tempered, and new patterns of consumer behavior emerge. Twenty-nine-inch Sony televisions in China, Avon cosmetics in South Korea, Wal-Mart discount stores in Argentina, Brazil, Mexico, China, and Thailand, McDonald's beefless Big Macs in India, Whirlpool washers and refrigerators in eastern Europe, Sara Lee food products in Indonesia, and Amway products in the Czech Republic represent the opportunities in emerging markets.

A pattern of economic growth and global trade that will extend well into the 21st century appears to be emerging. It consists of three multinational market regions that comprise major trading blocs: Europe, Asia, and the Americas. Within each trading bloc are fully industrialized countries, as typified by Germany, Japan, and the United States; rapidly industrializing countries such as Mexico, Poland, and South Korea that are close on the heels of the fully industrialized; and other countries that are achieving economic development but at more modest rates. Outside the triad of Europe, Asia, and the Americas are others at different levels of development striving to emulate their more prosperous neighbors. Indonesia, Malaysia, Thailand, and the Philippines are beginning to chase the leaders' tails, though from much lower levels of income. All four groups are creating enormous global markets. This chapter and the next explore the emerging markets and the multinational market regions and market groups that comprise the global trading blocs of the future.

Marketing and Economic Development

The economic level of a country is the single most important environmental element to which the foreign marketer must adjust the marketing task. The stage of economic growth within a country affects the attitudes toward foreign business activity,[1] the demand for goods, the distribution systems found within a country, and the entire marketing process.[2] In static economies, consumption patterns become rigid, and marketing is typically nothing more than a supply effort. In a dynamic economy, consumption patterns change rapidly. Marketing is constantly faced with the challenge of detecting and providing for new levels of consumption, and marketing efforts must be matched with ever-changing market needs and wants.

---

[1]Terrance H. Witkowski, "Antiglobal Challenges to Marketing in Developing Countries: Exploring the Ideological Divide," *Journal of Public Policy and Marketing* 24, no. 1 (2005), pp. 7–23.

[2]Ramarao Desiraju, Harikesh Nair, and Pradeep Chintagunta, "Diffusion of New Pharmaceutical Drugs in Developing and Developed Nations," *International Journal of Research in Marketing* 21, no. 4 (2004), pp. 341–357.

Economic development presents a two-sided challenge. First, a study of the general aspects of economic development is necessary to gain empathy regarding the economic climate within developing countries. Second, the state of economic development must be studied with respect to market potential, including the present economic level and the economy's growth potential. The current level of economic development dictates the kind and degree of market potential that exists, while knowledge of the dynamism of the economy allows the marketer to prepare for economic shifts and emerging markets.

Economic development is generally understood to mean an increase in national production that results in an increase in the average per capita gross domestic product (GDP).[3] Besides an increase in average per capita GDP, most interpretations of the concept also imply a widespread distribution of the increased income. Economic development, as commonly defined today, tends to mean rapid economic growth and increases in consumer demand—improvements achieved "in decades rather than centuries."

Stages of Economic Development

The best-known model for classifying countries by degree of economic development is the five-stage model presented by Walt Rostow.[4] Each stage is a function of the cost of labor, the technical capability of the buyers, the scale of operations, interest rates, and the level of product sophistication. Growth is the movement from one stage to another, and countries in the first three stages are considered to be economically underdeveloped. Briefly, the stages are as follows.

Stage 1: The traditional society. Countries in this stage lack the capability of significantly increasing the level of productivity. There is a marked absence of systematic application of the methods of modern science and technology. Literacy is low, as are other types of social overhead.

Stage 2: The preconditions for takeoff. This second stage includes those societies in the process of transition to the takeoff stage. During this period, the advances of modern science are beginning to be applied in agriculture and production. The development of transportation, communications, power, education, health, and other public undertakings has begun in a small but important way.

Stage 3: The takeoff. At this stage, countries achieve a growth pattern that becomes a normal condition. Human resources and social overhead have been developed to sustain steady development, and agricultural and industrial modernization lead to rapid expansion.

Stage 4: The drive to maturity. After takeoff, sustained progress is maintained and the economy seeks to extend modern technology to all fronts of economic activity. The economy takes on international involvement. In this stage, an economy demonstrates that it has the technological and entrepreneurial skills to produce not everything, but rather anything it chooses to produce.

Stage 5: The age of high mass consumption. The age of high mass consumption leads to shifts in the leading economic sectors toward durable consumer goods and services. Real income per capita rises to the point where a very large number of people have significant amounts of discretionary income.

Although Rostow's classification has met with some criticism because of the difficulty of distinguishing among the five stages, it provides the marketer with some indication of the relationship between economic development and the types of products a country needs, and of the sophistication of its industrial infrastructure.

---

[3]Gross domestic product (GDP) and gross national product (GNP) are two measures of a country's economic activity. GDP is a measure of the market value of all goods and services produced within the boundaries of a nation, regardless of asset ownership. Unlike gross national product, GDP excludes receipts from that nation's business operations in foreign countries, as well as the share of reinvested earnings in foreign affiliates of domestic corporations.

[4]Walt W. Rostow, *The Stages of Economic Growth*, 2nd ed. (London: Cambridge University Press, 1971), p. 10. See also W. W. Rostow, *The Stages of Economic Growth: A Non-Communist Manifesto* (London: Cambridge University Press, 1991).

Exhibit 9.1
Economic and Social Data for Selected Countries

Country	Consumer Spending				Health and Education		
	Food ($ millions)	Food Percentage of Total	Clothing ($ millions)	Clothing Percentage of Total	Hospital Beds (per 1000)	Physicians (per 1000)	Literacy (%)
United States	574,306	7.0	331,145	4.1	4.0	5.5	99.5
Argentina	15,559	24.2	4,476	7.4	3.3	3.0	97.0
Brazil	47,232	14.1	24,805	6.7	3.1	2.1	87.3
Colombia	16,275	26.7	3,315	5.5	1.5	1.4	92.1
Mexico	104,631	25.2	14,102	3.3	1.2	1.5	91.4
Venezuela	20,801	30.9	2,476	3.4	1.5	1.9	93.1

Source: World Bank, 2003. Copyright © 2003 World Bank. Reproduced with permission of World Bank via Copyright Clearance Center.

Alternatively, the United Nations classifies a country's stage of economic development based on its level of industrialization. It groups countries into three categories:

MDCs (more-developed countries). Industrialized countries with high per capita incomes, such as Canada, England, France, Germany, Japan, and the United States.

LDCs (less-developed countries). Industrially developing countries just entering world trade, many of which are in Asia and Latin America, with relatively low per capita incomes.

LLDCs (least-developed countries). Industrially underdeveloped, agrarian, subsistence societies with rural populations, extremely low per capita income levels, and little world trade involvement. LLDCs are found in Central Africa and parts of Asia. Violence and the potential for violence are often associated with LLDCs.[5]

The UN classification has been criticized because it no longer seems relevant in the rapidly industrializing world today. In addition, many countries that are classified as LDCs are industrializing at a very rapid rate, whereas others are advancing at more traditional rates of economic development. It is interesting to note in Exhibit 9.1 the differences in consumer spending among the Latin American countries and the United States.

Countries that are experiencing rapid economic expansion and industrialization and do not exactly fit as LDCs or MDCs are more typically referred to as *newly industrialized countries (NICs)*. These countries have shown rapid industrialization of targeted industries and have per capita incomes that exceed other developing countries. They have moved away from restrictive trade practices and instituted significant free market reforms; as a result, they attract both trade and foreign direct investment. Chile, Brazil, Mexico, South Korea, Singapore, and Taiwan are some of the countries that fit this description. NICs have become formidable exporters of many products, including steel, automobiles, machine tools, clothing, and electronics, as well as vast markets for imported products.

Brazil provides an example of the growing importance of NICs in world trade, exporting everything from alcohol to carbon steel. Brazilian orange juice, poultry, soybeans, and weapons (Brazil is the world's sixth-largest weapons exporter) compete with U.S. products for foreign markets. Embraer, a Brazilian aircraft manufacturer, has sold planes to over 60 countries and provides a substantial portion of the commuter aircraft used in the United States and elsewhere. Even in automobile production, Brazil is a world player; it ships more than 200,000 cars, trucks, and buses to Third World countries annually. Volkswagen has produced more than 3 million VW Beetles in Brazil and has invested more than $500 million in a project to produce the Golf and Passat automobiles. The firm also recently announced a deal to sell $500 million worth of auto parts to a Chinese partner. General

---

[5]See *Foreign Policy*'s "Failed States Index," July/August 2005, pp. 56–65.

Another sign of Vietnam's emergence in the world economy is the dramatic effect new production there (on the left) has had on world coffee prices in recent years. World prices crashed from a high of $1.85 per pound in 1997 to about $0.50 in 2001, adversely affecting growers in Brazil (on the right) and all other countries. (© *Christopher Anderson/Magnum Photos*)

Motors has invested $600 million to create what it calls "an industrial complex"—a collection of 17 plants occupied by suppliers such as Delphi, Lear, and Goodyear to deliver preassembled modules to GM's line workers. All in all, auto and auto parts makers are investing more than $2.8 billion aimed at the 200 million people in the Mercosur[6] market, the free trade group formed by Argentina, Brazil, Paraguay, and Uruguay.

Among the NICs, South Korea, Taiwan, Hong Kong, and Singapore have had such rapid growth and export performance that they are known as the "Four Tigers" of Southeast Asia. The Four Tigers have almost joined the ranks of developed economies in terms of GDP per head. These countries have managed to dramatically improve their living standards by deregulating their domestic economies and opening up to global markets. From typical Third World poverty, each has achieved a standard of living equivalent to that of industrialized nations, with per capita incomes in Hong Kong and Singapore rivaling those of the wealthiest Western nations.

These four countries began their industrialization as assemblers of products for U.S. and Japanese companies. They are now major world competitors in their own right. Korea exports such high-tech goods as petrochemicals, electronics, machinery, and steel, all of which are in direct competition with Japanese and U.S.-made products. In consumer products, Hyundai, Kia, Samsung, and Lucky-Goldstar are among the familiar Korean-made brand names in automobiles, microwaves, and televisions sold in the United States. Korea is also making sizable investments outside its borders. A Korean company recently purchased 58 percent of Zenith, the last remaining TV manufacturer in the United States. At the same time, Korea is dependent on Japan and the United States for much of the capital equipment and components needed to run its factories.

NIC Growth Factors

Both Rostow's and the UN's designations for stages of economic development reflect a static model in that they do not account for the dynamic changes in economic, political, and social conditions in many developing countries, especially among NICs. Why some countries have grown so rapidly and successfully while others with similar or more plentiful resources languish or have modest rates of growth is a question to which many have sought answers. Is it cultural values, better climate, more energetic population, or just an "Asian Miracle"? There is ample debate as to why the NICs have grown while other underdeveloped nations have not. Some attribute their growth to cultural values, others to cheap labor, and still others to an educated and literate population. Certainly all of these factors have contributed to growth, but other important factors are present in all the rapidly growing

---

[6]See www.guia.mercosur.com and/or www.mercosur.org.uy.

economies, many of which seem to be absent in those nations that have not enjoyed comparable economic growth.

One of the paradoxes of Africa is that its people are for the most part desperately poor while its land is extraordinarily rich. East Asia is the opposite: It is a region mostly poor in resources that over the last few decades has enjoyed an enormous economic boom. When several African countries in the 1950s (for example, Congo, the former Zaire) were at the same income level as many East Asian countries (for example, South Korea) and were blessed with far more natural resources, it might have seemed reasonable for the African countries to have prospered more than their Asian counterparts. Although there is no doubt that East Asia enjoyed some significant cultural and historical advantages, its economic boom relied on other factors that have been replicated elsewhere but are absent in Africa. The formula for success in East Asia was an outward-oriented, market-based economic policy coupled with an emphasis on education and health care. This is a model that most newly industrialized countries have followed in one form or another.

The factors that existed to some extent during the economic growth of NICs were as follows:

- Political stability in policies affecting their development.
- Economic and legal reforms. Poorly defined and/or weakly enforced contract and property rights are features the poorest countries have in common.
- Entrepreneurship. In all of these nations, free enterprise in the hands of the self-employed was the seed of the new economic growth.
- Planning. A central plan with observable and measurable development goals linked to specific policies was in place.
- Outward orientation. Production for the domestic market and export markets with increases in efficiencies and continual differentiation of exports from competition was the focus.
- Factors of production. If deficient in the factors of production—land (raw materials), labor, capital, management, and technology—an environment existed where these factors could easily come from outside the country and be directed to development objectives.
- Industries targeted for growth. Strategically directed industrial and international trade policies were created to identify those sectors where opportunity existed. Key industries were encouraged to achieve better positions in world markets by directing resources into promising target sectors.
- Incentives to force a high domestic rate of savings and to direct capital to update the infrastructure, transportation, housing, education, and training.
- Privatization of state-owned enterprises (SOEs) that placed a drain on national budgets. Privatization released immediate capital to invest in strategic areas and gave relief from a continuing drain on future national resources. Often when industries are privatized, the new investors modernize, thus creating new economic growth.

The final factors that have been present are large, accessible markets with low tariffs. During the early growth of many of the NICs, the first large open market was the United States, later joined by Europe and now, as the fundamental principles of the World Trade Organization (WTO) are put into place, by much of the rest of the world.

Although it is customary to think of the NIC growth factors as applying only to industrial growth, the example of Chile shows that economic growth can occur with agricultural development as its economic engine. Chile's economy has expanded at an average rate of 7.2 percent since 1987 and is considered one of the least risky Latin American economies for foreign investment. However, since 1976, when Chile opened up trade, the relative size of its manufacturing sector declined from 24.2 percent of GDP in 1973 to 13.2 percent in 2004.[7] Agriculture, on the other hand, has not declined. Exports of agricultural products

---

[7]World Bank, World Development Indicators, 2005.

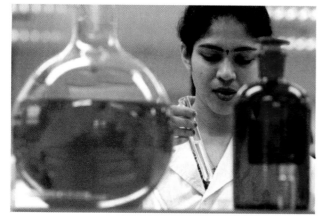

Despite world-class scientists, the Indian pharmaceutical industry (with its ownership restrictions, price controls, and weak intellectual property restrictions) does not benefit from innovations and international investments compared to more open emerging economies such as China. (*AP/Wide World Photos*)

have been the star performers. Chile went from being a small player in the global fruit market, exporting only apples in the 1960s, to one of the world's largest fruit exporters in 2000. Sophisticated production technology and management methods were applied to the production of table grapes, wine, salmon from fish farms, and a variety of other processed and semiprocessed agricultural products. Salmon farming, begun in the early 1980s, has made salmon a major export item. Salmon exports to the United States are 40,000 tons annually, whereas U.S. annual production of farm-raised salmon is only 31,000 tons. Chile is also a major exporter of the fishmeal that is fed to hatchery-raised salmon.

Chile's production technology has resulted in productivity increases and higher incomes. Its experience indicates that manufacturing is not the only way for countries to grow economically. The process is to continually adapt to changing tastes, constantly improve technology, and find new ways to prosper from natural resources. Contrast Chile today with the traditional agriculturally based economies that are dependent on one crop (e.g., bananas) today and will still be dependent on that same crop 20 years from now. This type of economic narrowness was the case with Chile a few decades ago when it depended heavily on copper. To expand its economy beyond dependency on copper, Chile began with what it did best—exporting apples. As the economy grew, the country invested in better education and infrastructure and improved technology to provide the bases to develop other economic sectors, such as grapes, wine, salmon, and tomato paste.

Regional cooperation and open markets are also crucial for economic growth. As will be discussed in Chapter 10, being a member of a multinational market region is essential if a country is to have preferential access to regional trade groups. As steps in that direction, in 2003 Chile and in 2005 Central American countries (including banana producers) signed free trade agreements with the United States.[8]

Information Technology, the Internet, and Economic Development

In addition to the growth factors previously discussed, a country's investment in information technology (IT) is an important key to economic growth.[9] The cellular phone, the Internet, and other advances in IT open opportunities for emerging economies to catch up with richer ones. New, innovative electronic technologies can be the key to a sustainable future for developed and developing nations alike.

Because the Internet cuts transaction costs and reduces economies of scale from vertical integration, some argue that it reduces the economically optimal size for firms. Lower transaction costs enable small firms in Asia or Latin America to work together to develop a global reach. Smaller firms in emerging economies can now sell into a global market. It is now easier, for instance, for a tailor in Shanghai to make a suit by hand for a lawyer in Boston, or a software designer in India to write a program for a firm in California. One of the big advantages that rich economies have is their closeness to wealthy consumers, which will be eroded as transaction costs fall.

The Internet accelerates the process of economic growth by speeding up the diffusion of new technologies to emerging economies. Unlike the decades required for many developing countries to benefit from railways, telephones, or electricity, the Internet is spreading rapidly throughout Asia, Latin America, and eastern Europe. IT can jump-start national economies and allow them to leapfrog from high levels of illiteracy to computer literacy.

The Internet also facilitates education, a fundamental underpinning for economic development. The African Virtual University, which links 24 underfunded and ill-equipped African campuses to classrooms and libraries worldwide, grants degrees in computer science, computer engineering, and electrical engineering. South Africa's School Net program

---

[8]"Chile and U.S. Sign Accord on Free Trade," *New York Times*, June 7, 2003, p. 3; David Armstrong, "CAFTA Signed into Law," *San Francisco Chronicle*, August 3, 2005, p. C1.

[9]Manjeet Kripalani, "The Digital Village," *BusinessWeek*, June 28, 2004, pp. 60–62.

links 1,035 schools to the Net, and the government's Distance Education program brings multimedia teaching to rural schools.

Mobile phones and other wireless technologies greatly reduce the need to lay down a costly telecom infrastructure to bring telephone service to areas not now served. In Caracas, Venezuela, for example, where half of the city's 5 million population lives in nonwired slums, cell phones with pay-as-you-go cards have provided service to many residents for the first time. The Grameen Bank, a private commercial enterprise in Bangladesh, has a program to supply phones to 300 villages. There are only five land phones lines for every 1,000 people in Bangladesh, one of the lowest phone-penetration rates in the world. The new network will be nationwide, putting every villager within two kilometers of a cellular phone. Already cell phone penetration has doubled from 4 per 1,000 to 10 per 1,000 during the last two years.[10]

The Internet allows for innovative services at a relatively inexpensive cost. For example, cyber post offices in Ghana offer e-mail service for the price of a letter. Telecenters in five African countries provide public telephone, fax, computer, and Internet services where students can read online books and local entrepreneurs can seek potential business partners. Medical specialists from Belgium help train local doctors and surgeons in Senegal via video linkups between classrooms and operating centers and provide them with Internet access to medical journals and databases. Traveling there to teach would be prohibitively expensive; via Internet technology, it costs practically nothing.

Substantial investments in the infrastructure to create easy access to the Internet and other aspects of IT are being made by governments and entrepreneurs. Hong Kong is investing in a $1.7 billion cyberport to house high-tech companies. If successful, it will create a new information economy and thousands of new jobs. Singapore's broadband network brings fast digital transmission capacity to homes and offices, allowing delivery of advanced multimedia services. Vietnam has entered the first stage of e-commerce development with the opening of a software zone in Hanoi and plans to spend $32.4 million to develop an information technology park.

India not only stands firmly at the center of many success stories in California's Silicon Valley (Indian engineers provide some 30 percent of the workforce there) but is also seeing Internet enthusiasm build to a frenzy on its own shores. Indian entrepreneurs and capital are creating an Indian Silicon Valley, dubbed "Cyberabad," in Bangalore. Exports there are growing 50 percent annually and each worker adds $27,000 of value per year, an extraordinary figure in a country where per capita GDP is about $500. After a little more than a decade of growth, the Indian industry has an estimated 280,000 software engineers in about 1,000 companies.

Similar investments are being made in Latin America and eastern Europe as countries see the technology revolution as a means to dramatically accelerate their economic and social development. As one economist commented, "Traditional economic reforms in the 1980s and 1990s managed to stop hyper-inflation and currency crises, but further change will not produce significant new growth needed to combat poverty. Governments must work to provide public access to the Internet and other information technologies."

The IT revolution is not limited to broad, long-range economic goals; as Crossing Borders 9.1 illustrates, it can have an almost immediate impact on the poorest inhabitants of an emerging country.

Objectives of Developing Countries

A thorough assessment of economic development and marketing should begin with a brief review of the basic facts and objectives of economic development.

Industrialization is the fundamental objective of most developing countries. Most countries see in economic growth the achievement of social as well as economic goals. Better education, better and more effective government, elimination of many social inequities, and improvements in moral and ethical responsibilities are some of the expectations of

---

[10]World Bank, World Development Indicators, 2005.

CROSSING BORDERS 9.1   The Benefits of Information Technology in Village Life

Delora Begum's home office is a corrugated-metal-and-straw hut in Bangladesh with a mud floor, no toilet, and no running water. Yet in this humble setting, she reigns as the "phone lady," a successful entrepreneur and a person of standing in her community. It's all due to a sleek Nokia cell phone. Mrs. Begum acquired the handset in 1999. Her telephone "booth" is mobile: During the day, it's the stall on the village's main dirt road; at night, callers drop by her family hut to use the cell phone.

Once the phone hookup was made, incomes and quality of life improved almost immediately for many villagers. For as long as he can remember, a brick factory manager had to take a two-and-a half-hour bus ride to Dhaka to order furnace oil and coal for the brick factory. Now, he avoids the biweekly trip: "I can just call if I need anything, or if I have any problems." The local carpenter uses the cell phone to check the current market price of wood, so he ensures a higher profit for the furniture he makes.

The only public telecom link to the outside world, this unit allows villagers to learn the fair value of their rice and vegetables, cutting out middlemen notorious for exploiting them. They can arrange bank transfers or consult doctors in distant cities and, in a nation where

only 45 percent of the population can read and write, the cell phone allows people to dispense with a scribe to compose a letter. It also earns some $600 a year for its owner—twice the annual per capita income in Bangladesh.

When members of the Grand Coast Fishing Operators cooperative salt and smoke the day's catch to prepare it for market, it may seem light years away from cyberspace, but for these women the Internet is a boon. The cooperative has set up a Web site that enables its 7,350 members to promote their produce, monitor export markets, and negotiate prices with overseas buyers before they arrive at markets in Senegal. Information technology has thus improved their economic position.

Finally, it seems that new technology can also breed new economic disputes. A disagreement over an unpaid $50 phone bill in a village 110 kilometers northeast of Dhaka, Bangladesh, turned into a gunfight between two groups of villagers that left 5 dead and 25 injured.

Sources: Miriam Jordan, "It Takes a Cell Phone," *Wall Street Journal*, June 25, 1999, p. B1; "Bangladesh—Five Killed in Shootout over Telephone Bill," *Los Angeles Times*, March 31, 2003, p. A17; World Bank, World Development Indicators, 2005.

---

developing countries. Thus economic growth is measured not solely in economic goals but also in social achievements.

Because foreign businesses are outsiders, they often are feared as having goals in conflict with those of the host country. Considered exploiters of resources, many multinational firms were expropriated in the 1950s and 1960s. Others faced excessively high tariffs and quotas, and foreign investment was forbidden or discouraged. Today, foreign investors are seen as vital partners in economic development. Experience with state-owned businesses proved to be a disappointment to most governments. Instead of being engines for accelerated economic growth, state-owned enterprises were mismanaged, inefficient drains on state treasuries. Many countries have deregulated industry, opened their doors to foreign investment, lowered trade barriers, and begun privatizing SOEs. The trend toward privatization is currently a major economic phenomenon in industrialized as well as in developing countries.

Infrastructure and Development

One indicator of economic development is the extent of social overhead capital, or infrastructure, within the economy. *Infrastructure* represents those types of capital goods that serve the activities of many industries. Included in a country's infrastructure are paved roads, railroads, seaports, communications networks, financial networks,[11] and energy supplies—all necessary to support production and marketing. The quality of an infrastructure directly affects a country's economic growth potential and the ability of an enterprise to engage effectively in business.[12] See Exhibit 9.2 for some comparisons of infrastructure among countries at different levels of economic development.

---

[11]"Consumer Lending in China, Safe as Houses?" *The Economist*, April 23, 2005, p. 73.

[12]"Shanghai's Evolving Architecture Reflects China's Growing Self-Confidence," *The Economist*, March 12, 2005, p. 46.

Exhibit 9.2
Infrastructure of Selected Countries

Country	Roads (1000 km)	Vehicles (per 1000 people)	Rail Lines (km)	Electrical Power (kwh per capita)	Mobile Phones (per 1000 people)	Personal Computers (per 1000 people)
United States	6,304	759	141,961	12,183	543	659
Brazil	1,724	79	30,403	1,776	264	75
China	1,765	12	60,627	987	215	28
Colombia	113	51	3,154	817	141	49
Germany	231	529	35,868	6,046	785	485
India	3,315	9	63,140	380	25	7
Japan	1,172	581	20,096	7,718	679	382
Kenya	64	13	2,634	120	50	6
Mexico	330	159	26,656	1,660	291	82
South Africa	276	143	20,041	3,860	364	73
Spain	664	539	13,866	5,048	909	196

Source: 2005 World Bank, World Development Indicators.

Infrastructure is a crucial component of the uncontrollable elements facing marketers. Without adequate transportation facilities, for example, distribution costs can increase substantially, and the ability to reach certain segments of the market is impaired. To a marketer, the key issue is the impact of a country's infrastructure on a firm's ability to market effectively. Business efficiency is affected by the presence or absence of financial and commercial service infrastructure found within a country—such as advertising agencies, warehousing storage facilities, credit and banking facilities, marketing research agencies, and satisfactory specialized middlemen. Generally speaking, the less developed a country is, the less adequate the infrastructure is for conducting business. Companies do market in less-developed countries, but often they must modify offerings and augment existing levels of infrastructure.

Countries begin to lose economic development ground when their infrastructure cannot support an expanding population and economy. A country that has the ability to produce commodities for export may be unable to export them because of an inadequate infrastructure. For example, Mexico's economy has been throttled by its archaic transport system. Roads and seaports are inadequate, and the railroad system has seen little modernization since the 1910 revolution. If it were not for Mexico's highway system (although it, too, is in poor condition), the economy would have come to a halt; Mexico's highways have consistently carried more freight than its railroads. Conditions in other Latin American countries are no better. Shallow harbors and inadequate port equipment make a container filled with computers about $1,000 more expensive to ship from Miami to San Antonio, Chile (about 3,900 miles), than the same container shipped from Yokohama, Japan, to Miami (8,900 miles).

Marketing's Contributions

How important is marketing to the achievement of a nation's goals? Unfortunately, marketing (or distribution) is not always considered meaningful to those responsible for planning. Economic planners frequently are more production oriented than marketing oriented and tend to ignore or regard distribution as an inferior economic activity. Given such attitudes, economic planners generally are more concerned with the problems of production, investment, and finance than the problems of efficiency of distribution.

While it is difficult to compete with China's low manufacturing costs, imagine marketing in a country with production but little disposable income, no storage, limited transportation that goes to the wrong markets, and no middlemen and facilitating agents to activate the flow of goods from the manufacturer to the consumer. When such conditions exist in developing markets, marketing and economic progress are retarded. To some

CROSSING **BORDERS 9.2** | Infrastructure: India

Animals in India provide 30,000 megawatts (MW) of power, more than the 29,000 MW provided by electricity.

Because of the religious ban on the slaughter of cattle in almost all states in the country, India has the highest cattle population in the world—perhaps as many as 360 million head. Bullocks are used for plowing fields, turning waterwheels, working crushers and threshers, and above all for hauling carts. The number of bullock carts has doubled to 15 million since India's independence in 1947. Bullocks haul more tonnage than the entire railway system (though over a much shorter distance); in many parts of rural India they are the only practical means of moving things about.

As a bonus, India's cattle produce enormous quantities of dung, which is used both as farmyard manure and, when dried in cakes, as household fuel. Each animal produces an estimated average of 3 kilograms of dung per day. Some studies suggest that these forms of energy are the equivalent of another 10,000 MW.

Although Indian farmers prefer machines for plowing and hauling carts, bullocks and other draft animals are still in demand. Because it will take a long time for farmers to replace these draft animals with machines and there is concern that the better breeds may degenerate or become extinct, the government has developed an artificial insemination program to preserve the best breeds.

Sources: "Bullock Manure," *The Economist*, October 17, 1981, p. 88; S. Rajendran, "India: Scheme to Preserve Local Cattle Breed on Anvil," *The Hindu*, August 9, 1997; "Not Enough Bulls to Till the Land," *Times of India*, May 9, 2000; Tim Sullivan, "India's Leader in a Beef over Dietary Insult," *Los Angeles Times*, April 6, 2003, p. A20.

degree, this is the problem in China and many of the republics of the former Soviet Union. In China, for example, most of the 1.2 billion potential consumers are not accessible because of a poor or nonexistent distribution network. Indeed, the true consumer market in China is probably limited to no more than 20 percent of those who live in the more affluent cities. No distribution and channel system exists to effectively distribute products, so companies must become resourceful to compensate for poor infrastructure.

For example, after nearly a decade of frustration in trying to effectively market and service its products in China, IBM took a bold step[13] and entered a venture with the Railways Ministry that allowed IBM to set up IBM service centers dubbed the "Blue Express." The agreement created a national network of service centers in railway stations that has enabled IBM to ship computer parts via the railroad around the country within 24 hours; competitors must book cargo space weeks in advance. In addition, the ministry's staff of more than 300 computer engineers helps out by providing customer services on IBM products.

Such innovative thinking by IBM and other marketers often accelerates the development of a more efficient market system.[14] IBM's service centers set an example of effective service before and after sales—important marketing activities. Management training for the thousands of employees of franchises such as Pizza Hut, McDonald's, and Kentucky Fried Chicken has spread expertise throughout the marketing system as the trainees move on to more advanced positions.

Marketing is an economy's arbitrator between productive capacity and consumer demand. The marketing process is the critical element in effectively utilizing production resulting from economic growth; it can create a balance between higher production and higher consumption. Although marketing may be considered a passive function, it is instrumental in laying the groundwork for effective distribution. An efficient distribution and channel system and all the attendant liaisons match production capacity and resources with consumer needs, wants, and purchasing power.

---

[13]MNCs are becoming more creative in their approaches to investment and operations in developing countries. See Ravi Ramamurti, "Developing Countries and MNEs: Extending and Enriching the Research Agenda," *Journal of International Business Studies* 35, no. 4 (2004), pp. 277–283.

[14]Klaus E. Meyer, "Perspectives on Multinational Enterprises in Emerging Economies," *Journal of International Business Studies* 35, no. 4 (2004), pp. 259–276.

Marketing in a Developing Country

A marketer cannot superimpose a sophisticated marketing strategy on an underdeveloped economy.[15] Marketing efforts must be keyed to each situation, custom tailored for each set of circumstances. A promotional program for a population that is 50 percent illiterate is vastly different from a program for a population that is 95 percent literate. Pricing in a subsistence market poses different problems from pricing in an affluent society. An efficient marketing program is one that provides for optimum utility given a specific set of circumstances. In evaluating the potential in a developing country, the marketer must make an assessment of the existing level of market development and receptiveness within the country.

Level of Market Development

The level of market development roughly parallels the stages of economic development. Exhibit 9.3 illustrates various stages of the marketing process as it evolves in a growing economy. The table is a static model representing an idealized evolutionary process. As discussed earlier, economic cooperation and assistance, technological change, and political, social, and cultural factors can and do cause significant deviations in this evolutionary process. However, the table focuses on the logic and interdependence of marketing and economic development. The more developed an economy, the greater the variety of marketing functions demanded, and the more sophisticated and specialized the institutions become to perform marketing functions. The evolution of the channel structure illustrates the relationship between market development and the stage of economic development of a country.

As countries develop, the distribution and channel systems develop. In the retail sector, specialty stores, supermarkets, and hypermarkets emerge, and mom-and-pop stores give way to larger establishments. In short, the number of retail stores declines and the volume of sales per store increases. Additionally, a defined channel structure from manufacturer to wholesaler to retailer develops and replaces the import agent that traditionally assumed all the functions between importing and retailing.

Advertising agencies, facilities for marketing research, repair services, specialized consumer-financing agencies, and storage and warehousing facilities are facilitating agencies created to serve the particular needs of expanded markets and economies. These institutions do not come about automatically, and the necessary marketing structure does not simply appear. Part of the marketer's task when studying an economy is to determine what in the foreign environment will be useful and how much adjustment will be necessary to carry out stated objectives. In some developing countries it may be up to the marketer to institute the foundations of a modern market system.

The limitation of Exhibit 9.3 in evaluating the market system of a particular country is that the system is in a constant state of flux. To expect a neat, precise progression through each successive growth stage, as in the geological sciences, is to oversimplify the dynamic nature of marketing development. A significant factor in the acceleration of market development is that countries or areas of countries have been propelled from the 18th to the 21st century in the span of two decades by the influence of borrowed technology.

Marketing structures of many developing countries are simultaneously at many stages. It is not unusual to find traditional marketing retail outlets functioning side by side with advanced, modern markets. This is especially true in food retailing, where a large segment of the population buys food from small produce stalls while the same economy supports modern supermarkets equal to any found in the United States. On the same street as the Wal-Mart store described in the Global Perspective are mom-and-pop food stands. Exhibit 9.4 (page 259) provides market indicators for selected countries.

Demand in a Developing Country

Estimating market potential in less-developed countries involves myriad challenges. Most of the difficulty arises from the coexistence of three distinct kinds markets in each country: (1) the traditional rural/agricultural sector,[16] (2) the modern urban/high-income sector, and

---

[15]Y. Luo, "Market-Seeking MNEs in an Emerging Market: How Parent–Subsidiary Links Shape Overseas Success," *Journal of International Business Studies* 35, no. 4 (2003), pp. 290–309.

[16]Leslie Chang, Chad Terhune, and Betsy McKay, "Rural Thing, Coke's Big Gamble in Asia: Digging Deeper in China, India," *Wall Street Journal*, August 11, 2004, pp. A1, A6.

Exhibit 9.3
Evolution of the Marketing Process

Stage	Substage	Example	Marketing Functions	Marketing Institutions	Channel Control	Primary Orientation	Resources Employed	Comments
Agricultural and raw materials	Self-sufficient	Nomadic or hunting tribes	None	None	Traditional authority	Subsistence	Labor Land	Labor intensive No organized markets
	Surplus commodity product	Agricultural economy, such as coffee, bananas	Exchange	Small-scale merchants, traders, fairs, export-import	Traditional authority	Entrepreneurial Commercial	Labor Land	Labor and land intensive Product specialization Local markets Import oriented
Manufacturing	Small scale	Cottage industry	Exchange Physical distribution	Merchants, wholesalers, export-import	Middlemen	Entrepreneurial Financial	Labor Land Technology Transportation	Labor intensive Product standardization and grading Regional and export markets Import oriented
	Mass production	U.S. economy, 1885–1914	Demand creation Physical distribution Market information	Merchants, wholesalers, traders, and specialized institutions	Producer	Production and finance	Labor Land Technology Transportation Capital	Capital intensive Product differentiation National, regional, and export markets
Marketing	Commercial—transition	U.S. economy, 1915–1929	Demand creation Physical distribution Market information	Large-scale and chain retailers	Producer	Entrepreneurial Commercial	Labor Land Technology Transportation Capital Communication	Capital intensive Changes in structure of distribution National, regional, and export markets
	Mass distribution	U.S. economy, 1950 to present	Demand creation Physical distribution Market information Market and product planning, development	Integrated channels of distribution Increase in specialized middlemen	Producer Retailer	Marketing	Labor Land Technology Transportation Capital Communication	Capital and land intensive Rapid product innovation National, regional, and export markets

CROSSING BORDERS 9.3   Got Distribution Problems? Call Grandma or Your Local University!

It may sound trivial, but in China's teeming cities, getting cold carbonated drinks into the hands of the young can be a struggle. Fierce competitors Coca-Cola and PepsiCo rely on Grandma and hip college students with space-age coolers to slake Chinese thirst.

Coca-Cola was having problems with Shanghai's two main shopping streets, Nanjing Lu and Huaihai Lu. The area was becoming too expensive for the small stores that offered Coke. Further, traffic regulations were constantly changing, downtown deliveries required a special pass, and street vendors were banned. So how did Coca-Cola get its product to market? Enter one of the lingering remnants of the old communist regime: that bastion of the geriatric busybody, the Chinese street committee.

Initially the Chinese street committee consisted of older people whose job was to make sure all within their territory were being "good Chinese citizens." If not, they scolded scofflaws, and if that didn't work, reported them to higher authorities. To carry out their jobs committee members had privileged status. People wearing the *zhi qin* (on-duty) armband could pretty much go where they liked and do whatever they wanted. As the Chinese experienced more personal freedom, however, they resented being spied on and bossed around by self-important old people—the traditional role of the street committee was becoming redundant.

The members, however, retained their privileged status, which, as Coca-Cola managers noted, meant they could push carts laden with ice-cold Coke around traffic and through street vendor–restricted areas of downtown Shanghai. So each committee was recruited to store, chill, and sell ice-cold Coke on an exclusive basis on its turf. Coca-Cola has signed up a fleet of 150 pushcarts and 300 specially designed tricycles.

PepsiCo, facing a similar problem, recruited young, energetic, and outgoing university students to roam through the hottest and most crowded shopping areas. Toting space-age coolers strapped to their backs, the students dispense cups of cold Pepsi stored at 2 degrees Celsius. With a cup dispenser on one shoulder strap, a money belt, and a dispensing gun snaking around from behind, the student sellers are mobile vending machines—and walking, talking billboards.

The latest Coke–Pepsi contest in China is over the rights to use NBA star Yao Ming's image in ads. Even though the 7-foot-5 center for the Houston Rockets has signed a deal with Pepsi and appeared in their TV ads for the Chinese market, his likeness concurrently appeared on bottles of Coke in Shanghai. It will be interesting to see how the companies decide to split the big guy—and we're sure the government will help "mediate" the dispute!

Sources: "Those Ever-Resourceful Coke Boys: Distribution Is It," *Business China*, April 28, 1997, p. 12; Bruce Gilley, "Pepsi Gets Street Smart: In Its Campaign to Win Over Young Chinese, Pepsi-Cola Is Drafting Student Ambassadors," *Far Eastern Economic Review*, June 2000, p. 37; Brook Larmer, "The Center of the World," *Foreign Policy*, September–October 2005, pp. 65–74.

(3) the often very large transitional sector usually represented by low-income urban slums. The modern sector is centered in the capital city and has jet airports, international hotels, new factories, and an expanding westernized middle class. The traditional rural sector tends to work in the countryside as it has for decades or centuries. Directly juxtaposed to the modern sector, the transitional sector contains those moving from the country to the large cities. Production and consumption patterns vary across the three sectors. India is a good example. The 11th largest industrial economy in the world, India has a population of approximately 1 billion, of which 200 million to 250 million are considered middle class. The modern sector demands products and services similar to those available in any industrialized country; the remaining 750 million in the transitional and rural sectors, however, demand items more indigenous and basic to subsistence. As one authority on India's markets observed, "A rural Indian can live a sound life without many products. Toothpaste, sugar, coffee, washing soap, bathing soap, kerosene are all bare necessities of life to those who live in semi-urban and urban areas." One of the greatest challenges of the 21st century is to manage and market to the transitional sector in developing countries. The large-city slums perhaps present the greatest problems for smooth economic development.

Developing countries thus have at least three different market segments. Each can prove profitable, but each requires its own marketing program and products and services appropriate for its market characteristics. Many companies market successfully to both the traditional and the modern market segments but often have problems in the transitional segments, where, for example, advertising targeting high-income consumers reaches low-income consumers.

Exhibit 9.4
Market Indicators in Selected Countries

Country	Population (millions)	GDP* (per capita)	Cars (per 1000 people)	TVs (per 1000 people)	Personal Computers (per 1000 people)
United States	290.8	$35,566	759	871	659
Argentina	36.8	7,165	181	326	82
Australia	19.9	21,688	601	722	565
Brazil	176.6	3,510	79	369	75
Canada	31.6	24,222	582	707	487
China	1,288.4	5,196	12	350	119
France	59.8	22,723	592	632	347
Germany	82.5	22,868	529	675	485
India	1,064.4	511	9	84	7
Indonesia	214.6	781	25	153	12
Italy	57.6	19,090	591	494	231
Japan	127.6	38,222	581	785	382
Kenya	31.9	341	13	44	6
South Korea	47.9	12,232	292	458	558
Mexico	102.3	5,792	159	282	82
Poland	38.2	4,634	307	229	142
South Africa	45.8	3,026	143	177	73
Spain	41.1	14,691	539	564	196
United Kingdom	59.3	25,742	424	950	406

Source: World Bank, 2003. Copyright © 2003 by World Bank. Reproduced with permission of World Bank via Copyright Clearance Center.

*Constant 2000 dollars.

Tomorrow's markets will include expansion in industrialized countries and the development of the transitional and traditional sectors of less-developed nations, as well as continued expansion of the modern sectors of such countries. The traditional sector offers the greatest long-range potential, but profits come only with a willingness to invest time and effort for longer periods. Market investment today is necessary to produce profits tomorrow.

New markets also mean that the marketer has to help educate the consumer. Procter & Gamble, Colgate, and Unilever are all aggressively pursuing dental health education programs—from school visits to scholarships at dental universities to sponsorship of oral care research. While creating new markets for their products they are also helping to spread more healthful practices. In China, for instance, only about 20 percent of the population in rural areas brushes daily—most view brushing as purely cosmetic, rather than medicinal. P&G's efforts may change that attitude as school children frolic with Crest's giant inflatable Tooth Mascot, which appears when the mobile dental van makes a stop in the countryside. Crest's program reaches 1 million children in China each year.[17]

The companies that will benefit in the future from emerging markets in eastern Europe, China, Latin America, and elsewhere are the ones that invest when it is difficult and initially unprofitable. In some of the less-developed countries, the marketer will institute the very foundations of a modern market system, thereby gaining a foothold in an economy that will someday be highly profitable. The price paid for entering in the early stages of development may be a lower initial return on investment, but the price paid for waiting until the market becomes profitable may be a blocked market with no opportunity for entry.

Bottom-of-the-Pyramid Markets (BOPMs)

C. K. Prahalad and his associates introduced a new concept into the discussion of developing countries and markets—bottom-of-the-pyramid markets (BOPMs)[18]—consisting of the 4 billion people across the globe with annual incomes of less than $1,200. These markets

---

[17]"P&G in Touch with Consumer Needs," *Chain Drug Review*, June 7, 1999; Normandy Madden, "China Warms Up to P&G," *Advertising Age*, April 7, 2003, p. S5.

[18]C. K. Prahalad, *The Fortune at the Bottom of the Pyramid* (Philadelphia: Wharton School Publishing, 2005).

are not necessarily defined by national borders, but rather the pockets of poverty across countries. These 4 billion consumers are, of course, most often concentrated in the LDCs and LLDCs, as defined in the aforementioned UN classification scheme.

Prahalad's basic point is that these consumers have been relatively ignored by international marketers because of misconceptions about their lack of resources (both money and technology) and the lack of appropriateness of products and services usually developed for more affluent consumers. Three cases well demonstrate the commercial viability of such markets and their long-term potential. CEMEX, the Mexican cement company with global operations, pioneered a profitable program to build better housing for the poor that includes innovative design, financing, and distribution systems. Similarly, Aravind Eye Care System in India began with the problem of blindness among the poor and developed an innovative organization of workflow—from patient identification to postoperative care—that has yielded better vision for consumers and profits for the company. Finally, in her wonderful book about the global economy, Pietra Rivoli[19] tells the story of how small entrepreneurs clothe East Africa with old American T-shirts. All three operations described include combinations of products, services, research, and promotions that are appropriate for the lowest-income neighborhoods on the planet.

A comprehensive study of the development of the leather-working industry in West Africa presents a new approach to creating industries and markets in BOPMs.[20] The authors describe how industry clusters evolve and can be supported by outside investments from commercial and governmental concerns. Exhibit 9.5 represents the ingredients and processes

---

[19]Pietra Rivoli, *The Travels of a T-Shirt in the Global Economy* (New York: Wiley, 2005).

[20]Eric Arnould and Jakki J. Mohr, "Dynamic Transformation for Base-of-the-Pyramid Market Clusters," *Journal of the Academy of Marketing Science* 3, no. 3 (2005), pp. 254–274.

Exhibit 9.5
Dynamic Transformation of BOPM Clusters

Source: Eric Arnould and Jakki J. Mohr, "Dynamic Transformation for Base-of-the-Pyramid Market Clusters," *Journal of the Academy of Marketing Science* 33, No. 3, July, 2005. Reprinted by permission of Sage Publications, Inc.

Note: BOPM = base-of-the-pyramid market

involved in establishing a viable industry cluster in a LLDC. Craftsmen must network and collaborate to attain efficiencies in production, domestic and international distribution,[21] and other marketing activities. Key to the vibrancy of the industry cluster will be a series of cluster characteristics, external inputs,[22] and macroenvironment factors. The scheme presented might serve as a checklist for stimulating economic development through marketing in BOPMS. Entrepreneurial activities that are networked appear to be perhaps the best way to stimulate economic development and growth from within[23] developing countries.[24] And marketing is key.

Developing Countries and Emerging Markets

As mentioned earlier, the U.S. Department of Commerce estimates that over 75 percent of the expected growth in world trade over the next two decades will come from the more than 130 developing and newly industrialized countries; a small core of these countries will account for more than half of that growth.[25] Commerce researchers also predict that imports to the countries identified as big emerging markets (BEMs),[26] with half the world's population and accounting for 25 percent of the industrialized world's GDP today, will by 2010 be 50 percent of that of the industrialized world. With a combined GDP of over $2 trillion, the BEMs already account for as large a share of world output as Germany and the United Kingdom combined, and exports to the BEMs exceed exports to Europe and Japan combined.

Big emerging markets share a number of important traits. They

- Are all physically large.
- Have significant populations.
- Represent considerable markets for a wide range of products.
- Have strong rates of growth or the potential for significant growth.
- Have undertaken significant programs of economic reform.
- Are of major political importance within their regions.
- Are "regional economic drivers."
- Will engender further expansion in neighboring markets as they grow.

Although these criteria are general and each country does not meet all the criteria, the Department of Commerce has identified those countries listed in Exhibit 9.6 as BEMs. Other countries such as Egypt,[27] Venezuela, and Colombia may warrant inclusion in the near future. The list is fluid because some countries will drop off while others will be added as economic conditions change. Inducements for those doing business in BEMs include Export-Import Bank loans and political-risk insurance channeled into these areas.

The BEMs differ from other developing countries in that they import more than smaller markets and more than economies of similar size. As they embark on economic development, demand increases for capital goods to build their manufacturing base and develop infrastructure. Increased economic activity means more jobs and more income to spend on products not yet produced locally. Thus, as their economies expand, there is an accelerated

---

[21]Jagdish Bhagwati, *In Defense of Globalization* (Oxford: Oxford University Press, 2004).

[22]John Daniszewski, "Debtor Nations Freed of Burdens," *Los Angeles Times*, June 12, 2005, pp. A1, A6.

[23]Debabrata Talukdar, Sumila Gulyani, and Lawrence F. Salmen, "'Customer-Orientation' in the Context of Development Projects: Insights from the World Bank," *Journal of Public Policy and Marketing* 24, no. 1 (2005), pp. 100–111.

[24]Alan J. Patricof and Julie E. Sunderland, "Big Ideas," *Milken Institute Review* 2 (2005), pp. 90–94.

[25]C. K. Prahalad and Allen Hammond, "Serving the World's Poor, Profitably," *Harvard Business Review* 80, no. 9 (September 2002), pp. 24–32.

[26]For more information on emerging markets see www.library.yale.edu/socsci/emerge/bigten.html.

[27]Amr Nabil, "Egypt, Catching Up with the 21st Century," *BusinessWeek*, May 30, 2005, pp. 50–51.

Exhibit 9.6
Big Emerging Markets

Country	Population (millions)	GDP* (billions)	GDP* (per capita)	Imports of Goods and Services (billions)	Exports of Goods and Services (billions)
Asia					
China	1,288.4	$1,375.2	$ 5,196	$441.8	$502.8
India	1,064.4	543.7	511	83.7	88.6
South Korea	47.9	586.1	12,232	213.8	266.4
Vietnam	81.3	38.2	470	28.6	23.9
Latin America					
Argentina	36.8	263.5	7,165	19.4	34.7
Brazil	176.6	619.9	3,510	63.8	88.0
Colombia	44.6	89.9	2,017	19.1	18.6
Mexico	102.3	592.5	5,792	189.2	177.9
Venezuela	25.7	102.9	4,009	12.9	27.7
Europe					
Poland	38.2	177.0	4,634	60.0	56.7
Turkey	70.7	210.5	2,997	69.5	66.3
Africa					
South Africa	45.8	138.7	3,026	37.6	37.4

Source: World Bank, 2005. World Development Indicators.

*Constant 2000 dollars.

growth in demand for goods and services, much of which must be imported. BEM merchandise imports are expected to be nearly $1 trillion higher than they were in 1990; if services are added, the amount jumps beyond the trillion-dollar mark.

Because many of these countries lack modern infrastructure, much of the expected growth will be in industrial sectors such as information technology, environmental technology, transportation, energy technology, healthcare technology, and financial services. India, for example, has less than 46 million telephone lines and 25 million mobile phones to serve a population of 1 billion, and Turkey's plans for improving health services will increase the demand for private hospital services and investments in new equipment.

What is occurring in the BEMs is analogous to the situation after World War II when tremendous demand was created during the reconstruction of Europe. As Europe rebuilt its

Old meets new in two big emerging markets. The Grand Bazaar in Istanbul is the oldest and largest covered marketplace in the world, dating back to the 15th century. In modern Istanbul it competes for customers with the ubiquitous McDonald's. Faint in the background is the Blue Mosque built in 1616. Of course, the pyramids at Giza near Cairo are much older. But new construction methods and development are competing for the skyline there as well. (*right: AP/Wide World Photos*)

CROSSING BORDERS 9.4

Marketing in the Third World: Teaching, Pricing, and Community Usage

Much of the marketing challenge in the developing world, which is not accustomed to consumer products, is to get consumers to use the product and to offer it in the right sizes. For example, because many Latin American consumers can't afford a seven-ounce bottle of shampoo, Gillette sells it in half-ounce plastic bottles. And in Brazil, the company sells Right Guard in plastic squeeze bottles instead of metal cans.

But the toughest task for Gillette is convincing Third World men to shave. Portable theaters called mobile propaganda units are sent into villages to show movies and commercials that tout daily shaving. In South African and Indonesian versions, a bewildered bearded man enters a locker room where clean-shaven friends show him how to shave. In the Mexican film, a handsome sheriff is tracking bandits who have kidnapped a woman. He pauses on the trail, snaps a double-edged blade into his razor, and lathers his face to shave. In the end, of course, the smooth-faced sheriff gets the woman. From packaging blades so that they can be sold one at a time to educating the unshaven about the joys of a smooth face, Gillette is pursuing a growth strategy in the developing world.

What Gillette does for shaving, Colgate-Palmolive does for oral hygiene. Video vans sent into rural India show an infomercial designed to teach the benefits of toothpaste and the proper method of brushing one's teeth. "If they saw the toothpaste tube, they wouldn't know what to do with it," says the company's Indian marketing manager. The people need to be educated about the need for toothpaste and then how to use the product. Toothpaste consumption has doubled in rural India in a six-year period.

There are more than 7 million PC and some 17 million Internet users in Indian households. Several companies are seeking to tap into this opportunity with community usage. One U.K.-based company has a contract with the state of Tamil Nadu to set up 13,000 community Internet cafes and is in discussions for similar installations with other state governments.

Sources: David Wessel, "Gillette Keys Sales to Third World Taste," *Wall Street Journal*, January 23, 1986, p. 30; "Selling to India," *The Economist*, May 1, 2000; Raja Ramachandran, "Understanding the Market Environment of India," *Business Horizons*, January/February 2000, p. 44; World Bank, World Development Indicators, 2005.

infrastructure and industrial base, demand for capital goods exploded; as more money was infused into its economies, consumer demand also increased rapidly. For more than a decade, Europe could not supply its increasing demand for industrial and consumer goods. During that period, the United States was the principal supplier because most of the rest of the world was rebuilding or had underdeveloped economies. Meeting this demand produced one of the largest economic booms the United States had ever experienced. As we shall see later in the chapter, consumer markets and market segments in the BEMs are already booming. Unlike the situation after World War II, however, the competition will be fierce as Japan, China, Europe, the NICs, and the United States vie for these big emerging markets.

Latin America   A political and economic revolution has been taking place in Latin America (see Exhibit 9.7) over the last two decades.[28] Most of the countries have moved from military dictatorships to democratically elected governments, and sweeping economic and trade liberalization is replacing the economic model most[29] Latin American countries followed for decades. Privatization of state-owned enterprises and other economic, monetary, and trade policy reforms show a broad shift away from the inward-looking policies of import substitution (that is, manufacturing products at home rather than importing them) and protectionism so prevalent earlier. The trend toward privatization of state-owned enterprises in the Americas

SOE's

---

[28]Several Web sites provide information on countries in the Americas: www.enterweb.org/latin.htm, www.oas.org, and www.lanic.utexas.edu.

[29]But not all: Marla Dickerson, "Cultivating Change to Take Back the Land," *Los Angeles Times*, December 12, 2004, pp. C1, C4.

Exhibit 9.7
Latin America

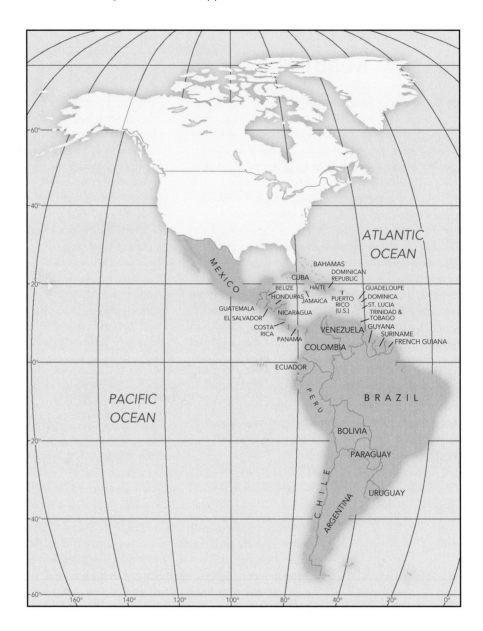

followed a period in which governments dominated economic life for most of the 20th century. State ownership was once considered the ideal engine for economic growth. Instead of economic growth, however, they ended up with inflated public-sector bureaucracies, complicated and unpredictable regulatory environments, the outright exclusion of foreign and domestic private ownership, and inefficient public companies.

Today many Latin American countries are at roughly the same stage of liberalization that launched the dynamic growth in Asia during the 1980s and 1990s. In a positive response to these reforms, investors have invested billions of dollars in manufacturing plants, airlines, banks, public works, and telecommunications systems. Because of its size and resource base, the Latin American market has always been considered to have great economic and market possibilities. The population of nearly 460 million is one-half greater than that of the United States and 100 million more than the European Community.

The strength of these reforms was tested during the last decade, a turbulent period both economically and politically for some countries. Argentina, Brazil, and Mexico, the three BEMs in Latin America, were affected by the economic meltdown in Asia and the continuing financial crisis in Russia. The Russian devaluation and debt default caused a rapid deterioration in Brazil's financial situation; capital began to flee the country, and Brazil

Exhibit 9.8
Eastern Europe and the
Baltic States

devalued its currency. Economic recession in Brazil—coupled with the sharp devaluation of the real—reduced Argentine exports, and Argentina's economic growth slowed. Mexico was able to weather the Russian debt default partly because of debt restructuring and other changes after the major devaluation and recession in the early 1990s. However, competition with Chinese manufacturing has yielded slower growth than predicted at the time of passage of the North American Free Trade Agreement (NAFTA).[30] Other Latin American countries suffered economic downturns that led to devaluations and in some cases political instability. Nevertheless, Latin America is still working toward economic reform.

Eastern Europe and the Baltic States

Eastern Europe and the Baltic states (see Exhibit 9.8), satellite nations of the former Soviet Union, have moved steadily toward establishing postcommunist market reforms.[31] New

---

[30]Marla Dickerson, "Mexico's Economy Posts Disappointing Growth," *Los Angeles Times*, August 17, 2005, pp. C1, C9.

[31]For detailed information on each of the eastern European countries (indeed, on any country), visit www.stat-usa.gov and click on Globus & NTDB, then click on the Country Commercial Guide.

As demand for tobacco declines in the more developed countries, manufacturers direct more marketing efforts in the direction of emerging economies. Indeed, recently Philip Morris published a report estimating the cost savings for the Czech government at $1,227 every time a smoker dies. Apparently, the company did not think through the public relations implications of this grisly bit of research. (*Courtesy American Legacy Foundation, American Cancer Society, and Campaign for Tobacco Free Kids*)

business opportunities are emerging almost daily, and the region is described as anywhere from chaotic with big risks to an exciting place with untold opportunities. Both descriptions fit as countries continue to adjust to the political, social, and economic realities of changing from the restrictions of a Marxist-socialist system to some version of free markets and capitalism. However, these countries have neither all made the same progress nor had the same success in economic reform and growth.

A little more than a decade after the fall of the Berlin Wall, several countries in central Europe[32] are fully integrated with the world economy and have joined the European Union, while some countries in the former Soviet Union, and the Balkans[33] are struggling. For example, Poland's economic output has continued at a steady pace upward since 1990, whereas Ukraine's has shrunk by half. And while Russian businesses struggle to raise cash at any price, companies in Hungary borrow at rates close to western European levels.

The differences can be explained in part by factors ranging from religion and culture to the political complexion of the countries' first post-1998 governments. However, a consensus is emerging that while these factors were important, the decisive factor has been sweeping economic change. Those countries that rapidly instituted the broadest free market policies and implemented the most radical reforms (such as extensive privatization of small and medium-size enterprises and banking reforms) have prospered most in the long run. Rapid liberalization of trade combined with their macroeconomic stabilization policies and broad institutional reforms created a supportive environment for the expansion and reorientation of their trade. Since the early 1990s eastern European countries' trade has been redirected away from dependence on former socialist countries and toward the more affluent western European markets, thus resulting in trade patterns that are more in tune with both historical (pre–World War II) and current market realities.

Eastern Europe.   It is dangerous to generalize beyond a few points about eastern Europe because each of the countries has its own economic problems and is at a different stage in its evolution from a socialist to a market-driven economy (see Exhibit 9.9). Most

[32]Gail Edmondson, William Boston, and Andrea Zammert, "Detroit East," *BusinessWeek*, July 25, 2005, pp. 48–52.

[33]Clifford J. Schultz II, Timothy J. Burkink, Bruno Grbac, and Natasa Renko, "When Policies and Marketing Systems Explode: An Assessment of Food Marketing in the War-Ravaged Balkans and Implications for Recovery, Sustainable Peace, and Prosperity," *Journal of Public Policy and Marketing* 24, no. 1 (2005), pp. 24–37.

Exhibit 9.9
Eastern European Markets

Country	Population (millions)	GDP* (billions)	GDP* (per capita)	Imports of Goods and Services (billions)	Exports of Goods and Services (billions)
Albania	3.1	$ 4.4	$1,916	$ 2.2	$ 1.0
Bosnia/Herzegovina	4.1	5.1	1,225	2.9	1.5
Bulgaria	7.8	14.4	1,835	10.6	8.9
Croatia	4.4	21.1	4,751	12.8	10.5
Czech Republic	10.2	59.8	5,866	48.1	43.8
Hungary	10.1	51.7	5,103	44.7	41.5
Macedonia	2.0	3.6	1,740	2.2	1.5
Poland	38.2	177.0	4,634	60.0	56.7
Romania	21.7	42.7	1,963	21.3	16.9
Slovak Republic	5.4	22.8	4,235	19.7	18.7
Slovenia	2.0	20.8	10,411	13.1	12.5

Source: World Bank, 2003. Copyright © 2003 by World Bank. Reproduced with permission of World Bank via Copyright Clearance Center.

*Constant 2000 dollars.

eastern European countries are privatizing state-owned enterprises, establishing free market pricing systems, relaxing import controls, and wrestling with inflation. The very different paths taken toward market economies have resulted in different levels of progress. Countries such as the Czech Republic, which moved quickly to introduce major changes, seem to have fared better than countries such as Hungary, Poland, and Romania, which held off privatizing until the government restructured internally. Moving quickly allows the transformation to be guided mainly by the spontaneity of innovative market forces rather than by government planners or technocrats. Those countries that took the slow road permitted the bureaucrats from communist days to organize effectively to delay and even derail the transition to a market economy.

Yugoslavia has been plagued with internal strife over ethnic divisions, and four of its republics (Croatia, Slovenia, Macedonia, and Bosnia/Herzegovina) seceded from the federation, leaving Serbia and Montenegro in the reduced Federal Republic of Yugoslavia. Soon after seceding, a devastating ethnic war broke out in Croatia and Bosnia/Herzegovina that decimated their economies. A tentative peace, maintained by United Nations peacekeepers, now exists, but for all practical purposes the economies of Croatia and Bosnia are worse now than ever before.

Nevertheless, most countries in the region continue to make progress in building market-oriented institutions and adopting legislation that conforms to that of advanced market economies. The Czech Republic, Hungary, the Slovak Republic, and Poland have become members of the OECD.[34] Joining the OECD means they accept the obligations of the OECD to modernize their economies and to maintain sound macroeconomic policies and market-oriented structural reforms. The four also became members of the European Union in 2004, and they are eager to stabilize their developing democracies and their westward tilt in foreign and security policies.

The Baltic States.

The Baltic states—Estonia, Latvia, and Lithuania—are a good example of the difference that the right policies can make. All three countries started off with roughly the same legacy of inefficient industry and Soviet-style command economies. Estonia quickly seized the lead by dropping the ruble, privatizing companies and land, letting struggling banks fail, and adopting the freest trading regime of the three countries. Its economic growth has handily outpaced Latvia's and Lithuania's. Since regaining independence in 1991, Estonia's economic reform policy has led to a liberalized, nearly tariff-free, open-market economy.

Although Latvia and Lithuania have made steady progress, government bureaucracy, corruption, and organized crime—common problems found in the countries of the former Soviet Union—continue. These represent the most significant hurdles to U.S. trade and investment. The governments and all major political parties support a free market system, yet traces of the Soviet methodology and regulatory traditions at the lower levels of bureaucracy remain visible. All three Baltic countries are WTO members and as of 2004 EU members.

Asia

Asia (see Exhibit 9.10) has been the fastest-growing area in the world for the past three decades, and the prospects for continued economic growth over the long run are excellent.[35] Beginning in 1996, the leading economies of Asia (Japan, Hong Kong, South Korea, Singapore, and Taiwan) experienced a serious financial crisis, which culminated in the meltdown of the Asian stock market. A tight monetary policy, an appreciating dollar, and a deceleration of exports all contributed to the downturn. Despite this economic adjustment, the 1993 estimates by the International Monetary Fund (IMF) that Asian economies would have 29 percent of the global output by the year 2000 were on target. Both as sources of new products and technology and as vast consumer markets, the

---

[34]www.oecd.org.

[35]Visit *Asia Week* for current information on Asian countries: www.asiaweek.com.

Exhibit 9.10
Asia

countries of Asia—particularly those along the Pacific Rim—are just beginning to gain their stride (see Exhibit 9.11).

Asian-Pacific Rim.   The most rapidly growing economies in this region are the group sometimes referred to as the Four Tigers (or Four Dragons): Hong Kong, South Korea, Singapore, and Taiwan. Often described as the "East Asian miracle," they were the first countries in Asia, besides Japan, to move from a status of developing countries to newly industrialized countries. They have grown from suppliers of component parts and assemblers of Western products to become major global competitors in electronics, shipbuilding, heavy machinery, and a multitude of other products. In addition, each has become a major influence in trade and development in the economies of the other countries within their spheres of influence. The rapid economic growth and regional influence of the member countries of the Association of Southeast Nations (ASEAN) over the last decade has

Exhibit 9.11
Asian Markets—Selected Countries

Country	Population (millions)	GDP* (billions)	GDP* (per capita)	Imports of Goods and Services (billions)	Exports of Goods and Services (billions)
Australia	19.9	$ 431.2	$21,688	$103.0	$ 87.7
China	1,288.4	1,375.2	5,196	441.8	502.8
Hong Kong	6.8	174.7	25,633	276.4	291.4
India	1,064.4	543.7	511	83.7	88.6
Indonesia	214.7	167.7	781	52.7	68.7
Japan	127.6	4,876.1	38,222	476.1	572.2
South Korea	47.9	586.1	12,232	233.5	266.4
Taiwan	22.7	282.2	12,261	108.1	125.6

Source: World Bank, Copyright © 2003 by World Bank. Reproduced with permission of World Bank via Copyright Clearance Center.

*Constant 2000 dollars.

A vendor delivers a Christmas tree in Beijing. Since China's reforms and loosening of controls on religion at the end of the 1970s, the number of Christians has risen from 2 million to 50 million. Although restrictions on freedom of religion continue as economic freedom grows so do political freedoms. (© *AFP/Getty Images*)

prompted the U.S. Trade Representative to discuss free-trade agreements—Singapore has already signed up. They are vast markets for industrial goods and, as will be discussed later, important emerging consumer markets.

The Four Tigers are rapidly industrializing and extending their trading activity to other parts of Asia. Japan was once the dominant investment leader in the area and was a key player in the economic development of China, Taiwan, Hong Kong, South Korea, and other countries of the region. But as the economies of other Asian countries have strengthened and industrialized, they are becoming more important as economic leaders. For example, South Korea is the center of trade links with north China and the Asian republics of the former Soviet Union. South Korea's sphere of influence and trade extends to Guangdong and Fujian, two of the most productive Chinese Special Economic Zones, and is becoming more important in interregional investment as well.

China.   Aside from the United States and Japan, there is no more important single market than China.[36] The economic and social changes occurring in China since it began actively seeking economic ties with the industrialized world have been dramatic. China's dual economic system, embracing socialism along with many tenets of capitalism, produced an economic boom with expanded opportunity for foreign investment that has resulted in annual GNP growth averaging nearly 10 percent since 1970. Most analysts predict that an 8 percent to 10 percent average for the next 10 to 15 years is possible. At that rate China's GNP should equal that of the United States by 2015. All of this growth is dependent on China's ability to deregulate industry, import modern technology, privatize overstaffed, inefficient SOEs, and continue to attract foreign investment. The prospects look good.

Two major events that occurred in 2000 are having a profound effect on China's economy: admission to the World Trade Organization and the United States' granting China normal trade relations (NTR) on a permanent basis (PNTR). PNTR and China's entry to the WTO cut import barriers currently imposed on American products and services. The United States is obligated to maintain the market access policies that it already applies to China, and has for over 20 years, and to make its normal trade relation status permanent. After years of procrastination, China has begun to comply with WTO provisions and has made a wholehearted and irrevocable commitment to creating a market economy that is tied to the world at large.

An issue that concerns many is whether China will follow WTO rules when it has to lower its formidable barriers to imported goods.[37] Enforcement of the agreement will not just happen. Experience with many past agreements has shown that to get compliance on some issues is often next to impossible. Some of China's concessions are repeats of unfulfilled agreements extending back to 1979. The United States has learned from its experience with Japan that the toughest work is yet to come. A promise to open markets to U.S. exports can be just the beginning of a long effort at ensuring compliance.

Because of China's size, diversity, and political organization, it can be more conveniently thought of as a group of six regions rather than a single country—a grouping of regional markets rather than a single market. There is no one-growth strategy for China. Each region is at a different stage economically and has its own link to other regions as well as links to other parts of the world. Each has its own investment patterns, is taxed differently, and has substantial autonomy in how it is governed. But while each region is separate enough to be considered individually, each is linked at the top to the central government in Beijing.

China has two important steps to take if the road to economic growth is to be smooth: improving human rights and reforming the legal system. The human rights issue has been a sticking point with the United States because of the lack of religious freedom, the Tiananmen Square massacre in 1989, the jailing of dissidents, and China's treatment of Tibet. The U.S. government's decision to award PNTR reflected, in part, the growing importance of China in the global marketplace and the perception that trade with China was

---

[36]"How China Runs the World Economy," *The Economist*, July 30, 2005, pp. 11, 61–63.

[37]Don Lee, "No Easy Answers on China Trade," *Los Angeles Times*, June 4, 2005, pp. C1, C2,

CROSSING BORDERS 9.5

In Developing Countries, Opportunity Means Creating It

There is an old story about two shoe salesmen from different companies sent to Zimara, an imaginary developing country, scouting for new markets. One cables headquarters, "Coming home tomorrow. No possibilities in Zimara. The natives don't wear shoes." The other cables home, "Fantastic sales opportunity!! Natives are all barefoot! Everyone here needs shoes."

Flexibility, patience, commitment, innovation, the right attitude, and the willingness to go the extra mile will often result in vast rewards in emerging markets. After 13 years of talks (patience), Nestlé was finally invited to help boost milk production in China. When Nestlé opened a powdered milk and baby cereal plant, it faced an inadequate source of milk and an overburdened infrastructure. Local trains and roads made it almost impossible to collect milk and deliver the finished product efficiently. Nestlé's solution was to develop its own infrastructure by weaving a distribution network known as the "milk roads" between 27 villages and the factory collection points (the extra mile). Farmers pushing wheelbarrows, pedaling bicycles, or walking delivered their milk and received payment on the spot, another innovation for China.

Suddenly the farms had an incentive to produce milk, and the district herds grew from 6,000 to 9,000 cows in a matter of months. To train the farmers in rudimentary animal health and hygiene, Nestlé hired retired teachers who were paid commissions on all sales to Nestlé (incentive). The result? Business took off. In three years, Nestlé factory production rose from 316 tons of powdered milk and infant formula to 10,000 tons. Capacity has tripled with the addition of two factories.

Seventeen years after talks began, Nestlé's $200 million sales were just barely profitable. However, a year later they had risen to $250 million (patience). Nestlé has exclusive rights to sell the output of its factories throughout China for 15 years (reward), and now sales of milk in China are more than $1 billion.

Sources: Carla Rapoport, "Nestle's Brand Building Machine," *Fortune*, September 19, 1994, pp. 147–156; Mark L. Clifford, Dexter Roberts, and Sherrie E. Zhan, "Penetrating Difficult Markets," *World Trade*, January 2000; Kathy Chen, "New Craze Seizes China's Consumers: A Glass of Milk," *Wall Street Journal*, February 28, 2003, p. A1.

too valuable to be jeopardized over a single issue. However, the issue remains delicate both within the United States and between the United States and China.

Meanwhile, China continues to reinvent itself. At the 2002 Communist Party's National Congress, Hu Jintao was selected as General Secretary. But perhaps more important than his selection was the admission of private entrepreneurs into the party. This signifies a huge transformation of the Chinese Communist Party from a class party representing workers and peasants into one representing the people as a whole.

Despite these positive changes, the American embassy in China has seen a big jump in complaints from disgruntled U.S. companies fed up with their lack of protection under China's legal system. Outside the major urban areas of Beijing, Shanghai, and Guangzhou, companies are discovering that local protectionism and cronyism make business tough even when they have local partners. Many are finding that Chinese partners with local political clout can rip off their foreign partner and, when complaints are taken to court, influence courts to rule in their favor.

Actually there are two Chinas—one a maddening, bureaucratic, bottomless money pit, the other an enormous emerging market. There is the old China, where holdovers of the Communist Party's planning apparatus heap demands on multinational corporations, especially in politically important sectors such as autos,[38] chemicals, and telecom equipment. Companies are shaken down by local officials, whipsawed by policy swings, railroaded into bad partnerships, and squeezed for technology. But there is also a new, market-driven China that is fast emerging. Consumer areas, from fast food to shampoo, are now wide open. Even in tightly guarded sectors, the barriers to entry are eroding as provincial authorities, rival ministries, and even the military challenge the power of Beijing's technocrats.

No industry better illustrates the changing rules than information technology. Chinese planners once limited imports of PCs and software to promote homegrown industries, but

---

[38]Brian Bremner and Kathleen Kerwin, "Here Come Chinese Cars," *BusinessWeek*, June 6, 2005, pp. 34–38.

the Chinese preferred smuggled imports to the local manufacturers. Beijing eventually loosened the restraints, and Microsoft is now the dominant PC operating system. A market whose modernization plan calls for imports of equipment and technology of over $100 billion per year, with infrastructure expenditures amounting to $250 billion through the remainder of the decade, is worth the effort. Indeed, China is now the second biggest market for personal computers, following only the United States.

In the long run the economic strength of China will not be as an exporting machine but as a vast market. The economic strength of the United States comes from its resources, productivity, and vast internal market that drives its economy. China's future potential might better be compared with America's economy, which is driven by domestic demand, than with Japan's, driven by exports. China is neither an economic paradise nor an economic wasteland, but a relatively poor nation going through a painfully awkward transformation from a socialist market system to a hybrid socialist–free market system, not yet complete and with the rules of the game still being written.

Hong Kong.   After 155 years of British rule, Hong Kong reverted to China in 1997 when it became a special administrative region (SAR) of the People's Republic of China. The Basic Law of the Hong Kong SAR forms the legal basis for China's "one country, two systems" agreement that guarantees Hong Kong a high degree of autonomy. The social and economic systems, lifestyle, and rights and freedoms enjoyed by the people of Hong Kong prior to the turnover were to remain unchanged for at least 50 years. The Hong Kong government negotiates bilateral agreements (which are then "confirmed" by Beijing) and makes major economic decisions on its own. The central government in Beijing is responsible only for foreign affairs and defense of the SAR.

The Hong Kong dollar continues to be freely convertible, and foreign exchange, gold, and securities markets continue to operate as before. Hong Kong is a free society with legally protected rights. The Hong Kong SAR government continues to pursue a generally noninterventionist approach to economic policy that stresses the predominant role of the private sector. The first test came when the Hong Kong financial markets had a meltdown in 1997 that reverberated around the financial world and directly threatened the mainland's interests. Beijing's officials kept silent; when they said anything, they expressed confidence in the ability of Hong Kong authorities to solve their own problems.

The decision to let Hong Kong handle the crisis on its own is considered strong evidence that the relationship is working for the best for both sides, considering that China has so much riding on Hong Kong. Among other things, Hong Kong is the largest investor in the mainland, investing more than $100 billion over the last few years for factories and infrastructure. The Hong Kong stock market is the primary source of capital for some of China's largest state-owned enterprises. China Telcom, for example, recently raised $4 billion in an initial public offering.

Most business problems that have arisen stem from fundamental concepts such as clear rules and transparent dealings that are not understood the same way on the mainland as they are in Hong Kong. Many thought the territory's laissez-faire ways, exuberant capitalism, and gung-ho spirit would prove unbearable for Beijing's heavy-handed communist leaders. But, except for changes in tone and emphasis, even opponents of communist rule concede that Beijing is honoring the "one country, two systems" arrangement.

The keys to Hong Kong's economic success—its free market philosophy, entrepreneurial drive, absence of trade barriers, well-established rule of law, low and predictable taxes, transparent regulations, and complete freedom of capital movement—all remain intact.

Taiwan.   The presidential victory of longtime Taiwan opposition leader and independence advocate Chen Shui-bian fanned fears in Beijing that the island, which it regards as part of China, would finally declare independence from the mainland. However, Chen quickly assuaged those fears when he promised not to formally declare independence unless China attacked Taiwan. Mainland–Taiwan economic ties are approaching a crossroads as both countries enter the World Trade Organization. As both sides implement WTO provisions, they will have to end many restrictions and implement direct trade—not that they have not been trading. Taiwanese companies have invested about $40 billion in China, and about 250,000 Taiwanese-run factories are responsible for about 12 percent of China's exports. Estimates of real trade are even higher if activities conducted through Hong Kong front companies are taken into consideration.

It is best to wrap future talks on the One China debate inside a bundle of more concrete issues, such as establishing the "three direct links"—in transportation, trade, and communications. The three-direct-links issue must be faced because each country has joined the WTO, and the rules insist that members should communicate over trade disputes and other issues. Trade fits well with both countries' needs. Taiwanese companies face rising costs at home; China offers a nearly limitless pool of cheap labor and engineering talent. Taiwan's tech powerhouses also crave access to China's market.

For Beijing, the Taiwanese companies provide plentiful jobs at a time when bloated state enterprises are laying off millions. They also bring the latest technology and management systems, which China needs as it joins the WTO. In any case, Taiwan continues to stand tall in the East Asian economy—indeed, as of 2004 the tallest building in the world is in Taipei, its capital.

India.   The wave of change that has been washing away restricted trade, controlled economies, closed markets, and hostility to foreign investment in most developing countries has finally reached India. Since its independence in 1950, the world's largest democracy had set a poor example as a model for economic growth for other developing countries and was among the last of the economically important developing nations to throw off traditional insular policies. As a consequence, India's growth had been constrained and shaped by policies of import substitution and an aversion to free markets. While other Asian countries were wooing foreign capital, India was doing its best to keep it out. Multinationals, seen as vanguards of a new colonialism, were shunned. Aside from textiles, Indian industrial products found few markets abroad other than in the former Soviet Union and eastern Europe.

Now, however, times have changed and India has embarked on the most profound transformation since it won political independence from Britain. A five-point agenda that includes improving the investment climate; developing a comprehensive WTO strategy; reforming agriculture, food processing, and small-scale industry; eliminating red tape; and instituting better corporate governance has been announced. Steps already taken include the following:

- Privatizing state-owned companies as opposed to merely selling shares in them. The government is now willing to reduce its take below 51 percent and to give management control of so-called strategic investors.

- Recasting the telecom sector's regulatory authority and demolishing the monopolies enjoyed by state-owned companies.

- Signing a trade agreement with the United States to lift all quantitative restrictions on imports.

- Maintaining the momentum in reform of the petroleum sector.

- Planning the opening of domestic long-distance phone services, housing, and real estate and retail-trading[39] sectors to foreign direct investment.

Leaders have quietly distanced themselves from campaign rhetoric that advocated "computer chips and not potato chips" in foreign investment and a "*swadeshi*" (made-in-India) economy. The new direction promises to adjust the philosophy of self-sufficiency that had been taken to extremes and to open India to world markets. India now has the look and feel of the next China or Latin America.

Foreign investors and Indian reformers still face problems, however. Although India has overthrown the restrictions of earlier governments, reforms meet resistance from bureaucrats, union members, and farmers, as well as from some industrialists who have lived comfortably behind protective tariff walls that excluded competition. Socialism is not dead in the minds of many in India, and religious, ethnic, and other political passions flare easily.

---

[39]Anand Giridharadas, "Megastores Gaze Longingly at India," *International Herald Tribune*, April 2, 2005, pp. 13, 15.

For a number of reasons, India still presents a difficult business environment. Tariffs are well above those of developing world norms, although they have been slashed to a maximum of 65 percent from 400 percent. Inadequate protection of intellectual property rights remains a serious concern. The antibusiness attitudes of India's federal and state bureaucracies continue to hinder potential investors and plague their routine operations. Policy makers have dragged their feet on selling money-losing state-owned enterprises, making labor laws flexible, and deregulating banking.

In addition, widespread corruption and a deeply ingrained system of bribery make every transaction complicated and expensive. One noted authority on India declared that corrupt practices are not the quaint custom of *baksheesh* but pervasive, systematic, structured, and degraded corruption running from the bottom to the top of the political order. Nevertheless, a survey of U.S. manufacturers shows that 95 percent of respondents with Indian operations plan on expanding and none say they are leaving. They are hooked on the country's cheap, qualified labor and the potential of a massive market.

Despite these uncertainties, being included among the BEMs reflects the potential of India's market. With a population now over 1 billion, India is second in size only to China, and both contain enormous low-cost labor pools. India has a middle class numbering some 250 million, about the population of the United States. Among its middle class are large numbers of college graduates, 40 percent of whom have degrees in science[40] and engineering. India has a diverse industrial base and is developing as a center for computer software. India may be on the threshold of an information technology boom. After establishing a reputation among foreign corporations by debugging computer networks in time for Y2K, Indian companies now supply everything from animation work to browsers used on new-generation wireless phones to e-commerce Web sites. As discussed earlier, India has been an exporter of technical talent to the U.S. Silicon Valley and now many of these individuals are returning to establish IT companies of their own.

India has the capacity to be one of the more prosperous nations in Asia[41] if allowed to develop and live up to its potential. Some worry, however, that the opportunity could be lost if reforms don't soon reach a critical mass—that point when reforms take on a life of their own and thus become irreversible.

Newest Emerging Markets

The United States' decision to lift the embargo against Vietnam and the United Nations' lifting of the embargo against South Africa resulted in the rapid expansion of these economies. Because of their growth and potential, the U.S. Department of Commerce designated both as BEMs.

Vietnam's economy and infrastructure were in a shambles after 20 years of socialism and years of war, but this country of more than 84 million is poised for significant growth. A bilateral trade agreement between the United States and Vietnam led to NTR status for Vietnam and will lower tariffs on Vietnamese exports to the United States from an average of 40 percent to less than 3 percent.[42] For example, Vietnamese coffee is now in almost every pantry in America, and the new competitiveness has caused prices to sharply decline on the world market. If Vietnam follows the same pattern of development as other Southeast Asian countries, it could become another Asian Tiger. Many of the ingredients are there: The population is educated and highly motivated, and the government is committed to economic growth. Some factors are a drag on development, however, including poor infrastructure, often onerous government restrictions, minimal industrial base, and a lack of capital and technology, which must come primarily from outside the country. Most of the

---

[40]Manjeet Kripalani, "Copycats No More, Indian Pharma Moves into Pure Research," *BusinessWeek*, April 18, 2005, p. 51.

[41]Even Disney appears interested? See "Disney Denies It Asked for India Land," *Associated Press*, May 2, 2005.

[42]Trade disputes still occur: "Shrimp Exporters [from Vietnam] Vow to Fight U.S. Suit," *Associated Press*, January 2, 2004.

capital and technology are being supplied by three of the Asian Tigers—Taiwan, Hong Kong, and South Korea. U.S. companies are beginning to make investments now that the embargo has been lifted.

South Africa's economic growth has increased significantly now that apartheid is officially over and the United Nations has lifted the economic embargo that isolated that nation from much of the industrialized world. Unlike Vietnam, South Africa has an industrial base that will help propel it into rapid economic growth, with the possibility of doubling its GNP in as few as 10 years. The South African market also has a developed infrastructure— airports, railways, highways, telecommunications—that makes it important as a base for serving nearby African markets too small to be considered individually but viable when coupled with South Africa.

Upbeat economic predictions, a stable sociopolitical environment, and reinforced vigor of the South African government in addressing the issues of privatization and deregulation[43] while maintaining the long-term goal of making the country more investor friendly bode well for U.S. businesses seeking trading, investment, and joint venture opportunities in South Africa. The country has a fair-sized domestic market of nearly $500 billion with significant growth potential and is increasingly becoming free market oriented. It has yet to develop to its full potential, however, because of years of isolation, former inward-looking trade and investment policies, a low savings rate, and a largely unskilled labor force with attendant low productivity.

Vietnam and South Africa have the potential to become the newest emerging markets, but their future development will depend on government action and external investment by other governments and multinational firms. In varying degrees, foreign investors are leading the way by making sizable investments.

Strategic Implications for Marketing

Surfacing in the emerging markets described earlier is a vast population whose expanding incomes are propelling them beyond a subsistence level to being viable consumers. As a country develops, incomes change, population concentrations shift, expectations for a better life adjust to higher standards, new infrastructures evolve, and social capital investments are made (see Exhibit 9.12). Market behavior changes and eventually groups of consumers with common tastes and needs (i.e., market segments) arise.[44]

When incomes rise, new demand is generated at all income levels for everything from soap to automobiles. Officially, per capita income in China is only about $1,000 a year. But nearly every independent study by academics and multilateral agencies puts incomes, adjusted for black market activity and purchasing power parity, at three or four times that level.[45] Further, large households can translate into higher disposable incomes. Young working people in Asia and Latin America usually live at home until they marry. With no rent to pay, they have more discretionary income and can contribute to household purchasing power. Countries with low per capita incomes are potential markets for a large variety of goods; consumers show remarkable resourcefulness in finding ways to buy what really matters to them. In the United States, the first satellite dishes sprang up in the poorest parts of Appalachia. Similarly, the poorest slums of Calcutta are home to 70,000 VCRs, and in Mexico, homes with color televisions outnumber those with running water.

As incomes rise to middle-class range, demand for more costly goods increases for everything from disposable diapers to automobiles. Incomes for the middle class in emerging markets are less than those in the United States, but spending patterns are different, so the middle class has more to spend than comparable income levels in the

---

[43]Nicole Itano, "After Industry Protests, South Africa Softens Mining Law," *New York Times*, May 1, 2003, p. W1.

[44]Peter G. P. Walters and Saeed Samiee, "Marketing Strategy in Emerging Markets: The Case of China," *Journal of International Marketing* 11, no. 1 (2003), pp. 97–106.

[45]The *CIA Factbook 2005* reports it to be $5,600, for example.

Exhibit 9.12

Living Standards in Selected Countries

Country	Households (millions)	Persons per Household	Color TV (per 100 households)	Passenger Car (per 100 households)	Refrigerator (per 100 households)	Shower (per 100 households)
Brazil	52	3.5	88	48	84	77
Chile	4	3.7	63	49	65	89
Colombia	12	3.8	87	37	68	98
Peru	6	4.8	50	20	49	62
Azerbaijan	3	2.5	54	22	57	67
China	378	3.5	46	3	7	43
Hong Kong	2	3.2	99	75	97	97
India	203	5.3	35	1	15	43
Indonesia	57	3.9	52	4	27	47
Japan	48	2.6	99	82	98	100
Kazakhstan	4	3.5	61	32	81	68
Malaysia	5	4.7	90	64	97	100
Pakistan	22	7.2	38	6	18	67
Philippines	17	4.9	67	8	44	84
Singapore	1	3.5	99	43	99	100
South Korea	17	2.8	94	44	97	95
Taiwan	7	3.2	99	51	100	98
Thailand	17	3.6	84	35	70	67
Vietnam	27	3.3	41	2	19	37
United States	110	2.6	100	93	100	100

Source: Euromonitor, 2005.

United States would indicate. For example, members of the middle class in emerging markets do not own two automobiles and suburban homes, and health care and housing in some cases are subsidized, freeing income to spend on refrigerators, TVs, radios, better clothing, and special treats. Exhibit 9.13 illustrates the percentage of household income spent on various classes of goods and services. More household money goes for food in emerging markets than in developed markets, but the next category of high expenditure for emerging and developed countries alike is appliances and other durable goods. Spending by the new rich, however, is a different story. The new rich want to display their new status; they want to wear status symbols such as Rolex watches, the high-end Swiss watch that costs more than $1,000.

A London securities firm says that a person earning $250 annually in a developing country can afford Gillette razors, and at $1,000, he or she can become a Sony television owner.

Exhibit 9.13

Consumption Patterns in Selected Countries (Percentage of Household Expenditures)

Country	Food	Alcohol and Tobacco	Clothing	Housing	Health/ Medical	Transportation	Communication	Leisure	Education
United States	7.0	2.2	4.1	18.2	19.1	11.0	1.8	9.1	2.6
Mexico	24.6	2.6	3.3	12.6	4.5	17.2	1.7	5.0	3.3
Azerbaijan	52.8	2.9	4.4	9.7	4.3	11.4	1.2	1.5	1.3
India	43.5	4.0	4.7	10.7	7.8	12.9	1.0	1.4	1.3
Malaysia	22.0	2.6	3.6	21.6	2.4	16.2	2.8	4.2	1.8
Singapore	12.3	1.6	3.8	15.2	6.2	17.9	2.4	7.1	6.9
Thailand	26.3	4.4	12.1	9.8	7.8	9.8	1.7	3.1	1.4
Algeria	36.1	3.0	4.7	18.9	4.7	11.3	2.8	3.5	1.1
South Africa	18.4	9.0	5.0	12.0	7.9	17.3	2.0	4.6	2.5

Source: Euromonitor, 2005.

A Nissan or Volkswagen could be possible with a $10,000 income. Whirlpool estimates that in eastern Europe a family with an annual income of $1,000 can afford a refrigerator, and with $2,000 they can buy an automatic washer as well. Estimates are that a sustainable growth in the car market will occur in China when average annual income of $5,000 is achieved. Even though that will not likely happen until 2010, more than one million cars were sold in 2005—making the Chinese market as large as all of South Asia combined.

Recognizing the growth in Asia, Whirlpool has invested $265 million to buy controlling interest in four competitors in China and two in India. The attraction is expanding incomes and low appliance ownership rates. Fewer than 10 percent of Chinese households have air conditioners, microwave ovens, or washers. At the same time, incomes are reaching levels where demand for such appliances will grow.

One analyst suggests that as a country passes the $5,000 per capita GNP level, people become more brand conscious and forgo many local brands to seek out foreign brands they recognize. At $10,000, they join those with similar incomes who are exposed to the same global information sources. They join the "$10,000 Club" of consumers with homogeneous demands who share a common knowledge of products and brands. They become global consumers. If a company fails to appreciate the strategic implications of the $10,000 Club, it will miss the opportunity to participate in the world's fastest-growing global consumer segment. More than one billion people in the world now have incomes of $10,000 or better. In Asia alone, Singapore's average income is over $27,000, Hong Kong is at $25,000, and Taiwan is just over $12,000.[46] Companies that look for commonalties among this 700 million will find a growing market for global brands.

Markets are changing rapidly, and identifiable market segments with similar consumption patterns are found across many countries. Emerging markets will be the growth areas of the 21st century.

Summary

The ever-expanding involvement in world trade of more and more people with varying needs and wants will test old trading patterns and alliances. The foreign marketer of today and tomorrow must be able to react to market changes rapidly and to anticipate new trends within constantly evolving market segments that may not have existed as recently as last year. Many of today's market facts will likely be tomorrow's historical myths.

Along with dramatic shifts in global politics, the increasing scope and level of technical and economic growth have enabled many nations to advance their standards of living by as much as two centuries in a matter of decades. As nations develop their productive capacity, all segments of their economies will feel the pressure to improve. The impact of these political, social, and economic trends will continue to be felt throughout the world, resulting in significant changes in marketing practices. Further, the impact of information technology will speed up the economic growth in every country. Marketers must focus on devising marketing plans designed to respond fully to each level of economic development. China and Russia continue to undergo rapid political and economic changes that have brought about the opening of most socialist-bloc countries to foreign direct investments and international trade. And though big emerging markets present special problems, they are promising markets for a broad range of products now and in the future. Emerging markets create new marketing opportunities for MNCs as new market segments evolve.

Questions

1. Define the following terms:

   underdeveloped   BEMs

   economic development   infrastructure

   NICs   BOPMs

2. Is it possible for an economy to experience economic growth as measured by total GNP without a commensurate rise in the standard of living? Discuss fully.

3. Why do technical assistance programs by more affluent nations typically ignore the distribution problem or relegate it to a minor role in development planning? Explain.

4. Discuss each of the stages of evolution in the marketing process. Illustrate each stage with a particular country.

5. As a country progresses from one economic stage to another, what in general are the marketing effects?

---

[46]World Bank and Euromonitor, 2005.

6. Select a country in the agricultural and raw materials stage of economic development and discuss what changes will occur in marketing when it passes to a manufacturing stage.

7. What are the consequences of each stage of marketing development on the potential for industrial goods within a country? For consumer goods?

8. Discuss the significance of economic development to international marketing. Why is the knowledge of economic development of importance in assessing the world marketing environment? Discuss.

9. The Internet accelerates the process of economic growth. Discuss.

10. Discuss the impact of the IT revolution on the poorest countries.

11. Select one country in each of the five stages of economic development. For each country, outline the basic existing marketing institutions and show how their stages of development differ. Explain why.

12. Why should a foreign marketer study economic development? Discuss.

13. The infrastructure is important to the economic growth of an economy. Comment.

14. What are the objectives of economically developing countries? How do these objectives relate to marketing? Comment.

15. Using the list of NIC growth factors, evaluate India and China as to their prospects for rapid growth. Which factors will be problems for India/for China?

16. What is marketing's role in economic development? Discuss marketing's contributions to economic development.

17. Discuss the economic and trade importance of the big emerging markets.

18. What are the traits of those countries considered big emerging markets? Discuss.

19. Discuss how the economic growth of BEMs is analogous to the situation after World War II.

20. Discuss the problems a marketer might encounter when considering the Marxist-socialist countries as a market.

21. One of the ramifications of emerging markets is the creation of a middle class. Discuss.

22. The needs and wants of a market and the ability to satisfy them are the result of the three-way interaction of the economy, culture, and the marketing efforts of businesses. Comment.

23. Discuss the strategic implications of marketing in India.

24. "Too much emphasis is usually laid—by Chinese policy makers as well as by foreign businessmen—on China's strength as an export machine. China is so big that its economic potential might more usefully be compared with continental America's." Discuss fully.

10

Multinational Market Regions and Market Groups

CHAPTER OUTLINE

Global Perspective: Might Free Trade Bring Peace
    to the Middle East?

La Raison d'Etre
    Economic Factors
    Political Factors
    Geographic and Temporal Proximity
    Cultural Factors

Patterns of Multinational Cooperation

Global Markets and Multinational Market Groups

Europe
    A Brief History of European Integration
    European Union
    Strategic Implications for Marketing in Europe
    Marketing Mix Implications
    The Commonwealth of Independent States

The Americas
    North American Free Trade Agreement (NAFTA)
    United States–Central American Free Trade Agreement–
        Dominican Republic Free Trade Agreement (CAFTA)
    Southern Cone Free Trade Area (Mercosur)
    Latin American Economic Cooperation
    NAFTA to FTAA or SAFTA?

Asian-Pacific Rim
    Association of Southeast Asian Nations
    Asia-Pacific Economic Cooperation

Africa

Middle East

Regional Trading Groups and Emerging Markets

CHAPTER LEARNING OBJECTIVES

What you should learn from Chapter 10:

- The reasons for economic union

- Patterns of international cooperation

- The evolution of the European Union

- Strategic implications for marketing in Europe

- Evolving patterns of trade as eastern Europe and
  the former Soviet states embrace the free-market
  system

- The trade linkage of NAFTA and South America and
  its regional effects

- The development of trade within the Asia-Pacific Rim

Global Perspective

MIGHT FREE TRADE BRING PEACE TO THE MIDDLE EAST?

The nearly complete destruction of the continental European economies by World War II seriously endangered the stability of Europe's social and political institutions. Europe's leaders knew that to rebuild from the ruins it was essential to form new kinds of international institutions to ensure prosperity, stability, and peace in the region. The first of these institutions was the European Coal and Steel Community established in 1952 to integrate the coal and steel industries of France, West Germany, Italy, Belgium, The Netherlands, and Luxembourg. Fifty years later, based on the success of this first small experiment in economic interdependence, we now see the European Union with twenty-five member nations and four candidate countries set to join during the next few years. The economies have burgeoned, but more importantly peace has persisted.

Might such an approach work in the war-torn Middle East? Let's consider the possibilities and potential of a Middle Eastern Union. The crux of the problem is Jerusalem. The holy Old City is a matter of faith to so many. For Christians it is sacred because of its associations with Christ. For Jews it has served as the center for their people—not only in a national way but, more importantly, in a religious sense. For Muslims only Mecca and Medina are more important spiritual places. And the fighting over the real estate that represents its spiritual events appears perpetual.

Jerusalem can be a primary part of the solution. But we must look beyond the bombing of the day. We must imagine a safe, prosperous, and peaceful place. Imagine an international shrine. Perhaps the Old City would be administered by Buddhists or Norwegians or the United Nations. Israel would have its grand capital to the west, in the New City, and the Palestinians to the east a bit.

Religious tourism would feed the economies in both countries, as well as the surrounding area. Imagine the possibilities! In 2000, before the most recent insanity of violence, tourism brought in $3.2 billion in revenues for Israel. Compare that to Disneyland in Orange County, California. That park's yearly 10 million visitors spend about $100 each on tickets, food, and souvenirs. Add in the transportation, hotel, and restaurant revenues appreciated in the neighborhood, and that's more than a couple of billion dollars a year coming to the Anaheim environs.

The Church of the Holy Sepulcher (built over the tomb of Jesus) would draw Christians. The Wailing Wall is a special place for Jews. Muslims would flock to the Dome of the Rock (Mohammed was carried by the angel Gabriel for a visit to Heaven after praying at the Rock). The most enlightened tourists would visit all three. Disney might consult on the queuing problems. And outside of the Old City are Bethlehem, Nazareth, Jericho, the Sea of Galilee, the Dead Sea, and Red Sea, to name only the more obvious attractions just in Israel. We're talking $10 billion to $20 billion in annual revenues if things are done right—that's about 10 to 15 percent of the current GDP of Israel.

To the east the new Hijaz Railway Corp. is already working on a line connecting Iran and Jordan via Syria and is talking about lines connecting Iraq, Turkey, and Europe as well—all for the sake of religious tourism. Indeed, the line's original purpose was taking pilgrims to Medina from Damascus; that was before Lawrence of Arabia severed it for carrying arms and troops during World War I. The current company executives reckon the two-day trip from Tehran to Amman will cost only about $30, and the Shiite Muslims of Iran will flock to their holy sights in the area. Why not run the line all the way to east Jerusalem?

How about Jerusalem as the site for the 2020 Olympic games? That's another $5 billion in revenues. And ignoring the dollars for a moment, please consider the sentiments associated with "the 2020 Jerusalem Games" juxtaposed with the disaster of Munich in 1972. And ignoring the dollars for another moment, imagine the spiritual splendor for so many millions visiting the sources of their faith, treading some of the original paths of David, Jesus, and Mohammed.

This little fantasy presumes a peaceful political division of Israel and Palestine along the lines reaffirmed in the Oslo Accords. It presumes a dropping of all commercial boycotts in the region. It presumes that Palestinians won't have to risk being shot while "hopping the fence" to work in Israel. It presumes that companies like Nestlé will be able to integrate the operations of their complementary plants in the area. It presumes that the United States and other countries will send to the region legions of tourists rather than boatloads of weapons. It presumes an open, international, and, most importantly, a whole Old City of Jerusalem. And it presumes free trade and travel among all nations in the region allowing all to prosper in new ways.

Finally, Pulitzer Prize–winner Jared Diamond points out that the Middle East, historically referred to as the Fertile Crescent, was the cradle of civilization. It became so so long ago because of innovation and trade in the region. One can only imagine what free trade in the area would produce now.

Source: John L. Graham, "Trade Brings Peace," paper delivered at the Global Ethics and Religion Forum; Clare Hall, Cambridge University conference, *War and Reconciliation: Perspectives of the World Religions*, May 26, 2003, in Cambridge, England; Jared Diamond, *Collapse: How Societies Choose to Fail or Succeed* (New York: Viking, 2005).

Following the success of aforementioned European Steel and Coal Community, a global economic revolution began in 1958 when the European Economic Community was ratified and Europe took the step that would ultimately lead to the present-day European Union (EU). Until then, skeptics predicted that the experiment would never work and that the alliance would fall apart quickly. It was not until the single market was established that the United States, Japan, and other countries gave serious thought to creating other alliances. The establishment of common markets, coupled with the trend away from planned economies to the free market system in Latin America, Asia, and eventually the former Soviet Union, created fertile ground that sparked the drive to form trade alliances and free markets the world over. Nation after nation embraced the free market system, implementing reforms in their economic and political systems with the desire to be part of a multinational market region in the evolving global marketplace. Traditions that are centuries old are being altered, issues that cannot be resolved by decree are being negotiated to an acceptable solution, governments and financial systems are restructuring, and companies are being reshaped to meet new competition and trade patterns.

The evolution and growth of *multinational market regions*—those groups of countries that seek mutual economic benefit from reducing interregional trade and tariff barriers— are the most important global trends today. Organizational form varies widely among market regions, but the universal goals of multinational cooperation are economic benefits for the participants and the associated peace. The world is awash in economic cooperative agreements as countries look for economic alliances to expand access to free markets.

Regional economic cooperative agreements have been around since the end of World War II. The most successful one is the European Union (EU), the world's largest multinational market region and foremost example of economic cooperation. Multinational market groups form large markets that provide potentially significant market opportunities for international business. As it became apparent in the late 1980s that the European Union was to achieve its long-term goal of a single European market, a renewed interest in economic cooperation followed, with the creation of several new alliances. The North American Free Trade Agreement (NAFTA) and Mercosur (Southern Cone Common Market) in the Americas and the Association of Southeast Asian Nations (ASEAN) and Asia-Pacific Economic Cooperation (APEC) in the Asian-Pacific Rim are all relatively new or reenergized associations that are gaining strength and importance as multinational market regions.

Along with the growing trend of economic cooperation, concerns about the effect of such cooperation on global competition are emerging. Governments and businesses worry that the EU, NAFTA, and other cooperative trade groups will become regional trading blocs without trade restrictions internally but with borders protected from outsiders. But as each of these trade groups continues to create new agreements with other countries and groups, the networked global economy and free trade are clearly on the ascendance. The benefits are clear for consumers; however, global companies face richer and more intense competitive environments.

La Raison d'Etre

Successful economic union requires favorable economic, political, cultural, and geographic factors as a basis for success. Major flaws in any one factor can destroy a union unless the other factors provide sufficient strength to overcome the weaknesses. In general, the advantages of economic union must be clear-cut and significant, and the benefits must greatly outweigh the disadvantages before nations forgo any part of their sovereignty. Many of the associations formed in Africa and Latin America have had little impact because perceived benefits were not sufficient to offset the partial loss of sovereignty.

In the past, a strong threat to the economic or political security of a nation was the impetus for cooperation. The cooperative agreements among European countries that preceded the EU had their roots in the need for economic redevelopment after World War II, the belief that economic integration created peace between[1] and within nations,[2] and the political concern for the perceived threat of communism. Many felt that if Europe was to survive there had to be economic unity; the agreements made then formed the groundwork for the European Union. The more recent creation of multinational market groups has been driven by the fear that not to be part of a vital regional market group is to be left on the sidelines of the global economic boom of the 21st century.

Economic Factors

Every type of economic union shares the development and enlargement of market opportunities as a basic orientation; usually, markets are enlarged through preferential tariff treatment for participating members, common tariff barriers against outsiders, or both. Enlarged, protected markets stimulate internal economic development by providing assured outlets and preferential treatment for goods produced within the customs union, and consumers benefit from lower internal tariff barriers among the participating countries. In many cases, external as well as internal barriers are reduced because of the greater economic security afforded domestic producers by the enlarged market.

Nations with complementary economic bases are least likely to encounter frictions in the development and operation of a common market unit. However, for an economic union to survive, it must have agreements and mechanisms in place to settle economic disputes. In addition, the total benefit of economic integration must outweigh individual differences that are sure to arise as member countries adjust to new trade relationships. The European Union includes countries with diverse economies, distinctive monetary systems, developed agricultural bases, and different natural resources. It is significant that most of the problems encountered by the EU have arisen over agriculture and monetary policy. In the early days of the European Community (now the European Union), agricultural disputes were common. The British attempted to keep French poultry out of the British market, France banned Italian wine, and the Irish banned eggs and poultry from other member countries. In all cases, the reason given was health and safety, but the probable motive was the continuation of the age-old policy of market protection. Such skirmishes are not unusual but they do test the strength of the economic union. In the case of the EU, the European Commission was the agency used to settle disputes and charge the countries that violated EU regulations.

The demise of the Latin American Free Trade Association (LAFTA) was the result of economically stronger members not allowing for the needs of the weaker ones. Many of the less well-known attempts at common markets have languished because of economic incompatibility that could not be resolved and the uncertainty of future economic advantage.

Political Factors

Political amenability among countries is another basic requisite for development of a supranational market arrangement. Participating countries must have comparable aspirations and general compatibility before surrendering any part of their national sovereignty. State sovereignty is one of the most cherished possessions of any nation and is relinquished only for a promise of significant improvement of the national position through cooperation.

Economic considerations are the basic catalyst for the formation of a customs union group, but political elements are equally important. The uniting of the original European Union countries was partially a response to the outside threat of the Soviet Union's great political and economic power; the countries of western Europe were willing to settle their family squabbles to present a unified front to the Russian bear. The communist threat no longer exists, but the importance of political unity to fully achieve all the benefits of economic integration has driven European countries to form the Union (EU).

---

[1]By far the strongest evidence for the trade-causes-peace notion is that provided by Solomon W. Polachek, "Why Democracies Cooperate More and Fight Less: The Relationship between International Trade and Cooperation," *Review of International Economics* 5, no. 3 (1997), pp. 295–309; additional evidence is supplied at www.cpbp.org, click on Peace Monitor, then Countries; Jonathan Schell, *The Unconquerable World* (New York: Metropolitan Books, 2003); and Thomas Friedman, *The World Is Flat* (New York: Farrar, Straus, and Giroux, 2005).

[2]New study of the causes of civil wars supports their belief; see Paul Collier, "The Market for Civil War," *Foreign Policy*, May/June 2003, pp. 38–45.

The geographic proximity allows Mexicans from Baja, California, to attend Padres baseball games in close-by San Diego. The team maintains this successful store just across the border in Plaza Rio shopping center in Tijuana. And, of course, historically Padre Junipero Serra had visited both places in the late 1700s while establishing the chain of missions in old Spanish California.

Geographic and Temporal Proximity   Although geographic and temporal proximity are not absolutely imperative for cooperating members of a customs union, such closeness does facilitate the functioning of a common market. Indeed, the most recent research demonstrates that more important than physical distance are differences across time zones.[3] That is, now trade tends to travel more easily in north–south directions than it did in ancient times. However, transportation networks (basic to any marketing system) are likely to be interrelated and well developed when countries are close together. Issues of immigration, legal and illegal, also promote closer economic integration between close neighbors. One of the first major strengths of the European Union was its transportation network; the opening of the tunnel between England and France further bound this common market. Countries that are widely separated geographically have major barriers to overcome in attempting economic fusion. However, with increasing efficiencies in communication and transportation the importance of such factors appears to be waning.

Cultural Factors   The United States has bilateral free trade agreements with, among others, Israel, Morocco, Chile, and Singapore.[4] These are in addition to its multilateral agreements such as NAFTA and CAFTA. But, generally, cultural similarity eases the shock of economic cooperation with other countries. The more similar the culture, the more likely an agreement is to succeed because members understand the outlook and viewpoints of their colleagues. Although there is great cultural diversity in the European Union, key members share a long-established Christian heritage and are commonly aware of being European. However, even this aspect of diversity may be unimportant as negotiations proceed with Turkey about EU membership.[5] Language, as a part of culture, has not created as much a barrier for EU countries as was expected. Nearly every educated European can do business in at least two or three languages, so the linguistic diversity of several major languages did not impede trade.

Patterns of Multinational Cooperation   Multinational market groups take several forms, varying significantly in the degree of cooperation, dependence, and interrelationship among participating nations. There are five fundamental groupings for regional economic integration, ranging from regional cooperation for development, which requires the least amount of integration, to the ultimate integration of political union.

Regional Cooperation Groups.   The most basic economic integration and cooperation is the *regional cooperation for development (RCD)*. In the RCD arrangement, governments agree to participate jointly to develop basic industries beneficial to each economy. Each country makes an advance commitment to participate in the financing of a new joint venture and to purchase a specified share of the output of the venture. An example is the project between Colombia and Venezuela to build a hydroelectric generating plant on the Orinoco River. They shared jointly in construction costs and they share the electricity produced.

Free Trade Area.   A *free trade area (FTA)* requires more cooperation and integration than the RCD. It is an agreement between two or more countries to reduce or eliminate

---

[3]Contrast Jared Diamond's *Guns, Germs, and Steel* (New York: W. W. Norton, 1999) and Jennifer Chandler and John L. Graham, "Corruption and the Attractiveness of International Markets," working paper, the Paul Merage School of Business, University of California, Irvine, 2006.

[4]www.ustr.gov/Trade_Agreements/, 2005.

[5]*The Economist*, "Turkey and the European Union: Bazaar Bargaining," September 3, 2005, pp. 46–47.

CROSSING **BORDERS 10.1**   Free Trade Means Losing Jobs—Or Does It?

"Is Your Job Next?" "Euro-skeptics Think the European Union Is Hostile to Free Markets." These and comparable headlines reflect the fears many have about free trade and multinational associations like the North American Free Trade Agreement (NAFTA), the European Union (EU), and other trade alliances among nations. Concerns range from jobs being exported to other countries to companies being closed out of once open, lucrative markets. In short, many fear that free trade will not live up to its promises of open markets, market growth, lower prices, more trade, and more jobs. Big multinational companies will not be hurt; the small company and the worker will suffer the brunt of free trade.

Since most trade alliances are still works in progress, it is much too early to make a definitive evaluation of their success or failure. However, consider the following "textbook examples" of how it is supposed to work.

Federal Express is a good example of how companies have benefited from the growth in trade. Prior to NAFTA, FedEx could service Mexico with only one daily flight in and out of Mexico City. Today, it flies three large-capacity planes daily, six times per week, in and out of Mexico City, Guadalajara, and Monterrey. Most recently FedEx began taking advantage of China's WTO entrance.

"Prior to NAFTA, the Mexican market was effectively shut to companies like ours because of high tariffs and import licenses," says the CEO of Quaker Fabric, a Massachusetts textile manufacturer. "NAFTA has reduced those obstacles and our sales to Mexico have grown sharply. Quaker's exports to our NAFTA partners now account for 8 percent to 10 percent of our business, worth $25 to 30 million a year." Without NAFTA, Quaker would probably have relocated to Mexico or to an even lower-wage country. NAFTA's rules of origin encourage the use of U.S. fabric and cloth in products made in Mexico for export. The increase in apparel imports from Mexico has come largely at the expense of Asian producers who do not use U.S. fabrics.

Yes, international business decisions can and do affect domestic jobs, but domestic business decisions also affect the job market. It is inherent in the course of commerce. When the meatpacking industry moved to the epicenter of the cattle market in the rural areas in Nebraska and Colorado, jobs were also lost. Fortunately for those displaced by NAFTA, the government provides federal aid to help offset job losses.

Exports by small companies have created thousands of new jobs in the last decade; many of these are a result of sales to new markets created by free trade and of products in markets where you would least expect sales. A Vermont company sells cheddar cheese in the village of Cheddar in southwest England. In France, imports of mozzarella cheese have tripled to 315,172 pounds from 92,568 pounds in six months. Poppers, maker of frozen appetizers such as mozzarella sticks and onion rings, exported 3.2 million pounds of appetizers to Europe in 1996, up from 800,000 pounds a year earlier.

Ten years ago, a Cape Cod, Massachusetts, entrepreneurial couple began a small business making kettle-fried chips. Today, the company is growing at 100 percent per year, selling in markets in Europe, South America, and Canada. Cape Cod Potato Chips are displayed among nearly 100 other stands hawking American food at the Salon International de l'Alimentation, one of the largest international food trade shows.

These are just a few examples of what is happening all over the United States. Some companies are moving offshore to Mexico and jobs are lost. In other cases, exports to Mexico and Canada are increasing and thus creating new jobs. It is much too early to gauge the success or failure of NAFTA, but as you explore the issues in this chapter, consider the consequences if the United States were not an active member of viable multinational trade regions.

Sources: David Wernick, "Next Generation NAFTA," *Latin America Trade Finance*, July 2000, p. 8; Pete Engardio, Aaron Bernstein, and Manjeet Kripalani, "Is Your Job Next? The New Global Job Shift," *BusinessWeek*, February 3, 2003, pp. 45–51; Patricia Sellers, "Bigger and BIGGER: How the Giants Keep Growing," *Fortune*, September 5, 2005, p. 105.

customs duties and nontariff trade barriers among partner countries while members maintain individual tariff schedules for external countries. Essentially, an FTA provides its members with a mass market without barriers to impede the flow of goods and services.

Customs Union.   A *customs union* represents the next stage in economic cooperation. It enjoys the free trade area's reduced or eliminated internal tariffs and adds a common external tariff on products imported from countries outside the union. The customs union is a logical stage of cooperation in the transition from an FTA to a common market. The European Union was a customs union before becoming a common market. Customs unions exist between France and Monaco, Italy and San Marino, and Switzerland and Liechtenstein, to name some examples.

Common Market. A *common market* agreement eliminates all tariffs and other restrictions on internal trade, adopts a set of common external tariffs, and removes all restrictions on the free flow of capital and labor among member nations. Thus a common market is a common marketplace for goods as well as for services (including labor) and for capital. It is a unified economy and lacks only political unity to become a political union. The Treaty of Rome, which established the European Economic Community (EEC) in 1957, called for common external tariffs and the gradual elimination of intramarket tariffs, quotas, and other trade barriers. The treaty also called for elimination of restrictions on the movement of services, labor, and capital; prohibition of cartels; coordinated monetary and fiscal policies; common agricultural policies; use of common investment funds for regional industrial development; and similar rules for wage and welfare payments. The EEC existed until the Maastricht Treaty created the European Union, an extension of the EEC into a political union.

Latin America boasts three common markets: the Central America Common Market (CACM), the Andean Common Market, and the Southern Cone Common Market (Mercosur). The three have roughly similar goals and seek eventual full economic integration.

Political Union. *Political union* is the most fully integrated form of regional cooperation. It involves complete political and economic integration, either voluntary or enforced. The most notable enforced political union was the Council for Mutual Economic Assistance (COMECON), a centrally controlled group of countries organized by the Soviet Union. With the dissolution of the Soviet Union and the independence of the Eastern European bloc, COMECON was disbanded.

A *commonwealth* of nations is a voluntary organization providing for the loosest possible relationship that can be classified as economic integration. The British Commonwealth comprises Britain and countries formerly part of the British Empire. Its members recognize the British monarch as their symbolic head, although Britain has no political authority over any commonwealth country. Its member states had received preferential tariffs when trading with Great Britain, but when Britain joined the European Community, all preferential tariffs were abandoned. A commonwealth can best be described as the weakest of political unions and is mostly based on economic history and a sense of tradition. Heads of state meet every three years to discuss trade and political issues they jointly face, and compliance with any decisions or directives issued is voluntary.

Two new political unions came into existence in the 1990s: the Commonwealth of Independent States (CIS), made up of the republics of the former Soviet Union, and the European Union (EU). The European Union was created when the 12 nations of the European Community ratified the Maastricht Treaty. The members committed themselves to economic and political integration. The treaty allows for the free movement of goods, persons, services, and capital throughout the member states; a common currency; common foreign and security policies, including defense; a common justice system; and cooperation between police and other authorities on crime, terrorism, and immigration issues. Although not all the provisions of the treaty have been universally accepted, each year the EU members become more closely tied economically and politically. Now that the Economic and Monetary Union is put in place and all participating members share a common currency, the EU is headed toward political union as well.

Global Markets and Multinational Market Groups

The globalization of markets, the restructuring of the Eastern European bloc into independent market-driven economies, the dissolution of the Soviet Union into independent states, the worldwide trend toward economic cooperation, and enhanced global competition make it important that market potential be viewed in the context of regions of the world rather than country by country. Formal economic cooperation agreements such as the EU are the most notable examples of multinational market groups, but many new coalitions are forming, old ones are being reenergized, and the possibility of many new cooperative arrangements is on the horizon.

This section presents basic information and data on markets and market groups in Europe, the Americas, Africa, Asia, and the Middle East. Existing economic cooperation agreements within each of these regions are reviewed. The reader must appreciate that the status of cooperative agreements and alliances among nations has been extremely fluid in some parts of the world. Many are fragile and may cease to exist or may restructure into a totally different form. Several decades will probably be needed for many of the new trading alliances that are now forming to stabilize into semipermanent groups.

Europe

Within Europe, every type of multinational market grouping exists. The European Union, European Economic Area, and the European Free Trade Association are the most established cooperative groups (see Exhibits 10.1 and 10.2).

Exhibit 10.1
European Market Regions

Association	Member	Population (millions)	GDP* (billions)	GDP* per Capita	Imports of Goods and Services (billions)	Exports of Goods and Services (billions)
European Union (EU)						
	Belgium	10.4	$ 233.9	$22,544	$200.2	$204.3
	Denmark	5.4	163.0	30,262	66.7	43.8
	Germany	82.5	1,887.5	22,868	641.3	702.7
	Greece	11.0	126.3	11,449	38.0	26.2
	Spain	41.1	603.8	14,691	205.2	182.3
	France	59.8	1,358.0	22,723	372.2	377.2
	Ireland	4.0	111.6	27,932	87.1	106.1
	Italy	57.6	1,100.5	17,298	292.3	286.8
	Luxembourg	0.4	20.6	46,067	26.7	30.9
	Netherlands	16.2	372.7	22,973	235.9	254.6
	Austria	8.1	195.9	24,217	106.9	107.8
	Portugal	10.4	107.4	10,284	45.7	35.0
	Finland	5.2	126.3	24,225	41.7	54.4
	Sweden	9.0	250.8	27,998	97.0	118.2
	United Kingdom	59.3	1,527.3	25,742	475.1	412.0
	Czech Republic	10.2	59.8	5,866	48.1	43.8
	Estonia	1.4	6.6	4,841	5.9	5.1
	Cyprus	0.8	9.7	12,647	—	—
	Latvia	2.3	9.6	4,116	5.2	3.9
	Lithuania	3.5	14.1	4,078	8.8	7.8
	Hungary	10.1	51.7	5,103	44.7	41.5
	Malta	0.4	3.8	9,568	—	—
	Poland	38.2	177.0	4,634	60.0	56.7
	Slovenia	2.0	20.8	10,411	13.1	12.5
	Slovak Republic	5.4	22.8	4,235	19.7	19.7
EU Candidate Countries						
	Bulgaria	7.8	14.4	1,835	10.6	8.9
	Croatia	4.4	21.5	4,751	12.8	10.7
	Romania	21.7	42.7	1,963	21.3	16.9
	Turkey	70.7	210.5	2,977	69.5	66.3
European Free Trade Area (EFTA)						
	Iceland	0.3	8.9	30,952	3.4	3.3
	Liechtenstein	0.03	—	—	—	—
	Norway	4.6	184.7	40,482	66.3	76.3
	Switzerland	7.4	248.2	33,765	97.2	112.0

*Constant 2000 dollars.

Exhibit 10.2
The European Economic
Area: EU, EFTA, and
Associates

Exhibit 10.2
The European Economic
Area: EU, EFTA, and
Associates

Of escalating economic importance are the fledgling capitalist economies of Eastern Europe and the three Baltic states that gained independence from the Soviet Union just prior to its breakup. Key issues center on their economic development and economic alliance with the EU. Also within the European region is the Commonwealth of Independent States. New and untested, this coalition of 12 former USSR republics may or may not survive in its present form to take its place among the other multinational market groups.

A Brief History of European Integration

Of all the multinational market groups, none is more secure in its cooperation or more important economically than the European Union (Exhibit 10.3). From its beginning, it has made progress toward achieving the goal of complete economic integration and, ultimately, political union. However, many people, including Europeans, had little hope for the success of the European Economic Community, or the European Common Market as it is often called, because of the problems created by integration and the level of national sovereignty that would have to be conceded to the community. After all, 1,000 years of economic separatism had to be overcome, and the European Common Market is quite heterogeneous. There are language differences, individual national interests, political differences, and centuries-old restrictions designed to protect local national markets.

Historically, standards have been used to effectively limit market access. Germany protected its beer market from the rest of Europe with a purity law requiring beer sold in Germany to be brewed only from water, hops, malt, and yeast. Italy protected its pasta market by requiring that pasta be made only from durum wheat. Incidentally, the European

Exhibit 10.3
From the European Coal
and Steel Community to
Monetary Union

Source: "Chronology of the EU,"
www.europa.eu.int/ (select Abc).
Reprinted with permission from the
European Communities.

1951	Treaty of Paris	European Coal and Steel Community (ECSC) (Founding members are Belgium, France, Germany, Italy, Luxembourg, and the Netherlands).
1957	Treaty of Rome	Blueprint, European Economic Community (EEC).
1958	European Economic Community	Ratified by ECSC founding members. Common Market is established.
1960	European Free Trade Association	Established by Austria, Denmark, Norway, Portugal, Sweden, Switzerland, and United Kingdom.
1973	Expansion	Denmark, Ireland, and United Kingdom join EEC.
1979	European monetary system	The European Currency Unit (ECU) is created. All members except the UK agree to maintain their exchange rates within specific margins.
1981	Expansion	Greece joins EEC.
1985	1992 Single Market Program	White paper for action introduced to European Parliament.
1986	Expansion	Spain and Portugal join EEC.
1987	Single European Act	Ratified, with full implementation by 1992.
1992	Treaty on European Union	Also known as Maastricht Treaty. Blueprint for Economic and Monetary Union (EMU).
1993	Europe 1992	Single European Act in force (January 1, 1992).
1993	European Union	Treaty on European Union (Maastricht Treaty) in force, with monetary union by 1999.
1994	European Economic Area	The EEA was formed with EU members and Norway and Iceland.
1995	Expansion	Austria, Finland, and Sweden join EU.
1997	Amsterdam Treaty	Established procedures for expansion to Central and Eastern Europe.
1999	Monetary union	Conversion rates are fixed, and euro used by banking and finance industry. Consumer prices are quoted in local currency and in euros.
2002	Banknotes and coins	Circulation of euro banknotes and coins begins January 1, and legal status of national banknotes and coins canceled July 1, 2002.
2004	Expansion	Ten new countries join EU.

Court of Justice has struck down both the beer and pasta regulations as trade violations. Such restrictive standards kept competing products, whether from other European countries or elsewhere, out of their respective markets. Skeptics, doubtful that such cultural, legal, and social differences could ever be overcome, held little hope for a unified Europe. Their skepticism has proved wrong. Today, many marvel at how far the European Economic Community has come. Although complete integration has not been fully achieved, a review of the structure of the EU, its authority over member states, the Single European Act, the European Economic Area, the Maastricht Treaty, and the Amsterdam Treaty will show why the final outcome of full economic and political integration seems certain.

The Single European Act. The Single European Act (1987) was the agreement designed to finally remove all barriers to trade and make the European Community a single internal market. The ultimate goal of the Treaty of Rome (1957), the agreement that founded the EC, was economic and political union, a United States of Europe. The Single European Act moved the EC one step closer to the goal of economic integration.

In addition to dismantling the existing barriers, the Single European Act proposed a wide range of new commercial policies, including single European standards, one of the more difficult and time-consuming goals to achieve. Technical standards for electrical products are a good example of how overwhelming the task of achieving universal standards is for the EU. EU member countries use 29 types of electrical outlets, 10 types

Each month the European Parliament meets for three weeks here in Brussels, Belgium, and then moves for one week to meet in Strasbourg, France. The inconvenience of the fourth week move was a concession to French pride—or perhaps the cheese is better there.

of plugs, and 12 types of cords. The estimated cost for all EU countries to change wiring systems and electrical standards to a single European standard is 90 billion euros, or about 95 billion U.S. dollars. Because of the time it will take to achieve uniform Euro-standards for health, safety, technical, and other areas, the Single European Act provides for a policy of harmonization and mutual recognition.

Under *harmonization,* the most essential requirements for protection of health, safety, the environment, and product standards are established. Once all members meet these EU-wide essential requirements (i.e., harmonization), each member state will be expected to recognize each other's national standards for nonessential characteristics (i.e., *mutual recognition*). In other words, all member countries must adopt the same essential requirements as a base but also accept any different national standards as adequate.

Among the first and most welcome reforms were the single customs document that replaced the 70 forms originally required for transborder shipments to member countries, the elimination of cabotage rules (which kept a trucker from returning with a loaded truck after delivery), and the creation of EU-wide transport licensing. More than 60,000 customs and tax formalities previously imposed at country borders have been eliminated. These changes alone were estimated to have reduced distribution costs 50 percent for companies doing cross-border business in the EU.

Even though several member states are not fully implementing all the measures, they are making progress. The proportion of directives not yet implemented in all 25 member states has fallen dramatically from 26.7 percent to 12.6 percent. Taxation is one of the areas where implementation lags and reform continues to be necessary. Value-added and registration taxes for automobiles, for example, range from 15 percent in Luxembourg to 218 percent in Denmark. A midsize Mercedes in Haderslev, Denmark, costs $90,000, nearly triple the amount you would pay in Flensburg, Germany, just 30 miles south. A Honda Civic costs the British consumer 89 percent more than it costs Continental customers. Scotch in Sweden has an $18 tax, nine times the amount levied in Italy. The EU finance ministers have addressed these issues and made some progress, even though tax-raising ability is a sacred power of the nation-state. The full implementation of the legislation is expected to take several years. Even though all proposals have not been met, the program for unification has built up a pace that cannot be reversed.

EU Institutions.   The European Union's institutions form a federal pattern with executive, parliamentary, and judicial branches: the European Commission, the Council of

Ministers, the European Parliament, and the Court of Justice. Their decision-making processes have legal status and extensive powers in fields covered by common policies. The European Union uses three legal instruments: (1) regulations binding the member states directly and having the same strength as national laws; (2) directives also binding the member states but allowing them to choose the means of execution; and (3) decisions addressed to a government, an enterprise, or an individual, binding the parties named. Over the years, the Union has gained an increasing amount of authority over its member states.

The European Commission initiates policy and supervises its observance by member states, and it proposes and supervises execution of laws and policies. Commission members act only in the interest of the EU, and their responsibilities are to ensure that the EU rules and the principles of the common market are respected.

The Council of Ministers is the decision-making body of the EU; it is the council's responsibility to debate and decide which proposals of the Single European Act to accept as binding on EU members. The council can enact into law all proposals by majority vote except for changes in tax rates on products and services, which require unanimous vote. The council, for example, drafted the Maastricht Treaty, which was presented to member states for ratification.

The European Parliament originally had only a consultative role that passed on most Union legislation. It can now amend and adopt legislation, although it does not have the power to initiate legislation. It also has extensive budgetary powers that allow it to be involved in major EU expenditures.

The European Court of Justice (ECJ) is the Union's Supreme Court. It is responsible for challenging any measures incompatible with the Treaty of Rome and for passing judgment, at the request of a national court, on interpretation or validity of points of EU law. The court's decisions are final and cannot be appealed in national courts. For example, Estée Lauder Companies appealed to the ECJ to overrule a German court's decision to prohibit it from selling its product Clinique. The German court had ruled that the name could mislead German consumers by implying medical treatment. The ECJ pointed out that Clinique is sold in other member states without confusing the consumer and ruled in favor of Estée Lauder. This was a landmark case because many member countries had similar laws that were in essence nontariff trade barriers designed to protect their individual markets. If the German court ruling against Estée Lauder had been let stand, it would have made it difficult for companies to market their products across borders in an identical manner. This is but one example of the ECJ's power in the EU and its role in eliminating nontariff trade barriers.

European Free Trade Association and European Economic Area.
Britain, not wanting to join the EEC, conceived the European Free Trade Association (EFTA) for those European nations not willing to join the EEC but wanting to participate in a free trade area. Britain and other EFTA countries later became members of the European Community in 1973. When Austria, Finland, and Sweden joined the EU in 1995 (see Exhibit 10.2), only Iceland, Liechtenstein, Norway, and Switzerland remained in EFTA.[6] EFTA will most probably dissolve as its members join either the European Economic Area (EEA) or the EU.

Because of the success of the EU and concern that they might be left out of the massive European market, five members of the European Free Trade Association elected to join the 12 members of the EU in 1994 to form the European Economic Area, a single market with free movement of goods, services, and capital. The EFTA countries joining the EEA adopted most of the EU's competition rules and agreed to implement EU rules on company law; however, they maintain their domestic farm policies. The EEA is governed by a special Council of Ministers composed of representatives from EEA member nations.

European Union[7]   The final step in the European Community's march to union was ratification of the Maastricht Treaty (1992). The treaty provided for the Economic and Monetary Union (EMU) and European Union. The treaty touched on all the missing links needed for a truly

---

[6]www.efta.int/, 2005.

[7]See http://europa.eu.int, 2005.

CROSSING BORDERS 10.2   There Are Myths and Then There Are Euromyths

The Austrians feared the European Union would force them to eat chocolate made with blood. The French worried about EU plans to ban certain maggots as bait because they suffer *"le stresse"* on a fishing hook. Italians complained about a fanciful plan to paint all taxis white. Others feared the EU would require nudity on beaches. Trendy Italian chefs cried foul when they heard that their cherished wood-burning ovens were to be banned. Brussels sprouted an edict on sexual harassment that struck down Valentine's Day cards. Then the EU wanted to do away with Britain's beloved double-decker buses and pull-chain toilets and classify carrots as fruit. In addition, Brussels outlawed asymmetrical Christmas trees and pronounced that donkeys must wear diapers. By the time EU packaging rules criminalized the curved cucumber, it was clear that the Eurocrats had lost their senses.

"There Is No Absurdity of Which the European Community Is Not Capable," "The Whole Thing Has Turned into a Mad, Bureaucratic Alice in Wonderland Crossed with Kafka," blared the headlines. Yet what is really Kafkaesque is that each of these stories has only a remote relationship to reality. The EU calls them "Euromyths."

The EU didn't actually ban skiing when snow is less than 20 centimeters deep—but the European Parliament did raise the possibility of such a prohibition. Brussels didn't require donkeys to wear diapers on Euro-beaches, but it won't award its Blue Flag to beaches that admit the animals.

Curved cucumbers aren't banned, just classified differently for packaging reasons. The guidelines lay down a "maximum height of arc, 10 mm per 10 cm length of cucumber." The official EU justification is that "if you have straight cucumbers, it's possible to know how many you are getting in a box." As for symmetrical Christmas trees, a trade association, not the EU, proposed something like this. Carrots *are* classified as fruit, which allows the Portuguese to continue their practice of making carrot jam.

Some myths are completely fanciful, like the one about the EU banning square gin bottles; this started as an April Fool's joke in the *Times*. Also in this category is the Valentine's Day warning that the sending of unwanted cards could qualify as sexual harassment under EU law; it was meant to be tongue in cheek.

At the extremes are stories likening those implementing European child safety standards to Nazi collaborators *(The Mirror)* or suggesting that EU grants have funded IRA arms bunkers *(Daily Mail)*. Both demonstrate nothing more than paranoia.

The EU has therefore hired grown men and women to spend their days reassuring an alarmed public that the EU has no plans to do away with paperboys, small bananas, knotty oak trees, saucy postcards, and any pizza that isn't 11 inches in diameter. Additionally, the European Commission publishes *Press Watch* to address press bias.

Sources: Dana Milbank, "Will Unified Europe Put Mules in Diapers and Ban Mini-Pizza?" *Wall Street Journal*, June 22, 1995, p.1; Peter Popham and Scott Hughes, "Could This Banana Be Straighter?" *Independent* (London), February 2, 1996, p.4; "Addressing the Bias," *Press Watch—The European Union*, April 2000, www.cec.org.uk/pubs/prwatch/pw00/pw0009.htm; "The Week that Was," *Times* (London), September 3, 2005, p. 51.

European political union, including foreign policy. Because procedures on how foreign policy and social legislation decisions are to be made are so complex, another round of negotiations, which was concluded in the Amsterdam Treaty (1997), was necessary. Initially, the viability of a European Union was in considerable doubt. Surrendering sovereignty beyond that already relinquished with the provisions of the Single European Act seemed too extreme for many. There was concern that monetary union would move monetary policy away from the individual countries to a central power. And even more sovereignty would be lost as the Court of Justice gained more power over business transactions. However, within months of the ratification of the treaty, the EU was expanded to include Austria, Finland, and Sweden—all members of the EEA. Norway voted not to join the EU but remains a member of the European Economic Area. Much of the concern persists even as the Economic and Monetary Union is put into place.

Economic and Monetary Union.   The EMU, a provision of the Maastricht Treaty, established the parameters of the creation of a common currency for the EU, the *euro,* and established a timetable for its implementation. In 2002, a central bank was established, conversion rates were fixed, circulation of euro banknotes and coins was completed (see Exhibit 10.4), and the legal tender status of participating members' banknotes

Exhibit 10.4
The Euro

Source: Euro, www.europa.eu.int/euro. Reprinted with permission from the European Communities.

Notes. There are seven euro notes in different colors and sizes, denominated in 500, 200, 100, 50, 20, 10 and 5 euros. The designs symbolize Europe's architectural heritage, with windows and gateways on the front side as symbols of the spirit of openness and cooperation in the EU. The reverse side features a bridge from a particular age, a metaphor for communication among the people of Europe and the rest of the world.

Coins. There are eight euro coins, denominated in 2 and 1 euros, then 50, 20, 10, 5, 2, and 1 cent. Every coin will carry a common European face—a map of the European Union against a background of transverse lines to which are attached the stars of the European flag. On the obverse, each member state will decorate the coins with their own motifs, for example, the King of Spain or some national hero. Regardless of the motif, every coin can be used and will have the same value in all the member states.

Sign. The graphic symbol for the euro was inspired by the Greek letter epsilon, in reference to the cradle of European civilization and to the first letter of the word *Europe*. It looks like an *E* with two clearly marked, horizontal parallel lines across it. The parallel lines are meant to symbolize the stability of the euro. The official abbreviation is "EUR."

and coins was canceled. To participate, members must meet strict limits on several financial and economic criteria, including a member's national deficit, debt, and inflation. The 12 member states employing the euro beginning in January 1, 2001, were Austria, Belgium, Finland, France, Germany, Greece, Ireland, Italy, Luxembourg, Netherlands, Portugal, and Spain. Denmark voted in 2000 not to join the monetary union, leaving Britain and Sweden still undecided. Denmark's rejection strengthened the antieuro groups in other countries[8] and means that the euro zone will not be expanded any further for several years. Denmark's rejection of the euro has serious implications for the broader debate on the EU's future. Antieuro advocates exploited fears of a "European superstate" and local interference from Brussels rather than relying on economic arguments when pushing for rejection.

Predictions of the impact of the euro range from its high costs and economic and political risk to its positive long-term impact. Its introduction is considered to be one of the most important economic events in postwar European history and one that will have a positive long-term impact, albeit a negative effect on economic growth in the short run. The cost for changing over to euros will be high for members as well as companies. As an example of the cost a company incurred to convert to euros, Philips, the Dutch-based MNC, had 35 groups involving about 250 people under a steering committee of 35 senior managers working to convert all intracompany transactions to euros. All companies of entering EU countries will have to convert as Philips did, and companies operating in the EU will have to convert prices, billing, and so forth because the euro will be the currency of the realm.

It took some selling for the Greeks to adopt the euro instead of the 2,500-year-old drachma. The truck seen here in Athens' Syntagma Square was equipped with video projectors and euro information stands and traveled to 40 Greek towns, informing folks about the new currency. (© AFP/Getty Images)

Treaty of Amsterdam.
The Treaty of Amsterdam, concluded in 1997, addressed some of the issues left undone in the Maastricht Treaty. It identifies the priority measures needed to bring the single market fully into effect and to lay a solid foundation for both the single currency and the enlargement into central and eastern Europe. The treaty's four objectives are to place employment and citizens' rights at the heart of the Union, to sweep away the last remaining obstacles to freedom of movement and strengthen security, to give Europe a stronger voice in world affairs, and to make the union's institutional structure more efficient with a view to enlarging the Union.

---

[8] Tracy Wilkinson, "In Italy, Bid to Revive the Lira Gains Currency," *Los Angeles Times*, June 9, 2005, p. A3.

CROSSING BORDERS 10.3   The Death of the Drachma

Having officially joined the European Union on January 1, 2001, Greece began phasing out the drachma, Europe's oldest currency and the survivor of some 2,500 years of war and economic turmoil. Below, highlights from its storied history.

—MEGAN JOHNSTON

Source: March 2001 *Money*. Used by permission of *Money Magazine*.

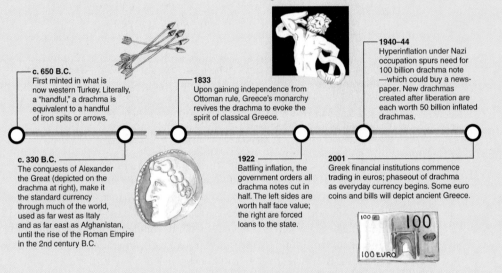

c. 650 B.C.
First minted in what is now western Turkey. Literally, a "handful," a drachma is equivalent to a handful of iron spits or arrows.

c. 330 B.C.
The conquests of Alexander the Great (depicted on the drachma at right), make it the standard currency through much of the world, used as far west as Italy and as far east as Afghanistan, until the rise of the Roman Empire in the 2nd century B.C.

1833
Upon gaining independence from Ottoman rule, Greece's monarchy revives the drachma to evoke the spirit of classical Greece.

1922
Battling inflation, the government orders all drachma notes cut in half. The left sides are worth half face value; the right are forced loans to the state.

1940–44
Hyperinflation under Nazi occupation spurs need for 100 billion drachma note —which could buy a newspaper. New drachmas created after liberation are each worth 50 billion inflated drachmas.

2001
Greek financial institutions commence trading in euros; phaseout of drachma as everyday currency begins. Some euro coins and bills will depict ancient Greece.

The original 40-year-old operating rules of the EC were proving to be inadequate in dealing with the problems that confront the EU today. Expansion beyond its present 25 members (see Exhibit 10.1), managing the conversion to the euro and EMU, and speaking with one voice on foreign policy that directly affects the European continent are all issues that require greater agreement among members and thus more responsibility and authority for the institutions of the EU. The Amsterdam Treaty increases the authority of the institutions of the EU and is designed to accommodate the changes brought about by the monetary union and the admission of new members.

Expansion of the European Union.
The process of enlargement has been the most important item on the EU's agenda. Ten new countries were added in 2004, some ahead of schedule.[9] The entry of Bulgaria and Romania is now planned for 2007, and talks with Turkey[10] and Croatia have begun. One of the main preoccupations is the prospect of illegal immigrants from former Soviet states surging across poorly guarded borders of the candidate states and making their way farther west within the EU. The EU is demanding that borders be sealed, but the candidate states are reluctant to jeopardize relations with neighboring communities. Further, the EU fears a flood of cheap labor even if the borders are closed; it wants a long transition period before freedom of movement of labor, whereas the applicants say their citizens should be allowed to work anywhere in the EU once they are members.

Strategic Implications for Marketing in Europe

The complexion of the entire world marketplace has been changed significantly by the coalition of nations into multinational market groups. To international business firms, multinational groups spell opportunity in bold letters through access to greatly enlarged markets with reduced or abolished country-by-country tariff barriers and restrictions. Production, financing, labor, and marketing decisions are affected by the remapping of the world into market groups.

---

[9]See *The Economist* special insert on EU expansion, "Meet the Neighbors," June 25, 2005, pp. 1–16.

[10]For a complete rundown on Turkey's entrance into the EU, see "Looking to Europe," *The Economist*, March 19, 2005, insert pp. 1–16.

World competition will intensify as businesses become stronger and more experienced in dealing with large market groups. European and non-European multinationals are preparing to deal with the changes in competition in a fully integrated Europe. In an integrated Europe, U.S. multinationals may have an initial advantage over expanded European firms because U.S. businesses are more experienced in marketing to large, diverse markets and are accustomed to looking at Europe as one market. U.S. firms do not carry the cumbersome baggage of multiple national organizations dealing in many currencies, with differentiated pricing and administration, with which most EU firms must contend. The advantage, however, is only temporary as mergers, acquisitions, and joint ventures consolidate operations of European firms in anticipation of the benefits of a single European market. Individual national markets will still confront international managers with the same problems of language, customs, and instability, even though they are packaged under the umbrella of a common market. However, as barriers come down and multicountry markets are treated as one common market, a global market will be one notch closer to reality.

Regulation of business activities has been intensified throughout multinational market groups; each group now has management and administrative bodies specifically concerned with business. In the process of structuring markets, rules and regulations common to the group are often more sophisticated than those of the individual countries. Despite the problems and complexities of dealing with the new markets, the overriding message to the astute international marketer continues to be opportunity and profit potential.

Opportunities.   Economic integration[11] creates large mass markets for the marketer. Many national markets, too small to bother with individually, take on new dimensions and significance when combined with markets from cooperating countries. Large markets are particularly important to businesses accustomed to mass production and mass distribution because of the economies of scale and marketing efficiencies that can be achieved. In highly competitive markets, the benefits derived from enhanced efficiencies are often passed along as lower prices that lead to increased purchasing power.

Most multinational groups have coordinated programs to foster economic growth as part of their cooperative effort. Such programs work to the advantage of marketers by increasing purchasing power, improving regional infrastructure, and fostering economic development. Despite the problems that are sure to occur because of integration, the economic benefits from free trade can be enormous.

Major savings will result from the billions of dollars now spent in developing different versions of products to meet a hodgepodge of national standards. Philips and other European companies invested a total of $20 billion to develop a common switching system for Europe's 10 different telephone networks. This compares with the $3 billion spent in the United States for a common system and $1.5 billion in Japan for a single system.

Market Barriers.   The initial aim of a multinational market is to protect businesses that operate within its borders. An expressed goal is to give an advantage to the companies within the market in their dealings with other countries of the market group. Analysis of the interregional and international trade patterns of the market groups indicates that such goals have been achieved. Intra-EU imports now account for 67.9 percent of total manufacturing imports compared with 61.2 percent before the 1992 program began. Intra-EU service imports also have increased somewhat, from 49.6 percent of the total to 50 percent. This increase of trade among the member states has not been at the expense of third countries.

Companies willing to invest in production facilities in multinational markets may benefit from protectionist measures because these companies become a part of the market. Exporters, however, are in a considerably weaker position. This prospect confronts many U.S. exporters who face the possible need to invest in Europe to protect their export markets in the European Union. The major problem for small companies may be adjusting to the EU standards. A company selling in one or two EU member countries and meeting standards there may find itself in a situation of having to change standards or be closed out when an EU-wide standard is adopted.

---

[11]Judy Dempsey, "Merkel Aide Seeks More EU Integration," *International Herald Tribune*, August 27, 2005, p. 1R.

A manufacturer of hoses used to hook up deep-fat fryers and other gas appliances to gas outlets faced such a problem when one of its largest customers informed the company that McDonald's was told it could no longer use that manufacturer's hoses in its British restaurants. The same thing happened at EuroDisney. Unfortunately, when the common standards were written, only large MNCs and European firms participated, so they had the advantage of setting standards to their benefit. The small company has only one choice: Change or leave. In this particular case, it appears that competitors are working to keep the company out of the market. There are, however, enough questions about threaded fittings and compatibility that the company worked with individual countries to gain entrance to their markets—just as it was before a single market existed.

The prospect of Europe as one unified internal market has many countries concerned about the EU becoming Fortress Europe—free trade within but highly protectionist to all others. Issues of protectionism will be apparent only after the EU has adjusted to the euro and its new directives and focuses more on external trade.

Reciprocity.   Reciprocity is an important part of the trade policy of a unified Europe. If a country does not open its markets to an EU firm, it cannot expect to have access to the EU market. Europeans see reciprocity as a fair and equitable way of allowing foreign companies to participate in the European market without erecting trade barriers, while at the same time giving Europeans equal access to foreign markets.

Marketing Mix Implications

Companies are adjusting their marketing mix strategies to reflect anticipated market differences in a single European market. In the past, companies often charged different prices in different European markets. Nontariff barriers between member states supported price differentials and kept lower-priced products from entering those markets where higher prices were charged. Colgate-Palmolive Company has adapted its Colgate toothpaste into a single formula for sale across Europe at one price. Before changing its pricing practices, Colgate sold its toothpaste at different prices in different markets.

Beddedas Shower Gel is priced in the middle of the market in Germany and as a high-priced product in the United Kingdom. As long as products from lower-priced markets could not move to higher-priced markets, such differential price schemes worked. Now, however, under the EU rules, companies cannot prevent the free movement of goods, and parallel imports from lower-priced markets to higher-priced markets are more likely to occur. Price standardization among country markets will be one of the necessary changes to avoid the problem of parallel imports. With the adoption of the euro, price differentials are much easier to spot, and the consumer can search for the best bargains in brand-name products more easily. Further, the euro will make marketing on the Internet a much simpler task for the European firm than it presently is. On balance, a single currency will make competition in Europe a lot fairer and also a lot tougher.

In addition to initiating uniform pricing policies, companies are reducing the number of brands they produce to focus advertising and promotion efforts. For example, Nestlé's current three brands of yogurt in the EU will be reduced to a single brand. Unilever began to winnow its 1,600 brands down to focus on 400 core brands. It plans to develop master brands in certain markets such as the EU and to market others globally. A major benefit from an integrated Europe is competition at the retail level. Europe lacks an integrated and competitive distribution system that would support small and midsize outlets. The elimination of borders could result in increased competition among retailers and the creation of Europe-wide distribution channels.

The Commonwealth of Independent States

Europe has one other trade group that has emerged and persisted since the dissolution of the Soviet Union: the Commonwealth of Independent States (CIS).[12] The series of events after the aborted coup against Mikhail Gorbachev led to the complete dissolution of the USSR. The first Soviet republics to declare independence were the Baltic states, which

---

[12]www.cisstat.com, 2005.

Exhibit 10.5
The Newly Independent States

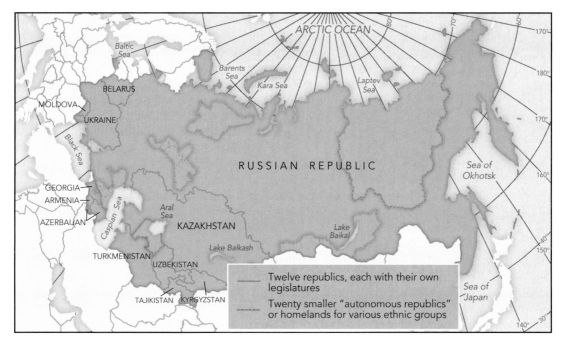

quickly gained recognition by several Western nations. The remaining 12 republics of the former USSR, collectively known as the Newly Independent States (NIS), regrouped into the Commonwealth of Independent States (see Exhibits 10.5 and 10.6).

The CIS is a loose economic[13] and political alliance with open borders but no central government. The main provisions of the commonwealth agreement are to repeal all Soviet laws and assume the powers of the old regimes; launch radical economic reforms, including freeing most prices; keep the ruble, but allow new currencies; establish a European

---

[13]"CIS Should Develop New Model of Integration—Official," *RAI Novosty*, September 1, 2005.

Exhibit 10.6
Commonwealth of Independent States (CIS)

Country	Population (millions)	GDP* (billions)	GDP* per Capita	Imports of Goods and Services (billions)	Exports of Goods and Services (billions)
Russia	143.4	$306.7	$2,138	$101.5	$148.7
Ukraine	48.4	39.3	812	22.3	24.2
Belarus	9.9	15.0	1,513	11.4	11.4
Armenia	3.1	2.7	884	1.4	0.9
Moldova	4.2	1.6	370	1.7	1.0
Azerbaijan	8.2	8.2	865	4.7	3.0
Uzbekistan	25.6	7.1	610	3.0	3.3
Turkmenistan	4.9	4.8	989	3.2	3.7
Tajikistan	6.3	1.3	208	0.9	1.0
Kazakhstan	14.9	24.9	1,673	8.7	13.3
Kyrgyzstan	5.1	1.5	305	0.6	0.6
Georgia	5.1	3.7	729	1.3	0.8

*Constant 2000 dollars.

Source: World Bank, 2003. Copyright © 2003 by World Bank. Reproduced with permission of World Bank via Copyright Clearance Center.

The hammer and sickle logo of the old USSR has been replaced by signs of free enterprise in Russia. Here in the main shopping district of St. Petersburg, Nike Sport is prominent along with the Coca-Cola advertising.

Union–style free trade association; create joint control of nuclear weapons; and fulfill all Soviet foreign treaties and debt obligations.

The 12 members of the CIS share a common history of central planning, and their close cooperation could make the change to a market economy less painful, but differences over economic policy, currency reform, and control of the military may break them apart. How the CIS will be organized and what its ultimate importance will be is anyone's guess.

The three Slavic republics of Russia,[14] Ukraine, and Belarus have interests and history in common, as do the five Central Asian republics. But the ties between these two core groups of the CIS are tenuous and stem mainly from their former Soviet membership. The CIS is by no means coming apart, although it has not solidified to the point of having a stable membership and purpose.[15] Under Vladimir Putin, Russia has shown renewed interest in the CIS, and a free trade zone, which Russia had blocked since the CIS was created, may become a reality.

Of all the former republics, Azerbaijan, Georgia, and Armenia have been the most economically successful since leaving the former USSR. After the USSR collapsed, their economies had all imploded to less than half their peak size during Soviet days. Now, however, they are showing sustained signs of commercial renewal—and multinational icons like Intel are pouring investment into the area.[16] Despite Russia's economic problems, all members of the CIS have had economic growth, and inflation has been held between a high of 5.9 percent for Tajikistan and a low of 0.2 percent for Kazakhstan.

The Americas[17]

Within the Americas, the United States, Canada, Central America, and South America have been natural if sometimes contentious trading partners. As in Europe, the Americas are engaged in all sorts of economic cooperative agreements, with NAFTA being the most significant and Mercosur and CAFTA[18] gaining in importance.

North American Free Trade Agreement

Preceding the creation of the North American Free Trade Agreement (NAFTA), the United States and Canada had the world's largest bilateral trade agreement; each was the other's largest trading partner. Despite this unique commercial relationship, tariff and other trade barriers hindered even greater commercial activity. To further support trade activity, the two countries established the United States–Canada Free Trade Area (CFTA), designed to eliminate all trade barriers between the two countries. The CFTA created a single, continental commercial market for all goods and most services. The agreement between the United States and Canada was not a customs union like the European Community; no economic or political union of any kind was involved. It provided only for the elimination of tariffs and other trade barriers.

Shortly after both countries had ratified the CFTA, Mexico announced that it would seek free trade with the United States. Mexico's overtures were answered positively by the United States, and talks on a U.S.–Mexico free trade area began. Mexico and the United States had been strong trading partners for decades, but Mexico had never officially expressed an interest in a free trade agreement until the president of Mexico, Carlos Salinas de Gortari, announced that Mexico would seek such an agreement with the United States and Canada.

---

[14]Guy Chazan, Gregory L. White, and Betsy McKay, "Coke Expands Russian Presence with a Juice Deal," *Wall Street Journal Europe*, April 1–3, 2005, p. 1.

[15]The Economist Intelligence Unit, "Kazakhstan: Transport and Communications," *Views Wire*, September 1, 2005, p. 15.

[16]Andy Reinhardt and Paul Starobin, "Intel Inside—Russia That Is," *BusinessWeek*, June 23, 2003, p. 48.

[17]For a comprehensive list of all trade agreements in the Americas, with links to specific documents, visit www.sice.oas.org and select Trade Agreements.

[18]Thomas Bell and Brian Faler, "They Stuck Out Their Necks—Now It's Their Hands," *Washington Post*, September 4, 2005, p. A5.

CROSSING **BORDERS 10.4**   Americans Obey European Rules

Americans may not realize it, but rules governing the food they eat, the software they use, and the cars they drive increasingly are set by the European Union. The European Union regulates more frequently and more rigorously than the United States, especially when it comes to consumer protection. So, even though the American market is bigger, the EU, as the jurisdiction with the tougher rules, tends to call the shots for the world's farmers and manufacturers.

Because of the EU, Microsoft Corp. has modified contracts with software makers and Internet service providers to give consumers a wider choice of technologies, and McDonald's Corp. has stopped serving soft plastic toys with its Happy Meals. Carrier air conditioners are redesigned to comply with pending European recycling rules, which are tougher than U.S. standards. The EU initiative requires electrical-equipment makers to eschew certain hard-to-recycle plastics and chemicals, such as brominated flame retardants. For many of GE's businesses, ranging from light bulbs to plastics, "almost 99 percent" of new regulations will come from the EU over time, says GE's chief executive.

Regulators on both sides of the Atlantic are trying to figure out how to protect consumers' online privacy. But while the United States has mostly promoted industry self-regulation, the EU, in October 1998, laid down the law: Europe's residents have the right to know what data has been collected about them online and to get that information changed, if it is inaccurate, or force the collector to delete it. The EU threatened to cut off trans-Atlantic e-mail traffic if U.S. companies failed to guarantee those rights. But during the past two years, voluntary agreements to abide by the EU rules have been signed by 176 companies, ranging from film manufacturer Eastman Kodak Co. to chewing-gum maker Wm. Wrigley Jr. Co. As global businesses, they didn't want to go to the expense of creating special Web sites or data-processing procedures just for Europeans. "There's only one program of privacy protection at Microsoft," and it's Europe's, says Microsoft's director of corporate privacy.

Another EU initiative targets automakers. A preliminary agreement between the European Commission and automakers in Europe, the United States, and Japan would require car hoods and bumpers to be redesigned so they would cause fewer injuries in accidents with pedestrians. Metal "bull bars"—the protruding curved pipes that help make the fronts of many sport-utility vehicles look rugged—would be banned on any new vehicles sold in Europe, because the rigid bars could make the vehicles more deadly if they struck a pedestrian. Automakers signed the deal because they figured it would be less onerous than binding legislation. The executive director of safety for General Motors Corp. says the bumper rule could force GM to retool its Corvette factory because the cost of designing and using special parts for the European market would be hard to justify.

U.S. farmers cater to European tastes, too. While the U.S. Food and Drug Administration has approved the use of most crops employing genetically modified organisms (GMOs) in human food, the EU has placed strict limits on which genetically modified seeds can be planted and how they can be used. What causes trouble for American farmers is the EU's labeling requirements for food containing even 1 percent of a genetically modified ingredient. Thus some U.S. food processors won't buy genetically modified corn or soybeans because they sell their products internationally, and making special non-GMO batches just for Europe isn't practical. Some food processors won't even buy conventional grain from farmers who also plant GMO varieties. Worried about trade with Europe, the Illinois Department of Agriculture last year asked farmers not to plant a Monsanto Co. corn that isn't approved in the EU. Kraft Foods Inc. says it won't use genetically modified vegetable oil in the Toblerone chocolate and Milka candy bars that it exports from Europe to 150 other countries, including the United States. Most recently the U.S. government tired of the "food fight" and decided to sue the EU over what it sees as breaches of WTO rules.

Sources: Brandon Mitchener, "Increasingly, Rules of Global Economy Are Set in Brussels," *Wall Street Journal*, April 23, 2002, p. A1; "Genetic Food Fight," *Wall Street Journal*, May 15, 2003, p. A16; *The Economist*, "The Luddites Make Ground—GM Foods and Trade," July 2, 2005, p. 37.

Despite the disparity between Mexico's economy and the economies of the other two countries, there were sound reasons for such an alliance. Canada is a sophisticated industrial economy, resource rich, but with a small population and domestic market. Mexico, on the other hand, desperately needs investment, technology, exports, and other economic reinforcement to spur its economy.[19] Even though Mexico has an abundance of

---

[19] John O'Dell, "A Toyota Factory Revs Up in Tijuana," *Los Angeles Times*, February 23, 2005, pp. C1, C4.

oil and a rapidly growing population, the number of new workers is increasing faster than its economy can create new jobs. The United States needs resources (especially oil) and, of course, markets. The three need each other to compete more effectively in world markets, and they need mutual assurances that their already dominant trading positions in each other's markets are safe from protection pressures. When NAFTA was ratified and became effective in 1994, a single market of 360 million people with a $6 trillion GNP emerged.

NAFTA requires the three countries to remove all tariffs and barriers to trade over 15 years, but each country will have its own tariff arrangements with nonmember countries. All changes already occurring under CFTA will stand and be built on under NAFTA. Some of the key provisions of the agreement can be found in Exhibit 10.7.

NAFTA is a comprehensive trade agreement that addresses, and in most cases improves, all aspects of doing business within North America. The elimination of trade and investment barriers among Canada, Mexico, and the United States creates one of the largest and richest markets in the world. Cross-border cooperation seems to ameliorate other long-standing areas of conflict such as legal and illegal immigration. NAFTA has paved the way for Wal-Mart to move into Mexico and Mexican supermarket giant Gigante to move into the United States. Other cross-border services are also thriving, including entertainment and health care.

NAFTA has its detractors, and it is safe to say that there has been constant turmoil since its inception. Mexico had a serious financial crisis that led to the devaluation of the peso, and the expansion of NAFTA became a political hot potato in the United States when it was severely politicized during the 1996 presidential election. Unfortunately, all the candidates presented a distorted picture. Opponents painted a picture of economic doom. One candidate claimed that NAFTA would produce a "giant sucking sound" of jobs running from the United States to Mexico. Proponents created an equally distorted picture of economic bliss. Neither side presented a factual picture. First, it was much too early to estimate accurately the effects of NAFTA; second, it was expected that jobs would be lost and companies displaced in the short run. Misinformation prevailed and the general public turned sour on NAFTA. With public opinion turning against the expansion of NAFTA to Chile, the next stage in the agreement, it became obvious that a request for fast-track authorization was in jeopardy; the Clinton administration lost interest, and NAFTA progress languished. Although none of its members advocated disbanding NAFTA, the U.S. administration had directed its attention elsewhere and did not follow through to the second stage—expansion beyond Mexico.

Depending on the source, NAFTA has been a "wash," a costly creator of deep U.S. trade deficits and job losses, or a success.[20] A survey taken three years after its beginning revealed that 67 percent of the Mexicans surveyed believed that Mexico had had little or no success with NAFTA. In another study, 57 percent of U.S. citizens said they were against any new trade pacts with Latin American countries. Our own quick look at the consequences of NAFTA suggest that unemployment has declined while GDP per capita, foreign direct investment inflows, and exports have risen for all three countries in the 10 years since passage.[21]

U.S. and foreign investors with apparel and footwear factories in Asia have been encouraged to relocate their production operations to Mexico. For example, Victoria's Secret lingerie chain opened a new manufacturing plant near Mexico City. The company previously had used contractors in Asia for its lingerie line. Even with wages in Mexico three times the monthly wages in Sri Lanka, the company will still come out ahead because moving goods from Mexico City to the United States is cheaper and faster than moving them from Colombo—the time needed to make a sample can be cut from weeks to days. Further, Mexican goods have no tariffs, whereas Sri Lankan goods carry a 19 percent duty.

Total foreign direct investment in Mexico has averaged $11 billion a year since 1995 as companies from all over the world poured money into auto and electronics plants, telecommunications, petrochemicals, and a host of other areas. A large chunk of investment

[20]David T. Griswold, "NAFTA at 10," *World Trade*, March 2003, p. 10; Julie Demers, "Learning from NAFTA," *CMA Management*, April 2003, pp. 48–50; Rob Portman, "Washington Speaks: Good Neighbors Must Talk," *Toronto Globe and Mail*, September 3, 2005, p. A23.

[21]World Bank, 2005.

Exhibit 10.7
Key Provisions of NAFTA*

Market access
Within 10 years of implementation, all tariffs will be eliminated on North American industrial products traded between Canada, Mexico, and the United States. All trade between Canada and the United States not already duty free will be duty free as provided for in CFTA. Mexico will immediately eliminate tariffs on nearly 50 percent of all industrial goods imported from the United States, and remaining tariffs will be phased out entirely within 15 years.

Nontariff barriers
In addition to elimination of tariffs, Mexico will eliminate nontariff barriers and other trade-distorting restrictions. U.S. exporters will benefit immediately from the removal of most import licenses that have acted as quotas, essentially limiting the importation of products into the Mexican market. NAFTA also eliminates a host of other Mexican barriers, such as local-content, local-production, and export-performance requirements that have limited U.S. exports.

Rules of origin
NAFTA reduces tariffs only for goods made in North America. Tough rules of origin will determine whether goods qualify for preferential tariff treatment under NAFTA. Rules of origin are designed to prevent free riders from benefiting through minor processing or transshipment of non-NAFTA goods. For example, Japan could not assemble autos in Mexico and avoid U.S. or Canadian tariffs and quotas unless the auto had a specific percentage of Mexican (i.e., North American) content. For goods to be traded duty free, they must contain substantial (62.5 percent) North American content. Because NAFTA rules of origin have been strengthened, clarified, and simplified over those contained in the U.S.–Canada Free Trade Agreement, they supersede the CFTA rules.

Customs administration
Under NAFTA, Canada, Mexico, and the United States have agreed to implement uniform customs procedures and regulations. Uniform procedures ensure that exporters who market their products in more than one NAFTA country will not have to adapt to multiple customs procedures. Most procedures governing rules-of-origin documentation, record-keeping, and verification will be the same for all three NAFTA countries. In addition, the three will issue advanced rulings, on request, on whether or not a product qualifies for tariff preference under the NAFTA rules of origin.

Investment
NAFTA will eliminate investment conditions that restrict the trade of goods and services to Mexico. Among conditions eliminated are the requirements that foreign investors export a given level or percentage of goods or services, use domestic goods or services, transfer technology to competitors, or limit imports to a certain percentage of exports.

Services
NAFTA establishes the first comprehensive set of principles governing services trade. U.S. and Canadian financial institutions are permitted to open wholly owned subsidiaries in Mexico, and all restrictions on the services they offer will be lifted. NAFTA opens Mexico's market for international truck, bus, and rail transport and eliminates the requirement to hand off cargo to a Mexican vehicle upon entry into Mexico, saving U.S. industry both time and money. U.S. truck and bus companies will have the right to use their own drivers and equipment for cross-border cargo shipment and passenger service with Mexico.

Intellectual property
NAFTA will provide the highest standards of protection of intellectual property available in any bilateral or international agreement. The agreement covers patents, trademarks, copyrights, trade secrets, semiconductor integrated circuits, and copyrights for North American movies, computer software, and records.

Government procurement
NAFTA guarantees businesses fair and open competition for procurement in North America through transparent and predictable procurement procedures. In Mexico, PEMEX (the national oil company), CFE (the national electric company), and other government-owned enterprises will be open to U.S. and Canadian suppliers.

Standards
NAFTA prohibits the use of standards and technical regulations used as obstacles to trade. However, NAFTA provisions do not require the United States or Canada to lower existing health, environmental, or safety regulations, nor does NAFTA require the importation of products that fail to meet each country's health and safety standards.

*A complete description of NAFTA provisions can be found at www.mac.doc.gov/nafta/3001.htm.

is earmarked for factories that will use Mexico as an export platform for the rest of North America, and increasingly the rest of Latin America.

The investment boom in Mexico has been a major source of new demand for U.S. manufacturers of capital goods. The largest post-NAFTA gains in U.S. exports to Mexico have been in such high-technology manufacturing sectors as industrial machinery, transportation and electronic equipment, plastics, rubber, fabricated metal products, and chemicals.

Job losses have not been as drastic as once feared, in part because companies such as Lucent Technologies have established *maquiladora* plants in anticipation of the benefits from NAFTA. The plants have been buying more components from U.S. suppliers, while cutting back on Asian sources. Miles Press, a $2 million maker of directory cards, saw orders from Lucent grow 20 percent in just a few months. Berg Electronics, a $700 million component maker, expects to triple sales to Lucent's Guadalajara plant next year. This ripple effect has generated U.S. service-sector jobs as well. Fisher Price shifted toy production for the U.S. market from Hong Kong to a plant in Monterrey. Celadon Trucking Services, which moves goods produced for Fisher Price from Mexico to the United States, has added 800 new U.S. drivers to the payroll.

For Valley Drive Systems, manufacturer of automobile front-wheel-drive assemblies, NAFTA has been a success. Because Canadian tariffs on its products were lowered, Valley Drive products are now competitive with those from Taiwan. The company made its first-ever exports in 1996 and now exports 17 percent of its products.

NAFTA is a work in progress. It is still too early to pass judgment; after all, the EU has been in existence for more than 40 years and has had its ups and downs. NAFTA is a mere babe in arms in comparison. What is happening is that economic relationships among the three countries are becoming more intense each day, for the most part quietly and profitably. In short, at least 10 to 15 years are needed for an objective evaluation of NAFTA to be possible.

Most recently, during the protracted economic slump following the dot-com bust in the United States, *maquiladora* plants have been closing at an uncomfortable rate. Manufacturing is migrating to other low-paying countries such as China,[22] Guatemala, and Vietnam. However, the firms operating in Tijuana and other border cities are responding with investments in technology and increased marketing efforts.

United States–Central American Free Trade Agreement–Dominican Republic Free Trade Agreement (CAFTA)

In August 2005, President Bush signed into law a comprehensive free trade agreement among Costa Rica, Dominican Republic, El Salvador, Guatemala, Honduras, Nicaragua, and the United States. The agreement includes a wide array of tariff reductions aimed at increasing trade and employment among the seven signatories. CAFTA represents another important step toward the ultimate goal of a free trade agreement encompassing all the Americas.

Southern Cone Free Trade Area (Mercosur)[23]

Mercosur (including Argentina, Bolivia, Brazil, Chile, Paraguay, and Uruguay) is the second-largest common-market agreement in the Americas after NAFTA. The Treaty of Asunción, which provided the legal basis for Mercosur, was signed in 1991 and formally inaugurated in 1995. The treaty calls for a common market that would eventually allow for the free movement of goods, capital, labor, and services among the member countries, with a uniform external tariff. Because Mercosur members were concerned about sacrificing sovereign control over taxes and other policy matters, the agreement envisioned no central institutions similar to those of the European Union institutions.

Since its inception, Mercosur has become the most influential and successful free trade area in South America. With the addition of Bolivia and Chile in 1996, Mercosur became a market of 220 million people with a combined GDP of nearly $1 trillion and is the third largest free trade area in the world. Mercosur has demonstrated greater success than many observers expected. The success can be attributed to the willingness of the region's governments to confront some very tough issues caused by dissimilar economic policies related to the automobile and textile trade and to modify antiquated border customs procedures that initially created a bottleneck to smooth border crossings. The lack of surface and

---

[22]Geri Smith, "Wasting Away: Despite SARS, Mexico Is Still Losing Export Ground to China," *BusinessWeek*, June 2, 2003, pp. 42–44.

[23]See www.mercosur.org.uy/.

transportation infrastructure to facilitate trade and communications is a lingering problem that is being addressed at the highest levels.

Mercosur has pursued agreements aggressively with other countries and trading groups. For example, there are concrete negotiations under way to create a free trade program with Mexico, talks with Canada regarding a free trade agreement, and talks between Chile and Mercosur aimed at gradual and reciprocal trade liberalization.

In addition, negotiations have been under way since 1999 for a free trade agreement between the EU and Mercosur, the first region-to-region free trade accord. A framework agreement was signed in 1995, and the long-term objective is to reach convergence in all areas—cooperation, trade, market access, intellectual property, and political dialogue—by 2006.[24] The two blocs propose the largest free trade area in the world. The advantages of the accord to Mercosur will mainly come from lifting trade barriers on agricultural and agro-industrial products, which account for the lion's share of Mercosur exports to Europe. However, that will also be a major stumbling block if the EU is unwilling to open its highly protected agricultural sector to Brazilian and Argentine imports. Nevertheless, one official of the EU indicated that the EU was already in the process of reforming its Common Agricultural Policy. Although negotiations will not be easy, Mercosur and the EU should be able to reach an accord. As we shall see in the next section, Mercosur has assumed the leadership in setting the agenda for the creation of a free trade area of the Americas or, more likely, a South American Free Trade Area (SAFTA).

Latin American Economic Cooperation

Besides the better-known NAFTA and Mercosur, other Latin American market groups (Exhibit 10.8) have had varying degrees of success. Plagued with tremendous foreign debt, protectionist economic systems, triple-digit inflation, state ownership of basic industries, and overregulation of industry, most Latin American countries were in a perpetual state of economic chaos. Under such conditions, trade or integration among member countries stagnated. But, as discussed earlier, sparked by the success of Mercosur and NAFTA, Latin America has seen a wave of genuine optimism about the economic miracle under way spurred by political and economic reforms from the tip of Argentina to the Rio Grande. Coupled with these market-oriented reforms is a desire to improve trade among neighboring countries by reviving older agreements or forming new ones. In fact, many of the trade groups are seeking ties to Mercosur, the European Union, or both.

Keeping track of all the proposed free trade areas in Latin America is a major endeavor, because almost every country has either signed some type of trade agreement or is involved in negotiations. In addition to new trade agreements, many of the trade accords that have been in existence for decades have moved from a moribund to an active state. For example, the first and most ambitious, the Latin American Free Trade Association (LAFTA), gave way to the Latin American Integration Association (LAIA or ALADI), with new rules of organization that revitalized that group.

Latin American Integration Association.
The long-term goal of the LAIA, better known by its Spanish acronym, ALADI,[25] is a gradual and progressive establishment of a Latin American common market. One of the more important aspects of LAIA that differs from LAFTA, its predecessor, is differential treatment of member countries according to their level of economic development. Over the years, negotiations among member countries have lowered duties on selected products and eased trade tensions over quotas, local-content requirements, import licenses, and other trade barriers. An important feature of LAIA is the provision that permits members to establish bilateral trade agreements among member countries. It is under this proviso that trade agreements have been developed among LAIA members.

Caribbean Community and Common Market (CARICOM).[26]
The success of the Caribbean Free Trade Association led to the creation of the Caribbean

[24]"EU, Mercosur Extend Trade Talks Timetable into 2006," *Reuters*, September 2, 2005.

[25]www.aladi.org, 2005.

[26]www.caricom.org, 2005.

Exhibit 10.8
Market Regions of the Americas

Association	Member	Population (millions)	GDP* (billions)	GDP* per Capita	Imports of Goods and Services (billions)	Exports of Goods and Services (billions)
North American Free Trade Agreement (NAFTA)						
	United States	290.8	$10,343.0	$35,566	$1,484.7	$1,014.2
	Mexico	102.3	592.5	5,792	189.1	177.9
	Canada	31.6	766.1	24,222	275.0	318.4
Central American Free Trade Agreement (CAFTA)						
	Guatemala	12.3	20.6	1,675	6.4	3.8
	Costa Rica	4.0	17.6	4,410	8.0	8.2
	El Salvador	6.5	13.9	2,129	6.2	3.9
	Nicaragua	5.5	4.2	767	2.1	1.1
	Honduras	7.0	6.5	927	3.6	2.6
	Dominican Republic	8.7	21.1	2,413	11.3	10.3
	United States	as above	—	—	—	—
Caribbean Community and Common Market (CARICOM)						
	Antigua and Barbuda	0.1	0.7	9,198	0.5	0.4
	Barbados	0.3	2.5	9,256	1.4	1.3
	Belize	0.3	1.0	3,635	0.7	0.5
	Dominica	0.1	0.2	3,447	0.1	0.1
	Grenada	0.1	0.4	3,861	0.3	0.2
	Guyana	0.8	0.7	942	0.8	0.7
	Haiti	8.4	3.9	298	1.9	0.6
	Jamaica	2.6	8.3	3,156	4.9	3.4
	Montserrat St. Kitts-Nevis	0.05	0.3	7,427	0.2	0.1
	St. Lucia	0.2	0.7	4,178	—	—
	Surinam	0.4	1.0	2,257	0.5	0.2
	Trinidad-Tobago	1.3	9.9	7,520	4.1	5.2
Latin American Integration Association (LAIA)						
	Argentina	36.8	263.5	7,165	19.4	34.7
	Bolivia	8.8	9.0	1,017	2.3	2.1
	Brazil	176.6	619.9	3,510	63.8	88.0
	Chile	15.8	82.0	5,196	22.6	26.8
	Colombia	44.6	90.0	2,017	19.1	18.6
	Ecuador	13.0	17.8	1,368	6.8	6.1
	Mexico	as above	—	—	—	—
	Paraguay	5.6	7.9	1,407	3.0	2.6
	Peru	27.1	57.8	2,131	10.4	10.4
	Uruguay	3.4	17.7	5,235	2.9	3.3
	Venezuela	25.7	102.9	4,009	12.9	27.7

*Constant 2000 dollars.

Source: World Bank, 2003. Copyright © 2003 by World Bank. Reproduced with permission of World Bank via Copyright Clearance Center.

Community and Common Market. CARICOM member countries continue in their efforts to achieve true regional integration. The group has worked toward a single-market economy and in 2000 established the CSME (CARICOM Single Market and Economy) with the goal of a common currency for all members. The introduction of a common external tariff structure was a major step toward that goal, but there is some unease as to whether the CSME will actually come into full existence in 2001, the date set for its implementation. CARICOM continues to seek stronger ties with other groups in Latin America and has signed a trade agreement with Cuba.

NAFTA to FTAA or SAFTA?

Initially NAFTA was envisioned as the blueprint for a free trade area extending from Alaska to Argentina. The first new country to enter the NAFTA fold was to be Chile, then membership was to extend south until there was a Free Trade Area of the Americas (FTAA) by 2005. The question now is whether there will be an FTAA or whether there will be a tri-country NAFTA in the north and a South American Free Trade Area (SAFTA) led by Brazil and the other member states of Mercosur in the south. The answer to this question rests in part with the issue of fast-track legislation and the policies of the Bush administration. Although the Clinton administration was successful in gaining legislation to create NAFTA, its policies toward Latin America and NAFTA drifted aimlessly afterward. As discussed earlier, NAFTA was severely politicized during the 1996 presidential elections, and the perceived lack of interest on the part of the United States created doubt among Latin American leaders about the sincerity of U.S. leadership. Although NAFTA remains a solid tricountry free trade area, it may or may not become a part of a larger trade area of the Americas.

Asian-Pacific Rim

Now, after decades of dependence on the United States and Europe for technology and markets, countries in the Asian-Pacific Rim are preparing for the next economic leap driven by trade, investment, and technology aided by others in the region. Though few in number, trade agreements among some of the Asian newly industrialized countries (NICs) are seen as movement toward a regionwide, intra-Asian trade area, with Japan and China at the center of this activity.

While the United States is Japan's single largest trading partner, markets in China and Southeast Asia are increasingly more important in Japanese corporate strategy for trade and direct investment. Once a source of inexpensive labor for products shipped to Japan or to third markets, these countries are now seen as viable markets. Further, Japanese investment across a number of manufacturing industries is geared toward serving local customers and building sophisticated local production and supplier networks.

Present trade agreements include one multinational trade group, the Association of Southeast Asian Nations (ASEAN), which is evolving into the ASEAN Free Trade Area (AFTA); ASEAN+3, a forum for ASEAN ministers plus ministers from China, Japan, and South Korea; and the Asia-Pacific Economic Cooperation (APEC), a forum that meets annually to discuss regional economic development and cooperation.

Association of Southeast Asian Nations

The primary multinational trade group in Asia is ASEAN.[27] The goals of the group are economic integration and cooperation through complementary industry programs; preferential trading, including reduced tariff and nontariff barriers; guaranteed member access to markets throughout the region; and harmonized investment incentives. Like all multinational market groups, ASEAN has experienced problems and false starts in attempting to unify the combined economies of its member nations. Most of the early economic growth came from trade outside the ASEAN group. Similarities in the kinds of products they had to export, in their natural resources, and other national assets hampered earlier attempts at intra-ASEAN trade. The steps countries took to expand and diversify their industrial base in order to foster intraregional trade when ASEAN was first created have resulted in the

---

[27]See www.aseansec.org.

Exhibit 10.9
Far Eastern Market Group

Association	Member	Population (millions)	GDP* (billions)	GDP* per Capita	Imports of Goods and Services (billions)	Exports of Goods and Services (billions)
ASEAN Free Trade Area (AFTA)						
	Brunei	0.4	$ —	$ —	$ —	$ —
	Cambodia	13.4	4.2	313	3.3	2.9
	Indonesia	214.7	167.7	781	52.7	68.7
	Laos	5.7	2.0	352	—	—
	Malaysia	24.8	99.4	4,011	96.3	115.5
	Myanmar	49.4	—	—	—	—
	Philippines	81.5	85.3	2,131	48.6	43.5
	Singapore	4.3	93.2	21,941	—	—
	Thailand	62.0	141.2	2,276	82.5	94.1
	Vietnam	81.3	38.3	470	28.6	23.9
Plus Three						
	China	1,288.4	1,375.2	1,067	441.8	502.8
	Japan	127.6	4,876.1	38,222	476.2	572.2
	South Korea	47.9	586.1	12,232	233.5	266.4

*Constant 2000 dollars.

Source: World Bank, 2003. Copyright © 2003 by World Bank. Reproduced with permission of World Bank via Copyright Clearance Center.

fastest-growing economies in the region and an increase in trade among members (see Exhibit 10.9).[28]

Four major events account for the vigorous economic growth of the ASEAN countries and their transformation from cheap-labor havens to industrialized nations: (1) the ASEAN governments' commitment to deregulation, liberalization, and privatization of their economies; (2) the decision to shift their economies from commodity based to manufacturing based; (3) the decision to specialize in manufacturing components in which they have a comparative advantage (this created more diversity in their industrial output and increased opportunities for trade); and (4) Japan's emergence as a major provider of technology and capital necessary to upgrade manufacturing capability and develop new industries.[29]

Although there has never been an attempt to duplicate the supranational government of the European Union, each year the group becomes more interrelated. ASEAN Vision 2020 is the most outward-looking commitment to regional goals ever accepted by the group. Among the targets that will lead to further integration is the commitment to implementing fully and as rapidly as possible the ASEAN Free Trade Area.

Just as was the case in the EU, businesses are drafting plans for operation within a free trade area. The ability to sell in an entire region without differing tariff and nontariff barriers is one of the important changes that will affect many parts of the marketing mix. Distribution can be centralized at the most cost-effective point rather than having distribution points dictated by tariff restrictions. Some standardization of branding will be necessary because large customers will buy at the regional level rather than bit by bit at the country level. Pricing can be more consistent, which will help reduce the smuggling and parallel importing that occur when different tariff schedules create major price differentials among countries. In essence, marketing can become more regionally and centrally managed.

---

[28]Mahathir Mohamad, "Cooperation to Enhance Development in East Asia: Former Malaysian Premier," *Xinhua News Agency*, September 5, 2005.

[29]Shisei Kaku, "Japan Walks the Path of Peace," *The Age*, September 6, 2005, p. 13.

One result of the Asian financial crisis of 1997 to 1998 was the creation of ASEAN+3 (ASEAN plus China, Japan, and South Korea) to deal with trade and monetary issues facing Asia. Most of East Asia felt that they were both let down and put upon by the West, who they felt created much of the problem by pulling out in the midst of the crisis. It was felt that the leading financial powers either declined to take part in the rescue operations, as the United States did in Thailand, or that they proposed unattainable solutions. The result was the creation of ASEAN+3, consisting of the foreign and finance ministers of each country, which meets annually after ASEAN meetings. The first meeting was devoted to devising a system whereby the member countries share foreign exchange reserves to defend their currencies against future attack. Although they were only tentative, the members of ASEAN+3 also discussed creating a common market and even a single currency or, perhaps, a new Asian entity encompassing both Northeast and Southeast Asia. Closer links between Southeast Asia and Northeast Asia are seen as a step toward strengthening Asia's role in the global economy and creating a global three-bloc configuration.

Asia-Pacific Economic Cooperation

The other important grouping that encompasses the Asian-Pacific Rim is the Asia-Pacific Economic Cooperation.[30] Formed in 1989, APEC provides a formal structure for the major governments of the region, including the United States and Canada, to discuss their mutual interests in open trade and economic collaboration. APEC is a unique forum that has evolved into the primary regional vehicle for promoting trade liberalization and economic cooperation. APEC includes all the major economies of the region and the most dynamic, fastest-growing economies in the world. APEC has as its common goal a commitment to open trade, to increase economic collaboration, to sustain regional growth and development, to strengthen the multilateral trading system, and to reduce barriers to investment and trade without detriment to other economies.

Representatives from APEC member nations meet annually to discuss issues confronting the group, to propose solutions to problems arising from the growing interdependence among their economies, and to continue their quest for ways to lower barriers to trade. Although APEC is still far from being a free trade area, each meeting seems to advance it another step in that direction, notwithstanding the objections of some members.

Africa

Africa's multinational market development activities can be characterized as a great deal of activity but little progress. Including bilateral agreements,[31] an estimated 200 economic arrangements exist between African countries (Exhibit 10.10). Despite the large number and assortment of paper organizations, there has been little actual economic integration because of the political instability that has characterized Africa in recent decades and the unstable economic base on which Africa has had to build. The United Nations Economic Commission for Africa (ECA) has held numerous conferences but has been hampered by governmental inexperience, undeveloped resources, labor problems, and chronic product shortages.

The Economic Community of West African States (ECOWAS) and the Southern African Development Community (SADC) are the two most active regional cooperative groups. A 15-nation group, ECOWAS has an aggregate gross domestic product of more than $57.9 billion and is striving to achieve full economic integration. The 20th ECOWAS summit in 1997 approved a plan to accelerate subregional economic integration and development, with emphasis on their full commitment to regional monetary integration and

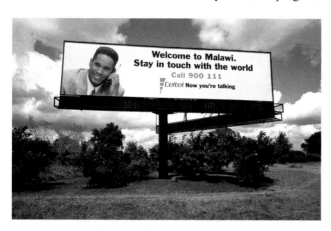

Cell phone service is available even in African countries with per capita incomes among the lowest in the world. (© Pers-Anders Pettersson/Getty Images)

---

[30]See www.apec.org.

[31]Isaya Muriwo Sithole, "Zimbabwe, SA in Perspective," *All Africa*, September 2, 2005, p. 16.

Exhibit 10.10
African Market Groups

Association	Member	Population (millions)	GDP* (billions)	GDP* per Capita	Imports of Goods and Services (billions)	Exports of Goods and Services (billions)
Afro-Malagasy Economic Union						
	Benin	6.7	$ 2.6	$ 392	$ 0.7	$ 0.4
	Burkina Faso	12.1	3.1	253	1.0	0.3
	Cameroon	16.1	10.2	634	2.8	2.9
	Central African Republic	3.9	1.0	229	—	—
	Chad	8.6	1.9	218	1.5	0.3
	Congo Dem. Rep.	53.2	4.6	87	1.4	1.1
	Côte d'Ivoire	16.8	10.1	597	3.5	4.3
	Gabon	1.3	5.2	3,865	1.9	2.0
	Mali	11.7	3.0	258	1.1	1.0
	Mauritania	2.9	1.1	372	0.8	0.3
	Niger	11.8	2.1	178	—	—
	Senegal	10.2	5.0	485	1.7	1.4
	Togo	4.9	1.4	292	0.7	0.5
East African Customs Union						
	Ethiopia	68.6	7.0	102	2.5	1.4
	Kenya	31.9	10.9	341	3.7	3.2
	Sudan	33.5	14.5	433	1.9	2.2
	Tanzania	35.9	11.1	309	2.5	1.8
	Uganda	25.3	7.0	277	1.6	0.9
	Zambia	10.4	3.7	354	1.3	1.0
Union of Arab Maghreb						
	Algeria	31.8	60.1	1,916	—	—
	Libya	5.6	—	—	—	—
	Tunisia	9.9	21.9	2,214	10.3	9.5
	Morocco	30.1	38.5	1,278	15.4	11.7
	Mauritania	as above	—	—	—	—

Source: World Bank, 2003. Copyright © 2003 by World Bank. Reproduced with permission of World Bank via Copyright Clearance Center.

the eventual adoption of a single West African currency. Unfortunately, ECOWAS continues to be plagued with financial problems, conflict within the group, and inactivity on the part of some members. After 25 years, the ECOWAS treaty and its much-defined objectives and the way they are to be achieved over a 15-year period in three stages languishes; nothing has been achieved and free trade remains a deferred dream.

The Southern African Development Community is the most advanced and viable of Africa's regional organizations. Its 14 members encompass a landmass of 6.6 million square kilometers containing abundant natural resources and a population of over 199 million. South Africa, the region's dominant economy, has a GDP of $176 billion and accounts for 76.8 percent of SADC market share. After years of negotiations, 11 members of SADC approved a free trade agreement aimed at phasing out a minimum of 85 percent of tariffs within eight years, and all tariffs by the end of 2012.

Middle East

The Middle East has been less aggressive in the formation of successfully functioning multinational market groups. The Arab Common Market has set goals for free internal trade but has not succeeded. The aim is to integrate the economies of the 22 Arab countries, but before that will be feasible, a long history of border disputes and persisting ideological differences will have to be overcome. The idea is still alive, however, and is a topic of

Association	Member	Population (millions)	GDP* (billions)	GDP* per Capita	Imports of Goods and Services (billions)	Exports of Goods and Services (billions)
Economic Community of West African States						
	Benin	as above	—	—	—	—
	Burkina Faso	as above	—	—	—	—
	Cape Verde	0.5	$ 0.6	$1,290	$ 0.4	$ 0.2
	Côte d'Ivoire	as above	—	—	—	—
	Gambia	1.4	0.5	324	0.2	0.2
	Ghana	20.7	5.7	276	3.7	2.5
	Guinea	7.9	3.4	431	0.9	0.8
	Guinea-Bissau	1.5	0.2	135	0.1	0.1
	Liberia	3.4	0.4	123	—	—
	Mali	as above	—	—	—	—
	Mauritania	as above	—	—	—	—
	Niger	as above	—	—	—	—
	Nigeria	136.5	48.8	357	21.6	25.3
	Senegal	as above	—	—	—	—
	Sierra Leone	5.3	0.8	141	0.6	0.2
	Togo	as above	—	—	—	—
Southern African Development Community						
	Angola	13.5	11.0	814	—	—
	Botswana	1.7	6.1	3,532	2.0	2.8
	Congo	as above	—	—	—	—
	Lesotho	1.8	1.0	530	0.9	0.4
	Namibia	2.0	3.7	1,845	1.7	1.7
	Malawi	11.0	1.7	157	0.7	0.5
	Mauritius	1.2	5.1	4,161	3.0	3.2
	Mozambique	18.8	4.8	255	1.5	1.0
	Seychelles	0.1	0.6	6,881	0.6	0.5
	S. Africa	45.8	138.7	3,026	37.6	37.5
	Swaziland	1.1	1.5	1,358	1.4	1.3
	Tanzania	—	—	—	—	—
	Zambia	as above	—	—	—	—
	Zimbabwe	13.1	6.2	479	1.8	2.0

*Constant 2000 dollars.

Source: World Bank, 2005.

discussion whenever Arab foreign ministers meet. The Arab Gulf states, Egypt, and Morocco are focusing on the proposed establishment of an Arab Free Trade Area by 2007. This proposal may become a reality because several Arab nations now have bilateral free trade zones, and one report indicated that many Arab countries are refurbishing their economic infrastructures to prepare for membership.

Iran, Pakistan, and Turkey, formerly the Regional Cooperation for Development (RCD), have renamed their regional group the Economic Cooperation Organization (ECO). Since reorganizing, Afghanistan and six of the newly independent states were accepted into the ECO. Impressive strides in developing basic industrial production were being made when the RCD was first organized, but the revolution in Iran ended any economic activity. ECO has as its primary goal the development of its infrastructure in order to pave the way for regional cooperation. Unfortunately, trade volume among ECO members constitutes only 7 percent of their total trade. However, a recent announcement from ECO indicated that there has been an agreement to reduce tariff and nontariff barriers to boost trade.

The other activity in the region, led by Iran, is the creation of the Organization of the Islamic Conference (OIC), a common market composed of Islamic countries. A preferential tariff system among the member states of the OIC and the expansion of commercial services in insurance, transport, and transit shipping are among the issues to be debated at the next conference of Islamic countries. The OIC represents 60 countries and over 650 million Muslims worldwide. The member countries' vast natural resources, substantial capital, and cheap labor force are seen as the strengths of the OIC.

Regional Trading Groups and Emerging Markets

During the last decade two opposing views prevailed regarding the direction of global trade in the future. One view suggested that the world is dividing into major regional trading groups such as the European Union, NAFTA, and the ASEAN Free Trade Area that are now and will continue to be the major markets of the future. The other view was that global economic power may be shifting away from the traditional industrialized markets to the developing world and its emerging markets. China's ascendancy and the continuing networking among countries through bilateral and multilateral trade agreements such as the WTO are yielding a third view: The dominant trend is a new globalization of markets where the notion of nation is becoming less important and the desires of consumers begin to dominate.

The most important argument given in support of this last view is that developed countries have mature, stable markets dominated by global companies. Thus their economies will grow more slowly than emerging markets and offer less opportunity for new trade. Conversely, enormous demand will be created as emerging economies continue the rate of economic development experienced over the last decade. These emerging economies will need highways, communications networks, utilities, factories, and the other capital goods necessary for industrialization. And as their economies continue to prosper, consumer goods will be needed to satisfy the demands of a newly affluent consumer market. Rather than international trade being driven by the major industrialized countries, emerging economies may be the engine for global market growth. Many experts predict that over the next 50 years the majority of global economic growth will be in the developing world, principally in those countries identified as emerging markets. While most of the immediate growth will be accounted for by 10 countries now on the threshold of expansion, many of the 120 other developing countries in Europe, Latin America, and Asia are awakening to the desire for economic development and industrialization and may soon be among the future emerging markets.

Summary

The experiences of the multinational market groups developed since World War II point up both the successes and the hazards such groups encounter. The various attempts at economic cooperation represent varying degrees of success and failure, but almost without regard to their degree of success, the economic market groups have created great excitement among marketers. In the near future these regional grouping will continue to form trade agreement ties with other nations and regions, thus paving the way for truly globalized markets where consumers dominate.

For companies the economic benefits possible through cooperation relate to more efficient marketing and production. Marketing efficiency is effected through the development of mass markets, encouragement of competition, improvement of personal income, and various psychological market factors. Production efficiency derives from specialization, mass production for mass markets, and the free movement of the factors of production. Economic integration also tends to foster political harmony among the countries involved; such harmony leads to stability and peace, which are beneficial to the marketer.

The marketing implications of multinational market groups may be studied from the viewpoint of firms located inside the market or of firms located outside, which wish to sell to the markets. For each viewpoint the problems and opportunities are somewhat different; regardless of the location of the marketer, however, multinational market groups provide great opportunity for the creative marketer who wishes to expand volume. Market groupings make it economically feasible to enter new markets and to employ new marketing strategies that could not be applied to the smaller markets represented by individual countries. At the same time, market groupings intensify competition by protectionism within a market group but may foster greater protectionism between regional markets. Mercosur and ASEAN+3, for example, suggest the growing importance of economic cooperation and integration. Such developments will continue to confront the international marketer by providing continually growing market opportunities and challenges.

Questions

1. Define the following terms:

multinational market region	free trade area
EMU	customs union
Single European Act	common market
NAFTA	political union
AFTA	Maastricht Treaty
Mercosur	Treaty of Amsterdam
APEC	ASEAN+3

2. Elaborate on the problems and benefits that multinational market groups represent for international marketers.

3. Explain the political role of multinational market groups.

4. Identify the factors on which one may judge the potential success or failure of a multinational market group.

5. Explain the marketing implications of the factors contributing to the successful development of a multinational market group.

6. Imagine that the United States was composed of many separate countries with individual trade barriers. What marketing effects might be visualized?

7. Discuss the possible types of arrangements for regional economic integration.

8. Differentiate between a free trade area and a common market. Explain the marketing implications of the differences.

9. It seems obvious that the founders of the European Union intended it to be a truly common market, so much so that economic integration must be supplemented by political integration to accomplish these objectives. Discuss.

10. The European Commission, the Council of Ministers, and the Court of Justice of the European Union have gained power in the last decade. Comment.

11. Select any three countries that might have some logical basis for establishing a multinational market organization and illustrate their compatibility as a regional trade group. Identify the various problems that would be encountered in forming multinational market groups of such countries.

12. U.S. exports to the European Union are expected to decline in future years. What marketing actions might a company take to counteract such changes?

13. "Because they are dynamic and because they have great growth possibilities, the multinational markets are likely to be especially rough and tumble for the external business." Discuss.

14. Differentiate between a customs union and a political union.

15. Why have African nations had such difficulty in forming effective economic unions?

16. Discuss the implications of the European Union's decision to admit Eastern European nations to the group.

17. Discuss the consequences to the United States of not being a part of SAFTA.

18. Discuss the strategic marketing implications of NAFTA.

19. How is the concept of reciprocity linked to protectionism?

20. Visit the Web pages for NAFTA and Mercosur and locate each group's rules of origin. Which group has the most liberal rules of origin? Why is there a difference?

21. Using the factors that serve as the basis for success of an economic union (political, economic, social, and geographic), evaluate the potential success of the EU, NAFTA, AFTA, and Mercosur.

22. For each regional trade group—EU, NAFTA, AFTA, ASEAN+3, and Mercosur—cite which of the factors for success are the strongest and which are the weakest. Discuss each factor.

23. What is the motive behind ASEAN+3 and what are the probable implications for global trade?

24. NAFTA has been in existence for several years—how has it done? Read Exibit 10.7, which discusses the initial provisions of the agreement, and, using the Internet, evaluate how well the provisions have been met.

11

global marketing management:

PLANNING AND ORGANIZATION

CHAPTER OUTLINE

Global Perspective: Global Gateways

Global Marketing Management

    The Nestlé Way: Evolution Not Revolution
    Benefits of Global Marketing

Planning for Global Markets

    Company Objectives and Resources
    International Commitment
    The Planning Process

Alternative Market-Entry Strategies

    Exporting
    Contractual Agreements
    Strategic International Alliances
    Direct Foreign Investment

Organizing for Global Competition

    Locus of Decision
    Centralized versus Decentralized Organizations

CHAPTER LEARNING OBJECTIVES

What you should learn from Chapter 11:

- How global marketing management differs from international marketing management

- The increasing importance of international strategic alliances

- The need for planning to achieve company goals

- The important factors for each alternative market-entry strategy

Global Perspective

GLOBAL GATEWAYS

With their domestic market crowded with competitors, Yahoo!, Lycos, America Online (AOL), and others are rushing to establish their brands in Europe, Asia, and Latin America before local competitors can create dominant franchises of their own.

Recently, Lycos Europe, a joint venture between Lycos Inc. and Germany's Bertelsmann AG, had its initial public offering on Germany's Neuer Markt. Many more such offerings are expected because U.S. Web executives and investors believe that the Internet will continue to grow faster abroad than at home. The U.S. share of Internet users fell from 42 percent in 1997 to 19 percent in 2005.

The battle has been hottest in Europe among the portals that serve as starting points for Web surfers looking for news, shopping, and search services. Yahoo! and Lycos each operates about two dozen foreign portals, most with native-language news, shopping links, and other content custom tailored to the local population. Lycos's German site features tips on brewing beer at home and a program for calculating auto speeding fines. Yahoo!'s Singapore site offers real-time information on haze and smog in Southeast Asia. AOL has about a dozen international ventures, and Excite, the portal arm of At Home Corporation, has nine international partners.

The top U.S. players face tough home-grown competitors, who often have a better sense of local culture and Internet styles. In many countries, the dominant telephone companies offer portals, giving them a big leg up because customers are automatically sent to their home pages when they log on. Germany's leading portal, T-Online, is run by Deutsche Telekom. In France, No. 1 Wanadoo is operated by France Telecom.

U.S. portals risk being viewed as digital colonists trying to flex their muscles around the world, according to industry analysts. Many advise that American companies hoping to set up shop abroad are better served by forming partnerships with local outfits that understand the culture.

Sources: Jon G. Auerbach, Bernard Wysocki Jr., and Neal E. Boudette, "For U.S. Internet Portals, the Next Big Battleground Is Overseas," *Wall Street Journal,* March 23, 2000, p. B1; Daekwan Kim, "The Internationalization of U.S. Portals: Does It Fit the Model of Internationalization?" *Marketing Intelligence & Planning* 21, no. 1 (2003), pp. 23–36; Euromonitor 2005.

Confronted with increasing global competition for expanding markets, multinational companies are changing their marketing strategies and altering their organizational structures. Their goals are to enhance their competitiveness and to ensure proper positioning in order to capitalize on opportunities in the global marketplace.

A recent study of North American and European corporations indicated that nearly 75 percent of the companies are revamping their business processes, that most have formalized strategic-planning programs, and that the need to stay cost competitive was considered to be the most important external issue affecting their marketing strategies. Change is not limited to the giant multinationals but includes midsize and small firms as well.

In fact, the flexibility of a smaller company may enable it to reflect the demands of global markets and redefine its programs more quickly than larger multinationals. Acquiring a global perspective is easy, but the execution requires planning, organization, and a willingness to try new approaches—from engaging in collaborative relationships to redefining the scope of company operations.

This chapter discusses global marketing management, competition in the global marketplace, strategic planning, and alternative market-entry strategies. It also identifies the elements that contribute to an effective international or global organization.

Global Marketing Management

In the 1970s the market segmentation argument was framed as "standardization versus adaptation." In the 1980s it was "globalization versus localization," and in the 1990s it was "global integration versus local responsiveness." The fundamental question was whether the global homogenization of consumer tastes allowed global standardization of the marketing mix. The Internet revolution of the 1990s with its unprecedented global reach added a new twist to the old debate.

Even today, some companies are answering "global" as the way to go. For example, executives at Twix Cookie Bars recently tried out their first global campaign with a new global advertising agency, Grey Worldwide. With analysis, perhaps a global campaign does make sense for Twix. But look at the companies that are going in the other direction. Levi's jeans have faded globally in recent years. Ford has chosen to keep acquired nameplates such as Mazda, Jaguar, and Volvo. And perhaps the most global company of all, Coca-Cola, is peddling two brands in India—Coke and Thums-Up. Coke's CEO explained at the time, "Coke has had to come to terms with a conflicting reality. In many parts of the world, consumers have become pickier, more penny-wise, or a little more nationalistic, and they are spending more of their money on local drinks whose flavors are not part of the Coca-Cola lineup."[1]

Part of this trend back toward localization is caused by the new efficiencies of customization made possible by the Internet and increasingly flexible manufacturing processes. Indeed, a good example of the new "mass customization" is Dell Computer Corporation, which maintains no inventory and builds each computer to order. Also crucial has been the apparent rejection of the logic of globalism by trade unionists, environmentalists, and consumers so well demonstrated in Seattle during the World Trade Organization meetings in 2000. While there is a growing body of empirical research illustrating the risks and difficulties of global standardization,[2] contrary results also appear in the literature. Finally, prominent among firms' standardization strategies is Mattel's recently unsuccessful globalization of blonde Barbie. We correctly predicted in the last edition of this book that a better

---

[1]Rance Crain, "Agencies Press Get-Global Plans but Clients Face Local Realities," *Advertising Age*, February 14, 2000, p. 32.

[2]Carl Arthur Solbert, "The Perennial Issue of Adaptation or Standardization of International Marketing Communication: Organizational Contingencies and Performance," *Journal of International Marketing* 10, no. 3 (2002), pp. 1–21; Marios Theodosiou and Leonidas C. Leonidou, "Standardization versus Adaptation of International Marketing Strategy: An Integrative Assessment of the Empirical Research," *International Business Review* 12 (2003), pp. 141–171; Joan Enric Ricart, Michael J. Enright, Panjak Ghemawat, Stuart L. Hart, and Tarun Khanna, "New Frontiers in International Strategy," *Journal of International Business Studies* 35, no. 3 (2004), pp. 175–200.

The competition among soft drink bottlers in India is fierce. Here Coke and Pepsi combine to ruin the view of the Taj Mahal. Notice how the red of Coke stands out among its competitors in the picture. Of course, now Coca-Cola has purchased Thums Up, a prominent local brand—this is a strategy the company is applying around the world. But the red is a substantial competitive advantage both on store shelves and in outdoor advertising of the sort common in India and other developing countries. We're not sure who borrowed the "monsoon/thunder" slogans from whom.

approach was that of Disney, with its more culturally diverse line of "Disney Princesses" including Mulan (Chinese) and Jasmine (Arabic). Even though Bratz and Disney Princesses won this battle of the new "toy soldiers," the question is still not completely settled.[3]

Indeed, the debate itself is a wonderful example of the ethnocentrism of American managers and academics alike. That is, from the European or even the Japanese perspective markets are by definition international, and the special requirements of the huge American market must be considered from the beginning. Only in America can international market requirements be an afterthought.

Moreover, as the information explosion allows marketers to segment markets ever more finely, it is only the manufacturing or finance managers in companies who argue for standardization for the sake of economies of scale. From the marketing perspective customization is always best. The ideal market segment size, if customer satisfaction is the goal, is *one.* According to one expert, "Forward-looking, proactive firms have the ability and willingness . . . to accomplish both tasks [standardization and localization] simultaneously."[4]

---

[3]Erika Kinetz, "Putting Away Childish Things," *International Herald Tribune,* April 2–3, 2005, p. 16.

[4]Masaaki Kotabe, "Contemporary Research Trends in International Marketing: The 1960s," Chapter 17 in Alan Rugman and Thomas L. Brewer (eds.), *Oxford Handbook of International Business* (Oxford: Oxford University Press, 2001). Also consistent are the findings of Shouming Zou and S. Tamer Cavusgil, "The GMS: A Broad Conceptualization of Global Marketing Strategy and Its Effect on Firm Performance," *Journal of Marketing* 66, no. 4 (October 2002), pp. 40–57.

Items in the Disney Princess collection are on display at the Licensing International show at New York's Javits Convention Center. It will be interesting to see Barbie's (Mattel's) competitive response to the ethnic breadth of the Disney line. *(AP/Wide World Photos)*

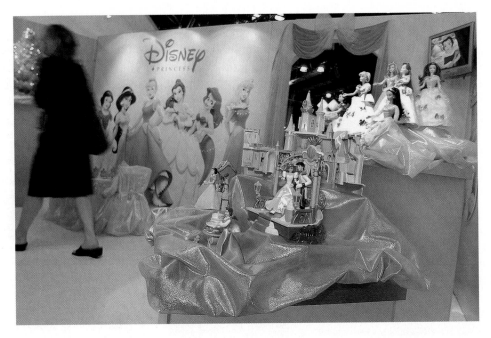

We believe things are actually simpler than that. As global markets continue to homogenize and diversify simultaneously, the best companies will avoid the trap of focusing on *country* as the primary segmentation variable. Other segmentation variables are often more important—for example, climate, language group, media habits, age, or income. The makers of Twix apparently think that media habits (that is, MTV viewership) supersede country, according to their latest segmentation scheme. At least one industry CEO concurred regarding media-based segmentation: "With media splintering into smaller and smaller communities of interest, it will become more and more important to reach those audiences wherever [whichever country] they may be. Today, media companies are increasingly delivering their content over a variety of platforms: broadcast—both TV and radio—and cable, online and print, big screen video, and the newest portable digital media. And advertisers are using the same variety of platforms to reach their desired audience." Finally, perhaps a few famous Italian brands are the best examples: Bruno Magli shoes, Gucci leather goods, and Ferrari cars sell to the highest-income segments globally. Indeed, for all three companies their U.S. sales are greater than their Italian sales.

In the 21st century, standardization versus adaptation is simply not the right question to ask.[5] Marketers will rightly always argue for the latter. Rather, the crucial question facing international marketers is what are the most efficient ways to segment markets. Country has been the most obvious segmentation variable, particularly for Americans. But as better communication systems continue to dissolve national borders, other dimensions of global markets are growing in salience.

The Nestlé Way: Evolution Not Revolution

Nestlé certainly hasn't been bothered by the debate on standardization versus adaptation. Nestlé has been international almost from its start in 1866 as a maker of infant formula. By 1920, the company was producing in Brazil, Australia, and the United States, and exporting to Hong Kong. Today, it sells more than 8,500 products produced in 489 factories in 193 countries. Nestlé is the world's biggest marketer of infant formula, powdered milk, instant coffee, chocolate, soups, and mineral water. It ranks second in ice cream, and in cereals it ties Ralston Purina and trails only Kellogg Company. Its products are sold in the most upscale supermarkets in Beverly Hills, California, and in huts in Nigeria, where women sell Nestlé bouillon cubes alongside homegrown tomatoes and onions. Although the company has no sales agents in North Korea, its products somehow find their way into stores there, too.

[5]Panjak Ghemawat, "Semiglobalization and International Business Strategy," *Journal of International Business Studies* 34 (2003), pp. 138–152.

The "Nestlé way" is to dominate its markets. Its overall strategy can be summarized in four points: (1) think and plan long term, (2) decentralize, (3) stick to what you know, and (4) adapt to local tastes. To see how Nestlé operates, take a look at its approach to Poland, one of the largest markets of the former Soviet bloc. Company executives decided at the outset that it would take too long to build plants and create brand awareness. Instead, the company pursued acquisitions and followed a strategy of "evolution not revolution." It purchased Goplana, Poland's second-best-selling chocolate maker (it bid for the No. 1 company but lost out) and carefully adjusted the end product via small changes every two months over a two-year period until it measured up to Nestlé's standards and was a recognizable Nestlé brand. These efforts, along with all-out marketing, put the company within striking distance of the market leader, Wedel. Nestlé also purchased a milk operation and, as it did in Mexico, India, and elsewhere, sent technicians into the field to help Polish farmers improve the quality and quantity of the milk it buys through better feeds and improved sanitation.

Nestlé's efforts in the Middle East are much longer term. The area currently represents only about 2 percent of the company's worldwide sales, and the markets, individually, are relatively small. Further, regional conflicts preclude most trade among the countries. Nevertheless, Nestlé anticipates that hostility will someday subside, and when that happens the company will be ready to sell throughout the entire region. Nestlé has set up a network of factories in five countries that can someday supply the entire region with different products. The company makes ice cream in Dubai and soups and cereals in Saudi Arabia. The Egyptian factory makes yogurt and bouillon, while Turkey produces chocolate. And a factory in Syria makes ketchup, a malted-chocolate energy food, instant noodles, and other products. If the obstacles between the countries come down, Nestlé will have a network of plants ready to provide a complete line to market in all the countries. In the meantime, factories produce and sell mostly in the countries in which they are located.

For many companies such a long-term strategy would not be profitable, but it works for Nestlé because the company relies on local ingredients and markets products that consumers can afford. The tomatoes and wheat used in the Syrian factory, for example, are major local agricultural products. Even if Syrian restrictions on trade remain, there are 14 million people to buy ketchup, noodles, and other products the company produces there. In all five countries and on all brands sold by Nestlé, the Nestlé name and the bird-in-a-nest trademark appear on every product.

Nestlé bills itself as "the only company that is truly dedicated to providing a complete range of food products to meet the needs and tastes of people from around the world, each hour of their day, throughout their entire lives."

Benefits of Global Marketing

Few firms have truly global operations balanced across major regional markets.[6] However, when large market segments can be identified, economies of scale in production and marketing can be important competitive advantages for global companies. As a case in point, Black & Decker Manufacturing Company—makers of electrical hand tools, appliances, and other consumer products—realized significant production cost savings when it adopted a pan-European strategy. It was able to reduce not only the number of motor sizes for the European market from 260 to 8 but also 15 different models to 8. Similarly, Ford estimates that by unifying product development, purchasing, and supply activities across several countries it can save up to $3 billion a year. Finally, while Japanese firms initially dominated the mobile phone business in their home market, international competitors pose growing challenges via better technologies developed through greater global penetration.[7]

Transfer of experience and know-how across countries through improved coordination and integration of marketing activities is also cited as a benefit of global operations. Global diversity in marketing talent leads to new approaches across markets. Unilever successfully introduced two global brands originally developed by two subsidiaries. Its South African subsidiary developed Impulse body spray, and a European branch developed a detergent

[6]Alan M. Rugman and Alaine Verbke, "A Perspective on Regional and Global Strategies of Multinational Enterprises," *Journal of International Business Studies* 35, no. 1 (2004), pp. 3–18.

[7]Kiyoshi Takenaka, "Japan Mobile Makers Face Challenges at Home, Abroad," *Reuters*, May 30, 2005.

CROSSING BORDERS 11.1   Swedish Takeout

Fifty years ago in the woods of southern Sweden, a minor revolution took place that has since changed the concept of retailing and created a mass market in a category where none previously existed. The catalyst of the change was and is IKEA, the Swedish furniture retailer and distributor that virtually invented the idea of self-service, takeout furniture. IKEA sells high-quality, reasonably priced, and innovatively designed furniture and home furnishings for a global marketplace.

The name was registered in Agunnaryd, Sweden, in 1943 by Ingvar Kamprad—the IK in the company's name. He entered the furniture market in 1950, and the first catalog was published in 1951. The first store didn't open until 1958 in Almhult. It became so incredibly popular that a year later the store had to add a restaurant for people who were traveling long distances to get there.

IKEA entered the United States in 1985. Although IKEA is global, most of the action takes place in Europe, with about 85 percent of the firm's $7 billion in sales. Nearly one-quarter of that comes from stores in Germany, while NAFTA units account for about $1 billion.

One reason for the relatively slow growth in the United States is that its stores are franchised by Netherlands-based Inter IKEA Systems, which carefully scrutinizes potential franchisees—individuals or companies—for strong financial backing and a proven record in retailing. The IKEA Group, based in Denmark, is a group of private companies owned by a charitable foundation in the Netherlands; they operate more than 100 stores. The Group also develops, purchases,

distributes, and sells IKEA products, which are available only in company stores. The items are purchased from more than 2,400 suppliers in 65 countries and shipped through 14 distribution centers.

Low price is built into the company's lines. Even catalog prices are guaranteed not to increase for one year. The drive to produce affordable products inadvertently put IKEA at the forefront of the environmental movement several decades ago. In addition to lowering costs, minimization of materials and packing addressed natural resource issues. Environmentalism remains an integral operational issue at IKEA. Even the company's catalog is completely recyclable and produced digitally rather than on film.

On the day that Russia's first IKEA store opened in 2000, the wait to get in was an hour. Highway traffic backed up for miles. More than 40,000 people crammed into the place, picking clean sections of the warehouse. The store still pulls in more than 100,000 customers per week. IKEA has big plans for Russia. Company officials dream of placing IKEA's simple shelves, kitchens, bathrooms, and bedrooms in millions of Russian apartments that haven't been remodeled since the Soviet days. And now IKEA is opening in Beijing.

Sources: Colin McMahon, "Russians Flock to IKEA as Store Battles Moscow," *Chicago Tribune*, May 17, 2000; Katarina Kling and Ingela Goteman, "IKEA CEO Anders Dahlvig on International Growth and IKEA's Unique Corporate Culture and Brand Identity," *Academy of Management Executive*, February 2003, pp. 31–37; Li Fangfang, "Ikea Revenue Up, Plans Giant Store in Beijing," *China Daily*, September 6, 2005.

---

that cleaned effectively in European hard water. Aluminum Company of America's (Alcoa) joint-venture partner in Japan produced aluminum sheets so perfect that U.S. workers, when shown samples, accused the company of hand-selecting the samples. Line workers were sent to the Japanese plant to learn the techniques, which were then transferred to the U.S. operations. Because of the benefits of such transfers of knowledge, Alcoa has changed its practice of sending managers overseas to "keep an eye on things" to sending line workers and managers to foreign locations to seek out new techniques and processes.

Marketing globally also ensures that marketers have access to the toughest customers. For example, in many product and service categories the Japanese consumer has been the hardest to please; the demanding customers are the reason that the highest-quality products and services often emanate from that country. Competing for Japanese customers provides firms with the best testing ground for high-quality products and services.

Diversity of markets served carries with it additional financial benefits.[8] Spreading the portfolio of markets served brings an important stability of revenues and operations to

---

[8]N. Capar and M. Kotabe have noted that for services firms the relationship between international diversification and firm performance can be curvilinear; see "The Relationship between International Diversification and Performance in Service Firms," *Journal of International Business Studies* 34, no. 4 (2003), pp. 345–355.

many global companies. Companies with global marketing operations suffered less during the Asian market downturn of the late 1990s than did firms specializing in the area. Firms that market globally are able to take advantage of changing financial circumstances in other ways as well. For example, as tax and tariff rates ebb and flow around the world, the most global companies are able to leverage the associated complexity to their advantage.

Planning for Global Markets

Planning is a systematized way of relating to the future. It is an attempt to manage the effects of external, uncontrollable factors on the firm's strengths, weaknesses, objectives, and goals to attain a desired end. Further, it is a commitment of resources to a country market to achieve specific goals. In other words, planning is the job of making things happen that might not otherwise occur.

Is there a difference between planning for a domestic company and for an international company? The principles of planning are not in themselves different, but the intricacies of the operating environments of the multinational corporation (i.e., host country, home, and corporate environments), its organizational structure, and the task of controlling a multi-country operation create differences in the complexity and process of international planning.

Planning allows for rapid growth of the international function, changing markets, increasing competition, and the turbulent challenges of different national markets. The plan must blend the changing parameters of external country environments with corporate objectives and capabilities to develop a sound, workable marketing program. A strategic plan commits corporate resources to products and markets to increase competitiveness and profits.

Planning relates to the formulation of goals and methods of accomplishing them, so it is both a process and a philosophy. Structurally, planning may be viewed as corporate, strategic, or tactical. International *corporate planning* is essentially long term, incorporating generalized goals for the enterprise as a whole. *Strategic planning* is conducted at the highest levels of management and deals with products, capital, and research, and long- and short-term goals of the company. *Tactical planning,* or market planning, pertains to specific actions and to the allocation of resources used to implement strategic planning goals in specific markets. Tactical plans are made at the local level and address marketing and advertising questions.

A major advantage to a multinational corporation (MNC) involved in planning is the discipline imposed by the process. An international marketer who has gone through the planning process has a framework for analyzing marketing problems and opportunities and a basis for coordinating information from different country markets. The process of planning may be as important as the plan itself because it forces decision makers to examine all factors that affect the success of a marketing program and involves those who will be responsible for its implementation. Another key to successful planning is evaluating company objectives, including management's commitment and philosophical orientation to international business. Finally, the planning process is a primary medium of organizational learning.

Company Objectives and Resources

Evaluation of a company's objectives and resources is crucial in all stages of planning for international operations.[9] Each new market can require a complete evaluation, including existing commitments, relative to the parent company's objectives and resources. As markets grow increasingly competitive, as companies find new opportunities, and as the cost of entering foreign markets increases, companies need such planning.

Defining objectives clarifies the orientation of the domestic and international divisions, permitting consistent policies. The lack of well-defined objectives has found companies rushing into promising foreign markets only to find activities that conflict with or detract from the companies' primary objectives.

Foreign market opportunities do not always parallel corporate objectives; it may be necessary to change the objectives, alter the scale of international plans, or abandon them.

---

[9]Peter J. Buckley and Niron Hashai, "A Global System View of Firm Boundaries," *Journal of International Business Studies* 35, no. 1 (2004), pp. 33–45.

CROSSING BORDERS 11.2 — There Was a Guy Riding a Bike and Talking on His Cell Phone

Bikers with cell phones are not an uncommon sight on streets throughout China—the problem for Lucent was how to get a piece of the action. As Aaron Fisher, general manager of wireless products for Lucent Microelectronics, explains, "There are a lot of screwdriver joint ventures in China, where a cell phone maker parachutes in a bag of parts and all the locals do is screw it together and ship it. There's no buildup of manufacturing know-how. The Chinese government is favoring companies that are doing more." There lay Lucent's chance, since "favoring" means choosing who does and who doesn't get a license to market cell phones in the country.

As a first step Lucent acquired more talent. In 1998 it bought Optima, a specialist in cell phone software based in Munich, Germany, for $65 million. Next it put together a team of Chinese nationals, including some working for other parts of its parent company, Lucent Technologies, which has six joint ventures, two wholly owned operations, and a new research center in China. The team then began approaching Chinese manufacturing companies with an offer they found hard to refuse: Let us put you in the cell phone business.

Lucent offered a basic design and production know-how for a phone circuit board with—no surprise—a three-piece Lucent chip. Most important, the circuit board met requirements for approval worldwide as a GSM phone. GSM, or Global System for Mobile Communications, is the most widely used cell phone technology in China as well as Europe. Admonished not to change a thing in the basic design, the Chinese company was free to dream up its own exterior plastic case, display, and keypad. Using Optima software, it could program the phone with special features: a visual display with Chinese characters, and, when keys are touched, notes from the Chinese musical scale, which differs from the Western one.

Sources: Philip Siekman, "The Secret of U.S. Exports: Great Products," *Fortune*, January 1, 2000, pp. 154–164; "Lucent Technologies Solves USB Bandwidth Bottleneck," *M2 Presswire*, May 23, 2000; "Lucent to Open Research Center in China," *New York Times*, June 6, 2003, p. 4; and most recently perhaps Lucent has done too much for its partners in China as it is being investigated for violations of the Foreign Corrupt Practices Act there—see Peter S. Goodman, "Kickbacks in China Can Cause Trouble," *Wall Street Journal Europe*, August 24, 2005, p. A3.

One market may offer immediate profit but have a poor long-run outlook, while another may offer the reverse.[10] Only when corporate objectives are clear can such differences be reconciled effectively.

International Commitment

The planning approach taken by an international firm affects the degree of internationalization to which management is philosophically committed. Such commitment affects the specific international strategies and decisions of the firm. After company objectives have been identified, management needs to determine whether it is prepared to make the level of commitment required for successful international operations—commitment in terms of dollars to be invested, personnel for managing the international organization, and determination to stay in the market long enough to realize a return on these investments.

The degree of commitment to an international marketing cause reflects the extent of a company's involvement. A company uncertain of its prospects is likely to enter a market timidly, using inefficient marketing methods, channels, or organizational forms, thus setting the stage for the failure of a venture that might have succeeded with full commitment and support by the parent company. Any long-term marketing plan should be fully supported by senior management and have realistic time goals set for sales growth. Occasionally, casual market entry is successful, but more often than not, market success requires long-term commitment.

The Planning Process

Whether a company is marketing in several countries or is entering a foreign market for the first time, planning is essential to success. The first-time foreign marketer must decide what products to develop, in which markets, and with what level of resource commitment. For the company that is already committed, the key decisions involve allocating effort and

---

[10]Farok J. Contractor, Sumit K. Kundu, and Chin-Chun Hsu, "A Three-Stage Theory of International Expansion: The Link between Multinationality and Performance in the Service Sector," *Journal of International Business Studies* 34, Issue 1 (2003), pp. 5–18.

Exhibit 11.1
International Planning Process

Information derived from each phase, market research, and evaluation of program performance

| **Phase 1** Preliminary analysis and screening: Matching company/country needs | **Phase 2** Adapting the marketing mix to target markets | **Phase 3** Developing the marketing plan | **Phase 4** Implementation and control |

Environmental factors, company character, and screening criteria

Matching mix requirements

Marketing plan development

Implementation, evaluation, and control

Company character
- Philosophy
- Objectives
- Resources
- Management style
- Organization
- Financial limitations
- Management and marketing skills
- Products
- Other

Home-country constraints
- Political
- Legal
- Economic
- Other

Host-country(s) constraints
- Economic
- Political/legal
- Competitive
- Level of technology
- Culture
- Structures of distribution
- Geography
- Competition

Product
- Adaptation
- Brand name
- Features
- Packaging
- Service
- Warranty
- Style
- Standards

Price
- Credit
- Discounts

Promotion
- Advertising
- Personal selling
- Media
- Message
- Sales promotion

Distribution
- Logistics
- Channels

- Situation analysis

- Objectives and goals

- Strategy and tactics

- Selecting mode of entry

- Budgets

- Action programs

- Objectives

- Standards

- Assign responsibility

- Measure performance

- Correct for error

resources among countries and product(s), deciding on new markets to develop or old ones to withdraw from, and determining which products to develop or drop. Guidelines and systematic procedures are necessary for evaluating international opportunities and risks and for developing strategic plans to take advantage of such opportunities. The process illustrated in Exhibit 11.1 offers a systematic guide to planning for the multinational firm operating in several countries.

Phase 1: Preliminary Analysis and Screening—Matching Company and Country Needs.
Whether a company is new to international marketing or heavily involved, an evaluation of potential markets is the first step in the planning process. A critical first step in the international planning process is deciding in which existing country market to make a market investment. A company's strengths and weaknesses, products, philosophies, and objectives must be matched with a country's constraining factors and market potential. In the first part of the planning process, countries are analyzed and screened to eliminate those that do not offer sufficient potential for further consideration. Emerging markets pose a special problem because many have inadequate marketing infrastructures, distribution channels are underdeveloped, and income level and distribution vary among countries.

The next step is to establish screening criteria against which prospective countries can be evaluated. These criteria are ascertained by an analysis of company objectives, resources, and other corporate capabilities and limitations. It is important to determine the reasons for entering a foreign market and the returns expected from such an investment.

A company's commitment to international business and its objectives for going international are important in establishing evaluation criteria. Minimum market potential, minimum profit, return on investment, acceptable competitive levels, standards of political stability, acceptable legal requirements, and other measures appropriate for the company's products are examples of the evaluation criteria to be established.

Once evaluation criteria are set, a complete analysis of the environment within which a company plans to operate is made. The environment consists of the uncontrollable elements discussed earlier and includes both home-country and host-country constraints, marketing objectives, and any other company limitations or strengths that exist at the beginning of each planning period. Although an understanding of uncontrollable environments is important in domestic market planning, the task is more complex in foreign marketing because each country under consideration presents the foreign marketer with a different set of unfamiliar environmental constraints. This stage in the planning process, more than anything else, distinguishes international from domestic marketing planning.

The results of Phase 1 provide the marketer with the basic information necessary to evaluate the potential of a proposed country market, identify problems that would eliminate the country from further consideration, identify environmental elements that need further analysis, determine which part of the marketing mix can be standardized and which part of and how the marketing mix must be adapted to meet local market needs, and develop and implement a marketing action plan.

Information generated in Phase 1 helps companies avoid the kinds of mistakes that plagued Radio Shack Corporation, a leading merchandiser of consumer electronic equipment in the United States, when it first went international. Radio Shack's early attempts at international marketing in western Europe resulted in a series of costly mistakes that could have been avoided had it properly analyzed the uncontrollable elements of the countries targeted for its first attempt at multinational marketing. The company staged its first Christmas promotion for December 25 in Holland, unaware that the Dutch celebrate St. Nicholas Day and give gifts on December 6. Furthermore, legal problems in various countries interfered with some plans; the company was unaware that most European countries have laws prohibiting the sale of citizen-band radios, one of Radio Shack's most lucrative U.S. products and one it expected to sell in Europe. German courts promptly stopped a free flashlight promotion in German stores because giveaways violate German sales laws. In Belgium, the company overlooked a law requiring a government tax stamp on all window signs, and poorly selected store sites resulted in many of the new stores closing shortly after opening.

With the analysis in Phase 1 completed, the decision maker faces the more specific task of selecting country target markets and segments, identifying problems and opportunities in these markets, and beginning the process of creating marketing programs.

Phase 2: Adapting the Marketing Mix to Target Markets.

A more detailed examination of the components of the marketing mix is the purpose of Phase 2. When target markets are selected, the market mix must be evaluated in light of the data generated in Phase 1. Incorrect decisions at this point lead to products inappropriate for the intended market or to costly mistakes in pricing, advertising, and promotion. The primary goal of Phase 2 is to decide on a marketing mix adjusted to the cultural constraints imposed by the uncontrollable elements of the environment that effectively achieves corporate objectives and goals.

The process used by the Nestlé Company is an example of the type of analysis done in Phase 2. Each product manager has a country fact book that includes much of the information suggested in Phase 1. The country fact book analyzes in detail a variety of culturally related questions. In Germany, the product manager for coffee must furnish answers to a number of questions. How does a German rank coffee in the hierarchy of consumer products? Is Germany a high or a low per capita consumption market? (These facts alone can be of enormous consequence. In Sweden the annual per capita consumption of coffee is 7.5 kilograms, in the United States 2.2, and in Japan it's only 0.8!)[11] How is coffee used—in

---

[11]Euromonitor, 2005.

Given all the tea in China, it's particularly amazing that now you can buy a mocha frappuccino in the Forbidden City in Beijing. The yellow roof symbolizes imperial grounds, but we don't think the Emperor had grounds of the coffee sort in mind when he built the place in the 1400s. China joining the WTO has opened up the market in new ways to franchisers from around the world. However, the store opened in 2000 to strong protests by the local media.

bean form, ground, or powdered? If it is ground, how is it brewed? Which coffee is preferred—Brazilian Santos blended with Colombian coffee, or robusta from the Ivory Coast? Is it roasted? Do the people prefer dark roasted or blonde coffee? (The color of Nestlé's soluble coffee must resemble as closely as possible the color of the coffee consumed in the country.)

As a result of the answers to these and other questions, Nestlé produces 200 types of instant coffee, from the dark robust espresso preferred in Latin countries to the lighter blends popular in the United States. Almost $50 million a year is spent in four research laboratories around the world experimenting with new shadings in color, aroma, and flavor. Do the Germans drink coffee after lunch or with their breakfast? Do they take it black or with cream or milk? Do they drink coffee in the evening? Do they sweeten it? (In France, the answers are clear: In the morning, coffee with milk; at noon, black coffee—that is, two totally different coffees.) At what age do people begin drinking coffee? Is it a traditional beverage, as in France; is it a form of rebellion among the young, as in England, where coffee drinking has been taken up in defiance of tea-drinking parents; or is it a gift, as in Japan? There is a coffee boom in tea-drinking Japan, where Nescafé is considered a luxury gift item; instead of chocolates and flowers, Nescafé is toted in fancy containers to dinners and birthday parties. With such depth of information, the product manager can evaluate the marketing mix in terms of the information in the country fact book.

Phase 2 also permits the marketer to determine possibilities for applying marketing tactics across national markets. The search for similar segments across countries can often lead to opportunities for economies of scale in marketing programs. This was the case for Nestlé when research revealed that young coffee drinkers in England and Japan had identical motivations. As a result, Nestlé now uses principally the same message in both markets.

Frequently, the results of the analysis in Phase 2 indicate that the marketing mix would require such drastic adaptation that a decision not to enter a particular market is made. For example, a product may have to be reduced in physical size to fit the needs of the market, but the additional manufacturing cost of a smaller size may be too high to justify market entry. Also, the price required to be profitable might be too high for a majority of the market to afford. If there is no way to reduce the price, sales potential at the higher price may be too low to justify entry.

The answers to three major questions are generated in Phase 2:

1. Are there identifiable market segments that allow for common marketing mix tactics across countries?

2. Which cultural/environmental adaptations are necessary for successful acceptance of the marketing mix?

3. Will adaptation costs allow profitable market entry?

Based on the results in Phase 2, a second screening of countries may take place, with some countries dropped from further consideration. The next phase in the planning process is development of a marketing plan.

Phase 3: Developing the Marketing Plan.

At this stage of the planning process, a marketing plan is developed for the target market—whether it is a single country or a global market set. The marketing plan begins with a situation analysis and culminates in the selection of an entry mode and a specific action program for the market. The specific plan establishes what is to be done, by whom, how it is to be done, and when. Included are budgets and sales and profit expectations. Just as in Phase 2, a decision not to enter a specific market may be made if it is determined that company marketing objectives and goals cannot be met.

Phase 4: Implementation and Control.

A "go" decision in Phase 3 triggers implementation of specific plans and anticipation of successful marketing.

However, the planning process does not end at this point. All marketing plans require coordination and control during the period of implementation.[12] Many businesses do not control marketing plans as thoroughly as they could even though continuous monitoring and control could increase their success. An evaluation and control system requires performance-objective action, that is, bringing the plan back on track should standards of performance fall short. A global orientation facilitates the difficult but extremely important management tasks of coordinating and controlling the complexities of international marketing.

Although the model is presented as a series of sequential phases, the planning process is a dynamic, continuous set of interacting variables with information continuously building among phases. The phases outline a crucial path to be followed for effective, systematic planning.

Utilizing a planning process encourages the decision maker to consider all variables that affect the success of a company's plan. Furthermore, it provides the basis for viewing all country markets and their interrelationships as an integrated global unit. By following the guidelines presented in Part Six of this text, "The Country Notebook—A Guide for Developing a Marketing Plan," the international marketer can put the strategic planning process into operation.

As a company expands into more foreign markets with several products, it becomes more difficult to efficiently manage all products across all markets. Marketing planning helps the marketer focus on all the variables to be considered for successful global marketing. With the information developed in the planning process and a country market selected, the decision regarding the entry mode can be made. The choice of mode of entry is one of the more critical decisions for the firm because the choice will define the firm's operations and affect all future decisions in that market.

Alternative Market-Entry Strategies

When a company makes the commitment to go international, it must choose an entry strategy. This decision should reflect an analysis of market characteristics (such as potential sales, strategic importance, strengths of local resources,[13] cultural differences,[14] and country restrictions) and company capabilities and characteristics, including the degree of near-market knowledge, marketing involvement, and commitment that management is prepared to make.[15] Even so, many firms appear to simply imitate others in the industry or repeat their own successful entry strategies—this is not what we recommend. The approach to foreign marketing can range from minimal investment with infrequent and indirect exporting and little thought given to market development, to large investments of capital and management in an effort to capture and maintain a permanent, specific share of world markets.[16] Depending on the firm's objectives and market characteristics, either approach can be profitable.

---

[12]Janell D. Townsend, Sengun Yeniyurt, Z. Seyda Deligonul, and S. Tamer Cavusgil, "Exploring Marketing Program Antecedents of Performance in a Global Company," *Journal of International Marketing* 12, no. 4 (2004), pp. 1–24.

[13]Ted London and Stuart L. Hart, "Reinventing Strategies for Emerging Markets: Beyond the Transnational Model," *Journal of International Business Studies* 35, no. 5 (2004), pp. 350–370.

[14]Keith D. Brouthers, "Institutional, Cultural, and Transaction Cost Influences on Entry Mode Choice and Performance," *Journal of International Business Studies* 33, no. 2 (2002), pp. 203–231; Laszlo Tihanyi, David A. Griffith, and Craig Russell, "The Effect of Cultural Distance on Entry Mode Choice, International Diversification, and MNE Performance: A Meta-Analysis," *Journal of International Business Studies* 36, no. 3 (2005), pp. 270–283; Torben Pedersen and Bent Pedersen, "Learning about Foreign Markets: Are Entrant Firms Exposed to a 'Shock Effect?'" *Journal of International Marketing* 12, no. 1 (2004), pp. 103–123.

[15]Naresh K. Malhotra, James Agarwal, and Francis M. Ulgado, "Internationalization and Entry Modes: A Multitheoretical Framework and Research Propositions," *Journal of International Marketing* 11, no. 4 (2003), pp. 1–31.

[16]A. Delios and W. J. Henisz, "Policy Uncertainty and the Sequence of Entry by Japanese Firms, 1980–1998," *Journal of International Business Studies* 34, no. 3 (2003), pp. 227–241.

Exhibit 11.2
Alternative Market-Entry
Strategies

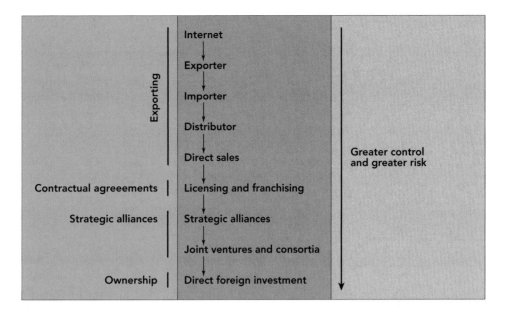

Companies most often begin with modest export involvement. As sales revenues grow the firms often proceed down through the series of steps listed in Exhibit 11.2.[17] Also, experience in larger numbers of foreign markets can increase the number of entry strategies used. In fact, a company in several country markets may employ a variety of entry modes because each country market poses a different set of conditions. For example, JLG Industries in Pennsylvania makes self-propelled aerial work platforms and sells them all over the world. The firm actually manufactured in Scotland and Australia beginning in the 1970s, but it was forced to close the plants in the 1990s. However, the company's international sales have burgeoned again. The growth in European business is allowing for a simplification of distribution channels through elimination of middlemen; dealerships have been purchased in Germany, Norway, Sweden, and the United Kingdom. JLG set up dealership joint ventures in Thailand and Brazil, and sales have been brisk despite economic problems in those countries. The company also has established sales and service businesses from scratch in Scotland, Italy, and South Africa.

A company has four different modes of foreign market entry from which to select: exporting, contractual agreements, strategic alliances, and direct foreign investment. The different modes of entry can be further classified on the basis of the equity or nonequity requirements of each mode. The amount of equity required by the company to use different modes affects the risk, return, and control that it will have in each mode. For example, indirect exporting requires no equity investment and thus has a low risk, low rate of return, and little control, whereas direct foreign investment requires the most equity of the four modes and creates the greatest risk, while offering the most control. Although direct foreign investment is the riskiest of the four modes, it has the potential for the highest return and affords the greatest control over all activities.

Exporting   Exporting accounts for some 10 percent of global economic activity.[18] Exporting can be either direct or indirect. With *direct exporting* the company sells to a customer in another country. This is the most common approach employed by companies taking their first international step because the risks of financial loss can be minimized. In contrast, *indirect exporting* usually means that the company sells to a buyer (importer or distributor) in the

[17]Mauro F. Guillen, "Experience, Imitation, and the Sequence of Foreign Entry: Wholly Owned and Joint-Venture Manufacturing by South Korean Firms and Business Groups in China, 1987–1995," *Journal of International Business Studies* 34, no. 2 (2003), pp. 185–198.

[18]Neil A. Morgan, Anna Kaleka, and Constantine S. Katsikeas, "Antecedents of Export Venture Performance: A Theoretical Model and Empirical Assessment," *Journal of Marketing* 68, no. 1 (2004), pp. 90–108.

home country, who in turn exports the product. Customers include large retailers such as Wal-Mart or Sears, wholesale supply houses, trading companies, and others that buy to supply customers abroad.

Early motives for exporting often are to skim the cream from the market or gain business to absorb overhead.[19] Early involvement may be opportunistic and come in the form of an inquiry from a foreign customer or initiatives from an importer in the foreign market. This is the case with Pilsner Urquell, the revered Czech beer, which for many years has sold in the United States through Guinness Bass Import Corporation (GBIC). However, recently the Czech firm severed its relationship with the importer because it wasn't getting the attention of the other imported beers in GBIC's portfolio. The firm is now establishing its own sales force of two dozen to handle five key metropolitan areas in the United States. Prices are being reduced and a global media plan is being developed with a British ad agency. The firm may import other brands from the Czech parent as well.

Exporting is also a common approach for mature international companies with strong marketing capabilities.[20] Some of America's largest companies engage in exporting as their major market-entry method. (Boeing is the best example, as America's largest exporter.) The mechanics of exporting and the different middlemen available to facilitate the exporting process are discussed in detail in Chapters 14 and 15.

The Internet.   The Internet is becoming increasingly important as a foreign market entry method. Initially, Internet marketing focused on domestic sales.[21] However, a surprisingly large number of companies started receiving orders from customers in other countries, resulting in the concept of international Internet marketing (IIM). PicturePhone Direct, a mail-order reseller of desktop videoconferencing equipment, posted its catalog on the Internet expecting to concentrate on the northeastern United States. To the company's surprise, PicturePhone's sales staff received orders from Israel, Portugal, and Germany.

Other companies have had similar experiences and are actively designing Internet catalogs targeting specific countries with multilingual Web sites. Dell Computer Corporation has expanded its strategy of selling computers over the Internet to foreign sites as well. Dell began selling computers via the Internet to Malaysia, Australia, Hong Kong, New Zealand, Singapore, Taiwan, and other Asian countries through a "virtual store" on the Internet. The same selling mode has been launched in Europe.

Amazon.com has jumped into the IIM game with both feet. It hired a top Apple Computer executive to manage its fast-growing international business. Just 15 months after setting up book and CD e-tailing sites in Germany and the United Kingdom, the new overseas Amazon Web sites have surged to become the most heavily trafficked commercial venues in both markets. Among the companies with the most profitable e-tailing businesses are former catalog companies such as Lands' End and L.L. Bean. However, Lands' End's successes in foreign markets have been tainted by recent problems in Germany. German law bans "advertising gimmicks"—and that's what regulators there call Lands' End's "unconditional lifetime guarantee." Indeed, the firm took the dispute all the way to the German supreme court and lost. Moreover, the uncertainty swirling around the EU's approach to taxing Internet sales is great cause for concern.

As discussed in Chapter 2, the full impact of the Internet on international marketing is yet to be determined. However, IIM should not be overlooked as an alternative market-entry strategy by the small or large company. Coupled with the international scope of credit card companies such as MasterCard and Visa and international delivery services such as UPS and Federal Express, deliveries to foreign countries can be relatively effortless.

---

[19]Luis Filipe Lages and Cristiana Raquel Lages, "The STEP Scale: A Measure of Short-Term Export Performance," *Journal of International Marketing* 12, no. 1 (2004), pp. 36–56.

[20]Shaoming Zou, Eric Fang, and Shuming Zhao, "The Effect of Export Marketing Capabilities on Export Performance: An Investigation of Chinese Exporters," *Journal of International Marketing* 11, no. 4 (2003), pp. 32–55.

[21]Ikechi Ekeledo and K. Sivakumar, "The Impact of E-Commerce on Entry-Mode Strategies of Services Firms: A Conceptual Framework and Research Propositions," *Journal of International Marketing* 12, no. 4 (2004), pp. 46–70.

Direct Sales. Particularly for high technology and big ticket industrial products, a direct sales force may be required in a foreign country. This may mean establishing an office with local and/or expatriate managers and staff, depending of course on the size of the market and potential sales revenues. Sales management is one of the topics covered in detail in Chapter 17.

Contractual Agreements

Contractual agreements are long-term, nonequity associations between a company and another in a foreign market. Contractual agreements generally involve the transfer of technology, processes, trademarks, or human skills. In short, they serve as a means of transfer of knowledge rather than equity.

Licensing.

A means of establishing a foothold in foreign markets without large capital outlays is *licensing*. Patent rights, trademark rights, and the rights to use technological processes are granted in foreign licensing. It is a favorite strategy for small and medium-sized companies, although by no means limited to such companies. Common examples of industries that use licensing arrangements in foreign markets are television programming and pharmaceuticals. Not many confine their foreign operations to licensing alone; it is generally viewed as a supplement to exporting or manufacturing, rather than the only means of entry into foreign markets. The advantages of licensing are most apparent when capital is scarce, import restrictions forbid other means of entry, a country is sensitive to foreign ownership, or patents and trademarks must be protected against cancellation for nonuse. The risks of licensing are choosing the wrong partner, quality and other production problems, payment problems, contract enforcement, and loss of marketing control.

Although licensing may be the least profitable way of entering a market, the risks and headaches are less than for direct investments. It is a legitimate means of capitalizing on intellectual property in a foreign market, and such agreements can also benefit the economies of target countries. Licensing takes several forms. Licenses may be granted for production processes, for the use of a trade name, or for the distribution of imported products. Licenses may be closely controlled or be autonomous, and they permit expansion without great capital or personnel commitment if licensees have the requisite capabilities. Not all experiences with licensing are successful because of the burden of finding, supervising, and inspiring licensees.

Franchising.

Franchising is a rapidly growing form of licensing in which the franchiser provides a standard package of products, systems, and management services, and the franchisee provides market knowledge, capital, and personal involvement in management. The combination of skills permits flexibility in dealing with local market conditions and yet provides the parent firm with a reasonable degree of control. The franchiser can follow through on marketing of the products to the point of final sale. It is an important form of vertical market integration. Potentially, the franchise system provides an effective blending of skill centralization and operational decentralization; it has become an increasingly important form of international marketing. In some cases, franchising is having a profound effect on traditional businesses. In England, for example, annual franchised sales of fast foods are estimated at nearly $2 billion, which accounts for 30 percent of all foods eaten outside the home.

Prior to 1970, international franchising was not a major activity. A survey by the International Franchising Association revealed that only 14 percent of its member firms had franchises outside of the United States, and the majority of those were in Canada. Now more than 30,000 franchises of U.S. firms are located in countries throughout the world. Franchises include soft drinks, motels (including membership "organizations" like Best Western International), retailing, fast foods, car rentals, automotive services, recreational services, and a variety of business services from print shops to sign shops. Canada is the dominant market for U.S. franchisers, with Japan and the United Kingdom second and third in importance. The Asia-Pacific Rim has seen rapid growth as companies look to Asia for future expansion.

Despite temporary setbacks during the global economic downturn right after the turn of the millennium, franchising is still expected to be the fastest-growing market-entry strategy.

CROSSING BORDERS 11.3 The Men Who Would Be Pizza Kings

"All the water served in the restaurant has been passed by the manager" states the message at the bottom of a menu in a Delhi eatery. Pizza menus won't boast of such startling messages, but you'll see eye-catching entries all the same—chatpata chana masala, a chettinad, or a chicken tikka.

In more senses than one, pizza outlets are set to mushroom all over India. The wait for pizza lovers in places like Surat, Kochi, and Bhubaneshwar is finally over. Domino's, the home delivery specialist, and Pizza Hut, a part of Yum! Brands, have plans to significantly increase the number of their restaurants. Chennai-based Pizza Corner, having established itself in the south, has now boldly ventured into the north—it has already opened three outlets in Delhi and is planning to increase the number to eight.

While Domino's is trying to dish out a pizza for every ethnic group, Pizza Hut is trying to expose Indians to the pizza's Chinese cousin. It has come up with the "Oriental," which has hot Chinese sauce, spring onions, and sesame seeds as its toppings. It's been developed based on the Indian fondness for Chinese food. This is not to say that Pizza Hut does not pay heed to the spice-soaked Indian version. Apart from the Oriental, it is also dishing out a spicy paneer tikka pizza. Milk shakes are on the menu, too. Most recently an Indian dairy company has been eating market share in both pizzas and ice cream. Things are getting interesting there fast. And, in spite of Kipling's prophesy that the two streams shall never meet, the Indianization of the pizza is truly here.

Sources: Smita Tripathi, "Butter Chicken Pizza in Ludhiana," *Business Standard*, June 17, 2000, p. 2; Rahul Chandawarkar, "Collegians Mix Money with Study Material," *Times of India*, June 22, 2000; Thomas L. Friedman, *The World Is Flat* (New York: Farrar, Straus, and Giroux, 2005).

Franchises were often among the first types of foreign retail business to open in the emerging market economies of Eastern Europe, the former republics of Russia, and China. McDonald's is in Moscow (its first store seated 700 inside and had 27 cash registers), and Kentucky Fried Chicken is in China (the Beijing KFC store has the highest sales volume of any KFC store in the world). The same factors that spurred the growth of franchising in the U.S. domestic economy have led to its growth in foreign markets. Franchising is an attractive form of corporate organization for companies wishing to expand quickly with low capital investment. The franchising system combines the knowledge of the franchiser with the local knowledge and entrepreneurial spirit of the franchisee. Foreign laws and regulations are friendly toward franchising because it tends to foster local ownership, operations, and employment.

Two types of franchise agreements are used by franchising firms—master franchise and licensing—either of which can have a country's government as one partner. The master franchise is the most inclusive agreement and the method used in more than half of the international franchises. The *master franchise* gives the franchisee the rights to a specific area (many are for an entire country), with the authority to sell or establish subfranchises. The McDonald's franchise in Moscow is a master agreement owned by a Canadian firm and its partner, the Moscow City Council Department of Food Services.

Licensing a local franchisee the right to use a product, good, service, trademark, patent, or other asset for a fee is a second type of franchise arrangement. Coca-Cola Company licenses local bottlers in an area or region to manufacture and market Coca-Cola using syrup sold by Coca-Cola. Rental-car companies often enter a foreign market by licensing a local franchisee to operate a rental system under the trademark of the parent company.

Lil'Orbits,[22] a Minneapolis-based company that sells donut-making equipment and ingredients to entrepreneurs, is an example of how a small company can use licensing and franchising to enter a foreign market. Lil'Orbits sells a donut maker that turns out 1.5-inch donuts while the customer waits. The typical buyer in the United States buys equipment and mix directly from the company without royalties or franchise fees. The buyer has a small shop or kiosk and sells donuts by the dozen for takeout or individually along with a beverage.

---

[22]www.lilorbits.com, 2005.

Successful in the United States, Lil'Orbits ran an advertisement in *Commercial News USA,* a magazine showcasing products and services in foreign countries, that attracted 400 inquiries. Pleased with the response, the company set up an international franchise operation based on royalties and franchise fees. Now a network of international franchised distributors markets the machines and ingredients to potential vendors. The distributors pay Lil'Orbits a franchise fee and buy machines and ingredients directly from Lil'Orbits or from one of the licensed vendors worldwide, from which Lil'Orbits receives a royalty. This entry strategy has enabled the company to enter foreign markets with minimum capital investment outside the home country. The company has over 20,000 franchised dealers in 85 countries. About 60 percent of the company's business is international.

Although franchising enables a company to expand quickly with minimum capital, there are costs associated with servicing franchisees. For example, to accommodate different tastes around the world, Lil'Orbits had to develop a more pastrylike, less-sweet mix than that used in the United States. Other cultural differences have had to be met as well. For example, customers in France and Belgium could not pronounce the trade name, Lil'Orbits, so Orbie is used instead. Toppings also had to be adjusted to accommodate different tastes. Cinnamon sugar is the most widely accepted topping, but in China, cinnamon is considered a medicine, so only sugar is used. In the Mediterranean region, the Greeks like honey, and chocolate sauce is popular in Spain. Powdered sugar is more popular than granulated sugar in France, where the donuts are eaten in cornucopia cups instead of on plates.

Strategic International Alliances

A *strategic international alliance (SIA)* is a business relationship established by two or more companies to cooperate out of mutual need and to share risk in achieving a common objective. Strategic alliances have grown in importance over the last few decades as a competitive strategy in global marketing management. SIAs are sought as a way to shore up weaknesses and increase competitive strengths. Firms enter into strategic international alliances for several reasons: opportunities for rapid expansion into new markets, access to new technology,[23] more efficient production and innovation,[24] reduced marketing costs, strategic competitive moves, and access to additional sources of products[25] and capital. Finally, evidence suggests that SIAs often contribute nicely to profits.[26]

Perhaps the most visible SIAs are now in the airlines industry. American Airlines, Cathay Pacific, British Airways, Canadian Airlines, Aer Lingus, and Quantas are partners in the Oneworld Alliance, which integrates schedules and mileage programs. Competing with Oneworld are the Star (led by United and Lufthansa) and SkyTeam (led by Air France, Northwestern, and KLM). These kinds of strategic international alliances imply that there is a common objective; that one partner's weakness is offset by the other's strength; that reaching the objective alone would be too costly, take too much time, or be too risky; and that together their respective strengths make possible what otherwise would be unattainable. For example, during the recent turmoil in the global airline industry Star Alliance began moving in the direction of buying aircraft, a new strategic innovation. In short, an SIA is a synergistic relationship established to achieve a common goal in which both parties benefit.

An SIA with multiple objectives involves C-Itoh (Japan), Tyson Foods (United States), and Provemex (Mexico). It is an alliance that processes Japanese-style yakitori (bits of marinated and grilled chicken on a bamboo stick) for export to Japan and other Asian countries. Each company had a goal and made a contribution to the alliance. C-Itoh's goal was to find a lower-cost supply of yakitori; because it is so labor intensive, it was becoming increasingly

[23]Bernard L. Simonin, "An Empirical Investigation of the Process of Knowledge Transfer in International Strategic Alliances," *Journal of International Business Studies* 35, no. 5 (2004), pp. 407–427.

[24]Diane Brady, "Reaping the Wind," *BusinessWeek*, October 11, 2004, pp. 201–202.

[25]Janet Y. Murray, Masaaki Kotabe, and Joe Nan Zhou, "Strategic Alliance–Based Sourcing and Market Performance: Evidence from Foreign Firms Operating in China," *Journal of International Business Studies* 36, no. 2 (2005), pp. 187–208.

[26]Africa Arino, "Measures of Strategic Alliance Performance: An Analysis of Construct Validity," *Journal of International Business Studies* 34, no. 1 (2003), pp. 66–79.

In the Wings strategic alliance, U.S.-based Northwest Airlines and Dutch KLM share several aspects of their operations including ticketing and reservations, catering, cargo, and airport slots. As the global airline industry consolidates after September 11, 2001, more strategic partnerships are being formed.

costly and noncompetitive to produce in Japan. C-Itoh's contribution was access to its distribution system and markets throughout Japan and Asia. Tyson's goal was new markets for its dark chicken meat, a by-product of demand for mostly white meat in the U.S. market. Tyson exported some of its excess dark meat to Asia and knew that C-Itoh wanted to expand its supplier base. But Tyson faced the same high labor costs as C-Itoh. Provemex, the link that made it all work, had as its goal expansion beyond raising and slaughtering chickens into higher value-added products for international markets. Provemex's contribution was to provide highly cost-competitive labor.

Through the alliance, they all benefited. Provemex acquired the know-how to bone the dark meat used in yakitori and was able to vertically integrate its operations and secure a foothold in a lucrative export market. Tyson earned more from the sale of surplus chicken legs than was previously possible and gained an increased share of the Asian market. C-Itoh had a steady supply of competitively priced yakitori for its vast distribution and marketing network. This is a collaborative relationship: Three companies with individual strengths created a successful alliance in which each contributes and each benefits.

Many companies also are entering SIAs to be in a strategic position to be competitive and to benefit from the expected growth in the single European market. As a case in point, when General Mills wanted a share of the rapidly growing breakfast-cereal market in Europe, it joined with Nestlé to create Cereal Partners Worldwide. The European cereal market was projected to be worth hundreds of millions of dollars as health-conscious Europeans changed their breakfast diet from eggs and bacon to dry cereal. General Mills' main U.S. competitor, Kellogg, had been in Europe since 1920 and controlled about half of the market.

For General Mills to enter the market from scratch would have been extremely costly. Although the cereal business uses cheap commodities as its raw materials, it is both capital and marketing intensive; sales volume must be high before profits begin to develop. Only recently has Kellogg earned significant profits in Europe. For General Mills to reach its goal alone would have required a manufacturing base and a massive sales force. Further, Kellogg's stranglehold on supermarkets would have been difficult for an unknown to breach easily. The solution was a joint venture with Nestlé. Nestlé had everything General Mills lacked—a well-known brand name, a network of plants, and a powerful distribution system—except for the one thing that General Mills could provide: strong cereal brands.

The deal was mutually beneficial. General Mills provided the knowledge in cereal technology, including some of its proprietary manufacturing equipment, its stable of proven brands, and its knack for pitching these products to consumers. Nestlé provided its name on the box, access to retailers, and production capacity that could be converted to making General Mills' cereals. In time, Cereal Partners Worldwide intends to extend its marketing effort beyond Europe. In Asia, Africa, and Latin America, Cereal Partners Worldwide will have an important advantage over the competition because Nestlé is a dominant food producer.

As international strategic alliances have grown in importance, more emphasis has been placed on a systematic approach to forming them. Most experts in the field agree that following the steps outlined in Exhibit 11.3 will lead to successful and high-performance strategic alliances.[27] Of course, in international business there are no guarantees. And a key activity in all the steps outlined in the exhibit is international negotiation, the subject of Chapter 19.[28]

International Joint Ventures. International joint ventures (IJVs) as a means of foreign market entry have accelerated sharply during the last 20 years. Besides serving as a

[27]Robert E. Spekman, Lynn A. Isabella, with Thomas C. MacAvoy, *Alliance Competence* (New York: Wiley, 2000).

[28]David G. Sirmon and Peter J. Lane, "A Model of Cultural Differences and International Alliance Performance," *Journal of International Business Studies* 35, no. 4 (2004), pp. 306–319.

Exhibit 11.3   Building Strategic Alliances

Primary Relationship Activity	Typical Actions, Interactions, Activities	Key Relationship Skill
Dating	Senior executives leveraging personal networks Wondering how to respond to inquiries Wondering how to seek out possibilities	Good radar; good relationship self-awareness
Imaging	Seeing the reality in possibilities Creating a shared vision from being together Involving trusted senior managers	Creating intimacy
Initiating	Bringing key executives into action Creating trust through face-to-face time	Trust building
Interfacing	Facilitating the creating of personal relationships at many levels Traveling to partner facilities and engaging in technical conversations Blending social and business time	Partnering
Committing	Demonstrating that managers are fully committed to the alliance and each other Managing the conflict inherent in making hard choices Accepting the reality of the alliance and its relationships	Commitment
Fine-tuning	Relying on mature and established relationships Facilitating interaction and relationships with future successors	Growing *with* another

Source: Adapted from Robert E. Spekman, Lynn A. Isabella, with Thomas C. MacAvoy, *Alliance Competence* (New York: Wiley, 2000), p. 81. Copyright © 2000, John Wiley & Sons, Inc. This material is used by permission of John Wiley & Sons, Inc.

means of lessening political and economic risks by the amount of the partner's contribution to the venture, IJVs provide a way to enter markets that pose legal and cultural barriers that is less risky than acquisition of an existing company.

A *joint venture* is differentiated from other types of strategic alliances or collaborative relationships in that a joint venture is a partnership of two or more participating companies that have joined forces to create a separate legal entity. Joint ventures are different from minority holdings by an MNC in a local firm.

Four characteristics define joint ventures: (1) JVs are established, separate, legal entities; (2) they acknowledge intent by the partners to share in the management of the JV; (3) they are partnerships between legally incorporated entities such as companies, chartered organizations, or governments, and not between individuals; and (4) equity positions are held by each of the partners.

IJVs can be hard to manage. The choice of partners and the qualities of the relationships[29] between the executives are important factors leading to success. Several other factors contribute to their success or failure as well: how control is shared,[30] relations with

[29]Steven C. Currall and Andrew C. Inkpen, "A Multilevel Approach to Trust in Joint Ventures," *Journal of International Business Studies* 33, no. 3 (2003), pp. 479–495.

[30]Nitin Pangarkar and Saul Klein, "The Impact of Control on IJV Performance: A Contingency Approach," *Journal of International Marketing* 12, no. 3 (2004), pp. 86–107; Chang-Bum Choi and Paul W. Beamish, "Split Management Control and IJV Performance," *Journal of International Business Studies* 35, no. 3 (2004), pp. 201–215; Yadong Luo and Seung H. Park, "Multiparty Cooperation and Performance in International Equity Joint Ventures," *Journal of International Business Studies* 35, no. 2 (2004), pp. 142–160; Jeffrey Q. Beardon, H. Kevin Steensma, and Marjorie A. Lyles, "The Influence of Parent Control Structure on Parent Conflict in Vietnamese IJVs: An Organizational Justice–Based Contingency Approach," *Journal of International Business Studies* 36, no. 2 (2005), pp. 156–174.

parents,[31] institutional (legal) environments,[32] and the extent that knowledge is shared across partners.[33] Despite this complexity, nearly all companies active in world trade participate in at least one international joint venture somewhere; many companies have dozens of joint ventures. A recent Conference Board study indicated that 40 percent of Fortune 500 companies were engaged in one or more international joint ventures. Particularly in telecommunications and Internet markets, joint ventures are increasingly favored. For example, Excite At Home has established joint venture relationships in Belgium, the Netherlands, Germany, Australia, and Japan.

In the Asia-Pacific Rim, where U.S. companies face unfamiliar legal and cultural barriers, joint ventures are preferred to buying existing businesses. Local partners can often lead the way through legal mazes and provide the outsider with help in understanding cultural nuances. A joint venture can be attractive to an international marketer when it enables a company to utilize the specialized skills of a local partner, when it allows the marketer to gain access to a partner's local distribution system, when a company seeks to enter a market where wholly owned activities are prohibited, when it provides access to markets protected by tariffs or quotas, and when the firm lacks the capital or personnel capabilities to expand its international activities.

In China, a country considered to be among the riskiest in Asia, more than 50,000 joint ventures have been established in the 25 years since the government began allowing IJVs there. Among the many reasons IJVs are so popular is that they offer a way of getting around high Chinese tariffs, allowing a company to gain a competitive price advantage over imports. Manufacturing locally with a Chinese partner rather than importing bypasses China's historically high tariffs. Manufacturing locally with a Chinese partner rather than importing achieves additional savings as a result of low-cost Chinese labor. Many Western brands are manufactured and marketed in China at prices that would not be possible if the products were imported.

Consortia. *Consortia* are similar to joint ventures and could be classified as such except for two unique characteristics: (1) they typically involve a large number of participants, and (2) they frequently operate in a country or market in which none of the participants is currently active. Consortia are developed to pool financial and managerial resources and to lessen risks. Often, huge construction projects are built under a consortium arrangement in which major contractors with different specialties form a separate company specifically to negotiate for and produce one job. One firm usually acts as the lead firm, or the newly formed corporation may exist independently of its originators.

Without doubt the most prominent international consortium has been Airbus, Boeing's European competitor in the global commercial aircraft market. Airbus Industrie was originally formed when four major European aerospace firms agreed to work together to build commercial airliners. The four partners are France's Aerospatiale Matra, Germany's Dasa aerospace unit of DaimlerChrysler, Britian's BAE Systems, and Spain's Construcciones. In 2000, the four agreed to transform the consortium into a global company to achieve operations efficiencies that would allow it to compete better against Boeing. Meanwhile, Boeing is joining together with its own consortium to develop new 7E7 aircraft.[34]

---

[31]Yaping Gong, Oded Shenkar, Yadong Luo, and Mee-Kau Nyaw, "Human Resources and International Joint Venture Performance: A System Perspective," *Journal of International Business Studies*, 2005 online.

[32]Yadong Luo, "Transactional Characteristics, Institutional Environment, and Joint Venture Contracts," *Journal of International Business Studies* 36, no. 2 (2005), pp. 209–230.

[33]Eric W. K. Tsang, Duc Tri Nguyen, and M. Krishna Erramilli, "Knowledge Acquisition and Performance in International Joint Ventures in the Transition Economy of Vietnam," *Journal of International Marketing* 12, no. 2 (2004), pp. 82–103; Charles Dhanaraj, Marjorie A. Lyles, H. Kevin Steensma, and Laszlo Tihanyi, "Managing Tacit and Explicit Knowledge Transfer in IJVs: The Role of Embeddedness and the Impact on Performance," *Journal of International Business Studies* 35, no. 5 (2004), pp. 428–442.

[34]Peter Pae, "Japanese Helping 787 Take Wing," *Los Angeles Times*, May 9, 2005, pp. C1, C5.

CROSSING BORDERS 11.4 — The Consortium Goes Corporate—Bad News for Boeing?

The partners in Airbus Industrie jacked up the competitive pressure on Boeing by turning their consortium into a corporation and officially starting to sell the A380 superjumbo jet. The announcement by the consortium companies came only hours before three of them launched the initial public offering of their merged company, the European Aeronautic Defence & Space Company (EADS), through which they planned to raise 3.5 billion euros.

Airbus was run by four companies—one French, one Spanish, one German, and one British. The four built planes as allied but independent companies and marketed them through their Airbus Industrie joint venture. Under the new agreement, they combined all their individual Airbus production assets and the joint venture (EADS) into a new French-registered company, the working name of which is Airbus Integrated Company (AIC).

The partners had said that creating the AIC was a prerequisite to launching the 550-seat A380. Developing the jet, which would be the world's largest passenger plane, will cost $12 billion, and the partners had said that the complex consortium structure was too inefficient to support such a large project.

The A380 has already drawn interest and orders from at least eight airlines, among them Quantas, Singapore Airlines, and Air France. The superjumbo jet will compete with Boeing's 400+-seat 747 jumbo jets, a major source of profit for the Seattle company because it had a monopoly on building the biggest jets. The consolidation of Airbus should make it more nimble and profitable as well as help it compete against Boeing. The A380 project should break even within 10 years on sales of 250 planes. Airbus already has booked orders for half that number. Are they sleepless in Seattle?

Sources: Daniel Michaels, "It's Official: Airbus Will Become a Company and Market A380 Jet," *Wall Street Journal Europe,* June 26, 2000, p. 6; Stanley Holmes, "Boeing Is Choking on Airbus' Fumes," *BusinessWeek,* June 30, 2003, p. 50; "Airbus Superjumbo Maiden Flight in Germany Draws 150,000," *Agence France Presse,* August 27, 2005.

Sematech, the other candidate for most prominent consortium, was originally an exclusively American operation. Sematech is an R&D consortium formed in Austin, Texas, during the 1980s to regain America's lead in semiconductor development and sales from Japan. Members included firms such as IBM, Intel, Texas Instruments, Motorola, and Hewlett-Packard. However, at the turn of the millennium even Sematech went international. Several of the founding American companies left and were replaced by firms from Taiwan, Korea, Germany, and the Netherlands (still none from Japan). The firm is also broadening its own investment portfolio to include a greater variety of international companies.

All such international contractual agreements can run into problems. Ford and Nissan launched a joint venture minivan in 1992 called the Mercury Villager/Nissan Quest. The car was mildly successful in the U.S. market, but in 2002 the joint venture stopped producing the cars—that's two years earlier than the original contract called for. Now that Nissan is controlled by French automaker Renault, it began producing its own minivan in 2003 for sale in the United States. When General Motors formed a joint venture with Daewoo, its purpose was to achieve a significant position in the Asian car market. Instead, Daewoo used the alliance to enhance its own automobile technology, and by the time the partnership was terminated GM had created a new global competitor for itself.

Nestlé has been involved in a particularly ugly dissolution dispute with Dabur India. The Swiss firm owned 60 percent and the Indian firm 40 percent of a joint venture biscuit company, Excelcia Foods. Following months of acrimony, in March 2000 Dabur filed a petition with the Indian government accusing Nestlé of indulging in oppression of the minority shareholder and of mismanaging the JV company. In particular, Dabur alleged that Nestlé was purposefully running Excelcia into bankruptcy so that Nestlé could wriggle out of its "non-compete obligations and go after the India-biscuit market using another brand." Nestlé countered that the problem had more to do with the partners' inability to agree on a mutually acceptable business plan. In June of that year the dispute was settled out of court by Nestlé buying Dabur's 40 percent interest, shortly after which Excelcia was closed in lieu of restructuring.

Direct Foreign Investment

A fourth means of foreign market development and entry is *direct foreign investment,* that is, investment within a foreign country. Companies may manufacture locally to capitalize on low-cost labor, to avoid high import taxes, to reduce the high costs of transportation to market, to gain access to raw materials, or as a means of gaining market entry. Firms may either invest in or buy local companies or establish new operations facilities. As with the other modes of market entry, several factors have been found to influence the structure and performance of direct investments: (1) timing—first movers have advantages but are more risky;[35] (2) the growing complexity[36] and contingencies of contracts;[37] (3) transaction cost structures;[38] (4) technology transfer;[39] (5) degree of product differentiation;[40] (6) the previous experiences and cultural diversity of acquired firms;[41] and (7) advertising and reputation barriers.[42] This mix of considerations and risks makes for increasingly difficult decisions about such foreign investments. But as legal restrictions continue to ease with WTO and other international agreements, more and more large firms are choosing to enter markets via direct investment.

The growth of free trade areas that are tariff free among members but have a common tariff for nonmembers creates an opportunity that can be capitalized on by direct investment. Similar to its Japanese competitors, Korea's Samsung has invested some $500 million to build television tube plants in Tijuana, Mexico, to feed the already huge NAFTA TV industry centered there. Kyocera Corporation, a Japanese high-tech company, bought Qualcomm's wireless consumer phone business as a means of fast entry into the American market. Yahoo! recently paid $1 billion for a 40 percent stake in Chinese competitor Alibaba.[43] Finally, Nestlé is building a new milk factory in Thailand to serve the ASEAN Free Trade Area.

A hallmark of global companies today is the establishment of manufacturing operations throughout the world.[44] This is a trend that will increase as barriers to free trade are eliminated and companies can locate manufacturing wherever it is most cost effective. The selection of an entry mode and partners are critical decisions because the nature of the firm's operations in the country market is affected by and depends on the choices made. The entry mode affects the future decisions because each mode entails an accompanying level of resource commitment, and changing from one entry mode to another without considerable loss of time and money is difficult.

---

[35]Andrew Delios and Shige Makino, "Timing of Entry and the Foreign Subsidiary Performance of Japanese Firms," *Journal of International Marketing* 11, no. 3 (2003), pp. 83–105.

[36]Peter J. Buckley and Pervez Ghauri, "Globalization, Economic Geography, and the Strategy of Multinational Enterprises," *Journal of International Business Studies* 35, no. 2 (2004), pp. 81–98.

[37]Jeffrey J. Reuer, Oded Shenkar, and Roberto Ragozzino, "Mitigating Risk in International Mergers and Acquisitions: The Role of Contingent Payouts," *Journal of International Business Studies* 35, no. 1 (2004), pp. 19–32.

[38]Hongxin Zhao, Yadong Luo, and Taewon Suh, "Transaction Cost Determinants and Ownership-Based Entry Mode Choice: A Meta-Analytic Review," *Journal of International Business Studies* 35, no. 6 (2004), pp. 524–544.

[39]Shih-Fen S. Chen, "Extending Internationalization Theory: A New Perspective on International Technology Transfer and Its Generalization," *Journal of International Business Studies* 36, no. 2 (2005), pp. 231–245.

[40]Lilach Nachum and Cliff Wymbs, "Product Differentiation, External Economies, and MNE Location Choices: M&A Global Cities," *Journal of International Business Studies*, 2005, online.

[41]Klaus Uhlenbruck, "Developing Acquired Foreign Subsidiaries: The Experience of MNEs in Transition Economies," *Journal of International Business Studies* 35, no. 2 (2004), pp. 109–123.

[42]Shin-Fen S. Chen and Ming Zeng, "Japanese Investors' Choice of Acquisition vs. Startups in the U.S.: The Role of Reputation Barriers and Advertising Outlays," *International Journal of Research in Marketing* 21, no. 2 (2004), pp. 123–136.

[43]Jason Dean and Jonathan Cheng, "Meet Jack Ma, Who Will Guide Yahoo in China," *Wall Street Journal*, August 12, 2005, pp. B1, B3.

[44]John A. Doukas and L. H. P. Lang, "Foreign Direct Investment, Diversification, and Firm Performance," *Journal of International Business Studies* 34, no. 2 (2003), pp. 153–172.

Organizing for Global Competition

An international marketing plan should optimize the resources committed to company objectives. The organizational plan includes the type of organizational arrangements to be used and the scope and location of responsibility. Because organizations need to reflect a wide range of company-specific characteristics—such as size, level of policy decisions, length of chain of command, staff support, source of natural and personnel resources, degree of control, centralization, and type or level of marketing involvement—devising a standard organizational structure is difficult. Many ambitious multinational plans meet with less than full success because of confused lines of authority, poor communications, and lack of cooperation between headquarters and subsidiary organizations.

An organizational structure that effectively integrates domestic and international marketing activities has yet to be devised.[45] Companies face the need to maximize the international potential of their products and services without diluting their domestic marketing efforts. Companies are usually structured around one of three alternatives: (1) global product divisions responsible for product sales throughout the world; (2) geographical divisions responsible for all products and functions within a given geographical area; or (3) a matrix organization consisting of either of these arrangements with centralized sales and marketing run by a centralized functional staff, or a combination of area operations and global product management.

Companies that adopt the global product division structure are generally experiencing rapid growth and have broad, diverse product lines. General Electric is a good example, having reorganized its global operations into six product divisions—infrastructure, industrial, commercial financial services, NBC Universal, health care, and consumer finance.[46] Geographic structures work best when a close relationship with national and local governments is important.

The matrix form—the most extensive of the three organizational structures—is popular with companies as they reorganize for global competition. A matrix structure permits management to respond to the conflicts that arise between functional activity, product, and geography. It is designed to encourage sharing of experience, resources, expertise, technology, and information among global business units. At its core is better decision making, in which multiple points of view affecting functional activity, product, and geography are examined and shared. A matrix organization can also better accommodate customers who themselves have global operations and global requirements.

A company may be organized by product lines but have geographical subdivisions under the product categories. Both may be supplemented by functional staff support. Exhibit 11.4 shows such a combination. Modifications of this basic arrangement are used by a majority of large companies doing business internationally.

The turbulence of global markets requires flexible organizational structures. Forty-three large U.S. companies studied indicated that they planned a total of 137 organizational changes for their international operations over a five-year period. Included were such changes as centralizing international decision making, creating global divisions, forming centers of excellence, and establishing international business units. Bausch & Lomb, one of the companies in the study, revamped its international organizational structure by collapsing its international division into a worldwide system of three regions and setting up business management committees to oversee global marketing and manufacturing strategies for four major product lines. Bausch & Lomb's goal was to better coordinate central activities without losing touch at the local level. "Global coordination is essential," according to the company's CEO, "but in a way that maintains the integrity of the foreign subsidiaries." More recently, General Motors dramatically revamped its global strategies through its network of strategic alliances.

---

[45]Kelly Hewett and William O. Beardon, "Dependence, Trust, and Relational Behavior on the Part of Foreign Subsidiary Marketing Operations: Implications for Managing Global Marketing Operations," *Journal of Marketing* 65, no. 4 (October 2001), pp. 51–66.

[46]Kathryn Kranhold, "GE Reorganizes into Six Units, Names Three New Vice Chairmen," *Wall Street Journal*, June 23, 2005, online.

Exhibit 11.4
Schematic Marketing Organization Plan Combining Product, Geographic, and Functional Approaches

To the extent that there is a trend, two factors seem to be sought, regardless of the organizational structure: a single locus for direction and control and the creation of a simple line organization that is based on a more decentralized network of local companies.

Locus of Decision

Considerations of where decisions will be made, by whom, and by which method constitute a major element of organizational strategy. Management policy must be explicit about which decisions are to be made at corporate headquarters, which at international headquarters, which at regional levels, and which at national or even local levels. Most companies also limit the amount of money to be spent at each level. Decision levels for determination of policy, strategy, and tactical decisions must be established. Tactical decisions normally should be made at the lowest possible level, without country-by-country duplication.[47] This guideline requires American headquarters managers to trust the expertise of their local managers.

Centralized versus Decentralized Organizations

An infinite number of organizational patterns for the headquarters activities of multinational firms exist, but most fit into one of three categories: centralized, regionalized, or decentralized organizations. The fact that all of the systems are used indicates that each has certain advantages and disadvantages. The chief advantages of centralization are the availability of experts at one location, the ability to exercise a high degree of control on both the planning and implementation phases, and the centralization of all records and information.[48]

Some companies effect extreme decentralization by selecting competent managers and giving them full responsibility for national or regional operations. These executives are in direct day-to-day contact with the market but lack a broad company view, which can mean partial loss of control for the parent company.

Multinationals are constantly seeking the "right" organizational structure that will provide them with flexibility, an ability to respond to local needs, and worldwide control over

[47]K. Hewett, M. S. Roth, and K. Roth, "Conditions Influencing Headquarters and Foreign Subsidiary Roles in Marketing Activities and Their Effects on Performance," *Journal of International Business Studies* 34, no. 6 (2003), pp. 567–585.

[48]Peter J. Buckley and Martin J. Carter, "A Formal Analysis of Knowledge Combinations in Multinational Enterprises," *Journal of International Business Studies* 35, no. 5 (2004), pp. 371–384.

far-flung business units. No single traditional organizational plan is adequate for today's global enterprise seeking to combine the economies of scale of a global company with the flexibility and marketing knowledge of a local company. Companies are experimenting with several different organizational schemes, but greater centralization of decisions is common to all.

In many cases, whether a company's formal organizational structure is centralized or decentralized, the informal organization reflects some aspect of all organizational systems. This is especially true relative to the locus of decision making. Studies show that even though product decisions may be highly centralized, subsidiaries may have a substantial amount of local influence in pricing, advertising, and distribution decisions. If a product is culturally sensitive, the decisions are more likely to be decentralized.

Summary

Expanding markets around the world have increased competition for all levels of international marketing. To keep abreast of the competition and maintain a viable position for increasingly competitive markets, a global perspective is necessary. Global competition also requires quality products designed to meet ever-changing customer needs and rapidly advancing technology. Cost containment, customer satisfaction, and a greater number of players mean that every opportunity to refine international business practices must be examined in light of company goals. Collaborative relationships, strategic international alliances, strategic planning, and alternative market-entry strategies are important avenues to global marketing that must be implemented in the planning and organization of global marketing management.

Questions

1. Define the following terms:

   global marketing management licensing
   corporate planning   franchising
   direct exporting   joint venture
   strategic planning   global market concept
   indirect exporting   SIA
   tactical planning

2. Define strategic planning. How does strategic planning for international marketing differ from domestic marketing?

3. Discuss the benefits to an MNC of accepting the global market concept. Explain the three points that define a global approach to international marketing.

4. Discuss the effect of shorter product life cycles on a company's planning process.

5. What is the importance of collaborative relationships to competition?

6. In Phases 1 and 2 of the international planning process, countries may be dropped from further consideration as potential markets. Discuss some of the conditions that may exist in a country that would lead a marketer to exclude a country in each phase.

7. Assume that you are the director of international marketing for a company producing refrigerators. Select one country in Latin America and one in Europe and develop screening criteria to use in evaluating the two countries. Make any additional assumptions that are necessary about your company.

8. "The dichotomy typically drawn between export marketing and overseas marketing is partly fictional; from a marketing standpoint, they are but alternative methods of capitalizing on foreign market opportunities." Discuss.

9. How will entry into a developed foreign market differ from entry into a relatively untapped market?

10. Why do companies change their organizations when they go from being an international to a global company?

11. Formulate a general rule for deciding where international business decisions should be made.

12. Explain the popularity of joint ventures.

13. Compare the organizational implications of joint ventures versus licensing.

14. Visit the Web sites of General Motors and Ford, both car manufacturers in the United States. Search their sites and compare their international involvement. How would you classify each—as exporter, international, or global?

15. Using the sources in question 14, list the different entry modes each company uses.

16. Visit the Nestlé Corporation Web site (www.nestle.com/) and the Unilever Web site (www.unilever.com/). Compare their strategies toward international markets. In what ways (besides product categories) do they differ in their international marketing?

12

products and services for consumers

CHAPTER OUTLINE

Global Perspective: Hong Kong—Disney Rolls the
  Dice Again

Quality

   Quality Defined
   Maintaining Quality
   Physical or Mandatory Requirements
     and Adaptation
   Green Marketing and Product Development

Products and Culture

   Innovative Products and Adaptation
   Diffusion of Innovation
   Production of Innovations

Analyzing Product Components for Adaptation

   Core Component
   Packaging Component
   Support Services Component

Marketing Consumer Services Globally

   Services Opportunities in Global Markets
   Barriers to Entering Global Markets for Consumer Services

Brands in International Markets

   Global Brands
   National Brands
   Country-of-Origin Effects and Global Brands
   Private Brands

CHAPTER LEARNING OBJECTIVES

What you should learn from Chapter 12:

- The importance of offering a product suitable for the intended market

- The relationship between product acceptance and the market into which it is introduced

- The importance of quality and how quality is defined

- Country-of-origin effects on product image

- Physical, mandatory, and cultural requirements for product adaptation

- The need to view all attributes of a product in order to overcome resistance to acceptance

Global Perspective

HONG KONG—DISNEY ROLLS THE DICE AGAIN

With the opening of Disneyland in Anaheim in 1955 the notion of the modern theme park was born. The combination of the rides, various other attractions, and the Disney characters has remained irresistible. Tokyo Disneyland has also proved to be a big success, making modest money for Disney through licensing and major money for its Japanese partners. Three quarters of the visitors at the Tokyo park are repeat visitors, the best kind.

Then came EuroDisney. Dissatisfied with the ownership arrangements at the Tokyo park, the EuroDisney deal was structured very differently. Disney negotiated a much greater ownership stake in the park and adjacent hotel and restaurant facilities. Along with the greater control and potential profits came a higher level of risk.

Even before the park's grand opening ceremony in 1992, protestors decried Disney's "assault" on the French culture. The location was also a mistake—the Mediterranean climate of the alternative Barcelona site not chosen seemed much more attractive on chilly winter days in France. Managing both a multicultural workforce and clientele proved daunting. For example, what language was most appropriate for the Pirates of the Caribbean attraction—French or English? Neither attendance nor consumer purchases targets were achieved during the early years: Both were off by about 10 percent. By the summer of 1994 EuroDisney had lost some $900 million. Real consideration was given to closing the park.

A Saudi prince provided a crucial cash injection that allowed for a temporary financial restructuring and a general reorganization, including a new French CEO and a new name, Paris Disneyland. The Paris park returned to profitability, and attendance increased. However, the temporary holiday on royalties, management fees, and leases is now expired and profits are dipping again. Disney's response was to expand with a second "Disney Studios" theme park and an adjacent retail and office complex at the Paris location. Again in 2005 the Saudi prince injected another $33 million into the park.

In 2006 Hong Kong Disneyland opened for business. The Hong Kong government provided the bulk of the investment for the project (almost 80 percent of the $3 billion needed). As in Europe, the clientele is culturally diverse, even though primarily Chinese. Performances are done in Cantonese (the local dialect), Mandarin (the national language), and English. Disney also inked a new joint venture agreement for online delivery of entertainment services to customers in China. Indeed, it will be quite interesting to follow Mickey's international adventures in the new millennium!

Sources: www.disney.go.com; "Disney to Build Hong Kong Theme Park; Euro Disney's Profit Slumped," *Dow Jones News Service,* November 2, 1999; Richard Verrier, "Saudi Prince Helps Out EuroDisney," *Los Angeles Times,* January 12, 2005, p. C2; Don Lee, "Disneyland Opens in Hong Kong," *Los Angeles Times,* September 13, 2005, pp. C1, C6.

The opportunities and challenges for international marketers of consumer goods and services today have never been greater or more diverse. New consumers are springing up in emerging markets in eastern Europe, the Commonwealth of Independent States, China and other Asian countries, India, Latin America—in short, globally. Although some of these emerging markets have little purchasing power today, they promise to be huge markets in the future. In the more mature markets of the industrialized world, opportunity and challenge also abound as consumers' tastes become more sophisticated and complex, and as increases in purchasing power provide them with the means of satisfying new demands.

As described in the Global Perspective, Disney is the archetypal American exporter for global consumer markets. The distinction between products and services for such companies means little. Their DVDs are *products,* whereas cinema performances of the same movies are *services.* Consumers at the theme parks (including foreign tourists at domestic sites) pay around $40 to get in the gate, but they also spend about the same amount on hats, T-shirts, and meals while there. And the movies, of course, help sell the park tickets and the associated toys and clothing. Indeed, this lack of distinction between products and services has led to the invention of new terms encompassing both products and services, such as *market offerings*[1] and *business-to-consumer marketing.* However, the governmental agencies that keep track of international trade still maintain the questionable product–service distinction, and thus so do we in this chapter and the next.[2] The reader should also note that when it comes to U.S. exports targeting consumers, the totals are about evenly split among the three major categories of durable goods (such as cars and computers), nondurable goods (mainly food, drugs, toys), and services (for example, tourism and telecommunications).

Never has the question "Which products/services should we sell?" been more critical than it is today. For the company with a domestic market extension orientation like Ben & Jerry's Ice Cream, the answer generally is "Whatever we are selling at home." The company with a multidomestic market orientation develops different products and services to fit the uniqueness of each country market; the global company ignores frontiers and seeks commonalties in needs among sets of country markets and responds with global market offerings.

The trend for larger firms is toward becoming global in orientation and strategy. However, product adaptation is as important a task in a smaller firm's marketing effort as it is for global companies. As competition for world markets intensifies and as market preferences become more global, selling what is produced for the domestic market in the same manner as it is sold at home proves to be increasingly less effective. Some products cannot be sold at all in foreign markets without modification; others may be sold as is, but their acceptance is greatly enhanced when tailored specifically to market needs. In a competitive struggle, quality products and services that meet the needs and wants of consumers at an affordable price should be the goal of any marketing firm.

Quality

Global competition is placing new emphasis on some basic tenets of business. It is shortening product life cycles and focusing on the importance of quality, competitive prices, and innovative products. The power in the marketplace is shifting from a sellers' to a customers' market, and the latter have more choices because more companies are competing for their attention. More competition, more choices, puts more power in the hands of the customer, and that, of course, drives the need for quality. Gone are the days when the customer's knowledge was limited to one or at best just a few different products. Today the customer knows what is best, cheapest, and highest quality. It is the customer who defines quality in terms of his or her needs and resources. For example, cell phones that don't roam don't sell

---

[1]For example, Philip Kotler and Kevin Lane Keller, *Marketing Management,* 12th ed. (Upper Saddle River, NJ: Prentice Hall, 2002).

[2]We hope that it is obvious that many of the points we make regarding the development of consumer products are pertinent to consumer services as well, and vice versa. Of course, some distinctions are still substantive. These are focused upon in the section of the chapter entitled Marketing Consumer Services Globally.

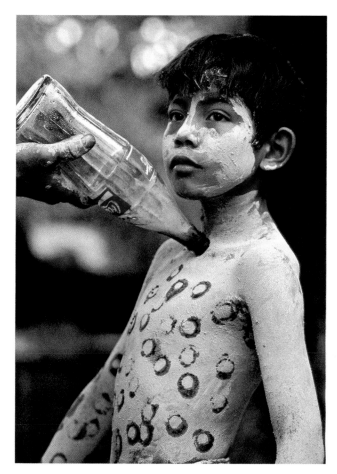

Products are not used in the same ways in all markets. Here a boy in an eastern Mexican village is prepared for a "Jaguar dance" to bring rain. Clay, ashes, and the globally ubiquitous Coke bottle make for the best cat costumes. (© Kenneth Garrett/National Geographic Image Collection)

in Japan at any price, but in China they do very well indeed. Just ask the folks at UTStarcom, a California firm that will soon be selling in India and Vietnam, as well as China.[3]

American products have always been among the world's best, but competition is challenging us to make even better products. In most global markets the cost and quality of a product are among the most important criteria by which purchases are made. For consumer and industrial products alike, the reason often given for preferring one brand over another is better quality at a competitive price. Quality, as a competitive tool, is not new to the business world, but many believe that it is the deciding factor in world markets. However, we must be clear about what we mean by quality.

Quality Defined   *Quality* can be defined on two dimensions: market-perceived quality and performance quality.[4] Both are important concepts, but consumer perception of a quality product often has more to do with market-perceived quality[5] than performance quality.[6] The relationship of quality conformance to customer satisfaction is analogous to an airline's delivery of quality. If viewed internally from the firm's perspective (performance quality), an airline has achieved quality conformance with a safe flight and landing. But because the consumer expects performance quality to be a given, quality to the consumer is more than compliance (a safe flight and landing). Rather, cost, timely service, frequency of flights, comfortable seating, and performance of airline personnel from check-in to baggage claim are all part of the customer's experience that is perceived as being of good or poor quality. Considering the number of air miles flown daily, the airline industry is approaching zero defects in quality conformance, yet who will say that customer satisfaction is anywhere near perfection? These market-perceived quality attributes are embedded in the total product, that is, the physical or core product and all the additional features the consumer expects.

In a competitive marketplace where the market has choices, most consumers expect performance quality to be a given. Naturally, if the product does not perform up to standards, it will be rejected. When there are alternative products, all of which meet performance quality standards, the product chosen is the one that meets market-perceived quality attributes. Interestingly, China's leading refrigerator maker recognized the importance of these market-perceived quality attributes when it adopted a technology that enabled it to let consumers choose from 20 different colors and textures for door handles and moldings. For example, a consumer can design an off-white refrigerator with green marble handles and moldings. Why is this important? Because it lets consumers "update their living rooms" where most of the refrigerators are parked. The company's motive was simple: It positioned its product for competition from multinational brands by giving the consumer another expression of quality.

---

[3]Peter Burrows, "Ringing off the Hook in China," *BusinessWeek*, June 9, 2003, pp. 80–81; *The Economist*, "Calling an End to Poverty," July 9, 2005, pp. 52, 52.

[4]Xiaohua Lin and Richard Germain, "Product Quality Orientation and Its Performance Implications in Chinese State-Owned Enterprises," *Journal of International Marketing* 11, no. 2 (2003), pp. 59–78.

[5]There is much evidence that perceptions of quality vary across cultures. For example, see Terrence Witkowski and Mary Wolfinbarger, "Comparative Service Quality: German and American Ratings of Five Different Service Settings," *Journal of Business Research*, November 2002, pp. 875–881.

[6]Michael Laroche, Linda C. Ueltschy, Shuzo Abe, Mark Cleveland, and Peter P. Yannopoulos, "Service Quality Perceptions and Customer Satisfaction: Evaluating the Role of Culture," *Journal of International Marketing* 13, no. 3 (2004), pp. 58–85.

CROSSING **BORDERS 12.1**   The Quality of Food Is a Matter of Taste

Food preferences vary not only across countries, but within them as well. For example, many Vietnamese still have to eat whatever they can lay their hands on. Pet birds and dogs are kept indoors to save them from the cooking pot. In 1998, the government tried to reduce the consumption of snakes and cats by banning their sale since the exploding rat population was damaging crops. Instead, peasants simply took to eating rats as well. The dwindling number of rats, in turn, has caused an explosion in the numbers of another tasty treat: snails.

Meanwhile, in nearby Ho Chi Minh City, the country's commercial capital, a recent survey found that 12.5 percent of children were obese—and the figure is rising. Local restaurants vie with one another in expense and luxury. Hoang Khai, a local businessman, recalls how his family always celebrated at home when he was young, because there was nowhere to go out. He decided to change all

that by plowing the returns from his textile business into a restaurant lavish enough to suit the city's business elite. The result is *Au Manoir de Khai*, a colonial villa smothered in gilt and silk where a meal with imported wine can set you back more than most Vietnamese earn in a year.

One has to wonder how ice cream from Fugetsudo, a small confectionary shop in northern Japan, would sell in either neighborhood in Vietnam. You can get fish, sea slug, whale meat, turtle, or cedar chip–flavored ice cream there. Fugetsudo's competition sells pickled-orchid, chicken-wing, shrimp, eel, and short-necked clam flavors. Yum!

Sources: "Eating Out in Vietnam," *The Economist*, December 21, 2002, pp. 49–50; Phred Dvorak, "Something Fishy Is Going On in Japan in the Ice-Cream Biz," *Wall Street Journal*, September 4, 2002, p. 1; Eric Johnston, "Savour the Whale," *The Guardian*, July 4, 2005, p. 6.

Quality is also measured in many industries by objective third parties. In the United States, JD Power and Associates has expanded its auto quality ratings based on consumer surveys to other areas, such as computers. Customer satisfaction indexes developed first in Sweden are now being used to measure customer satisfaction across a wide variety of consumer products and services.[7] Finally, the U.S. Department of Commerce annually recognizes American firms for the quality of their international offerings—the Ritz Carlton Hotel chain has won the prestigious award twice.

Maintaining Quality   Maintaining performance quality is critical,[8] but frequently a product that leaves the factory at performance quality is damaged as it passes through the distribution chain. This is a special problem for many global brands for which production is distant from the market and/or control of the product is lost because of the distribution system within the market. When Mars Company's Snickers and other Western confectioneries were introduced to Russia, they were a big hit. Foreign brands such as Mars, Toblerone, Waldbaur, and Cadbury were the top brands—indeed, only one Russian brand placed in the top 10. But within five years the Russian brands had retaken eight of the top spots, and only one U.S. brand, Mars's Dove bars, was in the top 10.

What happened? A combination of factors caused the decline. Russia's Red October Chocolate Factory got its act together, modernized its packaging, product mix, and equipment, and set out to capture the market. Performance quality was also an issue. When the Russian market opened to outside trade, foreign companies eager to get into the market dumped surplus out-of-date and poor-quality products. In other cases, chocolates were smuggled in and sold on street corners and were often mishandled in the process. By the time they made it to consumers, the chocolates were likely to be misshapen or discolored—poor quality compared with Russia's Red October chocolate.

[7]Claes Fornell, Michael D. Johnson, Eugene W. Anderson, Jaesung Cha, and Barbara Everitt Bryant, "The American Consumer Satisfaction Index: Nature, Purpose, and Findings," *Journal of Marketing* 60, no. 4 (October 1996), pp. 35–46; Jon E. Hilsenrath, "Satisfaction Theory: Mixed Yield—Professor's Portfolio Shows Strategy Linking Returns to Reputation Isn't Perfect," *Wall Street Journal*, February 19, 2003, p. A2.

[8]Duncan I. Simester, John R. Hauser, Birger Wernerfelt, and Roland T. Rust, "Implementing Quality Improvement Programs Designed to Enhance Customer Satisfaction: Quasi-Experiments in the United States and Spain," *Journal of Marketing Research* 37 (February 2000), pp. 102–112; Mark Landler, "Missteps Haunt Smart Car," *International Herald Tribune*, April 2–3, 2005, pp. 1, 4.

Market-perceived quality was also an issue. Russian chocolate has a different taste because of its formulation—more cocoa and chocolate liqueur are used than in Western brands, which makes it grittier. Thus the Red October brand appeals more to Russian taste even though it is generally priced above Western brands. As evinced by this example, quality is not just desirable, it is essential for success in today's competitive global market, and the decision to standardize or adapt a product is crucial in delivering quality.

Physical or Mandatory Requirements and Adaptation

A product may have to change in a number of ways to meet the physical or mandatory requirements of a new market, ranging from simple package changes to total redesign of the physical core product. In many countries the term *product homologation* is used to describe the changes mandated by local product and service standards. A recent study reaffirmed the often-reported finding that mandatory adaptations were more frequently the reason for product adaptation than adapting for cultural reasons.

Some changes are obvious with relatively little analysis; a cursory examination of a country will uncover the need to rewire electrical goods for a different voltage system, simplify a product when the local level of technology is not high, or print multilingual labels where required by law. Electrolux, for example, offers a cold-wash-only washing machine in Asian countries where electric power is expensive or scarce. Other necessary changes may surface only after careful study of an intended market.

Legal, economic, political, technological, and climatic requirements of the local marketplace often dictate product adaptation. During a period in India when the government strongly opposed foreign investment, Pepsi-Cola changed its product name to Lehar-Pepsi (in Hindi, *lehar* means "wave") to gain as much local support as possible. The name returned to Pepsi-Cola when the political climate turned favorable. Laws that vary among countries usually set specific package sizes and safety and quality standards. The European Union bans products with forms of genetically modified food content. The World Health Organization is beginning to regulate the marketing of high-carcinogen American cigarettes. But, most interesting, videogame content is regulated around the world according to violence levels and sexual content. To make a purchase more affordable in low-income countries, the number of units per package may have to be reduced from the typical quantities offered in high-income countries. Razor blades, cigarettes, chewing gum, and other multiple-pack items are often sold singly or two to a pack instead of the more customary 10 or 20. Cheetos, a product of PepsiCo's Frito-Lay, is packaged in 15-gram boxes in China so it can be priced at 1 yuan, about 12 cents. At this price, even children with little spending money can afford Cheetos.

Changes may also have to be made to accommodate climatic differences.[9] General Motors of Canada, for example, experienced major problems with several thousand Chevrolet automobiles shipped to a Middle Eastern country; GM quickly discovered they were unfit for the hot, dusty climate. Supplementary air filters and different clutches had to be added to adjust for the problem. Similarly, crackers have to be packaged in tins for humid areas.

The less economically developed a market is, the greater degree of change a product may need for acceptance. One study found that only one in ten products could be marketed in developing countries without modification of some sort. Because most products sold abroad by international companies originate in home markets and most require some form of modification, companies need a systematic process to identify products that need adaptation.

Green Marketing and Product Development

A quality issue of growing importance the world over, especially in Europe and the United States, is green marketing. Europe has been at the forefront of the "green movement," with strong public opinion and specific legislation favoring environmentally friendly marketing and products. *Green marketing* is a term used to identify concern with the environmental consequences of a variety of marketing activities. In the United States, Japanese car manufacturers are taking advantage of their gas-guzzling American cousins as consumers become more concerned about the environmental effects of SUVs like the General Motors

---

[9]Philip M. Parker and Nader T. Tavossoli, "Homeostasis and Consumer Behavior across Cultures," *International Journal of Research in Marketing* 17, no. 1 (March 2000), pp. 33–53.

CROSSING BORDERS 12.2
In Germany, Video Games Showing Frontal Nudity Are OK, but Blood Is Verboten

Video game heroine Lara Croft is an adrenaline junkie unafraid of getting bloody. But in Germany, the buxom starlet of the "Tomb Raiders" series doesn't bleed—even if she's being mauled by a tiger.

Although the $25 billion video game industry is global, the games themselves aren't. They reflect the distinct cultures and traditions of different markets, and game publishers carefully tweak their titles and other details to tone down offensive materials. And "offensive" varies from country to country.

Red blood in a game sold in the United States turns green in Australia. A topless character in a European title acquires a bikini in the United States. Human enemies in an American game morph into robots in Germany. Violent sex scenes in a Japanese game disappear in the American versions.

Of all countries, Germany is one of the trickiest to tackle, publishers say. The country has spent five decades developing one of the world's strictest decency standards for virtually all media, from books and comics to music and games.

If a game features blood splatterings, decapitations, or death cries, it runs the risk of being placed on a government list known as "the index." Being indexed means it can't be sold to anyone under 18, displayed in stores, or advertised on television, in newspapers, and in magazines. Games containing pornography or glorifications of war, Nazism, and racial hatred face the same fate.

The scariest part of this story is not the games themselves, but the newest use of them as political tools. A game indexed in Germany involves a prisoner of war camp for Turkish detainees. On the other side, Hizbollah, the terrorist organization known for killing 240 American marines in Lebanon in 1983, has also published a new "click-and-kill" game. When are such games more than just entertainment?

Sources: A. Phan and S. Sandell, "Germany, Video Games Showing Frontal Nudity Are OK, but Blood Is *Verboten*," *Los Angeles Times*, June 9, 2003, p. C1; Maija Pesola, "Gunning for Players," *Financial Times*, February 1, 2005, p. 14.

Hummer. The European Commission has passed legislation to control all kinds of packaging waste throughout the European Union. Two critical issues that affect product development are the control of the packaging component of solid waste and consumer demand for environmentally friendly products.

The European Commission issued guidelines for ecolabeling that became operational in 1992. Under the directive, a product is evaluated on all significant environmental effects throughout its life cycle, from manufacturing to disposal—a cradle-to-grave approach. A detergent formulated to be biodegradable and nonpolluting would be judged friendlier than a detergent whose formulation would be harmful when discharged into the environment. Aerosol propellants that do not deplete the ozone layer are another example of environmentally friendly products. No country's laws yet require products to carry an ecolabel to be sold, however. The designation that a product is "environmentally friendly" is voluntary, and environmental success depends on the consumer selecting the ecology-friendly product.

Since the introduction of the ecolabel idea, Hoover washing machines have been the only products that have gained approval for the ecolabel. Interestingly enough, the benefits of winning the symbol have resulted in Hoover tripling its market share in Germany and doubling its share of the premium sector of the U.K. washing-machine market. The approval process seems to be deterring many European manufacturers, many of whom are using their own, unofficial symbols. The National Consumer Council, a consumer watchdog group, reports that many consumers are so confused and cynical about the myriad symbols that they are giving up altogether on trying to compare the green credentials of similar products.

Laws that mandate systems to control solid waste, while voluntary in one sense, do carry penalties. The EU law requires that packaging material through all levels of distribution, from the manufacturer to the consumer, be recycled or reused. Currently, between 50 percent and 65 percent of the weight of the packaging must be recovered, and between 25 percent and 45 percent of the weight of the totality of packaging materials contained in packaging waste will be recycled.

Each level of the distribution chain is responsible for returning all packaging, packing, and other waste materials up the chain. The biggest problem is with the packaging the customer takes home; by law the retailer must take back all packaging from the customer if no central recycling locations are available. For the manufacturer's product to participate in direct collection and not have to be returned to the retailer for recycling, the manufacturer must guarantee financial support for curbside or central collection of all materials. The growing public and political pressure to control solid waste is a strong incentive for compliance.

Although the packaging and solid waste rules are burdensome, there have been successful cases of not only meeting local standards but also being able to transfer this approach to other markets. Procter & Gamble's international operations integrated global environmental concerns as a response to increasing demands in Germany. It introduced Lenor, a fabric softener in a superconcentrated form, and sold it in a plastic refill pouch that reduced packaging by 85 percent. This move increased brand sales by 12 percent and helped set a positive tone with government regulators and activists. The success of Lenor was transferred to the United States, where P&G faced similar environmental pressures. A superconcentrated Downy, the U.S. brand of fabric softener, was repackaged in refill pouches that reduced package size by 75 percent, thereby costing consumers less and actually increasing Downy market share. The global marketer should not view green marketing as a European problem; concern for the environment is worldwide and similar legislation is sure to surface elsewhere. This is another example of the need to adapt products for global marketing.

Products and Culture

To appreciate the complexity of standardized versus adapted products, one needs to understand how cultural influences are interwoven with the perceived value and importance a market places on a product. A product is more than a physical item: It is a bundle of satisfactions (or *utilities*) that the buyer receives. These include its form, taste, color, odor, and texture; how it functions in use; the package; the label; the warranty; the manufacturer's and retailer's servicing; the confidence or prestige enjoyed by the brand; the manufacturer's reputation; the country of origin; and any other symbolic utility received from the possession or use of the goods. In short, the market relates to more than a product's physical form and primary function.[10] The values and customs within a culture confer much of the importance of these other benefits. In other words, a product is the sum of the physical and psychological satisfactions it provides the user.

A product's physical attributes generally are required to create its primary function. The primary function of an automobile, for example, is to move passengers from point A to point B. This ability requires a motor, transmission, and other physical features to achieve its primary purpose. The physical features or primary function of an automobile is generally in demand in all cultures where there is a desire to move from one point to another other than by foot or animal power. Few changes to the physical attributes of a product are required when moving from one culture to another. However, an automobile has a bundle of psychological features that are as important in providing consumer satisfaction as its physical features. Within a specific culture, other automobile features (color, size, design, brand name, price) have little to do with its primary function—the movement from point A to B—but do add value to the satisfaction received.

The meaning and value imputed to the psychological attributes of a product can vary among cultures and are perceived as negative or positive.[11] To maximize the bundle of satisfactions received and to create positive product attributes rather than negative ones, adaptation of the nonphysical features of a product may be necessary. Coca-Cola, frequently touted as a global product, found it had to change Diet Coke to Coke Light when it was introduced in Japan. Japanese women do not like to admit to dieting, and, further, the idea

---

[10]C. K. Prahalad, *The Fortune at the Bottom of the Pyramid* (Philadelphia: Wharton School Publishing, 2005).

[11]Amberin Zaman, "Islamic-Style Swimsuits Give Women Freedom to Dive In," *Los Angeles Times*, August 21, 2005, p. A3.

Cola Turka holds a surprisingly large percentage of shelf space vis-à-vis Coke and Pepsi in this supermarket in Istanbul. The 2-liter bottle is priced at 2.00 lira, just under Coke's 2.05 lira. Cola Turka's TV ads featuring American actor Chevy Chase speaking Turkish seem to be working well.

of diet implies sickness or medicine. So instead of emphasizing weight loss, "figure maintenance" is stressed. Anti-American sentiment is also causing Coke problems with Muslim consumers. At least four new competitors have popped up recently—Mecca Cola, Muslim Up, Arab Cola, and Cola Turka. McDonald's is also responding to such problems with its new McArabia sandwich.

Adaptation may require changes of any one or all of the psychological aspects of a product. A close study of the meaning of a product shows the extent to which the culture determines an individual's perception of what a product is and what satisfaction that product provides.

The adoption of some products by consumers can be affected as much by how the product concept conforms with norms, values, and behavior patterns as by its physical or mechanical attributes. For example, only recently have Japanese consumers taken an interest in dishwashers—they simply didn't have room in the kitchen. However, very compact designs by Mitsubishi, Toto (a Japanese toilet company), and others are making new inroads into Japanese kitchens. A novelty always comes up against a closely integrated cultural pattern, and this is primarily what determines whether, when, how, and in what form it gets adopted. Some financial services have been difficult to introduce into Muslim countries because the pious have claimed they promoted usury and gambling, both explicitly forbidden in the Koran. The Japanese have always found all body jewelry repugnant. The Scots have a decided resistance to pork and all its associated products, apparently from days long ago when such taboos were founded on fundamentalist interpretations of the Bible. Filter cigarettes have failed in at least one Asian country because a very low life expectancy hardly places many people in the age bracket most prone to fears of lung cancer—even supposing that they shared Western attitudes about death.

When analyzing a product for a second market, the extent of adaptation required depends on cultural differences in product use and perception between the market the product was originally developed for and the new market. The greater these cultural differences between the two markets, the greater the extent of adaptation that may be necessary.

An example of this rule of thumb involves an undisputed American leader in cake mixes, which tacitly admitted failure in the English market by closing down operations after five unsuccessful years. Taking its most successful mixes in the U.S. market, the company introduced them into the British market. Considerable amounts of time, money, and effort were expended to introduce its variety of cake mixes to this new market. Hindsight provides several probable causes for the company's failure. Traditionalism was certainly among the most important. The British eat most of their cake with tea instead of dinner and have always preferred dry sponge cake, which is easy to handle; the fancy, iced cakes favored in the United States were the type introduced. Fancy iced cakes are accepted in Britain, but they are considered extra special and are purchased from a bakery or made with much effort and care at home. The company introduced what it thought to be an easy cake mix. This easy cake mix was considered a slight to domestic prowess. Homemakers felt guilty about not even cracking an egg, and there was suspicion that dried eggs and milk were not as good as fresh ones. Therefore, when the occasion called for a fancy cake, an easy cake mix was simply not good enough.

Ironically, this same company had faced almost identical problems, which it eventually overcame, when introducing new easy cake mixes in the U.S. market. There was initial concern about the quality of mixes and the resulting effect on the homemaker's reputation as a baker. Even today the feeling that "made-from-scratch" cakes are of special quality and significance and should be made for extra-important occasions persists—in spite of the uniform quality of results from almost all mixes and the wide variety of flavors that certainly equal, if not exceed, the ability of most to bake from scratch.

Such a cultural phenomenon apparently exists in other cultures as well. When instant cake mixes were introduced in Japan, the consumers' response was less than enthusiastic.

Not only do Japanese reserve cakes for special occasions, but they prefer the cakes to be beautifully wrapped and purchased in pastry shops. The acceptance of instant cakes was further complicated by another cultural difference: Many Japanese homes do not have ovens. An interesting sidebar to this example is the company's attempt to correct for that problem by developing a cake mix that could be cooked in a rice cooker, which all Japanese homes have. The problem with that idea was that in a Japanese kitchen rice and the manner in which it is cooked have strong cultural overtones, and to use the rice cooker to cook something other than rice is a real taboo.

Examples are typically given about cultures other than American, but the need for cultural adaptation is often necessary when a foreign company markets a product in the United States. A major Japanese cosmetics company, Shiseido, attempted to break into the U.S. cosmetic market with the same products sold in Japan. After introducing them in more than 800 U.S. stores, the company realized that American taste in cosmetics is very different from Japanese. The problem was that Shiseido's makeup required a time-consuming series of steps, a point that does not bother Japanese women. Success was attained after designing a new line of cosmetics as easy to use as American products.

The problems of adapting a product to sell abroad are similar to those associated with the introduction of a new product at home. Products are not measured solely by their physical specifications. The nature of the new product is in what it does to and for the customer—to habits, tastes, and patterns of life. The problems illustrated in the cake mix example have little to do with the physical product or the user's ability to make effective use of it, but more with the fact that acceptance and use of the cake mixes would have required upsetting behavior patterns considered correct or ideal.

What significance, outside its intended use, might a product have in a different culture? When product acceptance requires changes in patterns of life, habits, or tastes, the understanding of new ideas, the acceptance of the difficult to believe, or the acquisition of completely new tastes or habits, special emphasis must be used to overcome natural resistance to change.

Finally, there are some interesting surprises in the area of adaptation. The most recent example is Harry Potter. About 20 percent of the sales of his newest adventure book in Japan are in English. It ends up that Japanese consumers are looking for ways to augment English lessons, and the books and associated audiotapes fill that particular need very well. For them Potter is not just entertainment, it's education.[12]

Innovative Products and Adaptation

An important first step in adapting a product to a foreign market is to determine the degree of newness as perceived by the intended market. How people react to newness and how new a product is to a market must be understood. In evaluating the newness of a product, the international marketer must be aware that many products successful in the United States, having reached the maturity or even decline stage in their life cycles, may be perceived as new in another country or culture and thus must be treated as innovations. From a sociological viewpoint, any idea perceived as new by a group of people is an innovation.

Whether or not a group accepts an innovation, and the time it takes to do so, depends on the product's characteristics. Products new to a social system are innovations, and knowledge about the _diffusion_ (i.e., the process by which innovation spreads) of innovation is helpful in developing a successful product strategy. Sony's marketing strategies for the U.S. introduction of its PlayStation 2 were well informed by its wild successes achieved six months earlier during the product's introduction in Japan. Conversely, mid-1990s dips in Japanese sales of Apple computers were preceded by dips in Apple's home U.S. market.[13] Marketing strategies can guide and control to a considerable degree the rate and extent of new-product diffusion because successful new-product diffusion is dependent on the ability to communicate relevant product information and new-product attributes.

---

[12]"Potter's Japanese Adventure," _The Economist_, February 16, 2002, p. 39.

[13]Joel West, "Standards Competition and Apple Computers," unpublished doctoral dissertation, Graduate School of Management, University of California, Irvine, 2000.

A critical factor in the newness of a product is its effect on established patterns of consumption and behavior. In the preceding cake mix example, the fancy, iced cake mix was a product that required both acceptance of the "difficult to believe," that is, that dried eggs and milk are as good in cake as the fresh products, and the acquisition of new ideas, that is, that easy-to-bake fancy cakes are not a slight to one's domestic integrity. In this case, the product directly affected two important aspects of consumer behavior, and the product innovation met with sufficient resistance to convince the company to leave the market. Had the company studied the target market before introducing the product, perhaps it could have avoided the failure.

Another U.S. cake mix company entered the British market but carefully eliminated most of the newness of the product. Instead of introducing the most popular American cake mixes, the company asked 500 British housewives to bake their favorite cake. Since the majority baked a simple, very popular dry sponge cake, the company brought to the market a similar easy mix. The sponge cake mix represented familiar tastes and habits that could be translated into a convenience item and did not infringe on the emotional aspects of preparing a fancy product for special occasions. Consequently, after a short period of time, the second company's product gained 30 to 35 percent of the British cake mix market. Once the idea of a mix for sponge cake was acceptable, the introduction of other flavors became easier.

The goal of a foreign marketer is to gain product acceptance by the largest number of consumers in the market in the shortest span of time. However, as discussed in Chapter 4 and as many of the examples cited have illustrated, new products are not always readily accepted by a culture; indeed, they often meet resistance. Although they may ultimately be accepted, the time needed for a culture to learn new ways, to learn to accept a new product, is of critical importance to the marketer because planning reflects a time frame for investment and profitability. If a marketer invests with the expectation that a venture will break even in three years and seven are needed to gain profitable volume, the effort may have to be prematurely abandoned. The question comes to mind of whether the probable rate of acceptance can be predicted before committing resources and, more critically, if the probable rate of acceptance is too slow, whether it can be accelerated. In both cases, the answer is a qualified yes. Answers to these questions come from examining the work done in diffusion research—research on the process by which innovations spread to the members of a social system.

Diffusion of Innovations

Everett Rogers notes that "crucial elements in the diffusion of new ideas are (1) an innovation, (2) which is communicated through certain channels, (3) over time, (4) among the members of a social system."[14] Rogers continues with the statement that it is the element of time that differentiates diffusion from other types of communications research. The goals of the diffusion researcher and the marketer are to shorten the time lag between introduction of an idea or product and its widespread adoption.

Rogers and others[15] give ample evidence of the fact that product innovations have a varying rate of acceptance. Some diffuse from introduction to widespread use in a few years; others take decades. Patterns of alcoholic beverage consumption are seen to be converging across Europe only when a 50-year time frame is considered. Microwave ovens, introduced in the United States initially in the 1950s, took nearly 20 years to become widespread; the contraceptive pill was introduced during that same period and gained acceptance in a few years. In the field of education, modern math took only five years to diffuse through U.S. schools, whereas the idea of kindergartens took nearly 50 years to gain total

[14]Everett M. Rogers, *Diffusion of Innovations*, 4th ed. (New York: Free Press, 1995). This is a book that should be read by anyone responsible for product development and brand management, domestic or international.

[15]Marnik G. Dekimpe, Philip M. Parker, and Miklos Sarvary, "Global Diffusion and Technological Innovations: A Couple-Hazard Approach," *Journal of Marketing Research* 38 (February 2000), pp. 47–59; Gerard J. Tellis, Stefan Stremersch, and Eden Yin, "The International Takeoff of New Products: The Role of Economics, Culture, and Country Innovativeness," *Marketing Science* 22, no. 2 (2003), pp. 188–208; Sean Dwyer, Hani Mesak, and Maxwell Hsu, "An Exploratory Examination of the Influence of National Culture on Cross-National Product Diffusion," *Journal of International Marketing* 13, no. 2 (2005), pp. 1–27.

The Japanese and the Dutch are the world's champions in toilet innovations. Japan's long history of crowding has prompted the culture to focus on cleanliness, frequent bathing, and high-tech bathrooms. Thus, Matsushita's toilet reads your body weight, temperature, and blood pressure. Soon you will also be able to get a readout on glucose and protein levels in your urine! The Dutch are also worried about plumbing—much of their country is below sea level. Sphinx in Maastricht produces a urinal for women and a fly imbedded in the porcelain for their men's urinal. The latter reduces maintenance costs as the company's research has shown that most men will aim for the fly, which is strategically placed to minimize splash. Either Dutch innovation can be seen in Schiphol Airport outside of Amsterdam. *(top: © Michael Edrington/The Image Works)*

acceptance. A growing body of evidence suggests that the understanding of diffusion theory may provide ways in which the process of diffusion can be accelerated. Knowledge of this process may provide the foreign marketer with the ability to assess the time it takes for a product to diffuse—before a financial commitment is necessary.[16] It also focuses the marketer's attention on features of a product that provoke resistance, thereby providing an opportunity to minimize resistance and hasten product acceptance.

At least three extraneous variables affect the rate of diffusion of an object: the degree of perceived newness,[17] the perceived attributes of the innovation, and the method used to

[16]Stefan Stremersch and Gerard J. Tellis, "Understanding and Managing International Growth of New Products," *International Journal of Research in Marketing* 21, no. 4 (2004), pp. 421–438.

[17]Stanley Holmes, "The Machine of a New Shoe," *BusinessWeek*, March 14, 2005, pp. 99–100.

CROSSING BORDERS 12.3   So This Is What Is Called an Innovation—But Does It Flush?

An American diplomat was at a dinner party in a Japanese home when he excused himself to go to the bathroom. He completed his errand, stood up, and realized he didn't have a clue about how to flush the toilet.

The diplomat spoke Japanese, but he was still baffled by the colorful array of buttons on the complicated keypad on the toilet. This super-high-tech toilet had a control panel that looked like the cockpit of a plane. So he just started pushing.

He hit the noisemaker button, which makes a flushing sound to mask any noise you might be making in the john. He hit the button that starts the blow dryer for your bottom. Then he hit the bidet button and watched helplessly as a little plastic arm, sort of a squirt gun shaped like a toothbrush, appeared from the back of the bowl and began shooting a stream of warm water across the room and onto the mirror.

And that's how one of America's promising young Foreign Service officers ended up frantically wiping down a Japanese bathroom with a wad of toilet paper.

Other buttons he could have tried automatically open and close the lid: The button for men lifts the lid and seat; the button for women lifts the lid only. Some toilets even have a handheld remote control, sort of a clicker for the loo.

What confounded this diplomat was one of Japan's recent additions to the bathroom: the Toto "Washlit," a toilet of the future sold for $2,000 to $4,000, depending on the number of functional features. The company sells about $400 million annually of these technological wonders and has successfully entered the U.S. market with a less complicated, less expensive model called a Niagra—it features only the seat warmer, bottom washer, and deodorizing fan for $400.

Sources: Mary Jordan and Kevin Sullivan, "But Do They Flush?" *Washington Post*, May 15, 1997, p. 1; Anthony Paul, "Made in Japan, the Country's R&D Labs Are Busy Inventing the 21st Century," *Fortune*, December 6, 1999, pp. 190–202; Robert P. Mader, "Toilet Test Results Clash," *Contractor*, December 2002, p. 7.

communicate the idea.[18] Each variable has a bearing on consumer reaction to a new product and the time needed for acceptance. An understanding of these variables can produce better product strategies for the international marketer.

The more innovative a product is perceived to be, the more difficult it is to gain market acceptance. That is, at a fundamental level, innovations can be disruptive.[19] Consider alternative-fuel cars in the United States. Although they are popular with consumers, dealers did not appreciate their low maintenance requirements, which reduced after-sale service revenues. Further, the infrastructure to support hydrogen fuel cell cars has been expensive to build. Thus, some suggest that the technology is inappropriate for the United States, whereas China, without the established infrastructure, may be able to leapfrog the older, gasoline-fueled options.[20] Additionally, the perception of innovation can often be changed if the marketer understands the perceptual framework of the consumer. This has certainly proved to be the case with the fast global diffusion of Internet use, e-tailing, and health- and beauty-related products and services.

Analyzing the five characteristics of an innovation can assist in determining the rate of acceptance or resistance of the market to a product. A product's (1) *relative advantage* (the perceived marginal value of the new product relative to the old); (2) *compatibility* (its compatibility with acceptable behavior, norms, values, and so forth); (3) *complexity* (the degree of complexity associated with product use); (4) *trialability* (the degree of economic and/or social risk associated with product use); and (5) *observability* (the ease with which the product benefits can be communicated) affect the degree of its acceptance or resistance.

---

[18]Anita Elberse and Jehoshua Eliashberg, "Demand and Supply Dynamics for Sequentially Released Products in International Markets: The Case of Motion Pictures," *Marketing Science* 22, no. 3 (2003), pp. 329–354.

[19]Jared Diamond, *Collapse* (New York: Viking, 2005).

[20]Jane Lanhee Lee, "The Leapfrog Strategy: Fuel-Cell Advocates Say China Is Uniquely Positioned to Jump Past Petroleum," *Wall Street Journal*, July 25, 2005, p. R6.

In general, the rate of diffusion can be postulated as positively related to relative advantage, compatibility, trialability, and observability, but negatively related to complexity.

By analyzing a product within these five dimensions, a marketer can often uncover perceptions held by the market that, if left unchanged, would slow product acceptance. Conversely, if these perceptions are identified and changed, the marketer may be able to accelerate product acceptance.

The evaluator must remember that it is the perception of product characteristics by the potential adopter, not the marketer, that is crucial to the evaluation. A market analyst's self-reference criterion (SRC) may cause a perceptual bias when interpreting the characteristics of a product. Thus, instead of evaluating product characteristics from the foreign user's frame of reference, the marketer might analyze them from his or her frame of reference, leading to a misinterpretation of the product's cultural importance.

Once the analysis has been made, some of the perceived newness or causes for resistance can be minimized through adroit marketing. The more congruent that product perceptions are with current cultural values, the less resistance there will be and the more rapid product diffusion or acceptance will be.

Production of Innovations

Some consideration must be given to the inventiveness of companies[21] and countries.[22] For example, it is no surprise that most of the new ideas associated with the Internet are being produced in the United States.[23] The 160 million American users of the Internet far outnumber the 62 million Japanese users.[24] Similarly, America wins the overall R&D expenditure contest. Expenditures are about the same across member countries of the Organization for Economic Cooperation and Development at about 2 to 3 percent of GDP, so America's large economy supports twice the R&D spending as does Japan, for example. This spending yields about three times the U.S. patents granted to American firms versus Japanese firms. Most interestingly, the Japanese government had diagnosed the problem as a lack of business training. Japanese engineers are not versed in marketing and entrepreneurship, and American-style educational programs are being created at a record pace to fill the gap. Many Japanese firms also take advantage of American innovativeness by establishing design centers in the United States—most notable are the plethora of foreign auto design centers in southern California. At the same time American automobile firms have established design centers in Europe. Recent studies have shown that innovativeness varies across cultures and companies are placing design centers worldwide. Indeed, the Ford Taurus, the car that saved Ford in the 1980s, was a European design.

While increasing numbers of Japanese at the largest and most diversified firms are going back to business school, their Korean conglomerate competitors are leveraging their vertical integration more successfully at the lower end of the consumer electronics business. Samsung has created a number of very successful innovations by tying together product development teams across semiconductors, telecom, digital appliance, and digital media units. Finally, it must be recognized that new ideas come from a growing variety of sources, countries,[25] acquisitions,[26] and even global collaborations.[27]

---

[21]Rhohit Despande and John U. Farley, "Organizational Culture, Innovativeness, and Market Orientation in Hong Kong Five Years after Handover: What Has Changed?" *Journal of Global Marketing* 17, no. 4 (2004), pp. 53–75.

[22]Anyone interested in a wonderful book on this topic should read the Pulitzer Prize–winning *Guns, Germs, and Steel—The Fates of Human Societies* by Jared Diamond (New York: Norton, 1999); Subin Im, Cheryl Nakata, Heungsooa Park, and Young-Won Ha, "Determinants of Korean and Japanese New Product Performance: An Interrelational and Process View," *Journal of International Marketing* 11, no. 4 (2003), pp. 81–112. Also, one approach to innovation is copying—see Dexter Roberts, "Did Spark Spark a Copycat?" *BusinessWeek*, February 7, 2005, p. 64.

[23]Thomas L. Friedman, *The World Is Flat* (New York: Farrar, Straus, and Giroux, 2005).

[24]World Bank, 2005.

[25]Gail Edmondson, "Designer," *BusinessWeek*, February 16, 2004, pp. 56–62.

[26]Karen Ruckman, "Technology Sourcing through Acquisitions: Evidence from the U.S. Drug Industry," *Journal of International Business Studies* 36, no. 1 (2005), pp. 89–103.

[27]Several reporters, "The World of Ideas," *Fortune*, July 25, 2005, insert.

Analyzing Product Components for Adaptation

A product is multidimensional, and the sum of all its features determines the bundle of satisfactions (utilities) received by the consumer. To identify all the possible ways a product may be adapted to a new market, it helps to separate its many dimensions into three distinct components as illustrated in Exhibit 12.1, the *Product Component Model.* By using this model, the impact of the cultural, physical, and mandatory factors (discussed previously) that affect a market's acceptance of a product can be focused on the core component, packaging component, and support services component. These components include all a product's tangible and intangible elements and provide the bundle of utilities the market receives from use of the product.

Core Component

The *core component* consists of the physical product—the platform that contains the essential technology—and all its design and functional features. It is on the product platform that product variations can be added or deleted to satisfy local differences. Major adjustments in the platform aspect of the core component may be costly because a change in the platform can affect product processes and thus require additional capital investment. However, alterations in design, functional features, flavors, color, and other aspects can be made to adapt the product to cultural variations. In Japan, Nestlé originally sold the same kind of corn flakes it sells in the United States, but Japanese children ate them mostly as snacks instead of for breakfast. To move the product into the larger breakfast market, Nestlé reformulated its cereals to more closely fit Japanese taste. The Japanese traditionally eat fish and rice for breakfast, so Nestlé developed cereals with familiar tastes—seaweed, carrots and zucchini, and coconuts and papaya. The result was a 12 percent share of the growing breakfast-cereal market.

For the Brazilian market, where fresh orange juice is plentiful, General Foods changed the flavor of its presweetened powdered juice substitute, Tang, from the traditional

Exhibit 12.1
Product Component
Model

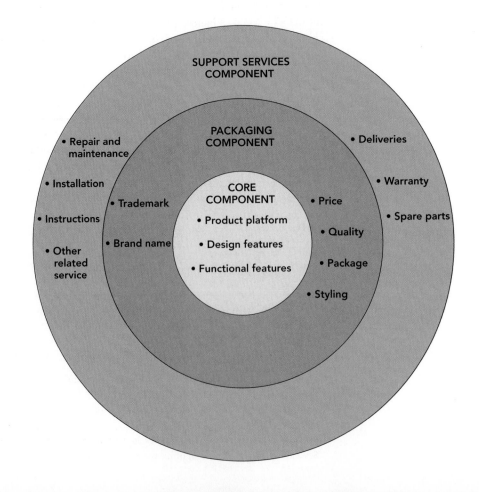

orange to passion fruit and other flavors. Changing flavor or fragrance is often necessary to bring a product in line with what is expected in a culture. Household cleansers with the traditional pine odor and hints of ammonia or chlorine popular in U.S. markets were not successful when introduced in Japan. Many Japanese sleep on the floor on futons with their heads close to the surface they have cleaned, so a citrus fragrance is more pleasing. Rubbermaid could have avoided missteps in introducing its line of baby furniture in Europe with modest changes in the core component. Its colors were not tailored to European tastes, but worst of all, its child's bed didn't fit European-made mattresses!

Functional features can be added or eliminated depending on the market. In markets where hot water is not commonly available, washing machines have heaters as a functional feature. In other markets, automatic soap and bleach dispensers may be eliminated to cut costs or to minimize repair problems. Additional changes may be necessary to meet safety and electrical standards or other mandatory (homologation) requirements. The physical product and all its functional features should be examined as potential candidates for adaptation.

Packaging Component

The *packaging component* includes style features, packaging, labeling, trademarks, brand name, quality, price, and all other aspects of a product's package. Apple Computer found this out the hard way when it first entered the Japanese market. Some of its Macintosh computers were returned unused after customers found the wrapping on the instruction manual damaged! As with the core component, the importance of each of the elements in the eyes of the consumer depends on the need that the product is designed to serve.

Packaging components frequently require both discretionary and mandatory changes. For example, some countries require labels to be printed in more than one language, while others forbid the use of any foreign language. At Hong Kong Disneyland the jungle cruise ride commentary is delivered in Cantonese, Mandarin, and English.[28] Several countries are now requiring country-of-origin labeling for food products. Elements in the packaging component may incorporate symbols that convey an unintended meaning and thus must be changed. One company's red-circle trademark was popular in some countries but was rejected in parts of Asia, where it conjured up images of the Japanese flag. Yellow flowers used in another company trademark were rejected in Mexico, where a yellow flower symbolizes death or disrespect.

A well-known baby-food producer that introduced small jars of baby food in Africa complete with labels featuring a picture of a baby experienced the classic example of misinterpreted symbols: The company was absolutely horrified to find that consumers thought the jars contained ground-up babies. In China, although not a problem of literacy per se, Brugel, a German children's cereal brand that features cartoon drawings of dogs, cats, birds, monkeys, and other animals on the package, was located in the pet foods section of a supermarket. The label had no Chinese, and store personnel were unfamiliar with the product. It is easy to forget that in low-literacy countries, pictures and symbols are taken literally as instructions and information.

Package size and price have an important relationship in bottom of the pyramid countries. Companies find that they have to package in small units to bring the price in line with spending norms. Unilever makes its Sunsilk brand shampoo affordable in India by packaging it in tiny plastic bags, enough for one shampoo.

Care must be taken to ensure that corporate trademarks and other parts of the packaging component do not have unacceptable symbolic meanings. Particular attention should be given to translations of brand names and colors used in packaging. When Ford tried to sell its Pinto automobile in Brazil, it quickly found out that the car model's name translated to "tiny male genitals." White, the color symbolizing purity in Western countries, is the color for mourning in others. In China, P&G packaged diapers in a pink wrapper. Consumers shunned the pink package—pink symbolized a girl, and in a country with a one-child-per-family

---

[28]Don Lee and Kim Christensen, "Translating Anaheim for Asia," *Los Angeles Times*, September 6, 2005, pp. C1, C5.

CROSSING BORDERS 12.4   D'oh! Or Just Dough in Dubai?

Both FOX and Microsoft are "Arabizing" their offerings for the Middle East market. At a trade show in Dubai the latter recently announced three new services and applications specifically targeting the Arab market. In the Windows XP Theme Pack are: MSN Arabia Souk Windows, Microsoft Keyboard Convert Service, and Mircosoft Match-Up Game.

When the Dubai-based Arab satellite TV network, MBC, decided to introduce FOX's *The Simpsons* to the Middle East, they knew the family would have to make some fundamental lifestyle changes.

"Omar Shamshoon," as he is called on the show, looks like the same Homer Simpson, but he has given up beer and bacon, which are both against Islam, and he no longer hangs out at "seedy bars with bums and lowlifes." In Arabia, Homer's beer is soda, and his hot dogs are barbequed Egyptian beef sausages. And the donut-shaped snacks he gobbles are the traditional Arab cookies called kahk.

An Arabized *Simpsons*—called *Al Shamshoon*—made its debut in the Arab world earlier this month, in time for Ramadan, a time of high TV viewership. It uses the original *Simpsons* animation, but the voices are dubbed into Arabic and the scripts have been adapted to make the show more accessible, and acceptable, to Arab audiences.

The family remains, as the producers describe them, "dysfunctional." They still live in Springfield, and "Omar" is still lazy and works at the local nuclear power plant. Bart (now called "Badr") is constantly cheeky to his parents and teachers and is always in trouble. Providing the characters' voices are several popular Egyptian actors, including Mohamed Heneidy, considered the Robert De Niro of the Middle East.

Al Shamshoon is currently broadcast daily during an early-evening prime-time slot, starting with the show's first season. If it is a hit, MBC envisions Arabizing the other 16 seasons.

But there's no guarantee of success. Many Arab blogs and Internet chat sessions have become consumed with how unfunny *Al Shamshoon* is. "They've ruined it! Oh yes they have, *sob*. . . . Why? Why, why oh why?!!!!" wrote a blogger, "Noors," from Oman.

Few shows have more obsessed fans than *The Simpsons*, and their vast online community is worried about whether classic Simpsons' dialogue can even be translated. One blogger wrote, "'Hi-diddly-ho, neighbors!' How the h— are they going to translate that? Or this great quote: Mr. Burns: Oooh, so Mother Nature needs a favor?! Well maybe she should have thought of that when she was besetting us with droughts and floods and poison monkeys! Nature started the fight for survival, and now she wants to quit because she's losing. Well I say, hard cheese."

A blogger, who uses the name "Nibaq," wrote, "I am sure the effort [of] the people who made this show to translate it to Arabic could have made a good original show about an Egyptian family living in Egypt, dealing with religion, life and work and trying to keep a family together. That way they can proudly say Made in Egypt, instead of Made in USA Assembled in Egypt."

Indeed, it will be interesting to watch if "D'oh!" can be converted into dough in Dubai.

Sources: Yasmine El-Rashidi, "D'oh! Arabized Simpsons Aren't Getting Many Laughs," *Wall Street Journal*, October 14, 2005, pp. B1, B2; and "Microsoft Launches New Arabized Solutions and Localized Windows XP Theme Packs at Gitex 2005," *AME Info/Middle East Company News*, September 27, 2005.

rule where males are preferred, you do not want anyone to think you have a girl, even if you do.

Reasons why a company might have to adapt a product's package are countless. In some countries, laws stipulate specific bottle, can, and package sizes and measurement units. If a country uses the metric system, it will probably require that weights and measurements conform to the metric system. Such descriptive words as "giant" or "jumbo" on a package or label may be illegal. High humidity or the need for long shelf life because of extended distribution systems may dictate extra-heavy packaging for some products. As is frequently mentioned, Japanese attitudes about quality include the packaging of a product. A poorly packaged product conveys an impression of poor quality to the Japanese. It is also important to determine if the packaging has other uses in the market. Lever Brothers sells Lux soap in stylish boxes in Japan because more than half of all soap cakes there are purchased during the two gift-giving seasons. Size of the package is also a factor that may make a difference to success in Japan. Soft drinks are sold in smaller-size cans than in the United States to accommodate the smaller Japanese hand. In Japan, most food is sold fresh or in clear packaging, while cans are considered dirty. So when Campbell introduced soups to the Japanese market, it decided to go with a cleaner, more expensive pop-top opener.

Labeling laws vary from country to country and do not seem to follow any predictable pattern. In Saudi Arabia, for example, product names must be specific. "Hot Chili" will not do; it must be "Spiced Hot Chili." Prices are required to be printed on the labels in Venezuela, but in Chile putting prices on labels or in any way suggesting retail prices is illegal. South Africa and the European Union have been engaged in disputes over the labeling of alcoholic beverages. Coca-Cola ran into a legal problem in Brazil with its Diet Coke. Brazilian law interprets *diet* to have medicinal qualities. Under the law, producers must give the daily recommended consumption on the labels of all medicines. Coca-Cola had to get special approval to get around this restriction. Until recently in China, Western products could be labeled in a foreign language with only a small temporary Chinese label affixed somewhere on the package. Under the new Chinese labeling law, however, food products must have their name, contents, and other specifics listed clearly in Chinese printed directly on the package—no temporary labels are allowed.

Labeling laws create a special problem for companies selling products in various markets with different labeling laws and small initial demand in each. In China, for example, there is a demand for American- and European-style snack foods even though the demand is not well developed at this time. The expense of labeling specially to meet Chinese law often makes market entry cost prohibitive. Forward-thinking manufacturers with wide distribution in Asia are adopting packaging standards comparable to those required in the European Union, by providing standard information in several different languages on the same package. A template is designed with a space on the label reserved for locally required content, which can be inserted depending on the destination of a given production batch.

Marketers must examine each of the elements of the packaging component to be certain that this part of the product conveys the appropriate meaning and value to a new market. Otherwise they may be caught short, as was the U.S. soft-drink company that incorporated six-pointed stars as decoration on its package labels. Only when investigating weak sales did they find they had inadvertently offended some of their Arab customers, who interpreted the stars as symbolizing pro-Israeli sentiments.

The most controversial labeling and product contents issue of all regards genetically modified (GM) foods, or what the critics are calling "Frankenfood." The disputes, primarily with the European Union, have huge implications for American firms, which lead the world in this technology. Japan, Australia, and New Zealand are adopting labeling requirements, and other countries are implementing bans and boycotts. And the problem has now spread to the United States itself, with government considering new labeling laws for domestic GM foods and products.

Support Services Component

The *support services* component includes repair and maintenance, instructions, installation, warranties, deliveries, and the availability of spare parts. Many otherwise successful marketing programs have ultimately failed because little attention was given to this product component. Repair and maintenance are especially difficult problems in developing countries. In the United States, a consumer has the option of company service as well as a score of competitive service retailers ready to repair and maintain anything from automobiles to lawn mowers. Equally available are repair parts from company-owned or licensed outlets or the local hardware store. Consumers in a developing country and in many developed countries may not have even one of the possibilities for repair and maintenance available in the United States.

CROSSING BORDERS 12.5   So Your Computer Isn't Working?

Most people have two options when the desk beast starts acting up. Call the service center or read the manual. Both are becoming cross-cultural activities. With increasing frequency, service call centers are being staffed by folks in the Philippines, India, and other developing countries where English is commonly spoken. The savings for the companies can be in the 90 percent range. But for consumers it was tough enough bridging the technician–lay gap. Now a cross-cultural layer is being added to the interaction.

At least many manufacturers are getting more adept at adapting user manuals. Indeed, in some countries the manuals are treasured for their entertainment value. Mike Adams of translation and marketing firm Arial Global Reach explains, "Japanese people really enjoy reading documentation, but that's because Japanese documentation is actually fun to look at." Japanese manuals are often jazzed up with creative cartoons. Even program interfaces are animated. Microsoft's much-maligned Clippy the Paperclip is replaced in Japan with an animated dolphin. "And even highly technical Japanese engineers don't feel at all childish when they view or interact with these animations."

Put those cute characters in manuals in other countries and the customer will doubt the seriousness of the firm. Mark Katib, general manager of Middle East Trans-

lation Services, says most customers in that part of the world, as do Americans, prefer uncluttered, nontechnical explanations. He spends most of his time making sure that information is presented in an acceptable manner, not impinging on people's beliefs.

Apparently you cannot give an Italian a command such as "never do this." The consequences for that kind of language are calls from Italians who have broken their machines by doing exactly "this." Instead, Italian manuals must use less demanding language, like "you might consider . . ."

The Germans will reject manuals with embedded humor. Hungarians like to fix things themselves, so their manuals are more like machine shop guides. Finally, one software maker that developed a WAN (wide-area network) used a flowing stream of text, "WAN WAN WAN WAN" on the package. To a Japanese that's the sound a dog makes, and in Japan no one would buy a product advertising itself by a barking dog.

The main point here is that "technobabble" is hard to translate in any language.

Sources: Michelle Delio, "Read the F***ing Story, then RTFM," *Wired News* (www.wired.com), June 4, 2002; Pete Engardio, Aaron Bernstein, and Manjeet Kripalani, "Is Your Job Next?" *BusinessWeek*, February 3, 2003, pp. 50–60.

In some countries, the concept of routine maintenance or preventive maintenance is not a part of the culture. As a result, products may have to be adjusted to require less-frequent maintenance, and special attention must be given to features that may be taken for granted in the United States.

Literacy rates and educational levels of a country may require a firm to change a product's instructions. A simple term in one country may be incomprehensible in another. In rural Africa, for example, consumers had trouble understanding that Vaseline Intensive Care lotion is absorbed into the skin. *Absorbed* was changed to *soaks into,* and the confusion was eliminated. The Brazilians have successfully overcome the low literacy and technical skills of users of the sophisticated military tanks it sells to Third World countries. The manufacturers include videocassette players and videotapes with detailed repair instructions as part of the standard instruction package. They also minimize spare parts problems by using standardized, off-the-shelf parts available throughout the world. And, of course, other kinds of cultural preferences come into play even in service manuals. For example, Japanese consumers actually read software manuals, some even find them entertaining, and the manuals often include cartoon characters and other diversions.

Although it may seem obvious to translate all instructions into the language of the market, many firms overlook such a basic point. "Do Not Step Here," "Danger," or "Use No Oil" has little meaning to an Arab unfamiliar with the English language. And marketers are now facing a new challenge of this sort. The costs of a customer service call center in the Philippines or India can be 10 percent of those in Omaha. Companies around the world, like

Delta Airlines and General Electric, are flooding such English-speaking countries with call center business. Despite the fluent English of these new, less-expensive employees, all the cross-cultural problems of angry American consumers "talking" to service representatives halfway around the world do crop up. Investments in training will be key if the cost savings are to make up for the quality of services provided.

The Product Component Model can be a useful guide in examining adaptation requirements of products destined for foreign markets. A product should be carefully evaluated on each of the three components for mandatory and discretionary changes that may be needed.

Marketing Consumer Services Globally

As mentioned at the beginning of the chapter, much of the advice regarding adapting products for international consumer markets also applies to adapting services. Moreover, some services are closely associated with products. Good examples are the support services just described or the customer services associated with the delivery of a Big Mac to a consumer in Moscow. However, many consumer services are distinguished by four unique characteristics—intangibility, inseparability, heterogeneity, and perishability—and thus require special consideration.[29]

Products are often classified as tangible, whereas services are *intangible.* Automobiles, computers, and furniture are examples of products that have a physical presence; they are things or objects that can be stored and possessed, and their intrinsic value is embedded within their physical presence. Insurance, dry cleaning, hotel accommodations, and airline passenger or freight service are intangible and have intrinsic value resulting from a process, a performance, or an occurrence that exists only while it is being created.

The intangibility of services results in characteristics unique to a service: It is *inseparable* in that its creation cannot be separated from its consumption;[30] it is *heterogeneous* in that it is individually produced and is thus unique; it is *perishable* in that once created it cannot be stored but must be consumed simultaneously with its creation. Contrast these characteristics with a tangible product that can be produced in one location and consumed elsewhere, that can be standardized, whose quality assurance can be determined and maintained over time, and that can be produced and stored in anticipation of fluctuations in demand.

As is true for many tangible products, a service can be marketed both as an industrial (business-to-business) or a consumer service, depending on the motive of, and use by, the purchaser. For example, travel agents and airlines sell industrial or business services to a businessperson and a consumer service to a tourist. Financial services, hotels, insurance, legal services, and others may each be classified as either a business or consumer service. As one would suspect, the unique characteristics of services result in differences in the marketing of services and the marketing of consumer products.

Services Opportunities in Global Markets

International tourism is by far the largest services export of the United States, ranking behind only capital goods and industrial supplies when all exports are counted. Spending by foreign tourists visiting American destinations such as Orlando or Anaheim is roughly double that spent by foreign airlines on Boeing's commercial jets. Worldwide tourists spent some $3.5 trillion last year, and an agency of the United Nations projects that number will grow to four times that by 2020. The industry employs some 200 million people all around the world. That same agency predicts that China will be followed by the United States, France, Spain, Hong Kong, Italy, Britain, Mexico, Russia, and the Czech Republic as the most popular destinations in the next century. Currently, France, Spain, the United States, Italy, and China are numbers one through five in that order. Most tourists will be, as they are today, Germans, Japanese, and Americans; Chinese will be the fourth largest group. Currently, Japanese tourists contribute the most to U.S. tourism income, at some $20 billion. SARS and the

---

[29]Valarie A. Zeithaml and Mary Jo Bitner, *Services Marketing*, 3rd ed. (New York: McGraw-Hill, 2002).

[30]Bruce D. Keillor, G. Tomas, M. Hult, and Destan Kandemir, "A Study of the Service Encounter in Eight Countries," *Journal of International Marketing* 12, no. 1 (2004), pp. 9–35.

conflicts in the Middle East have had their temporary impacts on otherwise viable tourist destinations. But overall the business is still expected to grow at its traditionally brisk pace.[31]

The dramatic growth in tourism has prompted American firms and institutions to respond by developing new travel services. For example, the Four Seasons Hotel in Philadelphia offers a two-day package including local concerts and museum visits. In addition to its attractions for kids, Orlando, Florida, now sells its opera company with performances by world-class singers. The cities of Phoenix, Las Vegas, and San Diego have formed a consortium and put together a $500,000 marketing budget specifically appealing to foreign visitors to stop at all three destinations in one trip. Even the smallest hotels are finding a global clientele on the Internet.

Other top consumer services exports include transportation, financial services, education, telecommunications, entertainment, information, and health care, in that order. Consider the following examples of each:

- American airlines are falling all over themselves to capture greater shares of the fast-expanding Latin American travel market through investments in local carriers.[32]

- Insurance sales are also burgeoning in Latin America, with joint ventures between local and global firms making the most progress.

- Financial services in China are undergoing a revolution,[33] with new services being offered at an incredible pace—new sources of investor information and National Cash Register ATMs popping up everywhere. Poles are just getting acquainted with ATMs as well.[34]

- Merrill Lynch is going after the investment-trust business that took off after Japan allowed brokers and banks to enter that business for the first time in 1998.

- Almost 600,000 foreign students (63,000 from China) spend some $11 billion a year in tuition to attend American universities and colleges.[35] Executive training is also a viable export for U.S. companies.[36]

- Currently, phone rates in markets such as Germany, Italy, and Spain are so high that American companies cannot maintain toll-free information hotlines or solicit phone-order catalog sales. Other telecommunications markets are deregulating, creating opportunities for foreign firms. Wireless communications are taking Japan and Europe by storm.

- *Buffy the Vampire Slayer*, *Xena, Hercules,* and comparably "dumbed-down" (i.e., heavy on action, violence, and sex) video-game heroes are conquering electronic screens worldwide. Even movies on Pearl Harbor are successfully being exhibited in Japan.

- Cable TV is exploding in Latin America.

- The latest Gallup poll in China indicates that 43 percent of Beijing residents are aware of the Internet.

- Sporting events are being sold all over the world—Mexican football in Los Angeles,[37] American football in Scotland, American baseball in Mexico, and professional soccer in China.

---

[31]Although tourists seem to be ignoring travel warnings more frequently: "Who Do We Trust?" *Conde Nast Traveler*, March 2005, pp. 53–62.

[32]Chris Kraul and James F. Peltz, "Low-Cost Carriers Set to Enter Mexican Airspace," *Los Angeles Times*, August 1, 2005, pp. C1, C5.

[33]Don Lee, "BofA Gains Foothold in China," *Los Angeles Times*, June 12, 2005, pp. C1, C9.

[34]For a good summary of the burgeoning international trade in financial services, see *The Economist*, "Open Wider: A Survey of International Banking," May 21, 2005, insert.

[35]"Free Degrees to Fly," *The Economist*, February 26, 2005, pp. 67–69.

[36]David M. Montgomery, "Asian Management Education: Some 21st Century Issues," *Journal of Public Policy and Marketing* 24, no. 1 (2005), pp. 150–154.

[37]David Davis, "Conquistador in Cleats," *Los Angeles Times Magazine*, March 13, 2005, pp. 8–11.

CROSSING BORDERS 12.6 Even the Old Technology and a Telemarketer Can Save Your Life

Usually, outbound telemarketers are left out in the cold, saleswise. But Maria del Pilar Basto, a telemarketing agent for Bell South, recently reached a customer who was himself out in the cold—Colombian hiker Leonardo Diaz, trapped in an Andes mountain blizzard at an altitude above 12,500 feet. Stuck in the storm for 24 hours, Diaz had tried to call out on his cell phone but discovered that his prepaid minutes had run out. Basto's well-timed call initially was simply to offer to sell him more minutes. Once on the phone, though, she and her co-workers kept Diaz talking, to keep him awake and help stave off hypothermia, until rescuers arrived.

Imagine if Senor Diaz had packed some of the new stuff available in Japan. How about Sanyo's picture phone with voice dialing (he wouldn't have had to take his hands out of his gloves), an electronic organizer (maybe he wouldn't have gotten lost in the first place), and a built-in answering machine (Senorita del Pilar's call would have gone through even if he was frozen solid). How about a wearable PC with a headband-mounted display? Even in a blizzard that would be entertaining. Pokemon at 12,000 feet! A MiniDisc player? That would have provided some music with which to while away the time, or a method of leaving a "last-words" message for his relatives. And then there's the Dick Tracey watch–phone combination, voice activated, with headphones. Perhaps Mr. Diaz might have kept better track of his minutes with that gadget.

Too bad Sanyo, Sony, or Samsung hadn't already come up with a combination compass–radar–hand warmer for Senor Diaz. Maybe Apple will develop that product after the Nano.

Sources: Lisa M. Keefe, "Strange but True, Nice Save," *Marketing News*, December 9, 2002, p. 16; Janice Brand, "Beyond Pokemon, Hot Products," *CIO*, January 1, 2003, p. 62; Lev Grossman and Sora Song, "Stevie's Little Wonder Honey, He Shrunk the I-Pod," *Technology*, September 19, 2005, p. 63.

- Finally, not only are foreigners coming to the United States for healthcare services in fast-growing numbers, but North American firms are building hospitals abroad as well. Recently two infants, one from Sweden and one from Japan, received heart transplants at Loma Linda Hospital in California—laws in both their countries prohibit such life-saving operations. Beijing Toronto International Hospital will soon open its doors for some 250 Chinese patients; the services include a 24-hour satellite link for consultations with Toronto. Asian[38] and Mexican[39] competitors are also now competing for this global market as well. Of course, the negative side of this trend is represented by the growing illegal global trade in organs for transplant.[40]

Barriers to Entering Global Markets for Consumer Services

Most other services—automobile rentals, airline services, entertainment, hotels, and tourism, to name a few—are inseparable and require production and consumption to occur almost simultaneously; thus exporting is not a viable entry method for them. The vast majority of services (some 85 percent) enter foreign markets by licensing, franchising, or direct investment. Four kinds of barriers face consumer services marketers in this growing sector of the global marketplace: protectionism, controls on transborder data flows, protection of intellectual property, and cultural requirements for adaptation.

Protectionism. The European Union is making modest progress toward establishing a single market for services. However, exactly how foreign service providers will be treated as unification proceeds is not clear. Reciprocity and harmonization, key concepts in the Single European Act, possibly will be used to curtail the entrance of some service industries into Europe. The U.S. film and entertainment industry seems to be a particularly difficult sector, although Vivendi's (a French company) purchase of Universal Studios made things a bit more interesting. A directive regarding transfrontier television broadcasting created

---

[38]Frederik Balfour, Manjeet Kripalani, Kerry Capell, and Laura Cohen, "Sand, Sun, and Surgery," *BusinessWeek*, February 16, 2004, pp. 48–49.

[39]Debora Vrana, "Health Net to Expand Coverage for Cross-Border Care," *Los Angeles Times*, September 11, 2004, pp. C1, C3.

[40]Nancy Scheper-Hughes, "Organs without Borders," *Foreign Policy*, January/February 2005, pp. 26–27.

CROSSING BORDERS 12.7   Just to Go to School

Kofi Annan, the secretary-general of the United Nations, did it; so did Vicente Fox of Mexico, Jacques Chirac of France, and King Abdullah of Jordan. All of them went to "college" in America (the French president enhanced his experience with a job scooping ice cream). Moreover, one-third of U.S. Nobel Prize winners were foreign born. But as the war for talent has given way to the war against terrorism, the welcome America extends to foreigners on its campuses is becoming much more guarded.

Last year, nearly 600,000 foreign students were enrolled at American universities and colleges. According to the Institute of International Education (IIE), about half came from Asia, mainly China and India. Fewer than 7 percent came from the Middle East. Students account for under 2 percent of all nonimmigrant visas (though they have the right to stay for much longer than tourists). They spend $11 billion a year on tuition and living expenses, helping to make higher education America's fifth-largest service export. And, as any visit to a Silicon Valley start-up reveals, they bring huge talent to the American economy.

Until September 11, 2001, the chief complaint was that America did not fully exploit this human capital.

Like other countries, it limits the amount of time foreign students can work in the country after they graduate. The IIE frets that America's share of the foreign-student market has dropped from 40 percent to under 30 percent in the past decade. It blames not only higher university fees in the United States and greater competition from Europe and Australia, but also America's cumbersome visa process.

For college students from mostly Muslim Malaysia it used to take about two weeks to get a student visa, but last year 20 Malay freshmen had to wait six months. They missed the fall semester. Undergraduate applications are declining nationwide. White House science adviser John H. Marburber III argues the delays do not reflect policies to exclude. However, Representative Dana Rohrabacher (R-Calif.) says that the appropriate objective is "to reduce the need to attract such a high percentage of foreign students."

Sources: "Student Visas: Chillier on Campus," *The Economist*, November 24, 2001, pp. 31–32; Catherine Arnst, "How the War on Terror Is Damaging the Brain Pool," *BusinessWeek*, May 19, 2003, pp. 72–73; James Boone, "Visa Crackdown Cost US Cream of Foreign Students," *The Times* (London), November 29, 2004, p. 33.

---

a quota for European programs, requiring EU member states to ensure that at least 50 percent of entertainment air time is devoted to "European works." The European Union argues that this set-aside for domestic programming is necessary to preserve Europe's cultural identity. The consequences for the U.S. film industry are significant, since over 40 percent of U.S. film industry profits come from foreign revenues.

Restrictions on Transborder Data Flows.   There is intense concern about how to deal with the relatively new "problem" of transborder data transfers. The European Commission is concerned that data on individuals (such as income, spending preferences, debt repayment histories, medical conditions, and employment data) are being collected, manipulated, and transferred between companies with little regard to the privacy of the affected individuals. A proposed directive by the Commission would require the consent of the individual before data are collected or processed. A wide range of U.S. service companies would be affected by such a directive—insurance underwriters, banks, credit reporting firms, direct marketing companies, and tour operators are a few examples. The directive would have broad effects on data processing and data analysis firms because it would prevent a firm from electronically transferring information about individual European consumers to the United States for computer processing. Hidden in all the laws and directives are the unstated motives of most countries: a desire to inhibit the activities of multinationals and to protect local industry. As the global data transmission business continues to explode into the new century, regulators will focus increased attention in that direction.

Protection of Intellectual Property.   An important form of competition that is difficult to combat arises from pirated trademarks, processes, copyrights, and patents.

Computer design and software, trademarks, brand names, and other intellectual properties are easy to duplicate and difficult to protect. The protection of intellectual property rights is a major problem in the services industries. Countries seldom have adequate—or any— legislation, and any laws they do have are extremely difficult to enforce. The Trade-Related Intellectual Property Rights (TRIPs) part of the GATT agreement obligates all members to provide strong protection for copyright and related rights, patents, trademarks, trade secrets, industrial designs, geographic indications, and layout designs for integrated circuits. The TRIPs agreement is helpful, but the key issue is that enforcement is very difficult without the full cooperation of host countries.

The situation in China has been particularly bad because that country has not been active in combating piracy of intellectual property. The annual cost of pirated software, CDs, books, and movies in China alone is estimated to be more than $1 billion. Worldwide, industry estimates are that U.S. companies lose $60 billion annually on piracy of all types of intellectual property. Because duplicating software, electronically recorded music, and movies is so easy, pirated copies often are available within a few days of their release. In Thailand, for example, illegal copies of movies are available within 10 days of their release in the United States. In Russia, pirated movies are sometimes available before their (legal) U.S. debut!

Cultural Barriers and Adaptation.   Because trade in services frequently involves people-to-people contact, culture plays a much bigger role in services than in merchandise trade. Examples are many: Eastern Europeans are perplexed by Western expectations that unhappy workers put on a "happy face" when dealing with customers. But McDonald's requires Polish employees to smile whenever they interact with customers. Such a requirement strikes many employees as artificial and insincere. The company has learned to encourage managers in Poland to probe employee problems and to assign troubled workers to the kitchen rather than to the food counter. Japanese Internet purchasers often prefer to pay in cash and in person rather than trust the Internet transaction or pay high credit card fees.

As another example, notice if the Japanese student sitting next to you in class ever verbally disagrees with your instructor. Classroom interactions vary substantially around the world. Students in Japan listen to lectures, take notes, and ask questions only after class, if then. In Japan the idea of grading class participation is nonsense. Conversely, because Spaniards are used to large undergraduate classes (hundreds rather than dozens), they tend to talk to their friends even when the instructor is talking. Likewise, healthcare delivery systems and doctor–patient interactions reflect cultural differences. Americans ask questions and get second opinions. Innovative healthcare services are developed on the basis of extensive marketing research. However, in Japan the social hierarchy is reflected heavily in the patients' deference to their doctors. While Japanese patient compliance is excellent and longevity is the best in the world, the healthcare system there is relatively unresponsive to the expressed concerns of consumers.

Japanese also tend to take a few long vacations—7 to 10 days is the norm. Thus vacation packages designed for them are packed with activities. Phoenix, Las Vegas, and San Diego or Rome, Geneva, Paris, and London in 10 days makes sense to them. The Four Seasons Hotel chain provides special pillows, kimonos, slippers, and teas for Japanese guests. Virgin Atlantic Airways and other long-haul carriers now have interactive screens available for each passenger, allowing viewing of Japanese (or American, French, etc.) movies and TV.

Managing a global services workforce is certainly no simple task. Just ask the folks at UPS. Some of the surprises UPS ran into included indignation in France when drivers were told they couldn't have wine with lunch, protests in Britain when drivers' dogs were banned from delivery trucks, dismay in Spain when it was found that the brown UPS trucks resembled the local hearses, and shock in Germany when brown shirts were required for the first time since 1945.

And while tips of 10 to 15 percent are an important part of services workers' incentives in the United States, this is not the case in Germany, where tips are rounded to the nearest deutsche mark. Thus closer management of service personnel is required in those countries to maintain high levels of customer satisfaction.

Clearly, opportunities for the marketing of consumer services will continue to grow in the 21st century. International marketers will have to be quite creative in responding to the legal and cultural challenges of delivering high-quality services in foreign markets and to foreign customers at domestic locales.

Brands in International Markets

Hand in hand with global products and services are global brands. A *global brand* is defined as the worldwide use of a name, term, sign, symbol (visual and/or auditory),[41] design, or combination thereof intended to identify goods or services of one seller and to differentiate them from those of competitors. Much like the experience with global products, the question of whether or not to establish global brands has no single answer. However, the importance of a brand name, even in the nonprofit sector, is unquestionable.[42] Indeed, Exhibit 12.2 lists the estimated worth (equity) of the 20 top global brands. And, as indicated in previous chapters, protecting brand names is also a big business.

[41]Nader T. Tavassoli and Jin K. Han, "Auditory and Visual Brand Identifiers in Chinese and English," *Journal of International Marketing* 10, no. 2 (November 2002), pp. 13–28.

[42]John A. Quelch and Nathalie Laidler-Kylander, *The New Global Brands* (Mason, OH: Southwestern, 2006).

Exhibit 12.2
Top Twenty Brands

Rank 2005/2004	2005 Brand Value (millions)	2004 Brand Value (millions)	Change (%)	Country of Ownership	Description
1/1 Coca-Cola	$67,525	$67,394	0%	U.S.	While Coke struggles to add new diet and energy drinks, it is still searching for a zippier global advertising message.
2/2 Microsoft	59,941	61,372	−2	U.S.	It continues to reach into hot consumer markets such as TV set-top box software, video games, and mobile phones.
3/3 IBM	53,376	53,791	−1	U.S.	The sale of the notebook business to Lenovo continues the transformation from a computer manufacturer to a services and consulting company.
4/4 GE	46,996	44,111	7	U.S.	Hawking itself as a center of cutting-edge innovation and source of earth-friendly products has enhanced GE's brand image.
5/5 Intel	35,588	33,499	6	U.S.	Thanks to its Pentium chips and Centrino wireless notebooks, Intel is a household name worldwide.
6/8 Nokia	26,452	24,041	10	Finland	Looking to take on Apple's iPod as cell phones and MP3 players converge into one device.
7/6 Disney	26,441	27,113	−2	U.S.	New CEO Bob Iger must develop new offerings. The trend is toward edgier fare even for kids.
8/7 McDonald's	26,014	25,001	4	U.S.	Who's not lovin' it? Big Mac has reconnected with moms and teens thanks to new offerings like salads and a hipper image.
9/9 Toyota	24,837	22,673	10	Japan	Poised to pass GM globally, Toyota's image gets a big boost from its growing stable of hybrids.
10/10 Marlboro	21,189 **2005**	22,128 **2004**	−4	U.S.	Still tops in the U.S., the world's biggest cigarette brand has struggled in Europe of late, losing share in France and in Germany.

A successful brand is the most valuable resource a company has. The brand name[43] encompasses the years of advertising, good will, quality evaluation, product experience, and other beneficial attributes the market associates with the product. Brand image is at the very core of business identity and strategy. Customers everywhere respond to images,[44] myths, and metaphors that help them define their personal and national identities within a global context of world culture and product benefits.[45] Global brands play an important role in that process. The value of Kodak, Sony, Coca-Cola, McDonald's, Toyota, and Marlboro is indisputable. One estimate of the value of Coca-Cola, the world's most valuable brand, places it at over $67 billion and growing. In fact, one authority speculates that brands are so valuable that companies will soon include a "statement of value" addendum to their balance sheets to include intangibles such as the value of their brands.

---

[43]Yih Hwai Lee and Kim Soon Ang, "Brand Name Suggestiveness: A Chinese Language Perspective," *International Journal of Research in Marketing* 20, no. 4 (2003), pp. 323–335.

[44]Pamela W. Henderson, Joseph A. Cote, Siew Meng Leong, and Berd Schmitt, "Building Strong Brands in Asia: Selecting the Visual Components of Image to Maximize Brand Strength," *International Journal of Research in Marketing* 20, no. 4 (2003), pp. 297–313.

[45]Douglas B. Holt, "What Becomes an Icon Most?" *Harvard Business Review*, March 2003, pp. 43–49.

Rank 2005/2004	2005 Brand Value (millions)	2004 Brand Value (millions)	Change (%)	Country of Ownership	Description
11/11 Mercedes-Benz	20,006	21,331	−6	Germany	Quality problems and strategic errors have punctured Mercedes' sales for two years. Will the new S-Class sedan help buff its image?
12/13 Citi	19,967	19,971	0	U.S.	A history in global markets that often helps it trump local players has helped to shield Citi from recent scandals.
13/12 Hewlett-Packard	18,866	20,978	−10	U.S.	Printer king HP faces increased competition, and new CEO Mark Hurd must figure a way to improve performance against computer rivals Dell and IBM.
14/14 American Express	18,559	17,683	5	U.S.	AmEx's star is rising since it won the right to let banks issue its cards. AmEx invested heavily in marketing spending worldwide.
15/15 Gillette	17,534	16,723	5	U.S.	The King of Blades is on a roll, with its battery-powered M3Power razor helping produce record results. Now it's getting ready to merge with P&G.
16/17 BMW	17,126	15,886	8	Germany	BMW is in the fast-lane, proving that the right mix of engineering and marketing can propel an auto maker's performance even in tough markets.
17/16 Cisco	16,592	15,948	4	U.S.	Partnered with Microsoft to tackle Internet security and limit damage from viruses. A new focus on small business is paying off.
18/44 Louis Vuitton	16,077	NA	NA	France	With Uma Thurman promoting its hot new Monogram Cerises collection, the world's richest luxury brand seems unstoppable.
19/18 Honda	15,788	14,874	6	Japan	Consumers can't get enough of Honda. Now it plans to boost annual North American production to 1.4 million vehicles by 2007.
20/21 Samsung	14,956	12,553	19	S. Korea	One big brand marketed everywhere, plus an explosion of popular cell phones, is boosting sales of all its gadgets.

Source: Robert Berner and David Kiley, "Global Brands," *BusinessWeek*, August 1, 2005, p. 90–91.

Copying is the highest form of flattery? Not so in the car business. The new QQ model from Chinese company Chery (left) resembles the *Matiz* or *Spark* from GM's Daewoo (right) perhaps a bit too much. (© *KEVIN LEE/BLOOMBERG NEWS/Landov*)

Global Brands

Naturally, companies with such strong brands strive to use those brands globally.[46] In fact, even perceived "globalness" appears to lead to increases in sales.[47] The Internet and other technologies accelerate the pace of the globalization of brands. Even for products that must be adapted to local market conditions, a global brand can be successfully used with careful consideration.[48] Heinz produces a multitude of products that are sold under the Heinz brand all over the world. Many are also adapted to local tastes. In the United Kingdom, for example, Heinz Baked Beans Pizza (available with cheese or sausage) was a runaway hit, selling over 2.5 million pizzas in the first six months after its introduction. In the British market, Heinz's brand of baked beans is one of the more popular products. The British consumer eats an average of 16 cans annually, for a sales total of $1.5 billion a year. The company realizes that consumers in other countries are unlikely to rush to stores for bean pizzas, but the idea could lead to the creation of products more suited to other cultures and markets.

Ideally a global brand gives a company a uniform worldwide image that enhances efficiency and cost savings when introducing other products associated with the brand name, but not all companies believe a single global approach is the best. Indeed, we know that the same brand does not necessarily hold the same meanings in different countries. In addition to companies such as Apple,[49] Kellogg, Coca-Cola, Caterpillar, and Levi's, which use the same brands worldwide, other multinationals such as Nestlé, Mars, Procter & Gamble,[50] and Gillette have some brands that are promoted worldwide and others that are country specific. Among companies that have faced the question of whether to make all

---

[46]Isabelle Schuiling and Jean-Noel Kapferer, "Real Differences Between Local and International Brands: Strategic Implications for International Marketers," *Journal of International Marketing* 12, no. 4 (2004), pp. 97–112.

[47]Jan-Benedict E. M. Steenkamp, Rajeev Batra, and Dana L. Alden, "How Perceived Brand Globalness Creates Brand Value," *Journal of International Business Studies* 34 (2003), pp. 53–65.

[48]Shi Zhang and Bernd H. Schmitt, "Creating Local Brands in Multilingual International Markets," *Journal of Marketing Research* 38 (August 2001), pp. 313–325; Brand Name Translation: Language Constraints, Product Attributes, and Consumer Perceptions in East and Southeast Asia," *Journal of International Marketing* 10, no. 2 (November 2002), pp. 29–45; Giana M. Eckhardt and Michael J. Houston, "Cultural Paradoxes Reflected in Brand Meaning: McDonald's in Shanghai, China," *Journal of International Marketing* 10, no. 2 (November 2002), pp. 68–82.

[49]Deborah L. Vence, "Not Taking Care of Business," *Marketing News*, March 15, 2005, pp. 19–21.

[50]"The Rise of Superbrands," *The Economist*, February 5, 2005, pp. 63–65.

Caterpillar shoes and clothing—apparently Norwegian consumers like the industrial strength of this brand.

their brands global, not all have followed the same path.[51] For example, despite BMW's worldwide successes, only recently did the company create its first global brands position.

Companies that already have successful country-specific brand names must balance the benefits of a global brand against the risk of losing the benefits of an established brand. And some brand names simply do not translate.[52] The cost of reestablishing the same level of brand preference and market share for the global brand that the local brand has must be offset against the long-term cost savings and benefits of having only one brand name worldwide. In those markets where the global brand is unknown, many companies are buying local brands of products that consumers want and revamping, repackaging, and finally relaunching them with a new image. Unilever purchased a local brand of washing powder, Biopan, which had a 9 percent share of the market in Hungary; after relaunching, market share rose to about 25 percent.

When Mars, a U.S. company that includes candy and pet food among its product lines, adopted a global strategy, it brought all its products under a global brand, even those with strong local brand names. In Britain, the largest candy market in Europe, M&Ms were sold as Treets and Snickers candy was sold under the name Marathon to avoid association with *knickers,* the British word for women's underpants. To bring the two candy products under the global umbrella, Mars returned the candies to their original names. The pet food division adopted Whiskas and Sheba for cat foods and Pedigree for dog food as the global brand name replacing KalKan. To support this global division that accounts for over $4 billion annually, Mars also developed a Web site for the pet food brands. The site functions as a "global infrastructure" that can be customized locally by any Pedigree Petfoods branch worldwide. For instance, Pedigree offices can localize languages and information on subjects such as veterinarians and cat-owner gatherings.

National Brands

A different strategy is followed by the Nestlé Company, which has a stable of global and country-specific national brands in its product line. The Nestlé name itself is promoted globally, but its global brand expansion strategy is two-pronged. In some markets it acquires well-established national brands when it can and builds on their strengths—there are 7,000 local brands in its family of brands. In other markets where there are no strong brands it can acquire, it uses global brand names. The company is described as preferring brands to be local, people to be regional, and technology to be global. It does, however, own some of the world's largest global brands; Nescafé is but one.

Unilever is another company that follows a similar strategy of a mix of national and global brands. In Poland, Unilever introduced its Omo brand detergent (sold in many other countries), but it also purchased a local brand, Pollena 2000. Despite a strong introduction of two competing brands, Omo by Unilever and Ariel by Procter & Gamble, a refurbished Pollena 2000 had the largest market share a year later. Unilever's explanation was that eastern European consumers are leery of new brands; they want brands that are affordable and in keeping with their own tastes and values. Pollena 2000 is successful not just because it is cheaper but because it chimes with local values.

Multinationals must also consider rises in nationalistic pride that occur in some countries and their impact on brands. In India, for example, Unilever considers it critical that its

---

[51]Prominent among those arguing against global brands are David A. Aaker and Erich Joachimsthaler, "The Lure of Global Branding," *Harvard Business Review*, November–December 1999; Aysegul Ozsomer and Gregory E. Prussia, "Competing Perspectives in International Strategy: Contingency and Process Models," *Journal of International Marketing*, January 1, 2000, pp. 27–50. For an interesting view of the arguments for and against globalization of brands see Anand P. Raman, "The Global Face Off," *Harvard Business Review*, June 2003, pp. 35–46.

[52]June Francis, Janet P. Y. Lam, and Jan Walls, "The Impact of Linguistic Differences on International Brand Name Standardization: A Comparison of English and Chinese Brand Names of Fortune 500 Companies," *Journal of International Marketing* 10, no. 1 (2002), pp. 98–116.

brands, such as Surf detergent and Lux and Lifebuoy soaps, are viewed as Indian brands. Just as is the case with products, the answer to the question of when to go global with a brand is "It depends—the market dictates." Use global brands where possible and national brands where necessary.

Country-of-Origin Effect and Global Brands

As discussed earlier, brands are used as external cues to taste, design, performance, quality, value, prestige, and so forth. In other words, the consumer associates the value of the product with the brand. The brand can convey either a positive or a negative message about the product to the consumer and is affected by past advertising and promotion, product reputation, and product evaluation and experience. In short, many factors affect brand image. One factor that is of great concern to multinational companies that manufacture worldwide is the country-of-origin effect on the market's perception of the product.

Country-of-origin effect (COE) can be defined as any influence that the country of manufacture, assembly, or design has on a consumer's positive or negative perception of a product. A company competing in global markets today manufactures products worldwide; when the customer becomes aware of the country of origin, there is the possibility that the place of manufacture will affect product or brand image.[53]

The country, the type of product, and the image of the company and its brands all influence whether the country of origin will engender a positive or negative reaction. A variety of generalizations can be made about country-of-origin effects on products and brands.[54] Consumers tend to have stereotypes about products and countries that have been formed by experience, hearsay, and myth. Following are some of the more frequently cited generalizations.

Consumers have broad but somewhat vague stereotypes about specific countries and specific product categories that they judge "best": English tea, French perfume, Chinese silk, Italian leather, Japanese electronics, Jamaican rum, and so on. Stereotyping of this nature is typically product specific and may not extend to other categories of products from these countries.

The importance of these types of stereotypes was emphasized recently as a result of a change in U.S. law that requires any cloth "substantially altered" (woven, for instance) in another country to identify that country on its label. Designer labels such as Ferragamo, Gucci, and Versace are affected in that they now must include on the label "Made in China" because the silk comes from China. The lure to pay $195 and up for scarves "Made in Italy" by Ferragamo loses some of its appeal when accompanied with a "Made in China" label. As one buyer commented, "I don't care if the scarves are made in China as long as it doesn't say so on the label." The irony is that 95 percent of all silk comes from China, which has the reputation for the finest silk but also a reputation of producing cheap scarves. The "best" scarves are made in France or Italy by one of the *haute couture* designers.

Ethnocentrism can also have country-of-origin effects; feelings of national pride—the "buy American" effect, for example—can influence attitudes toward foreign products. Honda, which manufactures one of its models almost entirely in the United States, recognizes this phenomenon and points out how many component parts are made in America in some of its advertisements. On the other hand, others have a stereotype of Japan as producing the "best" automobiles. A recent study found that U.S. automobile producers may suffer comparatively tarnished images regardless of whether they actually produce superior products.

---

[53]Svein Ottar Olsen and Ulf H. Olsson, "Multientity Scaling and the Consistency of Country-of-Origin Attitudes," *Journal of International Business Studies* 33, no. 1 (2002), pp. 149–167; Jill Gabrielle Klein, "Us Versus Them, or Us Versus Everyone? Delineating Consumer Aversion to Foreign Goods," *Journal of International Business Studies* 33, no. 2 (2002), pp. 345–363.

[54]Peeter W.J. Verleigh, Jan-Benedict E.M. Steenkamp, and Matthew T.G. Meulenberg, "Country-of-Origin Effects in Consumer Processing of Advertising Claims," *International Journal of Research in Marketing* 22, no. 2 (2005), pp. 127–139.

Countries are also stereotyped on the basis of whether they are industrialized, in the process of industrializing, or developing. These stereotypes are less product specific; they are more a perception of the quality of goods and services in general produced within the country. Industrialized countries have the highest quality image, and products from developing countries generally encounter bias.

In Russia, for example, the world is divided into two kinds of products: "ours" and "imported." Russians prefer fresh, homegrown food products but imported clothing and manufactured items. Companies hoping to win loyalty by producing in Russia have been unhappily surprised. Consumers remain cool toward locally produced Polaroid cameras and Philips irons. On the other hand, computers produced across the border in Finland are considered high quality. For Russians, country of origin is more important than brand name as an indicator of quality. South Korean electronics manufacturers have difficulty convincing Russians that their products are as good as Japanese ones. Goods produced in Malaysia, Hong Kong, or Thailand are more suspect still. Eastern Europe is considered adequate for clothing, but poor for food or durables. Turkey and China are at the bottom of the heap.

One might generalize that the more technical the product, the less positive is the perception of one manufactured in a less-developed or newly industrializing country. There is also the tendency to favor foreign-made products over domestic-made in less-developed countries. Foreign products fare not so well because consumers in developing countries have stereotypes about the quality of foreign-made products even from industrialized countries. A survey of consumers in the Czech Republic found that 72 percent of Japanese products were considered to be of the highest quality, German goods followed with 51 percent, Swiss goods with 48 percent, Czech goods with 32 percent, and, last, the United States with 29 percent.

One final generalization about COE involves fads that often surround products from particular countries or regions in the world. These fads are most often product specific and generally involve goods that are themselves faddish in nature. European consumers' affection for American products is quite fickle. The affinity for Jeep Cherokees, Budweiser beer, and Bose sound systems of the 1990s has faded to outright animosity[55] to American brands as a protest of American political policies. This echoes the 1970s and 1980s backlash against anything American, but in the 1990s American was in. In China, anything Western seems to be the fad. If it is Western, it is in demand, even at prices three and four times higher than those of domestic products. In most cases such fads wane after a few years as some new fad takes over.

There are exceptions to the generalizations presented here, but it is important to recognize that country of origin can affect a product or brand's image significantly. Further, not every consumer is sensitive to a product's country of origin. A finding in a recent study suggested that more knowledgeable consumers are more sensitive to a product's COE than those less knowledgeable. Another study report that COE varies across consumer groups; Japanese were found to be more sensitive than American consumers.[56] The multinational company needs to take these factors into consideration in product development and marketing strategy because a negative country stereotype can be detrimental to a product's success unless overcome with effective marketing.

Once the market gains experience with a product, negative stereotypes can be overcome. Nothing would seem less plausible than selling chopsticks made in Chile to Japan, but it happened. It took years for a Chilean company to overcome doubts about the quality of its product, but persistence, invitations to Japanese to visit the Chilean poplar forests that

---

[55]Lys S. Amine, Mike C. H. Chao, and Mark J. Arnold, "Exploring the Practical Effects of Origin, Animosity, and Price-Quality Issues: Two Case Studies of Taiwan and Acer in China," *Journal of International Marketing* 13, no. 2 (2005), pp. 114–150; Edwin J. Nijssen and Susan P. Douglas, "Examining the Animosity Model in a Country with a High Level of Foreign Trade," *International Journal of Research in Marketing* 21, no. 1 (2004), pp. 23–38; Kevin Allison, "World Turning Its Back on Brand America," *Financial Times*, August 1, 2005, p. 3.

[56]Zeynep Gurhan-Canli and Durariraj Maheswaran, "Cultural Variations in Country of Origin Effects," *Journal of Marketing Research* 37 (August 2000), pp. 309–317.

provided the wood for the chopsticks, and a high-quality product finally overcame doubt; now the company cannot meet the demand for chopsticks.

Country stereotyping can be overcome with good marketing. The image of Korean electronics and autos improved substantially in the United States once the market gained positive experience with Korean brands. All of this stresses the importance of building strong global brands like Sony, General Electric, and Levi's. Brands effectively advertised and products properly positioned can help ameliorate a less-than-positive country stereotype.

Private Brands

Private brands owned by retailers are growing as challengers to manufacturers' brands, whether global or country specific. Store brands are particularly important in Europe compared to the United States.[57] In the food-retailing sector in Britain and many European countries, private labels owned by national retailers increasingly confront manufacturers' brands. From blackberry jam and vacuum-cleaner bags to smoked salmon and sun-dried tomatoes, private-label products dominate grocery stores in Britain and in many of the hypermarkets of Europe. Private brands have captured nearly 30 percent of the British and Swiss markets and more than 20 percent of the French and German markets. In some European markets, private-label market share has doubled in just the past five years.

Sainsbury, one of Britain's largest grocery retailers with 420 stores, reserves the best shelf space for its own brands. A typical Sainsbury store has about 16,000 products, of which 8,000 are Sainsbury labels. These labels account for two-thirds of store sales. The company avidly develops new products, launching 1,400 to 1,500 new private-label items each year, and weeds out hundreds of others no longer popular. It launched its own Novon brand laundry detergent; in the first year, its sales climbed past Procter & Gamble's and Unilever's top brands to make it the top-selling detergent in Sainsbury stores and the second-best seller nationally, with a 30 percent market share. The 15 percent margin on private labels claimed by chains such as Sainsbury helps to explain why their operating profit margins are as high as 8 percent, or eight times the profit margins of their U.S. counterparts.

Private labels are formidable competitors. They provide the retailer with high margins; they receive preferential shelf space and strong in-store promotion; and, perhaps most important for consumer appeal, they are quality products at low prices. Contrast this with manufacturers' brands, which traditionally are premium priced and offer the retailer lower margins than they get from private labels.

To maintain market share, global brands will have to be priced competitively and provide real consumer value. Global marketers must examine the adequacy of their brand strategies in light of such competition. This may make the cost and efficiency benefits of global brands even more appealing.

---

[57]Tulin Erdem, Ying Zhao, and An Valenzuela, "Performance of Store Brands: A Cross-Country Analysis of Consumer Store-Brand Preferences, Perceptions, and Risk," *Journal of Marketing Research* 41, no. 1 (2004), pp. 59–72.

Summary

The growing globalization of markets that gives rise to standardization must be balanced with the continuing need to assess all markets for those differences that might require adaptation for successful acceptance. The premise that global communications and other worldwide socializing forces have fostered a homogenization of tastes, needs, and values in a significant sector of the population across all cultures is difficult to deny. However, more than one authority has noted that in spite of the forces of homogenization, consumers also see the world of global symbols, company images, and product choice through the lens of their own local culture and its stage of development and market sophistication. Each product must be viewed in light of how it is perceived by each culture with which it comes in contact. What is acceptable and comfortable within one group may be radically new and resisted within others, depending on the experiences and perceptions of each group. Understanding that an established product in one culture may be considered an innovation in another is critical in planning and developing consumer products for foreign markets. Analyzing a product as an innovation and using the Product Component Model may provide the marketer with important leads for adaptation.

Questions

1. Define the following terms:

   product diffusion   homologation

   Product Component Model innovation

   global brand   green marketing

   quality

2. Debate the issue of global versus adapted products for the international marketer.

3. Define the country-of-origin effect and give examples.

4. The text discusses stereotypes, ethnocentrism, degree of economic development, and fads as the basis for generalizations about country-of-origin effect on product perception. Explain each and give an example.

5. Discuss product alternatives and the three marketing strategies: domestic market extension, multidomestic markets, and global market strategies.

6. Discuss the different promotional/product strategies available to an international marketer.

7. Assume you are deciding to "go international." Outline the steps you would take to help you decide on a product line.

8. Products can be adapted physically and culturally for foreign markets. Discuss.

9. What are the three major components of a product? Discuss their importance to product adaptation.

10. How can knowledge of the diffusion of innovations help a product manager plan international investments?

11. Old products (that is, old in the U.S. market) may be innovations in a foreign market. Discuss fully.

12. "If the product sells in Dallas, it will sell in Tokyo or Berlin." Comment.

13. How can a country with a per capita GNP of $100 be a potential market for consumer goods? What kinds of goods would probably be in demand? Discuss.

14. Discuss the characteristics of an innovation that can account for differential diffusion rates.

15. Give an example of how a foreign marketer can use knowledge of the characteristics of innovations in product adaptation decisions.

16. Discuss "environmentally friendly" products and product development.

13

products and services for businesses

CHAPTER OUTLINE

Global Perspective: Intel, the Boom and the Inescapable Bust

Demand in Global Business-to-Business Markets

    The Volatility of Derived Demand
    Stages of Economic Development
    Technology and Market Demand

Quality and Global Standards

    Quality Is Defined by the Buyer
    ISO 9000 Certification: An International Standard of Quality

Business Services

    After-Sale Services
    Other Business Services

Trade Shows: A Crucial Part of Business-to-Business Marketing

Relationship Marketing in Business-to-Business Contexts

CHAPTER LEARNING OBJECTIVES

What you should learn from Chapter 13:

- The importance of derived demand in industrial markets

- How demand is affected by technology

- Characteristics of an industrial product

- The importance of ISO 9000 certification

- The growth of business services and nuances of their marketing

- The importance of trade shows in promoting industrial goods

- The importance of relationship marketing for industrial products and services

Global Perspective

INTEL, THE BOOM AND THE INESCAPABLE BUST

This is what we wrote here in the 1999 edition of this book:

Fortune's cover story, "Intel, Andy Grove's Amazing Profit Machine—and His Plan for Five More Years of Explosive Growth" is capped only by *Time*'s Man of the Year story, "Intel's Andy Grove, His Microchips Have Changed the World—and Its Economy." 1997 was the eighth consecutive year of record revenue ($25.1 billion) and earnings ($6.5 billion) for the company Grove helped found. Yet at the beginning of 1998 the real question was, Will the world change Intel? Judging from Intel's own forecasts for a flat first quarter in 1998, Chairman of the Board Grove and his associates were concerned that the financial meltdown in Asian markets would affect Intel's plans for "five more years of explosive growth." Some 30 percent of the firm's record 1997 revenues had come from Asian markets. Indeed, one pundit had earlier predicted, "I see no clear technology threats. The biggest long-term threat to Intel is that the market growth slows." Others warned there's something wrong out there: computer-industry overcapacity.

Actually Intel had an even longer list of threats all posted as a disclaimer to its published forecast: "Other factors that could cause actual results to differ materially are the following: business and economic conditions, and growth in the computing industry in various geographic regions; changes in customer order patterns, including changes in customer and channel inventory levels, and seasonal PC buying patterns; changes in the mixes of microprocessor types and speeds, motherboards, purchased components and other products; competitive factors, such as rival chip architectures and manufacturing technologies, competing software-compatible microprocessors and acceptance of new products in specific market segments; pricing pressures; changes in end users' preferences; risk of inventory obsolescence and variations in inventory valuation;

timing of software industry product introductions; continued success in technological advances, including development, implementation and initial production of new strategic products and processes in a cost-effective manner; execution of manufacturing ramp; excess storage of manufacturing capacity; the ability to successfully integrate any acquired businesses, enter new market segments and manage growth of such businesses; unanticipated costs or other adverse effects associated with processors and other products containing errata; risks associated with foreign operations; litigation involving intellectual property and consumer issues; and other risk factors listed from time to time in the company's SEC reports."

Time's Man of the Year had a lot to worry about—most of all that industrial market booms are always followed by busts. Will the rise truly last five more years?

How is it that the brilliant Mr. Grove didn't see the inescapable bust coming? Hadn't he been in this cyclic business from the beginning? His boom did last another three and a half years beyond his 1997 prediction, not five. And the bust has been an ugly thing. Sales revenues declined by more than 20 percent during 2001, the stock price crashed from a high of $75 a share to below $20, shedding 80 percent of the company's value along the way, and 11,000 layoffs were announced. Ouch!

The lesson here is a simple one: In industrial markets, including the global ones, what goes up must come down!

Sources: David Kirkpatrick, "Intel Andy Grove's Amazing Profit Machine—And His Plan for Five More Years of Explosive Growth," *Fortune*, February 17, 1997, pp. 60–75; "Man of the Year," *Time*, January 5, 1998, pp. 46–99; Peter Burrow, Gary McWilliams, Paul C. Judge, and Roger O. Crockett, "There's Something Wrong Out There," *BusinessWeek*, December 29, 1997, pp. 38–49. More recently, Intel is seeing strong growth in revenues; see Eric Auchard, "4-Intel Profit Up, but Capacity Tight and Shares Sag," *Reuters*, July 20, 2005.

Exhibit 13.1
Major Categories U.S. Exports

Category	Percentage
Services total	**29.6**
Travel (hotels, etc.)	6.4
Transportation (fares, freight, and port services)	5.0
Commercial, professional, and technical services (advertising, accounting, legal, construction, engineering)	6.0
Financial services (banking and insurance)	2.1
Education and training services (mostly foreign student tuition)	1.1
Entertainment (movies, books, records)	1.0
Royalties and license fees	4.5
Insurance	0.5
Telecommunications	0.4
Other categories (telecommunications, information, health care)	7.6
Merchandise total	**70.4**
Foods, feeds, and beverages (wheat, fruit, meat)	4.8
Industrial supplies (crude oil, plastics, chemicals, metals)	17.5
Capital goods (construction equipment, aircraft, computers, telecommunications)	28.5
Automotive vehicles, engines, and parts	7.6
Consumer goods (pharmaceuticals, tobacco, toys, clothing)	8.8
Other categories	7.7

Note: The United States exports approximately $1.2 trillion worth of services and goods each year. Services exports are the more understated, so these percentages are only reasonable approximations of the importance of each category listed. Each U.S. Commerce Department category comprises many kinds of products or services, including (but certainly not limited to) those listed in parentheses.

Source: U.S. Department of Commerce, www.doc.gov, 2005.

While everyone is familiar with most of the consumer brands described in Chapter 12, sales of such products and services do not constitute the majority of export sales for industrialized countries. Take the United States, for example. As can be seen in Exhibit 13.1, the main product the country sells for international consumption is *technology*. This is reflected in categories such as capital goods and industrial supplies, which together account for some 46 percent of all U.S. exports of goods and services.[1] Technology exports are represented by both the smallest and the largest products—semiconductors and commercial aircraft, the latter prominently including America's export champions, Boeing's 747s. The two most valuable companies in the world at this writing—Microsoft and General Electric[2]—are sellers of high-technology industrial products.

The issues of standardization versus adaptation discussed in Chapter 12 have less relevance to marketing industrial goods than consumer goods because there are more similarities in marketing products and services to businesses across country markets than there are differences. The inherent nature of industrial goods and the sameness in motives and behavior among businesses as customers create a market where product and marketing mix standardization are commonplace. Photocopy machines are sold in Belarus for the same reasons as in the United States: to make photocopies. Some minor modification may be necessary to accommodate different electrical power supplies or paper size but, basically, photocopy machines are standardized across markets, as are the vast majority of industrial goods. For industrial products that are basically custom made (specialized steel, customized machine tools, and so on), adaptation takes place for domestic as well as foreign markets.

---

[1] Internet jargon seems to be morphing the manager's lexicon toward B2B and B2C distinctions (that is, business-to-business and business-to-consumer) and away from the traditional industrial and consumer goods distinctions. International trade statistics, categories, and descriptors haven't kept up with these changes. Consequently, we use the adjectives *industrial* and *business-to-business* interchangeably in this book.

[2] See "Forbes 500," www.forbes.com, 2005.

CROSSING **BORDERS 13.1**   Trade Statistics Don't Tell the Whole Story

One reason U.S. manufacturers don't trumpet their export successes is that large companies no longer distinguish carefully between sales to Texas and to Thailand. The totals could be worked up, but why bother? It's one world, after all. Besides, it's incredibly complicated in some cases to determine the net contribution a manufacturer makes to the U.S. balance of trade. Lucent Technologies' Microelectronics Group, which exports half of what it makes to customers in Europe and Asia, is an extreme example. A wafer of Lucent's integrated circuits is often designed at its laboratories in England or China, made in its plants in Pennsylvania,

Florida, or Ireland, then shipped to Bangkok to be tested, diced, and packaged. After that the finished chips might move on to Germany to be used by Siemens in telecommunications equipment that, in turn, is shipped to BellSouth and installed in Charlotte, North Carolina.

Sources: Philip Siekman, "Industrial Management & Technology/Export Winners," *Fortune*, January 10, 2000, pp. 154–163; "Lucent CEO Sees China as Important Growth Area for Global Business," *Xinhua News Agency*, August 19, 2005; John Collins, "Buying in Ideas Gives Irish Firms License to Stay Ahead," *Irish Times*, September 9, 2005, p. 6.

Two basic factors account for greater market similarities among industrial goods customers than among consumer goods customers. First is the inherent nature of the product: Industrial products and services are used in the process of creating other goods and services; consumer goods are in their final form and are consumed by individuals. Second, the motive or intent of the user differs: Industrial consumers are seeking profit, whereas the ultimate consumer is seeking satisfaction. These factors are manifest in specific buying patterns and demand characteristics, and in a special emphasis on relationship marketing as a competitive tool. Whether a company is marketing at home or abroad, the differences between business-to-business and consumer markets merit special consideration.

Along with industrial goods, business services are a highly competitive growth market seeking quality and value. Manufactured products generally come to mind when we think of international trade. Yet the most rapidly growing sector of U.S. international trade today consists of business services—accounting, advertising, banking, consulting, construction, hotels, insurance, law, transportation, and travel sold by U.S. firms in global markets. The intangibility of services creates a set of unique problems to which the service provider must respond. A further complication is a lack of uniform laws that regulate market entry. Protectionism, although prevalent for industrial goods, can be much more pronounced for the service provider.

This chapter discusses the special problems in marketing goods and services to businesses internationally, the increased competition and demand for quality in those goods and services, and the implications for the global marketer.

Demand in Global Business-to-Business Markets   Gauging demand in industrial

markets can involve some huge bets. Shanghai's 30-kilometer, $1.2 billion bullet train line is one example. This product of a Sino-German joint venture is really a prototype for fast things to come in mass transit–dependent China. Indeed, plans are being drawn up for a 1,307-kilometer bullet train line from Shanghai to Beijing and that's probably a $100 billion bet![3] And China does change its mind—in 2005 a multi-billion-dollar upgrade of its wireless networks was substantially scaled back.[4] A big bet that did go bad was Iridium LLC—its 72-satellite, $5 billion communications system may be in orbit but the company can't sell the associated phones. Iridium badly miscalculated demand for its approach to global telecommunications, and the entire system is currently in disuse and is now classified by investors as space refuse.

---

[3]Eric Ng, "French Energy Giant in Talks on China Ventures," *South China Morning Post*, June 20, 2005, p. 4.

[4]Rebecca Buckman, "China Shrinks Wireless Plan," *Washington Post*, June 30, 2005, p. D5.

Three factors seem to affect the demand in international industrial markets differently than in consumer markets. First, demand in industrial markets is by nature more volatile. Second, stages of industrial and economic development affect demand for industrial products. Finally, the level of technology of products and services makes their sale more appropriate for some countries than others.

The Volatility of Industrial Demand

Consumer products firms have numerous reasons to market internationally—exposure to more-demanding customers, keeping up with the competition, extending product life cycles, and growing sales and profits, to name a few. Firms producing products and services for industrial markets have an additional crucial reason for venturing abroad: dampening the natural volatility of industrial markets.[5] Indeed, perhaps the single most important

[5]"The CEMEX Way," *The Economist*, June 16, 2001, pp. 75–76; Alan Clendenning, "Latin American Exporters Angling to Profit from Katrina Rebuilding, Get Tariffs Suspended," *Associated Press*, September 16, 2005.

Servers are sold to companies, thus the demand for them is more volatile than the demand for personal computers being sold to individual consumers. Here Microsoft acknowledges the technology bust of 2000 in its ads for servers in both the United States and Japan. In both countries, the pressure was on CIOs to "do more with less." Both executives faced "larger projects" and "shrinking budgets." The American executive is working late; everyone else has gone home. The focus on the Japanese individual executive may look odd to older, more collectivistic Japanese managers. However, Microsoft acknowledged that things were changing in Japan—particularly information technology decisions were more focused and less consensus-oriented. Younger Japanese will like the independence reflected in the image. Finally, do you think it's a coincidence that both executives are standing near windows? *(top: Courtesy Microsoft Corporation. Photographer: Kiran Masters; bottom: Courtesy Microsoft Corporation. Photographer: Tadayuki Minamoto; Talent: Takushi Yasumoto; CD/AD: Jun Asano; CW: Kenichi Okubo)*

The latest global campaign for Microsoft B2B products mentions nothing about the IT bust and uses the universal slogan "Your potential. Our passion" for both the Mexican and German markets, as in the United States. (*Courtesy Microsoft Corporation.*)

difference between consumer and industrial marketing is the huge, cyclical swings in demand inherent in the latter.[6] It is true that demand for consumer durables such as cars, furniture, or home computers can be quite volatile. In industrial markets, however, two other factors come into play that exacerbate both the ups and downs in demand: Professional buyers tend to act in concert, and derived demand accelerates changes in markets.

Purchasing agents at large personal computer manufacturers such as IBM, Apple, Acer, Samsung, and Toshiba are responsible for obtaining component parts for their firms as cheaply as possible and in a timely manner. They monitor demand for PCs and prices of components such as microprocessors or disk drives, and changes in either customer markets or supplier prices directly affect their ordering. Declines in PC demand or supplier prices can cause these professionals to slam on the brakes in their buying; in the latter case they wait for further price cuts. And because the purchasing agents at all the PC companies, here and abroad, are monitoring the same data, they all brake (or accelerate) simultaneously. Consumers monitor markets as well, but not nearly to the same degree. Purchases of cola, clothing, and cars tend to be steadier.

For managers selling capital equipment and big-ticket industrial services, understanding the concept of derived demand is absolutely fundamental to their success. *Derived demand* can be defined as demand dependent on another source. Thus the demand for Boeing 747s is derived from the worldwide consumer demand for air travel services, and the demand for Fluor Daniel's global construction and engineering services to design and build oil refineries in China is derived from Chinese consumers' demands for gasoline. Minor changes in consumer demand mean major changes in the related industrial demand. In the example in Exhibit 13.2, a 10 percent increase in consumer demand for shower stalls in year 2 translates into a 100 percent increase in demand for the machines to make shower stalls. The 15 percent decline in consumer demand in year 5 results in a complete shutdown of demand for

---

[6]Russ Arensman, "When Slower Is Better," *Electronic Business*, March 2003, pp. 52–57.

Exhibit 13.2
Derived Demand Example

Time Period	Consumer Demand for Premolded Fiberglass Shower Stalls			Number of Machines in Use to Produce the Shower Stalls			Demand for the Machines		
Year	Previous Year	Current Year	Net Change	Previous Year	Current Year	Net Change	Replacement	New	Total
1	100,000	100,000	—	500	500	—	50	—	50
2	100,000	110,000	+10,000	500	550	+50	50	50	100
3	110,000	115,000	+5,000	550	575	+25	50	25	75
4	115,000	118,000	+3,000	575	590	+15	50	15	65
5	118,000	100,000	−18,000	590	500	−90	—	−40	−40
6	100,000	100,000	—	500	500	—	10	—	10

Source: Adapted from R. L. Vaile, E. T. Grether, and R. Cox, *Marketing in the American Economy* (New York: Ronald Press, 1952), p. 16. Appears in Robert W. Haas, *Business Marketing*, 6th ed. (Cincinnati, OH: Southwestern, 1995), p. 115.

shower-stall-making machines. For Boeing, the September 11 terrorist attacks, the continuing threat of more of the same, and the subsequent armed conflicts in the Middle East combined to dramatically reduce air travel (both vacation and commercial) worldwide, which in turn caused cancellations of orders for aircraft. Moreover, the airlines not only canceled orders, they also mothballed parts of their current fleets. During August 2003 there were 310 jetliners stored in a Mojave Desert facility awaiting demand to pick up again.[7] The commercial aircraft industry has always been and will continue to be one of the most volatile of all.

Industrial firms can take several measures to manage this inherent volatility, such as maintaining broad product lines, raising prices faster and reducing advertising expenditures during booms, ignoring market share as a strategic goal, eschewing layoffs,[8] and focusing on stability. For most American firms, where corporate cultures emphasize beating competitors, such stabilizing measures are usually given only lip service. Conversely, German and Japanese firms value employees and stability more highly and are generally better at managing volatility in markets.[9]

Some U.S. companies, such as Microsoft and especially General Electric,[10] have been quite good at spreading their portfolio of markets served. Late-1990s declines in Asian markets were somewhat offset by strong American markets, just as late-1980s increases in Japanese demand had offset declines in the United States. Indeed, one of the strange disadvantages of having the previously command economies go private is their integration into the global market. That is, prior to the breakup of the USSR, Soviets bought industrial products according to a national five-year plan that often had little to do with markets outside of the communist bloc. Their off-cycle ordering tended to dampen demand volatility for companies able to sell there. Now privately held Russian manufacturers watch and react to world markets just as their counterparts do all over the globe. The increasing globalization of markets will tend to increase the volatility in industrial markets as purchasing agents around the world act with even greater

---

[7]Edward Wong, "Airlines' Unwanted Fleet Grows in the Desert," *New York Times*, June 7, 2003, p. C1; now demand has picked up and the latest Mojave inventory number we can find is around 200 jets on the ground there.

[8]Southwest Airlines management, different from almost all their competitors, has avoided layoffs during the recent bust in the industry. Refusing to make layoffs has been a founding principle of the organization. "Southwest Airlines Traffic Rises," *Wall Street Journal*, June 4, 2003, p. B4.

[9]Cathy Anterasian, John L. Graham, and R. Bruce Money, "Are American Managers Superstitious about Market Share?" *Sloan Management Review*, Summer 1996, pp. 667–677; John L. Graham, "Culture and Human Resources Management," Chapter 18 in Alan Rugman and Thomas L. Brewer (eds.), *The Oxford Handbook of International Business* (Oxford: Oxford University Press, 2001); Raji Srinivasan, Arvind Rangaswamy, Gary L. Lilien, "Turning Adversity into Advantage: Does Proactive Marketing During a Recession Pay Off?" *International Journal of Research in Marketing* 22, no. 2 (2005), pp. 109–125.

[10]Stanley Holmes, "GE: Little Engines that Could," *BusinessWeek*, January 20, 2003, pp. 62–63; Paul Meller, "Europe Extends Deadline on GE's Finnish Deal," *New York Times*, May 13, 2003, p. W7.

simultaneity. Managing this inherent volatility will necessarily affect all aspects of the marketing mix, including product/service development.

Stages of Economic Development

Perhaps the most significant environmental factor affecting the international market for industrial goods and services is the degree of industrialization. Although generalizing about countries is almost always imprudent, the degree of economic development can be used as a rough measure of a country's industrial market. Please recall Rostow's[11] five-stage model of economic development presented in Chapter 9; demand for industrial products and services can be classified correspondingly.

> **Stage 1** (*the traditional society*). The important industrial demand will be associated with natural resources extraction—think parts of Africa and the Middle East.
>
> **Stage 2** (*preconditions for takeoff*). Manufacturing is beginning. Primary needs will be related to infrastructure development—for example, telecommunications, construction, and power generation equipment and expertise. Vietnam would fit this category.
>
> **Stage 3** (*takeoff*). Manufacturing of both semidurable and nondurable consumer goods has begun. Goods demanded related to equipment and supplies to support manufacturing. Russian and eastern European countries fit this category.
>
> **Stage 4** (*drive to maturity*). These are industrialized economies such as Korea and the Czech Republic. Their focus is more on low-cost manufacturing of a variety of consumer and some industrial goods. They buy from all categories of industrial products and services.
>
> **Stage 5** (*the age of mass consumption*). These are countries where design activities are going on and manufacturing techniques are being developed, and they are mostly services economies. Japan and Germany are obvious examples of countries that purchase the highest-technology products and services mostly from other Stage 5 suppliers and consumer products from Stage 3 and 4 countries.

Technology and Market Demand

Another important approach to grouping countries is on the basis of their ability to benefit from and use technology, particularly now that countries are using technology as economic leverage to leap several stages of economic development in a very short time. Perhaps the best indicator of this dimension of development is the quality of the educational system. Despite relatively low levels of per capita GDP, many countries (e.g., China, the Czech Republic, and Russia) place great emphasis on education, which affords them the potential to leverage the technology that is transferred.

Not only is technology the key to economic growth, but for many products it is also the competitive edge in today's global markets. As precision robots and digital control systems take over the factory floor, manufacturing is becoming more science oriented and access to inexpensive labor and raw materials is becoming less important. The ability to develop the latest information technology and to benefit from its application is a critical factor in the international competitiveness of managers, countries, and companies. Three interrelated trends spur demand for technologically advanced products: (1) expanding economic and industrial growth in Asia, particularly China and India; (2) the disintegration of the Soviet empire; and (3) the privatization of government-owned industries worldwide.

Beginning with Japan, many Asian countries have been in a state of rapid economic growth over the last 30 years. Although this growth has recently slowed, the long-term outlook for these countries remains excellent. Japan has become the most advanced industrialized country in the region, while South Korea, Hong Kong, Singapore, and Taiwan (the "Four Tigers") have successfully moved from being cheap labor sources to becoming industrialized nations. The Southeast Asian countries of Malaysia, Thailand, Indonesia, and the Philippines are exporters of manufactured products to Japan and the United States now, and now that they have overcome most of their 1990s financial problems they are continuing to gear up for greater industrialization. Countries at each of the first three levels of industrial development demand

---

[11]Walt W. Rostow, *The Stages of Economic Growth*, 2nd ed. (London: Cambridge University Press, 1971).

technologically advanced products for further industrialization, which will enable them to compete in global markets.

As a market economy develops in the Commonwealth of Independent States (CIS, former republics of the USSR) and other eastern European countries, new privately owned businesses will create a demand for the latest technology to revitalize and expand manufacturing facilities. The BEMs (big emerging markets) discussed in Chapter 9 are expected to account for more than $1.5 trillion of trade by 2010. These countries will demand the latest technology to expand their industrial bases and build modern infrastructures.

Concurrent with the fall of communism, which fueled the rush to privatization in eastern Europe, Latin Americans began to dismantle their state-run industries in hopes of reviving their economies. Mexico, Argentina, and Venezuela are leading the rest of Latin America in privatizing state-owned businesses. The move to privatization will create enormous demand for industrial goods as new owners invest heavily in the latest technology. Telmex, a $4 billion joint venture between Southwestern Bell, France Telecom, and Teléfonos de Mexico, is investing hundreds of millions of dollars to bring the Mexican telephone system up to the most advanced standards. Telmex is only one of scores of new privatized companies from Poland to Paraguay that are creating a mass market for the most advanced technology.

The return to economic growth in Asia, the creation of market economies in eastern Europe and the republics of the former Soviet Union, and the privatization of state-owned enterprises in Latin America and elsewhere will create an expanding demand, particularly for industrial goods and business services, well into the 21st century. The competition to meet this global demand will be stiff; the companies with the competitive edge will be those whose products are technologically advanced, of the highest quality, and accompanied by world-class service.

Quality and Global Standards

As discussed in Chapter 12, the concept of quality encompasses many factors, and the perception of quality rests solely with the customer. The level of technology reflected in the product, compliance with standards that reflect customer needs, support services and follow-through, and the price relative to competitive products are all part of a customer's evaluation and perception of quality. As noted, these requirements are different for consumers versus industrial customers because of differing end uses. The factors themselves also differ among industrial goods customers because their needs are varied.

Business-to-business marketers frequently misinterpret the concept of quality. Good quality as interpreted by a highly industrialized market is not the same as that interpreted by standards of a less-industrialized nation. For example, an African government had been buying hand-operated dusters for farmers to distribute pesticides in cotton fields. The duster supplied was a finely machined device requiring regular oiling and good care. But the fact that this duster turned more easily than any other on the market was relatively unimportant to the farmers. Furthermore, the requirement for careful oiling and care simply meant that in a relatively short time of inadequate care the machines froze up and broke. The result? The local government went back to an older type of French duster that was heavy, turned with difficulty, and gave a poorer distribution of dust, but which lasted longer because it required less care and lubrication. In this situation, the French machine possessed more relevant quality features and therefore, in marketing terms, possessed the higher quality.

Likewise, when commercial jet aircraft were first developed, European and American designs differed substantially. For example, American manufacturers built the engines slung below the wings, whereas the British competitor built the engines into the wings. The American design made for easier access and saved on repair and servicing costs, and the British design reduced aerodynamic drag and saved on fuel costs. Both designs were "high quality" for their respective markets. At the time, labor was relatively expensive in the United States and fuel was relatively expensive in the United Kingdom.

Quality Is Defined by the Buyer

One important dimension of quality is how well a product meets the specific needs of the buyer. When a product falls short of performance expectations, its poor quality is readily apparent. However, it is less apparent but nonetheless true that a product that exceeds performance expectations is also of poor quality. A product whose design exceeds the wants of the buyer's intended use generally has a higher price, which reflects the extra capacity. Quality for many goods is assessed in terms of fulfilling specific expectations—no more and no less. Thus a product that produces 20,000 units per hour when the buyer needs one that produces only 5,000 units per hour is not a quality product, in that the extra capacity is unnecessary to meet the buyer's use expectations. Indeed, this is one of the key issues facing personal computer makers. Many business buyers are asking the question, "Do we really need the latest $1,000 PC for everyone?" And more and more often the answer is no, the $500 machines will do just fine.

This price–quality relationship is an important factor in marketing in developing economies, especially those in the first three stages of economic development described earlier. Standard quality requirements of industrial products sold in the U.S. market that command commensurately higher prices may be completely out of line for the needs of the less developed markets of the world. Labor-saving features are of little importance when time has limited value and labor is plentiful. Also of lesser value is the ability of machinery to hold close tolerances where people are not quality-control conscious, where large production runs do not exist, and where the wages of skillful workers justify selective fits in assembly and repair work. Features that a buyer does not want or cannot effectively use do not enhance a product's quality rating.

This does not mean quality is unimportant or that the latest technology is not sought in developing markets. Rather, it means that those markets require products designed to meet their specific needs, not products designed for different uses and expectations, especially if the additional features result in higher prices. This attitude was reflected in a study of purchasing behavior of Chinese import managers, who ranked product quality first, followed in importance by price. Timely delivery was third and product style/features ranked 11th out of 17 variables studied. Hence a product whose design reflects the needs and expectations of the buyer—no more, no less—is a quality product.

The design of a product must be viewed from all aspects of use. Extreme variations in climate create problems in designing equipment that is universally operable. Products that function effectively in western Europe may require major design changes to operate as well in the hot, dry Sahara region or the humid, tropical rain forests of Latin America. Trucks designed to travel the superhighways of the United States almost surely will experience operational difficulties in the mountainous regions of Latin America on roads that often barely resemble Jeep trails. Manufacturers must consider many variations in making products that will be functional in far-flung markets.

In light of today's competition, a company must consider the nature of its market and the adequacy of the design of its products. Effective competition in global markets means that overengineered and overpriced products must give way to products that meet the specifications of the customer at competitive prices. Success lies in offering products that fit a customer's needs—technologically advanced for some and less sophisticated for others, but all of high quality. To be competitive in today's global markets, the concept of total quality management (TQM)[12] must be a part of all MNCs' management strategy, and TQM starts with talking to customers.[13] Indeed, more and more frequently industrial customers, including foreign ones, are directly involved in all aspects of the product development process, from generating new ideas to prototype testing.

A lack of universal standards is another problem in international sales of industrial products. The United States has two major areas of concern in this regard for the industrial goods exporter: a lack of common standards for manufacturing highly specialized equipment such as machine tools and computers; and the use of the inch-pound, or English, system of measurement. Conflicting standards are encountered in test methods for materials and equipment, quality control systems, and machine specifications. In the telecommunications industry, the vast differences in standards among countries create enormous problems for expansion of that industry.

---

[12]Juan A. Magana-Campos and Elaine Aspinwall, "Comparative Study of Western and Japanese Improvement Systems," *TQM & Business Excellence* 14, no. 4 (June 2003), pp. 423–436.

[13]Ching-Chow Yang, "The Establishment of a TQM System for the Health Care Industry," *TQM Magazine* 15, no. 2 (2003), pp. 93–98.

CROSSING **BORDERS 13.2**   Your Hoses Are a Threat to Public Security!

Universal standards have made life miserable for Evan Segal. He is president of Dormont Manufacturing Company, which makes hoses that hook up deep-fat fryers and the like to gas outlets and which once sold these hoses throughout Europe. Then, one day one of his top customers, Frymaster Corporation of Shreveport, Louisiana, called to alert him that McDonald's was being told it could no longer use his hoses in its British restaurants. Similar problems popped up elsewhere, including EuroDisney outside Paris; shortly before the theme park opened, French inspectors demanded that Dormont's hoses be replaced with French-approved equipment.

The disparate national standards stemmed from the fact that the hoses are crucial to safe operation of gas appliances and thus fell under the product-safety provisions, allowing each country to set up its own standards. In Dormont's case, the specifications were written by committees often dominated by domestic European producers. They spell out minutiae of each country's acceptable gas hose design—such as the color of plastic coating or how the end pieces should be attached to the rest of the hose.

Mr. Segal thought he had made a major breakthrough when the British Standards Institute, one of the European agencies that test equipment and hand out approvals, issued Dormont a certificate authorizing the company to paste a seal of approval on its products signifying that the hoses conformed with European Union rules for gas appliances, enabling the company to sell them throughout the region. But the victory was short-lived. A miffed German competitor fired off a formal complaint to the European Commission, the EU's Brussels-based executive body. Commission officials familiar with the case say the rival argued that the British office erred because hoses are not really part of a gas appliance. The approval was withdrawn.

Sources: Timothy Aeppel, "Europe's Unity Undoes a U.S. Exporter," *Wall Street Journal,* April 1, 1996, p. B1; Brandon Mitchener, "Standard Bearers: Increasingly, Rules of Global Economy Are Set in Brussels," *Wall Street Journal,* April 23, 2002, p. A1.

Efforts are being made through international organizations to create international standards. For example, the International Electrotechnical Commission is concerned with standard specifications for electrical equipment for machine tools. The search has also been engaged for ways in which an international roaming umbrella can be established for wireless communications. The U.S. Department of Commerce participates in programs to promote U.S. standards and is active in the development of the Global Harmonization Task Force, an international effort to harmonize standards for several industry sectors. The U.S. Trade Representative participates in negotiations to harmonize standards as well. Recently a key agreement was signed with the European Union to mutually recognize one another's standards in six sectors. The agreements will eliminate the need for double testing (once each on both sides of the Atlantic) and address inspection or certification in telecommunications, medical devices, electromagnetic compatibility, electrical safety, recreation craft, and pharmaceuticals. The agreements cover approximately $50 billion in two-way trade and are expected to equate to a 2 percent to 3 percent drop in tariffs.

In addition to industry and international organizations setting standards, countries often have standards for products entering their markets. Saudi Arabia has been working on setting standards for everything from light bulbs to lemon juice, and it has asked its trading partners for help. The standards, the first in Arabic, will most likely be adopted by the entire Arab world. Most countries sent representatives to participate in the standard setting. For example, New Zealand sent a representative to help write the standards for the shelf life of lamb. Unfortunately, the United States failed to send a representative until late in the discussions, and thus many of the hundreds of standards written favor Japanese and European products. Also, Saudi Arabia adopted the new European standard for utility equipment. The cost in lost sales to two Saudi cities by just one U.S. company, Westinghouse, was from $15 million to $20 million for U.S.-standard distribution transformers. Increasingly, American firms are waking up to the necessity of participating in such standards discussions early on.

In the United States, conversion to the metric system and acceptance of international standards have been slow. Congress and industry have dragged their feet for fear conversion

CROSSING **BORDERS 13.3**   Yes, Opinions Do Differ about the Metric System

In Canada, feelings about the metric system run high, as evinced by the following newspaper column:

A generation has not passed since Canada's traditional system of weights and measures was suppressed by bureaucratic edict, in a direct assault on the public will. Countless millions have since been spent—most of it imposed in costs to industry, but millions more taxed to feed Ottawa's metric police and propaganda machine. And after years of the most audacious brainwashing campaign ever attempted on our nation's children, this alien system has made some progress. I said "alien" not because metric is French, but because it is inhuman.

The metric system was originally imposed on France by the blood-soaked operatives of the Revolutionary Terror. It was then dragged across Europe by the armies of Napoleon. It met popular resistance wherever it appeared, and everywhere that resistance was quelled by force.

Yet to this day, in France, as in our old monarchist citadel of Quebec, there are workmen calculating in *pieds* (feet) and *pouces* (inches), in *livres* (pounds) and *onces* (ounces)—quietly, beyond the reach of the metric police and their informers. These are masons and carpenters and the like. Their eyes are wistful and they smile to themselves.

Ten is the magical number of tyranny. It can be halved only once, and can never go into thirds. It allows the deceptive ease of calculating in decimal places, such that when right we only approxi-

mately hit the boat, but when wrong we land in another ocean.

In America, metric boosters insist that the switch is happening, but in stealthy ways. More than 2,000 American businesses use the metric system in research, development, and marketing, according to the U.S. Metric Association, a California advocacy group. All of Eastman Kodak's product development is done in the metric system; Procter & Gamble's Scope mouthwash is sold in incremental liter bottles. The reason is financial. Making deals in pounds isn't easy when you're negotiating with someone who speaks in grams

Britain duly converted to the metric system, selling its gasoline in liters and, more recently, its supermarket goods in grams. But small shopkeepers remained exempt until January 1, 2000. It was then that the new government regulations took effect, requiring every seller of loose goods—things like fruits, vegetables, carpets, window shades, loose candy, and meat—to begin selling in metric units.

The point, of course, was to harmonize with the rest of the European Union, a concept that is dear to the government of Prime Minister Tony Blair. But a healthy percentage of the country's 96,000 small shopkeepers do not feel much like harmonizing, especially not with the Germans and the French.

Sources: David Warren, "Ten: The Magical Number of Tyranny," *National Post* (Montreal), July 8, 2000, p. A14; Reed Tucker, "Why Don't We Use the Metric System?" *Fortune,* May 29, 2000, p. 56; Robin Paice, "Prepare to Name the (Metric) Day," *Financial Times,* August 31, 2005, p. 14.

would be too costly. But the cost will come from *not* adopting the metric system; the General Electric Company had a shipment of electrical goods turned back from a Saudi port because its connecting cords were six feet long instead of the required standard of two meters.

As foreign customers on the metric system account for more and more American industrial sales, the cost of delaying standardization mounts. Measurement-sensitive products account for one-half to two-thirds of U.S. exports, and if the European Union bars non-metric imports, as expected, many U.S. products will lose access to that market just as the European Union is on the threshold of major economic expansion. About half of U.S. exports are covered by the EU's new standards program.

To spur U.S. industry into action, the Department of Commerce indicated that accepting the metric system will not be mandatory unless you want to sell something to the U.S. government; all U.S. government purchases will be conducted exclusively in metric. All federal buildings are now being designed with metric specifications, and highway construction funded by Washington uses metric units. Because the U.S. government is the nation's largest customer, this directive may be successful in converting U.S. business to the metric system. The Defense Department now requires metric specifications for all new weapons systems as well.

Despite the edicts from Washington, the National Aeronautics and Space Administration (NASA), which presides over some of the most advanced technology in the world, resists metrification. The $100 billion-plus[14] space station contains some metric parts, but most of the major components are made in the United States and are based on inches and pounds. NASA's excuse was that it was too far into the design and production to switch. Unfortunately, the space station is supposed to be an international effort with Russia as one of the partners, and this decision created large problems for systems integration. Worse yet, the cause of the 1999 failure of the $125 million Mars Climate Orbiter was a mix-up between metric and English measurement systems. It is hard to believe that the only two countries not officially on the metric system are Myanmar and the United States. It is becoming increasingly evident that the United States must change or be left behind.

ISO 9000 Certification: An International Standard of Quality

With quality becoming the cornerstone of global competition, companies are requiring assurance of standard conformance from suppliers just as their customers are requiring the same from them. ISO 9000 certification has also been found to positively affect the performance[15] and stock prices[16] of firms.

ISO 9000s, a series of five international industrial standards (ISO 9000–9004) originally designed by the International Organization for Standardization in Geneva to meet the need for product quality assurances in purchasing agreements, are becoming a quality assurance certification program that has competitive and legal ramifications when doing business in the European Union and elsewhere.[17] The original ISO 9000 system was promulgated in 1994. In 2000 the system was streamlined, as it will be again in 2006. ISO 9000 concerns the registration and certification of a manufacturer's quality system. It is a certification of the existence of a quality control system a company has in place to ensure it can meet published quality standards. ISO 9000 standards do not apply to specific products. They relate to generic system standards that enable a company, through a mix of internal and external audits, to provide assurance that it has a quality control system. It is a certification of the production process only, and does not guarantee that a manufacturer produces a "quality" product or service. The series describes three quality system models, defines quality concepts, and gives guidelines for using international standards in quality systems.

To receive ISO 9000 certification,[18] a company requests a certifying body (a third party authorized to provide an ISO 9000 audit) to conduct a registration assessment—that is, an audit of the key business processes of a company. The assessor will ask questions about everything from blueprints to sales calls to filing. "Does the supplier meet promised delivery dates?" and "Is there evidence of customer satisfaction?" are two of the questions asked and the issues explored. The object is to develop a comprehensive plan to ensure that minute details are not overlooked. The assessor helps management create a quality manual, which will be made available to customers wishing to verify the organization's reliability. When accreditation is granted, the company receives certification. A complete assessment for recertification is done every four years, with intermediate evaluations during the four-year period.

Although ISO 9000 is generally voluntary, except for certain regulated products, the EU Product Liability Directive puts pressure on all companies to become certified. The directive holds that a manufacturer, including an exporter, will be liable, regardless of fault or negligence, if a person is harmed by a product that fails because of a faulty component. Thus customers in the EU need to be assured that the components of their products are free of defects or deficiencies. A manufacturer with a well-documented quality system will be better able to prove that products are defect free and thus minimize liability claims.

---

[14]The original cost estimate was $16 billion. Nick Anderson and David Holley, "International Space Station Proves a Diplomatic Success, if Nothing Else," *Los Angeles Times*, May 3, 2003, p. A16.

[15]Mile Terziovski, Damien Power, and Amrik S. Sohal, "The Longitudinal Effects of the ISO 9000 Certification Process on Business Performance," *European Journal of Operational Research*, May 1, 2003, pp. 580–595.

[16]Muli Rajan and Nabil Tamimi, "Payoff to ISO 9000 Registration," *Journal of Investing* 12, no. 1 (Spring 2003), pp. 71–77.

[17]Brandon Mitchener, "Standard Bearers: Increasingly, Rules of Global Economy Are Set in Brussels," *Wall Street Journal*, April 23, 2003, p. A1.

[18]Tammy Landon, "13 Steps to Certification in Less than a Year," *Quality Progress* 36, no. 3 (March 2003), pp. 32–41.

The Japanese manufacturer is quite proud of the ISO quality ratings for its plant in San Jose, Costa Rica.

A strong level of interest in ISO 9000 is being driven more by marketplace requirements than by government regulations, and ISO 9000 is now an important competitive marketing tool in Europe and around the world.[19] As the market demands quality and more and more companies adopt some form of TQM, manufacturers are increasingly requiring ISO 9000 registration of their suppliers. Companies manufacturing parts and components in China are quickly discovering that ISO 9000 certification is a virtual necessity, and the Japanese construction industry now requires ISO 9000 as part of the government procurement process. More and more buyers, particularly those in Europe, are refusing to buy from manufacturers that do not have internationally recognized third-party proof of their quality capabilities. ISO 9000 may also be used to serve as a means of differentiating "classes" of suppliers, particularly in high-tech areas where high product reliability is crucial. In other words, if two suppliers are competing for the same contract, the one with ISO 9000 registration may have a competitive edge.

Although more and more countries (now more than 100) and companies continue to adopt ISO 9000 standards, many have complaints about the system and its spread. For example, 39 electronics companies battled against special Japanese software criteria for ISO 9000. Electronics companies also protested against the establishment of a new ISO Health and Safety Standard. Still others are calling for more comprehensive international standards along the lines of America's Malcolm Baldrige Award, which considers seven criteria—leadership, strategic planning, customer and market focus, information and analysis, human resource development, management, and business results. The telecommunications industry recently promulgated an industry-specific TL 9000 certification program, which combines aspects of ISO 9000 and several other international quality standards.

Perhaps the most pertinent kind of quality standard is now being developed by the University of Michigan Business School and the American Society for Quality Control.[20] Using survey methods, their American Customer Satisfaction Index (ACSI) measures customers' satisfaction and perceptions of quality of a representative sample of America's goods and services. The approach was actually developed in Sweden and is now being used in other European and Asian countries as well.[21] The appeal of the ACSI approach is its focus on results, that is, quality as perceived by product and service users. So far the ACSI approach has been applied only in consumer product and service contexts; however, the fundamental notion that customers are the best judges of quality is certainly applicable to international business-to-business marketing settings as well. Individual industrial marketing firms are seeking even better ways to implement quality improvement programs.[22]

Business Services

For many industrial products the revenues from associated services exceed the revenues from the products. Perhaps the most obvious case is cellular phones, in which the physical product is practically given away to gain the phone services contract. Or consider how inexpensive printers may seem until the costs of operation (i.e., ink cartridges) are considered. Indeed, for many capital equipment manufacturers the margins on after-sale services (i.e., maintenance contracts, overhauls, repairs, and replacement parts) are much higher than the margins on the machinery itself. Further, when companies lease capital equipment to

[19]"China to Establish Industrial Garden in Nigeria," *Xinhua News Agency*, August, 22, 2005.

[20]Claes Fornell, Michael D. Johnson, Eugene W. Anderson, Jaesung Cha, and Barbara Everitt Bryant, "The American Consumer Index: Nature, Purpose, and Findings," *Journal of Marketing* 60, no. 4 (October 1996), pp. 35–46; Mary Wisniewski, "Consumer Satisfaction Down 1.75%," *Chicago Sun-Times*, May 17, 2005, p. 59; www.asq.org.

[21]Arti Mulchand, "Singapore's Own Quality Indicator," *Straits Times*, August 27, 2005.

[22]Duncan I. Simester, John R. Hauser, Birger Wernerfelt, and Roland T. Rust, "Implementing Quality Improvement Programs Designed to Enhance Customer Satisfaction: Quasi-Experiments in the United States and Spain," *Journal of Marketing Research* 37 (February 2000), pp. 102–112.

CROSSING BORDERS 13.4   Garbage Collection an International Service? Perhaps!

Having persuaded hundreds of local governments in the United States to contract out street cleaning and trash collection, WMX Technologies is collecting trash, cleaning streets, and constructing sanitary landfills in 20 countries, including Argentina, New Zealand, and Saudi Arabia. It also has a 15-year contract to run a hazardous-waste treatment plant that will process all of Hong Kong's industrial and chemical waste.

Even the French are handling British trash. Sita Group, a subsidiary of Suez Lyonnaise des Eaux, recently won a 25-year contract for waste collection in Surrey, England. With Surrey's population of around 1 million creating 500,000 tons of waste per year, the contract is worth some €1.5 billion. At the same time, Sita Group sold its subsidiaries in Australia and New Zealand to Waste Management of Houston, Texas.

More recently, because of financial problems at home, Waste Management has begun to shed its foreign acquisitions. The firm is even having trouble in close-by Mexico. Mexico is creating mountains of trash and industrial waste that it cannot safely manage, which should be a great opportunity for American waste management expertise and technology. However, of all the

American firms that rushed into the market right after the NAFTA signing, few are left, and even those few have scaled back operations.

Problems have been the lack of clear rules, bureaucratic snafus, and unanticipated political opposition to new dumps. One of the biggest U.S. firms, Waste Management, sold its share of Mexico's leading waste hauler and sought a $60 million judgment against the Mexican government for breaking NAFTA obligations to protect American businesses. Other U.S. firms have filed similar suits. Mexican governmental officials fault the companies. At least now with NAFTA, the American firms can seek redress in a systematic and transparent way. Many on both sides of the border await the outcomes. Waste management continues to be a burgeoning international business.

Sources: Joel Millman, "Waste Management Concerns Get Trashed in Mexico," *Wall Street Journal*, May 26, 1999, p. A17; "Waste Management CEO Says Sale of International Units Imminent," *Dow Jones Business News*, January 25, 2000; Oke Epia, "As Bauchi Seeks Opportunities Abroad. . ." *All Africa—Comtex*, September 9, 2005.

customers, the distinction between products and services almost disappears completely. When a business customer leases a truck, is it purchasing a vehicle or transportation services?

Businesses also buy a variety of services that are not associated with products. Our favorite examples are the at-sea-satellite-launch services now provide Boeing[23] and the Russian navy, the latter by submarine.[24] We also appreciate the Ukrainian cargo company that charges $24,000 an hour to rent space on its giant jets.[25] Other professional services are purchased from advertising and legal agencies, transportation and insurance companies, oil field services, banks and investment brokers,[26] and healthcare providers, to name only a few. Both categories of business services are discussed in this section.

After-Sale Services   Effective competition abroad requires not only proper product design but effective service, prompt deliveries, and the ability to furnish spare and replacement parts without delay.[27] For example, GE Medical Systems provides a wide range of after-sale services for hospitals that buy MRIs and other equipment—training, information technologies, associated healthcare services, and parts and accessories.[28] In the highly competitive European Union, it is imperative to give the same kind of service a domestic company or EU company can give. One U.S. export management firm warned that U.S. businesses may be too apathetic about Europe, treating it as a subsidiary market not worthy of "spending time to develop." It cites the case of an American firm with a $3 million potential sale in Europe that did not

---

[23]"Spaceport Southbound," *Orange County Register*, June 9, 2005, pp. 1, B1.

[24]"Sail of the Century," *The Economist*, June 18, 2005, pp. 77–78.

[25]Philip Shishkin, "A Cold-War Plane Lifts Ukrainians in Cargo Market," *Wall Street Journal*, January 19, 2005, pp. A1, A6.

[26]John U. Farley, Andrew F. Hayes, and Praveen K. Kopalle, "Choosing and Upgrading Financial Services Dealers in the U.S. and U.K.," *International Journal of Research in Marketing* 21, no. 4 (2004), pp. 359–375.

[27]John Conley, "What Happened to Customer Service?" *Risk Management*, April 2003, pp. 22–26.

[28]See www.gehealthcare.com.

even give engineering support to its representatives, although the same sale in the United States would have brought out "all the troops."

For many technical products, the willingness of the seller to provide installation and training may be the deciding factor for the buyers in accepting one company's product over another's.[29] South Korean and other Asian businesspeople are frank in admitting they prefer to buy from American firms but that Japanese firms often get the business because of outstanding after-sales service. Frequently heard tales of conflicts between U.S. and foreign firms over assistance expected from the seller are indicative of the problems of after-sales service and support. A South Korean executive's experiences with an American engineer and some Japanese engineers typify the situation. The Korean electronics firm purchased semiconductor-chip-making equipment for a plant expansion. The American engineer was slow in completing the installation; he stopped work at five o'clock and would not work on weekends. The Japanese, installing other equipment, understood the urgency of getting the factory up and running; without being asked they worked day and night until the job was finished.

Unfortunately this is not an isolated case. In another example, Hyundai Motor Company bought two multimillion-dollar presses to stamp body parts for cars. The presses arrived late, even more time was required to set up the machines, and Hyundai had to pay the Americans extra to get the machines to work correctly. Such problems translate into lost business for U.S. firms. Samsung Electronics Company, Korea's largest chipmaker, used U.S. equipment for 75 percent of its first memory-chip plant; when it outfitted its most recent chip plant, it bought 75 percent of the equipment from Japan. Of course, not all American companies have such problems. Indeed, in India Intel recently opened a data center comprising an Internet server farm of hundreds of servers. Already customers in many countries connect and store their servers and have them serviced by Intel at such centers.

Customer training is rapidly becoming a major after-sales service when selling technical products in countries that demand the latest technology but do not always have trained personnel. China demands the most advanced technical equipment but frequently has untrained people responsible for products they do not understand. Heavy emphasis on training programs and self-teaching materials to help overcome the common lack of skills to operate technical equipment is a necessary part of the after-sales service package in much of the developing world. While perhaps McDonald's Hamburger University is the most famous international customer training center, industrial sellers may soon catch up. Cisco Systems, collaborating with the government and a university in Singapore,[30] recently established the first Cisco Academy Training Centre to serve that region of the world, and Intel established e-Business Solutions Centers in five European countries.

A recent study of international users of heavy construction equipment revealed that, next to the manufacturer's reputation, quick delivery of replacement parts was of major importance in purchasing construction equipment. Furthermore, 70 percent of those questioned indicated they bought parts not made by the original manufacturer of the equipment because of the difficulty of getting original parts. Smaller importers complain of U.S. exporting firms not responding to orders or responding only after extensive delay. It appears that the importance of timely availability of spare parts to sustain a market is forgotten by some American exporters. When companies are responsive, the rewards are significant. U.S. chemical production equipment manufacturers dominate sales in Mexico because, according to the International Trade Administration, they deliver quickly. The ready availability of parts and services provided by U.S. marketers can give them a competitive edge.

Some international marketers also may be forgoing the opportunity of participating in a lucrative aftermarket. Certain kinds of machine tools use up to five times their original value in replacement parts during an average life span and thus represent an even greater market. One international machine tool company has capitalized on the need for direct service and available parts by changing its distribution system from "normal" to one of stressing rapid service and readily available parts. Instead of selling through independent distributors, as do most machine tool manufacturers in foreign markets, this company established a series of

---

[29]Brian Bremner, Peter Burrows, Moon Ihlwan, and Manjeet Kripalani, "Will Cisco Rewire Asia?" *BusinessWeek*, February 7, 2005, pp. 50–51.

[30]"SMEs Set to Boost IT Services in Asia," *Business Times Singapore*, August 22, 2005.

company stores and service centers similar to those found in the United States. The company can render service through its system of local stores, whereas most competitors must dispatch service people from their home-based factories. The service people are kept on tap for rapid service calls in each of its network of local stores, and each store keeps a large stock of standard parts available for immediate delivery. The net result of meeting industrial needs quickly is keeping the company among the top suppliers in foreign sales of machine tools.

International small-package door-to-door express air services and international toll-free telephone service have helped speed up the delivery of parts and have made after-sales technical service almost instantly available. Amdahl, the giant mainframe computer maker, uses air shipments almost exclusively for cutting inventory costs and ensuring premium customer service, which is crucial to competing against larger rivals. With increasing frequency, electronics, auto parts, and machine parts sent by air have become a formidable weapon in cutting costs and boosting competitiveness. Technical advice is only a toll-free call away, and parts are air-expressed immediately to the customer. Not only does this approach improve service standards, but it also is often more cost-effective than maintaining an office in a country, even though foreign-language speakers must be hired to answer calls.

After-sales services are not only crucial in building strong customer loyalty and the all-important reputation that leads to sales at other companies, but they are also almost always more profitable than the actual sale of the machinery or product.

Other Business Services

Trade creates demands for international services. Most U.S. business services companies enter international markets to service their U.S. clients abroad. Accounting and advertising firms were among the early companies to establish branches or acquire local affiliations abroad to serve their U.S. multinational clients. Hotels and auto-rental agencies followed the business traveler abroad. Most recently, healthcare services providers have been following firms abroad—Blue Cross is now selling HMO services to American companies operating in Mexico. Once established, many of these *client followers,* as one researcher refers to them, expand their client base to include local companies as well. As global markets grow, creating greater demand for business services, service companies become international market seekers. Indeed, notice in Exhibit 13.3 how American law firms have expanded (or contracted) overseas in recent years.[31]

As mentioned in Chapter 12, the mode of entry for most consumer services firms is licensing, franchising, or direct investment. This is so because of the inseparability of the creation and consumption of the services. However, because some business services have intrinsic value that can be embodied in some tangible form (such as a blueprint or architectural design),

---

[31]Mary K. Pratt, "International Fare: Lawyers Find Reach Expands Abroad," *Boston Business Journal,* March 10, 2003, p. 1.

Exhibit 13.3
Expansion of U.S. Law Firms in Selected Cities Worldwide

Source: *National Law Journal,* "Top 250 Report," 2003.

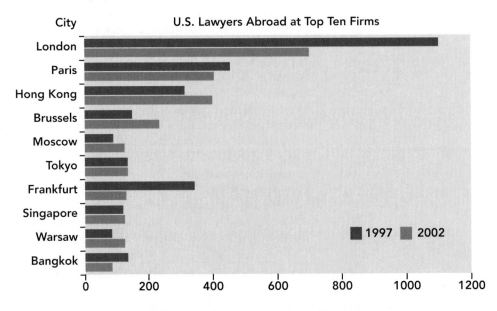

they can be produced in one country and exported to another. Data processing and data analysis services are good examples. The analysis or processing is completed on a computer located in the United States, and the output (the service) is transmitted via the Internet to a distant customer. Architecture and engineering consulting services are exportable when the consultant travels to the client's site and later returns home to write and submit a report or a design.

Business services firms face most of the same constraints and problems confronting merchandise traders. Protectionism is the most serious threat to the continued expansion of international services trade. The growth of international services has been so rapid during the last decade it has drawn the attention of local companies, governments, and researchers.[32] As a result, direct and indirect trade barriers have been imposed to restrict foreign companies from domestic markets. Every reason, from the protection of infant industries to national security, has been used to justify some of the restrictive practices. A list of more than 2,000 instances of barriers to the free flow of services among nations was recently compiled by the U.S. government. In response to the threat of increasing restriction, the United States has successfully negotiated to open business services markets through both NAFTA and GATT.

Until the GATT and NAFTA agreements, few international rules of fair play governed trade in services. Service companies faced a complex group of national regulations that impeded the movement of people and technology from country to country. The United States and other industrialized nations want their banks, insurance companies, construction firms, and other business service providers to be allowed to move people, capital, and technology around the globe unimpeded. Restrictions designed to protect local markets range from not being allowed to do business in a country to requirements that all foreign professionals pass certification exams in the local language before being permitted to practice. In Argentina, for example, an accountant must have the equivalent of a high school education in Argentinean geography and history before being permitted to audit the books of a multinational company's branch in Buenos Aires.

Restrictions on cross-border data flows are potentially the most damaging to both the communications industry and other MNCs that rely on data transfers across borders to conduct business. Some countries impose tariffs on the transmission of data, and many others are passing laws forcing companies to open their computer files to inspection by government agencies or are tightly controlling transmission domestically. Most countries have a variety of laws to deal with the processing and electronic transmission of data across borders. In many cases, concern stems from not understanding how best to tax cross-border data flows.

As mentioned earlier, competition in all sectors of the services industry is increasing as host-country markets are invaded by many foreign firms. The practice of following a client into foreign markets and then expanding into international markets is not restricted to U.S. firms. Service firms from Germany, Britain, Japan, and other countries follow their clients into foreign markets and then expand to include local business as well. Telecommunications, advertising, and construction are U.S. services that face major competition, not only from European and Japanese companies but also from representatives of Brazil, India, and other parts of the world.

Clearly opportunities for the marketing of business services will continue to grow well into the 21st century. International marketers will have to be quite creative in responding to the legal and cultural challenges of delivering high-quality business services in foreign markets and to foreign customers.

Trade Shows: A Crucial Part of Business-to-Business Marketing

The promotional problems encountered by foreign industrial marketers are little different from the problems faced by domestic marketers. Until recently there has been a paucity of specialized advertising media in many countries.[33] In the last decade, however, specialized industrial media

---

[32]Farok J. Contractor, Sumit K. Kundu, and Chin-Chun Hsu, "A Three-Stage Theory of International Expansion: The Link between Multinationality and Performance in the Service Sector," *Journal of International Business Studies* 34 (2003), pp. 5–19.

[33]Of course, it should be noted that some industrial companies still use nonspecialized media building brand awareness at all levels. Perhaps the best example is Intel's sponsorship of the official Web site of the Tour de France in 2002.

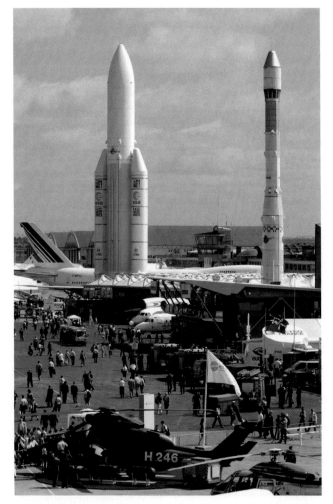

So you want to buy a jet fighter? How about kicking the tires of one at the Paris Air Show, the world's biggest aerospace trade show? (© AFP/Getty Images)

have been developed to provide the industrial marketer with a means of communicating with potential customers, especially in western Europe and to some extent in eastern Europe, the Commonwealth of Independent States (CIS), and Asia.

In addition to advertising in print media and reaching industrial customers through catalogs, Web sites,[34] and direct mail, the trade show or trade fair has become the primary vehicle for doing business in many foreign countries. As part of its international promotion activities, the U.S. Department of Commerce sponsors trade fairs in many cities around the world. Additionally, local governments in most countries sponsor annual trade shows. African countries, for example, host more than 70 industry-specific trade shows.

Trade shows serve as the most important vehicles for selling products, reaching prospective customers, contacting and evaluating potential agents and distributors, and marketing in most countries. Firms that have successfully integrated trade show attendance and follow-up personal selling efforts have been consistently shown to be more profitable.[35] Although important in the United States, trade shows serve a much more important role in other countries. They have been at the center of commerce in Europe for centuries and are where most prospects are found. European trade shows attract high-level decision makers who are attending not just to see the latest products but to buy. Preshow promotional expenditures are often used in Europe to set formal appointments. The importance of trade shows to Europeans is reflected in the percentage of their media budget spent on participating in trade events and how they spend those dollars. On average, Europeans spend 22 percent of their total annual media budget on trade events, whereas comparable American firms typically spend less than 5 percent. Europeans tend not to spend money on circuslike promotions, gimmicks, and such; rather, they focus on providing an environment for in-depth dealings. More than 2,000 major trade shows are held worldwide every year (although the largest U.S. trade show, Comdex, was canceled in 2004 after the IT meltdown).[36] The Hanover Industry Fair (Germany), the largest trade fair in the world, has nearly 6,000 exhibitors, who show a wide range of industrial products to 600,000 visitors.

Trade shows provide the facilities for a manufacturer to exhibit and demonstrate products to potential users and to view competitors' products. They are an opportunity to create sales and establish relationships with agents, distributors, franchisees,[37] and suppliers that can lead to more nearly permanent distribution channels in foreign markets.[38] In fact, a trade show may be the only way to reach some prospects. Trade show experts estimate that 80 to 85 percent of the people seen on a trade show floor never have a salesperson call on them. Several Web sites now specialize in virtual trade shows. They often include multimedia and elaborate product display booths that can be virtually toured. Some of these virtual trade shows last only a few days during an associated actual trade show.

The number and variety of trade shows are such that almost any target market in any given country can be found through this medium. Most remarkable was the Medical

[34]For illustrative examples of the burgeoning information available to industrial customers on Web sites, see www.caterpillar.com, www.fluor.com, www.hewlett-packard.com, and www.qualcom.com.

[35]Timothy Smith, Srinath Gopalakrishna, and Paul M. Smith, "The Complementary Effect of Trade Shows on Personal Selling," *International Journal of Research in Marketing* 21, no. 1 (2004), pp. 61–76.

[36]John Markoff, "Comdex Called Off for at Least a Year," *International Herald Tribune*, June 25, 2004, p. 15.

[37]Brad Fishman, "International Trade Shows: The Smartest Ticket for Overseas Research," *Franchising World*, April 2003, pp. 25–26.

[38]"As Aircraft Leases Rebound, Morgan Stanley Sets Sale," *AFX News*, August 17, 2005.

CROSSING **BORDERS 13.5** No More Aching Feet, but What about the 15-Ton Russian Tank?

During April 2000, the first stand-alone virtual trade show was staged by ISP Virtual Show. It was aimed at an appropriate audience—Internet service providers (ISPs). The address was (and will be) ISPVirtualShow.com. Technology for the show was provided by iTradeFair.com, a Web site worth the visit.

According to the promoters, "The advantages of a virtual trade show far outweigh those of the physical model. Exhibitors (booths start at $1,995) and attendees (tickets are $99) from all over the world will now be able to exhibit and attend direct from their desktops. There are endless benefits of a virtual show; including massive reductions in costs both in exhibiting and manpower terms, savings on booth space and buildings, accommodations, flights, expenses, the obligatory bar bills and costs of time spent out of the office."

The virtual trade show offers a fresh alternative to the traditional model. Using advanced technology, anyone anywhere in the world can visit the virtual show and access information in his or her own language—making language barriers a thing of the past. Also, if attendees

and exhibitors would like to continue a discussion offline, clocks displaying times from all over the world make scheduling easy. Finally, weary executives attending the same trade shows year in, year out will no longer have to suffer aching feet, hot stuffy rooms without air conditioning, and overpriced, plastic food.

Although this pitch sounds great, the authors of this book believe that an aspect of real trade shows that the virtual ones miss is the face-to-face contact and the all-important interpersonal relationship building that goes on over drinks or during those plastic meals. And there is no virtual way to achieve the same effect as a Russian software developer who recently displayed a 15-ton Russian tank in his booth at Comtek Trade Show in Moscow. We shall see how this new promotional medium evolves.

Sources: "ISP Virtual Show: World's First Virtual Trade Show," *M2 Presswire*, October 26, 1999; Jeanette Borzo, "Moscow's Comtek Trade Show Confronts Internet Challenge," *Dow Jones News Service*, April 19, 2000; "ICUEE Is the Demo Expo," *Transmission & Distribution*, August 1, 2005, p. 74.

Expo in Havana in 2000—the first trade show to be sanctioned by both the U.S. and Cuban governments in more than four decades.[39] Over 8,000 Cuban doctors, nurses, technicians, and hospital administrators attended. This initial event was followed in 2002 with a major food products trade show in Havana.[40] In eastern Europe, fairs and exhibitions offer companies the opportunity to meet new customers, including private traders, young entrepreneurs, and representatives of nonstate organizations. The exhibitions in countries such as Russia and Poland offer a cost-effective way of reaching a large number of customers who might otherwise be difficult to target through individual sales calls. Specialized fairs in individual sectors such as computers, the automotive industry, fashion, and home furnishings regularly take place.

In difficult economic and/or political circumstances online trade shows become a useful, but obviously less than adequate substitute.[41] A good example of the kinds of services being developed can be found in Crossing Borders 13.5. During the weakened global economy at the turn of the century slimmer travel budgets and SARS scares dramatically reduced attendance, and even forced cancellations, of traditionally popular international trade fairs.[42] Political conflicts between the EU and the United States over Middle East policies resulted in the U.S. Department of Defense discouraging American attendance at the 2003 Paris Air Show.[43] Top American executives at Boeing, Lockheed, and the like dutifully stayed away. Exhibit space declined by 5 percent and orders announced dropped from $45 billion in 2001

---

[39]Mark Fineman, "U.S. Medical Expo in Cuba Fuels Hope for Healthy Ties," *Los Angeles Times*, January 26, 2000, p. A1.

[40]Paul Richter, "Cuba Trade Show Kicks Off with a Hearty Welcome from Castro," *Los Angeles Times*, September 27, 2002, p. A3.

[41]Jennifer Saranow, "The Show Goes On: Online Trade Shows Offer Low-Cost, Flexible Alternatives for Organizers, Especially in These Days of Tight Travel Budgets," *Wall Street Journal*, April 28, 2003, p. R4.

[42]James Zoltak, "AEE Confab Cancelled Due to SARS," *Amusement Business*, April 28, 2003, p. 1.

[43]Daniel Michaels, "Paris Air Show May Sputter—Economic, Political Factors Stifle Aerospace Industry," *Wall Street Journal*, June 13, 2003, p. B4.

to $32 billion.[44] It is hard to estimate what the costs in terms of international orders are for firms such as Boeing when their top executives cannot mix with potential customers at such a crucial event. We do know that Airbus inked orders for dozens of commercial aircraft from customers in Qatar and the Arab Emirates. Not even the best online trade show imaginable can make up for this apparent step backward in international trade and cooperation.[45]

Relationship Marketing in Business-to-Business Contexts

The characteristics that define the uniqueness of industrial products and services lead naturally to relationship marketing.[46] The long-term relationships with customers that define relationship marketing fit the characteristics inherent in industrial products and are a viable strategy for business-to-business marketing. The first and foremost characteristic of industrial goods markets is the motive of the buyer: to make a profit. Industrial products fit into a business or manufacturing process, and their contributions will be judged on how well they contribute to that process. For an industrial marketer to fulfill the needs of a customer, the marketer must understand those needs as they exist today and how they will change as the buyer strives to compete in global markets that call for long-term relationships.

The industrial customer's needs in global markets are continuously changing, and suppliers' offerings must also continue to change. The need for the latest technology means that it is not a matter of selling the right product the first time but rather of continuously changing the product to keep it right over time. The objective of relationship marketing is to make the relationship an important attribute of the transaction, thus differentiating oneself from competitors. It shifts the focus away from price to service and long-term benefits. The reward is loyal customers that translate into substantial long-term profits.

Focusing on long-term relationship building will be especially important in most international markets where culture dictates stronger ties between people and companies. Particularly in countries with collectivistic and high-context cultures such as those in Latin America or Asia,[47] trust will be a crucial aspect of commercial relationships. Constant and close communication with customers will be the single most important source of information about the development of new industrial products and services. Indeed, in a recent survey of Japanese professional buyers a key choice criterion for suppliers was a trait they called "caring" (those who defer to requests without argument and recognize that in return buyers will care for the long-term interests of sellers). Longer-term and more communication-rich relationships are keys to success in international industrial markets.

As in all areas of international business, the Internet is facilitating relationship building and maintenance in new ways.[48] Cisco Systems is a leader in this area; it not only supplies the hardware that allows B2B commerce to work, but its relationship management practices and process also serve as models for the industry. Cisco's international customers can visit its Web site to check out product specs and to order. That information is then routed on the Internet through Cisco to its suppliers. A full 65 percent of the orders move directly from the supplier to the customer—Cisco never touches them. Things are built only after they are ordered; thus little, if any, inventory is kept in warehouses. Based on Cisco's success, businesses around the world are beginning to reorganize themselves accordingly.

---

[44]"Plane Makers Land Fewer Deals at Paris Air Show," *Los Angeles Times*, June 23, 2003, p. C3.

[45]Information about trade shows is available from the following sources: the U.S. Trade Information Center's *Export Promotion Calendar*, which lists dates and locations of trade shows worldwide; *Europe Trade Fairs*, which lists European shows, including the U.S. Department of Commerce–sponsored shows; *Trade Shows Worldwide* (published by Gale Research), a comprehensive listing of more than 6,000 trade shows worldwide; and *International Trade Fairs and Conferences* (published by Co-Mar Mangement Services), which lists 5,000 trade shows worldwide.

[46]Jagdish Sheth and Atul Parvatiyar, "Evolving Relationship Marketing into a Discipline," *Journal of Relationship Marketing* 1, no. 1 (2002), pp. 3–16.

[47]Alfred Wong, Dean Tjosvold, and Zhang Pengzhu, "Commitment and Conflict Management for Relational Marketing in China," *Journal of Technology Management* 24, no. 1 (2002), pp. 88–105.

[48]Sheena Leek, Peter W. Turnbull, and Peter Naude, "How Is Information Technology Affecting Business Relationships? Results from a U.K. Survey," *Industrial Marketing Management* 32, no. 2 (February 2003), pp. 119–126.

solar turbines inc.
a global industrial marketer

With more than 80 percent of its sales outside the United States, Solar Turbines Inc. is the most global subsidiary of one of America's most global companies. About half of Caterpillar's 2005 sales of over $30 billion were to customers outside the United States, making the parent corporation one of the country's leading exporters. Pictured here is work on the world's largest earthmoving project, the Three Gorges Dam site in China.

Solar® industrial gas turbines are used by customers in 86 countries worldwide, in the oil and gas industries, electrical power generation, and marine propulsion. Solar promotes its products on the Internet (see www.solarturbines.com) and in brochures and print media around the world, as represented below:

An ad appearing in a French trade publication. It emphasizes the energy-saving and low-pollution attributes of the products. Notice the Caterpillar yellow in the logo and the phone number for the European subsidiary offices.

The compact size makes Solar gas turbines ideally suited for offshore oil applications in places like the North Sea, the Gulf of Mexico, and offshore Malaysia and Latin America.

A Russian-language brochure. The former Soviet Union and now the Russian oil and gas industry has remained an important customer for Solar for more than 30 years.

(Courtesy Solar Turbines Inc.)

the project team

The Customer is involved as a vital member of the Project Team from the initial inquiry to final acceptance. The Customer works with and issues project specifications to our . . .

Sales Engineer, who maintains initial Customer contact, prompts analysis of Customer needs, submits a comprehensive proposal to the Customer, monitors execution of the order, and submits the order to the assigned . . .

Application Engineer, who is responsible for determining the best product match for Customer requirements and recommending alternative approaches as appropriate. The Application Engineer works closely with . . .

Engineering and Control Systems, where gas turbines, gas compressors, and controls are designed and gas turbine packages are customized for the customers based on proven designs.

Solar Turbines sells its products and services through Project Teams that include both customer personnel and vendors. Solar has followed its American customers around the world, supplying equipment and services for their global ventures. Of course, the firm sells directly to a wide variety of foreign firms as well.

Personal selling is the most important aspect of the promotions mix for industrial companies like Solar. In addition to calling on clients directly, sales engineers attend key trade shows around the world, such as this one in Amsterdam.

Project Manager handles all aspects of the order, maintains liaison with the Customer, controls documentation, arranges quality audits, and is responsible for on-time shipment and scheduling equipment commissioning at the Customer site.

Manufacturing Technicians produce, assemble, and test industrial gas turbines and turbomachinery packages designed to meet specific Customer needs. Manufacturing also arranges shipment of equipment to the Customer site where . . .

Customer Services handles installation and start-up of the turbomachinery, trains personnel, and provides a wide range of vital services to support Customer and operating requirements.

Suppliers are a critical element of all project teams; they provide materials and components that must meet Solar's demanding Quality Standards.

The Venezuelan offshore oil and gas platform pictured here is about a $40 million project for Solar; it includes four sets of turbomachinery. Close coordination among customer, subcontractors, and Solar is required from initial designs through powering up the facility.

(Courtesy Solar Turbines Inc.)

Solar's sales and services efforts don't stop when the machine has been turned on. After-sales services (maintenance contracts, overhaul, and spare parts) often account for a third of some industrial manufacturers' revenues, and Solar is no exception to that rule. Pictured are company overhaul operations in Indonesia.

solar's marketing affiliates

Solar sells and distributes its products through a variety of kinds of affiliates around the world. Most firms would prefer to keep things simple—direct sales worldwide. However, Solar has learned to be flexible and makes distribution decisions based on the level of business and local regulations.

Solar has packaging agreements with three Japanese companies, Mitsui Zosen, Niigata, and Yanmar. The one pictured, Yanmar, buys the turbine engines from Solar, then packages them with generators to suit Japanese regulations and customer specifications.

Delcom is Solar's distributor in Malaysia. Almost all the manufacturing is done in the United States, and Delcom's principal role is marketing in Southeast Asia. Pictured is Delcom's booth at a Malay trade show.

Solar has a variety of sales and manufacturing operations and affiliations in Mexico, including a maquiladora plant in Tijuana, offices in Mexico City, and a technology-sharing agreement with Turbinas Solar. The last facility is located in Veracruz and is pictured above.

Solar has also signed long-term alliance agreements with some of its major customers like Shell Oil. Pictured here are the Solar and Shell executives who worked on the agreement and then signed it at Solar's San Diego headquarters.

(Courtesy Solar Turbines Inc.)

IBM of Brazil stresses stronger ties with its customers by offering planning seminars that address corporate strategies, competition, quality, and how to identify marketing opportunities. One of these seminars showed a food import-export firm how it could increase efficiency by decentralizing its computer facilities to better serve its customers. The company's computers were centralized at headquarters, while branches took orders manually and mailed them to the home office for processing and invoicing. Several days elapsed before the customer's order was entered, adding several days to delivery time. The seminar helped the company realize it could streamline its order processing by installing branch-office terminals that were connected to computers at the food company's headquarters. A customer could then place an order and receive an invoice on the spot, shortening the delivery time by several days or weeks. Helping clients or suppliers identify problems and their solutions also helps IBM sell equipment to the attending companies. Not all participants who attend the 30 different seminars offered annually become IBM customers, but the seminars create a continuing relationship with potential customers.

Summary

Industrial (business-to-business) marketing requires close attention to the exact needs of customers. Basic differences across various markets are less than for consumer goods, but the motives behind purchases differ enough to require a special approach. Global competition has risen to the point that industrial goods marketers must pay close attention to the level of economic and technological development of each market to determine the buyer's assessment of quality. Companies that adapt their products to these needs are the ones that should be most effective in the marketplace.

The demand for products and services in business-to-business markets is by nature more volatile than in most consumer markets. The demand also varies by level of economic development and the quality of educational systems across countries. Ultimately, product or service quality is defined by customers, but global quality standards such as ISO 9000 are being developed that provide information about companies' attention to matters of quality. After-sale services are a hugely important aspect of industrial sales. The demand for other kinds of business services (e.g., banking, legal services, advertising) is burgeoning around the world. Trade shows are an especially important promotional medium in business-to-business marketing.

Questions

1. Define the following terms:

   derived demand   ISO 9000
   price–quality relationship   relationship marketing
   client followers

2. What are the differences between consumer and industrial goods and what are the implications for international marketing?

3. Discuss how the various stages of economic development affect the demand for industrial goods.

4. "Industrialization is typically a national issue, and industrial goods are the fodder for industrial growth." Comment.

5. "The adequacy of a product must be considered in relation to the general environment within which it will be operated rather than solely on the basis of technical efficiency." Discuss the implications of this statement.

6. Why hasn't the United States been more helpful in setting universal standards for industrial equipment? Do you feel that the argument is economically sound? Discuss.

7. What roles do service, replacement parts, and standards play in competition in foreign marketing? Illustrate.

8. Discuss the role industrial trade fairs play in international marketing of industrial goods.

9. Describe the reasons an MNC might seek an ISO 9000 certification.

10. What ISO 9000 legal requirements are imposed on products sold in the EU? Discuss.

11. Discuss the competitive consequences of being ISO 9000 certified.

12. Discuss how the characteristics that define the uniqueness of industrial products lead naturally to relationship marketing. Give some examples.

13. Discuss some of the more pertinent problems in pricing industrial goods.

14. What is the price–quality relationship? How does this affect a U.S. firm's comparative position in world markets?

15. Select several countries, each at a different stage of economic development, and illustrate how the stage affects demand for industrial goods.

16. England has almost completed the process of shifting from the inch-pound system to the metric system. What effect do you think this will have on the traditional U.S. reluctance to make such a change? Discuss the economic implications of such a move.

17. Discuss the importance of international business services to total U.S. export trade. How do most U.S. service companies become international?

18. Discuss the international market environment for business services.

14

international marketing channels

CHAPTER OUTLINE

Global Perspective: A Single Stick of Doublemint Today—18 Billion Tomorrow

Channel-of-Distribution Structures

    Import-Oriented Distribution Structure
    Japanese Distribution Structure
    Trends: From Traditional to Modern Channel Structures

Distribution Patterns

    General Patterns
    Retail Patterns

Alternative Middleman Choices

    Home-Country Middlemen
    Foreign-Country Middlemen
    Government-Affiliated Middlemen

Factors Affecting Choice of Channels

    Cost
    Capital Requirements
    Control
    Coverage
    Character
    Continuity

Locating, Selecting, and Motivating Channel Members

    Locating Middlemen
    Selecting Middlemen
    Motivating Middlemen
    Terminating Middlemen
    Controlling Middlemen

The Internet

CHAPTER LEARNING OBJECTIVES

What you should learn from Chapter 14:

- The variety of distribution channels and how they affect cost and efficiency in marketing

- The Japanese distribution structure and what it means to Japanese customers and to competing importers of goods

- How distribution patterns affect the various aspects of international marketing

- The growing importance of e-commerce as a distribution alternative

- The functions, advantages, and disadvantages of various kinds of middlemen

- The importance of middlemen to a product's success and the importance of selecting and maintaining middlemen

Global Perspective

A SINGLE STICK OF DOUBLEMINT TODAY—18 BILLION TOMORROW

Outside a corner candy stand in Shanghai, 10-year-old Zhang Xiaomei folds a piece of Wrigley's Doublemint gum into her mouth—one of 18 billion sticks the Wm. Wrigley Jr. Company will sell in China this year. To reach the flimsy blue plywood stand that serves this customer in pigtails, the minty stick traveled a thousand miles by truck, rusting freighter, tricycle cart, and bicycle—and it is still freshly soft and sugar-dusted at the time it is sold. That's something of a wonder given the daunting scale and obstacles in the world's largest developing country.

Mastering the distribution system is the single most important challenge of China's economic revolution. The task facing every consumer products company trying to reach the giant Chinese market is how to get the product to the consumer at a convenient location, in salable condition, properly displayed, and aggressively sold. That, at least, is the ideal.

Western goods can effectively reach only about 200 million of China's 1.2 billion people today. But the number of accessible Chinese consumers is increasing rapidly as companies become more adept at meeting the challenges of navigating where roads are poor, rivers are jammed, and railways are clogged.

Finding reliable distributors, usually by word of mouth, is the first challenge, but seldom the last. Distributors are often state owned and have little incentive to position a brand, let alone an understanding of how to do so. Market coverage, maintaining product quality, and effective presentation at the point of sale are Wrigley's goals. Wrigley wants its gum consumed within eight months of manufacture; otherwise, the gum dries out or sugar bleeds through the packaging.

Let's follow the route taken by Zhang Xiaomei's stick of Doublemint from a factory in Guangzhou on the southern coast of China to a corner stand in Shanghai. The gum is shipped to Shanghai from Guangzhou on a coastal freighter. But off the coast of Zhejiang province, a marine patrol seizes the ship; along with 960,000 packs of gum, the ship is loaded with smuggled cars. The gum and other cargo are seized by customs, while Wrigley waits and frets the whole time about aging. Finally, the gum is released and loaded onto a truck at the Shanghai port, only to face a complicated bribe-strewn journey through the distribution system on its way to market. Wrigley-hired trucks are often stopped not only by bandits but also by provincial gendarmes demanding exorbitant fees before they let the vehicles pass.

Once the gum gets into Shanghai, Wrigley loses control. Distribution now depends on one of the firms spun off from China's once-mighty state-owned trading companies. Wholesalers in China do not do much delivering; instead, like Wrigley wholesaler Chen Tuping, they wait in their warehouses for buyers to arrive.

So how does that stick of gum get to Zhang Xiaomei? Wrigley's legwork, that's how. Teams of Wrigley representatives walk the streets, talking to shop owners, handing out free Wrigley posters and plastic display stands. Among the targets is Xu Meili, who runs a booth at the Beautiful & Rich Wholesale Market. After a successful sales call, she begins to stock Wrigley's gum, which she fetches with a tricycle cart from Mr. Chen, the wholesaler, or one of his competitors.

Wrigley salesmen continue visiting small kiosks, like the blue plywood stand in Shanghai. Inside the stand, a young woman who calls herself Little Yan naps on her folded arms between sales. When stocks run low, she rides her bike the few blocks to Ms. Xu's booth to buy more gum or candy. All of this just to get Zhang Xiaomei a stick of gum.

"The margin isn't great," says Wrigley's international business chief. But for now, he says, the company is content to build market share. He adds: "We're a very patient company." To quote a statement on distribution from Wrigley's Web site, "The modest price of chewing gum means almost everybody can afford to buy it." The global market for gum is vast and Wrigley seeks markets in every country it can enter, even where consumers don't yet chew gum. For example, Wrigley recently invested in new plants in India, where only a very small number of Indians chew gum. But with a population almost as large as China's, it means big growth if only a small percentage of the one billion people buy the product. Wrigley's global distribution strategy is to ensure that everyone in the world can get gum wherever and whenever he or she wants.

Effort pays off—Doublemint chewing gum has a 91 percent market share in China, and that translates into sales of about 18 billion sticks per year! That's up from 400 million sticks just a decade ago.

Sources: Craig S. Smith, "Doublemint in China: Distribution Isn't Double the Fun," *Wall Street Journal,* December 5, 1995, p. B1; David Shook, "Wrigley: Solid Growth by Gum," *BusinessWeek Online*, April 11, 2003; www.wrigley.com, 2006.

If marketing goals are to be achieved, a product must be made accessible to the target market at an affordable price. Getting the product to the target market can be a costly process if inadequacies within the distribution structure cannot be overcome. Forging an aggressive and reliable channel of distribution may be the most critical and challenging[1] task facing the international marketer. Moreover, some argue that meeting such challenges is a key catalyst to economic development.[2]

Each market contains a distribution network with many channel choices whose structures are unique and, in the short run, fixed. In some markets the distribution structure is multilayered, complex, inefficient, even strange, and often difficult for new marketers to penetrate; in others, there are few specialized middlemen except in major urban areas; and in yet others, there is a dynamic mixture of traditional and new, evolving distribution systems available on a global scale. Regardless of the predominating distribution structure, competitive advantage will reside with the marketer best able to build the most efficient channel from among the alternatives available. And as global trade continues to burgeon and physical distribution infrastructures lag, the challenges will be even greater in the 21st century.[3]

This chapter discusses the basic points involved in making channel decisions: channel structures; distribution patterns; available alternative middlemen; factors affecting choice of channels; and locating, selecting, motivating, and terminating middlemen.

Channel-of-Distribution Structures

In every country and in every market, urban or rural, rich or poor, all consumer and industrial products eventually go through a distribution process. The *distribution process* includes the physical handling and distribution of goods, the passage of ownership (title), and—most important from the standpoint of marketing strategy—the buying and selling negotiations between producers and middlemen and between middlemen and customers.

A host of policy and strategic channel-selection issues confronts the international marketing manager. These issues are not in themselves very different from those encountered in domestic distribution, but the resolution of the issues differs because of different channel alternatives and market patterns.

Each country market has a *distribution structure* through which goods pass from producer to user. Within this structure are a variety of middlemen whose customary functions, activities, and services reflect existing competition, market characteristics, tradition, and economic development.

In short, the behavior of channel members is the result of the interactions between the cultural environment and the marketing process. Channel structures range from those with little developed marketing infrastructure such as those found in many emerging markets to the highly complex, multilayered system found in Japan.

Import-Oriented Distribution Structure

Traditional channels in developing countries evolved from economies with a strong dependence on imported manufactured goods. In an *import-oriented* or *traditional distribution structure,* an importer controls a fixed supply of goods and the marketing system develops around the philosophy of selling a limited supply of goods at high prices to a small number of affluent customers. In the resulting seller's market, market penetration and mass distribution are not necessary because demand exceeds supply and, in most cases, the customer seeks the supply from a limited number of middlemen.

---

[1]Indeed, David Ford argues that this challenge hasn't abated with new technologies, etc. See "Distribution, Internationalization and Networks: Solving Old Problems, Learning New Things, and Forgetting Most of Them," *International Marketing Review* 19, no. 2–3 (2002), pp. 225–235.

[2]Paul Ellis, "Are International Trade Intermediaries Catalysts in Economic Development? A New Research Agenda," *Journal of International Marketing* 11, no. 1 (2003), pp. 73–96.

[3]Ronald D. White, "Bracing for a Tighter Fit," *Los Angeles Times*, November 29, 2004, pp. C1, C5; Chip Cummins, "Istanbul Moment: Sir, There's a Ship in Your Bedroom," *Wall Street Journal*, July 28, 2005, pp. A1, A7.

They're in China, but they aren't Peking ducks. The birds are for sale in Guangzhou's free market, the first farmers' market to be opened in China after the Cultural Revolution. This was the place where free enterprise found its rebirth after the cultural revolution. Every kind of food is for sale here—from ducks to dogs, from scorpions to dried lizards on sticks.

This configuration affects the development of intermediaries and their functions. Distribution systems are local rather than national in scope, and the relationship between the importer and any middleman in the marketplace is considerably different from that found in a mass-marketing system. The idea of a channel as a chain of intermediaries performing specific activities and each selling to a smaller unit beneath it until the chain reaches the ultimate consumer is not common in an import-oriented system.[4]

Because the importer-wholesaler traditionally performs most marketing functions, independent agencies that provide advertising, marketing research, warehousing and storage, transportation, financing, and other facilitating functions found in a developed, mature marketing infrastructure are nonexistent or underdeveloped. Thus few independent agencies to support a fully integrated distribution system develop.

Contrast this with the distribution philosophy of mass consumption that prevails in the United States and other industrialized nations. In these markets, one supplier does not dominate supply, supply can be increased or decreased within a given range, and profit maximization occurs at or near production capacity. Generally a buyer's market exists and the producer strives to penetrate the market and push goods out to the consumer, resulting in a highly developed channel structure that includes a variety of intermediaries, many of which are unknown in developing markets.

Obviously, few countries fit the import-oriented model today, although the channel structure for chewing gum illustrated in the Global Perspective comes closest to describing a traditional import-oriented structure. As China develops economically, its market system and distribution structure will evolve as well. As already discussed, economic development is uneven, and various parts of an economy may be at different stages of development. Channel structures in countries that have historically evolved from an import-oriented base will usually have vestiges of their beginnings reflected in a less than fully integrated system. At the other extreme is the Japanese distribution system with multiple layers of specialized middlemen.

Japanese Distribution Structure

Distribution in Japan has long been considered the most effective nontariff barrier to the Japanese market.[5] Even though the market is becoming more open as many traditional modes of operation are eroding in the face of competition from foreign marketers, it still serves as an excellent case study for the pervasive impact culture plays on economic institutions such as national distribution systems. The Japanese distribution structure is different enough from its U.S. or European counterparts that it should be carefully studied by anyone contemplating entry. The Japanese system has four distinguishing features: (1) a structure dominated by many small middlemen dealing with many small retailers, (2) channel control by manufacturers, (3) a business philosophy shaped by a unique culture,[6] and (4) laws that protect the foundation of the system—the small retailer.

[4]Some progress is being made in e-commerce in some of the least developed countries. See William Wresh, "Initial e-Commerce Efforts in Nine Least Developed Countries," *Journal of Global Information Management*, April–June 2003, pp. 67–78.

[5]For a detailed study on this subject, see Frank Alpert, Michael Kamins, Tokoaki Sakano, Naoto Onzo, and John L. Graham, "Retail Buyer Decision Making in Japan: What U.S. Sellers Need to Know," *International Business Review* 6, no. 2 (1997), pp. 91–104; Yoshinobu Sato, "Some Reasons Why Foreign Retailers Have Difficulties in Succeeding in the Japanese Market," *Journal of Global Marketing* 18, no. 1/2 (2004), pp. 21–44.

[6]Keysuk Kim and Changho Oh, "On Distributor Commitment in Marketing Channels for Industrial Products: Contrast between the United States and Japan," *Journal of International Marketing* 10, no. 1 (2002), pp. 72–97.

Exhibit 14.1

Comparison of Distribution Channels between the United States and Japan

Automobile parts: Japan

Automobile parts: United States

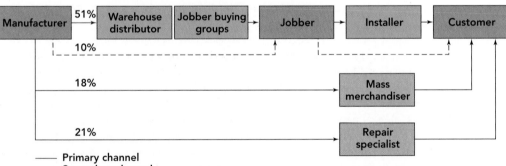

—— Primary channel
- - - Secondary channel

High Density of Middlemen.
The density of middlemen, retailers, and whole-salers in the Japanese market is unparalleled in any Western industrialized country.[7] The traditional Japanese structure serves consumers who make small, frequent purchases at small, conveniently located stores. An equal density of wholesalers supports the high density of small stores with small inventories. It is not unusual for consumer goods to go through three or four intermediaries before reaching the consumer—producer to primary, secondary, regional, and local wholesaler, and finally to retailer to consumer. Exhibit 14.1 illustrates the contrast between shorter U.S. channels and the long Japanese channels.

---

[7]Junji Nishimura, "The Linkage of Trades in Terms of Wholesale Business Formats in Japanese Distribution Systems," *Journal of Global Marketing* 18, no. 1 (2004), pp. 167–186.

Exhibit 14.2
Retail Structure in
Three Countries

Source: Euromonitor, 2003.

	Retail Outlets (000s)		
	Germany	**Japan**	**United States**
Food Stores			
Supermarkets	9.0	15.0	43.7
Hypermarkets	2.3	1.5	3.1
Discounters	15.4	1.0	29.1
Independent grocers	34.2	62.0	9.7
Bakers	47.2	74.7	2.8
Butchers	44.3	16.4	8.0
Fishmongers	27.1	27.0	1.6
Greengrocers	16.1	27.7	3.3
Nonfood Stores			
Booksellers	25.6	37.0	12.7
Chemists	39.4	83.3	47.4
Department stores	1.2	0.3	13.5
Electronics, computers	30.6	61.9	30.3
Home furnishings	11.7	38.7	28.2
Sporting goods	8.3	19.3	23.2
Toy shops	3.6	12.1	18.0

While other countries have large numbers of small retail stores, the major difference between small stores (nine or fewer employees) in Japan and the United States is the percentage of total retail sales accounted for by small retailers. In Japan, small stores (95.1 percent of all retail food stores) account for 57.7 percent of retail food sales; in the United States, small stores (69.8 percent of all retail food stores) generate 19.2 percent of food sales. A disproportionate percentage of nonfood sales are made in small stores in Japan as well. In the United States, small stores (81.6 percent of all stores) sell 32.9 percent of nonfood items; in Japan, small stores (94.1 percent of all stores) sell 50.4 percent. Such differences are also reflected in Exhibit 14.2. Notice the American emphasis on supermarkets, discount food stores, and department stores versus the Japanese prevalence of independent groceries and bakers.

As we shall see in a later section, profound changes in retailing are occurring in Japan. Although it is still accurate to describe the Japanese market as having a high density of middlemen, the number of small stores is declining as they are being replaced by larger discount and specialty stores. The number of retail stores is down more than 10 percent since 2000, and the number of retail stores with a staff of four or fewer dropped more than 15 percent. These small stores serve an important role for Japanese consumers. High population density, the tradition of frequent trips to the store, an emphasis on service, freshness, and quality, and wholesalers who provide financial assistance, frequent deliveries of small lots, and other benefits combine to support the high number of small stores.

Channel Control.   Manufacturers depend on wholesalers for a multitude of services to other members of the distribution network. Financing, physical distribution, warehousing, inventory, promotion, and payment collection are provided to other channel members by wholesalers. The system works because wholesalers and all other middlemen downstream are tied to manufacturers by a set of practices and incentives designed to ensure strong marketing support for their products and to exclude rival competitors from the channel. Wholesalers typically act as agent middlemen and extend the manufacturer's control through the channel to the retail level.

Control is maintained through the following elements:

1. **Inventory financing.** Sales are made on consignment with credits extending for several months.

2. **Cumulative rebates.** Rebates are given annually for any number of reasons, including quantity purchases, early payments, achieving sales targets, performing services, maintaining specific inventory levels, participating in sales promotions,

remaining loyal to suppliers, maintaining manufacturer's price policies, cooperating, and contributing to overall success.

3. **Merchandise returns.** All unsold merchandise may be returned to the manufacturer.

4. **Promotional support.** Intermediaries receive a host of displays, advertising layouts, management education programs, in-store demonstrations, and other dealer aids that strengthen the relationship between the middleman and the manufacturer.

Business Philosophy.   Coupled with the close economic ties and dependency created by trade customs and the long structure of Japanese distribution channels is a relationship-oriented business philosophy that emphasizes loyalty, harmony, and friendship. The value system supports long-term dealer–supplier relationships that are difficult to change as long as each party perceives economic advantage. The traditional partner, the insider, generally has the advantage.

A general lack of price competition, the provision of costly services, and other inefficiencies render the cost of Japanese consumer goods among the highest in the world. Indeed, when you just compare paychecks at current exchange rates (that is, GDP per capita), Japanese at $39,195 outearn Americans at $36,790. However, if you take into consideration what those paychecks will buy [that is, GDP per capita at purchase price parity (PPP)], then Americans at $36,665 do better than Japanese at $27,338.[8] Such prices create a perfect climate for discounting, which is beginning to be a major factor. The Japanese consumer contributes to the continuation of the traditional nature of the distribution system through frequent buying trips, small purchases, favoring personal service over price, and a proclivity for loyalty to brands perceived to be of high quality. Additionally, Japanese law gives the small retailer enormous advantage over the development of larger stores and competition. All these factors have supported the continued viability of small stores and the established system, although changing attitudes among many Japanese consumers are beginning to weaken the hold traditional retailing has on the market.

Large-Scale Retail Store Law and Its Successor.   Competition from large retail stores had been almost totally controlled by *Daitenho*—the Large-Scale Retail Store Law (and its more recent incarnations). Designed to protect small retailers from large intruders into their markets, the law required that any store larger than 5,382 square feet (500 square meters) must have approval from the prefecture government to be "built, expanded, stay open later in the evening, or change the days of the month they must remain closed." All proposals for new "large" stores were first judged by the Ministry of International Trade and Industry (MITI). Then, if all local retailers *unanimously* agreed to the plan, it was swiftly approved. However, without approval at the prefecture level the plan was returned for clarification and modification, a process that could take several years (10 years was not unheard of) for approval. Designed to protect small retailers against competition from large stores, the law had been imposed against both domestic and foreign companies. One of Japan's largest supermarket chains needed 10 years to get clearance for a new site. Toys "R" Us[9] fought rules and regulations for over three years before it gained approval for a store. Besides the *Daitenho,* there were myriad licensing rules. One investigation of retail stores uncovered many different laws, each requiring a separate license that had to be met to open a full-service store.

Businesspeople in Japan and the United States see the Japanese distribution system as a major nontariff barrier, and Japanese see it as a major roadblock to improvement of the Japanese standard of living. However, pressure from the United States and the Structural Impediments Initiative (SII) negotiations to pry open new markets for American companies has resulted in large cracks in the system. The most recent is the Large-Scale Retail Store Location Act of June 2000, which replaced the Large-Scale Retail Store Law.

The new law takes MITI out of the approval process. Under the new law, restrictions on the opening of large retailers near smaller shops are relaxed and the restriction on the

---

[8]World Development Indicators, World Bank, 2005.

[9]Jungyim Baek, "How Does the Global Retailer Localize Its Format? The Case of Toys 'R' Us and Carrefour in Japan," *Journal of Global Marketing* 18, no. 1/2 (2004), pp. 151–166.

CROSSING **BORDERS** 14.1   Mitsukoshi Department Store, Established 1611—But Will It Be There in 2011?

Japanese department stores have a long history in Japanese retailing; indeed, Mitsukoshi department store, the epitome of Japanese retailing, began as a dry goods store in 1611. Department stores were Japan's first big corporations, which created Japan's first banks. Those banks in turn spawned the *keiretsu* system of corporate family groups that drove Japan's transformation into an economic power. But are their days numbered?

To visit a Japanese department store is to get a glimpse of Japanese life. In the basements and sub-basements, food abounds, with everything from crunchy Japanese pickles to delicate French pastry and soft-colored, seasonally changing forms of Japanese candies. Besides the traditional floors for women's and men's apparel and furniture, most stores have a floor devoted to kimonos and related accessories and another floor dedicated to children's needs and wants. On the roof there may be miniature open-air amusement parks for children.

But wait, there's more. Department stores are not content merely to dazzle with variety, delight with imaginative displays, and accept large amounts of yen for clothes and vegetables. They also seek to serve up a bit of culture. Somewhere between the floors of clothing and the roof, you are likely to find a banquet hall, an art gallery, an exhibition hall, and one or two floors of restaurants serving everything from *doria* (creamy rice with cheese) to tempura. Department stores aim to be "total life-style enterprises," says one manager. "We try to be all-inclusive, with art, culture, shopping and fashion. We stress the philosophy of *i-shoku-ju*, the three big factors in life: what you wear, what you eat, and how you live."

Two kinds of stores dominate Japanese retailing: giant department stores like Mitsukoshi and small neighborhood shops, both kept alive by a complex distribution system that translates into high prices for the Japanese consumer. In exchange for high prices,

the Japanese consumer gets variety, services, and, what may be unique to Japanese department stores, cultural enlightenment.

But there are winds of change. Department stores' sales fell for 45 straight months from 1992 to late 1995. There was a slight increase prior to a sales tax increase, but a downward trend started by mid-1997. The Japanese like the amenities of department stores, but they are beginning to take notice of the wave of "new" discount stores that are challenging the traditional retail system by offering quality products at sharply reduced prices. Aoyama Trading Company, which opened a discount men's suit store in the heart of Ginza, where Tokyo's most prestigious department stores are located, may be the future. The owner says he can sell suits for two-thirds the department store price by purchasing directly from manufacturers. Fast Retailing Company, which operates the spectacularly successful Uni-Qlo clothing brand stores, has taken a Gap-like approach to clothes by selling simple and casual wear. Many people weave through its aisles to pay rock-bottom prices. Another omen may be Toys "R" Us, which had opened 100 discount toy stores by 2000 and is now the largest toy retailer in Japan. Department store response has been to discount toy prices, for the first time, by as much as 30 percent. As one discounter after another "cherry picks" item after item to discount, can department stores continue to be "total life-style enterprises"? Will there be a Mitsukoshi, as we know it today, in 2011?

Sources: "Tokyo Department Store Sales Slip 0.6% in April," *Kyodo World News Service*, May 16, 2000; "Japanese Retailers Still Struggling to Make a Sale," *Reuters*, May 24, 2000; Fred Crawford, "Business without Borders," *Chain Store Age*, December 2001, pp. 86–96; Lee Tee Jong, "Where the Customer Is King," *The Straits Times* (Singapore), September 3, 2005.

number of days stores must be closed has been abolished. However, local government has the authority to block construction if it thinks the new project will exacerbate pollution, traffic congestion, or noise. There is concern that the real impact of the new law depends on how it is interpreted by local governments. Whether they will use environmental protection as an excuse to limit new store openings and thus be more restrictive rather than less restrictive remains to be seen.

Changes in the Japanese Distribution System.
The Structural Impediments Initiative, deregulation, and most recently Wal-Mart[10] are causing changes in Japanese

---

[10] Ann Zimmerman and Martin Fackler, "Wal-Mart's Foray into Japan Spurs a Retail Upheaval," *Wall Street Journal*, online, September 19, 2003; Kay Itoi and George Wehrfritz, "A Dying Zombie," *NewsWeek*, August 30, 2004, pp. 34–35.

distribution practices. Ultimately, however, only local merchants challenging the traditional ways by giving the consumer quality products at competitive, fair prices can bring about the demise of the traditional distribution system. Specialty discounters are sprouting up everywhere, and entrepreneurs are slashing prices by buying direct and avoiding the distribution system altogether. For example, Kojima, a consumer electronics discounter, practices what it calls "global purchasing" and buys merchandise anywhere in the world as cheaply as possible. Kojima's tie with General Electric enables it to offer a 410-liter GE refrigerator for $640, down from the typical price of $1,925, and to reduce the 550-liter model from $3,462 to $1,585.

The "new" retailers are relatively small and account for no more than 5 percent of retail sales, compared with 14 percent for all specialty discounters in the United States. But the impact extends beyond their share of market because they are forcing the system to change.[11] Traditional retailers are modifying marketing and sales strategies in response to the new competition as well so as to take advantage of changing Japanese lifestyles. There are also indications that some wholesalers are modernizing and consolidating operations as more retailers demand to buy direct from the manufacturer or from the largest wholesalers. The process is slow because the characteristics of the distribution system are deeply rooted in the cultural history of Japan. However, the long supply chain consisting of many layers of middlemen in Japan is vulnerable to the efficiencies that business-to-business (B2B) commerce provides. Because the Internet allows suppliers and retailers to seek the cheapest price in the global market, it will be harder for the many Japanese middlemen to maintain the control they have had.

Similarly, traditional Japanese retailing is slowly giving ground to specialty stores, supermarkets, discounters, and convenience stores. Fast Retailing, a casual-clothing retailer, features good clothes at bargain prices. The store can sell cheaply without lowering quality because it shuns the traditional middlemen and designs its own clothes and sources them directly from factories in China. In 12 months, Fast Retailing's sales jumped by a third to $927 million, just as Japanese retail sales showed their 36th consecutive monthly drop.

Konbini, as convenience stores are called in Japan, are among those retailers bringing about a revolution in Japanese retailing. Besides the traditional array of convenience goods, *konbini* are adding an Internet feature whereby customers can pay bills, bank, or purchase travel packages, music, and merchandise on in-store terminals or over the Internet at home. Seven-Eleven Japan, with 8,000 outlets, has a joint venture with www.7dream.com. Instead of offering door-to-door delivery, 7dream wants to lure customers to the nearest 7-Eleven store to pay and pick up purchases. What seemed to be an impenetrable tradition-bound distribution system just a few years ago now appears to be on the verge of radical change. Japanese retailing seems to be following a direction similar to that of the United States decades earlier and may not be recognizable in a decade or two.

Trends: From Traditional to Modern Channel Structures

Today, few countries are sufficiently isolated to be unaffected by global economic and political changes. These currents of change are altering all levels of the economic fabric, including the distribution structure. Traditional channel structures are giving way to new forms, new alliances, and new processes—some more slowly than others, but all are changing.[12] Pressures for change in a country come from within and without. Multinational marketers are seeking ways to profitably tap market segments that are served by costly, traditional distribution systems. Direct marketing, door-to-door selling, hypermarkets, discount houses, shopping malls, catalog selling, the Internet, and other distribution methods are being introduced in an attempt to provide efficient distribution channels.

Some important trends in distribution will eventually lead to greater commonality than disparity among middlemen in different countries. Wal-Mart, for example, is expanding all

---

[11]Adrian Slywotzky and Richard Wise, "An Unfinished Revolution," *Sloan Management Review,* Spring 2003, pp. 94–95.

[12]Suk-Ching Ho, "Evolution versus Tradition in Marketing Systems: The Hong Kong Food Retailing Experience," *Journal of Public Policy and Marketing* 24, no. 1 (2005), pp. 90–99.

CROSSING **BORDERS 14.2**   Big-Box Cookie-Cutter Stores Don't Always Work

Wal-Mart, JCPenney, and Office Depot are all going global with their successful U.S. operating strategies. However, adaptation is still important, and many have had to adapt their operating strategy to accommodate cultural and business differences. Growth strategies must be supported by three foundations: (1) the retailer must offer a competitively superior product as defined by local customers, (2) the retailer must be able to develop superior economies across the value chain that delivers the product to the local consumer, and (3) global retailers must be able to execute in the local environment.

Consider, for example, some of the problems U.S. retailers have had when building their global strategies on these three pillars.

- In fashion and clothing markets, personal taste is critical in the buying decision. Distinctions in culture, climate, and even physiology demand that products be tailored to each market. Tight skirts, blouses, and any other article that tightly hugs the female silhouette are sure sellers in southern Europe and are sure losers in the north. Dutch women bicycle to work, so tight skirts are out. French men insist that trousers be suitable for cuffs; German men cannot be bothered with cuffs. Rayon and other artificial fabrics are impossible to sell in Germany, but next door in Holland artificial fabrics are popular because they are much cheaper.

- The best-selling children's lines in northern Europe don't have a significant following in France; the French dress their children as little adults, not as kids. One of the best sellers is a downsized version of a women's clothing line for girls.

- The lack of sunshine in northern Europe means that lime green fashions don't sell well there; consumers sense that the color leaves a rather sickly impression. But in the south, lime green looks great with a St. Tropez tan.

- Operational costs vary too. Costs in the United States, where the minimum wage is $5.15 per hour, are dramatically different than in France, where the minimum wage is over $10.00, including employer social charges. As a consequence, Toys "R" Us has been forced to adapt its operating structure in France, where it uses one-third fewer employees per store than it does in the United States.

- The image of Sam Walton's English setter on packages of its private-label dog food, Ol'Roy, was replaced with a terrier after Wal-Mart's German executives explained that terriers are popular in Germany, while setters aren't familiar.

- JCPenney is closing its five home-furnishing stores in Japan, in part because so many products, from curtains to bed sheets, had to be made differently there.

- Office Depot closed its U.S.-style cookie-cutter stores in Japan and reopened stores one-third the size of the larger ones. Customers were put off by the warehouselike atmosphere and confused by the English-language signs. The new stores have signs in Japanese and are stocked with office products more familiar to Japanese and purchased locally, such as two-ring loose-leaf binders rather than the typical three-ring binders sold in the United States.

- After initially doing well, Starbucks' profits temporarily fell in Japan. It appeared to be a matter of taste. One consumer reported, "The coffee tasted artificial." Ironically, since sales have been below expectations, customer service at Starbucks is reported to have gotten closer now to Japanese expectations.

Sources: Ernest Beck and Emily Nelson, "As Wal-Mart Invades Europe, Rivals Rush to Match Its Formula," *Wall Street Journal*, October 6, 1999; Stanley Holmes, Irene M. Kunii, Jack Ewing, and Kerry Capell, "For Starbucks, There's No Place Like Home," *BusinessWeek*, June 9, 2003, p. 48; "Sales Begin to Recover at Major Restaurant Chains," *Nikkei Report*, September 13, 2005.

over the world—from Mexico to Brazil and from Europe to Asia.[13] Avon is expanding into eastern Europe; Mary Kay Cosmetics and Amway into China; and L.L. Bean and Lands' End have successfully entered the Japanese market. The effect of all these intrusions into the traditional distribution systems is change that will make discounting, self-service, supermarkets, mass merchandising and e-commerce concepts common all over the world, elevating the competitive climate to a level not known before.

---

[13] Anand Giridharadas, "Megastores Gaze Longingly at India," *International Herald Tribune*, April 2–3, 2005, pp. 13, 15.

As U.S. retailers have invaded Europe, staid nationally based retailers have been merging with former competitors and companies from other countries to form Europe-wide enterprises.[14] Carrefour, a French global marketer, merged with Promodes, one of its fierce French competitors, to create, in the words of its CEO, "a worldwide retail leader." The U.K. supermarket giant Sainsbury has entered an alliance with Esselunga of Italy (supermarkets), Docks de France (hypermarkets, supermarkets, and discount stores), and Belgium's Delhaize (supermarkets). The alliance provides the four companies the opportunity to pool their experience and buying power to better face growing competition and opportunity afforded by the single European market and the euro.

While European retailers see a unified Europe as an opportunity for pan-European expansion, foreign retailers are attracted by the high margins and prices. Costco, the U.S.-based warehouse retailer, saw the high gross margins that British supermarkets command (7 to 8 percent compared with 2.5 to 3 percent in the United States) as an opportunity. Costco prices will initially be 10 to 20 percent cheaper than rival local retailers.

Expansion outside the home country, as well as new types of retailing, is occurring throughout Europe. El Corte Inglés, Spain's largest department store chain, not only is moving into Portugal and other European countries but also was one of the first retailers to offer a virtual supermarket on the Internet (www.elcorteingles.es) and to sponsor two 24-hour home shopping channels in Spain. It may very well be that the Internet will be the most important trend affecting distribution.

One of Wal-Mart's strengths is its internal Internet-based system, which makes its transactions with suppliers highly efficient and lowers its cost of operations. Indeed, it is buying ailing retailers around the world with the intention of "saving them" with its distribution technologies. This same type of system is available on the Internet for both business-to-business and business-to-consumer transactions. For example, General Motors, Ford Motor Company, and DaimlerChrysler have created a single online site called Covisint (www.covisint.com) for purchasing automotive parts from suppliers, which is expected to save the companies millions of dollars. A typical purchase order costs Ford $150, whereas a real-time order via Covisint will cost about $15. Sears, Roebuck and Carrefour of France have created GlobalNetXchange (www.gnx.com), a retail exchange that allows retailers and their suppliers to conduct transactions online. Any company with a Web browser can access the exchange to buy, sell, trade, or auction goods and services. Described as "one of the most dramatic changes in consumer-products distribution of the decade," the exchange is expected to lower costs for both buyer and supplier. As more such exchanges evolve, one can only speculate about the impact on traditional channel middlemen.

We have already seen the impact on traditional retailing within the last few years caused by e-commerce retailers such as Amazon.com, Dell Computer, e-Toys, eBay, and others—all of which are expanding globally. Most brick-and-mortar retailers are experimenting with or have fully developed Web sites, some of which are merely extensions of their regular stores, allowing them to extend their reach globally. L.L. Bean, Eddie Bauer, and Lands' End are examples.

One of the most challenging aspects of Web sales is delivery of goods. As discussed earlier, one of the innovative features of the 7dream program at 7-Eleven stores in Japan is the use of convenience stores for pick-up points for Web orders. It has worked so well in Japan that Ito-Yokado Corporation, owner of Seven-Eleven Japan and 72 percent of the U.S. chain, is exporting the idea to U.S. stores. In the Dallas–Fort Worth area, 250 stores have installed ATM-like machines tied into a delivery and payment system that promises to make 7-Elevens a depot for e-commerce. FedEx, UPS, and other package delivery services that have been the backbone of e-commerce delivery in the United States are offering similar services for foreign customers of U.S. e-commerce companies as well as for foreign-based e-commerce companies. When goods cross borders, UPS and others offer seamless shipments, including customs and brokerage. Most of these service companies are established in Europe and Japan and are building networks in Latin America and China.

---

[14]John Dawson, "New Cultures, New Strategies, New Formats, and New Relationships in European Retailing: Some Implications for Asia," *Journal of Global Marketing* 18, no. 1/2 (2004), pp. 73–98.

Now that Russians can own their homes, they're spending fast in home improvement stores like this one in St. Petersburg. In English it would be called "Super Home."

The impact of these and other trends will change traditional distribution and marketing systems.[15] While this latest retailing revolution is in flux, new retailing and middlemen systems will be invented, and established companies will experiment, seeking ways to maintain their competitive edge. These changes will resonate throughout the distribution chain before new concepts are established and the system stabilizes. Not since the upheaval that occurred in U.S. distribution after World War II that ultimately led to the "big box" type of retailer has there been such potential for change in distribution systems. This time, however, such change will not be limited mostly to the United States—it will be worldwide. Competition will translate efficiencies into lower consumer prices and force distribution to become even more innovative.

Distribution Patterns

Even though patterns of distribution are in a state of change and new patterns are developing, international marketers need a general awareness of the traditional distribution base. The "traditional" system will not change overnight, and vestiges of it will remain for years to come. Nearly every international firm is forced by the structure of the market to use at least some middlemen in the distribution arrangement. It is all too easy to conclude that, because the structural arrangements of foreign and domestic distribution seem alike, foreign channels are the same as or similar to domestic channels of the same name. This is misleading. Only when the varied intricacies of actual distribution patterns are understood can the complexity of the distribution task be appreciated. The following description should convey a sense of the variety of distribution patterns.

General Patterns

Generalizing about internal distribution channel patterns of various countries is almost as difficult as generalizing about behavior patterns of people. Despite similarities, marketing channels are not the same throughout the world. Marketing methods taken for granted in the United States are rare in many countries.

Middlemen Services.   The service attitudes of people in trade vary sharply at both the retail and wholesale levels from country to country. In Egypt, for example, the primary purpose of the simple trading system is to handle the physical distribution of available goods. On the other hand, when margins are low and there is a continuing battle for customer preference, both wholesalers and retailers try to offer extra services to make their goods attractive to consumers. When middlemen are not interested in promoting or selling individual items of merchandise, the manufacturer must provide adequate inducement to

---

[15]Jung-Hee Lee and San-Chul Choi, "The Effects of Liberalization in Retail Markets on Economy and Retail Industry," *Journal of Global Marketing* 18, no. 1/2 (2004), pp. 121–132.

the middlemen or undertake much of the promotion and selling effort. In China, for example, wholesalers see their function as storing the goods and waiting for their customers to come to them. Exhibit 14.2 gives an idea of the relative importance of different types of middlemen in the United States, Germany, and Japan.

Line Breadth.   Every nation has a distinct pattern relative to the breadth of line carried by wholesalers and retailers. The distribution system of some countries seems to be characterized by middlemen who carry or can get everything; in others, every middleman seems to be a specialist dealing only in extremely narrow lines. Government regulations in some countries limit the breadth of line that can be carried by middlemen, and licensing requirements to handle certain merchandise are not uncommon.

Costs and Margins.   Cost levels and middleman margins vary widely from country to country, depending on the level of competition, services offered, efficiencies or inefficiencies of scale, and geographic and turnover factors related to market size, purchasing power, tradition, and other basic determinants. In India, competition in large cities is so intense that costs are low and margins thin; in rural areas, however, the lack of capital has permitted the few traders with capital to gain monopolies, with consequent high prices and wide margins.

Channel Length.   Some correlation may be found between the stage of economic development and the length of marketing channels. In every country, channels are likely to be shorter for industrial goods and high-priced consumer goods than for low-priced products. In general, there is an inverse relationship between channel length and the size of the purchase. Combination wholesaler-retailers or semiwholesalers exist in many countries, adding one or two links to the length of the distribution chain. In China, for example, the traditional distribution system for over-the-counter drugs consists of large local wholesalers divided into three levels. First-level wholesalers supply drugs to major cities such as Beijing and Shanghai. The second level services medium-sized cities, and the third level distributes to counties and cities with 100,000 or fewer people. It can be profitable for a company to sell directly to the two top-level wholesalers and have them sell to the third level, which is so small that it would be unprofitable for the company to seek out.

Nonexistent Channels.   One of the things companies discover about international channel-of-distribution patterns is that in many countries adequate market coverage through a simple channel of distribution is nearly impossible. In many instances, appropriate channels do not exist; in others, parts of a channel system are available but other parts are not. In Peru, for example, the informal distribution network accounts for almost a quarter of all retail cash sales. The ubiquitous street markets and ambulatory sellers offer far wider market penetration than formal distribution companies. Further, their prices are generally lower than traditional retailers, partly because of lower overhead costs compared with the higher costs generated by the overextended formal distribution chain of the traditional retailer. Thus several distinct distribution channels are necessary to reach different segments of a market; channels suitable for distribution in urban areas seldom provide adequate rural coverage.

Blocked Channels.   International marketers may be blocked from using the channel of their choice. Blockage can result from competitors' already-established lines in the various channels or from trade associations or cartels having closed certain channels. The classic example of blocked channels is Japan, as discussed earlier, but it is by no means the only example. In China FedEx and DHL initially ran into the Chinese government's own mail service as a "blocking" competitor.

Associations of middlemen sometimes restrict the number of distribution alternatives available to a producer. Druggists in many countries have inhibited distribution of a wide range of goods through any retail outlets except drugstores. The drugstores, in turn, have been supplied by a relatively small number of wholesalers that have long-established relationships with their suppliers. Thus, through a combination of competition and association, a producer may be kept out of the market completely. In the United Kingdom, simple magnifying reading glasses that can be purchased in a dozen different types of stores in the

PEMEX (Petróleos Mexicanos), the Mexican national oil company, will not let foreign firms distribute there. However, in Malaysia a Mobil station sits right across the boulevard from a government-owned PETRONAS (Petroliam Nasional) station.

United States can be purchased only by prescription through registered optical stores, which are controlled by a few large companies.

Stocking.
The high cost of credit, the danger of loss through inflation, a lack of capital, and other concerns cause foreign middlemen in many countries to limit inventories. This often results in out-of-stock conditions and sales lost to competitors. Physical distribution lags intensify the problem so that in many cases the manufacturer must provide local warehousing or extend long credit to encourage middlemen to carry large inventories. Often large inventories are out of the question for small stores with limited floor space. Considerable ingenuity, assistance, and perhaps pressure are required to induce middlemen in most countries to carry adequate or even minimal inventories. BMW has taken a unique step to alleviate this problem in Germany. It encourages its customers to pick up their new cars at the factory by providing an amusement park for the kids adjacent to the plant.

Power and Competition.
Distribution power tends to concentrate in countries where a few large wholesalers distribute to a mass of small middlemen. Large wholesalers generally finance middlemen downstream. The strong allegiance they command from their customers enables them to effectively block existing channels and force an outsider to rely on less effective and more costly distribution.

Retail Patterns

Retailing shows even greater diversity in its structure than does wholesaling.[16] In Italy and Morocco, retailing is composed largely of specialty houses that carry narrow lines, whereas in Finland most retailers carry a more general line of merchandise. Retail size is represented at one end by Japan's giant department store Mitsukoshi, which reportedly enjoys the patronage of more than 100,000 customers every day, and at the other extreme by the market of Ibadan, Nigeria, where some 3,000 one- or two-person stalls serve not many more customers. Some manufacturers sell directly to consumers through company-owned stores such as Cartier and Disney,[17] and some sell through a half-dozen layers of middlemen.

Size Patterns.
The extremes in size in retailing are similar to those that predominate in wholesaling. Exhibit 14.3 dramatically illustrates some of the variations in size and

---

[16]Nobukazu J. Azuma, "The Paradox of Competition in the World of Volatility: An Analysis of the Drivers in the Middle Market of International Fashion Retailing," *Journal of Global Marketing* 18, no. 1/2 (2004), pp. 45–72.

[17]Richard Verrier, "Children's Place in Talks with Disney," *Los Angeles Times*, June 4, 2004, p. C2.

Exhibit 14.4
International Channel-
of-Distribution Alternatives

The channel process includes all activities, beginning with the manufacturer and ending with the final consumer. This means the seller must exert influence over two sets of channels: one in the home country and one in the foreign-market country. Exhibit 14.4 shows some of the possible channel-of-distribution alternatives. The arrows show those to whom the producer and each of the middlemen might sell. In the home country, the seller must have an organization (generally the international marketing division of a company) to deal with channel members needed to move goods between countries. In the foreign market, the seller must supervise the channels that supply the product to the end user. Ideally, the company wants to control or be directly involved in the process through the various channel members to the final user. To do less may result in unsatisfactory distribution and the failure of marketing objectives. In practice, however, such involvement throughout the channel process is not always practical or cost effective. Consequently, selection of channel members and effective controls are high priorities in establishing the distribution process.

Once the marketer has clarified company objectives and policies, the next step is the selection of specific intermediaries needed to develop a channel. External middlemen are differentiated on whether or not they take title to the goods: *Agent middlemen* represent the principal rather than themselves, whereas *merchant middlemen* take title to the goods and buy and sell on their own account. The distinction between agent and merchant middlemen is important because a manufacturer's control of the distribution process is affected by who has title to the goods in the channel.

Agent middlemen work on commission and arrange for sales in the foreign country but do not take title to the merchandise. By using agents, the manufacturer assumes trading risk but maintains the right to establish policy guidelines and prices and to require its agents to provide sales records and customer information.

Merchant middlemen actually take title to manufacturers' goods and assume the trading risks, so they tend to be less controllable than agent middlemen. Merchant middlemen provide a variety of import and export wholesaling functions involved in purchasing for their own account and selling in other countries. Because merchant middlemen primarily are concerned with sales and profit margins on their merchandise, they are frequently criticized for not representing the best interests of a manufacturer. Unless they have a franchise or a strong and profitable brand, merchant middlemen seek goods from any source and are likely to have low brand loyalty. Ease of contact, minimized credit risk, and elimination of all merchandise handling outside the United States are some of the advantages of using merchant middlemen.

Middlemen are not clear-cut, precise, easily defined entities. A firm that represents one of the pure types identified here is rare. Thus intimate knowledge of middlemen functions is especially important in international activity because misleading titles can fool a marketer unable to look beyond mere names. What are the functions of a British middleman called a stockist, or one called an exporter or importer? One exporter may, in fact, be an agent middleman, whereas another is a merchant. Many, if not most, international middlemen wear several hats and can be clearly identified only in the context of their relationship with a specific firm.

Only by analyzing middlemen functions in skeletal simplicity can the nature of the channels be determined. Three alternatives are presented: first, middlemen physically located in the manufacturer's home country; next, middlemen located in foreign countries; and finally, government-affiliated middlemen.

Home-Country Middlemen

Home-country middlemen, or *domestic middlemen,* located in the producing firm's country, provide marketing services from a domestic base. By selecting domestic middlemen as intermediaries in the distribution processes, companies relegate foreign-market distribution to others. Domestic middlemen offer many advantages for companies with small international sales volume, those inexperienced with foreign markets, those not wanting to become immediately involved with the complexities of international marketing, and those wanting to sell abroad with minimal financial and management commitment. A major trade-off when using home-country middlemen is limited control over the entire process. Domestic middlemen are most likely to be used when the marketer is uncertain or desires to minimize financial and management investment. A brief discussion of the more frequently used types of domestic middlemen follows.

Manufacturers' Retail Stores.
An important channel of distribution for a large number of manufacturers is the owned, or perhaps franchised, retail store. Disney, Benetton, and many of the classic Italian luxury goods makers take this approach.

Remember for a moment the scene in the Pixar movie *Monsters Inc.*—millions of doors on conveyor belts. That scene is reminiscent of the inside of the Nike's European distribution center in Laakdal, Belgium. The shoes come from a variety of Asian low-cost manufacturers and arrive at the center via Rotterdam and Antwerp and the adjacent canal. Twelve hundred people work at the heavily automated facility where 8 million pairs of shoes are sorted and then shipped to customers all over the continent via truck. Even as sales grow the company will not need to expand the center, because the trend is for the factories to ship directly to the major European retailers including the Nike Sport in St. Petersburg pictured in Chapter 10.

Global Retailers.
As global retailers like Ikea, Costco, Sears Roebuck, Toys "R" Us, and Wal-Mart expand their global coverage, they are becoming major domestic middlemen for international markets.[21] Wal-Mart, with more than 1,600 stores in nine foreign markets, is an attractive entry point to international markets for U.S. suppliers. Wal-Mart offers an effective way to enter international markets with a minimum of experience. For example, Pacific Connections, a California manufacturer of handbags with $70 million in sales, ventured into overseas markets in Argentina, Brazil, Canada, and Mexico through its ties to Wal-Mart. And as trade restrictions are eased through alliances such as NAFTA, new global retailers are being created—Gigante from Mexico is a good example of this trend.[22]

Export Management Companies.
The *export management company (EMC)* is an important middleman for firms with relatively small international volume or for those unwilling to involve their own personnel in the international function. EMCs range in size from 1 person upward to 100 and handle about 10 percent of the manufactured goods exported. An example of an EMC is a Washington, D.C.–based company that has exclusive agreements with 10 U.S. manufacturers of orthopedic equipment and markets these products on a worldwide basis.

[21]Peter Gwynne, "The Myth of Globalization?" *Sloan Management Review* 44, no. 2 (Winter 2003), p. 11.
[22]Denise Bonilla, "Latino Market Arrives with Giant Aspirations," *Los Angeles Times*, May 7, 2003, p. B3.

Exhibit 14.5

How Does an EMC
Operate?

Source: "The Export Management
Company," U.S. Department of
Commerce, Washington, DC.

Most export management companies offer a wide range of services and assistance, including the following:

Researching foreign markets for a client's products. Traveling overseas to determine the best method of distributing the product. Appointing distributors or commission representative as needed in individual foreign countries, frequently within an already existing overseas network created for similiar goods. Exhibiting the client's products at international trade shows, such as U.S. Department of Commerce–sponsored commercial exhibitions at trade fairs and U.S. Export Development Offices around the world.

Handling the routine details in getting the product to the foreign customer—export declarations, shipping and customs documentation, insurance, banking, and instructions for special export packing and marking.

Granting the customary finance terms to the trade abroad and ensuring payment to the manufacturer of the product.

Preparing advertising and sales literature in cooperation with the manufacturer and adapting it to overseas requirements for use in personal contacts with foreign buyers. Corresponding in the necessary foreign languages.

Making sure that goods being shipped are suitable for local conditions and meet overseas legal and trade norms, including labeling, packaging, purity, and electrical characteristics. Advising on overseas patent and trademark protection requirements.

Typically, the EMC becomes an integral part of the marketing operations of its client companies. Working under the names of the manufacturers, the EMC functions as a low-cost, independent marketing department with direct responsibility to the parent firm. The working relationship is so close that customers are often unaware they are not dealing directly with the export department of the company (see Exhibit 14.5).

The export management company may take full or partial responsibility for promotion of the goods, credit arrangements, physical handling, market research, and information on financial, patent, and licensing matters. An EMC's specialization in a given field often enables it to offer a level of service that could not be attained by the manufacturer without years of groundwork. Traditionally, the EMC works on commission, although an increasing number are buying products on their own account.

Two of the chief advantages of EMCs are minimum investment on the part of the company to get into international markets, and no commitment of company personnel or major expenditure of managerial effort. The result, in effect, is an extension of the market for the firm with negligible financial or personnel commitments.

The major disadvantage is that EMCs seldom can afford to make the kind of market investment needed to establish deep distribution for products because they must have immediate sales payout to survive. Such a situation does not offer the market advantages gained by a company that can afford to use company personnel. Carefully selected EMCs can do an excellent job, but the manufacturer must remember that the EMC is dependent on sales volume for compensation and probably will not push the manufacturer's line if it is spread too thinly, generates too small a volume from a given principal, or cannot operate profitably in the short run. In such cases the EMC becomes an order taker and not the desired substitute for an international marketing department.

Trading Companies.   Trading companies have a long and honorable history as important intermediaries in the development of trade between nations. *Trading companies* accumulate, transport, and distribute goods from many countries. In concept, the trading company has changed little in hundreds of years.

The British firm Gray MacKenzie and Company is typical of companies operating in the Middle East. It has some 70 salespeople and handles consumer products ranging from toiletries to outboard motors and Scotch whiskey. The key advantage to this type of trading company is that it covers the entire Middle East.

Large, established trading companies generally are located in developed countries; they sell manufactured goods to developing countries and buy raw materials and unprocessed goods. Japanese trading companies *(sogo shosha)* date back to the early 1700s and operate both as importers and exporters.[23] Some 300 are engaged in foreign and domestic trade through 2,000 branch offices outside Japan and handle over $1 trillion in trading volume annually. Japanese trading companies account for 61 percent of all Japanese imports and 39 percent of all exports, or about one-fifth of Japan's entire GDP.

For companies seeking entrance into the complicated Japanese distribution system, the Japanese trading company offers one of the easiest routes to success. The omnipresent trading companies virtually control distribution through all levels of channels in Japan. Because trading companies may control many of the distributors and maintain broad distribution channels, they provide the best means for intensive coverage of the market.[24]

U.S. Export Trading Companies.
The Export Trading Company (ETC) Act allows producers of similar products to form export trading companies. A major goal of the ETC Act was to increase U.S. exports by encouraging more efficient export trade services to producers and suppliers in order to improve the availability of trade finance and to remove antitrust disincentives to export activities. By providing U.S. businesses with an opportunity to obtain antitrust preclearance for specified export activities, the ETC Act created a more favorable environment for the formation of joint export ventures. Through such joint ventures, U.S. firms can take advantage of economies of scale, spread risk, and pool their expertise. In addition, through joint selling arrangements, domestic competitors can avoid interfirm rivalry in foreign markets. Prior to the passage of the ETC Act, competing companies could not engage in joint exporting efforts without possible violation of antitrust provisions. The other important provision of the ETC Act permits bank holding companies to own ETCs.

Immediately after passage of the ETC Act, several major companies (General Electric, Sears Roebuck, Kmart, and others) announced the development of export trading companies. In most cases, these export firms did not require the protection of the ETC Act since they initially operated independently of other enterprises. They provided international sales for U.S. companies to a limited extent, but primarily they operated as trading companies for their own products. To date, many of the trading companies (particularly the bank-owned ones) established after passage of the ETC Act have closed their doors or are languishing.

Complementary Marketers.
Companies with marketing facilities or contacts in different countries with excess marketing capacity or a desire for a broader product line sometimes take on additional lines for international distribution; although the formal name for such activities is *complementary marketing,* it is commonly called *piggybacking.* General Electric Company has been distributing merchandise from other suppliers for many years. It accepts products that are noncompetitive but complementary and that add to the basic distribution strength of the company itself.

Most piggyback arrangements are undertaken when a firm wants to fill out its product line or keep its seasonal distribution channels functioning throughout the year. Companies may work either on an agency or merchant basis, but the greatest volume of piggyback business is handled on an ownership (merchant) purchase-and-resale arrangement. The selection process for new products for piggyback distribution determines whether (1) the product relates to the product line and contributes to it, (2) the product fits the sales and distribution channel presently employed, (3) the margin is adequate to make the undertaking worthwhile, and (4) the product will find market acceptance and profitable volume. If these requirements are met, piggybacking can be a logical way of increasing volume and profit for both the carrier and the piggybacker.

---

[23]Roy Larke, "Expansion of Japanese Retailers Overseas," *Journal of Global Marketing* 18, no. 1/2 (2004), pp. 99–120.

[24]J. McGuire and S. Dow, "The Persistence and Implications of Japanese Keiretsu Organization," *Journal of International Business Studies* 34, no. 4 (2003), pp. 374–388; "The Mitsubishi Group, All in the Family," *The Economist*, May 29, 2004, p. 67.

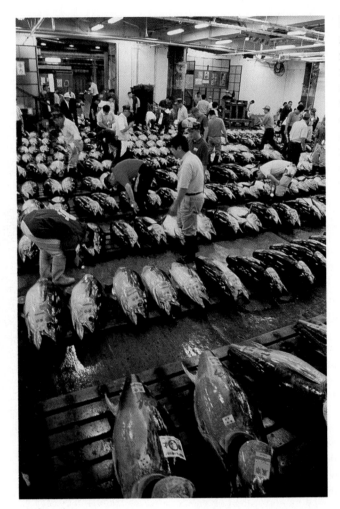

Recall that the Japanese are the world-champion fish consumers at nearly 60 kg per person per year—see Exhibit 4.2. Consequently, just as world prices for cut flowers are set at the Aalsmeer Flower Auction in the Netherlands, world prices for fish are set at the Tsukigi fish market in Tokyo. A big fresh bluefin tuna caught in the Atlantic, iced and shipped by air to Tokyo, can bring $10,000 at auction, and then be shipped by air back to Boston for hungry sushi consumers.

Manufacturer's Export Agent.   The *manufacturer's export agent (MEA)* is an individual agent middleman or an agent middleman firm providing a selling service for manufacturers. Unlike the EMC, the MEA does not serve as the producer's export department but has a short-term relationship, covers only one or two markets, and operates on a straight commission basis. Another principal difference is that MEAs do business in their own names rather than in the name of the client. Within a limited scope of operation, the MEAs provide services similar to those of the EMC.

Home-Country Brokers.   The term *broker* is a catchall for a variety of middlemen performing low-cost agent services. The term is typically applied to import-export brokers who provide the intermediary function of bringing buyers and sellers together and who do not have a continuing relationship with their clients. Most brokers specialize in one or more commodities, for which they maintain contact with major producers and purchasers throughout the world.

Buying Offices.   A variety of agent middlemen may be classified simply as buyers or buyers for export. Their common denominator is a primary function of seeking and purchasing merchandise on request from principals; as such, they do not provide a selling service. In fact, their chief emphasis is on flexibility and the ability to find merchandise from any source. They do not often become involved in continuing relationships with domestic suppliers and do not provide a continuing source of representation.

Selling Groups.   Several types of arrangements have been developed in which various manufacturers or producers cooperate in a joint attempt to sell their merchandise abroad. This may take the form of complementary exporting or of selling to a business combine such as a Webb-Pomerene export association. Both are considered agency arrangements when the exporting is done on a fee or commission basis.

Webb-Pomerene Export Associations.   *Webb-Pomerene export associations (WPEAs)* are another major form of group exporting. The Webb-Pomerene Act of 1918 allowed American business firms to join forces in export activities without being subject to the Sherman Antitrust Act. WPEAs cannot participate in cartels or other international agreements that would reduce competition in the United States, but they can offer four major benefits: (1) reduction of export costs, (2) demand expansion through promotion, (3) trade barrier reductions, and (4) improvement of trade terms through bilateral bargaining. Additionally, WPEAs set prices, standardize products, and arrange for disposal of surplus products. Although they account for less than 5 percent of U.S. exports, WPEAs include some of America's blue-chip companies in agricultural products, chemicals and raw materials, forest products, pulp and paper, textiles, rubber products, motion pictures, and television.

Foreign Sales Corporation.   A *foreign sales corporation (FSC)* is a sales corporation set up in a foreign country or U.S. possession that can obtain a corporate tax exemption on a portion of the earnings generated by the sale or lease of export property. Manufacturers and export groups can form FSCs. An FSC can function as a principal, buying and selling for its own account, or as a commissioned agent. It can be related to a manufacturing parent or can be an independent merchant or broker. The WTO in 2003 ruled FSCs to be in violation of international trade rules, thus starting a major trade dispute with the European Union that still simmers and occasionally sizzles.[25]

Export Merchants.

Export merchants are essentially domestic merchants operating in foreign markets. As such, they operate much like the domestic wholesaler. Specifically, they purchase goods from a large number of manufacturers, ship them to foreign countries, and take full responsibility for their marketing. Sometimes they utilize their own organizations, but more commonly they sell through middlemen. They may carry competing lines, have full control over prices, and maintain little loyalty to suppliers, although they continue to handle products as long as they are profitable. Canadian wholesalers selling low-cost pharmaceuticals to American consumers is an increasingly important, albeit controversial, example.

Export Jobbers.

Export jobbers deal mostly in commodities; they do not take physical possession of goods but assume responsibility for arranging transportation. Because they work on a job-lot basis, they do not provide a particularly attractive distribution alternative for most producers.

Exhibit 14.6 summarizes information pertaining to the major kinds of domestic middlemen operating in foreign markets. No attempt is made to generalize about rates of commission, markup, or pay because many factors influence compensation. Services offered or demanded, market structure, volume, and product type are some of the key determinants. The data represent the predominant patterns of operations; however, individual middlemen of a given type may vary in their operations.

Foreign-Country Middlemen

The variety of agent and merchant middlemen in most countries is similar to that in the United States. International marketers seeking greater control over the distribution process may elect to deal directly with middlemen in the foreign market. They gain the advantage of shorter channels and deal with middlemen in constant contact with the market.

Using foreign-country middlemen moves the manufacturer closer to the market and involves the company more closely with problems of language, physical distribution, communications, and financing. Foreign middlemen may be agents or merchants, they may be associated with the parent company to varying degrees, or they may be hired temporarily for special purposes. Some of the more important foreign-country middlemen are manufacturer's representatives and foreign distributors.

Manufacturer's Representatives.

Manufacturer's representatives are agent middlemen who take responsibility for a producer's goods in a city, regional market area, entire country, or several adjacent countries. When responsible for an entire country, the middleman is often called a *sole agent.* As in the United States, the well-chosen, well-motivated, well-controlled manufacturer's representative can provide excellent market coverage for the manufacturer in certain circumstances. The manufacturer's representative is widely used in distribution of industrial goods overseas and is an excellent representative for any type of manufactured consumer goods.

Foreign manufacturer's representatives have a variety of titles, including sales agent, resident sales agent, exclusive agent, commission agent, and indent agent. They take no credit, exchange, or market risk but deal strictly as field sales representatives. They do not arrange for shipping or for handling and usually do not take physical possession. Manufacturers who wish the type of control and intensive market coverage their own sales force would afford, but who cannot field one, may find the manufacturer's representative a satisfactory choice.

Distributors.

A *foreign distributor* is a merchant middleman. This intermediary often has exclusive sales rights in a specific country and works in close cooperation with the manufacturer. The distributor has a relatively high degree of dependence on the supplier

---

[25]"World Watch," *Wall Street Journal,* July 25, 2005, p. A3.

Exhibit 14.6
Characteristics of Domestic Middlemen Serving Overseas Markets

Type of Duties	Agent					Merchant				
	EMC	MEA	Broker	Buying Offices	Selling Groups	Norazi	Export Merchant	Export Jobber	Importers and Trading Companies	Complementary Marketers
Take title	No*	No	No	No	No	Yes	Yes	Yes	Yes	Yes
Take possession	Yes	Yes	No	Yes	Yes	Yes	Yes	No	Yes	Yes
Continuing relationship	Yes	Yes	No	Yes	Yes	No	No	Yes	Yes	Yes
Share of foreign output	All	All	Any	Small	All	Small	Any	Small	Any	Most
Degree of control by principal	Fair	Fair	Nil	Nil	Good	Nil	None	None	Nil	Fair
Price authority	Advisory	Advisory	Yes (at market level)	Yes (to buy)	Advisory	Yes	Yes	Yes	No	Some
Represent buyer or seller	Seller	Seller	Either	Buyer	Seller	Both	Self	Self	Self	Self
Number of principals	Few to many	Few to many	Many	Small	Few	Several per transaction	Many sources	Many sources	Many sources	One per product
Arrange shipping	Yes	Yes	Not usually	Yes	Yes	Yes	Yes	Yes	Yes	Yes
Type of goods	Manufactured goods and commodities	Staples and commodities	Staples and commodities	Staples and commodities	Complementary to their own lines	Contraband	Manufactured goods	Bulky and raw materials	Manufactured goods	Complementary to line
Breadth of line	Specialty to wide	All types of staples	All types of staples	Retail goods	Narrow	n.a.	Broad	Broad	Broad	Narrow
Handle competitive lines	No	No	Yes	Yes—utilizes many sources	No	Yes	Yes	Yes	Yes	No
Extend to promotion and selling effort	Good	Good	One shot	n.a.	Good	Nil	Nil	Nil	Good	Good
Extend credit to principal	Occasionally	Occasionally	Seldom	Seldom	Seldom	No	Occasionally	Seldom	Seldom	Seldom
Market information	Fair	Fair	Price and market conditions	For principal, not for manufacturer	Good	No	Nil	Nil	Fair	Good

Note: n.a. = not available.

*The EMC may take title and thus become a merchant middleman.

companies, and arrangements are likely to be on a long-run, continuous basis. Working through distributors permits the manufacturer a reasonable degree of control over prices, promotional effort, inventories, servicing, and other distribution functions. If a line is profitable for distributors, they can be depended on to handle it in a manner closely approximating the desires of the manufacturer.

Foreign-Country Brokers. Like the export broker discussed in an earlier section, *foreign-country brokers* are agents who deal largely in commodities and food products. The foreign brokers are typically part of small brokerage firms operating in one country or in a few contiguous countries. Their strength is in having good continuing relationships with customers and providing speedy market coverage at a low cost. Atypical, but still part of this category, are art auction houses such as those in China and in the Netherlands. At the latter you can spend $85,000,000 for Rembrandt if you can spare the change.[26]

Managing Agents and Compradors. A *managing agent* conducts business within a foreign nation under an exclusive contract arrangement with the parent company. The managing agent in some cases invests in the operation and in most instances operates under a contract with the parent company. Compensation is usually on the basis of cost plus a specified percentage of the profits of the managed company. In some countries, managing agents may be called *compradors* and there are some differences in duties performed (see Exhibit 14.7).

Dealers. Generally speaking, anyone who has a continuing relationship with a supplier in buying and selling goods is considered a dealer. More specifically, *dealers* are middlemen selling industrial goods or durable consumer goods direct to customers; they are the last step in the channel of distribution. Dealers have continuing, close working relationships with their suppliers and exclusive selling rights for their producer's products within a given geographic area. Finally, they derive a large portion of their sales volume from the products of a single supplier firm.

Some of the best examples of dealer operations include Massey Ferguson, with a vast, worldwide network of dealers, and Caterpillar Tractor Company, with dealers in every major city of the world.

Import Jobbers, Wholesalers, and Retailers. *Import jobbers* purchase goods directly from the manufacturer and sell to wholesalers and retailers and to industrial customers. Large and small wholesalers and retailers engage in direct importing for their own outlets and for redistribution to smaller middlemen. The combination retailer-wholesaler is more important in foreign countries than in the United States. It is not uncommon to find large retailers wholesaling goods to local shops and dealers. Exhibit 14.7 summarizes the characteristics of foreign-country middlemen.

Government-Affiliated Middlemen

Marketers must deal with governments in every country of the world. Products, services, and commodities for the government's own use are always procured through government purchasing offices at federal, regional, and local levels. In the Netherlands, the state's purchasing office deals with more than 10,000 suppliers in 20 countries. About one-third of the products purchased by that agency are produced outside the Netherlands. Finally, regarding the efficiency of the public sector versus the private sector, an important lesson was learned during the 2005 Hurricane Katrina disaster—Wal-Mart planned for and delivered aid better than FEMA (the U.S Federal Emergency Management Agency).[27]

---

[26]The European Fine Arts Fair (TEFAF) is in Maastricht every spring. "A Taste of Money," *Go Dutch*, March 2003, pp. 44–45.

[27]Ann Zimmerman and Valerie Bauerlein, "At Wal-Mart Emergency Plan Has a Big Payoff," *Wall Street Journal*, September 12, 2005, pp. B1, B3.

Exhibit 14.7

Characteristics of Foreign-Country Middlemen

	Agent				Merchant			
Type of Duties	**Broker**	**Manufacturer's Representative**	**Managing Agent**	**Comprador**	**Distributor**	**Dealer**	**Import Jobber**	**Wholesaler and Retailer**
Take title	No	No	No	No	Yes	Yes	Yes	Yes
Take possession	No	Seldom	Seldom	Yes	Yes	Yes	Yes	Yes
Continuing relationship	No	Often	With buyer, not seller	Yes	Yes	Yes	No	Usually not
Share of foreign output	Small	All or part for one area	n.a.	All, for one area	All, for certain countries	Assignment area	Small	Very small
Degree of control by principal	Low	Fair	None	Fair	High	High	Low	Nil
Price authority	Nil	Nil	Nil	Partial	Partial	Partial	Full	Full
Represent buyer or seller	Either	Seller	Buyer	Seller	Seller	Seller	Self	Self
Number of principals	Many	Few	Many	Few	Small	Few major	Many	Many
Arrange shipping	No	No	No	No	No	No	No	No
Type of goods	Commodity and food	Manufactured goods	All types	Manufactured goods	Manufactured goods	Manufactured goods	Manufactured goods	Manufactured consumer goods
Breadth of line	Broad	Allied lines	Broad	Varies	Narrow to broad	Narrow	Narrow to broad	Narrow to broad
Handle competitive lines	Yes	No	Yes	No	No	No	Yes	Yes
Extent of promotion and selling effort	Nil	Fair	Nil	Fair	Fair	Good	Nil	Nil usually
Extend credit to principal	No	No	No	Sometimes	Sometimes	No	No	No
Market information	Nil	Good	Nil	Good	Fair	Good	Nil	Nil

Note: n.a. = not available.

Factors Affecting Choice of Channels

The international marketer needs a clear understanding of market characteristics and must have established operating policies before beginning the selection of channel middlemen. The following points should be addressed prior to the selection process:

1. Identify specific target markets within and across countries.
2. Specify marketing goals in terms of volume, market share, and profit margin requirements.
3. Specify financial and personnel commitments to the development of international distribution.
4. Identify control, length of channels, terms of sale, and channel ownership.

Once these points are established, selecting among alternative middlemen choices to forge the best channel can begin. Marketers must get their goods into the hands of consumers and must choose between handling all distribution or turning part or all of it over to various middlemen.[28] Distribution channels vary depending on target market size, competition, and available distribution intermediaries.

Key elements in distribution decisions include the functions performed by middlemen (and the effectiveness with which each is performed), the cost of their services, their availability, and the extent of control that the manufacturer can exert over middlemen activities.

Although the overall marketing strategy of the firm must embody the company's profit goals in the short and long run, channel strategy itself is considered to have six specific strategic goals. These goals can be characterized as the six Cs of channel strategy: cost, capital, control, coverage, character, and continuity. In forging the overall channel-of-distribution strategy, each of the six Cs must be considered in building an economical, effective distribution organization within the long-range channel policies of the company. It should also be noted that many firms use multiple or hybrid[29] channels of distribution because of the trade-offs associated with any one option.[30] Indeed, both Dell selling computers at kiosks inside Japan's Jusco supermarkets and Toys "R" Us selling toys in food stores are good examples.

Cost

The two kinds of channel cost are (1) the capital or investment cost of developing the channel and (2) the continuing cost of maintaining it. The latter can be in the form of direct expenditure for the maintenance of the company's selling force or in the form of margins, markup, or commissions of various middlemen handling the goods. Marketing costs (a substantial part of which is channel cost) must be considered as the entire difference between the factory price of the goods and the price the customer ultimately pays for the merchandise. The costs of middlemen include transporting and storing the goods, breaking bulk, providing credit, and local advertising, sales representation, and negotiations.

Despite the old truism that you can eliminate middlemen but you cannot eliminate their functions or cost, creative, efficient marketing does permit channel cost savings in many circumstances. Some marketers have found, in fact, that they can reduce cost by eliminating inefficient middlemen and thus shortening the channel. Mexico's largest producer of radio and television sets has built annual sales of $36 million on its ability to sell goods at a low price because it eliminated middlemen, established its own wholesalers, and kept margins low. Conversely, many firms accustomed to using their own sales forces in large-volume domestic markets have found they must lengthen channels of distribution to keep costs in line with foreign markets.

---

[28]Alex Rialp, Catherine Axxin, and Sharon Tach, "Exploring Channel Internalization among Spanish Exporters," *International Marketing Review* 19, no. 2–3 (2002), pp. 133–155.

[29]Mika Gabrielsson, V. H. Manek Kirpalani, and Reijo Luostarinen, "Multiple Channel Strategies in the European Personal Computer Industry," *Journal of International Marketing* 10, no. 3 (2002), pp. 73–95.

[30]Rod B. McNaughton, "The Use of Multiple Export Channels by Small Knowledge-Intensive Firms," *International Marketing Review* 19, no. 2–3 (2002), pp. 190–203.

Capital Requirements

The financial ramifications of a distribution policy are often overlooked. Critical elements are capital requirement and cash-flow patterns associated with using a particular type of middleman. Maximum investment is usually required when a company establishes its own internal channels, that is, its own sales force. Use of distributors or dealers may lessen the capital investment, but manufacturers often have to provide initial inventories on consignment, loans, floor plans, or other arrangements. Coca-Cola initially invested in China with majority partners that met most of the capital requirements. However, Coca-Cola soon realized that it could not depend on its local majority partners to distribute its product aggressively in the highly competitive, market-share-driven business of carbonated beverages. To assume more control of distribution, it had to assume management control, and that meant greater capital investment from Coca-Cola. One of the highest costs of doing business in China is the capital required to maintain effective distribution.

Control

The more involved a company is with the distribution, the more control it exerts. A company's own sales force affords the most control, but often at a cost that is not practical. Each type of channel arrangement provides a different level of control;[31] as channels grow longer, the ability to control price,[32] volume, promotion, and type of outlets diminishes. If a company cannot sell directly to the end user or final retailer, an important selection criterion for middlemen should be the amount of control the marketer can maintain.[33]

Coverage

Another major goal is full-market coverage to gain the optimum volume of sales obtainable in each market, secure a reasonable market share, and attain satisfactory market penetration. Coverage may be assessed by geographic segments, market segments, or both. Adequate market coverage may require changes in distribution systems from country to country or time to time. Coverage is difficult to extend both in highly developed areas and in sparse markets—the former because of heavy competition and the latter because of inadequate channels.

Many companies do not attempt full-market coverage but seek significant penetration in major population centers. In some countries, two or three cities constitute the majority of the national buying power. For instance, 60 percent of the Japanese population lives in the Tokyo-Nagoya-Osaka market area, which essentially functions as one massive city.

At the other extreme are many developing countries with a paucity of specialized middlemen except in major urban areas. Those that do exist are often small, with traditionally high margins. In China, for example, the often-cited billion-person market is, in reality, confined to fewer than 25 to 30 percent of the population of the most affluent cities. Even as personal income increases in China, distribution inadequacies limit marketers in reaching all those who have adequate incomes. In both extremes, the difficulty of developing an efficient channel from existing middlemen plus the high cost of distribution may nullify efficiencies achieved in other parts of the marketing mix.

To achieve coverage, a company may have to use many different channels—its own sales force in one country, manufacturers' agents in another, and merchant wholesalers in still another.

Character

The channel-of-distribution system selected must fit the character of the company and the markets in which it is doing business. Some obvious product requirements, often the first considered, relate to perishability or bulk of the product, complexity of sale, sales service required, and value of the product.

---

[31]Daniel C. Bello, Cristian Chelariu, and Li Zhang, "The Antecedents and Performance Consequences of Relationalism in Export Distribution Channels," *Journal of Business Research* 56, no. 1 (January 2003), pp. 1–16.

[32]Ting-Jui Chou and Fu-Tang Chen, "Retail Pricing Strategies in Recession Economies: The Case of Taiwan," *Journal of International Marketing* 12, no. 1 (2004), pp. 82–102.

[33]Michael Harvey and Milorad M. Novicevic, "Selecting Marketing Managers to Effectively Control Global Channels of Distribution," *International Marketing Review* 19, no. 4–5 (2002), pp. 525–544.

You can buy just about anything at Stockmann's Department Store in Helsinki—men's and women's fashions, hardware (hammers, etc.) and software, bakery goods and garden supplies, fillet of reindeer and furniture, televisions—yes, everything from Audi A3s to artichokes. It even has cold storage services for your mink. But Stockmann's doesn't stock Samsung cell phones. The Korean company hasn't yet penetrated Nokia's home market. Of course, the product line is thin but rich at Cartier's in Paris. And you can find the Samsung at the Grand Bazaar (Kapali Carsi) in Istanbul, billed as the oldest and largest covered marketplace on the planet. The 15th-century mall competes for customers with its 20th-century cousin, Akmerkez Etiler, in a high-income neighborhood about 10 miles away.

Channel commanders must be aware that channel patterns change; they cannot assume that once a channel has been developed to fit the character of both company and market, no more need be done. Great Britain, for example, has epitomized distribution through specialty-type middlemen, distributors, wholesalers, and retailers; in fact, all middlemen have traditionally worked within narrow product specialty areas. In recent years, however, there has been a trend toward broader lines, conglomerate merchandising, and mass marketing. The firm that neglects the growth of self-service, scrambled merchandising, or discounting may find it has lost large segments of its market because its channels no longer reflect the character of the market.

Continuity   Channels of distribution often pose longevity problems. Most agent middlemen firms tend to be small institutions. When one individual retires or moves out of a line of business, the company may find it has lost its distribution in that area. Wholesalers and especially retailers are not noted for their continuity in business either. Most middlemen have little loyalty to their vendors. They handle brands in good times when the line is making money, but quickly reject such products within a season or a year if they fail to produce during that period. Distributors and dealers are probably the most loyal middlemen, but even with them, manufacturers must attempt to build brand loyalty downstream in a channel lest middlemen shift allegiance to other companies or other inducements.

Locating, Selecting, and Motivating Channel Members

The actual process of building channels for international distribution is seldom easy, and many companies have been stopped in their efforts to develop international markets by their inability to construct a satisfactory system of channels.

Construction of the middleman network includes seeking out potential middlemen, selecting those who fit the company's requirements, and establishing working relationships with them.[34] In international marketing, the channel-building process is hardly routine. The closer the company wants to get to the consumer in its channel contact, the larger the sales force required. If a company is content with finding an exclusive importer or selling agent for a given country, channel building may not be too difficult; however, if it goes down to the level of subwholesaler or retailer, it is taking on a tremendous task and must have an internal staff capable of supporting such an effort.

Locating Middlemen

The search for prospective middlemen should begin with study of the market and determination of criteria for evaluating middlemen servicing that market. The checklist of criteria differs according to the type of middlemen being used and the nature of their relationship with the company. Basically, such lists are built around four subject areas: productivity or volume, financial strength, managerial stability and capability, and the nature and reputation of the business. Emphasis is usually placed on either the actual or potential productivity of the middleman.

The major problems are locating information to aid in the selection and choice of specific middlemen and discovering middlemen available to handle one's merchandise. Firms seeking overseas representation should compile a list of middlemen from such sources as the following: the U.S. Department of Commerce; commercially published directories; foreign consulates; chamber-of-commerce groups located abroad; other manufacturers producing similar but noncompetitive goods; middlemen associations; business publications; management consultants; carriers—particularly airlines; and Internet-based services such as Unibex, a global technology services provider. Unibex provides a platform for small-to-medium-sized companies and larger enterprises to collaborate in business-to-business commerce.

Selecting Middlemen

Finding prospective middlemen is less a problem than determining which of them can perform satisfactorily. Low volume or low potential volume hampers most prospects, many are underfinanced, and some simply cannot be trusted.[35] In many cases, when a manufacturer is not well known abroad, the reputation of the middleman becomes the reputation of the manufacturer, so a poor choice at this point can be devastating.

Screening.   The screening and selection process itself should include the following actions: an exploratory letter including product information and distributor requirements in the native language sent to each prospective middleman; a follow-up to the best respondents for specific information concerning lines handled, territory covered, size of firm, number of salespeople, and other background information; check of credit and references from other clients and customers of the prospective middleman; and, if possible, a personal check of the most promising firms. Obtaining financial information on prospective middlemen has become easier via such Internet companies as Unibex, which provides access to Dun & Bradstreet and other client information resources.

Experienced exporters suggest that the only way to select a middleman is to go personally to the country and talk to ultimate users of your product to find who they consider to be the best distributors. Visit each possible middleman once before selecting the one to

---

[34]Stephen Keysuk Kim, "A Cross-National Study of Interdependence Structure and Distributor Attitudes: The Moderating Effect of Group Orientation," *International Journal of Research in Marketing* 20, no. 2 (2003), pp. 193–214.

[35]C. Zhang, S. T. Cavusgil, and A. S. Roath, "Manufacturer Governance of Foreign Distributor Relationships: Do Relational Norms Enhance Competitiveness in the Export Market?" *Journal of International Business Studies* 34, no. 6 (2003), pp. 550–566.

represent you; look for one with a key person who will take the new product to his or her heart and make it a personal objective to make the sale of that line a success. Further, exporters stress that if you cannot sign one of the two or three customer-recommended distributors, you might be better off having no distributor in that country, because having a worthless one costs you time and money every year and may cut you out when you finally find a good one.

The Agreement.   Once a potential middleman has been found and evaluated, the task of detailing the arrangements with that middleman begins.[36] So far the company has been in a buying position; now it must shift into a selling and negotiating position to convince the middleman to handle the goods and accept a distribution agreement that is workable for the company. Agreements must spell out specific responsibilities of the manufacturer and the middleman, including an annual sales minimum. The sales minimum serves as a basis for evaluation of the distributor; failure to meet sales minimums may give the exporter the right of termination.

Some experienced exporters recommend that initial contracts be signed for one year only. If the first year's performance is satisfactory, they should be reviewed for renewal for a longer period. This permits easier termination, and, more important, after a year of working together in the market, a more suitable arrangement generally can be reached.

Motivating Middlemen

The level of distribution and the importance of the individual middleman to the company determine the activities undertaken to keep the middleman motivated. On all levels the middleman's motivation is clearly correlated with sales volume. Motivational techniques that can be employed to maintain middleman interest and support for the product may be grouped into five categories: financial rewards, psychological rewards, communications, company support, and corporate rapport.

Obviously, financial rewards must be adequate for any middleman to carry and promote a company's products. Margins or commissions must be set to meet the needs of the middleman and may vary according to the volume of sales and the level of services offered. Without a combination of adequate margin and adequate volume, a middleman cannot afford to give much attention to a product.

Being human, middlemen and their salespeople respond to psychological rewards and recognition of their efforts. A trip to the United States or to the parent company's home or regional office is a great honor. Publicity in company media and local newspapers also builds esteem and involvement among foreign middlemen.

In all instances, the company should maintain a continuing flow of communication in the form of letters, newsletters, and periodicals to all its middlemen. The more personal these are, the better. One study of exporters indicated that the more intense the contact between the manufacturer and the distributor, the better the performance from the distributor. More and better contact naturally leads to less conflict and a smoother working relationship.

Finally, considerable attention must be paid to the establishment of close rapport between the company and its middlemen. In addition to methods noted earlier, a company should be certain that the conflicts that arise are handled skillfully and diplomatically. Bear in mind that all over the world business is a personal and vital thing to the people involved.

Terminating Middlemen

When middlemen do not perform up to standards or when market situations change, requiring a company to restructure its distribution, it may be necessary to terminate relationships. In the United States, this is usually a simple action regardless of the type of middlemen; they are simply dismissed. However, in other parts of the world, the middleman

---

[36]S. Tamer Cavusgil, Seyda Deligonul, and Chun Zhang, "Curbing Foreign Distributor Opportunism: An Examination of Trust, Contracts, and the Legal Environment in International Channel Relationships," *Journal of International Marketing* 12, no. 2 (2004), pp. 7–27.

CROSSING **BORDERS** 14.4   No More Roses for My Miami Broker

Eight out of ten flowers you buy this year will have come from Colombia, our nation's leading supplier of cut flowers. Colombia's cut-flower industry now amounts to $580 million in exports annually. The majority of the flowers coming to the United States arrive in Miami aboard jets, bound for Miami flower brokers who then hold them on consignment until U.S. wholesalers and retailers negotiate on price and place orders. Growers often financed the supply chain and had no idea what a shipment would bring until sales were negotiated in Miami by brokers who charged an average of 15 percent for their services. That was the situation until the creation of the Flower Purchase Network (FNP) and its Floraplex Web site (www.floraplex.com), the first electronic marketplace where flower growers, wholesalers, retailers, and consumers can meet online to conduct e-business.

FPN allows buyers to negotiate directly with the growers; the FPN system provides growers an opportunity to expand their markets and increase profits quickly and efficiently. Users can buy from Holland, Africa, and Israel with service through the Dutch auctions (refer to Chapter 4, pages 100–101), and from South and North America with service through self-provided

logistics providers. Floraplex members who utilize the marketplace receive all their invoices, orders, sales history, purchase history, and more by using the one-stop account summary page. This seamless link between buyer and seller means sellers can negotiate directly with buyers while simultaneously reducing the cost of middlemen. Floraplex applies a 3 percent to 8 percent service fee for system usage, depending on volume, whereas Miami brokers charge an average of 15 percent commission.

FPN, owned by World Commerce Online, handles roughly one million stems of flowers per week and actively trades flowers on six continents—and that's after being on the Web for less than a year. The next Web launch will be Freshplex, designed to do for the entire produce industry what Floraplex is doing for the flower industry.

Sources: "Colombia's Hope: Less Coca, More Carnations," *Christian Science Monitor*, March 24, 2000; Floraplex home page, www.floraplex.com; Mike Candelaria, "Changing the Way the Fresh-Cut Flower Industry Does Business," *Latin Trade*, June 2000; T. Christian Miller, "Everything Is Coming Up Roses for Colombia's Flower Industry," *Los Angeles Times*, February 14, 2003, p. A3.

often has some legal protection that makes termination difficult. In Colombia, for example, if you terminate an agent, you are required to pay 10 percent of the agent's average annual compensation, multiplied by the number of years the agent served, as a final settlement.

Competent legal advice is vital when entering distribution contracts with middlemen. But as many experienced international marketers know, the best rule is to avoid the need to terminate distributors by screening all prospective middlemen carefully. A poorly chosen distributor may not only fail to live up to expectations but may also adversely affect future business and prospects in the country.

Controlling Middlemen

The extreme length of channels typically used in international distribution makes control of middlemen especially important. Marketing objectives must be spelled out both internally and to middlemen as explicitly as possible. Standards of performance should include sales volume objective, inventory turnover ratio, number of accounts per area, growth objective, price stability objective, and quality of publicity. Cultural differences enter into all these areas of management.[37]

Control over the system and control over middlemen are necessary in international business. The first relates to control over the distribution network. This implies overall

---

[37]Jody Evans and Felix T. Mavondo, "Psychic Distance and Organizational Performance: An Empirical Examination of International Retailing Operations," *Journal of International Business Studies* 33, no. 3 (2002), pp. 515–532; David A. Griffith and Matthew B. Myers, "The Performance Implications of Strategic Fit of Relational Norm Governance Strategies in Global Supply Chain Relationships," *Journal of International Business Studies* 36, no. 3 (2005), pp. 254–269.

controls for the entire system to be certain the product is flowing through desired middlemen. Some manufacturers have lost control through "secondary wholesaling" or parallel imports.[38] A company's goods intended for one country are sometimes diverted through distributors to another country, where they compete with existing retail or wholesale organizations.

The second type of control is at the middleman level. When possible, the parent company should know (and to a certain degree control) the activities of middlemen with respect to their volume of sales, market coverage, services offered, prices, advertising, payment of bills, and even profit. Quotas, reports, and personal visits by company representatives can be effective in managing middleman activities at any level of the channel.

The Internet

The Internet is an important distribution method for multinational companies and a source of products for businesses and consumers. Indeed, a good argument can be made that the Internet has finally put the consumer in control of marketing and distribution globally.[39] Computer hardware and software companies and book and music retailers were the early e-marketers to use this method of distribution and marketing. More recently there has been an expansion of other types of retailing and business-to-business (B2B) services into e-commerce. Technically, e-commerce is a form of direct selling; however, because of its newness and the unique issues associated with this form of distribution, it is important to differentiate it from other types of direct marketing.

E-commerce is used to market business-to-business services, consumer services, and consumer and industrial products via the World Wide Web. It involves the direct marketing from a manufacturer, retailer, service provider, or some other intermediary to a final user. Some examples of e-marketers that have an international presence are Dell Computer Corporation[40] (www.dell.com), which generates nearly 50 percent of its total sales, an average of about $69 million a day, online, and Cisco Systems (www.cisco.com), which generates more than $1 billion in sales annually. Cisco's Web site appears in 14 languages and has country-specific content for 49 nations. Gateway has global sites in Japan, France, the Netherlands, Germany, Sweden, Australia, the United Kingdom, and the United States, to name a few (www.gateway.com). Sun Microsystems and its after-marketing company, SunExpress, have local-language information on more than 3,500 aftermarket products. SunPlaza enables visitors in North America, Europe, and Japan to get information online on products and services and to place orders directly in their native languages.

Besides consumer goods companies such as Lands' End, Levi, and Nike, many smaller[41] and less well-known companies have established a presence on the Internet beyond their traditional markets. An Internet customer from the Netherlands can purchase a pair of brake levers for his mountain bike from California-based Price Point. He pays $130 instead of the $190 that the same items would cost in a local bike store.

For a Spanish shopper in Pamplona, buying sheet music used to mean a 400-kilometer trip to Madrid. Now he crosses the Atlantic to shop—and the journey takes less time than a trip to the corner store. Via the Internet he can buy directly from specialized stores and high-volume discounters in New York, London, and almost anywhere else.

E-commerce is more developed in the United States than the rest of the world partly because of the vast number of people who own personal computers and because of the

---

[38]See the discussion of parallel imports in Chapter 18.

[39]"Crowned at Last, A Survey of Consumer Power," *The Economist*, April 2, 2005, insert pp. 1–16.

[40]Evan Ramstad and Gary McWilliams, "For Dell, Success in China Tells a Tale of Maturing Market," *Wall Street Journal*, July 5, 2005, pp. A1, A8.

[41]Oystein Moen, Iver Endresen, and Morten Gavlen, "Use of the Internet in International Marketing: A Case Study of Small Computer Software Firms," *Journal of International Marketing* 11, no. 4 (2003), pp. 129–149.

much lower cost of access to the Internet than found elsewhere. (See Exhibit 14.3.) Besides language, legal, and cultural differences, the cost of local phone calls (which are charged by the minute in most European countries) initially discouraged extensive use and contributed to slower Internet adoption in Europe. However, according to some estimates Europeans actually spend more on e-commerce than Americans, both at about $16 billion.[42]

The largest B2B players today are U.S.-based brick-and-mortar companies that generate a significant percentage of revenue internationally from sales via the Internet. Global B2B commerce is forecasted to reach $4 billion in the United States in 2006 and surpass $9 trillion worldwide. The expansion of B2B transactions will be fueled by growth in industrial inputs, such as steel, chemicals, and car components; transactions by smaller firms; and an increased number of business services offered over the Internet.

Small and middle-sized firms are expected to generate substantial growth in Internet transactions, as well as pooling their purchases through various Internet exchanges for everything from telephone services and office furniture to electricity. Although each order is individually small, such purchases combined account for 30 to 60 percent of firms' total nonlabor costs and are usually bought inefficiently and expensively. Reduced prices by bulk buying through an online intermediary and the savings resulting from placing and processing orders online, which is much cheaper and faster than the traditional way, could reduce costs by 10 to 20 percent. One study estimates that if all small- and medium-sized firms in Britain used the Internet to buy indirect inputs, they could save up to $36 billion a year.

Services, the third engine for growth, are ideally suited for international sales via the Internet. All types of services—banking, education, consulting, retailing, gambling— can be marketed through a Web site that is globally accessible. As outsourcing of traditional in-house tasks such as inventory management, quality control, and accounting, secretarial, translation, and legal services has become more popular among companies, the Internet providers of these services have grown both in the United States and internationally.

B2B enables companies to cut costs in three ways. First, it reduces procurement costs by making it easier to find the cheapest supplier, and it cuts the cost of processing the transactions. Estimates are that a firm's possible savings from purchasing over the Internet vary from 2 percent in the coal industry to up to 40 percent in electronic components. British Telecom claims that procuring goods and services online will reduce the average cost of processing a transaction by 90 percent and reduce the direct costs of goods and services it purchases by 11 percent. The Ford, GM, and DaimlerChrysler exchange network for buying components from suppliers could reduce the cost of making a car by as much as 14 percent. Second, it allows better supply-chain management. For example, more than 75 percent of all Cisco orders now occur online, up from 4 percent in 1996. This connection to the supply chain allowed Cisco to reduce order cycle time from six to eight weeks to one to three weeks, and to increase customer satisfaction as well.

And third, it makes possible tighter inventory control. With Wal-Mart's direct Internet links between its inventory control system and its suppliers, each sale automatically triggers a replenishment request. Fewer out-of-stock situations, the ability to make rapid inventory adjustments, and reduced ordering and processing costs have made Wal-Mart one of the industry's most efficient companies.

The worldwide potential for firms operating on the Internet is extraordinary, but only if they are positioned properly. The World Wide Web, as a market, is rapidly moving

---

[42]Such estimates vary considerably and must be taken with a grain of salt. These numbers come from "Europeans Outspend Americans," *Time*, December 23, 2002, p. A3. In "Santa's Little Helper," *The Economist*, December 4, 2002, p. 1, lower estimates are attributed to Forrester Research: $7.6 billion for Europeans and $9.5 billion for Americans. One thing is certain, Europeans and others outside of North America are adopting the Internet at a much faster rate as American use is nearing saturation.

through the stage where the novelty of buying on the Web is giving way to a more so-phisticated customer who has more and constantly improving Web sites to choose from. In short, Web merchants are facing more competition, and Web customers have more choice. This means that if a company is going to be successful in this new era of mar-keting, the basics of good marketing cannot be overlooked. For example, Forrester Re-search has discovered that nearly half the international orders received by U.S. companies go unfilled even though a typical U.S. company can expect 30 percent of its Web traffic to come from foreign countries and 10 percent of its orders to come from abroad.

By its very nature, e-commerce has some unique issues that must be addressed if a do-mestic e-vendor expects to be a viable player in the international cybermarketplace. Inter-national legal issues were discussed in Chapter 7.[43] Many other issues arise because the host-country intermediary who would ordinarily be involved in international marketing is eliminated. An important advantage of selling direct is that total costs can be lowered so that the final price overseas is considerably less than it would have been through a local-country middleman. However, such activities as translating prospective customer inquiries and orders into English and replying in the customer's language, traditionally done by a lo-cal distributor, have to be done by someone. When intermediaries are eliminated, someone, either the seller or the buyer, must assume the functions they performed. Consequently, an e-vendor must be concerned with the following issues.

1. Culture. The preceding chapters on culture should not be overlooked when doing business over the Web. The Web site and the product must be culturally neutral or adapted to fit the uniqueness of a market, because culture does matter.[44] In Japan, the pickiness of Japanese consumers about what they buy and their reluctance to deal with merchants at a distance must be addressed when marketing on the Web. Even a Japanese-language site can offend Japanese sensibilities. As one e-commerce consultant warns, in a product description, you wouldn't say "Don't turn the knob left," because that's too direct. In-stead, you would say something like: "It would be much better to turn the knob to the right." To many Europeans, American sites come off as having too many bells and whis-tles because European sites are more consumer oriented. The different cultural reactions to color can be a potential problem for Web sites designed for global markets. While red may be highly regarded in China or associated with love in the United States, in Spain it is associated with socialism. The point is that when designing a Web site, culture cannot be forgotten.

2. Adaptation. Ideally, a Web site should be translated into the languages of the tar-get markets. This may not be financially feasible for some companies, but at least the most important pages of the site should be translated. Simple translation of important pages is only a stopgap, however. If companies are making a long-term commitment to sales in an-other country, Web pages should be designed (in all senses of the term—color, use fea-tures, etc.) for that market. One researcher suggests that if a Web site does not have at least multiple languages, a company is losing sales. It is the company's responsibility to bridge the language and cultural gap; the customer will not bother—he or she will simply go to a site that speaks his or her language. As discussed earlier, culture does count, and as com-petition increases, a country-specific Web site may make the difference between success and failure.[45]

[43]Matthew Newman, "E-Commerce: The Rules—So Many Countries, So Many Laws," *Wall Street Journal*, April 28, 2003, p. R8.

[44]Kai H. Lim, Kwok Leung, Choon Ling Sia, and Matthew KO Lee, "Is eCommerce Boundary-less? Effects of Individualism-Collectivism and Uncertainty Avoidance on Internet Shopping," *Journal of International Business Studies* 35, no. 6 (2004), pp. 545–559.

[45]Patrick Y. K. Chau, Melissa Cole, Anne P. Massey, Mitzi Montoya-Weiss, and Robert O'Keefe, "Cultural Differences in the On-Line Behavior of Consumers," *Communications of the ACM* 45, no. 10 (2002), pp. 138–143.

Just imagine what you could do with extra money to spend at any Marriott hotel in the world. Enjoy a sparkling spa break. Relax by the pool with a bottle of bubbly. Or simply pay for your next night away. Just buy our *Stay for Breakfast* package with Visa and we'll give you Extra Euro™ coupons worth:

- €100 at Marriott hotels
- €50 at Courtyard by Marriott hotels

To be used on your next stay. So go on, treat yourself. It's all on us. Going above and beyond. IT'S THE MARRIOTT WAY™

Stay for Breakfast™ with Marriott and pay with Visa this summer and we'll give you up to €100 to spend on your next stay at any Marriott hotel worldwide

CHECK IN. CHILL OUT. Then do it all again, with up to €100 to spend on your next stay with us

To book your Stay for Breakfast call Toll free 1 800 40 9929 or visit Marriott.ie Promotional code: OTP

CHECK IN. CHILL OUT. Then do it all again, with up to £100 to spend on your next stay with us

CHECK IN. CHILL OUT. Stay for Breakfast™ with Visa this summer and get up to $100 off your next stay.

BOOK NOW **Marriott.com**

IT'S THE MARRIOTT WAY.

The primary means of distribution of travel services is now the Internet. Shafiq Khan, Marriott's senior vice president for eCommerce, describes important considerations and challenges he faces in the global marketing and distribution of Marriott's hotel services:

- **Major differences in Internet adoption rates across the globe** . . . which make the Web a more or less effective part of the marketing mix in different markets—until adoption becomes universal. Even for advanced EU economies, the variability of adoption is great, ranging from 73% in Sweden to 42% in France. The average for the entire continent of Africa is around 1%.

- **Unique issues caused by technology** . . . e.g., broad-band vs. narrow-band, which drive what products and services can be marketed, and how. In the world of narrow-band, highly graphic and video products are not viable. An example is the elaborate photo tours of our hotels on Marriott.com, which download quickly on broadband connections but take inordinately long on narrow-band. Therefore, a site designed for one market could be ineffective in another.

- **Costs to globalize** . . . can be enormous if multiple language sites need to be built. For example, translating the over 50,000-page Marriott.com Web site is a very costly undertaking to start with, both on a one-time and ongoing basis. Add to that the costs to translate the internal back-end systems which feed the site, and costs rise exponentially. For sites with a lot of content and heavy dependence on back-end systems, these costs can be prohibitive.

- **Implications of differing labor costs** . . . have an impact on ROI. For example, for Marriott in the

CROSSING BORDERS 14.5   *(Continued)*

U.S., the cost of an online booking is about half that of a phone booking using a reservations agent. That differential may not apply in China, where labor costs are very low, making it difficult to justify a Web site investment.

- **Different approaches to privacy, access, and infrastructure investment** . . . also require changes to strategy by market.

  - On privacy . . . for example, EU laws are much more stringent than U.S. laws; as a result, our e-mail marketing strategy in the European Union is much more cautious than in the United States.

  - On access . . . some countries regulate access to the Internet. For example, China only allows access to approved sites, while the United States does not limit Internet access.

  - On infrastructure investment . . . some countries have private investment fueling the development of the telecom technology systems required to enable Internet access (the U.S.), while

in other countries state-owned phone companies have this responsibility. In general, markets that have depended on state investment have been laggards in the Internet space.

Apart from all of the above issues, a very significant challenge for companies contemplating a global Internet presence is to decide whether they want to build "foreign market sites" or "foreign language sites." This was a key issue for Marriott International when we were deciding global Web site strategy. Quite simply, using French as an example, the question for us was:

Should we have a global site in French that caters to all French speaking customers, no matter which country they live in?

OR

Should we have a site in the French language, which addresses the needs of the local market in France?

Having a French language site for a global French-speaking market has significant benefits, since there is a sizable French-speaking population in the world, which includes major parts of North and Central Africa. However, we decided in favor of the latter approach. In summary, we found that:

- Local markets for lodging differ significantly in needs . . . e.g., vacation packages are very popular with U.K. customers, but not in the United States. Thus, even our English language site for the United States did not meet U.K. needs.

- Interests of each markets vary significantly . . . Germans are interested in different destinations than the French.

- Promotional approaches vary by country . . . e.g., sweepstakes are far more popular and accepted in the United States than in Europe.

In the company print advertising you can see reference to the country-specific Web sites and the differences in the currencies. Also, please notice eighteen country markets now served by separate Web sites for each.

Sign In | Create an Account | Look Up Reservations   Home | International Sites | Help | Contact Us | Site Map

Marriott

Find & Reserve | Specials & Packages | Destinations | Events & Meetings | Marriott Rewards

International Sites

Select Your Country of Residence
Marriott operates a growing list of Web sites around the world. Visit the site of your choice to view hotel information, special offers and local information in the local language.

Marriott International operates more than 2,600 hotels and resorts around the world and a growing list of web sites in support of our worldwide operations. We invite you to visit one of our global sites to reserve accommodations, view special offers and information about Marriott Rewards, the program that lets you get to the places you dream of 30% faster!

North America >>	Asia/Pacific
USA	Australia
	China
	Japan
	New Zealand
	South Korea

Europe	Latin America & Caribbean >>
France	Argentina
Germany	Brazil
Ireland	Chile
UK	Costa Rica
	Dominican Republic
	Mexico
	Peru
	Venezuela

International Sites | Travel Agents | Corporate Information | Careers | Help | Contact Us | Site Map

Source: Shafiq Khan, Senior Vice President, eCommerce, Marriott International, Inc., October 2005.

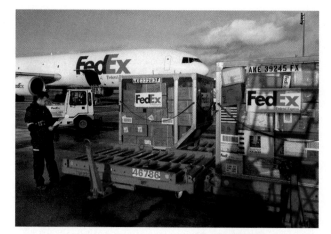

A FedEx employee checks cargo being loaded at the Roissy Airport north of Paris near its European dispatch center. More than 1,000 employees there move more than 500 tons of parcels each day. Notice the white arrow embedded in the company's logo between the E and the x—FedEx means motion. (© AFP/Getty Images)

3. Local contact. Companies fully committed to foreign markets are creating virtual offices abroad; they buy server space and create mirror sites, whereby a company has a voice mail or fax contact point in key markets. Foreign customers are more likely to visit sites in their own country and in the local language. In Japan, where consumers seem particularly concerned about the ability to easily return goods, companies may have outlets where merchandise can be returned and picked up. These so-called click-and-mortar models have gained a large following.

4. Payment. The consumer should be able to use a credit card number—by e-mail (from a secure page on the Web site), by fax, or over the phone.

5. Delivery. For companies operating in the United States, surface postal delivery of small parcels is most cost effective but takes the longest time. For more rapid but more expensive deliveries, Federal Express, United Parcel Service, and other private delivery services provide delivery worldwide. For example, Tom Clancy's bestseller *Executive Orders,* shipped express to Paris from Seattle-based Amazon.com, would cost a reader $55.52. The same book delivered in 4 to 10 weeks via surface mail costs $25.52, which is a substantial savings over the cost of the book in a Paris bookstore, where it sells for $35.38.

Once sufficient volume in a country or region is attained, container shipments to free trade zones or bonded warehouses can be used for distribution of individual orders via local delivery services within the region. These same locations can also be used for such after-sale services as spare parts, defective product returns, and supplies. Companies such as FedEx, UPS, and similar small-package delivery services also have overseas storage and fulfillment centers for individual orders that e-commerce companies can use to provide faster and less costly in-country delivery.

6. Promotion. Although the Web is a means of promotion, if you are engaging in e-commerce you also need to advertise your presence and the products or services offered. The old adage "Build a better mouse trap and the world will beat a path to your door" does not work for e-commerce, just as it does not work with other products unless you tell your target market about the availability of the "better mouse trap." How do you attract visitors from other countries to your Web site? The same way you would at home—except in the local language. Search engine registration, press releases, local newsgroups and forums, mutual links, and banner advertising are the traditional methods. A Web site should be seen as a retail store, with the only difference between it and a physical store being that the customer arrives over the Internet instead of on foot.

When discussing the Internet and international channels of distribution, the question of how traditional channels will be changed by the Internet must be considered. Already, comparison shopping across the Continent via the Internet is wrenching apart commercial patterns cobbled together over centuries. Before the Internet, Europeans rarely shopped across borders, and car companies, exempt from EU antitrust laws in distribution, offered cars at price differentials of up to 40 percent. The Internet has blown this system apart and allows the European customer to shop easily for the best price.

Not only will the traditional channels change, but so will the Internet, which is still evolving. Much of what is standard practice today may well be obsolete tomorrow as new means of data transmission are achieved, costs of accessing the Web decrease, and new e-commerce models are invented. The Web is rapidly growing and changing as it grows.

Summary

The international marketer has a broad range of alternatives for developing an economical, efficient, high-volume international distribution system. To the uninitiated, however, the variety may be overwhelming. Careful analysis of the functions performed suggests more similarity than difference between international and domestic distribution systems; in both cases the three primary alternatives are using agent middlemen, merchant middlemen, or government-affiliated middlemen. In many instances, all three types of middlemen are employed on the international scene, and channel structure may vary from nation to nation or from continent to continent.

The neophyte company in international marketing can gain strength from the knowledge that information and advice are available relative to the structuring of international distribution systems and that many well-developed and capable middleman firms exist for the international distribution of goods. Although international middlemen have become more numerous, more reliable, and more sophisticated within the past decade, traditional channels are being challenged by the Internet, which is rapidly becoming an important alternative channel to many market segments. Such growth and development offer an ever-wider range of possibilities for entering foreign markets.

Questions

1. Define the following terms:

   distribution process   agent middlemen

   distribution structure   merchant middlemen

   distribution channel   home-country middlemen

   dealer   trading company

   import jobber   complementary marketing

   Export Trading Company   Large-Scale Retail Store
      Act   Location Act

   facilitating agency

2. Discuss the distinguishing features of the Japanese distribution system.

3. Discuss the ways Japanese manufacturers control the distribution process from manufacturer to retailer.

4. Describe Japan's Large-Scale Retail Store Law and discuss how the Structural Impediments Initiative (SII) is bringing about change in Japanese retailing.

5. "Japanese retailing may be going through a change similar to that which occurred in the United States after World War II." Discuss and give examples.

6. Discuss how the globalization of markets, especially Europe after 1992, affects retail distribution.

7. To what extent, and in what ways, do the functions of domestic middlemen differ from those of their foreign counterparts?

8. Why is the EMC sometimes called an independent export department?

9. Discuss how physical distribution relates to channel policy and how they affect one another.

10. Explain how and why distribution channels are affected as they are when the stage of development of an economy improves.

11. In what circumstances is the use of an EMC logical?

12. In which circumstances are trading companies likely to be used?

13. How is distribution-channel structure affected by increasing emphasis on the government as a customer and by the existence of state trading agencies?

14. Review the key variables that affect the marketer's choice of distribution channels.

15. Account, as best you can, for the differences in channel patterns that might be encountered in a highly developed country and an underdeveloped country.

16. One of the first things companies discover about international patterns of channels of distribution is that in most countries it is nearly impossible to gain adequate market coverage through a simple channel-of-distribution plan. Discuss.

17. Discuss the various methods of overcoming blocked channels.

18. What strategy might be employed to distribute goods effectively in the dichotomous small/large middleman pattern, which characterizes merchant middlemen in most countries?

19. Discuss the economic implications of assessing termination penalties or restricting the termination of middlemen. Do you foresee such restrictions in the United States?

20. Discuss why Japanese distribution channels can be the epitome of blocked channels.

21. What are the two most important provisions of the Export Trading Company Act?

15

Exporting and Logistics:

SPECIAL ISSUES FOR BUSINESS

CHAPTER OUTLINE

Global Perspective: An Export Sale: From Trade Show
    to Installation

Export Restrictions

    Determining Export Requirements
    ELAIN, STELA, ERIC, and SNAP

Import Restrictions

    Tariffs
    Exchange Permits
    Quotas
    Import Licenses
    Standards
    Boycotts
    Voluntary Agreements
    Other Restrictions

Terms of Sale

Getting Paid: Foreign Commercial Payments

    Letters of Credit
    Bills of Exchange
    Cash in Advance
    Open Accounts
    Forfaiting

Export Documents

Packing and Marking

Customs-Privileged Facilities

    Foreign Trade Zones
    Offshore Assembly (Maquiladoras)

Logistics

    Interdependence of Physical Distribution Activities
    Benefits of a Physical Distribution System

    Export Shipping and Warehousing
    Foreign Freight Forwarder
    International Logistics and Supply Chain Management

Terrorism and Logistics

    Cargo and Container Security Initiative
    Customs–Trade Partnership against Terrorism
    Electronic Tracking

CHAPTER LEARNING OBJECTIVES

What you should learn from Chapter 15:

- How the U.S. government helps exporters

- The steps necessary to move goods across country borders

- How various import restrictions are used politically

- Means of reducing import taxes to remain competitive

- The mechanics of export documents and their importance

- The main instruments of foreign commercial payments

- The logistics and problems of the physical movement of goods

- The impact of antiterrorism regulations on the export-import process

Global Perspective

AN EXPORT SALE: FROM TRADE SHOW TO INSTALLATION

February 3: The Trade Show and the Order

This account of the sale of paper-converting machinery, called a case maker, between Austin Inc., a New Hampshire–based manufacturer, and China Books, a Chinese book publisher, details the steps of an international export sale. It begins in Germany at DRUPA, the largest trade show in the world for the printing and paper market. Mr. Kang, a representative for China Books, approaches Austin's booth and thinks, "Well, it took a week to find the Americans' booth, but watching their machines run has made it easier to see which equipment serves us best." Kang also muses that it was nice to meet the people who actually design and build the machine and to see the solid relationship with their Far Eastern sales agent. Kang likes the equipment and signs an order for $500,000, which stipulates a 15 percent deposit ($75,000) and the pledge of a letter of credit for the rest.

March 3: The Financing

Once Mr. Kang returns home, he applies for financing and an import license. The import license requirements make the whole deal a chicken-and-egg situation. Kang can't complete the financing until he gets the import license, and once he gets the license, he has a specified time in which to complete the transaction.

July 3: Import License and the Letter of Credit

Four months later, Mr. Kang finally gets the import license. Because it is good for only six months, he has to be careful that the letter of credit's latest ship and expiry dates are within the effective time of the import permit. He applies for financing and the letter of credit.

In the United States, Mr. Roberts, Austin's controller, is concerned about the sale to China Books. "It's been more than four months since the sales department sent a copy of the signed order, and yet the company still hasn't received the 15 percent deposit," Roberts thinks. "Until they send the money, the customer isn't really committed. Nevertheless, the general manager has decided to release a stock machine to the manufacturing department to begin the necessary adaptations that the Chinese buyer wants. If the company doesn't begin work now, the equipment will not be ready as promised on the order. If this customer doesn't come through, the company will be stuck with a product finished to China Books' specifications and no cash."

Over the past four months there was a flurry of fax messages between Austin and China Books. Before the instructions for the letter of credit can be completed, details on the proposed shipment dates (before December 31), terms of sale (CIF—cost, insurance, and freight), and lists of Export-Import (Ex-Im) Bank facilities from the trade resource center in Portsmouth, New Hampshire (China Books wants to finance part of the cost of the purchase with an Ex-Im Bank–guaranteed loan), have to be confirmed by both parties.

Roberts chooses CIF as the terms of sale so his company can select its regular freight forwarder to handle all the details. This is the company's first sale to China, so CIF gives Roberts some peace of mind—he won't have to rely on unknown people to collect on the letter of credit. It also means Austin controls selection of the shipping carrier and presumably will get the best shipping rate.

In addition, China Books was able to use one of the banks on the Ex-Im Bank list, so the financing should go smoothly, and Roberts is satisfied that China Books will qualify for a loan.

August 1: Closing the Deal

The bank just called Mr. Kang with loan approval. "Now I've got to get wire instructions for the letter of credit and send the 15 percent deposit. They said delivery this December. I'll put down December 31 as the latest shipment date, with an expiry of January 31."

Roberts receives the request for wire instructions from Kang. "It will probably take about three weeks for everything to clear the bank," he thinks. "But the wire instructions must go out now since nothing can be shipped until the original letter of credit is received." Shipping had advised Roberts that shipping the machinery through Montreal could avoid some stiff harbor maintenance fees that shipping out of New York would entail. Thus, when Roberts sends the wire instructions to Kang, he asks the Chinese buyer to permit shipment through Montreal.

September 4: Production and Shipment

Mr. Kang thinks to himself, "This faxing across the world is awkward but more efficient than telephoning, because while I'm writing in mid-morning, they're going to bed. Now we just need to wait for the machine to get here." Kang begins planning for the integration of the new case maker into China Book's production line, and realizes they need to add a counter stacker option to the machine. The plant efficiency that will be gained should be worth the extra $20,000. Mr. Kang starts to call the bank to have the counter stacker added to the letter of credit but hesitates and thinks, "I'm sick of bank rhetoric, so we'll just wire them the additional funds before shipment. The amendment to the letter of credit will cost too much time and money."

Because a lot rides on this order, Mr. Kang decides he will schedule a trip to New Hampshire for the final acceptance test. He wants to be sure the machine will handle the paper stock the company uses. No one wants the machine to be delivered and then find out it won't work the way they expect. Too many complications arise if the equipment is paid for and delivered and it needs major adjustments.

Back in New Hampshire, Roberts is checking details to make sure the case maker will be shipped on time. "Things are getting hectic—so much to do, so little time. If they expect to ship this year, the customer must accept the machine by December 16. That gives us a week to break it down and skid it (bolt the machine to a wooden pallet) and a week to get it on a boat. We have very little room for error because of the holidays. Besides, the customer wants special packing in desiccant because of climatic conditions. So we'll need to send the shipment to a packing specialist before it goes to port."

November 1: Letter of Credit

Roberts sends the original letter of credit to his freight forwarder by second-day air and includes the bank invoice forms and marine insurance certificate.

December 2: Final Inspection and Shipping Schedules

In China, Kang thinks, "Roberts faxed me possible vessel dates. They're going for Friday, December 20, out of Montreal, and I'm booked to be in New Hampshire December 11–15. The vessel arrives in Shanghai January 25. That would be just right. I hope they'll be ready for the test run because our material will be a challenge for them to run."

Meanwhile, Roberts is thinking, "I'm glad our general manager decided to release the case maker as a stock machine during the DRUPA show. He OK'd it because the China Books deal looked firm. We'd never be able to ship it this year otherwise. Kang seems like a decent person—very bright. They got their material here two weeks ago for us to try, and since then manufacturing has been working hard trying to meet their specs. I hope we have a good week."

December 13: The Test Run

"The machine looks impressive," Kang observes after he watches the test run take place. "But I'm not convinced we can run a consistent 120 per minute. I insist we come in tomorrow for one more demo. They're close, so if they don't quite do it, I won't pay the installation bill until we're comfortable with production at our plant. Besides, Roberts told me the boat would probably leave late, so they have a little extra time to get the container to the pier."

A second test run takes place the next day. Kang asks for a few minor adjustments but is otherwise satisfied that China Books will get consistently good production from Austin's case maker.

In his office, Roberts wonders why all foreign shipments seem to occur at year-end. "Cheryl at Fast Forwarder (Austin's freight forwarder) said we should be ready first thing on Monday, December 16, if we want to get the container on board for a December 31 sailing. Since nothing happens during the last week of the year, it needs to be there this Friday morning to be processed by the line. The steamship companies will probably start the holidays at noon on the 24th. Red alert! Call Cheryl immediately and tell her the 40-footer (container) must have a wooden floor—with no room for surprises!"

January 2: It's on the Way

Kang is ecstatic. "Roberts just faxed me the ocean bill of lading. The case maker was on board the vessel *Tiger Shark* December 31, with an estimated arrival in Shanghai on January 30. They just made it!"

Analysis

Although this scenario may seem staggering, it is not intended to overwhelm you or make you wary of exporting. The point is that specific export mechanics occur when goods are shipped from one country to another, and although they may be tedious, you cannot escape them. The good news is that assistance is available for the exporter from government and private sources. This scenario occurred prior to widespread use of the Internet, and many of the steps can either be completed on the Internet or sped up by using the Internet, but they *cannot be eliminated*. According to one source, a bank's role in handling the risks in shipping and paying for goods has not changed much since the 17th century. What has changed is technology. Banks are adapting their trade finance to the electronic age. Instead of faxes, telegraph, and postal service as used in the Global Perspective, many banks take a direct feed from a client's purchase-order system, extract the data, use it to create a letter of credit, and provide real-time information on transaction status. For example, Bank One offers an Internet-based tool for creating, modifying, and sending letters of credit and collections. And, in the future, banks will act as a hub to all parties involved in transactions—buyer, seller, bank, carrier, freight forwarder, insurance company, and customs authorities. The rules and regulations remain the same but the process is expedited, thanks to the benefits of the Internet. As you read this chapter, identify each of the places in this scenario where the Internet could be used to expedite the process.

Sources: Robert R. Costa, "Tales of Foreign Sales," *Financial Executive,* January–February 1997, pp. 43–46; Steve Marlin, "Banks Link Their Trade Platforms with the International Movement of Goods," *Information Week,* May 12, 2003, p. 48.

Exhibit 15.1
The Exporting Process

Leaving the Exporting Country	Physical Distribution	Entering the Importing Country
Licenses	International shipping and logistics	Tariffs, taxes
General	Packing	**Nontariff barriers**
Validated	Insurance	Standards
Documentation		Inspection
Export declaration		Documentation
Commercial invoice		Quotas
Bill of lading		Fees
Consular invoice		Licenses
Special certificates		Special certificates
Other documents		Exchange permits
		Other barriers

Exporting is an integral part of all international business, whether the company is large or small, or whether it markets in one country or is a global marketer. Goods manufactured in one country and destined for another must be moved across borders to enter the distribution system of the target market.

Most countries control the movement of goods crossing their borders, whether leaving (exports) or entering (imports). Export and import documents, tariffs, quotas, and other barriers to the free flow of goods between independent sovereignties are requirements that must be met by the exporter, the importer, or both.[1]

In addition to selecting a target market, designing an appropriate product, establishing a price, planning a promotional program, and selecting a distribution channel, the international marketer must meet the legal requirements involved in moving goods from one country to another. The exporting process (see Exhibit 15.1) includes the licenses and documentation necessary to leave the country, an international carrier to transport the goods, and fulfillment of the import requirements necessary to get the shipment legally into another country.[2]

Firms often have staff experienced in dealing with export mechanics, but agencies, government and private, are available to provide expert assistance to firms confronted with unfamiliar situations or a task that is too burdensome.[3] More and more, companies are finding it cost-effective to outsource many exporting activities, especially since the terrorist attack on New York's World Trade Center (9/11) called new security and compliance requirements into play.[4] In cases when exports are processed in-house, the necessary mechanics for exporting can be largely completed using the Internet. These mechanics of exporting are sometimes considered the essence of foreign marketing; however, although their importance cannot be minimized, they should not be seen as the primary task of international marketing but as a necessary step in completing the process of marketing.

Countries impose some form of regulation and restriction on the exporting and importing of goods for many reasons. *Export regulations* may be designed to conserve scarce goods for home consumption or to control the flow of strategic goods to actual or potential enemies. *Import regulations* may be imposed to protect health, conserve foreign exchange, serve as economic reprisals, protect home industry, provide revenue in the form of tariffs, and ensure national security. To comply with various regulations, the exporter may have to acquire export licenses or permits from the home country and ascertain that the potential

---

[1]For a comprehensive review of trade barriers, see "2004 National Trade Estimate Report on Foreign Trade Barriers," www.ustr.gov, select Search for Trade Barriers.

[2]Leonidas C. Leonidou, "An Analysis of the Barriers Hindering Small Business Export Development," *Journal of Small Business Management,* July 2004, discusses these issues in more detail.

[3]For a thorough discussion of the entire export-import process, see Evelyn Thomchick, Richard R. Young, and Kusumal Ruamsook, "Importing and Exporting: A Longitudinal Study of Process Component Importance and Expertise," *Transportation Journal,* Summer 2004, pp. 34–48.

[4]See, for example, Thomas A. Cook, Rennie Alston, and Kelly Raia, *Mastering Import and Export Management* (New York: American Management Association, 2004).

customer has the necessary permits for importing the goods. The rules and regulations that cover the exportation and importation of goods and their payment, and the physical movement of those goods between countries, are the special concerns of this chapter.

Export Restrictions

Although the United States requires no formal or special license to engage in exporting as a business, permission or a license to export may be required for certain commodities and certain destinations. Export licensing controls apply to exports of commodities and technical data from the United States; re-exports of U.S.-origin commodities and technical data from a foreign destination to another foreign destination; U.S.-origin parts and components used in foreign countries to manufacture foreign products for exports; and, in some cases, foreign products made from U.S.-origin technical data. Most items requiring special permission or a license for exportation are under the control of the Bureau of Industry and Security (BIS)[5] of the Department of Commerce.[6]

The volume of exports and the number of companies exporting from the United States have grown spectacularly over the last decade. In an effort to alleviate many of the problems and confusions of exporting and to expedite the process, the Department of Commerce has published a revised set of export regulations known as the *Export Administration Regulations (EAR)*. They are intended to speed up the process of granting export licenses by removing a large number of items from specific export license control and by concentrating licensing on a specific list of items, most of which affect national security, nuclear nonproliferation, terrorism, or chemical and biological weapons. Along with these changes comes a substantial increase in responsibility on the part of the exporter since the exporter must now ensure that Export Administration Regulations are not violated.

The export control provisions of the Export Administration Regulations are intended to serve the national security, foreign policy, and nonproliferation interests of the United States and, in some cases, to carry out its international obligations.[7] The EAR also includes some export controls to protect the United States from the adverse impact of the unrestricted export of commodities in short supply, such as Western cedar. Items that do not require a license for a specific destination can be shipped with the notation NLR (no license required) on the Shipper's Export Declaration.

Determining Export Requirements

The first step when complying with export licensing regulations is to determine the appropriate license for your product. Products exported from the United States require a general or a validated export license, depending on the product, where it is going, the end use, and the final user. The *general license* permits exportation of certain products that are not subject to EAR control with nothing more than a declaration of the type of product, its value, and its destination. The *validated license,* issued only on formal application, is a specific document authorizing exportation within specific limitations designated under the EAR.

The responsibility of determining if a license is required rests with the exporter. The steps necessary to determine the type of license required and/or if an item can be shipped are as follows:

- The exporter is responsible for selecting the proper classification number, known as the *Export Control Classification Number (ECCN)*, for the item to be exported. The ECCN leads to a description in the *Commerce Control List (CCL)*, which indicates the exportability status of the item.

- The exporter must decide from the CCL if the items have end-use restrictions, for example, use in nuclear, chemical, and biological weapons. The exporter must also determine if the product has a dual use, that is, if it can be used in both commercial and restricted applications.

---

[5]Formerly known as the Bureau of Export Administration (BXA).

[6]"BIS Norms Now Cover 24 More Import Items," *Economic Times*, April 19, 2003.

[7]For a primer on Commerce Department export controls, see "Introduction to Commerce Department Export Controls," www.bis.doc.gov and select Export Control basics.

- The exporter is responsible for determining the ultimate end customer and ultimate end uses of the product, regardless of the initial buyer. This step includes carefully screening end users and end uses of the product to determine if the final destination of the product is to an unapproved user or for an unapproved use. U.S. law requires firms to avoid shipments if the firm has knowledge that customers will use its products for illegal purposes or resell the product to unauthorized end users.

To illustrate, suppose you are an exporter of shotguns and you are beginning the process of fulfilling orders from Argentina (20-inch barrel shotguns), Australia (23-inch and 26-inch barrels), and Sudan (26-inch barrels).[8] The first step is to determine the proper Export Control Classification Number (ECCN) for the commodity to be exported. Each ECCN consists of five characters that identify its category, product group, type of control, and country group level. There are three general ways to determine a product's ECCN:

- If you are the exporter of the product but not its manufacturer, you can contact the manufacturer or developer to see if that firm already has an ECCN.
- Compare the general characteristics of the product to the Commerce Control List and find the most appropriate product category. Once the category is identified, you go through the entire category and identify the appropriate ECCN by determining the product's particular functions.
- Request a classification from the BIS. The request must include the end use, end user, and/or destination. The BIS will advise you whether a license is required or likely to be granted for a particular transaction. This type of request is known as an *advisory opinion.* An advisory opinion does not bind the BIS to issuing a license in the future, since government policies may change before a license is actually granted.

Once the proper ECCN has been obtained (in this illustration 0A984, see Exhibit 15.2), the second step is to locate the number in the Commerce Control List. Consulting the

---

[8]This is an abbreviated example intended to illustrate the general idea of the steps necessary to determine licensing requirements.

Exhibit 15.2

Illustration of Commerce Control List Requirements for ECCN 0A984

Source: Abstracted from Export Administration Regulations Database, Bureau of Industry and Security, www.bis.doc.gov.

0A984   Shotguns, barrel length 18 inches (45.72 cm) or over; buckshot shotgun shells; except equipment used exclusively to treat or tranquilize animals, and except arms designed solely for signal, flare, or saluting use; and parts, n.e.s.

License Requirements
Reason for Control: CC, FC, UN

Control(s)		*Country Chart*
FC applies to firearms		FC Column 1
CC 1	applies to shotguns with a barrel length greater than or equal to 18 in. (45.72 cm), but less than 24 in. (60.96 cm) or buckshot, shotgun shells controlled by this entry, regardless of end-user.	CC Column 1
CC 2	applies to shotguns with a barrel length greater than or equal to 24 in. (60.96 cm), regardless of end-user.	CC Column 2
CC 3	applies to shotguns with a barrel length greater than or equal to 24 in. (60.96 cm) if for sale or resale to police or law enforcement.	CC Column 3
UN	applies to UN sanctions that ban shipments of all firearms, regardless of type, to countries listed.	Rwanda; Serbia and Montenegro (formerly Yugoslavia)

List of Items Controlled
Unit: $ value
Related Controls: this entry does not control shotguns with a barrel length of less than 18 inches (45.72 cm). These items are subject to the export licensing authority of the Department of State.

Exhibit 15.3

Commerce Country Chart: Reasons for Control (Selected Countries)

Country	Chemical & Biological Weapons			Nuclear Nonproliferation		National Security		Missile Tech	Regional Stability		Firearms Convention	Crime Control			Antiterrorism	
	CB 1	CB 2	CB 3	NP 1	NP 2	NS 1	NS 2	MT 1	RS 1	RS 2	FC 1	CC 1	CC 2	CC 3	AT 1	AT 2
Albania	x*	x		x		x	x	x	x	x		x	x			
Argentina	x					x	x	x	x	x	x	x		x		
Australia	x					x		x	x							
Canada	x										x					
China	x	x	x	x		x	x	x	x	x		x		x		
France	x					x		x	x							
India	x	x	x	x	x	x	x	x	x	x		x		x		
Mexico	x	x		x		x	x	x	x	x	x	x		x		
Sudan	x	x		x		x	x	x	x	x		x		x	x	x
Syria	x	x	x	x		x	x	x	x	x		x		x	x	

*x = special license required.

Source: Abstracted from Commerce Country Chart, www.bxa.doc.gov. Under *Rules, Regulations and Lists* select *Go Direct to the Regs* and then select *part name, 738spir,* June 20, 2000.

(CCL) for shotguns (see Exhibit 15.2), the description shows that the reasons for control are Crime Control (CC), Firearms Convention (FC), and UN sanctions (UN) and that there are different restrictions depending on the length of the shotgun barrel.

The third step is to consult the *Commerce Country Chart (CCC)* (Exhibit 15.3), which helps you determine, based on the reason(s) for control associated with your item, if you need a license to export or re-export your item to a particular destination. In combination with the Commodity Control List, the CCC allows you to determine whether a license is required for items on the CCL exported to any country in the world.

In checking the CCC (Exhibit 15.3), you find Argentina, Australia, and Sudan all listed. Looking at the Crime Control and Firearms Convention columns and referencing the product description in the Commodity Control List, you see that the Argentinian order for shotguns with 20-inch barrels falls into CC Column 1 and FC Column 1, where the *x* indicates that the order cannot be shipped without a special license. The Australian orders for 23-inch and 26-inch shotguns (CC Columns 1 and 2) do not require special licenses.

Finally, an examination of the Sudanese order for 26-inch shotguns reveals in CC Column 2 that the product can be exported without a special license; however, CC Column 3 indicates that if the guns are for sale or resale to police or law enforcement, a special license is required. Because you are not sure if the shotguns are to be resold, more information will be needed before the order can be processed. If you determine that the guns will not be resold to police or law enforcement, they can be shipped without special license; otherwise, a license will have to be obtained before the shipment can take place.

But the challenge is not yet over. An exporter also must establish that the end user is not listed in the List of Denied Persons,[9] which lists those denied export privileges; no shipments may be made to any person or company on the denied persons list. In addition to checking the denial list, the exporter needs to make a general check to be sure there are no indications that the end user's intentions will lead to an unauthorized use of the product.

Unfortunately, you cannot always rely on the buyer's word. Sun Microsystems sold one of its supercomputers to a Hong Kong firm that claimed the computer was destined for a scientific institute near Beijing, an authorized sale. A trace of the final destination revealed that the computer's final destination was a military research facility in China, an unauthorized end use and end user. Because Sun Microsystems monitored the sale and reported the

---

[9]A database of all prohibited parties can be found on the "Prohibited Parties Database," which, in addition to the Denied Persons List, includes Debarred Parties, Entity List, and Specially Designated Nationals, Terrorists, Narcotics Traffickers, Blocked Persons and Vessels—all of whom must be screened before completing an export order. The list of denied persons can be found at www.bsi.doc.gov and select Denied Persons List under Rules, Regulations and Lists.

Chinese air force officers undergo a training session on the latest command center instruments at a training school in Beijing. China successfully test-fired a new type of long-range ground-to-ground missile within its territory as tensions between China and Taiwan intensified after Taiwan's president declared that relations between Taipei and Beijing should be regarded as "special state-to-state relations." Much of the electronic technology used in long-range missiles is dual-use; that is, the technology can be used for both nonmilitary and military applications. It is the exporter's responsibility to ensure that the final user of restricted dual-use products complies with exports restrictions. (© *Roger Ressmeyer/CORBIS*)

diversion, there were no legal consequences. Negotiations between China and the U.S. government resulted in the return of the computer to Sun Microsystems. To be alert to possible problems like the one Sun faced, the Export Administration Regulations suggest looking for red flags (Exhibit 15.4), which may give a clue that your customer is planning an unlawful diversion.

Exhibit 15.4
Red Flags

Source: www.bxa.doc.gov and select *Red Flags*.

The exporter has an important role to play in preventing exports and re-exports that might be contrary to the national security and foreign policy interests of the United States and to ensure that the shipment is not in violation of Bureau of Export Administration regulations. To assist in determining the motives of a buyer, the BXA proposes these indicators as possible signs that a customer is planning an unlawful diversion:

1. The customer or purchasing agent is reluctant to offer information about the end use of a product.

2. The product's capabilities do not fit the buyer's line of business; for example, a small bakery places an order for several sophisticated lasers.

3. The product ordered is incompatible with the technical level of the country to which the product is being shipped. For example, semiconductor-manufacturing equipment would be of little use in a country without an electronics industry.

4. The customer has little or no business background.

5. The customer is willing to pay cash for a very expensive item when the terms of the sale call for financing.

6. The customer is unfamiliar with the product's performance characteristics but still wants the product.

7. The customer declines routine installation, training, or maintenance services.

8. Delivery dates are vague, or deliveries are planned for out-of-the-way destinations.

9. A freight-forwarding firm is listed as the product's final destination.

10. The shipping route is abnormal for the product and destination.

11. Packaging is inconsistent with the stated method of shipment or destination.

12. When questioned, the buyer is evasive or unclear about whether the purchased product is for domestic use, export, or re-export.

Exhibit 15.5
Examples of Violations
and Penalties of BIS
Export Controls

Sources: "Don't Let This Happen to
You—An Introduction to U.S. Export
Control Law," Bureau of Industry and
Security, U.S. Department of
Commerce, April 2005,
www.bis.doc.gov.

End Use/End User Violation

A $12 million civil penalty was imposed against McDonnell Douglas as part of a settlement of charges that the company violated federal export control laws by submitting false and misleading statements about the end use and end user of machine tools. In a related case, the BIS imposed a $1.32 million civil penalty and a denial of export privileges on a group of Chinese government–owned companies and their U.S. affiliates that had received the machine tools from McDonnell Douglas.

Facilitating Export to Denied Persons

The Commerce Department imposed a $15,000 penalty on Federal Express (FedEx) for allegedly facilitating the export of U.S.-origin semiconductor test equipment from the United States to Taiwan to a Denied Person and failure to maintain records of the subject transaction.

Duel-Use Products

Bushnell Corporation, which does business as Worldwide Sports & Recreation, pleaded guilty to conspiracy and violation of export regulations. For a period of two years, more than 500 Night Ranger night vision devices were shipped to Japan and 14 other countries without the required export license. The U.S. attorney warned that "distributors of equipment with potential military use must be vigilant about compliance with export restrictions. . . . Willful blindness and deliberate ignorance of the law is not an excuse when national security is at issue." Under a plea agreement, Bushnell agreed to pay a criminal fine of $650,000 and receive five years of corporate probation.

Violation of Antiboycott Provisions

St. Jude Medical Export GmbH agreed to pay a $30,000 penalty for violating the EAR when it failed to report in a timely manner its receipt of three requests from an Iraqi government agency to adhere to the rules of the Arab League boycott of Israel during a reporting period. On four occasions, St. Jude also violated the antiboycott provisions of the EAR by agreeing to refuse to do business with persons blacklisted by the Arab League.

Illegal Transshipping

All export privileges were denied for eight years to David Portnoy, convicted of violating the International Emergency Economic Powers Act by transshipping electronic components and telecommunications equipment through Switzerland to Libya (a U.S. boycott of Libya was in force) without the required export licenses.

As is true of all the export mechanics that an exporter encounters, the details of exporting must be followed to the letter. Good record keeping, as well as verifying the steps undertaken in establishing the proper ECCN and in evaluating the intentions of end users and end uses, is important should a disagreement arise between the exporter and the Bureau of Industry and Security. Penalties can entail denial of export privileges, fines, or both. For example, a five-year denial of export privileges was imposed on a resident of Pittsfield, Massachusetts, based on his conviction of illegally exporting 150 riot shields to Romania without the required export license. At the time of the shipment, the riot shields were controlled for export worldwide for foreign policy reasons. See Exhibit 15.5 for examples of violations and penalties.

ELAIN, STELA, ERIC, and SNAP

Although the procedure for acquiring an export license may seem tedious on first reading, four electronic services facilitate the paperwork and reduce the time necessary to acquire export licenses.

- **ELAIN** (Export License Application and Information Network) enables exporters that have authorization to submit license applications via the Internet for all commodities except supercomputers to all free-world destinations. When approved, licensing decisions are conveyed back to the exporters via the Internet.

- **STELA** (System for Tracking Export License Applications), an automated voice-response system for tracking applications, can be accessed using a touch-tone phone. It provides applicants with the status of their license and classification applications and is available 24 hours a day, seven days a week. STELA can give exporters authority to ship their goods for those licenses approved without conditions.

- **ERIC** (Electronic Request for Item Classification), a supplementary service to ELAIN, allows an exporter to submit commodity classification requests via the Internet to the Bureau of Export administration.

- **SNAP** (Simplified Network Application Process), an alternative to paper license submissions, enables an exporter to submit export and re-export applications, high-performance computer notices, and commodity classification requests via the Internet. Acknowledgments of submissions will be received the same day, and electronic facsimiles of export licenses and other validations can be obtained online. SNAP is one of the changes made by the Department of Commerce to move it from being a paper-based bureaucracy to an all-digital department.

Import Restrictions

An exporter planning a sale to a foreign buyer must examine the export restrictions of the home country as well as the import restrictions and regulations of the importing country. Although the responsibility of import restrictions may rest with the importer, the exporter does not want to ship goods until it is certain that all import regulations of the destination country have been met. Goods arriving without proper documentation can be denied entry and returned to the shipper.[10]

Besides import tariffs, many other trade restrictions are imposed by foreign countries. A few examples from the 30 basic barriers to exporting considered important by *Business International* include import licenses, quotas, and other quantitative restrictions; currency restrictions and allocation of exchange at unfavorable rates on payments for imports; devaluation; prohibitive prior import deposits, prohibition of collection-basis sales, and insistence on cash letters of credit; arbitrarily short periods in which to apply for import licenses; and delays resulting from pressure on overworked officials or from competitors' influence on susceptible officials.[11]

Trading with the European Union from outside the European Union or within member states, an exporter continues to be confronted with market barriers that have yet to be eliminated. One study of 20,000 EU exporting firms indicated that the most troublesome barriers were administrative roadblocks, border-crossing delays, and capital controls. The French government imposed one such barrier against Japanese VCRs. All Japanese VCRs were directed to land only at one port, where only one inspector was employed; hence, just 10 to 12 VCRs could enter France each day. Generally such barriers are challenged and ultimately dropped. As the European Union becomes more fully integrated, many of the barriers that exist among member countries will be eliminated, although not as rapidly as some expect.

The most frequently encountered trade restrictions, besides tariffs, are such nontariff barriers (NTBs) as exchange permits, quotas, import licenses, standards, boycotts, and voluntary agreements.

Tariffs

Recall that tariffs are the taxes or customs duties levied against goods imported from another country. All countries have tariffs for the purpose of raising revenue and protecting home industries from competition with foreign-produced goods.[12] Tariff rates are based on value or quantity or a combination of both. In the United States, for example, the types of customs duties used are classified as follows: (1) *ad valorem duties,* which are based on a

---

[10]"Report Outlines Foreign Trade Barriers," *Industry Week*, May 2004.

[11]For a complete discussion of foreign trade barriers, see "2005 National Trade Estimate Report on Foreign Barriers, USTR, 2005, www.ustr.gov and select Foreign Trade Barriers.

[12]"Shrimp Import Tariffs Imposed to Curb Dumping," *Associated Press,* December 1, 2004.

percentage of the determined value of the imported goods; (2) *specific duties,* a stipulated amount per unit weight or some other measure of quantity; and (3) a *compound duty,* which combines both specific and ad valorem taxes on a particular item, that is, a tax per pound plus a percentage of value. Because tariffs frequently change, published tariff schedules for every country are available to the exporter on a current basis.[13]

Exchange Permits

Especially troublesome to exporters are exchange restrictions placed on the flow of currency by some foreign countries. To conserve scarce foreign exchange and alleviate balance-of-payment difficulties, many countries impose restrictions on the amount of their currency they will exchange for the currency of another country—in effect, they ration the amount of currency available to pay for imports. Exchange controls may be applied in general to all commodities, or a country may employ a system of multiple exchange rates based on the type of import. Essential products might have a very favorable exchange rate, while nonessentials or luxuries would have a less favorable rate of exchange. South Africa, for example, has a two-tier system for foreign exchange: Commercial Rand and Financial Rand.[14] At times, countries may not issue any exchange permits for certain classes of commodities.

In countries that use exchange controls, the usual procedure is for the importer to apply to the control agency of the importing country for an import permit; if the control agency approves the request, an import license is issued. On presentation to the proper government agency, the import license can be used to have local currency exchanged for the currency of the seller.

Receiving an import license, or even an exchange permit, however, is not a guarantee that a seller can exchange local currency for the currency of the seller. If local currency is in short supply—a chronic problem in some countries—other means of acquiring home-country currency are necessary. For example, in a transaction between the government of Colombia and a U.S. truck manufacturer, there was a scarcity of U.S. currency to exchange for the 1,000 vehicles Colombia wanted to purchase. The problem was solved through a series of exchanges. Colombia had a surplus of coffee that the truck manufacturer accepted and traded in Europe for sugar; the sugar was traded for pig iron, and finally the pig iron was traded for U.S. dollars.

This somewhat complicated but effective countertrade transaction is not uncommon. As will be discussed in Chapter 18, countertrade deals are often a result of the inability to convert local currency into home-country currency or of the refusal of a government to issue foreign exchange.

Quotas

Countries may also impose limitations on the quantity of certain goods imported during a specific period. These quotas may be applied to imports from specific countries or from all foreign sources in general. The United States, for example, has specific quotas for importing sugar, wheat, cotton, tobacco, textiles, and peanuts; in the case of some of these items, the amount imported from specific countries is also limited.[15] The most important reasons to set quotas are to protect domestic industry and to conserve foreign exchange. Some importing countries also set quotas to ensure an equitable distribution of a major market among friendly countries.

Import Licenses

As a means of regulating the flow of exchange and the quantity of a particular imported commodity, countries often require import licenses. The fundamental difference between quotas and import licenses as a means of controlling imports is the greater flexibility of import licenses over quotas. Quotas permit importing until the quota is filled; licensing limits quantities on a case-by-case basis.

---

[13]The entire Harmonized Tariff Schedule of the United States can be downloaded, or accessed via an interactive tariff database, at USITC: www.usitc.gov, select Harmonized Tariff Schedule.

[14]Moin Siddiqi, "End of South African ForEx Controls in Sight," *African Business,* November 2004.

[15]"U.S. Begins Probe to Limit Imports of Chinese Textiles, Apparel," *Kyodo News International, Inc.,* April 11, 2005.

CROSSING **BORDERS** 15.1

Major Smuggling Ring Busted—A Sweet Deal

The United States maintains an artificial price for sugar to protect the cane and beet sugar industry. This feat is accomplished by placing a quota on sugar imports. The amount of sugar imported annually is determined by estimating the annual consumption less estimated U.S. production. In 2004, consumption was 10.2 tons, production was 8.4 tons; thus the quota for that year was 1.8 tons. This held U.S. domestic raw sugar prices to 23 cents per pound compared to 9 cents on the world market. This means that U.S. consumers spend about $2 billion more yearly in higher prices for sugar and food items that contain sugar than if we had a free market in sugar. But while this means sugar costs more for the average citizen, it also means that if you could figure a way to buy sugar at 9 cents on the world market and sell it at 23 cents in the United States, you could make a pot full of money—but then there is that nasty quota standing in the way. Well, there may be a way around those quotas if we read the law carefully.

Eureka! After a careful reading of the categories of sugar and derivatives covered by the sugar quota, an enterprising importer spotted a category not included in the quota, a gooey brown sugar–based molasses that is good for little more than animal feed. The Customs Department was contacted about the molasses product and agreed that it was not covered by the sugar restrictions, and gave its explicit approval to import the mixture without paying high tariffs. The company built a processing plant in Canada to turn Brazilian sugar into the molasses and a refinery across the border in Michigan to reverse the process and produce precisely the sort of sugar syrup covered by the tariffs. It then sold the product to its usual customers: big makers of ice cream, confectionery, and breakfast cereals.

All went well until the ever-vigilant sugar lobby, one of the strongest lobbies in the United States, put pressure on prominent politicians from sugar-producing states to stop those "smugglers"—causing Customs to reverse itself. Alarmed that it might see its tariffs rise by some 7,000 percent, the company challenged the decision in the Court of International Trade (CIT). The court sided with the firm, dismissing the government's action as "arbitrary, capricious, and abuse of discretion," citing the precedent that products are classified according to the way they are imported, not their ultimate use. More pointedly, the court maintained that an importer had the right to design products specifically to get a lower duty. An internal memo from the agency said that under long-standing policy, what happened to a product after it was across the border didn't matter. The fact that, after importation, the product may be processed to allow it to compete directly with sugar subject to the quota is not relevant to classification. The agency has always tolerated a certain amount of tariff engineering. The judge said that carmakers routinely import parts they later assemble in the United States in order to avoid high tariffs. The judge noted that even when pearls are imported ready for stringing, with holes already drilled in them, Customs classifies them as pearls, not jewelry, which carries a higher tax rate.

A month after the ruling, the litigators began an appeal to Congress to change the definition of the sugar syrup to one of ultimate use, rather than what it is when imported. This would make the Customs ruling and the court case irrelevant. It would also put the company out of business. However, until the law is rewritten, truckloads of molasses goop cross the border into the United States to become clear sugar syrup that is used, among other things, as a coating for your breakfast cereal.

Tariff structures in other countries are just as tangled as in the United States—import a station wagon into China and pay a 38 percent tariff, import the body, bumpers, and engine separately, and pay 17 percent.

Sources: Bill Walsh, "Smart or Smuggling?" *New Orleans Times-Picayune*, April 30, 2000, p. F9; David Whelan, "Even the Biggest Companies Screw Up on Export Rules," *Forbes*, May 2004; "CAFTA Cornucopia," *Washington Times*, May 5, 2005, p. A18; "Sugar Farmers Waging a Life-or-Death Battle against Trade Pact," *Chicago Tribune*, May 12, 2005.

Standards   Like many nontariff barriers, standards have legitimacy. Health standards, safety standards, and product quality standards are necessary to protect the consuming public, and imported goods are required to comply with local laws. Unfortunately, standards can also be used to slow down or restrict the procedures for importing to the point that the additional time and cost required to comply become, in effect, trade restrictions.

Safety standards are a good example. Most countries have safety standards for electrical appliances and require that imported electrical products meet local standards. However, safety standards can be escalated to the level of an absolute trade barrier by manipulating the procedures used to determine if products meet the standards. The simplest process is for the importing nation to accept the safety standard verification used by the exporting country, such as Underwriters Laboratories (UL) in the United States. If the product is certified for sale in the United States, and if U.S. standards are the same as the importing country's, then U.S. standards and certification are accepted and no further testing is necessary. Most countries not interested in using standards as a trade barrier follow such a practice.

The extreme situation occurs when the importing nation does not accept the same certification procedure required by the exporting nation and demands all testing be done in the importing country. Even more restrictive is the requirement that each item be tested instead of accepting batch testing. In this case, the effect is the same as a boycott. Until recently, Japan required all electrical consumer products to be tested in Japan or tested in the United States by Japanese officials. Japan now accepts the UL's safety tests except for medical supplies and agricultural products, which still must be tested in Japan.

Boycotts

A boycott[16] is an absolute restriction against trade with a country or trade of specific goods. American firms must honor boycotts sanctioned by the U.S. government; however, a U.S. company participating in an unauthorized boycott could be fined for violating the U.S. antiboycott law. For example, U.S. companies are prohibited from participating in the Arab League boycott on trade with Israel. U.S. law forbids U.S. firms to comply with such unauthorized boycotts. If an American firm refuses to trade with Israel in order to do business with an Arab nation, or in any other way participates in the Arab League boycott, it faces stiff fines. Boycotts are the most restrictive NTB because they ban all trade, whereas other types of restrictions permit some trade.[17]

Voluntary Agreements

Foreign restrictions of all kinds abound, and the United States can be counted among those governments using restrictions. For over a decade, U.S. government officials have been arranging "voluntary" agreements with the Japanese steel and automobile industries to limit sales to the United States. Japan entered these voluntary agreements under the implied threat that if it did not voluntarily restrict the export of automobiles or steel to an agreed limit, the United States might impose even harsher restrictions, including additional import duties. Similar negotiations with the governments of major textile producers have limited textile imports as well. The cost of tariffs, quotas, and voluntary agreements on all fibers is estimated to be as much as $40 billion at the retail level. This works out to be a hidden tax of almost $500 a year for every American family.

Other Restrictions

Restrictions may be imposed on imports of harmful products, drugs, medicines, and immoral products and literature. Products must also comply with government standards set for health, sanitation, packaging, and labeling. For example, in the Netherlands all imported hen and duck eggs must be marked in indelible ink with the country of origin; in Spain, imported condensed milk must be labeled to show fat content if it is less than 8 percent fat; and in the European Union, strict import controls have been placed on beef and beef products imported from the United Kingdom because of mad cow disease. Add to this list all genetically modified foods, which are meeting stiff opposition from the European Union as well as activists around the world.

Failure to comply with regulations can result in severe fines, penalties, and delays in clearing customs. A shipment of pork sausages was delayed clearing customs for four

---

[16]Also referred to as an embargo.

[17]"The Case against Embargoes," *BusinessWeek*, April 25, 2005.

months because the proper permit was not issued, even though prior shipments had cleared with a similar permit. Because requirements vary for each country and change frequently, regulations for all countries must be consulted individually and on a current basis. *Overseas Business Reports,* issued periodically by the Department of Commerce, provides the foreign marketer with the most recent foreign trade regulations of each country as well as U.S. regulations regarding each country.

Although sanitation certificates, content labeling, and similar regulations serve a legitimate purpose, countries can effectively limit imports by using such restrictions as additional trade barriers. Most of the economically developed world encourages foreign trade and works through the World Trade Organization (WTO) to reduce tariffs and nontariff barriers to a reasonable rate.[18] Yet in times of economic recession, countries revert to a protectionist philosophy and seek ways to restrict the importing of goods. Nontariff barriers have become one of the most potent ways for a country to restrict trade. The elimination of nontariff barriers has been a major concern of GATT negotiations in both the Tokyo and Uruguay Rounds and continues with the WTO.

Terms of Sale

Terms of sale, or *trade terms,* differ somewhat in international marketing from those used in the United States. In U.S. domestic trade, it is customary to ship FOB (free on board, meaning that the price is established at the door of the factory), freight collect, prepaid, or COD (cash, or collect, on delivery). International trade terms often sound similar to those used in domestic business but generally have different meanings. International terms indicate how buyer and seller divide risks and obligations and, therefore, the costs of specific kinds of international trade transactions. When quoting prices, it is important to make them meaningful. The most frequently used international trade terms include the following:[19]

- **CIF** (cost, insurance, freight) to a named overseas port of import. A CIF quote is more meaningful to the overseas buyer because it includes the costs of goods, insurance, and all transportation and miscellaneous charges to the named place of debarkation.

- **C&F** (cost and freight) to a named overseas port. The price includes the cost of the goods and transportation costs to the named place of debarkation. The cost of insurance is borne by the buyer.

- **FAS** (free alongside) at a named U.S. port of export. The price includes cost of goods and charges for delivery of the goods alongside the shipping vessel. The buyer is responsible for the cost of loading onto the vessel, transportation, and insurance.

- **FOB** (free on board) at a named inland point, at a named port of exportation, or at a named vessel and port of export. The price includes the cost of the goods and delivery to the place named.

- **EX** (named port of origin). The price quoted covers costs only at the point of origin (for example, EX Factory). All other charges are the buyer's concern.

A complete list of terms and their definitions can be found in *Incoterms,* a booklet published by the International Chamber of Commerce.[20] It is important for the exporter to understand exactly the meanings of terms used in quotations. A simple misunderstanding regarding delivery terms may prevent the exporter from meeting contractual obligations or make that person responsible for shipping costs he or she did not intend to incur. Exhibit 15.6 indicates who is responsible for a variety of costs under various terms.

---

[18]"The WTO: Free Trade's Best Friend," *The Economist,* January 20, 2005.

[19]"Exporting to Europe: ME Survey Reveals 57% of U.S. Exporters Use 6 Terms," *Managing Exports,* April 1, 2003.

[20]A list of *Intercoms* can be found at www.iccbooks.com.

Exhibit 15.6
Who's Responsible for Costs under Various Terms?

Cost Items/Terms	FOB, Inland Carrier at Factory	FOB, Inland Carrier at Point of Shipment	FAS, Vessel or Plane at Port of Shipment	CIF, at Port of Destination
Export packing*	Buyer	Seller	Seller	Seller
Inland freight	Buyer	Seller	Seller	Seller
Port charges	Buyer	Buyer	Seller	Seller
Forwarder's fee	Buyer	Buyer	Buyer	Seller
Consular fee	Buyer	Buyer	Buyer	Buyer†
Loading on vessel or plane	Buyer	Buyer	Buyer	Seller
Ocean freight	Buyer	Buyer	Buyer	Seller
Cargo insurance	Buyer	Buyer	Buyer	Seller
Customs duties	Buyer	Buyer	Buyer	Buyer
Ownership of goods passes	When goods on board an inland ocean carrier (truck, rail, etc.) or in hands of inland carrier	When goods unloaded by inland carrier	When goods alongside carrier, in hands of air or ocean carrier	When goods on board air or carrier at port of shipment

*Who absorbs export packing? This charge should be clearly agreed on. Charges are sometimes controversial.

†The seller has responsibility to arrange for consular invoices (and other documents requested by the buyer's government). According to official definitions, the buyer pays fees, but sometimes as a matter of practice, the seller includes fees in quotations.

Getting Paid: Foreign Commercial Payments
The sale of goods in other countries is further complicated by additional risks encountered when dealing with foreign customers.[21] Risks from inadequate credit reports on customers, problems of currency exchange controls, distance, and different legal systems, as well as the cost and difficulty of collecting delinquent accounts, require a different emphasis on payment systems.[22] In U.S. domestic trade, the typical payment procedure for established customers is an *open account*—that is, the goods are delivered and the customer is billed on an end-of-the-month basis. However, the most frequently used term of payment in foreign commercial transactions for both export and import sales is a letter of credit, followed closely in importance by commercial dollar drafts or bills of exchange drawn by the seller on the buyer. Internationally, open accounts are reserved for well-established customers, and cash in advance is required of only the poorest credit risks or when the character of the merchandise is such that not fulfilling the terms of the contract may result in heavy loss. Because of the time required for shipment of goods from one country to another, advance payment of cash is an unusually costly burden for a potential customer and places the seller at a definite competitive disadvantage.

Terms of sales are typically arranged between the buyer and seller at the time of the sale. The type of merchandise, amount of money involved, business custom, credit rating of the buyer, country of the buyer, and whether the buyer is a new or old customer must be considered in establishing the terms of sale. The five basic payment arrangements—letters of credit, bills of exchange, cash in advance, open accounts, and forfaiting—are discussed in this section.

Letters of Credit
Export *letters of credit* opened in favor of the seller by the buyer handle most American exports. Letters of credit shift the buyer's credit risk to the bank issuing the letter of credit. When a letter of credit is employed, the seller ordinarily can draw a draft against the bank issuing the credit and receive dollars by presenting proper shipping documents. Except for cash in advance, letters of credit afford the greatest degree of protection for the seller.

---

[21]"International Payment Risk," *Financial Management*, March 2005.

[22]William Atkinson, "The International Obstacle Course," *Collections and Credit Risk*, January 2005.

Exhibit 15.7
A Letter-of-Credit Transaction

Here is what typically happens when payment is made by an irrevocable letter of credit confirmed by a U.S. bank. Follow the steps in the illustration below.

1. Exporter and customer agree on terms of sale.
2. Buyer requests its foreign bank to open a letter of credit.
3. The buyer's bank prepares an irrevocable letter of credit (LC), including all instructions, and sends the irrevocable letter of credit to a U.S. bank.
4. The U.S. bank prepares a letter of confirmation and letter of credit and sends to seller.
5. Seller reviews LC. If acceptable, arranges with freight forwarder to deliver goods to designated port of entry.
6. The goods are loaded and shipped.
7. At the same time the forwarder completes the necessary documents and sends documents to the seller.
8. Seller presents documents, indicating full compliance, to the U.S. bank.
9. The U.S. bank reviews the documents. If they are in order, issues seller a check for amount of sale.
10. The documents are airmailed to the buyer's bank for review.
11. If documents are in compliance, the bank sends documents to buyer.
12. To claim goods, buyer presents documents to customs broker.
13. Goods are released to buyer.

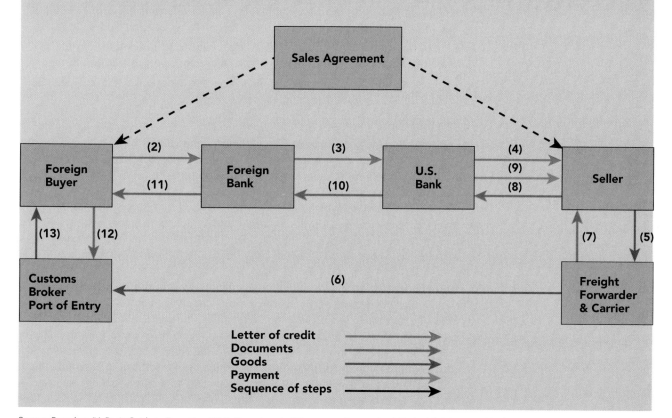

Source: Based on "A Basic Guide to Exporting," U.S. Department of Commerce, International Trade Administration, Washington, DC.

The procedure for a letter of credit begins with completion of the contract. (See Exhibit 15.7 for the steps in a letter-of-credit transaction.) The buyer then goes to a local bank and arranges for the issuance of a letter of credit; the buyer's bank notifies its correspondent bank in the seller's country that the letter has been issued. After meeting the requirements set forth in the letter of credit, the seller can draw a draft against the credit (in effect, the bank issuing the letter) for payment for the goods. The precise conditions of the letter of credit are detailed in it and usually also require presentation of certain documents along with the draft before the correspondent bank will honor it. The documents usually required are a commercial invoice, a consular invoice (when requested), a clean bill of lading, and an insurance policy or certificate.

Letters of credit can be revocable or irrevocable. An *irrevocable letter of credit* means that once the seller has accepted the credit, the buyer cannot alter it in any way without permission of the seller. Added protection is gained if the buyer is required to confirm the letter of credit through a U.S. bank. This irrevocable, confirmed letter of credit means that a U.S. bank accepts responsibility to pay regardless of the financial situation of the buyer or foreign bank. From the seller's viewpoint, this eliminates the foreign political risk and replaces the commercial risk of the buyer's bank with that of the confirming bank. The confirming bank ensures payment against a confirmed letter of credit. As soon as the documents are presented to the bank, the seller receives payment.

The international department of a major U.S. bank cautions that a letter of credit is not a guarantee of payment to the seller. Rather, payment is tendered only if the seller complies exactly with the terms of the letter of credit. Since all letters of credit must be exact in their terms and considerations, it is important for the exporter to check the terms of the letter carefully to be certain that all necessary documents have been acquired and properly completed. Some of the discrepancies found in documents that cause delay in honoring drafts or letters of credit include the following:

- Insurance defects such as inadequate coverage, no endorsement or countersignature, and a dating later than the bill of lading.
- Bill-of-lading defects such as the bill lacking an "on board" endorsement or signature of carrier, missing an endorsement, or failing to specify prepaid freight.
- Letter-of-credit defects such as an expired letter or one that is exceeded by the invoice figure, or one including unauthorized charges or disproportionate charges.
- Invoice defects such as missing signatures or failure to designate terms of shipment (C&F, CIF, FAS) as stipulated in the letter of credit.
- Documents that are missing, stalemated, or inaccurate.

As illustrated in the Global Perspective at the beginning of this chapter, the process of getting a letter of credit can take days, if not weeks.[23] Fortunately, this process is being shortened considerably as financial institutions provide letters of credit on the Internet. As one example, AVG Letter of Credit Management LLC uses eTrade Finance Platform (ETFP), an e-commerce trade transaction system that enables exporters, importers, freight forwarders, carriers, and trade banks to initiate and complete trade transactions over the Internet. The company advertises that the efficiencies afforded by the Internet make it possible to lower the cost of an export Letter of Credit from $500-plus to $25.[24]

Bills of Exchange

Another important form of international commercial payment is *bills of exchange* drawn by sellers on foreign buyers. In letters of credit, the credit of one or more banks is involved, but with bills of exchange (also known as *dollar drafts*), the seller assumes all risk until the actual dollars are received. The typical procedure is for the seller to draw a draft on the buyer and present this with the necessary documents to the seller's bank for collection. The documents required are principally the same as for letters of credit. On receipt of the draft, the U.S. bank forwards it with the necessary documents to a correspondent bank in the buyer's country; the buyer is then presented with the draft for acceptance and immediate or later payment. With acceptance of the draft, the buyer receives the properly endorsed bill of lading that is used to acquire the goods from the carrier.

Bills of exchange or dollar drafts can have one of three time periods—sight, arrival, or date. A *sight draft* requires acceptance and payment on presentation of the draft and often

---

[23]John L. Amos, Rowena Gates, and Gen. Merril A. McPeak, USAF (Ret.), "New Thoughts on Documenting Trade," *World Trade*, November 1, 2002.

[24]"New Web Technology Reduces LC Costs under e-UCP Rules," *Managing Exports*, May 2003.

before arrival of the goods. An *arrival draft* requires payment be made on arrival of the goods. Unlike the other two, a *date draft* has an exact date for payment and in no way is affected by the movement of the goods. Time designations may be placed on sight and arrival drafts to stipulate a fixed number of days after acceptance when the obligation must be paid. Usually this period is 30 to 120 days, thus providing a means of extending credit to the foreign buyer.

Dollar drafts have advantages for the seller because an accepted draft frequently can be discounted at a bank for immediate payment. Banks, however, usually discount drafts only with recourse; that is, if the buyer does not honor the draft, the bank returns it to the seller for payment. An accepted draft is firmer evidence in the case of default and subsequent litigation than an open account would be.

Cash in Advance The volume of international business handled on a cash-in-advance basis is not large. Cash places unpopular burdens on the customer and typically is used when credit is doubtful, when exchange restrictions within the country of destination are such that the return of funds from abroad may be delayed for an unreasonable period, or when the American exporter for any reason is unwilling to sell on credit terms. Although full payment in advance is employed infrequently, partial payment (from 25 to 50 percent) in advance is not unusual when the character of the merchandise is such that an incomplete contract can result in heavy loss. For example, complicated machinery or equipment manufactured to specification or special design would necessitate advance payment, which would be, in fact, a nonrefundable deposit.

Open Accounts Sales on open accounts are not generally made in foreign trade except to customers of long standing with excellent credit reputations or to a subsidiary or branch of the exporter. Open accounts obviously leave sellers in a position where most of the problems of international commercial finance work to their disadvantage. Sales on open accounts are generally not recommended when the practice of the trade is to use some other method, when special merchandise is ordered, when shipping is hazardous, when the country of the importer imposes difficult exchange restrictions, or when political unrest requires additional caution.

Forfaiting Inconvertible currencies and cash-short customers can kill an international sale if the seller cannot offer long-term financing. Unless the company has large cash reserves to finance its customers, a deal may be lost. *Forfaiting* is a financing technique for such a situation.

The basic idea of a forfaiting transaction is fairly simple: The seller makes a one-time arrangement with a bank or other financial institution to take over responsibility for collecting the account receivable. The exporter offers a long financing term to its buyer but intends to sell its account receivable, at a discount, for immediate cash. The forfaiter buys the debt, typically a promissory note or bill of exchange, on a nonrecourse basis. Once the exporter sells the paper, the forfaiter assumes the risk of collecting the importer's payments. The forfaiting institution also assumes any political risk present in the importer's country.[25]

Forfaiting is similar to factoring, but it is not the same. In *factoring* a company has an ongoing relationship with a bank that routinely buys its short-term accounts receivable at a discount—in other words, the bank acts as a collections department for its client. In forfaiting, however, the seller makes a one-time arrangement with a bank to buy a specific account receivable.[26]

Export Documents

Each export shipment involves many documents to satisfy government regulations controlling exporting as well as to meet requirements for international commercial payment transactions. The most frequently required documents are export declarations, consular invoices or certificates of origin, bills of lading, commercial invoices, and insurance

---

[25]For more information about forfaiting, visit www.afia-forfaiting.org.

[26]Margrit Lutschg-Emmenegger, "Forfaiters and Credit Insurers—Co-operation or Competition?" *Credit Control* 25, no. 1 (2004).

Exhibit 15.8
Principal Export
Documents

Source: Department of Commerce.

Export Documents Presented at the port of exit, includes the names and addresses of the principals involved, the destination of the goods, a full description of the goods, and their declared value.

Consular Invoice or Certificate of Origin Some countries require consular invoices obtained from the country's consulate and returned with two to eight copies in the language of the country, along with copies of other required documents (e.g., import license, commercial invoice, and/or bill of lading), before certification is granted. Preparation of the document should be handled with extreme care because fines are levied for any errors uncovered. In most countries, the fine is shared with whoever finds the errors, so few go undetected.

Bill of Lading The bill of lading is the most important document required for establishing legal ownership and facilitating financial transactions. It serves the following purposes: (1) as a contract for shipment between the carrier and shipper, (2) as a receipt from the carrier for shipment, and (3) as a certificate of ownership or title to the goods.

Commercial Invoice Every international transaction requires a commercial invoice, that is, a bill or statement for the goods sold. This document often serves several purposes; some countries require a copy for customs clearance, and it is one of the financial documents required in international commercial payments.

Insurance Policy or Certificate The insurance policy or certificate of insurance is considered a key document in export trade.

Licenses Export or import licenses are additional documents frequently required in export trade. In those cases where import licenses are required by the country of entry, a copy of the license or license number is usually required to obtain a consular invoice. Whenever a commodity requires an export license, it must be obtained before an export declaration can be properly certified.

Other Documents Sanitary and health inspection certificates attesting to the absence of disease and pests may be required for certain agricultural products before a country allows goods to enter its borders. Packing lists with correct weights are also required in some cases.

certificates. Additional documents such as import licenses, export licenses, packing lists, and inspection certificates for agricultural products are often necessary.

The paperwork involved in successfully completing a transaction is considered by many to be the greatest of all nontariff trade barriers. There are 125 different documents in regular or special use in more than 1,000 different forms. A single shipment may require over 50 documents and involve as many as 28 different parties and government agencies or require as few as five. Luckily, software is available that takes some of the burden out of this task. In one such program, the export information is entered once and the program automatically completes more than two dozen standard export forms, which can then be either printed or e-mailed to freight forwarders, customs brokers, or customers.

Although documents can be prepared routinely, their importance should not be minimized; incomplete or improperly prepared documents lead to delays in shipment. For example, a Mexican Customs official noticed that a certain piece of documentation out of all the paperwork required for a complete trainload of containers lacked a required signature—just one signature. The officer held the train up for almost two days until every container was unloaded and opened to verify that the contents matched the contents listed on the manifest.[27] In some countries, penalties, fines, or even confiscation of the goods could have resulted from errors in documentation.

Export documents are the result of requirements imposed by the exporting government, of requirements set by commercial procedures established in foreign trade, and, in some cases, of the supporting import documents required by the importing government. See Exhibit 15.8 for descriptions of the principal export documents.

---

[27]Michael D. White, *International Marketing Blunders* (Novato, CA., World Trade Press, 2002), p. 80.

Packing and Marking

In addition to completing all documentation, special packing and marking requirements must be considered for shipments destined to be transported over water, subject to excessive handling, or destined for parts of the world with extreme climates or unprotected outdoor storage. Packing that is adequate for domestic shipments often falls short for goods subject to the conditions mentioned. Protection against rough handling, moisture, temperature extremes, and pilferage may require heavy crating, which increases total packing costs as well as freight rates because of increased weight and size. Because some countries determine import duties on gross weight, packing can add a significant amount to import fees. To avoid the extremes of too much or too little packing, the marketer should consult export brokers, export freight forwarders, or other specialists.

All countries regulate the marking of imported goods and containers, and noncompliance can result in severe penalties. Recently announced Peruvian regulations require all imported foreign products to bear a brand name, country of origin, and an expiration date clearly inscribed on the product. In the case of imported wearing apparel, shoes, electric appliances, automotive parts, liquors, and soft drinks, the name and tax identity card number of the importer must also be added. Peruvian Customs refuse clearance to foreign products not fulfilling these requirements, and the importer has to reship the goods within 60 days of the customs appraisal date or they are seized and auctioned as abandoned goods. Further, goods already in Peru must meet the provisions of the decree or be subject to public auction.

The exporter must be careful that all markings on the container conform exactly to the data on the export documents because Customs officials often interpret discrepancies as an attempt to defraud. A basic source of information for American exporters is the Department of Commerce pamphlet series entitled *Preparing Shipment to [Country],* which details the necessary export documents and pertinent U.S. and foreign government regulations for labeling, marking, packing, and customs procedures.

Customs-Privileged Facilities

To facilitate export trade, countries designate areas within their borders as *customs-privileged facilities,* that is, areas where goods can be imported for storage and/or processing with tariffs and quota limits postponed until the products leave the designated areas. Foreign trade zones (also known as free trade zones), free ports, and in-bond arrangements are all types of customs-privileged facilities that countries use to promote foreign trade.[28]

Foreign Trade Zones

The number of countries with foreign trade zones (FTZs)[29] has increased as trade liberalization has spread through Africa, Latin America, eastern Europe, and other parts of Europe and Asia. Most FTZs function in a similar manner regardless of the host country.

In the United States, FTZs extend their services to thousands of firms engaged in a spectrum of international trade-related activities ranging from distribution to assembly and manufacturing. More than 300 foreign trade zones are located throughout the United States,[30] including New York, New Orleans, San Francisco, Seattle, Toledo, Honolulu, Mayagües (Puerto Rico), Kansas City, Little Rock, and Sault St. Marie. Goods subject to U.S. customs duties and quota restrictions can be landed in these zones for storage or such processing as repackaging, cleaning, and grading before being brought into the United States or reexported to another country.[31] Merchandise can be held in an FTZ even if it is subject to U.S. quota restrictions. When a particular quota opens up, the merchandise may then be immediately shipped into the United States. Merchandise subject to quotas may also be substantially transformed within a zone into articles that are not covered by quotas, and then shipped into the United States free of quota restrictions.

---

[28]Japan's version of the FTZ is called a foreign access zone (FAZ). It operates much like an FTZ. A complete description can be found on the JETRO Web site www.jetro.go.jp (search for FAZ).

[29]For a review of FTZs, see www.ia.ita.doc.gov/ftzpage.

[30]Matt Myerhoff, "Duty-Free Designation Seen as Lure to Business, Development," *Los Angeles Business Journal,* March 14, 2005.

[31]Andrew P. Doornaert, "New Way to Reduce Costs with Foreign Trade Zones," *Kansas City Daily News,* March 10, 2005.

CROSSING BORDERS 15.2 — Underwear, Outerwear, Sony Playstations, and Pointed Ears—What Do They Have in Common?

What do underwear, outerwear, pointed ears, and Sony Playstation2 have in common? Quotas, that's what!

Call the first one the Madonna Effect. Madonna, the voluptuous pop star, affected the interpretation of outerwear/underwear when the ever-vigilant U.S. Customs Service stopped a shipment of 880 bustiers at the U.S. border. The problem was quota and tariff violations. The shipper classified them as underwear, which comes into the United States without quota and tariff. Outerwear imports, however, have a quota and the Customs official classified the fashion item inspired by Madonna as "outerwear" and demanded the appropriate quota certificates.

"It was definitely outerwear. I've seen it; and I've seen the girls wearing it, and they're wearing it as outerwear." It took the importer three weeks to obtain sufficient outerwear quota allowances to cover the shipment; by that time, several retailers had canceled their orders.

Call the second the Video/Computer Effect. EU officials originally classified Sony's Playstation2 a video game and thus subject to a higher tariff than it would be if it were classified as a computer, which was Sony's desired classification. The Court of First Instance ruled that "it is intended mainly to be used to run video games," thus subject to millions of euros in customs duties as a video game. The appeals court sided with Sony on a technical error and reversed the decision. It really didn't make much difference since EU customs classifications were set to change six months later to allow computers and games consoles into the European Union with zero tariff.

Call the third the Vulcan Effect. EU officials applied the Vulcan death grip to Star Trek hero Spock. Likenesses of the pointy-eared Spock and other "nonhuman creatures" have fallen victim to an EU quota on dolls made in China. The EU Council of Ministers slapped a quota equivalent to $81.7 million on nonhuman dolls from China—but it left human dolls alone.

British Customs officials are in the unusual position of debating each doll's humanity. They have blacklisted teddy bears but cleared Batman and Robin. And although they have turned away Spock because of his Vulcan origins, they have admitted Star Trek's Captain Kirk. The Official Fan Club for Star Trek said the Customs officials "ought to cut Spock some slack" because his mother, Amanda, was human. But Britain's Customs office said, "We see no reason to change our interpretation. You don't find a human with ears that size."

Sources: Rosalind Resnick, "Busting Out of Tariff Quotas," *North American International Business* (now published as *International Business*), February 1991, p. 10; Dana Milbank, "British Customs Officials Consider Mr. Spock Dolls to Be Illegal Aliens," *Wall Street Journal*, August 2, 1994, p. B1; "EU Rejects Sony Customs Claim," *(Salt Lake City) Deseret News*, October 6, 2003.

In situations in which goods are imported into the United States to be combined with American-made goods and re-exported, the importer or exporter can avoid payment of U.S. import duties on the foreign portion and eliminate the complications of applying for a *drawback,* that is, a request for a refund from the government of 99 percent of the duties paid on imports later re-exported. Other benefits for companies utilizing foreign trade zones include lower insurance costs, because greater security is required in FTZs; more working capital, since duties are deferred until goods leave the zone; the opportunity to stockpile products when quotas are filled or while waiting for ideal market conditions; significant savings on goods or materials rejected, damaged, or scrapped, for which no duties are assessed; and exemption from paying duties on labor and overhead costs incurred in an FTZ, which are excluded in determining the value of the goods.[32]

Offshore Assembly (Maquiladoras)

Maquiladoras, in-bond companies, or *twin plants* are names given to a special type of customs-privileged facility that originated in Mexico in the early 1970s.[33] This type of facility has since expanded to other countries that have abundant, low-cost labor. Even though in-bond operations vary from country to country, the original arrangement between Mexico and the United States remains the most typical. In 1971, the Mexican and U.S. governments established an in-bond program that created a favorable opportunity for U.S. companies to use low-cost Mexican labor.

---

[32]See Chapter 18 for a discussion on using FTZs to help reduce price escalation.

[33]For a detailed explanation of maquiladoras, visit the U.S Treasury Department's site at www.itds.treas.gov/maquiladora.html.

The Mexican government allows U.S. processing, packaging, assembling, and/or repair plants located in the in-bond area to import parts and processed materials without import taxes, provided the finished products are re-exported to the United States or to another foreign country. In turn, the U.S. government permits the re-importation of the packaged, processed, assembled, or repaired goods with a reasonably low import tariff applied only to the value added while in Mexico. Originally goods processed in maquiladoras could not be sold in Mexico without first being shipped back to the United States and re-imported at regular Mexican tariffs. However, Mexican law was changed to allow maquiladoras, with special permission, the right to sell a maximum of 50 percent of their products in Mexico if they use some Mexican-made components.

The passage of NAFTA resulted in some changes in the rules governing maquiladoras. Preferential tariff treatment and all export performance requirements (for example, trade and foreign exchange balancing) have been eliminated for NAFTA countries. Also, 100 percent of all maquiladora-manufactured goods can be sold in Mexico versus the 50 percent permitted prior to NAFTA.[34]

More than 2,600 companies participate in the maquiladoras program, with finished products valued at more than $30 billion annually. Although still dominated by U.S. companies, the maquiladoras are no longer only American. Heavy investments are pouring in from Asia and Europe, spurring expansion at close to 7 percent annually. Products made in maquiladoras include electronics, healthcare items, automotive parts, furniture, clothing, and toys. In most in-bond arrangements, special trade privileges are also part of the process. The maquiladora arrangement is becoming more cost efficient for many companies that previously operated in Asia as Asian wage rates increase. Higher costs in Mexico are offset by the wage increases in Asia and increased shipping costs from Asia to the United States rather than from Mexico.

Logistics

When a company is primarily an exporter from a single country to a single market, the typical approach to the physical movement of goods is the selection of a dependable mode of transportation that ensures safe arrival of the goods within a reasonable time for a reasonable carrier cost.[35] As a company becomes global, such a solution to the movement of products could prove costly and highly inefficient for seller and buyer. As some global marketers say, the hardest part is not making the sale but getting the correct quantity of the product to customers in the required time frame at a cost that leaves enough margins for a profit.[36]

At some point in the growth and expansion of an international firm, costs other than transportation are such that an optimal cost solution to the physical movement of goods cannot be achieved without thinking of the physical distribution process as an integrated system. When an international marketer begins producing and selling in more than one country and becomes a global marketer, it is time to consider the concept of *logistics management,* a total systems approach to management of the distribution process that includes all activities involved in physically moving raw material, in-process inventory, and finished goods inventory from the point of origin to the point of use or consumption.[37]

Interdependence of Physical Distribution Activities

A *physical distribution system* involves more than the physical movement of goods. It includes location of plants and warehousing (storage), transportation mode, inventory quantities, and packing. The concept of physical distribution takes into account the interdependence of the costs of each activity; a decision involving one activity affects the cost

[34]See: "Maquiladoras," www.itds.treas.gov/maquiladora.html, 2004.

[35]Douglas J. Coates, "International Logistics," *World Trade,* March 2003, p. 28.

[36]Clyde E. Witt, "International Hires Global Trade Management Specialists," *Material Handling Management,* May 2005.

[37]An excellent source on this subject is Donald F. Wood et al., *International Logistics,* 2nd ed. (New York: Amacom, 2002).

Getting the product to market can mean multi-transportation modes from motorcycle delivery of moon cakes in Hanoi, to cargo containers in a U.S. port waiting to be loaded on to trucks, to air express service in Malaysia. More than 15 million containers are in use globally, and, by value, account for about 90 percent of the world's internationally traded cargo. For products using high value and time sensitive component parts manufactured worldwide, such air express services as provided by this DHL Worldwide Express Boeing 737 in Kuala Lumpur are vital. *(top: © Hoang Dinh Nam/AFP/Getty Images; left: © Macduff Everton/CORBIS; right: © Jimin Lai/AFP/Getty Images)*

and efficiency of one or all others. In fact, because of their interdependence, the sum of each of the different activity costs entails an infinite number of "total costs." (*Total cost* of the system is defined as the sum of the costs of all these activities.)

The idea of interdependence can be illustrated by the classic example of airfreight. Exhibit 15.9 is an illustration of an actual company's costs of shipping 44,000 peripheral boards worth $7.7 million from a Singapore plant to the U.S. West Coast using two modes of transportation—ocean freight and the seemingly more expensive airfreight. When considering only rates for transportation and carrying costs for inventory in transit, air transportation costs were approximately $57,000 higher than ocean freight. But notice that when total costs are calculated, airfreight was actually less costly than ocean freight because of other costs involved in the total physical distribution system.

To offset the slower ocean freight and the possibility of unforeseen delays and to ensure prompt customer delivery schedules, the company had to continuously maintain 30 days of inventory in Singapore and another 30 days' inventory at the company's distribution

Exhibit 15.9

Real Physical Distribution Costs between Air and Ocean Freight—Singapore to the United States

Source: Adapted from "Air and Adaptec's Competitive Strategy," *International Business*, September 1993, p. 44.

In this example, 44,000 peripheral boards worth $7.7 million are shipped from a Singapore plant to the U.S. West Coast. Cost of capital to finance inventories is 10 percent annually or $2,109 per day to finance $7.7 million.

	Ocean	**Air**
Transport costs	$ 31,790 (in transit 21 days)	$127,160 (in transit 3 days)
In-transit inventory financing costs	$ 44,289	$ 6,328
Total transportation costs	$ 76,179	$133,488
Warehousing inventory costs, Singapore and U.S.	(60 days @ $2,109 per day) $126,540	
Warehouse rent	$ 6,500	
Real physical distribution costs	$209,219	$133,488

centers. The costs of financing 60 days of inventory and of additional warehousing at both points—that is, real physical distribution costs—would result in the cost of ocean freight exceeding air by more than $75,000. And ocean freight may even entail additional costs such as higher damage rate, higher insurance, and higher packing rates.

Substantial savings can result from systematic examination of logistics costs and the calculation of total physical distribution costs. A large multinational firm with facilities and customers around the world shipped parts from its U.S. Midwest plant to the nearest East Coast port, then by water route around the Cape of Good Hope (Africa), and finally to its plants in Asia, taking 14 weeks. Substantial inventory was maintained in Asia as a safeguard against uncertain water-borne deliveries. The transportation carrier costs were the least expensive available; however, delivery delays and unreliable service caused the firm to make emergency air shipments to keep production lines going. As a result, air shipment costs rose to 70 percent of the total transport bill. An analysis of the problem in the physical distribution system showed that trucking the parts to West Coast ports using higher-cost motor carriers and then shipping them to Asia by sea could lower costs. Transit time was reduced, delivery reliability improved, inventory quantities in Asia lowered, and emergency air shipments eliminated. The new distribution system produced annual savings of $60,000.

Although a cost difference will not always be the case, the examples illustrate the interdependence of the various activities in the physical distribution mix and the total cost. A change of transportation mode can effect a change in packaging and handling, inventory costs, warehousing time and cost, and delivery charges.

The concept behind physical distribution is the achievement of the optimum (lowest) system cost consistent with customer service objectives of the firm. If the activities in the physical distribution system are viewed separately, without consideration of their interdependence, the final cost of distribution may be higher than the lowest possible cost (optimum cost) and the quality of service may be adversely affected. Additional variables and costs that are interdependent and must be included in the total physical distribution decision heighten the distribution problems confronting the international marketer. As the international firm broadens the scope of its operations, the additional variables and costs become more crucial in their effect on the efficiency of the distribution system.

One of the major benefits of the European Union's unification is the elimination of transportation barriers among member countries. Instead of approaching Europe on a country-by-country basis, a centralized logistics network can be developed. The trend in Europe is toward pan-European distribution centers. Studies indicate that companies operating in Europe may be able to cut 20 warehousing locations to 3 and maintain the same level of customer service. A German white goods manufacturer was able to reduce its European warehouses from 39 to 10, as well as improve its distribution and enhance customer service. By cutting the number of warehouses, it reduced total distribution and warehousing costs, brought down staff numbers, held fewer items of stock, provided greater access to regional markets, made better use of transport networks, and improved service to customers, all with a 21 percent reduction of total logistics costs.

Benefits of a Physical Distribution System

A system of physical distribution offers more benefits than cost advantages. An effective physical distribution system can result in optimal inventory levels and, in multiplant operations, optimal production capacity, both of which can maximize the use of working capital. In making plant-location decisions, a company with a physical distribution system can readily assess operating costs of alternative locations to serve various markets.

A physical distribution system may also result in better (more dependable) delivery service to the market; when production occurs at different locations, companies are able to determine quickly the most economical source for a particular customer. As companies expand into multinational markets and source these markets from multinational production facilities, they are increasingly confronted with cost variables that make it imperative to employ a total systems approach to the management of the distribution process to achieve efficient operation. Finally, a physical distribution system can render the natural obstructions created by geography less economically critical for the multinational marketer. Getting the product to market can mean multiple transportation modes, such as canal boats in China, pedal power in Vietnam, and speed trains in Japan or Europe.

Export Shipping and Warehousing

Whenever and however title to goods is transferred, those goods must be transported. Shipping goods to another country presents some important differences from shipping to a domestic site. The goods can be out of the shipper's control for longer periods of time than in domestic distribution, more shipping and collections documents are required, packing must be suitable, and shipping insurance coverage is necessarily more extensive. The task is to match each order of goods to the shipping modes best suited for swift, safe, and economical delivery. Ocean shipping, airfreight, air express, and parcel post are all possibilities. Ocean shipping is usually the least expensive and most frequently used method for heavy bulk shipment. For certain categories of goods, airfreight can be the most economical and certainly the speediest.

Shipping costs are an important factor in a product's price in export marketing, and the transportation mode must be selected in terms of the total impact on cost. One estimate is that logistics account for between 19 and 23 percent of the total cost of a finished product sold internationally. One of the important innovations in ocean shipping in reducing or controlling the high cost of transportation is the use of containerization.[38] Containerized shipments, in place of the traditional bulk handling of full loads or break-bulk operations, have resulted in intermodal transport between inland points, reduced costs, reduced losses from pilferage and damage, and simplified handling of international shipments.

With increased use of containerization, rail container service has developed in many countries to provide the international shipper with door-to-door movement of goods under seal, originating and terminating inland. This eliminates several loadings, unloading, and changes of carriers and reduces costs substantially. Unfortunately, such savings are not always possible for all types of cargo.

For many commodities of high unit value and low weight and volume, international airfreight is a reasonable choice. Airfreight has shown the fastest growth rate for freight transportation even though it accounts for only a fraction of total international shipments.[39] Although airfreight can cost two to five times the surface charges for general cargo, some cost reduction is realized through reduced packing requirements, paperwork, insurance, and the cost of money tied up in inventory. Although usually not enough to offset the higher rates charged for airfreight, it can, as illustrated in Exhibit 15.9, be a justifiable alternative if the commodity has high unit value or high inventory costs, or if delivery time is a concern. Many products moving to foreign markets meet these criteria.

---

[38]Joe DiRenzo and Chris Doane, "Shipping Containers—A Linchpin Issue in Maritime Security," *Naval Forces* 26, no. 1 (2005).

[39]"FedEx Is Top Cargo Airline," *Sunday Mail (Kuala Lumpur)*, December 4, 2004.

CROSSING **BORDERS 15.3**   If the Shoe Fits, Wear It . . . or Abandon It

Pilferage and theft are ongoing problems in shipping. These problems are constantly being addressed with different security strategies. Using containers for shipping is one of the more successful strategies, but containers also can be stolen. Such was the case in Los Angeles when thieves cut through security fencing at a major container terminal, drove a truck tractor into the area, and broke open a few containers until they found one with sports shoes that sell for $140 a pair in retail stores. They hooked up the container and drove out with their booty.

But the police had the last laugh. A week later, they found the container abandoned with its cargo intact. The U.S.-based shoe importer routinely ships all its left shoes in one container and all its right shoes in another. The thieves had stolen the container with left shoes.

Source: Adapted from John Davies, "Sneaking Up on Security," *International Business,* February 1997, p. 18.

In the last decade, the services available to the international shipper have continuously improved both in the home market and abroad. *Intermodal services,*[40] a transportation system that unites various modes of transportation into one seamless movement of goods from factory to the customer's port of entry, have become more efficient as deregulation has allowed the coupling of various modes of transportation. In addition, intermodal marketing companies (IMCs) have evolved to broker transportation services so that an exporter can make one transaction with an IMC that takes care of the movement of goods from factory to customer, rivaling the simplicity of single-mode freight transportation. The IMC stitches together each of the transportation modes involved in freight movements, which may reach as many as four separate transportation modes. All of this can be done within guaranteed periods, with 98 percent on-time performance schedules more the norm than the exception. As one logistics specialist commented, "No matter how fast or timely the ship carrying a 45 foot container from Shenzhen to Long Beach, it is the speed and dependability of the whole pipeline—the underlying modes and logistics functions to achieve the door-to-door requirements of the shipper that matters."[41]

Intermodal services in other parts of the world are not as advanced as in the United States. Europe is closest to providing similar services; however, deregulation and barriers that existed before unification have yet to be eliminated. Unlike truck transportation, Europe's 26 railways have not capitalized on the removal of borders in Europe's single market. Progress is being made as railroads are beginning to restructure, and a pan-European intermodal marketing company similar to those in the United States has been formed. Before long it will be possible to extend the services in the United States to European customers so that one transaction can be made to ensure freight delivery from a factory in the United States to a final customer in Europe. Such services are now becoming available in Asia and Latin America as improvements in transportation services are being made in both areas.

Rail transportation between the United States and Mexico improved with investments by Kansas City Southern and Union Pacific that have created a direct route from Chicago to Mexico City. Further, the proposed merger between Canadian National and Burlington Northern Santa Fe will establish a North American rail line from Canada into Mexico. U.S. railroad companies' investments in Brazil, New Zealand, and Britain call for major investments in the improvement of these rail systems. Moving goods rapidly and on a timely schedule is more important today than ever before, and the improvement of rail systems and the development of intermodal systems will go a long way toward making that possible.

Another innovation in transportation and logistics is the service provided by United Parcel Service (UPS), Federal Express (FedEx), and similar companies. In addition to providing airexpress service for packages, these companies are offering complete logistics management

[40]John V. Broadhurst, "From Highways to Skyways and Seaways—The Intermodal Challenge," *Public Roads,* July/August 2004.

[41]J. Douglas Coates, "International Logistics," *World Trade,* March 1, 2003, p. 28.

Two giant pandas, four-year-old male Le Le and two-year-old female Ya Ye, are being loaded onto the Panda Express, a FedEx plane, that is airlifting them from China to the Memphis, Tennessee, zoo for a ten-year visit. Whether it's pandas, time-sensitive deliveries, or cost-saving solutions, FedEx delivers high-value shipments door-to-door to as many as 210 countries. *(AP/Wide World Photos)*

services including support services for their clients—truly door-to-door delivery around the world. For example, FedEx will take a manufacturer's product, warehouse it, keep inventory, provide all the labor and technology, and move it throughout the world. FedEx can warehouse a computer system made in Malaysia, move it to Japan to be coupled with components from Taiwan, and then deliver a completed product to the final destination in yet another country. One client's experience illustrates how such a service can improve a company's distribution costs and service. The computer parts repair center of this company moved into a FedEx Express Distribution Center in Japan and was able to cut average total turnaround time from 45 days to 5 days while lowering cost. FedEx took over storage, control, and shipment of the parts using its own networks and aircraft. UPS offers similar services, including local parts stocking and defective return services in Europe, the Pacific Rim, and the Americas.

Distribution and its costs are an important part of every international transaction. Cheap labor may make Chinese clothing competitive in the United States, but if delays in shipment tie up working capital and cause winter coats to arrive in April, the advantage may be lost. Similarly, production machinery disabled for lack of a part can affect cost throughout the system, all of which might be avoided with a viable logistics system.

The globalization of marketing and manufacturing, in which component parts are made in several countries, assembled in some others, and serviced the world over, puts tremendous pressure on a company's ability to physically move goods. A narrow solution to physical movement of goods is the selection of transportation; a broader application is the concept of logistics management or physical distribution. When customers value broad product assortment, holding a great number of products or component parts in inventory increases the costs of the supplier. Although the need for warehousing can be reduced with direct deliveries from manufacturers, the value of direct deliveries is diminished when orders are received in several shipments and at different times. One solution to this problem is merge-in-transit, a distribution method in which goods shipped from several supply locations are consolidated into one final customer delivery point while they are in transit and then shipped as a unit to the customer.[42] As distribution systems become more complex and

---

[42]Mikko Karkkainen, Timo Ala-Risku, and Jan Holmstrom, "Increasing Customer Value and Decreasing Distribution Costs with Merge-in-Transit," *International Journal of Physical Distribution and Logistics Management* 33, no. 2 (2003), p. 132.

costly, merge-in-transit is one system designed to increase customer value and decrease distribution costs.

Foreign Freight Forwarder

The *foreign freight forwarder,* licensed by the Federal Maritime Commission, arranges for the shipment of goods as the agent for an exporter. The forwarder is an indispensable agent for an exporting firm that cannot afford an in-house specialist to handle paperwork and other export trade mechanics.[43]

Even in large companies with active export departments capable of handling documentation, a forwarder is useful as a shipment coordinator at the port of export or at the destination port. Besides arranging for complete shipping documentation, the full-service foreign freight forwarder provides information and advice on routing and scheduling, rates and related charges, consular and licensing requirements, labeling requirements, and export restrictions. Further, the agent offers shipping insurance, warehouse storage, packing and containerization, and ocean cargo or airfreight space.

An astute freight forwarder will also double-check all assumptions made on the export declaration, such as commodity classifications, and will check the list of denied parties and end uses. Both large and small shippers find freight forwarders' wide range of services useful and well worth the fees normally charged. In fact, for many shipments, forwarders can save on freight charges because they can consolidate shipments into larger, more economical quantities. Although many forwarders are available, more and more companies are using those that have joined alliances with shippers and become part of the larger multifaceted integrators discussed earlier. Experienced exporters regard the foreign freight forwarder as an important addition to in-house specialists.[44]

International Logistics and Supply Chain Management

As discussed previously, the essence of international logistics is to integrate all the steps necessary to move goods from supplier to manufacturer to customer. This means that a logistics system has to deal with an often disparate set of agents and activities—carriers, warehouses, export regulations, import regulations, customs agents, freight forwarders, and so on—each of which must be accessed individually by the logistics manager.[45] The goals are multidimensional and include cost minimization, increased levels of service, improved communication among customers or suppliers, and increased flexibility in terms of delivery and response time. The ability of firms to achieve these goals has been limited until recently because existing communication and knowledge links did not bring together all of the players in the process. The advent of information technology (IT) has allowed communication with the participants in real time via a single connection point.[46]

As illustrated in Crossing Borders 15.4, integrated software application systems like NextLinx[47] in conjunction with the Internet have enabled large companies such as Cisco Systems to manage their imports and exports more efficiently. Such software capabilities also afford companies such as UPS, FedEx, and DHL the means to integrate their core services with other service providers to offer a fully integrated logistics system to customers.

When a computer manufacturer has to coordinate supply chains that reach into China and Malaysia and Mexico and Portugal, software such as that provided by NextLinx, Descartes,[48] and others is used to fully automate its supply chain systems. Trucks, ships, trains, and planes cannot be made to travel much faster than they presently do; thus any additional speed has to come from better logistics management. An automated supply chain system can cut the time needed for deliveries from the Far East to warehouses in the United Kingdom from months to just 25 days.

---

[43]Marisa Mohd Isa, "International Freight Forwarding Made Easy," *New Straits Times,* January 17, 2005.

[44]For insight on all that a fully integrated freight forwarder can provide for a shipper, visit www.ups-scs.com.

[45]Annie Gregory, "Avoiding Supply Chain Strangulation," *Works Management,* Spring 2005.

[46]Clyde E. Witt, "Online Interface Eases Global Distribution," *Material Handling Management,* May 2005.

[47]See "NextLinx-Trade Collaborator: Software for Import and Export," at www.nextlinx.com/trd_col.html.

[48]For more information on these two software applications, visit www.nextlinx.com and www.descartes.com.

CROSSING BORDERS 15.4 | Global Trade Compliance

Besides the labyrinth of regulations, documentation requirements, and customs regulations that have traditionally been a part of export and import trade, stricter customs rules necessitated by national security further complicate the export/import process. Violation of these rules, even if inadvertent, can result in trade sanctions, fines, or imprisonments of executives.

The NextLinx Trade Import (NTI) Solution and the NextLinx Restricted Party (RPS) Screening Engine are two services offered by NextLinx that provide end-to-end visibility of the trade information used in processing entries through customs. They provide the user with prevalidated entry data and automatic shipping documentation for its network of global suppliers and carriers, and they identify whether a party to a shipment has been placed on any official denied persons or illegal transshipper list, blocked from import or export transactions, or sanctioned by a government for illegal acts such as child labor or convicted labor

violations. They also determine whether the user is transacting with an illegal, blocked, or sanctioned customer.

A user can expect to maximize opportunities for reducing costs in the customs entry process as well as improve overall operational efficiency by increasing its workload without increasing workforce. This service also provides an audit trail of all import transaction activities that encompasses the wide range of information necessary to help ensure compliant customs processing on the part of every import/export shipment made through the system.

Sources: "Global Knowledge," "Global Trade Applications," "Global Markets," and "White Paper," www.nextlinx.com; John Berry, "NextLinx Helps Sites Sell Globally," *InternetWeek*, June 5, 2000, p. 41; "Quova, NextLinx Partner to Enhance Global Trade Compliance," *PR Newswire*, February 24, 2005; "Leggett and Platt Selects NextLinx to Streamline Imports," *Business Wire*, March 15, 2005.

For companies not wishing to maintain a fully automated supply chain system in-house, 3PL providers[49] or integrators such as UPS Logistics Group[50] can process and store all inventory and then ship it within two hours to the precise plant location where it is needed.[51] They can also handle such tasks as customs clearance and return and repair of certain merchandise. Manufacturers can shift their supply chain structures much more rapidly and with less pain than is the case with vertically integrated operations.[52]

By providing inventory management, order fulfillment, and collections, integrators can assist e-commerce customers to more quickly enter new markets without having to invest in warehousing and distribution centers. The scramble is on to be able to fulfill orders that come from anywhere in the world without having to set up significant operations in such markets. The less onerous the process of moving products across a particular border, the easier it becomes for manufacturers to set up where it makes sense for business. Speed is perhaps the most essential goal for any manufacturer looking to develop a 21st-century supply chain.[53]

Terrorism and Logistics

Before the terrorist attack on New York's World Trade Center (9/11), international marketers had to contend with myriad details of exporting. Most companies had internal systems to manage documentation, customs, shipping, and other activities necessary to comply with cross-border marketing. "Security" referred to prevention of theft or pilferage.

---

[49]A. Michael Knemeyer and Paul R. Murphy, "Exploring the Potential Impact or Relationship Characteristics and Customer Attributes on the Outcomes of Third-Party Logistics Arrangements," *Transportation Journal*, Winter 2005.

[50]For a survey of the various services provided by UPS, visit www.ups-scs.com/logistics.

[51]John D. Schultz, "Four Questions to Ask Before Hiring a 3PL," *Transport Topics*, March 21, 2005.

[52]See, for example, Edmund Prater and Soumen Ghosh, "Current Operational Practices of U.S. Small and Medium-Sized Enterprises in Europe," *Journal of Small Business Management*, April 2005.

[53]Annie Gregory, "Avoiding Supply Chain Strangulation," *Works Management*, Spring 2005.

After 9/11, homeland security added a crucial step in logistics management—vigilance at each point in the export/import process. With more than 23 million sea, truck, and rail containers entering the United States each year,[54] guarding against the possibility that shipping will be used as a conduit into the United States for terrorists' weapons is critical. The Cargo and Container Security Initiative (CSI) is one of the U.S. government's first efforts to enhance post-9/11 security.[55]

Cargo and Container Security Initiative

CSI (24-hour rule) requires sea carriers and NVOCC (Non-Vessel Operating Common Carriers)[56] to provide U.S. Customs with detailed descriptions (manifests) of the contents of containers bound for the United States 24 hours before a container is loaded on board a vessel. Trucking companies are also bound by the 24-hour rule and are expected to provide a manifest 4 hours before trucks are loaded with products entering the United States and 24 hours in advance when leaving the United States.

United States Customs officer helps direct the use of a mobile gamma ray scanner to reveal the contents of a steel-shipping container, one of the 20 million closed containers that carry cargo into the United States each year. The device, used to help reveal nuclear, biological, or chemical threats inside, is one of more than 100 gamma and x-ray inspection devices deployed at major ports and border crossings into the United States. (*AP/Wide World Photos*)

The rule allows U.S. Customs officers time to analyze the contents of the container or truck and identify potential terrorist threats before the U.S.-bound shipment is loaded at a foreign port rather than after it arrives at a U.S. port. Cargo manifests must use precise terms as parts of the 24-hour rule; "Freight-All-Kinds" and "Said-to-Contain" or "General Merchandise," descriptions often used in the past, are no longer acceptable.[57] If any discrepancy appears on the manifest and if it is not presented 24 hours before loading, the shipment can be denied loading and entry into a U.S. port. Whenever an invalid cargo description is used, a "Do Not Load" message is posted and loading is denied. Cargo bound for a foreign port loaded on a vessel with cargo bound for the United States must also have a valid manifest presented within 24 hours or it will not be allowed to be shipped. A violation of the 24-hour rule may prevent the vessel from loading cargo or from unloading any cargo even if the violation applies to only one container.[58]

In an effort to safeguard food against bioterrorism, U.S. Customs and Border Protection (CBP) requires the Food and Drug Administration (FDA) to receive prior notice of all food for humans and animals imported or offered for import into the United States. Carriers must file notice two hours before reaching a port of entry. Without prior notification, CBP will hold the goods at the port of entry or at an FDA-registered secure facility.[59] Food offered for import with no prior notice or inadequate prior notice will be refused admission. Similar rules apply to drugs and medical devices.

Ports became the gatekeepers for the entire supply chain in preventing illegal entry of terrorists and weapons of mass destruction. They were expected to accomplish this task without interruption of service and without additional cost to shippers. Early on, government regulators saw that if the burden of compliance was not going to slow the movement of goods across borders to a snail's pace,[60] cooperation and compliance throughout the supply chain was necessary.

[54]"Customs to Ratchet Up C-TPAT Requirements for Importers," *Logistics Management,* February 2005.

[55]"U.S. Senator Calls for Enhanced Security at U.S. Seaports," *Xinhua News Agency*, February 24, 2005.

[56]Trucks, railroads, and other nonocean carriers.

[57]"Customs Issues 'No-Load' Directives on the 24-Hour Rule," *Customs & Border Protection, U.S. Department of Homeland Security,* www.cbp.gov, February 13, 2003.

[58]"Severe Penalty for Violation of U.S. Customs Rule," *Business Times (Malaysia)*, February 17, 2003.

[59]Terrence Nguyen, "Food Haulers Face Border Regs," *Fleet Owner,* July 2004.

[60]James A. Cooke, "Customs to Ratchet Up C-TPAT Requirements for Importers," *Logistics Management,* February 2005.

Customs–Trade Partnership against Terrorism

The Customs–Trade Partnership against Terrorism (C-TPAT) is a joint initiative between government and business designed to augment the 24-hour rule by extending security procedures throughout the supply chain. C-TPAT requires importers to establish a documented program for security-risk assessment of overseas suppliers. By requiring importers to establish a documented program for security-risk assessment of overseas suppliers throughout the supply chain, companies will ensure a more secure supply chain for their employees, suppliers, and customers, thus improving the flow of trade. Participation in C-TPAT means faster cargo processing at the border, reduced number of inspections, dedicated commercial lanes for more rapid border crossings, and an emphasis on self-policing rather than customs verification. Without C-TPAT accreditation, an importer will encounter countless inspections and delays.

C-TPAT certification requires members to:

- Conduct a comprehensive self-assessment of supply-chain security using C-TPAT guidelines jointly developed by U.S. Customs and the trade community.
- Submit a supply-chain security questionnaire to U.S. Customs.
- Identify and complete security checks of vendors and suppliers.[61]
- Record customs clearance documents and purchase orders.
- Ensure minimum-security standards and procedures for employee screening and facilities security by suppliers.
- Implement a program to communicate C-TPAT guidelines to companies in the supply chain and work toward building the guidelines into relationships with these companies.
- Maintain strict container security procedures, including security seals that are subject to periodic rigorous integrity examination and physical access controls in storage areas to eliminate unauthorized entry, pilferage, and sabotage.[62]

Even though C-TPAT applies only to U.S. importers, it is important for exporters outside the United States to know that they must also comply in order to be certified to remain in the supply chain[63] and thus benefit from faster processing at U.S. borders.

C-TPAT is an evolving process and customs is continually seeking ways to ensure that suppliers and intermediaries, such as freight forwarders and carriers, have systems and processes in place to promote trustworthiness and to document shipments fully and precisely.[64] Innovative software,[65] advances in information technology (IT), and electronic tracking are integral components in the successful implementation of C-TPAT.

Electronic Tracking

To further strengthen C-TPAT, U.S. Customs and Border Protection (CBP) announced plans for electronic container tracking as an integral part of the process. C-TPAT-Plus, as it is called, offers shippers immediate turnaround with no inspection upon arrival in exchange for including technologies that can electronically track incoming containers, monitor them for tampering from the point of origin, and provide a record of events[66] while in transit. Such tracking can include RFID[67] (radio frequency identification), GPS (global positioning systems), cellular, satellite, ultra-wide-band, "Bluetooth," bar codes,[68] and optical character

[61]"6 Areas Define Purchasing Role in Import Compliance" *Managing Exports*, June 2005.

[62]Raphael Madarang, "Tax Wise or Otherwise Stricter U.S. Customs Rules," *Business World,* May 12, 2005.

[63]A fact sheet with additional specific data about C-TPAT can be found at: "C-TPAT Fact Sheet and Frequently Asked Questions," May 2005 www.customs.gov search: C-TPAT facts.

[64]"C-TPAT Must Succeed—Or World Trade Faces the Consequences," *Material Handling Management,* www.mhmonline.com.

[65]"New UPS Software Simplifies Trade by Tackling Compliance Obstacles," *Business Wire,* May 23, 2005.

[66]"Government Mandates Key to Electronic Container Tracking Success," *Microwave Journal,* March 2005.

[67]For a discussion of how RFID works and some of the problems and benefits associated with this system, see: Perry A. Trunick and Dan Williams, "Stay Loose for the RFID Stretch Run," *Logistics Today,* March 2005.

[68]Elena Malykhina, "Bar Codes Expected to Have a Long Life," *Information Week,* October 21, 2004.

Exhibit 15.10
Radio Frequency Identification

As potential for a security breach, each of the 42 million containers imported annually is a Trojan horse. Companies and customs are seeking ways to ensure the security of cargo without causing undue delays in the movement of goods. RFID is a flexible system that is adaptable to different needs and has the potential to provide both the shipper and customs with information in real time as goods move through the supply chain.

By attaching an RFID tag, any item—shipping container, pallet, packing crate, or package—can be located and/or tracked from point of origin to final destination, gathering information along the way.

An RFID network consists of two primary components—a transponder and a reader. The transponder, commonly referred to as the tag, is a device that generates electrical signals interpreted by the reader. Transponders can be active (self-powered by internal battery) or passive (powered by magnetic field). Transponders can be read only or they can be read/write for applications that require data to be updated dynamically and stored in the transponder. Read–write tags allow identification data to be changed during normal operations when variable data are more important than a unique identity

The reader is a transmitter–receiver combination (transceiver) that activates and reads the identification signals from the transponder. A part of the reader is a microprocessor that can decode, perform simple calculations, and forward the information to a centrally located computer system for recordkeeping and processing.

The transponder (tag) is the backbone of the RFID system. It stores an identification code and other pertinent data and then transmits the data when the transceiver sends activation signals to it and receives identification data from the tag.

A read-only tag has an ID code plus other information such as the manifest, destination, shipping port, receiving port, and any other pertinent information the shipper desires. Each tag carries a mini-databank that identifies a particular item and contains accounting and inventory system information. Up to 70 pages of text can be coded on a tag. When a container with a tag passes an entry–exit point equipped with readers, its location is precisely recorded so managers can respond to any unanticipated changes. Further, any data desired can be accessed and sent to the shipper, customs, or anyone else needing the information.

RFID is ideal for a shipping company. Multiton cargo containers in an Asian port, for example, can be tracked daily using RFID to assist in loading and unloading at numerous ship berths and countless truck loading areas. Transponders are embedded in the ground throughout the port. When cranes hoist cargo on and off ships and trucks, the lifting arm–mounted readers interrogate each transponder and match the code with the yard location. Managers have real-time information on the location and destination of each container, and these data can be relayed to customs authorities before the arrival, thereby expediting border crossings.

Besides the basic read-only tag, transponders can also have read and write capabilities, which allow for data to be changed dynamically at any time. Read–write tags have the ability to receive information from a variety of sensors that can also be installed in a container. Sensors to detect changes in humidity within a container and others that detect changes in pressure and light to detect if the door has been opened can feed information to the RFID tag, which can then alert operators to the possibility of tampering or theft. An integrated environmental sensor module monitors temperature, humidity, and shock throughout the container's journey, allowing shippers, carriers, and logistics providers to detect spoilage or damage to goods. One system under development includes sensors that detect specific chemical, biological, and nuclear threats. The sensor data is sent in real time to a powerful transmitter on the ship, which can transmit the data via a satellite to authorities on shore. The system can also include sensors that monitor light, heat, motion, and shock, allowing it to detect conditions that might damage cargo. In addition, each container is monitored by GPS, so its location can be tracked worldwide.

Tags can verify that a container was loaded at a secure loading point, significantly reducing the likelihood that tampering will occur in transit, gather enough data to conduct a "virtual inspection" in advance of arrival, and guarantee that shipping containers meet governmental security regulations. Shipments that satisfy government regulations will avoid extensive delays in shipment and receipt and minimize cost of handling.

Sources: Mary Davis, "Smart Tags Bring Security to Containers Entering U.S.," *Modern Bulk Transporter,* July 2004; Tom Kevan, "High-Tech Container Security: Pressed to Protect Cargo from Damage, Theft, and Terrorists Threats, Business and Government Turn to Wireless Sensors and RFID Tags," *Frontline Solutions,* July 2004; Dick Caro, "RFID Unites the Supply Chain," *Instrument Society of America,* March 2005; Diane Brady, "Secure Containers for $10 a Pop," *BusinessWeek,* January 12, 2005.

recognition. Although numerous technological devices are available, none has been more widely implemented than bar codes and RFID.

For nearly 10 years, the U.S. Department of Defense has been using RFID tags on freight containers (see Exhibit 15.10). The Defense Department asks its suppliers to affix RFID tags on cases and pallets they ship to key receiving sites.[69] RFID tags provide different monitoring capabilities, but all track a container or pallet while in transit and in some cases communicate with a receiver at the border or elsewhere. Substantial disruptions in transit are avoided if security questions relating to a cargo shipment have been addressed prior to a vessel being loaded and sailing and then monitored while in transit.[70] RFID promises to deliver cost savings of up to $1.8 trillion globally. Domestically, Wal-Mart,[71] Gillette, Procter &Gamble, and Unilever are all adopting RFID.[72]

Satellite-based positioning systems that register when a container is taken off its predetermined route, weight sensors that register when a container weighs more than originally logged onto shipping documents, and radio tags that automatically report any in-transit intrusion to the destination customs and port authorities[73] are examples of some of the more advanced systems being developed and implemented.

Another promising tracking system, the Tamper Evident Secure Container (TESC), a palm-size device that is embedded in a container's wall, detects unauthorized access to any part of the door (including hinges) through a wireless network.[74] The technology can also be adapted to detect holes around the perimeter as well as humans inside the containers. Upon the delivery of a container, an inspector can use a wireless reader to check and disarm the device.[75]

Even with all the checking and vetting, people in the supply chain are the weakest link and without vigilance among warehouse managers, shippers, and port operators, technology can provide only part of the security needed to protect our borders.[76] We are entering a security economy where everybody has to take responsibility for the safety of the supply chain.

---

[69]For a detailed discussion of how RFID was used successfully in Afghanistan and Iraq, see Peter Galuszka, "Lessons from Baghdad," *Chief Executive,* May 2005.

[70]"World Shipping Council President Chris Koch Testifies before Senate Committee; Urges Enhance Cargo Container Screening Overseas," *PR Newswire,* May 18, 2005.

[71]John S. McClenahen, "Wal-Mart's Big Gamble," *Industry Week,* April 2005.

[72]"Business Must Tune In to the Radio Frequency," *Sunday Herald (Glasgow, UK),* October 10, 2004.

[73]"Avante to License and Deploy Its RFID Cargo Seal to Secure Container Shipping," *Business Wire,* April 6, 2005.

[74]Diane Brady, "Secure Containers for $10 a Pop," *BusinessWeek,* January 12, 2005.

[75]Ann Keeton, "Sensors on Containers May Offer Safer Shipping," *Wall Street Journal,* March 31, 2005, p. B-4.

[76]Henry E. Teitelbaum, "Focus: Continued Risk Seen in Global Cargo Shipping," *Wall Street Journal,* May 16, 2005.

Summary

An awareness of the mechanics of export trade is indispensable to the foreign marketer who engages in exporting goods from one country to another. Although most marketing techniques are open to interpretation and creative application, the mechanics of exporting are exact; they offer little room for interpretation or improvisation with the requirements of export licenses, quotas, tariffs, export documents, packing, marking, and the various uses of commercial payments. The very nature of the regulations and restrictions surrounding importing and exporting can lead to frequent and rapid change. In handling the mechanics of export trade successfully, the manufacturer must keep abreast of all foreign and domestic changes in requirements and regulations pertaining to the product involved. For firms unable to maintain their own export staffs, foreign freight forwarders can handle many details for a nominal fee.

With paperwork completed, the physical movement of goods must be considered. Transportation mode affects total product cost because of the varying requirements of packing, inventory levels, time requirements, perishability, unit cost, damage and pilfering losses, and customer service. Transportation for each product must be assessed in view of the interdependent nature of all these factors. To ensure optimum distribution at minimal cost, a physical distribution system determines everything from plant location to final customer delivery in terms of the most efficient use of capital investment, resources, production, inventory, packing, and transportation. The seemingly endless rules, regulations of exporting, the demands of efficient global logistics and the absolute necessity to comply with national security regulations can be daunting. Fortunately, the continuous innovations in information technology, the Internet, and software programs can minimize much of the burden associated with global marketing.

Questions

1. Define and show the significance to international marketing of the following terms:

Commerce Control List (CCL)	CSI
Classification Number (ECCN)	RFID
	bill of lading
Commerce Country Chart (CCC)	commercial invoice
	customs-privileged facilities
export regulations	foreign-trade zone
import regulations	maquiladora
Export Administrative Regulations (EAR)	export control
	forfaiting
logistics management	physical distribution system
consular invoice	merge-in-transit
letter of credit	SNAP
bill of exchange	ELAIN
24-hour rule	STELA
C-TPAT	ERIC

2. Explain the reasoning behind the various regulations and restrictions imposed on the exportation and importation of goods.

3. What determines the type of license needed for exportation? Discuss.

4. Discuss the most frequently encountered trade restrictions.

5. What is the purpose of an import license? Discuss.

6. Explain foreign-trade zones and illustrate how an exporter may use them. How do foreign-trade zones differ from bonded warehouses?

7. How do in-bond areas differ from foreign-trade zones? How would an international marketer use an in-bond area?

8. Explain each of the following export documents:
   a. Bill of lading
   b. Consular invoice
   c. Commercial invoice
   d. Insurance certificate

9. Why would an exporter use the services of a foreign freight forwarder? Discuss.

10. Besides cost advantages, what are the other benefits of an effective physical distribution system?

11. Explain how merge-in-transit can be beneficial to all parties in the distribution process.

12. Discuss customs-privileged facilities. How are they used?

13. Why would a company engage the services of an intermodal transportation service instead of performing activities in-house?

14. You are the manager of a small company that manufactures and sells various types of personal restraints (e.g., handcuffs and leg irons). Your customers are law enforcement agencies, private security companies, and novelty stores. You receive a large order from an importer in Madrid that you have never done business with, although you have previously sold your product in Spain. Do you need a special export license? Outline the steps you would take to ensure that your transaction is legal. (Note: The solution to this problem cannot be completely answered from information in the text. Additional information will have to be obtained from sources on the Internet.)

15. You are the sales manager of a small company with sales in the United States. About 30 percent of your business is mail order and the remainder is from your two retail stores. You recently created an e-store on the Web and a few days later received an order from a potential customer from a city near Paris, France. The shipping charges listed on the Web are all for locations in the United States. You don't want to lose this $350 order. You know you can use the postal service but the customer indicated she wanted the item in about a week. Air express seems logical, but how much will it cost? Consult both the FedEx home page (www.fedex.com) and the UPS home page (www.ups.com) to get some estimates on shipping costs. Here are some details you will need: value $350; total weight of the package, 2.5 pounds; package dimensions, 4 inches high by 6 inches wide; U.S. zip code, 97035; and French zip code, 91400. (Note: It's not fair to call UPS or FedEx—use the Internet.)

16. Based on the information collected in question 15, how practical would it be to encourage foreign sales? Your average order ranges from about $250 to $800. All prices are quoted plus shipping and handling. You handle a fairly exclusive line of Southwestern Indian jewelry that sells for about 15 to 20 percent higher in Europe than in the United States. The products are lightweight and high in value.

17. Discuss the principal requirements for gaining C-TPAT certification.

18. The Global Perspective illustrates a shipment from the United States to a Chinese customer. If the shipment had been from a Chinese manufacturer to a U.S. company, what would the U.S. company have to do to ensure compliance with all U.S. antiterrorism requirements?

16

integrated marketing communications and international advertising

CHAPTER OUTLINE

Global Perspective: Barbie versus Mulan

Sales Promotions in International Markets

International Public Relations

International Advertising

Advertising Strategy and Goals
> Product Attribute and Benefit Segmentation
> Regional Segmentation

The Message: Creative Challenges
> Global Advertising and the Communications Process
> Legal Constraints
> Linguistic Limitations
> Cultural Diversity
> Media Limitations
> Production and Cost Limitations

Media Planning and Analysis
> Tactical Considerations

Campaign Execution and Advertising Agencies

International Control of Advertising: Broader Issues

CHAPTER LEARNING OBJECTIVES

What you should learn from Chapter 16:

- Local market characteristics that affect the advertising and promotion of products

- The strengths and weaknesses of sales promotion and public relations in global marketing

- When global advertising is most effective; when modified advertising is necessary

- The effects of a single European market on advertising

- The effect of limited media, excessive media, paper and equipment shortages, and government regulations on advertising and promotion budgets

- The communication process and advertising misfires

Global Perspective

BARBIE VERSUS MULAN

For years, Barbie dolls sold in Japan looked different from their U.S. counterparts. They had Asian facial features, black hair, and Japanese-inspired fashions. Then Mattel Inc. conducted consumer research around the world and learned something surprising: The original Barbie, with her yellow hair and blue eyes, played as well in Hong Kong as it did in Hollywood. Girls didn't care if Barbie didn't look like them. "It's all about fantasies and hair," says Peter Broegger, general manager of Mattel's Asian operations. "Blond Barbie sells just as well in Asia as in the U.S."

Major toy makers are rethinking one of the basic tenets of their $55 billion global industry—that children in different countries want different playthings. The implications are significant for both kids and companies. In the past, giants such as Mattel, Hasbro Inc., and Lego Co. produced toys and gear in a variety of styles. Increasingly, they are designing and marketing one version worldwide. This has led to a series of massive merchandise blitzkriegs, with companies deluging boys and girls around the globe simultaneously with identical dolls, cars, and gadgets.

For example, Mattel's Rapunzel Barbie, whose ankle-length blonde locks cascade down her pink ball gown, was released on the same day last fall in 59 countries including the United States—the company's biggest product launch ever. Since then, Rapunzel Barbie and related merchandise has generated $200 million in global sales, nearly half of that outside the United States. Mattel no longer makes Asian-featured Barbies.

Two recent developments are changing kids' tastes. One is the rapid worldwide expansion of cable and satellite TV channels, which along with movies and the Internet expose millions of kids to the same popular icons. For example, Walt Disney Co. now operates 24 Disney-branded cable and satellite channels in 67 countries outside the United States—up from zero eight years ago. The other development is the widening international reach of retailing giants such as Wal-Mart Stores Inc., Toys "R" Us Inc., and Carrefour SA, which have opened some 2,300 stores outside their home markets. Increasingly, the mass retailers enter into exclusive deals with toy and consumer-products companies, allowing them to stage huge, coordinated promotional campaigns.

For example, when Rapunzel Barbie had its debut, Wal-Mart stores in South Korea and China hired local women to dress up like the doll and greet children as they entered. At the same time, the Mattel TV ad campaign was broadcast around the world in 15-, 20-, and 30-second spots—in 35 different languages. Mattel's Barbie Web site, which has eight language options, featured Rapunzel stories and games. A computer-animated movie, called *Barbie as Rapunzel,* was broadcast on TV and released on video and DVD around the world, and it was even shown in some theaters overseas.

In Madrid, the launch was accompanied by a "premiere" of the movie and special promotions of comb sets and other accessories at Carrefour stores across Spain. After attending the premiere, the kids could and did buy the dolls. For some parents this means Christmas shopping later in the year at the often frenetic Toys "R" Us in Madrid for stuffed dragons from the movie or a Barbie laptop computer, a Barbie kitchen set, a Barbie travel van, and a host of other Barbie gadgets and accessories.

Some toys, games, and animated characters don't cross national boundaries. German children, for example, rarely play with action figures. According to the NPD Group, which tracks toy sales, action figures make up just 1 percent of the German toy market, compared with 5 percent of the U.S. and 6 percent of the U.K. toy markets. American kids want Nascar toy cars, while European kids want Formula One models. Cheerleader-themed anything is irrelevant outside the United States. And few American companies sell toys in the Islamic world. Mattel, the world's largest toy company, has no plans to do so.

Perhaps Disney's Jasmine will well sell there, although she's actually inappropriately dressed for many of Islamic faith. Jasmine is just one of the new series of "Princess" dolls aimed directly at Barbie's dominance of the doll category. Snow White, Pocahontas, and Mulan are others in the band. Their diversity may have broader appeal. Disney uses pink in the packaging and Mattel objects. Disney is also mindful of the fashion-conscious Barbie critics. Disney Princess is more about tiaras and wands rather than handbags and high heels. Where Barbie is more a role model, and therefore objectionable to parents, Disney is putting its emphasis on the fantasy. Too bad someone isn't emphasizing education.

Indeed, too bad for Mattel—despite the comprehensiveness of the integrated marketing communications plan described above, the sales of Barbie declined sharply. Competitors' more ethnically diverse product lines sold better, including Mulan, Bratz, and Fulla, as described in Chapter 5.

Sources: Lisa Bannon and Carlta Vitshum, "One-Toy-Fits-All: How Industry Learned to Love the Global Kid," *Wall Street Journal,* April 29, 2003, p. A1; "A Challenge to Barbie, Toy Franchises," *The Economist,* April 19, 2003, p. 66; Christopher Palmeri, "Hair-Pulling in the Dollhouse," *BusinessWeek*, May 2, 2005, pp. 76–77.

Integrated marketing communications (IMC) are composed of advertising, sales promotions, trade shows, personal selling, direct selling, and public relations—almost all are included in the Barbie campaign described in the Global Perspective. Indeed, even the original *Wall Street Journal* story itself was most likely prompted by a company press release. All these mutually reinforcing elements of the promotional mix have as their common objective the successful sale of a product or service. In many markets the availability of appropriate communication channels to customers can determine entry decisions. For example, most toy manufacturers would agree that toys cannot be marketed profitably in countries without commercial television advertising directed toward children. Thus product and service development must be informed by research regarding the availability of communication channels. Once a market offering is developed to meet target market needs, intended customers must be informed of the offering's value and availability. Often different messages are appropriate for different communications channels, and vice versa.

For most companies, advertising and personal selling are the major components in the marketing communications mix. In this chapter, the other elements of IMC not covered in previous chapters are briefly discussed first. The goal of most companies is to achieve the synergies possible when sales promotions, public relations efforts, and advertising are used in concert. However, the primary focus of this chapter is on international advertising. The topic of the next chapter is global sales management.

Sales Promotions in International Markets

Sales promotions are marketing activities that stimulate consumer purchases and improve retailer or middlemen effectiveness and cooperation. Cents off, in-store demonstrations, samples, coupons, gifts, product tie-ins, contests, sweepstakes, sponsorship of special events such as concerts and fairs (even donut parades), and point-of-purchase displays are types of sales promotion devices designed to supplement advertising and personal selling in the promotional mix. The Rapunzel Barbie movie premiere is too.

Sales promotions are short-term efforts directed to the consumer or retailer to achieve such specific objectives as consumer-product trial or immediate purchase, consumer introduction to the store, gaining retail point-of-purchase displays, encouraging stores to stock the product, and supporting and augmenting advertising and personal sales efforts. For example, Procter & Gamble's introduction of Ariel detergent in Egypt included the "Ariel Road Show," a puppet show (not the Little Mermaid!) that was taken to local markets in villages, where more than half of all Egyptians still live. The show drew huge crowds, entertained people, told about Ariel's better performance without the use of additives, and sold the brand through a distribution van at a nominal discount. Besides creating brand awareness for Ariel, the road show helped overcome the reluctance of the rural retailers to handle the premium-priced Ariel. Perhaps our all-time favorite example in this genre is the Simpsons' international festival sponsored by Fox in Hollywood in 2000. Spain's Simpson trivia champion defeated 11 other global contestants in the "Bart Bowl World Finals."

In markets where the consumer is hard to reach because of media limitations, the percentage of the promotional budget allocated to sales promotions may have to be increased. In some less-developed countries, sales promotions constitute the major portion of the promotional effort in rural and less-accessible parts of the market. In parts of Latin America, a portion of the advertising-sales budget for both Pepsi-Cola and Coca-Cola is spent on carnival trucks, which make frequent trips to outlying villages to promote their products. When a carnival truck makes a stop in a village, it may show a movie or provide some other kind of entertainment; the price of admission is an unopened bottle of the product purchased from the local retailer. The unopened bottle is to be exchanged for a cold bottle plus a coupon for another bottle. This promotional effort tends to stimulate sales and encourages local retailers, who are given prior notice of the carnival truck's arrival, to stock the product. Nearly 100 percent coverage of retailers in the village is achieved with this type of promotion. In other situations, village merchants may be given free samples, have the outsides of their stores painted, or receive clock signs in attempts to promote sales.

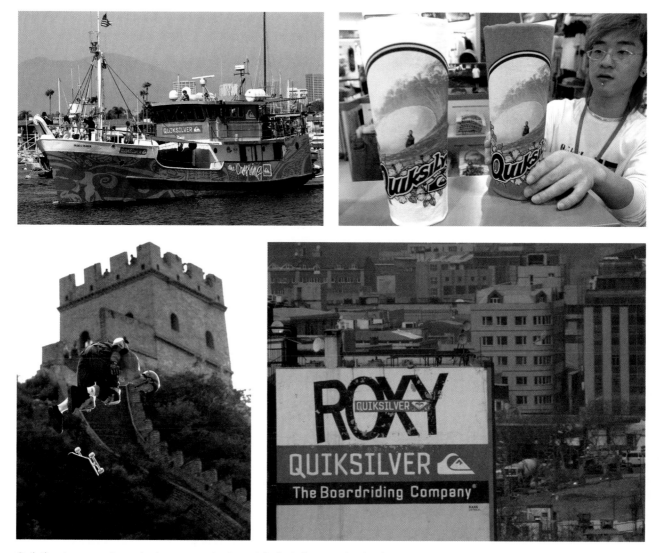

Quiksilver integrates its marketing communications globally. At home in the OC the company supports the Ocean Institute financially and with a visit from its Indies Trader boat, which travels the world promoting clean water environments and, of course, the company image. Quiksilver sponsored the 2005 Great Wall of China first-ever leap by Danny Way, a southern California skateboarder. The firm uses perhaps the broadest array of advertising media as well—T-shirts displayed in Shanghai and walls in Istanbul. *(top left: © tomcozad/newportsurfshot. com; top right: AP/Wide World Photos; bottom left: AP/Wide World Photos)*

An especially effective promotional tool when the product concept is new or has a very small market share is product sampling. Nestlé Baby Foods faced such a problem in France in its attempt to gain share from Gerber, the leader. The company combined sampling with a novel sales promotion program to gain brand recognition and to build goodwill. Since most French people take off for a long vacation in the summertime, piling the whole family into the car and staying at well-maintained campgrounds, Nestlé provided rest-stop structures along the highway where parents could feed and change their babies. Sparkling clean *Le Relais Bébés* are located along main travel routes. Sixty-four hostesses at these rest stops welcome 120,000 baby visits and dispense 600,000 samples of baby food each year. There are free disposable diapers, a changing table, and high chairs for the babies to sit in while dining. Finally, while all software firms decry piracy in foreign markets as a costly crime, most recognize that in some senses it is actually a form of product trial.[1]

---

[1]Ashutosh Prasad and Vijay Mahajan, "How Many Pirates Should a Software Firm Tolerate? An Analysis of Piracy Protection on the Diffusion of Software," *International Journal of Research in Marketing* 20, no. 4 (2003), pp. 337–353.

As is true in advertising, the success of a promotion may depend on local adaptation. Further, research has shown that responses to promotions can vary across promotional types[2] and cultures. Major constraints are imposed by local laws, which may not permit premiums or free gifts to be given. Some countries' laws control the amount of discount given at retail, others require permits for all sales promotions, and in at least one country, no competitor is permitted to spend more on a sales promotion than any other company selling the product. Effective sales promotions can enhance the advertising and personal selling efforts and, in some instances, may be effective substitutes when environmental constraints prevent full utilization of advertising.

International Public Relations

Creating good relationships with the popular press and other media to help companies communicate messages to their publics—customers, the general public, and governmental regulators—is the role of *public relations (PR)*.[3] The job consists of not only encouraging the press to cover positive stories about companies (as in the Barbie story), but also of managing unfavorable rumors, stories, and events. Regarding the latter, the distinction between advertising and public relations has become an issue now considered by the United States Supreme Court. Nike was criticized for using "sweatshop" labor in Asia and responded to critics with paid advertising. The Court decided that freedom of speech issues did not pertain to the ads, and the associated civil suit against the firm for false advertising could go forward. Indeed, Nike appears to have exacerbated and extended the problem from a public relations standpoint by taking the case all the way to the Supreme Court.

The importance of public relations in international marketing is perhaps best demonstrated by the Bridgestone/Firestone Tires safety recall disaster of 2000. The Japanese company was blamed for over 100 deaths in the United States because of its defective tires. True to form in such corporate disasters, the Japanese CEO of the American subsidiary "declared his full and personal responsibility" for the deaths at a U.S. Senate hearing. Such an approach is good public relations in Japan. However, in Washington the senators were not interested in apologies. Moreover, the company blamed its customer, Ford Motor Company, for the problems as well, accusing Ford of telling customers to underinflate the tires for a smoother ride. The problem spread to other markets—Saudi Arabia banned imports of vehicles equipped with Firestone tires. Unbelievably, the company's response to the Saudi action has been to denounce it as a violation of WTO agreements. The global impact of this product-quality and public relations disaster is certain to be great and long lasting. Perhaps the company would have been better off promoting its ISO 9000 rating—refer to the picture in Chapter 13 on page 381.

Public relations firms' billings in the international arena have been growing at double-digit rates for some years. Handling such international PR problems as global workplace standards has become big business for companies serving corporate clients such as Mattel Toys, McDonald's, and of course Nike. Fast growth is also being fueled by the expanding international communications industry. New companies need public relations consultation for "building an international profile," as the marketing manager of VDSL Systems explained when hiring MCC, a prominent British firm. Surprising growth is occurring in emerging markets like Russia as well. The industry itself is experiencing a wave of mergers and takeovers, including the blending of the largest international advertising agencies and the most well-established PR firms.

Corporate sponsorships might be classified as an aspect of public relations, although their connections to advertising are also manifest. The tobacco companies have been

---

[2]Lenard C. Huff and Dana L. Alden, "A Model of Managerial Response to Sales Promotions: A Four-Country Analysis," *Journal of Global Marketing* 13, no. 3 (2000), pp. 7–28.

[3]The story about how the Mayo brothers traveled the world makes for an interesting example of early, and quite effective public relations. See Misty Hathaway and Kent Seltman, "International Market Research at the Mayo Clinic," *Marketing Health Services*, Winter 2001, pp. 18–23.

CROSSING **BORDERS 16.1**   PR in the PRC

In 1999 an industry was born in China when the Ministry of Labor and Social Security recognized public relations as a profession. These excerpts from the *China Daily* illustrate how institutions evolve in emerging economies:

> More laws are needed to regulate China's fledgling public relations profession, an industry leader said yesterday in Beijing. "To seize the enormous business opportunities promised by China's upcoming entry in the World Trade Organization, we need specific laws to regulate the market, curb malpractice and promote competency of local PR firms," said Li Yue, vice-director of the China International Public Relations Association. Her comments were made during a national symposium on public relations, also know as PR.
>
> Symposium delegates said they were concerned about the disorder in the PR industry and the frequent personnel changes in PR firms. They urged the passage of more laws to put an end to what many consider to be the chaos in the profession. Industry insiders cited a limited talent pool, cut-throat price wars and low professional standards as the industry's major problems.
>
> In the 1980s, most Chinese people would think of reception girls, lavish banquets and the use of connections when public relations were mentioned. Now, public relations firms are seen as helping their clients gain better name recognition of their companies. They also manage corporate images.
>
> To help the industry develop, the Labor and Social Security Ministry this year instituted a nationwide qualifying exam for PR professionals. In 1999, the industry reported a total business volume of $120 million, while employing 3,000 people. In 2005 there are now 2000 PR *firms* and business volume is over $500 million.

Sources: "China: More Regulation of PR Sought," *China Daily*, January 20, 2000, p. 3; "PRW: The Top European PR Consultancies 2000," *PR Week*, June 23, 2000, p. 7; "PR Firms Gaining Experience by Working with Multinational Firms," *Industry Updates*, June 20, 2005.

particularly creative at using sports event sponsorships in avoiding countries' advertising regulations associated with more traditional media. Other prominent examples are Coca-Cola's sponsorship of European football (soccer) matches or Ford's sponsorship of the Australian Open tennis tournament. McDonald's executed a huge international IMC campaign surrounding its sponsorship of the 2000 Sydney Olympics. Included were Olympic-themed food promotions, packaging and in-store signs, TV and print ads, and Web chats with superstar athletes such as American basketball player Grant Hill. In addition to the various promotions targeting the 43 million daily customers in their 27,000 restaurants around the world, the firm targeted the athletes themselves. As the official restaurant partner, McDonald's got to operate seven restaurants in Sydney, including the two serving the Olympic Village. During the three weeks of the Games nearly 1.5 million burgers were served to the athletes, officials, coaches, media staffers, and spectators. Similarly, one of the more innovative sponsorship arrangements was Intel's agreement with the Tour de France to support the official Tour Web site, www.letour.com, in 2003. Of course, all these aspects of IMC work best when coordinated and reinforced with a consistent advertising campaign, the topic covered in the rest of the chapter.

International Advertising

Since the turn of the century, growth in global advertising expenditures has slowed with the global economy. Most estimates of total expenditures for 2005 are in the neighborhood of $400 billion.[4] A 4 percent annual growth rate is predicted through 2006, but that of course depends on a resurgence of growth in the general global economy. In this slow-growth global economic environment the advertising industry continues to undergo substantial restructuring. Global mass media advertising is a powerful tool for cultural change, and as such it receives continuing scrutiny by a wide variety of institutions. Even

---

[4]www.medialifemagazine.com, 2005.

Exhibit 16.1

Top 20 Global Advertisers ($ millions)*

2003	2002	Advertiser	Headquarters	2003	Percent Change
1	1	Procter & Gamble Co.	Cincinnati	$5,762	29.0
2	3	Unilever	London/Rotterdam	3,540	13.3
3	2	General Motors	Detroit	3,412	4.1
4	4	Toyota Motor Co.	Toyota City	2,669	9.2
5	5	Ford Motor Co.	Detroit	2,537	3.9
6	6	Time Warner	New York	2,378	9.9
7	7	Daimler-Chrysler	Stuttgart/Detroit	2,230	15.7
8	8	L'Oreal	Paris	2,180	37.3
9	10	Nestlé	Vevey, Switzerland	1,737	19.5
10	12	Sony Corp.	Tokyo	1,684	17.7
11	14	Walt Disney Co.	Burbank, CA	1,680	22.4
12	15	Nissan Motor Co.	Tokyo	1,674	27.7
13	9	Johnson & Johnson	New Brunswick, NJ	1,665	14.1
14	11	Honda Motor Co.	Tokyo	1,542	6.9
15	13	Altria Group	New York	1,514	9.2
16	16	Volkswagen	Wolfsburg, Germany	1,435	13.1
17	19	PepsiCo	Purchase, NY	1,255	9.5
18	20	Pfizer	New York	1,229	9.0
19	18	McDonald's Corp.	Oak Brook, IL	1,213	3.3
20	17	Coca-Cola Co.	Atlanta	1,195	0.8

*Figures are U.S. dollars in millions and are *AdvertisingAge* estimates.

Source: "Special Report Global Marketing," Reprinted with permission from the November 8, 2004 issue of *Advertising Age*. Copyright © 2004 Crain Communications, Inc.

so, most scholars agree that we are just beginning to understand some of the key issues involved in international advertising.

Exhibits 16.1 and 16.2 illustrate the biggest companies and product categories for international advertising. While the automotive companies dominate the lists, Proctor & Gamble was the global champion of spending. Also, notice the lack of growth across many of the categories and companies. We also broke out the spending patterns for two emerging markets in Exhibit 16.3. Demonstrated is a key difference in stage of development between China and Russia. While the latter is dominated by foreign food firms, China is creating its own home-grown brands of pharmaceuticals. Judging the relative progress of the two

Exhibit 16.2

Top 100 Advertisers' Global Spending by Category ($ millions)

Source: "Special Report Global Marketing," Reprinted with permission from the November 8, 2004 issue of *Advertising Age*. Copyright © 2004 Crain Communications, Inc.

Category	2003	Percent Change from 2002	Percent Total
Automotive	$20,928	8.8	25.3
Personal care	15,294	22.8	18.5
Entertainment and media	9,431	9.4	11.4
Food	7,786	17.3	9.4
Drugs	5,599	15.0	6.8
Soft drinks	2,916	4.5	3.5
Computers	2,904	19.1	3.5
Electronics and imaging	2,860	22.1	3.5
Telecommunications	2,822	31.3	3.4
Restaurants	2,471	2.2	3.0
Retail	2,210	25.3	2.7
Cleaners	2,063	16.5	2.5
Beer, wine, and liquor	1,682	−1.4	2.0
Financial	1,624	29.6	2.0
Candy	474	1.2	0.6

Exhibit 16.3a
Russia's Top Ten
Advertisers ($ millions)

Source: "Special Report Global Marketing," Reprinted with permission from the November 8, 2004 issue of *Advertising Age.* Copyright © 2004 Crain Communications, Inc.

Advertiser	2003	Percent Change from 2002
Procter & Gamble Co.	$167.6	39.5
Nestlé	78.2	27.1
Unilever	75.9	19.6
Wimm-Bill-Dann Foods	73.7	24.9
Mars Inc.	71.2	31.3
L'Oreal	57.1	62.7
Henkel	50.5	52.2
Wrigley	44.6	32.8
Mobile Telesystems	42.2	85.4
PepsiCo	40.6	30.6

Exhibit 16.3b
China's Top Ten
Advertisers ($ millions)

Source: "Special Report Global Marketing," Reprinted with permission from the November 8, 2004 issue of *Advertising Age.* Copyright © 2004 Crain Communications, Inc.

Advertiser	2003	Percent Change from 2002
Procter & Gamble Co.	$611.0	279.3
Naobaijin Health Products	140.1	45.5
Gai Zhong Gai	130.7	7.4
Arche	128.5	408.2
Huangjindadang	124.2	277.6
Puxue Oran Solution	123.5	NA
Guangzhou Wuzhou Aoqili Group Co.	97.3	NA
Jiuxin Group Daily Chemical Co.	93.4	296.8
Diaopai	90.4	237.2
Medical Treatment Information	87.7	18.1

countries on this single criterion, China looks like it is further up the ladder of economic development.

Of all the elements of the marketing mix, decisions involving advertising are those most often affected by cultural differences among country markets. Consumers respond in terms of their culture, its style, feelings, value systems, attitudes, beliefs, and perceptions. Because advertising's function is to interpret or translate the qualities of products and services in terms of consumer needs, wants, desires, and aspirations, the emotional appeals, symbols, persuasive approaches, and other characteristics of an advertisement must coincide with cultural norms if the ad is to be effective.

Reconciling an international advertising campaign with the cultural uniqueness of markets is the challenge confronting the international or global marketer. The basic framework and concepts of international advertising are essentially the same wherever employed. Seven steps are involved:

1. Perform marketing research.
2. Specify the goals of the communication.
3. Develop the most effective message(s) for the market segments selected.
4. Select effective media.
5. Compose and secure a budget.
6. Execute the campaign.
7. Evaluate the campaign relative to the goals specified.

Of these seven steps, developing messages almost always represents the most daunting task for international marketing managers, so that topic is emphasized here. Nuances of international media are then discussed. Advertising agencies are ordinarily involved in all seven steps and are the subject of a separate section. Finally, the chapter closes with a discussion of broader issues of governmental controls on advertising.

These vehicular ads make an effective advertising medium even in a dense London fog. Because most London cabs are black, the Snickers ad catches the eye immediately.

Advertising Strategy and Goals

The goals of advertising around the world vary substantially. For example, Chinese manufacturers are establishing new brands as their economy expands; Unilever is introducing a new product-line extension, Dove Shampoo, in East Asian markets; and Russia's airline Aeroflot is seeking to upgrade its quality image. All these marketing problems require careful marketing research and thoughtful and creative advertising campaigns in country, regional, and global markets, respectively.

Intense competition for world markets and the increasing sophistication of foreign consumers have led to a need for more sophisticated advertising strategies. Increased costs, problems of coordinating advertising programs in multiple countries, and a desire for a broader company or product image have caused multinational companies (MNCs) to seek greater control and efficiency without sacrificing local responsiveness. In the quest for more effective and responsive promotion programs, the policies covering centralized or decentralized authority,[5] use of single or multiple foreign or domestic agencies, appropriation and allocation procedures, copy, media, and research are being examined. More and more multinational companies can be seen to be managing the balance between standardization of advertising themes and customization.[6] And recently, as described in Chapter 12, more companies are favoring the latter.

A case in point is the Gillette Company, which sells 800 products in more than 200 countries. Gillette has a consistent worldwide image as a masculine, sports-oriented company, but its products have no such consistent image. Its razors, blades, toiletries, and cosmetics are known by many names. Trac II blades in the United States are more widely known worldwide as G-II, and Atra blades are called Contour in Europe and Asia. Silkience hair conditioner is known as Soyance in France, Sientel in Italy, and Silkience in Germany. Whether or not global brand names could have been chosen for Gillette's many existing products is speculative. However, Gillette's current corporate philosophy of globalization provides for an umbrella statement, "Gillette, the Best a Man Can Get," in all advertisements for men's toiletries products in the hope of providing some common image.

A similar situation exists for Unilever, which sells a cleaning liquid called Vif in Switzerland, Viss in Germany, Jif in Britain and Greece, and Cif in France. This situation is a result of Unilever marketing separately to each of these countries. At this point, it would be difficult for Gillette or Unilever to standardize their brand names because each brand is established in its market. Nortel Networks has used a "local heroes" approach in its international advertising. The company picks local celebrities to pitch standardized messages across national markets for their telecommunications services.

[5] Carl Solberg, "The Perennial Issue of Adaptation or Standardization of International Marketing Communications: Organizational Contingencies and Performance," *Journal of International Marketing*, 10, no. 3 (2002), pp. 1–21.

[6] Ali Kanso and Richard Alan Nelson, "Advertising Localization Overshadows Stardardization," *Journal of Advertising Research* 42, no. 1 (January–February 2002), pp. 79–89.

In many cases standardized products may be marketed globally. But, because of differences in cultures, they still require a different advertising appeal in different markets.[7] For instance, Ford's model advertising varies by nation because of language and societal nuances. Ford advertises the affordability of its Escort in the United States, where the car is seen as entry level. But in India, Ford launched the Escort as a premium car. "It's not unusual to see an Escort with a chauffeur there," said a Ford executive.

Finally, many companies are using market-segment strategies that ignore national boundaries—business buyers or high-income consumers across the globe are often targeted, for example.[8] Others are proposing newer global market segments defined by "consumer cultures" related to shared sets of consumption-related symbols—convenience, youth, America, internationalism, and humanitarianism are examples.[9] Other, more traditional segments are product and region related; those are discussed next.

Product Attribute and Benefit Segmentation

As discussed in the chapters on product and services development (Chapters 12 and 13), a market offering really is a bundle of satisfactions the buyer receives. This package of satisfactions, or utilities, includes the primary function of the product or service along with many other benefits imputed by the values and customs of the culture. Different cultures often seek the same value or benefits from the primary function of a product; for example, the ability of an automobile to get from point A to point B, a camera to take a picture, or a wristwatch to tell time. But while usually agreeing on the benefit of the primary function of a product, other features and psychological attributes of the item can have significant differences.

Consider the different market-perceived needs for a camera. In the United States, excellent pictures with easy, foolproof operation are expected by most of the market; in Germany and Japan, a camera must take excellent pictures, but the camera must also be state of the art in design. In Africa, where penetration of cameras is less than 20 percent of the households, the concept of picture taking must be sold. In all three markets, excellent pictures are expected (i.e., the primary function of a camera is demanded), but the additional utility or satisfaction derived from a camera differs among cultures. Many products produce expectations beyond the common benefit sought by all.

Dannon's brand of yogurt promotes itself as the brand that understands the relationship between health and food, but it communicates the message differently, depending on the market.[10] In the United States, where Dannon yogurt is seen as a healthy, vibrant food, the brand celebrates its indulgent side. In France, however, Dannon was seen as too pleasure oriented. Therefore, Dannon created the Institute of Health, a real research center dedicated to food and education. The end result is the same message but communicated differently—a careful balance of health and pleasure.

The Blue Diamond Growers Association's advertising of almonds is an excellent example of the fact that some products are best advertised only on a local basis. Blue Diamond had a very successful ad campaign in the United States showing almond growers knee-deep in almonds while pleading with the audience, "A can a week, that's all we ask." The objective of the campaign was to change the perception of almonds as a special-occasion treat to an everyday snack food. The campaign was a success; in addition to helping change the perception of almonds as a snack food, it received millions of dollars worth of free publicity for Blue Diamond from regional and national news media. The successful U.S. ad was tested in Canada for possible use outside the United States. The Canadian reaction was

[7]Henry F.L. Chung, "International Standardization Strategies: The Experiences of Australian and New Zealand Firms Operating in the Greater China Markets," *Journal of International Marketing* 11, no. 3 (2003), pp. 48–82.

[8]Greg Harris and Suleiman Attour, "The International Advertising Practices of Multinational Companies: A Content Analysis Study," *European Journal of Marketing* 37, no. 1–2 (2003), pp. 154–168.

[9]David A. Griffin, Aruna Chandra, and John K. Ryans Jr., "Examining the Intricacies of Promotion Standardization: Factors Influencing Advertising Message and Packaging," *Journal of International Marketing* 11, no. 3 (2003), pp. 30–47.

[10]Jae H. Pae, Saeed Samiee, and Susan Tai, "Global Advertising Strategy: The Moderating Role of Brand Familiarity and Execution Style," *International Marketing Review* 19, no. 2–3 (2002), pp. 176–189.

MICROSOFT annually spends

more than a billion dollars on its global advertising. The company has 75 subsidiaries around the world. The management processes used to develop the "Windows Office" campaign are instructive.

Things begin with marketing research in individual countries regarding key market segments, most attractive product features, and potential themes. The data collected by the international subsidiaries are then sent to McCann-Erickson's San Francisco offices for the development of a set of universal themes. McCann-Erickson Worldwide has more than 200 offices in 111 countries and is ideally suited for global clients such as Microsoft, Coca-Cola, DuPont, and Lucent Technologies. The San Francisco office is closest to Redmond, Washington, where Microsoft is headquartered, and, of course, it is also adjacent to the Silicon Valley.

The agency sends the appropriate core concepts, video footage, photographic layouts, and copy themes that comprise the set of universal materials. Then, in cooperation with their local agencies, managers at each subsidiary choose the most appropriate materials for their particular consumers and markets. The most customization is required in Brazil, China, India, and Russia—all are plagued by major piracy problems. Also, since Japan is the firm's second largest market behind only the United States, executives there are given more freedom to adapt to local requirements and tastes.

corporate/brand image campaign

The purpose behind this corporate campaign is to complement the firm's heavy product-oriented marketing with a program that explains Microsoft's broader corporate mission. That is, "to help people and businesses throughout the world reach their full potential." The campaign serves to soften the image of the firm and emphasizes the contribution its products and services have made to technology and the practical applications of personal computing in business, science, education, and so on. The program runs in more than 30 countries (here you see the versions used in the United States, Japan, and Mexico) including TV ads with local copy, voice-over, and other adaptations to the global theme. The majority of the ads are pre- and post-tested in multiple countries to check for cultural nuance. Some $19 million a year is spent just on this aspect of the research. The print and TV ads are complemented by an associated PR, government, and community affairs campaign. The campaign is in its third year with positive results reflected in measured improving consumers' views about the company.

product-specific advertising

Here Microsoft Office is pitted against its toughest competitor—earlier versions of itself. So the goal of the campaign is to break up the inertia and facilitate an upgrade cycle. The key message is the way the world (of information workers) works is much different today than it was three to five years ago, or one or two versions ago of Office. The ads focus on scenarios around mobility, collaboration, and controlling sensitive data.

Since there is so much complacency (85 percent satisfaction with Office), the firm needs to do something different or risk just reinforcing with customers the previous version of Office. The dinosaur heads proved to do that in most markets, but they needed local adaptations—photos were used in the United States, cartoons in Korea, and other treatments based on local cultures. This theme was supplemented by a heavy public relations campaign including speeches by Bill Gates about the changing information worker environment. The program was run in more than 30 countries, but not in China. Companies in that market are often in the "product trial" (that is, piracy) stage of the buyer–seller relationship, and different programs are therefore appropriate.

Notice the similarity of the campaigns across the countries, and notice the differences. For the Mexican version, after the "We See," "the king of the skies" is transformed into "imagine what heights you can reach." The tagline for all the ads was developed originally for the corporate campaign, but is now used almost universally. You will also notice that the ad targeting French buyers is the only one with no English in it (except for the product name).

The translations are done locally, so, for example, the copy is different between Mexico and Spain. A variety of themes and media (print and outdoor) are used across countries. And, in any one country, several themes and media may be used, particularly in the larger, more diverse markets.

Finally, the executions are then tested in each market and adjustments are made. This global approach makes sense for Microsoft because the product, its uses, and its market share are virtually the same across markets. This integrated approach has saved some $30 million in worker-hours and production costs over previous similar campaigns.

(Courtesy Microsoft Corporation)

vastly different; to them, the whole idea was just too silly. And further, Canadians prefer to buy products from Canadian farmers, not American farmers. This led to the decision to study each market closely and design an advertisement for each country market. The only similarity between commercials airing in markets in New York, Tokyo, Moscow, Toronto, or Stockholm is the Blue Diamond logo.

In Japan, the Blue Diamond brand of almonds was an unknown commodity until Blue Diamond launched its campaign of exotic new almond-based products that catered to local tastes. Such things as almond tofu, almond miso soup, and Clamond—a nutritional snack concocted from a mixture of dried small sardines and slivered almonds—were featured in magazine ads and in promotional cooking demonstrations. Television ads featured educational messages on how to use almonds in cooking, their nutritional value, the versatility of almonds as a snack, and the California mystique and health benefits of almonds. As a result, Japan is now the Association's largest importer of almonds.

In Korea, the emphasis was on almonds and the West. Commercials featured swaying palms, beach scenes, and a guitar-playing crooner singing "Blue Diamond" to the tune of "Blue Hawaii." And so it goes in the 94 countries where Blue Diamond sells its almonds. Blue Diamond assumes that no two markets will react the same, that each has its own set of differences—be they "cultural, religious, ethnic, dietary, or otherwise"—and that each will require a different marketing approach, a different strategy. The wisdom of adapting its product advertising for each market is difficult to question since two-thirds of all Blue Diamond's sales are outside the United States.

Regional Segmentation

The emergence of pan-European communications media is enticing many companies to push the balance toward more standardized promotional efforts. As media coverage across Europe expands, it will become more common for markets to be exposed to multiple messages and brands of the same product. To avoid the confusion that results when a market is exposed to multiple brand names and advertising messages, as well as for reasons of efficiency, companies will strive for harmony in brand names, advertising, and promotions across Europe.

Mars, the candy company, traditionally used several brand names for the same product but has found it necessary to select a single name to achieve uniformity in its standardized advertising campaigns. As a result, a candy bar sold in some parts of Europe under the brand name Raider was changed to Twix, the name used in the United States and the United Kingdom.

IBM has gradually created a pan-European promotional strategy by moving away from campaigns individually tailored for each European country. Broadcast and print advertisements for its personal computers feature an identical image with text that is translated into local languages. To ensure uniformity in its promotional materials, IBM developed a manual to provide step-by-step instructions on how to achieve a common theme in the design of all the company's product and service brochures. An important reason for uniform promotional packaging across country markets is cost savings. In IBM's case, one set of European ads versus one set for each country for one of its personal computers saved an estimated $2 million. The company also estimates that a completely unified European advertising strategy will result in stretching its $150 million European budget by an extra 15 to 20 percent.

Along with changes in behavior patterns, legal restrictions are slowly being eliminated, and viable market segments across country markets are emerging. Although Europe will never be a single homogeneous market for every product, that does not mean that companies should shun the idea of developing Europe-wide promotional programs. A pan-European promotional strategy would mean identifying a market segment across all European countries and designing a promotional concept appealing to market segment similarities. IBM and Mars candy are good examples of this strategy.

With a common language (Brazil being the one exception), Latin America also lends itself to regionwide promotion programs. Eveready Battery has successfully developed a 16-country campaign with one message instead of the patchwork of messages that previously existed. Cable and satellite TV channels also provide regionwide media. For example, HBO promotes American cable-TV hit *Six Feet Under* using a pan-Asian campaign.

The Message: Creative Challenges

Global Advertising and the Communications Process

International communications may fail for a variety of reasons: A message may not get through because of media inadequacy, the message may be received by the intended audience but not be understood because of different cultural interpretations, or the message may reach the intended audience and be understood but have no effect because the marketer did not correctly assess the needs and wants or even the thinking processes[11] of the target market.

The effectiveness of promotional strategy can be jeopardized by so many factors that a marketer must be certain no controllable influences are overlooked. Those international executives who understand the communications process are better equipped to manage the diversity they face in developing an international promotional program.

In the international communications process, each of the seven identifiable steps can ultimately affect the accuracy of the process. As illustrated in Exhibit 16.4, the process consists of the following:

1. **An information source.** An international marketing executive with a product message to communicate.

2. **Encoding.** The message from the source converted into effective symbolism for transmission to a receiver.

3. **A message channel.** The sales force and/or advertising media that convey the encoded message to the intended receiver.

4. **Decoding.** The interpretation by the receiver of the symbolism transmitted from the information source.

5. **Receiver.** Consumer action by those who receive the message and are the target for the thought transmitted.

6. **Feedback.** Information about the effectiveness of the message that flows from the receiver (the intended target) back to the information source for evaluation of the effectiveness of the process.

7. **Noise.** Uncontrollable and unpredictable influences such as competitive activities and confusion that detract from the process and affect any or all of the other six steps.

Unfortunately, the process is not as simple as just sending a message via a medium to a receiver and being certain that the intended message sent is the same one perceived by the receiver. In Exhibit 16.4, the communications-process steps are encased in Cultural Context A and Cultural Context B to illustrate the influences complicating the process when the message is encoded in one culture and decoded in another. If not properly considered, the different cultural contexts can increase the probability of misunderstandings. Research in the area suggests that effective communication demands the existence of a "psychological overlap" between the sender and the receiver; otherwise, a message falling outside the receiver's perceptual field may transmit an unintended meaning. It is in this area that even the most experienced companies make blunders.

Most promotional misfires or mistakes in international marketing are attributable to one or several of these steps not properly reflecting cultural influences or to a general lack of knowledge about the target market. Referring to Exhibit 16.4, the information source is a marketer with a product to sell to a specific target market. The product message to be conveyed should reflect the needs and wants of the target market; however, often the actual market needs and the marketer's perception of them do not coincide. This is especially true when the marketer relies more on the self-reference criterion (SRC) than on effective research. It can never be assumed that "if it sells well in one country, it will sell in another." For instance, bicycles designed and sold in the United States to consumers fulfilling recreational exercise needs are not sold as effectively for the same reason in a market where the

---

[11]Jennifer Aaker, "Accessibility or Diagnosticity? Disentangling the Influence of Culture on Persuasion Processes and Attitudes," *Journal of Consumer Research* 26, no. 4 (March 2000), pp. 340–357.

Exhibit 16.4
The International
Communications Process

primary use of the bicycle is transportation. Cavity-reducing fluoride toothpaste sells well in the United States, where healthy teeth are perceived as important, but has limited appeal in markets such as Great Britain and the French areas of Canada, where the reason for buying toothpaste is breath control. From the onset of the communications process, if basic needs are incorrectly defined, communications fail because an incorrect or meaningless message is received even though the remaining steps in the process are executed properly.

The encoding step causes problems even with a "proper" message. At this step such factors as color,[12] timing, values,[13] beliefs, humor,[14] tastes, and appropriateness of spokespersons can cause the international marketer to symbolize the message incorrectly. For example, the marketer wants the product to convey coolness so the color green is used; however, people in the tropics might decode green as dangerous or associate it with disease. Another example of the encoding process misfiring was a perfume presented against a backdrop of rain that, for Europeans, symbolized a clean, cool, refreshing image, but to Africans was a symbol of fertility. The ad prompted many viewers to ask if the perfume was effective against infertility. David Beckham may be a wonderful spokesperson in most of the world, but in the United States even the greatest soccer players get little recognition.[15]

Problems of literacy,[16] media availability, and types of media create challenges in the communications process at the encoding step. Message channels must be carefully selected if an encoded message is to reach the consumer. Errors such as using the Internet as a medium when only a small percentage of an intended market has access to the Internet, or using print media for a channel of communications when the majority of the intended users cannot read or do not read the language in the medium, are examples of ineffective media channel selection in the communications process.

[12]Thomas J. Madden, Kelly Hewett, and Martin S. Roth, "Managing Images in Different Cultures: A Cross-National Study of Color Meanings and Preferences," *Journal of International Marketing* 8, no. 4 (2000), pp. 108–121.

[13]Cheng Lu Wang and Allan K. K. Chan, "A Content Analysis of Connectedness vs. Separateness Themes Used in U.S. and PRC Print Advertisements," *International Marketing Review* 18, no. 2 (2001), pp. 145–160.

[14]Robert Guy Matthews, "KFC 'Soul' Ad Poses Global Issue," *Wall Street Journal*, January 27, 2005, p. B6.

[15]Erin White and Maureen Tkacik, "Spend It Like Beckham," *Wall Street Journal*, June 19, 2003, p. B1.

[16]Ivonne Torres, Betsy Gelb, and Jaime L. Noriega, "Warning and Informing the Domestic International Market," *Journal of Public Policy and Marketing* 22, no. 2 (2003), pp. 216–222.

(© AFP Getty/Images)   *(AP/Wide World Photos)*

Red Works! Notice the Coke advantage at work—the red contrasts with the outdoor environment while the Cristal aqua blends more with the blue sky. Cristal is a popular brand of bottled water actually owned by Coca-Cola and sold here in the Yucatan Peninsula in Mexico. The Coke ads are emblazoned on a café in the central plaza of Canas, Costa Rica. Spend it like Beckham—in addition to Vodafone and Nike on his jersey, David Beckham, here in his Manchester United red, also represents Pepsi, Adidas, Castrol, Upper Deck, Marks & Spencer, Police, Meiji, Tokyo Beauty Center, etc., etc., etc. Most recently the Spanish soccer power Real Madrid spent $40 million buying Mr. Beckham's contract from his British home team. One disadvantage of the move south—the white jersey of the Spanish team won't catch the eye as did the Manchester United red. Finally, the world's most famous athlete is not Beckham, it's Formula 1 racecar driver Michael Schumacher. The 35-year-old German makes more money than any other sports figure as he dominates the sport most watch on television globally. And the flamboyant red jumpsuit and red Ferraris help. The other red brands—Marlboro and Vodafone—love him, too.

Decoding problems are generally created by improper encoding, which caused such errors as Pepsi's "Come Alive" slogan being decoded as "Come out of the grave." Chevrolet's brand name for the Nova model (which means new star) was decoded into Spanish as No Va!, meaning "it doesn't go." In another misstep, a translation that was supposed to be decoded as "hydraulic ram" was instead decoded as "wet sheep." In a Nigerian ad, a platinum blonde sitting next to the driver of a Renault was intended to enhance the image of the automobile. However, the model was perceived as not respectable and so created a feeling of shame. An ad used for Eveready Energizer batteries with the Energizer bunny was seen by Hungarian consumers as touting a bunny toy, not a battery.

Decoding errors may also occur accidentally, as was the case with Colgate-Palmolive's selection of the brand name Cue for toothpaste. The brand name was not intended to have

CROSSING BORDERS 16.2   Arnold Terminates Site Leaking Foreign TV Ads

It's hard to say no to Arnold Schwarzenegger, or so a Victoria-based Web site learned. The site, dedicated to showing celebrities pitching products to Japanese audiences, was forced to terminate an overseas commercial featuring the brawny movie star-politician.

The three cofounders of the parody Internet site decided to say *hasta la vista* to the ad, never meant for release in North America, after receiving a cease-and-desist order from lawyers in Tokyo threatening legal action.

But the publicity surrounding the Web video of Mr. Schwarzenegger, the star of action movies including *The Terminator*, resulted in an unprecedented number of visits to the Gaijin, a Go-Go Café site set up by the small Canadian Web company Zero One Design. "I don't understand what all the hubbub is about," Jonathan

Lathigee, the site's 26-year-old cofounder, said. "We were a little blown away by all the attention."

The commercial at the center of the controversy was made for DirecTV, a Japanese satellite TV channel that broadcasts U.S. movies and programs. It shows Mr. Schwarzenegger playing several characters, including a reporter and a politician, and revisits his famous *Terminator* role.

The Web site downloads Japanese commercials featuring U.S. celebrities such as Demi Moore, Keanu Reeves, and Leonardo DiCaprio, who hawk everything from whiskey to beauty cream in lucrative overseas commercials not meant for North American audiences.

Sources: Kim Lunman, "Arnold Terminates Site Leaking Foreign TV Ads," *Toronto Globe and Mail*, August 11, 2000, p. A3; see www.gaijinagogo.com for details, 2005.

any symbolism; nevertheless, it was decoded by the French into a pornographic word. In some cases, the intended symbolism has no meaning to the decoder. In an ad transferred from the United States, the irony of tough-guy actor Tom Selleck standing atop a mountain with a steaming mug of Lipton tea was lost on eastern Europeans.

Errors at the receiver end of the process generally result from a combination of factors: an improper message resulting from incorrect knowledge of use patterns, poor encoding producing a meaningless message, poor media selection that does not get the message to the receiver, or inaccurate decoding by the receiver so that the message is garbled or incorrect. Even bad luck comes into play. French's mustard was boycotted (along with French wines, fries, etc.) by Americans when the Paris government did not go along with the attack in Iraq in 2003. This was so, even though the brand name has nothing to do with the country—the company founder's name was Robert T. French.[17]

Finally, the feedback step of the communications process is important as a check on the effectiveness of the other steps. Companies that do not measure their communications efforts are likely to allow errors of source, encoding, media selection, decoding, or receiver to continue longer than necessary. In fact, a proper feedback system (ad testing) allows a company to correct errors before substantial damage occurs.

In addition to the problems inherent in the steps outlined, the effectiveness of the international communications process can be impaired by noise. *Noise* comprises all other external influences, such as competitive advertising, other sales personnel, and confusion at the receiving end, that can detract from the ultimate effectiveness of the communication. Noise is a disruptive force interfering with the process at any step and is frequently beyond the control of the sender or the receiver. As Exhibit 16.4 illustrates with the overlapping cultural contexts, noise can emanate from activity in either culture or be caused by the influences of the overlapping of the cultural contexts.

The model's significance is that one or all steps in the process, cultural factors,[18] or the marketer's SRC can affect the ultimate success of the communication. For example, the message,

---

[17]Floyd Norris, "It's French's Mustard. What's in a Name these Days?" *International Herald Tribune*, March 29, 2003, p. 13.

[18]Donnel A. Briley and Robert S. Wyer Jr., "The Effect of Group Membership Salience on the Avoidance of Negative Outcomes: Implications for Social and Consumer Research," *Journal of Consumer Research* 29, no. 3 (December 2002), pp. 400–415.

City streets in Singapore are alive with advertising. California Fitness Centers in Southeast Asia are owned by America's 24-hour Fitness Centers. Obviously the image of "bodyland" southern California sells well around the world. However, there's an interesting irony in that brand name for Muslim customers. The word *California* first appears in the eleventh-century epic poem *The Song of Roland;* there it literally means the "caliph's domain"—the Caliph of Baghdad ruled the Islamic Empire then. The Spaniards who named California in the early 1500s thought they were in Asia! Moreover, the deeper meaning of the brand name is lost even on the modern Muslims who comprise 15% of Singapore's current population!

encoding, media, and the intended receiver can be designed perfectly but the inability of the receiver to decode may render the final message inoperative. In developing advertising messages, the international marketer can effectively use this model as a guide to help ensure that all potential constraints and problems are considered so that the final communication received and the action taken correspond with the intent of the source.

The growing intensity of international competition, coupled with the complexity of multinational marketing, demands that the international advertiser function at the highest creative level. The creative task is made more daunting by other kinds of barriers to effective communications—legal, linguistic, cultural, media, production, and cost considerations.

Legal Constraints   Laws that control comparative advertising vary from country to country in Europe. In Germany, it is illegal to use any comparative terminology; you can be sued by a competitor if you do. Belgium and Luxembourg explicitly ban comparative advertising, whereas it is clearly authorized in the United Kingdom, Ireland, Spain, and Portugal. The directive covering comparative advertising allows implicit comparisons that do not name competitors, but bans explicit comparisons between named products. The European Commission issued several directives to harmonize the laws governing advertising. However, member states are given substantial latitude to cover issues under their jurisdiction. Many fear that if the laws are not harmonized, member states may close their borders to advertising that does not respect their national rules.

Comparative advertising is heavily regulated in other parts of the world, as well. In Asia, an advertisement showing chimps choosing Pepsi over Coke was banned from most satellite television; the phrase "the leading cola" was accepted only in the Philippines. An Indian court ordered Lever to cease claiming that its New Pepsodent toothpaste was "102% better" than the leading brand. Colgate, the leading brand, was never mentioned in the advertisement, although a model was shown mouthing the word "Colgate" and the image was accompanied by a "ting" sound recognized in all Colgate ads as the ring of confidence. Banning explicit comparisons will rule out an effective advertising approach heavily used by U.S. companies at home and in other countries where it is permitted.

A variety of restrictions on advertising of specific products exist around the world. Advertising of pharmaceuticals is restricted in many countries. For example, critics in Canada complain that laws there haven't been revised in 50 years and have been rendered obsolete by the advent of TV and more recently the Internet. Toy, tobacco, and liquor advertising is restricted in numerous countries. The French government until recently forbade TV ads for retailers, publishing, cinema, and the press.

Advertising on television is strictly controlled in many countries.[19] China is relaxing some regulations[20] while strengthening others. For example, only recently has the government begun to require concrete proof of ad claims.[21] In Kuwait, the government-controlled TV network allows only 32 minutes of advertising per day, in the evening. Commercials are

---

[19]Sunil Erevelles, Fred Morgan, Ilkim Buke, and Rachel Nguyen, "Advertising Strategy in China: An Analysis of Cultural and Regulatory Factors," *Journal of International Consumer Marketing* 15, no. 1 (2002), pp. 91–123.

[20]Frederik Balfour and David Kiley, "Ad Agencies Unchained," *BusinessWeek*, April 25, 2005, pp. 50–51.

[21]Jonathan Cheng, "China Demands Concrete Proof of Ad Claims," *Wall Street Journal*, July 8, 2005, pp. B1, B4.

CROSSING BORDERS 16.3 | Joe Canuck Bashes America

Standing foursquare in front of a screen flashing Canadian symbols—beavers, Ottawa's Peace Tower, the Maple Leaf flag—an average Joe Canuck in a checked flannel shirt rips into American misperceptions about his country.

"I have a prime minister, not a president. I speak English or French, not American," he says, voice swelling with emotion. "And I pronounce it 'about,' not 'aboot.'"

"I believe in peacekeeping, not policing; diversity, not assimilation," he goes on in the 60-second television spot as the national icons loom over his shoulder. "And that the beaver is a proud and noble animal."

Strangely, in a country known for its aversion to the sort of rah-rah jingoism associated with its southern neighbor, this nationalistic tirade became an overnight sensation: taped and shown in bars, filling megascreens at hockey games, performed live in movie theaters.

Stranger still was the revved-up public reaction the ad evoked in this notoriously reticent land: wild cheers, stamping feet, frantic flag waving, and fists punching the air. And perhaps strangest of all, the spot was not the cunning propaganda of some ultrapatriot cabal, but a commercial for Molson Canadian beer.

The irony—the director of the commercial is an American, Kevin Donovan. Perhaps they'll make him an honorary Canuck!

Sources: Colin Nickerson, "Anti-U.S. Beer Ad Is So Canada," *Orange County Register*, April 15, 2000, pp. 29, 42; Paula Lyon Andruss, "Understanding Canada," *Marketing News*, March 15, 2001, pp. 1, 11.

controlled to exclude superlative descriptions, indecent words, fearful or shocking shots, indecent clothing or dancing, contests, hatred or revenge shots, ethnic derision,[22] and attacks on competition. Russian law forbids subliminal advertising, but it is still prevalent because enforcement resources are lacking.[23] Regulations regarding levels of violence in ads also vary around the world, as a division of Mitsubishi recently discovered in Spain.[24]

Some country laws against accessibility to broadcast media seem to be softening. Australia ended a ban on cable television spots, and Malaysia is considering changing the rules to allow foreign commercials to air on newly legalized satellite signals. However, with rare exceptions, all commercials on Malaysian television still must be made in Malaysia.

Companies that rely on television infomercials and television shopping are restricted by the limitations placed on the length and number of television commercials permitted when their programs are classified as advertisements. The levels of restrictions in the European Community vary widely, from no advertising on the BBC in the United Kingdom to member states that limit advertising to a maximum of 15 percent of programming daily. The Television without Frontiers directive permits stricter or more detailed rules to the broadcasters under jurisdiction of each member state. In Germany, for example, commercials must be spaced at least 20 minutes apart and total ad time may not exceed 12 minutes per hour. Commercial stations in the United Kingdom are limited to 7 minutes per hour.

Internet services are especially vulnerable as EU member states decide which area of regulation should apply to these services. Barriers to pan-European services will arise if some member states opt to apply television-broadcasting rules to the Internet while other countries apply print-media advertising rules. The good news is that the European Union is addressing the issue of regulation of activities on the Internet. Although most of the attention will be focused on domain names and Internet addresses, the Commission does recognize that online activities will be severely hampered if subject to fragmented regulation.

Some countries have special taxes that apply to advertising, which might restrict creative freedom in media selection. The tax structure in Austria best illustrates how advertising taxation can distort media choice by changing the cost ratios of various media: Federal states,

---

[22]Arundhati Parmar, "Objections to Indian Ad Not Taken Lightly," *Marketing News*, June 9, 2003, p. 4.

[23]Robyn Dixon, "Abusing the Power of Suggestion in Russian Ads," *Los Angeles Times*, August 25, 2002, p. A5.

[24]Ivan Castono, "Mitsubishi to Appeal Court Ruling on 'Violent' Ad," *AdAgeGlobal*, October 18, 2002.

with the exception of Bergenland and Tyrol, tax ad insertions at 10 percent; states and municipalities tax posters at 10 to 30 percent. Radio advertising carries a 10 percent tax, except in Tyrol, where it is 20 percent. Salzburg, Steiermark, Karnten, and Voralbert impose no tax. There is a uniform tax of 10 percent throughout the country on television ads. Cinema advertising has a 10 percent tax in Vienna, 20 percent in Bergenland, and 30 percent in Steiermark. There is no cinema tax in the other federal states.

Linguistic Limitations   Language is one of the major barriers to effective communication through advertising.[25] The problem involves different languages of different countries, different languages[26] or dialects within one country, and the subtler problems of linguistic nuance, vernacular, and even accent. Indeed, recently an Irish accent was voted "sexiest" in Britain and Ireland, beating the competition from the Scots, Welsh, Geordies, Brummies, West Country, and "posh English" contenders.[27] For many countries language is a matter of cultural pride and preservation—France is the best example, of course.[28]

Incautious handling of language has created problems in all countries.[29] Some examples suffice. Chrysler Corporation was nearly laughed out of Spain when it translated its U.S. theme that advertised "Dart Is Power." To the Spanish, the phrase implied that buyers sought but lacked sexual vigor. The Bacardi Company concocted a fruity bitters with a made-up name, Pavane, suggestive of French chic. Bacardi wanted to sell the drink in Germany, but Pavane is perilously close to *pavian,* which means "baboon." A company marketing tomato paste in the Middle East found that in Arabic the phrase "tomato paste" translates as "tomato glue." In Spanish-speaking countries you have to be careful of words that have different meanings in the different countries. The word *ball* translates in Spanish as *bola,* which means ball in one country, revolution in another, a lie or fabrication in another, and is an obscenity in yet another.

Tropicana brand orange juice was advertised as *jugo de China* in Puerto Rico, but when transported to Miami's Cuban community, it failed. To the Puerto Rican, *China* translated into *orange,* but to the Cuban it was China the country—and the Cubans were not in the market for Chinese juice. One Middle East advertisement featured an automobile's new suspension system, which, in translation, said the car was "suspended from the ceiling." Since there are at least 30 dialects among Arab countries, there is ample room for error. What may appear as the most obvious translation can come out wrong. For example, "a whole new range of products" in a German advertisement came out as "a whole new stove of products."

Language raises innumerable barriers that impede effective, idiomatic translation and thereby hamper communication. This is especially apparent in advertising materials and on the Internet.[30] Abstraction, terse writing, and word economy, the most effective tools of the advertiser, pose problems for translators. Communication is impeded by the great diversity of cultural heritage and education that exists within countries and which causes varying interpretations of even single sentences and simple concepts. Some companies have tried to solve the translation problem by hiring foreign translators who live in the United States. This often is not satisfactory because both the language and the translator change, so the expatriate in the United States is out of touch after a few years. Everyday words have

---

[25]Shi Zhang and Bernd H. Schmitt, "Creating Local Brands in Multilingual International Markets," *Journal of Marketing Research* 38 (August 2001), pp. 313–325; Yih Hwai Lee and Kim Soon Ang, "Brand Name Suggestiveness: A Chinese Language Perspective," *International Journal of Research in Marketing* 20, no. 4 (2003), pp. 323–335.

[26]David Luna and Laura A. Peracchio, "Advertising to Bilingual Consumers: The Impact of Code-Switching on Persuasion," *Journal of Consumer Research* 31, no. 2 (2005), pp. 57–73.

[27]Nicola Anderson, "Sexy Accent Makes Us Talk of the Town," *Irish Independent,* March 27, 2004, p. 7.

[28]Paul Johnson, "Current Events," *Forbes,* June 10, 2002, p. 13; Clifford Krauss, "Quebec Seeking to End Its Old Cultural Divide," *New York Times,* April 13, 2003, p. A12.

[29]See www.engrish.com for a wide range of (mostly) humorous translation problems related to the use of English for Japanese products, signage, and so on.

[30]Clyde A. Warden, Mengkuan Lai, and Wann-Yih Wu, "How Worldwide Is Marketing Communication on the World Wide Web," *Journal of Advertising Research* 42, no. 5 (September–October 2002), pp. 72–84.

different meanings in different cultures. Even pronunciation causes problems: Wrigley had trouble selling its Spearmint gum in Germany until it changed the spelling to Speermint.

In addition to translation challenges, low literacy in many countries seriously impedes communications and calls for greater creativity and use of verbal media. Multiple languages within a country or advertising area pose another problem for the advertiser. Even a tiny country such as Switzerland has four separate languages. The melting-pot character of the Israeli population accounts for some 50 languages. A Jerusalem commentator says that even though Hebrew "has become a negotiable instrument of daily speech, this has yet to be converted into advertising idiom." Advertising communications must be perfect, and linguistic differences at all levels cause problems. In-country testing with the target consumer group is the only way to avoid such problems.

Cultural Diversity

The problems associated with communicating to people in diverse cultures present one of the great creative challenges in advertising.[31] One advertising executive puts it bluntly: "International advertising is almost uniformly dreadful mostly because people don't understand language and culture." Communication is more difficult because cultural factors largely determine the way various phenomena are perceived.[32] If the perceptual framework is different, perception of the message itself differs.[33]

Knowledge of cultural diversity must encompass the total advertising project. General Mills had two problems with one product. When it introduced instant cake mixes in the United States and England, it had the problem of overcoming the homemaker's guilt feelings. When General Mills introduced instant cake mixes in Japan, the problem changed. Cakes were not commonly eaten in Japan, so there was no guilt feeling, but the homemaker was concerned about failing. She wanted the cake mix as complete as possible. In testing TV commercials promoting the notion that making a cake is as easy as making rice, General Mills learned it was offending the Japanese homemaker, who believes the preparation of rice requires great skill.

Existing perceptions based on tradition and heritages are often hard to overcome. For example, marketing researchers in Hong Kong found that cheese is associated with *Yeung-Yen* (foreigners) and rejected by some Chinese. The concept of cooling and heating the body is important in Chinese thinking—malted milk is considered heating, whereas fresh milk is cooling; brandy is sustaining, whiskey harmful. Toyota introduced the Prado SUV in China only to learn that the name sounded like the Chinese word for "rule by force." This reminded some Chinese of the 1937 invasion by Japan—not a nice memory at all.[34]

Procter & Gamble's initial advertisement for Pampers brand diapers failed because of cultural differences between the United States and Japan. A U.S. commercial that showed an animated stork delivering Pampers diapers to homes was dubbed into Japanese with the U.S. package replaced by the Japanese package and was put on the air. To P&G's dismay the advertisement failed to build the market. Some belated consumer research revealed that consumers were confused about why this bird was delivering disposable diapers. According to Japanese folklore, giant peaches that float on the river bring babies to deserving parents, not storks.

In addition to concerns with differences among nations, advertisers find subcultures within a country require attention as well. People in Hong Kong have 10 different patterns of breakfast eating. The youth of a country almost always constitute a different consuming culture from the older people, and urban dwellers differ significantly from rural dwellers.

---

[31]Elzbieta Lepkowska-White, "Polish and American Print Ads: Functional, Individualistic, Collectivistic, and Experiential Appeals," *Journal of Global Marketing* 17, no. 4 (2004), pp. 75–92.

[32]Nader T. Tavassoli and Yih Hwai Lee, "The Differential Interaction of Auditory and Visual Advertising Elements with Chinese and English," *Journal of Marketing Research* 40, no. 4 (2003), pp. 468–480.

[33]Some of the most important work being done in the area of culture and advertising is represented by Jennifer Aaker and Patti Williams's "Empathy and Pride: The Influence of Emotional Appeals across Cultures," *Journal of Consumer Research* 25 (December 1998), pp. 241–261; Ulrich R. Orth and Denisa Holancova, "Men's and Women's Responses to Sex Role Portrayals in Advertisements," *International Journal of Research in Marketing* 21, no. 1 (2004), pp. 77–88.

[34]Geoffrey A. Fowler, "China's Cultural Fabric Is a Challenge to Marketers," *Wall Street Journal*, January 21, 2004, p. B7.

CROSSING **BORDERS 16.4**   Objections to Indian Ad Not Taken Lightly

A financially strapped father laments his fate, saying, "Kaash agar mera beta hota," ("If I only had a son") while his dark-skinned, plain Jane daughter looks on, helpless and demoralized because she can't bear the financial responsibility of her family. Fast-forward and plain Jane has been transformed into a gorgeous light-skinned woman through the use of a "fairness cream." Now clad in a miniskirt, the woman is a successful flight attendant and can take her father to dine at a five-star hotel. She's happy and so is her father.

All's well that end's well—except not so for Hindustan Lever Ltd. (HLL). The company, a subsidiary of Unilever, launched this television campaign to promote its Fair & Lovely fairness cream in India. It withdrew the campaign two months later amid severe criticism for its portrayal of women. The incident underscores the changing social mores in India and highlights tensions between the government, consumer groups, and the industry regulatory agencies.

While tanning is the rage in Western countries, skin lightening treatments have been historically popular in Asia. The Japanese market for such products is estimated to be around $6 billion and in India about $150 million.

It may be safe for the skin, but not for society, says the All India Women's Democratic Association. Three things

were objectionable about the campaign to the group. It was racist, it promoted the son preference, and it was insulting to working women. A government ministry found the ads to be in violation of the Cable and Television Act of 1995, which in part forbids ads that "deride any race, caste, color, creed, and nationality." Industry regulators agreed and pressured the company to stop airing the ad. The company admitted no wrong, but complied.

If you haven't already, for an interesting discussion you might juxtapose this grim tale to our story about Barbie in the Global Perspectives at the start of the chapter. If you think that the $55-billion-global-toy, $100-billion-global-cosmetics, and $500-billion-advertising industries are unrelated, you need to go back and reread Chapter 4. And, finally, you might want to consider how different cultures have solved the "problem" of the appearance of women by juxtaposing the global expenditures on cosmetics and on burkas. Unfortunately, Euromonitor doesn't provide an estimate of the latter.

Sources: Arundhati Parmar, "Objections to Indian Ad Not Taken Lightly," *Marketing News*, June 9, 2003, pp. 4–5; Mike McPhate, "Skin Bias Sets Tone for Sales Blitz, Bleaching Creams and Skin-Sloughing Treatments Are Big Business in India," *Philadelphia Enquirer*, July 11, 2005, p. A1.

Besides these differences, there is the problem of changing traditions. In all countries, people of all ages, urban or rural, cling to their heritage to a certain degree but are willing to change some areas of behavior. A few years ago, trying to market coffee in Japan was unthinkable, but coffee has become the fashionable drink for younger people and urban dwellers who like to think of themselves as European and sophisticated. Coffee drinking in Japan was introduced with instant coffee, and there is virtually no market for anything else.

Media Limitations

Media are discussed at length later, so here we note only that limitations on creative strategy imposed by media may diminish the role of advertising in the promotional program and may force marketers to emphasize other elements of the promotional mix. A marketer's creativity is certainly challenged when a television commercial is limited to 10 showings a year with no two exposures closer than 10 days, as is the case in Italy. Creative advertisers in some countries have even developed their own media for overcoming media limitations. In some African countries, advertisers run boats up and down the rivers playing popular music and broadcasting commercials into rural areas as they travel.

Production and Cost Limitations

Creativity is especially important when a budget is small or where there are severe production limitations, such as poor-quality printing and a lack of high-grade paper. For example, the poor quality of high-circulation glossy magazines and other quality publications in eastern Europe has caused Colgate-Palmolive to depart from its customary heavy use of print media in the West for other media. Newsprint is of such low quality in China that a color ad used by Kodak in the West is not an option. Kodak's solution has been to print a single-sheet color insert as a newspaper supplement.

The necessity for low-cost reproduction in small markets poses another problem in many countries. For example, hand-painted billboards must be used instead of printed sheets because the limited number of billboards does not warrant the production of printed sheets. In Egypt, static-filled television and poor-quality billboards have led companies such as Coca-Cola and Nestlé to place their advertisements on the sails of feluccas, boats that sail along the Nile. Feluccas, with their triangle sails, have been used to transport goods since the time of the pharaohs and serve as an effective alternative to attract attention to company names and logos.

Media Planning and Analysis

Tactical Considerations

Although nearly every sizable nation essentially has the same kinds of media, a number of specific considerations, problems, and differences are encountered from one nation to another. In international advertising, an advertiser must consider the availability, cost, coverage, and appropriateness of the media. And the constant competitive churn among the media makes for a tricky and dynamic landscape in which decisions must be made.[35] For example, billboard ads next to highways cannot include paragraphs of text. Moreover, recent research has demonstrated that media effectiveness varies across cultures and product types. Local variations and lack of market data require added attention. Major multinationals are beginning to recognize the importance of planning communications channels as media companies continue to rationalize and evolve. Indeed, media giants such as Disney and Time Warner cover an increasingly broad spectrum of the electronic media, necessitating that MNCs rethink relationships with media service providers.

Imagine the ingenuity required of advertisers confronted with these situations:

- In Brazil, TV commercials are sandwiched together in a string of 10 to 50 commercials within one station break.
- National coverage in many countries means using as many as 40 to 50 different media.
- Specialized media reach small segments of the market only. In the Netherlands, there are Catholic, Protestant, socialist, neutral, and other specialized broadcasting systems.
- In Germany, TV scheduling for an entire year must be arranged by August 30 of the preceding year, with no guarantee that commercials intended for summer viewing will not be run in the middle of winter.
- In Vietnam, advertising in newspapers and magazines is limited to 10 percent of space, and to 5 percent of time, or three minutes an hour, on radio and TV.

Availability.   One of the contrasts of international advertising is that some countries have too few advertising media and others have too many. In some countries, certain advertising media are forbidden by government edict to accept some advertising materials. Such restrictions are most prevalent in radio and television broadcasting. In many countries there are too few magazines and newspapers to run all the advertising offered to them. Conversely, some nations segment the market with so many newspapers that the advertiser cannot gain effective coverage at a reasonable cost. One head of an Italian advertising agency commented about his country: "One fundamental rule. You cannot buy what you want."

In China the only national TV station, CCTV, has one channel that must be aired by the country's 27 provincial/municipal stations. Recently CCTV auctioned off the most popular break between the early evening news and weather; a secured year-long, daily five-second billboard ad in this break went for $38.5 million. For this price, advertisers are assured of good coverage—over 70 percent of households have TV sets. One of the other options for advertisers is with the 2,828 TV stations that provide only local coverage.

Cost.   Media prices are susceptible to negotiation in most countries. Agency space discounts are often split with the client to bring down the cost of media. The advertiser may

[35]Manjeet Kripalani, "Read All about It: India's Media Wars," *BusinessWeek*, May 16, 2005, p. 47.

find that the cost of reaching a prospect through advertising depends on the agent's bargaining ability. The per-contract cost varies widely from country to country. One study showed that the cost of reaching 1,000 readers in 11 different European countries ranged from $1.58 in Belgium to $5.91 in Italy; in women's service magazines, the page cost per 1,000 circulation ranged from $2.51 in Denmark to $10.87 in Germany. Shortages of advertising time on commercial television in some markets have caused substantial price increases. In Britain, prices escalate on a bidding system. They do not have fixed rate cards; instead, there is a preempt system in which advertisers willing to pay a higher rate can bump already-scheduled spots.

Coverage. Closely akin to the cost dilemma is the problem of coverage. Two points are particularly important: One relates to the difficulty of reaching certain sectors of the population with advertising and the other to the lack of information on coverage. In many world marketplaces, a wide variety of media must be used to reach the majority of the markets. In some countries, large numbers of separate media have divided markets into uneconomical advertising segments. With some exceptions, a majority of the population of less-developed countries cannot be reached readily through the traditional mass medium of advertising. In India, video vans are used to reach India's rural population with 30-minute infomercials extolling the virtues of a product. Consumer goods companies deploy vans year-round except in the monsoon season. Colgate hires 85 vans at a time and sends them to villages that research has shown to be promising.

Because of the lack of adequate coverage by any single medium in eastern European countries, companies must resort to a multimedia approach. In the Czech Republic, for example, TV advertising rates are high, and the lack of available prime-time spots has forced companies to use billboard advertising. In Slovenia the availability of adequate media is such a problem that companies resort to some unique approaches to get their messages out. For example, in the summer lasers are used to project images onto clouds above major cities. Vehicle advertising includes cement-mixers, where Kodak ads have appeared. On the positive side, crime is so low that products can be displayed in freestanding glass cabinets on sidewalks; Bosch Siemens (Germany) and Kodak have both used this method.

Lack of Market Data. Verification of circulation or coverage figures is a difficult task. Even though many countries have organizations similar to the Audit Bureau of Circulation in the United States, accurate circulation and audience data are not assured. For example, the president of the Mexican National Advertisers Association charged that newspaper circulation figures are grossly exaggerated. He suggested that as a rule, agencies should divide these figures in two and take the result with a grain of salt. The situation in China is no better; surveys of habits and market penetration are available only for the cities of Beijing, Shanghai, and Guangzhou. Radio and television audiences are always difficult to measure, but at least in most countries, geographic coverage is known. Research data are becoming more reliable as advertisers and agencies demand better-quality data.

Even where advertising coverage can be measured with some accuracy, there are questions about the composition of the market reached. Lack of available market data seems to characterize most international markets; advertisers need information on income, age, and geographic distribution, but such basic data seem chronically elusive except in the largest markets. Even the attractiveness of global television (satellite broadcasts) is diminished somewhat because of the lack of media research available.

An attempt to evaluate specific characteristics of each medium is beyond the scope of this discussion. Furthermore, such information would quickly become outdated because of the rapid changes in the international advertising media field. It may be interesting, however, to examine some of the unique international characteristics of various advertising media. In most instances, the major implications of each variation may be discerned from the data presented.

Newspapers. The newspaper industry is suffering from lack of competition in some countries and choking because of it in others. Most U.S. cities have just one or two major daily newspapers, but in many countries, there are so many newspapers that an advertiser has trouble achieving even partial market coverage. Uruguay, population 3 million, has 21 daily newspapers with a combined circulation of 553,000. Turkey has 380 newspapers, and an advertiser must consider the political position of each newspaper so that the product's reputation is not harmed through affiliation with unpopular positions. Japan has only five national daily newspapers, and the complications of producing a Japanese-language newspaper are such that they each contain just 16 to 20 pages. Connections are necessary to buy advertising space; *Asahi,* Japan's largest newspaper, has been known to turn down over a million dollars a month in advertising revenue.

In many countries there is a long time lag before an advertisement can be run in a newspaper. In India and Indonesia, paper shortages delay publication of ads for up to six months. Furthermore, because of equipment limitations, most newspapers cannot be made larger to accommodate the increase in advertising demand.

Separation between editorial and advertising content in newspapers provides another basis for contrast on the international scene. In some countries, it is possible to buy editorial space for advertising and promotional purposes; the news columns are for sale to anyone who has the price. Because there is no indication that the space is paid for, it is impossible to tell exactly how much advertising appears in a given newspaper.

Magazines.

The use of foreign national consumer magazines by international advertisers has been notably low for many reasons. Few magazines have a large circulation or provide dependable circulation figures. Technical magazines are used rather extensively to promote export goods but, as with newspapers, paper shortages cause placement problems. Media planners are often faced with the largest magazines accepting up to twice as many advertisements as they have space to run them in—then the magazines decide what advertisements will go in just before going to press by means of a raffle.

Such local practices may be key factors favoring the growth of so-called international media that attempt to serve many nations. Increasingly, U.S. publications are publishing overseas editions. *Reader's Digest International* has added a new Russian-language edition to its more than 20 other language editions. Other American print media available in international editions range from *Playboy* to *Scientific American,* and even include the *National Enquirer,* recently introduced to the United Kingdom. Advertisers have three new magazines through which to reach women in China: Hachette Filipachi Presse, the French publisher, is expanding Chinese-language editions of *Elle,* a fashion magazine; *Woman's Day* is aimed at China's "busy modern" woman; and *L'Evénement Sportif* is a sports magazine. These media offer alternatives for multinationals as well as for local advertisers.

Radio and Television.

Possibly because of their inherent entertainment value, radio and television have become major communications media in most nations. Most populous areas have television broadcasting facilities. In some markets, such as Japan, television has become almost a national obsession and thus finds tremendous audiences for its advertisers. Now high-definition television (HDTV) appears to be starting to take off worldwide as well.[36] In China, virtually all homes in major cities have a television and most adults view television and listen to radio daily. Radio has been relegated to a subordinate position in the media race in countries where television facilities are well developed. In many countries, however, radio is a particularly important and vital advertising medium when it is the only one reaching large segments of the population.

Television and radio advertising availability varies between countries. Three patterns are discernible: competitive commercial broadcasting, commercial monopolies, and noncommercial broadcasting. Countries with free competitive commercial radio and television normally encourage competition and have minimal broadcast regulations. Elsewhere, local or national monopolies are granted by the government, and individual stations or networks may then accept radio or TV commercials according to rules established by the government. In some countries, commercial monopolies may accept all the advertising they wish;

---

[36]Tim Burt, "Electronics Groups and Broadcasters Push the Button on HDTV," *Financial Times,* October 15, 2004, p. 15.

CROSSING BORDERS 16.5

Advertising Themes That Work in Japan, Including a Polite Duck

Respect for tradition: Mercedes ads stress that it was the first to manufacture passenger cars.

Mutual dependence: Shiseido ads emphasize the partnership (with their beauty consultants) involved in achieving beauty.

Harmony with nature: Toyotas are shown in front of Mt. Fuji.

Use of seasons: Commercials are often set in and products are often used in specific seasons only.

Newness and evolution: Products are shown to evolve from the current environment slowly.

Distinctive use of celebrities, including gaijin *(foreigners):* A recent study showed that 63 percent of all Japanese commercials featured hired celebrities. See Crossing Borders 16.2 for more details.

Aging of society: Seniors are featured often.

Changing families: The changing role of fathers—more time spent at home—is a common theme.

Generation gaps and individualism: Younger characters are shown as more individualistic.

Self-effacing humor: A dented Pepsi can was used in an ad to demonstrate its deference to more-popular Coke.

Polite ducks: The AFLAC duck is going to Japan, but with a softer quack. Instead of the American versions abrasive quack, the Japanese actor portrays the duck with a more soothing tone. "The Japanese culture does not like being yelled at," says the AFLAC spokeswoman. About 70 percent of the firm's international revenues come from Japan, some $8 billion last year. Although this campaign is the first to be shot specifically for Japan, the Japanese have met the duck before. In 2001 the company used dubbed voices of American ads including the loud "quacker."

Sources: George Fields, Hotaka Katahira, and Jerry Wind, *Leveraging Japan, Marketing to the New Asia* (San Francisco: Jossey-Bass, 2000); "ALFAC Tames Its Duck for Japanese Market," *Los Angeles Times*, May 13, 2003, p. C7; "Burger Campaign Larded with Jokes," *Associated Press*, December 7, 2004.

---

in others, only spot advertising is permissible and programs may not be sponsored. Live commercials are not permitted in some countries; in still others, commercial stations must compete for audiences against the government's noncommercial broadcasting network.

Some countries do not permit any commercial radio or television, but several of the traditional noncommercial countries have changed their policies in recent years because television production is so expensive. Until recently, France limited commercials to a daily total of 18 minutes, but now has extended the time limit to 12 minutes per hour per TV channel. South Korea has two television companies, both government owned, which broadcast only a few hours a day. They do not broadcast from midnight to 6 A.M. and they usually cannot broadcast between 10 A.M. and 5:30 P.M. on weekdays. Commercials are limited to 8 percent of airtime and are shown in clusters at the beginning and end of programs. One advertiser remarked, "We are forced to buy what we don't want to buy just to get on."

Lack of reliable audience data is another major problem in international marketing via radio and television. Measurement of radio and television audiences is always a precarious business, even with highly developed techniques. In most countries, either audience size is not audited or the existing auditing associations are ineffective. Despite the paucity of audience data, many advertisers use radio and television extensively. Advertisers justify their inclusion in the media schedule on the inherent logic favoring the use of these media, or defend their use on the basis of sales results.

Satellite and Cable TV.

Of increasing importance in TV advertising is the growth and development of satellite TV broadcasting. Sky Channel, a United Kingdom–based commercial satellite television station, beams its programs and advertising into most of Europe to cable TV subscribers. The technology that permits households to receive broadcasts directly from the satellite via a dish the size of a dinner plate costing about $350 is adding greater coverage and the ability to reach all of Europe with a single message. The expansion of TV coverage will challenge the creativity of advertisers and put greater

Exhibit 16.5

Media Penetration in Selected Countries (per 1,000 persons)

Country	TV	Cable TV	Satellite TV	Telephone Lines	Internet Users	Newspapers (per day)
United States	871	255	284	621	551	153
Canada	707	253	280	629	513	236
Argentina	326	163	169	219	112	96
Germany	675	251	283	657	473	388
Poland	229	94	117	319	232	194
Israel	342	190	258	458	301	250
South Africa	177	58	96	107	68	31
China	350	75	57	209	63	49
Japan	785	193	182	472	483	462
Australia	722	76	102	542	567	241

Source: Euromonitor, World Bank (World Development Indicators), 2005.

emphasis on global standardized messages. For a comparison of penetration rates by cable TV, computers, and the Internet in the several countries, see Exhibit 16.5.

Advertisers and governments are both concerned about the impact of satellite TV. Governments are concerned because they fear further loss of control over their airwaves and the spread of "American cultural imperialism." European television programming includes such U.S. shows as *Roseanne. Wheel of Fortune* is the most popular foreign show in the United Kingdom and in France, where both the U.S. and French versions are shown. U.S. imports are so popular in France and Germany that officials fear lowbrow U.S. game shows, sitcoms, and soap operas will crush domestic producers. This battle has even reached political levels associated with differences in worldviews represented in the news. France is investing in developing, not surprisingly, a French-language "CNN." Al-Jazeera, initially subsidized by Qatar government loans, is currently struggling to break even. Nevertheless, it is the now widely recognized Arabic "CNN" and is commensurately influential in the Middle East.

Parts of Asia and Latin America receive TV broadcasts from satellite television networks. Univision and Televisa are two Latin American satellite television networks broadcasting via a series of affiliate stations in each country to most of the Spanish-speaking world, including the United States. *Sabado Gigante,* a popular Spanish-language program broadcast by Univision, is seen by tens of millions of viewers in 16 countries. Star TV, a new pan-Asian satellite television network, has a potential audience of 2.7 billion people living in 38 countries from Egypt through India to Japan, and from Russia to Indonesia. Star TV was the first to broadcast across Asia but was quickly joined by ESPN and CNN. The first Asian 24-hour all-sports channel was followed by MTV Asia and a Mandarin Chinese–language channel that delivers dramas, comedies, movies, and financial news aimed at the millions of overseas Chinese living throughout Asia. Programs are delivered through cable networks but can be received through private satellite dishes.

One of the drawbacks of satellites is also their strength, that is, their ability to span a wide geographical region covering many different country markets. That means a single message is broadcast throughout a wide area. This may not be desirable for some products; further, with cultural differences in language, preferences, and so on, a single message may not be as effective. PVI (Princeton Video Imaging) is an innovation that will make regional advertising in diverse cultures easier than it presently is when using cable or satellite television. PVI allows ESPN, which offers this service, to fill visual real estate—blank walls, streets, stadium sidings—with computer-generated visuals that look like they belong in the scene. For instance, if you are watching the "street luge" during ESPN's X-games, you will see the racers appear to pass a billboard advertising Adidas shoes that really is not there. That billboard can say one thing in Holland and quite another in Cameroon. And if you are watching in Portland, Oregon, where Adidas might not advertise, you will see the scene as

Given the ubiquitous Guinness advertising in Dublin, it's not surprising that Irish livers need assurance. Ireland is behind only the Czech Republic when it comes to per capita consumption of beer. Actually, Royal Liver Assurance is a British pension/insurance company with offices in Dublin (it was established in the 1850s as the Liverpool Liver Burial Society). "Hurling" is a rather brutal form of field hockey popular in Ireland. The Irish government does recognize the causal effects of advertising on consumption—beer ads are not allowed on radio or TV before sports programs and may not be shown more than once per night on any one channel. See www.eurocare.org/profiles/irelnatpol.htm for more on the consumption of alcohol in Ireland.

it really appears—without the billboard. These commercials can play in different languages, in different countries, and even under different brand names.

Most satellite technology involves some government regulation. Singapore, Taiwan, and Malaysia prohibit selling satellite dishes, and the Japanese government prevents domestic cable companies from rebroadcasting from foreign satellites. Such restrictions seldom work for long, however. In Taiwan, an estimated 1.5 million dishes are in use and numerous illicit cable operators are in business. Through one technology or another, Asian households will be open to the same kind of viewing choice Americans have grown accustomed to and the advertising that it brings with it.

Direct Mail. Direct mail is a viable medium in an increasing number of countries. It is especially important when other media are not available. As is often the case in international marketing, even such a fundamental medium is subject to some odd and novel quirks. For example, in Chile, direct mail is virtually eliminated as an effective medium because the sender pays only part of the mailing fee; the letter carrier must collect additional postage for every item delivered. Obviously, advertisers cannot afford to alienate customers by forcing them to pay for unsolicited advertisements. Despite some limitations with direct mail, many companies have found it a meaningful way to reach their markets. The Reader's Digest Association has used direct mail advertising in Mexico to successfully market its magazines.

In Southeast Asian markets, where print media are scarce, direct mail is considered one of the most effective ways to reach those responsible for making industrial goods purchases, even though accurate mailing lists are a problem in Asia as well as in other parts of the world. In fact, some companies build their own databases for direct mail. Industrial advertisers are heavy mail users and rely on catalogs and sales sheets to generate large volumes of international business. Even in Japan, where media availability is not a problem, direct mail is successfully used by marketers such as Nestlé Japan and Dell Computer. To promote its Buitoni fresh-chilled pasta, Nestlé is using a 12-page color direct mail booklet of recipes, including Japanese-style versions of Italian favorites.

In Russia, the volume of direct mail has gone from just over 150,000 letters per month to over 500,000 per month in one year. Although small by U.S. standards, the response rate to direct mailings is as high as 10 to 20 percent, compared with only 3 to 4 percent or less in the United States. One suggestion as to why it works so well is that Russians are flattered by the attention—needless to say, that will probably change as use of the medium grows.

The Internet.   Though still evolving, the Internet has emerged as a viable medium for advertising and should be included as one of the media in a company's possible media mix. Its use in business-to-business communications and promotion via catalogs and product descriptions is rapidly gaining in popularity.[37] Because a large number of businesses have access to the Internet, the Internet can reach a large portion of the business-to-business market.

Although limited in its penetration of households globally,[38] the Internet is being used by a growing number of companies as an advertising medium for consumer goods. Many consumer goods companies have e-stores, and others use the Internet as an advertising medium to stimulate sales in retail outlets. Waterford Crystal of Ireland has set up its Web site specifically to drive store traffic. The aim is to promote its products and to attract people into stores that sell Waterford crystal. Sites list and display almost the entire catalog of the Waterford collection, while stores like Bloomingdale's that stock Waterford support the promotional effort by also advertising on the Internet.

For consumer products, the major limitation of the Internet is coverage (see Exhibit 16.5). In the United States growing numbers of households have access to a computer, but there are fewer in other countries. However, the growing number of Internet households accessible outside the United States generally constitutes a younger, better-educated market segment with higher-than-average incomes. For many companies, this group is an important market niche. Furthermore, this limitation is only temporary as new technology allows access to the Internet via television and as lower prices for personal computers expand the household base.

As the Internet continues to grow and countries begin to assert control over what is now a medium with few restrictions, increasing limitations will be set. Besides control of undesirable information, issues such as pay-per-view,[39] taxes, unfair competition, import duties, and privacy are being addressed all over the world. In Australia, local retailers are calling for changes in laws because of loss of trade to the Internet; under current law Internet purchases do not carry regular import duties. The Internet industry is lobbying for a global understanding on regulation to avoid a crazy quilt of confusing and contradictory rules.

Another limitation that needs to be addressed soon is the competition for Web surfers. The sheer proliferation of the number of Web sites makes it increasingly difficult for a customer to stumble across a particular page. Search engines have now become crucial directors of Web surfers' attention. Also, serious Internet advertisers or e-marketers will have to be more effective in communicating the existence of their Internet sites via other advertising media. Some companies are coupling their traditional television spots with a Web site; IBM, Swatch Watches, AT&T, and Samsung electronics are among those going for a one-two punch of on-air and online presences. TV spots are used to raise brand awareness of product regionally and to promote the company's Web site. Additionally, a company can buy ad banners on the Web that will lead enthusiastic consumers to the company's site, which also promotes the product. Some TV networks offer a package deal: a TV spot and ad banners on the network's Web site. For example, the EBN (European Business News) channel offers a cross-media program that includes TV spots and the advertiser's ad banner on the EB Interactive page for $15,000 a quarter.

---

[37]Oystein Moen, Iver Endresen, and Morten Gavlen, "Use of the Internet in International Marketing: A Case Study of Small Computer Software Firms," *Journal of International Marketing* 11, no. 4 (2003), pp. 129–149.

[38]See *The Economist*'s insert, "A Perfect Match, a Survey of E-Commerce," May 15, 2004.

[39]Ashutosh Prasad, Vijay Mahajan, and Bart Bronnenberg, "Advertising versus Pay-Per-View in Electronic Media," *International Journal of Research in Marketing* 20, no. 1 (March 2003), pp. 13–30.

Two novel media here: (1) Not only do the Russians sell space for space tourists on their rockets; they also sell advertising space! (2) Japanese beverage company Suntory promotes its products with "Monitor Man" during a football match at National Stadium. "Monitor Man" puts on an LCD display showing ads for Pepsi and other products and walks around the stadium. The job requires some muscle as the equipment weighs about 15 pounds. All this is perhaps purposely reminiscent of the Simpson's "Duff Man." Ohhh yaaaa! *(left: AP/Wide World Photos; right: © Tatsuyuki Tayama/Fujifotos/The Image Works)*

The online advertising business itself—for example, a banner ad for Amazon.com placed on a *Wall Street Journal* Web site—has come into its own. The industry is now conducting international festivals annually in Cannes, France. In 2005 over $8 billion was spent worldwide on online ads; continued dramatic growth is forecasted.[40] Of course, the creative possibilities (with global reach, hyperlinks, and such) are endless.

Other Media.   Restrictions on traditional media or their availability cause advertisers to call on lesser media to solve particular local-country problems. The cinema is an important medium in many countries, as are billboards and other forms of outside advertising. Billboards are especially useful in countries with high illiteracy rates. Hong Kong is clearly the neon capital of the world, with Tokyo's Ginza and New York's Times Square running close seconds. Indeed, perhaps the most interesting "billboard" was the Pizza Hut logo that appeared on the side of a Russian Proton rocket launched to carry parts of the international space station into orbit—can extraterrestrials read? Do they like Pizza?

In Haiti, sound trucks equipped with powerful loudspeakers provide an effective and widespread advertising medium. Private contractors own the equipment and sell advertising space much as a radio station would. This medium overcomes the problems of illiteracy, lack of radio and television set ownership, and limited print media circulation. In Ukraine, where the postal service is unreliable, businesses have found that the most effective form of direct business-to-business advertising is direct faxing.

In Spain, a new medium includes private cars that are painted with advertisements for products and serve as moving billboards as they travel around. This system, called *Publicoche* (derived from the words *publicidad,* meaning advertising, and *coche,* meaning car), has 75 cars in Madrid. Car owners are paid $230 a month and must submit their profession and "normal" weekly driving patterns. Advertisers pay a basic cost of $29,000 per car per month, and can select the type and color of car they are interested in and which owners are most suited to the campaign based on their driving patterns.

---

[40]*AdvertisingAge Factbook,* February 28, 2005, insert; and www.medialifemagazine.com, 2005.

Campaign Execution and Advertising Agencies

The development of advertising campaigns and their execution are managed by advertising agencies. Just as manufacturing firms have become international, so too have U.S., Japanese, and European advertising agencies expanded internationally to provide sophisticated agency assistance worldwide.[41] Local agencies also have expanded as the demand for advertising services by MNCs has developed. Thus the international marketer has a variety of alternatives available. In most commercially significant countries, an advertiser has the opportunity to employ a local domestic agency, its company-owned agency, or one of the multinational advertising agencies with local branches. There are strengths and weaknesses associated with each. The discussion regarding firm and agency relations in Chapter 8 on pages 236–237 and Exhibit 8.3 are quite pertinent here. Moreover, the agency–company relationships can be complicated and fragile in the international context—Ford and Disneyland Paris recently changed agencies, for example.

A local domestic agency may provide a company with the best cultural interpretation in situations where local modification is sought, but the level of sophistication can be weak. Moreover, the cross-cultural communication between the foreign client and the local agency can also be problematic. However, the local agency may have the best feel for the market, especially if the multinational agency has little experience in the market. Eastern Europe has been a problem for multinational agencies that are not completely attuned to the market. In Hungary, a U.S. baby care company advertisement of bath soap showing a woman holding her baby hardly seemed risqué. But where Westerners saw a young mother, scandalized Hungarians saw an unwed mother. The model was wearing a ring on her left hand; Hungarians wear wedding bands on the right hand. It was obvious to viewers that this woman wearing a ring on her left hand was telling everybody in Hungary she wasn't married. This is a mistake a local agency would not have made. Finally, in some emerging markets like Vietnam, local laws require a local partner.

The best compromise is the multinational agency with local branches because it has the sophistication of a major agency with local representation. Further, the multinational agency with local branches is better able to provide a coordinated worldwide advertising campaign. This has become especially important for firms doing business in Europe. With the interest in global or standardized advertising, many agencies have expanded to provide worldwide representation. Many companies with a global orientation employ one, or perhaps two, agencies to represent them worldwide.

---

[41]"Advertising, Consumer Republic," *The Economist,* March 19, 2005, pp. 69–70.

Exhibit 16.6
World's Top Ten Advertising Agency Organizations

2004	Agency	Headquarters	Global Revenues 2004	Percent Change from 2003	U.S. Revenues 2004
1	Omnicom Group	New York	$9,747	13.1	$5,223
2	WPP Group	London	9,370	16.2	3,552
3	Interpublic Group	New York	6,200	5.8	3,437
4	Publicis Groupe	Paris	4,777	8.4	2040
5	Dentsu	Tokyo	2,851	19.1	48
6	Havas	Suresnes, France	1,866	−0.6	731
7	Aegis Group	London	1,373	28.7	428
8	Hakuhodo DY Holdings	Tokyo	1,357	16.4	0.0
9	Asatsu-DK	Tokyo	473	14.3	3
10	Carlson Marketing Group	Minneapolis	347	7.6	247

Source: "Special Report Global Marketing," Reprinted with permission from the November 8, 2004 issue of *Advertising Age.* Copyright © 2004 Crain Communications, Inc.

Compensation arrangements for advertising agencies throughout the world are based on the U.S. system of 15 percent commissions. However, agency commission patterns throughout the world are not as consistent as they are in the United States; in some countries, agency commissions vary from medium to medium. Companies are moving from the commission system to a reward-by-results system, which details remuneration terms at the outset. If sales rise, the agency should be rewarded accordingly. This method of sharing in the gains or losses of profits generated by the advertising is gaining in popularity and may become the standard. Services provided by advertising agencies also vary greatly, but few foreign agencies offer the full services found in U.S. agencies.

Even a sophisticated business function such as advertising may find it is involved in unique practices. In some parts of the world, advertisers often pay for the promotion with the product advertised rather than with cash. Kickbacks on agency commissions are prevalent in some parts of the world and account in part for the low profitability of international advertising agencies. In Mexico, India, and Greece, the advertiser returns half the media commissions to the agencies. In many developing countries, long-term credit is used to attract clients.

International Control of Advertising: Broader Issues
In a previous section specific legal restrictions on advertising were presented. Here broader issues related to the past, present, and future of the international regulation of advertising are considered.

Consumer criticisms of advertising are not a phenomenon of the U.S. market only. Consumer concern with the standards and believability of advertising may have spread around the world more swiftly than have many marketing techniques. A study of a representative sample of European consumers indicated that only half of them believed advertisements gave consumers any useful information. Six of ten believed that advertising meant higher prices (if a product is heavily advertised, it often sells for more than brands that are seldom or never advertised); nearly eight of ten believed advertising often made them buy things they did not really need, and that ads often were deceptive about product quality. In Hong Kong, Colombia, and Brazil, advertising fared much better than in Europe. The non-Europeans praised advertising as a way to obtain valuable information about products; most Brazilians consider ads entertaining and enjoyable.

European Community officials are establishing directives to provide controls on advertising as cable and satellite broadcasting expands. Deception in advertising is a thorny issue since most member countries have different interpretations of what constitutes a misleading advertisement. Demands for regulation of advertising aimed at young consumers is a trend appearing in both industrialized and developing countries.

Decency and the blatant use of sex in advertisements also are receiving public attention. One of the problems in controlling decency and sex in ads is the cultural variations found around the world. An ad perfectly acceptable to a Westerner may be very offensive to someone from the Mideast, or, for that matter, another Westerner. Standards for appropriate behavior as depicted in advertisements vary from culture to culture. Regardless of these variations, concern about decency, sex, and ads that demean women and men is growing. International advertising associations are striving to forestall laws by imposing self-regulation, but it may be too late; some countries are passing laws that will define acceptable standards.

The difficulty that business has with self-regulation and restrictive laws is that sex can be powerful in some types of advertisements. European advertisements for Häagen-Dazs, a premium U.S. ice cream marketer, and LapPower, a Swedish laptop computer company, received criticism for being too sexy. Häagen-Dazs's ad showed a couple in various stages of undress, in an embrace, feeding ice cream to one another. Some British editorial writers and radio commentators were outraged. One commented that "the ad was the most blatant and inappropriate use of sex as a sales aid." The ad for LapPower personal computers that the Stockholm Business Council on Ethics condemned featured the co-owner of the company with an "inviting smile and provocative demeanor displayed." (Wearing a low-cut dress, she was bending over a LapPower computer.) The bottom line for both these companies was increased sales. In Britain, ice cream sales soared after the "Dedicated to Pleasure" ads appeared, and in Sweden, the co-owner stated, "Sales are increasing daily."

CROSSING BORDERS 16.6   Subliminal Advertising in Russia

Deep within a Russian television advertisement for a local beer, Klinskoye, lurked a split-second message for another thirst quencher: Pepsi. An image of Palmolive Fruit Essentials soap was there and gone in the blink of an eye on the NTV television network. Young viewers of Russian MTV unconsciously absorbed marketing messages for Secret deodorant, the New Musical Express newspaper, and the Red Hot Chili Peppers album *By The Way*.

In fact, according to Russian scientists, subliminal television advertising, although illegal in Russia, is strewn across the airwaves. Russian television stations insist they have no way of knowing whether video material provided by advertising agencies contains subliminal messages. Advertising firms and the companies whose products appear in subliminal messages deny any involvement. Such advertising is also outlawed in the United States, but the majority of marketing researchers deny its potency anyway.

"There are very many cases. I'm surprised by the quantity," said Svetlana Nemstova, deputy director-general of the All Russian Research Institute for TV and Radio Broadcasting, a state agency. "There are channels that are impossible to watch," she said, referring to the amount of subliminal advertising broadcast. "There are channels that don't overdo it, and there are also channels that don't do it at all." She declined to describe the list of offenders.

But time is running out for them. Nemstova and other Russian scientists at the broadcasting institute have developed equipment to trace subliminal messages that will constantly monitor Russian TV airwaves.

Sources: Robyn Dixon, "Abusing the Power of Suggestion in Russian Ads," *Los Angeles Times*, August 25, 2002, p. A5; Kerry Gill, "Adverts Should be Simple—Not Subliminal," *Daily Express*, June 13, 2005, p. 12.

Whether laws are passed or the industry polices itself, advertising and its effect on people's behavior have engendered international concern.

Advertising regulations are not limited to Europe; there is an enhanced awareness of the expansion of mass communications and the perceived need to effect greater control in developing countries as well. Malaysia consistently regulates TV advertising to control the effect of the "excesses of Western ways." The government has become so concerned that it will not allow "Western cultural images" to appear in TV commercials. No bare shoulders or exposed armpits are allowed, nor are touching or kissing, sexy clothing, or blue jeans. These are just a few of the prohibitions spelled out in a 41-page advertising code that the Malaysian government has been compiling for more than 10 years.

The assault on advertising and promotion of tobacco products is escalating. In the United States, the tobacco firms have agreed to curtail promotion as part of government-supported class-action lawsuits. The European Union Parliament approved larger health warnings on cigarette packs. Most significantly, the World Health Organization (WHO) launched a global campaign against the tobacco industry.[42] Dr. Gro Harlem Brundtland, director-general of the WHO, explains, "Tobacco is a communicable disease—it's communicated through advertising, marketing and making smoking appear admirable and glamorous." A worldwide ban of tobacco advertising is just one of the stated goals of the new WHO action.

Product placement within TV programming is another area of advertising receiving the attention of regulators. In the United States, complaints have been aired regarding cigarette smoking in movies and on TV. The product placements avoid some of the regulations in markets like China, where ad time is limited. Because these practices are new to China, the growth rate has been initially dramatic. It will be interesting to follow how product placement advertising will be regulated as the practice proliferates.

The advertising industry is sufficiently concerned with the negative attitudes and skepticism of consumers and governments and with the poor practices of some advertisers that the International Advertising Association and other national and international industry groups have developed a variety of self-regulating codes. Sponsors of these codes feel that

---

[42]"Global Tobacco Treaty," *All Africa/COMTEX*, April 12, 2005.

unless the advertisers themselves come up with an effective framework for control, governments will intervene. This threat of government intervention has spurred interest groups in Europe to develop codes to ensure that the majority of ads conform to standards set for "honesty, truth, and decency." In those countries where the credibility of advertising is questioned and in those where the consumerism movement exists, the creativity of the advertiser is challenged. The most egregious control, however, may be in Myanmar (formerly Burma), where each medium has its own censorship board that passes judgment on any advertising even before it is submitted for approval by the Ministry of Information. There is even a censorship board for calendars. Content restrictions are centered on any references to the government or military, other political matters, religious themes, or images deemed degrading to traditional culture.

In many countries, there is a feeling that advertising, and especially TV advertising, is too powerful and persuades consumers to buy what they do not need, an issue that has been debated in the United States for many years. South Korea, for example, has threatened to ban advertising of bottled water because the commercials may arouse public mistrust of tap water!

Summary

An integrated marketing communications (IMC) program includes coordination among advertising, sales management, public relations, sales promotions, and direct marketing. Global marketers face unique legal, language, media, and production limitations in every market. These must be considered when designing an IMC program. During the late 1990s many large firms moved toward an advertising strategy of standardization. However, more recently even the most multinational companies have changed emphasis to strategies based on national, subcultural, demographic, or other market segments.

The major problem facing international advertisers is designing the best messages for each market served. The potential for cross-cultural misunderstandings is great in both public relations and the various advertising media. The availability and quality of advertising media also vary substantially around the world. Marketers may be unable to profitably enter markets for lack of appropriate advertising media—for example, some products require the availability of TV.

Advances in communication technologies (particularly the Internet) are causing dramatic changes in the structure of the international advertising and communications industries. New problems are being posed for government regulators as well. Despite these challenges, the industry is experiencing dramatic growth as new media are developed and as new markets open to commercial advertising.

Questions

1. Define the following terms:

   integrated marketing
     communications
   public relations
   noise

   advertising
   sales promotions
   market segment

2. "Perhaps advertising is the side of international marketing with the greatest similarities from country to country throughout the world. Paradoxically, despite its many similarities, it may also be credited with the greatest number of unique problems in international marketing." Discuss.

3. Someone once commented that advertising is America's greatest export. Discuss.

4. With satellite TV able to reach many countries, discuss how a company can use satellite TV and deal effectively with different languages, different cultures, and different legal systems.

5. Outline some of the major problems confronting an international advertiser.

6. Defend either side of the proposition that advertising can be standardized for all countries.

7. Review the basic areas of advertising regulation. Are such regulations purely foreign phenomena?

8. How can advertisers overcome the problems of low literacy in their markets?

9. What special media problems confront the international advertiser?

10. After reading the section in this chapter on direct mail, develop guidelines to be used by a company when developing a direct mail program.

11. Will the ability to broadcast advertisements over TV satellites increase or decrease the need for standardization of advertisements? What are the problems associated with satellite broadcasting? Comment.

17

personal selling and sales management

CHAPTER OUTLINE

Global Perspective: International Assignments Are Glamorous, Right?

Designing the Sales Force

Recruiting Marketing and Sales Personnel

    Expatriates
    Virtual Expatriates
    Local Nationals
    Third-Country Nationals
    Host-Country Restrictions

Selecting Sales and Marketing Personnel

Training for International Marketing

Motivating Sales Personnel

Designing Compensation Systems

    For Expatriates
    For a Global Sales Force

Evaluating and Controlling Sales Representatives

Preparing U.S. Personnel for Foreign Assignments

    Overcoming Reluctance to Accept a Foreign Assignment
    Reducing the Rate of Early Returns
    Successful Expatriate Repatriation

Developing Cultural Awareness

The Changing Profile of the Global Manager

Foreign-Language Skills

CHAPTER LEARNING OBJECTIVES

What you should learn from Chapter 17:

- The role of interpersonal selling in international marketing

- The considerations in designing an international sales force

- The steps to recruiting three types of international sales people

- Selection criteria for international sales and marketing positions

- The special training needs of international personnel

- Motivation techniques for international sales representatives

- How to design compensation systems for an international sales force

- How to prepare Americans for foreign assignments

- The changing profile of the global sales and marketing manager

Global Perspective

INTERNATIONAL ASSIGNMENTS ARE GLAMOROUS, RIGHT?

"Glamorous" is probably not the adjective the following executives would use.

> The problem as I see it with the company's talk about international managers is that they were just paying lip service to it. When I applied for the posting to Malaysia they gave me all this stuff about the assignment being a really good career move and how I'd gain this valuable international experience and so on. And don't get me wrong, we really enjoyed the posting. We loved the people and the culture and the lifestyle and when it came back to returning home, we weren't really all that keen . . . The problem was that while I had been away, the company had undergone a wholesale restructuring . . . This meant that when I got back, my job had been effectively eliminated.

> We have been in the United States for eleven months and I reckon it will be another six to twelve months before my wife and the kids are really settled here. I'm still learning new stuff every day at work and it has taken a long time to get used to American ways of doing things . . . I mean if the company said, "Oh, we want you to move to South Africa in a year's time," I would really dig my heels in because it was initially very disruptive for my wife when she first came here.

And "glamorous" would not be on the tip of these expatriate spouses' tongues either:

> I found I haven't adapted to Spanish hours. I find it a continual problem because the 2–5 P.M. siesta closure is really awkward. I always find myself where I have to remind myself that from 2–5 I have a blank period that I can't do anything . . . We started adjusting to the eating schedule. Whether we like it or not, we eat a lot later.

> Well we went down to Club Med for a vacation and the French were all topless and my 8-year-old son didn't say anything but my 4-year-old daughter now refuses to wear a top. I will not let her get away with it back in the U.S.

> We've been really fortunate we haven't had to use health care services here . . . The thought of going to, needing to go to a doctor is scary because for me it would have to be someone English speaking or I wouldn't, you know, feel comfortable.

Given these kinds of problems, is that international sales position being offered to you as attractive as it looks? Will it really help your career?

Sources: Nick Forster, "The Myth of the 'International Manager,'" *International Journal of Resource Management* 11, no. 1 (February 2000), pp. 126–142; Mary C. Gilly, Lisa Penaloza, and Kenneth M. Kambara, "The Role of Consumption in Expatriate Adjustment and Satisfaction," working paper, The Paul Merage School of Business, University of California, Irvine, 2006.

The salesperson is a company's most direct tie to the customer; in the eyes of most customers, the salesperson is the company. As presenter of company offerings and gatherer of customer information, the sales representative is the final link in the culmination of a company's marketing and sales efforts.

Growing global competition coupled with the dynamic and complex nature of international business increases both the need and the means for closer ties with both customers and suppliers. Particularly in relationship cultures such as China, relationship marketing, built on effective communications between the seller and buyer, focuses on building long-term alliances rather than treating each sale as a one-time event.[1] Advances in information technology are allowing for increasingly higher levels of coordination across advertising, marketing research, and personal selling efforts, yielding new roles and functions in customer relationship management (CRM).[2] Similarly, such advances are changing the nature of personal selling and sales management, leading some to forecast substantial reductions in field sales efforts.

In this ever-changing environment of international business, the tasks of designing, building, training, motivating, and compensating an international sales group generate unique problems at every stage of management and development. This chapter discusses the alternatives and problems of managing sales and marketing personnel in foreign countries. Indeed, these problems are among the most difficult facing international marketers. In one survey of CEOs and other top executives, the respondents identified "establishing sales and distribution networks" and "cultural differences" as major difficulties in international sales and operations.

Designing the Sales Force

The first step in managing a sales force is its design. Based on analyses of current and potential customers, the selling environment, competition, and the firm's resources and capabilities, decisions must be made regarding the numbers, characteristics, and assignments of sales personnel. All these design decisions are made more challenging by the wide variety of pertinent conditions and circumstances in international markets. Moreover, the globalization of markets and customers, as illustrated by the IBM–Ford story in Crossing Borders 17.1, makes the job of international sales manager quite interesting.

As described in previous chapters, distribution strategies will often vary from country to country. Some markets may require a direct sales force, whereas others may not. How customers are approached can differ as well. For example, banks are placing sales representatives in Russian appliance stores to sell credit, a new concept there. The hard sell that may work in some countries can be inappropriate in others. Automobiles have been sold door to door in Japan for years, and only recently have stocks been sold over the Internet in Europe. More than 100,000 of Singapore's 6 million inhabitants are involved in home product sales and other forms of multilevel marketing. The size of accounts certainly makes a difference as well—notice in Crossing Borders 17.1 that an IBM sales representative works inside Ford. Selling high-technology products may allow for the greater use of American expatriates, whereas selling consulting services will tend to require more participation by native sales representatives. Selling in information-oriented cultures such as Germany may also allow for greater use of expatriates. However, relationship-oriented countries such as Japan will require the most complete local knowledge possessed only by natives. Writing about Japan, two international marketing experts agree: "Personal selling as a rule has to be localized for even the most global of corporations and industries."[3]

---

[1]Xueming Luo, David A. Griffith, Sandra S. Liu, and Yi-Zheng Shi, "The Effects of Customer Relationships and Social Capital on Firm Performance: A Chinese Business Approach," *Journal of International Marketing* 12, no. 4 (2004), pp. 25–47.

[2]Linda H. Shi, Shaoming Zou, J. Chris White, Regina C. McNally, and S. Tamer Cavusgil, "Global Account Management Capability: Insights from Leading Suppliers," *Journal of International Marketing* 13, no. 2 (2005), pp. 93–113.

[3]Johny K. Johansson and Ikujiro Nonaka, *Relentless: The Japanese Way of Marketing* (New York: Harper Business, 1997), p. 97; Klaus Brune agrees with regard to Europe, "U.S. Firms Get Success Recipe in Germany," *Wall Street Journal*, February 12, 2003, p. B5F.

CROSSING BORDERS 17.1   Sales Force Management and Global Customers

Did IBM really need a new sales compensation plan? For proof, just ask Kevin Tucker. Tucker, an IBM global account manager dedicated to Ford Motor Company, closed a $7 million sale with the automotive giant's European operations. Ford wanted Tucker and his team of IBM representatives to install networking systems in its engineering facilities. The systems would run the applications that design the company's automobiles.

Ford's installation required help from an IBM sales executive in Germany, the project's headquarters. So Tucker, whose office sits in Ford's Dearborn, Michigan, headquarters, sent an e-mail requesting the executive's assistance. And that's when things turned ugly. Although the rep in Germany didn't turn his back on the project, his initial reaction was less than enthusiastic. Ford wanted the systems installed throughout Europe, yet the compensation plan for IBM's Germany-based reps rewarded only the systems that were installed in that country. With 80 percent of the work scheduled outside of Germany, the executive was left wondering: Where's the payoff? Tucker and other IBM sales incentive managers wasted three weeks discussing ways to maximize the rep's incentive. Energy that could have been focused on the customer was wasted on a pay plan. "Ford was world-centric, we were country-centric," Tucker says. "The team in Germany was asking, 'Kevin, how can you make us whole?'"

They weren't the only salespeople asking that question at IBM. Tucker's predicament represents just one of many problems that were rooted in IBM's "$72 billion" sales incentive plan—a plan that had been obviously put on the back burner as the company giant tinkered with its vision.

Bob Wylie, manager of incentive strategies for IBM Canada, says, "There was the attitude that if it's outside my territory and outside my measurements, I don't get paid for it, and I don't get involved. What's in my pay plan defines what I do." Not the best setup for a company that operates in 165 countries.

Apparently, IBM has solved many of these problems. Ford signed contracts for more than $300 million with IBM to create almost all of the car company's software, including Internet and e-commerce applications in Europe and North America. Details about IBM's new sales compensation program are provided later in this chapter.

Sources: Michele Marchetti, "Gamble: IBM Replaced Its Outdated Compensation Plan with a Worldwide Framework. Is It Paying Off?" *Sales & Marketing Management*, July 1996, pp. 65–69; "Ford Motor and IBM," *Wall Street Journal Europe*, January 13, 1999, p. UK5A; William M. Bulkeley, "IBM and Dassault Capture Software Job from EDS," *Wall Street Journal*, February 6, 2003, p. B5.

Once decisions have been made about how many expatriates, local nationals, or third-country nationals a particular market requires, then more intricate aspects of design can be undertaken, such as territory allocation and customer call plans. Many of the most advanced operations research tools developed in the United States can be applied in foreign markets, with appropriate adaptation of inputs, of course. For example, one company has provided tools to help international firms create balanced territories and find optimal locations for sales offices in Canada, Mexico, and Australia.[4] However, the use of such high-tech resource allocation tools requires intricate knowledge of not only geographical details but also appropriate call routines. Many things can differ across cultures—the length of sales cycles, the kinds of customer relationships, and the kinds of interactions with customers. Indeed, more than one study has identified substantial differences in the importance of referrals in the sales of industrial services in Japan vis-à-vis the United States.[5] The implications are that in Japan sales calls must be made not only on customers, but also on the key people, such as bankers, in the all-important referral networks.

---

[4] See the Web site for The TerrAlign Group, www.terralign.com, for more detailed information.

[5] R. Bruce Money, Mary C. Gilly, and John L. Graham, "National Culture and Referral Behavior in the Purchase of Industrial Services in the United States and Japan," *Journal of Marketing* 62, no. 4 (October 1998), pp. 76–87; Chanthika Pornpitakpan, "Trade in Thailand: A Three-Way Cultural Comparison," *Business Horizons*, March–April 2000, pp. 61–70.

Recruiting Marketing and Sales Personnel

The number of marketing management personnel from the home country assigned to foreign countries varies according to the size of the operation, the availability of qualified locals, and other firm characteristics.[6] Increasingly, the number of U.S. home-country nationals (expatriates) assigned to foreign posts is smaller as the pool of trained, experienced locals grows.[7]

The largest personnel requirement abroad for most companies is the sales force, recruited from three sources: expatriates, local nationals, and third-country nationals. A company's staffing pattern may include all three types in any single foreign operation, depending on qualifications, availability, and a company's needs. Sales and marketing executives can be recruited via the traditional media of advertising (including newspapers, magazines, job fairs, and the Internet), employment agencies or executive search firms,[8] and the all-important personal referrals. The last source will be crucial in many foreign countries, particularly the relationship-oriented ones.

Expatriates

The number of companies relying on expatriate personnel is declining as the volume of world trade increases and as more companies use locals to fill marketing positions. However, when products are highly technical, or when selling requires an extensive background of information and applications, an expatriate sales force remains the best choice. The expatriate salesperson may have the advantages of greater technical training, better knowledge of the company and its product line, and proven dependability. Because they are not locals, expatriates sometimes add to the prestige of the product line in the eyes of foreign customers. And, perhaps most important, expatriates usually are able to effectively communicate with and influence headquarters personnel.

The chief disadvantages of an expatriate sales force are the high cost, cultural and legal barriers, and the limited number of high-caliber personnel willing to live abroad for extended periods. Companies in the United States are finding it difficult to persuade outstanding employees to take overseas posts. Employees are reluctant to go abroad for many reasons: Some find it difficult to uproot families for a two- or three-year assignment, increasing numbers of dual-career couples often require finding suitable jobs for spouses, and many executives believe such assignments impede their subsequent promotions at home. Recall the comments of the executives in the Global Perspective. The loss of visibility at corporate headquarters plus the belief that "out of sight is out of mind" are major reasons for the reluctance to accept a foreign assignment. Companies with well-planned career development programs have the least difficulty. Indeed, the best international companies make it crystal clear that a ticket to top management is an overseas stint. Korn/Ferry International reports in a survey of 75 senior executives from around the world that "international experience" is the attribute identified as second most important for CEOs—experience in marketing and finance positions were first and third, respectively.[9]

Expatriates commit to foreign assignments for varying lengths of time, from a few weeks or months to a lifetime. Some expatriates have one-time assignments (which may last for years), after which they are returned to the parent company; others are essentially professional expatriates, working abroad in country after country. Still another expatriate assignment is a career-long assignment to a given country or region; this is likely to lead to assimilation of the expatriate into the foreign culture to such an extent that the person may more closely resemble a local than an expatriate. Because expatriate marketing personnel are likely to cost substantially more than locals, a company must be certain of their effectiveness.

---

[6]Rene A. Belderbos and Marielle G. Heijltjes, "The Determinants of Expatriate Staffing by Japanese Multinationals in Asia: Control, Learning, and Vertical Business Groups," *Journal of International Business Studies* 36, no. 3 (2005), pp. 341–354.

[7]An interesting sign of the shrinking expat populations is the demise of the only English-language paper sold in Mexico City. See Reed Johnson, "English Paper in Mexico Folds," *Los Angeles Times*, January 17, 2003, p. A3.

[8]The largest international executive search firm is Korn/Ferry International (www.kornferry.com).

[9]See "Marketing Is Fastest Route to the Executive Suite," Korn/Ferry International, www.kornferry.com.

CROSSING **BORDERS 17.2**   The New Risks of International Travel

It's bad enough that sleep becomes a luxury because of jet lag. Your yawns at important meetings aren't the only dangers. Personal safety can also be a consideration for international sales representatives and expatriates. The U.S. State Department has long issued warnings for travelers (www.travel.state.gov). Here's a recent one:

Nigeria—Exercise extreme caution. Avoid demonstrations against U.S. policies. Visitors may be victims of armed robberies. Possible shakedowns at checkpoints.

The new terrorism yields advice like the following:

Stay in establishments that don't necessarily attract Americans. In planning for a recent trip to London, for example, a software executive changed her reservation from a Holiday Inn to a small place outside the city.

And then there's SARS (severe acute respiratory syndrome). The deaths are tragic and the macroeconomic effects are huge on the affected areas and companies. In the first affected places the economists knocked a percentage point off annual growth rates. Cathay Pacific, Singapore Air, and Qantas grounded 40 percent of their flights. But the inconvenience for sales representatives was more than just a bother. Here's one person's account from Hong Kong:

The Amoy Plaza shopping mall is brightly lit but deserted. A big Kentucky Fried Chicken restaurant

in the center is cordoned off with tape. Out back, men in protective suits are spraying each other with disinfectant. In front, almost everybody on the sidewalk is wearing a surgical mask . . .

This is a city living in fear. You can see it in people's eyes when somebody starts coughing on the bus or in the elevator. Nobody is prepared to risk their health and the health of their family and colleagues to be polite. Change seats or get off on the next floor, that's the best policy . . .

The biggest complaints come from those who have to travel for work. On the plane you sit helplessly breathing recirculated air that could be laden with the mystery virus. And then at your destination you will be shunned like a leper.

Finally, there's the ill-omened irony of the Tourist Boards' public relations slogan issued right before the SARS outbreak—Hong Kong will take your breath away!

Sources: Pete Engardio, Mark L. Clifford, and Michael Shari, "Epidemics and Economics," *BusinessWeek*, April 28, 2003, pp. 44–45; Jennifer Chandler and John L. Graham, "Corruption and the Attractiveness of International Markets," working paper, Merage School of Business, University of California, Irvine, 2006.

More and more American companies are taking advantage of American employees who are fluent in languages other than English. For example, many U.S. citizens speak Spanish as their first language. The large number of Puerto Ricans working for American multinationals in places like Mexico City is well documented. Recent immigrants and their sons and daughters who learn their parents' languages and about their native cultures will continue to be invaluable assets for firms wishing to enter such markets. Certainly ethnic Chinese- and Vietnamese-Americans are serving as cultural bridges for commerce with those two nations. Indeed, throughout history patterns of commerce have always followed paths of immigration.

Virtual Expatriates   The Internet and other advances in communications technologies, along with the growing reluctance of executives to move abroad, are creating a new breed of expatriate, the virtual one. According to a PricewaterhouseCoopers survey of 270 organizations, there has been a substantial increase in shorter-term, commuter, and virtual assignments in recent years. Virtual expatriates manage operations in other countries but don't move there. They stay in hotels, make long visits, and maintain their families at home. Some spend up to 75 percent of their working time traveling. None leave home without the ubiquitous laptop and cell phone.

Close contact with subordinates and customers is, of course, tougher for virtual expatriates. Moreover, the travel can be a killer—that is, foreign bugs are often more virulent and easier to catch on long international flights (indeed, one doctor calls airplanes "germ tubes"), crime against expatriates and travelers in foreign cities is a real hazard, and living

Exhibit 17.1
Risks of Violence in the International Marketplace

The best source of information we can find on comparative violence levels across countries is the World Health Organization (WHO) Mortality Statistics. The agency collects data from 69 countries on causes of death. Among the more than 100 causes listed, three are pertinent: "Homicide and injury purposely inflicted by other persons," "Other violence," and "Other external causes." We add these three numbers together and combine them with the WHO Estimated Mortality Coverage (Table 4) data to produce the "Deaths by Violence" statistics reported below.

Rank	Country	Deaths by Violence per 100,000	Rank	Country	Deaths by Violence per 100,000
1	Norway	1.2	36	Albania	6.2
2	Spain	1.3	37	U.K. (Scotland)	7.0
3	Greece	1.4	38	Slovenia	7.1
4	Netherlands	1.7	38	Switzerland	7.1
5	Austria	1.7	40	Cuba	7.6
6	New Zealand	2.0	41	United States	7.9
6	Japan	2.0	42	Poland	8.1
8	Australia	2.1	43	Israel	8.3
9	Luxembourg	2.3	44	Costa Rica	8.5
10	Ireland	2.5	45	Singapore	8.7
11	Iceland	2.6	46	Tajikistan	9.0
12	Malta	2.7	47	Azerbaijan	9.1
12	Canada	2.7	48	Uzbekistan	9.2
14	Italy	2.8	49	Thailand	10.2
15	Yugoslav Republic	3.0	50	Turkmenistan	10.6
16	Mauritius	3.1	51	Mexico	13.6
17	U.K. (Northern Ireland)	3.4	52	Armenia	15.1
18	Kuwait	3.8	53	Portugal	15.6
19	Germany	3.9	54	Argentina	16.8
20	Hungary	4.0	55	Lithuania	19.1
20	France	4.0	56	Chile	19.6
22	U.K. (England, Wales)	4.2	57	Kyrgyzstan	22.0
23	Croatia	4.4	58	Brazil	22.4
24	San Marino	4.5	59	Georgia	22.5
25	U.K.	4.6	60	Latvia	22.9
26	Czech Republic	4.7	61	Belize	23.5
26	Belgium	4.7	62	Estonia	24.8
26	Sweden	4.7	63	Republic of Moldova	25.1
29	Romania	5.0	64	Belarus	31.3
30	Finland	5.1	65	Kazakhstan	36.1
31	Slovakia	5.5	66	Ukraine	36.3
31	Denmark	5.5	67	Venezuela	45.5
33	Republic of Korea	5.7	68	Philippines	58.1
34	Bulgaria	5.9	69	Russian Federation	77.4
35	Uruguay	6.0			

Source: The Economist Intelligence Unit, July 2005. Reprinted with permission.

in hotels is lonely. However, virtual expatriates' families don't have to be uprooted, and executives can stay in closer touch with the home office. Finally, from the firm's perspective a virtual assignment may be the only option and often a good way to avoid the extra expenses of an actual executive move.

Local Nationals   The historical preference for expatriate managers and salespeople from the home country is giving way to a preference for local nationals. At the sales level, the picture is clearly biased in favor of the locals because they transcend both cultural and legal barriers. More knowledgeable about a country's business structure than an expatriate would be, local salespeople are better able to lead a company through the maze of unfamiliar distribution

A worker cleans an American Airlines plane detained at San Jose International Airport in California after a nonstop flight from Tokyo in which several passengers complained of symptoms similar to SARS, or severe acute respiratory syndrome. Officials found no threat after isolating passengers and crew for two hours. International travel can be a lot of work! *(© David Paul Morris/ Getty Images)*

systems and referral networks. Furthermore, pools of qualified foreign personnel available in some places cost less to maintain than a staff of expatriates.

In Europe and Asia, many locals have earned MBA degrees in the United States; thus a firm gets the cultural knowledge of the local meshed with an understanding of U.S. business management systems. Although expatriates' salaries may be no more than those of their national counterparts, the total cost of keeping comparable groups of expatriates in a country can be considerably higher (often three times the expense) because of special cost-of-living benefits, moving expenses, taxes, and other costs associated with keeping an expatriate abroad. As can be seen in Exhibit 17.2, only four of the most expensive cities in the world are in the United States.

The main disadvantage of hiring local nationals is the tendency of headquarters personnel to ignore their advice. Even though most foreign nationals are careful to keep relationships at the home office warm, their influence is often reduced by their limited English communication skills and lack of understanding of how home-office politics influence decision making. Another key disadvantage can be their lack of availability; one CEO of a consulting firm that specializes in recruiting managers in China reports that ten openings exist for every one qualified applicant. Moreover, whereas in the United States hiring experienced salespeople from competitors, suppliers, or vendors is common practice, the

Locals hit the road. Japanese salesmen saving on expenses in this "capsule hotel" in Osaka. Meanwhile, the Avon Lady calls on a customer in rural Brazil. *(left: © Roger Ressmeyer/CORBIS; right: © John Maier, Jr./The Image Works)*

CROSSING BORDERS 17.3   Avon Calling—or Not?

In a gold-mining town near an Amazon tributary, Maria de Fatima Nascimento ambles among mud shacks hawking Honesty and Care Deeply, two beauty products by Avon. She is part of a several-thousand-member Avon army that travels via foot, kayak, riverboat, and small plane through the Amazon basin. Latin America accounts for 35 percent of Avon's total sales, and its success can be attributed to the company's willingness to adapt to local conditions. Cash payments aren't required; many Brazilian customers barter for products with fruit, eggs, flour, or wood. Two dozen eggs buys a Bart Simpson roll-on deodorant, and miners pay from 1 to 4 grams of gold powder or nuggets for fragrances like Sweet Crystal Splash. "Ladies of the evening," who regard the cosmetics as a cost of doing business, are some of Nascimento's better customers. But then, so are miners. One commented, "It's worth 1½ grams of gold to smell nice."

Despite the success of the Bart Simpson roll-on in some parts of the world, Avon is not rolling along in the old-fashioned way in others. In 1998 at least ten people were killed in China during antigovernment rioting in several cities. Many of the rioters were from among the country's 200,000 Avon ladies. The Chinese government had banned direct selling, complaining in a directive that such practices spawn "weird cults, triads, superstitious groups, and hooliganism." Worse yet, the authorities criticized meetings of direct marketers that involved singing, chanting, and inspirational sermons. The *Peoples' Daily* once even complained that direct sales encouraged "excessive hugging"!

The latest and perhaps most serious threat to the 2.6 million Avon ladies working worldwide in 135 countries is the Internet. Many fret that Avon.com may replace "Ding dong, it's Avon calling." But, no matter what, Avon's international sales keep rolling along.

Sources: "Avon Calling Near the Amazon," *U.S. News & World Report*, October 25, 1994, pp. 16–17; Andrew Higgins, "Avon Calling? Not in China," *The Guardian*, May 1, 1998, p. 18; Kate Quill, "Ding Dong, Gone . . . Farewell Avon Lady?" *Times* (London), February 7, 2000, p. 7; "Avon Conducts Worldwide Dialogue with 20,000 Women in 22 Countries," *PR Newswire*, September 2, 2005.

same approach in other countries may not work. In places like Japan, employees are much more loyal to their companies and therefore are difficult to lure away even for big money. College recruits can also be hard to hire in Japan because the smartest students are heavily recruited by the largest Japanese firms. Smaller firms and foreign firms are seen in Japan as much more risky employment opportunities.

One other consideration makes recruiting of local nationals as sales representatives more difficult in many foreign countries. We all know about Americans' aversion to being a "salesman." Personal selling is often derided as a career and represented in a negative light in American media—Arthur Miller's *Death of a Salesman* is of course the best example. Despite the bad press, however, personal selling is the most common job in the United States. Indeed, the United States has been described as "a nation of salesmen."[10] But, as negatively as the selling profession is viewed in the United States, in many other countries it's viewed in even worse ways. Particularly in the more relationship-oriented cultures such

---

[10]See Earl Shorris's excellent and still pertinent book, *A Nation of Salesmen* (New York: Norton, 1994).

Exhibit 17.2

The 20 Most Expensive Cities to Live in on the Planet (in order)

Source: The Economist Intelligence Unit, July 2005. The cities are listed in order, Tokyo is the most expensive and Sydney the least.

Tokyo	Milan
Osaka	Paris
London	New York
Moscow	Dublin
Seoul	St. Petersburg
Geneva	Vienna
Zurich	Rome
Copenhagen	Stockholm
Hong Kong	Beijing
Oslo	Sydney

as France, Mexico, and Japan, sales representatives tend to be on the bottom rung of the social ladder. Thus recruiting the brightest people to fill sales positions in foreign operations can be very difficult indeed.

Third-Country Nationals

The internationalization of business has created a pool of third-country nationals (TCNs), expatriates from their own countries working for a foreign company in a third country. TCNs are a group whose nationality has little to do with where they work or for whom. An example would be a German working in Argentina for a U.S. company. Historically, few expatriates or TCNs spent the majority of their careers abroad, but now a truly "global executive" has begun to emerge. The recently appointed chairman of a division of a major Netherlands company is a Norwegian who gained that post after stints in the United States, where he was the U.S. subsidiary's chairman, and in Brazil, where he held the position of general manager. At one time, Burroughs Corporation's Italian subsidiary was run by a Frenchman, the Swiss subsidiary by a Dane, the German subsidiary by an Englishman, the French subsidiary by a Swiss, the Venezuelan subsidiary by an Argentinean, and the Danish subsidiary by a Dutchman.

American companies often seek TCNs from other English-speaking countries to avoid the double taxation costs of their American managers. Americans working in Spain, for example, must pay both Spanish and U.S. income taxes, and most American firms' compensation packages for expatriates are adjusted accordingly. So, given the same pay and benefits, it is cheaper for an American firm to post a British executive in Spain than an American.

Overall, the development of TCN executives reflects not only a growing internationalization of business but also an acknowledgment that personal skills and motivations are not the exclusive property of one nation. TCNs often are sought because they speak several languages and know an industry or foreign country well. More and more companies feel that talent should flow to opportunity regardless of one's home country.

Host-Country Restrictions

The host government's attitudes toward foreign workers often complicate selecting expatriate U.S. nationals over locals. Concerns about foreign corporate domination, local unemployment, and other issues cause some countries to restrict the number of non-nationals allowed to work within the country. Most countries have specific rules limiting work permits for foreigners to positions that cannot be filled by a national. Further, the law often limits such permits to periods just long enough to train a local for a specific position. Such restrictions mean that MNCs have fewer opportunities for sending home-country personnel to management positions abroad.

In earlier years, personnel gained foreign-country experience by being sent to lower management positions to gain the necessary training before eventually assuming top-level foreign assignments. Most countries, including the United States, control the number of foreigners allowed to work or train within their borders. Since September 11, 2001, U.S. immigration authorities have clamped down even harder on the issuance of all kinds of work visas.

Selecting Sales and Marketing Personnel

To select personnel for international marketing positions effectively, management must define precisely what is expected of its people. A formal job description can aid management in expressing long-range needs as well as current needs. In addition to descriptions for each marketing position, the criteria should include special requirements indigenous to various countries.

People operating in the home country need only the attributes of effective salespersons, whereas a transnational management position can require skills and attitudes that would challenge a diplomat. International personnel requirements and preferences vary considerably.[11] However, some basic requisites leading to effective performance should be considered

---

[11]Dominique Rouzies, Michael Segalla, and Barton A. Weitz, "Cultural Impact on European Staffing Decisions in Sales Management," *International Journal of Research in Marketing* 20, no. 1 (2003), pp. 67–85.

because effective executives and salespeople, regardless of what foreign country they are operating in, share certain personal characteristics, skills, and orientations.

Maturity is a prime requisite for expatriate and third-country personnel. Managers and sales personnel working abroad typically must work more independently than their domestic counterparts. The company must have confidence in their ability to make ethical[12] decisions and commitments without constant recourse to the home office or they cannot be individually effective.

International personnel require a kind of *emotional stability* not demanded in domestic sales positions.[13] Regardless of location, these people are living in cultures dissimilar to their own; to some extent they are always under scrutiny and always aware that they are official representatives of the company abroad. They need sensitivity to behavioral variations in different countries, but they cannot be so hypersensitive that their behavior is adversely affected.

Managers or salespeople operating in foreign countries need considerable *breadth of knowledge* of many subjects both on and off the job. The ability to speak one or more other languages is always preferable.

The marketer who expects to be effective in the international marketplace needs to have a *positive outlook* on an international assignment. People who do not like what they are doing and where they are doing it stand little chance of success, particularly in a foreign country. Failures usually are the result of overselling the assignment, showing the bright side of the picture and not warning about the bleak side.

An international salesperson must have a high level of *flexibility*, whether working in a foreign country or at home. Expatriates working in a foreign country must be particularly sensitive to the habits of the market; those working at home for a foreign company must adapt to the requirements and ways of the parent company.

Successful adaptation in international affairs is based on a combination of attitude and effort. A careful study of the customs of the market country should be initiated before the marketer arrives and should be continued as long as facets of the culture are not clear. One useful approach is to listen to the advice of national and foreign businesspeople operating in that country. *Cultural empathy* is clearly a part of the basic orientation because anyone who is antagonistic or confused about the environment is unlikely to be effective.[14]

Finally, international sales and marketing personnel must be *energetic* and *enjoy travel*. Many international sales representatives spend about two-thirds of their nights in hotel rooms around the world. Going through the long lines of customs and immigration after a 15-hour flight requires a certain kind of stamina not commonly encountered. Some even argue that frequent long flights can damage your health. Even the seductive lights of Paris nights fade after the fifth business trip there.

Most of these traits can be assessed during interviews and perhaps during role-playing exercises. Paper-and-pencil ability tests, biographical information, and reference checks are of secondary importance. Indeed, as previously mentioned, in many countries referrals will be the best way to recruit managers and sales representatives, making reference checks during evaluation and selection processes irrelevant.

There is also evidence that some traits that make for successful sales representatives in the United States may not be important in other countries. In one study sales representatives in the electronics industries in Japan and the United States were compared. For the American representatives, pay and education were both found to be positively related to performance and job satisfaction. In Japan they were not. That is, the Americans who cared more about

[12]Kam-hon Lee, Gong-ming Qian, Julie H. Yu, and Ying Ho, "Trading Favors for Marketing Advantage: Evidence from Hong Kong, China, and the United States," *Journal of International Marketing* 13, no. 1 (2005), pp. 1–35; Sergio Roman and Salvador Ruiz, "Relationship Outcomes of Perceived Ethical Sales Behavior: the Customer's Perspective," *Journal of Business Research* 58, no. 4 (2005), pp. 439–452.

[13]Willem Verbeke and Richard P. Bagozzi, "Exploring the Role of Self- and Customer-Provoked Embarrassment in Personal Selling," *International Journal of Research in Marketing* 20, no. 3 (2003), pp. 233–258.

[14]Don Y. Lee and Philip L. Dawes, "Gaunxi, Trust, and Long-Term Orientation in Chinese Business Markets," *Journal of International Marketing* 13, no. 2 (2005), pp. 28–56.

International sales is hard work. A typical week for this Canadian executive looks like this: Leaves Singapore with the flu. Arrives home in Toronto to discover that a frozen pipe has burst. Immediately boards a plane for a two-day trip to Chicago. Back to Toronto. On to Detroit, battling jet lag and the flu. Back to Toronto, running through the Detroit airport "like O.J. in the Hertz commercial" and throwing his briefcase into a closing door. Takes a brief break in flooded house before boarding another plane to China. Reports having woken up in a plane and asked his seatmate where they were landing. Seventeen flights in two weeks left him a bit confused. (© David McIntyre/Black Star)

money and were more educated tended to perform better in and be more satisfied with their sales jobs. Conversely, the Japanese sales representatives tended to be more satisfied with their jobs when their values were consistent with those of their company.[15] The few systematic studies in this genre suggest that selection criteria must be localized, and American management practices must be adapted to foreign markets.

Selection mistakes are costly. When an expatriate assignment does not work out, hundreds of thousands of dollars are wasted in expenses and lost time. Getting the right person to handle the job is also important in the selection of locals to work for foreign companies within their home country. Most developing countries and many European countries have stringent laws protecting workers' rights. These laws are specific as to penalties for the dismissal of employees. Perhaps Venezuela has the most stringent dismissal legislation: With more than three months of service in the same firm, a worker gets severance pay amounting to one month's pay at severance notice plus 15 days' pay for every month of service exceeding eight months plus an additional 15 days' pay for each year employed. Further, after an employee is dismissed, the law requires that person be replaced within 30 days at the same salary. Colombia and Brazil have similar laws that make employee dismissal a high-cost proposition.

Finally, new evidence indicates that a manager's culture affects personnel decisions. In a new line of international sales management research, one study reports "that managers given an identical [personnel selection] problem do not make the same decisions nor do they value the criteria often used in recruitment and promotion decisions equally. For example, they found that Austrian and German managers are more likely to hire compatriots than Italian managers."[16] Thus we are just scratching the surface of a variety of issues in the area of international sales management research.

[15]R. Bruce Money and John L. Graham, "Salesperson Performance, Pay, and Job Satisfaction: Tests of a Model Using Data Collected in the U.S. and Japan," *Journal of International Business Studies* 30, no. 1 (1999), pp. 149–172.

[16]Dominique Rouzies, Michael Segalla, and Barton A. Weitz, "Cultural Impact on European Staffing Decisions in Sales Management," *International Journal of Research in Marketing* 20, no. 1 (March 2003), pp. 67–85.

Training for International Marketing

The nature of a training program depends largely on both the home culture of the sales person[17] and the culture of the business system in the foreign market.[18] Also important is whether expatriate or local personnel will be representing the firm. Training for the expatriates focuses on the customs and the special foreign sales problems that will be encountered, whereas local personnel require greater emphasis on the company, its products, technical information, and selling methods. In training either type of personnel, the sales training activity is burdened with problems stemming from long-established behavior and attitudes. Local personnel, for instance, cling to habits continually reinforced by local culture. Nowhere is the problem greater than in China or Russia, where the legacy of the communist tradition lingers. The attitude that whether you work hard or not, you get the same rewards has to be changed if training is going to stick. Expatriates are also captives of their own habits and patterns. Before any training can be effective, open-minded attitudes must be established.

Continual training may be more important in foreign markets than in domestic ones because of the lack of routine contact with the parent company and its marketing personnel. In addition, training of foreign employees must be tailored to the recipients' ways of

[17]Richard P. Bagozzi, Willem Verbeke, and Jacinto C. Gavino Jr., "Culture Moderates the Self-Regulation of Shame and Its Effects on Performance: The Case of Salespersons in the Netherlands and the Philippines," *Journal of Applied Psychology* 88, no. 2 (2003), pp. 219–233.

[18]Sergio Roman and Salvador Ruiz, "A Comparative Analysis of Sales Training in Europe: Implications for International Sales Negotiations," *International Marketing Review* 20, no. 3 (2003), pp. 304–326.

Exhibit 17.3
Personal Selling Tips, from Brussels to Bangkok

The best training programs are much more than just a list of tips. But a quick read of such tips provides a glimpse of the cultural variation facing sales representatives around the globe.

Belgium—Be able to identify the decision makers. In Flanders (Dutch-speaking region) group decisions are common, but in Wallonia (French-speaking region) the highest-level execs have the final say.

China—Expect to continue negotiations after a deal is inked. To Chinese, signing a contract is just the beginning of the business relationship; therefore, they expect both sides to continue working together to fix problems that arise.

Colombia—Business counterparts want to get to know you personally and form a strong friendship with you. Be sure not to change reps in midstream, because often a switch puts an end to negotiations.

Germany—Be prepared with data and empirical evidence that supports your sales proposition. German businesspeople are unimpressed by flashy advertising and brochures, so keep them serious and detailed, with unexaggerated information.

India—Make sure your schedule remains flexible. Indians are more casual about time and punctuality. Because of India's rigid hierarchy, decisions are made only by the highest-level boss.

Mexico—When planning a meeting, breakfast and lunch are preferable. Take your time and cultivate relationships with business contacts. Those relationships are generally considered more important than professional experience.

Peru—Peruvians relate to individuals and not corporate entities. Establish personal rapport and don't switch your representative in the middle of negotiations.

Russia—Your first meeting will be just a formality. Your Russian counterparts will take this time to judge your credibility, so it's best to be warm and approachable.

Scotland—Scottish people tend to be soft-spoken and private. It takes time to build relationships, but business counterparts seem friendlier after bonds are established. (By the way, Scotch is a drink, not a nationality—it's Scottish.)

South Korea—Status is important. Make sure your business card clearly indicates your title. Don't send a rep to meet with a Korean executive of higher status—it could be viewed as disrespectful.

Thailand—The Thai culture emphasizes nonconflict, so don't make assertive demands when making sales pitches.

Source: *Sales & Marketing Management* publishes these tips regularly in its magazine and on its Web site (www.salesandmarketing.com).

learning and communicating. For example, the Dilbert cartoon characters theme that worked so well in ethics training courses with a company's American employees did not translate well in many of its foreign offices.

One aspect of training is frequently overlooked: Home-office personnel dealing with international marketing operations need training designed to make them responsive to the needs of the foreign operations. In most companies, the requisite sensitivities are expected to be developed by osmosis in the process of dealing with foreign affairs. However, the best companies provide home-office personnel with cross-cultural training and send them abroad periodically to increase their awareness of the problems of the foreign operations.

The Internet now makes some kinds of sales training much more efficient. Users can study text on-screen and participate in interactive assessment tests. Sun Microsystems estimates that its use of the Internet can shorten training cycles by as much as 75 percent. And in some parts of the world where telecommunications facilities are more limited, CD-ROM approaches have proven quite successful. Lockheed Martin uses an interactive CD-ROM–based system to train its employees worldwide on the nuances of the Foreign Corrupt Practices Act and associated corporate policies and ethics.

Motivating Sales Personnel

Motivation is especially complicated because the firm is dealing with different cultures, different sources, and different philosophies.[19] Marketing is a business function requiring high motivation regardless of the location of the practitioner. Marketing managers and sales managers typically work hard, travel extensively, and have day-to-day challenges. Selling is hard, competitive work wherever undertaken, and a constant flow of inspiration is needed to keep personnel functioning at an optimal level. National differences must always be considered in motivating the marketing force.[20] In one study, sales representatives in comparable Japanese and American sales organizations were asked to allocate 100 points across an array of potential rewards from work.[21] As shown in Exhibit 17.4, the results were surprisingly similar. The only real difference between the two groups was in social recognition, which, predictably, the Japanese rated as more important. However, the authors of the study concluded that although individual values for rewards may be similar, the social and competitive contexts still require different motivational systems.

---

[19]James P Neelankavil, Anil Mathur, and Yong Zang, "Determinants of Managerial Performance: A Cross-Cultural Comparison of the Perceptions of Middle-Level Managers in Four Countries," *Journal of International Business Studies* 31, no. 1 (2000), pp. 121–140; Evert Van de Vliert, "Thermoclimate, Culture, and Poverty as Country-Level Roots of Workers' Wages," *Journal of International Business Studies* 34, no. 1 (2003), pp. 40–52.

[20]Ping Ping Fu, Jeff Kennedy, Jasmine Tata, Gary Yukl, Michael Harris Bond, Tai-Kuang Peng, Ekkirala S. Srinivas, John P. Howell, Leonel Prieto, Paul Koopman, Jaap J. Boonstra, Selda Pasa, Marie-Francoise Lacassagne, Hiro Higashide, and Adith Cheosakul, "The Impact of Societal Cultural Values and Individual Social Beliefs on the Perceived Effectiveness of Managerial Influence Strategies: A Meso Approach," *Journal of International Business Studies* 35 (2004), pp. 284–305.

[21]R. Bruce Money and John L. Graham, "Salesperson Performance, Pay, and Job Satisfaction: Tests of a Model Using Data Collected in the U.S. and Japan," *Journal of International Business Studies* 30, no. 1 (1999), pp. 149–172.

Exhibit 17.4

Salespeople's Distribution of 100 Points among Rewards in Terms of Their Importance

Source: R. Bruce Money and John L. Graham, "Salesperson Performance, Pay, and Job Satisfaction: Tests of a Model Using Data Collected in the U.S. and Japan," *Journal of International Business Studies* 30, no. 1 (1999).

Rewards	Relative Importance (mean)	
	Japanese	Americans
Job security	18.5	17.6
Promotion	13.7	14.9
Merit increase in pay	24.7	26.2
Feeling of worthwhile accomplishment	18.5	18.2
Social recognition (sales club awards)	8.1	5.2
Personal growth and development	16.6	17.8

CROSSING BORDERS 17.4   How Important Are Those Meetings?

In Japan, they're real important. A former American sales manager tells this story:

> I worked as general manager of the Japanese subsidiary of an American medical equipment company. Our office was in downtown Tokyo, which made for a two-hour commute for most of our salesmen. Rather than have them come into the office before beginning sales calls every day, I instructed them to go to their appointments directly from home and to come to the office only for a weekly sales meeting. Although this was a common way for a U.S. sales force to operate, it was a disaster in Japan. Sales fell, as did morale. I quickly changed the policy and had everyone come to the office every day. Sales immediately climbed as the salesmen reinforced their group identity.

Now contrast that with how sales representatives are managed at Hewlett-Packard in the United States, as described by one of its sales executives: "We're really looking at this issue of work/family balance. If someone wants to work at home, they can, and we'll outfit their home offices at our expense, provided they have a good reason to want to work at home. If you want to

drive productivity, getting people's work lives and home lives in balance is key."

Sam Palmisano, IBM's new CEO, puts it even more strongly, "To win, our players have to be on the field. We can't win the game in the locker room . . . We want our people on the field in front of the customers, not in conference rooms talking to their managers or other staff organizations." At IBM a new corporate policy limits sales meeting to one per week.

Or consider the following statement from IBM's employment Web site: "Because when you walk through the door at IBM, you're going to be presented not just with attractive compensation, but also with educational reimbursement plans, flexible work schedules, global opportunities, activities, clubs, child care options—to help you learn, play and work the way you want. After all, it's about time. How do you want to spend yours?"

Sources: Clyde V. Prestowitz, *Trading Places—How We Are Giving Away Our Future to Japan and How to Reclaim It* (New York: Basic Books, 1989); Geoffrey Brewer et al., "The Top (25 Best Sales Forces in the U.S.)," *Sales & Marketing Management*, November 1, 1996, p. 38; Erin Strout, "Blue Skies Ahead?" *Sales & Marketing Management*, March 1, 2003, pp. 24–26; www.ibm.com, 2005.

Because the cultural differences reviewed in this and earlier chapters affect the motivational patterns of a sales force, a manager must be extremely sensitive to the personal behavior patterns of employees. Individual incentives that work effectively in the United States can fail completely in other cultures. For example, with Japan's emphasis on paternalism and collectivism and its system of lifetime employment and seniority, motivation through individual incentive does not work well because Japanese employees seem to derive the greatest satisfaction from being comfortable members of a group. Thus an offer of an individual financial reward for outstanding individual effort could be turned down because an employee would prefer not to appear different from peers and possibly attract their resentment. Japanese bonus systems are therefore based on group effort, and individual commission systems are rare. Japanese sales representatives are motivated more by the social pressure of their peers than by the prospect of making more money based on individual effort. Likewise, compensation packages in eastern European countries typically involve a substantially greater emphasis on base pay than in the

Part of the corporate culture (some say peer pressure) that motivates Japanese sales representatives is the morning calisthenics. (© Tom Wagner/CORBIS SABA)

United States, and performance-based incentives have been found to be less effective. Although some point out that motivational practices are changing even in Japan, such patterns do not change very quickly or without substantial efforts.

Communications are also important in maintaining high levels of motivation; foreign managers need to know that the home office is interested in their operations, and, in turn, they want to know what is happening in the parent country. Everyone performs better when well informed. However, differences in languages, culture, and communication styles[22] can make mutual understanding between managers and sales representatives more difficult.

Because promotion and the opportunity to improve status are important motivators, a company needs to make clear the opportunities for growth within the firm. In truly global firms, foreign nationals can aspire to the highest positions in the firm. Likewise, one of the greatest fears of expatriate managers, which can be easily allayed, is that they will be forgotten by the home office. Blending company sales objectives and the personal objectives of the salespeople and other employees is a task worthy of the most skilled manager. The U.S. manager must be constantly aware that many of the techniques used to motivate U.S. personnel and their responses to these techniques are based on the seven basic cultural premises discussed in Chapter 5. Therefore, each method used to motivate a foreigner should be examined for cultural compatibility.

Designing Compensation Systems

For Expatriates Developing an equitable and functional compensation plan that combines balance, consistent motivation, and flexibility is extremely challenging in international operations. This is especially true when a company operates in a number of countries, when it has individuals who work in a number of countries, or when the sales force is composed of expatriate and local personnel.[23] Fringe benefits play a major role in many countries. Those working in high-tax countries prefer liberal expense accounts and fringe benefits that are nontaxable instead of direct income subject to high taxes. Fringe-benefit costs are high in Europe, ranging from 35 to 60 percent of salary.

Pay can be a significant factor in making it difficult for a person to be repatriated. Often those returning home realize they have been making considerably more money with a lower cost of living in the overseas market; returning to the home country means a cut in pay and a cut in standard of living.

Conglomerate operations that include domestic and foreign personnel cause the greatest problems in compensation planning.[24] Expatriates tend to compare their compensation with what they would have received at the home office during the same time, and local personnel and expatriate personnel are likely to compare notes on salary. Although any differences in the compensation level may be easily and logically explained, the group receiving the lower amount almost always feels aggrieved and mistreated.

Short-term assignments for expatriates further complicate the compensation issue, particularly when the short-term assignments extend into a longer time. In general, short-term assignments involve payments of overseas premiums (sometimes called separation allowances if the family does not go along), all excess expenses, and allowances for tax differentials. Longer assignments can include home-leave benefits or travel allowances for the spouse.

Besides rewarding an individual's contribution to the firm, a compensation program can be used effectively to recruit, develop, motivate, or retain personnel. Most recommendations for developing a compensation program suggest that a program focus on whichever one of these purposes fits the needs of a particular situation. If all four purposes are targeted, it can result in unwieldy programs that become completely unmanageable. International compensation programs also provide additional payments for hardship locations and special inducements to reluctant personnel to accept overseas employment and to remain in the position.

---

[22]Alma Mintu-Wimsatt and Julie B. Gassenheimer, "The Moderating Effects of Cultural Context in Buyer-Seller Negotiation," *Journal of Personal Selling and Sales Management* 20, no. 1 (Winter 2000), pp. 1–9.

[23]Bronwyn Fryer, "In a World of Pay," *Harvard Business Review*, November 2003, pp. 31–40.

[24]For a still excellent discussion of the problems of constructing a compensation plan for expatriates, nationals, and third-country nationals, see Michael Harvey, "Empirical Evidence of Recurring International Compensation Problems," *Journal of International Business Studies*, 4th Quarter, 1993, pp. 785–799. Chao C. Chen, Jaepil Choi, and Shu-Chen Chi, "Making Sense of Local–Expatriate Compensation Disparity," *Academy of Management Journal* 45, no. 4 (August 2002), pp. 807–817; Anna Healy Fenton, "Expats Get Seven Times the Perks of Local Workers," *South China Morning Post*, February 7, 2003, p. 5.

Exhibit 17.5
Global Similarity to U.S. Compensation Plans

Countries/Regions		Degree of Plan Similarity with the United States					
		Eligibility	Performance Measures	Weighting	Plan Mechanics	Mix/ Leverage	Payout Frequency
Europe	United Kingdom						
	Scandinavia						
	France						
	Germany						
	Spain/Italy						
Southeast Asia	Hong Kong						
	Korea						
	Taiwan						
	Malaysia						
	Indonesia						
	(Singapore)						
	Australia						
Japan							
Canada							
South America							

☐ Similar   ☐ Varies   ☐ Dissimilar

Data represent multiple client projects conducted by The Alexander Group Inc. for primarily high-technology industry sales organizations.

Source: David G. Schick and David J. Cichelli, "Developing Incentive Compensation Strategies in a Global Sales Environment," *ACA Journal*, Autumn 1996; updated based on interview with David J. Cichelli, Vice President of the Alexander Group, in August 2005.

For a Global Sales Force

Compensation plans of American companies vary substantially around the globe, reflecting the economic and cultural differences[25] in the diverse markets served. As reflected in Exhibit 17.5, some experts feel compensation plans in Japan and southern Europe are most different from the standard U.S. approach. Those same experts believe that generally compensation schemes around the world are becoming more similar to the U.S. system with its emphasis on commissions based on individual performance. However, the data in Exhibit 17.5 still reflect the locations of the larger differences.[26]

One company has gone to great lengths to homogenize its worldwide compensation scheme. Beginning in the late 1990s IBM rolled out what is perhaps the most global approach to compensating a worldwide sales force.[27] The main features of that plan, which applies to 140,000 sales executives in 165 countries, are presented in Exhibit 17.6. The plan was developed in response to "global" complaints from sales representatives that the

[25]Nigel F. Piercy, George S. Low, and David W. Cravens, "Consequences of Sales Management's Behavior- and Compensation-Based Control Strategies in Developing Countries," *Journal of International Marketing* 12, no. 3 (2004), pp. 36–57; Marta M. Elvira and Anabella Davila, *Managing Human Resources in Latin America* (London: Routledge, 2005).

[26]Personal interview with David J. Cichelli, Vice President Alexander Group, August 2005.

[27]Michele Marchetti, "Gamble: IBM Replaces Its Outdated Compensation Plan with a World Wide Framework. Will It Pay Off?" *Sales & Marketing Management*, July 1996, pp. 65–69. IBM continues to globalize its sales management practices—see Erin Strout, "Blue Skies Ahead? IBM Is Transforming the Way Its Sales Force Does Business," *Sales & Marketing Management*, March 1, 2003, pp. 24–27.

Exhibit 17.6

A Compensation
Blueprint: How IBM Pays
140,000 Sales Executives
Worldwide

Source: Adapted from Michele
Marchetti, "Gamble: IBM Replaces Its
Outdated Compensation Plan with a
World Wide Framework. Will It Pay
Off?" *Sales and Marketing
Management*, July 1996, pp. 65–69.

Total Compensation		Plan Components	Payout Frequency	Pay Measurements	Number of Measurements Used to Calculate
Benefits					
Variable Pay →		Corporate Objectives	Annually	Bonus payment (based on) • Profit • Customer satisfaction	2
Incentive Compensation →		Teamwork	Monthly	20% of incentive compensation • Work team performance • Industry performance	2
		Personal Contribution	Quarterly	60% of incentive compensation • Growth • Solutions • Channels/partners • Profit contribution	1–2
		Challenges/ Contests	As earned	20% of incentive compensation • National • Local	1–4
Recognition					
Base Salary					

old plan was confusing and did not provide for work done outside one's territory (such as in the scenario presented in Crossing Borders 17.1), and that it therefore did not promote cross-border teamwork. IBM sales incentive managers from North America, Latin America, Asia Pacific, and Europe worked together with consultants on the design for some nine months. At first glance it may appear that IBM is making the cardinal error of trying to force a plan developed centrally onto sales offices literally spread around the world and across diverse cultures; however, the compensation plan still allows substantial latitude for local managers. Compensation managers in each country determine the frequency of incentive payouts and the split between base and incentive pay, while following a global scheme of performance measures. Thus the system allows for a high incentive component in countries like the United States and high base-salary components in countries like Japan.

Perhaps the most valuable information gained during IBM's process of revamping its sales compensation scheme was the following list of the "do's and don'ts" of global compensation:[28]

1. Do involve representatives from key countries.
2. Do allow local managers to decide the mix between base and incentive pay.
3. Do use consistent performance measures (results paid for) and emphasis on each measure.
4. Do allow local countries flexibility in implementations.
5. Do use consistent communication and training themes worldwide.
6. Don't design the plan centrally and dictate to local offices.
7. Don't create a similar framework for jobs with different responsibilities.
8. Don't require consistency on every performance measure within the incentive plan.
9. Don't assume cultural differences can be managed through the incentive plan.
10. Don't proceed without the support of senior sales executives worldwide.

---

[28]Ibid.

Evaluating and Controlling Sales Representatives

Evaluation and control of sales representatives in the United States is a relatively simple task. In many sales jobs, emphasis is placed on individual performance, which can easily be measured by sales revenues generated (often compared with past performance, forecasts, or quotas). In short, a good sales representative produces big numbers. However, in many countries the evaluation problem is more complex, particularly in relationship-oriented cultures, where teamwork is favored over individual effort. Performance measures require closer observation and may include the opinions of customers, peers, and supervisors. Of course, on the other hand, managers of sales forces operating in relationship-oriented cultures may see measures of individual performance as relatively unimportant.

One study comparing American and Japanese sales representatives' performance illustrates such differences.[29] Supervisors' ratings of the representatives on identical performance scales were used in both countries. The distribution of performance of the Japanese was statistically normal—a few high performers, a few low, but most in the middle. The American distribution was different—a few high, most in the middle, but almost no low performers. In the United States, poor performers either quit (because they are not making any money) or they are fired. In Japan the poor performers stay with the company and are seldom fired. Thus sales managers in Japan have a problem their American counterparts do not: how to motivate poor performers. Indeed, sales management textbooks in the United States usually include material on how to deal with "plateaued" salespeople but say little about poor performers because the latter are not a problem.

The primary control tool used by American sales managers is the incentive system. Because of the Internet and fax machines, more and more American sales representatives operate out of offices in their homes and see supervisors infrequently. Organizations have become quite flat and spans of control increasingly broad in recent years. However, in many other countries spans of control can be quite narrow by American standards—even in Australia and particularly in Japan. In the latter country, supervisors spend much more time with fewer subordinates. Corporate culture and frequent interactions with peers and supervisors are the means of motivation and control of sales representatives in relationship-oriented cultures like Japan.

Preparing U.S. Personnel for Foreign Assignments

Estimates of the annual cost of sending and supporting a manager and his or her family in a foreign assignment range from 150 to 400 percent of base salary. The cost in money (some estimates are in the $300,000 to $600,00 range) and morale increases substantially if the expatriate requests a return home before completing the normal tour of duty (a normal stay is two to four years). In addition, if repatriation into domestic operations is not successful and the employee leaves the company, an indeterminately high cost in low morale and loss of experienced personnel results. To reduce these problems, international personnel management has increased planning for expatriate personnel to move abroad, remain abroad, and then return to the home country.[30] The planning process must begin prior to the selection of those who go abroad and extend to their specific assignments after returning home. Selection, training, compensation, and career development policies (including repatriation) should reflect the unique problems of managing the expatriate.

Besides the job-related criteria for a specific position, the typical candidate for an international assignment is married, has two school-aged children, is expected to stay overseas three years, and has the potential for promotion into higher management levels. These characteristics of the typical expatriate are the basis of most of the difficulties associated with getting the best-qualified personnel to go overseas, keeping them there, and assimilating them on their return.

---

[29]R. Bruce Money and John L. Graham, "Salesperson Performance, Pay, and Job Satisfaction: Tests of a Model Using Data Collected in the U.S. and Japan," *Journal of International Business Studies* 30, no. 1 (1999), pp. 149–172.

[30]Jeffrey P. Shay and Sally A. Baack, "Expatriate Assignment, Adjustment and Effectiveness: An Empirical Examination of the Big Picture," *Journal of International Business Studies* 35, no. 3 (2004), pp. 216–232.

Overcoming Reluctance to Accept a Foreign Assignment

Concerns for career and family are the most frequently mentioned reasons for a manager to refuse a foreign assignment. The most important career-related reservation is the fear that a two- or three-year absence will adversely affect opportunities for advancement. This "out of sight, out of mind" fear (as exemplified in the opening Global Perspective) is closely linked to the problems of repatriation. Without evidence of advance planning to protect career development, better-qualified and ambitious personnel may decline the offer to go abroad. However, if candidates for expatriate assignments are picked thoughtfully, returned to the home office at the right moment, and rewarded for good performance with subsequent promotions at home, companies find recruiting of executives for international assignments eased.

Even though the career development question may be adequately answered with proper planning, concern for family may interfere with many accepting an assignment abroad. Initially, most potential candidates are worried about uprooting a family and settling into a strange environment. Questions about the education of the children, isolation from family and friends, proper health care, and, in some countries, the potential for violence reflect the misgivings a family faces when relocating to a foreign country. Special compensation packages have been the typical way to deal with this problem. A hardship allowance, allowances to cover special educational requirements that frequently include private schools, housing allowances, and extended all-expense-paid vacations are part of compensation packages designed to overcome family-related problems with an overseas assignment. Ironically, the solution to one problem creates a later problem when that family returns to the United States and must give up those extra compensation benefits used to induce them to accept the position.

Reducing the Rate of Early Returns

Once the employee and family accept the assignment abroad, the next problem is keeping them there for the assigned time. The attrition rate of those selected for overseas positions can be very high, although some studies have suggested it is declining overall. One firm with a hospital management contract experienced an annualized failure rate of 20 percent— not high when compared with the construction contractor who started out in Saudi Arabia with 155 Americans and was down to 65 after only two months.

American expatriates flock to stores like this one in Amsterdam. Inside you'll find not only books in English, but also Kraft macaroni and cheese, Bisquick, and other hard-to-find-in-Europe staples of the American diet.

The most important reasons a growing number of companies are including an evaluation of an employee's family among selection criteria are the high cost of sending an expatriate abroad and increasing evidence that unsuccessful family adjustment is the single most important reason for expatriate dissatisfaction and the resultant request for return home.[31] In fact, a study of personnel directors of over 300 international firms found that the inability of the manager's spouse to adjust to a different physical or cultural environment was the primary reason for an expatriate's failure to function effectively in a foreign assignment. One researcher estimated that 75 percent of families sent to a foreign post experience adjustment problems with children or have marital discord. One executive suggests that there is so much pressure on the family that if there are any cracks in the marriage and you want to save it, think long and hard about taking a foreign assignment.

Dissatisfaction is caused by the stress and trauma of adjusting to new and often strange cultures. The employee has less trouble adjusting than family members; a company's expatriate moves in a familiar environment even abroad and is often isolated from the cultural differences that create problems for the rest of the family. And about half of American expatriate employees receive cross-cultural training before the trip—much more often than their families.[32] Family members have far greater daily exposure to the new culture but are often

[31]Greg Hardesty, "Crash Course on Life in Japan," *Orange County Register*, July 20, 2005, pp. 1, 10.

[32]Visit www.natwestoffshore.com for a quick view of the kinds of services provided by expatriate preparation companies.

not given assistance in adjusting. New consumption patterns must be learned, from grocery shopping to seeking healthcare services.[33] Family members frequently cannot be employed and, in many cultures, female members of the family face severe social restrictions. In Saudi Arabia, for example, the woman's role is strictly dictated. In one situation, a woman's hemline offended a religious official who, in protest, sprayed black paint on her legs. In short, the greater problems of culture shock befall the family. Certainly any recruiting and selection procedure should include an evaluation of the family's ability to adjust.[34]

Families that have the potential and the personality traits that would enable them to adjust to a different environment may still become dissatisfied with living abroad if they are not properly prepared for the new assignment. More and more companies realize the need for cross-cultural training to prepare families for their new homes. One- or two-day briefings to two- or three-week intensive programs that include all members of the family are provided to assist assimilation into new cultures. Language training, films, discussions, and lectures on cultural differences, potential problems, and stress areas in adjusting to a new way of life are provided to minimize the frustration of the initial cultural shock. This cultural training helps a family anticipate problems and eases adjustment. Once the family is abroad, some companies even provide a local ombudsman (someone experienced in the country) to whom members can take their problems and get immediate assistance. Although the cost of preparing a family for an overseas assignment may appear high, it must be weighed against estimates that the measurable cost of prematurely returned families could cover cross-cultural training for 300 to 500 families. Companies that do not prepare employees and their families for culture shock have the highest incidence of premature return to the United States.

Successful Expatriate Repatriation

A Conference Board study reported that many firms have sophisticated plans for executives going overseas but few have comprehensive programs to deal with the return home. Many have noted that too often repatriated workers are a valuable resource neglected or wasted by inexperienced U.S. management.[35]

Low morale and a growing amount of attrition among returning expatriates have many causes. Some complaints and problems are family related, while others are career related. The family-related problems generally deal with financial and lifestyle readjustments. Some expatriates find that, in spite of higher compensation programs, their net worths have not increased, and the inflation of intervening years makes it impossible to buy a home comparable to the one they sold on leaving. The hardship compensation programs used to induce the executive to go abroad also create readjustment problems on the return home. Such compensation benefits frequently permitted the family to live at a much higher level abroad than at home (employing yard boys, chauffeurs, domestic help, and so forth). Because most compensation benefits are withdrawn when employees return to the home country, their standard of living decreases and they must readjust. Unfortunately, little can be done to ameliorate these kinds of problems short of transferring the managers to other foreign locations. Current thinking suggests that the problem of dissatisfaction with compensation and benefits upon return can be lessened by reducing benefits when overseas. Rather than provide the family abroad with hardship payments, some companies are considering reducing payments on the premise that the assignment abroad is an integral requirement for growth, development, and advancement within the firm.

Family dissatisfaction, which causes stress within the family on returning home, is not as severe a problem as career-related complaints. A returning expatriate's dissatisfaction

[33]Mary C. Gilly, Lisa Penaloza, and Kenneth M. Kambara, "The Role of Consumption in Expatriate Adjustment and Satisfaction," working paper, The Paul Merage School of Business, University of California, Irvine, 2006.

[34]James T. Areddy, "Deep Inside China American Family Struggles to Cope," *Wall Street Journal*, August 2, 2005, pp. A1, A6.

[35]Joann S. Lublin, "Making the Transition Back to Local Work after an Overseas Job," *Wall Street Journal*, April 1, 2003, p. B1; Gretchen Lang, "Going Home Isn't Always Best Option," *International Herald Tribune*, June 26–27, 2004, p. 18.

with the perceived future is usually the reason many resign their positions after returning to the United States. The problem is not unique to U.S. citizens; Japanese companies have similar difficulties with their personnel. The most frequently heard complaint involves the lack of a detailed plan for the expatriate's career when returning home. New home-country assignments are frequently mundane and do not reflect the experience gained or the challenges met during foreign assignment. Some feel their time out of the mainstream of corporate affairs has made them technically obsolete and thus ineffective in competing immediately on return. Finally, there is some loss of status requiring ego adjustment when an executive returns home.

Companies with the least amount of returnee attrition differ from those with the highest attrition in one significant way: personal career planning for the expatriate.[36] This planning begins with the decision to send the person abroad. The initial transfer abroad should be made in the context of a long-term company career plan. Under these circumstances, the individual knows not only the importance of the foreign assignment but also when to expect to return and at what level. Near the end of the foreign assignment, the process for repatriation is begun. The critical aspect of the return home is to keep the executive completely informed regarding such matters as the proposed return time, new assignment and an indication of whether it is interim or permanent, new responsibilities, and future prospects. In short, returnees should know where they are going and what they will be doing next month and several years ahead.

A report on what MNCs are doing to improve the reentry process suggests five steps:

1. Commit to reassigning expatriates to meaningful positions.
2. Create a mentor program. Mentors are typically senior executives who monitor company activities, keep the expatriate informed on company activities, and act as liaison between the expatriate and various headquarters departments.
3. Offer a written job guarantee stating what the company is obligated to do for the expatriate on return.
4. Keep the expatriate in touch with headquarters through periodic briefings and headquarters visits.
5. Prepare the expatriate and family for repatriation once a return date is set.

Some believe the importance of preparing the employee and family for culture shock upon return is on a par with preparation for going abroad.

Developing Cultural Awareness

Many businesses focus on the functional skills needed in international marketing, overlooking the importance of cultural intelligence.[37] Just as the idea "if a product sells well in Dallas it will sell well in Hong Kong" is risky, so is the idea that "a manager who excels in Dallas will excel in Hong Kong." Most expatriate failures are not caused by lack of management or technical skills but rather by lack of an understanding of cultural differences and their effect on management skills. As the world becomes more interdependent and as companies become more dependent on foreign earnings, there is a growing need for companies to develop cultural awareness among those posted abroad.

Just as we remark that someone has achieved good social skills (i.e., an ability to remain poised and be in control under all social situations), so too good cultural skills can be developed. These skills serve a similar function in varying cultural situations; they provide the individual with the ability to relate to a different culture even when the individual is

---

[36]Aimin Yan, Guorong Zhu, and Douglas T. Hall, "International Assignments for Career Building," *Academy of Management Review* 27, no. 3 (July 2002), pp. 373–391.

[37]P. Christopher Earley and Elaine Mosakowski, "Cultural Intelligence," *Harvard Business Review*, October 2004, pp. 139–146.

unfamiliar with the details of that particular culture. Cultural skills can be learned just as social skills can be learned. People with cultural skills can:

- Communicate respect and convey verbally and nonverbally a positive regard and sincere interest in people and their culture.

- Tolerate ambiguity and cope with cultural differences and the frustration that frequently develops when things are different and circumstances change.

- Display empathy by understanding other people's needs and differences from their point of view.

- Remain nonjudgmental about the behavior of others, particularly with reference to their own value standards.

- Recognize and control the SRC, that is, recognize their own culture and values as an influence on their perceptions, evaluations, and judgment in a situation.

- Laugh things off—a good sense of humor helps when frustration levels rise and things do not work as planned.

The Changing Profile of the Global Manager

Until recently the road to the top was well marked. Surveys of chief executives consistently reported that more than three-quarters had finance, manufacturing, or marketing backgrounds. As the post–World War II period of growing markets and domestic-only competition fades, however, so too does the narrow one-company, one-industry chief executive. In the new millennium increasing international competition, the globalization of companies, technology, demographic shifts, and the speed of overall change will govern the choice of company leaders. It will be difficult for a single-discipline individual to reach the top in the future.[38]

The executive recently picked to head Procter & Gamble's U.S. operations is a good example of the effect globalization is having on businesses and the importance of experience, whether in Japan, Europe, or elsewhere. The head of all P&G's U.S. business was born in the Netherlands, received an MBA from Rotterdam's Eramus University, then rose through P&G's marketing ranks in Holland, the United States, and Austria. After proving his mettle in Japan, he moved to P&G's Cincinnati, Ohio, headquarters to direct its push into East Asia, and then to his new position. Speculation is that if he succeeds in the United States, as he did in Japan, he will be a major contender for the top position at P&G.

Fewer companies today limit their search for senior-level executive talent to their home countries. Coca-Cola's former CEO, who began his ascent to the top in his native Cuba, and the former IBM vice chairman, a Swiss national who rose through the ranks in Europe, are two prominent examples of individuals who rose to the top of firms outside their home countries.

Some companies, such as Colgate-Palmolive, believe that it is important to have international assignments early in a person's career, and international training is an integral part of their entry-level development programs. Colgate recruits its future managers from the world's best colleges and business schools. Acceptance is highly competitive, and successful applicants have a BA or MBA with proven leadership skills, fluency in at least one language besides English, and some experience living abroad. A typical recruit might be a U.S. citizen who has spent a year studying in another country, or a national of another country who was educated in the United States.

Trainees begin their careers in a two-year, entry-level, total-immersion program that consists of stints in various Colgate departments. A typical rotation includes time in the finance, manufacturing, and marketing departments and an in-depth exposure to the company's marketing system. During that phase, trainees are rotated through the firm's ad agency, marketing research, and product management departments and then work seven months as field salespeople. At least once during the two years, trainees accompany their mentors on

---

[38]Erin White, "Future CEOs May Need to Have Broad Liberal-Arts Foundation," *Wall Street Journal*, April 12, 2005, p. B4.

CROSSING **BORDERS 17.5**   Iberia Grinds Airbus and Boeing

The principal characters were (1) Spain's Iberia Airlines CFO, Enrique Dupuy de Lome, (2) Boeing's top salesman (American), Toby Bright, and (3) Airbus's top salesman, John Leahy (American). In the crashed commercial jet market of 2003 the two Americans were fighting fiercely for the Spaniard's business.

And Senor Dupuy was having a great time, "Everything [in the negotiations] has been structured to maintain tension up to the last minute." The Americans were sweating. The order was for 12 wide-body jets for a total price of about $2 billion.

Leahy thought he had the inside edge being the European supplier. But Dupuy put the heat on him by shopping for used 747s in Singapore. Terrorism threats, the war in Iraq, and SARS were killing air travel markets, and the airlines were grounding older jets with higher operating costs. Next, Dupuy had to woo a skeptical Toby Bright into the game, and he succeeded in doing so over an expensive dinner in London.

Mr. Leahy not only sells jets, he also spends most of his time sitting in one—about 220 days each year. During the negotiations he made several trips from Airbus headquarters in Toulouse, France, to Madrid only to sit long hours into the night arguing with the Iberia team about the number of seats you can fit into a Boeing 777. Iberia argued they could put 30 more seats in the Boeing than the Airbus A340.

Meanwhile Dupuy used another lever on Leahy. Back in 1995 Leahy had conceded an asset-value guarantee to Iberia to consummate another 18-jet sale. That previous guarantee was haunting Leahy now as Dupuy threatened to make Airbus buy back the older planes at a high, promised price if he didn't cut prices further. Moreover, a new internal analysis by Iberia staff members favored the Boeing jets over the Airbus.

Senor Dupuy continued to keep all three options on the table. He interrupted a skiing vacation with his family in the Pyrenees for a four-hour lunch with Leahy. Then he flew to Seattle to further encourage Bright. And he kept talking about the Singapore Airlines 747s. As the global airline market sank deeper, both the companies cut prices further. Dupuy was enjoying himself immensely.

The deal clincher was a phone conversation between the CEOs of Iberia and Airbus. The two Europeans made what Boeing's Toby Bright criticized as the "easiest decision." John Leahy had won the day. However, Iberia's news release crowed about Airbus's new price guarantees, and Dupuy bragged he had won "extraordinary conditions." Personal selling is tough business, even when you win!

Sources: Daniel Michaels, "In Clandestine World of Airplane Contracts, An Inside Look at a Deal," *Wall Street Journal Europe*, March 10, 2003, p. A1; Stanley Holmes, "A Plastic Dream Machine," *BusinessWeek*, June 20, 2005, pp. 32–36.

business trips to a foreign subsidiary. The company's goal is to develop in their trainees the skills they need to become effective marketing managers, domestically or globally.

On completion of the program, trainees can expect a foreign posting, either immediately after graduation or soon after an assignment in the United States. The first positions are not in London or Paris, as many might hope, but in developing countries such as Brazil, the Philippines, or maybe Zambia. Because international sales are so important to Colgate (60 percent of its total revenues are generated abroad), a manager might not return to the United States after the first foreign assignment but rather move from one overseas post to another, developing into a career internationalist, which could open to a CEO position.

Companies whose foreign receipts make up a substantial portion of their earnings, and who see themselves as global companies rather than as domestic companies doing business in foreign markets, are the most active in making the foreign experience an integrated part of a successful corporate career. Indeed, for many companies a key threshold seems to be that when overseas revenues surpass domestic revenues, then the best people in the company want to work on international accounts. Such a global orientation then begins to permeate the entire organization—from personnel policies to marketing and business strategies. This was the case with Gillette, which in the 1990s made a significant recruitment and management-development decision when it decided to develop managers internally. Gillette's international human resources department implemented its international-trainee program, designed to supply a steady stream of managerial talent from within its own ranks. Trainees are recruited from all over the world, and when their training is complete they will return to their home countries to become part of Gillette's global management team.

CROSSING BORDERS 17.6

A Look into the Future: Tomorrow's International Leaders? An Education for the 21st Century

A school supported by the European Union teaches Britons, French, Germans, Dutch, and others to be future Europeans. The European School in a suburb of Brussels has students from 12 nations who come to be educated for life and work, not as products of motherland or fatherland but as Europeans. The European Union runs 10 European Schools in western Europe, enrolling 17,000 students from kindergarten to 12th grade. Graduates emerge superbly educated, usually trilingual, and very, very European.

The schools are a linguistic and cultural melange. Native speakers of 36 different languages are represented in one school alone. Each year students take fewer and fewer classes in their native tongue. Early on, usually in first grade, they begin a second language, known as the "working language," which must be English, French, or German. A third language is introduced in the seventh year, and a fourth may be started in the ninth.

By the time students reach their 11th year, they are taking history, geography, economics, advanced math, music, art, and gym in the working language. When the students are in groups talking, they are constantly switching languages to "whatever works."

Besides language, students learn history, politics, literature, and music from the perspective of all the European countries—in short, European cultures. The curriculum is designed to teach the French, German, Briton, and those of other nationalities to be future Europeans.

This same approach is being taken at the MBA level as well. The well-respected European School of Management has campuses in several cities—Berlin, Paris, Oxford, and Madrid. Students spend part of their time at each of the campuses. American MBA programs are beginning to imitate such programs. The University of Chicago School of Business now has campuses in Barcelona, Spain, and Singapore. The Fuqua School at Duke offers a unique executive MBA program involving travel to several foreign countries, and a substantial percentage of teaching delivered interactively over the Internet. This last program attracts students from all over the world who are willing to pay a six-figure tuition.

Sources: Glynn Mapes, "Polyglot Students Are Weaned Early Off Mother Tongue," *Wall Street Journal*, March 6, 1990, p. A1. Reprinted by permission of *The Wall Street Journal*, © 1990 Dow Jones & Company, Inc. All Rights Reserved Worldwide; Kevin Cape, "Tips on Choosing the Right One, International Schools," *International Herald Tribune*, January 25, 2003, p. 7; Victoria Griffith, "A Degree that Bridges the World," *Financial Times*, March 10, 2003, p. 13.

Foreign-Language Skills

Reviews are mixed on the importance of a second language for a career in international business. There are those whose attitude about another language is summed up in the statement that "the language of international business is English." Indeed, one journalist quipped, "Modern English is the Wal-Mart of languages: convenient, huge, hard to avoid, superficially friendly, and devouring all rivals in its eagerness to expand."[39] Others feel that even if you speak one or two languages, you may not be needed in a country whose language you speak. So, is language important or not?

Proponents of language skills argue that learning a language improves cultural understanding and business relationships.[40] Others point out that to be taken seriously in the business community, the expatriate must be at least conversational in the host language. Particularly when it comes to selling in foreign countries, languages are important. Says a Dutch sales training expert, "People expect to buy from sales reps they can relate to, and who understand their language and culture. They're often cold towards Americans trying to sell them products."

Some recruiters want candidates who speak at least one foreign language, even if the language will not be needed in a particular job. Having learned a second language is a strong signal to the recruiter that the candidate is willing to get involved in someone else's culture.

Though most companies offer short, intensive language-training courses for managers being sent abroad, many are making stronger efforts to recruit people who are bilingual or multilingual. According to the director of personnel at Coca-Cola, when his department

---

[39]Mark Abley, journalist.

[40]Kathyrn Kranhold, Dan Bilefsky, Matthew Karnitschnig, and Ginny Parker, "Lost in Translation?" *Wall Street Journal*, May 18, 2004, pp. B1, B6; "Know Thine Enemy," *The Economist*, May 7, 2005, p. 28.

searches its database for people to fill overseas posts, the first choice is often someone who speaks more than one language.

The authors feel strongly that language skills are of great importance; if you want to be a major player in international business in the future, learn to speak other languages or you might not make it—your competition will be those European students described in Crossing Borders 17.6. A joke that foreigners tell about language skills goes something like this: What do you call a person who speaks three or more languages? Multilingual. What do you call a person who speaks two languages? Bilingual. What do you call a person who speaks only one language? An American! Maybe the rest of the world knows something we don't.

Summary

An effective international sales force constitutes one of the international marketer's greatest concerns. The company's sales force represents the major alternative method of organizing a company for foreign distribution and, as such, is on the front line of a marketing organization.

The role of marketers in both domestic and foreign markets is rapidly changing, along with the composition of international managerial and sales forces. Such forces have many unique requirements that are being filled by expatriates, locals, third-country nationals, or a combination of the three. In recent years, the pattern of development has been to place more emphasis on local personnel operating in their own lands. This, in turn, has highlighted the importance of adapting U.S. managerial techniques to local needs.

The development of an effective marketing organization calls for careful recruiting, selecting, training, motivating, and compensating of expatriate personnel and their families to ensure maximization of a company's return on its personnel expenditures. The most practical method of maintaining an efficient international sales and marketing force is careful, concerted planning at all stages of career development.

Questions

1. Define the following terms:

   relationship marketing   TCN

   expatriate   repatriation

   local nationals   separation allowance

2. Why may it be difficult to adhere to set job criteria in selecting foreign personnel? What compensating actions might be necessary?

3. Why does a global sales force cause special compensation problems? Suggest some alternative solutions.

4. Under which circumstances should expatriate salespeople be utilized?

5. Discuss the problems that might be encountered in having an expatriate sales manager supervising foreign salespeople.

6. "To some extent, the exigencies of the personnel situation will dictate the approach to the overseas sales organization." Discuss.

7. How do legal factors affect international sales management?

8. How does the sales force relate to company organization? To channels of distribution?

9. "It is costly to maintain an international sales force." Comment.

10. Adaptability and maturity are traits needed by all salespeople. Why should they be singled out as especially important for international salespeople?

11. Can a person develop good cultural skills? Discuss.

12. Describe the attributes of a person with good cultural skills.

13. Interview a local company that has a foreign sales operation. Draw an organizational chart for the sales function and explain why that particular structure was used by that company.

14. Evaluate the three major sources of multinational personnel.

15. Which factors complicate the task of motivating the foreign sales force?

16. Why do companies include an evaluation of an employee's family among selection criteria for an expatriate assignment?

17. "Concerns for career and family are the most frequently mentioned reasons for a manager to refuse a foreign assignment." Why?

18. Discuss and give examples of why returning U.S. expatriates are often dissatisfied. How can these problems be overcome?

19. If "the language of international business is English," why is it important to develop a skill in a foreign language? Discuss.

20. The global manager of 2020 will have to meet many new challenges. Draw up a sample résumé for someone who could be considered for a top-level executive position in a global firm.

18

pricing for international markets

CHAPTER OUTLINE

Global Perspective: The Price War

Pricing Policy
> Pricing Objectives
> Parallel Imports

Approaches to International Pricing
> Full-Cost versus Variable-Cost Pricing
> Skimming versus Penetration Pricing

Price Escalation
> Costs of Exporting
> Taxes, Tariffs, and Administrative Costs
> Inflation
> Deflation
> Exchange Rate Fluctuations
> Varying Currency Values
> Middleman and Transportation Costs

Sample Effects of Price Escalation

Approaches to Reducing Price Escalation
> Lowering Cost of Goods
> Lowering Tariffs
> Lowering Distribution Costs
> Using Foreign Trade Zones to Lessen Price Escalation
> Dumping

Leasing in International Markets

Countertrade as a Pricing Tool
> Types of Countertrade
> Problems of Countertrading
> The Internet and Countertrading
> Proactive Countertrade Strategy

Transfer Pricing Strategy

Price Quotations

Administered Pricing
> Cartels
> Government-Influenced Pricing

CHAPTER LEARNING OBJECTIVES

What you should learn from Chapter 18:

- Components of pricing as competitive tools in international marketing

- The pricing pitfalls directly related to international marketing

- How to control pricing in parallel imports or gray markets

- Price escalation and how to minimize its effect

- Countertrading and its place in international marketing practices

- The mechanics of price quotations

Global Perspective

THE PRICE WAR

The battle between Procter & Gamble and Kimberly-Clark is bringing Pampers and Huggies, respectively, to places they have never been, forcing down diaper prices worldwide, and expanding the global market for disposable diapers. A battle in Brazil between the two giants gives an interesting glimpse of the global markets of tomorrow. Disposable diapers are still considered a luxury by the vast majority of Brazil's 160 million people, whose average annual income is under $4,000. Before P&G and Kimberly arrived, rich and poor alike generally made do with cloth or nothing at all. The disposables that were available were expensive, bulky, and leaky.

When less than 5 percent of the Brazilian mass market used disposable diapers, P&G launched Pampers Uni, a no-frills, unisex diaper. Before Uni, it cost more to pay for disposable diapers than to pay for a maid to wash the cloth ones. The introduction of the relatively cheap, high-quality Uni fundamentally changed the economics of the diaper market for most middle-class Brazilians.

The plan was to put such nonessentials as disposable diapers within the reach of millions of Brazilians for the first time. At the same time, the Brazilian economy was on the upswing—inflation had subsided and overnight the purchasing power of the poor increased by 20 percent. Low-priced products flew off the shelves. P&G had to truck in diapers from Argentina as it struggled to open new production lines.

But the good days didn't last. Kimberly-Clark entered the market and began importing Huggies from Argentina. With the help of a Unilever unit as its Brazilian distributor, Kimberly gained immediate distribution across the country and quickly made deep inroads into the market. Unilever agreed to work with Kimberly-Clark because its archrival in soap was P&G, and Kimberly-Clark's archrival in diapers was P&G. The two companies had earlier entered into a global alliance to look for win-win situations where it was in both their best interests to partner and help each other, from a competitive standpoint, against the dominant P&G. The Brazilian market was the perfect case for cooperation.

With Unilever's help, Kimberly "push girls" invaded markets to demonstrate the diaper's absorption. Sales rose rapidly and began to exceed production. To gain more product, Kimberly formed an alliance with Kenko do Brazil, P&G's largest home-grown rival, and created the "Monica" brand. "Monica's Gang," a comic strip similar to "Peanuts" in the United States, sells four million copies monthly. São Paulo malls were crowded with thousands of kids waiting to get an Easter photo taken with actors in Monica suits, an honor that required the purchase of three packs of diapers. Monica diapers were a big hit, and Kimberly became number one in the Brazilian market.

It was a tough blow to P&G. The company had devoted an entire page of its annual report to how Pampers Uni had tripled its market share in Brazil, helping P&G "retain the number one position in a market that has grown fivefold." Now it suddenly found itself on the defensive. First it cut prices, a step P&G loathes. "Price cutting is like violence: No one wins," says the head of its Brazilian operation. Then it broadened its product range, rolling out an up-market diaper called Super-Seca, priced 25 percent higher than Pampers Uni. Later, in a flanking move, it also unveiled Confort-Seca, a bikini-style diaper originally developed for Thailand and priced 10 to 15 percent lower than the already-inexpensive Uni.

Kimberly fired back, matching the price cut and then introducing a cheaper version of Monica called Tippy Basic. Four weeks later P&G cut prices another 10 percent on Super-Seca and Confort-Seca. Despite the price cuts, the two brands were still relatively expensive; then a wave of really cheap diapers arrived. Carrefour, a French retailer that is now Brazil's biggest supermarket chain, sells crudely made Bye-Bye Pipi diapers from Mexico. Despite their inferior quality, the cheap imports pulled down diaper prices across the board.

The real war started when lower prices became so attractive that consumers who otherwise could not afford diapers came into the market. As prices continued to drop, the market grew; that attracted more producers, which were mostly small, local Brazilian companies that offered even lower-priced competitive diapers. One such company, Mili, saw its market share increase from 4.8 percent in 1999 to 16.2 percent in 2002. What accounts for growth of these smaller companies? One analyst suggests that the multinationals are too sophisticated and, thus, too expensive for the Brazilian market. "Smaller companies are just supplying what consumers need at a price they can afford." But it also can be said that as prices drop, products become more attractive to a larger segment of the total market.

Sources: Raju Narisetti and Jonathan Friedland, "Disposable Income: Diaper Wars of P&G and Kimberly-Clark Now Heat Up in Brazil," *Wall Street Journal*, June 4, 1997, p. A1; "Brazil: Procter & Gamble Increased Market Share," *SABI* (South American Business Information), May 31, 2000; Brendan M. Case, "Irving Firm to Cut Jobs, Kimberly-Clark Says Savings Will Be Used toward New Products," *Business*, July 23, 2005, p. 1D. For more information, see Kimberly-Clark's Web site at www.kimberly-clark.com and Procter & Gamble's at www.pg.com.

Prices both evaluate and communicate in international markets.[1] For example, initially Hong Kong Disneyland's early attendance was lower than expected, in part driven by what some called an unaffordable opening-day price of $32 a ticket.[2] Setting the right price for a product or service can be the key to success or failure. Even when the international marketer produces the right product, promotes it correctly, and initiates the proper channel of distribution, the effort fails if the product is not properly priced. Although the quality of U.S. products is widely recognized in global markets, foreign buyers, like domestic buyers, balance quality and price in their purchase decisions. An offering's price must reflect the quality and value the consumer perceives in the product. Of all the tasks facing the international marketer, determining what price to charge is one of the most difficult. It is further complicated when the company sells its product to customers in different country markets.

As the globalization of world markets continues, competition intensifies among multinational and home-based companies. All are seeking a solid competitive position so they can prosper as markets reach full potential. The competition for the diaper market between Kimberly-Clark, P&G, and the smaller companies illustrates how price becomes increasingly important as a competitive tool and how price competition changes the structure of a market. Whether exporting or managing overseas operations, the manager's responsibility is to set and control the actual price of goods in different markets in which different sets of variables are to be found: different tariffs, costs, attitudes, competition, currency fluctuations, and methods of price quotation.

This chapter focuses on the basic pricing policy questions that arise from the special cost, market, and competitive factors found in foreign markets. A discussion of price escalation and its control and factors associated with price setting and leasing is followed by a discussion of the use of countertrade as a pricing tool and a review of the mechanics of international price quotation.

Pricing Policy

Active marketing in several countries compounds the number of pricing problems and variables relating to price policy. Unless a firm has a clearly thought-out, explicitly defined price policy, expediency rather than design establishes prices. The country in which business is being conducted, the type of product, variations in competitive conditions, and other strategic factors affect pricing activity. Price and terms of sale cannot be based on domestic criteria alone.

Pricing Objectives

In general, price decisions are viewed two ways: pricing as an active instrument of accomplishing marketing objectives, or pricing as a static element in a business decision. If prices are viewed as an active instrument, the company uses price to achieve a specific objective, whether a targeted return on profit, a targeted market share, or some other specific goal.[3] The company that follows the second approach, pricing as a static element, probably exports only excess inventory, places a low priority on foreign business, and views its export sales as passive contributions to sales volume. When U.S. and Canadian international businesses were asked to rate, on a scale of 1 to 5, several factors important in price setting, total profits received an average rating of 4.7, followed by return on investment (4.41), market share (4.13), and total sales volume (4.06). Liquidity ranked the lowest (2.19).

The more control a company has over the final selling price of a product, the better it is able to achieve its marketing goals. However, controlling end prices is not always possible. The broader the product line and the larger the number of countries involved, the more complex the process of controlling prices to the end user.[4]

---

[1]Lorraine Eden and Peter Rodriguez, "How Weak Are the Signals? International Price Indices and Multinational Enterprises," *Journal of International Business Studies* 36, no. 1 (2004), pp. 61–74.

[2]Don Lee, "Disneyland's Cost a Hurdle for Chinese," *Los Angeles Times*, September 10, 2005, pp. C1, C3.

[3]S. Tamer Cavusgil, Kwog Chan, and Chun Zhang, "Strategic Orientations in Export Pricing: A Clustering Approach to Create Firm Taxonomies," *Journal of International Marketing* 11, no.1 (2003), p. 47.

[4]Matthew B. Meyers and Michael Harvey, "The Value of Pricing Control in Export Channels: A Governance Perspective," *Journal of International Marketing* 9, no. 4 (2001), p. 1.

CROSSING BORDERS 18.1 How Do Levi's 501s Get to International Markets?

Levi Strauss sells in international markets; how else would 501 jeans get to market? The answer is via the gray market, or "diverters." Diverters are enterprising people who legally buy 501s at retail prices, usually during sales, and then resell them to foreign buyers. It is estimated that Levi Strauss sells millions of dollars of Levi's abroad at discount prices—all authorized sales. U.S. retail prices for Levi's 501s are $30 to $40 a pair; in Germany, they are sold to authorized wholesalers for about $40, and authorized retailers sell them at about $80. The difference of $40 or so makes it economically possible for a diverter to buy 501s in the United States and sell them to unauthorized dealers who then sell them for $60 to $70, undercutting authorized German retailers. Similar practices happen around the world. How do diverters work?

Here is an example of what is repeated in city after city all over the United States. "They come into a store in groups and buy every pair of Levi's 501 jeans they can," says one store manager. He says he has seen two or three vans full of people come to the store when there is a sale and buy the six-pair-a-day limit, returning day after day until the sale is over. In another retail chain store, where a similar thing was happening, a month-long storewide sale was stopped, at the behest of Levi's, after only two weeks. The Levi's are then channeled to a diverter, who exports them to unauthorized buyers throughout the world. Many eventually end up in discount stores and are sold at discounted prices relative to those distributed through approved channels. This is but one way diverters acquire merchandise. Another is for wholesalers to buy quantities in excess of their needs and then divert the excess to foreign buyers.

What makes these practices feasible are the lower markups and prices of U.S. and other retailers

compared with the higher costs and the resulting higher markups and prices that retailers charge in many other countries (Levi's has a higher wholesale price for foreign sales than for domestic sales).

Retail prices in the United States are often more competitive than in other countries where, historically, price competition is not as fierce. For example, besides Levi's 501s, which sell for $73 in Britain versus $45 in the United States, a Mariah Carey CD costs $23 versus $16, and Windows Office is $243 versus $118. Some, but not all, of the price differences can be attributed to price escalation, that is, tariffs, shipping, and other costs associated with exporting, but that portion of the difference attributable to higher margins creates an opportunity for profitable diverting.

In an attempt to stop discount stores not in the manufacturer's official distribution channel from selling "unauthorized" Levi's, Tesco, a U.K. supermarket chain, was sued by Levi-Strauss & Company. After a four-year court battle, Levi won when a London judge ruled that the supermarket had been selling Levi's illegally. However, Tesco, Costco, Wal-Mart, and other mass retailers cater to a vast market interested in value-priced, quality products—a market Levi's misses if its products are not sold there. Consequently, Levi's developed a Signature line for Tesco that sells for about £25 a pair—£20 less than ordinary Levis. I guess the old adage "If you can't beat them, join them" applies.

Sources: Jim Hill, "Flight of the 501s," *Oregonian*, June 27, 1993, p. G1; "Diversion!" *Journal of Commerce*, June 26, 2000, p. WP; Jean Eaglesham and Deborah Hargreaves, "Court Left to Iron Out Brand Import Wrinkle: Levis v. Tesco," *National Post*, January 24, 2001, p. C3; Tracy Nesdoly, "I'm Still Pursuing Jeans of My Dreams," *Toronto Star*, September 17, 2005, p. M07.

Parallel Imports

Besides having to meet price competition country by country and product by product, companies have to guard against competition with their own subsidiaries or branches. Because of the different prices possible in different country markets, a product sold in one country may be exported to another and undercut the prices charged in that country. For example, to meet economic conditions and local competition, an American pharmaceutical company might sell its drugs in a developing country at a low price and then discover that these discounted drugs are being exported to a third country, where, as parallel imports, they are in direct competition with the same product sold for higher prices by the same firm.

Parallel imports develop when importers buy products from distributors in one country and sell them in another to distributors who are not part of the manufacturer's regular distribution system. This practice is lucrative when wide margins exist between prices for the same products in different countries. A variety of conditions can create a profitable opportunity for a parallel market.

Restrictions brought about by import quotas and high tariffs also can lead to parallel imports and make illegal imports attractive. India has a three-tier duty structure on computer parts ranging from 50 to 80 percent on imports. As a result, estimates are that as much as 35 percent of India's domestic computer hardware sales are accounted for by the gray market.

The possibility of a parallel market occurs whenever price differences are greater than the cost of transportation between two markets. In Europe, because of different taxes and competitive price structures, prices for the same product vary between countries. When this occurs, it is not unusual for companies to find themselves competing in one country with their own products imported from another European country at lower prices. Pharmaceutical companies face this problem in Italy, Greece, and Spain because of price caps imposed on prescription drugs in those countries. For example, the ulcer drug Losec sells for only $18 in Spain but goes for $39 in Germany. The heart drug Plavix costs $55 in France and sells for $79 in London. Presumably such price differentials were to cease once all restrictions to trade were eliminated in the European Union, and in most cases this is true. However, the European Union does not prevent countries from controlling drug prices as part of their national health plans.

The drug industry has tried to stop parallel trade in Europe but has been overruled by European authorities. This time the industry is trying a different approach, restricting supplies to meet only local demand according to formulas based on prior demand and anticipated growth. The idea is that a country should receive just enough of a drug for its citizens. Wholesalers that order more with the intention of shipping the drugs to higher-price markets would not have enough to do so. A number of major pharmaceutical companies have imposed similar restrictions. The companies say these measures are intended to streamline distribution, help prevent medicine shortages, and curtail excess inventory, whereas distributors claim the strategy is aimed at thwarting cross-border drug trading. The fact is, "half of all demand in Britain of several products is being met by imports from low-priced countries" and companies are attempting to curtail parallel imports.

Gray market pharmaceuticals from Canada to the United States are estimated to be about $427 million annually. Not a large amount when compared to the $135 billion U.S. drug market, but it can be substantial for specific drugs like Paxil, Zyban, and Viagra. Although importing prescription drugs from a foreign country, including Canada, is against U.S. law, a person can travel to Canada or Mexico to make purchases or can buy over the Internet. Technically, buying over the Internet and having the drugs mailed to the United States is illegal. However, the government has taken a relatively lax view toward such purchases provided the supply does not exceed 90 days. Thanks to the low value of the Canadian dollar and government price caps on drugs, an American can often save 50 percent to 70 percent by ordering from the 70 or more Internet pharmacies operating across Canada.

Naturally, drug companies that have been hit the hardest want to put a stop to the traffic. Glaxo SmithKline, the prescription drug maker, has asked all Canadian pharmacies and wholesalers to "self-certify" that they are not exporting its drugs outside Canada. The company also is warning U.S. customers about imported drugs in a new advertising campaign.[5] Those that fail to comply will have their Glaxo supplies cut off—"Glaxo products are approved by Health Canada for sale in Canada only." Some feel that this move will not solve the problem even if Glaxo is able to stop Canadian sales since Americans will be able to find less expensive drugs in other markets, like Australia and Ireland. The Internet trade will be hard to shut down as long as large price differentials persist among markets. Further, U.S. legislators are passing laws that allow such drug imports.[6]

Exclusive distribution, a practice often used by companies to maintain high retail margins in order to encourage retailers to provide extra service to customers, to stock large assortments, or to maintain the exclusive-quality image of a product, can create a favorable condition for parallel importing. Perfume and designer brands such as Gucci and Cartier are especially prone to gray markets. To maintain the image of quality and exclusivity, prices for such products traditionally include high profit margins at each level of distribution; characteristically, there are differential prices among markets and limited quantities of product, and distribution is restricted to upscale retailers. Wholesale prices for exclusive brands of fragrances are often 25 percent more in the United States than wholesale prices

---

[5]Barrie McKenna, "New Shot Fired in Net Drug Battle," *Toronto Globe and Mail*, June 2, 2005, p. B3.
[6]"Senate Passes Bill to Keep Drug Import Bans Out of Trade Deals," *FDA Week* 11, no. 37 (September 16, 2005). 11(37).

Exhibit 18.1
How Gray-Market Goods End Up in U.S. Stores

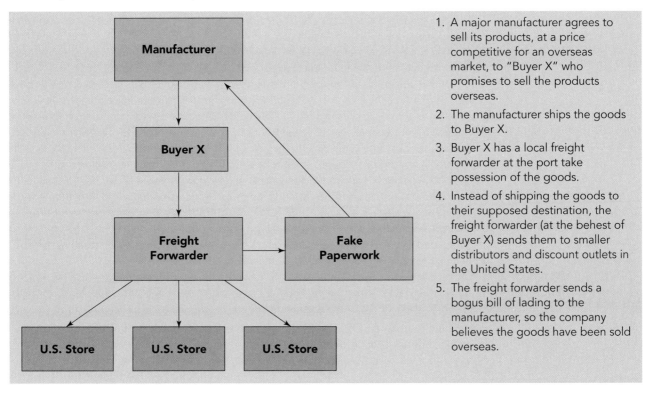

1. A major manufacturer agrees to sell its products, at a price competitive for an overseas market, to "Buyer X" who promises to sell the products overseas.

2. The manufacturer ships the goods to Buyer X.

3. Buyer X has a local freight forwarder at the port take possession of the goods.

4. Instead of shipping the goods to their supposed destination, the freight forwarder (at the behest of Buyer X) sends them to smaller distributors and discount outlets in the United States.

5. The freight forwarder sends a bogus bill of lading to the manufacturer, so the company believes the goods have been sold overseas.

in other countries. These are ideal conditions for a lucrative gray market for unauthorized dealers in other countries who buy more than they need at wholesale prices lower than U.S. wholesalers pay. They then sell the excess at a profit to unauthorized U.S. retailers, but at a price lower than the retailer would have to pay to an authorized U.S. distributor.

The high-priced designer sportswear industry is also vulnerable to such practices. Nike, Adidas, and Calvin Klein were incensed to find their products being sold in one of Britain's leading supermarket chains, Tesco. Nike's Air Max Metallic trainers, which are priced at £120 ($196) in sports shops, could be purchased at Tesco for £50 ($80). Tesco had bought £8 million in Nike sportswear from overstocked wholesalers in the United States (Exhibit 18.1). To prevent parallel markets from developing when such marketing and pricing strategies are used, companies must maintain strong control over distribution and prices.

Companies that are serious about restricting the gray market must establish and monitor controls that effectively police distribution channels. In some countries they may get help from the courts. A Taiwan court ruled that two companies that were buying Coca-Cola in the United States and shipping it to Taiwan were violating the trademark rights of both the Coca-Cola Company and its sole Taiwan licensee. The violators were prohibited from importing, displaying, or selling products bearing the Coca-Cola trademark. In other countries, the courts have not always come down on the side of the trademark owner. The reasoning is that once the trademarked item is sold, the owner's rights to control the trademarked item are lost. In a similar situation in Canada, the courts did not side with the Canadian exporter who was buying 50,000 cases of Coke a week and shipping them to Hong Kong and Japan. The exporter paid $4.25 a case plus shipping of $1.00 a case and sold them at $6.00, a nifty profit of 75 cents a case. Coca-Cola sued, but the court ruled that the product was bought and sold legally. The reasoning was that once a trademarked item is sold, the owner's right to control the trademarked item is lost.

Where differences in prices between markets occur, the Internet makes it easy for individuals to participate in the gray market. Music CDs are especially vulnerable because of price differentials. Six foreign-owned record companies that maintain high prices through limited distribution dominate the Australian market and create a situation ripe for the gray market.

CDs retail there for an average of $24 but can be purchased for about 25 to 30 percent less from the many e-stores on the Internet. It is estimated that CDs purchased directly from the United States over the Internet have led to a 5 percent fall in Australian retail sales. In the United Kingdom, gray-market CDs come from Italy, where they are about 50 percent cheaper and account for between 15 and 20 percent of sales in some releases. Sony believes that over 100,000 copies of one of Celine Dion's best-selling albums sold in the United Kingdom were from parallel imports. The Internet has truly become a global price equalizer.

Parallel imports can do long-term damage in the market for trademarked products. Customers who unknowingly buy unauthorized imports have no assurance of the quality of the item they buy, of warranty support, or of authorized service or replacement parts. Purchasers of computers, for example, may not be able to get parts because authorized dealers have no obligation to service these computers. In the case of software, the buyer may be buying a counterfeit product and will not be authorized for technical support. Further, when a product fails, the consumer blames the owner of the trademark, and the quality image of the product is sullied.

With global brands and the euro making price comparison easier and the Internet facilitating purchasing, it is increasingly difficult to differentiate in prices among European markets. Companies will either have to harmonize prices among member states or contend with parallel imports where differences in selling prices are profitable. Brand harmonization and price harmonization must be addressed simultaneously.

Approaches to International Pricing

Whether the orientation is toward control over end prices or over net prices, company policy relates to the net price received. Cost and market considerations are important; a company cannot sell goods below cost of production and remain in business, and it cannot sell goods at a price unacceptable in the marketplace. Firms unfamiliar with overseas marketing and firms producing industrial goods orient their pricing solely on a cost basis. Firms that employ pricing as part of the strategic mix, however, are aware of such alternatives as market segmentation from country to country or market to market, competitive pricing in the marketplace, and other market-oriented pricing factors[7] including cultural differences in perceptions of pricing.[8]

Full-Cost versus Variable-Cost Pricing

Firms that orient their price thinking around cost must determine whether to use variable cost or full cost in pricing their goods. In *variable-cost pricing,* the firm is concerned only with the marginal or incremental cost of producing goods to be sold in overseas markets. Such firms regard foreign sales as bonus sales and assume that any return over their variable cost makes a contribution to net profit. These firms may be able to price most competitively in foreign markets, but because they are selling products abroad at lower net prices than they are selling them in the domestic market, they may be subject to charges of dumping. In that case, they open themselves to antidumping tariffs or penalties that take away from their competitive advantage. Nevertheless, variable-cost (or *marginal-cost*) pricing is a practical approach to pricing when a company has high fixed costs and unused production capacity. Any contribution to fixed cost after variable costs are covered is profit to the company.

On the other hand, companies following the *full-cost pricing* philosophy insist that no unit of a similar product is different from any other unit in terms of cost and that each unit must bear its full share of the total fixed and variable cost.[9] This approach is suitable when a company has high variable costs relative to its fixed costs. In such cases, prices are often set on a cost-plus basis, that is, total costs plus a profit margin. Both variable-cost and full-cost policies are followed by international marketers.

---

[7]Pradeep K. Chintagunta and Ramaroa Desiraju, "Strategic Pricing and Detailing Behavior in International Markets," *Marketing Science* 24, no. 1 (2005), pp. 67–80.

[8]Lee C. Simmons and Robert M. Schindler, "Cultural Superstitions and the Price Endings Used in Chinese Advertising," *Journal of International Marketing* 11, no. 2 (2003), pp. 101–111; Manoj Thomas and Vick Morwitz, "Penny Wise and Pound Foolish: The Left-Digit Effect in Price Cognition," *Journal of Consumer Research* 32, no. 2 (2005), pp. 54–64.

[9]For a research report on cost variables that influence price strategy, see Mary Anne Raymond, John F. Tanner Jr., and Joghoon Kim, "Cost Complexity of Pricing Decisions for Exporters in Developing and Emerging Markets," *Journal of International Marketing* 9, no. 3 (2001), p. 19.

CROSSING BORDERS 18.2   Don't Squeeze the Charmin, Mr. Whipple—Or Change the Color

The British pay twice as much as the Germans and the French, and nearly two-and-a-half times as much as Americans, for a standard four-roll pack of toilet paper. Why? Is it price gouging, the impact of the euro, the relative value of the English pound, or just culture?

The answer is rather simple: British consumers insist on a softer, more luxurious texture than their less discriminating continental and America cousins. British toilet paper is four grams heavier per square meter because it contains more fiber than European tissues. Extensive consumer testing has established that British consumers are not willing to be fobbed off with anything less.

Another factor distinguishes the British preference for a special toilet paper roll. Go to any supermarket and you will be confronted by an extraordinary choice of more than 50 colors, sizes, and brands. Honeysuckle, warm pink, summer peach, pearl white, meadow green, breeze blue, and magnolia are just some of the shades on offer.

The reason for this variety apparently is that the British shopper insists that toilet paper match the color scheme of the bathroom. On the continent, consumers settle happily for white, with pink thrown in as a wild alternative.

Procter & Gamble captured 10 percent of the market in less than five months after offering a stronger Charmin, but it may have gone too far. There were complaints that the "wet strength" of Charmin was unsuitable for U.K. toilets. The U.K. sewage system could handle Charmin alone, but the issue was whether the system would get clogged if several rival tissues adopted the stronger tissue. Procter & Gamble agreed to halve the strength of its Charmin toilet tissue, but will the price come down?

Sources: "Going Soft," *The Economist,* March 4, 2000; "P&G Unblocks Sewage Row with Toilet Paper Revamp," *Reuters,* May 10, 2000; Timothy Kenny, "Eurasia: Of Toilet Paper, Escalators and Hope," *Wall Street Journal Europe,* September 16, 2005, p. A9.

Skimming versus Penetration Pricing

Firms must also decide when to follow a skimming or a penetration pricing policy. Traditionally, the decision of which policy to follow depends on the level of competition, the innovativeness of the product, market characteristics, and company characteristics.[10]

A company uses *skimming* when the objective is to reach a segment of the market that is relatively price insensitive and thus willing to pay a premium price for the value received. If limited supply exists, a company may follow a skimming approach in order to maximize revenue and to match demand to supply. When a company is the only seller of a new or innovative product, a skimming price may be used to maximize profits until competition forces a lower price. Skimming often is used in markets with only two income levels: the wealthy and the poor. Costs prohibit setting a price that will be attractive to the lower-income market, so the marketer charges a premium price and directs the product to the high-income, relatively price-insensitive segment. Apparently this was the policy of Johnson & Johnson's pricing of diapers in Brazil before the arrival of P&G. Today, such opportunities are fading away as the disparity in income levels is giving way to growing middle-income market segments. The existence of larger markets attracts competition and, as is often the case, the emergence of multiple product lines, thus leading to price competition.

A *penetration pricing policy* is used to stimulate market and sales growth by deliberately offering products at low prices.[11] Penetration pricing most often is used to acquire and hold share of market as a competitive maneuver. However, in country markets experiencing rapid and sustained economic growth, and where large shares of the population are moving into middle-income classes, penetration pricing may be used to stimulate market growth even with minimum competition. Penetration pricing may be a more profitable strategy than skimming if it maximizes revenues as a base for fighting the competition that is sure to come.

Regardless of the formal pricing policies and strategies a company uses, it must be remembered that the market sets the effective price for a product. Said another way, the price has to be set at a point at which the consumer will perceive value received, and the price

---

[10]S. Tamer Cavusgil, Kwong Chan, and Chun Zhang, "Strategic Orientations in Export Pricing: A Clustering Approach to Creating Firm Taxonomies," *Journal of International Marketing* 11, no. 1 (2003), pp. 47–72.

[11]Eric Bellman and Deborah Ball, "Unilever, P&G Wage Price War for Edge in India," *Wall Street Journal,* August 11, 2004, pp. B1, B3.

Chinese wait to enter Beijing's first Wal-Mart outlet. Thousands crowded the Sam's Club store on the far western edge of Beijing as the world's biggest retailer made its first foray into a major Chinese city. Wal-Mart has more than 20 stores elsewhere in China; the first was opened in 1996. The low-price-for-good-quality strategy of Wal-Mart and other mass retailers such as Costco and Carrefour, the French supermarket chain, have resulted in lowering retail prices in China, Japan, and other Asian countries they have entered. *(AP/Wide World Photos)*

must be within reach of the target market. As a consequence, many products are sold in very small units in some markets in order to bring the unit price within reach of the target market. Warner-Lambert's launch of its five-unit pack of Bubbaloo bubble gum in Brazil failed—even though bubble gum represents over 72 percent of the overall gum sector—because it was priced above the target market. A relaunch of a single-unit "pillow" pack brought the price within range and enabled the brand to quickly gain a respectable level of sales.

As a country's economy grows and distribution of wealth becomes more equitable, multiple income levels develop, distinct market segments emerge, and multiple price levels and price/quality perceptions will increase in importance. As an example, the market for electronic consumer goods in China changed in just a few years. Instead of a market for imported high-priced and high-quality electronic goods aimed at the new rich and cheaper, poorer-quality Chinese-made goods for the rest of the market, a multitiered market reflecting the growth of personal income has emerged.

Sony of Japan, the leading foreign seller of the high-priced consumer electronic goods, was upstaged in the Chinese market when Aiwa, a competitor, recognized the emergence of a new middle-tier market for good-quality, modestly priced electronic goods. As part of a global strategy focused on slim margins and high turnover, Aiwa of Korea began selling hi-fi systems at prices closer to Chinese brands than to Sony's. Aiwa's product quality was not far behind that of Sony and was better than top Chinese brands, and the product resembled Sony's high-end systems. Aiwa's recognition of a new market segment and its ability to tap into it resulted in a huge increase in overall demand for Aiwa products.

Pricing decisions that were appropriate when companies directed their marketing efforts toward single market segments will give way to more sophisticated practices. As incomes rise in many foreign markets, the pricing environment a company encounters will be similar to that in the United States. As countries prosper and incomes become more equitably distributed, multiple market segments develop. As these segments emerge, Wal-Mart, Carrefour, and other mass retailers enter the market to offer price-conscious customers good value at affordable prices. This scenario seems to repeat itself in country after country. Within these markets an effective pricing strategy becomes crucial.

Price Escalation

People traveling abroad often are surprised to find goods that are relatively inexpensive in their home country priced outrageously high in other countries. Because of the natural tendency to assume that such prices are a result of profiteering, manufacturers often resolve to begin exporting to crack these new, profitable foreign markets only to find that, in most cases, the higher prices reflect the higher costs of exporting. A case in point is a pacemaker for heart patients that sells for $2,100 in the United States. Tariffs and the Japanese distribution system add substantially to the final price in Japan. Beginning with the import tariff, each time the pacemaker changes hands an additional cost is incurred. The product passes first through the hands of an importer, then to the company with primary responsibility for sales and service, then to a secondary or even a tertiary local distributor, and finally to the hospital. Markups at each level result in the $2,100 pacemaker selling for over $4,000 in Japan. Inflation results in price escalation, one of the major pricing obstacles facing the MNC marketer. This is true not only for technical products like the pacemaker but for such products as crude oil, soft drinks, and beer. Estimates are that if tariffs and trade barriers on these products were abolished, the consumer would enjoy savings of 6.57 trillion yen.

Costs of Exporting

Excess profits exist in some international markets, but generally the cause of the disproportionate difference in price between the exporting country and the importing country, here termed *price escalation,* is the added costs incurred as a result of exporting products from one country to another. Specifically, the term relates to situations in which ultimate prices are raised by shipping costs, insurance, packing, tariffs, longer channels of distribution, larger middlemen margins, special taxes, administrative costs, and exchange rate fluctuations. The majority of these costs arise as a direct result of moving goods across borders from one country to another and often combine to escalate the final price to a level considerably higher than in the domestic market.

Taxes, Tariffs, and Administrative Costs

"Nothing is surer than death and taxes" has a particularly familiar ring to the ears of the international trader because taxes include tariffs, and tariffs are one of the most pervasive features of international trading. Taxes and tariffs affect the ultimate consumer price for a product; in most instances, the consumer bears the burden of both. Sometimes, however, consumers benefit when manufacturers selling goods in foreign countries reduce their net return in order to gain access to a foreign market. Absorbed or passed on, taxes and tariffs must be considered by the international businessperson.

A tariff, or duty, is a special form of taxation. Like other forms of taxes, a tariff may be levied for the purpose of protecting a market or for increasing government revenue. A tariff is a fee charged when goods are brought into a country from another country. Recall from Chapter 15 that the level of tariff is typically expressed as the rate of duty and may be levied as specific, ad valorem, or compound. A specific duty is a flat charge per physical unit imported, such as 15 cents per bushel of rye. Ad valorem duties are levied as a percentage of the value of the goods imported, such as 20 percent of the value of imported watches. Compound duties include both a specific and an ad valorem charge, such as $1 per camera plus 10 percent of its value. Tariffs and other forms of import taxes serve to discriminate against all foreign goods.

Fees for import certificates or for other administrative processing can assume such levels that they are, in fact, import taxes. Many countries have purchase or excise taxes, which apply to various categories of goods; value-added or turnover taxes, which apply as the product goes through a channel of distribution; and retail sales taxes. Such taxes increase the end price of goods but, in general, do not discriminate against foreign goods. Tariffs are the primary discriminatory tax that must be taken into account in reckoning with foreign competition.

In addition to taxes and tariffs, a variety of administrative costs are directly associated with exporting and importing a product. Export and import licenses, other documents, and the physical arrangements for getting the product from port of entry to the buyer's location mean additional costs. Although such costs are relatively small, they add to the overall cost of exporting.

Inflation

In countries with rapid inflation or exchange variation, the selling price must be related to the cost of goods sold and the cost of replacing the items. Goods often are sold below their cost of replacement plus overhead, and sometimes are sold below replacement cost. In these instances, the company would be better off not to sell the products at all. When payment is likely to be delayed for several months or is worked out on a long-term contract, inflationary factors must be figured into the price. Inflation and lack of control over price were instrumental in an

Shoppers look at stacks of discount clothing jutting out on a sidewalk to attract potential buyers at Tokyo's Sugamo shopping district. With the stock market plunging to 16-year lows, talk of deflationary dangers, and a morass of confusion in its political leadership, Japan appears to be headed toward a serious economic crisis. The central bank played down the possibility of deflation, saying that falling prices show the market is finally opening up to competition. However, consumer prices have fallen so precipitously that most believe that Japan's economy is experiencing serious deflation. *(AP/Wide World Photos)*

unsuccessful new-product launch in Brazil by the H. J. Heinz Company; after only two years, Heinz withdrew from the market. Misunderstandings with the local partner resulted in a new fruit-based drink being sold to retailers on consignment; that is, they did not pay until the product was sold. Faced with a rate of inflation of over 300 percent at the time, just a week's delay in payment eroded profit margins substantially. Soaring inflation in many developing countries (Latin America in particular) makes widespread price controls a constant threat.

Because inflation and price controls imposed by a country are beyond the control of companies, they use a variety of techniques to inflate the selling price to compensate for inflation pressure and price controls. They may charge for extra services, inflate costs in transfer pricing, or break up products into components and price each component separately.

Inflation causes consumer prices to escalate and the consumer is faced with ever-rising prices that eventually exclude many consumers from the market. On the other hand, deflation results in ever-decreasing prices creating a positive result for consumers, but both put pressure to lower costs on everyone in the supply chain.

Deflation   The Japanese economy has been in a deflationary spiral for a number of years. In a country better known for $10 melons and $100 steaks, McDonald's now sells hamburgers for 52 cents, down from $1.09; a flat screen 32-inch color television is down from $4,000 to $2,400; and clothing stores compete to sell fleece jackets for $8, down from $25 two years earlier.[12] Consumer prices have dropped to a point where they are similar to those Japanese once found only on overseas shopping trips. The high prices prevalent in Japan before deflation allowed substantial margins for everyone in the distribution chain. As prices continued to drop over several years, those less able to adjust costs to allow some margin with deflated prices fell by the wayside. Entirely new retail categories—100-yen discount shops, clothing chains selling low-cost imported products from China, and warehouse-style department stores—have become the norm. Sales at discount stores grew by 78 percent in the late 1990s. Discounting is the way to prosper in Japan, which again helps fuel deflation. While those in the distribution chain adjusted to a different competitive environment or gave up, Japanese consumers were reveling in their newfound spending power. Japanese tourists used to travel to the United States to buy things at much cheaper prices, but, as one consumer commented, "Nowadays, I feel prices in Japan are going down and America is no longer cheaper." Although she was accustomed to returning from trips to the United States carrying suitcases of bargains, she returned from her last two-week vacation with purchases that fit in one fanny pack.

In a deflationary market, it is essential for a company to keep prices low and raise brand value to win the trust of consumers. Whether deflation or inflation, an exporter has to place emphasis on controlling price escalation.

Exchange Rate Fluctuations   At one time, world trade contracts could be easily written because payment was specified in a relatively stable currency. The American dollar was the standard and all transactions could be related to the dollar. Now that all major currencies are floating freely relative to one another, no one is quite sure of the future value of any currency.[13] Increasingly, companies are insisting that transactions be written in terms of the vendor company's national

---

[12]At least one exception in Japan is the Louis Vuitton brand of handbags, leather, and other luxury goods, which has managed to raise prices twice in one year despite Japan's severe deflation. See Philippe Ries, "French Luxury Goods Hold Their Own in Japan Despite Euro's Rise," *Agence France-Presse,* March 2, 2003.

[13]Even China has begun to let its currency float within a defined range; Michael M. Phillips, "China Drops Yuan's Dollar Peg, Will Let Currency Float in Band," *Wall Street Journal*, July 21, 2005, p. A1.

currency, and forward hedging is becoming more common. If exchange rates are not carefully considered in long-term contracts, companies find themselves unwittingly giving 15 to 20 percent discounts. The added cost incurred by exchange rate fluctuations on a day-to-day basis must be taken into account, especially where there is a significant time lapse between signing the order and delivery of the goods. Exchange rate differentials mount up. Whereas Hewlett-Packard gained nearly half a million dollars additional profit through exchange rate fluctuations in one year, Nestlé lost a million dollars in six months. Other companies have lost or gained even larger amounts.[14]

Varying Currency Values

In addition to risks from exchange rate variations, other risks result from the changing values of a country's currency relative to other currencies.[15] Consider the situation in Germany for a purchaser of U.S. manufactured goods from mid-2001 to mid-2003. During this period, the value of the U.S. dollar relative to the euro went from a strong position (U.S.$1 to €1.8315) in mid-2001 to a weaker position in mid-2003 (U.S.$1 to €0.8499). A strong dollar produces price resistance because a larger quantity of local currency is needed to buy a U.S. dollar. Conversely, when the U.S. dollar is weak, demand for U.S. goods increases because fewer units of local currency are needed to buy a U.S. dollar. The weaker U.S. dollar, compared with most of the world's stronger currencies, that existed in mid-2003 stimulated exports from the United States. Consequently, when the dollar strengthens U.S. exports will soften.

When the value of the dollar is weak relative to the buyer's currency (i.e., it takes fewer units of the foreign currency to buy a dollar), companies generally employ cost-plus pricing. To remain price competitive when the dollar is strong (i.e., when it takes more units of the foreign currency to buy a dollar), companies must find ways to offset the higher price caused by currency values. When the rupee in India depreciated significantly against the U.S. dollar, PC manufacturers faced a serious pricing problem. Because the manufacturers were dependent on imported components, their options were to absorb the increased cost or raise

---

[14]Mark A. Stein, "Dollar's Fall Helps Some," *International Herald Tribune*, March 25, 2005, p. 17.

[15]Annually *The Economist* publishes its BigMac index, which predicts currency fluctuations: "Fast Food and Strong Currencies," June 11, 2005, p. 70.

During the mid-1990s, Mexico knocked three zeroes off the peso in response to a major devaluation. In 2005 Turkey knocked six zeroes off its lira toward its potential alignment with the European Union. Both actions affected perceptions of key constituencies. Both bills are worth about 75¢.

Exhibit 18.2
Export Strategies under Varying Currency Conditions

When Domestic [American] Currency Is WEAK . . .	When Domestic [American] Currency Is STRONG . . .
Stress price benefits	Engage in nonprice competition by improving quality, delivery, and aftersale service
Expand product line and add more-costly features	Improve productivity and engage in vigorous cost reduction
Shift sourcing and manufacturing to domestic market	Shift sourcing and manufacturing overseas
Exploit export opportunities in all markets	Give priority to exports to relatively strong-currency countries
Conduct conventional cash-for-goods trade	Deal in countertrade with weak-currency countries
Use full-costing approach, but use marginal-cost pricing to penetrate new/competitive markets	Trim profit margins and use marginal-cost pricing
Speed repatriation of foreign-earned income and collections	Keep the foreign-earned income in host country and slow collections
Minimize expenditures in local, host-country currency	Maximize expenditures in local, host-country currency
Buy needed services (advertising, insurance, transportation, etc.) in domestic market	Buy needed services abroad and pay for them in local currencies
Minimize local borrowing	Borrow money needed for expansion in local market
Bill foreign customers in domestic currency	Bill foreign customers in their own currency

Source: S. Tamer Cavugil, "Unraveling the Mystique of Export Pricing," Chapter 71 in Sidney J. Levy, George R. Frerichs, and Howard L. Gordon (eds.), *The Dartnell Marketing Manager's Handbook* (Chicago: Dartnell Corporation 1994), Figure 2, p. 1362. Reprinted with permission of Dartnell Corporation. All rights reserved.

the price of PCs. Exhibit 18.2 focuses on the different price strategies a company might employ under a weak or strong domestic currency. U.S. companies marketing in those countries with strong currencies have a choice between lowering prices even further, and thereby expanding their market share, or maintaining prices and accumulating larger profits.

Currency exchange rate swings are considered by many global companies to be a major pricing problem. Because the benefits of a weaker dollar are generally transitory, firms need to take a proactive stance one way or the other. For a company with long-range plans calling for continued operation in foreign markets yet wanting to remain price competitive, price strategies need to reflect variations in currency values.

Innumerable cost variables can be identified depending on the market, the product, and the situation. The cost, for example, of reaching a market with relatively small potential may be high. High operating costs of small specialty stores like those in Mexico and Thailand lead to high retail prices. Intense competition in certain world markets raises the cost or lowers the margins available to world business. Even small things like payoffs to local officials can introduce unexpected costs to the unwary entrepreneur. Only experience in a given marketplace provides the basis for compensating for cost differences in different markets. With experience, a firm that prices on a cost basis operates in a realm of reasonably measurable factors.

Middleman and Transportation Costs

Channel length and marketing patterns vary widely, but in most countries channels are longer and middleman margins higher than is customary in the United States. The diversity of channels used to reach markets and the lack of standardized middleman markups leave many producers unaware of the ultimate price of a product.

Besides channel diversity, the fully integrated marketer operating abroad faces various unanticipated costs because marketing and distribution channel infrastructures are underdeveloped in many countries. The marketer can also incur added expenses for warehousing and handling of small shipments and may have to bear increased financing costs when dealing with underfinanced middlemen.

Because no convenient source of data on middleman costs is available, the international marketer must rely on experience and marketing research to ascertain middleman costs. The Campbell Soup Company found its middleman and physical distribution costs in the United

A woman looks at a poster offering a half-priced bacon and lettuce hamburger, reduced from U.S.$3.20 to $1.60 during a monthly discount at a McDonald's restaurant in downtown Tokyo. McDonald's Japan announced that it would reduce the price of hamburgers by 30 percent for a month to return to customers the profit the company made by the strong yen against U.S. dollars in importing the raw materials from abroad. McDonald's move creates goodwill among its customers at a time when they are forced to lower prices to "hike" sales in an economy that is suffering a major downturn. This is a good example of how differences in the value of currencies can be positive for a company, as in this case, or negative when the value of the dollar is much stronger than the local currency. *(AP/Wide World Photos)*

Kingdom to be 30 percent higher than in the United States. Extra costs were incurred because soup was purchased in small quantities—small English grocers typically purchase 24-can cases of assorted soups (each case being hand-packed for shipment). In the United States, typical purchase units are 48-can cases of one soup purchased by the dozens, hundreds, or carloads. The purchase habits in Europe forced the company into an extra wholesale level in its channel to facilitate handling small orders.

Exporting also incurs increased transportation costs when moving goods from one country to another. If the goods go over water, insurance, packing, and handling are additional costs not generally added to locally produced goods. Such costs add yet another burden because import tariffs in many countries are based on the landed cost, which includes transportation, insurance, and shipping charges. These costs add to the inflation of the final price. The next section details how a reasonable price in the home market may more than double in the foreign market.

Sample Effects of Price Escalation

Exhibit 18.3 illustrates some of the effects the factors discussed previously may have on the end price of a consumer item. Because costs and tariffs vary so widely from country to country, a hypothetical but realistic example is used. It assumes that a constant net price is received by the manufacturer, that all domestic transportation costs are absorbed by the various middleman and reflected in their margins, and that the foreign middlemen have the same margins as the domestic middlemen. In some instances, foreign middleman margins are lower, but it is equally probable that these margins could be greater. In fact, in many instances, middlemen use higher wholesale and retail margins for foreign goods than for similar domestic goods.

Notice that the retail prices in Exhibit 18.3 range widely, illustrating the difficulty of price control by manufacturers in overseas retail markets. No matter how much the manufacturer may wish to market a product in a foreign country for a price equivalent to U.S. $10, there is little opportunity for such control. Even assuming the most optimistic conditions for Foreign Example 1, the producer would need to cut net by more than one-third to absorb freight and tariff costs if the goods are to be priced the same in both foreign and domestic markets. Price escalation is everywhere: A man's dress shirt that sells for $40 in the United States retails for $80 in Caracas. A $20 U.S. electric can opener is priced in Milan at $70; a $35 U.S.-made automatic toaster is priced at $80 in France. The Cadillac Catera, which sells in the United States for $30,000, sells for $46,644 in Switzerland.

Unless some of the costs that create price escalation can be reduced, the marketer is faced with a price that may confine sales to a limited segment of wealthy, price-insensitive customers. In many markets, buyers have less purchasing power than in the United States and can be easily priced out of the market. Further, once price escalation is set in motion it can spiral upward quickly. When the price to middlemen is high and turnover is low, they may insist on higher margins to defray their costs, which, of course, raises the price even higher. Unless price escalation can be reduced, marketers find that the only buyers left are the wealthier ones. If marketers are to compete successfully in the growth of markets around the world, cost containment must be among their highest priorities. If costs can be reduced anywhere along the chain from manufacturer's cost to retailer markups, price escalation will be reduced. A discussion of some of the approaches to reducing price escalation follows.

Japanese wholesale store manager of a meat market in Tokyo arranges packs of beef imported from Australia. Earlier in the day, the government said Japan plans to raise its tariff on refrigerated beef imports to 50 percent from 38.5 percent, following a spike in imports. The price tag reads: Premium beef, sirloin steak from Australia @ 258 yen (U.S.$2.20) per 100 grams. Tariffs are one of the main causes of price escalation for imported products. *(AP/Wide World Photos)*

Exhibit 18.3
Sample Causes and Effects of Price Escalation

	Domestic Example	Foreign Example 1: Assuming the Same Channels with Wholesaler Importing Directly	Foreign Example 2: Importer and Same Margins and Channels	Foreign Example 3: Same as 2 but with 10 Percent Cumulative Turnover Tax	
Manufacturing net	$ 5.00	$ 5.00	$ 5.00	$ 5.00	
Transport, CIF	n.a.	6.10	6.10	6.10	
Tariff (20 percent CIF value)	n.a.	1.22	1.22	1.22	
Importer pays	n.a.	n.a.	7.32	7.32	
Importer margin when sold to wholesaler (25 percent on cost)	n.a.	n.a.	1.83	1.83 +0.73	turnover tax
Wholesaler pays landed cost	5.00	7.32	9.15	9.88	
Wholesaler margin (33⅓ percent on cost)	1.67	2.44	3.05	3.29 +0.99	turnover tax
Retailer pays	6.67	9.76	12.20	14.16	
Retail margin (50 percent on cost)	3.34	4.88	6.10	7.08 +1.42	turnover tax
Retail price	$10.01	$14.64	$18.30	$22.66	

Notes: All figures in U.S. dollars; CIF = cost, insurance, and freight; n.a. = not applicable. The exhibit assumes that all domestic transportation costs are absorbed by the middleman. Transportation, tariffs, and middleman margins vary from country to country, but for purposes of comparison, only a few of the possible variations are shown.

Approaches to Reducing Price Escalation

Three methods used to reduce costs and lower price escalation are lowering cost of goods, lowering tariffs, and lowering distribution costs.

Lowering Cost of Goods If the manufacturer's price can be lowered, the effect is felt throughout the chain. One of the important reasons for manufacturing in a third country is an attempt to reduce manufacturing costs and thus price escalation. The impact can be profound if you consider that the hourly cost of skilled labor in a Mexican maquiladora is less than $3 an hour including benefits, compared with more than $10 in the United States.

In comparing the costs of manufacturing microwave ovens in the United States and in Korea, the General Electric Company found substantial differences. A typical microwave oven cost GE $218 to manufacture compared with $155 for Samsung, a Korean manufacturer. A breakdown of costs revealed that assembly labor cost GE $8 per oven, and Samsung only 63 cents. Perhaps the most disturbing finding for GE was that Korean laborers delivered more for less cost: GE produced four units per person, whereas the Korean company produced nine.

Although Korea remains an important offshore manufacturing location, China is emerging as a global manufacturing powerhouse backed by an inexpensive labor force, rapidly improving production quality, new sources of capital, a more dynamic private sector, and a deliberately undervalued currency. China supplies a growing range of products to the global marketplace. Japan, the land of zero-defect quality control, is increasingly happy with the competence of Chinese workers. Star Manufacturing, a Japanese precision machine tool manufacturing company, moved 30 percent of its production to China because China's cheap labor and cheap resources reduces production cost by 20 percent.

Eliminating costly functional features or even lowering overall product quality is another method of minimizing price escalation. For U.S.-manufactured products, the quality and additional features required for the more developed home market may not be necessary in countries that have not attained the same level of development or consumer demand. In the price war between P&G and Kimberly-Clark in Brazil, the quality of the product was lowered in order to lower the price. Remember that the grandmother in the grocery store chose the poorest-quality and the lowest-priced brand of diaper. Similarly, functional features on washing machines

CROSSING BORDERS 18.3   When Is a Car a Truck and a Daily Planner a Diary? When the U.S. Customs Says So

How an import is classified can mean a big difference in the tariffs paid. But how a product should be classified is not always apparent, at least to the U.S. Customs Service. Here are two cases.

The U.S. Customs Service classified multipurpose vehicles as trucks, that is, vehicles designed to transport cargo or other goods. Trucks pay a 25 percent tariff, whereas passenger vehicles pay only a 2.5 percent tariff. The two-door Nissan Pathfinder was initially classified as a truck rather than as a passenger vehicle, but Nissan challenged the classification. The Justice Department argued that the Pathfinder was built with the same structural design as the Nissan pickup truck despite all the options added later in production, and it should therefore be considered a truck for tariff purposes. The court said that doesn't matter; it's how the vehicle is used that counts. The judge declared that the Pathfinder "virtually shouts to the consumer, 'I am a car, not a truck!'" The ruling means a $225 saving for every $1,000 the consumer spends on a Pathfinder.

The Mead Corporation imports what it considers to be a looseleaf daily planner that contains a section for daily notes, phone numbers, and addresses. Customs classified the planners as "Bound Diaries" on which a 4 percent duty applies. Mead challenged the decision and contended that the product should be classified as a daily planner on which there is no duty. The U.S. Supreme Court ruled in favor of Mead.

Sources: "Nissan Wins U.S. Customs Suit," *Associated Press*, September 9, 1994; "U.S. High Court: No Deference to Customs on Tariffs," *Reuters News Service*, June 18, 2001.

made for the United States, such as automatic bleach and soap dispensers, thermostats to provide four different levels of water temperature, controls to vary water volume, and bells to ring at appropriate times, may be unnecessary for many foreign markets. Eliminating them means lower manufacturing costs and thus a corresponding reduction in price escalation. Lowering manufacturing costs can often have a double benefit: The lower price to the buyer may also mean lower tariffs, since most tariffs are levied on an ad valorem basis.

Lowering Tariffs   When tariffs account for a large part of price escalation, as they often do, companies seek ways to lower the rate. Some products can be reclassified into a different, and lower, customs classification. An American company selling data communications equipment in Australia faced a 25 percent tariff, which affected the price competitiveness of its products. It persuaded the Australian government to change the classification for the type of products the company sells from "computer equipment" (25 percent tariff) to "telecommunication equipment" (3 percent tariff). Like many products, this company's products could be legally classified under either category. One complaint against customs agents in Russia is the arbitrary way in which they often classify products. Russian customs, for instance, insists on classifying Johnson & Johnson's 2 in 1 Shower Gel as a cosmetic with a 20 percent tariff rather than as a soap substitute, which the company considers it, at a 15 percent tariff.

How a product is classified is often a judgment call. The difference between an item being classified as jewelry or art means paying no tariff for art or a 26 percent tariff for jewelry. For example, a U.S. customs inspector could not decide whether to classify a $2.7 million Fabergé egg as art or jewelry. The difference was zero tariff versus $700,000. An experienced freight forwarder/customs broker saved the day by persuading the customs agent that the Fabergé egg was a piece of art. Because the classification of products varies among countries, a thorough investigation of tariff schedules and classification criteria can result in a lower tariff. See Crossing Borders 18.4 for some examples of various tariffs rules in the United States.

Besides having a product reclassified into a lower tariff category, it may be possible to modify a product to qualify for a lower tariff rate within a tariff classification. In the footwear industry, the difference between "foxing" and "foxlike" on athletic shoes makes a substantial difference in the tariff levied. To protect the domestic footwear industry from an onslaught of cheap sneakers from the Far East, the tariff schedules state that any canvas or vinyl shoe with a foxing band (a tape band attached at the sole and overlapping the shoe's upper by more than one-quarter inch) be assessed at a higher duty rate. As a result, manufacturers design shoes so that the sole does not overlap the upper by more than one-quarter inch. If the overlap exceeds one-quarter inch, the shoe is classified as having a foxing band;

CROSSING BORDERS 18.4

What Does It Mean To Be Human?
5.2 Percent, That's What

"What does it mean to be human?" asked Judge Barzilay in her chambers at the U.S. Court of International Trade. At the heart of the problem were some 60 little plastic figures of Marvel Enterprises' X-Men and other comic figures.

Marvel subsidiary Toy Biz Inc. sought to have its heroes from a range of comic characters declared nonhuman. At the time, tariffs were higher on dolls (12 percent) than toys (6.8 percent). According to the U.S. tariff code, human figures are dolls, whereas figures representing animals or "creatures," such as monsters and robots, are deemed toys.

Thus began the great debate over the figures' true being. Barbie is a doll. Pooh Bear's a toy. That much is easy. But what about Wolverine, the muscular X-Man with the metal claws that jut out from his fists? Wolverine has known many forms in his more than 40 years as a Marvel character. But is he human? Or Kraven, a famed hunter, who once vanquished Spiderman, thanks in part to the strength gained from drinking secret jungle elixirs.

Toy Biz argued that the figures "stand as potent witnesses for their status as nonhuman creatures." How could they be humans if they possessed "tentacles, claws, wings or robotic limbs"? The U.S. Customs Service argument was that each figure had a "distinctive individual personality." Some were Russians, Japanese, black, white, women, even handicapped. Wolverine, the government insisted, was simply "a man with prosthetic hands."

To weigh the question, Judge Barzilay sat down with a sheaf of opposing legal briefs and more than 60 action figures, including Wolverine, Storm, Rogue, Kraven, and Bonebreaker. Judge Barzilay described in her ruling how she subjected many of the figures to "comprehensive examinations." At times, that included "the need to remove the clothes of the figure." The X-Men, oddly, gave her the least trouble. They are mutants, she declared, who "use their extraordinary and unnatural powers on the side of good or evil." Thus the X-Men are "something other than human." Tougher for the judge were figures from the Fantastic Four and Spiderman series. After careful examination and thought, the judge found Kraven exhibited "highly exaggerated muscle tone in arms and legs." He wore a "lion's mane-like vest." Both features helped relegate him to the netherworld of robots, monsters, and devils. Case closed.

Toy Biz Inc. was elated but the fans were incensed—no way are X-Men mere creatures. "Marvel's superheroes are supposed to be as human as you or I. They live in New York. They have families and go to work. And now they're no longer human?" The current author of Marvel's "Uncanny X-Men" comic-book series is also incredulous. He worked hard for a year, he says, to emphasize the X-Men's humanity, to show "that they're just another strand in the evolutionary chain." "Don't fret, Marvel fans, a decision that the X-Men figures indeed do have 'nonhuman' characteristics further proves our characters have special, out-of-this world powers."

Although this scenario may seem trivial, it highlights just how arbitrary tariff classification can be. It pays to argue your case if you believe a product can be classified at a lower rate. For every $100,000 of plastic figures Toy Biz imports, the reclassification saves them $5,200. Not a bad day's work considering the hundreds of thousands of dollars worth of figures the company imports annually. Not to mention the undisclosed sum Toy Biz can recoup of years of overpaid tariffs.

Sources: Niel King Jr., "Is Wolverine Human? A Judge Answers No; Fans Howl in Protest," *Wall Street Journal*, January 20, 2003; Larry Williams, "X-Men Not Human? That's Inhumane," *South Florida Sun-Sentinel*, May 6, 2003; Stanford W. Carpenter, "Man or Mutant? A Matter of Import," *Baltimore Sun*, May 26, 2003, p. 13A.

less than one-quarter inch, a foxlike band. A shoe with a foxing band is taxed 48 percent and one with a foxlike band (one-quarter inch or less overlap) is taxed a mere 6 percent.

There are often differential rates between fully assembled, ready-to-use products and those requiring some assembly, further processing, the addition of locally manufactured component parts, or other processing that adds value to the product and can be performed within the foreign country. For example, a ready-to-operate piece of machinery with a 20 percent tariff may be subject to only a 12 percent tariff when imported unassembled. An even lower tariff may apply when the product is assembled in the country and some local content is added.

Repackaging also may help to lower tariffs. Tequila entering the United States in containers of one gallon or less carries a duty of $2.27 per proof gallon; larger containers are assessed at only $1.25. If the cost of rebottling is less than $1.02 per proof gallon, and it probably would be, considerable savings could result. As will be discussed shortly, one of the more important activities in foreign trade zones is the assembly of imported goods, using local and frequently lower-cost labor.

An actor portraying Wolverine, an X-Men fictional character from Marvel Enterprises. A tariff classification issue arose when the company declared the imported toy characters as nonhuman toys and U.S. Customs said that they were human figure dolls—tariffs on dolls at that time were 12 percent versus 6.8 percent for toys. U.S. Customs alleged that the X-Men figures were human figures and thus should be classified as dolls and were not figures featuring animals or creatures, which would mean that they could be classified as toys. Product classifications are critical when tariffs are determined. See Crossing Borders 18.4 for more details on this case. *(20th Century Fox/Marvel Entertainment Group/The Kobal Collection/Dory, Attila)*

Lowering Distribution Costs   Shorter channels can help keep prices under control. Designing a channel that has fewer middlemen may lower distribution costs by reducing or eliminating middleman markup. Besides eliminating markups, fewer middlemen may mean lower overall taxes. Some countries levy a value-added tax on goods as they pass through channels. Goods are taxed each time they change hands. The tax may be cumulative or noncumulative. A cumulative value-added tax is based on total selling price and is assessed every time the goods change hands. Obviously, in countries where value-added tax is cumulative, tax alone provides a special incentive for developing short distribution channels. Where that is achieved, tax is paid only on the difference between the middleman's cost and the selling price. While many manufacturers have had to cut prices in wake of Japan's deflation, Louis Vuitton, a maker of branded boutique goods, was able to increase prices instead. A solid brand name and direct distribution have permitted Vuitton's price strategy. Vuitton's leather monogrammed bags have become a Japanese buyer's "daily necessity" and Vuitton distributes directly and fixes its own prices.

Using Foreign Trade Zones to Lessen Price Escalation   Some countries have established foreign or free trade zones (FTZs) or free ports to facilitate international trade.[16] More than 300 of these facilities operate throughout the world, storing or processing imported goods. As free trade policies in Africa, Latin America, eastern Europe, and other developing regions expand, an equally rapid expansion has taken place in the creation and use of foreign trade zones.

Recall from Chapter 15 that in a free port or FTZ, payment of import duties is postponed until the product leaves the FTZ area and enters the country. An FTZ is, in essence, a tax-free enclave and not considered part of the country as far as import regulations are concerned. When an item leaves an FTZ and is imported officially into the host country of the FTZ, all duties and regulations are imposed.

Utilizing FTZs can to some extent control price escalation resulting from the layers of taxes, duties, surcharges, freight charges, and so forth. Foreign trade zones permit many of these added charges to be avoided, reduced, or deferred so that the final price is more competitive. One of the more important benefits of the FTZ in controlling prices is the exemption from duties on labor and overhead costs incurred in the FTZ in assessing the value of goods.

By shipping unassembled goods to an FTZ in an importing country, a marketer can lower costs in a variety of ways:

- Tariffs may be lower because duties are typically assessed at a lower rate for unassembled versus assembled goods.

- If labor costs are lower in the importing country, substantial savings may be realized in the final product cost.

- Ocean transportation rates are affected by weight and volume; thus unassembled goods may qualify for lower freight rates.

- If local content, such as packaging or component parts, can be used in the final assembly, tariffs may be further reduced.

---

[16]Liu Li, "Free Trade Zone in Pipeline in Xinjiang," *China Daily*, September 20, 2005.

Exhibit 18.4
How Are Foreign Trade Zones Used?

There are more than 100 foreign trade zones (FTZs) in the United States, and FTZs exist in many other countries as well. Companies use them to postpone the payment of tariffs on products while they are in the FTZ. Here are some examples of how FTZs in the United States are used.

- A Japanese firm assembles motorcycles, jet skis, and three-wheel all-terrain vehicles for import as well as for export to Canada, Latin America, and Europe.

- A U.S. manufacturer of window shades and miniblinds imports and stores fabric from Holland in an FTZ, thereby postponing a 17 percent tariff until the fabric leaves the FTZ.

- A manufacturer of hair dryers stores its product in an FTZ, which it uses as its main distribution center for products manufactured in Asia.

- A European-based medical supply company manufactures kidney dialysis machines and sterile tubing using raw materials from Germany and U.S. labor. It then exports 30 percent of its products to Scandinavian countries.

- A Canadian company assembles electronic teaching machines using cabinets from Italy; electronics from Taiwan, Korea, and Japan; and labor from the United States, for export to Colombia and Peru.

In all these examples, tariffs are postponed until the products leave the FTZ and enter the United States. Further, in most situations the tariff is at the lower rate for component parts and raw materials versus the higher rate that would be charged if products were imported directly as finished goods. If the finished products are not imported into the United States from the FTZ but are shipped to another country, no U.S. tariffs apply.

Sources: Lewis E. Leibowitz, "An Overview of Foreign Trade Zones," *Europe*, Winter–Spring 1987, p. 12; "Cheap Imports," *International Business*, March 1993, pp. 98–100; "Free-Trade Zones: Global Overview and Future Prospects," www.stat-usa.gov.

All in all, a foreign or free trade zone is an important method for controlling price escalation. Incidentally, all the advantages offered by an FTZ for an exporter are also advantages for an importer. U.S. importers use over 100 FTZs in the United States to help lower their costs of imported goods. See Exhibit 18.4 for illustrations of how FTZs are used.

Dumping

A logical outgrowth of a market policy in international business is goods priced competitively at widely differing prices in various markets. Marginal (variable) cost pricing, as discussed earlier, is a way prices can be reduced to stay within a competitive price range. The market and economic logic of such pricing policies can hardly be disputed, but the practices often are classified as dumping and are subject to severe penalties and fines. Various economists define *dumping* differently. One approach classifies international shipments as dumped if the products are sold below their cost of production. Another approach characterizes dumping as selling goods in a foreign market below the price of the same goods in the home market.[17]

World Trade Organization (WTO) rules allow for the imposition of a dumping duty when goods are sold at a price lower than the normal export price or less than the cost in the country of origin increased by a reasonable amount for the cost of sales and profits, when this is likely to be prejudicial to the economic activity of the importing country. A *countervailing duty* or *minimum access volume (MAV),* which restricts the amount a country will import, may be imposed on foreign goods benefiting from subsidies whether in production, export, or transportation.

For countervailing duties to be invoked, it must be shown that prices are lower in the importing country than in the exporting country and that producers in the importing country are being directly harmed by the dumping. A report by the US. Department of Agriculture indicated that levels of dumping by the United States hover around 40 percent for wheat and between 25 and 30 percent for corn, and levels for soybeans have risen steadily over the past four years to nearly 30 percent. These percentages, for example, mean that wheat is selling up to 40 percent below the cost of production. For cotton, the level of dumping for 2001 rose to a remarkable 57 percent, and for rice it has stabilized at around 20 percent. The study indicated that these commodities are being dumped onto international markets by the United States in violation of WTO rules. The report found that after many years of accepting

---

[17]"U.S. Places Duties on TVs from China," *Bloomberg News*, May 15, 2005.

agricultural dumping, a few countries have begun to respond by investigating whether some U.S. agricultural exports are dumped. Brazil is considering a case against U.S. cotton before the WTO. In 2001, Canada briefly imposed both countervailing and antidumping duties on U.S. corn imports; the United States did the same for Chinese apple juice concentrate.[18]

Dumping is rarely an issue when world markets are strong. In the 1980s and 1990s dumping became a major issue for a large number of industries when excess production capacity relative to home-country demand caused many companies to price their goods on a marginal-cost basis. In a classic case of dumping, prices are maintained in the home-country market and reduced in foreign markets.

Today, tighter government enforcement of dumping legislation is causing international marketers to seek new routes around such legislation. Assembly in the importing country is a way companies attempt to lower prices and avoid dumping charges. However, these *screw-driver plants,* as they are often called, are subject to dumping charges if the price differentials reflect more than the cost savings that result from assembly in the importing country. Another subterfuge is to alter the product so that the technical description will fit a lower duty category. To circumvent a 16.9 percent countervailing duty imposed on Chinese gas-filled, nonrefillable pocket flint lighters, the manufacturer attached a useless valve to the lighters so that they fell under the "nondisposable" category, thus avoiding the duty. Countries do see through many such subterfuges and impose taxes. For example, the European Union imposed a $27 to $58 dumping duty per unit on a Japanese firm that assembled and sold electronic typewriters in the European Union. The firm was charged with valuing imported parts for assembly below cost.

The U.S. market is currently more sensitive to dumping than in the recent past. In fact, the Uruguay Round of the GATT included a section on antidumping that grew out of U.S. insistence on stricter controls on dumping of foreign goods in the United States at prices below those charged at home. Changes in U.S. law have enhanced the authority of the Commerce Department to prevent circumvention of antidumping duties and countervailing duties that have been imposed on a country for dumping. The United States and the European Union have been the most ardent users of antidumping duties. A question asked by many: Are dumping charges just a cover for protectionism? Previously, when an order was issued to apply antidumping and countervailing duties on products, companies charged with the violation would get around the order by slightly altering the product or by doing minor assembly in the United States or a third country. This created the illusion of a different product not subject to the antidumping order. The new authority of the Department of Commerce closes many such loopholes.

Leasing in International Markets

An important selling technique to alleviate high prices and capital shortages for capital equipment is the leasing system. The concept of equipment leasing has become increasingly important as a means of selling capital equipment in overseas markets. In fact, an estimated $50 billion worth (original cost) of U.S.-made and foreign-made equipment is on lease in western Europe.

The system of leasing used by industrial exporters is similar to the typical lease contracts used in the United States. Terms of the leases usually run one to five years, with payments made monthly or annually; included in the rental fee are servicing, repairs, and spare parts. Just as contracts for domestic and overseas leasing arrangements are similar, so are the basic motivations and the shortcomings. For example:

- Leasing opens the door to a large segment of nominally financed foreign firms that can be sold on a lease option but might be unable to buy for cash.
- Leasing can ease the problems of selling new, experimental equipment, because less risk is involved for the users.
- Leasing helps guarantee better maintenance and service on overseas equipment.
- Equipment leased and in use helps to sell other companies in that country.
- Lease revenue tends to be more stable over a period of time than direct sales would be.

---

[18]Shannon Dininny, "Commerce Department Supports Continued Duties on Chinese Apple Juice Concentrate," *Associated Press*, September 9, 2005.

The disadvantages or shortcomings take on an international flavor. Besides the inherent disadvantages of leasing, some problems are compounded by international relationships. In a country beset with inflation, lease contracts that include maintenance and supply parts (as most do) can lead to heavy losses toward the end of the contract period. Further, countries where leasing is most attractive are those where spiraling inflation is most likely to occur. The added problems of currency devaluation, expropriation, or other political risks are operative longer than if the sale of the same equipment is made outright. In light of these perils, leasing incurs greater risk than does outright sale; however, there is a definite trend toward increased use of this method of selling internationally.

Countertrade as a Pricing Tool

Countertrade is a pricing tool that every international marketer must be ready to employ, and the willingness to accept a countertrade will often give the company a competitive advantage. The challenges of countertrade must be viewed from the same perspective as all other variations in international trade. Marketers must be aware of which markets will likely require countertrades just as they must be aware of social customs and legal requirements. Assessing this factor along with all other market factors will enhance a marketer's competitive position.

One of the earliest barter arrangements occurred between Russia and PepsiCo before the ruble was convertible and before most companies were trading with Russia. PepsiCo wanted to beat Coca-Cola into the Russian market. The only way possible was for PepsiCo to be willing to accept vodka (sold under the brand name Stolichnaya) from Russia and bottled wines (sold under the brand name of Premiat) from Romania to finance Pepsi-Cola bottling plants in those countries. From all indications, this has been a very profitable arrangement for Russia, Romania, and PepsiCo. PepsiCo continues to use countertrade to expand its bottling plants. In a recent agreement between PepsiCo and Ukraine, Pepsi agreed to market $1 billion worth of Ukrainian-made commercial ships over an eight-year period. Some of the proceeds from the ship sales will be reinvested in the shipbuilding venture, and some will be used to buy soft-drink equipment and build five Pepsi bottling plants in Ukraine. PepsiCo dominates the cola market in Russia and all the former Soviet republics in part because of its exclusive countertrade agreement with Russia, which locked Coca-Cola out of the Russian cola market for more than 12 years. After the Soviet Union was dismembered, the Russian economy crashed and most of the Russian payment system broke down into barter operations. Truckloads of aspirin were swapped by one company, then traded for poultry, which in turn was bartered for lumber, in turn to be exchanged for X-ray equipment from Kazakhstan—all to settle debts. Many of these transactions involved regional electricity companies that were owed money by virtually everyone.

Although cash may be the preferred method of payment, countertrades are an important part of trade with eastern Europe, the newly independent states, China, and, to a varying degree, some Latin American and African nations. Barter or countertrades still constitute between 20 and 40 percent of all transaction in the economies of the former Soviet bloc. Corporate debts to suppliers, payment and services, even taxes—all have a noncash component or are entirely bartered. Many of these countries constantly face a shortage of hard currencies with which to trade and thus resort to countertrades when possible. A recent purchase of 48 F-16 Falcons from Lockheed Martin was pegged at $3.5 billion. The financial package included soft loans and a massive offset program—purchases from Polish manufacturers that more than erased the costs of the deal in foreign exchange. With an economy short of hard currency, Russia is offering a wide range of products in barter for commodities it needs. For example, Russian expertise in space technology is offered for Malaysian palm oil and rubber, and military equipment is exchanged for crude palm oil or rice from Indonesia.[19] Exhibit 18.5 illustrates the many reasons countries demand countertrades. Today, an international company must include in its market-pricing tool kit some understanding of countertrading.

---

[19]Zakki P. Hakim, "Ministry Eyes Rice-for-Planes Trade Deal," *Jakarta Post*, September 20, 2005, p. 13.

Exhibit 18.5
Why Purchasers Impose Countertrade

To preserve hard currency. Countries with nonconvertible currencies look to countertrade as a way of guaranteeing that hard currency expenditures (for foreign imports) are offset by hard currency (generated by the foreign party's obligation to purchase domestic goods).

To improve balance of trade. Nations whose exports have not kept pace with imports increasingly rely on countertrade as a means to balance bilateral trade ledgers.

To gain access to new markets. As a nonmarket or developing country increases its production of exportable goods, it often lacks a sophisticated marketing channel to sell the goods to the West for hard currency. By imposing countertrade demands, foreign trade organizations utilize the marketing organizations and expertise of Western companies to market their goods for them.

To upgrade manufacturing capabilities. By entering compensation arrangements under which foreign (usually Western) firms provide plant and equipment and buy back resultant products, the trade organizations of less-developed countries can enlist Western technical cooperation in upgrading industrial facilities.

To maintain prices of export goods. Countertrade can be used as a means to dispose of goods at prices that the market would not bear under cash-for-goods terms. Although the Western seller absorbs the added cost by inflating the price of the original sale, the nominal price of the counterpurchased goods is maintained, and the seller need not concede what the value of the goods would be in the world supply-and-demand market. Conversely, if the world price for a commodity is artificially high, such as the price of crude oil, a country can barter its oil for Western goods (e.g., weapons) so that the real "price" the Western partner pays is below the world price.

To force reinvestment of proceeds from weapons deals. Many Arab countries require that a portion of proceeds from weapons purchases be reinvested in facilities designated by the buyer—everything from pipelines to hotels and sugar mills.

Source: Leo G. B. Welt, "Countertrade? Better Than No Trade," *Export Today*, Spring 1985, p. 54; Anne Marie Squeo and Daniel Pearl, "The Big Sell: How a Gulf Sheikdom Landed Its Sweet Deal with Lockheed Martin," *Wall Street Journal*, April 20, 2000.

Types of Countertrade

Countertrade includes four distinct transactions: barter, compensation deals, counterpurchase, and buyback. *Barter* is the direct exchange of goods between two parties in a transaction. For example, the Malaysian government bought 20 diesel-electric locomotives from General Electric. Officials of the government said that GE will be paid with palm oil to be supplied by a plantation company. The company will supply about 200,000 metric tons of palm oil over a period of 30 months. This was GE's first barter deal for palm oil and palm products, although its division GE Trading has several other countertrade agreements worldwide. No money changed hands, and no third parties were involved. Obviously, in a barter transaction, the seller must be able to dispose of the goods at a net price equal to the expected selling price in a regular, for-cash transaction. Further, during the negotiation stage of a barter deal, the seller must know the market and the price for the items offered in trade. In the General Electrical example, palm oil has an established price and a global market for palm oil and palm products. But not all bartered goods have an organized market and products can range from hams to iron pellets, mineral water, furniture, or olive oil—all somewhat more difficult to price and to find customers.

Barter may also be used to reduce a country's foreign debt. To save foreign exchange reserves, the Philippine government offered some creditors canned tuna to repay part of a state $4-billion debt. If tuna is not enough, coconut oil and a seaweed extract, carrageenan, used as an additive in foods, toothpaste, cosmetics and ice cream, were offered. The seaweed and tuna exporters will be paid with pesos so no currency leaves the country.

Compensation deals involve payment in goods and in cash. A seller delivers lathes to a buyer in Venezuela and receives 70 percent of the payment in convertible currency and 30 percent in tanned hides and wool. In an actual deal, General Motors Corporation sold $12 million worth of locomotives and diesel engines to Yugoslavia and took cash and $4 million in Yugoslavian cutting tools as payment. McDonnell Douglas agreed to a compensation deal with Thailand for eight top-of-the-range F/A-18 strike aircraft. Thailand agreed to pay $578 million of the total cost in cash, and McDonnell Douglas agreed to accept $93 million in a mixed bag of goods including Thai rubber, ceramics, furniture, frozen chicken, and canned fruit. In a move to reduce its current account deficit, the Thai government requires that 20 to 50 percent of the value of large contracts be paid for in raw and processed agricultural goods.

An advantage of a compensation deal over barter is the immediate cash settlement of a portion of the bill; the remainder of the cash is generated after successful sale of the goods received. If the company has a use for the goods received, the process is relatively simple and uncomplicated. On the other hand, if the seller has to rely on a third party to find a buyer, the cost involved must be anticipated in the original compensation negotiation if the net proceeds to the seller are to equal the market price.

Counterpurchase, or *offset trade,* is probably the most frequently used type of countertrade. For this trade, the seller agrees to sell a product at a set price to a buyer and receives payment in cash. However, two contracts are negotiated. The first contract is contingent on a second contract that is an agreement by the original seller to buy goods from the buyer for the total monetary amount involved in the first contract or for a set percentage of that amount. This arrangement provides the seller with more flexibility than the compensation deal because there is generally a time period—6 to 12 months or longer—for completion of the second contract. During the time that markets are sought for the goods in the second contract, the seller has received full payment for the original sale. Further, the goods to be purchased in the second contract are generally of greater variety than those offered in a compensation deal. Even greater flexibility is offered when the second contract is nonspecific; that is, the books on sales and purchases need to be cleared only at certain intervals. The seller is obligated to generate enough purchases to keep the books balanced or clear between purchases and sales.

Offset trades are becoming more prevalent among economically weak countries. Several variations of a counterpurchase or offset have developed to make it more economical for the selling company. For example, the Lockheed Martin Corporation entered into an offset trade with the United Arab Emirates (UAE) in a $6.4 billion deal for 80 F-16 fighter planes called Desert Falcons. Lockheed agreed to make a $160 million cash investment in a gas pipeline running from Qatar to UAE industrial projects and then on to Pakistan. The UAE requires that some of the proceeds from weapon sales be reinvested in the UAE. Such offsets are a common feature of arms deals, in which sellers build facilities ranging from hotels to sugar mills at the request of the buyer.

Product buyback agreement is the fourth type of countertrade transaction. This type of agreement is made when the sale involves goods or services that produce other goods and services, that is, production plant, production equipment, or technology. The buyback agreement usually involves one of two situations: The seller agrees to accept as partial payment a certain portion of the output, or the seller receives full price initially but agrees to buy back a certain portion of the output. One U.S. farm equipment manufacturer sold a tractor plant to Poland and was paid part in hard currency and the balance in Polish-built tractors. In another situation, General Motors built an auto manufacturing plant in Brazil and was paid under normal terms but agreed to the purchase of resulting output when the new facilities came online. Levi Strauss took Hungarian blue jeans, which it sells abroad, in exchange for setting up a jeans factory near Budapest.

An interesting buyback arrangement has been agreed on between the Rice Growers Association of California (RGAC) and the Philippine government. The RGAC will invest in Philippine farmlands and bring new technologies to enhance local rice production. In return, the RGAC will import rice and other food products in payment. A major drawback to product buyback agreements comes when the seller finds that the products bought back are in competition with its own similarly produced goods. On the other hand, some have found that a product buyback agreement provides them with a supplemental source in areas of the world where there is demand but where they have no available supply.

Problems of Countertrading

The crucial problem confronting a seller in a countertrade negotiation is determining the value of and potential demand for the goods offered. Frequently there is inadequate time to conduct a market analysis; in fact, it is not unusual to have sales negotiations almost completed before countertrade is introduced as a requirement in the transaction.

Although such problems are difficult to deal with, they can be minimized with proper preparation. In most cases where losses have occurred in countertrades, the seller has been unprepared to negotiate in anything other than cash. Some preliminary research should be done in anticipation of being confronted with a countertrade proposal. Countries with a history of countertrading are identified easily, and the products most likely to be offered in a countertrade often can be ascertained. For a company trading with developing countries, these facts and some background on handling countertrades should be a part of every pricing tool kit. Once goods are acquired, they can be passed along to institutions that assist companies in selling bartered goods.

Barter houses specialize in trading goods acquired through barter arrangements and are the primary outside source of aid for companies beset by the uncertainty of a countertrade. Although barter houses, most of which are found in Europe, can find a market for bartered goods, this requires time, which puts a financial strain on a company because capital is tied up longer than in normal transactions.

In the United States, there are companies that assist with bartered goods and their financing. Citibank has created a countertrade department to allow the bank to act as a consultant as well as to provide financing for countertrades. It is estimated that there are now about 500 barter exchange houses in the United States, many of which are accessible on the Internet. Some companies with a high volume of barter have their own in-house trading groups to manage countertrades. The 3M Company (Minnesota Mining and Manufacturing), for example, has a wholly owned division, 3M Global Trading (www.3m.com/globaltrading), which offers its services to smaller companies.

The Internet and Countertrading

The Internet may become the most important venue for countertrade activities. Finding markets for bartered merchandise and determining market price are two of the major problems with countertrades. Several barter houses have Internet auction sites, and a number of Internet exchanges are expanding to include global barter.

Some speculate that the Internet may become the vehicle for an immense online electronic barter economy, to complement and expand the offline barter exchanges that take place now. In short, some type of electronic trade dollar would replace national currencies in international trade transactions. This would make international business considerably easier for many countries because it would lessen the need to acquire sufficient U.S. currency or other hard currency to complete a sale or purchase.

TradeBanc, a market-making service, has introduced a computerized technology that will enable members of trade exchanges to trade directly, online, with members of other trade exchanges anywhere in the world, as long as their barter company is a TradeBanc affiliate (www.tradebanc.com). The medium of exchange could be the Universal Currency proposed by the International Reciprocal Trade Association (IRTA; www.irta.com), an association of trade exchanges with members including Russia, Iceland, Germany, Chile, Turkey, Australia, and the United States. The IRTA has proposed to establish and operate a Universal Currency Clearinghouse, which would enable trade exchange members to easily trade with one another by using this special currency. When the system is in full swing all goods and services from all the participating affiliates would be housed in a single database. The transactions would be cleared by the local exchanges, and settlement would be made using IRTA's Universal Currency, which could be used to purchase anything from airline tickets to potatoes.[20]

Proactive Countertrade Strategy

Currently most companies have a reactive strategy; that is, they use countertrade when they believe it is the only way to make a sale. Even when these companies include countertrade as a permanent feature of their operations, they use it to react to a sales demand rather than using countertrade as an aggressive marketing tool for expansion. Some authorities suggest, however, that companies should have a defined countertrade strategy as part of their marketing strategy rather than be caught unprepared when confronted with a countertrade proposition

A proactive countertrade strategy is the most effective strategy for global companies that market to exchange-poor countries. Economic development plans in eastern European countries, the Commonwealth of Independent States (CIS), and much of Latin America will put unusual stress on their ability to generate sufficient capital to finance their growth. Further, as countries encounter financial crises such as in Latin America in 1996 and Asia

---

[20]You may want to visit the American Countertrade Association, www.countertrade.org, for a detailed discussion of the services offered a countertrader.

in 1998, countertrade becomes especially important as a means of exchange. To be competitive, companies must be willing to include some countertraded goods in their market planning. Companies with a proactive strategy make a commitment to use countertrade aggressively as a marketing and pricing tool. They see countertrades as an opportunity to expand markets rather than as an inconvenient reaction to market demands.

Successful countertrade transactions require that the marketer accurately establish the market value of the goods being offered and dispose of the bartered goods once they are received. Most unsuccessful countertrades result from not properly resolving one or both of these factors.

In short, unsuccessful countertrades are generally the result of inadequate planning and preparation. One experienced countertrader suggests answering the following questions before entering into a countertrade agreement: (1) Is there a ready market for the goods bartered? (2) Is the quality of the goods offered consistent and acceptable? (3) Is an expert needed to handle the negotiations? (4) Is the contract price sufficient to cover the cost of barter and net the desired revenue?

Capital-poor countries striving to industrialize will account for much of the future demand for goods. Indonesia, for instance, requires any foreign purchase exceeding $500 million to have a portion in a countertrade. Companies not prepared to seek this business with a proactive countertrade strategy will miss important market opportunities.

Transfer Pricing Strategy

As companies increase the number of worldwide subsidiaries, joint ventures, company-owned distributing systems, and other marketing arrangements, the price charged to different affiliates becomes a preeminent question. Prices of goods transferred from a company's operations or sales units in one country to its units elsewhere, known as *intracompany pricing* or *transfer pricing,* may be adjusted to enhance the ultimate profit of the company as a whole. The benefits are as follows:

- Lowering duty costs by shipping goods into high-tariff countries at minimal transfer prices so that duty base and duty are low.

- Reducing income taxes in high-tax countries by overpricing goods transferred to units in such countries; profits are eliminated and shifted to low-tax countries. Such profit shifting may also be used for "dressing up" financial statements by increasing reported profits in countries where borrowing and other financing are undertaken.

- Facilitating dividend repatriation when dividend repatriation is curtailed by government policy. Invisible income may be taken out in the form of high prices for products or components shipped to units in that country.

Government authorities have not overlooked the tax and financial manipulation possibilities of transfer pricing.[21] Transfer pricing can be used to hide subsidiary profits and to escape foreign-market taxes. Intracompany pricing is managed in such a way that profit is taken in the country with the lowest tax rate. For example, a foreign manufacturer makes a VCR for $50 and sells it to its U.S. subsidiary for $150. The U.S. subsidiary sells it to a retailer for $200, but spends $50 on advertising and shipping so that it shows no profit and pays no U.S. taxes. Meanwhile, the parent company makes a $100 gross margin on each unit and pays at a lower tax rate in the home country. If the tax rate were lower in the country where the subsidiary resides, the profit would be taken in the foreign country and no profit taken in the home country.[22]

When customs and tax regimes are high, companies have a strong incentive to trim fiscal liabilities by adjusting the transaction value of goods and services between subsidiaries.

---

[21]Susan C. Borkowski, "Transfer Pricing Documentation and Penalties: How Much Is Enough?" *International Tax Journal,* Spring 2003, p. 31; Lorraine Eden, Luis F. Juarez, and Dan Li, "Talk Softly but Carry a Big Stick: Transfer Pricing Penalties and the Market Valuation of Japanese Multinationals in the United States," *Journal of International Business Studies,* 2005, prepublished online.

[22]For a detailed report on transfer pricing methods and their importance to an MNC with divisions located in different countries, see Thomas H. Stevenson and David W. E. Cabell, "Integrating Transfer Pricing Policy and Activity-Based Costing," *Journal of International Marketing* 10, no. 4 (2002), p. 77.

Pricing low cuts exposure to import duties; declaring a higher value raises deductible costs and thereby lightens the corporate tax burden. The key is to strike the right balance that maximizes savings overall.

The overall objectives of the intracompany pricing system include maximizing profits for the corporation as a whole; facilitating parent-company control; and offering management at all levels, both in the product divisions and in the international divisions, an adequate basis for maintaining, developing, and receiving credit for their own profitability. Transfer prices that are too low are unsatisfactory to the product divisions because their overall results look poor; prices that are too high make the international operations look bad and limit the effectiveness of foreign managers.

An intracompany pricing system should employ sound accounting techniques and be defensible to the tax authorities of the countries involved. All of these factors argue against a single uniform price or even a uniform pricing system for all international operations. Four arrangements for pricing goods for intracompany transfer are as follows:

1. Sales at the local manufacturing cost plus a standard markup.
2. Sales at the cost of the most efficient producer in the company plus a standard markup.
3. Sales at negotiated prices.
4. Arm's-length sales using the same prices as quoted to independent customers.

Of the four, the arm's-length transfer is most acceptable to tax authorities and most likely to be acceptable to foreign divisions, but the appropriate basis for intracompany transfers depends on the nature of the subsidiaries and market conditions.

Although the practices described in this section are not necessarily improper, they are being scrutinized more closely by both home and host countries concerned about the loss of potential tax revenues from foreign firms doing business in their countries as well as domestic firms underreporting foreign earnings. The U.S. government is paying particular attention to transfer pricing in tax audits, as are other countries. This has led to what some have described as a "tax war" between the United States and Japan over transfer pricing by its MNCs, with each country bringing charges against foreign MNCs for underpayment of taxes because of transfer pricing practices. For example, the United States claimed that Nissan U.S. had inflated the prices it paid to its parent for finished cars it was importing to lower U.S. taxes. As a result, the United States levied a hefty multimillion-dollar tax penalty against Nissan. Japan retaliated by hitting Coca-Cola with a $145 million tax deficiency charge.

Governments are seeking tax revenues from their domestic MNCs as well. Prior to PepsiCo's decision to spin off its restaurant division into a separate company, the IRS charged PepsiCo $800 million after an audit of its foreign operations of Taco Bell, Pizza Hut, and Kentucky Fried Chicken indicated an underreporting of profits of their foreign operations. Penalties can be as high as 40 percent of the amount underreported. The only certain way to avoid such penalties is to enter an *advanced pricing agreement (APA)* with the IRS. An APA is an agreement between the IRS and a taxpayer on transfer pricing methods that will be applied to some or all of a taxpayer's transactions with affiliates. Such agreements generally apply for up to five years and offer better protection against penalties than other methods. Otherwise, once the IRS charges underreporting, the burden of proof that a transfer price was fair rests with the company.

Price Quotations

In quoting the price of goods for international sale, a contract may include specific elements affecting the price, such as credit, sales terms, and transportation. Parties to the transaction must be certain that the quotation settled on appropriately locates responsibility for the goods during transportation and spells out who pays transportation charges and from what point. Price quotations must also specify the currency to be used, credit terms, and the type of documentation required. Finally, the price quotation and contract should define quantity and quality. A quantity definition might be necessary because different countries use different units of measurement. In specifying a ton, for example, the contract should identify it as a metric or an English ton, and as a long or short ton. Quality specifications can also be misunderstood if not completely spelled out. Furthermore, there should be complete agreement on quality standards to be used in evaluating the product. For example, "customary merchantable quality" may be clearly understood among U.S. customers but have a completely different interpretation in another country. The international trader must review all terms of the contract; failure to do so may have the effect of modifying prices even though such a change was not intended.

Administered Pricing

Administered pricing is an attempt to establish prices for an entire market. Such prices may be arranged through the cooperation of competitors, through national, state, or local governments, or by international agreement. The legality of administered pricing arrangements of various kinds differs from country to country and from time to time. A country may condone price fixing for foreign markets but condemn it for the domestic market, for instance.

In general, the end goal of all administered pricing activities is to reduce the impact of price competition or eliminate it. Price fixing by business is not viewed as an acceptable practice (at least in the domestic market), but when governments enter the field of price administration, they presume to do it for the general welfare to lessen the effects of "destructive" competition.

The point at which competition becomes destructive depends largely on the country in question. To the Japanese, excessive competition is any competition in the home market that disturbs the existing balance of trade or gives rise to market disruptions. Few countries apply more rigorous standards in judging competition as excessive than Japan, but no country favors or permits totally free competition. Economists, the traditional champions of pure competition, acknowledge that perfect competition is unlikely and agree that some form of workable competition must be developed.

The pervasiveness of price-fixing attempts in business is reflected by the diversity of the language of administered prices; pricing arrangements are known as agreements, arrangements, combines, conspiracies, cartels, communities of profit, profit pools, licensing, trade associations, price leadership, customary pricing, or informal interfirm agreements.[23] The arrangements themselves vary from the completely informal, with no spoken or acknowledged agreement, to highly formalized and structured arrangements. Any type of price-fixing arrangement can be adapted to international business, but of all the forms mentioned, cartels are the most directly associated with international marketing.

Cartels

A *cartel* exists when various companies producing similar products or services work together to control markets for the types of goods and services they produce. The cartel association may use formal agreements to set prices, establish levels of production and sales for the participating companies, allocate market territories, and even redistribute profits. In some instances, the cartel organization itself takes over the entire selling function, sells the goods of all the producers, and distributes the profits.

The economic role of cartels is highly debatable, but their proponents argue that they eliminate cutthroat competition and rationalize business, permitting greater technical progress and lower prices to consumers. However, most experts doubt that the consumer benefits very often from cartels.

The Organization of Petroleum Exporting Countries (OPEC) is probably the best-known international cartel. Its power in controlling the price of oil resulted from the percentage of oil production it controlled. In the early 1970s, when OPEC members provided the industrial world with 67 percent of its oil, OPEC was able to quadruple the price of oil. The sudden rise in price from $3 a barrel to $11 or more a barrel was a primary factor in throwing the world into a major recession. In 2000, OPEC members lowered production, and the oil price rose from $10 to over $30, creating a dramatic increase in U.S. gasoline prices.[24] Non-OPEC oil-exporting countries benefit from the price increases while net importers of foreign oil face economic repercussions.

---

[23]Dana Nunn and Miklos Sarvary, "Pricing Practices and Firms' Market Power in International Cellular Markets, an Empirical Study," *International Journal of Research in Marketing* 21, no. 4 (2004), pp. 377–395.

[24]www.eia.doe.gov/emeu/cabs/chron.html, 2005.

Oil prices quadrupled in the mid-1970s because of OPEC's control of supplies. The $60/barrel oil you see in this picture has been caused by burgeoning demand in China and around the world circa 2005. Pertamina is the Indonesian national oil company. *(Dadang Tri/Reuters/Landov)*

One important aspect of cartels is their inability to maintain control for indefinite periods. Greed by cartel members and other problems generally weaken the control of the cartel. OPEC members tend to maintain a solid front until one decides to increase supply, and then others rapidly follow suit. In the short run, however, OPEC can affect global prices. Indeed, at this writing world oil prices are above $60 a barrel, but most analysts attribute this more to burgeoning demand than OPEC's ability to control supply.[25]

A lesser-known cartel, but one that has a direct impact on international trade, is the shipping cartel that exists among the world's shipping companies. Every two weeks about 20 shipping-line managers gather for their usual meeting to set rates on tens of billions of dollars of cargo. They do not refer to themselves as a cartel but rather operate under such innocuous names as "The Trans-Atlantic Conference Agreement," (www.tacaconf.com). Regardless of the name, they set the rates on about 70 percent of the cargo shipped between the United States and northern Europe. Shipping between the United States and Latin American ports and between the United States and Asian ports also is affected by shipping cartels. Not all shipping lines are members of cartels, but a large number are; thus they have a definite impact on shipping. Although legal, shipping cartels are coming under scrutiny by the U.S. Congress, and new regulations may soon be passed.

Another cartel is the diamond cartel controlled by De Beers. For more than a century, De Beers has smoothly manipulated the diamond market by keeping a tight control over world supply. The company mines about half the world's diamonds and takes in another 25 percent through contracts with other mining companies. In an attempt to control the other 25 percent, De Beers runs an "outside buying office" where it spends millions buying

---

[25]Evelyn Iritani, "Asian Economies Starting to Feel Effect of Oil Prices," *Los Angeles Times*, August 29, 2005, pp. C1, C5.

The De Beers company is one of the world's largest cartels and, for all practical purposes, it controls most of the world's diamonds and thus is able to maintain artificially high prices for diamonds. One of the ways in which it maintains control is illustrated by a recent agreement with Russia's diamond monopoly where De Beers will buy at least $550 million in rough gem diamonds from Russia, or about half of the country's annual output. By controlling supply from Russia, the second largest producer of diamonds, the South African cartel can keep prices high. *(© Susan Van Etten/Photo Edit)*

up diamonds to protect prices. The company controls most of the world's trade in rough gems and uses its market power to keep prices high.

The legality of cartels at present is not clearly defined. Domestic cartelization is illegal in the United States, and the European Union also has provisions for controlling cartels. The United States does permit firms to take cartel-like actions in foreign markets, although it does not allow foreign-market cartels if the results have an adverse impact on the U.S. economy. Archer Daniels Midland Company, the U.S. agribusiness giant, was fined $205 million for its role in fixing prices for two food additives, lysine and citric acid. German, Japanese, Swiss, and Korean firms were also involved in the cartel. The group agreed on prices to charge and then allocated the share of the world market each company would get down to the tenth of a decimal point. At the end of the year, any company that sold more than its allotted share was required to purchase in the following year the excess from a coconspirator that had not reached its volume allocation target.

Although the EU member countries have had a long history of tolerating price fixing, the European Union is beginning to crack down on cartels in the shipping, automobile, and cement industries, among others. The unified market and the single currency have prompted the move. As countries open to free trade, powerful cartels that artificially raise prices and limit consumer choice are coming under closer scrutiny. However, the EU trustbusters are fighting tradition—since the trade guilds of the Middle Ages, cozy cooperation has been the norm. In each European country, companies banded together to control prices within the country and to keep competition out.

Government-Influenced Pricing

Companies doing business in foreign countries encounter a number of different types of government price setting. To control prices, governments may establish margins, set prices and floors or ceilings, restrict price changes, compete in the market, grant subsidies, and act as a purchasing monopsony, or selling monopoly. The government may also influence prices by permitting, or even encouraging, businesses to collude in setting manipulative prices.

The Japanese government traditionally has encouraged a variety of government-influenced price-setting schemes, However, in a spirit of deregulation that is gradually moving through Japan, Japan's Ministry of Health and Welfare will soon abolish regulation of business hours and price setting for such businesses as barbershops, beauty parlors, and laundries. Under the current practice, 17 sanitation-related businesses can establish such price-setting schemes, which are exempt from the Japanese Anti-Trust Law.

Governments of producing and consuming countries seem to play an ever-increasing role in the establishment of international prices for certain basic commodities. There is, for example, an international coffee agreement, an international cocoa agreement, and an international sugar agreement. And the world price of wheat has long been at least partially determined by negotiations between national governments.

Despite the pressures of business, government, and international price agreements, most marketers still have wide latitude in their pricing decisions for most products and markets.

Summary

Pricing is one of the most complicated decision areas encountered by international marketers. Rather than deal with one set of market conditions, one group of competitors, one set of cost factors, and one set of government regulations, international marketers must take all these factors into account, not only for each country in which they are operating, but often for each market within a country. Market prices at the consumer level are much more difficult to control in international than in domestic marketing, but the international marketer must still approach the pricing task on a basis of established objectives and policy, leaving enough flexibility for tactical price movements. Controlling costs that lead to price escalation when exporting products from one country to another is one of the most challenging pricing tasks facing the exporter. Some of the flexibility in pricing is reduced by the growth of the Internet, which has a tendency to equalize price differentials between country markets.

The continuing growth of Third World markets coupled with their lack of investment capital has increased the importance of countertrades for most marketers, making countertrading an important tool to include in pricing policy. The Internet is evolving to include countertrades, which will help eliminate some of the problems associated with this practice.

Pricing in the international marketplace requires a combination of intimate knowledge of market costs and regulations, an awareness of possible countertrade deals, infinite patience for detail, and a shrewd sense of market strategy.

Questions

1. Define the following terms:

   dumping
   parallel imports
   exclusive distribution
   buyback agreement
   administered pricing
   variable-cost pricing
   full-cost pricing
   skimming
   price escalation
   barter

   countervailing duty
   compensation deal
   subsidy
   cartel
   counterpurchase
   transfer pricing
   advanced pricing agreement
   countertrade

2. Discuss the causes of and solutions for parallel imports and their effect on price.

3. Why is it so difficult to control consumer prices when selling overseas?

4. Explain the concept of price escalation and tell why it can mislead an international marketer.

5. What are the causes of price escalation? Do they differ for exports and goods produced and sold in a foreign country?

6. Why is it seldom feasible for a company to absorb the high cost of international transportation and reduce the net price received?

7. Price escalation is a major pricing problem for the international marketer. How can this problem be counteracted? Discuss.

8. Changing currency values have an impact on export strategies. Discuss.

9. "Regardless of the strategic factors involved and the company's orientation to market pricing, every price must be set with cost considerations in mind." Discuss.

10. "Price fixing by business is not generally viewed as an acceptable practice (at least in the domestic market), but when governments enter the field of price administration, they presume to do it for the general welfare to lessen the effects of 'destructive' competition." Discuss.

11. Do value-added taxes discriminate against imported goods?

12. Explain specific tariffs, ad valorem tariffs, and compound tariffs.

13. Suggest an approach a marketer may follow in adjusting prices to accommodate exchange rate fluctuations.

14. Explain the effects of indirect competition and how they may be overcome.

15. Why has dumping become such an issue in recent years?

16. Cartels seem to rise, phoenixlike, after they have been destroyed. Why are they so appealing to business?

17. Discuss the different pricing problems that result from inflation versus deflation in a country.

18. Discuss the various ways in which governments set prices. Why do they engage in such activities?

19. Discuss the alternative objectives possible in setting prices for intracompany sales.

20. Why do governments so carefully scrutinize intracompany pricing arrangements?

21. Why are costs so difficult to assess in marketing internationally?

22. Discuss why countertrading is on the increase.

23. Discuss the major problems facing a company that is countertrading.

24. If a country you are trading with has a shortage of hard currency, how should you prepare to negotiate price?

25. Of the four types of countertrades discussed in the text, which is the most beneficial to the seller? Explain.

26. Why should a "knowledge of countertrades be part of an international marketer's pricing tool kit"? Discuss.

27. Discuss the various reasons purchasers impose countertrade obligations on buyers.

28. Discuss how FTZs can be used to help reduce price escalation.

29. Why is a proactive countertrade policy good business in some countries?

30. Differentiate between proactive and reactive countertrade policies.

31. One free trade zone is in Turkey. Visit www.esbas.com.tr and discuss how it might be used to help solve the price escalation problem of a product being exported from the United States to Turkey.

32. Visit Global Trading (a division of 3M) at www.mmm.com/globaltrading/edge.html and select "The Competitive Edge" and "Who We Are." Then write a short report on how Global Trading could assist a small company that anticipates having merchandise from a countertrade.

19

Negotiating with International customers, partners, and Regulators

CHAPTER OUTLINE

Global Perspective: A Japanese *Aisatsu*

The Dangers of Stereotypes

The Pervasive Impact of Culture on Negotiation
    Behavior
        Differences in Language and Nonverbal Behaviors
        Differences in Values
        Differences in Thinking and Decision-Making Processes

Implications for Managers and Negotiators
        Negotiation Teams
        Negotiation Preliminaries
        At the Negotiation Table
        After Negotiations

Conclusions

CHAPTER LEARNING OBJECTIVES

What you should learn from Chapter 19:

- The problems associated with cultural stereotypes

- How culture influences behaviors at the
  negotiation table

- Common kinds of problems that crop up during
  international business negotiations

- The similarities and differences in communication
  behaviors in several countries

- How differences in values and thinking processes
  affect international negotiations

- The important factors in selecting a negotiation team

- How to prepare for international negotiations

- Managing all aspects of the negotiation process

- The importance of follow-up communications
  and procedures

Global Perspective

A JAPANESE *AISATSU*

It is not so much that speaking only English is a disadvantage in international business. Instead, it's more that being bilingual is a huge advantage. Observations from sitting in on an *aisatsu* (a meeting or formal greeting for high-level executives typical in Japan) involving the president of a large Japanese industrial distributor and the marketing vice president of an American machinery manufacturer are instructive. The two companies were trying to reach an agreement on a long-term partnership in Japan.

Business cards were exchanged and formal introductions made. Even though the president spoke and understood English, one of his three subordinates acted as an interpreter for the Japanese president. The president asked everyone to be seated. The interpreter sat on a stool between the two senior executives. The general attitude between the parties was friendly but polite. Tea and a Japanese orange drink were served.

The Japanese president controlled the interaction completely, asking questions of all Americans through the interpreter. Attention of all the participants was given to each speaker in turn. After this initial round of questions for all the Americans, the Japanese president focused on developing a conversation with the American vice president. During this interaction an interesting pattern of nonverbal behaviors developed. The Japanese president would ask a question in Japanese. The interpreter then translated the question for the American vice president. While the interpreter spoke, the American's attention (gaze direction) was given to the interpreter. However, the Japanese president's gaze direction was at the American. Thus the Japanese president could carefully and unobtrusively observe the American's facial expressions and nonverbal responses. Conversely, when the American spoke the Japanese president had twice the response time. Because the latter understood English, he could formulate his responses during the translation process.

What is this extra response time worth in a strategic conversation? What is it worth to be able to carefully observe the nonverbal responses of your top-level counterpart in a high-stakes business negotiation?

Source: James Day Hodgson, Yoshihiro Sano, and John L. Graham, *Doing Business with the New Japan* (Boulder, CO: Rowman & Littlefield, 2000).

I (John Graham) had been in China a couple of weeks. I was tired. The fog had delayed my flight from Xian to Shanghai by four hours. I was standing in a long line at the counter to check in *again.* I started chatting with the older chap in line ahead of me. Juhani Kari introduced himself as a Finnish sales manager at ABB. He asked me what I did for a living. I responded, "I teach international business." He replied, "There is no such thing as international business. There's only interpersonal business." A wise man, indeed!

Face-to-face negotiations are an omnipresent activity in international commerce.[1] Once global marketing strategies have been formulated, once marketing research has been conducted to support those strategies, and once product/service, pricing, promotion, and place decisions have been made, then the focus of managers turns to implementation of the plans. In international business such plans are almost always implemented through face-to-face negotiations with business partners and customers from foreign countries. The sales of goods and services, the management of distribution channels, the contracting for marketing research and advertising services, licensing and franchise agreements, and strategic alliances all require managers from different cultures to sit and talk with one another to exchange ideas and express needs and preferences.[2]

Executives must also negotiate with representatives of foreign governments who might approve a variety of their marketing actions or in fact be the actual ultimate customer for goods and services. In many countries governmental officials may also be joint venture partners, and in some cases vendors. For example, negotiations for the television broadcast rights for the 2008 Summer Olympics in Beijing, China, included NBC, the International Olympic Committee, and Chinese governmental officials. Some of these negotiations can become quite complex, involving several governments, companies, and cultures.[3] Good examples are the European and North American talks regarding taxing the Internet, the ongoing interactions regarding global environmental issues, or the ongoing WTO negotiations begun in Doha, Qatar, in 2001. All these activities demand a new kind of "business diplomacy."

One authority on international joint ventures suggests that a crucial aspect of all international commercial relationships is the negotiation of the original agreement. The seeds of success or failure often are sown at the negotiation table, vis-à-vis (face-to-face), where not only are financial and legal details agreed to but, perhaps more important, the ambiance of cooperation is established. Indeed, the legal details and the structure of international business ventures are almost always modified over time, usually through negotiations. But

---

[1]Several excellent books have been published on the topic of international business negotiations. Among them are Camille Schuster and Michael Copeland, *Global Business, Planning for Sales and Negotiations* (Fort Worth, TX: Dryden, 1996); Robert T. Moran and William G. Stripp, *Dynamics of Successful International Business Negotiations* (Houston: Gulf, 1991); Pervez Ghauri and Jean-Claude Usunier (eds.), *International Business Negotiations* (Oxford: Pergamon, 1996); Donald W. Hendon, Rebecca Angeles Henden, and Paul Herbig, *Cross-Cultural Business Negotiations* (Westport, CT: Quorum, 1996); Sheida Hodge, *Global Smarts* (New York: Wiley, 2000); and Jeanne M. Brett, *Negotiating Globally* (San Francisco: Jossey-Bass, 2001). Additionally, Roy J. Lewicki, David M. Saunders, and John W. Minton's *Negotiation: Readings, Exercises, and Cases,* 3rd ed. (New York: Irwin/McGraw-Hill, 1999) is an important book on the broader topic of business negotiations. The material from this chapter draws extensively on John L. Graham, "Vis-à-Vis International Business Negotiations," Chapter 3, pp. 69–91, in the Ghauri and Usunier book; James Day Hodgson, Yoshihiro Sano, and John L. Graham, *Doing Business with the New Japan* (Boulder, CO: Rowman & Littlefield, 2000); and John L. Graham, "Culture and Human Resources Management," in Alan M. Rugman and Thomas L. Brewer (eds.), *The Oxford Handbook of International Business* (Oxford: Oxford University Press, 2001), pp. 503–536.

[2]David G. Sirmon and Peter J. Lane, "A Model of Cultural Differences and International Alliance Performance," *Journal of International Business Studies* 345, no. 4 (2004), pp. 306–319.

[3]R. Bruce Money provides an interesting theoretical perspective on the topic in "International Multilateral Negotiations and Social Networks," *Journal of International Business Studies* 29, no. 4 (1998), pp. 695–710. Lively anecdotes are included in Jiang Feng, "Courting the Olympics: Beijing's Other Face," *Asian Wall Street Journal,* February 26, 2001, p. 6; and Ashling O'Connor, "After 54 Years, the Olympic Clock Is Ticking," *Times of London,* February 10, 2003, p. 35.

the atmosphere of cooperation initially established face-to-face at the negotiation table persists—or the venture fails.

Business negotiations between business partners from the same country can be difficult. The added complication of cross-cultural communication can turn an already daunting task into an impossible one.[4] On the other hand, if cultural differences are taken into account, oftentimes wonderful business agreements can be made that lead to long-term, profitable relationships across borders. The purpose of this final chapter is to help prepare managers for the challenges and opportunities of international business negotiations. To do this, we will discuss the dangers of stereotypes, the impact of culture on negotiation behavior, and the implications of cultural differences for managers and negotiators.

The Dangers of Stereotypes

The images of John Wayne, the cowboy, and the samurai, the fierce warrior, often are used as cultural stereotypes in discussions of international business negotiations.[5] Such representations almost always convey a grain of truth—an American cowboy kind of competitiveness versus a samurai kind of organizational (company) loyalty. One Dutch expert on international business negotiations argues, "The best negotiators are the Japanese because they will spend days trying to get to know their opponents. The worst are Americans because they think everything works in foreign countries as it does in the USA."[6] There are, of course, many Americans who are excellent international negotiators and some Japanese who are ineffective. The point is that negotiations are not conducted between national stereotypes; negotiations are conducted between people, and cultural factors often make huge differences.

Recall our discussion on the cultural diversity *within* countries from Chapter 4 and consider its relevance to negotiation. For example, we might expect substantial differences in negotiation styles between English-speaking and French-speaking Canadians. The genteel style of talk prevalent in the American Deep South is quite different from the faster speech patterns and pushiness more common in places like New York City. Experts tell us that negotiation styles differ across genders in America as well. Still others tell us that the urbane negotiation behaviors of Japanese bankers are very different from the relative aggressiveness of those in the retail industry in that country. Finally, age and experience can also make important differences. The older Chinese executive with no experience dealing with foreigners is likely to behave quite differently from her young assistant with undergraduate and MBA degrees from American universities.

The focus of this chapter is culture's influence on international negotiation behavior. However, it should be clearly understood that individual personalities and backgrounds and a variety of situational factors also heavily influence behavior at the negotiation table—and it is the manager's responsibility to consider these factors.[7] Remember: Companies and countries do not negotiate—people do. Consider the culture of your customers and business partners, but treat them as individuals.

---

[4]James K. Sebenius, "The Hidden Challenge of Cross-Border Negotiations," *Harvard Business Review*, March–April, 2002, pp. 76–82.

[5]Nurit Zaidman discusses how stereotypes are formed in "Stereotypes of International Managers: Content and Impact on Business Interactions," *Group & Organizational Management*, March 1, 2000, pp. 45–54.

[6]Samfrits Le Poole comments on the American stereotype in "John Wayne Goes to Brussels," in Roy J. Lewicki, Joseph A. Litterer, David M. Saunders, and John W. Minton (eds.), *Negotiation: Readings, Exercises, and Cases,* 2nd ed. (Burr Ridge, IL: Irwin, 1993). The quote is from the Spanish newspaper *Expansion,* November 29, 1991, p. 41.

[7]Stephen E. Weiss provides the most complete recent review of the international negotiations literature—"International Business Negotiations Research," in B. J. Punnett and O. Shenkar (eds.), *Handbook for International Management Research* (Ann Arbor: University of Michigan Press, 2004), pp. 415–474.

The Europeans stereotype themselves. This postcard was purchased at the European Parliament gift store in Brussels. Of course, not all Dutch are cheap; there are sober Irish, etc., etc., etc. Now that the European Union has expanded to 25 countries a larger card will be required. But we're fairly certain they'll have a humorous perspective on all the new entrants. (© *J N Hughes-Wilson*)

The Pervasive Impact of Culture on Negotiation Behavior

The primary purpose of this section is to demonstrate the extent of cultural differences in negotiation styles and how these differences can cause problems in international business negotiations. The material in this section is based on a systematic study of the topic over the last three decades in which the negotiation styles of more than 1,000 businesspeople in 16 countries (19 cultures) were considered.[8] The countries studied were Japan, Korea, Taiwan, China (Tianjin, Guangzhou, and Hong Kong), the Philippines, Russia, Norway, the Czech Republic, Germany, France, the United Kingdom, Spain, Brazil, Mexico, Canada (English-speaking and French-speaking), and the United States. The countries were chosen because they constitute America's most important present and future trading partners.

---

[8]The following institutions and people provided crucial support for the research upon which this material is based: U.S. Department of Education; Toyota Motor Sales USA, Inc.; Solar Turbines, Inc. (a division of Caterpillar Tractors Co.); the Faculty Research and Innovation Fund and the International Business Educational Research (IBEAR) Program at the University of Southern California; Ford Motor Company; The Marketing Science Institute; Madrid Business School; and Professors Nancy J. Adler (McGill University), Nigel Campbell (Manchester Business School), A. Gabriel Esteban (University of Houston, Victoria), Leonid I. Evenko (Russian Academy of the National Economy), Richard H. Holton (University of California, Berkeley), Alain Jolibert (Université des Sciences Sociales de Grenoble), Dong Ki Kim (Korea University), C. Y. Lin (National Sun-Yat Sen University), Hans-Gunther Meissner (Dortmund University), Alena Ockova (Czech Management Center), Sara Tang (Mass Transit Railway Corporation, Hong Kong), Kam-hon Lee (The Chinese University of Hong Kong), and Theodore Schwarz (Monterrey Institute of Technology).

Looking broadly across the several cultures, two important lessons stand out. The first is that regional generalizations very often are not correct.[9] For example, Japanese and Korean negotiation styles are quite similar in some ways, but in other ways they could not be more different. The second lesson learned from this study is that Japan is an exceptional place: On almost every dimension of negotiation style considered, the Japanese are on or near the end of the scale. Sometimes Americans are on the other end. But actually, most of the time Americans are somewhere in the middle. The reader will see this evinced in the data presented in this section. The Japanese approach, however, is most distinct, even *sui generis.*

Cultural differences cause four kinds of problems in international business negotiations, at the levels of:[10]

1. Language
2. Nonverbal behaviors
3. Values
4. Thinking and decision-making processes

The order is important; the problems lower on the list are more serious because they are more subtle. For example, two negotiators would notice immediately if one were speaking Japanese and the other German. The solution to the problem may be as simple as hiring an interpreter or talking in a common third language, or it may be as difficult as learning a language. Regardless of the solution, the problem is obvious. Cultural differences in nonverbal behaviors, on the other hand, are almost always hidden below our awareness. That is to say, in a face-to-face negotiation participants nonverbally—and more subtly—give off and take in a great deal of information. Some experts argue that this information is more important than verbal information. Almost all this signaling goes on below our levels of consciousness.[11] When the nonverbal signals from foreign partners are different, negotiators are most likely to misinterpret them without even being conscious of the mistake. For example, when a French client consistently interrupts, Americans tend to feel uncomfortable without noticing exactly why. In this manner, interpersonal friction often colors business relationships, goes undetected, and, consequently, goes uncorrected. Differences in values and thinking and decision-making processes are hidden even deeper and therefore are even harder to cure. We discuss these differences here, starting with language and nonverbal behaviors.

Differences in Language and Nonverbal Behaviors

Americans are clearly near the bottom of the languages skills list, although Australians assert that Australians are even worse. It should be added, however, that American undergrads recently have begun to see the light and are flocking to language classes and study-abroad programs. Unfortunately, foreign language teaching resources in the United States are inadequate to satisfy the increasing demand. In contrast, the Czechs are now throwing away a hard-earned competitive advantage: Young Czechs will not take Russian anymore. It is easy to understand why, but the result will be a generation of Czechs who cannot leverage their geographic advantage because they will not be able to speak to their neighbors to the east.

The language advantages of the Japanese executive in the description of the *aisatsu* that opened the chapter were quite clear. However, the most common complaint heard from American managers regards foreign clients and partners breaking into side conversations in their native languages. At best, this is seen as impolite, and quite often American negotiators

[9]Rohit Deshpande and John Farley, "High Performance Firms in a Complex New China: A Tale of Six Cities," *Journal of Global Marketing* 16, no. 1–2 (2002), pp. 207–209.

[10]For additional details see John L. Graham, "Culture and Human Resources Management," in Alan M. Rugman and Thomas L. Brewer (eds.), *The Oxford Handbook of International Business* (Oxford: Oxford University Press, 2001), pp. 503–536.

[11]Jan Ulijn, Anne Francoise Rutowski, Rajesh Kumar, and Yunxia Zhu, "Patterns of Feelings in Face-to-Face Negotiation: A Sino-Dutch Pilot Study," *Cross Cultural Management* 12, no. 3 (2005), pp. 103–118.

Japanese negotiators exchange business cards at the front end of a meeting. Even more important than the nonverbal demonstration of respect in the "little ritual" is the all-important information about the relative status of the negotiators clearly communicated by job title and company. Japanese executives literally do not know how to talk to one another until the status relationship is determined, because proper use of the language depends on knowledge of the relative status of the negotiators. (© Photodisc Green/ Getty Images)

are likely to attribute something sinister to the content of the foreign talk—"They're plotting or telling secrets."

This is a frequent American mistake. The usual purpose of such side conversations is to straighten out a translation problem. For instance, one Korean may lean over to another and ask, "What'd he say?" Or the side conversation can regard a disagreement among the foreign team members. Both circumstances should be seen as positive signs by Americans— that is, getting translations straight enhances the efficiency of the interactions, and concessions often follow internal disagreements. But because most Americans speak only one language, neither circumstance is appreciated. By the way, people from other countries are advised to give Americans a brief explanation of the content of their first few side conversations to assuage the sinister attributions.

Data from simulated negotiations are also informative. In our study, the verbal behaviors of negotiators in 14 of the cultures (six negotiators in each of the 14 groups) were videotaped. The numbers in the body of Exhibit 19.1 represent the percentages of statements that were classified into each category listed. That is, 7 percent of the statements made by Japanese negotiators were classified as promises, 4 percent as threats, 7 percent as recommendations, and so on. The verbal bargaining behaviors used by the negotiators during the simulations proved to be surprisingly similar across cultures. Negotiations in all 14 cultures studied were composed primarily of information-exchange tactics—questions and self-disclosures. Note that the Japanese appear on the low end of the continuum of self-disclosures. Their 34 percent (along with the Spaniards and the English-speaking Canadians) was the lowest across all 14 groups, suggesting that they are the most reticent about giving information. Overall, however, the verbal tactics used were surprisingly similar across the diverse cultures.

Exhibit 19.2 provides analyses of some linguistic aspects and nonverbal behaviors for the 14 videotaped groups. Although these efforts merely scratch the surface of these kinds of behavioral analyses, they still provide indications of substantial cultural differences.[12] Note that, once again, the Japanese are at or next to the end of the continuum on almost every dimension of the behaviors listed. Their facial gazing and touching are the least among the 14 groups. Only the northern Chinese used the word *no* less frequently, and only the Russians used more silent periods than did the Japanese.

A broader examination of the data in Exhibits 19.1 and 19.2 reveals a more meaningful conclusion: The variation across cultures is greater when comparing linguistic aspects of language and nonverbal behaviors than when the verbal content of negotiations is considered. For example, notice the great differences between Japanese and Brazilians in Exhibit 19.1 vis-à-vis Exhibit 19.2.

Following are further descriptions of the distinctive aspects of each of the 14 cultural groups videotaped. Certainly, conclusions about the individual cultures cannot be drawn from an analysis of only six businesspeople in each culture, but the suggested cultural differences are worthwhile to consider briefly.

Japan.   Consistent with most descriptions of Japanese negotiation behavior, the results of this analysis suggest their style of interaction is among the least aggressive (or most polite). Threats, commands, and warnings appear to be deemphasized in favor of the more positive promises, recommendations, and commitments. Particularly indicative of their polite conversational style was their infrequent use of *no* and *you* and facial gazing, as well as more frequent silent periods.

---

[12]Thomas W. Leigh and John O. Summers, "An Initial Evaluation of Industrial Buyers' Impressions of Salespersons' Nonverbal Cues," *Journal of Personal Selling & Sales Management*, Winter 2002, pp. 41–53.

Exhibit 19.1
Verbal Negotiatation Tactics (The "What" of Communications)

Bargaining Behaviors and Definitions	JPN	KOR	TWN	CHN*	RUSS	GRM	UK	FRN	SPN	BRZ	MEX	FCAN	ECAN	USA
Promise. A statement in which the source indicated its intention to provide the target with a reinforcing consequence, which the source anticipates the target will evaluate as pleasant, positive, or rewarding.	7†	4	9	6	5	7	11	5	11	3	7	8	6	8
Threat. Same as promise, except that the reinforcing consequences are thought to be noxious, unpleasant, or punishing.	4	2	2	1	3	3	3	5	2	2	1	3	0	4
Recommendation. A statement in which the source predicts that a pleasant environmental consequence will occur to the target. Its occurrence is not under source's control.	7	1	5	2	4	5	6	3	4	5	8	5	4	4
Warning. Same as recommendation, except that the consequences are thought to be unpleasant.	2	0	3	1	0	1	1	3	1	1	2	5	0	1
Reward. A statement by the source that is thought to create pleasant consequences for the target.	1	3	2	0	3	4	5	3	3	2	1	1	3	2
Punishment. Same as reward, except that the consequences are thought to be unpleasant.	1	5	1	0	1	2	0	3	2	3	0	2	1	3
Positive normative appeal. A statement in which the source indicates that the target's past, present, or future behavior was or will conform with social norms.	1	1	0	1	0	0	0	0	0	0	0	1	0	1
Negative normative appeal. Same as positive normative appeal except that the target's behavior is in violation of social norms.	3	2	1	0	0	1	1	0	1	1	1	2	1	1
Commitment. A statement by the source to the effect that its future bids will not go below or above a certain level.	15	13	9	10	11	9	13	10	9	8	9	8	14	13
Self-disclosure. A statement in which the source reveals information about itself.	34	36	42	36	40	47	39	42	34	39	38	42	34	36
Question. A statement in which the source asks the target to reveal information about itself.	20	21	14	34	27	11	15	18	17	22	27	19	26	20
Command. A statement in which the source suggests that the target perform a certain behavior.	8	13	11	7	7	12	9	9	17	14	7	5	10	6

Cultures (in each group, n = 6)

*Northern China (Tianjin and environs).

†Read "7 percent of the statements made by Japanese negotiators were promises."

Exhibit 19.2
Linguistic Aspects of Language and Nonverbal Behaviors ("How" Things Are Said)

Bargaining Behaviors (per 30 minutes)	Cultures (in each group, n = 6)													
	JPN	KOR	TWN	CHN*	RUSS	GRM	UK	FRN	SPN	BRZ	MEX	FCAN	ECAN	USA
Structural Aspects														
"No's." The number of times the word *no* was used by each negotiator.	1.9	7.4	5.9	1.5	2.3	6.7	5.4	11.3	23.2	41.9	4.5	7.0	10.1	4.5
"You's." The number of times the word *you* was used by each negotiator.	31.5	34.2	36.6	26.8	23.6	39.7	54.8	70.2	73.3	90.4	56.3	72.4	64.4	54.1
Nonverbal Behavior														
Silent periods. The number of conversational gaps of 10 seconds or longer.	2.5	0	0	2.3	3.7	0	2.5	1.0	0	0	1.1	0.2	2.9	1.7
Conversational overlaps. Number of interruptions.	6.2	22.0	12.3	17.1	13.3	20.8	5.3	20.7	28.0	14.3	10.6	24.0	17.0	5.1
Facial gazing. Number of minutes negotiators spent looking at opponent's face.	3.9	9.9	19.7	11.1	8.7	10.2	9.0	16.0	13.7	15.6	14.7	18.8	10.4	10.0
Touching. Incidents of bargainers touching one another (not including handshaking).	0	0	0	0	0	0	0	0.1	0	4.7	0	0	0	0

*Northern China (Tianjin and environs).

Source: From James Day Hodgson, Yoshihiro Sano, and John L. Graham, *Doing Business with the New Japan*, 2000, Rowman and Littlefield. Reprinted with permission.

CROSSING **BORDERS** 19.1   Poker Faces and Botox Injections

We often hear from American executives the complaint that their Japanese counterparts are "hard to read" at the negotiation table; that is, they are "poker faced." However, when we videotape and count negotiators' facial movements (smiles and frowns) we see no differences between Japanese and Americans. It appears that because of differences in the timing and meaning of facial expressions across the two cultures, the Americans are unable to intepret the Japaneaese facial expressions, so they mistakenly report seeing nothing.

Now it seems that American executives are seeking their own poker-face advantage through the new wonder of science, Botox. Shots of the new drug are being used to freeze and sculpt their faces into "semipermanent serenity." Says one American executive, "When you look strong and tough and not afraid, people respect you more . . . showing less expression really makes a statement."

Paul Ekman, a University of California psychologist who studies facial expressions, describes this trend as "very scary." Facial expressions have evolved to serve a purpose, to aid in the formation of basic human bonds through subconscious facial movements. Take those away and how can we tell friend or foe, mate or murderer?

And there are other hazards. An overzealous doctor pumped too much Botox into one executive's forehead, causing paralysis in the upper third of her face. Her underlings kept asking whether she was tired or sick. Until the treatment wore off she was forced to avoid any animated conversations inside and outside the company.

Rather than preparing for your international negotiations using Botox, we instead recommend a good book, a nice round of golf, or perhaps a good, old-fashioned facial!

Sources: James D. Hodgson, Yoshihiro Sano, and John L. Graham, *Doing Business with the New Japan* (Bolder, CO: Rowman & Littlefield, 2000); Suein L. Hwang, "Some Type A Staffers Dress for Success with a Shot of Botox," *Wall Street Journal*, June 31, 2002, p. B1.

Korea.   Perhaps one of the more interesting aspects of the analysis is the contrast of the Asian styles of negotiations. Non-Asians often generalize about Asians; the findings demonstrate, however, that this is a mistake. Korean negotiators used considerably more punishments and commands than did the Japanese. Koreans used the word *no* and interrupted more than three times as frequently as the Japanese. Moreover, no silent periods occurred between Korean negotiators.

China (Northern).   The behaviors of the negotiators from northern China (i.e., in and around Tianjin) were most remarkable in the emphasis on asking questions[13] (34 percent). Indeed, 70 percent of the statements made by the Chinese negotiators were classified as information-exchange tactics. Other aspects of their behavior were quite similar to the Japanese, particularly the use of *no* and *you* and silent periods.[14]

Taiwan.   The behavior of the businesspeople in Taiwan was quite different from that in China and Japan but similar to that in Korea. The Chinese in Taiwan were exceptional in the time of facial gazing—on the average, almost 20 of 30 minutes. They asked fewer questions and provided more information (self-disclosures) than did any of the other Asian groups.

---

[13]The Chinese emphasis on questions is consistent with other empirical findings: Dean Tjosvold, Chun Hui, and Haifa Sun, "Can Chinese Discuss Conflicts Openly? Field and Experimental Studies of Face Dynamics," *Group Decision and Negotiation* 13 (2004), pp. 351–373.

[14]There is a burgeoning literature on negotiations with Chinese. See Catherine H. Tinsley and Jeanne M. Brett, "Managing Workplace Conflict in the U.S. and Hong Kong," *Organizational Behavior and Human Decision Process*, forthcoming; Pervez Ghauri and Tony Fang, "Negotiating with the Chinese: A Socio-Cultural Analysis," *Journal of World Business*, September 22, 2001, pp. 303–312; Vivian C. Sheer and Ling Chen, "Successful Sino-Western Business Negotiation: Participants' Accounts of National and Professional Cultures," *Journal of Business Communication*, January 1, 2003, pp. 50–64; Rajesh Kumar and Verner Worm, "Social Capital and the Dynamics of Business Negotiations between the Northern Europeans and the Chinese," *International Marketing Review* 20, no. 3 (2003), pp. 262–286; John L. Graham and N. Mark Lam, "The Chinese Negotiation," *Harvard Business Review*, October 2003, pp. 82–91; Anna Stark, Kim-Shyan Fam, David S. Waller, and Zhilong Tian, "Chinese Negotiation Practice, Perspective from New Zealand Exporters," *Cross Cultural Management* 12, no. 3 (2005), pp. 85–102.

Russia.   The Russians' style was quite different from that of any other European group, and, indeed, was quite similar in many respects to the style of the Japanese. They used *no* and *you* infrequently and used the most silent periods of any group. Only the Japanese did less facial gazing, and only the Chinese asked a greater percentage of questions.

Germany.   The behaviors of the Germans are difficult to characterize because they fell toward the center of almost all the continua. However, the Germans were exceptional in the high percentage of self-disclosures (47 percent) and the low percentage of questions (11 percent).

United Kingdom.   The behaviors of the British negotiators were remarkably similar to those of the Americans in all respects.

Spain.   *Diga* is perhaps a good metaphor for the Spanish approach to negotiations evinced in our data. When you make a phone call in Madrid, the usual greeting on the other end is not *hola* ("hello") but is, instead, *diga* ("speak"). It is not surprising, then, that the Spaniards in the videotaped negotiations likewise used the highest percentage of commands (17 percent) of any of the groups and gave comparatively little information (self-disclosures, only 34 percent). Moreover, they interrupted one another more frequently than any other group, and they used the terms *no* and *you* very frequently.

France.   The style of the French negotiators was perhaps the most aggressive of all the groups. In particular, they used the highest percentage of threats and warnings (together, 8 percent). They also used interruptions, facial gazing, and *no* and *you* very frequently compared with the other groups, and one of the French negotiators touched his partner on the arm during the simulation.

Brazil.   The Brazilian businesspeople, like the French and Spanish, were quite aggressive. They used the second-highest percentage of commands of all the groups. On average, the Brazilians said the word *no* 42 times, *you* 90 times, and touched one another on the arm about 5 times during 30 minutes of negotiation. Facial gazing was also high.

Mexico.   The patterns of Mexican behavior in our negotiations are good reminders of the dangers of regional or language-group generalizations.[15] Both verbal and nonverbal behaviors were quite different from those of their Latin American (Brazilian) or continental (Spanish) cousins. Indeed, Mexicans answer the telephone with the much less demanding *bueno* (short for "good day"). In many respects, the Mexican behavior was very similar to that of the negotiators from the United States.

French-Speaking Canada.   The French-speaking Canadians behaved quite similarly to their continental cousins. Like the negotiators from France, they too used high percentages of threats and warnings, and even more interruptions and eye contact. Such an aggressive interaction style would not mix well with some of the more low-key styles of some of the Asian groups or with English speakers, including English-speaking Canadians.

English-Speaking Canada.   The Canadians who speak English as their first language used the lowest percentage of aggressive persuasive tactics (threats, warnings, and punishments totaled only 1 percent) of all 14 groups. Perhaps, as communications researchers suggest, such stylistic differences are the seeds of interethnic discord as witnessed in Canada over the years. With respect to international negotiations, the English-speaking Canadians used noticeably more interruptions and *no*'s than negotiators from either of Canada's major trading partners, the United States and Japan.

United States.   Like the Germans and the British, the Americans fell in the middle of most continua. They did interrupt one another less frequently than all the others, but that was their sole distinction.

---

[15]T. Lenartowicz and J. P. Johnson, "A Cross-National Assessment of the Values of Latin American Managers: Contrasting Hues or Shades of Gray?" *Journal of International Business Studies* 34, no. 3 (May 2003), pp. 266–281.

These differences across the cultures are quite complex, and this material by itself should not be used to predict the behaviors of foreign counterparts. Instead, great care should be taken with respect to the aforementioned dangers of stereotypes. The key here is to be aware of these kinds of differences so that the Japanese silence, the Brazilian "no, no, no . . . ," or the French threat is not misinterpreted.

Differences in Values   Four values—objectivity, competitiveness, equality, and punctuality—that are held strongly and deeply by most Americans seem to frequently cause misunderstandings and bad feelings in international business negotiations.

Objectivity.   "Americans make decisions based upon the bottom line and on cold, hard facts." "Americans don't play favorites." "Economics and performance count, not people." "Business is business." Such statements well reflect American notions of the importance of objectivity.

The single most important book on the topic of negotiation, *Getting to Yes,*[16] is highly recommended for both American and foreign readers. The latter will learn not only about negotiations but, perhaps more important, about how Americans think about negotiations. The authors are emphatic about "separating the people from the problem," and they state, "Every negotiator has two kinds of interests: in the substance and in the relationship." This advice is probably worthwhile in the United States or perhaps in Germany, but in most places in the world such advice is nonsense. In most places in the world, particularly in collectivistic, high-context cultures, personalities and substance are not separate issues and cannot be made so.

For example, consider how important nepotism is in Chinese or Hispanic culture. Experts tell us that businesses don't grow beyond the bounds and bonds of tight family control in the burgeoning "Chinese Commonwealth." Things work the same way in Spain, Mexico, and the Philippines by nature. And, just as naturally, negotiators from such countries not only will take things personally but will be personally affected by negotiation outcomes. What happens to them at the negotiation table will affect the business relationship regardless of the economics involved.

Competitiveness and Equality.   Simulated negotiations can be viewed as a kind of experimental economics wherein the values of each participating cultural group are roughly reflected in the economic outcomes. The simple simulation used in our research represented the essence of commercial negotiations—it had both competitive and cooperative aspects. At least 40 businesspeople from each culture played the same buyer–seller game, negotiating over the prices of three products. Depending on the agreement reached, the "negotiation pie" could be made larger through cooperation (as high as $10,400 in joint profits) before it was divided between the buyer and seller. The results are summarized in Exhibit 19.3.

The Japanese were the champions at making the pie big. Their joint profits in the simulation were the highest (at $9,590) among the 18 cultural groups involved. The American pie was more average sized (at $9,030), but at least it was divided relatively equitably (51.8 percent of the profits went to the buyers). Conversely, the Japanese (and others) split their pies in strange (perhaps even unfair)[17] ways, with buyers making higher percentages of the profits (53.8 percent). The implications of these simulated business negotiations are completely consistent with the comments of other authors and the adage that in Japan the buyer is "kinger." By nature, Americans have little understanding of the Japanese practice of giving complete deference to the needs and wishes of buyers. That is not the way things work in America. American sellers tend to treat American buyers more as equals, and the egalitarian values of American society support this behavior. Moreover, most Americans will, by nature, treat Japanese buyers more frequently as equals. Likewise, American buyers will

---

[16]Roger Fisher, William Ury, and Bruce Patton, *Getting to Yes: Negotiating Agreement without Giving In* (New York: Penguin, 1991).

[17]Concepts of fairness clearly vary across cultures: see Nancy R. Buchan, Rachael T. S. Croson, and Eric J. Johnson, "When Do Fair Beliefs Influence Bargaining Behavior: Experimental Bargaining in Japan and the United States," *Journal of Consumer Research* 31, no. 2 (2004), pp. 181–190.

Exhibit 19.3
Cultural Differences in
Competitiveness and
Equality

Source: From James Day Hodgson,
Yoshihiro Sano, and John L. Graham,
Doing Business with the New Japan,
2000, Rowman and Littlefield.
Reprinted with permission.

Based upon at least 40 businesspeople in each cultural group.

generally not "take care of" American sellers or Japanese sellers. The American emphasis on competition and individualism represented in these findings is quite consistent with the work of Geert Hofstede[18] detailed in Chapter 4, which indicated that Americans scored the highest among all the cultural groups on the individualism (versus collectivism) scale. Moreover, values for individualism/collectivism have been shown to directly influence negotiation behaviors in several other countries.[19]

Finally, not only do Japanese buyers achieve higher results than American buyers, but compared with American sellers ($4,350), Japanese sellers also get more of the commercial pie ($4,430) as well. Interestingly, when shown these results, Americans in executive seminars still often prefer the American seller's role. In other words, even though the American sellers make lower profits than the Japanese, many American managers apparently prefer lower profits if those profits are yielded from a more equal split of the joint profits.

Time.   "Just make them wait." Everyone else in the world knows that no negotiation tactic is more useful with Americans, because no one places more value on time, no one has less patience when things slow down, and no one looks at their wristwatches more than Americans do. The material from Chapter 5 on P-time versus M-time is quite pertinent here. Edward T. Hall[20] in his seminal writing is best at explaining how the passage of time is viewed differently across cultures and how these differences most often hurt Americans.

Even Americans try to manipulate time to their advantage, however. As a case in point, Solar Turbines Incorporated (a division of Caterpillar) once sold $34 million worth of industrial gas turbines and compressors for a Russian natural gas pipeline project. Both parties agreed that final negotiations would be held in a neutral location, the south of France. In previous negotiations, the Russians had been tough but reasonable. But in Nice, the Russians were not nice. They became tougher and, in fact, completely unreasonable, according to the Solar executives involved.

The Americans needed a couple of discouraging days to diagnose the problem, but once they did, a crucial call was made back to headquarters in San Diego. Why had the Russians turned so cold? They were enjoying the warm weather in Nice and weren't interested in

---

[18]Geert Hofstede, *Culture's Consequences,* 2nd ed. (Thousand Oaks, CA: Sage, 2001).

[19]John L. Graham, "Culture's Influence on Business Negotiations: An Application of Hofstede's and Rokeach's Ideas," in Farok J. Contractor and Peter Lorange (eds.), *Cooperative Strategies and Alliances* (Amsterdam: Pergamon, 2002), pp. 461–492. Also see Roy J. Lewicki, David M. Saunders, and John W. Minton, *Essentials of Negotiation,* 2nd ed. (New York: McGraw-Hill, 2001).

[20]Edward T. Hall, "The Silent Language in Overseas Business," *Harvard Business Review,* May–June 1960, pp. 87–96.

CROSSING BORDERS 19.2 | A Russian and an Indonesian Manager Talk about Negotiations

The new Russian business managers are traders. Many got their start in the black markets of the old Soviet system. They will promise you the world, but these promises often lack substance. Although they are inexperienced in Western business practices, they are often very shrewd negotiators. In many instances, the stubborn Russian negotiator gets the best of his Western counterpart who is in a rush to close the deal.

However, those who live in Russia and get used to the Russian bargaining techniques often come to enjoy the intricacies of negotiating there. Formalized games of power politics and posturing can provide hours of enjoyment for the entire office staff. To negotiate successfully in Russia, you must be thick-skinned, bullheaded, and warmhearted. And always remember that Russians are the world's greatest chess players.

—Marina Volobueva

I grew up outside my native Indonesia but went back to do an internship in the family business.

One day I had the privilege of accompanying my father during a fairly important negotiation. We met first for lunch, but we never discussed the business deal at all. Instead, the person my father was meeting spent the entire time asking questions about my education in the United States. Apparently he intended to send his son to school there. After spending what seemed to me two unproductive hours, we agreed to play golf that Saturday morning. Afterward, my father told me that most important business deals take place on the golf course. That Saturday, we met on the course, but it was not until the 10th hole that they finally got around to discussing business. After the game was over, they agreed to meet again at the office to finish up the details of the deal.

—Aidil A. Madjid

Source: From Sheida Hodge, *Global Smarts* (New York: Wiley, 2000), pp. 191, 196. Reprinted with permission of John Wiley & Sons, Inc.

---

making a quick deal and heading back to Moscow! The call to California was the key event in this negotiation. Solar's headquarters people in San Diego were sophisticated enough to allow their negotiators to take their time. From that point on, the routine of the negotiations changed to brief, 45-minute meetings in the mornings, with afternoons at the golf course, beach, or hotel, making calls and doing paperwork. Finally, during the fourth week, the Russians began to make concessions and to ask for longer meetings. Why? They could not go back to Moscow after four weeks on the Mediterranean without a signed contract. This strategic reversal of the time pressure yielded a wonderful contract for Solar.

Differences in Thinking and Decision-Making Processes

When faced with a complex negotiation task, most Westerners (notice the generalization here) divide the large task up into a series of smaller tasks. Issues such as prices, delivery, warranty, and service contracts may be settled one issue at a time, with the final agreement being the sum or the sequence of smaller agreements. In Asia, however, a different approach is more often taken wherein all the issues are discussed at once, in no apparent order, and concessions are made on all issues at the end of the discussion. The Western sequential approach and the Eastern holistic approach do not mix well.[21]

That is, American managers often report great difficulties in measuring progress in Japan. After all, in America, you are half done when half the issues are settled. But in Japan, nothing seems to get settled. Then, surprise, you are done. Often Americans make unnecessary concessions right before agreements are announced by the Japanese. For example, one American department store buyer traveling to Japan to buy six different consumer products for his chain lamented that negotiations for his first purchase took an entire week. In the United States, such

---

[21]Other East–West differences in thinking are studied in detail in Joel Brockner, Ya-Ru Chen, Elizabeth A. Mannix, Kwok Leung, and Daniel P. Skarlicki, "Culture and Procedural Fairness: When the Effects of What You Do Depend on How You Do It," *Administrative Science Quarterly,* March 1, 2000, pp. 138–157. Most important is Richard E. Nisbett, *The Geography of Thought, How Asians and Westerners Think Differently . . . and Why* (New York: Free Press, 2003).

a purchase would be consummated in an afternoon. So, by his calculations, he expected to have to spend six weeks in Japan to complete his purchases. He considered raising his purchase prices to try to move things along faster. But before he was able to make such a concession, the Japanese quickly agreed on the other five products in just three days. This particular business-man was, by his own admission, lucky in his first encounter with Japanese bargainers.

This American businessman's near-blunder reflects more than just a difference in decision-making style. To Americans, a business negotiation is a problem-solving activity, the best deal for both parties being the solution. To a Japanese businessperson, on the other hand, a business negotiation is a time to develop a business relationship with the goal of long-term mutual benefit. The economic issues are the context, not the content, of the talks. Thus settling any one issue really is not that important. Such details will take care of themselves once a viable, harmonious business relationship is established. And, as happened in the case of our retail goods buyer, once the relationship was established—signaled by the first agreement—the other "details" were settled quickly.

American bargainers should anticipate such a holistic approach and be prepared to discuss all issues simultaneously and in an apparently haphazard order. Progress in the talks should not be measured by how many issues have been settled. Rather, Americans must try to gauge the quality of the business relationship. Important signals of progress can be the following:

- Higher-level foreigners being included in the discussions
- Their questions beginning to focus on specific areas of the deal
- A softening of their attitudes and position on some of the issues—"Let us take some time to study this issue"
- At the negotiation table, increased talk among themselves in their own language, which may often mean they're trying to decide something
- Increased bargaining and use of the lower-level, informal, and other channels of communication

Implications for Managers and Negotiators

Considering all the potential problems in cross-cultural negotiations, particularly when you mix managers from relationship-oriented cultures with those from information-oriented ones, it is a wonder that any international business gets done at all. Obviously, the economic imperatives of global trade make much of it happen despite the potential pitfalls. But an appreciation of cultural differences can lead to even better international commercial transactions—it is not just business deals but highly profitable business relationships that are the real goal of international business negotiations.

Four steps lead to more efficient and effective international business negotiations. They are as follows: (1) selection of the appropriate negotiation team;[22] (2) management of preliminaries, including training, preparations, and manipulation of negotiation settings; (3) management of the process of negotiations, that is, what happens at the negotiation table; and (4) appropriate follow-up procedures and practices. Each is discussed in this section.

Negotiation Teams

One reason for global business successes is the large numbers of skillful international negotiators. These are the managers who have lived in foreign countries and speak foreign languages. In many cases, they are immigrants to the United States or those who have been immersed in foreign cultures in other capacities (Peace Corps volunteers and Mormon missionaries are common examples). More business schools are beginning to reemphasize language training and visits abroad. Indeed, it is interesting to note that the original Harvard Business School catalog of 1908–1909 listed German, French, and Spanish correspondence within its curriculum.

The selection criteria for international marketing and sales personnel previously detailed in Chapter 17 are applicable in selecting negotiators as well. Traits such as maturity, emotional stability, breadth of knowledge, optimism, flexibility, empathy, and stamina are all

---

[22]Leonidas C. Leonidou, Constantine S. Katsikeas, and John Hadjimarcou, "Building Successful Export Business Relationships," *Journal of International Marketing*, January 1, 2002, pp. 96–101.

important, not only for marketing executives involved in international negotiations, but also for the technical experts who often accompany and support them. In studies conducted at Ford Motor Company and AT&T, three additional traits were found to be important predictors of negotiator success with international clients and partners: willingness to use team assistance, listening skill, and influence at headquarters.

Willingness to use team assistance is particularly important for American negotiators. Because of a cultural heritage of independence and individualism, Americans often make the mistake of going it alone against greater numbers of foreigners. One American sitting across the negotiation table from three or four Chinese negotiators is unfortunately an all too common sight. The number of brains in the room does make a difference. Moreover, business negotiations are social processes, and the social reality is that a larger number of nodding heads can exercise greater influence than even the best arguments. It is also much easier to gather detailed information when teams are negotiating rather than individuals. For example, the Japanese are quite good at bringing along junior executives for the dual purposes of careful note taking and training via observation. Compensation schemes that overly emphasize individual performance can also get in the way of team negotiating—a negotiation team requires a split commission, which many Americans naturally eschew. Finally, negotiators may have to request the accompaniment of senior executives to better match up with client's and partner's negotiation teams. Particularly in relationship-oriented cultures, rank speaks quite loudly in both persuasion and the demonstration of interest in the business relationship.

The single most important activity of negotiations is listening. The negotiator's primary job is collecting information with the goal of enhancing creativity. This may mean assigning one team member the sole responsibility of taking careful notes and not worrying about speaking during the meetings. This may also mean that knowing the language of clients and partners will be crucial for the most complete understanding of their needs and preferences. The importance of listening skills in international business negotiations cannot be overstated.

Bringing along a senior executive is important because influence at headquarters is crucial to success. Indeed, many experienced international negotiators argue that half the negotiation is with headquarters. The representatives' lament goes something like this: "The better I understand my customer, the tougher time I have with headquarters." Of course, this misery associated with boundary-spanning roles is precisely why international negotiators and sales executives make so much money.

Women can get the job done. Here Chile's Foreign Minister, Maria Soledad Alvear, at a news conference with former U.S. Trade Representative (now Undersecretary of State) Robert Zoellick discusses the free trade pact between the two nations. Zoellick was preceded in his job by two American women, both quite successful in opening up foreign markets. Indeed, Charlene Barshefsky earned the nickname "Velvet Crowbar" from her Asian counterparts while she served as USTR during President Clinton's second term. *(AP/Wide World Photos)*

Finally, it is also important to reiterate a point made in Chapter 5: Gender should not be used as a selection criterion for international negotiation teams. This is so despite the great differences in the roles of women across cultures. Even in countries where women do not participate in management, American women negotiators are treated as foreigners first. For obvious reasons it may not be appropriate for women managers to participate in some forms of business entertainment—common baths in locker rooms at Japanese golf course clubhouses, for example. However, it is still important for women executives to establish personal rapport at restaurants and other informal settings. Indeed, one expert on cross-gender communication suggests that women may actually have some advantages in international negotiations:

> In general, women are more comfortable talking one-on-one. The situation of speaking up in a meeting is a lot closer to boys' experience of using language to establish their position in a large group than it is to girls' experience using language to maintain intimacy. That's something that can be exploited. Don't wait for the meeting; try to make your point in advance, one-to-one. This is what the Japanese do, and in many ways American women's style is a lot closer to the Japanese style than to American men's.[23]

---

[23]Deborah Tannen, *You Just Don't Understand: Men and Women in Conversation* (New York: William Morrow, 1990).

En los negocios no se consigue lo que se merece, se consigue lo que se negocia.

Ahora, más que nunca, la gente de éxito acude a Karrass.

La revista **Forbes** lo dijo en pocas palabras: "Claro, hay docenas de tipos –demasiados –que corren de acá para allá dando cursos, pero la lista de clientes de Karrass es de otra casta: Mobil, General Motors, Ford, IBM, General Electric, Arco, Shell, ITT, Phillips Petroleum, –9 de las 15 empresas más grandes de los Estados Unidos –y 140 más." Añadió **Forbes:**

Kaiser Aluminum & Chemical, que gastó en el transcurso de varios años, cerca de $15,000 dólares en cursos de Karrass, pidió que sus empleados identificaran ahorros específicos logrados al negociar mejor. El total sumó millones de dólares. Un ejecutivo de ventas de Boeing dijo lo mismo acerca de una sola negociación en el Medio Oriente. En General Electric, reconocida por sus programas internos de capacitación, el 90 por ciento de los empleados se

Dr. Chester L. Karrass

Continúa en la siguiente página

Through his books and training courses, Chester Karrass has taught more people to negotiate than anyone else on earth. His firm offers seminars in dozens of countries and advertises in in-flight magazines here in Spanish. *(Copyrighted and used by permission of KARRASS, LTD. Beverly Hills, California)*

Negotiation Preliminaries   Many companies in the United States provide employees with negotiations training.[24] For example, through his training programs, Chester Karrass[25] has taught more people (some 400,000) to negotiate than any other purveyor of the service[26]—see his ads in almost all in-flight magazines of domestic American air carriers. However, very few companies provide training for negotiations with managers from other countries. Even more surprising is the lack of cultural content in the training of the government's diplomats. Instead, in most schools of diplomacy the curricula cover language skills, social and diplomatic skills, and knowledge specific to the diplomatic profession, including diplomatic history and international relations, law, economics, politics, international organizations, and foreign policies. Cultural differences in negotiation and communication styles are seldom considered.

Things are different at Ford Motor Company. Ford does more business with Japanese companies than any other firm. Ford owns 33 percent of Mazda, it built a successful minivan with Nissan, and it buys and sells component parts and completed cars from and to Japanese companies. But perhaps the best measure of Ford's Japanese business is the 8,000 or so U.S.-to-Japan round-trip airline tickets the company buys annually. Ford has made a large investment in training its managers with Japanese responsibilities. Over 2,000 of its executives have attended a three-day program on Japanese history and culture and the company's Japanese business strategies. Further, more than 1,000 Ford managers who work face-to-face with Japanese have attended a three-day program entitled "Managing Negotiations: Japan" (MNJ). The MNJ program includes negotiation simulations with videotape feedback, lectures with cultural differences demonstrated via videotapes of Japanese–American interactions, and rehearsals of upcoming negotiations. The company also conducts similar programs on Korea and the People's Republic of China.

In addition to MNJ, the broader Japan training efforts at Ford must be credited for Ford's successes in Japan. Certainly, MNJ alumni can be seen exercising influence across and up the ranks regarding Japanese relationships. But the organizational awareness of the cultural dimensions of the Japanese business system was quickly raised as well by its broader, three-day program on Japanese business strategies. Remember the story about the Russians in Nice? Two critical events took place. First, the Solar Turbines negotiators

[24]The Harvard Program on Negotiations provides a range of negotiations courses (www.pon.harvard.edu). Also, negotiations courses are the most popular in MBA programs around the country; see Leigh Thompson and Geoffrey J. Leonardelli, "Why Negotiation Is the Most Popular Business Course," *Ivey Business Journal Online*, July/August 2004, p. 1.

[25]See Karrass's Web site for information regarding his programs: www.karrass.com. Other Web sites providing information about publically offered training programs and information on international negotiation styles are www.pon.harvard.edu, www.usip.org, www.iimcr.org, www.executiveplanet.com, and www.etiquetteintl.com. See Marisa Mohd Isa, "Learning the Art of Refined Behavior," *New Straits Times*, March 17, 2003, p. 23.

[26]Lee Edison provides an interesting description of what he calls "The Negotiation Industry," in an article he wrote in *Across the Board* 37, no. 4 (April 2000), pp. 14–20. Other commentators on training for international business negotiators are Yeang Soo Ching, "Putting a Human Face on Globalization," *New Straits Times*, January 16, 2000, p. 10; A. J. Vogl, "Negotiation: The Advanced Course," *Across the Board*, April 1, 2000, p. 21; and R. V. Veera, "MIT Preparing Students for New Millennium," *New Straits Times*, July 21, 2002, p. 5.

CROSSING BORDERS 19.3   Ford Trains Executives for Negotiations with Japanese

"Proactive and direct" is the approach Ford uses to develop competence in employees who interact with the Japanese. This occurs through a variety of practices, including programs that help Ford personnel better understand the Japanese culture and negotiating practices, and by encouraging the study of the spoken language. By designing training that highlights both the pitfalls and the opportunities in negotiations, Ford increases the chance "to expand the negotiation pie."

The key personnel on our minivan team attended one of the first sessions of the Managing Negotiations: Japan's (MNJ) program at the Ford Executive Development Center. Its negotiations with the Nissan team improved immediately. But perhaps the best measure of the usefulness of the MNJ program is the success of the Nissan joint venture product itself. Reflected in the Villager/Quest are countless hours of effective face-to-face meetings with Ford's Japanese partners.

Not everyone negotiating outside the United States has the advantages of in-house training. However, many sources of information are available—books (particularly, on Japan), periodicals, and colleagues with first-hand experience. To succeed, I believe negotiators have to be truly interested in and challenged by the international negotiating environment. Structuring negotiations to achieve win–win results and building a long-term relationship take thoughtful attention and commitment.

—Joe Gilmore
(Ford executive in charge of the minivan project with Nissan)

Source: James Day Hodgson, Yoshihiro Sano, and John L. Graham, *Doing Business with the New Japan* (Boulder, CO: Rowman & Littlefield, 2000), p. 81.

diagnosed the problem. Second, and equally important, their California superiors appreciated the problem and approved the investments in time and money to outwait the Russians. So it is that the Ford programs have targeted not only the negotiators working directly with the Japanese but also their managers, who spend most of their time in the company's Detroit headquarters. Negotiators need information specific to the cultures in which they work. Just as critical, their managers back in the United States need a basic awareness and appreciation for the importance of culture in international business so that they will be more amenable to the "odd-sounding" recommendations coming from their people in Moscow, Rio, or Tokyo.

Any experienced business negotiator will tell you that there is never enough time to get ready. Given the time constraints of international negotiations, preparations must be accomplished efficiently—the homework must be done before the bargaining begins. We recommend the following checklist to ensure proper preparation and planning for international negotiations:

1. Assessment of the situation and the people
2. Facts to confirm during the negotiation
3. Agenda
4. Best alternative to a negotiated agreement (BATNA)[27]
5. Concession strategies
6. Team assignments

---

[27]The most instructive story we have ever seen regarding how to build one's BATNA is found in Daniel Michael, "In Clandestine World of Airplane Contracts, An Inside Look at a Deal," *Wall Street Journal*, March 10, 2003, p. A1. It is a must read for anyone interested in the topic of international business negotiations.

Preparation and planning skill is at the top of almost everyone's list of negotiator traits, yet it seems many Americans are still planning strategies during over-ocean flights when they should be trying to rest. Quick wits are important in business negotiations, and arduous travel schedules and jet lag dull even the sharpest minds. Obviously, information about the other side's goals and preferences should be sought ahead of time. Also important are clear directions from headquarters and detailed information about market conditions.

No matter how thorough the preliminary research, negotiators should always make a list of key facts to reconfirm at the negotiation table. Information gathered about foreign customers and markets almost always includes errors, and things can change during those long airline flights. Next, anticipate that managers from other cultures may put less emphasis on a detailed agenda, but having one to propose still makes sense and helps to organize the meetings.

The most important idea in *Getting to Yes* is the notion of the *best alternative to a negotiated agreement (BATNA)*.[28] This is how power in negotiations is best measured. Even the smallest companies can possess great power in negotiations if they have many good alternatives and their large-company counterparts do not. It is also important to plan out and write down concession strategies. Concessions can often snowball, and writing them down ahead of time helps negotiators keep them under control.

Finally, specific team assignments should be made clear—who handles technical details, who takes notes, who plays the tough guy, who does most of the talking for the group, and so forth. Also, in relationship-oriented cultures selection of intermediaries and the seniority of negotiators will be crucial considerations.

At least seven aspects of the negotiation setting should be manipulated ahead of time if possible:

1. Location
2. Physical arrangements
3. Number of parties
4. Number of participants
5. Audiences (news media, competitors, fellow vendors, etc.)
6. Communications channels
7. Time limits

---

[28]Roger Fisher, William Ury, and Bruce Patton, *Getting to Yes* (New York: Penguin, 1991).

Different negotiation settings have different advantages and disadvantages. Of course, teleconferencing saves money, but meetings tend to be rushed. Golf course negotiations are perhaps the most leisurely, but thoughtful responses are more likely as golfers can consider reactions to statements made at the tee as they chase down their errant shots. E-mail also allows for thoughtful reactions in a similar way. Here an executive "negotiates" a putt at China's first golf course, the Chuan Shan Hot Spring Golf Club. (*left: © Charles Gupton/CORBIS; right: © Macduff Everton/CORBIS*)

Location speaks loudly about power relations. Traveling to a negotiating counterpart's home turf is a big disadvantage, and not just because of the costs of travel in money and fatigue. A neutral location may be preferred—indeed, many trans-Pacific business negotiations are conducted in Hawaii. The weather and golf are nice and the jet lag is about equal. Location is also an important consideration because it may determine legal jurisdiction if disputes arise. If you must travel to your negotiating counterpart's city, then a useful tactic is to invite clients or partners to work in a meeting room at your hotel. You can certainly get more done if they are away from the distractions of their offices.

Physical arrangements can affect cooperativeness in subtle ways. In high-context cultures the physical arrangements of rooms can be quite a source of embarrassment and irritation if handled improperly. To the detriment of their foreign business relationships, Americans tend to be casual about such arrangements. Furthermore, views about who should attend negotiations vary across cultures. Americans tend to want to get everyone together to "hammer out an agreement" even if opinions and positions are divergent. Japanese prefer to talk to everyone separately, then, once everyone agrees, to schedule inclusive meetings. Russians tend toward a cumulative approach, meeting with one party and reaching an agreement, then both parties calling on a third party, and so on. In addition, the importance of not being outnumbered in international business negotiations has already been mentioned.

Audiences can have crucial influences on negotiation processes. Purchasing executives at PetroBras, the Brazilian national oil company, are well known for putting competitive bidders in rooms adjacent to one another to increase competitive pressures on both vendors. Likewise, news leaks to the press played a crucial role in pushing along the negotiations between General Motors and Toyota regarding a joint venture production agreement.

As electronic media become more available, efficient, and sometimes necessary (e.g., the war in Iraq or the SARS outbreak mentioned in Chapter 17), more business can be conducted without face-to-face communication. However, Americans should recognize that their counterparts in many other countries do not necessarily share their attraction to the Internet[29] and teleconferencing.[30] Indeed, recent research has shown that when using e-mail trust is harder to build,[31] and in Hong Kong businesspeople tend to negotiate more competitively.[32] A conversation over a long dinner may actually be the most efficient way to communicate with clients and partners in places like Mexico, Malaysia, and China.

Finally, it is important to manipulate time limits. Recall the example about the Russians and Americans in Nice. The patience of the home office may be indispensable, and major differences in time orientation should be planned for when business negotiations are conducted in most other countries.

At the Negotiation Table

The most difficult aspect of international business negotiations is the actual conduct of the face-to-face meeting. Assuming that the best representatives have been chosen, and assuming those representatives are well prepared and that situational factors have been manipulated in one's favor, things can still go sour at the negotiation table. Obviously, if these other preliminaries have not been managed properly, things will go wrong during the meetings. Even with great care and attention to preliminary details, managing the dynamics of the

---

[29]Jan M. Uljn, Andreas Lincke, and Yunus Karakaya, "Non-Face-to-Face International Business Negotiation: How Is National Culture Reflected in This Medium," *IEEE Transactions on Professional Communication* 44, no. 2 (June 2001), pp. 126–137.

[30]Tim Ambler and Chris Styles, *The Silk Road to International Marketing* (London: Financial Times and Prentice Hall, 2000).

[31]Charles E. Naquin and Gaylen D. Paulson, "Online Bargaining and Interpersonal Trust," *Journal of Applied Psychology* 88, no. 1 (2003), pp. 113–120.

[32]Guang Yang, *The Impact of Computer Mediated Communication on the Processes and Outcomes of Buyer–Seller Negotiations*, unpublished doctoral dissertation, Merage School of Business, University of California, Irvine, 2003.

CROSSING BORDERS 19.4   The Digital Impact on International Negotiations

All in all, e-commerce is good for global marketing. It allows domestic firms to internationalize more quickly and at less cost. It allows international firms to communicate internally and externally with greater efficiency. Fax replaced telex, which, in turn, replaced the telegram. But e-mail is only partly replacing mail, fax, and phone. It is better seen as a different, more informal medium than fax and more convenient than phone. For networking purposes, e-mail is easily copied and relayed, though excess should be avoided. Many of us have learned to screen out e-mails addressed to multiple recipients.

Above all, e-mail can nurture, but not create, the long-term relationships so crucial to international marketing. The decision by Boeing to enter into an automated relationship with Dell was made not by two machines, but by personal contact between executives on both sides. The success of the P&G/Wal-Mart relationship rests with the personal relationships and interactions between P&G's key account team and Wal-Mart's buyers. Although non-Thais can learn a great deal about Thailand from the Internet, they can never really understand Thai customers, the way they do business, and their feelings toward products unless they interact directly. Understanding culture requires personal experiential learning, the wellspring of social information.

Sources: Reprinted with permission from Tim Ambler and Chris Styles, *The Silk Road to International Marketing* (London: The Financial Times/Prentice Hall, 2000); Guang Yang, *The Impact of Computer Mediated Communication on the Process and Outcomes of Buyer–Seller Negotiations*, unpublished doctoral dissertation, Merage School of Business, University of California, Irvine, 2003.

negotiation process is almost always the greatest challenge facing Americans seeking to do business in other countries.

Going into a business negotiation, most people have expectations about the "proper" or normal process of such a meeting.[33] Based on these expectations, progress is measured and appropriate bargaining strategies are selected. That is, things may be done differently in the latter stages of a negotiation than they were in the earlier. Higher-risk strategies may be employed to conclude talks—as in the final two minutes of a close soccer match. But all such decisions about strategy are made relative to perceptions of progress through an expected course of events.

Differences in the expectations held by parties from different cultures are one of the major difficulties in any international business negotiation. Before these differences are discussed, however, it is important to point out similarities. Everywhere around the world we have found that business negotiations proceed through four stages:

1. Nontask sounding
2. Task-related exchange of information
3. Persuasion
4. Concessions and agreement

The first stage, nontask sounding, includes all those activities that might be described as establishing a rapport or getting to know one another, but it does not include information related to the "business" of the meeting. The information exchanged in the second stage of business negotiations regards the parties' needs and preferences. The third stage, persuasion, involves the parties' attempts to modify one another's needs and preferences through the use of various persuasive tactics. The final stage of business negotiations involves the consummation of an agreement, which is often the summation of a series of concessions or smaller agreements.

---

[33]Sometimes these expectations are referred to as "the spirit of the deal" or the "social contract." See Ron S. Fortgang, David A. Lax, and James K. Sebenius, "Negotiating the Spirit of the Deal," *Harvard Business Review*, January–February 2003, pp. 66–74.

Exhibit 19.4
Summary of Japanese and American Business Negotiation Styles

Category	Japanese	Americans
Language	Most Japanese executives understand English, although interpreters are often used.	Americans have less time to formulate answers and observe Japanese nonverbal responses because of a lack of knowledge of Japanese.
Nonverbal behaviors	The Japanese interpersonal communication style includes less eye contact, fewer negative facial expressions, and more periods of silence.	American businesspeople tend to "fill" silent periods with arguments or concessions.
Values	Indirectness and face saving are important. Vertical buyer/seller relationships, with sellers depending on goodwill of buyers (amae), is typical.	Speaking one's mind is important. Buyer/seller relationships are horizontal.

Four Stages of Business Negotiations

1. Nontask sounding	Considerable time and expense devoted to such efforts is the practice in Japan.	Very short periods are typical.
2. Task-related exchange of information	This is the most important step—high first offers with long explanations and in-depth clarifications.	Information is given briefly and directly. "Fair" first offers are more typical.
3. Persuasion	Persuasion is accomplished primarily behind the scenes. Vertical status relations dictate bargaining outcomes.	The most important step: Minds are changed at the negotiation table and aggressive persuasive tactics are often used.
4. Concessions and agreement	Concessions are made only toward the end of negotiations—a holistic approach to decision making. Progress is difficult to measure for Americans.	Concessions and commitments are made throughout—a sequential approach to decision making.

Source: James Day Hodgson, Yoshihiro Sano, and John L. Graham, *Doing Business with the New Japan* (Boulder, CO: Rowman & Littlefield, 2000), p. 45. Used by permission of Rowman & Littlefield.

Despite the consistency of this process across diverse cultures, the content and duration of the four stages differ substantially. For example, Exhibit 19.4 details procedural differences in Japan and the United States, as well as differences in language, nonverbal behavior, and values.

Nontask Sounding.   Americans always discuss topics other than business at the negotiation table (for example, the weather, family, sports, politics, and business conditions in general), but not for long. Usually the discussion is moved to the specific business at hand after 5 to 10 minutes. Such preliminary talk, known as *nontask sounding,* is much more than just friendly or polite; it helps negotiators learn how the other side feels that particular day. During nontask sounding one can determine if a client's attention is focused on business or distracted by other matters, personal or professional.

Learning about a client's background and interests also provides important cues about appropriate communication styles. To the extent that people's backgrounds are similar, communication can be more efficient. Engineers can use technical jargon when talking to other engineers. Sports enthusiasts can use sports analogies. Those with children can compare the cash drain of "putting a kid through college," and so on.

During these initial stages of conversation, judgments, too, are made about the "kind" of person(s) with whom one is dealing: Can this person be trusted?[34] Will he be reliable? How much power does she have in her organization? All such judgments are made before business discussions ever begin.

These preliminary nontask discussions have a definite purpose. Although most people are often unaware of it, such time almost always is used to size up one's clients. Depending on the results of this process, proposals and arguments are formed using different jargon and analogies. Or if clients are distracted by other personal matters or if the other people seem untrustworthy, the decision may be to discuss no business at all. This sounds like a lot to accomplish in 5 to 10 minutes, but that's how long it usually takes in the information-oriented United States. This is not the case in relationship-oriented countries like China or Brazil; the goals of the nontask sounding are identical, but the time spent is much, much longer.

In the United States, firms resort to the legal system and their lawyers when they've made a bad deal because of a mistake in sizing up a customer or vendor. In most other countries the legal system cannot be depended upon for such purposes. Instead, executives in places like Korea and Egypt spend substantial time and effort in nontask sounding so that problems do not develop later. Americans need to reconsider, from the foreigner's perspective, the importance of this first stage of negotiations if they hope to succeed in Seoul or Cairo.

Task-Related Information Exchange.
Only when nontask sounding is complete and a trusting personal relationship is established should business be introduced. American executives are advised to let foreign counterparts decide when such substantive negotiations should begin, that is, to let them bring up business.

A *task-related information exchange* implies a two-way communication process. However, observations suggest that when Americans meet executives from some cultures across the negotiation table, the information flow is unidirectional. Japanese, Chinese, and Russian negotiators all appear to ask "thousands" of questions and to give little feedback. The barrage of questions severely tests American negotiators' patience, and the lack of feedback causes them great anxiety. Both can add up to much longer stays in these countries, which means higher travel expenses.

Certainly an excellent negotiation tactic is to "drain" information from one's negotiation counterparts. But the oft-reported behaviors of Chinese, Japanese, and Russians may not necessarily represent a sophisticated negotiation ploy. Indeed, reference to Exhibit 19.2 provides some hints that differences in conversational styles—silent periods occurred more frequently in negotiations in all three cultures—may be part of the explanation. Indeed, in careful studies of conversational patterns of Americans negotiating with Japanese, the Americans seem to fill the silent periods and do most of the talking. These results suggest that American negotiators must take special care to keep their mouths shut and let foreign counterparts give them information.

Exchanging information across language barriers can be quite difficult as well. Most of us understand about 80 to 90 percent of what our same-culture spouses or roommates say—that means 10 to 20 percent is misunderstood or misheard. That latter percentage goes up dramatically when someone is speaking a second language, no matter the fluency levels or length of acquaintance. And when the second language capability is limited, entire conversations may be totally misunderstood. Using multiple communication channels during presentations—writing, exhibits, speaking, repetition—works to minimize the inevitable errors.

In many cultures negative feedback is very difficult to obtain. In high-context cultures such as Mexico and Japan, speakers are reluctant to voice objections lest they damage the all-important personal relationships. Some languages themselves are by nature indirect and indefinite. English is relatively clear, but translations from languages like Japanese can leave much to be understood. In more collectivistic cultures like China, negotiators may be reluctant to

---

[34]Trust is a key negotiation concept that is receiving growing attention in diverse areas. See Alaka N. Rao, Jone L. Pearce, and Katherine Xin, "Governments, Reciprocal Exchange, and Trust among Business Associates," *Journal of International Business Studies* 36, no. 1 (2005), pp. 104–118; on the chemical basis of trust, see Michael Kosfeld, Markus Heinrichs, Paul J. Zak, Urs Fischbacher, and Ernst Fehr, "Oxytocin Increases Trust in Humans," *Nature* 435 (June 2005), pp. 673–676.

CROSSING BORDERS 19.5 | Fishing for Business in Brazil

How important is nontask sounding? Consider this description about an American banker's meeting in Brazil, as told by an observer.

Introductions were made. The talk began with the usual "How do you like Rio?" questions—Have you been to Ipanema, Copacabana, Corcovado, etc? There was also talk about the flight down from New York. After about five minutes of this chatting, the senior American quite conspicuously glanced at his watch, and then asked his client what he knew about the bank's new services.

"A little," responded the Brazilian. The senior American whipped a brochure out of his briefcase, opened it on the desk in front of the client, and began his sales pitch.

After about three minutes of "fewer forms, electronic transfers, and reducing accounts receivables," the Brazilian jumped back in, "Yes, that should make us more competitive . . . and competition is important here in Brazil. In fact, have you been following the World Cup *fútbol* (soccer) matches recently? Great games." And so the reel began to whir, paying out that monofilament line, right there in that hot high-rise office.

After a few minutes' dissertation on the local *fútbol* teams, Pélé, and why *fútbol* isn't popular in the United States, the American started to try to crank the Brazilian back in. The first signal was the long look at his watch, then the interruption, "Perhaps we can get back to the new services we have to offer."

The Brazilian did get reeled back into the subject of the sale for a couple of minutes, but then the reel started to sing again. This time he went from efficient banking transactions to the nuances of the Brazilian financial system to the Brazilian economy. Pretty soon we were all talking about the world economy and making predictions about the U.S. presidential elections.

Another look at his Rolex, and the American started this little "sport fishing" ritual all over again. From my perspective (I wasn't investing time and money toward the success of this activity), this all seemed pretty funny. Every time the American VP looked at his watch during the next 45 minutes, I had to bite my cheeks to keep from laughing out loud. He never did get to page two of his brochure. The Brazilian just wasn't interested in talking business with someone he didn't know pretty well.

Source: Reprinted from John L. Graham, *International Business Negotiations*, copyright 1996, pp. 69–91, with permission from Elsevier Science; also see Philip R. Harris and Robert T. Moran, *Managing Cultural Differences* (Houston: Gulf Publishing, 2000).

speak for the decision-making group they represent, or they may not even know how the group feels about a particular proposal. All such problems suggest the importance of having natives of customer countries on your negotiation team and of spending extra time in business and informal entertainment settings trying to understand better the information provided by foreign clients and partners. Conversely, low-context German executives often complain that American presentations include too much "fluff"—they are interested in copious information only, not the hyperbole and hedges so common in American speech. Negative feedback from Germans can seem brutally frank to higher-context Americans.

A final point of potential conflict in information exchange has to do with first offers. Price padding varies across cultures, and Americans' first offers tend to come in relatively close to what they really want. "A million dollars is the goal, let's start at $1.2 million" seems about right to most Americans. Implicit in such a first offer is the hope that things will get done quickly. Americans do not expect to move far from first offers. Negotiators in many other countries do not share the goal of finishing quickly, however. In places like China, Brazil, or Spain, the expectation is for a relatively longer period of haggling, and first offers are more aggressive to reflect these expectations. "If the goal is one million, we better start at two," makes sense there. Americans react to such aggressive first offers in one of two ways: They either laugh or get mad. And when foreign counterparts' second offers reflect deep discounts, Americans' ire increases.

A good example of this problem regards an American CEO shopping for a European plant site. When he selected a $20 million plot in Ireland, the Spanish real estate developer he had visited earlier called wondering why the American had not asked for a lower price for the Madrid site before choosing Dublin. He told the Spaniard that his first offer "wasn't even in the ballpark." He wasn't laughing when the Spaniard then offered to beat the Irish price. In fact, the American executive was quite mad. A potentially good deal was forgone because of different expectations about first offers. Yes, numbers were exchanged, but information was not. Aggressive first offers made by foreigners should be met with questions, not anger.

Persuasion.   In Japan, a clear separation does not exist between task-related information exchange and persuasion. The two stages tend to blend together as each side defines and refines its needs and preferences. Much time is spent in the task-related exchange of information, leaving little to "argue" about during the persuasion stage. Conversely, Americans tend to lay their cards on the table and hurry through the information exchange to persuasion. After all, the persuasion is the heart of the matter. Why hold a meeting unless someone's mind is to be changed? A key aspect of sales training in the United States is "handling objections." So the goal in information exchange among Americans is to quickly get those objections out in the open so they can be handled.

This handling can mean providing clients with more information. It can also mean getting mean. As suggested by Exhibit 19.2, Americans make threats and issue warnings in negotiations.[35] They do not use such tactics often, but negotiators in many other cultures use such tactics even less frequently and in different circumstances. For example, notice how infrequently the Mexicans and English-speaking Canadians used threats and warnings in the simulated negotiations. Others have found Filipino and Chinese negotiators to use a less aggressive approach than Americans.[36] Indeed, in Thailand or China the use of such aggressive negotiation tactics can result in the loss of face and the destruction of important personal relationships. Such tough tactics may be used in Japan, but by buyers only and usually only in informal circumstances—not at the formal negotiation table. Americans also get mad during negotiations and express emotions that may be completely inappropriate in foreign countries. Such emotional outbursts may be seen as infantile or even barbaric behavior in places like Hong Kong and Bangkok.

You want him on your side! Banana salespeople such as this fellow in Agra, India, are known worldwide for their negotiation skills—they're hawking a perishable product that shows the wear. In Japan they even have a negotiation strategy named for them. That is, outrageously high first offers are derogated as *"banana no tataki uri,"* the banana sale approach.

The most powerful persuasive tactic is actually asking more questions. Foreign counterparts can be politely asked to explain why they must have delivery in two months or why they must have a 10 percent discount. Chester Karrass, in his still useful book *The Negotiation Game,*[37] suggests that it is "smart to be a little dumb" in business negotiations. Repeat questions; for example, "I didn't completely understand what you meant—can you please explain that again?" If clients or potential business partners have good answers, then perhaps a compromise on the issue is best. Often, however, under close and repeated scrutiny their answers are not very good. When their weak position is exposed, they are obliged to concede. Questions can elicit key information, being the most powerful yet passive persuasive device. Indeed, the use of questions is a favored Japanese tactic, one they use with great effect on Americans.

---

[35]For more details see Deborah A. Cai and Edward L. Fink, "Conflict Style Differences between Individualists and Collectivists," *Communication Monographs*, March 1, 2002, pp. 67–75.

[36]X. Michael Song, Jinhong Xie, and Barbara Dyer, "Antecedents and Consequences of Marketing Managers' Conflict Handling Procedures," *Journal of Marketing* 64 (January 2000), pp. 50–66; Alma Mintu-Wimsatt and Julie B. Gassenheimer, "The Moderating Effects of Cultural Context in Buyer–Seller Negotiation," *Journal of Personal Selling & Sales Management* 20, no. 1 (Winter 2000), pp. 1–9.

[37]Chester Karrass, *The Negotiation Game* (New York: Crowell, 1970).

Third parties and informal channels of communication are the indispensable media of persuasion in many countries, particularly the more relationship-oriented ones. Meetings in restaurants or meetings with references and mutual friends who originally provided introductions may be used to handle difficult problems with partners in other countries. The value of such informal settings and trusted intermediaries is greatest when problems are emotion laden. They provide a means for simultaneously delivering difficult messages and saving face. Although American managers may eschew such "behind the scenes" approaches, they are standard practice in many countries.

Concessions and Agreement.   Comments made previously about the importance of writing down concession-making strategies and understanding differences in decision-making styles—sequential versus holistic—are pertinent here. Americans often make concessions early, expecting foreign counterparts to reciprocate. However, in many cultures no concessions are made until the end of the negotiations. Americans often get frustrated and express anger when foreign clients and partners are simply following a different approach to concession making, one that can also work quite well when both sides understand what is going on.

After Negotiations   Contracts between American firms are often longer than 100 pages and include carefully worded clauses regarding every aspect of the agreement. American lawyers go to great lengths to protect their companies against all circumstances, contingencies, and actions of the other party. The best contracts are written so tightly that the other party would not think of going to court to challenge any provision. The American adversarial system requires such contracts.

In most other countries, particularly the relationship-oriented ones, legal systems are not depended upon to settle disputes. Indeed, the term *disputes* does not reflect how a business relationship should work. Each side should be concerned about mutual benefits of the relationship and therefore should consider the interests of the other. Consequently, in places like Japan written contracts are very short—two to three pages—are purposely loosely written, and primarily contain comments on principles of the relationship. From the Japanese point of view, the American emphasis on tight contracts is tantamount to planning the divorce before the wedding.

In other relationship-oriented countries, such as China, contracts are more a description of what business partners view their respective responsibilities to be. For complicated business relationships they may be quite long and detailed. However, their purpose is different from the American understanding. When circumstances change, then responsibilities must also be adjusted, despite the provisions of the signed contract. The notion of enforcing a contract in China makes little sense.

Informality being a way of life in the United States, even the largest contracts between companies are often sent through the mail for signature. In America, ceremony is considered a waste of time and money. But when a major agreement is reached with foreign companies, their executives may expect a formal signing ceremony involving CEOs of the respective companies. American companies are wise to accommodate such expectations.

Tung Chee Hwa, Chief Executive of the Hong Kong Special Administrative Region, consummated the deal with the Mouse for Asia's new Walt Disney World, that opened in 2005. *(AP/Wide World Photos)*

Finally, follow-up communications are an important part of business negotiations with partners and clients from most foreign countries. Particularly in high-context cultures, where personal relationships are crucial, high-level executives must stay in touch with their counterparts. Letters, pictures, and mutual visits remain important long after contracts are signed. Indeed, warm relationships at the top often prove to be the best medicine for any problems that may arise in the future.

Conclusions

Despite the litany of potential pitfalls facing international negotiators, things are getting better. The stereotypes of American managers as "innocents abroad" or cowboys are becoming less accurate. Likewise, we hope it is obvious that the stereotypes of the reticent Japanese or the pushy Brazilian evinced in the chapter may no longer hold so true. Experience levels are going up worldwide, and individual personalities are important. So you can find talkative Japanese, quiet Brazilians, and effective American negotiators. But culture still does, and always will, count. We hope that it is fast becoming the natural behavior of American managers to take culture into account.

English author Rudyard Kipling said some one hundred years ago: "Oh, East is East, and West is West, and never the twain shall meet." Since then most have imbued his words with an undeserved pessimism. Some even wrongly say he was wrong.[38] The problem is that not many have bothered to read his entire poem, *The Ballad of East and West:*

> Oh, East is East, and West is West, and never the twain shall meet,
> Till Earth and Sky stand presently at God's great Judgment Seat;
> But there is neither East nor West, border, nor breed, nor birth,
> When two strong men stand face to face, though they come from the ends of the earth!

The poem can stand some editing for these more modern times. It should include the other directions—North is North and South is South. And the last line properly should read, "When two strong *people* stand face to face." But Kipling's positive sentiment remains. Differences between countries and cultures, no matter how difficult, can be worked out when people talk to each other in face-to-face settings. Kipling rightly places the responsibility for international cooperation not on companies or governments, but instead directly on the shoulders of individual managers, present and future, like you. Work hard!

---

[38]Michael Elliot, "Killing off Kipling," *Newsweek*, December 29, 1977, pp. 52–55.

Summary

Because styles of business negotiations vary substantially around the world, it is important to take cultural differences into account when meeting clients, customers, and business partners across the international negotiation table. In addition to cultural factors, negotiators' personalities and backgrounds also influence their behavior. Great care should be taken to get to know the individuals who represent client and customer companies. Cultural stereotypes can be quite misleading.

Four kinds of problems frequently arise during international business negotiations—problems at the level of language, nonverbal behaviors, values, and thinking and decision-making processes. Foreign-language skills are an essential tool of the international negotiator. Nonverbal behaviors vary dramatically across cultures, and because their influence is often below our level of awareness, problems at this level can be serious. Whereas most Americans value objectivity, competitiveness, equality, and punctuality, many foreign executives may not. As for thinking and decision making, Western business executives tend to address complex negotiations by breaking deals down into smaller issues and settling them sequentially; in many Eastern cultures a more holistic approach is taken in discussions.

Much care must be taken in selecting negotiation teams to represent companies in meetings with foreigners. Listening skills, influence at headquarters, and a willingness to use team assistance are important negotiator traits. Americans should be careful to try to match foreign negotiation teams in both numbers and seniority. The importance of cross-cultural training and investments in careful preparations cannot be overstated. Situational factors such as the location for meetings and the time allowed must also be carefully considered and managed.

All around the world business negotiations involve four steps: nontask sounding, task-related information exchange, persuasion, and concessions and agreement. The time spent on each step can vary considerably from country to country. Americans spend little time on nontask sounding or getting to know foreign counterparts. Particularly in relationship-oriented cultures, it is important to let the customers bring up business when they feel comfortable with the personal relationship. Task-related information goes quickly in the United States as well. In other countries, such as Japan, the most time is spent on the second stage, and careful understandings of partners are focused upon. Persuasion is the most important part of negotiations from the American perspective. Aggressive persuasive tactics (threats and warnings) are used frequently. Such persuasive tactics, although they may work well in some cultures, will cause serious problems in others. Finally, because Americans tend to be deal oriented, more care will have to be taken in follow-up communications with foreign clients and partners who put more emphasis on long-term business relationships.

Questions

1. Define the following terms:

   BATNA
   nontask sounding

   task-related information exchange

2. Why can cultural stereotypes be dangerous? Give some examples.

3. List three ways that culture influences negotiation behavior.

4. Describe the kinds of problems that usually come up during international business negotiations.

5. Why are foreign-language skills important for international negotiators?

6. Describe three cultural differences in nonverbal behaviors and explain how they might cause problems in international business negotiations.

7. Why is time an important consideration in international business negotiations?

8. What can be different about how a Japanese manager might address a complex negotiation compared with an American negotiator?

9. What are the most important considerations in selecting a negotiation team? Give examples.

10. What kinds of training are most useful for international business negotiators?

11. Name three aspects of negotiation situations that might be manipulated before talks begin. Suggest how this might be done.

12. Explain why Americans spend so little time on nontask sounding and Brazilians so much.

13. Why is it difficult to get negative feedback from counterparts in many foreign countries? Give examples.

14. Why won't getting mad work in Mexico or Japan?

15. Why are questions the most useful persuasive tactic?

country notebook

THE COUNTRY NOTEBOOK—A GUIDE FOR DEVELOPING A MARKETING PLAN

THE COUNTRY NOTEBOOK OUTLINE

Cultural Analysis

Economic Analysis

Market Audit and Competititve Market Analysis

Preliminary Marketing Plan

The first stage in the planning process is a preliminary country analysis. The marketer needs basic information to evaluate a country market's potential, identify problems that would eliminate a country from further consideration, identify aspects of the country's environment that need further study, evaluate the components of the marketing mix for possible adaptation, and develop a strategic marketing plan. One further use of the information collected in the preliminary analysis is as a basis for a country notebook.

Many companies, large and small, have a *country notebook* for each country in which they do business. The country notebook contains information a marketer should be aware of when making decisions involving a specific country market. As new information is collected, the country notebook is continually updated by the country or product manager. Whenever a marketing decision is made involving a country, the country notebook is the first database consulted. New-product introductions, changes in advertising programs, and other marketing program decisions begin with the country notebook. It also serves as a quick introduction for new personnel assuming responsibility for a country market.

This section presents four separate guidelines for collection and analysis of market data and preparation of a country notebook: (1) guideline for cultural analysis, (2) guideline for economic analysis, (3) guideline for market audit and competitive analysis, and (4) guideline for preliminary marketing plan. These guidelines suggest the kinds of information a marketer can gather to enhance planning.

The points in each of the guidelines are general. They are designed to provide direction to areas to explore for relevant data. In each guideline, specific points must be adapted to reflect a company's products. The decision as to the appropriateness of specific data and the depth of coverage depends on company objectives, product characteristics, and the country market. Some points in the guidelines are unimportant for some countries or some products and should be ignored. Preceding chapters of this book provide specific content suggestions for the topics in each guideline.

I. Cultural Analysis

The data suggested in the cultural analysis include information that helps the marketer make market planning decisions. However, its application extends beyond product and market analysis to being an important source of information for someone interested in understanding business customs and other important cultural features of the country.

The information in this analysis must be more than a collection of facts. Whoever is responsible for the preparation of this material should attempt to interpret the meaning of cultural information. That is, how does the information help in understanding the effect on the market? For example, the fact that almost all the populations of Italy and Mexico are Catholic is an interesting statistic but not nearly as useful as understanding the effect of Catholicism on values, beliefs, and other aspects of market behavior. Furthermore, even though both countries are predominantly Catholic, the influence of their individual and unique interpretation and practice of Catholicism can result in important differences in market behavior.

Guideline

I. Introduction

Include short profiles of the company, the product to be exported, and the country with which you wish to trade.

II. Brief discussion of the country's relevant history

III. Geographical setting

 A. Location

 B. Climate

 C. Topography

IV. Social institutions

 A. Family

 1. The nuclear family

 2. The extended family

     3. Dynamics of the family
       a. Parental roles
       b. Marriage and courtship
     4. Female/male roles (changing or static?)
  B. Education
     1. The role of education in society
       a. Primary education (quality, levels of development, etc.)
       b. Secondary education (quality, levels of development, etc.)
       c. Higher education (quality, levels of development, etc.)
     2. Literacy rates
  C. Political system
     1. Political structure
     2. Political parties
     3. Stability of government
     4. Special taxes
     5. Role of local government
  D. Legal system
     1. Organization of the judiciary system
     2. Code, common, socialist, or Islamic-law country?
     3. Participation in patents, trademarks, and other conventions
  E. Social organizations
     1. Group behavior
     2. Social classes
     3. Clubs, other organizations
     4. Race, ethnicity, and subcultures
  F. Business customs and practices
V. Religion and aesthetics
  A. Religion and other belief systems
     1. Orthodox doctrines and structures
     2. Relationship with the people
     3. Which religions are prominent?
     4. Membership of each religion
     5. Any powerful or influential cults?
  B. Aesthetics
     1. Visual arts (fine arts, plastics, graphics, public art, colors, etc.)
     2. Music
     3. Drama, ballet, and other performing arts
     4. Folklore and relevant symbols
VI. Living conditions
  A. Diet and nutrition
     1. Meat and vegetable consumption rates
     2. Typical meals
     3. Malnutrition rates
     4. Foods available
  B. Housing
     1. Types of housing available
     2. Do most people own or rent?
     3. Do most people live in one-family dwellings or with other families?
  C. Clothing
     1. National dress
     2. Types of clothing worn at work
  D. Recreation, sports, and other leisure activities
     1. Types available and in demand
     2. Percentage of income spent on such activities
  E. Social security
  F. Health care

VII. Language
    A. Official language(s)
    B. Spoken versus written language(s)
    C. Dialects
VIII. Executive summary

After completing all of the other sections, prepare a *two-page* (maximum length) summary of the major points and place it at the front of the report. The purpose of an executive summary is to give the reader a brief glance at the critical points of your report. Those aspects of the culture a reader should know to do business in the country but would not be expected to know or would find different based on his or her SRC should be included in this summary.

IX. Sources of information
 X. Appendixes

II. Economic Analysis

The reader may find the data collected for the economic analysis guideline are more straightforward than for the cultural analysis guideline. There are two broad categories of information in this guideline: general economic data that serve as a basis for an evaluation of the economic soundness of a country, and information on channels of distribution and media availability. As mentioned earlier, the guideline focuses only on broad categories of data and must be adapted to particular company and product needs.

Guideline

  I. Introduction
 II. Population
    A. Total
       1. Growth rates
       2. Number of live births
       3. Birthrates
    B. Distribution of population
       1. Age
       2. Sex
       3. Geographic areas (urban, suburban, and rural density and concentration)
       4. Migration rates and patterns
       5. Ethnic groups
 III. Economic statistics and activity
    A. Gross national product (GNP or GDP)
       1. Total
       2. Rate of growth (real GNP or GDP)
    B. Personal income per capita
    C. Average family income
    D. Distribution of wealth
       1. Income classes
       2. Proportion of the population in each class
       3. Is the distribution distorted?
    E. Minerals and resources
    F. Surface transportation
       1. Modes
       2. Availability
       3. Usage rates
       4. Ports
    G. Communication systems
       1. Types
       2. Availability
       3. Usage rates

H. Working conditions
   1. Employer–employee relations
   2. Employee participation
   3. Salaries and benefits
I. Principal industries
   1. What proportion of the GNP does each industry contribute?
   2. Ratio of private to publicly owned industries
J. Foreign investment
   1. Opportunities?
   2. Which industries?
K. International trade statistics
   1. Major exports
      a. Dollar value
      b. Trends
   2. Major imports
      a. Dollar value
      b. Trends
   3. Balance-of-payments situation
      a. Surplus or deficit?
      b. Recent trends
   4. Exchange rates
      a. Single or multiple exchange rates?
      b. Current rate of exchange
      c. Trends
L. Trade restrictions
   1. Embargoes
   2. Quotas
   3. Import taxes
   4. Tariffs
   5. Licensing
   6. Customs duties
M. Extent of economic activity not included in cash income activities
   1. Countertrades
      a. Products generally offered for countertrading
      b. Types of countertrades requested (i.e., barter, counterpurchase, etc.)
   2. Foreign aid received
N. Labor force
   1. Size
   2. Unemployment rates
O. Inflation rates
IV. Developments in science and technology
   A. Current technology available (computers, machinery, tools, etc.)
   B. Percentage of GNP invested in research and development
   C. Technological skills of the labor force and general population
V. Channels of distribution (macro analysis)
   This section reports data on all channel middlemen available within the market. Later, you will select a specific channel as part of your distribution strategy.
   A. Retailers
      1. Number of retailers
      2. Typical size of retail outlets
      3. Customary markup for various classes of goods
      4. Methods of operation (cash/credit)
      5. Scale of operation (large/small)
      6. Role of chain stores, department stores, and specialty shops

      B. Wholesale middlemen
        1. Number and size
        2. Customary markup for various classes of goods
        3. Method of operation (cash/credit)
      C. Import/export agents
      D. Warehousing
      E. Penetration of urban and rural markets
  VI. Media
      This section reports data on all media available within the country or market.
      Later, you will select specific media as part of the promotional mix and strategy.
      A. Availability of media
      B. Costs
        1. Television
        2. Radio
        3. Print
        4. Other media (cinema, outdoor, etc.)
      C. Agency assistance
      D. Coverage of various media
      E. Percentage of population reached by each medium
 VII. Executive summary
      After completing the research for this report, prepare a two-page (maximum)
      summary of the major economic points and place it at the front
VIII. Sources of information
  IX. Appendixes

III. Market Audit and Competitive Market Analysis

Of the guidelines presented, this is the most product or brand specific. Information in the other guidelines is general in nature, focusing on product categories, whereas data in this guideline are brand specific and are used to determine competitive market conditions and market potential.

Two different components of the planning process are reflected in this guideline. Information in Parts I and II, Cultural Analysis and Economic Analysis, serve as the basis for an evaluation of the product or brand in a specific country market. Information in this guideline provides an estimate of market potential and an evaluation of the strengths and weaknesses of competitive marketing efforts. The data generated in this step are used to determine the extent of adaptation of the company's marketing mix necessary for successful market entry and to develop the final step, the action plan.

The detailed information needed to complete this guideline is not necessarily available without conducting a thorough marketing research investigation. Thus another purpose of this part of the country notebook is to identify the correct questions to ask in a formal market study.

Guideline

  I. Introduction
 II. The product
      A. Evaluate the product as an innovation as it is perceived by the intended market
        1. Relative advantage
        2. Compatibility
        3. Complexity
        4. Trialability
        5. Observability
      B. Major problems and resistances to product acceptance based on the preceding
        evaluation
III. The market
      A. Describe the market(s) in which the product is to be sold
        1. Geographical region(s)
        2. Forms of transportation and communication available in that (those) region(s)

    3. Consumer buying habits
       a. Product-use patterns
       b. Product feature preferences
       c. Shopping habits
    4. Distribution of the product
       a. Typical retail outlets
       b. Product sales by other middlemen
    5. Advertising and promotion
       a. Advertising media usually used to reach your target market(s)
       b. Sales promotions customarily used (sampling, coupons, etc.)
    6. Pricing strategy
       a. Customary markups
       b. Types of discounts available
  B. Compare and contrast your product and the competition's product(s)
    1. Competitor's product(s)
       a. Brand name
       b. Features
       c. Package
    2. Competitor's prices
    3. Competitor's promotion and advertising methods
    4. Competitor's distribution channels
  C. Market size
    1. Estimated industry sales for the planning year
    2. Estimated sales for your company for the planning year
  D. Government participation in the marketplace
    1. Agencies that can help you
    2. Regulations you must follow
IV. Executive summary
  Based on your analysis of the market, briefly summarize (two-page maximum) the major problems and opportunities requiring attention in your marketing mix, and place the summary at the front of the report.
V. Sources of information
VI. Appendixes

IV. Preliminary Marketing Plan

Information gathered in guidelines I through III serves as the basis for developing a marketing plan for your product or brand in a target market. How the problems and opportunities that surfaced in the preceding steps are overcome or exploited to produce maximum sales and profits are presented here. The action plan reflects, in your judgment, the most effective means of marketing your product in a country market. Budgets, expected profits and losses, and additional resources necessary to implement the proposed plan are also presented.

Guideline

I. The marketing plan
  A. Marketing objectives
    1. Target market(s) (specific description of the market)
    2. Expected sales year 20—
    3. Profit expectations year 20—
    4. Market penetration and coverage
  B. Product adaptation or modification—Using the product component model as your guide, indicate how your product can be adapted for the market.
    1. Core component
    2. Packaging component
    3. Support services component

   C. Promotion mix
      1. Advertising
         a. Objectives
         b. Media mix
         c. Message
         d. Costs
      2. Sales promotions
         a. Objectives
         b. Coupons
         c. Premiums
         d. Costs
      3. Personal selling
      4. Other promotional methods
   D. Distribution: From origin to destination
      1. Port selection
         a. Origin port
         b. Destination port
      2. Mode selection: Advantages/disadvantages of each mode
         a. Railroads
         b. Air carriers
         c. Ocean carriers
         d. Motor carriers
      3. Packing
         a. Marking and labeling regulations
         b. Containerization
         c. Costs
      4. Documentation required
         a. Bill of lading
         b. Dock receipt
         c. Air bill
         d. Commercial invoice
         e. Pro forma invoice
         f. Shipper's export declaration
         g. Statement of origin
         h. Special documentation
      5. Insurance claims
      6. Freight forwarder

         If your company does not have a transportation or traffic management department, then consider using a freight forwarder. There are distinct advantages and disadvantages to hiring one.

   E. Channels of distribution (micro analysis)

     This section presents details about the specific types of distribution in your marketing plan.

      1. Retailers
         a. Type and number of retail stores
         b. Retail markups for products in each type of retail store
         c. Methods of operation for each type (cash/credit)
         d. Scale of operation for each type (small/large)
      2. Wholesale middlemen
         a. Type and number of wholesale middlemen
         b. Markup for class of products by each type
         c. Methods of operation for each type (cash/credit)
         d. Scale of operation (small/large)

      3. Import/export agents
      4. Warehousing
        a. Type
        b. Location
   F. Price determination
      1. Cost of the shipment of goods
      2. Transportation costs
      3. Handling expenses
        a. Pier charges
        b. Wharfage fees
        c. Loading and unloading charges
      4. Insurance costs
      5. Customs duties
      6. Import taxes and value-added tax
      7. Wholesale and retail markups and discounts
      8. Company's gross margins
      9. Retail price
   G. Terms of sale
      1. EX works, FOB, FAS, C&F, CIF
      2. Advantages/disadvantages of each
   H. Methods of payment
      1. Cash in advance
      2. Open accounts
      3. Consignment sales
      4. Sight, time, or date drafts
      5. Letters of credit
II. Pro forma financial statements and budgets
   A. Marketing budget
      1. Selling expense
      2. Advertising/promotion expense
      3. Distribution expense
      4. Product cost
      5. Other costs
   B. Pro forma annual profit and loss statement (first year and fifth year)
III. Resource requirements
   A. Finances
   B. Personnel
   C. Production capacity
IV. Executive summary

After completing the research for this report, prepare a two-page (maximum) summary of the major points of your successful marketing plan, and place it at the front of the report.

 V. Sources of information
VI. Appendixes

The intricacies of international operations and the complexity of the environment within which the international marketer must operate create an extraordinary demand for information. When operating in foreign markets, the need for thorough information as a substitute for uninformed opinion is equally important as it is in domestic marketing. Sources of information needed to develop the country notebook and answer other marketing questions are discussed in Chapter 8 and its appendix.

Summary

Market-oriented firms build strategic market plans around company objectives, markets, and the competitive environment. Planning for marketing can be complicated even for one country, but when a company is doing business internationally, the problems are multiplied. Company objectives may vary from market to market and from time to time; the structure of international markets also changes periodically and from country to country; and the competitive, governmental, and economic parameters affecting market planning are in a constant state of flux. These variations require international marketing executives to be especially flexible and creative in their approach to strategic marketing planning.

cases 1

AN OVERVIEW

OUTLINE OF CASES

1-1 Starbucks—Going Global Fast

1-2 Nestlé: The Infant Formula Controversy

1-3 Coke and Pepsi Learn to Compete in India

1-4 Marketing Microwave Ovens to a New Market Segment

CASE 1–1 Starbucks—Going Global Fast

The Starbucks coffee shop on Sixth Avenue and Pine Street in downtown Seattle sits serene and orderly, as unremarkable as any other in the chain bought 15 years ago by entrepreneur Howard Schultz. A little less than three years ago, however, the quiet storefront made front pages around the world. During the World Trade Organization talks in November, 1999, protesters flooded Seattle's streets, and among their targets was Starbucks, a symbol, to them, of free-market capitalism run amok, another multinational out to blanket the earth. Amid the crowds of protesters and riot police were black-masked anarchists who trashed the store, leaving its windows smashed and its tasteful green-and-white decor smelling of tear gas instead of espresso. Says an angry Schultz: "It's hurtful. I think people are ill-informed. It's very difficult to protest against a can of Coke, a bottle of Pepsi, or a can of Folgers. Starbucks is both this ubiquitous brand and a place where you can go and break a window. You can't break a can of Coke."

The store was quickly repaired, and the protesters have scattered to other cities. Yet cup by cup, Starbucks really is caffeinating the world, its green-and-white emblem beckoning to consumers on three continents. In 1999, Starbucks Corp. had 281 stores abroad. Today, it has about 1,200—and it's still in the early stages of a plan to colonize the globe. If the protesters were wrong in their tactics, they weren't wrong about Starbucks' ambitions. They were just early.

The story of how Schultz & Co. transformed a pedestrian commodity into an upscale consumer accessory has a fairy-tale quality. Starbucks has grown from 17 coffee shops in Seattle 15 years ago to 5,689 outlets in 28 countries. Sales have climbed an average of 20 percent annually since the company went public 10 years ago, to $2.6 billion in 2001, while profits bounded ahead an average of 30 percent per year, hitting $181.2 million last year. And the momentum continues. In the first three quarters of this fiscal year, sales climbed 24 percent, year to year, to $2.4 billion, while profits, excluding onetime charges and capital gains, rose 25 percent, to $159.5 million.

Moreover, the Starbucks name and image connect with millions of consumers around the globe. It was one of the fastest-growing brands in a *BusinessWeek* survey of the top 100 global brands published August 5. At a time when one corporate star after another has crashed to earth, brought down by revelations of earnings misstatements, executive greed, or worse, Starbucks hasn't faltered. The company confidently predicts up to 25 percent annual sales and earnings growth this year. On Wall Street, Starbucks is the last great growth story. Its stock, including four splits, has soared more than 2,200 percent over the past decade, surpassing Wal-Mart, General Electric, PepsiCo, Coca-Cola, Microsoft, and IBM in total return. Now at $21, it is hovering near its all-time high of $23 in July, before the overall market drop.

And after a slowdown last fall and winter, when consumers seemed to draw inward after September 11, Starbucks is rocketing ahead once again. Sales in stores open at least 13 months grew by 6 percent in the 43 weeks through July 28, and the company predicts monthly same-store sales gains as high as 7 percent through the end of this fiscal year. That's below the 9 percent growth rate in

2000, but investors seem encouraged. "We're going to see a lot more growth," says Jerome A. Castellini, president of Chicago-based CastleArk Management, which controls about 300,000 Starbucks shares. "The stock is on a run."

But how long can that run last? Already, Schultz's team is hard-pressed to grind out new profits in a home market that is quickly becoming saturated. Amazingly, with 4,247 stores scattered across the United States and Canada, there are still eight states in the United States with no Starbucks stores. Frappuccino-free cities include Butte, Mont., and Fargo, N.D. But big cities, affluent suburbs, and shopping malls are full to the brim. In coffee-crazed Seattle, there is a Starbucks outlet for every 9,400 people, and the company considers that the upper limit of coffee-shop saturation. In Manhattan's 24 square miles, Starbucks has 124 cafés, with four more on the way this year. That's one for every 12,000 people—meaning that there could be room for even more stores. Given such concentration, it is likely to take annual same-store sales increases of 10 percent or more if the company is going to match its historic overall sales growth. That, as they might say at Starbucks, is a tall order to fill.

Indeed, the crowding of so many stores so close together has become a national joke, eliciting quips such as this headline in *The Onion,* a satirical publication: "A New Starbucks Opens in Rest-Room of Existing Starbucks." And even the company admits that while its practice of blanketing an area with stores helps achieve market dominance, it can cut sales at existing outlets. "We probably self-cannibalize our stores at a rate of 30 percent a year," Schultz says. Adds Lehman Brothers Inc. analyst Mitchell Speiser: "Starbucks is at a defining point in its growth. It's reaching a level that makes it harder and harder to grow, just due to the law of large numbers."

To duplicate the staggering returns of its first decade, Starbucks has no choice but to export its concept aggressively. Indeed, some analysts give Starbucks only two years at most before it saturates the U.S. market. The chain now operates 1,200 international outlets, from Beijing to Bristol. That leaves plenty of room to grow. Indeed, about 400 of its planned 1,200 new stores this year will be built overseas, representing a 35 percent increase in its foreign base. Starbucks expects to double the number of its stores worldwide, to 10,000 in three years. During the past 12 months, the chain has opened stores in Vienna, Zurich, Madrid, Berlin, and even in far-off Jakarta. Athens comes next. And within the next year, Starbucks plans to move into Mexico and Puerto Rico. But global expansion poses huge risks for Starbucks. For one thing, it makes less money on each overseas store because most of them are operated with local partners. While that makes it easier to start up on foreign turf, it reduces the company's share of the profits to only 20 percent to 50 percent.

Moreover, Starbucks must cope with some predictable challenges of becoming a mature company in the United States. After riding the wave of successful baby boomers through the '90s, the company faces an ominously hostile reception from its future consumers, the twenty- or thirtysomethings of Generation X. Not only are the activists among them turned off by the power and image of the well-known brand, but many others say that Starbucks' latte-sipping sophisticates and piped-in Kenny G music are a real turnoff. They don't feel wanted in a place that sells designer coffee at $3 a cup.

Even the thirst of loyalists for high-price coffee can't be taken for granted. Starbucks' growth over the past decade coincided with a remarkable surge in the economy. Consumer spending has continued strong in the downturn, but if that changes, those $3 lattes might be an easy place for people on a budget to cut back. Starbucks executives insist that won't happen, pointing out that even in the weeks following the terrorist attacks, same-store comparisons stayed positive while those of other retailers skidded.

Starbucks also faces slumping morale and employee burnout among its store managers and its once-cheery army of baristas. Stock options for part-timers in the restaurant business was a Starbucks innovation that once commanded awe and respect from its employees. But now, though employees are still paid better than comparable workers elsewhere—about $7 per hour—many regard the job as just another fast-food gig. Dissatisfaction over odd hours and low pay is affecting the quality of the normally sterling service and even the coffee itself, say some customers and employees. Frustrated store managers among the company's roughly 470 California stores sued Starbucks in 2001 for allegedly refusing to pay legally mandated overtime. Starbucks settled the suit for $18 million this past April, shaving $0.03 per share off an otherwise strong second quarter. However, the heart of the complaint—feeling overworked and underappreciated—doesn't seem to be going away.

To be sure, Starbucks has a lot going for it as it confronts the challenge of maintaining its growth. Nearly free of debt, it fuels expansion with internal cash flow. And Starbucks can maintain a tight grip on its image because stores are company-owned: There are no franchisees to get sloppy about running things. By relying on mystique and word-of-mouth, whether here or overseas, the company saves a bundle on marketing costs. Starbucks spends just $30 million annually on advertising, or roughly 1 percent of revenues, usually just for new flavors of coffee drinks in the summer and product launches, such as its new in-store Web service. Most consumer companies its size shell out upwards of $300 million per year. Moreover, unlike a McDonald's or a Gap Inc., two other retailers that rapidly grew in the United States, Starbucks has no nationwide competitor.

Starbucks also has a well-seasoned management team. Schultz, 49, stepped down as chief executive in 2000 to become chairman and chief global strategist. Orin Smith, 60, the company's numbers-cruncher, is now CEO and in charge of day-to-day operations. The head of North American operations is Howard Behar, 57, a retailing expert who returned last September, two years after retiring. The management trio is known as H2O, for Howard, Howard, and Orin.

Schultz remains the heart and soul of the operation. Raised in a Brooklyn public-housing project, he found his way to Starbucks, a tiny chain of Seattle coffee shops, as a marketing executive in the early '80s. The name came about when the original owners looked to Seattle history for inspiration and chose the moniker of an old mining camp: Starbo. Further refinement led to Starbucks, after the first mate in *Moby-Dick,* which they felt evoked the seafaring romance of the early coffee traders (hence the mermaid logo). Schultz got the idea for the modern Starbucks format while visiting a Milan coffee bar. He bought out his bosses in 1987 and began expanding. Today, Schultz has a net worth of about $700 million, including $400 million of company stock.

Starbucks has come light years from those humble beginnings, but Schultz and his team still think there's room to grow in the United States—even in communities where the chain already has dozens of stores. Clustering stores increases total revenue and market share, Smith argues, even when individual stores poach on each other's sales. The strategy works, he says, because of Starbucks' size. It is large enough to absorb losses at existing stores as new ones open up, and soon overall sales grow beyond what they would have with just one store. Meanwhile, it's cheaper to deliver to and manage stores located close together. And by clustering, Starbucks can quickly dominate a local market.

The company is still capable of designing and opening a store in 16 weeks or less and recouping the initial investment in three years. The stores may be oases of tranquility, but management's expansion tactics are something else. Take what critics call its "predatory real estate" strategy—paying more than market-rate rents to keep competitors out of a location. David C. Schomer, owner of Espresso Vivace in Seattle's hip Capitol Hill neighborhood, says Starbucks approached his landlord and offered to pay nearly double the rate to put a coffee shop in the same building. The landlord stuck with Schomer, who says: "It's a little disconcerting to know that someone is willing to pay twice the going rate." Another time, Starbucks and Tully's Coffee Corp., a Seattle-based coffee chain, were competing for a space in the city. Starbucks got the lease but vacated the premises before the term was up. Still, rather than let Tully's get the space, Starbucks decided to pay the rent on the empty store so its competitor could not move in. Schultz makes no apologies for the hardball tactics. "The real estate business in America is a very, very tough game," he says. "It's not for the faint of heart."

Still, the company's strategy could backfire. Not only will neighborhood activists and local businesses increasingly resent the tactics, but customers could also grow annoyed over having fewer choices. Moreover, analysts contend that Starbucks can maintain about 15 percent square-footage growth in the United States—equivalent to 550 new stores—for only about two more years. After that, it will have to depend on overseas growth to maintain an annual 20 percent revenue growth.

Starbucks was hoping to make up much of that growth with more sales of food and other noncoffee items, but has stumbled somewhat. In the late '90s, Schultz thought that offering $8 sandwiches, desserts, and CDs in his stores and selling packaged coffee in supermarkets would significantly boost sales. The specialty business now accounts for about 16 percent of sales, but growth has been less than expected. A healthy 19 percent this year, it's still far below the 38 percent growth rate of fiscal 2000. That suggests that while coffee can command high prices in a slump, food—at least at Starbucks—cannot. One of Behar's most important goals is to improve that record. For instance, the company now has a test program of serving hot breakfasts in 20 Seattle stores and may move to expand supermarket sales of whole beans.

What's more important for the bottom line, though, is that Starbucks has proven to be highly innovative in the way it sells its main course: coffee. In 800 locations it has installed automatic espresso machines to speed up service. And in November, it began offering prepaid Starbucks cards, priced from $5 to $500, which clerks swipe through a reader to deduct a sale. That, says the company, cuts transaction times in half. Starbucks has sold $70 million of the cards.

In early August, Starbucks launched Starbucks Express, its boldest experiment yet, which blends java, Web technology, and faster service. At about 60 stores in the Denver area, customers can pre-order and prepay for beverages and pastries via phone or on the Starbucks Express Web site. They just make the call or click the mouse before arriving at the store, and their beverage will be waiting—with their name printed on the cup. The company will decide in January on a national launch.

And Starbucks is bent on even more fundamental store changes. On August 21, it announced expansion of a high-speed wireless Internet service to about 1,200 Starbucks locations in North America and Europe. Partners in the project—which Starbucks calls the world's largest Wi-Fi network—include Mobile International, a wireless subsidiary of Deutsche Telekom, and Hewlett-Packard. Customers sit in a store and check e-mail, surf the Web, or download multimedia presentations without looking for connections or tripping over cords. They start with 24 hours of free wireless broadband before choosing from a variety of monthly subscription plans.

Starbucks executives hope such innovations will help surmount their toughest challenge in the home market: attracting the next generation of customers. Younger coffee drinkers already feel uncomfortable in the stores. The company knows that because it once had a group of twentysomethings hypnotized for a market study. When their defenses were down, out came the bad news. "They either can't afford to buy coffee at Starbucks, or the only peers they see are those working behind the counter," says Mark Barden, who conducted the research for the Hal Riney & Partners ad agency (now part of Publicis Worldwide) in San Francisco. One of the recurring themes the hypnosis brought out was a sense that "people like me aren't welcome here except to serve the yuppies," he says. Then there are those who just find the whole Starbucks scene a bit pretentious. Katie Kelleher, 22, a Chicago paralegal, is put off by Starbucks' Italian terminology of grande and venti for coffee sizes. She goes to Dunkin' Donuts, saying: "Small, medium, and large is fine for me."

As it expands, Starbucks faces another big risk: that of becoming a far less special place for its employees. For a company modeled around enthusiastic service, that could have dire consequences for both image and sales. During its growth spurt of the mid- to late-1990s, Starbucks had the lowest employee turnover rate of any restaurant or fast-food company, largely thanks to its then unheard-of policy of giving health insurance and modest stock options to part-timers making barely more than minimum wage.

Such perks are no longer enough to keep all the workers happy. Starbucks' pay doesn't come close to matching the workload it requires, complain some staff. Says Carrie Shay, a former store manager in West Hollywood, Calif.: "If I were making a decent living, I'd still be there." Shay, one of the plaintiffs in the suit against the company, says she earned $32,000 a year to run a store with 10 to 15 part-time employees. She hired employees, managed their schedules, and monitored the store's weekly profit-and-loss statement. But she was also expected to put in significant time behind the counter and had to sign an affidavit pledging to work up to 20 hours of overtime a week without extra pay—a requirement the company has dropped since the settlement. Smith says that Starbucks offers better pay, benefits, and training than comparable companies, while it encourages promotions from within.

For sure, employee discontent is far from the image Starbucks wants to project of relaxed workers cheerfully making cappuccinos. But perhaps it is inevitable. The business model calls for lots of low-wage workers. And the more people who are hired as Starbucks expands, the less they are apt to feel connected to the original mission of high service—bantering with customers and treating them like family. Robert J. Thompson, a professor of popular culture at Syracuse University, says of Starbucks: "It's turning out to be one of the great 21st century American success stories—complete with all the ambiguities."

Overseas, though, the whole Starbucks package seems new and, to many young people, still very cool. In Vienna, where Starbucks had a gala opening for its first Austrian store last December, Helmut Spudich, a business editor for the paper *Der Standard,* predicted that Starbucks would attract a younger crowd than the established cafés. "The coffeehouses in Vienna are nice, but they are old. Starbucks is considered hip," he says.

But if Starbucks can count on its youth appeal to win a welcome in new markets, such enthusiasm cannot be counted on indefinitely. In Japan, the company beat even its own bullish expectations, growing to 368 stores after opening its first in Tokyo in 1996. Affluent young Japanese women like Anna Kato, a 22-year-old Toyota Motor Corp. worker, loved the place. "I don't care if it costs more, as long as it tastes sweet," she says, sitting in the world's busiest Starbucks, in Tokyo's Shibuya district. Yet same-store sales growth has fallen in the past 10 months in Japan, Starbucks' top foreign market, as rivals offer similar fare. Add to that the depressed economy, and Starbucks Japan seems to be losing steam. Although it forecasts a 30 percent gain in net profit, to $8 million, for the year started in April, on record sales of $516 million, same-store sales are down 14 percent for the year ended in June. Meanwhile in England, Starbucks' second-biggest overseas market, with 310 stores, imitators are popping up left and right to steal market share.

Entering other big markets may be tougher yet. The French seem to be ready for Starbucks' sweeter taste, says Philippe Bloch, cofounder of Columbus Cafe, a Starbucks-like chain. But he wonders if the company can profitably cope with France's arcane regulations and generous labor benefits. And in Italy, the epicenter of European coffee culture, the notion that the locals will abandon their own 200,000 coffee bars en masse for Starbucks strikes many as ludicrous. For one, Italian coffee bars prosper by serving food as well as coffee, an area where Starbucks still struggles. Also, Italian coffee is cheaper than U.S. java and, say Italian purists, much better. Americans pay about $1.50 for an espresso. In northern Italy, the price is 67 cents; in the south, just 55 cents. Schultz insists that Starbucks will eventually come to Italy. It'll have a lot to prove when it does. Carlo Petrini, founder of the antiglobalization movement Slow Food, sniffs that Starbucks' "substances served in styrofoam" won't cut it. The cups are paper, of course. But the skepticism is real.

As Starbucks spreads out, Schultz will have to be increasingly sensitive to those cultural challenges. In December, for instance, he flew to Israel to meet with Foreign Secretary Shimon Peres and other Israeli officials to discuss the Middle East crisis. He won't divulge the nature of his discussions. But subsequently, at a Seattle synagogue, Schultz let the Palestinians have it. With Starbucks outlets already in Kuwait, Lebanon, Oman, Qatar, and Saudi Arabia, he created a mild uproar among Palestinian supporters. Schultz quickly backpedaled, saying that his words were taken out of context and asserting that he is "pro-peace" for both sides.

There are plenty more minefields ahead. So far, the Seattle coffee company has compiled an envious record of growth. But the giddy buzz of that initial expansion is wearing off. Now, Starbucks is waking up to the grande challenges faced by any corporation bent on becoming a global powerhouse.

Profit at Starbucks Coffee Japan fell 70 percent in the first nine months of the year because of growing competition from rival coffee chains. Sales at stores open more than one year fell 16 percent. The firm expects a loss for the full year.

In a 2005 bid to boost sales in its largest international market, Starbucks Corp. is expanding its business in Japan beyond cafes and into convenience stores with a line of chilled coffee in plastic cups. The move gives the Seattle-based company a chance to grab a chunk of Japan's $10 billion market for coffee sold in cans, bottles or vending machines, rather than made-to-order at cafés. It is a lucrative but fiercely competitive sector, but Starbucks, which has become a household name since opening its first Japanese store nine years ago, is betting on the power of its brand to propel sales of the new drinks.

Starbucks, working with Japanese beverage maker and distributor Suntory Ltd., is launching the drinks, called Starbucks Discoveries, here today, with plans to extend sales to a total of 10,000 stores in the coming weeks. Starbucks says it hasn't decided yet whether to launch the product nationwide. Tomorrow, the company also plans to start selling the product in Taiwan.

The Discoveries line is the company's first foray into the ready-to-drink market outside North America, where it sells a line of bottled and canned coffee. It also underscores Starbucks' determination to expand its presence in Asia by catering to local tastes. For instance, the new product comes in two variations—espresso and latte—that are less sweet than their U.S. counterparts, as the coffee maker developed them to suit Asian palates.

Starbucks officials said they hope to establish their product as the premium chilled cup brand, which, at 210 yen ($1.87), will be priced at the upper end of the category.

Starbucks faces steep competition. Japan's "chilled cup" market is teeming with rival products, including Starbucks lookalikes. One of the most popular brands, called Mt. Rainier, is emblazoned with a green circle logo that closely resembles that of Starbucks. Convenience stores also are packed with canned coffee drinks, including Coca-Cola Co.'s Georgia brand and brews with extra caffeine or made with gourmet coffee beans.

Starbucks Chairman Howard Schultz declined to speculate on exactly how much coffee Starbucks might sell through Japan's convenience stores. "We wouldn't be doing this if it wasn't important both strategically and economically," he said.

The company has no immediate plans to introduce the beverage in the United States, although it has in the past brought home products launched in Asia. A green tea frappuccino, first launched in Asia, was introduced in the United States and Canada this past summer, where company officials say it was well-received.

Starbucks has done well in Japan, although the road hasn't always been smooth. After cutting the ribbon on its first Japan store in 1996, the company began opening stores at a furious pace, and it now has 570. New shops attracted large crowds, but the effect wore off as the market became saturated. Sales began to slow, forcing the company to post a loss in Japan in the fiscal year ended March 2003.

The company has since returned to profitability, and for the fiscal year ended March 31 net profit jumped more than sixfold from the previous fiscal year to 1.17 billion yen. In August, it cleared another hurdle when sales at stores open at least 13 months rose from a year earlier for the first time in four years. It is focusing on continuing this trend by renovating stores and improving service.

Mr. Schultz says Japan is ripe for development, including further store openings. "The wind is at our back here," Mr. Schultz says.

QUESTIONS

As a guide use Exhibit 1.3 and its description in Chapter 1, and do the following:

1. Identify the controllable and uncontrollable elements that Starbucks has encountered in entering global markets.

2. What are the major sources of risk facing the company and discuss potential solutions.

3. Critique Starbucks' overall corporate strategy.

4. How might Starbucks improve profitability in Japan?

Visit www.starbucks.com for more information.

Sources: Stanley Holmes, Drake Bennett, Kate Carlisle, and Chester Dawson, "Planet Starbucks: To Keep Up the Growth It Must Go Global Quickly," *BusinessWeek*, December 9, 2002, pp. 100–110; Ken Belson, "Japan: Starbucks Profit Falls," *New York Times*, February 20, 2003, p. 1; and Ginny Parker Woods, "Starbucks Bets Drinks Will Jolt Japan Sales," *Asian Wall Street Journal*, September 27, 2005, p. A7.

CASE 1–2 Nestlé: The Infant Formula Controversy

Nestlé Alimentana of Vevey, Switzerland, one of the world's largest food-processing companies with worldwide sales of over $8 billion, has been the subject of an international boycott. For over 20 years, beginning with a Pan American Health Organization allegation, Nestlé has been directly or indirectly charged with involvement in the death of Third World infants. The charges revolve around the sale of infant feeding formula, which allegedly is the cause for mass deaths of babies in the Third World.

In 1974 a British journalist published a report that suggested that powdered-formula manufacturers contributed to the death of Third World infants by hard-selling their products to people incapable of using them properly. The 28-page report accused the industry of encouraging mothers to give up breast feeding and use powdered milk formulas. The report was later published by the Third World Working Group, a lobby in support of less-developed countries. The pamphlet was entitled "Nestlé Kills Babies," and accused Nestlé of unethical and immoral behavior.

Although there are several companies that market infant baby formula internationally, Nestlé received most of the attention. This incident raises several issues important to all multinational companies. Before addressing these issues, let's look more closely at the charges by the Infant Formula Action Coalition and others and the defense by Nestlé.

THE CHARGES

Most of the charges against infant formulas focus on the issue of whether advertising and marketing of such products have discouraged breast feeding among Third World mothers and have led to misuse of the products, thus contributing to infant malnutrition and death. Following are some of the charges made:

- A Peruvian nurse reported that formula had found its way to Amazon tribes deep in the jungles of northern Peru. There, where the only water comes from a highly contaminated river—which also serves as the local laundry and toilet—formula-fed babies came down with recurring attacks of diarrhea and vomiting.

- Throughout the Third World, many parents dilute the formula to stretch their supply. Some even believe the bottle itself has nutrient qualities and merely fill it with water. The result is extreme malnutrition.

- One doctor reported that in a rural area, one newborn male weighed 7 pounds. At four months of age, he weighed 5 pounds. His sister, aged 18 months, weighed 12 pounds, what one would expect a four-month-old baby to weigh. She later weighed only 8 pounds. The children had never been breast fed, and since birth their diets were basically bottle feeding. For a four-month-old baby, one can of formula should have lasted just under three days. The mother said that one can lasted two weeks to feed both children.

- In rural Mexico, the Philippines, Central America, and the whole of Africa, there has been a dramatic decrease in the incidence of breast feeding. Critics blame the decline largely on the intensive advertising and promotion of infant formula. Clever radio jingles extol the wonders of the "white man's powder that will make baby grow and glow." "Milk nurses" visit nursing mothers in hospitals and their homes and provide samples of formula. These activities encourage mothers to give up breast feeding and resort to bottle feeding because it is "the fashionable thing to do or because people are putting it to them that this is the thing to do."

THE DEFENSE

The following points are made in defense of the marketing of baby formula in Third World countries:

- First, Nestlé argues that the company has never advocated bottle feeding instead of breast feeding. All its products carry a statement that breast feeding is best. The company states that it "believes that breast milk is the best food for infants and encourages breast feeding around the world as it has done for decades." The company offers as support of this statement one of Nestlé's oldest educational booklets on "Infant Feeding and Hygiene," which dates from 1913 and encourages breast feeding.

- However, the company does believe that infant formula has a vital role in proper infant nutrition as a supplement, when the infant needs nutritionally adequate and appropriate foods in addition to breast milk, and as a substitute for breast milk when a mother cannot or chooses not to breast feed. One doctor reports, "Economically deprived and thus dietarily deprived mothers who give their children only breast milk are raising infants whose growth rates begin to slow noticeably at about the age of three months. These mothers then turn to supplemental feedings that are often harmful to children. These include herbal teas and concoctions of rice water or corn water and sweetened, condensed milk. These feedings can also be prepared with contaminated water and are served in unsanitary conditions."

- Mothers in developing nations often have dietary deficiencies. In the Philippines, a mother in a poor family who is nursing a child produces about a pint of milk daily. Mothers in the United States usually produce about a quart of milk each day. For both the Filipino and U.S. mothers, the milk produced is equally nutritious. The problem is that there is less of it for the Filipino baby. If the Filipino mother doesn't augment the child's diet, malnutrition develops.

- Many poor women in the Third World bottle feed because their work schedules in fields or factories will not permit breast feeding. The infant feeding controversy has largely to do with the gradual introduction of weaning foods during the period between three months and two years. The average well-nourished Western woman, weighing 20 to 30 pounds more than most women in less-developed countries, cannot feed only breast milk beyond five or six months. The claim that Third World women can breast feed exclusively for one or two years and have healthy, well-developed children is outrageous. Thus, all children beyond the ages of five to six months require supplemental feeding.

- Weaning foods can be classified as either native cereal gruels of millet or rice, or commercial manufactured milk formula. Traditional native weaning foods are usually made by mixing maize, rice, or millet flour with water and then cooking the mixture. Other weaning foods found in use are crushed crackers, sugar and water, and mashed bananas.

There are two basic dangers to the use of native weaning foods. First, the nutritional quality of the native gruels is low. Second, microbiological contamination of the traditional weaning foods is a certainty in many Third World settings. The millet or the flour is likely to be contaminated, the water used in cooking will most certainly be contaminated, and the cooking containers will be contaminated; therefore, the native gruel, even after it is cooked, is frequently contaminated with colon bacilli, staph, and other dangerous bacteria. Moreover, large batches of gruel are often made and allowed to sit, inviting further contamination.

- Scientists recently compared the microbiological contamination of a local native gruel with ordinary reconstituted milk formula prepared under primitive conditions. They found both were contaminated to similar dangerous levels.

- The real nutritional problem in the Third World is not whether to give infants breast milk or formula, but how to supplement mothers' milk with nutritionally adequate foods when they are needed. Finding adequate locally produced, nutritionally sound supplements to mothers' milk and teaching people how to prepare and use them safely are the issues. Only effective nutrition education along with improved sanitation and good food that people can afford will win the fight against dietary deficiencies in the Third World.

THE RESOLUTION

In 1974, Nestlé, aware of changing social patterns in the developing world and the increased access to radio and television there, reviewed its marketing practices on a region-by-region basis. As a result, mass media advertising of infant formula began to be phased out immediately in certain markets and, by 1978, was banned worldwide by the company. Nestlé then undertook to carry out more comprehensive health education programs to ensure that an understanding of the proper use of their products reached mothers, particularly in rural areas.

"Nestlé fully supports the WHO [World Health Organization] Code. Nestlé will continue to promote breast feeding and ensure that its marketing practices do not discourage breast feeding anywhere. Our company intends to maintain a constructive dialogue with governments and health professionals in all the countries it serves with the sole purpose of servicing mothers and the health of babies." This quote is from *Nestlé Discusses the Recommended WHO Infant Formula Code*.

In 1977, the Interfaith Center on Corporate Responsibility in New York compiled a case against formula feeding in developing nations, and the Third World Institute launched a boycott against many Nestlé products. Its aim was to halt promotion of infant formulas in the Third World. The Infant Formula Action Coalition (INFACT, successor to the Third World Institute), along with

several other world organizations, successfully lobbied the World Health Organization to draft a code to regulate the advertising and marketing of infant formula in the Third World. In 1981, by a vote of 114 to 1 (three countries abstained and the United States was the only dissenting vote), 118 member nations of WHO endorsed a voluntary code. The eight-page code urged a worldwide ban on promotion and advertising of baby formula and called for a halt to distribution of free product samples or gifts to physicians who promoted the use of the formula as a substitute for breast milk.

In May 1981 Nestlé announced it would support the code and waited for individual countries to pass national codes that would then be put into effect. Unfortunately, very few such codes were forthcoming. By the end of 1983, only 25 of the 157 member nations of the WHO had established national codes. Accordingly, Nestlé management determined it would have to apply the code in the absence of national legislation, and in February 1982 it issued instructions to marketing personnel that delineated the company's best understanding of the code and what would have to be done to follow it.

In addition, in May 1982 Nestlé formed the Nestlé Infant Formula Audit Commission (NIFAC), chaired by former Senator Edmund J. Muskie, and asked the commission to review the company's instructions to field personnel to determine if they could be improved to better implement the code. At the same time, Nestlé continued its meetings with WHO and UNICEF (United Nations Children's Fund) to try to obtain the most accurate interpretation of the code. NIFAC recommended several clarifications for the instructions that it believed would better interpret ambiguous areas of the code; in October 1982, Nestlé accepted those recommendations and issued revised instructions to field personnel.

Other issues within the code, such as the question of a warning statement, were still open to debate. Nestlé consulted extensively with WHO before issuing its label warning statement in October 1983, but there was still not universal agreement with it. Acting on WHO recommendations, Nestlé consulted with firms experienced and expert in developing and field testing educational materials, so that it could ensure that those materials met the code.

When the International Nestlé Boycott Committee (INBC) listed its four points of difference with Nestlé, it again became a matter of interpretation of the requirements of the code. Here, meetings held by UNICEF proved invaluable, in that UNICEF agreed to define areas of differing interpretation—in some cases providing definitions contrary to both Nestlé's and INBC's interpretations.

It was the meetings with UNICEF in early 1984 that finally led to a joint statement by Nestlé and INBC on January 25. At that time, INBC announced its suspension of boycott activities, and Nestlé pledged its continued support of the WHO code.

NESTLÉ SUPPORTS WHO CODE

The company has a strong record of progress and support in implementing the WHO code, including the following:

- Immediate support for the WHO code, May 1981, and testimony to this effect before the U.S. Congress, June 1981.

- Issuance of instructions to all employees, agents, and distributors in February 1982 to implement the code in all Third World countries where Nestlé markets infant formula.

- Establishment of an audit commission, in accordance with Article 11.3 of the WHO code, to ensure the company's compliance with the code. The commission, headed by

Edmund S. Muskie, was composed of eminent clergy and scientists.

- Willingness to meet with concerned church leaders, international bodies, and organization leaders seriously concerned with Nestlé's application of the code.
- Issuance of revised instructions to Nestlé personnel, October 1982, as recommended by the Muskie committee to clarify and give further effect to the code.
- Consultation with WHO, UNICEF, and NIFAC on how to interpret the code and how best to implement specific provisions, including clarification by WHO/UNICEF of the definition of children who need to be fed breast milk substitutes, to aid in determining the need for supplies in hospitals.

NESTLÉ POLICIES

In the early 1970s Nestlé began to review its infant formula marketing practices on a region-by-region basis. By 1978 the company had stopped all consumer advertising and direct sampling to mothers. Instructions to the field issued in February 1982 and clarified in the revised instructions of October 1982 to adopt articles of the WHO code as Nestlé policy include the following:

- No advertising to the general public
- No sampling to mothers
- No mothercraft workers
- No use of commission/bonus for sales
- No use of infant pictures on labels
- No point-of-sale advertising
- No financial or material inducements to promote products
- No samples to physicians except in three specific situations: a new product, a new product formulation, or a new graduate physician; limited to one or two cans of product
- Limitation of supplies to those requested in writing and fulfilling genuine needs for breast milk substitutes
- A statement of the superiority of breast feeding on all labels/materials
- Labels and educational materials clearly stating the hazards involved in incorrect usage of infant formula, developed in consultation with WHO/UNICEF

Even though Nestlé stopped consumer advertising, it was able to maintain its share of the Third World infant formula market. In 1988 a call to resume the seven-year boycott was made by a group of consumer activist members of the Action for Corporate Accountability. The group claimed that Nestlé was distributing free formula through maternity wards as a promotional tactic that undermined the practice of breast feeding. The group claimed that Nestlé and others, including American Home Products, have continued to dump formula in hospitals and maternity wards and that, as a result, "babies are dying as the companies are violating the WHO resolution." As late as 1997 the Interagency Group on Breastfeeding Monitoring (IGBM) claimed Nestlé continues to systematically violate the WHO code. Nestlé's response to these accusations is included on its Web site (see www.nestlé.com for details).

The boycott focus is Taster's Choice Instant Coffee, Coffee-mate Nondairy Coffee Creamer, Anacin aspirin, and Advil.

Representatives of Nestlé and American Home Products rejected the accusations and said they were complying with World Health Organization and individual national codes on the subject.

THE NEW TWISTS

A new environmental factor has made the entire case more complex: As of 2001 it was believed that some 3.8 million children around the world had contracted the human immunodeficiency virus (HIV) at their mothers' breasts. In affluent countries mothers can be told to bottle feed their children. However, 90 percent of the child infections occur in developing countries. There the problems of bottle feeding remain. Further, in even the most infected areas, 70 percent of the mothers do not carry the virus, and breast feeding is by far the best option. The vast majority of pregnant women in developing countries have no idea whether they are infected or not. One concern is that large numbers of healthy women will switch to the bottle just to be safe. Alternatively, if bottle feeding becomes a badge of HIV infection, mothers may continue breast feeding just to avoid being stigmatized. In Thailand, pregnant women are offered testing, and if found HIV positive, are given free milk powder. But in some African countries, where women get pregnant at three times the Thai rate and HIV infection rates are 25 percent compared with the 2 percent in Thailand, that solution is much less feasible. Moreover, the latest medical evidence indicates that extending breastfeeding reduces the risk of breast cancer. Most recently the demand for infant formula in South Africa has outstripped supply as HIV-infected mothers make the switch to formula. Demand grew 20 percent in 2004 and the government is investigating the shortages as Nestlé scrambles to catch up with demand. The firm reopened a shuttered factory and began importing formula from Brazil.

THE ISSUES

Many issues are raised by this incident and the ongoing swirl of cultural change. How can a company deal with a worldwide boycott of its products? Why did the United States decide not to support the WHO code? Who is correct, WHO or Nestlé? A more important issue concerns the responsibility of an MNC marketing in developing nations. Setting aside the issues for a moment, consider the notion that, whether intentional or not, Nestlé's marketing activities have had an impact on the behavior of many people. In other words, Nestlé is a cultural change agent. When it or any other company successfully introduces new ideas into a culture, the culture changes and those changes can be functional or dysfunctional to established patterns of behavior. The key issue is, What responsibility does the MNC have to the culture when, as a result of its marketing activities, it causes change in that culture? Finally, how might Nestlé now participate in the battle against the spread of HIV and AIDS in developing countries?

QUESTIONS

1. What are the responsibilities of companies in this or similar situations?
2. What could Nestlé have done to have avoided the accusations of "killing Third World babies" and still market its product?
3. After Nestlé's experience, how do you suggest it, or any other company, can protect itself in the future?

4. Assume you are the one who had to make the final decision on whether or not to promote and market Nestlé's baby formula in Third World countries. Read the section titled "Ethical and Socially Responsible Decisions" in Chapter 5 (pp. 148–149) as a guide to examine the social responsibility and ethical issues regarding the marketing approach and the promotion used. Were the decisions socially responsible? Were they ethical?

5. What advice would you give to Nestlé now in light of the new problem of HIV infection being spread via mothers' milk?

This case is an update of "Nestlé in LDCs," a case written by J. Alex Murray, University of Windsor, Ontario, Canada, and Gregory M. Gazda and Mary J. Molenaar, University of San Diego. The case originally appeared in the fifth edition of this text.

The case draws from the following: "International Code of Marketing of Breastmilk Substitutes" (Geneva: World Health Organization, 1981); *INFACT Newsletter*, Minneapolis, February 1979; John A. Sparks, "The Nestlé Controversy—Anatomy of a Boycott" (Grove City, PA: Public Policy Education Funds); "WHO Drafts a Marketing Code," *World Business Weekly*, January 19, 1981, p. 8; "A Boycott over Infant Formula," *BusinessWeek*, April 23, 1979, p. 137; "The Battle over Bottle-Feeding," *World Press Review*, January 1980, p. 54; "Nestlé and the Role of Infant Formula in Developing Countries: The Resolution of a Conflict" (Nestlé Company, 1985); "The Dilemma of Third World Nutrition" (Nestlé SA, 1985), 20 pp.; Thomas V. Greer, "The Future of the International Code of Marketing of Breastmilk Substitutes: The Socio-Legal Context," *International Marketing Review*, Spring 1984, pp. 33–41; James C. Baker, "The International Infant Formula Controversy: A Dilemma in Corporate Social Responsibility," *Journal of Business Ethics*, 1985, no. 4, pp. 181–190; and Shawn Tully, "Nestlé Shows How to Gobble Markets," *Fortune*, January 16, 1989, p. 75. For a comprehensive and well-balanced review of the infant formula issue, see Thomas V. Greer, "International Infant Formula Marketing: The Debate Continues," *Advances in International Marketing*, 1990, 4, pp. 207–225. For a discussion of the HIV complication, see "Back to the Bottle?" *Economist*, February 7, 1998, p. 50; Alix M. Freedman and Steve Stecklow, "Bottled Up: As UNICEF Battles Baby-Formula Makers, African Infants Sicken," *Wall Street Journal*, December 5, 2000; Rone Tempest, "Mass Breast-Feeding by 1,128 Is Called a Record," *Los Angeles Times*, August 4, 2002, p. B1; "South Africa: Erratic Infant Formula Supply Puts PMTCT at Risk, "*All Africa/COMTEX*, August 22, 2005.

CASE I-3 Coke and Pepsi Learn to Compete in India

THE BEVERAGE BATTLEFIELD

In 2003, Jagdeep Kapoor, chairman of Samsika Marketing Consultants in Mumbai (formerly Bombay), commented that "Coke lost a number of years over errors. But at last it seems to be getting its positioning right." Similarly, Ronald McEachern, PepsiCo's Asia chief, asserted "India is the beverage battlefield for 2003."

The experience of the world's two giant soft drinks companies in India during the 1990s and the beginning of the new millennium was not a happy one, even though the government had opened its doors wide to foreign companies. Both companies experienced a range of unexpected problems and difficult situations that led them to recognize that competing in India requires special knowledge, skills, and local expertise. In many ways, Coke and Pepsi managers had to learn the hard way that "what works here" does not always "work there." In spring 2003, Alex von Behr, the president of Coca-Cola India, admitted ruefully, "The environment in India is challenging, but we're learning how to crack it."

THE INDIAN SOFT DRINKS INDUSTRY

In India, over 45 percent of the soft drinks industry in 1993 consisted of small manufacturers. Their combined business was worth $3.2 million dollars. Leading producers included Parle Agro (hereafter "Parle"), Pure Drinks, Modern Foods, and McDowells. They offered carbonated orange and lemon-lime beverage drinks. Coca-Cola Corporation (hereafter "Coca-Cola") was only a distant memory to most Indians at that time. The company had been present in the Indian market from 1958 until its withdrawal in 1977, following a dispute with the government over its trade secrets. After decades in the market, Coca-Cola chose to leave India rather than cut its equity stake to 40 percent and hand over its secret formula for the syrup.

Following Coca-Cola's departure, Parle became the market leader and established thriving export franchise businesses in Dubai, Kuwait, Saudi Arabia, and Oman in the Gulf, along with Sri Lanka. It set up production in Nepal and Bangladesh, and served distant markets in Tanzania, Britain, the Netherlands, and the United States. Parle invested heavily in image advertising at home, establishing the dominance of its flagship brand, Thums Up.

Thums Up is a brand associated with a "job well done" and personal success. These are persuasive messages for its target market of young people aged 15 to 24. Parle has been careful in the past not to call Thums Up a cola drink, so it has avoided direct comparison with Coke and Pepsi, the world's brand leaders.

The soft drinks market in India is composed of six product segments: cola, "cloudy lemon," orange, "soda" (carbonated water), mango, and "clear lemon," in order of importance. Cloudy lemon and clear lemon together make up the lemon-lime segment. Prior to the arrival of foreign producers in India, the fight for local dominance was between Parle's Thums Up and Pure Drinks' Campa Cola.

In 1988, the industry had experienced a dramatic shakeout following a government warning that BVO, an essential ingredient in locally produced soft drinks, was carcinogenic. Producers either had to resort to using a costly imported substitute, estergum, or they had to finance their own R&D in order to find a substitute ingredient. Many failed and quickly withdrew from the industry.

Competing with the segment of carbonated soft drinks is another beverage segment composed of noncarbonated fruit drinks. These are a growth industry because Indian consumers perceive fruit drinks to be natural, healthy, and tasty. The leading brand has traditionally been Parle's Frooti, a mango-flavored drink, which was also exported to franchisees in the United States, Britain, Portugal, Spain, and Mauritius.

OPENING UP THE INDIAN MARKET IN 1991

In June 1991, India experienced an economic crisis of exceptional severity, triggered by the rise in imported oil prices following the first Gulf War (after Iraq's invasion of Kuwait). Foreign exchange reserves fell as nonresident Indians (NRIs) cut back on repatriation of their savings, imports were tightly controlled across all sectors, and industrial production fell while inflation was rising. A new government took office in June 1991 led by Prime Minister Narasimha Rao. Inspired by Finance Minister Dr. Manmohan Singh, the government introduced measures to stabilize the economy in the short term and launched a fundamental restructuring program to ensure medium-term growth. Results were dramatic. By 1994, inflation was halved, exchange reserves were greatly increased, exports were growing, and foreign investors were looking at India, a leading Big Emerging Market, with new eyes.

The turnaround could not be overstated; one commentator said "India has been in economic depression for so long that everything except the snake-charmers, cows and the Taj Mahal has faded from the memory of the world." For many years, the outside world had viewed the Indian government as unfriendly to foreign investors. Outside investment had been allowed only in high tech sectors and was almost entirely prohibited in consumer goods sectors. The "principle of indigenous availability" had specified that if an item could be obtained anywhere else within the country, imports of similar items were forbidden. As a result of this policy, India became self-reliant in its defense industry, developing both nuclear and space programs. In contrast, Indian consumers had little choice of products or brands, and no guarantees of quality or reliability.

Following liberalization of the Indian economy in 1991 and introduction of the New Industrial Policy intended to dismantle complicated trade rules and regulations, foreign investment increased dramatically. Beneficiary industries included processed foods, software, engineering plastics, electronic equipment, power generation, and petroleum generation. A commentator observed, "In the 1970s and 1980s, it was almost antinational to advocate foreign investment. Today the Prime Minister and Finance Minister are wooing foreign investors."

Foreign companies that had successfully pioneered entry into the Indian market many decades earlier, despite all the stringent rules, quickly increased their equity stakes under the new rules from 40 percent to 51 percent. These long-established companies included global giants such as Unilever, Procter & Gamble, Pfizer, Hoechst, BAT, and Philips (of the Netherlands).

COCA-COLA AND PEPSICO ENTER THE INDIAN MARKET

Despite its huge population, India had not been considered by foreign beverage producers to be an important market. In addition to the deterrents imposed by the government through its austere trade policies, rules and regulations, local demand for carbonated drinks in India was very low compared to countries at a similar stage of economic development. In 1989, the average Indian was buying only three bottles a year. This compared to per-capita consumption rates of 11 bottles a year in Bangladesh and 13 in Pakistan, India's two neighbors.

PepsiCo
PepsiCo lodged a joint venture application to enter India in July 1986. It had selected two local partners, Voltas and Punjab Agro. This application was approved under the name "Pepsi Foods Ltd." by the government of Rajiv Gandhi in September 1988. As expected, very stringent conditions were imposed on the venture. Sales of soft drink concentrate to local bottlers could not exceed 25 percent of total sales for the new venture. This limit also included processing of fruits and vegetables by Pepsi Foods Ltd. Robert Beeby, CEO of Pepsi-Cola International, said at that time: "We're willing to go so far with India because we wanted to make sure we get an early entry while the market is developing."

In May 1990, the government mandated that Pepsi Food's products be promoted under the name "Lehar Pepsi" ("lehar" meaning "wave"). Foreign collaboration rules in force at the time prohibited use of foreign brand names on products intended for sale inside India. Other examples of this policy were Maruti Suzuki, Carrier Aircon, L&T Honeywell, Wilkinson's Wiltech, Modi-Champion, and Modi-Xerox.

In keeping with local tastes, Pepsi Foods launched Lehar 7UP in the clear lemon category, along with Lehar Pepsi. Marketing and distribution were focused in the north and west around the major cities of Delhi and Mumbai. An aggressive pricing policy on the one-liter bottles had a severe impact on the local producer, Pure Drinks. The market leader, Parle, preempted any further pricing moves by Pepsi Foods by introducing a new 250-ml. bottle that sold for the same price as its 200-ml. bottle.

Pepsi Foods struggled to fight off local competition from Pure Drinks' Campa Cola, Duke's lemonade, and various brands of Parle. Aware of its difficulties, Pepsi Foods approached Parle in December 1991 to offer an alliance. Parle declined the offer, choosing to stand its ground and continuing to fight to preserve its number one position.

The fight for dominance intensified in 1993 with Pepsi Food's launch of two new brands, Slice and Teem, along with the introduction of fountain sales. At this time, market shares in the cola segment were 60 percent for Parle (down from 70 percent), 26 percent for Pepsi Foods, and 10 percent for Pure Drinks.

Coca-Cola
In May 1990, Coca-Cola attempted to reenter India by means of a proposed joint venture with a local bottling company owned by the giant Indian conglomerate, Godrej. The government of Rajiv Gandhi turned down this application just as PepsiCo's application was being approved. Undeterred, Coca-Cola made its return to India by joining forces with Britannia Industries India Ltd., a local producer of snack foods. The new venture was called "Britco Foods." In 1993 Coca-Cola filed an application to create a 100 percent-owned soft drinks company, Coca-Cola India.

The arrival of Coca-Cola in the Indian soft drinks industry forced local small producers to consider extreme survival measures. The small Delhi-based company, Pure Drinks, tried to revamp its bottling alliance with Coca-Cola from earlier years, even offering to withdraw its own leading brand, Campa Cola, as an inducement to Coca-Cola. Campa Cola's brand share at the time was 10 percent. However, Coca-Cola had its sights set on a different partner, Parle.

Among local producers, it was believed at that time that Coca-Cola would not take market share away from local companies because the beverage market was itself growing consistently from year to year. Yet this belief did not stop individual local producers from trying to align themselves with the market leader. Thus, in July 1993, Parle offered to sell Coca-Cola its bottling plants in the four key cities of Delhi, Mumbai, Ahmedabad, and Surat. In addition, Parle offered to sell its leading brands including Thums Up, Limca, Citra, Gold Spot, and Mazaa. It chose to retain ownership only of Frooti and a soda (carbonated water) called Bisleri.

As a result of Parle's offer, two new ventures were set up to bottle and market both companies' products. The marketing venture would provide advertising, media services, promotional and sales support. Parle's chief, Ramesh Chauhan, was named Chairman and Coca-Cola staffed the Managing Director's position. Parle held 49 percent of the marketing venture but took an equal 50 percent stake in the bottling venture.

FAST FORWARD TO THE NEW MILLENNIUM

Seasonal Sales Promotions—the 2000 Navratri Campaign
In India the summer season for soft drink consumption lasts 70 to 75 days from mid-April to June. During this time, over 50 percent of the year's carbonated beverages are consumed across the country. The second-highest season for consumption lasts only 20 to 25 days during the cultural festival of Navratri ("Nav" means nine and "ratri" means night). This is a traditional Gujarati festival and it goes on for nine nights in the state of Gujarat, in the western part of India. Mumbai also has a significant Gujarati population that is considered part of the target market for this campaign.

As Sunil Kapoor, Regional Marketing Manager for Coca-Cola India, stated, "As part of the 'think local—act local' business plan, we have tried to involve the masses in Gujarat with 'Thums Up Toofani Ramjhat,' with 20,000 free passes issued, one per Thums Up bottle. ('Toofan' means a thunderstorm and 'ramjhat' means 'let's dance,' so together these words convey the idea of a 'fast dance.') There are a number of (retail) on-site activities too, such as the 'buy one—get one free' scheme and lucky draws where one can win a free trip to Goa." (Goa is an independent Portuguese-speaking state on the west coast of India, that is famed for its beaches and tourist resorts.)

For its part, PepsiCo also participates in annual Navratri celebrations through massive sponsorships of "garba" competitions in selected venues in Gujarat. ("Garba" is the name of a dance, which is done by women during the Navratri festival.) In 2000 Deepak Jolly, Executive Vice-President for PepsiCo India, commented: "For the first time, Pepsi has tied up with the Gujarati TV channel,

Zee Alpha, to telecast 'Navratri Utsav 2000 at Mumbai' on all nine nights. ('Utsav' means festival.) Then there is the mega offer for the people of Ahmedabad, Baroda, Surat, and Rajkot where every refill of a case of Pepsi 300-ml. bottles will fetch one kilo of Basmati rice free." (These are four cities located in the state of Gujarat. Basmati rice is considered to be a premium quality rice. After the initial purchase of a 300-ml. bottle, consumers can get refills at reduced rates at select stores.)

During the Navratri festival, both companies are extremely generous with giveaways in their sales promotions. For example, in 2000 Pepsi Foods offered a free Kit Kat with every 1.5-liter bottle and a Polo (hard candies like "Lifesavers") with each 500-ml. bottle of Pepsi and Mirinda.

The 2002 Summer TV Campaign

In 2002 Pepsi Foods took the lead in the clear lime category with 7UP leading its category, followed by Coca-Cola's Sprite brand. On March 7, 2002, it launched a new summer campaign for 7UP. This date was chosen to coincide with the India–Zimbabwe One-Day cricket series. The new campaign slogan was "Keep It Cool" to emphasize the product attribute of refreshment.

A nationwide television advertising campaign was designed with the objectives of growing the category and building brand salience. The national campaign was to be reinforced with regionally adapted TV campaigns, outdoor activities, and retail promotions.

PepsiCo's ad spending for 7UP was not comparable to the level invested in its flagship brand, Pepsi-Cola, because the clear lime segment in 2002 was minuscule, accounting for just 4.5 percent of the total carbonated soft drinks market. This was equal to about 250–270 million cases. The cloudy lemon segment is more than twice this size, with 10 percent market share; carbonated orange drinks account for about 15 percent.

7UP was being sold in 250-ml., 300-ml., and 500-ml. bottles, and in 200-ml. bottles in southern states. The industry trend was pushing toward 200-ml. bottles in order to increase frequency of purchase and volume of consumption. Pepsi Foods rolled out its Mirinda Lemon, Apple and Orange in 200-ml. bottles in the Delhi market, following similar market launches in Punjab and Uttar Pradesh in the previous year.

In the past, celebrity actors Amitabh Bachchan and Govinda, who are famous male stars of the Indian movie industry, had endorsed Mirinda Lemon. This world-famous industry is referred to as "Bollywood" (the Hollywood of India based in Bombay).

Both Coca-Cola and PepsiCo routinely keep close track of the success of their seasonal advertising campaigns in India through use of marketing research agencies. Coca-Cola has used ORG-MARG, while Pepsi Foods has worked with IMRB. ORG-MARG uses its weekly "Ad Track" to study spontaneous ad recall among 1,000 male and female respondents aged 12–49 in 17 cities. IMRB's "Perception Analyzer System" surveys 15–30 year olds in four cities. Responses are sought on measures of likeability of the ad and intention to buy.

Pepsi's Sponsorship of Cricket and Football (Soccer)

After India won an outstanding victory in the 2002 India–England NatWest One-Day cricket series finals, PepsiCo launched a new ad campaign featuring the batting sensation, Mohammad Kaif. Although he had been signed up a year earlier, Kaif had not yet figured in Pepsi ads. The spotlight had been on Sachin Tendulkar and Amitabh Bachchan, who are famous icons as a cricket player and a movie star, respectively. Sachin Tendulkar is considered to be the best batsman in the history of cricket. He started his international cricket career at the age of 16, and now at age 29 he already figures in the list of top young billionaires in the country! Amitabh Bachchan has the distinction of having being the leading superstar in the Indian movie industry for the last 30 years. Even now, at 60 years of age, he commands the highest name rating any star has ever received in Bollywood.

PepsiCo's line-up of other cricket celebrities includes Saurav Ganguly, Rahul Dravid, Harbhajan Singh, Zaheer Khan, V.V.S. Laxman, and Ajit Agarkar. Saurav Ganguly is presently the captain of the Indian cricket team. All of these players were part of the Indian team for the 2003 World Cup Cricket held in South Africa, where they performed superbly, reaching the finals. They lost to Australia in the finals, but PepsiCo was able to capitalize on the overall team's performance during the month and a half long tournament.

Six months earlier, PepsiCo had taken advantage of World Cup soccer fever in India, featuring football heroes such as Baichung Bhutia in their celebrity and music-related advertising communications. These ads featured football players pitted against Sumo wrestlers. In addition, para football tournaments were held in selected cities.

In 2003, similar sports-themed promotions took place, centered on PepsiCo's sponsorship of the World Cup Series in cricket. During the two months of the Series, a new product, Pepsi Blue, was marketed nationwide. This was positioned as a "limited edition," icy-blue cola sold in 300-ml. returnable glass bottles and 500-ml. plastic bottles. These were priced at 8 rupees (Rs) and Rs. 15, respectively. In addition, commemorative, nonreturnable 250-ml. Pepsi bottles priced at Rs. 12 were introduced. (One rupee was equal to US 2.08 cents in 2003.)

To consolidate its investment in the 2003 campaign, PepsiCo also featured a music video with other celebrity endorsers including the Bollywood stars Amitabh Bachchan, Kareena Kapoor, Abishek Bachchan (the son of Amitabh Bachchan) and Fardeen Khan, as well as several cricketers. The new music video aired on SET Max, which is a satellite channel owned by Sony. This channel is popular among the 15–25 age group, mainly in the northern and western parts of India.

Coca-Cola's Lifestyle Advertising

In 2002 and 2003, Coca-Cola India used a strategy of "building a connect using the relevant local idioms," according to Rajesh Mani, Regional Marketing Manager. The ad strategy, developed by Orchard Advertising in Bangalore, was based on use of "gaana" music and ballet. ("Gaana" means to sing.)

The first ad execution, called "Bombay Dreams," featured A. R. Rahman, who is a famous music director. This approach was very successful among the target audience of young people, increasing sales by about 50 percent. It also won an Effi Award from the Mumbai Advertising Club. (Note: Even though the name of the city has been officially changed from Bombay to Mumbai, local people still continue to use Bombay.)

2003 saw the launch of a second execution of this regional strategy in Chennai (formerly Madras), called "Chennai Dreams." This ad featured Vijay, a youth icon who is famous as an actor in the regional movies of south India. The campaign targeted consumers in Tamil Nadu, located in the southern part of the country. Thomas Xavier, Executive Creative Director of Orchard Advertising, commented that the success of the ad was due to insight into needs of the target market. "We were clear that the need of the hour was not for an ad film, but for a Tamil feature film in 60 seconds."

In 2002 Coca-Cola India worked hard to build up a brand preference for its flagship brand, Coke, among young people in rural target markets. The campaign slogan was "thanda matlab Coca-Cola" (or "cool means Coca-Cola" in Hindi). Coca-Cola India calls its rural youth target market "India B." The prime objective in this market is to grow the generic soft drinks category and to develop brand preference for Coke. The "thanda" ("cold") campaign of 2002 successfully propelled Coke into the number three position in rural markets.

The urban youth target market, known as "India A," includes 18–24 year olds in the major metropolitan areas. In 2003, the urban youth market was targeted with a campaign developed by McCann Erickson. The TV ad ran for 60 seconds and featured actor Vivek Oberoi with Aishwarya Rai. Both are famous as Bollywood movie stars. Aishwarya was the winner of the Miss World crown in 1994 and became an instant hit in Indian movies after deciding on an acting career.

This ad showed Oberoi trying to hook up with Rai by deliberately leaving his mobile phone in the taxi that she hails, and then calling her. The ad message aimed to emphasize confidence and optimism, and a theme of "seize the day," according to Shripad Nadkarni, Vice-President of Marketing for Coca-Cola India. The 2003 campaign used a variety of media including television, print, outdoor, point-of-sale, restaurant and grocery chains, and local promotional events. "While awareness of soft drinks is high, there is a need to build a deeper brand connect" in urban centers, according to Sharda Agarwal, Director of Marketing for Coca-Cola India. "Vivek Oberoi—who's an up and coming star today, and has a wholesome, energetic image—will help build a stronger bond with the youth, and make them feel that it is a brand that plays a role in their life, just as much as Levi's or Ray-Ban."

Coca-Cola's specific marketing objectives for 2003 were to grow the per-capita consumption of soft drinks in the rural markets, and to capture a larger share in the urban market from competition and increase the frequency of consumption there, according to Ms. Agarwal. It was expected that a new "affordability plank" in the advertising strategy, along with introduction of a new 5-rupee bottle, would help to achieve all of these goals.

The "Affordability Plank"

In 2003, Coca-Cola India dramatically reduced prices of its soft drinks by 15 percent to 25 percent nationwide, in order to encourage consumption. This followed an earlier regional action in North India that reduced prices by 10–15 percent for its carbonated brands, Coke, Thums Up, Limca, Sprite and Fanta. In other regions such as Rajasthan, western and eastern Uttar Pradesh, and Tamil Nadu, prices were slashed to Rs. 5 for 200-ml. glass bottles and Rs. 8 for 300-ml. bottles from the existing Rs. 7 and Rs. 10 price points, respectively.

These price reductions were in keeping with Coca-Cola's goal of enhancing affordability of its products, bringing them within arm's reach of consumers and thereby promoting regular consumption. Given the very low per-capita consumption of soft drinks in India, it was expected that price reductions would expand both the consumer base and the market for soft drinks. PepsiCo was forced to match these price reductions, leading PepsiCo's Asia chief to conclude: "India is the beverage battlefield for 2003."

Another initiative by Coca-Cola was the introduction of a new size, the "Mini." This was expected to increase total volume of sales and account for the major chunk of Coca-Cola's carbonated soft drink sales, according to Rajesh Mani, Regional Marketing Manager for Coca-Cola India.

The price reduction and new production launch were announced together by means of a new television ad campaign for Fanta and Coke in Tamil. Lowe Chennai created the ad concept, with executions by Primary Colors for Fanta and Rajiv Menon Productions for Coke. Both agencies are based in Chennai.

The 30-second Fanta spot featured the brand ambassador, actress Simran, well-known for her dance sequences in Hindi movies. The ad showed Simran stuck in a traffic jam. Thirsty, she tosses a 5-rupee coin to a roadside stall and signals to the vendor that she wants a Fanta Mini by pointing to her orange dress. (Fanta is an orangeade drink.) She gets her Fanta and sets off a chain reaction on the crowded street, with everyone from school children to a traditional "nani" mimicking her action. ("Nani" is the Hindi word for grandmother.)

Rajesh Mani commented that the company wanted to make consumers "sit up and take notice." This was accomplished "by using a local star, with local insight, because Tamil Nadu is a big market for Fanta."

A NEW PRODUCT CATEGORY

In order to encourage growth in demand for bottled beverages in the Indian market, several producers have launched their own brand in a new category, bottled water. This market was valued at 1,000 Crore in 2003. (1 Crore = 10,000,000 Rupees, US$1 = Rs48, so 1,000 Crore = US$0.2083 million.)

Coca-Cola's brand, Kinley, was introduced in 2000. Ogilvy and Mather designed a two-ad television campaign. By 2002 Kinley had achieved a 28 percent market share and was being produced in 15 plants. The biggest of these are located in Mumbai, Delhi, Goa and Bangalore. In 2003 it was planned to double bottling capacity by adding another 10 to 15 production plants. These would be a combination of company-owned plants, franchisee operations, and contract packing companies.

The Kinley brand of bottled water sells in various pack sizes: 500 ml., 1 liter, 1.5 liter, 2 liter, 5 liter, 20 liter, and 25 liter. The smallest pack was priced at Rs. 6 for 500 ml., while the 2-liter bottle was Rs. 17.

The current market leader with 40 percent market share is the Bisleri brand, owned by Ramesh Chauhan, who is the CEO of Parle. Pepsi Foods' brand is Aquafina with about 11 percent market share. Aquafina is produced in six company-owned or franchised bottling plants in Roha (Maharashtra), Bangalore, Kolkata (formerly Calcutta), and New Delhi. Focusing on metropolitan areas, Pepsi Foods' ad campaign uses both television and outdoor media, and is managed by HTA, Pepsi Foods' agency.

Other competing brands in this segment include Bailley by Parle, Hello by Hello Mineral Waters Pvt. Ltd., Pure Life by Nestlé, and a new brand launched by Indian Railways, called Rail Neer.

COCA-COLA'S ATTEMPTS TO "CRACK" THE INDIAN MARKET

By 2002, Coca-Cola owned 30 bottling plants, 10 franchisees, and held a 56 percent market share of the national soft drink market in India. Yet despite creative and locally responsive marketing efforts and a total investment of some $840 million to build its distribution and manufacturing infrastructure, Coca-Cola had reported losses in India since its return there in 1993. In 2001 the company had written off a loss of $400 million. Total accumulated losses were estimated to be over 2,000 Crore (US$0.4166 million).

To make matters worse, in January 2002 the company was ordered by the government to sell 49 percent of Hindustan Coca-Cola Holding Pvt. Ltd. (HCCHPL), the wholly owned holding company for all Coca-Cola operations in India, to Indian investors. This move by the government followed action taken by Coca-Cola in 1996 when it had requested and received government permission to increase its investment in the Indian market. Under the new governmental policy passed that same year affecting all new soft drink investments, Coca-Cola had agreed to sell 49 percent of its equity to Indian partners within two years. This time limit had been extended once already, but a request for a second extension to 2007 was turned down on October 3, 2001. Coca-Cola was hoping that by 2007 it would be in a stronger financial position and would receive a better return on its forced disinvestment.

The government's response to the company's second request was that "entry conditions cannot be changed." This response might have been acceptable if investment rules in India were clear and unchanging, but this was not the case during the 1990s when implementation of government rules had been inconsistent. Some companies, like Coca-Cola, were required to reduce their equity in order to allow Indians into the industry. At the same time, other companies—like Philips (of the Netherlands), Carrier (of the United States), and Cadbury-Schweppes (of Britain)—were being allowed to buy back most of their outstanding shares and would likely delist their shares altogether, effectively making their Indian operations wholly owned subsidiaries. This was the status that Coca-Cola was being forced to give up.

Local market analysts commented that there is no apparent logic behind these government policies, other than to allow local investors to become bargain hunters at the expense of Coca-Cola.

Coca-Cola responded by trying to maintain some control over its operations. It applied for government approval from the Foreign Investment Promotion Board (FIPB) to deny voting rights to its new Indian shareholders. Again the government response was that the company had to abide by the legal provisions that were applicable on the date of its original foreign investment in the country. Since all equities back in 1996–1997 mandatorily had voting rights, it was considered normal that Indian shareholders in this case should receive voting rights. The Indian government in May 2002 turned down Coca-Cola's request for a waiver of the disinvestment rule.

Making things even more difficult for Coca-Cola at that time was a change of oversight of the FIPB, from the Ministry of Industry to the Department of Economic Affairs. This change would require Coca-Cola and other foreign companies to build new relationships with bureaucrats, rendering past lobbying efforts useless.

Local business observers faulted Coca-Cola for trying to obtain repeated waivers of the disinvestment rule, pointing to the favorable expectation of an oversubscription for shares in the company's initial public offering. One commentator said " This is in no way a priority industry, and when it (Coca-Cola) was permitted to do business in India, it was with the condition that it will dilute a 49 percent stake after five years. Foreign companies keep on saying that in India promises are not fulfilled. Why doesn't this multinational set an example by fulfilling its own commitment in this particular issue?" Another stated unsympathetically, "They went into this with their eyes open."

The Indian government had originally stipulated the 49 percent disinvestment clause as a condition for its agreement to allow Coca-Cola to buy out local Indian bottlers when the company first entered the market, instead of setting up greenfield bottling plants, as Coca-Cola had initially proposed. In contrast to Coca-Cola, PepsiCo had entered India in a different year under a different set of rules. Moreover, it was not held to a disinvestment rule because it had opted to set up several greenfield bottling units.

Coca-Cola India initiated its compliance with the government disinvestment rule in February 2003 by following the private placement route. It agreed to place 49 percent of equity from its wholly owned subsidiary Hindustan Coca-Cola Holdings Pvt. Ltd. (HCCHPL), worth $41 million, in its bottling subsidiary Hindustan Coca-Cola Beverages Pvt. Ltd. (HCCBPL). HCCBPL runs the bottling plants originally taken over from local Indian bottlers including Parle. Of the 49 percent equity placed by HCCHPL, 10 percent was placed in Hindustan Coca-Cola Beverages (HCCB), in favor of employee and welfare trusts.

THE SECOND GULF WAR

During spring 2003, as a result of the attack by the United States and Britain on Iraq, a call was launched by the All-India Anti-Imperialist Forum to boycott purchases of American and British goods. The boycott targeted specifically Pepsi, Coca-Cola, and McDonald's as a protest against the "unjust" war. The Forum's president is Justice V. R. Krishna Iyer, a former judge of the Indian Supreme Court. The Forum's general secretary, S. K. Mukherjee, said, "We give a call to all peace-loving people of the world and India to rise up in protest against the imperialist aggression against Iraq . . ." Within two weeks of the announcement of the boycott, sales of Coke and Pepsi in the southern Indian state of Kerala plummeted 50 percent.

Members of the Forum included more than 250 nongovernmental groups. These went on "shop-to-shop" campaigns to persuade retailers not to stock American products. They visited homes in Kerala, presenting the same plea to consumers. Other items on the boycott list included toothpaste, soap, cooking oil, and cosmetics. Retailers feared a public backlash if they stocked items on the boycott list. In place of brand name items, retailers were asked to promote local substitutes such as an herbal product in place of toothpaste and mango juice instead of colas. Sunil Gupta, vice-president of Hindustan Coca-Cola Beverages, commented that this action would hurt not only the Kerala region. "We have one million retail suppliers of our products (in India). In the event of a boycott, it is the Indian economy that will be hit."

LEARNING SOME HARD LESSONS

In 2002 Coca-Cola's overall sales reached $940 million and company products accounted for more than half the soft drinks market. A three-year cost-cutting program had brought dramatic results, reducing the company's payroll by 23 percent. Eight outdated plants, inherited from the Thums Up purchase, were closed. Local purchasing policies brought savings of 57 percent on import duties. Coca-Cola's well known but poorly supported Thums Up brand was reinvigorated with an infusion of $3.5 million spent on advertising and distribution. Market share for Thums Up, which had slipped from more than 60 percent of carbonated beverage sales down to a puny 15 percent, was regained. Within a year, Thums Up ranked second nationwide. Coke still trailed its arch-rival Pepsi, however, with a market share of only 16.5 percent versus 23.5 percent.

Compared with per-capita consumption rates in other Big Emerging Markets, India's rate was still very low in 2003 at seven (8 ounce) servings per person. This compared with 14 in Pakistan, 89 in China, 278 in South Africa, 471 in Brazil, 1,484 in Mexico, and 1,404 in the domestic U.S. market. Coca-Cola India's Director of Finance, N. Sridhar, stated confidently, however, "We have turned a corner." In a similar vein, Jagdeep Kapoor, chairman of Samsika Marketing Consultants in Mumbai, concluded "Coke lost a number of years over errors. But at last it seems to be getting its positioning right."

CONTAMINATION ALLEGATIONS AND WATER USAGE

Just as things began to look up, an environmental organization claimed that soft drinks produced in India by Coca-Cola and Pepsi contained significant levels of pesticide residue. Coke and Pepsi denied the charges and argued that extensive use of pesticides in agriculture had resulted in a minute degree of pesticide in sugar used in their drinks. The result of tests conducted by the Ministry of Health and Family Welfare showed that soft drinks produced by the two companies were safe to drink under local health standards.

In an attempt to regain public trust and credibility after allegations of pesticide contamination incited angry consumers in Bombay to smash thousands of Coke bottles in 2003, the company formed an advisory board led by a former Indian Cabinet Secretary to oversee Coca-Cola's practices in India. Coke also appointed a former Chief of the Supreme Court to lead an advisory body called the India Environment Council, which will guide Coca-Cola India's social-responsibility practices. The Coca-Cola Company and PepsiCo hoped the creation of the advisory boards and the purity tests conducted by the Indian government will put to rest consumer fears.

After all the bad press Coke got in India over the pesticide content in its soft drinks, an activist group in California launched a campaign directed at U.S. college campuses accusing Coca-Cola of India of using precious groundwater, lacing its drinks with pesticides and supplying farmers with toxic waste used for fertilizing their crops. According to one report, a plant that produces 300,000 liters of soda drink a day uses 1.5 million liters of water, enough to meet the requirements of 20,000 people.

The issue revolved around a bottling plant in Plachimada, India. Though the state government granted Coke permission to build its plant in 1998, the company was obliged to get the locally elected village council's go-ahead to exploit groundwater and other resources. The village council issued the required licenses to Coke in 1998 and 2000 but did not renew permission in 2002, claiming the bottling operation had depleted the farmers' drinking water and irrigation supplies. In 2003 Coke's plant was closed until the corporation won a court ruling allowing them to reopen.

The reopening of the plant and the activities of the activist group led to several colleges in the United States and even in Europe to ban or stop renewing their contract with Coke. Hundreds of people in the United States called on Coca-Cola to close its bottling plants because the plants drain water from communities throughout India. They contended that such irresponsible practice robs the poor of their fundamental right to drinking water, is a source of toxic waste, causes serious harm to the environment, and threatens the people's health.

QUESTIONS

1. The political environment in India has proven to be critical to company performance for both PepsiCo and Coca-Cola India. What specific aspects of the political environment have played key roles? Could these effects have been anticipated prior to market entry? If not, could developments in the political arena have been handled better by each company?

2. Timing of entry into the Indian market brought different results for PepsiCo and Coca-Cola India. What benefits or disadvantages accrued as a result of earlier or later market entry?

3. The Indian market is enormous in terms of population and geography. How have the two companies responded to the sheer scale of operations in India in terms of product policies, promotional activities, pricing policies, and distribution arrangements?

4. "Global localization" (glocalization) is a policy that both companies have implemented successfully. Give examples for each company from the case.

5. Some analysts consider that Coca-Cola India made mistakes in planning and managing its return to India. Do you agree? What or whom do you think was responsible for any mistakes?

6. How can Pepsi and Coke confront the issues of water use in the manufacture of their products? How can they defuse further boycotts or demonstrations against their products? How effective are activist groups like the one that launched the campaign in California? Should Coke address the group directly or just let the furor subside, as it surely will?

7. Which of the two companies do you think has better long-term prospects for success in India?

8. What lessons can each company draw from its Indian experience as it contemplates entry into other Big Emerging Markets?

This case was prepared by Lyn S. Amine, PhD, Professor of Marketing and International Business, Distinguished Fellow of the Academy of Marketing Science, President, Women of the Academy of International Business, Saint Louis University, and Vikas Kumar, Assistant Professor, Strategic Management Institute, Bocconi University, Milan, Italy. Dr. Lyn S. Amine and Vikas Kumar prepared this case from public sources as a basis for classroom discussion only. It is not intended to illustrate either effective or ineffective handling of administrative problems. The case was revised in 2005 with the authors' permission.

Sources: Lyn S. Amine and Deepa Raizada, "Market Entry into the Newly Opened Indian Market: Recent Experiences of US Companies in the Soft Drinks Industry," in *Developments in Marketing Science*, XVIII, proceedings of the annual conference of the Academy of Marketing Science, Roger Gomes (ed.) (Coral Gables, FL: AMS, 1995), pp. 287–292; Jeff Cioletti, "Indian Government Says Coke and Pepsi Safe," *Beverage World*, September 15, 2003; "Indian Group Plans Coke, Pepsi Protests After Pesticide Claims," *AFP*, December 15, 2004; "Fortune Sellers," *Foreign Policy*, May/June 2004; "International Pressure Grows to Permanently Close Coke Bottling Plant in Plachimada," *PR Newswire*, June 15, 2005; "Indian Village Refuses Coca-Cola License to Exploit Ground Water," *AFP*, June 14, 2005; and "Why Everyone Loves to Hate Coke," *Economist Times*, June 16, 2005.

CASE 1-4 Marketing Microwave Ovens to a New Market Segment

You are the Vice President of International Marketing for White Appliances, an international company that manufactures and markets appliances globally. The company has a line of microwave ovens—some manufactured in the United States and some in Asia—which are exported to the U.S. market and Europe. Your company markets several high-end models in India that are manufactured in the United States. Your presence in the Indian market is limited at this time.

After preliminary analysis, you and your team have come to the conclusion that, besides the market for high-end models, a market for microwave ovens at all price levels exists. Several international companies like Samsung, Whirlpool, and LG Electronics India are entering the market with the idea that demand can be expanded with the right product at the right price. There are, however, several challenges in the Indian market, not the least of which is the consumer's knowledge about microwaves and the manner in which they are perceived as appliances.

In conducting research on the market, your research team put together a summary of comments from consumers and facts about the market that should give you a feel for the market and the kinds of challenges that will have to be dealt with if the market is to grow and if White Appliances is to have a profitable market share.

- Five top consumer durable companies are in the race to sell the oven. But to sell the product, they must first sell the idea. The players don't even agree on the size of the market; fewer still on what the oven will do for the Indian family.

- It may be a convenient and efficient way to cook, but is has been invented with European food in mind. "Only when Indian eating habits change can the microwave ovens market grow in a big way," says one market leader in appliances.

- Some companies disagree with the statement above. Their contention is that all Indian dishes can be prepared in a microwave; people only need to know how to use one.

- Consumer comments were mixed. One housewife commented, "The microwave oven was the first purchase after my wedding. I bought it only because I liked it and I had the money. But I must say its performance surprised me."

- Men no longer have an excuse for not helping in cooking. My husband, who never used to enter the kitchen, now uses the microwave oven to cook routinely.

- Somebody gifted it to me but food doesn't taste the same when cooked in a microwave whatever the company people may claim.

- Microwave ovens will be very useful and they are fast becoming as essential as a fridge.

- Ovens are of great use to bachelors. They can make curries every day or sambhar every day. If you heat in a regular oven sambhar or dal for the second or third time it will have a burnt smell. The microwave oven will not get you any such problem. It will be heated and at the same time as fresh as if it was made now.

- Some people say that using a microwave oven is lazy and getting away from the traditional "Indian culture" of always fresh food. I say that microwaves are of greatest use when you are very busy and not lazy. There are times when piping hot food rapidly becomes cold, especially in Winter and a microwave is the easiest, quickest and cleanest way to heat up, so it even has applications in a traditional family running on "Indian Culture" mode.

- To the chagrin of microwave oven marketers, the Indian perception of the gadget remains grey. Yet, for the first time in the some seven years that it's been officially around optimism towards the microwave has been on the upswing.

- A microwave oven is beginning to replace the demand for a second television or a bigger refrigerator. The middle-income consumer comes looking for novelty, value, and competitive pricing.

- The penetration level of microwave ovens remains shockingly minuscule, under 1 percent. The top seven cities comprise nearly 70 percent of the market with Delhi and Mumbai (Bombay) recording the highest sales. But the good news is that the microwave is beginning to be seen in smaller towns.

- When asked about the nonurban market, one microwave oven company executive commented, "We know it's an alien concept for the rural consumer, but we want to do our homework now to reap the benefits years later. Once the consumer is convinced a microwave can actually be part of daily cooking, the category will grow immensely."

- Apart from styling and competitive pricing, marketers acknowledge that cracking the mindset that microwaves are not suited to Indian food holds the key to future growth.

- People who own microwaves usually have cooks who may not be using the gadget in any case. Even consumers who own microwave ovens don't use them frequently; usage is confined to cooking Western food or reheating.

- With consumers still unclear on how to utilize the microwave oven for their day-to-day cooking, marketers are shifting away from mass marketing to a more direct marketing–oriented approach to create awareness about the benefits of the product.

- The challenge in this category is to get the user to cook in the microwave oven rather than use it as a product for reheating food. Keeping this in mind, companies are expecting an increasing number of sales for microwave ovens to come from the semiurban/rural markets. We are seeing an increasing number of sales coming from the upcountry markets.

- "Elite fad or smoke-free chullah for low-fat paranthas? Which way will the microwave oven go in the Indian market?" asks one company representative.

- Most agree on a broadly similar strategy to expand the Indian market: product and design innovation to make the

Exhibit 1

A Customer's Evaluation
of the LG Robogrill
Microwave

One customer's lengthy evaluation of the LG Robogrill Microwave posted on MouthShut.com, India's first, largest, and most comprehensive Person to Person (P2P) Information Exchange follows:

"We bought our LG Robogrill Microwave about 10 months ago. The microwave has all the features mentioned in the official description, in addition to many other helpful features."

For a complete review by this customer, see www.mouthshut.com and select Microwave Ovens, then select LG on the menu, then select model # LGMH-685 HD.

microwave suited to Indian cooking; local manufacturing facility to promote innovation while continuing to import high-end models; reduce import content to cut cost; boost volumes; and bring down prices.

- Even as early as 1990, the microwave was touted as a way to cook Indian food. Julie Sahni, the nation's best know authority on Indian cooking, has turned her attention to the microwave. And her new cookbook sets a new threshold for the microwave cook. Simple cooked lentils, spicy dal, even tandoori chicken—with its distinctive reddish color—come steaming from the modern microwave with the spices and scents of an ancient cuisine. Cynics who think microwave cooking is bland and unimaginative will eat their words.

MARKET DATA

LG Electronics, the category leader, has a 41.5 percent share of the 1.6 lakh[1] units market; its eight models are priced in the range of Rs 8,500–19,000 with a marked presence in the Indian family size of 28–30 liter. LG Electronics and Samsung India dominated the segment with a collective market share of about 61 percent.

In the early days, microwave ovens did not figure at all in the consumer's purchase list. Kelvinator's Magicook made a high profile entry some seven years ago. What went wrong, according to the analyst, was the pricing, which was nothing less than Rs 20,000, and sizes which were too small to accommodate large Indian vessels.

Efforts to grow the market are concentrated in large urban areas with routine fare such as organizing cookery classes, recipe contests, and in-house demos, giving away accessories such as glass bowls, aprons, and gloves as freebies and hosting co-promotions

"To change the way you look, just change the way you cook" was a recent tagline by one of the companies.

What will really spur the category's growth will be a change in eating habits. One company piggybacks on "freshness," a tactic the company adopts for all its product lines.

Even though consumer durable sales fell in the first quarter of 2005, the microwave oven segment, which accounts for 70 percent of unit sales in the consumer durable industry, bucked the overall trend. The strength of microwave oven sales is attributed to the steady price reduction from Rs 7,000 for the lowest priced to Rs 5,000 over the last two years. While sales are predominantly in the urban areas, semiurban towns have emerged as a key growth driver for the category.

There is some difference of opinion on the right price for the ovens. For the microwave market to take off its price would have to be below Rs 7,000, says one company. During the time that microwave ovens have been introduced locally prices have been all over the waterfront. For example, one company prices its ovens between Rs 7,000 and Rs 18,000, another between Rs 12,500 and 15,000 and an oven with grill functions for Rs 17,900.

From wooing the supermom to courting the single male the journey of microwave ovens has just begun. Once perceived as a substitute to the OTG (Oven Toaster and Grill), companies with large shares of this segment now are portraying microwaves as more than just a reheating device.

According to one analyst, the product category is going through a transition period and the consumer today is more educated about an OTG than a microwave. The analyst believes there is demand for both microwave and OTG categories.

Microwave companies face a chicken-and-egg question on price and sales. Prices will not come down easily until volumes go up, while volumes depend on prices.

The product is a planned purchase and not an impulse buy. Samsung has set up call centers where the customers can call and get all their queries pertaining to the Samsung Microwave Oven answered.

Besides the basic, low-end models which lead sales, the combination models (convection and microwave) models are showing a steady increase in sales.

Though the concept of microwave ovens is Western, the fact is that microwave technology today has advanced to a level wherein even complex cooking like Indian cooking is very much possible.

One of the older company marketing managers, who has worked in microwave marketing most of his career, is somewhat skeptical about the prospects of rapid growth of the Indian market. He remarked that the microwave oven first introduced in the U.S. market in about 1950 did not become popular across all market segments until about the mid-1970s. Of course, now almost every household in the United States has at least one microwave.

Your task is to develop a strategy to market White Appliance's microwave ovens in India. Include target market(s), microwave oven features, price(s), promotion, and distribution in your program. You should also consider both short-term as well as long-term marketing programs. Some of the issues you may want to consider are:

- Indian food preparation versus Western food preparation.
- Values and customs that might affect opinions about microwave ovens.
- The effects of competition in the market.

You may also want to review the Country Notebook: A Plan for Developing a Marketing Plan, p. 585 of the text for some direction.

---

[1]A lakh is a unit in a traditional number system, still widely used in India. One lakh is equal to 100,000. A crore is also a traditional number system unit, and one crore is equal to 10 million.

cases 2

THE CULTURAL ENVIRONMENT OF GLOBAL MARKETING

OUTLINE OF CASES

2-1 The Not-So-Wonderful World of EuroDisney—
Things Are Better Now at Paris Disneyland

2-2 Cultural Norms, *Fair & Lovely,* and Advertising

2-3 Starnes-Brenner Machine Tool Company: To Bribe
or Not to Bribe?

2-4 Ethics and Airbus

2-5 Coping with Corruption in Trading with China

2-6 When International Buyers and Sellers Disagree

2-7 McDonald's and Obesity

CASE 2–1 The Not-So-Wonderful World of EuroDisney—Things Are Better Now at Paris Disneyland

BONJOUR, MICKEY!

In April 1992, EuroDisney SCA opened its doors to European visitors. Located by the river Marne some 20 miles east of Paris, it was designed to be the biggest and most lavish theme park that Walt Disney Company (Disney) had built to date—bigger than Disneyland in Anaheim, California; Disneyworld in Orlando, Florida; and Tokyo Disneyland in Japan.

Much to Disney management's surprise, Europeans failed to "go goofy" over Mickey, unlike their Japanese counterparts. Between 1990 and early 1992, some 14 million people had visited Tokyo Disneyland, with three-quarters being repeat visitors. A family of four staying overnight at a nearby hotel would easily spend $600 on a visit to the park. In contrast, at EuroDisney, families were reluctant to spend the $280 a day needed to enjoy the attractions of the park, including *les hamburgers* and *les milkshakes*. Staying overnight was out of the question for many because hotel rooms were so high priced. For example, prices ranged from $110 to $380 a night at the Newport Bay Club, the largest of EuroDisney's six new hotels and one of the biggest in Europe. In comparison, a room in a top hotel in Paris cost between $340 and $380 a night.

Financial losses became so massive at EuroDisney that the president had to structure a rescue package to put EuroDisney back on firm financial ground. Many French bankers questioned the initial financing but the Disney response was that their views reflected the cautious, Old World thinking of Europeans who didn't understand U.S.-style free market financing. After some acrimonious dealings with French banks a two-year financial plan was negotiated. Disney management rapidly revised their marketing plan and introduced strategic and tactical changes in the hope of "doing it right" this time.

A Real Estate Dream Come True
The Paris location was chosen over 200 other potential sites stretching from Portugal through Spain, France, Italy, and into Greece. Spain thought it had the strongest bid based on its yearlong, temperate, and sunny Mediterranean climate, but insufficient acreage of land was available for development around Barcelona.

In the end, the French government's generous incentives, together with impressive data on regional demographics, swayed Disney management to choose the Paris location. It was calculated that some 310 million people in Europe live within two hours' air travel of EuroDisney, and 17 million could reach the park within two hours by car—better demographics than at any other Disney site. Pessimistic talk about the dismal winter weather of northern France was countered with references to the success of Tokyo Disneyland, where resolute visitors brave cold winds and snow to enjoy their piece of Americana. Furthermore, it was argued, Paris is Europe's most-popular city destination among tourists of all nationalities.

Spills and Thrills
Disney had projected that the new theme park would attract 11 million visitors and generate over $100 million in operating earnings during the first year of operation. By summer 1994, EuroDisney had lost more than $900 million since opening. Attendance reached only 9.2 million in 1992, and visitors spent 12 percent less on purchases than the estimated $33 per head.

If tourists were not flocking to taste the thrills of the new EuroDisney, where were they going for their summer vacations in 1992? Ironically enough, an unforeseen combination of transatlantic airfare wars and currency movements resulted in a trip to Disneyworld in Orlando being cheaper than a trip to Paris, with guaranteed good weather and beautiful Florida beaches within easy reach.

EuroDisney management took steps to rectify immediate problems in 1992 by cutting rates at two hotels up to 25 percent, introducing some cheaper meals at restaurants, and launching a Paris ad blitz that proclaimed "California is only 20 miles from Paris."

An American Icon
One of the most worrying aspects of EuroDisney's first year was that French visitors stayed away; they had been expected to make up 50 percent of the attendance figures. A park services consulting firm framed the problem in these words: "The French see EuroDisney as American imperialism—plastics at its worst." The well-known, sentimental Japanese attachment to Disney characters contrasted starkly with the unexpected and widespread French scorn for American fairy-tale characters. French culture has its own lovable cartoon characters such as Astérix, the helmeted, pint-sized Gallic warrior who has a theme park located near EuroDisney.

Hostility among the French people to the whole "Disney idea" had surfaced early in the planning of the new project. Paris theater director Ariane Mnouchkine became famous for her description of EuroDisney as "a cultural Chernobyl." In fall 1989, during a visit to Paris, French Communists pelted Michael Eisner with eggs. The joke going around at the time was, "For EuroDisney to adapt properly to France, all seven of Snow White's dwarfs should be named Grumpy *(Grincheux)*."

Early advertising by EuroDisney seemed to aggravate local French sentiment by emphasizing glitz and size, rather than the variety of rides and attractions. Committed to maintaining Disney's reputation for quality in everything, more detail was built into EuroDisney. For example, the centerpiece castle in the Magic Kingdom had to be bigger and fancier than in the other parks. Expensive trams were built along a lake to take guests from the hotels to the park, but visitors preferred walking. Total park construction costs were estimated at FFr 14 billion ($2.37 billion) in 1989 but rose by $340 million to FFr 16 billion as a result of all these add-ons. Hotel construction costs alone rose from an estimated FFr 3.4 billion to FFr 5.7 billion.

EuroDisney and Disney managers unhappily succeeded in alienating many of their counterparts in the government, the banks, the ad agencies, and other concerned organizations. A barnstorming, kick-the-door-down attitude seemed to reign among the U.S. decision makers. "They had a formidable image and convinced everyone that if we let them do it their way, we would all have a marvelous adventure." One former Disney executive voiced the opinion, "We were arrogant—it was like 'We're building the Taj Mahal and people will come—on our terms.'"

STORM CLOUDS AHEAD

Disney and its advisors failed to see signs at the end of the 1980s of the approaching European recession. Other dramatic events included the Gulf War in 1991, which put a heavy brake on vacation travel for the rest of that year. Other external factors that Disney executives have cited were high interest rates and the devaluation of several currencies against the franc. EuroDisney also encountered difficulties with regard to competition—the World's Fair in Seville and the 1992 Olympics in Barcelona were huge attractions for European tourists.

Disney management's conviction that it knew best was demonstrated by its much-trumpeted ban on alcohol in the park. This proved insensitive to the local culture because the French are the world's biggest consumers of wine. To them a meal without *un verre de rouge* is unthinkable. Disney relented. It also had to relax its rules on personal grooming of the projected 12,000 cast members, the park employees. Women were allowed to wear redder nail polish than in the United States, but the taboo on men's facial hair was maintained. "We want the clean-shaven, neat and tidy look," commented the director of Disney University's Paris branch, which trains prospective employees in Disney values and culture. EuroDisney's management did, however, compromise on the question of pets. Special kennels were built to house visitors' animals. The thought of leaving a pet at home during vacation is considered irrational by many French people.

Plans for further development of EuroDisney after 1992 were ambitious. The initial number of hotel rooms was planned to be 5,200, more than in the entire city of Cannes on the Côte d'Azur. Also planned were shopping malls, apartments, golf courses, and vacation homes. EuroDisney would design and build everything itself, with a view to selling at a profit. As a Disney executive commented, "Disney at various points could have had partners to share the risk, or buy the hotels outright. But it didn't want to give up the upside."

"From the time they came on, Disney's Chairman Eisner and President Wells had never made a single misstep, never a mistake, never a failure," said a former Disney executive. "There was a tendency to believe that everything they touched would be perfect." The incredible growth record fostered this belief. In the seven years before EuroDisney opened, they took the parent company from being a company with $1 billion in revenues to one with $8.5 billion, mainly through internal growth.

Telling and Selling Fairy Tales   Mistaken assumptions by the Disney management team affected construction design, marketing and pricing policies, and park management, as well as initial financing. Disney executives had been erroneously informed that Europeans don't eat breakfast. Restaurant breakfast service was downsized accordingly, and guess what? "Everybody showed up for breakfast. We were trying to serve 2,500 breakfasts in a 350-seat restaurant [at some of the hotels]. The lines were horrendous. And they didn't just want croissants and coffee, they wanted bacon and eggs."

In contrast to Disney's American parks where visitors typically stay at least three days, EuroDisney is at most a two-day visit. Energetic visitors need even less time. One analyst claimed to have "done" every EuroDisney ride in just five hours. Typically many guests arrive early in the morning, rush to the park, come back to their hotel late at night, and then check out the next morning before heading back to the park.

Vacation customs of Europeans were not taken into consideration. Disney executives had optimistically expected that the arrival of their new theme park would cause French parents to take their children out of school in mid-session for a short break. It did not happen unless a public holiday occurred over a weekend. Similarly, Disney expected that the American-style short but more frequent family trips would displace the European tradition of a one-month family vacation, usually taken in August. However, French office and factory schedules remained the same, with their emphasis on an August shutdown.

In promoting the new park to visitors, Disney did not stress the entertainment value of a visit to the new theme park; the emphasis was on the size of the park, which "ruined the magic." To counter this, ads were changed to feature Zorro, a French favorite, Mary Poppins, and Aladdin, star of the huge moneymaking movie success. A print ad campaign at that time featured Aladdin, Cinderella's castle, and a little girl being invited to enjoy a "magic vacation," at the kingdom where all dreams come true." Six new attractions were added in 1994, the Temple of Peril, Storybook Land; and the Nautilus attraction. Donald Duck's birthday was celebrated on June 9. All in hopes of positioning EuroDisney as the No. 1 European destination of short duration, one to three days.

Tomorrowland   Faced with falling share prices and crisis talk among shareholders, Disney was forced to step forward in late 1993 to rescue the new park. Disney announced that it would fund EuroDisney until a financial restructuring could be worked out with lenders. However, it was made clear by the parent company, Disney, that it "was not writing a blank check."

In June 1994, EuroDisney received a new lifeline when a member of the Saudi royal family agreed to invest up to $500 million for a 24 percent stake in the park. The prince has an established reputation in world markets as a "bottom-fisher," buying into potentially viable operations during crises when share prices are low. The prince's plans included a $100 million convention center at EuroDisney. One of the few pieces of good news about EuroDisney is that its convention business exceeded expectations from the beginning.

MANAGEMENT AND NAME CHANGES

Frenchman Philippe Bourguignon took over at EuroDisney as CEO in 1993 and has navigated the theme park back to profitability. He was instrumental in the negotiations with the firm's bankers, cutting a deal that he credits largely for bringing the park back into the black.

Perhaps more important to the long-run success of the venture were his changes in marketing. The pan-European approach to marketing was dumped, and national markets were targeted separately. This new localization took into account the differing tourists' habits around the continent. Separate marketing offices were opened in London, Frankfurt, Milan, Brussels, Amsterdam, and Madrid, and each was charged with tailoring advertising and packages to its own market. Prices were cut by 20 percent for park admission and 30 percent for some hotel room rates. Special promotions were also run for the winter months.

The central theme of the new marketing and operations approach is that people visit the park for an "authentic" Disney day out. They may not be completely sure what that means, except that it entails something American. This is reflected in the transformation of the park's name. The "Euro" in EuroDisney was first shrunk in the logo, and the word "land" added. Then in October

1994 the "Euro" was eliminated completely; the park is now called Disneyland Paris.

In 1996, Disneyland Paris became France's most visited tourist attraction, ahead of both the Louvre Art Museum and the Eiffel Tower. 11.7 million visitors (a 9 percent increase from the previous year) allowed the park to report another profitable year.

THEME PARK EXPANSION IN THE TWENTY-FIRST CENTURY

With the recovery of Disneyland Paris, Disney embarked on an ambitious growth plan. In 2001 the California Adventure Park was added to the Anaheim complex at a cost of $1.4 billion and Walt Disney Studios Theme Park was added to Disneyland Paris. Through agreements with foreign partners, Disney will open Disney-Sea in Tokyo and plans are underway for a theme park in Shanghai that Chinese officials hope will open in time for the 2008 Olympic Games in Beijing, and a park in Hong Kong is to open in 2006.

A decade after being slammed for its alleged ignorance of European ways with EuroDisney, Disney is trying to prove it's gotten things right the second time around. The new movie-themed park, Walt Disney Studios adjacent to Disneyland Paris, is designed to be tribute to moviemaking—but not just the Hollywood kind. The Walt Disney Studios blends Disney entertainment and attractions with the history and culture of European film since French camera-makers helped invent the motion picture. The park's general layout is modeled after an old Hollywood studio complex, and some of the rides and shows are near replicas of Disney's first film park, Disney-MGM Studios. Rather than celebrating the history of U.S. Disney characters, the characters in the new theme park speak six different languages. A big stunt show features cars and motorcycles that race through a village modeled after the French resort town of St. Tropez.

Small details reflect the cultural lessons learned. "We made sure that all our food venues have covered seating," recalling that, when EuroDisney first opened, the open-air restaurants offered no protection from the rainy weather that assails the park for long stretches of the year.

On the food front, EuroDisney offered only a French sausage, drawing complaints from the English, Germans, Italians, and everyone else about why their local sausages weren't available. This time around, the park caters to the multiple indigenous cultures throughout Europe—which includes a wider selection of sausages.

Unlike Disney's attitude with their first park in France, "Now we realize that our guests need to be welcomed on the basis of their own culture and travel habits," says Disneyland Paris Chief Executive. Disneyland Paris today is Europe's biggest tourist attraction—even more popular than the Eiffel Tower—a turnaround that showed the park operators' ability to learn from their mistakes.

The root of Disney's problems in EuroDisney may be found in the tremendous success of Japan's Disneyland. The Tokyo Park was a success from the first day, and it has been visited by millions of Japanese who wanted to capture what they perceived as the ultimate U.S entertainment experience.

Disney took the entire U.S. theme park and transplanted it in Japan. It worked because of the Japanese attachment to Disney characters. Schools have field trips to meet Mickey and his friends to the point that the Disney experience has become ingrained in Japanese life. In the book *Disneyland as Holy Land,* University of Tokyo professor Masako Notoji wrote: "The opening of Tokyo Disneyland was, in retrospect, the greatest cultural event in Japan during the '80s." With such success, is there any wonder that Disney thought they had the right model when they first went to France? The Tokyo Disney constitutes a very rare case in that the number of visitors has not decreased since the opening.

While Disney Japan was a success the company also admitted making a major financial error when the park was launched. It had licensed its name and image to another company that actually owns and operates the park as well as the land where it sits. Disney collects only a small fraction of the revenues, which ran into hundreds of millions of dollars every year. Since they were not certain of the success of the first international venture, it was the price they were willing to pay; however, they vowed never to repeat that error and to never have their hands tied again. As a consequence, when they began the Paris park, they were fanatically intent on owning and controlling the park as well as enough adjacent property for its own exclusive hotels—"they were sure they had the right model and they were going to own it all." Thus, they began planning EuroDisney.

2005 Update—Bankruptcy Pending

In early 2005, EuroDisney was on the verge of bankruptcy. EuroDisney's newest park, called Walt Disney Studios, with Hollywood-themed attractions such a ride called "Armageddon—Special Effects" that it based on a movie starring Bruce Willis, flopped. Guests said it lacked attractions to justify the entrance price, and others complained it focused too much on American, rather than European, filmmaking. Disney blames other factors: the post-9/11 tourism slump, strikes in France and a summer heat wave in 2003. The French government came to the aid of EuroDisney with a state-owned bank contribution of around $500 million to save the company from bankruptcy.

A new EuroDisney's CEO, a former Burger King executive, has introduced several changes in hopes of bringing EuroDisney back from the edge of bankruptcy. To make EuroDisney a cheaper vacation destination, the CEO is lobbying the government to open up Charles de Gaulle airport to more low-cost airlines. Under his direction, EuroDisney has created its first original character tailored for a European audience: the Halloween-themed "L'Homme Citrouille," or "Pumpkin Man." He has also introduced a one-day pass giving visitors access to both parks in place of two separate tickets. He is also planning new rides including Tower of Terror rides and other new attractions. If these changes fail to bring in millions of new visitors, Disney and the French government might once again be forced to consider dramatic measures.

Even though French President Chirac calls the spread of American culture an "ecological disaster" and the French government imposes quotas on non-French movies to offset the influence of Hollywood and officially discourages the use of English words such as "e-mail," EuroDisney is important to the French economy. In light of France's 10 percent unemployment, EuroDisney is seen as a job-creation success. The company accounts for an estimated 43,000 jobs and its parks attract over 12 million visitors a year, more than the Louvre Museum and the Eiffel Tower combined.

REFERENCES

"An American in Paris," *BusinessWeek,* March 12, 1990, pp. 60–61, 64.

Asahi Shimbun, " Tokyo Disney Prospers In Its Own Way," *Asahi Evening News,* April 22, 2003.

Chester Dawson, "Will Tokyo Embrace Another Mouse?" *BusinessWeek*, September 10, 2001.

"Disney Characters in Europe Will Mark Quebec's National Holiday by Chowing Down on Poutine," *Broadcast News* (Canada), June 24, 2003.

"Euro Disney Gets Its Rights Issue Thanks to Underwriting Banks but Success in Balance," *Euroweek,* February 11, 2005.

"EuroDisney's Prince Charming?" *BusinessWeek,* June 13, 1994, p. 42.

"EuroDisney Tries to End Evil Spell," *Advertising Age,* February 7, 1994, p. 39.

Paul Herbig, "Disney's Mickey Mouse: N'est Ce Oas . . . Faux Pas," in Michael D. White, *International Marketing Blunders* (Novato, CA: World Trade Press, 2002), p. 4.

"The Kingdom inside the Republic (New Management Strategy at Euro-Disney)," *The Economist,* April 13, 1996, p. 66.

"The Mouse Isn't Roaring," *BusinessWeek,* August 24, 1992, p. 38.

"Mouse Trap: Fans Like EuroDisney but Its Parent's Goofs Weigh the Park Down," *Wall Street Journal,* March 10, 1994, p. A12.

Paulo Prada and Bruce Orwall, "A Certain 'Je Ne Sais Quoi' at Disney's New Park," *Wall Street Journal,* March 12, 2002, p. B1.

"Saudi to Buy as Much as 24% of EuroDisney," *Wall Street Journal,* June 2, 1994, p. A4.

Richard Verrier, "Disney May Add 2nd China Park," *Los Angeles Times,* July 20, 2002, p. C2.

Bernard J. Wolfson, "The Mouse That Roared Back," *Orange County Register,* April 9, 2000, pp. 1.

Jo Wrighton and Bruce Orwall, "Despite Losses and Bailouts, France Stays Devoted to Disney," *Wall Street Journal,* January 26, 2005.

James Zoltak, "Tokyo DisneySea Plans New Attractions," *Amusement Business,* May 26, 2003, p. 1.

QUESTIONS

1. What factors contributed to EuroDisney's poor performance during its first year of operation?

2. To what degree do you consider that these factors were (a) foreseeable and (b) controllable by either EuroDisney or the parent company, Disney?

3. What role does ethnocentrism play in the story of EuroDisney's launch?

4. How do you assess the cross-cultural marketing skills of Disney?

5. Why did success in Tokyo predispose Disney management to be too optimistic in their expectations of success in France? Discuss.

6. Do you think the new theme park would have encountered the same problems if a location in Spain had been selected? Discuss.

7. In light of the near-bankruptcy in 2005, evaluate the proposed plans to strengthen Disney's appeal to the French market.

8. Now that Disney has begun work on the new Hong Kong and Shanghai locations, where and when should it go next? Assume you are a consultant hired to give Disney advice on the issue of where and when to go next. Pick three locations and select the one you think will be the best new location for "Disneyland *X.*" Discuss.

9. Given your choice of locale *X* for the newest Disneyland, what are the operational implications of the history of EuroDisney for the new park?

Professor Lyn S. Amine prepared this case with graduate student Carolyn A. Tochtrop, Saint Louis University, Saint Louis, Missouri, as a basis for class discussion rather than to illustrate either effective or ineffective handling of a situation. The original case appearing in the 11th edition has been edited and updated to reflect recent developments.

CASE 2-2 Cultural Norms, *Fair & Lovely*, and Advertising

Fair & Lovely, a branded product of Hindustan Lever, LTD (HLL), is touted as a cosmetic that lightens skin color. On its Web site (www.hll.com) the company calls its product, "the miracle worker," which is "proven to deliver one to three shades of change." While tanning is the rage in Western countries, skin lightening treatments are popular in Asia.

According to industry sources, the top-selling skin lightening cream in India is *Fair & Lovely* from Hindustan Lever, followed by CavinKare's *Fairever* brand. HLL's *Fair & Lovely* brand was the undisputed monarch of the market with a 90 percent share until CavinKare Ltd (CKL) launched *Fairever*. In just two years, the *Fairever* brand gained an impressive 15 percent market share. HLL's share of market for the *Fair & Lovely* line generates about $60 million annually. The product sells for about 23 rupees ($0.29) for a 25-gram tube of cream.

The rapid growth of CavinKare's *Fairever* (www.cavinkare.com) brand prompted HLL to increase its advertising effort and to launch a series of ads depicting a "fairer girl gets the boy theme." One advertisement featured a financially strapped father lamenting his fate, saying, "If only I had a son," while his dark-skinned daughter looks on, helpless and demoralized because she can't bear the financial responsibility of her family. Fast-forward and plain Jane has been transformed into a gorgeous light-skinned woman through the use of a "fairness cream," *Fair & Lovely*. Now clad in a miniskirt, the woman is a successful flight attendant and can take her father to dine at a five-star hotel. She's happy and so is her father.

In another ad, two attractive young women are sitting in a bedroom; one has a boyfriend and, consequently, is happy. The darker-skinned woman, lacking a boyfriend, is not happy. Her friend's advice—Use a bar of soap to wash away the dark skin that's keeping men from flocking to her.

HLL's series of ads provoked CavinKare Ltd to counter with an ad that takes a dig at HLL's *Fair & Lovely* ad. CavinKare's ad has a father–daughter duo as the protagonists, with the father shown encouraging the daughter to be an achiever irrespective of her complexion. CavinKare maintained that the objective of its new commercial is not to take a dig at *Fair & Lovely* but to "reinforce *Fairever's* positioning."

"We have noticed attempts by *Fair & Lovely* to blur our positioning by changing its communication platform from 'wanting to get married' to 'achievement,' the principal *Fairever* theme. Since we don't have the spending power to match HLL, a tactical way for us to respond is to reinforce our brand positioning and 'the commercial will be aired until the company's "objective" is achieved,'" a CavinKare official said.

Skin color is a powerful theme in India and much of Asia where a lighter color represents a higher status. While Americans and Europeans flock to tanning salons, many across Asia seek ways to have "fair" complexions. Culturally, fair skin is associated with positive values that relate to class and beauty. One Indian lady commented that when she was growing up, her mother forbade her to go outdoors. She was not trying to keep her daughter out of trouble but was trying to keep her skin from getting dark.

Brahmins, the priestly caste at the top of the social hierarchy, are considered fair because they traditionally stayed inside, poring over books. The undercaste at the bottom of the ladder are regarded as the darkest people because they customarily worked in the searing sun. Ancient Hindu scriptures and modern poetry eulogize women endowed with skin made of white marble.

Skin color is closely identified with caste and is laden with symbolism. Pursue any of the "grooms" and "brides wanted" ads in newspapers or on the Web that families use to arrange suitable alliances and you will see that most potential grooms and their families are looking for "fair" brides; some even are progressive enough to invite responses from women belonging to a different caste. These ads, hundreds of which appear in India's daily newspapers, reflect attempts to solicit individuals with the appropriate religion, caste, regional ancestry, professional and educational qualifications, and, frequently, skin color. Even in the growing numbers of ads that announce "caste no bar," the adjective "fair" regularly precedes professional qualifications.

Bollywood (India's Hollywood) glorifies conventions on beauty by always casting a fair-skinned actress in the role of heroine, surrounded by the darkest extras. Women want to use whiteners because it is "aspirational, like losing weight."

Even the gods supposedly lament their dark complexion—Krishna sings plaintively, "Radha kyoon gori, main kyoon kala? (Why is Radha so fair when I'm dark?)." A skin deficient in melanin (the pigment that determines the skin's brown color) is an ancient predilection. More than 3,500 years ago, Charaka, the famous sage, wrote about herbs that could help make the skin fair.

Indian dermatologists maintain that fairness products cannot truly work as they reach only the upper layers of the skin and so do not affect melanin production. Nevertheless, "hope springs eternal" and for some *Fair & Lovely* is a "miracle worker." "The last time I went to my parents' home, I got compliments on my fair skin from everyone," one user gushes—but for others, only disappointment. One 26-year-old working woman has been a regular user for the past eight years but to no avail. "I should have turned into Snow White by now but my skin is still the same wheatish color."

The number of Indians who think lighter skin is more beautiful may be shrinking. Sumit Isralni, a 22-year-old hair designer in his father's salon, thinks things have changed in the last two years, at least in India's most cosmopolitan cities, Delhi, Mumbai, and Bangalore. Women now "prefer their own complexion, their natural way" Isralni says; he prefers a more "Indian beauty" himself. "I won't judge my wife on how fair her complexion is." Sunita Gupta, a beautician in the same salon, is more critical. "It's just foolishness!" she exclaimed. The premise of the ads that women could not become airline attendants if they are dark-skinned was wrong, she said. "Nowadays people like black beauty." It is a truism that women, especially in the tropics, desire to be a shade fairer no matter what their skin color. Although, unlike the approach used in India, advertisements elsewhere usually show how to use the product and how it works.

Shahnaz-Husain (www.shahnaz-husain.com), an herbal care company in India (which has for three decades been the greatest promoter of ayurveda, a holistic health system that originated around 5,000 years ago in India), introduced (2004) a new fairness cream for the masses. The founder says, "I have another fairness product which is a cream to cure skin pigmentation but that cost Rs 300 and people kept on telling me, 'Are you only for the rich? Can't the poor ever make use of your products? So I decided there has to be something for everyone. I have spent 34 years trying to figure out how to enter the mass market, I have spent 34 years in research and development and this is it—this white tube is the end result."

Commenting on the cultural bias toward fair skin, one critic states, "There are attractive people who go through life feeling inferior to their fairer sisters. And all because of charming grandmothers and aunts who do not hesitate to make unflattering comparisons. Kalee Kalooti is an oft-heard comment about women who happen to have darker skin. They get humiliated and mortified over the color of their skin, a fact over which they have no control. Are societal values responsible? Or advertising campaigns? Advertising moguls claim they only reflect prevailing attitudes in India. This is possibly true but what about ethics in advertising? Is it correct to make advertisements that openly denigrate a majority of Indian people—the dark-skinned populace? The advertising is blatant in their strategy. Mock any one who is not the right color and shoot down their self-image."

A dermatologist comments, "Fairness obtained with the help of creams is short-lived. The main reason being, most of these creams contain a certain amount of bleaching agent, which whitens facial hair, and not the skin, which leads people to believe that the cream worked." "In India the popularity of a product depends totally on the success of its advertising."

HLL launched its television ad campaign to promote *Fair & Lovely* in December 2001 and withdrew it in February 2003, amid severe criticism for its portrayal of women. Activists argued that one of the messages the company sends through its "air hostess" ads demonstrating the preference for a son who would be able to take on the financial responsibility for his parents is especially harmful in a country such as India where gender discrimination is rampant. Another offense is perpetuating a culture of discrimination in a society where "fair" is synonymous with "beautiful." AIDWA (All India Women's Democratic Association) lodged a complaint in March and April 2002 with HLL about their offensive ads, but Hindustan Lever failed to respond.

The women's association then appealed to the National Human Rights Commission alleging that the ad demeaned women. AIDWA objected to three things: (1) the ads were racist, (2) they were promoting son preference, and (3) they were insulting to working women. "The way they portrayed the young woman who, after using *Fair & Lovely,* became attractive and therefore lands a job suggested that the main qualification for a woman to get a job is the way she looks." The Human Rights Commission passed AIDWA's complaints on to the Ministry of Information and Broadcasting, which said the campaign violated the Cable and Television Network s Act of 1995—provisions in the Act state that no advertisement shall be permitted which "derides any race, caste, color, creed and nationality" and that "Women must not be portrayed in a manner that emphasized passive, submissive qualities and encourages them to play a subordinate secondary role in the family and society." The government issued notices of the complaints to HLL. After a year-long campaign led by the AIDWA, Hindustan Lever Limited discontinued two of its television advertisements for *Fair & Lovely* fairness cold cream in March 2003.

Shortly after pulling its ads off the air, and, coincidentally, on International Women's Day, HLL launched its "Fair & Lovely Foundation," vowing to "encourage economic empowerment of women across India" by providing resources in education and business. Millions of women "who, though immensely talented and capable, need a guiding hand to help them take the leap forward." Presumably into a fairer future.

HLL sponsored career fairs in over 20 cities across the country offering counseling in as many as 110 careers. It supported 100 rural scholarships for women students passing their 10th grade, a professional course for aspiring beauticians, and a three-month Home Healthcare Nursing Assistant's course catering to young women between the ages 18 and 30. According to HLL, the Fair & Lovely Academy for Home Care Nursing Assistants offers a unique training opportunity for young women who possess no entry level skills and, therefore, are not employable in the new economy job market. The Fair & Lovely Foundation plans to serve as a catalyst for the economic empowerment for women across India. The Fair & Lovely Foundation will showcase the achievements of these women not only to honor them, but also to set an example for other women to follow.

Fairness creams advertising on television registered a rise of nearly 56 percent in the first half of 2004 as compared to the same in 2003. Hindustan Lever rules the fairness creams category with nearly 84.4 percent of the advertising pie on television.

In 2004 *Fair & Lovely* redefined the route to fairness with the new advanced multivitamin Total Fairness cream which lightens skin complexion in four weeks. Total Fairness cream is formulated with the world's most advanced, patented fairness technology for regular every day use. It contains Vitamin C and Vitamin E plus a triple sunscreen system which protects the skin from the sun's darkening UVA and UVB rays.

A product review in www.mouthshut.com posted February 28, 2005, praises *Fair & Lovely* fairness cream: "[*Fair & Lovely*] contains fairness vitamins which penetrate deep down our skin to give us radiant fairness." "I dunno if it can change the skin color from dark to fair, but my personal experience is that it works very well, if you have a naturally fair color and want to preserve it without much headache." "I think Riya Sen has the best skin right now in Bollywood. It appears to be really soft and tender. So, to have a soft and fair skin like her I recommend *Fair & Lovely* Fairness Lotion or Cream." Although "skin color isn't a proof of greatness. Those with wheatish or dark skin are by no way inferior to those who have fair skin."

Here are a few facts about HLL taken from www.hll.com in 2003:

> Lever Limited is India's largest Packaged Mass Consumption Goods Company. We are leaders in Home and Personal Care Products and Food and Beverages including such products as Ponds and Pepsodent. We seek to meet everyday needs of people everywhere—to anticipate the aspirations of our consumers and customers and to respond creatively and competitively with branded products and services which raise the quality of life. It is this purpose which inspires us to build brands. Over the past 70 years, we have introduced about 110 brands.
>
> *Fair & Lovely* has been specially designed and proven to deliver one to three shades of change in most people. Also its sunscreen system is specially optimized for Indian skin. Indian skin unlike Caucasian skin tends to "tan" rather than

"burn" and, hence, requires a different combination of UVA & UVB sunscreens.

The fairness cream is marketed in over 38 countries through HLL Exports and local Unilever companies and is the largest selling skin lightening cream in the world. The brand today offers a substantive range of products to consumers including Fair & Lovely Fairness Reviving Lotion, Fair & Lovely Fairness Cold Cream and Fair & Lovely Fairness Soap.

The following statement was taken from HLL www.hhl.com in August 2005.

A woman's passion for beauty is universal and catering to this strong need is *Fair & Lovely*. Based on a revolutionary breakthrough in skin lightening technology, *Fair & Lovely* was launched in 1978.

The Hindustan Lever Research Centre [it is among the largest research establishments in India's private sector, including pharmaceutical companies, with facilities in Mumbai and Bangalore] deployed technology, based on pioneering research in the science of skin lightening, to develop *Fair & Lovely*. The formulation is patented. Its formulation acts safely and gently with the natural renewal process of the skin, making complexion fairer over a period of six weeks.

Fair & Lovely is formulated with optimum levels of UV sunscreens and niacinamide, which is known to control dispersion of melanin in the skin. It is a patented and proprietary formulation, which has been in the market for 25 years. Niacinamide (Vitamin B3) is a water-soluble vitamin and is widely distributed in cereals, fruits and vegetables—and its use in cosmetic formulations has been known for various end benefits. The UV components of the formulation are scientifically chosen and used at optimum levels to provide wide spectrum protection against UV rays of the sun. Specifically, this patented formulation offers a high UVA protection, which is more relevant to Asian skin than plain SPF protection creams sold in the West. All the active ingredients in the *Fair & Lovely* formulation function synergistically to lighten skin color through a process that is natural, reversible and totally safe.

The brand today offers a substantive range of products, including Ayurvedic *Fair & Lovely* Fairness cream, *Fair & Lovely* Anti-Marks Cream, *Fair & Lovely* Oil Control Fairness Gel, *Fair & Lovely* for Deep Skin and *Fair & Lovely* Fairness Soap. The latest has been the Perfect Radiance, a complete range of 12 premium skincare solutions from *Fair & Lovely*.

QUESTIONS

1. Is it ethical to sell a product that is, at best, only mildly effective? Discuss.

2. Is it ethical to exploit cultural norms and values to promote a product? Discuss

3. Is the advertising of Fair & Lovely demeaning to women or is it portraying a product not too dissimilar to cosmetics in general?

4. Will HLL's Fair & Lovely Foundation be enough to counter charges made by AIDWA? Discuss

5. In light of AIDWA's charges, how would you suggest Fair & Lovely promote its product? Discuss. Would your response be different if Fairever continues to use "fairness" as a theme of its promotion? Discuss.

6. Propose a promotion/marketing program that will counter all the arguments and charges against Fair & Lovely and be an effective program.

7. Comment on the change in the two statements by HLL between 2003 and 2005. Do the changes in the statements reflect a change in marketing/advertising strategy?

8. Comment on Shahnaz-Husain's introduction of "fairness cream for the masses" in 2004 in light of AIDWA's charges.

Sources: Nicole Leistikow, "Indian Women Criticize 'Fair and Lovely' Ideal," *Women's eNews*, April 28, 2003; Shuchi Sinha, "Skin Care: Fair & Growing," *India Today*, December 4, 2000, p. 48; Ratna Bhushan, "CavinKare Changes Tack to Challenge HLL Strategy," *Business Line (The Hindu)*, July 10, 2002; Arundhati Parmar, "Objections to Indian Ad Not Taken Lightly," *Marketing News*, June 9, 2003, p. 4; "Fair & Lovely Launches Foundation to Promote Economic Empowerment of Women," *Press Release Fair & Lovely Foundation* (www.hll.com and search for foundation), March 11, 2003; Cavinkare Changers Tack to Challenge HLL Strategy," *Indian Business Insight*, July 10, 2002; Shunu Sen, "A Fair Way of Advertising," *Business Line (The Hidu)*, August 1, 2002; "Ad Nauseam," *The Statesman-Asia Africa Intelligence Wire*, March 9, 2002; Rina Chandran, "All for Self-Control," *Business Line (The Hindu)*, April 24, 2003; Miriam Jordan, "Creams for a Lighter Skin Capture the Asian Market Especially in India as a Cultural Virtue," *International Herald Tribune*, May 24, 1998; Simon Robinson and Peter Hawthorne, "Color Blindness: Obsessed with Fair Skin, Many African Women Are Using Dangerous Lighteners," *Time*, July 30, 2001; Khozem Merchant and Edward Luce, "Not So Fair and Lovely," *Financial Times*, March 19, 2003; Bhanu Pande and Seema Shukla, "Big Brother Is Watching," *Economic Times*, May 9, 2003; "Herbal Queen Shahnaz Brings Mass Fairness Cream," *Indo-Asian News Service*, September 14, 2004; "Fair & Lovely Redefines Fairness with Multivitamin Total Fairness Cream," press release, Hindustan Lever Ltd., May 3, 2005; and Dr. Deepa Kanchankoti, "Do You Think Fairness Creams Work?" www.mid-day.com/metro, July 13, 2005.

CASE 2−3 Starnes-Brenner Machine Tool Company: To Bribe or Not to Bribe?

The Starnes-Brenner Machine Tool Company of Iowa City, Iowa, has a small one-man sales office headed by Frank Rothe in Latino, a major Latin American country. Frank has been in Latino for about 10 years and is retiring this year; his replacement is Bill Hunsaker, one of Starnes-Brenner's top salespeople. Both will be in Latino for about eight months, during which time Frank will show Bill the ropes, introduce him to their principal customers, and, in general, prepare him to take over.

Frank has been very successful as a foreign representative in spite of his unique style and, at times, complete refusal to follow company policy when it doesn't suit him. The company hasn't really done much about his method of operation, although from time to time he has angered some top company people. As President Jack McCaughey, who retired a couple of years ago, once remarked to a vice president who was complaining about Frank, "If he's making money—and he is (more than any of the other foreign offices)—then leave the guy alone." When McCaughey retired, the new chief immediately instituted organizational changes that gave more emphasis to the overseas operations, moving the company toward a truly worldwide operation into which a loner like Frank would probably not fit. In fact, one of the key reasons for selecting Bill as Frank's replacement, besides Bill's record as a top salesperson, is Bill's capacity to be an organization man. He understands the need for coordination among operations and will cooperate with the home office so that the Latino office can be expanded and brought into the mainstream.

The company knows there is much to be learned from Frank, and Bill's job is to learn everything possible. The company certainly doesn't want to continue some of Frank's practices, but much of his knowledge is vital for continued, smooth operation. Today, Starnes-Brenner's foreign sales account for about 25 percent of the company's total profits, compared with about 5 percent only 10 years ago.

The company is actually changing character, from being principally an exporter, without any real concern for continuous foreign market representation, to having worldwide operations, where the foreign divisions are part of the total effort rather than a stepchild operation. In fact, Latino is one of the last operational divisions to be assimilated into the new organization. Rather than try to change Frank, the company has been waiting for him to retire before making any significant adjustments in its Latino operations.

Bill Hunsaker is 36 years old, with a wife and three children; he is a very good salesperson and administrator, although he has had no foreign experience. He has the reputation of being fair, honest, and a straight shooter. Some back at the home office see his assignment as part of a grooming job for a top position, perhaps eventually the presidency. The Hunsakers are now settled in their new home after having been in Latino for about two weeks. Today is Bill's first day on the job.

When Bill arrived at the office, Frank was on his way to a local factory to inspect some Starnes-Brenner machines that had to have some adjustments made before being acceptable to the Latino government agency buying them. Bill joined Frank for the plant visit. Later, after the visit, we join the two at lunch.

Bill, tasting some chili, remarks, "Boy! This certainly isn't like the chili we have in America."

"No, it isn't, and there's another difference, too. The Latinos are Americans and nothing angers a Latino more than to have a 'Gringo' refer to the United States as America as if to say that Latino isn't part of America also. The Latinos rightly consider their country as part of America (take a look at the map), and people from the United States are North Americans at best. So, for future reference, refer to home either as the United States, States, or North America, but, for gosh sakes, not just America. Not to change the subject, Bill, but could you see that any change had been made in those S-27s from the standard model?"

"No, they looked like the standard. Was there something out of whack when they arrived?"

"No, I couldn't see any problem—I suspect this is the best piece of sophisticated bribe taking I've come across yet. Most of the time the Latinos are more 'honest' about their *mordidas* than this."

"What's a *mordida*?" Bill asks.

"You know, *kumshaw, dash, bustarella, mordida;* they are all the same: a little grease to expedite the action. *Mordida* is the local word for a slight offering or, if you prefer, bribe," says Frank.

Bill quizzically responds, "Do we pay bribes to get sales?"

"Oh, it depends on the situation, but it's certainly something you have to be prepared to deal with." Boy, what a greenhorn, Frank thinks to himself, as he continues, "Here's the story. When the S-27s arrived last January, we began uncrating them and right away the *jefe* engineer (a government official)—*jefe*, that's the head man in charge—began extra-careful examination and declared there was a vital defect in the machines; he claimed the machinery would be dangerous and thus unacceptable if it wasn't corrected. I looked it over but couldn't see anything wrong, so I agreed to have our staff engineer check all the machines and correct any flaws that might exist. Well, the *jefe* said there wasn't enough time to wait for an engineer to come from the States, that the machines could be adjusted locally, and we could pay him and he would make all the necessary arrangements. So, what do you do? No adjustment his way and there would be an order cancelled; and, maybe there was something out of line, those things have been known to happen. But for the life of me, I can't see that anything had been done since the machines were supposedly fixed. So, let's face it, we just paid a bribe, and a pretty darn big bribe at that—about $1,200 per machine. What makes it so aggravating is that that's the second one I've had to pay on this shipment."

"The second?" asks Bill.

"Yeah, at the border, when we were transferring the machines to Latino trucks, it was hot and they were moving slow as molasses. It took them over an hour to transfer one machine to a Latino truck and we had ten others to go. It seemed that every time I spoke to the dock boss about speeding things up, they just got slower. Finally, out of desperation, I slipped him a fistful of pesos and, sure enough, in the next three hours they had the whole thing loaded. Just one of the local customs of doing business. Generally, though, it comes at the lower level where wages don't cover living expenses too well."

There is a pause and Bill asks, "What does that do to our profits?"

"Runs them down, of course, but I look at it as just one of the many costs of doing business—I do my best not to pay, but when I have to, I do."

Hesitantly, Bill replies, "I don't like it, Frank. We've got good products, they're priced right, we give good service, and keep plenty of spare parts in the country, so why should we have to pay bribes? It's just no way to do business. You've already had to pay two bribes on one shipment; if you keep it up, the word's going to get around and you'll be paying at every level. Then all the profit goes out the window—you know, once you start, where do you stop? Besides that, where do we stand legally? The Foreign Bribery Act makes paying bribes like you've just paid illegal. I'd say the best policy is to never start: You might lose a few sales, but let it be known that there are no bribes; we sell the best, service the best at fair prices, and that's all."

"You mean the Foreign Corrupt Practices Act, don't you?" Frank asks, and continues, in an I'm-not-really-so-out-of-touch tone of voice, "Haven't some of the provisions of the Foreign Corrupt Practices Act been softened somewhat?"

"Yes, you're right, the provisions on paying a *mordida* or grease have been softened, but paying the government official is still illegal, softening or not," replies Bill.

Oh boy! Frank thinks to himself as he replies, "Look, what I did was just peanuts as far as the Foreign Corrupt Practices Act goes. The people we pay off are small, and, granted we give good service, but we've only been doing it for the last year or so. Before that I never knew when I was going to have equipment to sell. In fact, we only had products when there were surpluses stateside. I had to pay the right people to get sales, and besides, you're not back in the States any longer. Things are just done different here. You follow that policy and I guarantee that you'll have fewer sales because our competitors from Germany, Italy, and Japan will pay. Look, Bill, everybody does it here; it's a way of life, and the costs are generally reflected in the markup and overhead. There is even a code of behavior involved. We're not actually encouraging it to spread, just perpetuating an accepted way of doing business."

Patiently and slightly condescendingly, Bill replies, "I know, Frank, but wrong is wrong and we want to operate differently now. We hope to set up an operation here on a continuous basis; we plan to operate in Latino just like we do in the United States. Really expand our operation and make a long-range market commitment, grow with the country! And one of the first things we must avoid is unethical . . ."

Frank interrupts, "But really, is it unethical? Everybody does it, the Latinos even pay *mordidas* to other Latinos; it's a fact of life— is it really unethical? I think that the circumstances that exist in a country justify and dictate the behavior. Remember, man, 'When in Rome, do as the Romans do.'"

Almost shouting, Bill blurts out, "I can't buy that. We know that our management practices and relationships are our strongest point. Really, all we have to differentiate us from the rest of our competition, Latino and others, is that we are better managed and, as far as I'm concerned, graft and other unethical behavior have got to be cut out to create a healthy industry. In the long run, it should strengthen our position. We can't build our futures on illegal and unethical practices."

Frank angrily replies, "Look, it's done in the States all the time. What about the big dinners, drinks, and all the other hanky-panky that goes on? Not to mention PACs' [Political Action Committee] payments to congressmen, and all those high speaking fees certain congressmen get from special interests. How many congressmen have gone to jail or lost reelection on those kinds of things? What is that, if it isn't *mordida* the North American way? The only difference is that instead of cash only, in the United States we pay in merchandise and cash."

"That's really not the same and you know it. Besides, we certainly get a lot of business transacted during those dinners even if we are paying the bill."

"Bull, the only difference is that here bribes go on in the open; they don't hide it or dress it in foolish ritual that fools no one. It goes on in the United States and everyone denies the existence of it. That's all the difference—in the United States we're just more hypocritical about it all."

"Look," Frank continues, almost shouting, "we are getting off on the wrong foot and we've got eight months to work together. Just keep your eyes and mind open and let's talk about it again in a couple of months when you've seen how the whole country operates; perhaps then you won't be so quick to judge it absolutely wrong."

Frank, lowering his voice, says thoughtfully, "I know it's hard to take; probably the most disturbing problem in underdeveloped countries is the matter of graft. And, frankly, we don't do much advance preparation so we can deal firmly with it. It bothered me at first; but then I figured it makes its economic contribution, too, since the payoff is as much a part of the economic process as a payroll. What's our real economic role, anyway, besides making a profit, of course? Are we developers of wealth, helping to push the country to greater economic growth, or are we missionaries? Or should we be both? I really don't know, but I don't think we can be both simultaneously, and my feeling is that, as the company prospers, as higher salaries are paid, and better standards of living are reached, we'll see better ethics. Until then, we've got to operate or leave, and if you are going to win the opposition over, you'd better join them and change them from within, not fight them."

Before Bill could reply, a Latino friend of Frank's joined them and they changed the topic of conversation.

QUESTIONS

1. Is what Frank did ethical? By whose ethics—those of Latino or the United States?

2. Are Frank's two different payments legal under the Foreign Corrupt Practices Act as amended by the Omnibus Trade and Competitiveness Act of 1988?

3. Identify the types of payments made in the case; that is, are they lubrication, extortion, or subornation?

4. Frank seemed to imply that there is a similarity between what he was doing and what happens in the United States. Is there any difference? Explain.

5. Are there any legal differences between the money paid to the dockworkers and the money paid the *jefe* (government official)? Any ethical differences?

6. Frank's attitude seems to imply that a foreigner must comply with all local customs, but some would say that one of the contributions made by U.S. firms is to change local ways of doing business. Who is right?

7. Should Frank's behavior have been any different had this not been a government contract?

8. If Frank shouldn't have paid the bribe, what should he have done, and what might have been the consequences?

9. What are the company interests in this problem?

10. Explain how this may be a good example of the SRC (self-reference criterion) at work.

11. Do you think Bill will make the grade in Latino? Why? What will it take?

12. How can an overseas manager be prepared to face this problem?

CASE 2—4 Ethics and Airbus

In September last year, a fraud squad, led by Jean-Claude Van Espen, a Belgian magistrate, raided Airbus's headquarters in Toulouse. "They wanted to check whether there was possible falsification of documents, bribery or other infractions as part of the sale of Airbus aircraft to Sabena," says Mr. Van Espen's spokesman. The team of 20 Belgian and French investigators interviewed several Airbus employees during its three-day stay in Toulouse and carted away boxes of documents.

In November 1997 Sabena had approved an order for 17 Airbus A320s (narrow-bodied aircraft) which it did not need. Even more oddly, it had doubled the order at the last minute to 34, a move which helped trigger the airline's collapse four years later.

Though nominally controlled by the Belgian government, Sabena was run by the parent company of Swissair, SAirGroup, which had owned a stake of 49.5 percent since 1995 and which also went bust in 2001. A former Sabena manager, who arrived after the Airbus order was placed, says that the planes were not needed: "It was a fatal business decision." A Belgian parliamentary commission's recent report confirms that the Airbus order was a big cause of Sabena's collapse.

Mr. Van Espen's separate criminal investigation is continuing. According to the report, it started in October 2001 after Philippe Doyen, then a Sabena employee, lodged a complaint. Among other things, he suggested to Mr. Van Espen that he interview Peter Gysel, a former Swissair employee now working at Airbus, who put together Sabena's deal with Airbus. Mr. Gysel denies any impropriety. The former Sabena manager says: "I never got the slightest whiff that the decision was driven by kickbacks, side-payments and so on. But I cannot rule anything out." Neither does Mr. Van Espen.

Today airlines are ordering about 400 aircraft a year. But in good times 800 planes, worth around $60 billion, are sold a year. In the past ten years Airbus (originally a consortium, now owned 80 percent by EADS and 20 percent by BAE Systems) has caught up with Boeing, which had enjoyed two-thirds of the market since its 747 jumbo-jet entered commercial service in 1970.

Many aircraft are no doubt bought and sold in entirely conventional ways. But many are not. After all, lots of airlines are still state-owned and not subject to normal business rules. Commission payments (licit or illicit) on multi-million-dollar aircraft deals increase the capital cost of aircraft, which are therefore subject to higher depreciation or operating-lease charges, or both. But these extra costs are barely discernible in the pool of red ink created by the carriers' perennial losses.

Aircraft purchases drag on for years, as airlines play Boeing and Airbus off against each other. Especially in a buyer's market, deep discounts are common, performance guarantees are demanding and manufacturers have to offer all sorts of sweeteners (for instance, aircraft trade-ins, or unusual guarantees) to persuade an airline to switch to their aircraft.

Unsurprisingly, given the regulated nature of international air travel, politics plays a part. For instance, no sooner had Air Mauritius bought Airbus A340s in 1994 than it obtained an upgrade from Paris Orly to Charles de Gaulle airport, which is Air France's main base with better onward connections.

Aircraft purchases have long been associated with controversy. In the 1970s, when Lockheed was still making civil jets, it was caught bribing Japanese officials to buy its L1011 wide-bodied airliner. A Japanese prime minister was later charged and convicted in 1983 for taking a bribe. Prince Bernhard of the Netherlands was also disgraced for his involvement with Lockheed. This scandal led in 1977 to Congress passing the Foreign Corrupt Practices Act (FCPA), which forbids American companies, their officers or their representatives from bribing foreign officials.

Critics (including this newspaper) have often pointed out that American firms can sidestep the FCPA by using foreign subsidiaries and nationals to pay bribes. Boeing says that its policy is to adhere to the spirit and letter of the FCPA, that its systems of controls ensure employees comply with this policy, and that no Boeing employee has been charged under the FCPA. In 1982 Boeing pleaded guilty to false statements about commissions on the sale of commercial aircraft prior to 1977. Boeing also says that there have been public hearings in the Bahamas over allegations of bribery in the 1990 sale of deHavilland aircraft to Bahamas Air, during Boeing's ownership of deHavilland.

Airbus has not been subject to such constraints. France ratified an OECD convention to outlaw bribery of foreign public officials in 2000. Until then the government even permitted French companies tax deductions for giving bribes.

For years, as they steadily lost market share to the European challenger, the Americans have been outspokenly critical of Airbus. In the 1980s the beef was the huge subsidies that European governments poured into the industry. Now that Airbus repays such launch aid, that is less relevant, especially as Boeing receives indirect subsidies through America's defense budget and space program.

But the American government has also spoken out on the subject of bribery. Two years ago Grant Aldonas, an undersecretary for international trade, told a congressional committee: "Unfortunately this [aircraft manufacturing] is an industry where foreign corruption has a real impact . . . this sector has been especially vulnerable to trade distortions involving bribery of foreign public officials."

According to a European Parliament report, published in 2001, America's National Security Agency (NSA) intercepted faxes and phone calls between Airbus, Saudi Arabian Airlines and the Saudi government in early 1994. The NSA found that Airbus agents were offering bribes to a Saudi official to secure a lion's share for Airbus in modernizing Saudi Arabian Airlines' fleet. The planes were in a $6 billion deal that Edouard Balladur, France's then prime minister, had hoped to clinch on a visit to see King Fahd in January 1994. He went home empty-handed.

James Woolsey, then director of the Central Intelligence Agency, recounted in a newspaper article in 2000 how the American government typically reacted to intelligence of this sort. "When we have caught you [Europeans] . . . we go to the government you're bribing and tell its officials that we don't take kindly to such corruption," he wrote. Apparently this (and a direct sales pitch from Bill Clinton to King Fahd) swung the aircraft part of the deal Boeing's and McDonnell Douglas's way.

KUWAITI KICKBACKS?

Not even the NSA, however, knows about everything in the aircraft-manufacturing industry as it actually happens. Consider the history of an Airbus order placed by Kuwait Airways Corporation (KAC), another state-owned airline.

In November 1995, Reuters reported that Kuwaiti prosecutors had questioned Bader Mallalah, KAC's then chief financial officer, over allegations of embezzlement made against him by KAC. The firm's chairman, Ahmed al Mishari, had suspended Dr. Mallalah from his job the previous month. But KAC had trumped up the allegations against Dr. Mallalah to put the lid on a story of corruption in which its then chairman was himself involved.

That story began exactly five years earlier in Cairo, where KAC had set up temporary headquarters after Iraq's invasion of Kuwait in August 1990. Most of its planes would inevitably be lost or damaged, so Mr. al Mishari was planning a shiny new postwar fleet. Naturally, both Boeing and Airbus were asked to tender. Both firms expected politics to play a part in KAC's choice, especially after an American-led coalition had liberated Kuwait.

Shortly after the liberation of Kuwait, Boeing and KAC met in London. One person present says Mr. al Mishari gave the impression that the order would be Boeing's. After all, until then, American companies had won most of the large reconstruction contracts from a grateful government.

Airbus hoped otherwise. In 1991, shortly before the Paris Air Show, Jean Pierson, the then boss of Airbus, met Mr. al Mishari at the Churchill Hotel in London. The two talked in private for part of the time, so what they discussed is not known. Two clear inferences can, however, be drawn from subsequent events: Mr. al Mishari promised the order to Airbus; and Mr. Pierson pressed for an announcement at the imminent air show.

As substantial public funds were involved, KAC was supposed to follow the formal process in Kuwait before placing the order. This included approvals from the Ministry of Finance and the public-spending watchdog. None of these approvals was sought before the air show. In June 1991, at the show, Mr. al Mishari stunned Kuwaiti officials and Boeing, when he announced a firm order for 15 Airbus aircraft, worth $1.1 billion, and options for nine more, worth up to $900 million. A delighted Mr. Pierson trumpeted the deal as Airbus's first single order for all its aircraft types.

Most unusually, Boeing was not asked for its "best and final" offer, according to a former KAC employee. Boeing's response to the announcement was to offer generous discounts to KAC—so that its package was around $100 million cheaper than its rival's—but it was too late. The upshot of a meeting in the summer of 1991 between the boss of Boeing Commercial, furious American officials and the Crown Prince of Kuwait was a messy compromise. KAC would order the engines for the Airbuses from General Electric; Boeing would receive an order for two wide-bodied planes as a sop; and the firm order for 15 Airbus aircraft would go ahead provided that KAC bought from Boeing in future.

This left Mr. al Mishari in a rather awkward spot. KAC had an option to buy nine more aircraft from Airbus. An airline is usually able to walk away from an option deal if it forfeits the modest deposit paid. But this case was far from normal. The company that was to take up the option was not KAC itself but a subsidiary, Aviation Lease and Finance Company (ALAFCO), which Mr. al Mishari had set up in Bermuda in September 1992. ALAFCO was to buy the aircraft and lease them to KAC. In late 1992 Mr. al Mishari confirmed to Mr. Pierson that ALAFCO would buy the nine planes and sent off a $2.5 million deposit. By buying the planes through ALAFCO, Mr. al Mishari intended to bypass formal governmental approval.

There was more to the deal. Airbus chipped in a total of $450,000 between 1992 and 1994 to help with the costs of setting up and running ALAFCO. On December 15, 1992, ALAFCO appointed a part-time commercial adviser, Mohamed Habib El Fekih, a Tunisian national. His day job was then as head of sales in the Middle East—for Airbus. Under his ALAFCO contract of employment, a copy of which *The Economist* has and which is to run for three years from January 1993, Mr. El Fekih received $5,000 a month, and $80,000 in back pay for "services" rendered to ALAFCO from February 1, 1990—31 months before ALAFCO'S incorporation—to December 31, 1992. The $5,000 was paid each month from ALAFCO's account number 201-901-04 at the Commercial Bank of Kuwait in New York to Mr. El Fekih's personal account (number 0000003930B) at Crédit Lyonnais's branch in Blagnac, France, where Airbus is based on the outskirts of Toulouse.

By 1993 three of the nine aircraft under option, all cargo planes, were nearly ready for delivery. However, Dr. Mallalah, who was also ALAFCO's chief executive, insisted that the transaction be subject to formal procedure in Kuwait. This meant competitive tenders from Airbus and Boeing. Unsurprisingly, Airbus, with inside knowledge from its two-hatted vice-president, Mr. El Fekih, was able to match exactly offers from Boeing, after Boeing came in over $50 million cheaper. With nothing to choose between the offers, ALAFCO selected Airbus, on the grounds that KAC's fleet now comprised predominantly Airbus aircraft.

The deal sailed through KAC's board and the Ministry of Finance. However, Dr. Mallalah provided Kuwait's public spending watchdog with full details of ALAFCO's order for the cargo planes. It refused to sanction the deal. Consultants concluded in early 1995 that the purchase of the cargo aircraft was not justified. The Ministry of Finance told KAC not to proceed. After Dr. Mallalah submitted a report to KAC's board on the affair, Mr. El Fekih resigned from ALAFCO in March 1995.

Mr. El Fekih says that he acted in an honest way; Mr. Pierson approved his ALAFCO contract, as did the boards of KAC and ALAFCO; his ALAFCO contract had nothing to do with the sale of Airbus to KAC; KAC cancelled its option; ALAFCO never bought any Airbus aircraft; he acted as a consultant to help set up ALAFCO as an aircraft-financing company; and he declared his earnings to the taxman. Airbus says that it offers this sort of support to customers, when asked. The present owners of the ALAFCO business confirm that ALAFCO bought three Airbus aircraft.

Of the other six aircraft under option, three were not converted into firm orders. Two Airbus A320s were leased to Shorouk Air in Egypt. This joint-venture between KAC and EgyptAir was specifically set up to find a home for them, but is being liquidated because of massive losses. Kuwait's Ministry of Finance leased another.

Mr. al Mishari, sacked as the chairman of KAC in 1999 after spending almost his entire career with the airline, owns a shopping complex in the Salmiya district of Kuwait, which local wags have dubbed the "Airbus Centre." Mr. al Mishari, whose family is wealthy, suffered financial problems when the Kuwaiti stock-market collapsed in the early 1980s. Mr. al Mishari declines to comment, as does KAC.

It is not irrelevant to ask if the price of the Airbus aircraft was inflated to allow for kickbacks. No evidence of graft has ever come to light. However, no policeman, in Kuwait (or elsewhere), has looked for any.

INDIA INK

What about cases where police have carried out investigations? In March 1990 India's Central Bureau of Investigation (CBI) filed a first information report (FIR). It was investigating allegations that Airbus had bribed highly placed public servants and others to induce Indian Airlines (IA) to order its aircraft.

In March 1986 state-owned IA had ordered 19 Airbus A320s, worth $952 million, with an option for 12 more, later exercised. This was despite the fact that, when IA set up a committee in 1983 to recommend replacement aircraft for its aging Boeing fleet, the A320 was not considered—it had not then been launched or flown. With approval from the Indian government, IA had in July 1984 paid Boeing a deposit for 12 Boeing 757s, large narrow-bodied aircraft.

Several civil servants and IA officials were named in the FIR. One name not on the list was that of Rajiv Gandhi, India's prime minister in 1984–89, who was killed in a bomb explosion in May 1991.

How has the CBI's investigation progressed in the intervening 13 years? Hardly at all, despite the hounding on public-interest grounds of the CBI in Delhi's High Court since 1998 by B. L. Wadehra, an anti-corruption lawyer based in Delhi. *The Economist* has examined the publicly available court documents—the CBI's status reports on its investigation are secret—from Mr. Wadehra's litigation.

These papers allege, first, that in October 1984, weeks before Mr. Gandhi, a former pilot, succeeded his mother, IA received an offer from Airbus for A320 aircraft, a smaller and less expensive plane than Boeing's 757. It required urgent attention. Second, that in November, the aviation ministry gave IA just three days to appraise the offer for Mr. Gandhi's office.

Much later, in 1990, *Indian Express,* an Indian newspaper, reported a leaked manuscript note which showed that Mr. Gandhi had decided at a meeting on August 2, 1985, that IA "should go in for Airbus A320 aircraft."

Mr. Gandhi's correspondence file on the deal mysteriously vanished. The court papers show that civil servants reconstructed 29 pages of the missing file for the CBI by obtaining copy correspondence from government departments. Remarkably, this task took seven years—and even then the reconstruction was only partial.

After the green light from Mr. Gandhi, approvals from IA and government bodies were a formality. For instance, the IA board approved the Airbus order at a meeting on August 30, 1985, which started at noon. The quality of the analysis presented to the board on the competing offers was pitiful. The board considered only one criterion—comparative fuel efficiency. Even for that, the data were incomplete. The A320 with the engine chosen by IA had yet to be tried and tested anywhere; provisional data only were included in the report for Boeing 737s "since no technical data were supplied by the company."

But Boeing had not been asked for any. This was because two hours before the board meeting, at 9:50 AM, IA's managing director, who is named in the FIR as an alleged recipient of kickbacks, received a letter from Richard Elliott, then Boeing's regional sales director. Boeing offered to supply up to 35 of its 737 aircraft, its narrow-bodied rival to the A320, with a discount of $5 million per plane. This would reduce IA's investment in new planes by $140 million, stated Mr. Elliott. IA's board brushed the offer aside on the grounds that "if Boeing was [sic] too serious . . . they [sic] could have made the offer earlier."

The Delhi court has a withering opinion of the help Airbus has given the CBI. It allowed Mr. Wadehra to add Airbus's Indian subsidiary to his action on the grounds that Airbus in France was not cooperating. Airbus told Mr. Wadehra that French law forbade it from answering his questions. "[Airbus] sells its aircraft on their merits," the firm insisted.

The court has castigated the CBI for its dilatory approach. It took the Indian authorities until 1995 to contact Airbus for information, only to be told that such requests should be routed through the French government. The CBI told Mr. Wadehra, despite trying Interpol and diplomatic channels, it was not getting any help from the French government. The French embassy in Delhi in effect told Mr. Wadehra to get lost when he wrote to ask why France was not cooperating.

Mr. Wadehra's case is now topical. This is because in March last year, IA's board approved an order for 43 Airbus planes, worth around $2 billion. The order now needs government approval. However, in September 2000, the Delhi court ruled that the Indian government should not approve further purchases from Airbus until the CBI had obtained the information it wanted from the French.

The upshot of the IA story is that no serious attempt has been made to establish whether or not Airbus paid kickbacks to Mr. Gandhi and associates. The CBI has not answered our written questions.

MOUNTIES AND BANKS

But there are police forces which have shown rather more resolve and initiative than the CBI. One important case establishes that Airbus has paid "commissions" to individuals hiding behind shell companies in jurisdictions where ownership of companies is not a matter of public record, and where strict bank secrecy applies.

Airbus's first big sale in North America was a $1.5 billion deal, signed in 1988, to sell 34 aircraft to the then state-owned Air Canada. The middleman was Karlheinz Schreiber, a German-Canadian with connections to politicians in Germany and Canada. Mr. Schreiber emerged as a figure in the financing scandal that engulfed Germany's Christian Democrat party and its top politician, Helmut Kohl, a former chancellor, in the late 1990s.

In August 1999 the Royal Canadian Mounted Police, acting on a German arrest warrant, nabbed Mr. Schreiber. In 2000, Mr. Schreiber was charged in Germany with tax evasion on money he had received for the Airbus transaction and other deals. The *Süddeutsche Zeitung,* a German daily, has supplied a copy of Mr. Schreiber's indictment to *The Economist.* According to this document, Airbus signed a consultancy contract (amended four times) with International Aircraft Leasing (IAL) in March 1985. IAL, which was to help with the Air Canada deal, was a shell company based in Vaduz, Liechtenstein, and a subsidiary of another Liechtenstein-registered shell, Kensington Anstalt.

According to the indictment, between September 30, 1988, and October 21, 1993 (i.e., as Air Canada took delivery of Airbus planes), Airbus paid a total of $22,540,000 in "commissions" to IAL. $10,867,000 was paid into IAL's account number 235.972.037 at the Verwaltungs- und Privat-Bank in Vaduz and $11,673,000 into IAL's account number 18.679.4 at Swiss Bank Corporation (SBC) in Zurich. During extradition proceedings against Mr. Schreiber in 1999, Airbus admitted to these payments. In October 2000 Mr. Schreiber won a suspension of execution of his case.

The court ruled that IAL belonged to Mr. Schreiber, but also that, to the extent that Mr. Schreiber had paid out the Airbus "commissions" as *Schmiergelder* ("grease monies"), these payments could be tax deductible. Mr. Schreiber's German tax lawyer later told the court: "*Schmiergelder* were not openly paid to the 'greased' person by [Airbus]. It was through third persons to make reception anonymous and the *Schmiergelder* unrecognisable as such."

So who got the commissions? After years of police investigations in at least five jurisdictions, it is still not clear. According to *The Last Amigo*, a well-researched book on the affair by Harvey Cashore and Stevie Cameron, both Canadian journalists, a lot was withdrawn in cash. Mr. Cashore, a producer on "the fifth estate," Canadian Broadcasting Corporation's main investigative program, says that Mr. Schreiber's bank records and diaries showed that he usually followed a simple formula for dividing up the money: half for Canadians and half for Europeans.

The book alleges that there may have been a smaller scam within the bigger scam: an Airbus employee may have got some of the money. Some of the money was transferred into subaccounts at SBC in Zurich. One of the subaccounts, code-named "Stewardess," received as much as one-eighth of the commissions. The book suggests that this account was intended for Stuart Iddles, Airbus's senior vice-president from 1986 to 1994.

Mr. Iddles's wife bought Casa Las Estacas, a luxurious beachfront villa in Puerto Vallarta, Mexico, in September 1992. Documents in *The Economist*'s possession show the price was $1.5 million. According to a person involved in the deal, the money was wired from account number 154963-01-10 in the name of the Ciclon Foundation at the Zurich branch of Lloyds, a British bank. Mrs. Iddles confirms that she bought the villa in 1992, but says she has not the "foggiest idea" how much it cost, or which bank the money came from. Mr. Iddles has denied any impropriety. Airbus says it has not been indicted in any jurisdiction over the Air Canada deal, or over any other sales. It adds that no investigator has found unethical behavior on its part.

SYRIAN SCANDALS

Only one case of Airbus's colluding with a middleman apparently to bribe officials to buy its aircraft has led to convictions. According to Syria's state news agency, three people were sentenced in Syria in October 2001 to 22 years imprisonment each (later reduced to 10 years) for "serious irregularities" in connection with state-owned Syrianair's order for six Airbus A320s in 1996. The court also imposed a fine on the three of $268 million. They were a former minister for economic affairs, a former transport minister, and Munir Abu Khaddur, the middleman. Mr. Khaddur was sentenced in absentia, and is reportedly living in Spain. The court found that the men had forced the airline to buy the planes, worth $240 million, and as a result Syrianair had incurred "big financial losses."

The only inferences to be drawn are: either there was a miscarriage of justice; or bribes were paid. If the latter, the news agency did not release details of how much the men embezzled. Quite why bribes would have been necessary is puzzling. Because America deems Syria to be a sponsor of terrorism, Boeing has long been prohibited from exporting there. The Syrian government declines to comment.

The result of our investigations into instances of corruption or alleged corruption by Airbus suggests that Mr. Van Espen will have a very long haul as he tries to establish whether "commis-

sions" influenced Sabena's decision to buy Airbuses. The order for the 34 A320s could be viewed as incompetence. But nobody can predict the results of Mr. Van Espen's inquiry.

The parliamentary report says Sabena's board received some lacunary information that was misleading. The choice of Airbus supposedly meant Sabena was confident of strong sales growth. Yet a month after the order was placed, SAirGroup's chief executive, who also sat on Sabena's board, said: "We're now in the last year or years of the boom in air travel." (We do not mean to imply by inference that the chief executive was corrupt.)

Most of what is recounted in this article happened before Airbus's present top management team arrived, before it was established as a proper company, and before France adopted the OECD convention on bribery.

No one doubts the company's ability to compete across the whole product range with Boeing. By the time next week's Paris Air Show is over, Airbus will probably be well ahead of its rival in market share, thanks to an attractive range of planes. But if charges of corruption involving Airbus were to emerge from Mr. Van Espen's investigation of Sabena, that would deal the company's reputation a severe blow.

AIRBUS LOBBIES TO RELAX ANTI-BRIBERY RULES

Newly released documents have revealed how companies used their lobbying power to loosen official rules designed to stop corruption. In behind-the-scenes maneuvers, Rolls-Royce, BAE Systems and the aircraft giant Airbus persuaded trade secretary Patricia Hewitt to allow them to keep secret details of the middlemen used to secure international contracts.

She brushed aside the advice of Whitehall officials who argued that these middlemen are often used to channel bribes to foreign politicians and officials to win contracts. The government's Export Credits Guarantee Department (ECGD) had proposed that exporters had to disclose the identities of middlemen when they applied for financial support from the taxpayer. The government required the details as part of tougher measures to stop the payment of bribes overseas by British companies.

The documents were released by the ECGD following a freedom of information request from the *Guardian* and a recent court case. Minutes of a meeting on August 9 last year show that the three companies told the ECGD that information about these middlemen was "very commercially sensitive." The minutes continued: "The network of agents/intermediaries was a valuable asset built up over a number of years and offered important commercial advantages such as being able to open doors . . . The intermediaries themselves may have valid and justifiable reasons for wanting to remain anonymous."

The companies claimed that the names of the agents would leak from the ECGD, enabling competitors to poach them. Ms. Hewitt agreed that the companies did not have to give the names or addresses of these middlemen, provided the firms gave an explanation.

At a meeting on October 7, the companies wanted "confirmation that commercial confidentiality would be accepted as a valid reason for not identifying its agents." Ms. Hewitt has been forced to rethink the anti-bribery rules because of a legal victory by anti-corruption campaigners, the Corner House group. Susan Hawley, for the group, said: "Knowing who is the middleman is crucial to stopping corruption, otherwise the taxpayer will end up directly supporting bribery." BAE is alleged to have made corrupt payments through middlemen in Saudi Arabia, Qatar, and India. Rolls-Royce is accused of paying £15 million to win a contract in India.

QUESTIONS

1. In each of the cases described above who benefits and who suffers from the alleged ethical and legal lapses of Airbus?

2. How should the public relations staff at Airbus respond to the articles appearing in *The Economist* and *The Guardian*?

3. What steps might Boeing take to defend itself from this sort of competition?

4. Do you think that Boeing and Airbus behave differently in marketing their aircraft around the globe? How and why?

5. Had France adopted the OECD convention on bribery ahead of these transactions would the firm's behavior have differed? Why?

Sources: "Airbus' Secret Past—Aircraft and Bribery," *The Economist*, June 14, 2003, pp. 55–58; and Rob Evans and David Leigh, "Firms Can Keep Secret Agents: Minister Persuaded to Ease Anti-bribery Rules," *The Guardian*, January 25, 2005, p. 18.

CASE 2–5 Coping with Corruption in Trading with China

Corruption is a fact of life in China. In fact, Transparency International, a German organization that applies its "Corruption Perception Index"[1] (CPI) globally, rates China with a CPI of 3.4 and is number 71 of 145 countries rated. Finland is rated the least corrupt at number 1 with a CPI of 9.7, the United States at 17 with a CPI of 7.5, and Haiti the most corrupt at number 145 with a CPI of 1.5. The country's press frequently has detailed cases of corruption and of campaigns to crack down on bribery and other forms of corruption. The articles primarily have focused on domestic economic crimes among Chinese citizens and on local officials, who have been fired, sent to prison, or assessed other penalties.

There is strong evidence that the Chinese government is taking notice and issuing regulations to fight corruption. Newly issued Communist Party of China (CPC) regulations on internal supervision and disciplinary penalties have raised hopes that the new regulations will enhance efforts against corruption.[2] The regulations established 10 kinds of punishing mechanisms for acts of party members who violate political, personnel, and financial regulations and are involved in bribery, malfeasance and infringement of others' rights. Some believe that the execution of three bankers, for "a run-of-the-mill fraud," just before the Communist party's annual meeting, was an indication of how serious the government was about cracking down on corruption.[3]

Much of China's early efforts to stem corruption were focused on activities among domestic Chinese companies and not on China's foreign business community. Traders, trade consultants, and analysts have said that foreign firms are vulnerable to a variety of corrupt practices. Although some of these firms said they had no experience with corruption in China, the majority said they increasingly were asked to make payments to improve business, engage in black-market trade of import and export licenses, and bribe officials to push goods through customs or the Commodity Inspection Bureau, or engage in collusion to beat the system. The Hong Kong Independent Commission Against Corruption reports that outright bribes, as well as gifts or payment to establish *guanxi*, or "connections," average 3 to 5 percent of operating costs in the PRC, or $3 billion to $5 billion of the $100 billion of foreign investments that have been made there. The most common corrupt practices confronting foreign companies in China are examined here.

PAYING TO IMPROVE BUSINESS

Foreign traders make several types of payments to facilitate sales in China. The most common method is a trip abroad. Chinese officials, who rarely have a chance to visit overseas, often prefer foreign travel to cash or gifts. (This was especially true when few PRC officials had been abroad.) As a result, traders report that dangling foreign trips in front of their PRC clients has become a

regular part of negotiating large trade deals that involve products with a technological component. "Foreign travel is always the first inducement we offer," said an executive involved in machinery trade. In most cases, traders build these costs into the product's sale price. Some trips are "reasonable and bona fide expenditures directly related to the promotion, demonstration, or explanation of products and services, or the execution of a contract with a foreign government agency" but it may be another matter when officials on foreign junkets are offered large per diems and aren't invited specifically to gain technical knowledge.

Foreign travel isn't always an inducement—it also can be extorted. In one case, a PRC bank branch refused to issue a letter of credit for a machinery import deal. The Chinese customer suggested that the foreign trader invite the bank official on an overseas inspection tour. Once the invitation was extended, the bank issued the letter of credit.

ANGLING FOR CASH

Some MNCs are asked to sponsor overseas education for the children of trading officials. One person told a Chinese source that an MNC paid for that individual's U.S. $1,500-a-month apartment, as well as a car, university education, and expenses.

Firms find direct requests for cash payments—undeniably illegal—the most difficult. One well-placed source said that a major trader, eager for buyers in the face of an international market glut, had fallen into regularly paying large kickbacks into the Honduran, U.S., and Swiss accounts of officials at a PRC foreign trade corporation. Refusing to make payments may not only hurt sales, it can also be terrifying. A U.S. firm was one of several bidders for a large sale; a Chinese official demanded the MNC pay a 3 percent kickback. When the company representative refused, the official threatened: "You had better not say anything about this. You still have to do business in China, and stay in hotels here." Not surprisingly, the U.S. company lost the deal.

Traders of certain commodities may be tempted to resort to the black market for import and export licenses that are difficult to obtain legally. A fairly disorganized underground market, for instance, exists for licenses to export China-made garments to the United States.

Some branches of the Commodity Inspection Bureau (CIB) also have posed problems for traders. Abuses have emerged in the CIB since it started inspecting imports in 1987. A Japanese company, for instance, informed CIB officials of its intention to bring heavy industrial items into China—items that had met Japanese and U.S. standards. The officials responded that they planned to dismantle the products on arrival for inspection purposes. The problem was resolved only after the firm invited the officials to visit Japan.

Some traders get around such problems by purchasing inspection certificates on the black market. According to press accounts, these forms, complete with signatures and seals, can be bought for roughly U.S. $200.

Some claim that, for the appropriate compensation, customs officials in a southern province are very willing to reduce the

---

[1]See www.transparency.org for more details about their 2002 index.

[2]"CPC Regulations Lift Confidence in China's Corruption Fight," *Xinhua News Service (China)*, February 20, 2004.

[3]Julius Melinster, "China's Strict Bribery Laws Keep Sponsors Guessing," *Corporate Legal Times*, November 2004.

dutiable value of imports as much as 50 percent. Because the savings can far exceed transport costs, some imports that would logically enter China through a northern port are redirected through the southern province.

The new Communist Party of China (CPC) regulations address some of these problems but, unfortunately, the new law raises more questions than answers. Two kinds of bribes are covered under the new law: The "Criminal Law of the PRC," known as "common bribery," applies to the bribery of state officials and employees of state-owned enterprises, i.e., most of China's large companies. Anyone who demands or accepts money or property in return for benefits is guilty of bribery. Penalties can range from mandatory jail sentences to fines for bribes between $600 and $12,000.

The other is the "Law Against Unfair Competition of the PRC," known as commercial bribery. It prohibits businesses from giving money or property to customers to sell or purchase products. It imposes mandatory criminal detention for up to three years for amounts between $600 and $12,000 and three to ten years for larger transactions.

The law is confusing in that it says nothing about punishment for gifts and benefits costing less than $600 or even whether these transactions can amount to bribes. Thus, tickets to sports events, which can cost several hundred dollars, wining and dining executives, or even pharmaceutical samples to physicians remain in a gray area. The only clue is that Communist party guidelines prohibit members from accepting gifts exceeding $500 but that doesn't necessarily mean that gifts under $500 won't be considered a violation of the law. The trouble with China's bribery laws is that they can be interpreted to apply to any gift at all.

An interesting comment from a retired agent in the U.S. Foreign Service raises questions about how strictly the Foreign Corrupt Practices Act is enforced. The economics officer of the U.S. Foreign Service says he intentionally subverted the intent of the Foreign Corrupt Practices Act so U.S. investors and exporters would not lose out unfairly to companies and agencies from other foreign countries.

"I figured out how business was actually done in corrupt countries, who was on the take, whether the going rate for host country cooperation in a particular type of transaction was 10 percent or 25 percent and who was good or bad as a go between."

I would tell Americans trying to do business in the host country: "Don't tell me about any corrupt practices you are engaged in, because I am obliged to write that up and report you to Washington, but do tell me in detail about corrupt activities by competing foreign companies. In return, if your information is interesting, I'll give you my best guess on how corruption works here." By doing this I hope that I have helped level the playing field.[4]

QUESTIONS

1. List all the different types of bribes, payments, or favors represented in this case under (a) FCPA, (b) Criminal Law of PRC, and (c) Law Against Unfair Competition of the PRC. Why is each either legal or illegal?

2. For those practices that you listed as illegal, classify each as lubrication, extortion, or subornation, and explain your reasoning.

3. Which of the payments, favors, or bribes are illegal under the Foreign Corrupt Practices Act (FCPA)?

4. Assuming that the FCPA did not exist, what is the ethical response to each of the payments, favors, or bribes you have identified? Read the section titled "Ethical and Socially Responsible Decisions" in Chapter 5 as a guide to assist you in your decision.

5. Now that the OECD has approved an FCPA-like treaty to ban commercial bribery by firms in member countries, do you think bribery will become less prevalent in markets like China?

6. Discuss the ethical issues raised by the statement of the retired Foreign Service agent who hopes that "I have helped level the playing field."

7. List alternatives to paying bribes in international markets and discuss the pluses and minuses of each.

---

[4]Walter H. Drew, "Corrupt Thinking," *Foreign Policy*, May/June 2005.

CASE 2-6 When International Buyers and Sellers Disagree

No matter what line of business you're in, you can't escape sex. That may have been one conclusion drawn by an American exporter of meat products after a dispute with a German customer over a shipment of pork livers. Here's how the disagreement came about.

The American exporter was contracted to ship "30,000 lbs. of freshly frozen U.S. pork livers, customary merchantable quality, first rate brands." The shipment had been prepared to meet the exacting standards of the American market, so the exporter expected the transaction to be completed without any problem. But when the livers arrived in Germany, the purchaser raised an objection: "We ordered pork livers of customary merchantable quality—what you sent us consisted of 40 percent sow livers."

"Who cares about the sex of the pig the liver came from?" the exporter asked.

"We do," the German replied. "Here in Germany we don't pass off spongy sow livers as the firmer livers of male pigs. This shipment wasn't merchantable at the price we expected to charge. The only way we were able to dispose of the meat without a total loss was to reduce the price. You owe us a price allowance of $1,000."

The American refused to reduce the price. The determined resistance may have been partly in reaction to the implied insult to the taste of the American consumer. "If pork livers, whatever the sex of the animal, are palatable to Americans, they ought to be good enough for anyone," the American thought.

It looked as if the buyer and seller could never agree on eating habits.

QUESTIONS

1. In this dispute which country's law would apply, that of the United States or of Germany?

2. If the case were tried in U.S. courts, who do you think would win? In German courts? Why?

3. Draw up a brief agreement that would have eliminated the following problems before they could occur.

   a. Whose law applies

   b. Whether the case should be tried in U.S. or German courts

   c. The difference in opinion as to "customary merchantable quality"

4. Discuss how SRC may be at work in this case.

CASE 2-7 McDonald's and Obesity

THE PROBLEM

Governments and influential health advocates around the world, spooked that their nations' kids will become as fat as American kids, are cracking down on the marketers they blame for the explosion in childhood obesity. Across the globe, efforts are under way to slow the march of obesity.

In the United States roughly 30 percent of American children are overweight or obese. According the U.S. Centers for Disease Control and Prevention (CDC), an estimated 64.5 percent of Americans tip the scales as overweight or obese, the highest percentage of fat people of any country in the world. However, adults and kids in other countries are catching up.

THE WORLD

The World Health Organization (WHO) reports that globally there are now more than 1 billion overweight adults and that at least 300 million of those are obese, a 50 percent increase in the number of obese people from 1995, when there were 200 million. An estimated 17.6 million children under five are estimated to be overweight worldwide.

In many countries the worst increases in obesity have occurred in young people. About half a million children in Europe are suffering classic middle-aged health problems because they are too fat. Obesity among European children has been on the rise over the last 15 years. The number of overweight children in Europe did not change much from 1974 to 1984; then the rate started to creep up during the next 10 years, and it exploded after 1995.

In Britain, one in five children is overweight or obese, in Spain 30 percent, and in Italy, 36 percent. While less than 1 percent of the children in Africa suffer from malnutrition, 3 percent are overweight or obese.

Perhaps the most distressing data come from Asia, where the measure of being overweight used in Western countries may underestimate the seriousness of weight-related health problems faced by Asians. In Japan, for example, obesity is defined as a body mass index (BMI) level of 25 or more, not 30 as it is in Western countries. But Japanese health officials report that a BMI of 25 or more is already causing high rates of diabetes. About 290 million children in China are thought to be overweight, and researchers expect that number to double in the next 10 years. The World Health Organization has warned of an escalating global epidemic of overweight and obesity.

GLOBAL REACTIONS TO OBESITY

One of the perplexing questions is why the relatively sudden increase of obesity worldwide? Some opine that fast food portion sizes are partly to blame. The average size order of French fries has nearly tripled since 1955. Some people say advertising is to blame, particularly ads aimed at children, such as those ads that use celebrities to market high-calorie foods. According to *USA Today,* one study found that the average American child sees 10,000 food ads a year, mostly for high-fat or sugary foods and drinks.

Traditionally, in developing countries, the poorest people have been the thinnest, a consequence of hard physical labor and the consumption of small amounts of traditional foods. But when these people in poor countries migrate to cities, obesity rates rise fastest among those in the lowest socioeconomic group.

Even as food companies' battle U.S. lawsuits and legislators who blame them for inducing childhood obesity, they're being attacked on another front—Europe—which is threatening, among other things, to ban advertising icons such Tony the Tiger and Ronald McDonald. "I would like to see the industry not advertising directly to children," said one European health commissioner. "If this doesn't produce satisfactory results, we will proceed to legislation." The European Health Commission has called for the food industry to set its own regulations to curb so-called junk-food advertising aimed at the European Union's 450 million citizens—or face bans similar to the tobacco industry.

The ominous comparison to cigarettes is increasingly being made in the United States as well. Commenting on a McDonald's plan to send Ronald McDonald to schools to preach about nutrition, an aide to a U.S. senator said, "No matter what Ronald is doing, they are still using this cartoon character to sell fatty hamburgers to kids. Once upon a time, tobacco companies had Joe Camel and they didn't get it either."

Also under fire is TV advertising of kids' foods, as calls for curbs or bans rise around the world. "If the rise in [the] child obesity trend continues, within five years we'll be in the same situation as America is today," said a senior child nutritionist at the University of Copenhagen who sits on the board of Denmark's National Board of Nutritional Science. "Banning TV ads that are targeting kids is an important strategy to adopt." But there is an argument that those measures won't help. "In Sweden, Norway and Quebec, where food ads are banned from kids' TV, there's no evidence that obesity rates have fallen."

A new law in France will force food marketers to choose between adding a health message to commercials or paying a 1.5 percent tax on their ad budgets to fund healthy-eating messages. Other measures under consideration in Europe include banning celebrities and cartoon characters from food ads aimed at children and preventing food marketers from using cell phone jingles to reach kids.

Ireland bans celebrities from food and beverage ads aimed at children and requires confectionery and soft-drink spots broadcast in programs where half the audience is younger than 18 to carry a visual or voice-over warning that snacking on sugary foods and drinks can damage teeth. Ireland is a small market, but there are fears that these measures could spread to the United Kingdom and then to the rest of Europe, especially since many advertisers run the same campaigns in the United Kingdom and Ireland.

Unlike France and Ireland, the United Kingdom is trying a more carrot-and-stick approach, encouraging self-regulation with legislation as a last but threatened resort. In November 2004, the U.K. government published health recommendations giving the food and beverage industries until early 2007 to act more responsibly or face formal legislation. The document followed a high-profile

U.K. government inquiry into child obesity last year. Marketing and agency executives called to give evidence were grilled publicly over the use of celebrities in ads, inciting kids' "pester power" and high salt and sugar content in foods.

The paper's proposals include clamping down on using cartoon characters to appeal to kids in food and beverage ads, potentially dooming brand icons such as Kellogg's Tony the Tiger. There have also been calls for a ban, like Ireland's, on celebrity endorsement in "junk-food" advertising by 2006. In a country where the biggest grocery-store brand, PepsiCo's Walker's Crisps, relies on celebrities in its ad campaigns, that's a big deal.

The Nordic countries are the most militant about enacting laws to ban or restrict marketing of foods that they consider unhealthy to children, and fighting to extend those restrictions to the rest of Europe. The toughest laws against advertising to children have long been in Scandinavia, where the health risks of obesity and diabetes from high sugar consumption are sometimes compared to tobacco. The legislatures in Sweden, Finland, and Denmark are all considering even tighter controls on marketing sugary foods. Denmark's National Consumer Council has petitioned the government to ban marketing "unhealthy food products" to anyone under 16, and Finland's legislature is hearing from health groups that want a total ban on TV ads for sugar-laden food. Commenting on such proposals, the CEO of the Finnish Food and Drink Industries Federation said, "Implementing stricter controls on advertising food and drinks will not be a quick-fix answer to all these problems."

"The European Union is on it, Washington is on it, the ball is rolling now and the food companies have to do something," said one top advertising agency executive. But he added, "I hope food companies won't be bullied into doing things that play to the politicians," noting there are other contributing factors for obesity, such as low income. He said food marketers could truly contribute to a solution by putting money into programs like the USDA's Nutrition Program for Women, Infants and Children, a subsidized food and education program that also happens to be very good at driving sales for the products approved for the list. The key is to translate the hype to real solutions like physical education in schools and parents—the most important role models, according to substantiated research—reclaiming responsibility. "If a food has a right to exist, a marketer has the right to advertise it."

Marketers are struggling against a crackdown on food advertising amid growing concern over obesity throughout the world. Marketers are trying to avert a clampdown with greater self-regulation. But, despite a slew of individual company efforts to shift new-product and marketing focus to healthier offerings, the industry has, until now, largely shied away from defending itself more broadly.

MCDONALD'S RESPONSE

For the last few years, McDonald's has reacted to the obesity issues in several ways in the U.K. and other countries. Concerned about consumer reaction to the film *Super Size Me,*[1] McDonald's Corp.

broke a U.K. campaign called "Changes" with poster ads that omit the Golden Arches for the first time, replacing them with a question mark in the same typeface and the tagline "McDonald's. But not as you know it." Promoting ongoing menu changes, the posters feature items such as a salad, a pile of free-range eggshells, pieces of fruit and cups of cappuccino. The effort preceded a direct-mail campaign to 17 million households touting healthier menu items and smaller portion size.

McDonald's aim was to cause people to think differently about McDonald's and to make the public aware of new products. "There's no intention to abandon the Arches" but only to focus attention on the "healthy" additions to the menu. Despite the new campaign, research showed the chain hadn't received the hoped-for awareness for some of the newer items on its menu, including the all-white-meat Chicken Selects and the fruit bags. More worrisome, a research study revealed that frequent users didn't like to admit to friends that they ate at McDonald's. "We don't want to have closet loyalists."

One researcher urged more time for McDonald's "Changes" campaign to get traction. "The market position and market stature of McDonald's in the U.K. is not nearly as strong as it is in the U.S. and accordingly, you have to stick with the program longer," he said. But he warned that the "Changes" campaign could backfire. "Trying to suppress the logo is not likely to change the hearts and minds of many fast-food voters in Europe."

In anticipation of the release of the documentary *Super Size Me* in the United Kingdom, McDonald's in London went on the defensive with full-page newspaper ads discussing the film. The ads, headlined "If you haven't seen the film 'Super Size Me,' here's what you're missing," have appeared in the film-review sections of six newspapers to coincide with filmmaker Morgan Spurlock's appearance at the annual Edinburgh film festival. The copy describes it as "slick and well-made," and says McDonald's actually agrees with the "core argument" of the film—"If you eat too much and do too little, it's bad for you." However, it continues: "What we don't agree with is the idea that eating at McDonald's is bad for you." The ad highlights some of McDonald's healthier menu items such as grilled chicken salad and fruit bags. A spokeswoman for McDonald's said it ran the ads to ensure there was a "balanced debate" about the film. *Super Size Me* distributor Tartan Films has retaliated by running identical-looking ads in newspapers promoting the film.

As a direct response to government calls for food marketers to promote a more active lifestyle, McDonald's U.K. launched an ad campaign aimed at kids featuring Ronald McDonald and animated fruit and vegetable characters called Yums. In two-minute singing-and-dancing animated spots, the Yums urge, "It's fun when you eat right and stay active."

Even though McDonald's plans to expand its healthier menu offerings, it does so cautiously, so people remember that the Golden Arches at its core still means burgers and fries.

McDonald's, throughout Europe and elsewhere, is testing ways to address the obesity issue. In Scandinavia, for example, popular healthy local foods have been added to the McMenu, like cod wrapped in rye bread in Finland. In Norway, some outlets sell a salmon burger wrapped in rye bread. In Sweden, no salt is added to the food served.

In Australia, McDonald's took a different approach—it reduced its budget for ads directed to kids by 50 percent.

McDonald's French operation raised the ire of the parent company when it ran a print ad in a women's magazine quoting a

---

[1]*Super Size Me* is a documentary on the fast-food industry and the addictivness of fast food, its allure to children, etc. Scenes in the film feature Morgan Spurlock (the director and producer of the documentary), whose fast-food feat consists of eating some 5,000 calories a day, twice what his doctor says he needs to maintain his starting weight of 185 pounds. He also avoids exercise because, he says, that's what most Americans do. Spurlock gains weight—nearly 25 pounds over 30 days. His cholesterol goes up, and so does his blood pressure. His doctor describes his liver function test results as "obscene." Spurlock complains of sluggishness, depression, shortness of breath, impotence, chest pressure, and headaches.

nutritionist's suggestion that kids shouldn't eat at the restaurant more than once a week. While the ad was meant to promote McDonald's and seems reasonable since the French only visit quick-service restaurants every two weeks on average anyway, such a campaign would have been heresy in the United States. McDonald's Corp. later issued a statement claiming that "the majority of nutritionists" believe McDonald's can fit into a balanced diet. Later, the company recruited a pair of French nutritionists who declared the Big Mac and cheeseburger healthier than traditional French fare such as quiche.

Marketers in France have lobbied hard to be allowed to use positive lifestyle messages in ads—like emphasizing the importance of physical exercise and a balanced diet—rather than grim health warnings. France's Ministry of Health appears to be listening, and is now expected to let marketers choose among three or four positive health messages. Industry experts say the government changed its mind out of fear that strong warnings might backfire, causing anxiety among consumers about eating. Moreover, France may hope its new law, if not too extreme, will become a blueprint for Europe.

SNACK FOOD INDUSTRY RESPONSES

Snack food and beverage companies like PepsiCo have joined the fray along with the fast-food industry. PepsiCo's strategy includes adding products like Walker's Potato Heads, launched recently in the United Kingdom as a healthier snack for children, and encouraging exercise. In October 2004, Walker's did a pedometer giveaway through its Web site, backed by a $5.6 million TV campaign. "We want to demonstrate that we are taking a responsible approach and make governments aware of what we are doing. In our view it is entirely wrong to pin all the blame on advertising to children, and we think we have moved to the stage where most governments accept this."

In Canada, where about one-third of children aged 2–11 are overweight, Concerned Children's Advertisers, a group whose members include Nestlé Canada, Coca-Cola, General Mills, Kellogg, and Kraft, has just begun running the first of three 60-second spots featuring "Health Rock," a colorful animated figure on a T-shirt, who sings about balancing food and activity.

In the Asia/Pacific region, few countries except Australia have yet to make food marketing and childhood obesity an issue. In much of Asia, a Western fast-food meal or a cola is still an occasional treat rather than a daily overindulgence. As childhood obesity begins to register as a concern in China, though, McDonald's has started promoting healthier items such as high-calcium fruit yogurt and chocolate pudding and low-fat milk on in-store marketing materials like tray liners.

Marketers are also keeping an eye on Brazil. A São Paulo university recently analyzed children's programming and found that 1 out of every 10 minutes of advertising was a food commercial. That study is a starting point for the group appointed within a government health organization's ad unit to examine nutritional claims in advertising to children.

QUESTIONS

1. How should McDonald's respond when ads promoting healthy lifestyles featuring Ronald McDonald are equated with Joe Camel and cigarette ads? Should McDonald's eliminate Ronald McDonald in its ads?

2. Discuss the merits of the law proposed by France that would require fast-food companies either to add a health message to commercials or to pay a 1.5 percent tax on their ad budgets. Propose a strategy for McDonald's to pay the tax or add health messages, and defend your recommendation.

3. If there is no evidence that obesity rates fall in those countries that ban food advertising to children, why bother?

4. The broad issue facing McDonald's U.K. is the current attitude toward rising obesity. The company seems to have tried many different approaches to deal with the problem but the problem persists. List all the problems facing McDonald's and critique their various approaches to solve the problems.

5. Based on your response to question 4 above, recommend both a short-range and long-range plan for McDonald's to implement.

Sources: Alexandra Jardine and Laurel Wentz, "U.K. Not Feeling the Love; McD's Puts Slogan on Ice" *Advertising Age,* September 13, 2004; Kate McArthur, "Marketers Brace for Food-Ad Rules," *Advertising Age,* October 25, 2004; "Thinking Locally," *Advertising Age,* March 7, 2005; "The Weight of the World Obesity: A Global Epidemic," *Current Events,"* September 26, 2003; Alexandra Jardine and Laurel Wentz, "It's a Fat World After All," *Advertising Age,* March 7, 2005; Steven Gray and Janet Adamy, "McDonald's Gets Healthier—But Burgers Still Rule," *Wall Street Journal,* February 23, 2005; Alexandra Jardine and Laurel Wentz, "McD's Refutes Film in U.K. Ads," *Advertising Age,* September 30, 2004; Alexandra Jardine and Laurel Wentz, "McD's Rolls Ads sans Golden Arches," *Advertising Age,* October 18, 2004; Stephanie Thompson, "Europe Slams Icons as Food Fights Back" *Advertising Age,* January 31, 2005; "Thinking Locally," *Advertising Age,* March 7, 2005; Emma Ross, "Obesity Hurting Health of European Children," *Associated Press,* June 3, 2005; J. E. Brody, "Globesity," *New York Times,* April 19, 2005.

cases 3

ASSESSING GLOBAL MARKET OPPORTUNITIES

OUTLINE OF CASES

3-1 International Marketing Research at the Mayo Clinic

3-2 Swifter, Higher, Stronger, Dearer

3-3 easyCar.com

3-4 Marketing to the Bottom of the Pyramid

CASE 3–1 International Marketing Research at the Mayo Clinic

Mayo Clinic has a long international history and has been providing care to international patients since its inception. Despite its history and reputation, however, the marketing staff continues to monitor the international market to gauge the level of awareness, reputation, and attractiveness of Mayo Clinic around the world. Here's a look at how one institution has used word-of-mouth marketing to maintain its global reputation.

Marketing, as most formally defined, has historically not been a critical factor in delivering patients to Mayo Clinic. Indeed, the marketing department at Mayo Clinic has existed for only the past 15 years, and patients have been coming to us for care for more than a century. We like to believe the marketing department provides valuable information to physicians and their support staff, information that helps them deliver better care, highlights their patients' wants and needs, and educates them as to what's going on in the marketplace.

In reality, however, it's the providers themselves—the doctors, nurses, receptionists, and all the rest of the allied health staff—who bring in business by creating positive experiences for patients. Patients who leave Mayo Clinic highly satisfied with their care will return to their communities in the United States and elsewhere and say good things about us to their family and friends. And these family members and friends in turn travel to Mayo Clinic when they need tertiary or quaternary medical care. While we in marketing strive to provide excellent internal support, we know that it's the doctors and other care providers who have created and maintained a brand of health care excellence.

Despite the hype surrounding what has been presented as the highly lucrative international marketplace, "international" is not something new at Mayo Clinic. We know from experience and research that "international" is a part of who we are, as well as part of how the market defines us. Nearly 100 years ago, our founders, a family of physicians named "Mayo," created an international legacy by traveling around the world to compare notes and surgical approaches with physicians across the globe. In some cases, they even returned with international patients who were in need of additional expertise. As in so many other areas of our medical practice, we continue in their traditions.

In recent years, however, we've begun to more thoroughly study our international patient population in particular and the international marketplace in general. Our studies fall into a few categories and grow in number in proportion to our understanding (or perhaps our greater understanding of how much we don't know) of the international marketplace.

First of all, we track our international patient trends rather carefully. This seems like an obvious place to start. But as in most data tracking, the value of the concept is significantly more straightforward than the logistics of acquiring consistently reliable data. Internal data systems must be coordinated—a significant undertaking for any institution, and particularly hard, we believe, when dealing with a large and complicated infrastructure. To give a simple example, data fields must be made uniform—not just on one data system, but on all of them. Rather than a free-text field, for example, that allows a registrant to enter

Venzuela, or Venosuela, or Vensuala, or maybe even Venezuela, we push for a pre-defined field that gives us standardized information.

We monitor our international data by the quarter, carefully watching trends over time by country or region, tracking significant changes in volume, hospitalization rates, and percentage of new patients out of any given market. We know, for example, that we have between 9,000 and 10,000 patients, depending on the year, coming to us from more than 160 different countries annually. Some are third-generation patients—maybe their grandfather was cured here in the 1930s—and others are brand new. Some are our neighbors in Ontario or Monterrey; others come all the way from Indonesia. We know that some markets are significantly less predictable than others, and some countries deliver more "new" patients than others. We probe further to figure out why.

Second, we conduct research with our internal salespeople—the physicians and their support staff who deliver care to our international patients. Through carefully moderated focus groups, we identify the things that are going smoothly as well as the barriers to providing excellent care. And where appropriate, we make recommendations for change.

Third, just as with our U.S.-based patients, we conduct both quantitative and qualitative research in the international marketplace. This includes research with our patients, international physicians, and international health care consumers, designed to help us understand why people choose to leave their own communities for health care, why some of them come to Mayo Clinic, and why others do not. We work hard to understand how health care decisions are made, so we can better assist decision makers, physicians, and their staff in providing care. We position ourselves to perhaps offer counsel on where to best expend valuable institutional resources, both human and financial.

GLOBAL MARKET RESEARCH

The marketing department conducts periodic and ongoing patient satisfaction studies with our international patients, measuring their assessment of various aspects of the care we provide. To date, we have surveyed nearly 1,500 patients in 20 countries, in four different languages. As any market researcher knows, sound patient satisfaction research requires great attention to detail to ensure reliable data. We find, not surprisingly, that international data collection offers significant additional challenges:

The quality of our own data. The name and address fields designed for clean U.S. addresses often are not sufficient to hold reliable international detail. If we want to do it right, we must manually "clean" thousands of patient records before fielding our studies.

Varying quality of international postal and telecommunications infrastructure. This variance can create significant problems for either phone or mail surveys; consequently, international studies take a lot more time than U.S.-based studies and require much more patience.

Exhibit 1

Which Was Most
Important in Your Decision
to Choose Mayo Clinic?

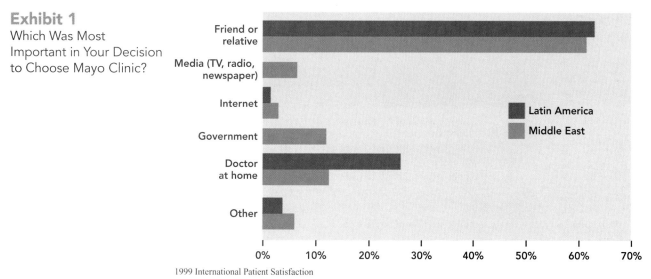

1999 International Patient Satisfaction

N = 331 Middle Eastern patients; 755 Latin American patients

Cultural dynamics. In some countries, individuals may be suspicious of an international call; in others, they may spend a lot of time outside of their homes. In still others, a nonfamily "gatekeeper" must be diplomatically convinced to transfer the call to the targeted respondents. These cultural dynamics pose further delays and require special sensitivities.

High standards for quality. Our own standards for quality compel us to maintain high quality language- and culture-specific fielding of our various research projects. These studies, whether managed internally or through an external vendor, require more oversight than we are accustomed to with U.S.-based research.

Despite these challenges, however, this international research has taught us a lot. International patient satisfaction studies demonstrate that the key driver of our patients' satisfaction seems to hold across borders. This is excellent care—manifested by listening, explaining, and thoroughness on the part of Mayo Clinic physicians. Other factors in the health care experience are important—for example, quality of language interpretation and waiting times—but they don't consistently correlate with overall satisfaction.

The power of word of mouth is also confirmed in the international marketplace. Most of our international patients indicate that friends or relatives provided their most important influence in choosing Mayo Clinic. This finding reminds us of our most powerful marketing "tool"—satisfied patients who say good things about Mayo Clinic and influence others' health care decisions. Exhibit 1 indicates the factors influencing choice of Mayo Clinic by patients from Latin America and the Middle East.

We conducted formal focus groups with international patients and non-patients in six cities around the world, probing to learn more about how those populations make health care decisions, and whether the process is the same or different from U.S. health care consumers. As it turns out, for most aspects of decision making, the process is very similar to that of U.S. consumers. However, for a few others the process is quite different.

The areas where we've found the most difference across borders relate to the role of health insurance. We've been involved in three cosponsored international research projects that have taught us some good lessons and demonstrated that international

health care insurance is as different from that in the United States as it is across countries and regions. Furthermore, many assumptions we take for granted in the U.S. market—for example, name recognition—simply don't hold in certain international markets. Exhibit 2 is a graph of responses from a satisfaction study of our patients from Latin America and the Middle East, showing the different history of Mayo Clinic brand awareness in those regions

We weren't surprised to learn that Mayo Clinic awareness among our patients was much more recent in the Middle East than in Latin America. From other studies, however, we have learned that awareness among nonpatients—even those who have purchased health insurance policies that offer them Mayo Clinic care as a benefit—is not as strong.

The international health care insurance market is expanding rapidly, and many providers view this expansion as a significant opportunity to glean additional patients from outside the United States. Commercial and noncommercial contracts comprise a significant body of business in U.S. health care. If this business could be expanded to provide patients from markets outside the United States, all the better. We know, however, that health care systems vary significantly from country to country, and knowledge and use of health insurance vary even more. To study these differences in detail, we cosponsored two quantitative studies of health care insurance policyholders—in particular, holders of policies that offer some degree of coverage for care at Mayo Clinic.

The first study consisted of face-to-face interviews with 400 policyholders in a particular country and delivered a great deal of information regarding policyholders' preferences, health care behavior, and demographics. In this country, as throughout most of the world, the public health care system exists as a universal "safety net" for all citizens. Even in markets where the private insurance market has expanded, the public system continues to offer care for all citizens. This means that if a private insurance policy does not offer adequate coverage, especially for high-cost procedures, the public system is used to reduce the consumer's financial burden.

The private policy might cover, for example, access to primary and secondary care at private rather than public clinics as well as the price of a private room, or the option of receiving care at a more upscale facility. But for high-cost, life-threatening procedures,

Exhibit 2
How Long Ago Did You First Hear of Mayo Clinic?

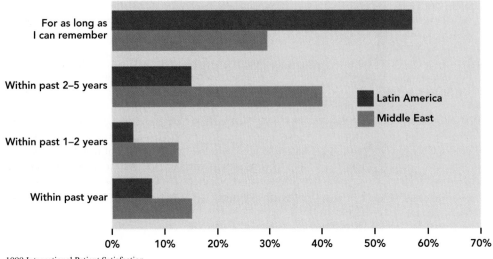

1999 International Patient Satisfaction
N = 331 Middle Eastern patients; 755 Latin American patients

the co-pay or deductible for having these procedures conducted exclusively in the private sector remains significant. The end result, of course, is that the lower cost procedures are transferred to the private system, while the higher cost procedures remain in the public safety net. The implication for U.S. tertiary providers is that, while private insurance might reduce some of the financial risk for traveling out of country for care, in many cases the risk is not completely eliminated. Therefore, the policies might not deliver the volume of patients initially anticipated.

Other factors, such as a lack of brand awareness and limited perceived need for U.S. medical care, may be impediments to attracting patients in the international health care insurance market. In our first study, when we probed for brand awareness among those 400 consumers who had purchased a health insurance policy touting Mayo Clinic coverage as a benefit, we discovered no unaided recall of that coverage as a benefit of the policy. (See Exhibit 3.) In an aided list, Mayo Clinic coverage was ranked as the least important benefit of the policy, on a par with eyeglass coverage at the bottom of the list.

Furthermore, when we asked policyholders to name a leading medical center in the United States, most (72 percent) didn't know a single one. Twenty-five percent (25 percent) named Mayo Clinic, and the other 2 percent named other U.S. medical centers. We were not particularly surprised that citizens in the studied country were not familiar with Mayo Clinic. However, we were surprised that policyholders who had purchased an insurance product that very publicly advertised the Mayo Clinic benefit were unable to name Mayo Clinic as a leading U.S. medical center.

Exhibit 3
Recall of Plan Benefits (unaided)

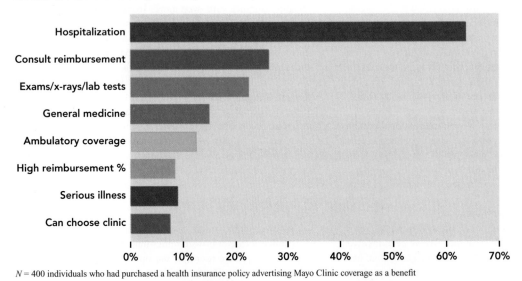

N = 400 individuals who had purchased a health insurance policy advertising Mayo Clinic coverage as a benefit

As it turned out, many of these policyholders had no intention of leaving their home country for medical care. They were buying insurance to facilitate care in the more desirable private system. Furthermore, most felt that the health care in their own country was very good and that there would be little if any reason to ever leave home to obtain care elsewhere. We've encountered this phenomenon repeatedly in our research with U.S. patients. Most believe in the abilities of their own doctor and feel very confident about medical care in their own community. Even though "quality" may be regionally or culturally defined, almost everyone considers his or her doctor to be a good one.

A second cosponsored study consisted of 353 telephone interviews with individuals who had purchased a health care insurance policy specifically for international coverage. Once again, confidence in local care was very high—in fact, significantly higher than in the country of our first study. Nonetheless, this group of individuals had purchased a product that offered them coverage for medical care outside their home country, should they decide it was necessary or appropriate. In this study, our aided brand recognition among policyholders was higher than in the first; when asked directly whether they'd heard of Mayo Clinic, 75 percent responded affirmatively. But when asked unaided to name the best medical centers in the United States, the vast majority (nearly 70 percent) of policyholders indicated they didn't know. And while the majority had heard of Mayo Clinic, fewer than 10 percent were aware of any benefit of their health insurance policy that related to Mayo Clinic.

In both of these studies, we learned substantially more about the nature of international insurance agreements, policyholders' wants and needs, and their disposition toward traveling out of country for medical care. But we also learned that the knowledge of our brand is limited outside the United States and that a high number of policyholders does not necessarily translate into a high number of patients. Our research has taught us to be more selective, to be cautious in expending significant resources to pursue insurance arrangements, and to conduct further research to expand our understanding.

THE FUTURE

We anticipate that "international" will continue to be part of who we are at Mayo Clinic. Our doctors, hailing from all corners of the globe, will continue to collaborate with their colleagues around the world. Mayo Clinic researchers will conduct clinical trials in collaboration with researchers on many continents. Our students and residents will continue to offer us rich diversity, as Mayo international alumni now number 1,500, representing 67 countries. But most important, Mayo Clinic will strive to provide the best medical care possible to those patients around the world who need us the most.

To support that mission, those of us in "marketing" will continue to support our medical staff by studying our patients' wants, needs, preferences, and behavior patterns, and learning all that we can about the ever-changing, rich and diverse worldwide health care market. In the end, outstanding medical care and sensitive service to patients and families will be our most productive marketing strategy, because it creates positive word-of-mouth about something very important—health care. As the stories of satisfied patients churn—sometimes for decades—in the minds of their friends and family, Mayo Clinic remains an option if they ever need the care we offer.

QUESTION

1. Assume you are the new marketing vice president at the Mayo Clinic. The CEO and the board have decided to expand their international sales revenues by 100 percent over the next five years. Write a memo to your staff outlining the marketing research that will be needed to support such a strategy. Be specific about sources of secondary data and the best places and media for gathering primary data. Also, be specific about the best methods to use.

Source: Misty Hathaway and Kent Seltman, "International Marketing Research at the Mayo Clinic," *Marketing Health Services,* Winter 2001, 21(4), pp. 18–23. Used with permission of American Marketing Association.

CASE 3–2 Swifter, Higher, Stronger, Dearer

Television and sport are perfect partners. Each has made the other richer. But is the alliance really so good for sport?

Back in 1948, the BBC, Britain's public broadcasting corporation, took a fateful decision. It paid a princely £15,000 (£27,000 in today's money) for the right to telecast the Olympic Games to a domestic audience. It was the first time a television network had paid the International Olympic Committee (IOC, the body that runs the Games) for the privilege. But not the last. The rights to the 1996 Summer Olympics, which opened in Atlanta on July 19, 1996, raised $900 million from broadcasters round the world. And the American television rights to the Olympiads up to and including 2008 have been bought by America's NBC network for an amazing $3.6 billion (see Exhibit 1).

The Olympics are only one of the sporting properties that have become hugely valuable to broadcasters. Sport takes up a growing share of screen time (as those who are bored by it know all too well). When you consider the popularity of the world's great tournaments, that is hardly surprising. *Sportsfests* generate audiences beyond the wildest dreams of television companies for anything else. According to Nielsen Media Research, the number of Americans watching the Super Bowl, the main annual football championship, averaged 94 million. The top eight television programs in America are all sporting events. Some 3 billion people watched some part of the 2000 Olympiad—over half of mankind.

The reason television companies love sport is not merely that billions want to tele-gawk at ever-more-wonderful sporting feats. Sport also has a special quality that makes it unlike almost any other sort of television program: immediacy. Miss seeing a particular episode of, say, *ER,* and you can always catch the repeat and enjoy it just as much. Miss seeing your team beat hell out of its biggest rival, and the replay will leave you cold. "A live sporting event loses almost all its value as the final whistle goes," says Steve Barnett, author of a British book on sport. The desire to watch sport when it is happening, not hours afterward, is universal: A study in South Korea by Spectrum, a British consultancy, found that live games get 30 percent of the audience while recordings get less than 5 percent.

This combination of popularity and immediacy has created a symbiotic relationship between sport and television in which each is changing the other. As Stephen Wenn, of Canada's Wilfrid Laurier University, puts it, television and the money it brings have had an enormous impact on the Olympic Games, including on the timing of events and their location. For instance, an Asian Olympics poses a problem for American networks: Viewers learn the results on the morning news.

The money that television has brought into professional basketball has put some of the top players among the world's highest-paid entertainers: A few are getting multiyear contracts worth over $100 million. Rugby has begun to be reorganized to make it more television friendly; other sports will follow. And, though soccer and American football draw the largest audiences, television has also promoted the popularity of sports that stir more local passions: rugby league in Australia, cricket in India, table tennis in China, snooker in Britain.

Exhibit 1
Chariots for Hire: Olympic Broadcast Rights Fees,* $bn (world totals)

Source: International Olympic Committee. Used by permission of the International Olympic Committee.

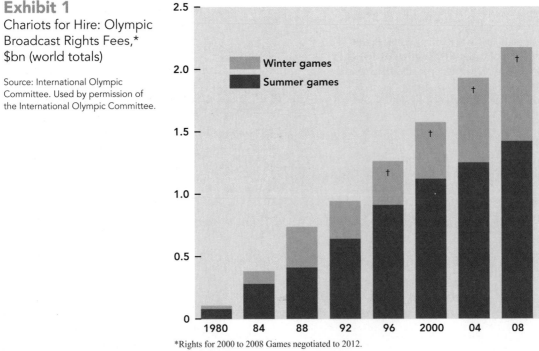

*Rights for 2000 to 2008 Games negotiated to 2012.
†Two years earlier

What is less often realized is that sport is also changing television. To assuage the hunger for sports, new channels are being launched at a tremendous pace. In America, ESPN, a cable network owned by Capital Cities/ABC, started a 24-hour sports news network in 1997; in Britain, BSkyB, a satellite broadcaster partly owned by Rupert Murdoch, has three sports channels. Because people seem more willing to pay to watch sport on television than to pay for any other kind of programming, sport has become an essential part of the business strategy of television empire-builders such as Mr. Murdoch. Nobody in the world understands the use of sports as a bait for viewers better than he.

In particular, sport suggests an answer to one of the big problems that will face television companies in the future: How can viewers, comfortable with their old analog sets, be persuaded to part with the hefty price of a new digital set and a subscription to an untried service? The answer is to create an exclusive chance to watch a desirable event, or to use the hundreds of channels that digital television provides to offer more variety of sports coverage than analog television can offer. This ploy is not new. "Radio broadcasts of boxing were once used to promote the sale of radios, and baseball to persuade people to buy television sets," points out Richard Burton, a sports marketing specialist at the Lundquist College of Business at Oregon University. In the next few years, the main new outlet for sports programs will be digital television.

GOING FOR GOLD

To understand how these multiple effects have come about, go back to those vast sums that television companies are willing to pay. In America, according to Neal Weinstock of Weinstock Media Analysis, total spending on sports rights by television companies is about $2 billion a year. Easily the most valuable rights are for American football. One of the biggest sporting coups in the United States was the purchase by Fox, owned by Mr. Murdoch's News Corporation, of the rights to four years of National Football League games for $1.6 billion, snatching them from CBS. Rights for baseball, basketball, and ice hockey are also in the billion-dollar range.

Americans are rare in following four main sports rather than one. America is also uncommon in having no publicly owned networks. As a result, bidding wars in other countries, though just as fierce as in America, are different in two ways: They are often fought between public broadcasters and new upstarts, many of them pay channels, and they are usually about soccer.

Nothing better illustrates the change taking place in the market for soccer rights than the vast deal struck in 1997 by Kirch, a German group owned by a secretive Bavarian media mogul. The group spent $2.2 billion for the world's biggest soccer-broadcasting rights: to show the finals of the World Cup in 2002 and 2006 outside America. That is over six times more than the amount paid for the rights to the World Cups of 1990, 1994, and 1998.

Such vast bids gobble up a huge slice of a television company's budget. In America, reckons London Economics, a British consultancy, sport accounts for around 15 percent of all television-program spending. For some television companies, the share is much larger. BSkyB spends £100 million ($155 million) a year on sports, about a third of its programming budget.

This seems to pose a threat to public broadcasting, for, in any bidding war outside America, public broadcasting companies are generally the losers. A consortium of mainly public broadcasters bought the rights to the 1990 to 1998 World Cups for a total of $344 million. This time around, the consortium raised its bid to around $1.8 billion, and still lost. Public broadcasters often do not have the money to compete. In Britain, the BBC spends about 4 percent of its program budget on sport in a non-Olympic year, about £15 million a year less than BSkyB.

The problem is that the value of sport to viewers ("consumer surplus," as economists would put it) is much larger than the value of most other sorts of programming. Public broadcasters have no way to benefit from the extra value that a big sporting event offers viewers. But with subscription television and with pay TV, where viewers are charged for each event, the television company will directly collect the value viewers put on being able to watch.

Because of this, many people (especially in Europe) worry that popular sports will increasingly be available only on subscription television, which could, they fear, erode the popular support upon which public broadcasters depend. In practice, these worries seem excessive. Although far more sport will be shown on subscription television, especially outside America's vast advertising market, the most popular events are likely to remain freely available for many years to come, for two reasons.

First, those who own the rights to sporting events are rarely just profit-maximizers: They also have an interest in keeping the appeal of their sport as broad as possible. They may therefore refuse to sell to the highest bidder. For example, the IOC turned down a $2 billion bid from Mr. Murdoch's News Corporation for the European broadcasting rights to the Olympic Games between 2000 and 2008 in favor of a lower bid from a group of public broadcasters. Sometimes, as with the sale of World Cup rights to Kirch, the sellers may stipulate that the games be aired on "free" television.

Second, the economics of televising sport means that the biggest revenues are not necessarily earned by tying up exclusive rights. Steven Bornstein, the boss of ESPN, argues that exclusive deals to big events are "not in our long-term commercial interest." Because showing sport on "free" television maximizes the audience, some advertisers will be willing to pay a huge premium for the big occasion. So will sponsors who want their names to be seen emblazoned on players' shirts or on billboards around the field.

It is not only a matter of audience size. Sport is also the most efficient way to reach one of the world's most desirable audiences from an advertiser's point of view: young men with cash to spend. Although the biggest audiences of young men are watching general television, sporting events draw the highest concentrations. Thus, advertisers of products such as beer, cars, and sports shoes can pay mainly for the people they most want to attract.

There are other ways in which sport can be indirectly useful to the networks. A slot in a summer game is a wonderful opportunity to promote a coming autumn show. A popular game wipes out the audience share of the competition. And owning the rights to an event allows a network plenty of scope to entertain corporate grandees who may then become advertisers.

For the moment, though, advertising revenue is the main recompense that television companies get for their huge investments in sport. Overall, according to *Broadcasting & Cable,* a trade magazine, sport generated $3.5 billion, or 10 percent, of total television advertising revenues in America last year. The biggest purchasers of sports rights by far in America are the national networks. NBC alone holds more big sports rights than any other body has held in the history of television. It can, obviously, recoup some of the bill by selling advertising: For a 30-second slot during the Super Bowl, NBC asked for $1.2 million.

Such deals, however, usually benefit the networks indirectly rather than directly. The Super Bowl is a rarity: It has usually made a profit for the network that airs it. "Apart from the Super Bowl, the World Series and probably the current Olympics, the big sports don't usually make money for the networks," says Arthur Gruen of Wilkowsky Gruen, a media consultancy. "But they are a boon for their affiliate stations, which can sell their advertising slots for two or three times as much as other slots." Although Fox lost money on its NFL purchase, it won the loyalty of affiliate stations (especially important for a new network) and made a splash.

Almost everywhere else, the biggest growth in revenues from showing sports will increasingly come from subscriptions or pay-per-view arrangements. The versatility and huge capacity of digital broadcasting make it possible to give subscribers all sorts of new and lucrative services.

In America, DirectTV and Primestar, two digital satellite broadcasters, have been tempting subscribers with packages of sporting events from distant parts of the country. "They have been creating season tickets for all the main events, costing $100–150 per season per sport," says John Mansell, a senior analyst with Paul Kagan, a California consultancy. In Germany, DF1, a satellite company jointly owned by Kirch and BSkyB, has the rights to show Formula One motor racing. It allows viewers to choose to follow particular teams, so that Ferrari fanatics can follow their drivers, and to select different camera angles.

In Italy, Telepiu, which launched digital satellite television in 1997, offers viewers a package in September that allows them to buy a season ticket to live matches played by one or more teams in the top Italian soccer leagues. The system's "electronic turnstile" is so sophisticated that it can shut off reception for subscribers living in the catchment area for a home game, to assuage clubs' worries that they will lose revenue from supporters at the gate. In fact, top Italian clubs usually have to lock out their fanatical subscribers to avoid overcapacity.

Most skillful of all at using sports rights to generate subscription revenue is BSkyB. It signed an exclusive contract with the English Premier League that has been the foundation of its success. Some of those who know BSkyB well argue that £5 billion of the business's remarkable capital value of £8 billion is attributable to the profitability of its soccer rights.

WINNER TAKE ALL

Just as the purchase of sporting rights enriches television companies, so their sale has transformed the finances of the sports lucky enough to be popular with viewers. On the whole, the biggest beneficiaries have not been the clubs and bodies that run sports, but the players. In the same way as rising revenues from films are promptly dissipated in vast salaries to stars in Hollywood, so in sport the money coming in from television soon flows out in heftier payments to players.

In America, the market for sportsmen is well developed and the cost of players tends to rise with the total revenues of the main sporting organizations. Elsewhere, the market is newer and so a bigger slice of the revenues tends to stick to the television companies. "The big difference between sports and movies is the operating margins," says Chris Akers, chairman of Caspian, a British media group, and an old hand at rights negotiations. "Hollywood majors have per-subscriber deals. No sports federation has yet done such a deal."

Guided by the likes of Mr. Akers, they soon will. Telepiu's latest three-year soccer contract gives the television firm enough revenue to cover its basic costs, guarantees the soccer league a minimum sum, and then splits the takings down the middle. In Britain, BSkyB is locked in dispute with the Premier League over the terms of the second half of its rights deal: Should the league then be able to opt for half the revenue from each subscriber on top of or instead of a fixed hunk of net profits?

The logical next step would be for some clubs or leagues to set up their own pay-television systems, distributing their games directly by satellite or cable. A few people in British soccer are starting to look with interest at America's local sports networks, such as the successful Madison Square Garden cable network, and to wonder whether Europe might move the same way.

If it does, not all teams will benefit equally. In America, football has an elaborate scheme to spread revenues from national television across teams. But in other sports, including baseball, the wealth and size of a team's local market mean large differences in rights from local television. The New York Yankees make almost $50 million a year from local television rights, says Brian Schechter, a Canadian media analyst. At the other end of the scale, the Kansas City Royals make $4 million to $5 million a year.

Not all players benefit equally, either. Television has brought to sport the "winner-take-all" phenomenon. It does not cost substantially more to stage a televised championship game than a run-of-the-week, untelevised match. But the size of the audience, and therefore the revenue generated, may be hugely different. As a result, players good enough to be in the top games will earn vastly more than those slightly less good, who play to smaller crowds.

THE REFEREE'S WHISTLE

The lure of money is already altering sport and will change it more. Increasingly, games will be reorganized to turn them into better television. British rugby-union officials are squabbling over the spoils from television rights. Rugby league, whose audiences had been dwindling, won a contract worth £87 million over five years from BSkyB earlier this year in exchange for switching its games from winter to summer. Purists were aghast.

Other reorganizations for the benefit of television will surely come. Mr. Murdoch wants to build a rugby superleague, allowing the best teams around the world to play each other. A European superleague for soccer is possible. "At the moment, Manchester United plays AC Milan every 25 years: it's a joke," complains one enthusiast.

Sports traditionalists resist changing their ways for the likes of Mr. Murdoch. So far, the big sporting bodies have generally held out against selling exclusive pay-television rights to their crown jewels, and have sometimes deliberately favored public broadcasters. Regulators have helped them, intervening in some countries to limit exclusive deals with pay-television groups. Britain passed a law to stop subscription channels tying up exclusive rights to some big events, such as the Wimbledon tennis championship. In Australia, a court threw out News Corporation's attempt to build a rugby superleague as the lynchpin of its pay-television strategy.

The real monopolists are not the media companies, however, but the teams. Television companies can play off seven or eight Hollywood studios against each other. But most countries have only one national soccer league, and a public that loves soccer above all other sports. In the long run, the players and clubs hold most of the cards. The television companies are more likely to be their servants than their masters.

QUESTIONS

1. The following are the prices paid for the *American* television broadcasting rights of the summer Olympics since 1980: Moscow—NBC agreed to pay $85 million; 1984 in Los Angeles—ABC paid $225 million; 1988 in Seoul—NBC paid $300 million; 1992 in Barcelona—NBC paid $401 million; 1996 through 2008—NBC will pay $3.6 billion; 2010—NBC will pay $820 million; 2012 in London—NBC will pay $1.18 billion for its American broadcast rights. You have been charged with the responsibility of determining the IOC and local Olympic Committee's asking prices for the London 2012 television broadcast rights for five different markets: Japan, China, Australia, the European Union, and Brazil. Determine a price for each and justify your decisions.

2. Your instructor may assign you to represent either the IOC or any one of the television networks in each of the five countries that have been asked to bid for the broadcast rights for the London 2012 Games. Prepare to negotiate prices and other organizational details.

3. The World Football League (WFL), a joint venture between the National Football League (NFL) and Fox Television (owned by Rupert Murdoch's News Corporation), has offered you the Edinburgh, Scotland, Claymores franchise. Your Scottish Claymores, should you choose to invest, will be playing against the other five WFL teams from London, Barcelona, Amsterdam, Frankfurt, and Düsseldorf. What would you be willing to pay for the Claymores? The interested investor will note that a previous incarnation of the WFL with three teams in Europe and seven in the United States folded in its second season in 1992 having lost $50 million.

Sources: Adapted from *The Economist,* July 20, 1996, pp. 17–19. Also see Mark Hyman, "The Jets: Worth a Gazillion?" *BusinessWeek,* December 6, 1999, pp. 99–100; Mark Hyman, "Putting the Squeeze on the Media," *BusinessWeek,* December 11, 2000, p. 75; www.worldleague.com/claymores/; and Alan Abrahamson, "NBC Wins Rights to 2010, 2012 Olympics," *Los Angeles Times,* June 7, 2003, p. C1.

CASE 3−3 easyCar.com

At easyCar we aim to offer you outstanding value for money. To us value for money means a reliable service at a low price. We achieve this by simplifying the product we offer, and passing on the benefits to you in the form of lower prices.[1]

This was the stated mission of car rental company easyCar.com. EasyCar was a member of the EasyGroup family of companies, founded by the flamboyant Greek entrepreneur Stelios Haji-Ioannou, who was known simply as Stelios to most. Stelios founded low-cost air carrier easyJet.com in 1995 after convincing his father, a Greek shipping billionaire, to loan him the £5 million (in January 2003, £1 = €1.52 = U.S.$1.61) needed to start the business.[2] EasyJet was one of the early low-cost, no-frills air carriers in the European market. It was built on a foundation of simple point to point flights, booked over the Internet, and the aggressive use of yield management policies to maximize the revenues it derived from its assets. The company proved highly successful, and as a result Stelios had expanded this business model to industries with similar characteristics as the airline industry. EasyCar, founded in 2000 on a £10 million investment on the part of Stelios, was one of these efforts.

EasyCar's approach, built on the easyJet model, was quite different from the approaches used by the traditional rental car companies. EasyCar rented only a single vehicle type at each location it operated, while most of its competitors rented a wide variety of vehicle types. EasyCar did not work with agents—over 95 percent of its bookings were made through the company's Web site, with the remainder of bookings being made directly through the company's phone reservation system (at a cost to the customer of €0.95/minute for the call). Most rental car companies worked with a variety of intermediaries, with their own Web sites accounting for less than 10 percent of their total booking.[3] And like easyJet, easyCar managed prices in an attempt to have its fleet rented out 100 percent of the time and to generate the maximum revenue from its rentals. EasyCar's information system constantly evaluated projected demand and expected utilization at each site, and it adjusted price accordingly. Because of its aggressive pricing, easyCar was able to achieve a fleet utilization rate in excess of 90 percent[4]— much higher than other major rental car companies. Industry leader Avis Europe, for example, had a fleet utilization rate of 68 percent.[5]

It was January 2003. EasyCar had broken even in the fiscal year ending September 2002[6] on revenues of £27 million.[7] This represented a significant improvement over 2001, when easyCar had lost £7.5 million on revenues of £18.5 million.[8] While pleased that the company had broken even in only its third year in operation, Stelios had set aggressive financial goals for easyCar for the next two years. Plans called for a quadrupling of revenues in the next two years in preparation for a planned initial public offering in the second half of 2004. EasyCar's goal was to reach £100 million in revenue and £10 million in profit for the year 2004. The £100 million revenue goal and £10 million profit goal were felt necessary to obtain the desired return from an initial public offering (IPO). It was thought that with this level of performance, the company might be worth about £250 million.[9] To achieve these financial goals, the company was pushing to open an average of 2 new sites a week through 2003 and 2004 to reach a total of 180 sites by the end of 2004.[10]

THE RENTAL CAR INDUSTRY IN WESTERN EUROPE

The western European rental car industry consisted of many different national markets that were only semi-integrated. Although many companies competed within this European rental car industry, a handful of companies held dominant positions, either across a number of national markets or within one or a few national markets. Industry experts saw the sector as ripe for consolidation.[11] Several international companies—notably Avis, Europcar, and Hertz—had strong positions across most major European markets. Within most countries, a primarily national or regional company had a strong position in its home market and perhaps a moderate market share in neighboring markets. Sixt was the market leader in Germany, for example, while Atesa (in partnership with National) was the market leader in Spain. Generally these major players accounted for more than half the market. In Germany, for example, Sixt, Europcar, Avis, and Hertz had a combined 60 percent of the €2.5 billion German rental car market.[12] In Spain, the top five firms accounted for 60 percent of the €920 million Spanish rental car market. Generally, these top firms targeted both business and vacation travelers and offered a wide range of vehicles for rent. Exhibit 1 provides basic information on these market-leading companies.

Many smaller rental companies operated in each market in addition to these major companies. In Germany, for example, there were over 700 smaller companies,[13] while in Spain there were more than 1,600 smaller companies. Many of these smaller companies

---

[1]EasyCar.com Web site.

[2]"The Big Picture—An Interview with Stelios," *Sunday Herald (UK)*, March 16, 2003.

[3]"Click to Fly," *The Economist*, May 13, 2004.

[4]E. Simpkins, "Stelios Isn't Taking It Easy," *Sunday Telegraph (UK)*, December 15, 2002.

[5]Avis Europe Plc. 2002 annual report, p. 10, accessed at ir.avis-europe.com/avis/reports on August 16, 2004.

[6]E. Simpkins, Stelios Isn't Taking It Easy," *Sunday Telegraph (UK)*, December 15, 2002.

[7]"Marketing: Former eBay UK Chief Lands Top easyCar Position," *Financial Times Information Limited*, January 9, 2003.

[8]T. Burt, "EasyCar Agrees to Deal with Vauxhall," *Financial Times*, April 30, 2002, p. 24.

[9]N. Hodgson, "Stelios Plans easyCar Float," *Liverpool Echo*, September 24, 2002.

[10]E. Simpkins, "Stelios Isn't Taking It Easy," *Sunday Telegraph (UK)*, December 15, 2002.

[11]"Marketing Week: Don't Write Off the Car Rental Industry," *Financial Times Information Limited*, September 26, 2002.

[12]"EasyCar Set to Shake Up German Car Rental Market," *European Intelligence Wire*, February 22, 2002.

[13]"EasyCar Set to Shake Up German Car Rental Market," *European Intelligence Wire*, February 22, 2002.

Exhibit 1

Information on easyCar's Major European Competitors

	easyCar	Avis Europe	Europcar	Hertz	Sixt
Number of rental outlets	46	3,100	2,650	7,000	1,250
2002 fleet size	7,000	120,000	220,000	700,000	46,700
Number of countries	5	107	118	150	50
Largest market	U.K.	France	France	U.S.	Germany
Company owner	EasyGroup/ Stelios Haji-Ioannou	D'Ieteren (Belgium) is majority shareholder	Volkswagen AG	Ford Motor Company	Publicly traded
European revenues	€41 million	€1.25 billion	€1.12 billion	€910 million	€600 million
Company Web site	www.easyCar.com	www.avis-europe.com	www.europcar.com	www.hertz.com	ag.sixt.com

Source: Information in this table came from each company's Web site and online annual reports. European revenues are for vehicle rental in Europe and are estimated based on market share estimates for 2001 from Avis Europe's Web site.

operated at only one or a few locations and were particularly prevalent in tourist locations. A number of brokers also operated in the sector, like Holiday Autos. Brokerage companies did not own their own fleet of cars, but basically managed the excess inventory of other companies and matched customers with rental companies with excess fleet capacity.

Overall, the rental car market could be thought of as composed of two broad segments, a business segment and a tourist/leisure segment. Depending on the market, the leisure segment represented somewhere between 45 and 65 percent of the overall market, and a large part of this segment was very price conscious. The business segment made up the remaining 35 to 55 percent of the market. It was less price sensitive than the tourist segment and more concerned about service quality, convenience, and flexibility.

THE GROWTH OF EASYCAR

EasyCar opened its first location in London on April 20, 2000, under the name easyRentacar. In the same week, easyCar opened locations in Glasgow and Barcelona. All three locations were popular easyJet destinations. Vehicles initially could be rented for as low as €15 a day plus a one-time car preparation fee of €8. Each of these locations had a fleet consisting entirely of Mercedes A-class vehicles. It was the only vehicle that easyCar rented at the time.

EasyCar had signed a deal with Mercedes, amid much fanfare, at the Geneva Motor Show earlier in the year to purchase a total of 5,000 A-class vehicles. The vehicles, which came with guaranteed buyback terms, cost easyCar's parent company a little over £6 million.[14] Many in the car rental industry were surprised by the choice, expecting easyCar to rely on less expensive models.[15]

In describing the acquisition of the 5,000 Mercedes vehicles, Stelios had said:

> The choice of Mercedes reflects the easyGroup brand. EasyRentacar will use brand new Mercedes cars in the same way that easyJet uses brand new Boeing aircraft. We do not compromise on the hardware, we just use innovation to substantially reduces costs. The car hire industry is where the airline industry was five years ago, a cartel feeding off the corporate client. EasyRentacar will provide a choice for consumers who pay out of their own pockets and who will not be ripped off for traveling mid-week.[16]

EasyCar quickly expanded to other locations, focusing first on those locations that were popular with easyJet customers, including Amsterdam, Geneva, Nice, and Malaga. By July 2001, a little over a year after its initial launch, easyCar had fleets of Mercedes A-class vehicles in 14 locations in the United Kingdom, Spain, France, and the Netherlands. At this point, EasyCar secured £27 million from a consortium of Bank of Scotland Corporate Banking and NBGI Private Equity to further expand its operations. The package consisted of a combination of equity and loan stock.

Although easyCar added a few sites in the second half of 2001 and early 2002, volatile demand in the wake of the September 11 attacks forced easyCar to roll out new rental locations somewhat slower than originally expected.[17] Growth accelerated, however, in the spring of 2002. Between May 2002 and January 2003, easyCar opened 30 new locations, to go from 18 sites to a total of 48 sites. This acceleration in growth also coincided with a change in easyCar's policy regarding the makeup of its fleet. By May 2002, easyCar's fleet consisted of 6,000 Mercedes A-class vehicles

[14]N. Hodgson, "Stelios Plans easyCar Float," *Liverpool Echo*, September 24, 2002.

[15]A. Felsted, "EasyCar Courts Clio for Rental Fleet," *Financial Times*, February 11, 2002, p. 26.

[16]EasyCar.com Web site news release, March 1, 2000.

[17]T. Burt, "EasyCar Agrees to Deal with Vauxhall," *Financial Times*, April 30, 2002, p. 24.

Exhibit 2
EasyCar Locations in January 2003

Source: easyCar.com Web site, January 2003.

Country	City	Number	Number Near an Airport
France	Nice	1	1
France	Paris	8	0
Netherlands	Amsterdam	3	1
Spain	Barcelona	2	0
Spain	Madrid	2	0
Spain	Majorca	1	1
Spain	Malaga	1	1
Switzerland	Geneva	1	1
UK	Birmingham	2	0
UK	Bromley	1	0
UK	Croydon	1	1
UK	Glasgow	2	1
UK	Kingston-upon-Thames	1	0
UK	Liverpool	2	1
UK	London	15	0
UK	Manchester	2	1
UK	Waterford	1	0
Total	5 countries, 17 cities	46	9

across 18 sites. Beginning in May, however, easyCar began to stock its fleet with other types of vehicles. It still maintained its policy of offering only a single vehicle at each location, but now the vehicle the customer received depended on the location. The first new vehicle easyCar introduced was the Vauxhall Corsa. According to Stelios,

> Vauxhall Corsas cost easyCar £2 a day less than Mercedes A-Class so we can pass this saving on to customers. Customers themselves will decide if they want to pay a premium for a Mercedes. EasyGroup companies benefit from economies of scale where relevant but we also want to create contestable markets among our suppliers so that we can keep the cost to our customers as low as possible.[18]

By January 2003, easyCar was also using Ford Focuses (4 locations), Renault Clios (3 locations), Toyota Yarises (3 locations), and Mercedes Smart cars (2 locations) in addition to the Vauxhall Corsas (7 locations) and the Mercedes A-Class vehicles (28 locations). Plans called for a further expansion of the fleet, from the 7,000 vehicles that easyCar had in January to 24,000 vehicles across 180 rental sites by the end of 2004.[19]

In addition to making vehicles available at more locations, easyCar had also changed its policies for 2003 to allow rentals for as little as one hour, and with as little as one hour's notice of rental. By making this change, Stelios felt that easyCar could be a serious competitor to local taxis, buses, trains, and even car ownership. EasyCar expected that if it made car rental simple enough and cheap enough, some people living in traffic-congested European cities who only use their car occasionally would give up the costs and hassles of car ownership and simply rent an easyCar when they needed a vehicle. Tapping into this broader transportation market would help the company reach its ambitious future sales goals.

FACILITIES

EasyCar had facilities in a total of 17 cities in 5 European countries, as shown in Exhibit 2. It primarily located its facilities near bus and train stations in the major European cities, seeking out sites that offered low lease costs. It generally avoided prime airport locations, as the cost for space at and in some cases near airports was significantly higher than most other locations. When easyCar did locate near an airport, it generally chose sites off the airport, to reduce the cost of the lease. Airport locations also tended to require longer hours to satisfy customers arriving on late flights or departing on very early flights. EasyCar kept its airport locations open 24 hours a day, whereas its other locations were generally open only from 7 A.M. to 11 P.M.

The physical facilities at all locations were kept to a minimum. In many locations, easyCar leased space in an existing parking garage. Employees worked out of a small, self-contained cubicle within the garage. The cubicle, depending on the location, might be no more than 15 square meters and included little more than a small counter and a couple of computers at which staff processed customers as they came to pick up or return their vehicles. EasyCar also leased a number of spaces within the garage for its fleet of cars. However, because easyCar's vehicles were rented 90 percent of the time, the number of spaces required at an average site, which had a fleet of about 150 cars, was only 15–20 spaces.[20] To speed up the opening of new sites, easyCar had equipped a number of vans with all the needed computer and telephone equipment to run a site.[21] From an operational perspective, it could open a new location by simply leasing 20 or so spaces in a parking garage, hiring a small staff, driving a van to the location, and adding the location to the company's Web site. Depending on the fleet size at a location, easyCar typically had only one or two people working at a site at a time.

---

[18]EasyCar.com Web site news release, May 2, 2002.

[19]"Marketing Week: EasyCar Appoints Head of European Marketing," *Financial Times Information Limited*, January 9, 2003.

[20]E. Simpkins, "Stelios Isn't Taking It Easy," *Sunday Telegraph (UK)*, December 15, 2002.

[21]E. Simpkins, "Stelios Isn't Taking It Easy," *Sunday Telegraph (UK)*, December 15, 2002.

VEHICLE PICKUP AND RETURN PROCESSES

Customers arrived to a site to pick up a vehicle within a pre-arranged one-hour time period. Each customer selected this time slot when booking the vehicle. EasyCar adjusted the first day's rental price based on the pickup time. Customers who picked their cars up early in the day or at popular times were charged more compared to customers picking up their cars late in the day or at less busy times. Customers were required to bring a printed copy of their contract, along with the credit card they used to make the booking and identification. Given the low staffing levels, customers occasionally had to wait 30 minutes or more to be processed and receive their vehicles, particularly at peak times of the day. Processing a customer began with the employee accessing the customer's contract on line. If the customer was a new easyCar customer to the site, the basic policies and possible additional charges were briefly explained. The employee then made copies of the customer's identification and credit card and took a digital photo of the customer. Customers were charged an €80 refundable deposit, signed the contract, and were on their way.

All vehicles were rented with more or less empty fuel tanks with the exact level dependent on how much gasoline was left in the vehicle when the previous renter returned it. Customers were provided with a small map of the immediate area around the rental site, showing the location and hours of nearby gas stations. Customers could return vehicles with any amount of gas in them as long as the low-fuel indicator light in the vehicle was not on. Customers who returned vehicles with the low-fuel indicator light on were charged a fueling fee of €16.

Customers were also expected to return the vehicle within a pre-arranged one-hour time period, which they also selected at the time of booking. While customers did not have to worry about refueling the car before returning it, they were expected to thoroughly clean the car. This clean-car policy had been implemented in May 2002 as a way to further reduce the price customers could pay for their vehicle. Prior to this change, all customers paid a fixed preparation fee of €11 each time they rented a vehicle (up from the €8 preparation fee when the company started operations in 2000). The new policy reduced this up-front preparation fee to €4 but required customers to either return the vehicle clean or pay an additional cleaning fee of €16. To avoid any misunderstanding about what it meant by a clean car, easyCar provided customers with an explicit description of what constituted a clean car, both for the interior and the exterior of the car. This included the appearance that the exterior of the car had been washed prior to returning the vehicle. The map that customers were provided when they picked up their cars that showed nearby gas stations also showed nearby car washes where they could clean the car before returning it. Although easyCar had received some bad press in relation to the policy,[22] 85 percent of customers returned their vehicles clean as a result of the policy.

When a customer returned the vehicle, an easyCar employee would check to make sure that the vehicle was clean and undamaged and that the low-fuel indicator light was not on. The employee would also check the kilometers driven. The customer would then be notified of any additional charges. These charges would be subtracted from the €80 deposit and the difference refunded to the customer's credit card (or, if additional charges exceeded the €80 deposit, the customer's credit card would be charged the difference).

PRICING

EasyCar clearly differentiated itself from its competitors with its low price. In addition, pricing played a key role in easyCar's efforts to achieve high utilization of its fleet of cars. EasyCar advertised prices as low as €5 per day plus a per-rental preparation fee of €4. Prices, however, varied by the location and dates of the rental, by when the booking was made, and by what time the car was to be picked up and returned. EasyCar's systems constantly evaluated projected demand and expected utilization at each site, and adjusted price accordingly. Achieving the €5 per day rate usually required customers to book well in advance, and these rates were typically available only on weekdays. Weekend rates, when booked well in advance, typically started a few euros higher than the weekday rates. As a given rental date approached, however, the price typically went up significantly as easyCar approached 100 percent fleet utilization for that day. Rates could literally triple overnight if there was sufficient booking activity. Generally, however, easyCar's price was less than half that of its major competitors. EasyCar, unlike most other rental car companies, required customers to pay in full at the time of booking and once a booking was made, it was nonrefundable.

EasyCar's base price covered only the core rental of the vehicle—the total price customers paid was in many cases much higher and depended on how the customer reserved, paid for, used, and returned the vehicle. EasyCar's price was based on customers booking through the company's Web site and paying for their rental with their easyMoney credit card. EasyMoney was the easyGroup's credit and financial services company. Customers who chose to book through the company's phone reservation system were charged an additional €0.95 each minute for the call and those who used other credit cards were charged €5 extra. All vehicles had to be paid for by a credit or debit card—cash was not accepted. The base rental price allowed customers to drive vehicles 100 kilometers per day; additional kilometers were charged at a rate of €0.12 per kilometer. In addition, customers were expected to return their cars clean and on time. Customers who returned cars that did not meet easyCar's standards for clean were charged a €16 cleaning fee. Those who returned their cars late were immediately charged €120 and subsequently charged an additional €120 for each subsequent 24-hour period in which the car was not returned. EasyCar explained the high late fee as representing the cost that they would likely incur in providing another vehicle to the next customer. Customers wishing to make any changes to their bookings were also charged a change fee of €16. Changes could be made either before the rental started or during the rental period but were limited to changing the dates, times, and location of the rental and were subject to the prices and vehicle availability at the time the change was being made. If the change resulted in an overall lower price for the rental, however, no refund was provided for the difference.

Beginning in 2003, all customers were also required to purchase loss-damage insurance for an additional charge of €4 each day, which eliminated the customer's liability for loss or damage to the vehicle (excluding damage to the tires or windshield of the vehicle). Through 2002, customers were able to choose whether or not to purchase additional insurance from easyCar to eliminate any financial liability in the event that the rental vehicle was damaged.

---

[22]J. Hyde, "Travel View: Clearing Up on the Extras," *The Observer (UK)*, July 7, 2002.

The cost of this insurance had been €6 per day, and approximately 60 percent of easyCar's customers purchased this optional insurance. Those not purchasing this insurance had either assumed the liability for the first €800 in damages personally or had their own insurance through some other means (e.g., some credit card companies provide this insurance to their cardholders at no additional charge for short-term rentals paid for with the credit card).

EasyCar's Web site attempted to make all of these additional charges clear to customers at the time of their booking. EasyCar had received a fair amount of bad press when it first opened for business after many renters complained about having to pay undisclosed charges when they returned their cars.[23] In response, easyCar had revamped its Web site in an effort to make these charges more transparent to customers and to explain the logic behind many of these charges.

PROMOTION

EasyCar's promotional efforts had through 2002 focused primarily on posters and press advertising. Posters were particularly prevalent in metro systems and bus and train stations in cities where easyCar had operations. All of this advertising focused on easyCar's low price. According to founder Stelios: "You will never see an advert for an easy company offering an experience—it's about price. If you create expectations you can't live up to then you will ultimately suffer as a result."[24] In 2002, easyCar spent £1.43 million on such advertising.[25]

EasyCar also promoted itself by displaying its name, phone number, and Web site address prominently on the doors and rear window of its entire fleet of vehicles, and it took advantage of free publicity when the opportunity presented itself. An example of seeking out such publicity occurred when Hertz complained that easyCar's comparative advertising campaign in the Netherlands, featuring the line "The best reason to use easyCar.com can be found at hertz.nl," violated Dutch law that required comparative advertising to be exact, not general. In response, Stelios and a group of easyCar employees, dressed in orange boiler suits and with a fleet of easyCar vehicles, protested outside the Hertz Amsterdam office with signs asking "What is Hertz frightened of?"[26]

In an effort to help reach its goal of quadrupling sales in the next two years, easyCar hired Jennifer Mowat into the new position of commercial director to take over responsibility for easyCar's European marketing. Ms. Mowat had previously been eBay's U.K. country manager and had recently completed an MBA in Switzerland. Previously, Stelios and easyCar's managing director, Andrew Fitzmaurice, had handled the marketing function themselves.[27] As part of this stepped-up marketing effort, easyCar also planned to double its advertising budget for 2003, to £3 million, and to begin to advertise on television. The television advertising campaign was to feature easyCar's founder, Stelios.[28]

LEGAL CHALLENGES

EasyCar faced several challenges to its approaches. The most significant dealt with a November 2002 ruling made by the Office of Fair Trading (OFT) that easyCar had to grant customers seven days from the time they made a booking to cancel their booking and receive a full refund. The OFT, a U.K. governmental agency, is responsible for protecting U.K. consumers from unfair and/or anti-competitive business practices. The ruling against easyCar was based on the 2000 Consumer Protection Distance Selling Regulations. These regulations stipulated that companies that sell at a distance (e.g., by Internet or phone) must provide customers with a seven-day cooling-off period, during which customers can cancel their contracts with the company and receive a full refund. The law exempted accommodation, transportation, catering, and leisure service companies from this requirement. The OFT's ruling concluded that easyCar did not qualify as a transportation service company because consumers had to drive themselves and thus were receiving not a transport service, but just a car.[29]

EasyCar appealed the OFT's decision to the U.K. High Court on the grounds that it was indeed a transportation service company and was entitled to an exemption from this requirement. EasyCar was hopeful that it would eventually win this legal challenge. EasyCar had argued that this ruling would destroy the company's book-early–pay-less philosophy and could lead to a tripling of prices.[30] Chairman Stelios said, "It is very serious. My fear is that as soon as we put in the seven-day cooling off periods our utilization rate will fall from 90% to 65%. That's the difference between a profitable company and an unprofitable one."[31] EasyCar was also concerned that prolonged legal action on this point could interfere with its plans for a 2004 IPO.

OFT, for its part, had also applied to the U.K. High Court for an injunction to make the company comply with the ruling. Other rental car companies were generally unconcerned about the ruling, as few offered big discounts for early bookings or nonrefundable bookings.[32]

EasyCar's new policy of posting the pictures of customers whose cars were 15 days or more overdue was also drawing legal criticism. EasyCar had recently received public warnings from lawyers that this new policy might violate data protection, libel, privacy, confidentiality, and human rights laws.[33] Of particular concern to some lawyers was the possibility that easyCar might post the wrong person's picture, given the large number of customers the company dealt with.[34] Such a mistake could open the company to costly libel suits. The policy of posting the pictures of overdue customers on the easyCar Web site, initiated in November 2002, was designed to reduce the losses associated with customers renting a vehicle and never returning it. The costs were significant, according to Stelios: "These cars are expensive, £15,000 each, and

---

[23]J. Stanton, "The Empire That's Easy Money," *Edinburgh Evening News*, November 26, 2002.

[24]"The Big Picture—An Interview with Stelios," *Sunday Herald (UK)*, March 16, 2003.

[25]"Marketing Week: EasyCar Appoints Head of European Marketing," *Financial Times Information Limited*, January 9, 2003.

[26]EasyCar.com Web site news release, April 22, 2002.

[27]"Marketing Week: EasyCar Appoints Head of European Marketing," *Financial Times Information Limited*, January 9, 2003.

[28]"Campaigning: EasyGroup Appoints Publicist for easyCar TV Advertising Brief," *Financial Times Information Limited*, January 31, 2003.

[29]J. Macintosh, "EasyCar Sues OFT Amid Threat to Planned Flotation," *Financial Times*, November 22, 2002, p. 4.

[30]"Marketing Week: EasyCar Appoints Head of European Marketing," *Financial Times Information Limited*, January 9, 2003.

[31]J. Mackintosh, "EasyCar Sues OFT Amid Threat to Planned Flotation," *Financial Times*, November 22, 2002, p. 4.

[32]J. Mackintosh, "EasyCar Sues OFT Amid Threat to Planned Flotation," *Financial Times*, November 22, 2002, p. 4.

[33]B. Sherwood and A. Wendlandt, "EasyCar May Be in Difficulty over Naming Ploy," *Financial Times*, November 14, 2002, p. 2.

[34]B. Sherwood and A. Wendlandt, "EasyCar May Be in Difficulty over Naming Ploy," *Financial Times*, November 14, 2002, p. 2.

we have 6000 of them. At any given time we are looking for as many as several tens which are overdue. If we don't get one back, it's a write-off. We are writing off an entire car, and its uninsurable."[35]

Stelios was also convinced of the legality of the new policy. In a letter to the editor responding to the legal concerns raised in the press, Stelios said:

> From a legal perspective, we have been entirely factual and objective and are merely reporting the details of the overdue car and the person who collected it. In addition, our policy is made very clear in our terms and conditions and the photo is taken both overtly and with the consent of the customer . . . I estimate the total cost of overdue cars to be 5% of total easyCar costs, or 50p on every car rental day for all customers. In 2004, when I intend to float easyCar, this cost will amount to £5 million unless we can reduce our quantity of overdue cars.[36]

In the past, easyCar had simply provided pictures to police when a rental was 15 or more days overdue. The company hoped that posting the picture would both discourage drivers from not returning vehicles and shame those drivers who currently had overdue cars into returning them. In fact, the first person who easyCar posted to its Web site did indeed return his car two days later. The vehicle was 29 days late.[37]

THE FUTURE

At the end of 2002, Stelios had stepped down as the CEO of easyJet so that he could devote more of his time to the other easyGroup companies, including easyCar. He had three priorities for the new year. One was to turn around the money-losing easyInternetCafe business, which Stelios had described as "the worst mistake of my career."[38] The 22-store chain had lost £80 million in the last two years. A second was to oversee the planned launch of another new easyGroup business, easyCinema, in the spring of 2003. And the third was to oversee the rapid expansion of the easyCar chain so that it would be ready for an initial public offering in the second half of 2004.

QUESTIONS

1. What are the characteristics of the car rental industry? How do these characteristics influence the design of service delivery processes in this industry in general?

2. EasyCar obviously competes on the basis of low price. What does it do in operations to support this strategy?

3. How would you characterize the level of quality that easyCar provides?

4. Is easyCar a viable competitor to taxis, buses, and trains, as Stelios claims? How does the design of its operations currently support this form of competition? How not?

5. What are the operational implications of the changes made by EasyCar.com in the last year?

6. How significant are the legal challenges that easyCar is facing?

7. What is your assessment of the likelihood that easyCar will be able to realize its goals for 2005?

Source: This case was written by John J. Lawrence (University of Idaho) and Luis Solis (Instituto de Empresa) and used with their permission.

---

[35]"e-business: Internet Fraudsters Fail to Steal Potter Movie's Magic & Other News," *Financial Times Information Limited*, November 19, 2002.

[36]S. Haji-loannou, "Letters to the Editor: Costly Effect of Late Car Return," *Financial Times*, November 16, 2002, p. 10.

[37]M. Hookham, "How Stelios Nets Return of His Cars," *Liverpool (UK) Daily Post*, November 14, 2002.

[38]S. Bentley, "The Worst Mistake of My Career, by Stelios," *Financial Times*, December 24, 2002.

CASE 3—4 Marketing to the Bottom of the Pyramid

Professor C. K. Prahalad's seminal publication, "The Fortune at the Bottom of the Pyramid,"[1] suggests there is an enormous market at the "bottom of the pyramid" (BOP)—that group of some 4 billion people who subsist on less than $2 a day. By some estimates, these "aspirational poor," who make up three-fourths of the world's population, represent $14 trillion in purchasing power, more than Germany, the United Kingdom, Italy, France, and Japan put together. Demographically, it's young and growing at 6 percent a year or more.

Traditionally, the poor are not considered an important market segment. "The poor can't afford most products"; "they will not accept new technologies"; and "except for the most basic products, they have little or no use for most products sold to higher income market segments"—these are some of the assumptions that have, until recently, caused most multinational firms to pay little or no attention to those at the bottom of the pyramid. Typical market analysis is limited to urban areas, thereby ignoring rural villages where, in markets like India, the majority of the population lives. However, as major markets become more competitive and in some cases saturated with resulting ever-thinning profit margins, marketing to the bottom of the pyramid is seen by some as having potential worthy of exploration.

One researcher suggested that American and European businesses have to go back and look at their own roots. Sears, Roebuck was created to serve the lower-income, sparsely settled rural market. Singer sewing machines fashioned a scheme to make consumption possible by allowing customers to pay $5 a month instead of $100 at once. The world's largest company today, Wal-Mart, was created to serve the lower-income market. A few examples of multinational company efforts to overcome the challenges in marketing to the BOP follow.

Designing products for the BOP is not about making cheap stuff but about making technologically advanced products affordable. For example, one company was inspired to invent the Freeplay, a windup self-power-generating radio, when it was learned that isolated, impoverished people in South Africa weren't getting information about AIDS because they had no electricity for radios and couldn't afford replacement batteries.

If a product requires the support of an advanced infrastructure, then the product has to be redesigned or the marketing program has to include infrastructure support. For example, Hindustan Lever, a subsidiary of Unilever, markets an inexpensive, reusable heat shield that can keep ice cream cold for 24 hours—permitting the use of vending machines in areas without affordable electricity. And Electrolux Kelvinator, another Indian subsidiary of a Western company, sells refrigerators that can keep contents frozen through six-hour blackouts.

Observers note that such innovations yield marketable products for middle-class consumers, too. For example, the Freeplay radio is now sold in wealthy nations as a standby radio for emergencies.

A Chinese appliance maker has captured a third of the world microwave oven market with designs originally intended for the tight spaces of Chinese kitchens.

The BOP market has a need for advanced technology, but to be usable, infrastructure support must often accompany the technology. For example, ITC, a $2.6 billion a year Indian conglomerate, decided to create a network of PC kiosks in villages. For years, ITC conducted its business with farmers through a maze of intermediaries, from brokers to traders. The company wanted farmers to be able to connect directly to information sources to check ITC's offer price for produce, as well as prices in the closest village market, in the state capital, and on the Chicago commodities exchange. With direct access to information, farmers would get the best price for their product, hordes of intermediaries were bypassed, and ITC gained a direct contact with the farmers, thus improving the efficiency of ITC's soybean acquisition. To achieve this goal, it had to do much more than just distribute PCs. It had to provide equipment for managing power outages, solar panels for extra electricity, and a satellite-based telephone hookup, and it had to train farmers to use the PCs. Without these steps the PCs would never have worked. The complex solution serves ITC very well. Now more than 10,000 villages and more than 1 million farmers are covered by its system. ITC is able to pay more to farmers and at the same time cut its costs because it has dramatically reduced the inefficiencies in logistics.

The vast market for cell phones among those at the BOP is not for phones costing $200 or even $100 but for phones costing less than $50. Such a phone cannot simply be a cut-down version of an existing handset. It must be very reliable and have lots of battery capacity, as it will be used by people who do not have reliable access to electricity Motorola went thorough four redesigns to develop a low-cost cell phone with battery life as long as 500 hours for villagers without regular electricity and an extra-loud volume for use in noisy markets. Motorola's low-cost phone, a no-frills cell phone priced at $40, has a standby time of two weeks and conforms to local languages and customs. The cell-phone manufacturer says it expects to sell 6 million cell phones in six months in markets including China, India, and Turkey.

There is also demand for personal computers but again, at very low prices. To meet the needs of this market, Advanced Micro Devices markets a $185 Personal Internet communicator—a basic computer for developing countries—and a Taiwan Company offers a similar device costing just $100.

For most products, demand is contingent on the customer having sufficient purchasing power. Companies have to devise creative ways to assist those at the BOP to finance larger purchases. For example, Cemex, the world's third-largest cement company, recognized an opportunity for profit by enabling lower-income Mexicans to build their own homes. The company's Patrimonio Hoy Programme, a combination builder's "club" and financing plan that targets homeowners who make less than $5 a day, markets building kits using its premium-grade cement. It recruited 510

[1]C. K. Prahalad, *The Fortune at the Bottom of the Pyramid* (Philadelphia: Wharton School Publishing, 2004).

promoters to persuade new customers to commit to building additions to their homes. The customers paid Cemex $11.50 a week and received building materials every 10 weeks until the room was finished (about 70 weeks—customers were on their own for the actual building). Though poor, 99.6 percent of the 150,000 Patrimonio Hoy participants have paid their bills in full. Patrimonio Hoy attracted 42,000 new customers and is expected to turn a $1.5 million profit in 2005.

One customer, Diega Chavero, thought the scheme was a scam when she first heard of it, but after eight years of being unable to save enough to expand the one-room home where her family of six lived, she was willing to try anything. Four years later, she has five bedrooms. "Now I have a palace."

Another deterrent to the development of small enterprises at the BOP is available sources of adequate financing for microdistributors and budding entrepreneurs. For years, those at the bottom of the pyramid needing loans in India had to depend on local moneylenders, at interest rates up to 500 percent a year. ICICI bank, the second-largest banking institution in India, saw these people as a potential market and critical to its future. To convert them into customers in a cost-effective way, ICICI turned to village self-help groups.

ICICI Bank met with microfinance-aid groups working with the poor and decided to give them capital to start making small loans to the poor—at rates that run from 10 percent to 30 percent. This sounds usurious, but it is lower than the 10 percent daily rate that some Indian loan sharks charge. Each group was composed of 20 women who were taught about saving, borrowing, investing, and so on. Each woman contributes to a joint savings account with the other members and, based on the self-help group track record of savings, the bank then lends money to the group, which in turn lends money to its individual members. ICICI has developed 10,000 of these groups reaching 200,000 women. ICICI's money has helped 1 million households get loans that average $120 to $140. The bank's executive directory says the venture has been "very profitable." ICICI is working with local communities and NGOs to enlarge its reach.

When Unilever saw that dozens of agencies were lending microcredit loans funds to poor women all over India, they thought that these would-be microentrepreneurs needed businesses to run. Unilever realized it couldn't sell to the bottom of the pyramid unless it found low-cost ways to distribute its product, so it created a network of hundreds of thousands of *Shakti Amma* ("empowered mothers") who sell Lever's products in their villages through an Indian version of Tupperware parties. Start-up loans enabled the women to buy stocks of goods to sell to local villagers. In one case, a woman who received a small loan was able to repay her start-up loan and has not needed to take another one. She now sells regularly to about 50 homes, and even serves as a miniwholesaler, stocking tiny shops in outlying villages a short bus ride from her own. She sells about 10,000 rupees ($230) of goods each month, keeps about $26 profit, and ploughs the rest back into new stock. While the $26 a month she earns is less than the average $40 monthly income in the area, she now has income, whereas before she had nothing.

Today about 1,300 poor women are selling Unilever's products in 50,000 villages in 12 states in India and account for about 15 percent of the company's rural sales in those states. Overall, rural markets account for about 30 percent of the company's revenue.

In another example, Nguyen Van Hon operates a floating sundries distributorship along the Ke Sat River in Vietnam's Mekong Delta—a maze of rivers and canals dotted with villages. His boat is filled with boxes containing small bars of Lifebuoy soap and single-use sachets of Sunsilk shampoo and Omo laundry detergent, which he sells to riverside shopkeepers for as little as 2.5 cents each. At his first stop he makes deliveries to a half dozen small shops. He sells hundred of thousands of soap and shampoo packets a month, enough to earn about $125—five times his previous monthly salary as a junior Communist party official. "It's a hard life, but its getting better." Now, he says, he "has enough to pay his daughter's schools fees and soon he will have saved enough to buy a bigger boat, so I can sell to more villages." Because of aggressive efforts to reach remote parts of the country through an extensive network of more than 100,000 independent sales representatives such as Hon, the Vietnam subsidiary of Unilever realized a 23 percent increase in sales in 2004 to more than $300 million.

As one observer noted, "the poor cannot be Wal-Martized." Consumers in rich nations use money to stockpile convenience. We go to Sam's Club, Costco, K-Mart, and so on, to get bargain prices and the convenience of buying shampoos and paper towels by the case. Selling to the poor requires just the opposite approach. They do not have the cash to stockpile convenience and they do not mind frequent trips to the village store. Products have to be made available locally and in affordable units; fully 60 percent of the value of all shampoo sold in India is in single-serve packets.

Nestlé is targeting China with a blitz of 29 new ice cream brands, many selling for as little as 12 cents with take-home and multipack products ranging from 72 cent to $2.30. It also features products specially designed for local tastes and preferences of Chinese consumers, such as Nestlé Snow Moji, a rice pastry filled with vanilla ice cream that resembles dim sum, and other ice cream flavors like red bean and green tea. The ice cream products are distributed through a group of small independent saleswomen, which the company aims to expand to 4,000 women by 2006. The project is expected to account for as much as 24 percent of the company's total rural sales within the next few years.

QUESTIONS

1. As a junior member of your company's committee to explore new markets, you have received a memo from the chairman telling you to be prepared at the next meeting to discuss key questions that need to be addressed if the company decides to look further into the possibility of marketing to the BOP segment. The ultimate goal of this meeting will be to establish a set of general guidelines to use in developing a market strategy for any one of the company's products to be marketed to the "aspirational poor." These guidelines need not be company or product specific at this time. In fact, think of the final guideline as a checklist—a series of questions that a company could use as a start in evaluating the potential of a specific BOP market segment for one of its products.

2. Marketing to the BOP raises a number of issues revolving around the social responsibility of marketing efforts. Write a position paper either pro or con on one of the following:

   a. Is it exploitation for a company to profit from selling soaps, shampoo, personal computers, and ice cream, and so on, to people with little disposable income?

b. Can making loans to customers whose income is less than \$100 monthly at interest rates of 20 percent to purchase TVs, cell phones, and other consumer durables be justified?

c. One authority argues that squeezing profits from people with little disposable income—and often not enough to eat—isn't capitalist exploitation but rather that it stimulates economic growth.

Sources: C. K. Prahalad, *The Fortune at the Bottom of the Pyramid* (Philadelphia: Wharton School Publishing, 2004); Stefan Stern, "How Serving the Poorest Can Bring Rich Rewards," *Management Today,* August 2004; Kay Johnson and Xa Nhon, "Selling to the Poor: There Is a Surprisingly Lucrative Market in Targeting Low-Income Consumers," *Time,* April 25, 2005; Cris Prystay, "India's Small Loans Yield Big Markets," *Asian Wall Street Journal,* May 25, 2005; C. K. Prahalad, "Why Selling to the Poor Makes for Good Business," *Fortune,* November 15, 2004; Alison Maitland, "A New Frontier in Responsibility," *Financial Times,* November 29, 2004; Normandy Madden, "Nestlé Hits Mainland with Cheap Ice Cream," *Advertising Age,* March 7, 2005; Ritesh Gupta, "Rural Consumers Get Closer to Established World Brands," *Ad Age Global,* June 2002; Alison Overholt, "A New Path to Profit," *Fast Company,* January 1, 2005; Patrick Whitney, "Designing for the Base of the Pyramid," *Design Management Review,* Fall 2004; C. K. Prahalad and Stuart Hart, "Fortune at the Bottom of the Pyramid," *Strategy & Business* 26 (2002); C. K. Prahalad and Aline Hammond, "Serving the World's Poor, Profitably," *Harvard Business Review,* September 2002; "The Invisible Market," *Across the Board,* September/October 2004; Anuradha Mittal and Lori Wallach, "Selling Out the Poor," *Foreign Policy,* September/October 2004; G. Pascal Zachary, "Poor Idea," *New Republic,* March 7, 2005; "Calling an End to Poverty," *The Economist,* July 9, 2005; Susanna Howard, "P&G, Unilever Court the World's Poor," *Wall Street Journal,* June 1, 2005; Rajiv Banerjee and N. Shatrujeet, "Shoot to the Heart," *Economic Times,* July 6, 2005; David Ignatius, "Pennies from the Poor Add Up to Fortune," *Korea Herald,* July 7, 2005; Rebecca Buckman, "Cell Phone Game Rings in New Niche: Ultra Cheap," *Wall Street Journal,* August 18, 2005, p. B4.

cases 4

DEVELOPING GLOBAL MARKETING STRATEGIES

OUTLINE OF CASES

4-1 McDonald's Great Britain—The Turnaround

4-2 Tambrands: Overcoming Cultural Resistance

4-3 Iberia Airlines Builds a BATNA

4-4 Sales Negotiations Abroad for MRI Systems

4-5 National Office Machines—Motivating Japanese Salespeople: Straight Salary or Commission?

4-6 AIDS, Condoms, and Carnival

4-7 Making Socially Responsible and Ethical Marketing Decisions: Selling Tobacco to Third World Countries

CASE 4–1 McDonald's Great Britain—The Turnaround

New menus, improved service, advertising, opening new stores, closing others, and refurbishing others have propelled McDonald's U.S. back into an active growth cycle after experiencing a slack period in 2003 and 2004—U.S. sales have climbed for 24 straight months. Sales in Great Britain have not shown a similar movement. Sales at McDonald's 1,235 British outlets have been sluggish for years, and the reasons are numerous. New chains such as Yo! Sushi and Nando's Chicken Restaurants, which features spicy Portuguese chicken, have outpaced McDonald's. Operators such as U.S.-based Subway Restaurants are pulling in customers with fresh salads and sandwiches on focaccia bread. Starbucks has made McDonald's outlets look sterile and out-of-date. And the 2001 scare over mad cow disease, along with concerns about rising obesity, make things worse.

In part because of lackluster performance in Great Britain, McDonald's European operations—the second biggest market after America, responsible for about 30 percent of profits, have suffered. In 2005, European sales fell 0.7 percent, while U.S. sales grew 4.7 percent. Further, same-store sales for European restaurants open more than a year registered a 3 percent decline.

To give you a flavor of what McDonald's U.K. faces, here are observations about McDonald's Britain.

COMMENTS FROM VARIOUS NEWS SOURCES

- A 24-year-old advertising sales representative in West London commented, "The McDonald's near where I work is really smart, with Internet access and everything, but I only go in there as a last resort."

- "Twenty-three years ago, or thereabouts, I had my first McDonald's. I was studying at Cambridge and a group of us drove to London to watch a football match. We stopped off at McDonald's in the Strand and I experienced the joys of a Big Mac with fries, to go. It felt like the height of cool. I was from Cumbria, and McDonald's, which came to this country only in 1974, hadn't yet penetrated that far north. My friends were Londoners, hip, dead trendy. They had cars at university, they drove to see the capital's smarter teams, and they ate at McDonald's.

  "Recently, I popped into the same outlet in Strand and clearly, it's not just fashion that shifts: my taste buds have altered too—either that or after two or three pints at a football ground, anything seems delicious. Eschewing the option—as most of its customers do—to go healthy and order a salad, I went for a traditional double cheeseburger. The burger bun tasted like cottonwood, the beef in the burger patty lacked texture. It was manufactured, processed and quick."

- Some opine that like all empires, McDonald's has had its day and is now on the slippery slope to oblivion. McDonald's could go the way of Howard Johnson's, another restaurant chain that once covered America but now has all but disappeared.

- Everything has been hurled at the company, from fears about contracting mad cow disease to two teenage girls suing the company for making them fat to a savagely critical best-selling book, *Fast Food Nation* (which revealed, among other things, that the beef in McDonald's patties can come from up to 100 different cows) and a hit film, *Super Size Me* (whose maker, Morgan Spurlock, did nothing except eat at McDonald's for a month with disastrous effects to his health, turning his liver into something approaching pâté). The result: profits fell, earnings per share were down, and the firm famous for its expansion was forced to close restaurants.

- A recently released documentary, called *McLibel*, reopened old wounds for McDonald's. *McLibel* recounts the story behind a decade-long court battle—the longest in British history—that pitted McDonald's against two Greenpeace activists whom the company accused of libel. McDonald's sued (1994) five London-based Greenpeace activists after they distributed leaflets that asked, "What's Wrong with McDonald's?" Three pulled out but two fought the chain. After initially being ordered to pay damages, the two appealed twice, then took their complaint to the U.K.'s Court of Human Rights, claiming that a lack of access to legal aid hurt their right to a fair trail. In February the court sided with the activists, giving the government three months to appeal. At the time of the decision McDonald's said the world has moved on since then and so has McDonald's.

- There are positives for McDonald's U.K. For all its perceived problems, McDonald's profits are £118 million a year. Nearly 3 million people visit its British branches every day and among teenagers, McDonald's is still the number one food brand.

- The company monitors news articles and television references to McDonald's in Britain, rating them "negative," "neutral," or "positive." In 2004, most reports were negative, but in 2005 opinion had moved to pretty much neutral ground.

STEPS TAKEN TO REVERSE THE TREND

- McDonald's has rolled out new offerings, including salads, yogurt, and other fare aimed at health-conscious diners. To develop new recipes, the company has opened a test kitchen in Europe. It's also planning facelifts for many of its 6,200 European outlets.

- McDonald's temporarily dropped its globally recognized Golden Arches logo in ads in the U.K. in an attempt to change customers' perception and emphasize a new "healthy menu." The two-week campaign is called "Change" and carries the tag line "McDonald's—But not as you know it." The ads show healthy meals such as fruits and salads.

- The Big Tasty, a burger on an oversize bun introduced last year, is selling well, the company says.

- April 2004 a Salads Plus menu, which features four varieties of main-course salads topped with warm chicken, a premium chicken sandwich, and a fruit-and-yogurt dessert, were introduced in Britain.

- In response to demands for more nutritional information on McDonald's menu, tray liners were used to convey dietary information. On the top of tray liners is an appeal for RMCC (Ronald McDonald Children's Charities) and on the flip side is a detailed breakdown of nutritional and allergy information. Every item available in a McDonald's is listed, from the obvious—a Big Mac at 493 calories, 22.9 grams of fat, and 5.9 grams of fiber—to the less obvious—mineral water comprises no nuts, no seafood, no gluten, and no egg and is suitable for vegetarians. No other restaurant chain goes in for this analytical overload. One observer's reaction to the nutritional detail was less than positive: "The amount of detail is mind-boggling, and disturbing. You come in for a fast burger and fries, knowing they aren't the healthiest foods on the planet, and you're assailed with a battery of facts and figures that merely confirm what you already know."

- McDonald's feels itself under siege from diet campaigners and food experts as well as competitors pushing "healthy" salads and even bread-free sandwiches. To some it seems that McDonald's has adopted a defense posture even though it is still the second best known brand in the world, behind Coca-Cola.

- Aiming to boost its popularity among women, McDonald's launched an ad program (April 2005) featuring performers Destiny's Child. The campaign features its Salads Plus menu with the addition of chicken salad with pasta, which includes roast peppers, basil, and cherry tomatoes. A low-fat, grilled-chicken Caesar flatbread will replace the grilled chicken flatbread item launched six months earlier. The company has also replaced its dressing on its Salad Plus, which had been criticized for its fat content, with lower-calorie, lower-fat versions.

- In response to the rise of coffee shops, McDonald's is serving coffee made from freshly ground Kenco beans. Since the restaurants started grinding beans, the response has been phenomenal. The same goes for the salads and fruit now offered. Ten percent of their profit mix is from salads and 10 million fruit bags were sold in the first year after introduction.

COMMENTS OF A NEWLY APPOINTED CEO OF MCDONALD'S U.K.

We're not innovating the way we used to, we're not leading the way we used to. The world is changing—our customers tell us they're changing and we've not been changing.

- We will upgrade the McDonald's experience and give more value to the customer.

- We've slipped. In the area of service, it has become spartan and inconsistent. Our cleanliness didn't just used to be good, it used to be great. We need to get back to basics. The first part of back to basics is giving the customers the choice they want. The second is making sure service and cleanliness are great. I'm finding out what's important and I'm reacting to it.

- We're the innovators, we're the leaders. Our customers are outspoken and they criticize. My job is to understand the problem and to lead. If we can get this right, our customers will reward us. We took our eye off the ball. Our customers have been changing and we haven't noticed. In the last four or five years, a raft of companies have come to the marketplace that have done a better job of identifying those changing tastes.

- I want McDonald's to be the U.K.'s breakfast restaurant. Households have been blitzed with new menus, including toasted bagels and toast, and sampling deals. I want people to try it, to compare us. Breakfast is a huge opportunity for us. We can use our drive-thru to offer lattes and toasted bagels to people on their way to work.

- One immediate task is to assuage the franchisees and owner-operators. If our performance is flat, they're flat. My philosophy is that we're like a three-legged stool—staff, suppliers, and owner-operators.

- Does he eat at McDonald's? Not every day, but three times a week. His favorite—double cheeseburger.

QUESTIONS

1. Identify the problems confronting McDonald's U.K. and list them from the most to the least critical. For each problem identified, explain your reasoning.

2. Some problems you identified in question 1 may require a "quick fix" in the short run while others may require a major shift in company strategy. Assuming that you cannot focus on all the problems at once, suggest the order in which the issues should be addressed and suggest an approach to solving each problem.

Sources: Carol Matlack, Laura Cohn, and Michael Arndt, "Can McDonald's Get Cooking in Europe?" *BusinessWeek,* April 26, 2004; "Healthier Options Help McDonald's to Fatter Profits," *The Times (London),* October 14, 2004; "Film Revisits McD's Libel Suit in U.K.," *Advertising Age,* June 20, 2005; Katherine Griffiths, "McDonald's Sales Fall in Europe," *The (London) Independent,* June 9, 2005; Chris Blackhurst, "Peter Beresford," *Management Today,* January 2005, p. 28; Mark Sweney, "McDonald's Unveils U.K. 8 Million Ads to Win Over Women," *Marketing (UK),* April, 6, 2005; Eric Herman, "McDonald's Europe Chief Quits after Sales Slide," *Chicago Sun-Times,* June 8, 2005; Richard Gibson, "McDonald's Names New Head of Its European Operations," *Wall Street Journal,* June 7, 2005.

CASE 4–2 Tambrands—Overcoming Cultural Resistance

Tampax, Tambrands' only product, is the best-selling tampon in the world with 44 percent of the global market. North America and Europe account for 90 percent of those sales. The company saw earnings drop 12 percent to $82.8 million on revenues of $662 million in 1996. The stakes are high for Tambrands because tampons are basically all it sells, and in the United States, which currently generates 45 percent of Tambrands' sales, the company is mired in competition with such rivals as Playtex Products and Kimberly-Clark. What's more, new users are hard to get because 70 percent of women already use tampons.

In the overseas market, Tambrands officials talk glowingly of a huge opportunity. Only 100 million of the 1.7 billion eligible women in the world currently use tampons. In planning for expansion into a global market, Tambrands divided the world into three clusters, based not on geography, but on how resistant women are to using tampons. The goal is to market to each cluster in a similar way.

Most women in Cluster 1, including the United States, the United Kingdom, and Australia, already use tampons and may feel they know all they need to know about the product. In Cluster 2, which includes countries such as France, Israel, and South Africa, about 50 percent of women use tampons. Some concerns about virginity remain and tampons are often considered unnatural products that block the flow. Tambrands enlists gynecologists' endorsements to stress scientific research on tampons. Potentially the most lucrative group—but infinitely more challenging—is Cluster 3, which includes countries like Brazil, China, and Russia. There, along with tackling the virginity issue, Tambrands must also tell women how to use a tampon without making them feel uneasy. While the advertising messages differ widely from country to country, Tambrands is also trying to create a more consistent image for its Tampax tampons. The ads in each country show consecutive shots of women standing outside declaring the tampon message, some clutching a blue box of Tampax. They end with the same tagline, "Tampax. Women Know." While marketing consultants say Tambrands' strategy is a step in the right direction, some caution that tampons are one of the most difficult products to market worldwide.

"The greatest challenge in the global expansion of tampons is to address the religious and cultural mores that suggest that insertion is fundamentally prohibited by culture," says the managing director of a consulting company. "The third market [Cluster 3] looks like the great frontier of tampons, but it could be the seductive noose of the global expansion objective."

A Tambrands spokeswoman says the company is aware that even within Cluster 3, cultural and religious barriers vary. While the company's sales are increasing in some countries like Russia, Tambrands isn't targeting Muslim countries, she says. As Tambrands gears up for international expansion, it is also increasing ad spending in its mainstay U.S. market. Its new focus in the United States—encouraging women to use tampons overnight. Using the Cluster 1 approach of pitching to an already educated and jaded audience, a new ad tries to tease women with a provocative question, "Should I sleep with it, or not?"

The company's new global campaign for Tambrands is a big shift from most feminine protection product ads, which often show frisky women dressed in white pants biking or turning cartwheels, while discreetly pushing messages of comfort. The new campaign features local women talking frankly about what had been a taboo subject in many countries. A recent Brazilian ad shows a close-up of a tampon while the narrator chirps, "It's sleek, smooth, and really comfortable to use."

For years Tambrands has faced a delicate hurdle selling Tampax tampons in Brazil because many young women fear they'll lose their virginity if they use a tampon. When they go to the beach in tiny bikinis, tampons aren't their choice. Instead, hordes of women use pads and gingerly wrap a sweater around their waist. Now, the No. 1 tampon maker hopes a bold new ad campaign will help change the mind-set of Brazilian women. "Of course, you're not going to lose your virginity," reassures one cheerful Brazilian woman in a new television ad. Tambrands's risky new ads are just part of a high-stakes campaign to expand into overseas markets where it has long faced cultural and religious sensitivities. The new ads feature local women being surprisingly blunt about such a personal product. In China, another challenging market for Tambrands, a new ad shows a Chinese woman inserting a tampon into a test tube filled with blue water. "No worries about leakage," declares another.

"In any country, there are boundaries of acceptable talk. We want to go just to the left of that," says the creative director of the New York advertising agency that is creating Tambrands' $65 million ad campaign worldwide. "We want them to think they have not heard frankness like this before." The agency planned to launch new Tampax ads in 26 foreign countries and the United States. However, being a single-product company, it is a risky proposition for Tambrands to engage in a global campaign and to build a global distribution network all at the same time.

Tambrands concluded that the company could not continue to be profitable if its major market was the United States and that to launch a global marketing program was too risky to do alone. The company approached Procter & Gamble about a buyout, and the two announced a $1.85 billion deal. The move puts Procter back in the tampon business for the first time since its Rely brand was pulled in 1980 after two dozen women who used tampons died from toxic shock syndrome. Procter plans to sell Tampax as a complement to its existing feminine-hygiene products, particularly in Asia and Latin America. P&G, known for its innovation in such mundane daily goods as disposable diapers and detergent, has grown in recent years by acquiring products and marketing them internationally. "Becoming part of P&G—a world-class company with global marketing and distribution capabilities—will accelerate the global growth of Tampax and enable the brand to achieve its full potential. This will allow us to take the expertise we've gained in the feminine protection business and apply it to a new market with Tampax." Market analysts applauded the deal. "P&G has the worldwide distribution that Tampax so desperately needs," said a stock market analyst. "Tambrands didn't have the infrastructure to tap into growth in the developing countries and P&G does."

P&G's efforts to build on Tambrands earlier marketing overseas have met with failure. The company abandoned its marketing in Brazil as too expensive and slow-growing, despite the promise the country initially seemed to offer with its beach culture and mostly urban population. The company also had dispatched marketers to southern India and Nanjing, China, but decided it couldn't justify the cost of expanding those tests. Most competitors, such as Playtex Products Inc. and Kimberly-Clark Corp., have basically written off creating new tampon markets as not worth the investment.

Regrouping and looking to build a marketing model that it could export to the rest of the globe, P&G began studying cities in Mexico. It figured Monterrey, an industrial hub of 4 million people—with 1.2 million women as its target customers—was a prime test spot. Research and focus groups of Mexican women led P&G to develop a new approach based on education.

"Everywhere we go, women say 'this is not for senoritas,'" says Silvia Davila, P&G's marketing director for Tampax Latin America. They're using the Spanish word for unmarried women as a modest expression for young virgins. This concern crops up in countries that are predominantly Catholic, executives say. In Italy, for instance, just 4 percent of women use tampons. P&G is finding that in countries where school health education is limited, that concept is difficult to overcome. P&G marketers say they often find open boxes of tampons in stores—a sign, P&G says, that women were curious about the product but unsure as to how it worked.

Hanging out in blue jeans and tank tops and sipping Diet Pepsi on a recent afternoon, Sandra Trevino and her friends seem very much in tune with American culture. But the young women are getting a lesson in Ms. Trevino's living room on how to use a product that is commonplace in the United States—and is a mystery to them.

"We're giving you the opportunity to live differently 'those days' of the month," Karla Romero tells the group. She holds up a chart of the female body, then passes out samples to the 10 women. Tampons will bring freedom and discretion, Ms. Romero says. "For me, it's the best thing that ever happened." A few of the women giggle. Ms. Romero is on the front lines of a marketing campaign for one of the world's most in-the-closet products. Procter & Gamble Co. pays Ms. Romero to give a primer on tampons in gatherings that resemble Tupperware parties.

Ms. Romero and other counselors run through a slide show about the stages of puberty. She pours blue liquid through a stand-up model of a woman's reproductive tract so the girls can see what happens inside their bodies when they have their periods. They see the tampon absorb the blue fluid. Ms. Romero points to the hymen on the model and explains they won't lose their virginity with a tampon. Still, when Maria brought home a sample from another session a few months ago, "my mother said don't use them," she reported. While the 18-year-old can be rebellious—she wears a tiny tank top, heavy-blue eye shadow, and three gold studs in each ear—she shares her mother's doubts. "You can lose your virginity. The norm here is to marry as a virgin," she says.

In addition to in-home demonstrations, counselors, in navy pantsuits or doctor's white coats embroidered with the Tampax logo, speak in stores, schools and gyms, anywhere women gather. One counselor met with 40 late-shift women workers in a cookie factory at midnight.

Counselors are taught to approach the subject in a dignified and sensitive manner. For example, they avoid using the word "tampon," which is too close to the Spanish word *tampone,* meaning plug. P&G calls its product an "internal absorbent" or simply Tampax.

Early results indicate its investment is paying off. Though tampons currently account for just 4 percent of the total Mexican market for feminine-protection products, that is up from 2 percent before the program. Tampax sales have tripled in the past 12 months.

Based on the success in Mexico, P&G picked Venezuela to be its next market because it's relatively small—23 million people—and its population is mostly urban. P&G gathered women in Caracas for focus groups where they expressed some cultural similarities with their Mexican counterparts, emphasizing the sanctity of virginity. But the tropical weather fostered some promising differences, too. There's a party culture where women seem comfortable with their bodies in skimpy skirts and clingy pants.

This attitude led P&G marketers to conclude that Tampax advertising could be racier in Venezuela. One slogan, though, misfires. On a list of common misconceptions headed by "will I lose my virginity?" P&G wrote, "La ignorancia es la madre de todo los mitos," which translates as "ignorance is the mother of all myths." Focus groups were offended. "In a Latin culture, ignorance and mother don't go together." The title was scrapped.

In the end, they unveiled ads like "Es Tiempo De Cambiar Las Reglas," for billboards, buses, and magazines. The company knows that Venezuelan women will catch the pun: "reglas" is the slang they use for their period, but the ad also translates as "It's time to change the rules."

P&G's advertising for Tampax has met with criticism and ridicule. For example, during the election of Russian President Putin, and as a response to the question of why he turned down free radio and television time, he was quoted as saying that "he won't be marketed like Tampax or Snickers."

P&G has always been an early and aggressive adopter of new media, dating back to radio and television. Continuing in this vein, Procter & Gamble is stepping up its Internet activity to use the Web as a marketing medium. P&G's idea is to attract consumers to interactive sites that will be of interest to particular target groups, with the hope of developing deeper relationships with consumers. Its first step was to launch a Web site for teenage girls with information on puberty and relationships, promoting products such as Clearasil, Sunny Delight, and Tampax. The Web site, www.beinggirl.com, was designed with the help of an advisory board of teenage girls. Visit Tampax's Web site at www.tampax.com for some examples of their Web advertising in various countries. Procter & Gamble can be found at www.pg.com.

QUESTIONS

1. Evaluate the wisdom of Tambrands becoming part of Procter & Gamble.

2. Tambrands indicated that the goal of its global advertising plan was to "market to each cluster in a similar way." Discuss this goal. Should P&G continue with Tambrands' original goal adapted to the new educational program? Why? Why not?

3. For each of the three clusters identified by Tambrands, identify the cultural resistance that must be overcome. Suggest possible approaches to overcoming the resistance you identify.

4. In reference to the approaches you identified in question 3, is there an approach that can be used to reach the goal of "marketing to each cluster in a similar way"?

5. P&G is marketing in Venezuela with their "Mexican" model. Would that work in Brazil as well? Discuss.

Sources: Yumiko Ono, "Tambrands Ads Aim to Overcome Cultural and Religious Obstacles," *Wall Street Journal,* March 17, 1997, p. B8; Sharon Walsh, "Procter & Gamble Bids to Acquire Tambrands; Deal Could Expand Global Sales of Tampax," *Washington Post,* April 10, 1997, p. C01; Ed Shelton, "P&G to Seek Web Friends," *The European,* November 16, 1998, p. 18; Emily Nelson and Miriam Jordan, "Sensitive Export: Seeking New Markets for Tampons, P&G Faces Cultural Barriers," *Wall Street Journal,* December 8, 2000, p. A1; *Weekend Edition Sunday (NPR),* March 12, 2000; "It's Hard to Market the Unmentionable," *Marketing Week,* March 13, 2002, p. 19; Richard Weiner, "A Candid Look at Menstrual Products—Advertising and Public Relations," *Public Relations Quarterly,* Summer 2004; "Procter & Gamble and Warner Bros. Pictures Announce 'Sisterhood' between New Movie and Popular Teen Web Site," *PR Newswire,* June 1, 2005.

CASE 4−3 Iberia Airlines Builds a BATNA

MADRID—One day last April, two model airplanes landed in the offices of Iberia Airlines.

They weren't toys. The Spanish carrier was shopping for new jetliners, and the models were calling cards from Boeing Co. and Airbus, the world's only two producers of big commercial aircraft.

It was the first encounter in what would become a months-long dogfight between the two aviation titans—and Iberia was planning to clean up.

Airbus and Boeing may own the jetliner market, with its projected sales of more than $1 trillion in the next 20 years, but right now they don't control it. The crisis in the air-travel industry makes the two manufacturers desperate to nail down orders. So they have grown increasingly dependent on airlines, engine suppliers and aircraft financiers for convoluted deals.

Once the underdog, Airbus has closed the gap from just four years ago—when Boeing built 620 planes to Airbus's 294—and this year the European plane maker expects to overtake its U.S. rival. For Boeing, Iberia was a chance to stem the tide. For Airbus, Iberia was crucial turf to defend.

Iberia and a few other airlines are financially healthy enough to be able to order new planes these days, and they are all driving hard bargains. Enrique Dupuy de Lome, Iberia's chief financial officer and the man who led its search for widebody jets, meant from the start to run a real horse race. "Everything has been structured to maintain tension up to the last 15 minutes," he said.

Throughout the competition, the participants at Iberia, Boeing and Airbus gave *The Wall Street Journal* detailed briefings on the pitches, meetings and deliberations. The result is a rarity for the secretive world of aircraft orders: an inside look at an all-out sales derby with globetrotting executives, huge price tags and tortuous negotiations over everything from seats to maintenance and cabin-noise levels. The rivals' offers were so close that on the final day of haggling, Iberia stood ready with multiple press releases and extracted last-minute concessions in a phone call between the airline's chairman and the winning bidder.

By that point, both suitors felt like they'd been through the wringer. "With 200 airlines and only two plane makers, you'd think we'd get a little more respect," said John Leahy, Airbus's top salesman.

Airbus, a division of European Aeronautic Defense & Space Co., reckoned it had a big edge. It had sold Iberia more than 100 planes since 1997. Mr. Leahy thought last summer that he might even bag the contract with minimal competition. In June he had clinched a separate deal with Iberia for three new Airbus A340 widebodies.

But Mr. Dupuy made Mr. Leahy fight for the order—and so enticed Boeing to compete more aggressively. Then, "just to make things interesting," Mr. Dupuy said, he upped the pressure by going shopping for secondhand airplanes. These are spilling onto the market at cut-rate prices as the airline industry's problems force carriers to ground older jets with their higher operating costs.

Iberia is one of the industry's few highly profitable carriers, thanks to a thorough restructuring before the national carrier was privatized in early 2001. The world's No. 18 in passenger traffic,

with a fleet of 145 planes, it has benefited by flying few routes to North America, where air travel is in tatters, and by dominating the large Latin American market.

The Spanish carrier was looking to replace six Boeing 747-200 jumbo jets more than 20 years old. It wanted as many as 12 new planes to complete a 10-year modernization program for Iberia's long-haul fleet. Based on list prices, the 12-plane order was valued at more than $2 billion.

Iberia's Mr. Dupuy, 45 years old, a soft-spoken career finance man, first needed to woo Boeing to the table. The U.S. producer had last sold Iberia planes in 1995, and since then the carrier had bought so many Airbus jets that Boeing considered not even competing. But in late July, Mr. Dupuy met Toby Bright, Boeing's top salesman for jets. Over dinner in London, according to both men, Mr. Dupuy told Mr. Bright that Iberia truly wanted two suppliers, not just Airbus.

The Boeing sales chief was skeptical, and he recalled thinking at the time, "You're running out of ways to show us." Having worked as Boeing's chief salesman in Europe, Airbus's home turf, he had heard similar lines from customers who eventually bought Airbus planes. So he wondered: "Are we being brought in as a stalking horse?"

Yet replacing Iberia's old 747s with new 777s would be Boeing's last chance for years to win back Iberia. The argument against Boeing was that an all-Airbus fleet would make Iberia's operations simpler and cheaper. Still, going all-Airbus might weaken Iberia's hand in future deals. Airbus would know that the carrier's cost of switching to Boeing would require big investments in parts and pilot training.

In early November, Airbus and Boeing presented initial bids on their latest planes. The four-engine Airbus A340-600 is the longest plane ever built. Boeing's 777-300ER is the biggest twin-engine plane.

The new A340 can fly a bit farther and has more lifting power than the 777. The new Boeing plane is lighter, holds more seats and burns less fuel. The Boeing plane, with a catalog price around $215 million, lists for some $25 million more than the A340.

Mr. Dupuy, whose conference room is decorated with framed awards for innovative aircraft-financing deals, set his own tough terms on price and performance issues including fuel consumption, reliability and resale value. He won't divulge prices, but people in the aviation market familiar with the deal say he demanded discounts exceeding 40 percent.

As negotiations began, Mr. Dupuy told both companies his rule: Whoever hits its target, wins the order. The race was on.

Mr. Bright, who had been appointed Boeing's top airplane salesman in January of 2002, pitched the Boeing 777 as a "revenue machine." He insisted that his plane could earn Iberia about $8,000 more per flight than the A340-600 because it can hold more seats and is cheaper to operate. A burly 50-year-old West Virginian, Mr. Bright joined Boeing out of college as an aerospace designer. He knew the new Airbus would slot easily into Iberia's fleet. But he also felt that Mr. Dupuy's target price undervalued his plane.

At Airbus, Mr. Leahy also fumed at Iberia's pricing demands. A New York City native and the company's highest-ranking American, he pursues one goal: global domination over Boeing. Last year he spent 220 days on sales trips.

To Iberia, he argued that his plane offered a better investment return because the A340 is less expensive to buy and is similar to Iberia's other Airbus planes. From a hodge-podge of 11 models in 1997, Iberia now flies five types, and replacing the old 747s with A340s would trim that to four—offering savings on parts, maintenance and pilot training.

Even before presenting Airbus's offer, Mr. Leahy had flown to Madrid in October to make his case. On Nov. 18, he once again took a chartered plane for the one-hour flight from Airbus headquarters in Toulouse, France, to Madrid. For two hours that evening, he and his team sat with Mr. Dupuy and other Iberia managers around a table in Mr. Dupuy's office, debating how many seats can fit on a 777. Those numbers were crucial to the deal because each seat represents millions of dollars in revenue over the life of a plane but also adds weight and cost.

Boeing had told Iberia that its 777 could hold 30 more seats than the 350 Iberia planned to put on the Airbus plane. Mr. Leahy argued that the Boeing carries at most five more seats. "Get guarantees from Boeing" on the seat count, Mr. Leahy prodded the Iberia managers.

At Boeing, Mr. Bright was eager to soften Iberia's pricing demand. His account manager, Steve Aliment, had already made several visits to pitch the plane, and in late November, Mr. Bright sent him once again to protest that Iberia didn't appreciate the 777's revenue potential. Boeing desperately wanted to avoid competing just on price, so Mr. Bright pushed operating cost and comfort.

On the Airbus side, Mr. Leahy also was feeling pressured because a past sales tactic was coming back to haunt him. In 1995, when Iberia was buying 18 smaller A340s and Mr. Dupuy expressed concern about their future value, Mr. Leahy helped seal the deal by guaranteeing him a minimum resale price, which kicks in after 2005. If Iberia wants to sell them, Airbus must cover any difference between the market price of the used planes and the guaranteed floor price.

The guarantee is one of the tools that Mr. Leahy has used to boost Airbus's share of world sales to about 50 percent today from 20 percent in 1995. Boeing rarely guarantees resale values.

Mr. Dupuy had wanted guarantees because they lower his risk of buying, and thus cut his cost of borrowing. What mattered now was that the guarantees also freed him to sell the planes at a good price. Early in the competition, he suggested to both Airbus and Boeing that he might eventually replace all of Iberia's A340s with Boeings—and potentially stick Airbus with most of the tab.

"If we didn't have the guarantees, the position of Airbus would be very strong," Mr. Dupuy said in an interview. Instead, "we have a powerful bargaining tool on future prices."

On Dec. 4, Mr. Leahy flew again to Madrid to try to persuade Iberia to close a deal by year's end. Running through a presentation in Mr. Dupuy's office, Mr. Leahy and five colleagues ticked off fuel and maintenance costs for their plane. They asserted that passengers prefer the plane because it is quieter than the 777 and has no middle seats in business class.

Mr. Dupuy then rattled Mr. Leahy's cage with a new scenario: Iberia managers would be flying off next week to look at used Boeing 747-400 jumbo jets. Singapore Airlines had stopped flying the planes and was offering to lease them at bargain prices.

Mr. Leahy chided Mr. Dupuy, saying that was "like buying a used car," where a bargain can easily backfire. Mr. Dupuy replied that sometimes buying used makes sense because it offers the flexibility of other options. The message: Iberia could dump its Airbus fleet.

Within Iberia, another debate was ending. Mr. Dupuy heard from his managers the results of a yearlong analysis of the rival planes. The Airbus was cheaper than the Boeing, and the A340's four engines help it operate better in some high-altitude Latin American airports. But Iberia managers had decided they could fit 24 more seats on the Boeing, boosting revenue. And Iberia engineers calculated that the 777 would cost 8 percent less to maintain than the A340. Maintenance on big planes costs at least $3 million a year, so the savings would be huge over the life of a fleet.

Unaware of Iberia's analysis, the Boeing team arrived in Mr. Dupuy's office on the morning of Dec. 11 with three bound selling documents. One contained Boeing's revised offer, titled "Imagine the Possibilities . . . Iberia's 777 Fleet." Knowing Mr. Dupuy as a numbers guy, the Boeing team peppered him with data showing passengers would choose Iberia because they prefer the 777.

Mr. Dupuy told the salesmen their price was still too high.

By mid-December, Iberia chairman Xabier de Irala was getting impatient and wanted a decision by the end of the year. On Dec. 18, Boeing's Mr. Bright flew to Madrid. Over a long lunch, Mr. Dupuy reiterated his price target.

"If that's your number, let's give this up," Mr. Bright said. Talks continued cordially, but the men left doubtful they could close the gap. That Friday, Dec. 20, Mr. Dupuy told Iberia's board that prices from Airbus and Boeing were still too high and he would push the used-plane option harder.

By the start of the year, Airbus's Mr. Leahy, growing frustrated, arranged a Saturday meeting with Mr. Dupuy. On Jan. 4, the Iberia executive interrupted a family skiing holiday in the Pyrenees and drove two hours along winding French roads to meet Mr. Leahy for lunch.

Mr. Leahy spent four hours trying to convince Mr. Dupuy and a colleague that Airbus couldn't offer a better deal. Mr. Dupuy argued that Airbus had just given steep discounts to British airline easyJet, so it should do the same for Iberia. Annoyed, Mr. Leahy said media reports of a 50 percent price cut for easyJet were nonsense.

"You get Boeing to give you a 50 percent discount and I'll send you a bottle of champagne," he told the Iberia executives.

Mr. Bright was frustrated too. In the first week of January, Mr. Dupuy proposed visiting Seattle, where Boeing builds passenger planes. Mr. Bright's reply: If Iberia was unwilling to budge, there was little reason to come. So, when Mr. Dupuy said he would make the 14-hour journey, Mr. Bright was encouraged.

On Jan. 14, Mr. Dupuy and two colleagues arrived in Seattle. In the private dining room of Cascadia, a high-end downtown restaurant, they met for dinner with the Boeing salesmen and Alan Mulally, the chief executive of Boeing's commercial-plane division. Mr. Dupuy was impressed by Mr. Mulally's eagerness and was pleased when he urged Mr. Bright's team to find a way to close the gap.

The next day, the Boeing salesmen offered a new proposal—including a slightly lower price, improved financing and better terms on spare parts, crew training and maintenance support from General Electric Co., maker of the plane's engines.

When Mr. Dupuy left Seattle on Jan. 16, Mr. Bright felt Iberia was relenting a bit on price and that Mr. Dupuy wanted to "find a way to do the deal." Mr. Dupuy was also optimistic about striking a deal with Boeing.

Back in Madrid the next day, he raced off to join Iberia's chairman, Mr. Irala, for a meeting with Mr. Leahy and Airbus President

Noel Forgeard. Mr. Irala, a bear of a man who is credited with saving Iberia from bankruptcy eight years ago, told the Airbus executives that Mr. Dupuy's price target remained firm. When the Airbus men relented on a few points, Mr. Irala yielded a bit, too, and spelled out Iberia's remaining targets for Airbus. Mr. Forgeard said a deal looked possible.

As the meeting broke up, Mr. Dupuy was pleased. He felt that Boeing and Airbus were digging deep. And no wonder. The world air-travel market was sinking deeper, and fears of war in Iraq and terrorism had slashed global bookings.

In the next few days, the sales teams from Boeing and Airbus each huddled to refine their offers. Both remained about 10 percent above Mr. Dupuy's price targets. Each called him several times daily, pushing for concessions. Mr. Dupuy didn't budge. On Jan. 23, he told Iberia's board that both companies could do better. The board scheduled a special meeting for the following Thursday, Jan. 30.

Energized by the Seattle meetings, Mr. Bright pushed his team "to go all out to win this bid," and they worked around the clock. Mr. Bright phoned Mr. Dupuy daily from Seattle and occasionally fielded his calls at 3 A.M., Pacific time. By late January, Boeing had cut its price by more than 10 percent after haggling over engine price with GE and financing with leasing firms. The 777 was now less than 3 percent above Mr. Dupuy's target—so close that Mr. Bright asked for a gesture of compromise from Iberia.

Mr. Dupuy was impressed by Boeing's new aggressiveness. But Airbus was also closing the gap so quickly, he said, that he could offer no concessions. To Mr. Leahy, he talked up Boeing's willingness to deal. "I was just talking to Toby . . ." Mr. Dupuy told Mr. Leahy during several conversations, referring to Mr. Bright. Airbus improved its offer further.

On Wednesday, the day before the deadline, Boeing and Airbus were running about even. In Seattle, Mr. Bright threw some clothes in his briefcase and proposed to Mr. Dupuy that he hop on a plane to Madrid. Mr. Dupuy said the choice was his, but what really mattered was the price target. That day, Mr. Dupuy told Messrs. Bright and Leahy that their bosses should call Mr. Irala with any final improvements before the board meeting.

On Thursday morning, Mr. Bright offered to trim Boeing's price further if Mr. Dupuy could guarantee that Boeing would win the deal. "I can't control Forgeard," Mr. Dupuy replied, referring to the Airbus president, who was due to talk soon with Mr. Irala. Mr. Bright made the price cut without the concession.

"You're very close," Mr. Dupuy told him.

Later, Mr. Forgeard got on the phone with Iberia's Mr. Irala, who said he still needed two concessions on the financial terms and economics of the deal. Airbus had already agreed to most of Mr. Dupuy's terms on asset guarantees and, with engine maker Rolls-Royce PLC, agreed to limit Iberia's cost of maintaining the jets. Mr. Forgeard asked if relenting would guarantee Airbus the deal. Mr. Irala replied yes, pending board approval—and looked over with a grin at Mr. Dupuy, who sat nearby with his laptop open. Mr. Forgeard acquiesced. Mr. Dupuy plugged the new numbers in his spreadsheet. Airbus had hit its target.

That evening, Boeing got a call from Iberia saying the airline would soon announce it had agreed to buy nine A340-600s and taken options to buy three more. Hours later, Boeing posted on its Web site a statement criticizing Iberia's choice as "the easiest decision." Mr. Bright said later that he simply couldn't hit Mr. Dupuy's numbers and "do good business."

In the end, Airbus nosed ahead thanks to its planes' lower price and common design with the rest of Iberia's fleet. By offering guarantees on the planes' future value and maintenance costs, plus attractive financing terms, Airbus edged out Boeing's aggressive package. The deal's final financial terms remain secret.

At Airbus, Mr. Leahy was relieved, but he faced one last slap. Iberia's news release crowed about Airbus's price guarantees on the planes—a detail Mr. Leahy considered confidential. Iberia's Mr. Dupuy said he wasn't rubbing it in. But he had, he boasted, won "extraordinary conditions."

QUESTIONS

1. Critique the negotiation strategies and tactics of all three key executive involved: Dupuy, Leahy, and Bright.

2. Critique the overall marketing strategies of the two aircraft makers as demonstrated in this case.

3. What were the key factors that ultimately sent the order in Airbus's direction?

4. Assume that Iberia again is on the market for jet liners. How should Bright handle a new inquiry? Be explicit.

Source: Daniel Michaels, "Boeing and Airbus in Dogfight to Meet Stringent Terms of Iberia's Executives," *Wall Street Journal Europe,* March 10, 2003, p. A1. Copyright 2003 by Dow Jones & Co. Inc. Reproduced with permission of Dow Jones & Co. Inc. via Copyright Clearance Center.

CASE 4—4 Sales Negotiations Abroad for MRI Systems

International sales of General Medical's Magnetic Resonance Imaging (MRI) systems have really taken off in recent months. Your representatives are about to conclude important sales contracts with customers in both Tokyo and Rio de Janeiro. Both sets of negotiations require your participation, particularly as final details are worked out. The bids you approved for both customers are identical (see tables). Indeed, both customers had contacted you originally at a medical equipment trade show in Las Vegas, and you had all talked business together over drinks at the conference hotel. You expect your two new customers will be talking together again over the Internet about your products and prices as they had in Las Vegas. The Japanese orders are potentially larger because the doctor you met works in a hospital that has nine other units in the Tokyo/Yokohama area. The Brazilian doctor represents a very large hospital in Rio, which may require more than one unit. Your travel arrangements are now being made. Your local representatives will fill you in on the details. Best of luck!

[*Note:* Your professor will provide you with additional material that you will need to complete this case.]

Table 1
Price Quotation

Deep Vision 2000 MRI (basic unit)	$1,200,000
Product options	
• 2D and 3D time-of-flight (TOF) angiography for capturing fast flow	150,000
• Flow analysis for quantification of cardiovascular studies	70,000
• X2001 software package	20,000
Service contract (2 years normal maintenance, parts, and labor)	60,000
Total price	$1,500,000

Table 2
Standard Terms and Conditions

Delivery	6 months
Penalty for late delivery	$10,000/month
Cancellation charges	10% of contract price
Warranty (for defective machinery)	parts, one year
Terms of payment	COD

CASE 4-5 National Office Machines—Motivating Japanese Salespeople: Straight Salary or Commission?

National Office Machines of Dayton, Ohio, manufacturers of cash registers, electronic data processing equipment, adding machines, and other small office equipment, recently entered into a joint venture with Nippon Cash Machines of Tokyo, Japan. Last year, National Office Machines (NOM) had domestic sales of over $1.4 billion and foreign sales of nearly $700 million. In addition to the United States, it operates in most of western Europe, the Mideast, and some parts of the Far East. In the past, it had no significant sales or sales force in Japan, although the company was represented there by a small trading company until a few years ago. In the United States, NOM is one of the leaders in the field and is considered to have one of the most successful and aggressive sales forces found in this highly competitive industry.

Nippon Cash Machines (NCM) is an old-line cash register manufacturing company organized in 1882. At one time, Nippon was the major manufacturer of cash register equipment in Japan, but it has been losing ground since 1970 even though it produces perhaps the best cash register in Japan. Last year's sales were 9 billion yen, a 15 percent decrease from sales the prior year. The fact that it produces only cash registers is one of the major problems; the merger with NOM will give them much-needed breadth in product offerings. Another hoped-for strength to be gained from the joint venture is managerial leadership, which is sorely needed.

Fourteen Japanese companies have products that compete with Nippon; other competitors include several foreign giants such as IBM, National Cash Register, and Unisys of the United States, and Sweda Machines of Sweden. Nippon has a small sales force of 21 men, most of whom have been with the company their entire adult careers. These salespeople have been responsible for selling to Japanese trading companies and to a few larger purchasers of equipment.

Part of the joint venture agreement included doubling the sales force within a year, with NOM responsible for hiring and training the new salespeople, who must all be young, college-trained Japanese nationals. The agreement also allowed for U.S. personnel in supervisory positions for an indeterminate period of time and for retaining the current Nippon sales force.

One of the many sales management problems facing the Nippon/American Business Machines Corporation (NABMC, the name of the new joint venture) was which sales compensation plan to use. That is, should it follow the Japanese tradition of straight salary and guaranteed employment until death with no individual incentive program, or the U.S. method (very successful for NOM in the United States) of commissions and various incentives based on sales performance, with the ultimate threat of being fired if sales quotas go continuously unfilled?

The immediate response to the problem might well be one of using the tried-and-true U.S. compensation methods, since they have worked so well in the United States and are perhaps the kind of changes needed and expected from U.S. management. NOM management is convinced that salespeople selling its kinds of products in a competitive market must have strong incentives to produce. In fact, NOM had experimented on a limited basis in the United States with straight salary about ten years ago and it was a

bomb. Unfortunately, the problem is considerably more complex than it appears on the surface.

One of the facts to be faced by NOM management is the traditional labor–management relations and employment systems in Japan. The roots of the system go back to Japan's feudal era, when a serf promised a lifetime of service to his lord in exchange for a lifetime of protection. By the start of Japan's industrial revolution in the 1880s, an unskilled worker pledged to remain with a company all his useful life if the employer would teach him the new mechanical arts. The tradition of spending a lifetime with a single employer survives today mainly because most workers like it that way. The very foundations of Japan's management system are based on lifetime employment, promotion through seniority, and single-company unions. There is little chance of being fired, pay raises are regular, and there is a strict order of job-protecting seniority.

Japanese workers at larger companies still are protected from outright dismissal by union contracts and an industrial tradition that some personnel specialists believe has the force of law. Under this tradition, a worker can be dismissed after an initial trial period only for gross cause, such as theft or some other major infraction. As long as the company remains in business, the worker isn't discharged, or even furloughed, simply because there isn't enough work to be done.

Besides the guarantee of employment for life, the typical Japanese worker receives many fringe benefits from the company. Bank loans and mortgages are granted to lifetime employees on the assumption that they will never lose their jobs and therefore the ability to repay. Just how paternalistic the typical Japanese firm can be is illustrated by a statement from the Japanese Ministry of Foreign Affairs that gives the example of A, a male worker who is employed in a fairly representative company in Tokyo.

> To begin with, A lives in a house provided by his company, and the rent he pays is amazingly low when compared with average city rents. The company pays his daily trips between home and factory. A's working hours are from 9 A.M. to 5 P.M. with a break for lunch which he usually takes in the company restaurant at a very cheap price. He often brings home food, clothing, and other miscellaneous articles he has bought at the company store at a discount ranging from 10 percent to 30 percent below city prices. The company store even supplies furniture, refrigerators, and television sets on an installment basis, for which, if necessary, A can obtain a loan from the company almost free of interest.
>
> In case of illness, A is given free medical treatment in the company hospital, and if his indisposition extends over a number of years, the company will continue paying almost his full salary. The company maintains lodges at seaside or mountain resorts where A can spend the holidays or an occasional weekend with the family at moderate prices . . . It must also be remembered that when A reaches retirement age (usually 55) he will receive a lump-sum retirement allowance or a pension, either of which will assure him a relatively stable living for the rest of his life.

Even though A is only an example of a typical employee, a salesperson can expect the same treatment. Job security is such an expected part of everyday life that no attempt is made to motivate the Japanese salesperson in the same manner as in the United States; as a consequence, selling traditionally has been primarily an order-taking job. Except for the fact that sales work offers some travel, entry to outside executive offices, the opportunity to entertain, and similar side benefits, it provides a young person with little other incentive to surpass basic quotas and drum up new business. The traditional Japanese bonuses are given twice yearly, can be up to 40 percent of base pay, and are no larger for salespeople than any other functional job in the company.

As a key executive in a Mitsui-affiliated engineering firm put it recently, "The typical salesman in Japan isn't required to have any particular talent." In return for meeting sales quotas, most Japanese salespeople draw a modest monthly salary, sweetened about twice a year by bonuses. Manufacturers of industrial products generally pay no commission or other incentives to boost their businesses.

Besides the problem of motivation, a foreign company faces other different customs when trying to put together and manage a sales force. Class systems and the Japanese distribution system with its penchant for reciprocity put a strain on the creative talents of the best sales managers, as Simmons, the U.S. bedding manufacturer, was quick to learn.

In the field, Simmons found itself stymied by the bewildering realities of Japanese marketing, especially the traditional distribution system that operates on a philosophy of reciprocity that goes beyond mere business to the core of the Japanese character. It's involved with *on,* the notion that regards a favor of any kind as a debt that must be repaid. To wear another's *on* in business and then turn against that person is to lose face, abhorrent to most Japanese. Thus, the owner of large Western-style apartments, hotels, or developments buys his beds from the supplier to whom he owes a favor, no matter what the competition offers.

In small department and other retail stores, where most items are handled on consignment, the bond with the supplier is even stronger. Consequently, all sales outlets are connected in a complicated web that runs from the largest supplier, with a huge national sales force, to the smallest local distributor, with a handful of door-to-door salespeople. The system is self-perpetuating and all but impossible to crack from the outside.

However, there is some change in attitude taking place as both workers and companies start discarding traditions for the job mobility common in the United States. Skilled workers are willing to bargain on the strength of their experience in an open labor market in an effort to get higher wages or better job opportunities; in the United States, it's called shopping around. And a few companies are showing a willingness to lure workers away from other concerns. A number of companies are also plotting how to rid themselves of deadwood workers accumulated as a result of promotions by strict seniority.

Toyo Rayon company, Japan's largest producer of synthetic fibers, started reevaluating all its senior employees every five years with the implied threat that those who don't measure up to the company's expectations have to accept reassignment and possibly demotion; some may even be asked to resign. A chemical engineering and construction firm asked all its employees over 42 to negotiate a new contract with the company every two years. Pay raises and promotions go to those the company wants to keep. For those who think they are worth more than the company is willing to pay, the company offers retirement with something less than the $30,000 lump-sum payment the average Japanese worker receives at age 55.

More Japanese are seeking jobs with foreign firms as the lifetime-employment ethic slowly changes. The head of student placement at Aoyama Gakuin University reports that each year the number of students seeking jobs with foreign companies increases. Bank of America, Japan Motorola, Imperial Chemical Industries, and American Hospital Supply are just a few of the companies that have been successful in attracting Japanese students. Just a few years ago, all Western companies were places to avoid.

Even those companies that are successful work with a multitude of handicaps. American companies often lack the intricate web of personal connections that their Japanese counterparts rely on when recruiting. Further, American companies have the reputation for being quick to hire and even quicker to fire, whereas Japanese companies still preach the virtues of lifelong job security. Those U.S. companies that are successful are offering big salaries and promises of Western-style autonomy. According to a recent study, 20- to 29-year-old Japanese prefer an employer-changing environment to a single lifetime employer. They complain that the Japanese system is unfair because promotions are based on age and seniority. A young recruit, no matter how able, has to wait for those above him to be promoted before he too can move up. Some feel that if you are really capable, you are better off working with an American company.

Some foreign firms entering Japan have found that their merit-based promotion systems have helped them attract bright young recruits. In fact, a survey done by *Nihon Keizai Shimbun,* Japan's leading business newspaper, found that 80 percent of top managers at 450 major Japanese corporations wanted the seniority promotion system abolished. But, as one Japanese manager commented, "We see more people changing their jobs now, and we read many articles about companies restructuring, but despite this, we won't see major changes coming quickly."

A few U.S. companies operating in Japan are experimenting with incentive plans. Marco and Company, a belting manufacturer and Japanese distributor for Power Packing and Seal Company, was persuaded by Power to set up a travel plan incentive for salespeople who topped their regular sales quotas. Unorthodox as the idea was for Japan, Marco went along. The first year, special one-week trips to Far East holiday spots like Hong Kong, Taiwan, Manila, and Macao were inaugurated. Marco's sales of products jumped 212 percent, and the next year sales were up an additional 60 percent.

IBM also has made a move toward chucking the traditional Japanese sales system (salary plus a bonus but no incentives). For about a year, it has been working with a combination that retains the semiannual bonus while adding commission payments on sales over preset quotas. "It's difficult to apply a straight commission system in selling computers because of the complexities of the product," an IBM Japan official said. "Our salesmen don't get big commissions because other employees would be jealous." To head off possible ill feeling, therefore, some nonselling IBM employees receive monetary incentives.

Most Japanese companies seem reluctant to follow IBM's example because they have doubts about directing older salesmen to go beyond their usual order-taking role. High-pressure tactics are not well accepted here, and sales channels are often pretty well set by custom and long practice (e.g., a manufacturer normally deals with one trading company, which in turn sells only to customers A, B, C, and D). A salesman or trading company, for that matter, is not often encouraged to go after customer Z and get him away from a rival supplier.

The Japanese market is becoming more competitive and there is real fear on the part of NOM executives that the traditional system just won't work in a competitive market. On the other hand,

Exhibit 1
Life Goals

	(Unit: %)						
Japan	35.4	5.8	41.2		6.8	10.8	
US	6.2	5.1	77.3			9.5	1.8
UK	11.2	13.9	63.4			8.6	2.9
Germany	9.0	17.8	60.6		5.5	7.5	
France	7.1	16.4	62.2			10.9	3.4
Switzerland	3.7	9.2	72.3			11.9	3.0
Sweden	2.5	1.7	84.8			7.5	3.4
Australia	6.7	5.1	76.0			10.5	1.6
India	22.3	33.3	16.2		26.3		1.8
Philippines	21.7	9.6	46.2		22.0		0.5
Brazil	7.7	16.7	63.2			11.9	0.5
Key:	To get rich	To acquire social position	To live as I choose		To work on behalf of society	No answer	

the proponents of the incentive system agree that the system really has not been tested over long periods or even adequately in the short term because it has been applied only in a growing market. In other words, was it the incentive system that caused the successes achieved by the companies or was it market growth? Especially there is doubt because other companies following the traditional method of compensation and employee relations also have had sales increases during the same period.

The problem is further complicated for NABMC because it will have both new and old salespeople. The young Japanese seem eager to accept the incentive method, but older ones are hesitant. How do you satisfy both since you must, by agreement, retain all the sales staff?

A study done by the Japanese government on attitudes of youth around the world suggests that younger Japanese may be more receptive to U.S. incentive methods than one would anticipate. In a study done by the Japanese prime minister's office, there were some surprising results when Japanese responses were compared with responses of similar-aged youths from other countries. Exhibit 1 summarizes some of the information gathered on life goals. One point that may be of importance in shedding light on the decision NOM has to make is a comparison of Japanese attitudes with young people in 11 other countries—the Japanese young people are less satisfied with their home life, school, and working situations, and are more passive in their attitudes toward social and political problems. Further, almost a third of those employed said they were dissatisfied with their present jobs primarily because of low income and short vacations. Asked if they had to choose between a difficult job with responsibility and authority or

an easy job without responsibility and authority, 64 percent of the Japanese picked the former, somewhat less than the 70 to 80 percent average in other countries.

Another critical problem lies with the nonsales employees; traditionally, all employees on the same level are treated equally, whether sales, production, or staff. How do you encourage competitive, aggressive salesmanship in a market unfamiliar with such tactics, and how do you compensate salespeople to promote more aggressive selling in the face of tradition-bound practices of paternalistic company behavior?

QUESTIONS

1. What should NABMC offer—incentives or straight salary? Support your answer.

2. If incentives are out, how do you motivate salespeople and get them to compete aggressively?

3. Design a U.S.-type program for motivation and compensation of salespeople. Point out where difficulties may be encountered with your plan and how the problems are to be overcome.

4. Design a pay system you think would work, satisfying old salespeople, new salespeople, and other employees.

5. Discuss the idea that perhaps the kind of motivation and aggressiveness found in the United States is not necessary in the Japanese market.

6. Develop some principles of motivation that could be applied by an international marketer in other countries.

CASE 4−6 AIDS, Condoms, and Carnival

Worldwide more than 3 million people died of AIDS in 2002 and more than 40 million are estimated to be living with HIV/AIDS.

BRAZIL

Half a million Brazilians are infected with the virus that causes acquired immunodeficiency syndrome (AIDS), and millions more are at high risk of contracting the incurable ailment, a federal study reported. The Health Ministry study is Brazil's first official attempt to seek an estimate of the number of residents infected with human immunodeficiency virus (HIV). Many had doubted the government's prior number of 94,997. The report by the National Program for Transmissible Diseases/AIDS said 27 million Brazilians are at high risk to contract AIDS, and another 36 million are considered to be at a medium risk. It said Brazil could have 7.5 million AIDS victims in the next decade.

"If we are going to combat this epidemic, we have to do it now," said Pedro Chequer, a health ministry official. Chequer said the Health Ministry would spend $300 million next year, distributing medicine and 250 million condoms and bringing AIDS awareness campaigns to the urban slums, where the disease is most rampant. Last month, Brazil became one of the few countries to offer a promising AIDS drug free to those who need it. The drug can cost as much as $12,000 a year per patient.

AIDS cases in Brazil have risen so dramatically for married women that the state of São Paulo decided that it must attack a basic cultural practice in Latin America: Their husbands don't practice safe sex. Last month, the government of Brazil's megalopolis started promoting the newly released female condom.

Many of the new AIDS cases in Brazil are married women who have children, according to a report released last month at the Pan-American Conference on AIDS in Lima, Peru. Worldwide, women constitute the fastest-growing group of those diagnosed with HIV. And of the 30.6 million people who are diagnosed with HIV, 90 percent live in poor countries.

One Brazilian mother, Rosana Dolores, knows well why women cannot count on male partners to use condoms. She and her late husband never thought of protecting their future children against AIDS. "We were married. We wanted to have kids," says Mrs. Dolores, both of whose children were born HIV positive. "These days, I would advise young people to always use condoms. But married couples . . . who is going to?"

Brazil, with its 155 million people and the largest population in South America, has the second-highest number of reported HIV infections in the Americas, after the United States, according to a report released by the United Nations agency UNAIDS.

Public health officials say one reason why AIDS prevention efforts have failed is that many Brazilians just don't like condoms. Although use in Brazil has quadrupled in the past six years, it is still the least popular method of birth control—a touchy issue in the predominantly Roman Catholic country. Another reason is that condoms cost about 75 cents each, making them more expensive here than anywhere else in the world, health officials say.

Plus, Latin-style machismo leaves women with little bargaining power. Only 14 percent of Brazilian heterosexual men used condoms last year, according to AIDSCAP, an AIDS prevention program funded by the U.S. Agency for International Development. In other studies, many women said they would not ask their partner to use a condom, even if they knew he was sleeping with others.

"Women are afraid of asking their men to have safe sex, afraid of getting beaten, afraid of losing their economic support," says Guido Carlos Levi, a director at the health department at Emilio Ribas Hospital. "This is not Mexico, but we're quite a machistic society here."

The frequency with which Latin men stray from monogamous relationships has compounded the problem. In studies conducted in Cuba by the Pan American Health Organization, 49 percent of men and 14 percent of women in stable relationships admitted they had had an affair in the past year.

In light of statistics showing AIDS as the number one killer of women of childbearing age in São Paulo state, public health officials here launched a campaign in December promoting the female condom. The hope is that it will help women—especially poor women—protect themselves and their children. But the female condom seemed unlikely to spark a latex revolution when it hit city stores January 1. The price is $2.50 apiece—more than three times the price of most male condoms.

The Family Health Association is asking the government to help subsidize the product and to cut the taxes on condoms that make them out of reach for many poor Brazilians. "We're looking for a pragmatic solution to prevent the transmission of HIV-AIDS," group President Maria Eugenia Lemos Fernandes said. "Studies show there is a high acceptance of this method because it's a product under the control of women."

While 75 percent of the women and 63 percent of the men in a pilot study on the female condom said they approved of the device, many women with AIDS say they would have been no more likely to have used a female condom than a conventional one.

Part of the problem is perception: 80 percent of women and 85 percent of men in Brazil believe they are not at risk of contracting HIV, according to a study conducted by the Civil Society for the Well-Being of the Brazilian Family.

Also at risk are married women, 40 percent of whom undergo sterilization as an affordable way of getting around the Catholic church's condemnation of birth control, health officials noted.

"It's mostly married women who are the victims. You just never think it could be you," says a former hospital administrator who was diagnosed with the virus after her husband had several extramarital affairs. He died two years ago. "I knew everything there was to know about AIDS—I worked in a hospital—but I never suspected he was going out like that. He always denied it," she says.

While HIV is making inroads in rural areas and among teenagers in Brazil, Fernandes says it doesn't have to reach epidemic proportions as in Uganda or Tanzania. "There is a very big window of opportunity here."

Brazil's Health Ministry is adding a new ingredient to the heady mix that makes up the country's annual Carnival—condoms. The ministry will distribute 10 million condoms next month, along with free advice on how to prevent the spread of AIDS, at places like Rio de Janeiro's sambadrome, where bare-breasted dancing girls attract millions of spectators every year.

"It's considered as a period of increased sexual activity," a spokeswoman at the ministry's AIDS coordination department said on Monday. "The euphoria provoked by Carnival and the excessive consumption of alcohol make it a moment when people are more likely to forget about prevention," she explained.

It is no coincidence that Rio de Janeiro was chosen to host this year's Conference on HIV Pathogenesis and Treatment. Brazil's handling of the epidemic is widely regarded as exemplary. In the early 1990s, the World Bank predicted that by 2000, HIV would have infected 1.2 million Brazilians. Today, five years after that deadline, the total is just half the Bank's prediction at about 600,000. So how did Brazil do it, and can other poor countries learn from what was done?

Perhaps the first lesson is don't be squeamish. Brazil, a predominantly Catholic country, hands out free condoms in abundance. Some 20 million are given away every month—a figure that is boosted by 50 percent in February to accommodate the exuberance of the country's famous carnivals. Drug users, too, are treated sensibly. Those who inject are offered regular supplies of clean needles and, as a result, three-quarters of them claim never to share needles with others. Nor are prostitutes neglected. Both ladies and gentlemen of the night are the targets of campaigns intended to promote condom use.

The second lesson is to treat freely. Brazilian law gives all residents the right to the best available drug treatment at no cost. This is important, because having to pay discourages people from complying with the full treatment and thus encourages the emergence of drug-resistant viruses. Providing free treatment is, of course, expensive. This year, the government will spend $395 million on anti-HIV drugs, almost two-thirds of it on three expensive patented drugs. This has brought it into conflict with foreign drug companies. Although it has never actually broken a drug-company patent, the government has exploited every available loophole to evade patents and buy or manufacture generic versions of drugs. For those patents that cannot legally be evaded, the government has played chicken with the patent owners over prices, knowing that manufacturers are desperate to avoid a patent-breaking precedent that others might follow. So far, it has been the companies that have blinked, though the latest sparring match, with Abbott Laboratories, an American firm, over a drug combination called Kaletra, has yet to be resolved.

The third lesson is to encourage voluntary action. In 1992, Brazil had 120 charities and voluntary groups devoted to AIDS. By the turn of the century, that had risen to 500. The virtues of voluntarism were recently confirmed when the Global Fund (the main multilateral distributor of anti-AIDS money to poor countries) audited the success of its donations. It found that spending by voluntary groups usually produced the best value for the money.

The fourth lesson is to do the sums. One of the arguments that has sustained Brazil's anti-AIDS program is "if you think action is expensive, try inaction." The government spent $1.8 billion on antiretroviral drugs between 1996 and 2002 but estimates that early treatment saved it more than $2.2 billion in hospital costs over the same period. Add that to the GDP loss that Brazil would have suffered if the World Bank had been right, and an aggressive program of prevention and treatment does not seem so costly after all.

INDIA

S. Mani's small barbershop in a southern Indian city looks like any other the world over. It's equipped with all the tools of the trade: scissors, combs, razors—and condoms, too.

A blue box full of free prophylactics stands in plain view of his customers as Mr. Mani trims hair and dispenses advice on safe sex, a new dimension to his 20-year career. "I start by talking about the family and children," Mr. Mani explains, snipping a client's moustache. "Slowly, I get to women, AIDS, and condoms."

Many Indian men are too embarrassed to buy condoms at a drugstore or to talk freely about sex with health counselors and family members. There's one place where they let down their hair: the barbershop. So, the state of Tamil Nadu is training barbers to be frontline soldiers in the fight against AIDS.

Programs like the barber scheme are what make Tamil Nadu, a relatively poor Indian state that's home to 60 million people, a possible model for innovative and cost-effective methods to contain AIDS in the developing world.

Six years after it was first detected in India, the AIDS virus is quickly spreading in the world's second most populous nation. Already, up to 5 million of India's 920 million people are infected with HIV—more than in any other country, according to UNAIDS, the United Nations' AIDS agency.

But faced with more immediate and widespread health woes, such as tuberculosis and malaria, officials in many Indian states are reluctant to make AIDS prevention a priority. And in some states, the acquired immunodeficiency syndrome is regarded as a Western disease of decadence; officials deny that prostitution and drug use even exist in their midst. "Some Indian states are still in total denial or ignorance about the AIDS problem," says Salim Habayeb, a World Bank physician who oversees an $84 million loan to India for AIDS prevention activities.

Tamil Nadu, the state with the third-highest incidence of HIV infection, has been open about its problem. Before turning to barbers for help, Tamil Nadu was the first state to introduce AIDS education in high school and the first to set up a statewide information hotline. Its comprehensive AIDS education program targets the overall population, rather than only high-risk groups.

In the past two years, awareness of AIDS in Tamil Nadu has jumped to 95 percent of those polled, from 64 percent, according to Operations Research Group, an independent survey group. "Just two years ago, it was very difficult to talk about AIDS and the condom," says P. R. Bindhu Madhavan, director of the Tamil Nadu State AIDS Control Society, the autonomous state agency managing the prevention effort.

The AIDS fighters take maximum advantage of the local culture to get the message across. Tamils are among the most ardent moviegoers in this film-crazed country. In the city of Madras, people line up for morning screenings even during weekdays. Half of the state's 630 theaters are paid to screen an AIDS-awareness short before the main feature. The spots are usually melodramatic musicals laced with warnings.

In the countryside, where cinemas are scarce, a movie mobile does the job. The concept mimics that used by multinationals, such as Colgate-Palmolive, for rural advertising. Bright red-and-blue trucks ply the back roads, blaring music from well-known movie soundtracks whose lyrics have been rewritten to address AIDS issues. In villages, hundreds gather for the show, on a screen that pops out of the rear of the truck.

In one six-minute musical, a young husband's infidelity leads to his death from AIDS, the financial ruin of his family, and then the death of his wife, also infected. The couple's toddler is left alone in the world. The heart-rending tale is followed by a brief lecture by an AIDS educator—and the offer of a free pack of condoms and an AIDS brochure.

Tamil Nadu's innovations have met with obstacles. It took several months for state officials to persuade Indian government television, Doordarshan, to broadcast an AIDS commercial featuring the Hindu gods of chastity and death. Even then, Mr. Madhavan says, Doordarshan "wouldn't do it as a social ad, so we have to pay a commercial rate."

Later, the network refused to air a three-minute spot in which a woman urges her husband, a truck driver, to use a condom when he's on the road. Safe infidelity was deemed "inappropriate for Indian living rooms," says Mr. Madhavan. A number of commercial satellite channels have been willing to run the ad.

Tamil Nadu has met little resistance recruiting prostitutes for the cause. For almost a year, 37-year-old prostitute Vasanthi has been distributing condoms to colleagues. With state funding, a non-governmental agency has trained her to spread the word about AIDS and other sexually transmitted diseases. As an incentive, the state pays participants like Ms. Vasanthi, a mother of three, the equivalent of $14 a month, about what she earns from entertaining a client.

Before Ms. Vasanthi joined the plan, she didn't know that the condom could help prevent HIV infection. These days, if any client refuses to wear a condom, "I kick him out, even if it takes using my shoes," she says. "I'm not flexible about this." More men are also carrying their own condoms, she says.

Thank barbers such as Mr. Mani for that. Especially in blue-collar areas of Madras, men "trim their hair and beard before frequenting a commercial sex worker," says Mr. Madhavan. They can pick up their condom on the way out.

Tamil Nadu launched the barber program in Madras last March. So far, it has enlisted 5,000 barbers, who receive AIDS education at meetings each Tuesday—the barbers' day off. The barbers aren't paid to be AIDS counselors, but they appear to take pride in their new responsibility.

Over the generations, India's barbers have been respected as traditional healers and trusted advisers. "If you want to get to the king's ears, you tell his barber," says Mr. Madhavan, the state AIDS director. Reinforcing the image of barbers as healers, the local trade group is called the Tamil Nadu Medical Barber Association.

"I first talked about AIDS with my barber," says Thiyagrajan, an electrician in his 40s. "I don't have multiple partners, so I don't need a condom, but I take them for my friends."

One recent night, a man in his 30s walked into Aruna Hair Arts, greeted Mr. Swami, then headed out the door with a fistful of condoms scooped from the plastic dispenser. "That's OK," Mr. Swami says approvingly. "He's a regular customer."

A local nongovernmental organization helps barbers replenish condom stocks by providing each shop with self-addressed order forms. But the central government hasn't always been able to meet supply, for reasons ranging from bureaucracy to price disputes with manufacturers.

Tamil Nadu has started sourcing condoms from elsewhere. But they're too expensive to give away. So the next stage of the barber scheme, just under way, is to charge two rupees (six cents) for a two-condom "pleasure pack." The barbers will get a 25 percent commission. Thus far, the only perk of participating has been a free wall calendar listing AIDS prevention tips.

Roughly 30 percent of barbers approached by Tamil Nadu have refused to participate in the AIDS program, fearing that they would alienate customers. But those who take part insist that carrying the AIDS message hasn't hurt business. "We give the message about AIDS, but we still gossip about women," says barber N. V. Durairaj at Rolex Salon.

Multinational soft drink giants Coke and Pepsi may soon become part of the Indian government's efforts to reach out to people in far-flung areas to spread awareness about HIV/AIDS and promote the use of condoms. Where social marketing efforts have failed in reaching supplies of condoms, the idea is to reach out through the soft drink firms that have managed to set up a marketing network estimated at more than 1 million outlets across the country. "Realizing their reach, we have appealed to the cola companies PepsiCo and Coca-Cola to allow us to piggyback on their advertisement, including possible slogans on their soft drinks bottles," a senior health ministry official said. "We have also asked them to help us with the distribution of condoms through their outlets in remote areas."

The requests have elicited encouraging response from both the multinationals. "We are planning to talk to them and hope that they will soon be on board with our awareness campaign and promotion of condom use," the official said.

What led to the National AIDS Control Organisation (NACO) looking to Coke and Pepsi for support was the encouraging response they received for advertisements featuring cricket stars advising on the need for preparedness. Some campaigns even had them carrying condoms along with the cricket gear. Backed by 10 countries, including India, the International Cricket Council (ICC) has been actively supporting efforts to promote awareness about HIV/AIDS through campaigns on safe sex. "So whether it is cricket stumps bearing condoms or cricketers themselves urging the need for preparedness, we are finding good response among the public." NACO also wants to take the campaign forward with celebrity endorsement at a time when sensitive films about HIV/AIDS like *Phir Milenge* ("We'll Meet Again") and *My Brother Nikhil* have struck a responsive chord among viewers.

The effort is to ensure that the number of HIV-positive cases in the country is contained at the official estimate of 5.13 million. Besides cola companies, several other multinational and national companies with large sales networks, such as banks, are now being looked at by NACO as potential vehicles for creating mass awareness and promotion of condoms.

LONDON INTERNATIONAL GROUP

London International Group (LIG) is recognized worldwide as a leader in the development of latex and thin-film barrier technologies. The Group has built its success on the development of its core businesses: the Durex family of branded condoms, Regent medical gloves, and Marigold household and industrial gloves. These are supported by a range of noncore health and beauty products.

With operational facilities in over 40 countries, 12 manufacturing plants, either wholly or jointly owned, and an advanced research and development facility based in Cambridge, England, LIG is well placed to expand into the new emerging markets of the world.

Durex is the world's No. one condom brand in terms of quality, safety, and brand awareness. The Durex family of condom brands includes Sheik, Ramses, Hatu, London, Kohinoor, Dua Lima, Androtex, and Avanti. Sold in over 130 countries worldwide and leader in more than 40 markets, Durex is the only global condom brand.

The development of innovative and creative marketing strategies is key to communicating successfully with target audiences. Consumer marketing initiatives remain focused on supporting the globalization of Durex. A series of innovative yet cost-effective projects have been used to communicate the global positioning "Feeling Is Everything" to the target young adult market, securing loyalty.

The Durex Global Survey, together with a unique multimillion-pound global advertising and sponsorship contract with MTV, has successfully emphasized the exciting and modern profile of Durex and presented significant opportunities for local public relations and event sponsorship, especially in emerging markets like Taiwan.

LIG continues to focus on education, using sponsorship of events such as the XI Annual AIDS Conference held in Vancouver and other educational initiatives to convey the safer sex message to governments, opinion formers, and educators worldwide.

JAPAN

London Okamoto Corporation, the joint venture company between London International Group and Okamoto Industries, announced the Japanese launch in Spring 1998 of Durex Avanti, the world's first polyurethane male condom.

This is the first time an international condom brand will be available in Japan, the world's most valuable condom market, which is estimated to be worth £260 million ($433 million). Durex Avanti has already been successfully launched in the United States and Great Britain, and will be launched in Italy and other selected European countries during the next 12 months.

Durex Avanti condoms are made from Duron, a unique polyurethane material twice as strong as latex, which enables them to be made much thinner than regular latex condoms, thereby increasing sensitivity without compromising safety. In addition, Durex Avanti condoms are able to conduct body heat, creating a more natural feeling, and are the first condoms to be totally odorless, colorless, and suitable for use with oil-based lubricants.

Commenting on the launch, Nick Hodges, chief executive of LIG, said; "Japan is a very important condom market; with oral contraceptives still not publicly available, per capita usage rates for condoms are among the highest in the world. Our joint venture with Okamoto, Japan's leading condom manufacturer, gives us instant access to this strategically important market."

The joint venture with Okamoto, which is the market leader in Japan with a 53 percent share, was established in 1994 with the specific purpose of marketing Durex Avanti. Added Mr. Takehiko Okamoto, president of Okamoto, "We are confident that such an innovative and technically advanced product as Durex Avanti, coupled with our strong market franchise, will find significant consumer appeal in Japan's sophisticated condom market."

Durex Avanti, which is manufactured at LIG's research and development center in Cambridge, England, has taken over ten years to develop and represents an investment by LIG of approximately £15 million.

QUESTIONS

1. Comment on the Brazilian and Indian governments' strategies for the prevention of AIDS via the marketing of condoms.

2. How is the AIDS problem different in the United States compared with Brazil and India?

3. Would the approaches described in Brazil and India work in the United States? Why or why not?

4. Suggest additional ways that London International Group could promote the prevention of AIDS through the use of condoms worldwide.

5. Do you think it would be a good idea for Coke and Pepsi to participate in a condom distribution program in India, Brazil, and the United States?

Sources: "Half a Million Brazilians Are Infected with the AIDS Virus," *Associated Press,* December 21, 1996; Andrea McDaniels, "Brazil Turns to Women to Stop Dramatic Rise in AIDS Cases. São Paulo Pushes Female Condom to Protect Married Women from Husbands, but Costs of Devices Are High," *Christian Science Monitor,* January 9, 1998, p. 7; "Brazil to Hand out 10 Million Condoms during Carnival," *Chicago Tribune,* January 19, 1998, p. 2; Miriam Jordan, "India Enlists Barbers in the War on AIDS," *Wall Street Journal,* September 24, 1996, p. A18; Caro Ezzzell, "Care for a Dying Continent," *Scientific American,* May 2000, pp. 96–105; Ginger Thompson, "In Grip of Aids, South Africa Cries for Equity," *New York Times,* p. 4; "Roll Out, Roll Out—AIDS in Brazil," *The Economist,* July 30, 2005, p. 376; "AIDS Campaign May Soon Piggyback on Pepsi, Coke," www.HindustanTimes.com, August 30, 2005. Also see the Web sites www.lig.com and www.durex.com.

CASE 4-7 Making Socially Responsible and Ethical Marketing Decisions: Selling Tobacco to Third World Countries

Strategic decisions move a company toward its stated goals and perceived success. Strategic decisions also reflect the firm's social responsibility and the ethical values on which such decisions are made. They reflect what is considered important and what a company wants to achieve.

Mark Pastin, writing on the function of ethics in business decisions, observes:

> There are fundamental principles, or ground rules, by which organizations act. Like the ground rules of individuals, organizational ground rules determine which actions are possible for the organization and what the actions mean. Buried beneath the charts of organizational responsibility, the arcane strategies, the crunched numbers, and the political intrigue of every firm are sound rules by which the game unfolds.

The following situations reflect different decisions made by multinational firms and governments and also reflect the social responsibility and ethical values underpinning the decisions. Study the following situations in the global cigarette marketplace carefully and assess the ground rules that guided the decisions of firms and governments.

EXPORTING U.S. CIGARETTE CONSUMPTION

In the United States, 600 billion cigarettes are sold annually, but sales are shrinking rapidly. Unit sales have been dropping at about 1 to 2 percent a year, and sales have been down by almost 5 percent in the last six years. The U.S. Surgeon General's campaign against smoking, higher cigarette taxes, and the concern Americans have about general health have led to the decline in tobacco consumption. Faced with various class-action lawsuits, the success of states in winning lawsuits, and the pending federal legislation, tobacco companies have stepped up their international marketing activities to maintain profits.

Even though companies have agreed to sweeping restrictions in the United States on cigarette marketing and secondhand smoke and to bolder cancer-warning labels, they are fighting as hard as ever in the Third World to convince the media, the public, and policy makers that similar changes are not needed. In seminars at luxury resorts worldwide, tobacco companies invite journalists, all expenses paid, to participate in programs that play down the health risks of smoking. It is hard to gauge the influence of such seminars, but, in the Philippines, a government plan to reduce smoking by children was "neutralized" by a public relations campaign from cigarette companies to remove "cancer awareness and prevention" as a "key concern." A slant in favor of the tobacco industry's point of view seemed to prevail.

At a time when most industrialized countries are discouraging smoking, the tobacco industry is avidly courting consumers throughout the developing world using catchy slogans, obvious image campaigns, and single-cigarette sales that fit a hard-pressed customer's budget. The reason is clear: the Third World is an expanding market. As an example, Indonesia's per capita cigarette consumption quadrupled in less than ten years. Increasingly, cigarette advertising on radio and television is being restricted in some countries but other means of promotion, especially to young people, are not controlled.

Recently, a major U.S. tobacco company signed a joint venture agreement with the Chinese government to produce cigarettes in China. The $21 million factory will employ 350 people and produce 2.5 billion cigarettes annually when fully operational. China, with more than 300 million smokers, produces and consumes about 1.4 trillion cigarettes per year, more than any other country in the world. The company projects that about 80 percent of the cigarettes produced under the joint venture will be for the domestic market, with the remainder for export.

By using China's low-cost labor, this factory will put cigarettes within easy reach of 1.1 billion consumers. The tobacco company estimates that China has more smokers than the United States has people. Just 1 percent of that 1.4 trillion cigarette market would increase the U.S. tobacco company's overseas sales by 15 percent and would be worth as much as $300 million in added revenue.

American cigarette companies have received a warm welcome in Russia, where at least 50 percent of the people smoke. Consumers are hungry for most things Western, and tobacco taxes are low. Unlike in the United States and other countries that limit or ban cigarette advertising, there are few effective controls on tobacco products in Russia. Russia, the world's fourth largest cigarette market, has proved extremely profitable territory for British American Tobacco (BAT). BAT Russia, which was established in 1949, sold 65 billion cigarettes in Russia last year (2005), giving it almost one-fifth of market share.

ADVERTISING AND PROMOTIONS

In Gambia, smokers send in cigarette boxtops to qualify for a chance to win a new car. In Argentina, smoking commercials fill 20 percent of television advertising time. And in crowded African cities, billboards that link smoking to the good life tower above the sweltering shantytowns. Such things as baby clothes with cigarette logos, health warnings printed in foreign languages, and tobacco-sponsored contests for children are often featured in tobacco ads in Third World countries. Latin American tobacco consumption rose by more than 24 percent over a ten-year period. In the same period, it rose by 4 percent in North America.

Critics claim that sophisticated promotions in unsophisticated societies entice people who cannot afford the necessities of life to spend money on a luxury—and a dangerous one at that. The sophistication theme runs throughout the smoking ads. In Kinshasa, Zaire, billboards depict a man in a business suit stepping out of a black Mercedes as a chauffeur holds the door. In Nigeria, promotions for Graduate brand cigarettes show a university student in his cap and gown. Those for Gold Leaf cigarettes have a barrister in a white wig and the slogan "A very important cigarette for very important people." In Kenya, a magazine ad for Embassy cigarettes shows an elegant executive officer with three young men and women equivalent to American yuppies. The most disturbing trend in developing countries is marketing that associates tobacco with American affluence and culture. Some women in Africa, in their struggle for women's rights, defiantly smoke cigarettes as a symbol of freedom. Billboards all over Russia feature pictures of skyscrapers and white sandy beaches and slogans like "Total Freedom" or "Rendezvous with America." They aren't advertising foreign travel but American cigarette brands.

Every cigarette manufacturer is in the image business, and tobacco companies say their promotional slant is both reasonable and common. They point out that in the Third World a lot of people cannot understand what is written in the ads anyway, so the ads zero in on the more understandable visual image. "In most of the world, the Marlboro Man isn't just a symbol of the Wild West; he's a symbol of the West." "You can't convince people that all Americans don't smoke." In Africa, some of the most effective advertising includes images of affluent white Americans with recognizable landmarks, such as the New York City skyline, in the background. In much of Africa, children as young as five are used to sell single cigarettes, affordable to other children, to support their own nicotine habits.

The scope of promotional activity is enormous. In Kenya, a major tobacco company is the fourth-largest advertiser. Tobacco-sponsored lotteries bolster sales in some countries by offering as prizes expensive goods that are beyond most people's budgets. Gambia has a population of just 640,000, but a tobacco company lottery attracted 1.5 million entries (each sent in on a cigarette boxtop) when it raffled off a Renault car.

Evidence is strong that the strategy of tobacco companies is to target young people as a means of expanding market demand. Report after report reveals that adolescents receive cigarettes free as a means of promoting the product. For example, in Buenos Aires, a Jeep decorated with the yellow Camel logo pulls up in front of a high school. The driver, a blond woman wearing khaki safari gear, begins handing out free cigarettes to 15- and 16-year-olds on lunch recess. Teens visiting the Music Television Network's Web sites in China, Germany, India, Poland, and Latin America were given the chance to click on a banner ad that led them to a questionnaire about their exposure to cigarette ads and other marketing tools in their countries. Some 10,000 teens responded to the banner ads. "In the past week, more than 62 percent of teenagers in these countries have been exposed to tobacco advertising in some form," the 17-year-old SWAT (Students Working Against Tobacco) chairman told Reuters. "The tobacco companies learned that marketing to teens and kids worked in this country, but since they can't do it here anymore, they've taken what they learned to other countries." At a video arcade in Taipei, free American cigarettes are strewn atop each game. "As long as they're here, I may as well try one," says a high school girl.

In Malaysia, *Gila-Gila,* a comic book popular with elementary school students, carries a Lucky Strike ad. Attractive women in cowboy outfits regularly meet teenagers going to rock concerts or discos in Budapest and hand them Marlboros. Those who accept a light on the spot also receive Marlboro sunglasses.

In Russia, a U.S. cigarette company sponsors disco parties where thousands of young people dance to booming music. Admission is the purchase of one pack of cigarettes. At other cigarette-sponsored parties, attractive women give cigarettes away free.

In many countries, foreign cigarettes have a status image that also encourages smoking. A 26-year-old Chinese man says he switched from a domestic brand to Marlboro because "You feel a higher social position" when you smoke foreign cigarettes.

"Smoking is a sign of luxury in Czechoslovakia as well as in Russia and other Eastern countries," says an executive of a Czech tobacco firm that has a joint venture with a U.S. company. "If I can smoke Marlboro, then I'm a well-to-do man."

The global tobacco companies insist that they are not attempting to recruit new smokers. They say they are only trying to encourage smokers to switch to foreign brands. "The same number of cigarettes are consumed whether American cigarettes or not," was the comment of one executive. Internal corporate documents reveal that British American Tobacco, the world's second-largest multinational tobacco company, secretly encouraged tax evasion and cigarette smuggling for decades in a global effort to secure market share and lure generations of new smokers. The company vehemently denied the accusations; however, the evidence strongly suggested otherwise.

Evidence showed that corporate executives in Britain, the United States, and other locales controlled the volumes, brands, marketing campaigns, timing, and price levels throughout the smuggling distribution networks they exploited. Company officials worked closely with their local agents—giving those perks such as tickets to soccer matches and vacation holidays. Researchers demonstrated that a large percentage of cigarettes were entering the black market by comparing annual global exports with global imports, about one-third of all cigarettes entering international commerce each year could not be accounted for. The industry's sanguine reaction to apparently losing a third of its inventory annually only fueled suspicions that companies knew more than they were willing to admit. "That cannot be happening without the knowledge of the producing companies."

In an apparent attempt to continue to target teens, the tobacco industry is offering candy-flavored cigarettes, according to the American Lung Association Tobacco Policy Trend Alert: "From Joe Camel to Kauai Kolada—The Marketing of Candy-Flavored Cigarettes" (see http://slati.lungusa.org). Advertising and promotion of these products uses hip-hop imagery, attractive women, and other imagery to appeal to youth in similar ways that Joe Camel did a decade ago. Marketing efforts for candy-flavored cigarettes came after the 1998 Master Settlement Agreement prohibited tobacco companies from using cartoon characters to sell cigarettes. Researchers recently released the results of several surveys that showed that 20 percent of smokers ages 17 to 19 smoked flavored cigarettes, while only 6 percent of smokers ages 17 to 20 did.

Over the past five years, as countries have increasingly limited the type of public advertising that cigarette companies can use, companies have sought other means of promoting their product. One of Philip Morris International's promotions was a contest and the prize was to be among the 42 young men and women from Asia, Latin America, and Europe selected to be part of the 2004 Adventure Team event in Utah. The event was part-vacation, part-Marlboro marketing extravaganza for smokers from around the world to play cowboy on beautiful public lands. No Americans were eligible to participate in the contest because of the agreement between the tobacco companies and attorneys-general of various U.S. states that prohibit this type of promotion within the United States. The real prize was the names, addresses, and other demographic information of the more than a million young smokers from all around the world who are starting their smoking careers and are susceptible to advertising—a value that can't be estimated as Philip Morris advertises directly to them over the next ten years. [1]

---
[1] Jennifer Ludden, "Interview with Charles Duhigg (*Los Angeles Times*) about an event in Utah Staged by Philip Morris," *Weekend Edition NPR News*, November 27, 2004.

Another source of concern is the tar and nicotine content of cigarettes. A 1979 study found three major U.S. brands with filters had 17 milligrams of tar in the United States, 22.3 in Kenya, 29.7 in Malaysia, and 31.1 in South Africa. Another brand with filters had 19.1 milligrams of tar in the United States, 28.8 in South Africa, and 30.9 in the Philippines.

Although cigarette companies deny they sell higher tar and nicotine cigarettes in the Third World, one British tobacco company does concede that some of its brands sold in developing countries contain more tar and nicotine than those sold in the United States and Europe. This firm leaves the tar- and nicotine-level decisions to its foreign subsidiaries, which tailor their products to local tastes. The firm says that Third World smokers are used to smoking their own locally made product, which might have several times more tar and nicotine.

C. Everett Koop, the retired U.S. Surgeon General, was quoted in a recent news conference as saying, "Companies' claims that science cannot say with certainty that tobacco causes cancer were flat-footed lies" and that "sending cigarettes to the Third World was the export of death, disease, and disability." An Oxford University epidemiologist has estimated that, because of increasing tobacco consumption in Asia, the annual worldwide death toll from tobacco-related illnesses will more than triple over the next two decades. He forecasts about 3 million a year to 10 million a year by 2050, a fifth of them in China.

GOVERNMENT INVOLVEMENT

Third World governments often stand to profit from tobacco sales. Brazil collects 75 percent of the retail price of cigarettes in taxes, some $100 million a month. The Bulgarian state-owned tobacco company, Bulgartabac, contributes almost $30 million in taxes to the government annually. Bulgartabac is a major exporter of cigarettes to Russia, exporting 40,000 tons of cigarettes in 1997.

Tobacco is Zimbabwe's largest cash crop. One news report from a Zimbabwe newspaper reveals strong support for cigarette companies. "Western anti-tobacco lobbies demonstrate unbelievable hypocrisy," notes one editorial. "It is relatively easy to sit in Washington or London and prattle on about the so-called evils of smoking, but they are far removed from the day-to-day grind of earning a living in the Third World." It goes on to comment that it doesn't dispute the fact that smoking is addictive or that it may cause diseases, but "smoking does not necessarily lead to certain death. Nor is it any more dangerous than other habits." Unfortunately, tobacco smoking has attracted the attention of a particularly "sanctimonious, meddling sector of society. They would do better to keep their opinions to themselves."

Generally, smoking is not a big concern of governments beset by debt, internal conflict, drought, or famine. It is truly tragic, but the worse famine becomes, the more people smoke—just as with war, when people who are worried want to smoke. "In any case," says one representative of an international tobacco company, "People in developing countries don't have a long enough life expectancy to worry about smoking-related problems. You can't turn to a guy who is going to die at age 40 and tell him that he might not live up to 2 years extra at age 70." As for promoting cigarettes in the Third World, "If there is no ban on TV advertising, then you aren't going to be an idiot and impose restrictions on yourself," says the representative, "and likewise, if you get an order and you know that they've got money, no one is going to turn down the business."

Cigarette companies figure China's self-interest will preserve its industry. Tobacco provides huge revenues for Beijing because all tobacco must be sold through the China National Tobacco Company monopoly. Duty on imported cigarettes is nearly 450 percent of their value. Consequently, tobacco is among the central government's biggest source of funding, accounting for more than $6 billion a year in income. China is also a major exporter of tobacco. In 2000, China's exports of tobacco were over $500 million, a substantial increase from a year earlier.

National self-interest is not limited to Third World countries alone. The United States sends mixed signals as well. On the one hand, the State Department sent a directive to all U.S. diplomatic posts in 1998 instructing them not to promote American tobacco products abroad. According to the directive, tobacco would be treated as a danger to health. At the same time, the directive also stated that the government would continue to oppose trade policies abroad that favor local tobacco products over those made in the United States. Unfortunately, even unambiguous directives have not always been followed. In 1994, the administration promised to work toward lowering smoking around the world but worked hand in hand with tobacco companies against an effort by the government of Thailand to require tobacco companies to disclose the ingredients in each brand of cigarettes. In 1994, the ambassador to Romania attended the opening of a new U.S. cigarette company plant and declared, "I'm sure that the splendid products of [company name] will prosper in Romania."

ASSESSING THE ETHICS OF STRATEGIC DECISIONS

Ethical decision making is not a simplistic "right" or "wrong" determination. Ethical ground rules are complex, tough to sort out and to prioritize, tough to articulate, and tough to use.

The complexity of ethical decisions is compounded in the international setting, which comprises different cultures, different perspectives of right and wrong, different legal requirements, and different goals. Clearly, when U.S. companies conduct business in an international setting, the ground rules become further complicated by the values, customs, traditions, ethics, and goals of the host countries, which have developed their own ground rules for conducting business.

Three prominent American ethicists have developed a framework to view ethical implications of strategic decisions by American firms. They identify three ethical principles that can guide American managers in assessing the ethical implications of their decisions and the degree to which these decisions reflect these ethical principles or ground rules. They suggest asking, "Is the corporate strategy acceptable according to the following ethical ground rules?"

Principles	Question
Utilitarian ethics (Bentham, Smith)	Does the corporate strategy optimize the "common good" or benefits of all constituencies?
Rights of the parties (Kant, Locke)	Does the corporate strategy respect the rights of the individuals involved?
Justice or fairness (Aristotle, Rawls)	Does the corporate strategy respect the canons of justice or fairness to all parties?

Exhibit 1

A Decision Tree for
Incorporating Ethical and
Social Responsibility Issues
into Multinational Business
Decisions

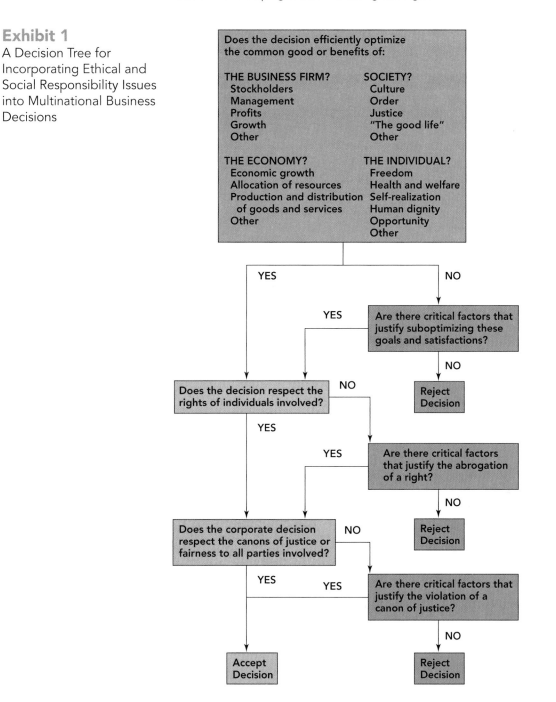

These questions can help uncover the ethical ground rules embedded in the tobacco consumption situation described in this case. These questions lead to an ethical analysis of the degree to which this strategy is beneficial or harmful to the parties and, ultimately, whether it is a "right" or "wrong" strategy, or whether the consequences of this strategy are ethical or socially responsible for the parties involved. These ideas are incorporated in the decision tree in Exhibit 1.

Laczniak and Naor discuss the complexity of international ethics or, more precisely, the ethical assumptions that underlie strategic decisions for multinationals.[2] They suggest that multinationals can develop consistency in their policies by using federal law as a baseline for appropriate behavior as well as respect for the host country's general value structure. They conclude with four recommendations for multinationals:

1. Expand codes of ethics to be worldwide in scope.

2. Expressly consider ethical issues when developing worldwide corporate strategies.

3. If the firm encounters major ethical dilemmas, consider withdrawal from the problem market.

4. Develop periodic ethics-impact statements, including impacts on host parties.

[2]Gene R. Laczniak and Jacob Naor, "Global Ethics: Wrestling with the Corporate Conscience," *Business,* July–September 1985.

See www.who.int, the World Health Organization Web site, for more details regarding the current tobacco controversy. See also www.getswat.com for a worldwide student initiative against smoking.

QUESTIONS

1. Use the model in Exhibit 1 as a guide and assess the ethical and social responsibility implications of the situation described.

2. Can you recommend alternative strategies or solutions to the dilemmas confronting the tobacco companies? To governments? What is the price of ethical behavior?

3. Should the U.S. government support U.S. tobacco company interests abroad?

4. Should a company be forced to stop marketing a product that is not illegal, e.g., cigarettes?

GLOSSARY

administered pricing The attempt to establish prices for an entire market through the cooperation of competitors, through national, state, or local governments, or by international agreement. Its legality differs from country to country and from time to time.

advanced pricing agreement (APA) An agreement made between a company and the Internal Revenue Service covering **transfer pricing** methods used by the company. Without such an agreement, if the IRS charges the company with underreporting income through its transactions with affiliates, the burden of proof that a transfer price was fair rests with the company.

aesthetics Philosophically, the creation and appreciation of beauty; collectively, the arts, including folklore, music, drama, and dance.

AFTA ASEAN (Association of Southeast Asian Nations) Free Trade Area; a multinational trade group that evolved from ASEAN. *See* **APEC; ASEAN+3**

agent middlemen In an international transaction, intermediaries who represent the principal (home manufacturer/marketer) rather than themselves; agent middlemen work on commission and arrange for sales in the foreign country but do not take title to the merchandise. *See* **home-country middlemen; merchant middlemen**

analogy A method of market estimation that assumes that demand for a product develops in much the same way in all countries as comparable economic development occurs in each country.

APEC The Asian-Pacific Economic Cooperation; a forum that meets annually to discuss regional economic development. *See* **AFTA; ASEAN+3**

arbitration A procedure, used as an alternative to **litigation,** in which parties in a dispute may select a disinterested party or parties as referee to determine the merits of the case and make a judgment that both parties agree to honor.

ASEAN+3 A forum for ministers of the Association of Southeast Asian Nations plus ministers from China, Japan, and South Korea. *See* **AFTA; APEC**

back translation The process in which a document, such as a questionnaire, or phrase is translated from one language to another and then translated by a second party into the original language. Back translations can be used to verify that the first translation, as of a marketing slogan, has the intended meeting for the targeted audience. *See* **decentering; parallel translation**

balance of payments The system of accounts that records a nation's international financial transactions.

balance of trade The difference in value over a period of time between a country's imports and exports.

barter The direct exchange of goods between two parties in a transaction. *See* **compensation deals; counterpurchase; countertrade**

BATNA Acronym for "best alternative to a negotiated agreement," a notion discussed in *Getting to Yes*, by Fisher, Ury, and Patton.

BEMs Big emerging markets; used to describe the core group of populous nations that will account for much of the growth in world trade among developing and newly industrialized countries.

bills of exchange A form of international commercial payment drawn by sellers on foreign buyers; in transactions based on bills of exchange, the seller assumes all risk until the actual dollars are received, making them riskier for the seller than **letters of credit.**

capital account The portion of a **balance of payments** statement that shows a record of direct investment, portfolio investment, and short-tern capital movements to and from countries.

cartel An arrangement in which various companies producing similar products or services work together to control markets for the goods and service they produce. The Organization of Petroleum Exporting Countries (OPEC) is the best-known international cartel.

client followers Companies, often providers of services, that follow companies that first moved into a foreign market; for example, an American insurance company setting up in Mexico to serve a U.S. auto company that had previously opened a factory there.

code law A legal system based on an all-inclusive system of written rules, or codes, of law; generally divided into three separate codes: commercial, civil, and criminal. In the United States, Louisiana is the one state to use code law. *See* **common law**

Commerce Control List (CCL) A directory, organized by a series of **Export Control Classification Numbers,** that indicates U.S. rules for the exportability of items. Exporters must use the list to determine if there are end-use restrictions on certain items, such as uses in nuclear, chemical, and biological weapons, and determine if a product has a dual use—that is, both in commercial and restricted applications. *See* **Export Administration Regulations**

Commerce Country Chart (CCC) A directory of information that a U.S. exporter needs to consult, along with the **Commerce Control List,** to determine if the exporter needs a license to export or reexport a product to a particular destination. *See* **Export Control Classification Numbers**

common law The body of law based on tradition, past practices, and legal precedents set by courts through interpretations of statutes, legal legislation, and past rulings. Common law, which is used in all states in the United States except Louisiana, uses past decisions to interpret statutes and apply them to present situations. Also known as English law. *See* **code law**

common market An agreement that eliminates all tariffs and other restrictions on internal trade, adopts a set of common external tariffs, and removes all restrictions on the free flow of capital and labor among member nations.

compensation deals Transactions that involve payment in both goods and cash. *See* **barter; counterpurchase; countertrade**

complementary marketing The process by which companies with excess marketing capacity in different countries or with a desire for a broader product line take on additional lines for international distribution; commonly called *piggybacking.*

conciliation A nonbinding agreement between parties to resolve disputes by asking a third party to mediate differences. Also known as *mediation. See* **arbitration; litigation**

confiscation   The seizing of a company's assets without payment. Prominent examples involving U.S. companies occurred in Cuba and Iran. *See* **domestication; expropriation**

controllable elements   The aspects of trade over which a company has control and influence; they include marketing decisions covering product, price, promotion, distribution, research, and advertising. *See* **uncontrollable elements**

corporate planning   The formulation of long-term, generalized goals for an enterprise as a whole. *See* **strategic planning; tactical planning**

counterpurchase   A type of **countertrade** in which a seller receives payment in cash but agrees in a contract to buy goods from the buyer for the total monetary amount involved in the first transaction or for a set percentage of that amount; also known as *offset trade*. *See* **barter; compensation deals**

countertrade   A type of transaction in which goods are imported and sold by a company from a country in exchange for the right or ability to manufacture and/or sell goods in that country. Countertrade can substitute for cash entirely or partially and is used extensively in trade between U.S. firms and the former Soviet bloc, along with other emerging markets. *See* **barter; compensation deals; counterpurchase**

countervailing duty   A fee that may, under **World Trade Organization** rules, be imposed on foreign goods benefiting from subsidies, whether in production, export, or transportation; may be applied in conjunction with *minimum access volume,* which restricts the amount of goods a country will import.

cultural borrowing   The phenomenon by which societies learn from other cultures' ways and borrow ideas to solve problems or improve conditions.

cultural congruence   A marketing strategy in which products are marketed in a way similar to the marketing of products already in the market in a manner as congruent as possible with existing cultural norms.

cultural elective   *See* **elective**

cultural exclusive   *See* **exclusive**

cultural imperative   *See* **imperative**

cultural sensitivity   An awareness of the nuances of culture so that a culture can be viewed objectively, evaluated, and appreciated; an important part of foreign marketing.

cultural values   The system of beliefs and customs held by a population in a given **culture.** A book by Geert Hofstede describes a study of 66 nations and divides the cultural values of those nations into four primary dimensions: the Individualized/Collectivism Index, the Power Distance Index, the Uncertainty Avoidance Index, and the Masculinity/Femininity Index (which is not considered as useful as the other three).

culture   The human-made part of human environment—the sum total of knowledge, beliefs, arts, morals, laws, customs, and any other capabilities and habits acquired by humans as members of society.

current account   The portion of a **balance of payments** statement that shows a record of all merchandise exports, imports, and services, plus unilateral transfers of funds.

customs-privileged facilities   Areas, as in international transactions, where goods can be imported for storage and/or processing with tariffs and quota limits postponed until the products leave the designated areas. *See* **foreign-trade zones**

customs union   A stage in economic cooperation that benefits from a **free trade area**'s reduced or eliminated internal tariffs and adds a common external tariff on products imported from countries outside the union. *See* **common market; political union**

cybersquatters   Persons or businesses that buy, usually for a nominal fee, and register as Web site names descriptive nouns, celebrity names, variations on company trademarks, geographic and ethnic group names, and pharmaceutical and other descriptors and then hold them until they can be sold at an inflated price. Sometimes called *CSQ.*

d

dealers   The middlemen selling industrial goods or durable goods directly to customers; they are the last step in the **distribution channel.**

decentering   A method of translation, a variation on **back translation,** that is a successive process of translation and retranslation of a document, such as a questionnaire, each time by a different translator. The two original-language versions are then compared, and if there are differences, the process is repeated until the second original-language version is the same as the first. *See* **parallel translation**

derived demand   Demand that is dependent on another source; it can be fundamental to the success of efforts to sell capital equipment and big-ticket industrial services.

direct exporting   The type of exporting in which a company sells to a customer in another country. *See* **indirect exporting**

distribution channels   The various routes through which marketers must negotiate their goods to deliver them to the consumer. Distribution channel structures range from those with little developed marketing infrastructure, as found in many emerging markets, to those with a highly complex, multilayered systems, as found in Japan. Consideration for channel structure involves "the six Cs": cost, capital, control, coverage, character, and continuity.

distribution process   The physical handling of goods, the passage of ownership (title), and—especially important from a marketing viewpoint—the buying and selling negotiations between the producers and middlemen and between middlemen and customers. *See* **distribution structure**

distribution structure   The system, present in every country's market, through which goods pass from producer to user; within the structure are a variety of middlemen. *See* **distribution process**

domestication   A process by which a host country gradually transfers foreign investments to national control and ownership through a series of government decrees mandating local ownership and greater national involvement in company management. *See* **confiscation; expropriation**

domestic environment uncontrollables   Factors in a company's home country over which the company has little or no control or influence. They include political and legal forces, the economic climate, level of technology, competitive forces, and economic forces. *See* **uncontrollable elements**

dumping An export practice, generally prohibited by laws and subject to penalties and fines, defined by some as the selling of products in foreign markets below the cost of production and by others as the selling of products at below the prices of the same goods in the home market.

e

economic development Generally, an increase in national production that results in an increase in average per capita gross domestic product.

economic dualism The coexistence of modern and traditional sectors within an economy, especially as found in less-developed countries.

ELAIN Export License Application and Information Network; an electronic service that enables authorized exporters to submit license applications via the Internet for all commodities except supercomputers and to all free-world destinations. *See* **ERIC; SNAP; STELA**

elective A business custom (as in a foreign country) to which adaptation is helpful but not necessary. *See* **exclusive; imperative**

EMU The Economic and Monetary Union; formed by the **Maastricht Treaty,** which also formed the European Union.

ERIC Electronic Request for Item Classification; a supplementary service to **ELAIN** that allows an exporter to submit commodity classification requests via the Internet to the Bureau of Export administration. *See* **SNAP; STELA**

exclusive A business custom (as in a foreign country) in which an outsider must not participate. *See* **elective; imperative**

exclusive distribution A practice in which a company restricts which retailers can carry its product; often used by companies to maintain high retail margins, to maintain the exclusive-quality image of a product, and to encourage retailers to provide extra service to customers.

expatriate A person living away from his or her own country. In international sales, expatriates from the selling company's home country may be the best choice for the sales force when products are highly technical or when selling requires an extensive knowledge of the company and its product line. *See* **local nationals**

expert opinion A method of market estimation in which experts are polled for their opinions about market size and growth rates; used particularly in foreign countries that are new to the marketer.

Export Administration Regulations (EAR) A set of rules issued by the U.S. Department of Commerce, designed to alleviate many of the problems and confusions of exporting; they are intended to speed up the process of granting export licenses by concentrating license control on a list of specific items, most of which involve national security. Exporters must ensure that their trade activities do not violate the provisions of EAR. *See* **Commerce Control List; Export Control Classification Number**

Export Control Classification Number (ECCN) Under the provisions of the U.S. **Export Administration Regulations (EAR),** a classification number that a U.S. exporter must select for an item to be exported; the number corresponds to a description in the **Commerce Control List,** which indicates the exportability of the item.

export documents The various items of documentation for an international transaction, as required by the exporting government, by established procedures of foreign trade, and, in some cases, as required by the importing government.

export regulations Restrictions placed by countries on the selling of goods abroad; among reasons they may be imposed are to conserve scarce goods for home consumption and to control the flow of strategic goods actual or potential enemies. *See* **import regulations**

Export Trading Company (ETC) Act An act allowing producers of similar products in the United States to form an export trading company; the act created a more favorable environment for the formation of joint export ventures, in part by removing antitrust disincentives to trade activities.

expropriation The seizure of an investment by a government in which some reimbursement is made to the investment owner; often the seized investment becomes nationalized. *See* **confiscation; domestication**

f

factual knowledge A type of knowledge or understanding of a foreign culture that encompasses different meanings of color, different tastes, and other traits of a culture that a marketer can study, anticipate, and absorb. *See* **interpretive knowledge**

FCPA Foreign Corrupt Practices Act. The act prohibits U.S. businesses from paying bribes openly or using middlemen as conduits for a bribe when the U.S. official knows that the middleman's payment will be used for a bribe.

foreign environment uncontrollables Factors in the foreign market over which a business operating in its home country has little or no control or influence. They include political and legal forces, economic climate, geography and infrastructure, level of technology, structure of distribution, and level of technology. *See* **domestic environment uncontrollables**

foreign-trade zones (FTZs) Regions or ports that act as holding areas for goods before quotas or customs duties are applied. In the United States, more than 150 FTZs allow companies to land imported goods for storage or various processing such as cleaning or packaging before the goods are officially brought into the United States or reexported to another country. *See* **customs-privileged facilities**

forfaiting A financing technique that may be used in an international transaction in which the seller makes a one-time arrangement with a bank or other financial institution to take over responsibility for collecting the account receivable.

franchising A form of **licensing** in which a company (the franchiser) provides a standard package of products, systems, and management services to the franchisee, which in foreign markets may have market knowledge. Franchising permits flexibility in dealing with local market conditions while providing the parent firm with a degree of control.

free trade area (FTA) A type of regional cooperation that involves an agreement between two or more countries to reduce or eliminate customs duties and nontariff trade barriers among partner countries while members maintain individual tariff schedules for external countries. An FTA requires more cooperation than the arrangement known as the regional cooperation for development.

full-cost pricing   A method of pricing based on the view that no unit of a similar product is different from any other unit of a similar product and that each unit must bear its full share of the total fixed and variable cost, whether sold in the home market or abroad. *See* **skimming; variable-cost pricing**

g

GATT   General Agreement on Tariffs and Trade; a trade agreement signed by the United States and 22 other countries shortly after World War II. The original agreement provided a process to reduce **tariffs** and created an agency to patrol world trade; the treaty and subsequent meetings have produced agreements significantly reducing tariffs.

global awareness   A frame of reference, important to the success of a businessperson, that embodies tolerance of cultural differences and knowledge of cultures, history, world market potential, and global economic, social, and political trends.

global brand   The worldwide use of a name, term, sign, symbol (visual or auditory), design, or a combination thereof to identify goods or services of a seller and to differentiate them from those of competitors.

global marketing   The performance of business activities designed to plan, price, promote, and direct the flow of a company's goods and services to consumers or users in more than one nation for a profit. The most profound difference between global and domestic marketing involves the orientation of the company toward markets and planning activities around the world.

global marketing concept   A perspective encompassing an entire set of country markets, whether the home market and one other country or the home market and 100 other countries, and viewing them as a unit, identifying groups of prospective buyers with similar needs as a global market segment, and developing a market plan that strives for standardization wherever it is effective in cost and cultural terms.

global orientation   A means of operating by which a company acts as if all the company's markets in a company's scope of operations (including the domestic market) were approachable as a single global market, with the company standardizing the marketing mix where culturally feasible and cost effective.

green marketing   Consideration and concern for the environmental consequences of product formulation, marketing, manufacturing, and packaging.

h

home-country middlemen   In international transactions, the intermediaries, located in the producer's home country, who provide marketing services from a domestic base; also known as *domestic middlemen*. Home-country middlemen offer advantages for companies with small international sales volume or for those inexperienced in international trade. *See* **agent middlemen; merchant middlemen**

homologation   A term used to describe changes in a product that are mandated by local standards for product and service **quality.**

i

IMF   The International Monetary Fund. A global institution that, along with the World Bank Group, was created to assist nations in becoming and remaining economically viable.

imperative   A business custom (as in a foreign country) that must be recognized and accommodated. *See* **elective; exclusive**

import jobbers   In international transactions, business entities that purchase goods directly from the manufacturer and sell to wholesalers and retailers and to industrial customers.

import regulations   Restrictions placed by countries on the sale of goods from outside markets; among the reasons they are imposed are to protect health, conserve foreign exchange, serve as economic reprisals, protect home industry, and provide revenue from tariffs. Exporters to markets under such regulations may have to go through various steps to comply with them. *See* **export regulations**

indirect exporting   The type of exporting in which a company sells to a buyer (an importer or distributor) in the home country; the buyer in turn exports the product. *See* **direct selling**

infrastructure   The collective assortment of capital goods that serve the activities of many industries and support production and marketing.

innovation   An idea perceived as new by a group of people; when applied to a product, an innovation may be something completely new or something that is perceived as new in a given country or culture. *See* **product diffusion**

integrated marketing communications (IMCs)   The collective arrangement of efforts and methods to sell a product or service, including advertising, sales promotions, trade shows, personal selling, direct selling, and public relations.

international marketing   The performance of business activities designed to plan, price, promote, and direct the flow of a company's goods and services to consumers or users in more than one nation for a profit.

international marketing research   The form of **marketing research** involving two additional considerations: (1) the need to communicate information across national boundaries, and (2) the challenge of applying established marketing techniques in the different environments of foreign markets, some of which may be strange or vexing milieus for the marketer.

interpretive knowledge   An ability to understand and to appreciate fully the nuances of different cultural traits and patterns. *See* **factual knowledge**

Islamic law   The *Shari'ah;* the legal system based on an interpretation of the Koran. Islamic law encompasses religious duties and obligations as well as the secular aspect of law regulating human acts. Among its provisions is a prohibition of the payment of interest.

ISO 9000s   A series of international industrial standards (ISO 9000–9004) originally designed by the International Organization for Standardization to meet the need for product quality assurances in purchasing agreements.

J

joint venture A partnership of two or more participating companies that join forces to create a separate legal entity. *See* **strategic international alliance**

justice or fairness One of three principles of ethics (the others are **utilitarian ethics** and **rights of the parties**); it tests an action by asking if the action respects the canons of justice or fairness to all parties involved.

l

Large-Scale Retail Store Location Act A regulatory act in Japan, implemented under pressure from the United States in 2000; it replaced the protective Large-Scale Retail Store Law and relaxed restrictions on the opening of large retailers near small shops and abolished the mandate on the number of days a store must be closed.

letters of credit Financing devices that, when opened by a buyer of goods, allow the seller to draw a draft against the bank issuing the credit and receive dollars by presenting proper shipping document. Except for cash in advance, letters of credit afford the seller the greatest degree of protection. *See* **bills of exchange**

licensing A contractual means by which a company grants patent rights, trademark rights, and the rights to use technology to another company, often in a foreign market; a favored strategy of small and medium-sized companies seeking a foothold in foreign markets without making large capital outlays. *See* **franchising**

linguistic distance The measure of difference between languages; an important factor in determining the amount of trade between nations.

litigation The process in which a dispute between parties is contested in a formal judicial setting; commonly instigated by a lawsuit asserting one party's version of the facts.

local nationals Persons living in their home country; historically the persons preferred by **expatriate** managers to form the sales force. Local nationals are more knowledgeable about a country's business structure than an expatriate would be, and they are generally less expensive to field and maintain.

logistics management A total systems approach to management of the distribution process that includes all activities involved in physically moving raw material, in-process inventory, and finished goods inventory from the point of origin to the point of use or consumption.

m

Maastricht Treaty Treaty signed by 12 nations of the European Community creating the European Union.

Manifest Destiny The notion that Americans were a chosen people ordained by God to create a model society; it was accepted as the basis for U.S. policy during much of the 19th and 20th centuries as the nation expanded its territory.

maquiladoras Also known as *in-bond companies* or *twin plants,* a type of customs-privileged facility that originated in Mexico in the 1970s and provided U.S. companies with a favorable means to use low-cost Mexican labor. They operate through an agreement with the Mexican government allowing U.S. companies to import parts and materials into Mexico without import taxes provided the finished products are reexported to the United States or another country. *See* **customs-privileged facilities**

marketing research The systematic gathering, recording, and analyzing of data to provide information useful in marketing decision making. *See* **international marketing research**

Marxist-socialist tenets The set of views in which law is subordinate to prevailing economic conditions. Marxist-socialist tenets influenced the legal systems of Russia and other republics of the former Soviet Union, as well as China, forcing these nations to revamp their commercial legal code as they become involved in trade with non-Marxist countries.

merchant middlemen In international transactions, the intermediaries, located in the foreign market, who take title to the home-country manufacturer's goods and sell on their own account. Manufacturers using merchant middlemen have less control over the **distribution process** than those using **agent middlemen.** *See* **home-country middlemen**

Mercosur An evolving South American union, also called the Southern Cone Free Trade Area, formed in 1991 with the goal of creating a **common market** and **customs union** among the participating countries. The original signers were Argentina, Brazil, Paraguay, and Uruguay; Bolivia and Chile later signed agreements with Mercosur.

merge-in-transit A distribution method in which goods shipped from several supply locations are consolidated into one final customer delivery point while they are in transit and then shipped as a unit to the customer.

Monroe Doctrine A cornerstone of U.S. foreign policy as enunciated by President James Monroe, it proclaimed three basic dicta: no further European colonization in the New World, abstention of the United States from European political affairs, and nonintervention of European governments in the governments of the Western Hemisphere. *See* **Roosevelt Corollary**

M-time Monochromatic time; describing a view of time, typical of most North Americans, Swiss, Germans, and Scandinavians, as something that is linear and can be saved, wasted, spent, and lost. M-time cultures tend to concentrate on one thing at a time and value promptness. *See* **P-time**

multicultural research Inquiry, analysis, and study of countries and cultures that takes into account differences in language, economic structure, social structure, behavior, and attitude patterns. Different methods of research may have varying reliability in different countries.

multinational market regions The groups of countries that seek mutual economic benefit from reducing interregional tariffs and barriers to trade.

n

NAFTA North American Free Trade Agreement. NAFTA is a comprehensive trade agreement that addresses, and in many cases improves all aspects of doing business within North America. By eliminating trade and investment barriers among Canada, the United States, and Mexico, it created one of the largest and richest markets in the world.

nationalism An intense feeling of national pride and unity; an awakening of a nation's people to pride in their country. Nationalism can take on an antiforeign business bias.

NICs Newly industrialized countries; countries that are experiencing rapid economic expansion and industrialization.

noise The term for an impairment to communications process comprising external influences, such as competitive advertising, other sales personnel, and confusion at the "receiving end." Noise can disrupt any step of the communications process and is frequently beyond the control of the sender or the receiver.

nontariff barriers Restrictions, other than **tariffs,** placed by countries on imported products; they may include quality standards, sanitary and health standards, **quotas,** embargoes, boycotts, and antidumping penalties.

nontask sounding The part of the negotiation process in which conversation covers topics other than the business at hand; nontask sounding is commonly a preliminary phase and precedes **task-related information exchange.**

O

open account In U.S. domestic trade, the typical payment procedure for established customers, in which the goods are delivered and the customer is billed on an end-of-the-month basis.

orderly market agreements (OMAs) Agreements, similar to **quotas,** between an importing country and an exporting country for a restriction on the volume of exports. Also known as **voluntary export restraints.**

P

parallel imports International transactions in which importers buy products from distributors in one country and sell them in another to distributors that are not part of the manufacturer's regular distribution system.

parallel translation A method of translation in which two translators are used to make a **back translation;** the results are compared, differences are discussed, and the most appropriate translation is used. The method addresses the use of common idioms in the languages being translated. *See* **decentering**

physical distribution system The overall network for the physical movement of goods, including plants and warehousing, transportation mode, inventory quantities, and packaging.

planned change A marketing strategy in which a company deliberately sets out to change those aspects of a foreign culture resistant to predetermined marketing goals. *See* **unplanned change**

political union A fully integrated form of regional cooperation that involves complete political and economic integration, either voluntary or enforced; the most notable example was the now-disbanded Council for Mutual Economic Assistance (COMECON), a centrally controlled group of countries organized by the Soviet Union.

predatory pricing A practice by which a foreign producer intentionally sells its products in another country for less than the cost of production to undermine the competition and take control of the market.

price escalation The pricing disparity in which goods are priced higher in a foreign market than in the home market; caused by the added costs involved in exporting products from one country to another.

price–quality relationship The balance between a product's price and how well the product performs. Often the price–quality of a product is ideal if it meets basic expectations and no more, allowing it to be priced competitively.

primary data Data collected, as in market research, specifically for a particular research project. *See* **secondary data**

principle of justice or fairness *See* **justice or fairness**

principle of rights of the parties *See* **rights of the parties**

principle of utilitarian ethics *See* **utilitarian ethics**

prior use versus registration The principle, as observed in the United States and other common-law nations, that ownership of intellectual property rights usually goes to whoever can establish first use.

product buyback agreement A type of **countertrade** in which the sale involves goods or services that produce other goods or services—that is, production plant, production equipment, or technology.

Product Component Model A tool for characterizing how a product may be adapted to a new market by separating the product's many dimensions into three components: support services, packaging, and core component.

product diffusion The process by which product **innovation** spreads; successful product diffusion may depend on the ability to communicate relevant product information and new product attributes.

protectionism The use by nations of legal barriers, exchange barriers, and psychological barriers to restrain entry of goods from other countries.

PSAs Political and social activists. PSAs are individuals who participate in efforts to change the practices and behaviors of corporations and governments, with tactics that can range from peaceful protest to terrorism.

P-time Polychromatic time; a view of time, as held in "high context" cultures, in which the completion of a human transaction is more important than holding to schedules. P-time is characterized by the simultaneous occurrence of many things. *See* **M-time**

public relations (PR) The effort made by companies to create positive relationships with the popular press and general media and to communicate messages to their publics, including customers, the general public, and government regulators.

Q

quality The essential character of something, such as a good or service; defined in two dimensions: market-perceived quality and performance quality. Consumer perception of a product's quality often has more to do with market-perceived quality than performance quality.

quotas Specific unit or dollar limits applied to a particular type of good by the country into which the good is imported. *See* **tariff**

r

relationship marketing   The aspect of marketing products that depends on long-term associations with customers; an important factor in business-to-business contexts and especially important in most international markets, where culture dictates strong ties between people and companies.

research process   The process of obtaining information; it should begin with a definition of the research problem and establishment of objectives, and proceed with an orderly approach to the collection and analysis of data.

reserves account   The portion of a **balance-of-trade** statement that shows a record of exports and imports of gold, increases or decreases in foreign exchange, and increases or decreases in liabilities to foreign banks.

rights of the parties   One of three principles of ethics (the others are **utilitarian ethics** and **justice or fairness**); it tests an action by asking if the action respects the rights of the individuals involved.

Roosevelt Corollary   An extension of U.S. policy applied to the Monroe Doctrine by President Theodore Roosevelt, stating that the United States would not only prohibit non-American intervention in Latin American affairs but would also police Latin America and guarantee that all Latin American nations would meet their international obligations. *See* **Monroe Doctrine**

S

sales promotion   Marketing activities that stimulate consumer purchases and improve retailer or middlemen effectiveness and cooperation.

secondary data   Data collected by an agency or individual other than the one conducting research; often useful in market research. *See* **primary data**

self-reference criterion (SRC)   An unconscious reference to one's own cultural values, experience, and knowledge as a basis for a decision.

separation allowances   Payment of overseas premiums to employees who take on short-term foreign assignments and travel without their families; allowances generally compensate for all excess expenses and any tax differential.

Silent Language   Term used by Edward T. Hall for the nonspoken and symbolic meanings of time, space, things, friendships, and agreements, and how they vary across cultures; from Hall's article "The Silent Language of Business."

Single European Act   An agreement, ratified in 1987, designed to remove all barriers to trade and to make the European Community a single internal market.

skimming   A method of pricing, generally used for foreign markets, in which a company seeks to reach a segment of the market that is relatively price insensitive and thus willing to pay a premium price for the value received; may be used to sell a new or innovative product to maximize profits until a competitor forces a lower price. *See* **full-cost pricing; variable-cost pricing**

SNAP   Simplified Network Application Process; an electronic service offered by the U.S. Department of Commerce as an alternative to paper license submissions that enables an exporter to submit export and reexport applications, high-performance computer notices, and commodity classification requests via the Internet. *See* **ELAIN; ERIC; STELA**

social institutions   The methods and systems, including family, religion, school, the media, government, and corporations, that affect the ways in which people relate to one another, teach acceptable behavior to succeeding generations, and govern themselves.

sovereignty   The powers exercised by a state in relation to other countries, as well as the supreme powers of a state as exercised over its own inhabitants.

special drawing rights (SDRs)   A means of monetary measurement that represents an average base of value derived from the value of a group of major currencies. Known as "paper gold," it is used by the **IMF** to report most monetary statistics in a unit more reliable than a single currency, such as dollars.

stage of economic development   A classification describing the (stage of) maturity and sophistication of a nation's economy as it evolves over time. The best-known model, by Walt Rostow, describes five stages, starting with the traditional society and finally reaching the age of high mass consumption.

STELA   System for Tracking Export License Applications; an automated voice response system for exporters that enables license applicants to track the status of their license and classification applications with U.S. authorities. *See* **ELAIN; ERIC; SNAP**

strategic international alliance (SIA)   A business relationship established by two or more companies to cooperate out of mutual need and to share risk in achieving a common objective.

strategic planning   A type of planning conducted at the highest levels of management, dealing with products, capital, and research and the long- and short-term goals of a company. *See* **corporate planning; tactical planning**

subornation   The giving of large sums of money—frequently not fully accounted for—designed to entice an official to commit an illegal act on behalf of the one offering the money.

sustainable development   An approach toward economic growth that has been described (by Joke Waller-Hunter) as a cooperative effort among businesses, environmentalists, and others to seek growth with "wise resource management, equitable distribution of benefits, and reduction of negative efforts on people and the environment from the process of economic growth."

t

tactical planning   A type of planning that pertains to specific actions and to the allocation of resources used to implement strategic planning goals in specific markets; also known as *market planning;* generally conducted at the local level. *See* **corporate planning; strategic planning**

tariff   A fee or tax that countries impose on imported goods, often to protect a country's markets from intrusion from foreign countries. *See* **nontariff barriers; quotas**

task-related information exchange   The point in the negotiation process at which nontask communication, or **nontask sounding,** is completed and substantial negotiations begin.

TCNs   Third-country nationals; expatriates from one country working for a foreign company in a third country. *See* **expatriate; local nationals**

terms of sale   The set of rules and costs applying to a transaction, covering such categories as price, freight, and insurance. In international trade, terms of sale often sound similar to those in domestic commerce but generally have different meanings. Also known as *trade terms*.

trading companies   Business entities that accumulate, transport, and distribute goods from many countries.

transfer pricing   The pricing of goods transferred from a company's operations or sales units in one country to its units elsewhere; also known as *intracompany pricing*. In transfer pricing, prices may be adjusted to enhance the ultimate profit of the company as a whole.

Treaty of Amsterdam   Treaty, concluded in 1997, that addressed issues left undone by the **Maastricht Treaty** and identified priority measures necessary to bring a single market in Europe fully into effect and to lay a solid foundation for both a single currency and an enlargement of the European Union into central and eastern Europe. *See* **Economic and Monetary Union; Single European Act**

24-Hour Rule   A U.S. requirement, part of the Cargo and Container Security Initiative, mandating that sea carriers and NVOCCs (Non-Vessel Operating Common Carriers) provide U.S. Customs with detailed descriptions (manifests) of the contents of containers bound for the United States 24 hours before a container is loaded on board a vessel.

U

uncontrollable elements   Factors in the business environment over which the international marketer has no control or influence; may include competition, legal restraints, government controls, weather, consumer preferences and behavior, and political events. *See* **controllable elements**

United States–Canada Free Trade Agreement   An agreement, known as CFTA, between the United States and Canada designed to eliminate all trade barriers between the two nations.

unplanned change   A marketing strategy in which a company introduces a product into a market without a plan to influence the way the market's culture responds to or resists the company's marketing message. *See* **planned change**

utilitarian ethics   One of three principles of ethics (the others are **rights of the parties** and **justice or fairness**); it tests an action by asking if it optimizes the "common good" or benefits of all constituencies.

V

variable-cost pricing   A method of pricing goods in foreign markets in which a company is concerned only with the marginal or incremental costs of producing goods for sale in those markets. Firms using variable-cost pricing take the view that foreign sales are bonus sales. *See* **full-cost pricing; skimming**

VERS   *See* **voluntary export restraints**

voluntary export restraints (VERS)   Agreements, similar to **quotas,** between an importing country and an exporting country for a restriction on the volume of exports. Also known as **orderly market agreements (OMAs).**

W

World Trade Organization   *See* **WTO**

WTO   World Trade Organization. The organization formed in 1994 that encompasses the **GATT** structure and extends it to new areas that had not been adequately covered previously. The WTO adjudicates trade disputes. All member countries have equal representation.

a

Aaker, David A., 363n
Aaker, Jennifer L., 96, 479n, 486n
Abdullah, King of Jordan, 358
Abe, Shuzo, 339n
Abley, Mark, 524n
Abrahamson, Alan, 643
Abu-Nasr, Donna, 182n
Adams, Mike, 354
Adler, Nancy J., 129n, 560n
Aeppel, Timothy, 378
Agarkar, Ajit, 606
Agarwal, James, 322n
Agarwal, Sharda, 607
Ahmad, Khurshid, 185n
Akers, Chris, 642
Ala-Risku, Timo, 458n
Alden, Dana L., 362n, 470n
Aldonas, Grant, 624
Alevear, Maria Soledad, 571
Allison, Kevin, 365n
Almond, Phil, 206n
Alpert, Frank, 225n, 397n
Alston, Rennie, 435n
Amador, Manuel, 55
Ambler, Tim, 575n, 576
Amine, Lyn S., 58, 365n, 609, 617
Amos, John L., 448n
Anderson, Brooke, 131n
Anderson, Eugene W., 340n, 381n
Anderson, Nick, 380n
Anderson, Nicola, 485n
Ang, Kim Soon, 361n, 485n
Anhalt, Karen Nickel, 37n
Annan, Kofi, 358
Anterasian, Cathy, 138, 374n
Appert, Nicolas, 35
Applebaum, Anne, 153n
Arbenz, Jacobo, 61
Archer, Michelle, 96
Areddy, James T., 520n
Arensman, Russ, 373n
Argawal, Manoj K., 232n
Arino, Africa, 327n
Aristotle, 101, 672
Armstrong, David, 251n
Arndt, Michael, 655
Arnold, Catherine, 230n
Arnold, Mark J., 365n
Arnould, Eric J., 82n, 260
Arnst, Catherine, 358
Asbell, Bernard, 90
Atkinson, William, 446n
Attour, Suleiman, 475n
Au, Kevin, 118n
Auchard, Eric, 369
Auer, Peter, 72n
Auerbach, Jon G., 311
Axxin, Catherine N., 237n, 419n
Azuma, Nobukazu J., 407n

b

Baack, Sally A., 518n
Bachchan, Abishek, 606
Bachchan, Amitabh, 606
Bacon, Francis, 32
Badenhausen, Kurt, 7
Baek, Jungyim, 400n
Bagozzi, Richard P., 510n, 511n
Bailey, Thomas A., 30n
Baker, James C., 603
Baker, Ted, 120n
Balfour, Frederick, 200n, 357n, 483n
Ball, Deborah, 533n
Balladur, Edouard, 624
Banderas, Antonio, 131
Banerjee, Rajiv, 652

Bannon, Lisa, 111, 130n, 218n, 467
Barboza, David, 245
Barden, Mark, 598
Barker, Garry, 213
Barnett, Steve, 640
Baron, Steve, 231n
Barone, Michael, 60n
Barroso, Manuel, 114
Barshefsky, Charlene, 571
Barzilay, Judge, 542
Bastiat, Frederic, 39
Basto, Maria del Pilar, 357
Bate, Roger, 197n
Batra, Rajeev, 362n
Bauerlein, Valerie, 417n
Baumgartner, Hans, 229n
Beamish, Paul W., 329n
Beardon, Jeffrey Q., 329n
Beardon, William O., 333n
Beck, Ernest, 403
Becker, Gary S., 159
Beckham, David, 480, 481
Beeby, Robert, 605
Begum, Delora, 253
Behar, Howard, 597
Belderbos, Rene A., 504n
Bell, Alexander Graham, 38, 62
Bell, Thomas, 296n
Bellman, Eric, 533n
Bello, Daniel C., 420n
Belson, Ken, 599
Benedict XVI, Pope, 131
Benito, G. R. G., 11n
Bennett, Drake, 599
Bentham, Jeremy, 672
Bentley, S., 649n
Berman, Paul Schiff, 187n
Berner, Robert, 361
Bernhard, Prince, 624
Bernstein, Aaron, 283, 354
Berry, John, 460
Bhagat, Rabi S., 138
Bhagwati, Jagdish, 3n, 261n
Bierderman, Patricia Ward, 41
Bijmolt, Tammo H. A., 215n
Bilefsky, Dan, 524n
Binkley, Christina, 224n
Bitner, Mary Jo, 355n
Blackhurst, Chris, 655
Blair, Tony, 114, 207–208, 379
Bloch, Philippe, 598
Block, Robert, 163
Block, Steven A., 150n
Blume, Mary, 98
Bolivar, Simon, 35
Bonaparte, Napoleon, 34, 35, 93, 379
Bond, Michael Harris, 94n, 513n
Bonilla, Denise M., 7, 8, 411n
Boone, James, 358
Boone, Paula Fitzgerald, 201n
Boonstra, Jaap J., 94n, 513n
Borkowski, Susan C., 550n
Bornstein, Steven, 641
Boroditsky, Lera, 99n
Borzo, Jeannette, 387
Boscariol, John W., 181
Boston, William, 266n
Boudette, Neal E., 311
Bourguignon, Philippe, 615
Bovard, James, 38
Bove, Jose, 6
Brady, Diane, 327n, 463, 464n
Brand, Janice, 357
Brauchli, Marcus W., 192
Bremner, Brian, 4n, 82n, 270n, 383n
Brett, Jeanne M., 558n, 565n
Brewer, Geoffrey, 514

Brewer, Thomas L., 97n, 229n, 313n, 374n, 558n, 561n
Bright, Toby, 523, 659–661
Briley, Donnel A., 482
Broadhurst, John V., 457n
Brockner, Joel, 569
Brody, J. E., 634
Broegger, Peter, 111, 467
Bronnenberg, Bart, 494n
Brouthers, Keith D., 322n
Brown, Stuart S., 7n
Brundtland, Gro Harlem, 498
Brune, Klaus, 502n
Bryant, Barbara Everitt, 381n
Buchan, Nancy R., 138, 567n
Buchholz, Todd G., 27
Buck, Trevor, 138
Buckley, Peter J., 317n, 332n, 334n
Buckman, Rebecca, 652
Buke, Ilkim, 483n
Bulkeley, William M., 503
Bunau-Varilla, Philippe Jean, 55
Burdett, Tony, 63n
Burkink, Timothy J., 3n, 266n
Burroughs, James E., 227n
Burrows, Peter, 339n, 369, 383n
Burt, Tim, 490n, 644n, 645n
Bush, George W., 300
Bush, Jason, 208n
Byrant, Barbara Levitt, 340n

c

Cabell, David W. E., 550n
Cai, Deborah A., 580n
Calantone, Roger J., 220n
Callighan, James, 60
Cameron, Stevie, 627
Campbell, Kerry, 137n
Campbell, Nigel, 560n
Campbell-Hunt, Colin, 23n
Candelaria, Mike, 424
Cao, A. D., 40
Capar, N., 316n
Cape, Kevin, 524
Capell, Kerry, 357n, 403
Carey, John, 5n, 38, 201n
Carey, Mariah, 529
Carlisle, Kate, 599
Carlson, Chester, 41n
Caro, Dick, 463
Carpenter, Stanford W., 542
Carter, Martin J., 334n
Case, Brendan M., 527
Casellas, Pam, 29
Cashore, Harvey, 627
Castellini, James A., 596
Castono, Ivan, 484n
Castro, Fidel, 41, 154, 158
Cavusgil, S. Tamer, 23n, 313n, 322n, 422n, 423n, 502n, 528n, 533n, 538
Cha Jaesung, 340n, 381n
Chan, Allan K. K., 480n
Chandawarkar, Rahul, 326
Chandler, Clay, 408n
Chandler, Jennifer D., 98n, 163n, 282n, 505
Chandra, Aruna, 475n
Chandran, Rina, 620
Chang, Leslie, 223, 256n
Chao, Mike C. H., 365n
Chase, Chevy, 344
Chase, Marilyn, 98n
Chau, Patrick Y. K., 427n
Chauhan, Ramesh, 605, 607
Chavero, Diega, 651
Chazan, Guy, 151n, 296n

Chelariu, Christian, 420n
Chen, Chao C., 515n
Chen, Kathy, 91n, 270
Chen, Shih-Fen S., 12n, 332n
Chen Fu-Teng, 420n
Cheng, Jonathan, 332n, 483n
Cheng Han-cheng, 119
Chen Jiangtian, 99n
Chen Shui-bian, 271
Chen Tuping, 395
Cheosakul, Adith, 94n, 513n
Chequer, Pedro, 666
Chetty, Sylvie, 23n
Chintagunta, Pradeep K., 246n, 531n
Chirac, Jacques, 358, 616
Choi Chang-Bum, 329n
Choi San-Chul, 405n
Chou Ting-Jui, 420n
Chow, Raymond P. M., 112n, 116n
Christensen, Kim, 351n
Chung, Henry F. L., 475n
Chung-Leung Luk, 116n
Chun Hui, 565n
Chun Zhang, 528n, 533n
Cichelli, David J., 516
Cioletti, Jeff, 609
Clancy, Tom, 430
Clark, William C., 67n
Clendenning, Alan, 372n
Cleveland, Mark, 339n
Clifford, Mark L., 219n, 270, 505
Clinton, Bill, 158, 571, 624
Cloodt, Danielle, 194n
Clusius, Carolus, 89
Coates, Douglas J., 453n, 457n
Cohen, Laura, 357n
Cohen, Lizabeth, 30n
Cohn, Laura, 655
Cole, Melissa, 427n
Colin, Michelle, 128n
Collier, Paul, 281n
Colling, Trevor, 206n
Collins, John, 371
Columbus, Christopher, 30n
Confucius, 99, 101, 119
Conley, John, 382n
Connor, Steve, 68
Connors, Richard, 41
Contractor, Farok J., 19n, 318n, 385n, 568n
Cook, John E., 197n
Cook, Thomas A., 435n
Cooke, James A., 461n
Copeland, Lennie, 103
Copeland, Michael, 558n
Cortés, Hernan, 31
Costa, Robert R., 434
Cote, Joseph A., 361n
Coviello, Nicole E., 18n
Cox, R., 374
Crain, Rance, 312n
Cravens, David W., 516n
Crockett, Roger O., 369
Croson, Rachel T. S., 567n
Cummins, Chip, 207n, 396n
Currall, Steven C., 329n
Cusack, Robert, 41
Cyrus the Great, 149

d

Daniszewski, John, 261n
Darling, Juanita, 56
Darrigrand, Maritxu, 21
David, King of Israel, 279
Davies, John, 457
Davila, Anabella, 91n, 516n
Davila, Sheila, 657

Davis, David, 8n, 356n
Davis, Mary, 463
Dawes, Philip L., 139n, 510n
Dawson, Chester, 37n, 99n, 599, 617
Dawson, John, 404n
Dean, Jason, 332n
Debanjan, Mitra, 215n
DeBlij, Harm J., 62
Decourse, Christopher R., 86n
Dekimpe, Marnik G., 346n
Delaney, Kevin J., 62
De la Torre, Jose, 78n
Deligonul, Z. Seyda, 322n, 423n
Delio, Michelle, 354
Delios, Andrew, 322n, 332n
Dellios, Hugh, 148n
Demers, Julie, 298n
Dempsey, Judy, 293
Deng Rong, 192
Deng Xiaopeng, 192
De Niro, Robert, 352
Denton, Carlos, 229n
Deshpande, Rohit, 112n, 561n
Desiraju, Ramarao, 246n, 531n
Despande, Rhohit, 349n
Dhanaraj, Charles, 330n
Dhume, Sadanand, 50n
Diamantopoulos, Adamantios, 225n, 237n
Diamond, Jared, 3n, 87–90, 279, 348n
Dias, Bartolomeu, 30n
Diaz, Leonardo, 357
Diaz, Porfirio, 58, 59
DiCaprio, Leonardo, 482
Dickerson, Marla, 148n, 263n, 265n
Dininny, Shannon, 545n
Dion, Celine, 532
DiRenzo, Joe, 456n
Dixon, Robyn, 484n, 498
Doane, Chris, 456n
Doh, Jonathan P., 159n
Dolores, Rosana, 666
Donlan, Thomas G., 57
Donnellan, Eithne, 121n
Donovan, Kevin, 484
Donthu, Naveen, 94n, 105n
Doornaert, Andrew P., 451n
Douglas, Susan P., 22n, 86n, 365n
Douglass, Elizabeth, 147n
Doukas, John A., 332n
Dove, Timothy, 145
Dow, S., 413n
Doyen, Philippe, 624
Dravid, Rahul, 606
Dresser, N., 219
Drew, Walter H., 630
Drucker, Peter F., 115, 214n
Duncan, Robert, 106n
Dunfee, Thomas W., 137n
Dupuy de Lome, Enrique, 523, 658–661
Durairaj, N. V., 668
Durden, Geoffrey R., 237n
Dvorak, Phred, 340
Dwyer, Sean, 346n
Dyer, Barbara, 115n, 580n

e

Eadington, William R., 207n
Eaglesham, Jean, 529
Earley, P. Christopher, 113n, 521n
Earnest, Leslie, 21
Echikson, William D., 81
Eckhardt, Giana M., 361n
Eckholm, Erik, 223
Eden, Lorraine, 528n, 550n
Edison, Lee, 572n
Edison, Thomas Alva, 38, 62
Edmondson, Gail, 266n, 349n
Efron, Sonni, 156n
Eig, Jonathan, 165n
Eisner, Michael, 614, 615

Ekeledo, Ikechi, 324n
Ekman, Paul, 565
Elberse, Anita, 348n
El Fekih, Mohamed Habib, 625
Eliasberg, Jehoshua, 348n
Elizabeth I, 32
Elliot, Michael, 582n
Elliott, Richard, 626
Ellis, Paul, 396n
Ellison, Sarah, 229n
El-Rashidi, Yasmine, 352
El-Tablawy, Tarek, 131n
Elvira, Marta M., 91n, 516n
Endresen, Iver, 425n, 494n
Engardio, Pete, 283, 354, 505
Engels, Friedrich, 36
Ennew, Christine T., 200n
Enright, Michael J., 312n
Epia, Oke, 382
Epstein, Gene, 70n
Erdem, Tulin, 366n
Erevelles, Sunil, 483n
Erez, Miriam, 138
Erramilli, M. Krishna, 330n
Esteban, A. Gabriel, 560n
Estrel, Mik, 155n
Evans, Jody, 424n
Evans, Rob, 628
Evenko, Leonid I., 560n
Ewing, Jack, 201n, 403
Ezzell, Caro, 669

f

Fackler, Martin, 401n
Fahd, King, 624
Fairlamb, David, 137n
Faler, Brian, 296n
Fam, Kim-Shyan, 565n
Fang, Eric, 324n
Fang, Tony, 565n
Fanning, Shawn, 16
Farley, John U., 112n, 349n, 382n, 561n
Farrell, Diana, 37n
Farzad, Roben, 16, 191
Fassihi, Farnaz, 83n
Fayerman, Pamela, 234
Fehr, Ernst, 578n
Felsted, A., 645n
Fenton, Anna Healy, 515n
Ferner, Anthony, 206n
Ferreira, Leandro V., 68
Fields, George, 491
Fineman, Mark, 387n
Fink, Edward L., 580n
Fischbacher, Urs, 578n
Fisher, Aaron, 318
Fisher, Roger, 567n, 574n
Fishman, Brad, 386n
Flanigan, James, 3n
Fleming, John, 39
Fock, Henry, 118n
Fogel, Marya, 195
Ford, David, 396n
Ford, Henry, 40
Forgeard, Noel, 661
Fornell, Claes, 340n, 381n
Forster, Nick, 501
Fortgang, Ron S., 576n
Fortuny, Mariangels, 72n
Foss, Nicoli Juul, 237n
Fowler, Geoffrey A., 200n, 486n
Fox, Vicente, 148
France, Karen Russo, 201n
Francis, June, 363n
Francis Ferdinand, Archduke, 40
Freedman, Alix M., 603
French, Robert T., 482
Frerichs, George R., 538
Friedland, Jonathan, 527
Friedman, Thomas L., 5n, 105n, 156n, 281n, 326, 349n
Friedman, Wayne, 101
Fryer, Bronwyn, 515n

Fuhrmans, Vanessa, 83n
Fukuyama, Francis, 90
Fuller, Thomas, 48n
Fulmer, Melinda, 111, 218n
Fulton, Robert, 34
Fu Ping Ping, 94n, 118n
Furness, Victoria, 99n
Fuyuno, Ichiko, 182n, 183

g

Gaines, Ann Graham, 56n
Galuszka, Peter, 464n
Gandhi, Indira, 72
Gandhi, Rajiv, 605, 626
Ganguly, Saurav, 606
Gannon, Martin J., 100
Gassenheimer, Julie B., 515n, 580n
Gates, Bill, 214, 477
Gates, Rowena, 448n
Gautam, Naik, 74n
Gavino, Jacinto C., Jr., 511n
Gavlen, Morten, 425n, 494n
Gazda, Gregory M., 603
Gedajlovic, Eric, 120n
Gelb, Betsy, 480n
Genghis Khan, 28
Georgoff, David M., 232n
Germain, Richard, 339n
Ghauri, Pervez, 332n, 558n, 565n
Ghemawat, Pankaj, 98n, 312n, 314n
Ghosh, Soumen, 460n
Ghosh, Sugata, 185n
Ghoshal, Sumantra, 22n
Gibson, Cristina B., 100n, 118n, 138
Gibson, Richard, 655
Gill, Kerry, 498
Gilland, Bernard, 56n
Gilley, Bruce, 258
Gilly, Mary C., 501, 503n, 520n
Gilmore, Joe, 573
Giridharadas, Anand, 72n, 272n, 403n
Giuliani, Rudolph, 69
Glader, Paul, 38
Glenn, David, 91n
Golder, Peter N., 94n, 215n
Gomes, Roger, 609
Gomez, Jim, 4n
Gong-ming Qian, 510n
Gonzales, Alberto, 197
Goodman, Peter S., 50n, 318
Gopalakrishna, Srinath, 386n
Gorbachev, Mikhail, 6, 294
Gordon, Howard L., 538
Gotman, Ingela, 316
Govinda, 606
Graham, Jefferson, 207n
Graham, John L., 3n, 8, 86n, 96, 97n, 98n, 99n, 119, 124n, 125n, 130n, 134n, 138, 139n, 156n, 158, 163n, 197n, 223n, 225n, 279, 374n, 397n, 503n, 505, 511n, 512, 513n, 518n, 557, 558, 561n, 562, 564, 565n, 568, 573, 577, 579
Grant, Jeremy, 198n
Grant, Ulysses S., 58
Granzin, Kent L., 151n
Grbac, Bruno, 3n, 266n
Green, Paul E., 222n
Greer, Thomas V., 603
Gregory, Annie, 459n, 460n
Gress, Stefan, 222n
Grether, E. T., 374
Griffith, David A., 12n, 322n, 424n, 475n, 502n
Griffith, Victoria, 524
Griffiths, Katherine, 655
Griggs, Lewis, 103
Grignon, Francois, 148n
Griswold, David T., 298n

Grogaard, B., 11n
Grossman, Lev, 357
Grossman, Terry, 83n
Grotius, Hugo, 32
Grove, Andrew, 369
Grow, Brian, 6, 208n
Gruen, Arthur, 642
Guang Yang, 125n, 575n, 576
Guillen, Mauro, 323n
Gulyani, Sumila, 261n
Gupta, Ritesh, 652
Gupta, Sunil, 608
Gupta, Sunita, 618
Gurhan-Canli, Zeynep, 365n
Gwynee, Peter, 411n
Gysel, Peter, 624

h

Ha, Oanh, 206n
Ha, Young-Won, 349n
Haas, Robert W., 374
Habayeb, Salim, 667
Hadjimarcou, John, 570n
Hagedoom, John, 194n
Haifa Sun, 565n
Haji-Ioannou, Stelios, 644, 646, 648, 649
Hakim, Zakki P., 546n
Hall, Douglas T., 521n
Hall, Edward T., 86, 97, 105, 122–123, 126, 139, 568
Hall, William, 202n
Hamilton, Gary G., 119
Hammerle, Ron, 234
Hammond, Aline, 652
Hammond, Allen, 261n
Han, Jin K., 360n
Hannibal, 65
Haq, Mahmudul, 135
Hardesty, Greg, 519n
Hargreaves, Deborah, 529
Harris, Greg, 475n
Harris, Philip R., 579
Harrison, Lawrence E., 24n, 86n, 140
Hart, Stuart L., 312n, 322n, 652
Hartnett, William M., 69
Harvey, Michael, 420n, 515n, 528n
Harzing, Anne-Wil, 22n
Hashai, Niron, 317n
Hathaway, Misty, 470n, 639
Hauser, John R., 340n, 381n
Havemann, Joel, 147n
Hawley, Susan, 627
Hawthorne, Peter, 620
Hayes, Andrew F., 382n
Healey, Jon, 197n
Healey, Nigel M., 231n
Hedlund, Kyle, 57
Heijltjes, Marielle G., 504n
Heinrichs, Markus, 578n
Henderson, Mark, 74n
Henderson, Pamela W., 361n
Hendon, Donald W., 558n
Hendon, Rebecca Angeles, 558n
Heneidy, Mohamed, 352
Henisz, W. J., 322n
Hennessy-Fiske, Molly, 69
Henry the Navigator, 30n
Henry VIII, 31
Herbig, Paul, 558n, 617
Herman, Eric, 655
Herskovitz, Melvin, 86n
Hewett, Kelly, 333n, 334n, 480n
Hewitt, Patricia, 627
Higashide, Hiro, 94n, 513n
Higgins, Andrew, 508
Hill, Grant, 471
Hill, Jim, 529
Hillman, Amy J., 165n
Hilsenrath, Jon E., 340n
Himmelsbach, Vawn, 63n
Hirsch, Jerry, 154n
Hodge, Robert W., 84n

Hodge, Sheila, 569
Hodges, Nick, 669
Hodgson, James Day, 86, 96, 111, 124n, 125n, 130n, 557, 558n, 563, 564, 565, 568, 573, 577
Hodgson, N., 644n, 645n
Hofstede, Frenkel ter, 20n, 95n
Hofstede, Geert, 86, 94, 95, 105, 112, 116, 118, 125, 138, 139, 140, 143, 568
Holancova, Denisa, 486n
Holley, David, 380n
Holmes, Stanley, 331, 347n, 374n, 403, 523, 599
Holmstrom, Jan, 458n
Holt, Douglas B., 361n
Holton, Richard H., 560n
Holtschneider, Petra, 21
Holzmuller, Hartmut H., 237n
Hon, Nguyen Van, 651
Honeycutt, Earl D., 93n
Hongxin Zhao, 332n
Hookham, M., 649n
Ho Suk-Ching, 402n
Houston, H. Rika, 134n, 139n
Houston, Michael J., 361n
Hovanesian, Der, 182n
Howard, Susanna, 652
Howell, John P., 94n, 513n
Hsee, Christopher K., 191
Hsu, Dau-lin, 119
Hsu, Maxwell, 346n
Hsu Chin-Chun, 19n, 318n, 385n
Huff, Leonard C., 470n
Hughes, Scott, 290
Hui, Michael K., 118n
Hui, Sylvia, 76n
Hu Jintao, 153, 270
Hult, Tomas M., 355n
Hunsaker, Bill, 621–622
Huntington, Samuel P., 24n, 86n, 140
Hurd, Mark, 361
Hussein, Saddam, 204
Huygen, Maarten, 98
Hwang, Suein L., 565
Hyde, J., 647n
Hyman, Mark, 643

Iddles, Stuart, 627
Iger, Bob, 360
Ignatius, David, 652
Ihlwan, Moon, 383n
Ilieva, Janet, 231n
Im, Subim, 349n
Inkpen, Andrew C., 329n
Irala, Xabier de, 660–661
Irano, Nicole, 274n
Iritani, Evelyn, 4n, 6n, 49n, 98n, 154n, 553n
Isa, Marisa Mohd, 459n, 572n
Isabella, Lynn A., 328n, 329
Islam, Nurul, 135
Isralni, Sumit, 618
Itoi, Kay, 401n
Iwata, Edward, 215n
Iyer, V. R. Krishna, 608

James, LeBron, 200
Jan, Amal Kumar, 44
Jardine, Alexandra, 634
Jefferson, Thomas, 35, 158
Jesus, 279
Jetter, Frances, 106
Jewkes, Stephen, 65n
Jiang Feng, 558n
Jimhong Xie, 580n
Joachimsthaler, Erich, 363n
Jobs, Steven, 213, 214
Johansson, Johny K., 502n
John, King of England, 29

Johnson, Eric J., 567n
Johnson, J. P., 118n, 566n
Johnson, Kay, 652
Johnson, Michael D., 340n, 381n
Johnson, Paul, 485n
Johnson, Reed, 504n
Johnston, Eric, 340
Johnston, Megan, 292
Jolibert, Alain, 560n
Jolly, Deepak, 605
Jones, Marian V., 18n
Jordan, Mary, 348
Jordan, Miriam, 64n, 253, 620, 658, 669
Juarez, Luis F., 550n
Judge, Paul C., 369
Jung, Kwon, 223n

Kadafi, Muammar el, 151n
Kaku, Shisei, 304n
Kaleka, Anna, 323n
Kambara, Kenneth M., 501, 520n
Kam-hon Lee, 133n, 510n, 560n
Kamins, Michael, 225n, 397n
Kamprad, Ingvar, 316
Kanchankoti, Deepa, 620
Kandemir, Destan, 355n
Kanso, Al, 474n
Kant, Emmanuel, 672
Kapferer, Jean-Noel, 362n
Kapoor, Jagdeep, 604, 609
Kapoor, Kareena, 606
Kapoor, Sunil, 605
Karakaya, Yunus, 575n
Kari, Juhani, 558
Karkkainen, Mikko, 458n
Karnitschnig, Matthew, 524n
Karp, Jonathan, 83n
Karrass, Chester, 572, 580
Katahira, Hotaka, 491
Katib, Mark, 354
Kato, Anna, 598
Katsikeas, Constantine S., 323n, 570n
Kawaguchi, Yoriko, 74n
Keefe, Lisa M., 357
Keeton, Ann, 464n
Keillor, Bruce D., 355n
Kelleher, Katie, 598
Keller, Kevin Lane, 338n
Kellner, Tomas, 27
Kennedy, David M., 30n
Kennedy, Jeff, 94n, 513n
Kennedy, John F., 58
Kenny, Timothy, 533
Kerr, Simeon, 131n
Kerwin, Kathleen, 4n, 270n
Kevan, Tom, 463
Khaddur, Munir Abu, 627
Khai, Hoang, 340
Khamenei, Ayatollah Ali, 150
Khan, Fardeen, 606
Khan, Shafiq, 428, 429
Khan, Zaheer, 606
Khanna, Tarun, 138, 312n
Khasru, Atahar, 135
Khomeini, Ayatollah Ruhollah, 150
Kiley, David, 200n, 361, 483n
Kim, Daekwan, 311
Kim, Dong Ki, 560n
Kim, Joghoon, 531n
Kim, Keysuk, 397n
Kim, Stephen Keysuk, 422n
Kinetz, Erika, 313n
King, Max, 126
King, Niel, Jr., 542
Kipling, Rudyard, 41, 582
Kirkpatrick, David, 369
Kirpalani, Manek, 419n
Klapper, Bradley S., 65n
Klein, Jill Gabrielle, 364n
Klein, Saul, 329n
Kling, Katrina, 316

Knemeyer, A. Michael, 460n
Knight, Gary A., 23n
Koch, Chris, 464n
Koh Chin Ling, 70n
Kohl, Helmut, 626
Koisumi, Junichiro, 153
Koop, G. Everett, 672
Koopman, Paul, 94n, 513n
Kopalle, Praveen K., 382n
Kopytoff, Vern, 181
Kosfeld, Michael, 578n
Kotabe, Masaski, 229n, 313n, 316n, 327n
Kotler, Philip, 338n
Kozak, John, 163
Kranenburg, Hans van, 194n
Kranhold, Kathryn, 205, 333n, 524n
Kras, Eva S., 116n
Krasner, Stephen D., 156n
Kraul, Chris, 56, 356n
Krauss, Clifford, 485n
Krieger, Abba M., 222n
Kripalani, Manjeet, 152, 251n, 273n, 283, 354, 357n, 383n, 408n, 488n
Kuber, Girish, 76
Kublai Khan, 29
Kumar, Rajesh, 561n, 565n
Kumar, Vikas, 609
Kundu, Sumit K., 19n, 318n, 385n
Kunii, Irene M., 403
Kurtenbach, Elaine, 46n
Kurzweil, Ray, 83n
Kwok Leong, 138, 569
Kwong Chan, 528n, 533n

Lacassagne, Marie-Francoise, 94n, 513n
Laczniak, Gene R., 673n
Lages, Cristiana Raquel, 324n
Lages, Luis Filipe, 324n
Lagnado, Alice, 6
Lai, Mengkuan, 485n
Laidler-Kylander, Nathalie, 160n, 360n
Lam, Janet P. Y., 363n
Lam, N. Mark, 119, 139n, 197n, 565n
Lama, Agnes, 6
Lambert, Richard, 61n
Landler, Mark, 202n, 340n
Landon, Tammy, 380n
Landro, Laura, 121n
Lang, Gretchen, 520n
Lang, Jack, 8
Lang, L. H. P., 332n
Lantz, Garold, 223n
Larke, Roy, 413n
Larmer, Brook, 258
Laroche, Michael, 339n
Larson, Gary, 217
Lathigee, Jonathan, 482
Lavery, Brian, 193n
Lawrence, John J., 649n
Lawrence (of Arabia), Thomas Edward, 279
Lax, David A., 576n
Laxman, V. V. S., 606
Leahy, John, 523, 659–661
Lebowitz, Lewis E., 544
Lee, Don Y., 139n, 166n, 191, 219n, 269n, 337, 351n, 356n, 510n, 528n
Lee, Jane Lanhee, 348n
Lee, Jenny, 112n
Lee, Matthew KO, 427n
Leeds, Jeff, 16
Lee Jung-Hee, 405n
Leek, Sheena, 388n
Lee Tee Jong, 401
Lee Yih Hwai, 361n, 485n, 486n
Leggett, Karby, 223
Leigh, David, 628

Leigh, Thomas W., 562n
Leistikow, Nicole, 620
Lemos Fernandes, Maria Eugenia, 666
Lenartowicz, T., 118n, 566n
Lenin, Vladimir, 40
Leonardelli, Geoffrey J., 572n
Leong, Siew Meng, 361n
Leonidou, Leonidas C., 312n, 435n, 570n
Lepkowska-White, Elzbieta, 486n
Le Poole, Samfrits, 559n
Leung, Kwok, 427n
Levey, David H., 7n
Levi, Guido Carlos, 666
Levine, Robert, 126, 127
Levy, Sidney J., 538
Lewicki, Roy J., 558n, 559n, 568n
Li, Dan, 550n
Li Fangfang, 316
Li Jianghong, 72n
Lilien, Gary L., 374n
Lim, Kai H., 427n
Lin, C. Y., 560n
Lincke, Andreas, 575n
Ling Chen, 565n
Linkin Park, 16
Linton, Ralph, 104n
Litterer, Joseph A., 559n
Liu, Sandra S., 502n
Liu Li, 543n
Livingstone, David, 36
Li Yue, 471
Li Zhang, 420n
Locke, John, 672
Locke, Mary, 50n
Loeb, Sandra G., 223n
Lohr, Steve, 191
London, Ted, 322n
Lopez-Bowlan, Ellie, 60
Lorange, Peter, 568n
Louis XI, 30n
Louis XV, 33
Lou Yadong, 187n, 329n, 330n, 332n
Lovely, William, 72n
Low, George S., 516n
Lubatkin, Michael, 120n
Lubetzky, Daniel, 3
Lublin, Joann S., 520n
Luce, Edward, 620
Ludden, Jennifer, 671n
Luhnow, David, 203n
Luna, Adriana, 221
Luna, David, 485n
Lunman, Kim, 482
Luo, Y., 256n
Luostarinen, Reijo, 419n
Lutscg-Emmenegger, Margrit, 449n
Luxner, Larry, 78n
Lyles, Marjorie A., 329n, 330n
Lynch, David J., 77n
Lyon, Paula, 484

MacAvoy, Thomas C., 328n, 329
Macdonald, Godfrey, 99
Macintosh, J., 648n
Madarang, Raphael, 462n
Madden, Normandy, 259n, 652
Madden, Thomas J., 480n
Mader, Robert P., 348
Madhavan, P. R. Bindhu, 667–668
Madjid, Aidil A., 569
Madonna, 192, 452
Magana-Campos, Juan A., 377n
Magnier, Mark, 152n, 208n, 234n
Magnusson, Paul, 5n, 147n
Mahajan, Vijay, 193n, 469n, 494n
Maheswaran, Durairaj, 365n
Maitland, Alison, 652
Maitland, Elizabeth, 18n
Makino, Shige, 332n
Malhotra, Naresh K., 322n

Malik, Huma Aamir, 72n
Mallalah, Bader, 625
Malouf, Mary Brown, 158n
Malykhina, Elena, 462n
Mani, Rajesh, 606, 607
Mani, S., 667
Mannix, Elizabeth A., 569
Mansell, John, 642
Mao Zedong, 42
Mapes, Glynn, 524
Marburber, John H., III, 358
Marchetti, Michele, 503, 516n, 517
Markoff, John, 386n
Marlin, Steve, 434
Marquand, Robert, 66n
Marshall, Tyler, 154n
Martin, Nancy M., 3n, 156n, 158
Marx, Karl, 36
Massey, Anne P., 427n
Mathur, Anil, 228n, 513n
Matlack, Carol, 137n, 655
Matthews, Robert Guy, 45n, 480n
Mavondo, Felix T., 424n
McArthur, Kate, 634
McCargo, Duncan, 56n
McCaughey, Jack, 621
McClelland, David C., 120, 122
McClenahen, John S., 464n
McDaniels, Andrea, 669
McEachern, Ronald, 604
McGuire, J., 413n
McKay, Betsy, 256n, 296n
McKee, Steve, 91n
McKenna, Barrie, 530n
McMahon, Colin, 316
McNally, Regina C., 502n
McNaughton, Rod B., 419n
McPeak, Merril A., 448n
McPhate, Mike, 487
McWilliams, Gary, 369, 425n
Meadows, Andrew, 157n
Mee-Kau Nyaw, 330n
Meissner, Hans-Gunther, 560n
Melinster, Julius, 629n
Meller, Paula, 98n, 202n, 374n
Menn, Joseph, 16, 208n
Merchant, Khozem, 620
Mesak, Haani, 346n
Meucci, Antonio, 62
Meulenberg, Matthew T. G., 364n
Meyer, Klaus E., 255n
Meyers, Matthew B., 528n
Michaels, Daniel, 331, 387n, 523, 573n, 661
Middlehoff, Thomas, 16
Mika Gabrielsson, V. H., 419n
Milbank, Dana, 290, 452
Mill, John Stuart, 36
Miller, Arthur, 508
Miller, Rich, 36n
Miller, T. Christian, 424
Millman, Joel, 83n, 382
Ming Zeng, 332n
Minton, John W., 558n, 568n
Mintu-Wimsatt, Alma, 515n, 580n
Mishari, Ahmed al, 625
Mitchener, Brandon, 202n, 297, 378, 380n
Mittal, Anuradha, 652
Mnouchkine, Ariane, 614
Moen, Oystein, 425n, 494n
Moffett, Sebastian, 75n, 81
Mohamad, Mahathir, 304n
Mohammed, 279
Mohr, Jakki J., 260
Molenaar, Mary J., 603
Money, R. Bruce, 138, 223n, 374n, 503n, 511n, 512, 513n, 518n, 558n
Monroe, James, 35, 60
Montgomery, David M., 356n
Montoya-Weiss, Mitzi, 427n
Moore, Demi, 482
Moran, Robert T., 558n, 579
Morgan, Fred, 483n

Morgan, Neil A., 323n
Morris, D., 44n
Morton, W. Scott, 104n
Morwitz, Vick, 531n
Mosakowski, Elaine, 113n, 521n
Moszynski, Peter, 65n
Mowat, Jennifer, 648
Moxon, Richard W., 78n
Mudambi, Ram, 237n
Muhammad II, 30n
Mukherjee, S. K., 608
Mulchand, Arti, 381n
Mun, Thomas, 31
Munoz, Lorenzo, 197n
Murdick, Robert G., 232n
Murdoch, Rupert, 641, 642
Murphy, Paul R., 460n
Murray, J. Alex, 603
Murray, Janet Y., 327n
Murray, Sarah, 153n
Muskie, Edmund J., 601, 602
Myerhoff, Matt, 451n
Myers, Gifford, 51
Myers, Matthew B., 220n, 424n

Nabil, Amr, 261n
Nachum, Lilach, 332n
Nadeau, Barbie, 67n
Nader, Ralph, 42
Nadkarni, Shripad, 607
Naidoo, Anand, 62
Naik, Gautam, 73n, 98n
Nair, Harsikesh, 246n
Nakata, Cheryl, 349n
Nanda, R., 11n
Nan Zhou, Joe, 327n
Naor, Jacob, 673n
Naquin, Charles E., 575n
Narisetti, Raju, 527
Naude, Peter, 388n
Navarro, Pietro, 237n
Neelankavil, James P., 228n, 513n
Nelson, Emily, 403, 658
Nelson, Richard Alan, 474n
Nemstova, Svetlana, 498
Nesdoly, Tracy, 529
Newman, Matthew, 209n, 427n
Newton, Isaac, 33
Ng, Eric, 371n
Ng, Loretta, 70n
Nguyen, Duc Tri, 330n
Nguyen, Rachel, 483n
Nguyen, Terrence, 461n
Nhon, Xa, 652
Niak, Gautam, 83n
Nicholas, Stephen, 18n
Nickerson, Colin, 484
Nijssen, Edwin J., 365n
Nisbett, Richard E., 87n, 101, 139n, 569
Nishimura, Junji, 398n
Nonaka, Ikujiro, 502n
Noriega, Jaime L., 480n
Noriega, Manuel, 61
Norris, Floyd, 153n, 482n
Notoji, Masako, 616
Novicevic, Milorad M., 420n
Nunes, Joseph C., 191
Nunn, Dana, 552n

Oberoi, Vivek, 607
Ochoa, Labastida, 148
Ockova, Alena, 560n
O'Connor, Ashling, 558n
O'Dell, John, 297n
Ogawa, Naohiro, 84n
O'Grady, Mary Anastasia, 61n
Oh, Changho, 397n
Okamoto, Takehiko, 669
O'Keefe, Robert, 427n

Okello, Brenda, 135
Olenik, J. Kenneth, 104n
Olsen, Svein Ottar, 364n
Olsson, Ulf H., 364n
Omidtar, Pierre, 81
Ono, Yumiko, 81, 658
Onzo, Naoto, 225n, 397n
Oon, Clarisa, 223
Orth, Ulrich R., 486n
Orwall, Bruce, 617
Overholt, Alison, 652
Ozsomer, Aysegul, 363n

Paarlberg, Robert L., 98n
Paas, Leo J., 215n
Pae, Jae H., 475n
Pae, Peter, 154n, 330n
Page, Thomas J., Jr., 220n
Paghunathan, V. K., 72n
Paice, Robin, 379
Painter, John J., 151n
Palepu, Krishna G., 138
Palmeri, Christopher, 131n, 467
Palmisano, Sam, 514
Pande, Bhanu, 620
Pangarkar, Nitin, 329n
Park, Heungsooa, 349n
Park, Seung H., 329n
Parker, Ginny, 524n
Parker, Philip M., 90, 232n, 341n, 346n
Parmar, Arundhati, 231n, 484n, 487, 620
Parvatiyar, Atul, 388n
Pasa, Selda, 94n, 513n
Pastin, Mark, 670
Patricof, Alan J., 49n, 261n
Patton, Bruce, 567n, 574n
Paul, Anthony, 348
Paulson, Gaylen D., 575n
Pearce, Jone L., 134n, 578n
Pearl, Daniel, 547
Pedersen, Bent, 322n
Pedersen, Torben, 237n, 322n
Pélé, 579
Peltz, James F., 356n
Penaloza, Lisa, 501, 520n
Peng, Mike W., 217n
Pengzhu Zhang, 388n
Peracchio, Laura A., 485n
Peres, Shimon, 598
Perlmutter, Howard, 22n
Peron, Juan, 61
Perry, Matthew C., 37, 56
Pesola, Maija, 342
Petrick, Joseph A., 185n
Petrini, Carlo, 598
Phan, A., 342
Phillips, Michael M., 153n, 536n
Piercy, Nigel F., 516n
Pierson, Jean, 625
Ping Ping Fu, 513n
Pirson, Jean, 625
Polachek, Solomon W., 281n
Pollay, Richard W., 200n
Polo, Marco, 29, 84
Pontoniere, Paolo, 76n
Pool, Brian, 358
Popham, Peter, 290
Pornpitakpan, Chanthika, 503n
Porter, Richard E., 219
Portman, Robert, 298n
Portnoy, David, 440
Postrel, Virginia, 159
Power, Damien, 380n
Prada, Paulo, 617
Prahalad, C. K., 259–260, 261n, 343n, 650, 652
Prasad, Ashutosh, 469n, 494n
Prater, Edmund, 460n
Pratt, Mary K., 384n
Prestowitz, Clyde V., 514
Price, Elizabeth, 154n
Prieto, Leonel, 94n, 513n

Prussia, Gregory E., 363n
Prystay, Cris, 652
Punnett, B. J., 559n
Putin, Vladimir, 150–151, 296, 657

Qian Gong-ming, 133n
Qin Jize, 183
Quelch, John A., 160n, 360n
Quesnay, Francois, 33

Ragozzino, Roberto, 332n
Rahman, A. R., 606
Rai, Aishwarya, 607
Raia, Kelly, 435n
Raizada, Deepa, 609
Rajan, Muli, 380n
Rajendran, S., 255
Ramachandran, Raja, 263
Ramamurti, Ravi, 255n
Raman, Anand P., 363n
Ramstad, Evan, 425n
Rangaswamy, Arvind, 374n
Rao, Alaka N., 134n, 578n
Rao, Narasimha, 604
Rapoport, Carla, 270
Rasad, Ashutosh, 193n
Ratnesar, Romesh, 56n
Rawls, John, 672
Raymond, Mary Anne, 531n
Rebello, Joseph, 154n
Redding, Gordon, 137n
Reddy, Sudeep, 37n
Red Hot Chili Peppers, 498
Reed, Susan E., 165n, 221
Reeves, Keanu, 482
Reid, Tim, 160m
Reinhardt, Andy, 202n, 296n
Renko, Natasa, 3n, 266n
Resnick, Rosalind, 452
Reuer, Jeffrey J., 332n
Reynolds, N. L., 225n
Rialp, Alex, 419n
Ricardo, David, 35
Ricart, Joan Enric, 312n
Rice-Osley, Mark, 51n
Richburg, Keith B., 245
Richter, Paul, 387n
Riding, Alan, 207n
Ries, Philippe, 536n
Rifkin, Jeremy, 68n
Rilian Qu, 200n
Rindfleisch, Aric, 227n
Rivoli, Pietra, 3n, 260
Roath, A. S., 422n
Roberts, Dexter, 191, 270, 349n
Roberts, Julia, 207–208
Robinson, Jonathan, 208n
Robinson, Simon, 620
Rodriguez, Peter, 528n
Rogers, Everett M., 106n, 346
Rohrbacher, Dana, 358
Rohter, Larry, 57
Rokeach, M., 568n
Roman, Sergio, 510n, 511n
Romero, Karla, 657
Roosevelt, Theodore, 55, 60, 202
Rose, Elizabeth L., 18n
Rosenthal, Elisabeth, 21, 131n
Ross, Emma, 634
Ross, William T., 137n
Rossant, John, 137n
Rostow, Walt W., 247, 249, 375
Roth, K., 334n
Roth, M. S., 334n
Roth, Martin S., 480n
Rothe, Frank, 621–622
Rouzies, Dominique, 509n, 511n
Row!ey, Ian, 99n
Ruamsook, Kusumal, 435n
Ruckman, Karen, 349n
Ruckman, Rebecca, 371n

Rugman, Alan M., 18n, 97n, 229n, 315n, 374n, 558n, 561n
Ruhlen, Merrit, 99n
Ruiz, Salvador, 510n, 511n
Runzo, Joseph, 3n, 156n, 158
Russell, Craig J., 12n, 322n
Rust, Roland T., 340n, 381n
Rutkowski, Anne Francoise, 561n
Ryan, Jordan, 40
Ryans, John K., Jr., 475n
Ryle, Sarah, 145

S

Saatsoglou, Paul, 222n
Saccomano, Ann, 77n
Sacks, Danielle, 222n
Sakano, Tokoaki, 225n, 397n
Sale, Nigel, 102
Salinas de Gotari, Carlos, 296
Salmen, Lawrence F., 261n
Salter, Jim, 188
Samiee, Saeed, 274n, 475n
Samovar, Larry A., 219
Samuelson, Robert J., 82n
Sanchez, Marcela, 61n
Sandell, S., 342
Sandholtz, Wayne, 134n
San Martin, Nancy, 159
Sano, Yoshihiro, 86n, 96, 124n, 125n, 130n, 557, 563, 564, 568, 568n, 573, 577
Santos-Dumont, Alberto, 57
Saranow, Jennifer, 387n
Sarvary, Miklos, 552n
Sato, Yoshinobu, 397n
Saunders, David M., 558n, 559n, 568n
Savary, Miklos, 346n
Schechter, Brian, 642
Scheer, Vivian C., 565n
Scheier, Rachel, 135
Schell, Jonathan, 281n
Scheper-Hughes, Nancy, 98n, 357n
Schick, David G., 516
Schindler, Robert M., 100n, 531n
Schlosser, Eric, 98n
Schmitt, Bernd H., 226n, 361n, 362n, 485n
Schomer, David C., 597
Schrage, Burkhard, 150n
Schreiber, Karlheinz, 626–627
Schuiling, Isabelle, 362n
Schultz, Clifford J., III, 3n, 266n
Schultz, Howard, 596–597, 599
Schultz, John D., 460n
Schumacher, Michael, 481
Schuster, Camille, 558n
Schut, Frederik T., 222n
Schwarz, Theodore, 560n
Schwarzenegger, Arnold, 482
Sciolino, Elaine, 5n, 200n
Scupin, Raymond, 86n
Sebenius, James K., 559n, 576n
Sebutinde, Julie, 135
Segal, Evan, 378
Segalla, Michael, 509n, 511n
Sell, Susan, 194n
Selleck, Tom, 482
Sellers, Patricia, 222n, 283
Seltman, Kent, 470n, 639
Semon, Thomas T., 216n
Sen, Shunu, 620
Serra, Junipero, 282n
Servan-Schreiber, J. J., 31
Shahrim, Azura, 138
Shakespeare, William, 31
Shaoming Zou, 324n, 502n
Shari, Michael, 505
Sharma, Subhash, 227n
Shatrujeet, N., 652
Shay, Carrie, 598
Shay, Jeffrey P., 518n
Shelton, Ed, 658
Shenkar, O., 559n

Shenkar, Oded, 330n, 332n
Sherwood, B., 648n
Sheth, Jagdish, 388n
Shi, Linda H., 502n
Shishkin, Philip, 382n
Shi Zhang, 226n, 362n, 485n
Shook, David, 164n, 395
Shorris, Earl, 508n
Shouming Zou, 313n
Shu Chen-Chi, 515n
Shukla, Seema, 620
Shuming Zhao, 324n
Sia Choon Ling, 427n
Siddiqi, Moin, 442n
Siekman, Philip, 318, 371
Siemens, Werner, 37
Simester, Duncan I., 340n, 381n
Simintiras, A. C., 225n
Simkins, E., 644n, 646n
Simmet, Heike, 237n
Simmons, Lee C., 100n, 531n
Simonin, Bernard L., 327n
Simpson, Glenn R., 135
Simran, 607
Sin, Leo Y. M., 112n, 116n
Singh, Harbhajan, 606
Singh, Manmohan, 604
Sinha, Shuchi, 620
Sinkula, James M., 237n
Sirmon, David G., 328n, 558n
Sithole, Isaya Muriwo, 305n
Sivakumar, K., 324n
Skirius, John, 58
Slater, Joanna, 83n
Slywotsky, Adrian, 402n
Smith, Adam, 33, 34, 35, 90, 117, 138, 672
Smith, Craig S., 395, 409
Smith, Geri, 5n, 147n, 300n
Smith, N. Craig, 137n
Smith, Orin, 597
Smith, Paul M., 386n
Smith, Timothy, 386n
Sohal, Amrik S., 380n
Sokal, Robert R., 99n
Solberg, Carl, 474n
Solbert, Carl Arthur, 312n
Solis, Luis, 649n
Solomon, Jay, 160m
Song, Michael, 115n
Song, Sora, 357
Song, X. Michael, 580n
Sonoda, Yoshitaka, 184
Souchon, Anne L., 237n
Sowers, Carol, 59n
Spagat, Elliott, 221
Sparks, John A., 603
Speiser, Mitchell, 596
Spekman, Robert E., 328n, 329
Spudlich, Helmut, 598
Spurlock, Morgan, 633n, 654
Squeo, Anne Marie, 547
Sridhar, N., 609
Srinivas, Ekkirala S., 94n, 513n
Srinivasan, Raji, 374n
Stamborski, 188
Standage, Tom, 90
Stanton, J., 648n
Stark, Anna, 565n
Starlicki, Daniel P., 569
Starobin, Paul, 296n
Stecklow, Steve, 157n, 603
Steenkamp, Jan-Benedict E. M., 20n, 95n, 229n, 362n, 364n
Steensma, H. Kevin, 329n, 330n
Stefani, Lisa A., 219
Stein, Mark A., 537n
Stelzer, Irwin, 145
Stephenson, George, 35
Stern, Stefan, 652
Stevenson, Thomas H., 550n
Stewart, Heather, 4n
Stojanovic, Jovan, 163
Stone, Andrea, 56n
Stone, Brad, 1243

Stremersch, Stefan, 233n, 346n, 347n
Stripp, William G., 558n
Strout, Erin, 514, 516n
Styles, Chris, 575n, 576
Suh Seong Mu, 409
Sullivan, Kevin, 348
Sullivan, Tim, 255
Summers, John O., 562n
Sunderland, Julie E., 49n, 261n
Swan, Joseph, 62
Sweney, Mark, 655

t

Taagerpera, Rein, 134n
Tach, Sharon, 419n
Taewon Suh, 332n
Tagliabue, John, 6
Tai, Susan, 475n
Tai-Kuang Peng, 94n, 513n
Takenaka, Kiyoshi, 315n
Talukdar, Debabrata, 261n
Tamimi, Nabil, 380n
Tang, Sara, 560n
Tannen, Deobrah, 571n
Tanner, John F., Jr., 531n
Tashiro, Hiroko, 82n, 99n
Tata, Jasmine, 94n, 513n
Tavassoli, Nader T., 232n, 341n, 360n, 486n
Taylor, Charles R., 220n
Teegen, Hildy, 159n
Teitelbaum, Henry E., 464n
Tellis, Gerard J., 233n, 346n, 347n
Tendulkar, Sachin, 606
Teresa, Maria, 33
Terhune, Chad, 256n
Terziovski, Mile, 380n
Thelen, Shawn T., 93n
Theodosiou, Marios, 312n
Thomas, Madeline, 210n
Thomas, Manoj, 531n
Thomchick, Evelyn, 435n
Thompson, Craig J., 82n
Thompson, Ginger, 16, 669
Thompson, Leigh, 572n
Thompson, Robert J., 598
Thompson, Stephanie, 634
Thomson, Adam, 50n
Thurman, Uma, 361
Thurow, Lester, 137
Thurow, Roger, 157n
Thyet, Nguyen Thi, 223n
Tihanyi, Laszlo, 12n, 322n, 330n
Timur Lang, 29
Tinsley, Catherine H., 565n
Tjosvold, Dean, 388n, 565n
Tkacik, Maureen, 480n
Tochtrop, Carolyn A., 617
Torres, Ivonne, 480n
Townsend, Jamell D., 322n
Trevino, Sandra, 457
Triandis, Harry C., 94n
Tripathi, Smita, 326
Trotsky, Leon, 40
Trunick, Perry A., 462n
Tsang, Eric W. K., 330n
Tse, Alan C. B., 112n, 116n
Tucker, Kevin, 503
Tucker, Reed, 379
Tully, Shawn, 603
Tung Chee Hwa, 581
Turnbull, Peter W., 388n
Tyson, Laura D'Andrea, 151n

U

Ueltschy, Linda C., 339n
Uhlenbruck, Klaus, 332n
Ulgado, Francis M., 322n
Ulijin, Jan M., 561n, 575n
Urban II, Pope, 28
Ury, William, 567n, 574n
Usorne, David, 74n
Usunier, Jean-Claude, 558n

V

Vaaler, Paul M., 150n
Vachani, Sushil, 159n
Vaile, R. L., 374
Van de Vliert, Evert, 90, 513n
Van Espen, Jean-Claude, 624
Van Gogh, Vincent, 89
Van Rijn, Rembrandt, 89
Veerz, R. V., 572n
Velenzuela, An, 366n
Vence, Deborah L., 361n
Verbeke, Willem, 510n, 511n
Verbke, Alaine, 11n, 18n, 315n
Verleigh, Peeter W. J., 364n
Vermunt, Jeroen K., 215n
Verrier, Richard, 337, 407n, 617
Victoria, Queen, 35
Vitshum, Carlta, 467
Vitzthum, Carlita, 130n, 218n
Vogl, A. J., 572n
Volobueva, Marina, 569
Von Behr, Alex, 604
Vrana, Debora, 357n

W

Wadehra, B. L., 626
Wain, Barry, 41
Walker, Marcus, 82n
Wallach, Lori, 652
Waller, David S., 565n
Walls, Jan, 363n
Walsh, Bill, 443
Walsh, Sharon, 658
Walt, Vivienne, 157n
Walters, Peter G. P., 274n
Walton, Sam, 403
Wan, William P., 165n
Wang Cheng Lu, 480n
Wang Hai, 192
Ward, Andrew, 198n
Warden, Clyde A., 485n
Warner, Susan, 27n
Warren, David, 379
Wasem, Juergen, 222n
Way, Danny, 469
Wayne, John, 559
Weathers, Danny, 227n
Weber, Elke U., 191
Weber, Max, 112, 120, 140
Weber, Melanie, 198n
Wedel, Michel, 20n, 95n
Weekly, James K., 241
Wehrfritz, George, 401n
Wei, Nasha, 21
Weiner, Richard, 658
Weinstock, Neal, 641
Weis, Kenneth R., 5n
Weisberger, Bernard A., 56
Weiss, Stephen E., 559n
Weitz, Barton A., 509n, 511n
Welt, Leo G. B., 547
Wendlandt, A., 648n
Wen Jiabao, 114
Wenn, Stephen, 640
Wentz, Laurel, 634
Wernerfelt, Birger, 340n, 381n
Wernick, David, 283
Wertheimer, Linda, 195
Wessel, David, 263
West, Joel, 99n, 345n
Whelan, David, 443
White, Erin, 229n, 480n, 522n
White, Gregory L., 296n
White, J. Chris, 502n
White, Michael D., 63n, 450n, 617
White, Ronald D., 396n
Whitney, Patrick, 652
Wilbert, Carol, 152
Wilke, John R., 202n
Wilkie, Ken, 84n
Wilkinson, Tracy, 291n
Williams, Dan, 462n
Williams, Larry, 542

Williams, Patti, 96, 486n
William the Conqueror, 28
Willis, Bruce, 616
Wind, Jerry, 491
Wind, Yoram, 22n, 222n
Winfrey, Oprah, 98
Wise, Richard, 402n
Wisniewski, Mary, 381n
Witkowski, Terrence H., 16, 246n, 339n
Witt, Clyde E., 453n, 459n
Wolfinbarger, Mary, 339n
Wolfson, Bernard J., 617
Wong, Alfred, 388n
Wong, Edward, 374n
Wong, Nancy, 227n
Wood, Andrew, 195
Wood, Donald F., 453n
Woods, Ginny Parker, 599
Woolsey, James, 624
Worm, Verner, 565n
Wragg, Ralph, 208n
Wresh, William, 397n
Wright, Orville, 39
Wright, Tom, 48n

Wright brothers, 57
Wrighton, Jo, 617
Wu Wann-Yih, 485n
Wyer, Robert S., Jr., 482
Wylie, Bob, 503
Wymbs, Cliff, 332n
Wysocki, Bernard, Jr., 311

X

Xavier, Thomas, 606
Xiaohua Lin, 339n
Xie Jinhong, 115n
Xin, Katherine, 134n, 578n
Xueming Luo, 502n
Xu Meili, 395

Y

Yan, Amina, 521n
Yancey, Kitty Bean, 21
Yang Ching-Chow, 377n
Yannopoulos, Peter P., 339n
Yao Ming, 258
Yaping Gong, 330n

Ya-Ru Chen, 569
Yau, Oliver H. M., 112n, 116n
Yaveroglu, Idil Sayrac, 105n
Yeang Soo Ching, 572n
Yeniyurt, Sengun, 322n
Yin, Eden, 233n, 346n
Ying Ho, 133n, 510n
Ying Zhao, 366n
Yi-Zheng Shi, 502n
Yong Zhang, 228n, 513n
Yoo, Boonghee, 94n
Young, Richard R., 435n
Young, Steve, 62
Yu, Julie H., 133n, 510n
Yukl, Gary, 94n, 513n
Yung, Katherine, 37n
Yunxia Zhu, 561n

Z

Zabarenko, Deborah, 205
Zacharia, Jannie, 206n
Zachary, G. Pascal, 652
Zaidman, Nurit, 559n
Zak, Paul J., 578n

Zaltman, Gerald, 106n, 214n, 227n
Zaman, Amberin, 343n
Zammert, Andrea, 266n
Zarembo, Alan, 126
Zarocostas, John, 213
Zedillo, Ernesto, 41n, 61, 148
Zeithaml, Valerie A., 355n
Zeller-Bruhn, Mary E., 100n, 118n
Zhai Ligong, 223
Zhan, Sherrie, 270
Zhang, C., 422n
Zhang Chun, 423n
Zhang Xiaomei, 395
Zhilong Tian, 565n
Zhu, Guorong, 521n
Zhu Zhe, 102
Zimmerman, Ann, 401n, 417n
Zoellick, Robert, 571
Zoltak, James, 387n, 617
Zworykin, Vladimir, 40

SUBJECT INDEX

a

Aalsmeer Flower Auction, 100, 101, 414
Abbott Laboratories, 667
ABI/INFORM, 243
Acculturation, 98
Aceh Besar, Indonesia, 64
Achievement, 134
Action for Corporate Accountability, 602
Adaptation, 14–15, 98, 338
    basic criteria, 125
    cultural barriers, 359–360
    cultural electives, 126–127
    cultural exclusives, 127
    cultural imperatives, 125–126
    cultural influences, 343–349
    degree of, 124–125
    in e-commerce, 427
    for global marketing, 320–321
    innovative products, 345–346
    of packaging, 351–353
    product analysis for, 350–355
    required, 124–127
    requirements, 341
Adidas, 481, 492, 531
Administered pricing
    cartels, 552–554
    definition, 552
    government-influenced pricing, 554
Administrative costs, 535
Ad valorem duties, 441–442, 535
Advanced Micro Devices, 650
Advanced pricing agreements, 551
Advertising; *see* International advertising
Advertising agencies, 496–497
Advertising campaign, 496–497
    by Microsoft, 476–477
Advertising measurement, 230
Advil, 602
Advisory opinion, 437
Aegis Group, 496
Aer Lingus, 327
Aeroflot, 217, 474
Aerospatiale Matra, 330
Aesthetics, 111–112
Affiliation, 133
Afghanistan, 45
    U.S. war in, 4, 170
Africa
    AIDS epidemic, 16
    instability in, 160
    paradoxes of, 250
    statistics on, 262
African market groups, 305–306
African Virtual University, 251
After-sale services, 382–384
Agency for International
    Development, 29, 179
Agent middlemen, 410
Agent's fees, 148
Agents of change, 94
Aging of populations, 74–75
AIDSCAP, 666
AIDS epidemic, 16, 99
AIDS prevention, 666–669
Airbus Industrie, 3n, 166, 330, 331,
    388, 523
    case, 624–628
    competition with Boeing, 659–661
Airbus Integrated Company, 331
Air Canada, 626
Air conditioning market, 20
Aircraft industry, 3
Air express services, 457–458
Air France, 327
Air freight, 456
Airline industry, 659–661
Airlines alliance, 327
Air Mauritius, 624
Aiwa, 534
Akmerkez Etiler, 421
Alcohol consumption, 96–97
Alien Claims Act, 206

Alien status of foreign business, 12–13
Al-Jazeera, 492
All India Women's Democratic
    Association, 487, 619
All Russian Research Institute for TV and
    Radio Broadcasting, 498
Alpo, 7
Al Qaeda, 89
Alternative-fuel cars, 348
Altria Group, 472
Aluminum Company of America, 316
Amana, 171
Amazon.com, 172, 324, 404, 430, 495
Amazonian rain forest, 68
Amdahl, 384
American Airlines, 227, 327, 508
American apple sales in Japan, 213
American Arbitration Association, 189
American Consumer Satisfaction Index, 381
American Export Register, 241
American Express, 361
American Free Trade Area, 33
American Home Products, 602
American Hospital Supply, 664
American Lung Association Tobacco Policy
    Trend Alert, 671
American management style, 127–130
American Society for Quality Control, 381
America Online, 311
Amnesty International, 171–172
Amway Corporation, 41, 246, 403, 408, 409
Anacin, 602
Analogy, 232–233
Andean Common Market, 284
Anderson Worldwide, 222
Anheuser-Busch Companies, 188
Animosity, targeted, 164–165
Antiboycott law, 205–206
Antibribery law, 144, 146, 148
Anti-Cyber Squatting Consumer
    Protection Act, 208
Antidumping duties, 49
Antidumping penalties, 44–45
Antiglobalization protests, 6, 51–52,
    169, 312
Antisweatshop campaign, 52
Antitrust law
    European Union, 202
    Japan, 554
    United States, 205, 414
Aoyama Trading Company, 401
Apartheid, 170
Apple Computer, 170, 213, 214, 233, 324,
    345, 351, 357, 360, 362, 373
    revenues, 9
Apple iPod, 193
Apple iTunes Music Store, 214
Application, 99
Arab Cola, 343
Arab Common Market, 306
Arab Free Trade Area, 307
Arab League boycott, 206
Arab world
    and American television, 352
    boycotts, 48
    and economic integration, 306
    and free trade, 279
    Islamic law, 185–186
    standardization in, 378
Aravind Eye Care System, 260
Arbitration, 189–190
Arbitration clauses in contracts, 190
Arche, 473
Archer Daniels Midland, 554
ARCO, 8
Arial Global Reach, 354
Ariel detergent, 363, 468
Arm's length transfer, 551
Arrival draft, 449
Art, 111–112
Artists Coalition Against Piracy, 209

Asahi, 490
Asatsu-DK, 496
Asea Brown Boveri, 558
ASEAN+3, 305
ASEAN Vision 2000, 304
Asia
    economic growth, 375–376
    economies of, 267–273
    financial crisis of 1997, 50, 305
    negotiating styles, 565
    satellite TV, 492
    statistics on, 262
Asian markets, 269
Asian-Pacific Rim, 268–269, 303–305
Asian Tigers, 249, 268–269, 274
Asia-Pacific Economic Cooperation
    Conference, 33, 305
Association of Southeast Asian Nations,
    268–269, 280, 303–305, 332
Atesa, 644
At Home Corporation, 311
AT&T, 571
Attorneys, number of, 182, 183
Audi, 421
Audit Bureau of Circulation, 489
Austin Inc., 433–434
Authority, 130–131
AVG Letter of Credit Management
    LLC, 448
Aviation history, 57
Aviation Lease and Finance Company, 625
Avis, 644
Avon Products Inc., 25, 246, 408, 507
    sales dangers, 508

b

Bacardi Company, 485
Back translation, 228
BAE Systems, 330, 624, 627
Bahamas Air, 624–625
Baksheesh, 273
Balance of merchandise trade, 32
Balance of payments accounts, 35–37
Balance of trade, 547
Ballad of East and West (Kipling), 582
Baltic States, 267
Banana wars, 157
Bangladesh, 147, 252, 253
Bankers Trust, 8
Banking, and Islamic law, 185
Bank of America, 664
Bank of Scotland Corporate Banking, 645
Bank One, 434
Barbie dolls, 123, 142–143, 218, 467
Barriers to entry
    cultural barriers, 359–360
    data flow restrictions, 358
    intellectual property protection,
        358–359
    protectionism, 357–358
Barter, 545–547
Barter houses, 549
Basel Convention, 67, 164
Basic Law of the Hong Kong SAR, 271
BATNA; *see* Best alternative to a
    negotiated agreement
Battle of San Jacinto, 59
Bausch & Lomb, 192, 333
Bayer AG, 195, 219
BBC, 484, 640
Beautiful & Rich Wholesale Market, 395
Beddedas Shower Gel, 294
Beijing Conciliation Center, 189
Beijing Toronto International Hospital, 357
Beliefs, 112–113
BellSouth, 371
BEM; *see* Big emerging markets
Ben & Jerry's Ice Cream, 7, 338
Benetton, 411
Berg Electronics, 300
Bertelsmann AG, 16, 311

Best alternative to a negotiated agreement,
    574
    case, 659–661
Bestfoods, 192
Best Western International, 325
Big emerging markets, 261–263
    Eastern Europe, 266
    India, 273
    Latin America, 264–265
    South Africa, 274
    statistics on, 262
    trade projections, 376
    traits, 261
    Vietnam, 273–274
Bilateral trade agreements, 49
Billboards, 495
Bill of lading, 450
Bills of exchange, 448–449
Bimbo, 8
Biopan, 363
Bisleri, 605, 607
Bisquick, 519
BitTorrent, 16
Black & Decker, 315
Blockbuster Video, 8
Blocked channels, 406–407
Blocked currency, 42
Bloomingdale's, 494
Blue Cross, 384
Blue Diamond Growers Association,
    475–478
BMG Entertainment, 16
BMW, 7, 8, 361, 363, 407
Boeing Company, 3, 4, 11, 46, 150, 166,
    324, 355, 370, 373–374, 382,
    387–388, 454, 523, 576
    competition with Airbus, 330, 331,
        624–626, 659–661
    revenues, 9
Book of Songs, 103–104
Book rip-offs, 192
BOPM; *see* Bottom-of-the-pyramid markets
Bosch Siemens, 64, 489
Bose, 365
Botox, 565
Bottom-of-the-pyramid markets, 259–261
    marketing to, 650–652
Bounty paper towels, 245
Boycotts, 42, 48, 169, 444
    and antiboycott law, 205–206
Brand image, 361
Brand name protection, 191
Brand name rip-off, 192
Brand names
    country-specific, 363
    international disputes, 188
    language problems, 15–17
    value of, 361
Brands
    county-of-origin effect, 364–366
    global, 360, 362–363
    in international marketing, 360–366
    national, 363–364
    private, 366
Brazil, 68, 248–249, 579
    AIDS prevention, 666–667
    negotiating style, 566
Breadth of knowledge, 510
Bribery, 203–204, 273
    agent's fees, 148
    cultural context, 146–147
    and extortion, 147
    Foreign Corrupt Practices Act, 46,
        146, 148, 203–204, 622, 624, 630
    political payoffs, 178
    Starnes-Brenner Machine Tool
        Company, 621–622
    subornation and lubrication, 148
    and types of culture, 151
    Western focus on, 144–145

Bridges, 65
Bridgestone/Firestone Tires, 470
British Airways, 327
British American Tobacco, 605, 670, 671
British Commonwealth, 284
British Petroleum, 8
British Standards Institute, 378
Broadcasting & Cable, 641
Brokers
    foreign-country, 417
    home-country, 414
Brother, 44
Brugel, 351
Bruno Magli, 314
BSkyB, 641, 642
Budejovicky Budvar N. P., 188
Budweiser, 192, 365
Buitoni, 493
Bulgartabac, 672
Bureau for International Registration of
    Trademarks, 196
Bureau of Export Administration
    regulations, 439
Bureau of Industry and Security, 436
    advisory opinions, 437
    violations and penalties, 440
Burger King, 7, 8, 119, 174
Burroughs Corporation, 509
Burlington Northern Santa Fe, 457
Bush administration, 61n, 303
Bushnell Corporation, 440
Business behavior/customs
    culture criteria, 124
    gender bias, 140–142
    influence of culture on, 149–161
    regional adaptation, 124–127
    responsible decision making, 149
Business briefings periodicals, 243
Business ethics
    agent's fees, 148
    Airbus case, 624–628
    Bribe Payers Index, 146
    bribery, 144–148
    Corruption Perception Index, 145–146,
        151, 153, 629
    corruption defined, 142–143
    extortion, 147–148
    Foreign Corrupt Practices Act, 46,
        146, 148, 203–204, 622, 624, 630
    Nestlé Infant Formula, 600–603
    principles of, 149
    social responsibility, 148–149
    Starnes-Brenner Machine Tool
        Company, 621–622
    subornation and lubrication, 148
    trading in China, 629–630
Business International, 441
Business negotiations; see International
    business negotiations
Business Operations Report, 243
Business philosophy, 400
Business regulation, 293, 297
Business schools, 522, 524
Business services, 371
    after-sale services, 382–384
    client followers, 384
    customer training, 383
    garbage pickup, 382
    international marketing of, 381–385
    law firms, 384
    and protectionism, 385
Business Software Alliance, 191–192
Business-to-business commerce, 136
Business-to-business marketing, 369–393
    brick-and-mortar companies, 426
    business services, 381–385
    characteristics, 370–371
    client followers, 384–385
    cutting costs, 426
    demand in, 371–376
    by Intel, 369
    on Internet, 494
    Internet distribution, 425–430
    inventory control, 426
    ISO 9000 certification, 380–381
    major U.S. exports, 370
    and metric system, 378–380
    and protectionism, 385
    purchasing agents, 373

quality in, 376–380
Solar Turbines Inc., 389–392
and stages of economic
    development, 375
standardization in, 378–381
technology and market demand,
    375–376
trade shows, 385–388
volatility of industrial demand, 372–375
Business-to-consumer marketing, 338; see
    also Products and services
BusinessWeek, 596
Buyback agreement, 548
Buyer panels, 230
Buyer-seller disagreements, 631
Buying office, 414
Buztronics Inc., 34

C

Cable and Television Act of 1995, 487
Cable and Television Networks Act of 1995
    (India), 619
Cable TV, 491–493
Cadbury, 96, 340
Cadbury-Schweppes, 608
Cadillac, 539
California Fitness Centers, 483
Calvin Klein, 52, 531
Campa Cola, 605
Campbell's Soup Company, 245, 353,
    538–539
Canada
    advertising laws, 483
    and metric system, 379
    negotiating style, 566
    product comparison law, 200
Canadian Airlines, 327
Canadian-American Commercial Arbitra-
    tion Commission, 189
Canadian Broadcasting Corporation, 627
Canadian law, 181
Canadian National, 457
C&F (cost and freight), 445–446
Canon, 11, 408
Cape Cod Potato Chips, 283
Capital account, 35
Capital Cities/ABC, 641
Capital cost, 419
Capitalism
    Chinese version, 151
    communitarian, 149–151
    individualistic, 149–151
Capital requirements, 420
CARE, 172
Cargo and Container Security Initiative, 461
Caribbean Community and Common
    Market, 301
Caribbean Free Trade Association, 301
Carlsberg, 169
Carlson Marketing Group, 496
Carnation, 6
Carrefour SA, 404, 467, 527, 534
Car rental business, 644–649
Carrier, 201, 608
Carrier Aircon, 605
Cartels, 552–554
Cartier, 191, 421, 540
Cases
    AIDS prevention, 666–669
    Airbus Industrie, 624–628
    buyer-seller disagreements, 631
    Coke and Pepsi in India, 604–609
    easyCar.com, 644–649
    EuroDisney, 614–617
    Fair & Lovely, 618–620
    Iberia Airlines, 659–661
    magnetic resonance imaging, 662
    marketing to the bottom of the
        pyramid, 650–652
    Mayo Clinic, 636–639
    McDonald's and obesity, 632–634
    McDonald's Great Britain, 654–655
    microwave ovens, 610–612
    National Office Machines, 663–665
    Nestlé Infant Formula, 600–603
    Starbucks Corporation, 596–599
    Starnes-Brenner Machine Tool
        Company, 621–623

Tambrands, 656–658
televised sports, 640–643
tobacco sales in Third World,
    670–674
trading in China, 629–630
Cash in advance, 449
Caspian, 642
Castle system, 103
CastleArk Management, 596
Castrol, 481
Caterpillar Tractor Company, 170, 222,
    362, 363, 389, 417, 568
Cathay Pacific, 327, 505
CavinKare, 618
CBS, 641
CCTV, 488
Celadon Trucking Services, 300
Cell phones, 252; see also Mobile phones
    Chinese market, 318
CEMEX, 8, 260, 650
Center for Combating Unfair Competition
    (Germany), 201
Centers for Disease Control and
    Prevention, 632
Central America Free Trade Agreement,
    157, 159
Central American Common Market, 284
Central American Free Trade Agreement–
    Dominican Republic Free Trade
    Agreement, 300
Central Bureau of Investigation
    (India), 626
Central Intelligence Agency, 162, 624
Centralized organizations, 334–335
Cereal Partners Worldwide, 328
Certificate of origin, 450
CFE, 299
Chain-ratio approach to forecasting, 232
Chanel, 104
Change; see Cultural change; Innovation
Channel control, 420
Channel control elements, 399–400
Channel costs, 419
Channel length, 406
Channel-of-distribution structure
    business philosophy, 400
    channel control, 399–400
    high density, 398–399
    import-oriented, 396–397
    in Japan, 397–398, 401–402
    Japan's retailing law, 400–401
    trend to modern structures, 402–405
Channel selection
    foreign-country middlemen, 415–417
    government-affiliated middlemen, 417
    home-country middlemen, 411–415
    middlemen choices, 409–418
    process, 410
Channels of distribution; see also
    International marketing channels;
    Logistics management
    blocked, 406–407
    capital requirements, 420
    character, 420–421
    in China, 258
    constructing, 422–425
    continuity, 421
    control, 420
    costs, 419
    coverage, 420
    in emerging markets, 256
    factors affecting selection, 419–421
    Internet, 425–430
    middlemen choices, 409–418
    nonexistent, 406
Channel Tunnel, 65
Charmin, 533
Cheetos, 341
Chef America, 7
Chery Company, 362
Chevrolet, 481
Child labor, 171
Children and television advertising, 198
Chile, 250–251
China, 308
    air conditioning market, 20
    alternative-fuel cars, 348
    arbitration in, 189
    bullet train, 371

car market, 276
cell phone market, 318
collectivism, 131
commercial law, 186
counterfeiting and piracy, 192–194
customer training, 383
distribution channels, 258
distribution inadequacies, 420
dogs in, 115
easing of trade barriers, 11
economic growth steps, 269–270
economy of, 267–271
energy use, 70
entry into World Trade Organization,
    48, 269
feng shui, 112–113
first golf course, 573
franchises in, 321
gross national product, 269
guanxi, 125–126, 151
and Hong Kong, 271
hostility toward Japan, 164–165
human rights violations, 269–270
information technology, 270–271
intellectual property rights, 195, 359
joint ventures, 330
legal environment, 12
legal system failures, 270
licensing marketing research, 223
male-female imbalance, 76
manufacturing powerhouse, 540
marketing in, 254–255
marketing laws, 200
Ministry of Health, 223
missile technology, 439
multiple income levels, 534
National Statistics Enforcement Office,
    219
national TV station, 488
negotiating style, 558–559, 565
number of Christians in, 269
One China policy, 272
and Panama Canal Zone, 56
Party National Congress, 270
permanently normalized trade
    relations, 170, 269
pollution problems, 67
population growth, 72
public relations in, 471
Railway Ministry, 255
rebirth of enterprise, 397
refrigerator makers, 339
regional markets, 269
return of Hong Kong and Macao, 33
Three Gorges Dam, 66, 389
tobacco industry, 672
top ten advertisers, 473
view of contracts, 581
and World Trade Organization
    loopholes, 49
China Books, 433–434
China Hand, 243
China International Public Relations
    Association, 471
China National Tobacco Company, 672
Chiquita Brands International, 157
Chrysler Corporation, 6, 7, 8, 485
Chusan Shan Hot Spring Golf Club,
    China, 573
Ciclon Foundation, 627
Cidesport, 195
CIF (cost, insurance, freight) quote, 433,
    445–446
Cigarette advertising, 498, 670–672
Cinema advertising, 495
Cisco Academy Training Centre, 383
Cisco Systems, 176, 361, 383, 388, 425,
    426, 459
Citibank, 206, 549
Cities, most expensive, 508
Citigroup, 361
    revenues, 9
C-Itoh, 327–328
Clean float, 50
Client followers, 384
Climate, 63–65
    El Niño, 84
Climate zones, 85
Climatic differences, 341

Clinique, 289
Clinton administration, 303
Club Med, 501
CNN, 27, 172, 492
Coach, 194
Coca-Cola Company, 12, 13, 23, 168, 191,
    202, 203, 206, 296, 312, 313, 326,
    343–344, 353, 360, 361, 362, 420,
    468, 471, 472, 476, 481, 488, 522,
    524, 531, 546, 551, 599, 634, 668
    in China, 258
    competition in India, 604–609
    as global company, 20
    in India, 164
    revenues, 9
    in Vietnam, 246
COD (cash on delivery), 445
Code law, 182, 183–185
Coffeemate Nondairy Coffee Creamer, 602
Coke, 339, 483
Coke Light, 343
Cola Turka, 343
Colgate-Palmolive Company, 192, 259,
    263, 294, 478, 487, 489, 522,
    523, 667
Colgate toothpaste, 483
Collectivism, 107
    national/regional index score, 154–155
Columbus Cafe, 598
Comdex, 386
Commerce Control List, 436–438
Commerce Country Chart, 438
Commercial Bank of Kuwait, 625
Commercial invoice, 450
Commercial law, 203; see also Legal
        environment
    antitrust law, 202–203
    case, 188
    dispute resolution procedures,
        187–191
    green marketing, 201–202
    international disputes, 186–187
    marketing laws, 198–201
    under socialism, 186
Commercial News, 327
Committee decision making, 131
Commodity Inspection Bureau, China, 629
Common law, 182, 183–185
Common market, 280
    characteristics, 284
    cultural factors, 292
    economic factors, 281
    geographic/temporal proximity, 292
    of Islamic countries, 306–308
    political factors, 281
Commonwealth of Independent States, 284,
    286, 376, 549
    description, 294–296
    map, 295
    membership statistics, 295
Commonwealth of nations, 284
Communication
    follow-up, 581
    high- or low-context culture, 135–136
    language, 109–111
    and language barriers, 226–228
    limited means of, 226
    nontask sounding, 577–578, 579
    of opinions, 224
    in sales management, 514–515
    symbols for, 109–112
    task-related information exchange,
        578–580
Communication process, 479–483
Communication styles, 134–137
    face-to-face, 135–136
    Internet, 136–137
Communication technology, 78
Communism, 102
Communist Party of China, 270, 629, 630
Communitarian capitalism, 149–151
Compadre, 125–126
Company-agency-customer relationship,
    237
Company objectives and resources,
    317–318
Comparative advertising, 483
Compatibility, 348
Compensation deals, 546–547

Compensation systems
    advertising agencies, 497
    case, 663–665
    expatriates, 515
    global sales force, 516–517
Competition, 6, 129–130, 333–335,
    338–339
    in business-to-business marketing, 377
    in domestic environment, 11–12
    and European Union, 293
    private brands, 366
    worldwide, 31
Competitive environment, 23, 28
Competitive market analysis, 590–591
Competitiveness, 567–568
Competitive situation, 215
Complementary marketing, 413
Complexity, 348
Compound duty, 442, 535
Compradors, 417
Computer hackers, 6
Computers
    cybercrime, 172–173
    diffusion rate, 233
    in Japanese market, 214
    for marketing research, 230–231
    national comparisons, 254
    support services, 354
Comtek Trade Show, Moscow, 387
Concessions and agreement, 581
Conciliation, 187–189
Confucian philosophy, 57, 131
Consortia, 330–331
Construcciones, 330
Consular invoice, 450
Consumer behavior
    and cultural values, 107–108
    Japan, 427
Consumer Europe, 242
Consumer identification systems, 230
Consumer products, 338–355
    compared to industrial goods,
        372–373
    international marketing of, 338–355,
        360–366
Consumer Protection Distance Selling
    Regulations (UK), 648
Consumers
    cost of tariffs, 39
    country stereotyping, 364–366
    criticisms of advertising, 497
    Japan vs. U.S., 400
    perception of newness, 345–346
Consumer services, 355–360
Consumers International, 169
Consumption, 203–204
    consequences of, 97–98
    national comparisons, 276
    patterns of, 96–98
Containerization, 456
Continental Can Company, 173
Contracts/Contractual agreements
    arbitration clauses, 190
    consortia, 331
    definition, 35
    franchising, 325–327
    licensing, 35
    from negotiations, 581
    performance of, 184–185
    validity of, 209–210
Controllable elements, 10, 11
Control of middlemen, 424–425
Control Risks Group, 179
Convenience stores, 402
Convention on the Recognition and
    Enforcement of Foreign Arbitral
    Awards, 190
Copyright law, 194
    China and Russia, 186
Core component, 350–351
Corner House, 627
Corona Extra, 203
Corporate philanthropy, 176
Corporate planning, 317
Corporate Social Responsibility, 149
Corporations, 105
    independent enterprise, 128

Corruption, 273; see also Bribery;
        Business ethics; Foreign Corrupt
        Practices Act
    Airbus case, 624–628
    definitions, 142–143
    extortion, 147
    overcoming, 148–149
    Starnes-Brenner Machine Tool
        Company, 621–622
    trading in China, 629–630
Corruption Perception Index, 145–146,
    151, 153, 629
Costco, 8, 404, 411, 529, 651
Cost of goods sold, 540–541
Cost of physical distribution, 454–456
Costs
    of advertising, 488–489
    of expatriates, 518
    of exporting, 535
    middleman, 538–539
    of transportation, 538–539
Council for Mutual Economic
    Assistance, 284
Council of Ministries (EU), 289
Counterfeiting, 191–194
Counterpurchase, 548
Countertrade, 442
    as barter, 546
    compensation deals, 546–547
    counterpurchase, 548
    definition, 546
    Internet, 549
    offset trade, 548
    proactive strategy, 549–550
    problems of, 548–549
    product buyback agreement, 548
    reasons for imposing, 547
    Russia and PepsiCo, 545
Countervailing duty, 45, 544–545
Country needs, 310–320
Country notebook, 585–594
    competitive market analysis, 590–591
    cultural analysis, 586–588
    definition, 586
    economic analysis, 588–590
    market audit, 590–591
    preliminary marketing plan, 591–593
Country-of-origin effect, 364–366
Country-specific brand names, 363
Country stereotyping, 364–366
Court of International Trade, 443
Coverage, 420
Coverage of advertising, 489
Covisint, 404
Cracker Jack, 43
Crédit Lyonnais, 625
Crest, 259
Cross-cultural analysis, 17
Cross-cultural communication, 135–137
Cross-cultural marketing research, 226–228
Cross-cultural misunderstandings, 14, 15
Cross-cultural negotiations; see International
        business negotiations
Cuban boycott, 169
Cuban embargo, 41, 42, 181
Cue toothpaste, 478
Cultural adjustments, 14
Cultural analysis, 586–588
Cultural awareness, 114, 126, 521–522
Cultural barriers, 237
    and adaptation, 359–360
Cultural borrowing, 110, 116
Cultural change
    consequences of innovation, 119–120
    cultural borrowing, 116
    ongoing process, 115–116
    planned or unplanned, 118–119
    resistance to change, 117–118
    similarities illusion, 116–117
Cultural conditioning, 15
Cultural congruence, 118–119
Cultural data, 215
Cultural differences, 151–152
    awareness of, 17–18
    case, 656–658
    channels of distribution, 502
    in collecting primary data, 224–225
    decision-making process, 569–570
    Euro Disney, 614–617

in European Union, 117
negotiation behavior, 560–570
obstacles to marketing, 15–17
in personal selling, 508–509, 512
sales force meetings, 514
sales force motivation, 513–515
on time, 568–569
in values, 567–569
Cultural diversity, 486–487
Cultural electives, 126–127
Cultural empathy, 510
Cultural exclusives, 127
Cultural heritage, 116
Cultural imperatives, 125–126
Cultural knowledge
    factual vs. interpretive, 114–115
    kinds of, 113–114
    sensitivity and tolerance, 115
Cultural nationalism, 163–164
Cultural sensitivity, 115
Cultural shock, 520
Cultural training, 520
Cultural uniqueness, 23
Cultural values
    affiliation and social acceptance, 133
    and consumer behavior, 107–108
    effect of religion, 104
    gift-giving, 108
    government influence on, 105
    Hofstede's indexes, 106–107
    individualism/collectivism, 107
    influence of geography, 99–102
    and Internet services, 93
    and language, 111
    power and achievement, 133
    power distance, 107
    security and mobility, 132
    uncertainty avoidance, 107
    work-personal life trade-off, 132–133
Culture
    and birthrate, 95–96
    as communication, 109
    and communications technology, 78
    customs, 126–127
    definition, 56
    definitions and origin of, 98–99
    dimensions of, 106
    elements of, 105–113
    ethnocentrism, 15–17, 313, 364
    food preferences, 340
    and geography, 63
    high-context, 135–136
    high vs. low context, 151
    historical perspectives, 56–62
    illusions of similarity, 116–117
    impact of geography, 99–102
    impact of technology, 102–103
    impact on negotiations, 560–570
    importance for marketing, 94
    importance of family, 72
    influence on strategic thinking,
        149–161
    information-oriented, 151–152
    local history, 62
    low-context, 135–136
    management style, 124
    national/regional index score, 154–155
    origin, elements, and consequences, 99
    patterns of consumption, 96–98
    perceptions of time, 138–140
    pervasive impact of, 94–98
    political economy, 102
    and product marketing, 343–349
    relationship-oriented, 151–152
    rituals, 108–109
    services marketing, 359–360
    shaping management objectives,
        132–134
    social institutions, 103–104
    symbols, 109–113
    thought processes, 113
    transmission of, 116
    and value judgments, 115
    values, 106–108
    views of corruption, 142–143
Culture Matters (Harrison &
    Huntington), 152
Cumulative rebates, 399–400

Currency speculation, 142
Currency value variations, 537–538
Current account, 35, 36
Customer relationship management, 502
Customer training, 383
Customization, 312
Custom-privileged facilities
   foreign trade zones, 451–452, 543–544
   maquiladoras, 452–453
Customs, 126–127
Customs administration, 299
Customs duties, 441–442
Customs-Trade Partnership against
   Terrorism, 462
Customs union, 283–284
Cyberabad (India), 252
Cybercrime, 172–173
Cyberlaw
   in China, 186
   contract validity, 209–210
   cybersquatters, 207–209
   domain names, 207–209
   jurisdiction of disputes, 209–210
   and tax collection, 209
Cybersquatters, 207–209
Cyberterrorism, 172–173
Czech Republic, 266

d

Dabur India, 331
Daewoo Motor Company, 168, 331, 362
Daewoo Motor Sales Company, 168
Daily Mail, 289
DaimlerChrysler, 330, 404, 426, 472
Daitenho, 400
Dams, 66
*D & B Principal International Business
   Directory,* 241
Dannon, 475
Dasa aerospace, 330
Date draft, 449
Dealers, 417
Death of a Salesman (Miller), 508
De Beers Company, 553
Decentering, 228
Decentralized decision making, 130–131
Decentralized organizations, 334–335
Decision makers, communicating with,
   236–237
Decision making, 334
   cultural differences, 569–570
   socially responsible, 149
   styles of, 130–131
   tobacco marketing, 670–674
   wide sharing in, 128–129
Decoding, 479
Deflation, 536
Delhaize, 404
Delivery options, 429–430
Dell Computer, 136, 312, 324, 361, 404,
   419, 425, 493, 576
Delphi, 249
Delta Air Lines, 355
Demand
   in business-to-business marketing,
      371–376
   derived demand, 373–374
   in emerging markets, 256–259
   market indicators, 259
   volatility of, 372–375
Demand shifts, 6
Demeanor, 126
Demographics; *see* Global population
Dentsu, 496
Department of Agriculture, 544
   Nutrition Program for Women, Infants,
      and Children, 633
Department of Commerce, 148, 178, 238,
   261, 273, 340, 379, 422, 545
   Bureau of Industry and Security, 436,
      437, 440
   Export Administration Regulations,
      436
   export violations and penalties, 440
   Global Harmonization Task
      Force, 378
   Overseas Business Reports, 445
   trade fairs, 386

Department of Defense, 379, 387
   radio frequency identification,
      463–464
Department of Justice, 204, 205
Department of State travel warnings, 505
Department stores, 401
Derived demand, 373–374
Descartes, 459
Design rip-off, 192
Deutsche Telekom, 311, 598
Developing countries; *see* Emerging
   markets
DHL Worldwide Express, 406, 454, 459
Diamond cartel, 553–554
Diaopai, 473
Diet change, 119
Diet Coke, 343, 353
Differential exchange rate, 42
Diffusion of innovation, 345, 346–349
Digital divide, 13
Direct exporting, 323–324
Direct foreign investment, 332
   in Mexico, 300
Direct mail advertising, 493–494
Direct marketing, 408–409
*Directory of American Firms Operating in
   Foreign Countries,* 241
Directory of U.S. Exporters, 241
Directory of U.S. Importers, 241
Direct sales, 325
DirecTV, 642
Dirty float, 50
Disease, incidence of, 97–98
Disneyland, 8, 279, 337
Disney Princesses, 313, 314
Disney-Sea, Tokyo, 616
Distribution agreement, 423
Distribution costs, 543
Distribution patterns; *see also* Channels
   of distribution; International
   marketing channels
   blocked channels, 406–407
   channel length, 406
   costs and margins, 406
   line breadth, 406
   middlemen services, 405–406
   nonexistent channels, 406
   power and competition, 407
   in retailing, 407–409
   stocking, 407
Distribution process, 396
Distribution structure, 396
Distribution systems, 397
   evolution of, 402–405
Distributors, 415–417
Docks de France, 404
Doctors' hours, 133
Doha Round, 558
Dole Food Company, 157
Dollar, weak, 537–538
Dollar draft, 448, 449
Domain names, 207–209
Domestication, 166
   planned, 177
Domestic environment, 11–12
   effect of competition, 11–12
   political decisions, 11
Domestic environment uncontrollables,
   11–12
Domestic market extension orientation, 22
Domestic marketing *vs.* international
   marketing, 9
Domestic middlemen; *see* Home-country
   middlemen
Domino's Pizza, 326
Dormont Manufacturing Company, 378
Dove bars, 340
Dove Shampoo, 474
Downy, 343
Drachma, 292
Drawback, 452
Dreyer's Grand Ice Cream, 202
Dristan, 193
Drive to maturity, 247, 375
DRUPA trade show, 433–434
Dual-purpose technology, 204–205
Due process of law, 182
Dumping, 44, 544–545
Dumping duty, 544

Dun & Bradstreet, 422
Dunkin' Donuts, 598
DuPont, 476
Durable goods, 338

e

EADS, 624
Early return rate of expatriates, 519–520
East Asian Business Intelligence, 243
eastCar.com, case, 644–649
Eastern Environmental Services, 69
Eastern Europe
   economic development, 376
   economies of, 265–267
   trade shows, 387
Eastman Kodak, 11–12, 195, 297, 361,
   487, 489
EasyGroup, 644
eBay, 93, 207, 404
e-Business Solutions Centers, 383
Ecolabeling, 202, 342
E-commerce, 425–430
   and adaptation, 427
   business-to-business advantages, 426
   and culture, 427
   delivery options, 429–430
   in European Union, 210
   example, 428–429
   impact on negotiations, 576
   local contact, 429
   payment, 429
   potential, 426–427
   promotion, 430
   and taxation, 209
   trade transaction system, 448
Economic analysis, 588–590
   Asian countries, 267–273
   Baltic States, 267
   Eastern Europe, 265–267
   Latin America, 263–265
   newest emerging markets, 273–274
Economic and Monetary Union, 290–291
Economic and social data, 248
Economic boom of 1990s, 3
Economic Bulletin Board, 238
Economic Community of West African
   States, 305–306, 307
Economic Cooperation Organization, 307
Economic data, 215
Economic development, 246–255
   in Brazil, 68
   categories of countries, 249
   challenges of, 247
   definition, 247
   demand factors, 256–258
   evolution of marketing process, 257
   five-stage model, 375
   and information technology,
      251–252, 253
   infrastructure, 253–254, 255
   levels of market development, 256
   marketing's contribution, 254–255
   newly industrialized countries,
      249–251
   objectives, 252–253
   regional cooperation, 282
   stages of, 247–249
   sustainable, 67–68
   technology uses, 375–376
Economic environment, 281
Economic growth, 375–376
   environmental management, 67–69
   geographic factors, 65–67
   natural resources for, 70–71
   projections, 33–34
Economic integration; *see* Multinational
   market regions; Regional trading
   groups
Economic nationalism, 163–164
Economic risks
   exchange controls, 167
   import restrictions, 167–168
   labor problems, 168
   local-content laws, 167
   price controls, 168
   tax controls, 168
Eddie Bauer, 404
Education, 104

EEJ-net, 210
Efficiency *versus* competition, 129–130
El Corte Inglés, 404
Electrolux, 341
Electrolux Kelvinator, 650
Electronic Request for Item Classification
   (ERIC), 440–441
Electronic tracking, 462–464
Elle, 490
El Niño, 84
E-mail, 136–137
E-mail marketing lists, 230
Embargoes, 41, 42, 170, 181
Embedded research, 230–231
Embraer, 248
Emerging markets
   Asia, 267–273
   Asia-Pacific Rim, 268–269
   Baltic States, 267
   big emerging markets, 261–263
   bottom-of-the-pyramid markets,
      259–261
   categories of countries, 248
   China, 269–271
   consumption patterns, 275
   creating opportunity, 270
   demand factors, 256–259
   developing countries, 261–274
   Eastern Europe, 265–267
   economic development, 246–258
   evolution of marketing process, 257
   examples, 245
   Hong Kong, 271
   India, 272–273
   information technology, 251–252, 253
   infrastructure, 253–254, 255
   Internet use, 251–252, 253
   Latin America, 263–265
   level of market development, 256
   liberalization of, 247
   living standards, 275
   marketing in Third World, 263
   marketing's contribution, 254–255
   marketing to the bottom of the pyra-
      mid, 650–652
   market potential estimation, 256–258
   market segments, 258–259
   multinational market regions, 247
   new consumers, 338
   newest, 273–274
   NIC growth factors, 249–251
   objectives, 252–253
   regional trading groups, 308
   South Africa, 274
   statistics on, 262
   strategic implications, 274–276
   Taiwan, 271–272
   tobacco sales, 670–674
   trade projections, 376
   Vietnam, 273–274
Emotional stability, 510
Encarta Encyclopedia, 62
Encoding, 479, 480
   decoding, 481–482
   noise, 482
   receiver, 482
Energy consumption, 71
Energy Group, 7
Energy production and consumption, 86
Energy sources, 70
English
   Internet use, 136–137
   as language of business, 524
   U.S. *vs.* U.K., 116–117
English, Welch & Scottish Railway, 7
English law, 183n
Enron, 4, 93, 144, 390
Entrepreneurship, 250
Environmental adaptation, 14–15
Environmental issues, 66–67
   and urbanization, 74
Environmental laws, 201–202, 342–343
Environmental management, 67–69
EPRG schema, 22, 23
E-protectionism, 209
Equality in negotiations, 567–568
ESPN, 492, 641
Espresso Vivace, 597
Esso, 15, 16

Estée Lauder Companies, 289
Estimating market demand, 232–234
Estonia, 267
Ethical marketing decisions, 670–674
Ethnocentrism, 15–17, 313, 364
eToys, 404
eTrade Finance Platform, 448
Euro, 290–291
    description, 291
    initial circulation, 287
    and price differentials, 294
    projected impact, 291
EuroDisney, 217, 294, 337, 378, 496
    case, 614–617
Euromonitor, 487
Europcar, 644
Europe
    aging populations, 74–75
    Marshall Plan for, 28–29
    protectionism in, 30–31
    statistics on, 262
    trade fairs, 386
European Aeronautic Defence & Space
    Company, 331, 659
European Business News, 494
European Coal and Steel Community,
    279, 280
European Commission, 48, 198, 288–289,
    342, 358
European Common Market, 286, 287
European Community, 30–31, 167,
    200–201, 280, 281, 455
European Court, 201, 289
European Data and Marketing Statistics, 242
European Economic Area, 287, 290
European Economic Community, 284,
    286, 287
European Fine Arts Fair, 417n
European Free Trade Area, 285
European Free Trade Association, 289
European Health Commission, 632
European market regions, 285
European monetary system, 287
European Parliament, 288, 289
European Patent Convention, 196
European School, Brussels, 524
European School of Management, 524
European self-stereotyping, 560
European Union, 5, 158
    advertising regulations, 483, 497–498
    after-sale services, 382–383
    agreement on standards, 378
    agriculture and monetary problems, 281
    antidumping duties, 545
    antitrust law, 202
    banana wars, 157
    ban on beef, 174
    bilateral trade agreements, 49
    birthrate decline, 74
    business regulation, 297
    business schools, 524
    candidate countries, 285
    commercial code, 200–201
    corporate social responsibility, 149
    cultural differences, 117
    and cyberlaw, 210
    Eastern Europe in, 267
    economic and monetary union,
        290–291
    environmental policies, 67
    example for Middle East, 279
    expansion of, 292
    harmonization standards, 288
    historical background, 286–289
    institutions of, 288–289
    job loss issue, 283
    Maastricht Treaty, 289–290
    map, 286
    market barriers, 293–294, 441
    marketing implications, 292–294
    marketing mix implications, 294
    membership statistics, 285
    and Mercosur, 301
    mutual recognition, 288
    myths about, 290
    opportunities, 293
    and political union, 284
    price fixing, 554
    price variations, 530

pricing policies, 294
Product Liability Directive, 380
protectionism in, 357–358
quotas, 452
reciprocity, 294
recycling and ecolabeling, 202
regulation of TV advertising, 484
Single European Act, 287–288
statistical data errors, 220
taxation of e-commerce, 209
taxes, 288
timeline, 287
trade war with U.S., 40–41
transportation network, 282
Treaty of Amsterdam, 291–292
tunnel and bridge building, 65
women managers, 141
worker/retiree ratio, 76
workers' rights laws, 511
and World Trade Organization, 48
European Union Commission, 209, 210
European Union Parliament, 198
Eveready Battery, 478, 481
Excelcia Foods, 331
Exchange-control restrictions, 42–43
Exchange controls, 167, 442
Exchange permits, 442
Exchange rate differentials, 42
Exchange-rate fluctuations, 37, 50,
    536–537
Exchange swings, 538
Excise taxes, 535
Excite At Home Corporation, 311, 330
Exclusive distribution, 530–531
EX (named port of origin), 445
Expatriates; *see also* Sales management
    attributes, 509–511
    candidate profile, 518
    compensation, 515
    cost of, 518
    cultural awareness, 521–522
    declining use of, 504
    disadvantages, 504
    early return rate, 519–520
    families of, 519–520
    host-country restrictions, 509
    language skills, 505, 524–525
    length of assignment, 504
    versus local nationals, 506–509
    most expensive cities for, 508
    overcoming reluctance, 519
    preparation of, 518–521
    reentry process, 521
    repatriation, 520–521
    returnee attrition, 520–521
    selection mistakes, 511
    training program, 512–513
    travel risk, 505, 506
    virtual, 505–506
Expert opinion, 232
Export Administration Regulations, 436, 439
Export Control Classification Number,
    436–438, 440
Export control system, 204–205
Export Credits Guarantee Department, 627
Export documents, 449–450
Exporters Encyclopedia, 242
Export expansion, 46
Export-Import Bank, 178, 261, 433
Exporting, 435–441
    bills of exchange, 448–449
    cash in advance, 449
    costs of, 535
    customs-privileged facilities, 451–452
    direct or indirect, 323–324
    factoring, 449
    foreign trade zones, 451–452
    forfaiting, 449
    global trade compliance, 460
    letters of credit, 446–448
    logistics management, 453–464
    maintaining prices, 547
    maquiladoras, 452–453
    market-entry strategy, 323–325
    open accounts, 446, 449
    packing and marking, 451
    payment arrangements, 446–449
    and pilferage, 457
    process, 435

terms of sale, 445–446
trade shows for, 433–434
transportation costs, 539
Export jobbers, 415
Export license, 46, 450
    general, 436
    validated, 436
Export License Application and
    Information Network
    (ELAIN), 440
Export licensing controls, 436
Export management companies, 411–412
Export Market Locator, 242
Export merchants, 415
Export regulations, 435–436
Export restrictions
    Commerce Control List, 437–438
    Commerce Country Chart, 438
    determining export requirements,
        436–440
    electronic services for, 440–441
    Export Administration
        Regulations, 436
    export license, 436–437
    List of Denied Persons, 438–439
    Prohibited Parties Database, 438n
    red flags, 439
    violations and penalties, 440
Exports
    African market groups, 306
    Asian countries, 268
    Asian-Pacific Rim, 304
    big emerging markets, 262
    Commonwealth of Independent
        States, 295
    Eastern Europe, 266
    European Free Trade Area, 285
    European Union, 285
    Latin America, 302
Export shipping, 456–459
Export trade, 46
Export Trading Company Act, 413
Export Yellow Pages, 240
Expropriation, 166–167
Extortion, 147
Extraterritoriality of U.S. laws, 181, 203,
    206–207
Exxon, 11
Eye contact, 126

f

Fabergé, 541
Face-to-face communication, 135–136
Face-to-face negotiations, 558–559
Factoring, 449
Factors of production, 250
Factual knowledge, 114–115
Failed State Index, 174, 175
Fair & Lovely, case, 618–620
Fairness, 149, 672
Families of expatriates, 519–520
Family
    forms and functions, 103–104
    importance of, 72
Family planning, 73
Fanta, 607
Fascism, 102
FAS (free alongside), 445–446
Fast-food restaurants, 173–174
Fast Forwarder, 434
Fast Retailing Company, 401, 402
Fear, targeted, 164–165
Fedders, 19–20, 23
Fedders Xinle, 20
Federal Emergency Management Agency,
    417
Federal Express, 209, 283, 324, 404, 406,
    430, 440, 457, 458, 459
Federal Express Distribution Center,
    Japan, 458
Federal Maritime Commission, 459
Federal Register, 157
Federal Trade Commission, 198
Feedback, 479, 482
Femininity, 154–155
Feng shui, 112–113
Ferragamo, 364
Ferrari, 314

Ferrero, 43
Fertility rates, 96
Fidelity Investments, 93, 118
Field surveys, 225–226
Firestone tires, 6, 7
First-name basis, 137
First-to-invent issue, 195
First-to-register issue, 195
Fisher Price, 300
Five-stage model of economic
    development, 375
Flexibility, 510
Floating exchange rates, 50
Floraplex Web site, 424
Flower industry, 100–101
Flower Purchase Network, 424
Fluor Daniel, 373
Focus groups, online, 230
Fomento Economico Mexicano SA, 203
Food and Drink Industries Federation,
    Finland, 633
Food and Drug Administration, 297, 461
Food quality, 340
Ford Focus, 646
Ford Motor Company, 7, 23, 123, 142, 235,
    312, 315, 331, 404, 426, 471, 472,
    475, 496, 571
    Executive Development Center, 573
    Firestone Tire problem, 470
    and IBM, 502, 503
    Managing Negotiations: Japan, 572
    revenues, 9
Ford Pinto, 351
Ford Taurus, 349
Forecasting
    chain-ratio approach, 232
    global health care market, 234
    market demand, 232–234
    by triangulation, 232
Foreign assignment
    candidate profile, 518
    cost of preparation, 518
    example, 501, 508
    expatriate repatriation, 520–521
    most expensive cities for, 508
    overcoming reluctance, 519
    qualifications for, 509–511
    reducing early return rate, 519–520
Foreign Corrupt Practices Act, 46, 146,
    148, 203–204, 622, 624, 630
Foreign-country brokers, 417
Foreign-country middlemen
    brokers, 417
    compradors, 417
    dealers, 417
    distributors, 415–417
    import jobbers, 417
    managing agents, 417
    manufacturer's representative, 415
    retailers, 417
    wholesalers, 417
Foreign Credit Insurance Association, 178
Foreign distributors, 415–417
Foreign economic assistance, 29–30
Foreign environment, 12–13
Foreign environment uncontrollables,
    12–13
Foreign exchange rates, 442
Foreign exchange shortages, 167
Foreign freight forwarder, 458
Foreign investment, 159, 166, 176, 178
Foreign Investment Promotion Board,
    India, 608
Foreign language skills, 505, 524–525
Foreign market development
    by direct foreign investment, 332
    by exporting, 323–325
    by franchising, 325–327
    by licensing, 325
    by strategic alliances, 327–331
Foreign markets
    avoidance of, 19
    barriers to entry, 357–360
    domestic extension concept, 22
    global marketing stage, 20–22
    global orientation to, 23
    infrequent involvement, 19
    multidomestic orientation to, 22–23

Foreign markets *(Continued)*
  regular involvement, 19
  transition to international marketing, 19–20
Foreign-owned U.S. companies, 6–8
Foreign policy
  decisions, 11
  Monroe Doctrine, 58–61
Foreign Policy, 158, 174
Foreign sales corporations, 414–415
Foreign students, 358
Foreign Trade Report FI 410, 240
Foreign Traders Index, 240
Foreign trade zones, 451–452
  to lessen price escalation, 543–544
  uses, 544
Forfaiting, 449
Formality, 137–138
Forrester Research, 427
Fortune 500 companies, 330
Forward hedging, 537
Four Seasons Hotels, 356, 359
Fox Network, 352, 641, 642
Fox Studios, 468
France
  animosity toward U.S., 165
  ban on English terms, 136
  birth bonus, 105
  consequences of consumption, 97
  equities trading, 93
  EuroDisney, 337
  farmers' union, 177
  formality in, 137
  language wars, 110
  nationalism, 8
  negotiating style, 566
  trade disputes with, 27
  uncertainty avoidance, 107
France Telecom, 311, 376
Franchising, 325–327
Frankenfood, 169, 174, 353
Free Burma Campaign, 169
Free-market system, 280
Freeplay radio, 650
Free trade, 33
  and Middle East, 279
  United States treaties, 282
Free Trade Area of the Americas, 303
Free trade areas, 332; *see also* European
  Union; North American Free
  Trade Agreement
  characteristics, 282–283
  and job loss, 283
Freight forwarder, 458
French Peasant Confederation, 6
French's mustard, 482
Freshplex, 424
Friendship, 125–126
Frito-Lay, 341
Frymaster Corporation, 378
Fugetsudo, 340
Fuji Photo Film, 7, 11
Full-cost pricing, 532
Functional features, 351
Fuqua School, Duke University, 524

g

Gaijin, 482
Gai Zhong Gai, 473
Gap, Inc., 52, 597
Garbage collection services, 382
Garbage disposal problem, 69
Gas fields, 86
Gateway Computer, 425
Gender
  imbalance in China, 76
  and negotiation teams, 571
Gender bias, 103–104, 140–142
General Agreement on Tariffs and Trade,
  28, 30, 46–48, 385, 445, 545
  skirting the spirit of, 49
General Agreement on Trade in Services, 47
General Electric, 171, 297, 333, 355, 360,
  365, 370, 374, 379, 402, 413, 540,
  547, 596, 660, 661
  Magnetic Resonance Imaging systems,
  662
  revenues, 9

General Electric Medical Systems, 382
General export license, 436
General Foods, 350–351
General Mills, 486, 634
  Nestlé partnership, 328
General Motors, 248–249, 297, 331, 333,
  341–342, 360, 362, 404, 426, 472,
  547, 548, 575
General Motors of Canada, 341
Genetically modified food/organisms, 118,
  169, 174, 297, 353
Geographic hurdles, 64–65
  overcoming, 66
Geographic proximity, 282
Geography
  climate and topography, 63–65
  and culture, 56, 99–102
  engineering projects, 66
  environmental management, 66–69
  garbage disposal problem, 69
  global markets, 62–71
  mountain ranges, 64–65
  physical barriers, 65
  resources, 70–71
  sustainable development, 67–68
  water supply, 63
Geography of Thought (Nisbett), 113
Gerber, 224
Germany
  Center for Combating Unfair Competition, 201
  communitarian capitalism, 150
  consequences of consumption, 97
  negotiating style, 566
  product comparison law, 200
  retail structures, 399
Getting to Yes (Fisher, Ury, & Patton),
  567, 574
Gift-giving, 108
Gigante supermarkets, 7, 8, 411
Gillette Company, 157, 263, 275, 361, 362,
  464, 474, 523
GlaxoSmithKline, 530
Global awareness, 17–18
Global brands
  characteristics, 362–363
  definition, 360
  top twenty, 360–361
  value of, 361
Global business
  communication links, 78
  geographic factors, 62–71
  government encouragement, 178–179
  historical perspective, 56–62
  political environment, 158
  world trade routes, 77–78
Global Business Procurement Opportunities, 238
Global business risks
  assessing vulnerability, 173–176
  confiscation, 166–167
  cyberterrorism/cybercrime, 172–173
  domestication, 166–167
  economic risks, 167–168
  expropriation, 166–167
  forecasting political risks, 174–176
  lessening vulnerability, 176–178
  from NGOs, 169–172
  political sanctions, 169
  from political/social activists, 169–172
  violence of terrorism, 172
Global communications, 88
Global companies, 22
  expanding reach, 34
Global competition, 333–335, 338–339
  effect on pricing, 528
  relationship marketing, 502
Global economy, 91
Global gross national product, 31
Global Harmonization Task Force, 378
Global health care market, 234
Globalization, 284–285, 308
  versus localization, 312–313
  protests against, 51–52
  ranking of nations, 24
Global managers, 522–524
Global marketing, 20–22; *see also* International marketing
  benefits, 315–317

  marketing mix, 320–321
  segmentation variables, 314
Global marketing concept, 23
Global marketing management, 310–335
  benefits of global marketing, 315–317
  brands in, 360–366
  centralized or decentralized organizations, 334–335
  characteristics, 312–314
  company objectives and resources, 317–318
  consortia, 330–331
  consumer services, 355–360
  contractual agreements, 325–327
  direct foreign investment, 332
  direct sales, 325
  exporting, 323–325
  franchising, 325–327
  gateways, 311–312
  by IKEA, 316
  implementation and control, 321–322
  international commitment, 318
  international joint ventures, 328–330
  Internet use, 324
  by Levi Strauss, 529
  licensing, 325
  localization trend, 312–313
  locus of decision, 334
  market-entry strategies, 322–332
  marketing mix adaptation, 320–321
  marketing plan, 321
  McDonald's, 654–655
  Nestlé Company, 314–315
  old *vs.* new debate, 312–314
  organizing for, 333–335
  planning for, 317–322
  preliminary analysis, 319–320
  proactive countertrade strategy, 549–550
  risks of violence, 506
  segmentation variables, 314
  Starbucks Corporation, 596–599
  strategic international alliances, 327–331
  tactical approaches, 315–317
Global market orientation, 23
Global markets
  cultural uniqueness in, 473
  homogenization/diversification, 314
GlobalNetXchange, 404
Global population
  Africa, 262
  African market groups, 306
  aging of populations, 74–75
  Asia, 262, 269
  Asian-Pacific Rim, 304
  big emerging markets, 262
  Commonwealth of Independent States, 295
  controlling growth of, 72–73
  current size, 72
  Eastern Europe, 266
  Europe, 262
  European Free Trade Area, 285
  European Union, 285
  female/male statistics, 140–141
  gender imbalance in China, 76
  immigration, 76–77
  Latin America, 262, 264, 302
  life expectancy, 73
  population decline, 74–75
  regional distribution, 73–74
  rural-urban migration, 73–74
  rural-urban population, 73
  worker shortage, 76–77
Global product division structure, 333
Global retailers, 411
Global sales force compensation, 516–517
Global System for Mobile Communications, 318
Global trade compliance, 460
Godiva chocolates, 171
Goldman, Sachs, 93
Goldstar TVs, 6
Goodyear Tire & Rubber Company, 249
Goplana, 315
Gotthard Tunnel, 65
Government, 105
  forms of, 161–162

Government-affiliated middlemen, 417
Government approval to secure foreign exchange, 42–43
Government encouragement, 178–179
Government-influenced pricing, 554
Government policy stability
  Africa, 160
  forms of government, 161–162
  Mexico, 159–160
  nationalism, 163–164
  political parties, 162–163
  Russia, 160–161
  targeted fear/animosity, 164–165
  trade disputes, 157, 165–166
Grameen Bank, 252
Grand Bazaar, Istanbul, 421
Grand Coast Fishing Operators, 253
Grand Tour, 114
Gray MacKenzie and Company, 412
Gray markets, 530–532
Great Depression, 30
Greece, end of drachma, 292
Green marketing, 201–202, 341–342
Greenpeace, 169, 654
Grey Worldwide, 312
Grokster, 16
Gross Domestic Product, 247; *see also* Per
  capita GDP
  African market groups, 306
  Asian countries, 268
  Asian-Pacific Rim, 304
  big emerging markets, 261, 262
  Chile, 250
  Commonwealth of Independent States, 295
  Eastern Europe, 266
  European Free Trade Area, 285
  European Union, 285
  Latin America, 302
Gross national product, 247n
  global, 31
  and living standards, 276
  of NAFTA area, 298
Group decision making, 131
Group identification, 133
Group of Eight, 173
Growth factors, 249–251
Grupo Modelo SA, 203
Guangzhou Wuzhou Aoqili Group Company, 473
Guanxi, 125–126, 151
Gucci, 191, 314, 364, 540
Guinness, 104, 493
Guinness Bass Import Corporation, 324

h

H. J. Heinz Company, 362, 536
Häagen-Dazs, 497
Habitat for Humanity, 172
Hachette Filipachi, 490
Hackers, 6
Hakuhoda DY Holdings, 496
Hal Riney & Partners, 598
Hanna Andersson, 409
Hanover Industry Fair, 386
Hard currency, 547
Harmonization, 288
Harry Potter books, 345
Harvard Business Review, 135
Harvard Business School, 570
Hasbro, Inc., 123, 207, 467
Haste, 137–138
Havas, 496
Hawg Heaven Bait Company, 11
Hazardous waste, 67
HBO, 478
Health Canada, 540
Health care, East *vs.* West, 219
Health care market, 234
Health issues, 174
Hedging, 537
Heineken, 169
Heinz Baked Beans Pizza, 362
Helms-Burton Act, 181
Henkel, 473
Hertz, 644
Heterogeneous services, 355
Hewlett-Packard, 331, 361, 514, 537, 598
  revenues, 9

Hierarchical cultures, 107
High-context culture, 135–136, 151
High-definition television, 490
Hijaz Railway Corporation, 279
Hindustan Coca-Cola Holding Pvt. Ltd., 608
Hindustan Lever LTD, 487, 650
    case, 618–620
Hindustan Lever Research Center, 620
History
    and culture, 102
    International trade, 29–34
    local, 62
    National mission, 56–62
    Panama, 55–56
    subjectivity in, 57–59
    timeline, 29–45
HIV/AIDS, 16, 99
Hoechst, 605
Holiday Autos, 645
Home-country brokers, 414
Home country laws, 206–207
Home-country middlemen
    brokers, 414
    buying office, 414
    complementary marketing, 413
    export jobbers, 415
    export management companies,
        411–412
    export merchant, 415
    foreign sales corporations, 414–415
    global retailers, 411
    manufacturer's export agent, 414
    manufacturers' retail stores, 411
    selling groups, 414
    trading companies, 412–413
    U.S. export trading companies, 413
    Web-Pomerene export associations, 414
Home-office personnel training, 513
Honda Civic, 288
Honda Motor Company, 7, 8, 361, 364, 472
Honda motorcycles, 192
Hong Kong, 271
Hong Kong Disneyland, 6, 113, 337, 351,
    528, 581
Hong Kong Independent Commission
        Against Corruption, 629
Honne, 136
Hoover washing machines, 342
Host-country restrictions, 509
Huangjindadang, 473
Huffy Corporation, 7
Hughes Aircraft, 46
Hummer, 342
Hyundai Motor Company, 249, 383

I

Iberia Airlines, 523
IBM, 11, 136, 170, 206, 255, 331, 360, 361,
        373, 393, 478, 494, 514, 522, 596,
        663, 664
    and Ford Motor Company, 502, 503
    worldwide compensation, 516–517
IBM Canada, 503
IBM Japan, 664
IBM Thinkpad, 7
ICICI Bank, 651
IKEA, 411
    global marketing, 316
Immigration, 76–77
Impatience, 137–138
Imperial Chemical Industries, 664
Import certificate fees, 535
Import jobbers, 417
Import license, 433, 442, 450
Import-oriented distribution structure,
        396–397
Import regulations, 435–436
Import relief, 46
Import restrictions, 167–168, 441–445
    boycotts, 444
    exchange permits, 442
    harmful products, 444–445
    import licenses, 442
    quotas, 442
    sanitation certificates, 445
    and smuggling, 443
    standards, 443–444
    tariffs, 441–442

violations, 452
    voluntary agreements, 444
Imports
    African market groups, 306
    Asian countries, 268
    Asian-Pacific Rim, 304
    big emerging markets, 262
    Commonwealth of Independent
        States, 295
    Eastern Europe, 266
    European Free Trade Area, 285
    European Union, 285
    Latin America, 302
Improvement, quest for, 129
In-bond companies, 452–453
Incentive system, 518
Incoterms, 445
Independent enterprise, 128
India
    advertising case, 618–620
    AIDS prevention, 667–668
    business environment, 273
    caste system, 103
    cattle dung for fuel, 72
    Central Bureau of Investigation, 626
    Coca-Cola in, 164
    Coke vs. Pepsi, 604–609
    demand in, 258
    economy of, 272–273
    electric power, 255
    information technology, 252, 273
    infrastructure, 255
    Internet users, 263
    middle class, 273
    Narmada Valley Dam Project, 66
    pharmaceutical industry, 251
    population growth, 72
    restrictions on investment, 163
Indirect exporting, 323–324
Individualism, 117, 124, 142
    national/regional index score, 154–155
Individualism/Collectivism Index, 106–107
Individual Retirement Accounts, 551
Indonesia, 569
Industrial corporations, largest, 31–32
Industrial goods
    after-sale services, 382–384
    derived demand, 373–374
    gauging demand for, 371–376
    ISO 9000 certification, 380–381
    and metric system, 378–380
    quality standards, 376–381
    standardization of, 370–371
    and stages of economic development,
        375
    volatility of demand, 372–375
Industrialization objective, 252–253
Industrial wastes, 67
Infant feeding formula, 120
Infant Formula Action Coalition, 601
Inflation, 535–536
Informality, 137
Information
    key to marketing research, 214
    types needed for marketing research,
        215
Information explosion, 313–314
Information-oriented cultures, 151–152
Information sources, 479
    bibliographies, 241
    demographic data, 242–243
    directories, 241
    marketing guides, 242
    periodical indexes, 243
    periodicals, 243
    U.S. government sources, 239–241
    Web sites, 238–239
Information technology
    in China, 270–271
    and economic development, 251–252
    in India, 273
    in village life, 253
Infrastructure
    in big emerging markets, 262–263
    definition, 253
    and economic development, 253–254
    in India, 255
    and Internet, 252
    national comparisons, 254

Innovation, 98
    acceptance of, 117–118
    consequences of, 119–120
    five characteristics of, 348–349
    impact on culture, 102–103
    perception of newness, 345–346, 348
Innovative products
    adaptation, 345–346
    diffusion of innovation, 345, 346–349
    production of, 349
INSEAD, 149
Inseparability of services, 355
Institute of Health, 475
Institute of International Education, 358
Institutional Revolutionary Party (Mexico),
        159–160
Insurance policy/certificate, 450
Intangibility of services, 355
Integrated marketing communications; see
        also International advertising
    definition, 468
    Mattel Inc., 467
    public relations, 470–471
    sales promotions, 468–470
Intel Corporation, 23, 331, 360, 369, 471
    e-Business Solutions Centers, 383
    revenues, 9
Intellectual property
    and cybersquatters, 208
    laws on, 142
    protection of, 358–359
Intellectual property rights, 16, 47
    code law vs. common law, 183–184
    counterfeiting and piracy, 191–194
    inadequate protection, 194
    in India, 273
    international conventions, 196–198
    and NAFTA, 299
    prior use vs. registration, 194–195
Interactive Tariff Database, 38
Interagency Group on Breastfeeding
        Monitoring, 602
Inter-American Commercial Arbitration
        Commission, 189
Inter-American Convention, 196
Inter-American Convention of International
        Arbitration, 190
Interest, prohibition of, 185
Interfaith Center on Corporate
        Responsibility, 601
Intermodal marketing companies, 457
International advertising
    advertising agencies, 496–497
    basic framework and concepts, 473
    benefit segmentation, 475–378
    campaign execution, 496–497
    communication process, 479–483
    comparative advertising, 483
    consumer criticisms, 497–498
    creative challenge, 479–488
    cultural diversity, 486–487
    and cultural uniqueness, 473
    decoding errors, 481–482
    direct mail, 493–494
    encoding problems, 480
    expenditure rate growth, 472
    Fair and Lovely case, 618–620
    and global competition, 474
    international control, 497–499
    Internet, 494–495
    language problems, 110
    laws on, 198–201
    legal constraints, 483–485
    linguistic limitations, 485–486
    literacy problems, 479
    magazine advertising, 490
    Mattel Inc., 467
    media limitations, 487
    media penetration, 492
    media planning/analysis, 488–495
    message, 479–488
    by Microsoft, 476–477
    newspaper advertising, 489–490
    noise impairment, 482
    other media, 495
    product attribute, 475–478
    production/cost limitations, 487–488
    product placement, 498
    promotional misfires/mistakes, 479–482

radio advertising, 490–491
    regional segmentation, 478
    satellite/cable TV, 491–493
    and self-reference criterion, 479–480
    self-regulation, 497–498
    sex in, 497
    strategy and goals, 474–478
    subliminal messages, 498
    tactical considerations, 488
    taxes, 484–485
    television advertising, 490–491
    tobacco ban, 498
    top ten advertisers, 473
    top twenty advertisers, 471
    total expenditures 2005, 471
International Advertising Association, 498
International Aircraft Leasing, 626
International Brands and Their Companies,
        241
International business
    challenge of, 5
    projected changes, 33–34
    purpose of antitrust law, 205
    scope of, 5
    trends, 5
International Business Handbook, 242
International business negotiations
    aftermath, 581
    audiences, 575
    BATNA, 574
    characteristics, 558–559
    checklist, 573
    competitiveness/equality, 567–568
    concessions and agreement, 581
    contracts, 581
    cross-cultural comparisons, 562–567
    danger of stereotypes, 559–560
    decision-making process, 569–570
    differences in thinking, 569–570
    digital impact, 576
    elements and attitudes, 140
    e-mail, 575
    follow-up communications, 581
    gender issue, 571
    Iberia Airlines case, 659–661
    impact of culture, 560–570
    improvements in, 582
    Japan aisatsu, 557
    Japan/U.S. comparisons, 567–568, 577
    language differences, 561–567
    linguistics, 564
    and local customs, 126–127
    location, 575
    MRI systems case, 662
    at the negotiating table, 575–581
    negotiating teams, 570–571
    nontask sounding, 577–578
    nonverbal behavior, 561–567
    objectivity, 567
    persuasion, 580–581
    physical arrangements, 575
    preliminaries, 572–575
    Russia/Indonesia, 569
    stages, 576
    task-related information exchange,
        578–580
    time factor, 568–569
    value differences, 567–569
    verbal tactics, 563
International Chamber of Commerce,
        189–190, 209, 445
International commitment, 318
International communication process,
        479–483
International conventions on property
        rights, 196–198
International corporate planning, 317
International Court of Justice, 187
International Cricket Council, 668
International Criminal Court, 158
International Directory of Business Infor-
        mation Sources and Services, 241
International Directory of Corporate
        Affiliations, 241
International Economic Indicators, 240
International Electrotechnical Commission,
        378
International Franchising Association, 325
International Herald Tribune, 140

International Internet marketing, 324
International joint ventures, 328–330
International Labor Organization, 141, 171
International law, 158
International legal disputes; see also Legal
    environment
    arbitration, 189–190
    case, 188
    conciliation, 187–189
    cyberlaw jurisdiction, 209–210
    jurisdiction in, 186–187
    litigation, 190–191
International legal environment; see Legal
    environment
International logistics management,
    459–460
International marketing
    bottom-of-the-pyramid markets,
      259–261
    brands in, 360–366
    cause of peace, 3–4
    characteristics, 9–10
    communication links, 78
    contribution to economic development,
      254–255
    cultural congruence strategy, 118–119
    disruptions, 6
    and economic development, 246–255
    effect of world events, 4
    in emerging markets, 256–274
    ethical decisions, 670–674
    and ethnocentrism, 15–17
    and European Union, 292–294
    government encouragement, 178–179
    gray markets, 530–532
    implications of emerging markets,
      274–276
    information sources, 238–243
    linguistic distance concept, 110
    opportunities and challenges, 338
    orientation of, 23–25
    pertinence of culture, 94
    public relations in, 470
    and self-reference criterion, 15–17
    small businesses in, 34
    stage of foreign marketing, 19–20
    strategic orientation, 22–23
    in Third World, 263
    by U.S. businesses, 6–9
    uncontrollable elements, 9–10
    websites for, 238–239
International marketing channels, 394–430;
    see also Channels of distribution;
    Logistics management
    channel choice, 419–421
    channel-of-distribution structure,
      396–405
    direct marketing, 408–409
    distribution costs, 543
    distribution patterns, 405–409
    example, 395–396
    exclusive distribution, 530–531
    foreign trade zones, 543–544
    import-oriented, 396–397
    Internet, 425–430
    in Japan, 397–398, 401–402
    locating/selecting middlemen, 422–425
    middleman costs, 538–539
    options, 409–418
    retailing, 407–409
    sales force design, 502
    six Cs of channel strategy, 419–421
    transportation costs, 538–539
International Marketing Data and
    Statistics, 242
International marketing environment, 9–10
    controllable elements, 10, 11
    domestic, 11–12
    foreign, 12–13
    impact of geography, 62–71
    need for adaptation, 14–15
    place of culture in, 94
    uncontrollable elements, 10, 11
International Marketing Information
    Sources, 240
International marketing involvement
    stages, 18–22
    global marketing, 20–22
    infrequent marketing, 19

international marketing, 19–20
    no direct foreign marketing, 19
    regular foreign marketing, 19
International marketing plan, 321–322
International marketing research, 214; see
    also Marketing research
International marketing task
    aspects of domestic environment,
      11–12
    aspects of foreign environment, 12–13
    marketing decision factors, 10–11
    uncertainties in, 10
International Monetary Fund, 49–50, 169,
    267
    protests against, 51–52
International Olympic Committee, 640
International Organization for
    Standardization, 380
    Health and Safety Standard, 381
International planning process, 319–322
International pricing, 526–554
    administered pricing, 552–554
    administrative costs, 535
    advanced pricing agreements, 551
    cartels, 552–554
    costs of exporting, 535
    costs of goods sold, 540–541
    countertrade, 546–550
    deflation, 535–536
    distribution costs, 543
    dumping, 544–545
    effects of price escalation, 539–540
    in European Union, 294
    exchange rate fluctuations, 536–537
    factors important to, 528
    foreign trade zones, 543–544
    full-cost vs. variable-cost, 532
    functions, 528
    government-influenced, 554
    gray market goods, 530–531
    inflation, 535–536
    international agreements, 554
    leasing, 545–546
    middleman costs, 538–539
    multiple-income levels, 534
    parallel imports, 529–532
    penetration pricing, 533–534
    price escalation, 534–545
    price fixing, 552
    price quotations, 551–552
    price war, 527
    pricing objectives, 528
    skimming policy, 533–534
    tariffs, 535, 541–542
    and taxes, 535
    transfer pricing, 550–551
    transportation costs, 538–539
    varying currency values, 537–538
International public relations, 470–471
International Reciprocal Trade
    Association, 549
International sales; see Sales management
International Space Station, 3
International standards, 378–381
International tourism, 355–357
International trade; see also Business-to-
    business marketing; Products and
    services; Trade barriers
    antidumping penalties, 44–45
    Asian countries, 268
    balance of merchandise trade, 32
    balance of payments, 33–37
    big emerging markets, 262
    boycotts or embargoes, 42
    China and U.S., 269
    competitive environment, 28
    disputes with Japan, 27–28
    dumping, 44, 544–545
    early 20th century, 33–35
    easing restrictions on, 45–49
    Eastern Europe, 266
    export control system, 204–205
    export trade, 46
    foreign commercial payments,
      446–449
    General Agreement on Tariffs and
      Trade, 46–48
    growth projections, 33–34
    historical overview, 29–35

intellectual property rights, 196
International Monetary Fund, 49–50
    and legal conflicts, 181
    map, 91
    Marshall Plan, 29–30
    nontariff barriers, 40, 42–45
    oil imports, 70
    Omnibus Trade and Competitiveness
      Act, 45–46
    opposing views on, 308
    permanently normalized trade
      relations, 11
    protectionism, 37
    protests against global institutions,
      51–52
    in services, 47
    skirting spirit of GATT/WTO, 49
    terms of sale, 445–446
    timeline, 28–45
    top U.S. trading partners, 28
    and U.S. multinationals, 30–33
    World Bank, 49–50
    World Trade Organization, 48–49
    world trade routes, 77–78
International Trade Administration,
    178, 238
International trade disputes, 157, 166–166
International Tradeshow, 242
International treaty regimes, 158
Internet, 78
    advertising on, 494–495
    in business-to-business context, 388
    countertrade, 549
    cybercrime, 172–173
    and cyberlaw, 207–210
    demographics of users, 230
    as distribution channel, 425–430
    and economic development, 251–252
    European Union regulation, 484
    in India, 263
    market-entry strategy, 324
    for marketing research, 230–231
    number of users, 230, 349
    online auctions, 93
    and taxes, 209
    tool of protesters, 169–170
Internet communication, 136–137
Internet Corporation for Assigned Names
    and Numbers, 208
Interpretive knowledge, 114–115
Interpublic Group, 496
Intracompany pricing, 550–551
Inventory control, 426
Inventory financing, 399
Investing Licensing and Trading Abroad,
    243
Investment; see also Direct foreign
    investment; Foreign investment
    and North American Free Trade
      Agreement, 299
    restrictions on, 47
Investment base, 177
Invisible hand, 129
iPod, 360
Iran, 162
Iran embargo, 42, 169
Iraq War, 4, 165
Iridium LLC, 371
Irrevocable letter of credit, 448
Islam, 104
Islamic law, 182, 185–186
ISO 9000 certification, 380–381
ISO Health and Safety Standard, 381
ISP Virtual Show, 387
Israel
    Arab League boycott, 206
    and free trade, 279
    Oslo Accords, 279
    and Palestinians, 56n
ITC, 650
Ito-Yokado Corporation, 404

J

Jaguar, 7, 312
Japan
    advertising themes, 491
    aging populations, 74–75
    AIDS prevention, 669

aisatsu, 557, 561
American apples, 213
antitrust law, 554
Apple Computer, 213
arbitration in, 189–190
birthrate decline, 74
birthrates, 95
blondes in, 123
business philosophy, 400
capital markets, 93
Chinese hostility toward, 164–165
communitarian capitalism, 150
consensus orientation, 124
consequences of consumption,
    97–98
consumer behavior, 14, 427
cultural characteristics, 57
deflation, 536
density of middlemen, 398–399
department stores, 401
diet change, 119
distribution structure, 397–398,
    401–402
energy use, 70
expatriates, 521
fertility rate, 96
Ford Motor Company in, 572–573
foreign access zones, 451n
government price-setting, 554
group identification, 133
high-context culture, 151
historical overview, 56–57
JETRO, 231
keiretsu system, 401
Korean competitors, 349
Large-Scale Retail Store Law,
    400–401
Ministry of Health and Welfare, 554
Ministry of International Trade and
    Industry, 400
nationalism in, 164
negotiating style, 557, 561–562,
    567–568, 577
Nestlé in, 350
ningen kankei, 125–126
number of lawyers, 182, 183
patent law, 184
retail structures, 399
sales force motivation, 513–514
sales force views, 513
stock trading, 93
Structural Impediments Initiative, 400,
    401–402
toilet innovations, 347, 348
trade disputes with, 27
trading companies, 413
truth, 136
U.S. design centers, 349
U.S. fear of, 8
U.S. trade sanctions, 170
uncertainty avoidance, 107
vacation time, 359
view of contracts, 581
voluntary export restraints, 42, 444
work ethic, 132
Japan Motorola, 664
JCPenney, 64, 403
JD Power & Associates, 340
Jeep Cherokee, 365
Jerusalem, 279
JETRO, Japan, 231
Jiuxin Group Daily Chemical Company,
    473
JLG Industries, 323
Job loss, and free trade, 283, 300
Job mobility, 132
Johns Hopkins Hospital, 234
Johnson & Johnson, 25, 27n, 472,
    533, 541
Joint ventures, 19–20, 177, 328–330
Joseph Paolino & Sons, 69
Jurisdiction
    case, 188
    and cyberlaw, 209–210
    international legal disputes, 186–187
    objective theory of, 203
    over online activity, 209
Jusco supermarkets, 419
Justice, 149, 672

K

KalKan, 363
Katrina, hurricane, 64
Kazaa, 16
Keiretsu system, 401
Kellogg Company, 191, 314, 328, 362, 633, 634
Kelvintaor, 611
Kenko do Brazil, 527
Kentucky Fried Chicken, 110, 172, 173–174, 255, 326, 505, 551
Khaker, 6
Khian Sea cargo ship, 69
Kia, 249
Kimberly-Clark Corporation, 528, 540, 656, 657
    competition with Procter & Gamble, 527
Kirch, 641, 642
Klinskoye, 498
KLM, 327, 328
Kmart, 413, 651
Knowledge, 113–114
Kodak, 191
Kojima, 402
Komsomolskaya Pravda, 218
Konbini, 402
Koran, 185
Korn/Ferry International, 504
KPMG Peat Marwick, 137
Kraft Foods, 297, 519, 634
Kuwait Airways Corporation, 625
Kyocera Corporation, 332
Kyoto Protocol, 158

L

L. L. Bean, 324, 404
Labeling laws, 342, 351, 353, 364
Labor-management relations, 150
Labor problems, 168
Landfills, 69
Lands' End, 324, 403, 404, 425
L&T Honeywell, 605
Language, 109–111
    differences in English, 116–117
    foreign-language skills, 524–525
    national/regional index score, 154–155
    of space, 134
Language barriers, 226–228, 485–486, 578–579
    back translation, 228
    decentering, 228
    literacy rates, 227
    parallel translation, 228
    as research problem, 226–227
    and research questionnaires, 227
Language differences, 15–16
    in negotiations, 561–567
Language family trees, 111
Language wars, 110
LapPower, 497
Large-Scale Retail Store Law, Japan, 400–401
Large-Scale Retail Store Location Act, Japan, 400–401
Latin America
    child labor, 171
    Chilean economy, 250–251
    compadre, 125–126
    economic cooperation, 301–303
    economic problems, 301
    economies of, 263–265
    infrastructure, 254
    marketing considerations, 64
    market regions, 302
    Mercosur, 300–301
    and Monroe Doctrine, 58–61
    regionwide promotion programs, 478
    satellite TV, 492
    statistics on, 262
    U.S. interventions, 61
    vocabulary differences, 110
Latin American Free Trade Association, 281, 301
Latin American Integration Association, 301–303
Latvia, 195, 267

Laura Ashley, 6
Law firm expansion, 384
Layoffs, 150
Lear Jet, 249
Leasing, 545–546
Least-developed countries, 248
Legal environment, 180–210
    advertising, 198–201
    alien status problem, 12–13
    antiboycott law, 205–206
    antitrust law, 202–203, 205
    bases for legal systems, 182–186
    Canadian law, 181
    case, 631, 632–634
    China, 12, 270
    code law, 182, 183–185
    commercial law, 198–203
    common law, 182, 183–185
    contract validity, 209–210
    counterfeiting and piracy, 191–194
    cyber/Internet law, 207–210
    dispute resolution, 187–191
    due process variations, 182
    ecolabeling, 342
    extraterritorial application, 181, 206–207
    Foreign Corrupt Practices Act, 203–204
    green marketing legislation, 201–202
    home country laws, 203
    intellectual property rights, 191–198
    international advertising, 483–485, 497–498
    international marketing issues, 183
    Islamic law, 185–186
    Japanese retailing, 400–401
    jurisdiction, 186–187, 209–210
    marketing laws, 198–201
    Marxist-socialist tenets, 186
    and national interest, 203
    national security laws, 204–205
    packaging, 342–343
    patent law, 184, 194–196
    product adaptation, 341
    product comparison laws, 200
    sales promotion regulation, 198–200
    satellite TV, 492
    trademark law, 194–196
    U.S. laws, 203–207
    videogame content, 342
    Wal-Mart case, 181
Legal systems
    bases for, 182–186
    complexity of, 182
    number of attorneys, 182, 183
Lego Company, 123, 467
Lehar Pepsi, 341, 605
Lehar 7UP, 605
Lehman Brothers, 596
Lenor, 482
Less-developed countries, 248; *see also* Emerging markets
Letters of credit, 433–434, 446–448
Level of market development, 256
L'Evénement Sportif, 490
Lever Brothers, 176, 353
Lever Limited, 619
Levi's jeans, 191, 312
Levi Strauss & Company, 362, 365, 425, 548
    global marketing, 529
LG Electronics, Inc., 6, 611
Licensing, 325
    local franchises, 326
    technology, 177
Lifebuoy, 364
Life expectancy, 73, 97
Lil' Orbits, franchising by, 326–327
Limca, 607
LimeWire, 16
Line breadth, 406
Linguistic distance, 110, 111, 152
Linguistic limitations, 485–486
Lipton tea, 482
List of Denied Persons, 438–439
Literacy problems, 479
Literacy rate, 104, 227, 354, 486
Lithuania, 267
Litigation, 190–191

and cyberlaw, 208
    against multinational corporations, 206
Liverpool Liver Burial Society, 493
Living standard comparisons, 276
L.L. Bean, 403
Lloyds Bank, 627
Local contact, 429
Local-content laws, 167
Localization trend, 312–313
Local nationals, 506–509
Lockheed Corporation, 148, 387, 624
Lockheed Martin, 513, 546, 548
Locus of decision, 334
Loetschberg tunnel, 65
Logistics management
    cargo and container security, 461
    customs-trade partnership, 462
    definition, 453
    electronic tracking, 462–464
    export shipping, 456–459
    foreign freight forwarder, 459
    international, 459–460
    physical distribution system, 453–456
    radio frequency identification, 462–464
    supply chain management, 459–460
    and terrorism, 460–464
    warehousing, 456–459
Loma Linda Hospital, California, 357
London Court of Arbitration, 189
London International Group, 668–669
London Okamoto Corporation, 668
Long- short-term orientation, 154–155
Long-term orientation, 106n
L'Oréal, 472, 473
Louis Vuitton, 157, 361, 536n, 543
Low-context culture, 135–136, 151
Lowe Chennai, 607
Lubrication, 148
Lucent Microelectronics, 318
Lucent Technologies, 300, 476
    in China, 318
    Microelectronics Group, 371
Lucky-Goldstar, 249
Lux, 353, 364
Lycos Inc., 311

M

Maastricht Treaty, 284, 287, 289–290
Macintosh computers, 351
Madrid Arrangement, 196
Maersk, 454
Magazine advertising, 490
Maintenance and repair, 353–354
Maintenance cost, 419
Malcolm Baldrige Award, 381
Management objectives and aspirations
    affiliation and social acceptance, 133
    personal life, 132–133
    power and achievement, 134
    security and mobility, 132
Management style, 123–140
    affiliation and social acceptance, 133
    around the world, 130–140
    authority, 130–131
    communication styles, 134–137
    competition, 129–130
    and culture, 124
    decision making, 130–131
    definition, 124
    formality and tempo, 137–138
    impact of U.S. culture, 127–130
    master of destiny philosophy, 127–128
    merit choices, 128
    mobility, 132
    in negotiations, 140
    objective analysis, 128
    objectives and aspirations, 132–134
    office location, 134
    personal life, 132–133
    power and achievement, 133
    quest for improvement, 129
    required adaptation, 124–127
    security, 132
    sharing decision making, 128–129
    time systems, 138–140
Managing agents, 417
Managing Negotiations: Japan, 572–573

Mañana attitude, 138, 139
M&Ms, 363
Manifest Destiny, 59–61
Manufacturer's export agent, 414
Manufacturer's representative, 415
Manufacturers' retail stores, 411
Manufacturing capability updates, 547
Maps; *see* World/Regional maps
Maquiladoras, 300, 452–453
Marathon candy, 363
Marco and Company, 664
Marginal-cost pricing, 532
Market access, 45, 46–47
Market analyst, 349
Market audit, 590–591
Market conditions, 215
Market data, 489
Market demand estimates
    analogy, 232–234
    expert opinion, 232
    global health care market, 234
Market development levels, 256
Market-entry strategies
    alternatives, 323
    consortia, 330–331
    contractual agreements, 325–327
    decision process, 322–323
    direct foreign investment, 332
    direct sales, 325
    exporting, 323–325
    franchising, 325–327
    international joint ventures, 328–330
    Internet use, 324
    licensing, 325
    strategic alliances, 327–331
Market indicators, 259
Marketing decision factors, 10–11
Marketing in Europe, 243
Marketing laws, 198–201
    in China, 200
    enforcement differences, 198–200
    in European Union, 200–201
    national discrepancies, 200
    product comparison laws, 200
Marketing mix
    adapted to global marketing, 320–321
    global perspective, 23
    strategies in European Union, 294
Marketing News, 236
Marketing plan, 321–322; *see also* Country notebook
Marketing program
    cross-cultural analysis for, 17
    environmental adaptation, 14–15
    and international marketing task, 10–13
    obstacles to, 15–17
Marketing research
    analyzing and interpreting data, 234–235
    apples and Apple Computer in Japan, 212–213
    breadth and scope of, 215–216
    communicating with decision makers, 236–237
    cross-cultural, 226–228
    decentralization trend, 236
    definition, 214
    environments of, 215
    establishing objectives, 217–218
    estimating market demand, 232–234
    field surveys, 225–226
    foreign *vs.* domestic, 215
    inadequate data, 489
    on Internet, 230–231
    language comprehension, 226–228
    managing cultural barriers, 237
    Mayo Clinic case, 636–639
    Microsoft problem in Mexico, 232
    multicultural research, 229–230
    national expenditure comparisons, 216
    need for information, 214
    primary data, 221–229
    problem definition, 217–218
    problems in China, 223
    process, 216
    qualitative research, 221–229
    quantitative research, 221–229
    responsibility for, 235–236

Marketing research (*continued*)
    secondary data, 218–221, 238–243
    self-reference criterion, 217
    types of information collected, 215
Marketing research firms, 236
Market offerings, 338
Market-perceived quality, 339
Market potential estimation, 256–258
Market Research International, 243
Markets, changing and evolving, 94
Market segmentation
    case, 610–611
    in emerging markets, 258–259
    old *vs.* new views, 312–313
    strategies, 475–478
    variables for global marketing, 314
Market Share Report, 240
Marks & Spencer, 481
Marlboro, 191, 360, 361, 481
Marriage, 108–109
Marriott Hotels, 428, 429
Mars Company, 340, 362, 363
Marshall Plan, 29–30
Mars Inc., 473, 478
Maruti Suzuki, 605
Marvel Enterprises, 542, 543
Marxism, 142
Marxist-socialist tenets, 182, 186
Mary Kay Cosmetics, 403
Masculinity, 154–155
Masculinity/Femininity Index, 106
Mass consumption, 247, 375, 397
Mass customization, 312
Massey Ferguson, 417
MasterCard, 324
Master franchise, 326
Master of destiny philosophy, 127–128
Master Settlement Agreement, 671
Matrix structure, 333
Matsushita, 20, 34, 133, 347
Mattel, Inc., 123, 142–143, 157, 218, 312, 467, 470
Maturity, 510
Mayo Clinic, 234
    case, 636–639
Mazda, 142, 312, 572
MBA degrees, 507, 522, 524
MBC, 352
McCann-Erickson, 476, 607
McDonald's Corporation, 4, 6, 16, 23, 52, 111, 119, 169, 172, 174, 194, 195, 196, 201, 226, 246, 255, 262, 294, 297, 326, 343, 359, 360, 361, 470, 471, 472, 536, 539, 597, 608
    in Great Britain, 654–655
    and obesity problem, 632–634
    problems in France, 177
    in Yugoslavia, 175
McDonald's Hamburger University, 383
McDonnell Douglas, 440, 547, 624
McDowell's, 604
McVitie's, 16, 17
Mead Corporation, 541
Mecca Cola, 343
Media, 105
Media limitations, 487
Media penetration, 492
Media planning/analysis
    availability, 488
    cable TV, 491–493
    costs, 488–489
    coverage, 489
    direct mail, 493–494
    Internet, 494–495
    lack of market data, 489
    magazines, 490
    newspapers, 489–490
    other media types, 493
    radio and television, 490–491
    satellite TV, 491–493
    tactical considerations, 488–489
Mediation, 187
Medical Expo, Havana, 386–387
Medical Treatment Information, 473
Meiji, 481
Mercedes, 7, 288, 491, 645, 646
Mercedes-Benz, 361

Merchandise exports, 370
Merchandise returns, 400
Merchant middlemen, 410
Merck & Company, 176
Mercosur, 280, 284, 300–301
Mercury Villager/Nissan Quest, 331
Merge-in-transit, 458
Mergers and acquisitions, 202
Merit, 128
Merrill Lynch, 93, 356
Message
    in advertising, 479–483
    construction of, 479
    decoding errors, 481–482
    encoding problems, 480
    feedback, 482
    linguistic limitations, 485–486
    literacy problems, 480
    noise, 482
    receiver problems, 482
    and self-reference criterion, 479–480
Message channel, 479
Messina Strait bridge, 65
Metaphors, 112
Meter-Man, 19, 22
Metric system, 379–380
Mexican-American War, 60
Mexican National Advertisers Association, 489
Mexican Revolution, 59
Mexico
    acquisitions in U.S., 8
    antitrust law, 202
    Catholicism in, 114
    child labor, 171
    foreign direct investment in, 300
    infrastructure, 254
    limits on ownership, 159
    maquiladoras, 300, 452–453
    Microsoft in, 221
    negotiating style, 566
    and NAFTA, 297–300
    perception of history, 58–62
    political parties, 159–160, 162
    Progresa program, 171
Mexico City, 74
MGA Entertainment, Inc., 143
Microlending, 651
Microsoft Corporation, 6, 136, 191, 192, 193, 195, 201, 202, 208, 214, 234, 271, 297, 352, 354, 360, 361, 370, 372, 373, 374, 596
    ad campaign, 476–477
    Mexican joint venture, 221
    product adaptation, 62
    technology training, 176
Middle class, 264–275
Middle East
    economic integration, 306–308
    and free trade, 279
    Nestlé Company in, 315
    Oslo Accords, 279
Middle East Translation Services, 354
Middleman costs, 538–539
Middlemen
    agent middlemen, 410
    analysis of functions, 411
    associations of, 406–407
    cash flow patterns, 420
    commonalities, 402–403
    competition, 407
    controlling, 424–425
    costs and margins, 406
    distribution agreement, 423
    foreign-country middlemen, 415–417, 418
    government-affiliated, 417
    high density of, 398–399
    home-country middlemen, 411–415, 416
    inventories, 407
    locating, 422
    merchant middlemen, 410
    motivating, 423
    retail patterns, 407–408
    screening, 422–423
    selecting, 422–423
    terminating, 423–424

Middlemen services, 405–406
Miles Press, 300
Milka, 297
Mini Disc, 357
Minimum access volume, 544
Ministry of International Trade and Industry, Japan, 400
Ministry of Labor and Social Security, China, 471
Mirror, 289
Missionaries, 142
Mitsubishi, 133, 343, 484
Mitsui Corporation, 664
Mitsui Zosen, 392
Mitsukoshi department store, 401, 407
Mobil, 407
Mobile International, 598
Mobile phone industry, 3
Mobile phones, 13, 252
    diffusion rate, 233
    national comparisons, 254
Mobile Telesystems, 473
Modelo, 203
Modern Foods, 604
Modi-Champion, 605
Modi-Xerox, 605
Molson Canadian beer, 484
Monetary trade barriers, 42–43
Monochronic time, 139
Monroe Doctrine, 58–61
    Roosevelt Corollary, 60
Monsanto Company, 297
Monsoon Wedding, 108–109
More-developed countries, 248
Morinaga Love restaurant chain, 119
Moshe & Ali's Gourmet Foods, 3n
Motivation
    middlemen, 423
    sales force, 513–515
Motorola, Inc., 3n, 11, 25, 176, 331, 650
Motorola Japan, 664
Mount Sinai Hospital, Miami, 234
Mrs. Baird's Bread, 8
M-time, 139
Multicountry research, 236
Multicultural research, 229–230
Multidomestic market orientation, 22–23
Multinational cooperation, 282–284
Multinational corporations, 30–33, 105
    advertising agencies, 496–497
    and emerging markets, 253
    expatriate reentry process, 521
    foreign acquisitions, 8
    global managers, 522–524
    global marketing planning, 317
    green marketing, 201–202
    and nationalistic pride, 363–364
    nationalist of largest firms, 32
    organizational structure, 334–335
    outperforming domestic companies, 8–9
    and piracy of products, 16
    political vulnerability, 176–178
    total quality management, 377–378
    transfer pricing, 551
    and U.S. laws, 206–207
Multinational market regions, 247; *see also* Regional trading groups
    Africa, 305–306
    the Americas, 296–303
    Asian-Pacific Rim, 303–305
    definition, 280
    global markets, 294–296
    Middle East, 306–308
    Middle East and free trade, 279
    patterns of cooperation, 282–284
    reasons for, 280–282
Multiple income levels, 534
Mumbai Advertising Club, 606
Music CD industry, 531–532
Music Television Network (MTV), 492, 498, 671
Muslim Up, 343
Mutual recognition, 288

Myanmar, 499
My Father, Deng Xiaopeng (Deng Rong), 192

n

N. V. Philips, 34
Nando's Chicken Restaurants, 654
Naobaijin Health Products, 473
Napoleonic Code, 183n
Napster, 16
Narmada Valley Dam Project, India, 66
National Aeronautics and Space Administration, 3, 4, 379–380
National AIDS Control Organization, 668
National Board of Nutritional Science, 632
National brands, 363–364
National Car Rental, 644
National Cash Register, 356, 663
National Consumer Council (Denmark), 633
National Consumer Council (EU), 342
National Enquirer, 490
National Football League, 641
National Human Rights Commission (India), 619
National interest, 203
Nationalism, 163–164
Nationalistic pride, 363–364
National mission, 56–62
National Office Machines, case, 663–665
National Security Agency, 624
National security laws, 204–205
National Statistics Enforcement Office, China, 219
National Trade Data Bank, 46, 238, 240–241
National Trade Estimates Report on Foreign Trade Barriers, 241
Natural disasters, 65–66
Natural resources, 70–71
NBC, 558, 640
NBC Universal, 333
NBGI Private Equity, 645
Negotiation Game (Karrass), 580
Negotiation preliminaries, 572–575
Negotiations training, 572–573
Negotiation table, 575–577
Negotiation teams, 570–571
Nescafé, 6, 363
Nestlé Baby Foods, 469
Nestlé Boycott Committee, 601
Nestlé Canada, 634
Nestlé Company, 34, 42, 43, 120n, 169, 202, 279, 294, 331, 332, 350, 362, 363, 472, 473, 488, 537, 651
    in China, 270
    General Mills partnership, 328
    global marketing by, 314–315
    global marketing mix, 320–321
    Infant Formula controversy, 600–603
Nestlé Infant Formula, 120n
Nestlé Infant Formula Audit Commission, 601
Nestlé Japan, 493
Netherlands, The, 100–101
Neutrogena, 27
New Balance, 193
Newly Independent States, 295–296
Newly industrialized countries, 31, 303–305
    characteristics, 248–249
    growth factors, 249–251
New Musical Express, 498
Newness or products, 345–346
New Pepsodent, 483
News Corporation, 641, 642
Newspaper advertising, 489–490
New York Convention, 190
New York Post, 7
NextLinx Trade Import Solution, 459, 460
Niagra, 348
Nielsen Media Research, 640
Nihon Keizai Shimbun, 664
Niigata, 392
Nike, Inc., 153, 169, 192, 200, 411, 425, 481, 531
    sweatshop controversy, 470
Nike Sport, 296, 411

Ningen kankei, 125–126
Nippon/American Business Machines
    Corporation, 663, 665
Nippon Cash Machines, 663
Nissan Motor Company, 222, 276, 331,
    472, 551, 573
Nissan Pathfinder, 541
Nivea, 195
No. 1 Wanadoo, 311
Nochar Inc., 34
Noise, 479
Nokia, 3n, 360, 421
No-license-required notation, 436
Nominet Dispute Resolution Service
    (UK), 208
Nondurable goods, 338
Nonexistent channels, 406
Nongovernmental organizations, 169–172
Nontariff barriers, 40, 42–50, 441
Nontask sounding, 577–578, 579
Nonverbal behaviors, 561–567
Non-Vessel Operating Common
    Carriers, 461
Norelco, 6
North American Free Trade Agreement, 5,
    8, 33, 43, 44, 61, 158, 159, 160,
    167, 265, 280, 296–300, 382, 385
    benefits and detractors, 298
    historical background, 296–298
    job loss issue, 283, 300
    key provisions, 299
    and maquiladoras, 453
    and production relocation,
        298–299
    and South American Free Trade
        Area, 303
North American Free Trade Area,
    33–34
North Atlantic Treaty Organization, 158
Northwestern Airlines, 327
Novon, 365
NPD Group, 467
Nynex, 222

Obesity problem, 632–634
Objective analysis, 128
Objective theory of jurisdiction, 203
Objectivity, 567
Observability, 348
Observational research, 231
Ocean currents, 84–85
Ocean Institute, 469
Office Depot, 403
Office of Fair Trading (UK), 648
Offset trade, 548
Ogilvy & Mather, 607
Oil prices, 552–553
Oil production areas, 86
Okamoto Industries, 668
Olympic Committee, 558
Olympic Games, 471
Omnibus Trade and Competitiveness Act,
    38, 45–46, 203–204
Omnicom Group, 496
Omo detergent, 363
One China policy, 272
Oneworld Alliance, 327
Online auctions, 93
Online electronic barter economy, 549
Online surveys, 230
Open account, 446, 449
Open markets, 39
Opinions, 224
Optima software, 318
Orange County, California, 21
Orchard Advertising, 606
Orderly market agreements, 42
Oresund Link, 65
Organizational structure
    centralized *vs.* decentralized,
        334–335
    flexible, 333
    international marketing alternatives,
        333
    locus of decision, 334
    matrix form, 333
    product divisions, 333

Organization for Economic Cooperation
    and Development, 29n, 33, 67,
    148, 218, 220, 267, 349
    convention of combating bribery,
        144–145
Organization of American States,
    145, 148
Organization of Petroleum Exporting
    Countries, 170, 552–553
Organization of the Islamic Conference,
    307–308
Oroweat, 7
Oslo Accords, 279
Overseas Business Reports, 240, 445
Overseas Investment Corporation, 179
Overseas premiums, 515
Oxfam, 172

Pacific Connections, 411
PacifiCorp, 7
Packaging
    component of products,
        351–353
    labeling, 351, 353
    legislation on, 342–343
    trademark on, 351–352
Pajama caper, 181
Palestinians, 56n, 279
Pampers, 486
Panama Canal Zone, 60
    and China, 56
Panama timeline, 55–56
Pan-European promotional strategy, 478
Parallel imports, 425
    definition, 529
    exclusive distribution, 530–531
    gray markets, 530–532
    reasons for, 529–530
    trademarked products, 532
Parallel translation, 228
Paris Air Show, 386, 387–388
Paris Convention for the Protection of
    Individual Property, 196
Parle Agro, 604, 605
Partido Accion Nacional (Mexico), 160
Patent Cooperation Treaty, 196
Patent law, 184
Patents, 194, 195, 196
Paul Kagan, 642
Pavane, 485
Payment options, 429
Peace from commerce, 3–4
Peace protests, 170
Peace Works, 3
Pearle Vision, 6
Pedigree Petfoods, 363
PEMEX, 299, 407
Peoples' Daily, 508
Pepsi, 343, 483, 498
PepsiCo, 160–161, 164, 168, 169, 198,
    203, 313, 341, 468, 472, 473, 481,
    491, 495, 546, 551, 596, 633, 634,
    668
    in China, 258
    competition in India, 604–609
Pepsodent, 176
Per capita GDP, 232–233
    African market groups, 306
    Asian countries, 268
    Asian-Pacific Rim, 304
    big emerging markets, 262
    Commonwealth of Independent
        States, 295
    Eastern Europe, 266
    European Free Trade Area, 285
    European Union, 285
    India, 252
    Japan *vs.* U.S., 400
    Latin America, 302
Performance measures, 518
Performance quality, 339, 340–341
Perishability, 355
Permanently normalized trade relations, 11,
    170
    with China, 269
Personal security, 132

Personal selling
    in different cultures, 502
    foreign views of, 508–509
    national comparisons, 512
Persuasion, 580–581
Pertamina, 553
Pet Milk, 16
PetroBras, 575
Petroleum, 70
PETRONAS, 407
Pfizer, Inc., 193, 472, 605
Pharmaceutical industry, 530
    in India, 251
Philip Morris International, 266, 671
Philips Electronics, 235, 291, 293, 365,
    605, 608
Physical barriers, 64–65
Physical distance, 15
Physical distribution system, 453–456; *see
    also* Logistics management
PicturePhone Direct, 324
Piggybacking, 413
Pilferage, 457
Pilsner Urquell, 324
Piracy, 16, 191–194, 209
    national comparisons, 193
    software, 359
Pixar, 411
Pizza Corner, 326
Pizza Hut, 169, 172, 174, 255, 326, 495
Planned change, 118–119
Planned domestication, 177
Planning
    adapting marketing mix, 320–321
    corporate, 317
    for global marketing, 317–322
    implementation and control, 321–322
    marketing plan, 321
    preliminary analysis, 319–320
    strategic, 317
    tactical, 317
Playboy, 490
Playtex Products, 656, 657
PNTR; *see* Permanently normalized
    trade relations
Pokemon, 357
Polaroid, 365
Police, 481
Political and social activists, 169–172
Political bargaining, 178
Political climate, 215
Political economy, 102
Political environment, 156–179
    alien status of foreign business, 12–13
    assessing vulnerability, 173–176
    case study, 157, 164
    China, 269–271
    confiscation threat, 166–167
    cyberterrorism, 172–173
    domestication, 166–167
    of domestic marketing, 11
    Eastern Europe, 266
    economic risks, 167–168
    expropriation threat, 166–167
    in foreign countries, 12
    forms of government, 161–162
    government policy stability, 159–166
    government encouragement, 178–179
    India, 272
    lessening political vulnerability,
        176–178
    nationalism, 163–164
    newly industrialized countries, 250
    NGOs, 169–172
    political parties, 162–163
    political sanctions, 169
    political/social activists, 169–172
    product adaptation, 341
    regional trading groups, 281
    risks of global business, 166–173
    sovereignty of nations, 158–159
    targeted fear/animosity, 164–165
    trade disputes, 165–166
    violence or terrorism, 172
Politically sensitive products, 173–174
Political parties, 162–163
Political payoffs, 178
Political risk, 174–176
Political sanctions, 168

Political union, 284
Political vulnerability
    assessing, 173–176
    forecasting risk, 174–176
    lessening, 176–178
    political sensitive products/issues,
        173–174
Pollena 2000, 363
Pollution regulations, 67
Polychronic time, 139
Poppers, 283
Population; *see* Global population
Population control, 72–73
Population decline, 74–75
Positive outlook, 510
Power, 134
Power distance, 117, 131
    national/regional index score, 154–155
Power Distance Index, 106, 107, 130, 137
Power Packing and Seal Company, 664
Predatory pricing, 44
Predicasts F & S Index Europe, 243
Predicasts F & S Index International, 243
Preliminary analysis and screening,
    310–320
Preliminary marketing plan, 591–593
Preliminary nontask discussions,
    577–578, 579
Press Watch, 289
Price controls, 168, 536
Price escalation, 534–545
    administrative costs, 535
    approaches to lessening, 540–545
    deflation, 536
    distribution costs, 543
    dumping, 544–545
    exchange rate fluctuations, 536–537
    exporting costs, 535
    foreign trade zones, 543–544
    inflation, 535–536
    lowering cost of goods sold, 540–541
    lowering tariffs, 541–542
    middleman costs, 538–539
    sample effects of, 539–540
    tariffs, 535
    taxes, 535
    transportation costs, 538–539
    varying currency values, 537–538
Price fixing, 552, 554
Price Point, 425
Price-quality relationship, 377
Price quotations, 551–552
Pricesmart, 245
Price war, 527
PricewaterhouseCoopers, 505
Pricing objectives, 528
Primary Colors, 607
Primary data
    ability to communicate opinions, 224
    analyzing and interpreting, 234–235
    definition, 221
    gathering, 221–223
    language comprehension, 226–228
    sampling in field surveys, 225–226
    willingness to respond, 224–225
Primestar, 642
Princeton Video Imaging, 492
Prior use *vs.* registration, 194–195
Private brands, 366
Privatization, 167–168, 250, 263–264,
    272, 376
Proactive countertrade strategy, 549–550
Problem definition, 217–218
Procter & Gamble, 23, 176, 192, 194,
    202, 223, 245, 259, 343, 351, 361,
    362, 363, 365, 379, 464, 468, 472,
    473, 486, 528, 533, 540, 576, 605,
    656–657
    competition with Kimberly-Clark, 527
    effect of globalization, 522
Product adaptation; *see* Adaptation
Product adoption, 119–120
Product attribute/benefit segmentation,
    475–478
Product buyback agreement, 548
Product comparison laws, 200
Product component model, 350
Product design, 377
Product diffusion, 119–120

Product homologation, 341
Production/cost limitations, 487–488
Product Liability Directive (EU), 380
Product-line structure, 333
Product placement, 498
Product platform, 350
Product rip-off, 192
Products
    counterfeiting, 191–194
    effects of climate, 63–65
    piracy, 191–194
    politically sensitive, 173–174
Product safety, 444–445
Products and services; see also
        Business-to-business marketing
    adaptation requirements, 338, 341
    barriers to entry, 357–360
    brands, 360–366
    business-to-consumer
        marketing, 338
    core component, 350–351
    country-of-origin effect, 364–366
    culture, 343–349
    diffusion of innovation, 346–349
    global competition, 338–339
    green marketing, 341–343
    innovative products, 345–349
    Internet distribution, 425–430
    labeling laws, 353
    marketing services, 355–360
    market offerings, 338
    opportunities and challenges, 338
    packaging, 351–353
    perception of newness, 345–346
    physical/mandatory
        requirements, 341
    product component model, 350
    quality, 338–343
    support services, 353–355
    utilities, 343
    Walt Disney Company, 337, 338
Product-testing laboratories, 222
Profit versus corruption, 142–143
Progresa program, 171
Prohibited Parties Database, 438n
Promodes, 404
Promotion
    in e-commerce, 430
    pan-European strategy, 478
Promotional mix, 468
Promotional support, 400
Promotion culture, 128
Protectionism
    and business services, 385
    cost to consumers, 39
    in European Union, 293–294, 357–358
    logic and illogic of, 37–39
    in postwar Europe, 30–31
    trade barriers, 39–46
Protestant work ethic, 132
Provemex, 327–328
Publicis Groupe, 496
Publicis Worldwide, 598
Public relations, 470–471
Punctuality, 138–139
Punjab Agro, 605
Purchasing agents, 373
Pure Drinks, 604, 605
Puxue Oran Solution, 473

q
Qantas Airlines, 327, 331, 505
Quaker Fabric, 283
Qualcomm, 332
Qualitative research, 221–223
Quality
    adaptation, 341
    in business-to-business marketing,
        376–381
    defined by buyer, 376–380
    of food, 340
    in global marketing, 338–343
    green marketing, 341–343
    international standards, 378–381
    kinds of, 339–340
    maintaining, 340–341
    measurement of, 340
    video game content, 342

Quantitative research, 221–223
Quicksilver, 21, 469
Quotas, 41, 442

r
Radio advertising, 490–491
Radio frequency identification, 462–464
Radio Shack Corporation, 320
Rail transportation, 457
Rajiv Menon Productions, 607
Ralston Purina, 314
Rampant consumerism, 142
Random House, 7, 8
Rapunzel Barbie, 467
Ray Ban, 192
RCA Corporation, 7
Reader's Digest, 228
Reader's Digest Association, 490, 493
Receiver, 479
Reciprocity, 294
Reckitt Benckiser PLC, 165n
Recruitment of sales force, 504–509
Recycling, 342–343
Red Crescent, 171
Red Cross, 171
Red October Chocolate Factory, 340–341
Reebok International, 192
Reference Book for World Traders, 242
Regional Cooperation for Development,
    282, 307
Regional segmentation, 478
Regional trading groups
    Africa, 305–306
    ASEAN, 303–305
    Asia-Pacific Economic Cooperation,
        305
    Caribbean Community, 301
    Central America - Dominican
        Republic, 300
    common market, 284
    Commonwealth of Independent States,
        294–296
    cultural factors, 282
    customs union, 283–284
    economic factors, 281
    emerging markets, 308
    Europe, 284–284
    free trade and Middle East, 279
    free trade areas, 283–283
    geographic proximity, 282
    Latin American Integration Associa-
        tion, 301–303
    Mercosur, 300–301
    Middle East, 206–208
    NAFTA, 296–300
    patterns of multinational cooperation,
        282–284
    political factors, 281
    political union, 284
    reasons for, 280–282
    regional cooperation groups, 282
    temporal proximity, 282
Registration assessment, 380
Reha Enterprises, 157
Reinvestment, 547
Relationship marketing, 502
    in business-to-business context,
        388–393
    Solar Turbines Inc., 389–392
Relationship-oriented cultures, 151–152
Relative advantage, 348
Religion, 104
    world map, 90
Renault, 331, 481
Renault Clios, 646
Repatriation, 520–521
Research and development expenditures, 349
Research departments, 236
Research objectives, 217–218
Research process, 216
Reserves account, 35–36
Resistance to change, 117–118
Retailers, 417; see also Middlemen
    costs and margins, 406
    global, 411
    line breadth, 406
    manufacturers' stores, 411
    private brands, 366

Retailing
    direct marketing, 408–409
    diversity of, 407
    global strategies, 403–405
    in Japan, 398–399, 400–402
    Japan's law on, 400–401
    national comparisons, 399, 408
    resistance to change, 409
    size patterns, 407–408
Revenue, global vs. domestic, 9
Revocable letter of credit, 448
Rice Growers Association of California,
    548
Ride, 245
Right Guard, 263
Rights of the parties, 149, 672
Risk assessment, 174–176
Rituals, 108–109
Ritz Carlton Hotel chain, 340
Rolex, 191, 275, 408
Rolls-Royce PLC, 627, 661
Ronald McDonald Children's Charities,
    655
Roosevelt Corollary, 60
Royal Liver Assurance, 493
R-rated American movies, 142
Rubbermaid, 351
Rules of origin, 299
Rural/urban migration, 73–74
Rural/urban population statistics, 73–74
Russia
    commercial law, 186
    computer hackers, 6
    negotiating style, 566, 569
    political parties, 162–163
    subliminal advertising, 498
    top ten advertisers, 473

s
Sabena Airlines, 624, 627
Sabre, 168
Safety standards, 444
Sainsbury, 365
St. Jude Medical Export GmbH, 440
St. Louis Post Dispatch, 188
SAirGroup, 624, 627
Sales force; see also Expatriates
    attributes, 509–511
    evaluation and control of, 518
    foreign-language skills, 524–525
    foreign views of, 508–509
    host-country restrictions, 509
    incentives, 514
    local nationals, 506–509
    rewards for work, 513
    third-country nationals, 509
Sales force meetings, 514
Sales for design, 502–503
Sales management, 501–525; see also
        Expatriates; Foreign assignments
    communication in, 514–515
    compensation system, 515–517
    cultural awareness, 521–522
    customer relationship management,
        502
    designing sales force, 502–503
    evaluation and control, 518
    foreign assignments, 501
    foreign-language skills, 524–525
    global customers, 503
    host-country restrictions, 509
    local nationals, 506–509
    motivating personnel, 513–515
    National Office Machine case,
        663–665
    preparation for foreign assignments,
        518
    profile of global managers, 522–524
    recruiting personnel, 504–509
    risks of international travel, 505,
        506, 508
    selecting personnel, 509–511
    third-country nationals, 509
    training program, 512–513
Sales promotion laws, 198–200
Sales promotions, 468–470
Sales territory assignments, 503
Salon International de l'Alimentation, 283

Sampling techniques, adequacy of, 226
Sam's Club, 534, 651
Samsika Marketing Consultants, 604
Samsung Electronics Company, 3n, 6, 34,
    249, 332, 349, 357, 361, 373, 383,
    421, 494
Samsung India, 611
San Antonio Living History Association,
    61
San Diego Padres, 282
Sanitation certificates, 445
San Patricios, 60
Sanyo, 357
Sara Lee, 246
SARS outbreak, 4, 99, 505, 575
Satellite-based positioning system, 464
Satellite TV, 491–493
Saudi Arabia, 378
Saudi Committee for the Propagation of
    Virtue and Prevention of Vice,
    147
Schematic marketing organization plan,
    334
School, 104, 105
Scientific American, 490
Scientific studies, 222
Screening criteria, 310–320
Screening middlemen, 422–423
Screwdriver plants, 545
Sears, Roebuck, 324, 404, 411, 413, 650
Seattle antiglobalization protests, 51, 52,
    169, 312
Secondary data
    analyzing and interpreting, 234–235
    availability of, 218–219
    comparability of, 220
    errors in reporting, 219–220
    foreign sources, 218
    reliability of, 219–220
    sources of, 238–243
    U.S. government sources, 218
    validating, 220–221
Secondary wholesaling, 425
Secret deodorant, 498
Section 301 investigations, 38
Securities and Exchange Commission,
    144, 225
Security, 132
Selection of sales force, 509–511
Self-reference criterion, 15–17, 57, 115, 125
    and advertising message, 479–480
    market analyst, 349
    and marketing research, 217
Selling groups, 414
Sematech, 331
Separation allowances, 515
Services, 338; see also Business services
    barriers in foreign markets, 357–360
    global marketing of, 355–360
    Internet sales, 426
    major U.S. exports, 370
    nature of, 355
    and NAFTA, 299
Services trade, 47
7dream program, 402, 404
7-Eleven, 6
Seven-Eleven Japan, 402, 404, 408
7UP, 606
Sex in advertising, 497–498
Shahnaz-Husain, 618–619
Shari'ah, 185
Sheba, 363
Shell Oil Company, 153, 392
Sherman Antitrust Act, 205, 414
Shipper's Export Declaration, 436
Shipping cartel, 553
Shipping costs, 456
Shiseido, 345, 491
Shop America, 408
Shorouk Air, 625
Siemens, 3n, 371
Sight draft, 448–449
"Silent Language of Overseas Business"
    (Hall), 134–135
Silicon Graphics Inc., 204
Silicon Valley, 252
Silkience, 474
Silk Road, 102
Similarities illusion, 116–117

Simmons, 664
Simplified Network Application Process (SNAP), 440–441
Simpsons, The, 105
Simulated negotiations, 567
Singapore, 95
Singapore Air, 505
Single European Act, 287–288, 289, 290, 357
Sita Group, 382
Six Cs of channel strategy, 419–421
Sixt, 644
Skimming price policy, 533–534
Skippy Peanut Butter, 192
Sky Channel, 491
SkyTeam, 327
Slow Food, 598
Small companies
    in global marketing, 312
    in international marketing, 34
Smart & Final, 8
Smith & Wesson, 6, 7
Smith Corona, 44
Smoot-Hawley Tariff of 1930, 30
Smuggling, 41, 443
Snickers, 340, 363
Social acceptance, 133
Social hierarchy, 131
Social inequality, 107
Social institutions
    characteristics, 103
    corporations, 105
    family, 103–104
    government, 105
    media, 105
    religion, 104
    schools, 104–105
Socialist law, 186
Socialization, 98
Social justice, 185
Social responsibility, 148–149
    environmental issues, 67–69
Sociological data, 215
Software piracy rates, 193
Solar Turbines Inc., 389–392, 568–569, 572–573
Sole agent, 415
Sony Corporation, 6, 246, 275, 345, 357, 365, 472, 532, 534, 606
Sony Ericsson, 3n
Sony Playstation2, 452
South Africa
    apartheid, 170
    economy of, 274
    foreign exchange system, 442
    GDP, 306
    School Net program, 251–252
South America, 64; *see also* Latin America
South American Free Trade Area, 301, 303
Southdown, 8
Southern African Development Community, 305, 306, 307
Southern Cone Common Market; *see* Mercosur
South Korea, 194, 249, 349
    negotiating style, 565
Southwest Airlines, 374n
Southwestern Bell, 376
Sovereignty of nations, 158–159
Soviet Union, 160–161, 284
    Afghan War, 170
    dissolution, 294–296
    post-collapse, 175–176
Space, language of, 134
Spain, 566
Special drawing rights, 50
Specific duties, 442
Specific duty, 535
Spectrum, 640
Sphinx, 347
Sponsorships, 471
Sports television, 640–643
Sportswear industry, 531
Sprite, 607
Spy Who Shagged Me, 117
SRC; *see* Self-reference criterion
Standardization *vs.* adaptation, 312–313

Standards, 293, 299
    in business-to-business marketing, 370–371
    conflicting, 377–378
    import restrictions, 443–444
    international, 378–381
    ISO 9000 certification, 380–381
    TL 9000 certification, 381
    as trade barriers, 43–44
Star, 327
Starbucks Corporation, 403
    case, 596–599
Star Manufacturing, 540
Starnes-Brenner Machine Tool Company, case, 621–623
State-owned enterprises, 31, 263–264
State Secrets Law (China), 186
STAT-USA, 238
Stereotypes
    danger of, 559–560
    European, 560
    of products, 364–366
Sterling Winthrop, 195
Stockholm Business Council on Ethics, 497
Stocking, 407
Stockmann's Department Store, 421
Strategic international alliances, 327–331
    building, 329
    consortia, 330–331
    joint ventures, 328–330
Strategic orientation
    domestic market extension, 22
    global, 23
    multidomestic, 22–23
Strategic planning, 317
Strategic thinking, 149–151
Strategy
    of cultural congruence, 118–119
    planned change, 118–119
    unplanned change, 118–119
Structural Impediments Initiative, 400, 401–402
Study abroad programs, 114
Subcultures, 486–487
Subliminal advertising, 498
Subordination, 124
Subornation, 148
Suez Canal, 62
Suez Lyonnaise des Eaux, 382
Suffrage laws, 161
Sugar price controls, 443
Sumitomo, 133
Sun Express, 425
Sun Microsystems, 425, 438–439, 513
Suntory, 495
Super Bowl, 640, 642
Supermarket, 220
Superstition, 113
Supply-chain management, 459–460
Support services, 353–355
Surf, 364
Surfwear industry, 21
Survey research, 222, 225–226
SurveySite, 231
Sustainable development, 6–68
Suzuki, 192
Swatch Watches, 494
Swissair, 624
Swiss Bank Corporation, 626
Symbols
    aesthetics, 111–112
    language, 109–111
System for Tracking Export License Applications (STELLA), 441

t

Taco Bell, 169
Tactical planning, 317
Taitmae, 136
Taiwan
    economy of, 271–272
    negotiating style, 565
Takeoff, 375
Takeoff preconditions, 247
Tambo, 110
Tambrands, case, 656–658
Tamper Evident Secure Containers, 464

Tang, 350–351
Tangibility of products, 355
Target markets, 320–321
Tariffs, 441–442
    cost to consumers, 39
    countervailing duties, 544–545
    EU-US trade war, 157
    operation of, 40–41
    and price escalation, 535
    product classifications, 541–542
    reductions in, 47–48
Task-related information exchange, 578–580
Taster's Choice Instant Coffee, 602
Tax controls, 168
Taxes
    on advertising, 484–485
    on e-commerce, 209
    in European Union, 288
    and price escalation, 535
    and transfer pricing, 550–551
Tax evasion, 224–225
Technological environment, 215
Technology
    dual-purpose, 204–205
    exports of, 370
    impact on culture, 102–103
    licensing, 177
    and market demand, 375–376
    as uncontrollable element, 12
Teléfonos de Mexico, 221, 376
Telemarketing, 357
Telepiu, 642
Televisa, 492
Television
    advertising on, 198, 490–491
    bans on advertising, 483–484
    product placement, 498
    regulation of advertising, 491
    satellite/cable, 491–493
    sportscasting, 640–643
Telmex, 376
Tempo, 137–138
Temporal proximity, 282
Terms of sale
    arranging, 446
    kinds of, 445–446
Terrorism, 172
    and logistics management, 460–464
    map, 89
    and travel warnings, 505
Terrorist attack of 2001, 4, 89, 204, 435
Tesco, 529, 531
Texas Commerce Bank, 222
Texas Instruments, 331
Theme parks, 337, 338
Thinking, cultural differences, 569–570
Third-country nationals, 509
Third-party logistics arrangement (3PL), 460
Third World tobacco sales, 670–674
Third World Working Group, 600
Thought processes, 113
Three Gorges Dam, China, 66, 389
3M Corporation, 549
3M Global Trading, 549
Thums Up, 312, 313, 604, 605, 607, 608
Time
    cultural perceptions, 138
    mañana attitude, 138, 139
    monochronic, 138–140
    polychronic, 138–140
Time frame of negotiations, 568–569
Time of India, 147
Time Warner, 472, 488
TL 9000 certification, 381
Tobacco advertising, 498
Tobacco sales in Third World, 670–674
Tobacco use, 96–97
Toblerone, 297, 340
Toilet paper preferences, 533
Tokyo Beauty Center, 481
Tokyo Disneyland, 217, 337
Tokyo Round, 46–47
Tolerance, 115
Tony Roma, 203
Top-level management, 130
Topography, 63–65

Toshiba, 373
Total costs, 454
Total quality management, 377, 381
Toto, 220, 343, 348
Tour de France, 471
Toxic waste disposal, 69
Toy Biz Inc., 542
Toyo Rayon, 664
Toyota Motor Company, 6, 8, 164, 178, 360, 361, 472, 486, 491, 575
Toyota Yaris, 646
Toys "R" Us, 400, 401, 403, 411, 419, 467
TradeBanc, 549
Trade barriers, 39–46
    antidumping penalties, 44–45
    boycotts and embargoes, 42
    on business services, 385
    and common markets, 284
    easing of, 11, 45–49
    and European Union, 293–294
    EU-US trade war, 157
    export restrictions, 436–441
    import restrictions, 167–168, 441–445
    marketer's minefield, 27–28
    monetary barriers, 42–43
    nontariff types, 40
    and NAFTA, 298, 299
    and parallel imports, 529–530
    protectionism, 37–39
    quotas, 41
    reasons for, 37
    standards, 43–44
    tariffs, 40–41
    U.S. hypocrisy, 38
    voluntary export restraints, 42
Trade blacklist, 170
Trade deficit, 35
Trade Directories of the World, 242
Trade disputes, 165–166
Trademark protection, 191
Trademarks, 192, 194–195, 196, 351–352
Trade Opportunity Program, 240
Trade-Related Aspects of Intellectual Property Rights agreement, 47, 194, 196, 359
Trade-Related Investment Measures, 47
Trade routes, 77–78
Trade sanctions, 48, 170
Trade shows
    in business-to-business marketing, 385–388
    and exporting, 433–434
    information sources on, 388n
    virtual trade shows, 387
Trade terms, 445–446
Trade war, 157
Trading blocs, 247
Trading companies, 412–413
Trading with the Enemy Act, 205, 206
Traditional channel structures, 402–405
Traditional distribution structure, 396
Traditional society, 247, 375
Training
    expatriates, 512–513
    for global managers, 522–524
    home-office personnel, 513
    for negotiations, 572–573
Trans-Atlantic Conference Agreement, 553
Transborder data flow restrictions, 358, 385
Transfer pricing strategy, 550–551
Transparency International, 145–146, 151–152, 153, 629
Transportation costs, 538–539
Travel and tourism industry, 355–357
Travel warnings, 172, 505
Treaty of Amsterdam, 287, 290, 291–292
Treaty of Asunción, 300
Treaty of Paris, 287
Treaty of Rome, 284, 288, 289
Treets, 363
Trialability, 348
Triangulation, 232
Tricon Restaurants, 326
TRIPS; *see* Trade-Related Aspects of Intellectual Property Rights
Tropicana, 485
Tsukigi fish market, 414

Tsunami of 2005, 64
Tulip growers, 100–101
Tully's Coffee Corporation, 597
Tunnels, 65
Turbinas Solar, 392
TV Guide, 7
24-hour rule, 461
Twin plants, 452–453
Twix Cookie Bars, 312, 314
Tyson Foods, 327–328

U

Uganda, 147
Uncertainty avoidance, 117
    national/regional index score, 154–155
Uncertainty Avoidance Index, 106, 107
Uncontrollable elements, 9–10, 12, 14,
    254, 320
Underwriters Laboratory, 444
Unibex, 422
UNICEF, 172
Uniform Dispute Resolution policy, 208
Uniformity, 124
Unilever, 259, 294, 315, 363, 365, 464,
    472, 473, 474, 527, 605, 651
Union Carbide, Bhopal, India incident, 174
Union Pacific, 457
Uni-Qlo stores, 401
Unisys Corporation, 215, 663
UNITE, 52
United Airlines, 4
United Arab Emirates, 548
United Kingdom
    cake mixes, 346
    consequences of consumption, 97
    Consumer Protection Distance Selling
        Regulations, 648
    English language in, 116–117
    and metric system, 379
    negotiating style, 566
    Nominet Dispute Resolution
        Service, 208
    Office of Fair Trading, 648
    political parties, 162
    toilet paper preferences, 533
United Nations, 67, 218
    country classification, 248
United Nations Economic Commission for
        Africa, 305
United Parcel Service, 324, 359, 404, 430,
        457, 458, 459
United Parcel Service Logistics Group, 460
United States
    aging populations, 74–75
    alternative-fuel cars, 348
    animosity toward Japan, 164
    birthrates, 95
    English language in, 116–117
    foreign students in, 358
    French animosity toward, 165
    historical overview, 58–62
    Internet users, 349
    interventions in Latin America, 61
    lawyers abroad, 384
    Mexican-American War, 60
    and Mexico, 58–62
    Monroe Doctrine, 58–61
    and Panama, 55–56
    patent law, 184
    statistical information, 218
    subcultures, 117
    territorial expansion, 59–61
United States–Canada Free Trade
        Area, 296
United States Court of International
        Trade, 542
United States Customs and Border
        Protection, 461
United States customs code, 38
United States Customs Service, 443,
        452, 541
United States economy
    balance of payments, 35–37
    bilateral trade agreements, 49

boom of 1990s, 3
    and cartels, 554
    changing role in trade, 32
    consequences of consumption, 97
    current account, 36–37
    distribution structure, 398
    exchange rate changes, 37
    export restrictions, 436–441
    focus on bribery, 144–146
    foreign investment in, 6–7
    foreign-owned companies, 6–8
    foreign trade zones, 451, 544
    free trade agreements, 282
    in global gross national product, 31
    in global rankings, 24
    hypocrisy on trade, 38
    import restrictions, 441–445
    international disruptions, 6
    internationalization of, 5
    internationalization of business, 6–9
    and international treaty regimes, 158
    maintaining competitive strength, 33
    major export categories, 370
    management style, 127–130
    and Marshall plan, 29–30
    and metric system, 379–380
    multinational corporations, 30–33
    negotiating style, 561–562, 566, 567,
        569–570, 577, 580
    oil imports, 70
    performance of contracts, 184–185
    ratification of World Trade
        Organization, 48
    retail structures, 399
    sales force views, 513
    sugar price controls, 443
    top grossing companies, 9
    top trading partners, 28
    trade blacklist, 170
    trade information sources, 239–241
    trade with China, 269
    worldwide competition for, 31
United States export trading companies,
        413
United States laws
    antiboycott law, 205–206
    antitrust law, 205
    extraterritoriality, 181, 203, 206–207
    Foreign Corrupt Practices Act,
        203–204
    national security laws, 204–205
United States Marines, 59
United States Metric Association, 379
United States State Department travel
        warnings, 172
United States Supreme Court, 541
United States Surgeon General, 670
United States Trade Representative, 157,
        269, 378
Universal Currency Clearinghouse, 549
Universal Studios, 6, 357
University of Chicago School of Business,
        524
University of Michigan Business School,
        381
University of Texas Cancer Center, 234
Univision, 492
Unocal Corporation, 159, 206
Unplanned change, 118–119
Upper Deck, 481
Urbanization, 73–74
Uruguay Round, 30, 46–48, 49, 445, 545
U.S. Cartoon Network, 8
U.S. Custom House Guide, 242
Utilitarian ethics, 149, 672
Utilities, 343
UTStarcom, 339

V

Validated export license, 436
Valley Drive Systems, 300
Value, 343–344
Value-added tax, 209, 288
Value differences, 567–569

Value judgments, 115
Vans sneakers, 21
Variable-cost pricing, 532, 544
Vaseline Intensive Care Lotion, 354
Vauxhall Corsa, 646
VDSL Systems, 470
Verbal communication, 135
Versace, 364
Verwalthungs-und Privat-Bank,
        Vaduz, 626
Vicks Company, 17
Victoria's Secret, 298–299
Video game content, 341, 342
Vietnam, 247, 249, 252
    economy of, 273–274
    food preferences, 340
Violence, 172
    national comparisons, 506
Virgin Atlantic Airways, 359
Virtual expatriates, 505–506
Virtual permanent establishment, 209
Virtual trade shows, 387
Visa, 324
Vivendi, 357
Vodafone, 481
Volcom, 21
Volkswagen, 8, 248, 276, 472
Voltas, 605
Voluntary export restraints, 42, 444
Volvo, 312
VP-Schickedanz AG, 202

W

Waldbaur, 340
Wall Street (film), 129
Wall Street Journal, 234, 468, 495
Wal-Mart, 165, 168, 207, 246, 298, 324,
        401–402, 402–403, 404, 411, 417,
        426, 464, 467, 524, 529, 534, 576,
        596, 650
    in China, 245
    and Cuba embargo, 181
    revenues, 9
Wal-Mart Canada, 181
Walt Disney Company, 6, 113, 217, 313,
        337, 338, 360, 411, 467, 472, 488
    case, 614–617
    revenues, 9
Walt Disney Studios Theme Park, 616
Warehousing, 456–459
Warner-Lambert, 534
Waste Management, 382
Waterford Crystal, 494
Water supply/shortage, 63, 74, 87
Wealth of Nations (Smith), 102, 129
Weapons of mass destruction, 204
Webb-Pomerene export associations, 414
Web site proliferation, 494
Web visitor tracking, 230
WebXpress, 118
Weddings, 108–109
Wedel, 315
Weinstock Media Analysis, 641
Westinghouse, 378
Whirlpool, 20, 34, 171, 246
    in Asia, 276
Whiskas, 363
White Appliance, case, 610–611
Wholesalers, 417; see also Middlemen
    costs and margins, 406
    importers, 397
    in Japan, 398–399
    line breadth, 406
Wilkinson's Wiltech, 605
Wilkowsky Gruen, 642
William Wrigley Jr. Company, 297, 395
Willingness to respond, 224–225
Wimm-Bill-Dann Foods, 473
Wimpy, 174
Wind directions, 84–85
Wireless Access Protocol, 233
Wisconsin Central Transportation, 7
WMX Technologies, 382
Woman's Day, 490

Women
    in European management, 141
    gender bias in business, 140–142
    in population statistics, 140–141
Worker shortages, 76–77
Work ethic, 132
Work-personal life trade-off, 132–133
World Bank, 33, 51, 169
    protests against, 51–52
WorldCom, 4, 93, 144
World Commerce Online, 424
World Commodity Forecasts: Industrial
        Raw Materials and Food, 243
World Court, 187
World Cup, 641
World Directory of Consumer Brands and
        Their Owners, 242
World Directory of Marketing Information
        Sources, 241
World Directory of Trade and Business
        Associations, 242
World Economic Forum, 51
World energy consumption, 71
World Factbook (CIA), 240
World Health Organization, 341, 498, 601,
        602, 632
World Intellectual Property Organization,
        196, 208–209
World Market Share Reporter, 243
World/regional maps
    the Americas, 264
    Asia, 268
    climate, 84–85
    Commonwealth of Independent States,
        295
    communications, 88
    Eastern Europe, 265
    economy, 91
    energy, 86
    Europe, 286
    religion, 90
    terrorism, 89
    trade flows, 91
    trade routes, 77
    water areas, 87
    world, 82–83
World Retail Directory Sourcebook, 242
World's largest industrial corporations,
        31–32
World Trade Center attack, 4, 435, 460–461
World Trade Organization, 5, 11, 28, 33,
        38, 46, 48–49, 157, 158–159, 169,
        174, 188, 196, 213, 250, 283, 308,
        312, 414–415, 445, 471, 558
    China's entry, 269
    on dumping, 544
    protests against, 51–52
    skirting the spirit of, 49
    Taiwan in, 271–272
World trade routes, 77–78
Worldwide Franchise Directory, 242
Worldwide Sports & Recreation, 440
WPP Group, 496
Wrigley, 473
WTO-TRIPS Agreement, 194

X

Xbox, 214

Y

Yahoo!, 172, 311
Yamaha, 192
Yanmar, 392
Yin and yang, 219
Yo! Sushi, 654
Yugoslavia, 267
Yugoslav Red Cross, 175

Z

Zambia, 13
ZDNet, 172
Zenith, 6, 249
Zero One Design, 482